COMPOSERS SINCE 1900

COMPOSERS SINCE 1900

A BIOGRAPHICAL AND CRITICAL GUIDE

Compiled and Edited by
DAVID EWEN

THE H. W. WILSON COMPANY · NEW YORK · 1969

COMPOSERS SINCE 1900

Introduction

COMPOSERS SINCE 1900 is the replacement for three volumes published between 1934 and 1954. The first was *Composers of Today*. After two editions and several printings this book became outdated and was allowed to go out of print. In 1949 it was supplanted by *American Composers Today*, which concentrated on composers in North America and Latin America, since the postwar period made it difficult, at times impossible, to gain accurate and up-to-date information about European composers. With the return of normal conditions in Europe, the editor, in several trips abroad, was able to gather the material for *European Composers Today*, which was published in 1954.

Now another biographical and critical guide to twentieth century composers is needed, brought up to date and taking advantage of the latest musicological findings and critical evaluations to give an accurate representation of musical creativity today. To achieve this aim a return to a single volume embracing both American and European composers was considered desirable. In COMPOSERS SINCE 1900, 70 North and South Americans, 147 Europeans, and 3 Australians are included.

COMPOSERS SINCE 1900 covers musicians who have been writing music since January 1, 1900. Many are no longer alive, and some belong to traditions and backgrounds long since vanished. Others, however, are of our own time, a cross-section of every significant trend and movement in twentieth century music from impressionism to serialism, from neoromanticism to neodadaism. Included among traditionalists, innovators, eclectics, and romanticists are composers who stand in the vanguard of the avant-garde–those who are doing significant work with aleatory music, electronic music, directional music, organized sound, and other modern methods of composition.

As in the earlier books, the selection of composers was based on the following factors: (1) the importance of their work; (2) the frequency with which their compositions are heard in the world's concert halls or opera houses and on recordings; (3) the interest and curiosity which the composers have aroused both for themselves and for their music. Musicians of exclusively local significance have been omitted, as well as musicians who have inspired only passing interest or whose works are not in general circulation.

The editor has felt strongly that the value of this publication would be in direct ratio to the comprehensiveness with which each composer is discussed. Consequently, this volume is confined to two hundred and twenty composers treated more or less fully, rather than many more treated sparingly. COMPOSERS SINCE 1900 will provide the music lover with information not readily available elsewhere. It discusses many composers from many different places in biographical, personal, and critical detail.

The practice of going to first-hand sources, which was inaugurated with the first volume in 1934, has been continued. More than half the composers have been personally interviewed. Three trips were made to Europe to gather new material from the composers themselves: to Italy, France, Switzerland, and Germany in 1964; to Austria, Hungary, France, and Germany in 1965; to England, Holland, and Scandinavia in 1966. American composers were also interviewed. These meetings were supplemented by extensive correspondence. The editor wishes to express his indebtedness to composers both in the United

Introduction

States and abroad for their patience in answering innumerable queries, for providing source material and photographs, and for correcting errors that have crept into other reference books. Various music societies, music publishing houses, foreign consulates, and libraries have also been extraordinarily cooperative.

The pronunciation of unusual or difficult names is indicated in footnotes to the biographies. The system follows that of *Webster's Biographical Dictionary*.

Miami, Florida
May 1969

DAVID EWEN

Contents

Jean Absil
1893–

Jean Absil was born in Péruwelz, Hainaut, Belgium, on October 23, 1893. As a pupil of Martin Lunssens and Léon Dubois at the Brussels Conservatory, he received first prizes in organ, harmony, and fugue. Later, he studied orchestration and composition privately with Paul Gilson.

In 1921 Absil's First Symphony won the Prix Agniez, and a year later his cantata *La Guerre* was awarded the second Prix de Rome. These and other early works were composed, wrote Joseph Dopp in *La Revue Musicale*, "according to scholastic principles in which the inspiration still submitted to abstract rules and academic form." The most remarkable of these early works were the tone poem *La Mort de Tintagiles* (1926) and the *Rhapsodie sur des Thèmes Populaires Flamands* (1928).

After 1929, with his first string quartet, Absil developed the style in which he produced some of his most significant music. Coming into contact with the music and principles of Milhaud, Schoenberg, and Hindemith, Absil was able to free himself from the restrictions of traditional harmony and rhythm while permitting himself greater independence through the use of atonality, polytonality, and polyrhythms. His music became complex and austere. It was characterized by the skill and inventiveness with which he employed modern resources in the formulation of his musical ideas. His compositions were extensively played throughout Europe and won several major awards, among them the Prix Rubens in 1934 and the Prix Ysaÿe in 1939. Florent Schmitt referred to Absil in *Le Temps* as "one of the leaders of the contemporary movement in Belgium, if not all of Europe."

Since 1939 Absil has produced major works for orchestra, chorus, chamber music groups, and the stage. His first ballet, *Le Miracle de Pan*, was produced in Brussels in 1949. Of the three ballets that followed, *Deux Danses Rituelles* enjoyed a substantial success when introduced in Brussels in 1960.

In his analysis of Absil's style, Joseph Dopp wrote: "His music, informed by deep emotion,

Absil: ȧp sēl'

is remarkable for its spontaneity, originality, and for purity of style. ... His music is contrapuntal throughout. He goes very far in the matter of irregular meters. ... He uses discords as consonances freely, but his music is always tonal or modal. ... He uses many new scales. ... The description of his technique and methods might suggest that his music is mainly cerebral, too abstract, deliberately calculated. In actual fact, it is profoundly human, quite accessible."

Richard De Guide has noted Absil's frequent use of the variation form, a form "enlarged and freshened through present-day techniques." De Guide finds a deeply moving religious sentiment and mysticism in such works as *Les Bénédictions* (1941), *Les Chants du Mort* (1943), and *Thrène pour le Vendredi Saint* (1945). In some of Absil's compositions for voice, De Guide discerns a delicate humor and a keen sense of irony.

JEAN ABSIL

Between 1923 and 1963 Absil was the director of music at the Academy of Etterbeek, and from 1930 to 1960 he was professor of harmony and fugue at the Royal Conservatory in Brussels. Since 1957 he has served as professor of fugue at the Chapelle Musicale de la Reine Elisabeth. He has also served as president of the Belgian section of the International Society for Contemporary Music, as president of the Société Nationale des Droits d'Auteurs, and as a member of the Royal Academy of Belgium. He was the founder of the distinguished

Brussels publication *Revue Internationale de Musique*.

MAJOR WORKS

Ballets—Le Miracle de Pan; Épouvantail; Les Météores; Deux Danses Rituelles.

Chamber Music—4 string quartets; 3 wind quintets; 3 quartets for saxophones; 2 piano quartets; 2 string trios; 2 cello quartets; Chaconne, for solo violin; Sonatine en Duo, for violin and viola; Concerto Grosso, for wind instruments; Fantaisie Concertante, for violin and piano.

Choral Music—Ulysse et les Sirènes; Philatélie; Les Bénédictions; Les Chants du Mort; Thrène pour le Vendredi Saint; Le Zodiaque; Pierre Breughel l'Ancien.

Operas—Peau d'Âne; Fansou; Les Voix de la Mer.

Orchestral Music—6 rhapsodies (including Rhapsodie Flamande); 5 suites; 3 symphonies; 2 tone poems (including Jeanne d'Arc); Five Pieces, for small orchestra; Concertino for Cello and Orchestra; Serenade; Variations Symphoniques; various concertos for solo instruments and orchestra (piano; violin; viola; cello).

Piano Music—Bagatelles, Esquisses, Impromptus, Pieces, Variations; Sonatina; Hommage à Schumann.

Vocal Music—Five Melodies; Nostalgie d'Arabella, for contralto and several instruments; Phantasmes, for contralto, saxophone, viola, piano, and percussion.

ABOUT

La Revue Musicale, October–December 1937.

Eugène d'Albert
1864–1932

Eugène Francis Charles d'Albert was born April 10, 1864 in Glasgow. The son of Charles Louis Napoléon d'Albert, a dancing master and prolific composer of dance music, he received his first musical training from his father. When Eugène was twelve, he was selected as a Newcastle scholar for the National Training School in London. There he made excellent progress in piano with Ernst Pauer, and in theory with Arthur Sullivan, John Stainer, and Ebenezer Prout.

On June 23, 1879, d'Albert's music (an orchestral overture) received its first performance at a students' concert at the St. James Hall. A year and a half later, on November 22, 1880, d'Albert made his concert debut as pianist at a Monday Night Popular Concert in London. He made such a good impression that he was engaged for two more appearances in 1881 at these Popular Concerts and was

d'Albert: dȧl bĕr′

particularly acclaimed for his performance of the Schumann Piano Concerto. He then combined his activities as pianist and composer in presenting the world première of his Piano Concerto in A major at a Royal Philharmonic concert conducted by Hans Richter on October 24, 1881.

EUGÈNE D'ALBERT

The winning of the Mendelssohn Scholarship enabled him late in 1881 to spend a year in travel. In Vienna he played the first movement of his piano concerto with the Vienna Philharmonic under Hans Richter. Franz Liszt, impressed by the young man's talent, accepted him as a pupil. Liszt greatly admired his student and often playfully referred to him as "Albertus Magnus" and "a young Tausig." (At that time, Karl Tausig was thought to be one of the foremost keyboard technicians.)

His studies with Liszt ended, d'Albert embarked on a career as concert pianist that took him around the world and placed him with the virtuosos of his generation. Beginning in 1882, d'Albert briefly filled a post as pianist in Weimar. He now made Germany his permanent homeland as well as the country of his allegiance, repudiating his British citizenship, which he had held up to this time. During World War I he openly expressed his hostility to England and prayed for a German military victory. This stand exposed him to considerable opposition and hostility when, after the war, he returned to England for concert appearances.

In 1895 d'Albert became the conductor of orchestral concerts in Weimar; and in 1907 he embarked upon a distinguished career as a music educator, succeeding Joseph Joachim as the director of the Berlin Hochschule für Musik.

D'Albert's first opera, *Der Rubin*, was a failure when introduced in Karlsruhe on October 12, 1893. Several more operas, introduced in various German cities, also failed. On November 15, 1903, *Tiefland*—now remembered as his greatest opera—received its première performance in Prague. It attracted little notice at the time and for a while seemed destined for the obscurity suffered by his earlier operas. But in a revised and abridged version, *Tiefland* was introduced at the Metropolitan Opera on November 23, 1908, with Emmy Destinn in the principal female role of Marta, and Alfred Hertz conducting. The opera was received enthusiastically. Its success was repeated in London on October 5, 1910, under Thomas Beecham's direction. After that, the opera was produced throughout Germany. Since then it has been revived intermittently in Europe. In 1913, in Oslo, Kirsten Flagstad made her singing debut in *Tiefland*; and with this opera, in 1959, she launched her career as the director of the National Opera in Oslo. The Opera was revived by the Century Opera Company in New York City in 1914 and by Opera '48 in New York City in 1948.

The libretto by Rudolf Lothar, based on a Catalan play by Ángel Guimera, follows the traditions of *verismo* opera in Italy. For this story of seduction, passion, and murder d'Albert created a score in which a Puccini-like style is married to Germanic dramatic values. In describing the music of *Tiefland*, Felix Borowski dwelt upon this union of Italian and German operatic methods: "In his score, d'Albert followed the Italians only partly down the road they had made. He, as they, caused the music to deepen and enhance the message of the play, but d'Albert did not open the sluices of vocal melody that caused Italian opera to be the synonym for song. With him, as with most German composers for the theatre, the orchestra carries the burden of the music, and the vocal element is declamation, only occasionally transmuted into tone. For the rest, the score is often charming and not infrequently stirring to the ear.

Originality may not stream richly through its pages, but that perhaps may explain some of the opera's success."

Of d'Albert's later operas, two were moderately successful: *Flauto Solo*, introduced in Prague on November 12, 1905, and *Die Toten Augen*, seen first in Dresden on March 5, 1916. The latter was produced in the United States in 1923, when the visiting Wagnerian Opera Company toured the country. D'Albert's last opera was *Mister Wu*, which he did not live to complete. Finished by Leo Blech, it was introduced posthumously—in Dresden on September 29, 1932.

D'Albert also wrote some instrumental music. In this field his most significant work was the Concerto for Cello and Orchestra, which was successfully revived at the Edinburgh Festival in 1949.

All his life d'Albert was an avid sports fan, his particular enthusiasms being cycling and tennis. The study of medicine was a favorite mental pastime.

He was married six times. His second wife was Hermine Finck, a singer; his third was Teresa Carreño, the world-famous pianist. His last divorce was obtained just before his death in Riga, Latvia, on March 3, 1932.

MAJOR WORKS

Chamber Music—2 string quartets.
Choral Music—Der Mensch und das Leben.
Operas—Kain; Tiefland; Flauto Solo; Die Toten Augen; Mister Wu (completed by Leo Blech).
Orchestral Music—2 piano concertos; 2 concert overtures; Symphony in F major; Concerto for Cello and Orchestra; Vier Gesange, for soprano and orchestra; Aschenputtel, suite.
Piano Music—Suite; Sonata in F-sharp minor; Pieces.

ABOUT

Raupp, W., Eugène d'Albert: Ein Künstler- und Menschenschicksal.

Musical Courier, March 12, 1932; Musical Times (London), November 1, 1904.

Franco Alfano
1876–1954

Franco Alfano was born at Posillipo, near Naples, on March 8, 1876. He studied music with Paolo Serrao and De Nardis at the

---

Alfano: äl fä′ nō

3

Alfano

Naples Conservatory, and with Jadassohn and Sitt at the Leipzig Conservatory. His musical horizon was broadened through his contacts with German music, and the solidity of form and an inventive harmonic language, found in some of his piano pieces published in Germany at this time, reveal the impact of this influence.

FRANCO ALFANO

His first opera, *Miranda*, introduced in 1896 in Leipzig, was received poorly, as was its immediate successor, *La Fonte di Enscir*, when it was given in Breslau on November 8, 1898. In 1900 Alfano visited Paris, where he became fascinated by French ballet and *opéra comique*. A folk ballet, *Napoli*, produced at the Folies Bergères on January 28, 1901, proved so successful that it had a run of one hundred and sixty performances.

After returning to Italy, Alfano completed the opera that made him famous throughout Europe. It was *Risurrezione*, with a libretto by Cesare Hanau based on Tolstoy's novel *Resurrection*. When first presented in Turin on November 4, 1904, the opera was a great success. Describing it as "a remarkable opera," Irving Schwerké wrote: "The significant aspects of the score are the utilization of Russian themes without imitative purports, the poetic melancholy which pervades the work as a whole, the richness of harmonic fabric, and the exalted characterization of the persons of the drama." *Risurrezione* was introduced in Chicago on December 31, 1925, with Mary

Garden in the leading role; at this presentation the opera was sung in French. It enjoyed a highly successful revival in Paris in 1954.

Subsequent Alfano operas fulfilled the promise of *Risurrezione*. *L'Ombra di Don Giovanni* (La Scala, Milan, April 3, 1914), *La Leggenda di Sakuntala* (Bologna, December 10, 1921), and *Madonna Imperia* (Turin, May 5, 1927) proved welcome additions to the contemporary Italian opera repertory. *Madonna Imperia* was produced at the Metropolitan Opera on February 8, 1928. Donald Jay Grout described this lyric comedy as a "charming Boccaccio-like libretto (by Arthur Rossato) with neo-Puccini music. . . . The voice lines alternate smoothly between melodic phrases and a most flexible, lively and expressive arioso, supported by luscious and delicate harmonies not unlike Ravel in many respects . . . and with beautiful impressionistic orchestration–a perfect match for the refinedly voluptuous text."

In most of his operas, Alfano carried on the traditions of the *verismo* school of Italian opera initiated by Mascagni and Leoncavallo and brought to its richest fulfillment by Puccini. Alfano's spiritual alignment with Puccini made him the logical choice to complete Puccini's last opera, *Turandot*, when the master died in 1924 leaving the final duet and the closing scene unwritten. The opera, without Alfano's ending, was heard for the first time at La Scala, on April 25, 1926, Arturo Toscanini conducting. All subsequent performances have been presented with Alfano's additions.

Alfano also composed two symphonies and some chamber and piano music. Nicolas Slonimsky has written that the symphonies were "in the characteristic expansive and grandiloquent idiom of his operas."

In the years 1919-1923 Alfano was the director of the Liceo Musicale in Bologna. From 1923 to 1939 he directed the Turin Conservatory, and from 1940 to 1942 he was superintendent of the Teatro Massimo in Palermo. From 1947 until his death he directed the Rossini Conservatory in Pesaro. He died in San Remo, Italy, on October 26, 1954.

MAJOR WORKS

Ballets—Napoli; Vesuvius.

Chamber Music—3 string quartets; Sonata for Violin and Piano; Sonata for Cello and Piano.

Choral Music—Hymn to Bolivar.

4

Operas—Risurrezione (Resurrection); L'Ombre di Don Giovanni; La Leggenda de Sakuntala; Madonna Imperia; L'Ultimo Lord; Cyrano de Bergerac; Il Dottor Antonio.

Orchestral Music—3 symphonies; Suite Romantica.

ABOUT

Della Corte, A., Rittrato di Franco Alfano; Schwerké, I., Kings Jazz and David.

Musical Times (London), March 1921.

Hugo Alfvén
1872–1960

Hugo Alfvén was born in Stockholm on May 1, 1872. He received his preliminary musical training from 1887 to 1891 at the Stockholm Conservatory; during the next five years he received violin instruction from Zetterquist and composition lessons with Lindegren. In the period between 1890 and 1897 Alfvén earned his living playing the violin in the Royal Orchestra, with which he occasionally appeared as violin soloist. His debut as a composer came in 1896 with his Violin Sonata, op. 1, and with his first symphony, in F minor, completed in 1897 and introduced in Stockholm on February 9 of the same year. After an additional period of violin study with César Thomson in Brussels, he returned to Sweden, where he achieved recognition as a composer with the successful performance of his second symphony, in E major, in Stockholm on May 2, 1899. On the strength of this achievement, in 1900 the government awarded him the Jenny Lind stipend, enabling him to spend three years of travel and study in France and Germany; during this period he studied conducting with Kutzschbach in Dresden.

Not long after his return to Sweden, Alfvén completed the first composition to bring him international renown: the rhapsody *Midsummer Vigil (Midsommarvaka)*, inspired by the St. John's Eve revel in small Swedish towns. Although strongly influenced by Brahms, Alfvén here evolved his own creative identity by tapping the vein of Swedish folk music. Alfvén's rhapsody is based mainly on native folk song and dance materials, along with some material from the Schleswig-Holstein region of

Alfvén: ăl vän´

Germany. Following a highly successful introduction in Sweden soon after completion in 1904, the rhapsody was eventually adapted into an important one-act ballet, *La Nuit de Saint-Jean*, introduced by the Ballets Suédois in Paris on October 25, 1920. It was presented 134 times during the first season and 119 times more in the next three years. Louis Schneider wrote that this ballet recreated "the personality of a people."

In 1906 Alfvén wrote the most popular of his five symphonies, the third, in E major, performed in Gothenburg, Sweden, on December 5, 1906. The composer described it as "a paean in praise of all the joys of life, sunshine, and the joy of living." Alfvén's last two symphonies were introduced in Stockholm —the C minor on November 16, 1918, and the F minor on April 30, 1952.

HUGO ALFVÉN

Among Alfvén's later symphonic works, the most successful was his third Swedish rhapsody (1937), entitled *Dalecarlian* because all its musical material is derived from the Dalecarlian region. The composer himself provided a description of his music: "The rhapsody is imbued with the serenity of the lake forests north of Lake Siljan. The basic theme is gloomy, melancholy, full of yearning." This is in sharp contrast to Alfvén's first rhapsody, *Midsummer Vigil*, which had been festive in mood and ebullient in spirit.

In 1908 Alfvén was elected to the Royal Academy of Music in Sweden. From 1910 to 1939 he was the music director of the Royal University of Uppsala, where he conducted the students' choir. He conducted other Swedish choral groups in concerts throughout Europe in the years 1910-1947 and made occasional guest appearances as symphony conductor in Scandinavia, Austria, and England. In 1938 he paid his only visit to the United States.

Additional recognition came in 1917 when he was given an honorary doctorate by Uppsala University. As one of Sweden's most distinguished composers, he was occasionally called upon to write compositions for special festive occasions and patriotic anniversaries. In 1927 he composed a cantata celebrating the 450th anniversary of the founding of Uppsala University; in 1935 he created another cantata to honor the 500th anniversary of the Swedish Parliament.

In 1957, as part of the festivities attending the celebration of Alfvén's eighty-fifth birthday in Stockholm, the Royal Swedish Opera performed the world première of his ballet *The Prodigal Son*. The choreography was by Ivo Cramer. A seven-movement suite from this ballet score has been performed at symphony concerts in Europe and the United States and has been recorded; in 1957 one of the numbers from this suite, "Roslag's Spring," became a hit in Sweden as a popular song.

Alfvén bears the same relationship to Swedish music that Grieg did to Norwegian and Sibelius to Finnish. All were essentially Romantic composers who respected traditional practices and structures, leaned on folk idioms, and created music that was strongly lyrical, energized by a powerful rhythmic drive. With Alfvén, polyphony played a significant role.

Hugo Alfvén published three volumes of memoirs in the period 1948-1952. He was married three times, the last time just one year before his death at Falum, Dalarna, Sweden, on May 8, 1960.

MAJOR WORKS

Ballet—The Prodigal Son.

Chamber Music—Elegy, for horn and piano; Sonata in C, for violin and piano; Romance, for violin and piano.

Choral Music—Baltic Exposition Cantata; Ode to Gustavus Vasa; Sten Sture, cantata; Manhem, cantata; Sveriges Flagga, for male voices.

Orchestral Music—10 cantatas for solo voice and orchestra; 5 symphonies; 3 rhapsodies (including Midsummer Vigil and Dalecarlian); The Bells, for baritone and orchestra; Ein Skargardssagen, tone poem; Festspiel.

ABOUT

Nyblom, C. G., Hugo Alfvén; Svensson, S. E., Hugo Alfvén.

Etude, March 1953.

Humberto Allende
1885–1959

Sarón Pedro Humberto Allende, Chile's foremost composer in the twentieth century, was the first Chilean composer to receive recognition outside his own country.

HUMBERTO ALLENDE

He was born in Santiago on June 29, 1885. In 1899 he entered the National Conservatory there. While still a student, he conducted two of his orchestral compositions at the Conservatory. In 1905 he was graduated as violinist, and in 1908 in composition. He then earned his living teaching in the Santiago public schools. In 1910 he completed his Symphony in B-flat, which received a prize of 1,500 Chilean pesos. With this money he made a tour of Europe to survey institutions of musical learning and methods of music education.

He returned to his country in 1911 and was

Allende: ä yĕn´ dä

appointed a member of the Chilean Folklore Society. From this time his preoccupation with Chilean folk music was repeatedly reflected in his compositions, many of which assumed a pronounced national character. In 1913 he wrote a tone poem, *Escenas Campesinas Chilenas*, utilizing native Chilean idioms. This work attracted interest and attention; Felipe Pedrell, the eminent scholar of Spanish folk music, praised it highly.

One of Allende's significant compositions was a set of twelve piano pieces, *Tonadas de Carácter Popular Chileno*, written during the years 1918–1922 and published in Paris in 1923. "What a delight are these little pages," wrote Florent Schmitt, "what sharp and deep sensibility is revealed here. . . . This music, which one can play fifty times without tiring, enjoying it anew, makes us think of Chopin's mazurkas, which these *tonadas* resemble in their nostalgic flavor."

Nicolas Slonimsky explains that the word *tonada* literally means "something to be intoned." He adds: "In its Latin American form *tonada* is a dance in two parts of which the first is slower than the second. . . . Allende's harmonic style is definitely established [in these pieces]. It is acridly bitonal, with considerable chromatic interweaving in the inner voices."

Several of these *tonadas* have been transcribed by the composer for orchestra and chorus, and in this version three were successfully introduced in Paris on January 30, 1930.

Another characteristic work by Allende is *La Voz de las Calles*, a brilliantly conceived tone poem for orchestra written in 1920 and introduced in Santiago on May 20, 1921. This composition derived its materials from the songs and cries of Chilean street vendors.

Allende wrote several impressive concertos. One written in 1915 for cello and orchestra elicited warm praise from Debussy when Pablo Casals introduced it in Paris. A later concerto, for violin and orchestra, received a prize at the Quadricentennial Music Contest in Santiago in November 1941; it was given its première performance in Santiago on December 4, 1942.

In 1922 and 1923 Allende toured France and Spain. From 1928 to 1945 he taught composition at the Santiago National Conservatory. On several occasions he was a Chilean representative at important folk-music conferences abroad: Kharkov in 1924; Prague in 1928 (under the auspices of the League of Nations); Barcelona in 1929. In 1945 Allende received a Chilean government prize for his lifelong musical achievements and contributions to Chilean culture.

Allende lived with his wife and two daughters on the outskirts of Santiago. One daughter, Tegualda, was a gifted sculptress. Towards the end of his life Allende was incapable of doing any creative work or teaching because of poor health. He died in Santiago on August 16, 1959.

MAJOR WORKS

Chamber Music—String Quartet.

Orchestral Music—Symphony in B-flat; Escenas Campesinas Chilenas, tone poem; Concerto for Cello and Orchestra; La Voz de las Calles, tone poem; La Despedida, for two sopranos, contralto and orchestra; Two Songs, for soprano and orchestra; Concerto in D major, for violin and orchestra.

Piano Music—3 sonatas; Tonadas de Carácter Popular Chileno, twelve pieces; Four Etudes.

ABOUT

Slonimsky, N., Music of Latin America.

Musical America, August 1942; Revista Musical Chilena, September 1945.

Hendrik Andriessen
1892–

Hendrik Andriessen was born in Haarlem, Holland, on September 17, 1892. The son of an organist and composer, he studied the organ first with his brother Willem, then with Louis Robert and J. B. De Pauw. He later attended the Amsterdam Conservatory where he was a member of Bernhard Zweers' class in composition.

In 1913, he wrote his first mature composition, a chorale for organ in which the influence of César Franck can be detected. In his later organ music, Andriessen helped to carry on the Franck tradition, extending it in new technical and aesthetic directions. In 1919, Andriessen became a church organist in his native city, and from 1934 to 1942 he was the organist of the Utrecht Cathedral. He grew famous not only for his virtuosity on the organ but also for his improvisations.

Andriessen: än′ drē sĕn

Andriessen

Andriessen's Catholic upbringing influenced his significant contributions to Dutch music, beginning with spiritual songs with organ (or orchestral) accompaniment and continuing with his Masses. "His ideal," wrote Wouter Paap, "was a calm, sober sound picture in which each discharge of emotion was avoided, and in which the content of the liturgical text can be reflected in a clear, simple manner."

HENDRIK ANDRIESSEN

Andriessen also wrote many distinguished works for the concert stage, among them a cello sonata in 1926, his first symphony in 1930, and a violin sonata in 1932. Jos Wouters finds that the most typical features of Andriessen's secular compositions are "a broadly flowing sense of melody, often based on modal scales, and a very personal use of harmonic sound effects in which there is usually a tonal basis, coupled with colorful instrumentation, which often betrays the organist in him."

During the Nazi occupation of Holland, Andriessen was prevented from pursuing his varied musical activities, and on one occasion was even imprisoned as a hostage. In 1946 Andriessen's *Te Deum* appeared on the program of the first concert by the Concertgebouw Orchestra in postwar Amsterdam.

Two major works in 1950 helped spread his fame outside Holland. The *Ricercare*, for orchestra, was written to commemorate the two hundredth anniversary of the death of Johann Sebastian Bach and was performed extensively throughout Europe. The second composition was his opera, *Philomela*, Andriessen's finest work for the stage, commissioned by the Dutch government to celebrate the fiftieth anniversary of Queen Wilhelmina's reign. *Philomela* was introduced at the Holland Music Festival in Amsterdam on June 23, 1950. The Dutch poet Jan Engelman based the libretto on an episode in the sixth book of Ovid's *Metamorphoses*. Reviewing the première performance for the New York *Times*, Daniel Schorr wrote that this opera "looks like one of the most successful contemporary Dutch productions, ranking with some of the best musical theatre of the day.... Packed with dramatic punch, the music has a supple, somewhat rhapsodic quality, moving rapidly to match each mood and punctuate every action, yet without ever appearing episodic or losing its strong melodic course."

Andriessen has had a long, productive career as a teacher and educator. From 1928 to 1934 he taught at the Amsterdam Conservatory. During the years 1937–1944 he was a member of the faculty of Utrecht Conservatory and after 1949 director of the Hague Royal Conservatory. He has also appeared as pianist and lecturer and has written on musical subjects. Among his publications is an excellent monograph on César Franck.

MAJOR WORKS

Chamber Music—Sonata for Cello and Piano; Sonata for Violin and Piano; Piano Trio; Pastorale, for flute, viola, and piano.

Choral Music—Masses; Qui Habitat, motet; Magnificat; Two Madrigals; Te Deum; Psalm 47.

Opera—Philomela.

Organ Music—Chorales; Intermezzi; Sonata da Chiesa; Passacaglia; Sinfonia.

Orchestral Music—4 symphonies; Ballade van de Merel, for narrator and orchestra; Capriccio; Ballet Suite; Concerto for Organ and Orchestra; Ricercare; Étude Symphonique; Variations and Fugue on a Theme by Johann Kuhnau; Mascherata.

Vocal Music—Trois Pastorales; Miroirs de Peine; L'Attente Mystique.

ABOUT

Lang, P. H. and Broder, N. (eds.), Contemporary Music in Europe; Reeser, E. (ed.), Music in Holland.

George Antheil
1900–1959

George Antheil was born in Trenton, New Jersey, on July 8, 1900, "of German-Polish ancestry, mostly Polish," as he wrote to this editor in the late 1940's. "My childhood was like that of most American kids except that I exhibited a great love for music at an early age, studying the violin when I was five. The piano came much later, when I was ten. The study of harmony was begun in my twelfth year. My first serious teacher was Constantine von Sternberg, former pupil of Liszt. He was an old man, but devoted to my talent; he insisted upon a strict contrapuntal basis. . . . I studied very intensively during those early adolescent years and was able to write passable, and even musical, fugues, when I was eighteen—also sonata-allegro movements.

"At several Philadelphia Orchestra concerts I heard Stravinsky's *Petrouchka*, which revolutionized all of my previous musical ideas. I began studying every piece of new music I could put my hands on. I left Sternberg in 1919, went to New York, and became a pupil of Ernest Bloch. It was while I was with Bloch that I composed my First Symphony. I wanted the symphony to express the part of America which I saw all around me: Trenton, the Delaware River, the people I knew, the sounds and emotions I felt.

"Sternberg introduced me to Mrs. Bok (later Mrs. Efrem Zimbalist). She gave me a scholarship for the Settlement School (the forerunner of the Curtis Institute). I studied there for a period, improving my piano playing amongst other things."

In 1922 Antheil toured Europe as a concert pianist, making his debut in London on June 22. He began to acquire the reputation of being a "bad boy of music," largely because of his insistence on playing the ultramodern piano music of that day. For a while he remained in Berlin, where his First Symphony was introduced by the Berlin Philharmonic conducted by Schultz von Dornberg. The audience reacted politely, but the critics were hostile.

The realization that he wanted to be a composer and not a concert pianist impelled him in 1923 to abandon his concert tours and devote

---

Antheil: ăn′ tīl

himself exclusively to composition. He went to Paris where he lived on the Rue de l'Odéon, above the Shakespeare Bookshop of Sylvia Beach (publisher of James Joyce's *Ulysses*). Here he wrote much chamber music and some orchestral compositions in an avant-garde style. His fame soared, especially in the more fashionable Parisian salons. His concerts were crowded. The avant-garde among the Parisian intellectuals adopted him as their favorite son. Jean Cocteau sang his praises; Ezra Pound spoke of him as a genius in *Antheil and the Treatise on Harmony*.

On October 4, 1925, George Antheil married Elizabeth (Böske) Markus, the niece of the famous Austrian novelist and playwright Arthur Schnitzler. The Antheils had a son, Peter Richard, born in California a decade after their marriage.

GEORGE ANTHEIL

In 1925 Antheil completed the *Ballet Mécanique* with which he attracted international attention. With this provocative work, one period in his development came to a close, a period in which he aspired to write music "of precision . . . strange, cold, dreamlike, ultraviolet music," as he himself described it. The *Ballet Mécanique* was neither a ballet nor an actual description of factories or machines. Scored for anvils, airplane propellers, electric bells, automobile horns, and sixteen pianos, it was described as a "mechanistic dance of life" by its composer: "My idea was to warn the age in which I am living of [the] simultaneous beauty and danger of its own unconscious mechanistic philosophy."

The *Ballet Mécanique* was introduced in Paris on June 19, 1926, Vladimir Golschmann conducting, and was a great success. On April 10, 1927, it was performed at Carnegie Hall with Eugene Goossens conducting and Aaron Copland as one of the pianists. Unfortunately, the concert emphasized the sensational; the propeller was visible, a gigantic eyesore on the stage; the number of pianos was doubled; the whole atmosphere was that of a circus. Because of the blatant publicity with which the concert was launched and the garishness with which it was realized, Antheil was severely criticized as a sensation-seeker. The notoriety of that performance almost wrecked his career; for years musicians and audiences refused to take him seriously. But Antheil had had nothing to do with launching this publicity, nor had he anticipated that his manager would indulge in such melodramatic effects.

Antheil's continued faith in the significance of the *Ballet Mécanique* was expressed in a letter to Nicolas Slonimsky in 1936: "I personally consider that the *Ballet Mécanique* was important in one particular: that it was conceived in a new form, that form specifically being the filling out of a certain time-canvas with musical abstractions and sound material composed and contrasted with one another with the thought of time values rather than tonal values. . . . In the *Ballet Mécanique* . . . my ideas were the most abstract of the abstract."

The revival of the *Ballet Mécanique* in New York on February 20, 1954, adhered more faithfully to Antheil's intentions—even though only four pianos were now used and the noise of a plane (this time that of a jet) was reproduced by a recording machine. By 1954 the work had lost its capacity to shock. It attracted little attention and no controversy, and was generally regarded by audience and critics as little more than a period piece.

The year 1927 brought Antheil other disappointments and frustrations besides the fiasco of the *Ballet Mécanique* in New York. His piano concerto was a failure when introduced in Budapest and repeated in Paris at the Concerts Golschmann. A period of discouragement followed. But the première of his opera *Transatlantic* at the Frankfurt Opera on May 25, 1930, was a splendid success. The first American opera introduced in Germany, it received twenty curtain calls on opening night. Built around a presidential candidate and his search for Helena, a beautiful woman, it proved a saga of America, racy with jazz effects and idioms—novel, modern, American. It spoke of hotels, Childs restaurants, department stores. One aria was sung in a bathtub. The German audiences—infected with the spirit of *Zeitkunst*—loved its jazzy atmosphere and exciting tempo.

In 1932 Antheil received a Guggenheim fellowship which enabled him to write another opera, *Helen Retires*, with a libretto by John Erskine. Introduced at the Juilliard School of Music in New York on February 28, 1934, the opera failed to make an impression. The book was wordy and dull; the music was described by one unidentified critic as "a tissue of contradictions," combining elements of jazz, Broadway musical comedy, and avant-garde discords.

After 1933 Antheil went to Hollywood to work on films. In 1937 he completed his Second Symphony, subtitled "American," with which a new creative era emerged for him, an era in which he established new values for himself through an intensive restudy of the masterworks of the past. "I began to realize," he wrote, "that no young artist starts the world all over again for himself, but merely continues . . . the heritage of the past, pushing it if possible on a little further."

Antheil's last three symphonies were his most important. The Fourth, inspired by World War II, was introduced by the NBC Symphony under Leopold Stokowski on February 13, 1944. "I put everything I knew into this symphony," the composer said. "Mostly into it had gone El Alamein, Stalingrad, and the new America I saw awakening. The feeling of it. You can put these big abstractions into music." Though the symphony is a mélange of many different styles and moods—including waltzes, military music, a fugue, choruses in the style of those sung by the Red Army, music for an eccentric dance—it was praised by many critics, and it was heard on the programs of a great many of the major American symphony orchestras.

The Fifth (1947) was first performed by the Philadelphia Orchestra under Eugene Ormandy on December 31, 1948. Antheil subtitled it "The Joyous." Three movements are permeated with an infectious gaiety which achieves a climax in the last movement. For Antheil this music expressed, as he explained, "a sort of youthful optimistic joy, not only of my boyhood, but of the people about me ... of America. ... This air of happiness is at times almost uncontained." But in the finale, as in the preceding slow movement, joyous moods alternate with slower, lyrical sections that carry for Antheil "the nostalgia of certain tunes we sang as boys in a summer camp on the upper Delaware."

The Sixth Symphony, completed in 1948 and. introduced by the San Francisco Symphony under Pierre Monteux on February 10, 1949, is regarded by many critics as Antheil's finest work in the symphonic form. Its first movement was inspired by Eugène Delacroix's painting "Liberty Leading the People." Antheil explained: "It is emotionally connected with this painting; there is the smoke of battle, courage, despair, and hope, all marching into the future." The second movement, a passage of extended lyricism, has for the composer "the breath of autumn, of sadness and optimism at once," while the finale means "the triumph of joy and optimism over despair, war, annihilation."

Antheil's most important creations in the 1950's were the ballet *Capital of the World*, with choreography by Eugene Loring, and the full-length opera *Volpone*. The ballet, created for television, had its première on December 6, 1953. (The first staged presentation was given by the Ballet Theatre in New York on December 27, 1953.) Set in Spain, it tells the tragic story of young Paco, who dreams of becoming a bullfighter and meets his death in a mock bullfight with Enrique, his friend.

Volpone is Antheil's most important opera. It is based on Ben Jonson's comedy, adapted for opera by Albert Perry. The first performance, in Los Angeles on January 9, 1953, lasted four hours. The composer and librettist then condensed the work into two hours of running time. This version was successfully introduced in New York in July 1953. Perry's shortened libretto was now suitable for comic opera, with which Antheil's tuneful score, which often carried echoes from the Broadway musical-comedy stage, was in complete har-

mony. Albert Goldberg wrote in his review: "The music runs a gamut of style including a number of waltzes *à la Rosenkavalier*." He also pointed out that many of the arias and ensembles were "extremely effective" and that the orchestration was "remarkably diverse."

"As I grow older," Antheil wrote to this editor in 1948, "I find myself more and more finding my true musical happiness in the works of the great masters of the past—particularly Beethoven." To the program annotator of the Philadelphia Orchestra, Antheil added in 1949: "The objective of my ... creative work has been to disassociate myself from the passé modern school of the last half century and create a music for myself and those around me which has no fear of developed melody, real development itself, tonality, or understandable forms."

Establishing his permanent home in Hollywood in the late 1930's, Antheil divided his creative activities among the concert hall, the opera house, and motion pictures. Among the screen productions for which he wrote the background music in the 1940's were *The Scoundrel*, *Once in a Blue Moon*, and *Make Way for Tomorrow*.

To discuss Antheil's music is to speak of only one facet of his diverse career. He also wrote articles for *Esquire* and conducted a lovelorn column ("Boy Meets Girl") syndicated to thirty-three newspapers. He wrote a mystery novel (under the pen name of Stacey Bishop), a political book (*The Shape of the War to Come*, published anonymously in 1940), and an autobiography, *Bad Boy of Music* (published in 1945). With the collaboration of the motion picture star Hedy Lamarr, he invented and patented a radio torpedo. He regarded himself also as an amateur endocrine criminologist – a student of the relationship between crime and glandular disturbances in the criminal.

George Antheil died in New York City on February 12, 1959. Among his last major works was a cantata, *Cabeza de Vaca*. It was performed posthumously over the CBS-TV network on June 10, 1962.

MAJOR WORKS

Ballets—Fighting the Waves; Dreams; Capital of the World.

Chamber Music—3 string quartets; 2 violin sonatas; Chamber Music for Eight Instruments; Concerto

Arnell

for Flute, Bassoon and Piano; Sonatina for Violin and Piano.

Operas—Transatlantic; Helen Retires; Volpone; The Brothers; The Wish; Venus in Africa.

Orchestral Music—6 symphonies; Ballet Mécanique; Concerto for Piano and Orchestra; Nocturne; Decatur at Algiers; Over the Plains; Concerto for Violin and Orchestra; Specter Waltzes; The Children's Symphony; McKonkey's Ferry; Tom Sawyer: A Mark Twain Overture.

Piano Music—4 sonatas.

Vocal Music—Cabeza de Vaca, cantata.

ABOUT

Antheil, G., Bad Boy of Music; Chase, G., America's Music; Pound, E., Antheil and the Treatise on Harmony.

Modern Music, May–June 1931.

Richard Arnell
1917–

Richard Anthony Sayer Arnell was born in Hampstead, London, on September 15, 1917. After attending the Hall School in Hampstead from 1925 to 1929 and the University College School from 1929 to 1935, he was admitted in 1935 to the Royal College of Music in London. There he studied composition with John Ireland and piano with St. John Dykes. In 1938 he received the Farrer Prize in composition.

He went to the United States in 1939, remaining for eight years. From 1943 to 1945 he was music consultant to the North American Service of the BBC, and in 1945 and 1946 he helped conduct the chorus of the International Ladies' Garment Workers' Union. During his long residence in America he completed his first important compositions, including two symphonies, a violin concerto and other orchestral compositions, and works for chamber music groups and solo instruments. In 1941 he wrote the score for *The Land*, a film documentary produced by the noted director Robert Flaherty for the United States Department of Agriculture.

Outstanding performances in the United States drew attention to his flowering creative talent. On January 21, 1941, Leon Barzin led the world première of an overture, *The New Age*, at a concert of the National Orchestral Association. A reviewer for *Musical America*

Arnell: är′něl

wrote: "[It] disclosed the virtues of well-balanced design, well-controlled orchestration and smooth writing." In 1944 Sir Thomas Beecham conducted the première of his Second Symphony in New York. On April 21, 1946, the National Orchestral Association presented Arnell's violin concerto with Harold Kohon as soloist, and on January 8, 1947, Vera Brodsky performed the première of his piano concerto with the CBS Symphony, Bernard Herrmann conducting. Other premières included those of two orchestral divertimentos, one given by the CBS Symphony under Victor Bray and a second broadcast over radio station WQXR, New York, under Leon Barzin's direction.

RICHARD ARNELL

In the United States Arnell received several commissions. One of these resulted in the writing of *Prelude and Flourish*, for brass instruments, created for and performed during the visit of Sir Winston Churchill to Columbia University in New York in 1946. Another commission came from the Ballet Society, which introduced Arnell's first ballet, *Punch and the Child*, in New York in November 1947.

Towards the end of 1947 Arnell returned to London. In 1948 he became professor of composition at the Trinity College of Music where two years later he was made Honorary Fellow. He resigned from Trinity College in 1964. In 1967–1968 he was Visiting Lecturer on Music at Bowdoin College in Brunswick, Maine.

Major presentations of his later music took place both in the United States and in England. In 1949 John Barbirolli led the première of Arnell's Fourth Symphony at the Cheltenham Festival in England, and in the same year Leopold Stokowski directed the first performance of *Black Mountain*, an orchestral prelude, with the New York Philharmonic Orchestra. Sadler's Wells Theatre Ballet produced *Harlequin in April* in April 1951; it received over 150 performances in the next few years. Two orchestral compositions were commissioned and performed by Sir Thomas Beecham: *Lord Byron*, a tone poem, heard at a concert of the Royal Philharmonic in London in 1952, and *Landscapes and Figures*, which Sir Thomas Beecham presented at the Edinburgh Festival in 1956. In 1955 Arnell wrote the music for a television opera, *Love in Transit*, probably the first such work written for that medium by an English composer. This opera was subsequently also produced over Belgian television. In 1962 a program of Arnell's music under his own direction was given at the International Festival of Contemporary Music.

Arnell belongs with the traditional composers whose music is essentially diatonic, but not devoid of modern idioms. "In the midst of the modern fashion of ear-lacerating compositions," said Noel Goodwin in the London *Daily Express*, "Mr. Arnell is almost a lone voice in writing descriptive music that is not afraid of melody." Roy Budden has written: "His music is always effectively written and well laid out for the medium; the style is basically diatonic, though there is a considerable use of 'modern' effects."

In *Music and Musicians* Richard Arnell clarified his ideas about music as follows: "I simply believe that it is mere prejudice and unclear thinking which rejects a work of art that has attached to it the stigma of 'program music.' Music is a complicated amalgam of meanings, an expression of man himself, and cannot be abstracted from him without becoming 'un-music' or sheer noise. Theorists and academicians who try to tear them apart would doom us to sterility and death."

MAJOR WORKS

Ballets—Punch and the Child; Harlequin in April; The Great Detective.

Chamber Music—5 string quartets; 3 trios; 2 cello sonatas; 2 sonatas for unaccompanied cello; various quintets; Flute Quartet; Piano Quartet; Four Serious Pieces, for cello and piano; Pieces, for clarinet and piano; Cassation, for wind quartet; Serenade, for eleven instruments; The Grenadiers, variations for wind ensemble; Passacaglia, for unaccompanied violin; Partita, for unaccompanied viola; Suite in Seven Movements, for unaccompanied cello.

Choral Music—Childhood Impressions; Pensum Latinum, madrigal.

Opera—Love in Transit (for television).

Orchestral Music—5 symphonies; 2 divertimentos; Classical Variations, for string orchestra; The New Age, concert overture; Sonata, for chamber orchestra; Concerto for Violin and Orchestra; Prelude and Flourish, for brass; Concerto for Piano and Orchestra; Canzona and Capriccio, for violin and string orchestra; Sinfonia Quasi Variazioni; Concertino for Harpsichord and Orchestra; Fantasia; Black Mountain, orchestral prelude; Abstract Forms, for string orchestra; Lord Byron, tone poem; Landscapes and Figures; Ode to the West Wind, for soprano and orchestra; Robert Flaherty Impressions; Concerto Capriccioso, for violin and orchestra.

Organ Music—2 sonatas; Baroque, Prelude and Fantasia; Fugal Flourish.

Piano Music—Twenty-two Variations; Four in D, a suite of simple piano pieces; Thoughts and Second Thoughts, for piano duet; Sonatina, for piano four hands.

Malcolm Arnold
1921–

Malcolm Henry Arnold was born in Northampton, England, on October 21, 1921. He attended several schools until he was thirteen; thereafter he concentrated on music study with private teachers. In 1938 he entered the Royal College of Music in London on a scholarship, specializing in trumpet and composition. In 1941 he received the Cobbett Prize for composition, and two years later he completed his first distinctive work, *Larch Trees*, a tone poem for orchestra. Meanwhile, in 1941, he had joined the trumpet section of the London Philharmonic Orchestra; one year later he took over the first chair.

He was mustered into the army in 1944 and discharged a year later for medical reasons. He returned to orchestral playing, serving as second trumpet for the BBC Symphony in 1945 and 1946. He then resumed his former post as first trumpet of the London Philharmonic. In 1947 the winning of the Mendelssohn Scholarship enabled him to go to Italy for further study. Out of this extended visit came several major works, among them the *Festival*

Arnold

Overture for orchestra (1948); his first symphony and a clarinet concerto, both in 1949; and his first opera, *The Dancing Master* (1951).

In 1953 he was commissioned to write music for a ballet performed during the coronation of Queen Elizabeth II. Entitled *Homage to the Queen*, it was seen first at Covent Garden on June 2, 1953, before a distinguished audience, including the Queen. The year 1953 saw the premières of two more compositions: his second symphony, in Bournemouth on May 25, and his Concerto for Oboe and String Orchestra, in London, on June 9.

MALCOLM ARNOLD

Arnold has written several delightful works based on old English and Scottish folk songs and dances. Probably his most popular work for orchestra is the *English Dances*, written in 1950–1951. This is an eight-movement suite (divided into two sets). Its second, third, fourth, and seventh movements utilize old modes (Mixolydian, Aeolian, Mixolydian, and Dorian, respectively) to recreate the remote and esoteric quality found in old English dance music. In the first movement a lilting dance tune is played by muted violins over an ostinato accompaniment. The fifth movement, the most extended in the suite, presents a gay dance melody in piccolo supported mainly by side drum. In the sixth movement, a rustic dance first heard in clarinets and bassoons is repeated five times; and in the finale, its main energetic subject is played twice.

After 1953 Arnold produced three symphonies, as well as other major compositions. In 1954 he composed a harmonica concerto for Larry Adler, who introduced it at a London Promenade Concert on August 14 of that year. In 1956 Arnold completed an opera, *The Open Window*, and on November 2, 1960, his fourth symphony was presented in London.

He represents, says Arthur Cohn, "the imaginative nonexperimentalist.... Though he refuses to burden his music with heaviness, he avoids the danger zone of sticky sentimentality."

Arnold has been a prolific contributor of screen music. Successful motion pictures for which he provided the background music include *The Captain's Paradise* (1953), *I Am a Camera* (1955), *Trapeze* (1956), *Island in the Sun* (1957), *The Bridge on the River Kwai* (1957), *Inn of the Sixth Happiness* (1958), *Roots of Heaven* (1958), and *Nine Hours to Rama* (1962). In his music for *The Bridge on the River Kwai* Arnold made effective use of a tune called "Colonel Bogey" which Kenneth Alford had written in 1914. Arnold developed it into a stirring march, adding to it a countermelody. His adaptation achieved extraordinary popularity both in the United States and in England; more than one million copies of the Columbia recording by Mitch Miller and his orchestra were sold in 1957.

MAJOR WORKS

Ballets—Homage to the Queen; Rinaldo and Armida; Solitaire; Sweeney Todd; Electra.

Chamber Music—Sonata for Violin and Piano; Sonata for Viola and Piano; Piano Trio; Trio, for flute, viola, and piano; Divertimento, for flute, oboe, and clarinet; Quintet, for flute, violin, viola, horn, and bassoon; Quintet, for two trumpets, horn, trombone, and tuba; Three Shanties, for wind quintet; Sonatina, for flute and piano; Oboe Quartet; Fantaisies, for solo wind instruments.

Choral Music—Two Ceremonial Psalms; John Clare, cantata for solo voices and piano duet; Song of Praise.

Operas—The Dancing Master; The Open Window.

Orchestral Music—5 symphonies; 2 sinfoniettas; various concertos for solo instruments and orchestra (flute; clarinet; oboe; horn; guitar; organ; harmonica); Larch Trees, tone poem; Festival Overture; Tam O'Shanter; Four Scottish Dances; Little Suite; English Dances; Concerto for Two Violins and String Orchestra.

Piano Music—Variations on a Ukrainian Folk Song; Children's Suite.

ABOUT

Cohn, A., Twentieth Century Music in Western Europe.

Kurt Atterberg
1887–

Kurt Atterberg was born in Gothenburg, Sweden, on December 12, 1887. He attended the Royal Swedish Technical School in preparation for a career in engineering. As a boy, however, he had learned to play the cello, and music remained his major interest. He later combined engineering studies with musical training and became a pupil of Andreas Hallén at the Royal Conservatory for ten months in 1910–1911. A government subsidy enabled Atterberg to spend two years in Germany, where he attended numerous performances of symphonic music and operas and pursued music study mainly by himself. Meanwhile, he had completed two symphonies and a violin concerto in the period between 1911 and 1913 and had begun to think seriously about composition. The First Symphony in B minor and the Violin Concerto were both introduced in Gothenburg, the former in 1912, the latter in 1914; the Second Symphony in F major received its première in Sondershausen in 1914.

After fulfilling military duty by serving as radio engineer at the Stockholm Naval Station, Atterberg found employment in the Royal Patent Office, where he remained until 1940. During this period he became involved in various musical activities. He completed his Third Symphony in D major in 1916, and his Fourth, *Sinfonia Piccola*, in 1919. Both were introduced successfully in Stockholm. He also completed an opera, *Härvard Harpolekare*, produced in Stockholm on September 29, 1919. But composition was not his sole musical interest. From 1913 to 1922 he was a conductor at the Royal Dramatic Theatre and from 1919 to 1957 the music critic of the Stockholm *Tidningen*. In the years 1940–1953 he was also the secretary of the Royal Academy of Music in Stockholm.

His reputation as one of Sweden's leading composers was established during the 1920's with a succession of highly important works that included his Fifth Symphony in D minor (*Sinfonia Funèbre*), a cello concerto (first heard in Berlin in 1923 with Emanuel Feuermann as soloist), and an opera, *Bäckahästen*, presented in Stockholm on January 23, 1925.

Atterberg: åt′ tĕr bär y'

Then, in 1928, what promised to be one of the triumphs of his career became the cause of his temporary disrepute, subjecting him to considerable unwarranted criticism. In that year his Sixth Symphony in C major won first prize of ten thousand dollars in an international competition sponsored by the Columbia Phonograph Company to commemorate the centenary of Franz Schubert's death. After its world première in Cologne on October 15, 1928, the symphony received worldwide circulation through performances by major orchestras everywhere. But the international fame that this symphony achieved for Atterberg soon brought notoriety as well. Some critics, disturbed by the derivative influences they found in the music, accused the composer of borrowing from others. Ernest Newman, in the London *Sunday Times*, suggested that these "borrowings" had been deliberate, an attempt by the composer to win favor with

KURT ATTERBERG

the distinguished judges either by imitating the mannerisms of some or by assuming the style to which others were partial. In rebuttal (*Musical Digest*, February 1929), Atterberg refuted these charges. He insisted that the only quotation of which he had been guilty was one from Schubert himself—an effort to honor Schubert in line with the purpose of the competition. He hotly denied he had intended to cater to the jury. "If I have fooled anyone," Atterberg concluded, "it must be the reminiscence-hunting critics who did not find the

Schubert citation, and some Swedish newspapers, who have showed that they have no interest in a prize won by a compatriot but very great interest in publishing scandalous matters and in trying to damage the reputation of Swedish music and Swedish musicians."

The scandal died down, and eventually was forgotten—particularly after the performance of Atterberg's symphonic work which to this day remains his most frequently played composition—*A Värmland Rhapsody*, written in 1933 to honor Selma Lagerlöf, the Swedish Nobel Prize novelist, on the occasion of her seventy-fifth birthday. All the folk melodies used in this score come from a region associated with Lagerlöf's masterwork, *Gösta Berlings Saga*. The rhapsody was introduced on the Swedish Radio on Selma Lagerlöf's birthday, November 20, 1933, and was an immediate success.

A Värmland Rhapsody is one of several major works by Atterberg to derive its melodic and rhythmic materials from Swedish folk songs. Two symphonies also have a national identity: the Fourth, in G minor (*Sinfonia Piccola*), and the Eighth, in E minor, the latter first heard in Stockholm in 1945. Generally, however, Atterberg has avoided musical nationalism, favoring a style described as "temperate, Nordic, neo-Romantic . . . with a strong feeling for form and colorful orchestration." This is the style of his later works, which include his opera *The Tempest*, based on Shakespeare (Stockholm, September 19, 1949); the Ninth Symphony (Helsinki, 1957); and the Concerto for Violin, Cello (or Viola) and Orchestra (Stockholm, 1961).

It was a decade before Atterberg's Ninth Symphony, which he regards as the summit of his symphonic output, received its first hearing. The Swedish première took place at Malmö on December 12, 1967, at a concert celebrating the composer's eightieth birthday. The symphony was inspired by the *Poetic Edda*, the tenth century Icelandic saga describing the creation and destruction of the world.

MAJOR WORKS

Ballets—Per Svinaherde; De Fåvitska Jungfrurna.
Chamber Music—2 string quartets; Suite, for string quartet; String Quintet; Bellaman Variations, for string quartet; Sonata for Cello and Piano.
Choral Music—Requiem; The Land of Iron Carriers.
Operas—Härvard Harpolekare (revised as Härvard der Harfner); Bäckahästen; Fanal; Aladdin; The Tempest.
Orchestral Music—9 symphonies; 9 suites; Concerto for Violin and Orchestra; Concerto for Cello and Orchestra; The Song; Rondeau Rétrospectif; A Värmland Rhapsody; Le Fleuve, tone poem; Concerto for Horn and Orchestra; Rondeau-Overture; Ballad Without Words; Concerto for Violin, Cello or Viola) and Orchestra.

ABOUT

Stuart, E. M., Kurt Atterberg.

Louis Aubert
1877–1968

Louis François Marie Aubert was born in Paramé, Ille-et-Vilaine, France, February 19, 1877. A prodigy, he entered the Paris Conservatory in his tenth year. There, as a pupil of Fauré, Vidal, and Vincent d'Indy, he won prizes in virtually every branch of music. While attending the Conservatory, and until his voice broke, he sang in the choirs of the Madeleine and Trinity churches.

His career as a composer began in 1892 with the song "Sous Bois." Two years later, in the song "Vieille Chanson Espagnole," he first revealed the influence of Spanish subjects and materials which later characterized some of his most popular compositions. *Rimes Tendres*, in 1896, was his first work to receive publication.

At the Conservatory, Aubert developed into such a promising pianist that his teacher, Louis Diémer, encouraged him to consider a career as virtuoso. For a while Aubert concertized in France. But composition soon absorbed most of his time and interest. His first successes as a composer finally influenced him to abandon the concert stage. These came with the *Fantaisie*, for piano and orchestra (1899), which Diémer introduced at a Concert Colonne on November 17, 1901; the *Suite Brève*, for two pianos, which made an excellent impression at the Paris Exposition in 1900; and the song "La Lettre," which became an extremely popular concert number.

On February 14, 1902, Aubert married Suzanne Mairot. During this same year he

Aubert: ō bâr′

completed *La Légende du Sang*, a series of historical scenes for narrator, chorus, and orchestra, which failed to make an impression when first introduced. The ballet *La Momie*, however, met a more favorable reaction when it was produced in Paris in 1903.

LOUIS AUBERT

Aubert worked six years on his opera *La Forêt Bleue*, with a libretto by Jacques Chenevière based on several of Perrault's fairy tales. This work, says Eric Blom, "has a certain delicacy and restrained grace which precludes it from any sensational success, and its undoubtedly great poetical qualities are a little pale and devoid of pronounced individuality." The opera was introduced in Geneva on January 7, 1913. This performance (which did not meet with the composer's approval) was received coldly. But the American première in Boston, on March 8, 1913, met Aubert's specifications and was well received. The opera did not reach Paris until after World War I, when it was performed at the Opéra-Comique on June 10, 1924.

During the years Aubert was occupied with writing his opera, he completed another significant composition, the song cycle *Crépuscules d'Automne* (1908), heard in Paris on February 20, 1909. After completion of the opera, Aubert finished a number of compositions with Spanish backgrounds and materials. First came *Nuit Mauresque*, for voice and orchestra (1911), followed by Aubert's most celebrated instrumental work, the tone

poem *Habanera*, introduced at a Pasdeloup concert in Paris on March 22, 1919, and from the beginning a major success.

During World War I, Aubert tried to enter military service but was turned down because of poor health. He then became organist and choirmaster at the Saint-Hippolyte Church in Paris. After the war Aubert joined the faculty of the Paris Conservatory. He is an Officier des Arts et des Lettres, and a member of the Legion of Honor.

World War II inspired Aubert to write *Offrande*, for orchestra, as a tribute "to all victims of the war." It was introduced in Luxembourg in 1947 and later the same year (on November 11) was heard in New York.

Aubert belonged with those composers who drew their inspiration and acquired their direction from Fauré. His best music has some of Fauré's sensitivity and refinement as well as his classic repose. But much of Aubert is also in the post-Impressionist style of Ravel. Like Ravel, Aubert found a good deal of his stimulation and inspiration in Spanish backgrounds; but Aubert's Spanish music is evocative in the manner of Manuel de Falla. Aubert died in Paris in January of 1968.

MAJOR WORKS

Ballets—La Moisson; La Momie; Chrysothémis; La Nuit Ensorcelée; Belebat; Cinéma.

Chamber Music—Piano Quintet; Introduction and Allegro, for flute and piano; Sonata for Violin and Piano; Madrigal, for flute and piano.

Choral Music—Tu Es Petrus; La Légende du Sang; Les Cloches; Saisons.

Opera—La Forêt Bleue.

Orchestral Music—Fantaisie in B minor, for piano and orchestra; Six Poèmes Arabes, song cycle for voice and orchestra; Nuit Mauresque, for voice and orchestra; Suite Brève (also for two pianos); Habanera; Dryade; Caprice, for violin and orchestra; Feuilles d'Images; Offrande; Le Tombeau de Châteaubriand.

Piano Music—Trois Esquisses; Sillages.

Vocal Music—Crépuscules d'Automne; individual songs for voice and piano including La Lettre, La Mauvaise Prière, and Tendresse.

ABOUT

Hill, E. B., Modern French Music; Vuillemin, L., Louis Aubert et Son Œuvre.

La Revue Musicale, February 1927.

Georges Auric
1899–

Georges Auric was born in the town of Lodève, Hérault, France, on February 15, 1899, and received his academic and musical education in Montpellier. He began writing songs and piano pieces when he was twelve. At fourteen, his family moved to Paris where he attended first the Paris Conservatory and then the Schola Cantorum; in the latter he was a pupil of Albert Roussel and Vincent d'Indy. By the time he was fifteen Auric had over two hundred compositions to his credit; one of these, a cycle of three songs entitled *Interludes*, was performed at a concert of the Société Nationale. When he was eighteen he completed the score for his first ballet, *Les Noces de Gamache*, and at nineteen, his first comic opera, *La Reine de Cœur*.

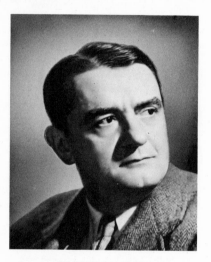

GEORGES AURIC

Like many other young French musicians of the time, Auric came under the influence of Erik Satie whose iconoclastic ideas about what the mission of music should be and the new techniques that composers should adopt made a profound impression on the younger man. Under the Satie influence Auric joined a group of young French composers who called themselves Les Nouveaux Jeunes, their aim being to carry on the innovations of Satie in achieving a music that was down to earth and of popular

Auric: ô rēk′

appeal—music that, in Auric's words, produced "auditory pleasure without demanding a disproportionate effort from the listener."

On June 6, 1917, several members of Les Nouveaux Jeunes, including Auric, gave a concert of their compositions at a painter's studio in the Rue Huyghens. A public concert followed on January 15, 1918, at the Vieux Colombier, its program made up of works by six young composers, all passionate followers of Satie: Germaine Tailleferre, Darius Milhaud, Arthur Honegger, Francis Poulenc, Roland-Manuel, and Georges Auric. Some time later there appeared in Paris an album of piano pieces by five of these composers (Roland-Manuel was absent), supplemented by a few compositions by a sixth newcomer, Louis Durey. Reviewing this album in *Comoedia* on January 16, 1920, Henri Collet referred to these young French composers as The French Six or Les Six, the first time they were thus designated. Collet wrote: "The Six Frenchmen have by magnificent and voluntary return to simplicity brought about a renaissance of French music, because they understood the lesson of Erik Satie and followed the precepts, so pure, of Jean Cocteau. . . . The different temperaments of the six composers jostle without jarring, and their works, individual and distinct, reveal a unity of approach to art, in conformity with the spokesman of the group, Jean Cocteau." One week later, Henri Collet published a second article in *Comoedia* in which he returned to the subject of modern French music and to the contributions made by The Six. The two articles caused the sobriquet The French Six to be applied to these young French composers, and it was as members of The French Six that each attracted considerable publicity, some realized their first successes.

Strictly speaking, The French Six were never an integrated school of composers in the way The Russian Five had been. It is true that all six Frenchmen were united by their rebellion against the excesses of post-Romanticism, but this was a nebulous tie. Each composer had his individual style; almost from the beginning, each pursued his own direction, uninfluenced by what his colleagues were doing. Darius Milhaud explained this in *Anbruch* by saying: "We, The Six, had different types of musical education, and this contributed to the independence of our individual thinking, taste, and style. . . . In view of this, how can we be regarded as slaves of a single code of aesthetics, or of one theory?" The career of The French Six therefore was short-lived. After a few attempts at giving concerts collaboratively and a single attempt to produce a ballet collectively, the six composers parted company.

If there was a unifying element in this group it was the fact that each of the six, at one time or another, wrote music that refused to take itself seriously, that borrowed its materials from the French music hall or from American ragtime and jazz, and that was light in style, slight in structure, with the aim to please at first contact. In 1920, for example, Georges Auric wrote *Adieu New York*, a fox-trot for piano that became popular. He also wrote a fox-trot for orchestra. Here Auric was following Satie's lead in trying to create a popular musical art. He continued following that lead in his music for ballet, a field which Auric cultivated with particular success.

Auric's first successful association with the ballet came in 1921 when he joined four other members of The Six to produce the score for *Les Mariés de la Tour Eiffel*, with a scenario by Jean Cocteau. Its première performance was given by the Ballet Russe de Monte Carlo in Paris on June 18, 1921. Auric's contribution to this musical collaboration of five composers was a sprightly overture entitled *The Fourteenth of July* which, as Jean Cocteau said, "evoked the powerful charm of the streets, the people on holiday, the little bandstands that resemble guillotines, drums and cornets inciting clerks and girls and sailors to dance. His soft trills accompany the miming in the same way that a circus orchestra repeats a tune interminably during an acrobatic act."

Without the benefit of composer-collaborators, Auric completed two important ballet scores for Sergei Diaghilev's Ballet Russe. *Les Fâcheux*, based on Molière, was produced in Monte Carlo on January 19, 1924. The light, popular, occasionally satiric music aroused considerable interest. More successful still was *Les Matelots*, seen first in Paris on June 17, 1925. With choreography by Léonide Massine and scenario by Boris Kochno, *Les Matelots* described the adventures of three sailors on leave who test the fidelity of a young girl engaged to one of them. They disguise themselves, and one of them tries to make love to her. When she resists, the sailors remove their disguises, and the lovers embrace. As one of the sailors, Serge Lifar made his first appearance in a leading dance role. Auric's racy score, spiced with popular tunes and rhythms, was a major contribution to the success of the ballet, not only in France but also in England (where it was introduced on June 29, 1925) and in New York City (March 9, 1934).

Auric produced other successful ballet scores. *La Pastorale* was seen on May 26, 1926; *Les Enchantements d'Alciné* on May 21, 1929; *La Concurrence*, on April 12, 1932; *Les Imaginaires*, on May 31, 1934.

Auric entered a new and fertile field of musical creativity in 1931 when he wrote the background score for René Clair's motion picture *À Nous la Liberté*. During the next quarter of a century and more Auric proved a prolific contributor to film music, in both French and English productions. Among the motion pictures for which he created the music were *Le Lac aux Dames*, *Orage*, *Sang d'un Poète*, *La Belle et la Bête*, *Orpheus*, *Symphonie Pastorale*, Bernard Shaw's *Caesar and Cleopatra*, *Passport to Pimlico*, *The Lavender Hill Mob*, and *Moulin Rouge*. In 1952 his score for *La Putaine Respectueuse* won first prize at the Venice Biennale cinema festival. Auric had previously won the Cannes award for *Symphonie Pastorale* and the Punta del Este award for *Orpheus*. *Moulin Rouge*, in 1952, yielded a major song hit in "The Song from Moulin Rouge" or "Where Is Your Heart?" It was sung on the soundtrack (for Zsa Zsa Gabor) by Muriel Smith; a Columbia recording by Percy Faith and his orchestra sold over a million disks.

Auric's later ballet scores included *Phèdre* (his first on a serious subject), which was seen at the Paris Opéra on May 23, 1950; *Coup de Feu*, given on May 7, 1952, during the Exposition of the Masterpieces of the Twentieth Century; and *Bal des Voleurs*, in 1959. In addition to his ballet music, he produced several interesting instrumental compositions.

Between 1954 and 1964, Auric was seven times president of the Société des Auteurs, Compositeurs et Éditeurs. He has been made Commandeur des Arts et des Lettres, Commandeur des Palmes Académiques, and Commandeur de la Légion d'Honneur.

Babbitt

In 1962 Auric assumed managerial responsibility when he became the single head of Paris's two major operatic institutions, the Paris Opéra and the Opéra-Comique. He resigned this post in 1968. The last night of his six-year regime was the opening night performance of the Roland Petit Ballet at the Opéra, in July. He was given a thunderous ovation. The occasion was reported as follows in *Variety* by Wolfe Kaufman: "Everyone in the theatre knew that Auric stood there quietly, hidden in the shadow of a box, watching, looking, listening. For the last time. You don't have to call him 'Monsieur l'Administrateur' any more. He's back where he started now, a composer. And happy, because he walked out on an upbeat."

Once considered in the avant-garde camp, Auric today has become conservative in his musical outlook. He has little sympathy for advanced tendencies in contemporary music and looks disdainfully on new musical systems. "It's all very well to escape from the classical tonal system," he says. "But to bind oneself to a system still more rigid – that is simply terrible!" His present-day musical interests reach far into the past, mainly to the music of the fifteenth and sixteenth centuries.

Auric was married to the portrait painter Nora Vilter on October 27, 1930.

MAJOR WORKS

Ballets—Les Fâcheux; Les Matelots; La Pastorale; Les Enchantements d'Alciné; La Concurrence; Le Peintre et Son Modèle; Phèdre; La Pierre Enchantée; Les Chaises Musicales; Coup de Feu; Chemin de Lumière; La Chambre; Bal des Voleurs.
Chamber Music—Sonata for Violin and Piano; Trio, for oboe, clarinet, and bassoon.
Choral Music—Songs on Fifteenth Century Poems.
Opera—Sous la Masque.
Orchestral Music—Overture; Suite Symphonique; Chandelles Romaines.
Piano Music—Adieu New York; Sonata; Impromptus; Partita, for two pianos; Trois Pastorales.
Vocal Music—Alphabet de Radiguet; Eight Poems of Jean Cocteau; Five Poems of Gérard de Nerval; Three Poems of Léon Paul Fargue; Six Poems of Paul Éluard; Three Poems of Max Jacob.

ABOUT

Goléa, A., Georges Auric.
La Revue Musicale, January 1926.

Milton Babbitt
1916–

Milton Byron Babbitt was born on May 10, 1916, in Philadelphia, Pennsylvania, where his father was employed as an actuary. He spent his youth in Jackson, Mississippi, where he attended the public schools, and was graduated from Central High School in 1931. He began to study the violin when he was five and the clarinet when he was eight. Almost from the time of his first music lessons he composed songs, the words as well as the music.

MILTON BABBITT

"Since my father was, and is, a professional mathematician, as is my younger and only brother," Babbitt explains in a sketch written for the editor of this book, "my early intellectual climate was predominantly mathematical. I entered college with the intention of becoming a mathematician and continuing music study only incidentally. At the college I was appalled by the 'engineering' mathematics to which I was subjected and by the philistine attitudes towards logic and abstract mathematics which I encountered. At the same time I became intrigued by the later music of Schoenberg, Webern, and Berg and the 'middle period' works of Stravinsky. I suddenly decided to exchange the degrees of emphasis that I would place upon my two domains of interest, and to concern myself particularly with composition and theory." He enrolled in New York University where he studied music with Marion Bauer, Martin Bernstein, and Philip James. After his graduation in 1935, he spent three years in the private study of composition with Roger Sessions in New York. Babbitt freely acknowledges that his greatest debt as a musician is to Sessions, who pointed out new directions for him.

In 1938, Babbitt joined the faculty of the music department of Princeton University. Four years later he became a member of the first group to receive from Princeton a graduate degree in music (Master of Fine Arts). Meanwhile, in 1941, his composition *Music for the Mass* received the Bearns Prize. "This work," he notes, "was a *pièce d'occasion* which embodied deliberately idiomatic conservatism, as a momentary respite from the twelve-tone composition with which I had already become deeply involved."

In 1942 and 1943, Babbitt was engaged in war-related activity "which is still classified as secret." During the summer of 1943 he returned to Princeton, to the mathematics department. He writes: "During those years of teaching mathematics there was little time for sustained musical composition; I did, however, 'think' myself through a whole stage in my compositional career, without producing a single completed work. The analytical, theoretical results of this period were contained in a monograph I wrote in 1946, *The Function of Set Structure in the Twelve-Tone System.* The first compositions which I regarded as satisfactorily embodying the theories expounded in my monograph were the *Three Compositions*, for piano (1946–1947) and *Composition for Four Instruments* (1947), the latter receiving a citation from the New York Music Critics Circle in 1949. These were the first compositions in which the principles of formation and transformation of the twelve-tone system were applied to other than pitch elements, primarily to temporal elements. All of these concerns have continued to characterize my music, as means of attempting to achieve a music in which each musical event, indeed each dimension of each musical event, possesses maximal functional multiplicity."

In 1950, Babbitt completed a setting of William Carlos Williams' "The Widow's Lament in Springtime," for the singer Bethany Beardslee. This, says the composer, was "an event of particular consequence, since it made

possible the beginning of my collaboration with this singularly gifted and devoted performer." In 1951, Babbitt was elected president of the United States branch of the International Society for Contemporary Music, and in 1952 he was a member of the faculty of the Salzburg Seminar in American Studies in Austria.

In 1957, Babbitt was commissioned by the Brandeis Festival of the Creative Arts in Waltham, Massachusetts, to write a work for jazz instrumentalists. The result was *All Set*, an unusual jazz work in that it employed the serial technique. On June 12, 1959, came another composition in serial technique—*Two Sonnets*, for baritone and three instruments, presented at the International Society for Contemporary Music festival in Rome.

During the summers of 1957 and 1958, Babbitt served on the composition faculty of the Berkshire Music Center at Tanglewood. The year 1958 was particularly significant, says Babbitt: "It was in January of 1958 that I was invited by RCA to acquaint myself actively with the Mark II Electronic Sound Synthesizer. This opportunity culminated over twenty years of concern on my part with the electronic production of sound, begun with tiny experiments in the late 1930's. My work on the Olsen-Belar Synthesizer, under the direction of Herbert Belar, was at first of a purely exploratory nature. But a grant of the Rockefeller Foundation made possible the founding of the Electronic Music Center of Columbia and Princeton Universities in 1959— the first center associated with universities entirely devoted both to research and composition in the field of electronically produced music."

Richard Kostelanetz described the music Synthesizer in the New York *Times Magazine:* "In contrast to most electronic music, which is produced by tape doctoring, Babbitt's electronic pieces are composed directly on the Synthesizer, a wholly singular instrument. . . . Some twenty feet long and seven feet high, the Synthesizer contains various sound-generating devices (tuning forks, oscillators, frequency multipliers, etc.) and about 1,700 tubes, all of which make it capable of producing sounds precisely to the composer's instructions. Potentially, Babbitt says, the machine can create any sound known to man; however, certain sounds, he admits, remain for the moment beyond his

21

capacity to specify their components. . . . On the face of the machine are switches that specify the following dimensions of a musical sound—frequency (pitch), octave, volume, timbre and envelope (degree of attack and decrease). When the composer assigns all the attributes of a note, the Synthesizer immediately produces the sound. If the composer finds that the result suits his intentions, he can affix it to the tape; if not, he can readjust the switches to make a new sound. . . . The composer can also place one sound atop another (as is standard in tape doctoring), transform live sounds and even program wholly original scales. . . . In short, unlike the tape laboratories, which require that sound be transferred from one machine to another, the Synthesizer does all its work itself."

Early in 1961, Babbitt completed *Composition for Synthesizer*, the first extended musical composition produced entirely on the RCA Electronic Sound Synthesizer. Later the same year, he completed the first composition ever written for a performer with synthesized accompaniment—*Vision and Prayer*, for soprano, based on a poem by Dylan Thomas, and commissioned by the Fromm Foundation. The song was introduced in New York City early in September 1961 by Bethany Beardslee, in a concert presented at the Eighth Congress of the International Musicological Society. In 1964 two other works for Synthesizer were heard: *Ensembles for Synthesizer*, featured at the Ojai Festival in California, and *Philomela*, for soprano, recorded soprano, and synthesized accompaniment, which had been commissioned by the Ford Foundation. The latter composition received a citation from the New York Music Critics Circle.

The Synthesizer, as Benjamin Boretz has explained, "made an enormous practical difference in Babbitt's compositional life, particularly in permitting the exploration of complex new rhythmic situations that lie within the bounds of perceptual possibility but beyond even the ultimate mechanical capacities of human performers. Perhaps even more important was the achievement—for once—of performance conditions under which the distinctive sonic and successional qualities that his idea had always presupposed could be realized. . . . In *Philomela* an entirely new level of electronic-musical possibility is revealed."

Babbitt's first composition for symphony orchestra was *Relata I*, given its world première in Cleveland on March 3, 1966, with Gunther Schuller conducting the Cleveland Orchestra. This is one of two single movement compositions entitled *Relata*, the other one being named *Relata II*, "so related," the composer explains, "that either may be performed separately or . . . the two may be performed together as a continuous single movement with I necessarily preceding II." Gunther Schuller explains that "*Relata* certainly represents an altogether new and radical way of using the orchestra. In its multileveled complexity it proposes a new set of relationships which the individual player must understand and master before the piece can fully work."

During the summers of 1959 and 1960, Babbitt belonged to the faculty of the Princeton Seminar for Advanced Musical Studies, and since 1959 he has been a member of the committee of direction at its Electronic Music Center. In 1964 he was on the faculty of the Internationale Ferienkurse at Darmstadt, Germany. In 1966 he succeeded Roger Sessions as professor of music at Princeton.

In 1959, Babbitt received an award from the National Institute of Arts and Letters, citing him for "imaginative compositions" and for revealing "an original and penetrating grasp of musical order that has had a great influence on many younger composers." He was elected to the National Institute of Arts and Letters in 1965. In 1960 and 1961 Babbitt held a Guggenheim fellowship for research in electronic music. His fiftieth birthday was celebrated in New Haven on May 14, 1966, at a festival of American music sponsored by the International Society for Contemporary Music.

Babbitt told an interviewer: "I believe in cerebral music. I never choose a note unless I know why it is there. . . . The structure idea is the idea from which I begin. . . . I have the end in mind as well as the beginning and the middle, and the piece ends when the possibilities or resources of the particular set are exhausted."

This is the way Benjamin Boretz has summed up Babbitt's contribution: "More than any other composer of our time, Milton Babbitt has accepted the twentieth century musical situation as an opportunity rather than a menace, and has enthusiastically taken up the challenge to create musical coherence and relevance within the prevailing vacuum of relativism. . . . Babbitt has demonstrated, with almost revelatory impact, the enormous potential for significant musical development possible through a searching reinterpretation of the fundamental principles of perception and relation on which the continuity of Western musical tradition has been based."

On December 27, 1939, Babbitt married Sylvia Miller. They have one child, a daughter, Betty Ann. "My hobbies and interests 'outside music' are not, I fear, outside my musical interests," he writes. "They are: mathematics (particularly finite group theory, combinatory theory, logic, time series analysis, statistical analysis in general, information theory, theory of automata, machine stimulation, pattern detection, scaling theory), audio electronics, computer logic, artificial intelligence, perception theory, mathematical learning theory, concept formation, philosophy of science, linguistic philosophy, structural linguistics, machine translation, and acoustics. I might add, no less justifiably, television (watching) and horse-racing (betting)."

MAJOR WORKS

Chamber Music—2 string quartets; Composition for Four Instruments; Composition for Twelve Instruments; Composition for Viola and Piano; Woodwind Quartet; All Set, for seven jazz instrumentalists; Sextets, for violin and piano.
Electronic Music—Composition for Synthesizer; Ensembles for Synthesizers; Vision and Prayer, for soprano and synthesized accompaniment; Philomela, monodrama for soprano, recorded soprano, and synthesized accompaniment.
Orchestral Music—Relata I and II; Correspondence, for strings and tape.
Piano Music—Three Compositions; Partitions; Semisimple Variations.
Vocal Music—Du, song cycle for soprano and piano; The Widow's Lament in Springtime, for soprano and piano; Composition, for tenor and six instruments; Sounds and Words, for soprano and piano; Two Sonnets, for baritone and three instruments.

ABOUT

Machlis, J., Introduction to Contemporary Music.
BMI: The Many Worlds of Music, July 1965; High Fidelity, August 1960; Musical America, February 1951; New York Times Magazine, January 15, 1967.

Henk Badings
1907–

Hendrik Herman (Henk) Badings, Dutch composer, was born in Bandoeng, Java, on January 17, 1907. His interest in music manifested itself early in study of the violin, followed by an intensive period of self-study in composition and five years of composition lessons from 1919 to 1924 with Willem Pijper, one of Holland's most distinguished musicians. Badings' original ambition was to become a mining engineer and he attended the Technical University in Delft, from which he received a diploma in engineering, *cum laude*, in 1931. From 1931 to 1937 he was an assistant there in the department of palaeontology and historic geology.

HENK BADINGS

Meanwhile, his musical interest had turned from performance to composition. His first major work was a violin concerto, completed in 1928. This was followed in 1930 by his first symphony, which was warmly received when it was introduced by the Concertgebouw Orchestra in Amsterdam. His first string quartet came in 1931, and his second symphony in 1932.

His early music was generally marked by a melancholy which permeated the slow movements of his first two symphonies and the first string quartet, occasionally even filtering

Badings: bä′dǐngs

Badings

through the pages of his heroic fast movements. This preoccupation with tragedy was also evident in his choice of sad texts for songs.

In 1934, he became a professor of composition at the Music Lyceum in Amsterdam where, in 1938, he was promoted to the post of codirector; during this same period he served as professor of composition at the Rotterdam Conservatory. During the Nazi occupation of Holland, he was director of the Conservatory at The Hague. He finally gave up pedagogy to devote himself entirely to composition.

The most important of his earlier compositions was his Third Symphony, completed in 1934, now considered a landmark in modern Dutch symphonic music. Here Badings makes skillful use of a monothematic technique, in which the main subjects of all four movements are based on the same material, the melodic nucleus of which is two rising seconds. In this symphony, as in several other large works of this period, he shows, as J. M. Meulenhoff pointed out, a "preference for broad, 'sung,' melody which he develops contrapuntally." The serious, tragic overtones so characteristic of Badings' music of this period are also present in this symphony.

Gradually, a lighter mood penetrated his writing. This first became apparent in 1941 in his ballet *Orpheus and Eurydice*, and in his comic opera *Love Intrigues*. From 1941 on, and for about another decade, this lighter touch was combined with an increasing economy of material, transparency of harmonic and instrumental texture, and simplification of style. Even the more complex of Badings' compositions make for pleasant listening, since he always combines advanced idioms in harmony and counterpoint with broad, spacious melodies.

Badings' most important compositions of the 1940's include the fourth symphony, first given in Rotterdam on October 13, 1947; the third and fourth violin concertos, in 1944 and 1946; the oratorio *Apocalypse*, introduced in Rotterdam on November 25, 1949; the fifth symphony, heard in Amsterdam on December 7, 1949; and the opera *The Night Watch* produced in Antwerp on May 13, 1950. The style here, according to Meulenhoff, "may be considered as a continuation of the line Brahms-Reger-Hindemith."

In 1946 Badings was accused of wartime collaboration with the Nazis. He was found guilty, and for two years was barred from all professional activities. When these charges were reexamined, Badings was completely exonerated.

For a long time Badings interested himself in new tuning systems. He built up his own harmonic system constructed from a scale of alternating major and minor seconds, and he wrote a number of compositions for Professor A. D. Fokker's thirty-one-keyed organ. After 1952 Badings became interested in electronic music. He built his own electronic studio at the Philips Research Laboratory at Eindhoven. When this studio was taken over by the University of Utrecht in 1960, Badings became its director. He wrote two ballets in which electronic effects are prominent—*Cain and Abel* (The Hague, June 21, 1956) and *The Woman of Andros* (Hanover, April 14, 1960); the opera *Salto Mortale* (Netherlands television, June 19, 1959); and *Genèse*, music for five oscillators (Brussels, October 7, 1958). The *Genèse* score was subsequently used for a ballet which was produced at Innsbruck, Austria, in 1959 under the title *Der Sechste Tag*, and at Linz in 1960 as *Mikrobiologisches*. He also wrote the electronic sequences for the background music used in the motion picture *Freud*, released in 1963.

Probably Badings' most successful use of electronic sounds is to be found in his opera *Martin Korda, D.P.* The première on June 15, 1960, was the opening performance that season of the Holland Festival. Albert von Heyk's libretto used as a setting a displaced persons' camp, and the plot highlighted the tragic negotiations between one of the inmates and his government. Badings uses electronics to suggest the nightmarish quality of a hallucination. Loudspeakers throughout the auditorium helped make the audience acutely conscious of the experience of terrifying unreality.

Despite his intense preoccupation with electronics, Badings did not abandon compositions using regular instruments. In 1953 he received the Paganini Award for his third violin sonata and two years after that a prize from the French radio for his choral music. His Symphony No. 6, the *Symphony of the Psalms*, was a major success when introduced at the Holland Music Festival in Haarlem on June 25, 1953. His Seventh Symphony, commissioned by the

Louisville Philharmonic in Kentucky, was introduced by that organization on February 26, 1955. In the years between 1955 and 1961 Badings completed three more symphonies and an excellent Concerto for Two Violins and Orchestra; the latter was heard at The Hague on January 19, 1955.

"His style," says Nicolas Slonimsky, "may be described as romantic modernism; his harmonic approach, polytonality; in his melodic material he often uses a scale of alternating whole tones and semitones."

Since 1962 Badings has served as professor of composition at the High School of Music at Stuttgart, Germany. He is married to Olly Folge Fonden, a former concert violinist.

MAJOR WORKS

Ballets—Orpheus and Eurydice; Cain and Abel (electronic); Evolutions (electronic); The Woman of Andros (electronic).

Chamber Music—3 string quartets; 2 piano trios; 2 violin sonatas; 2 cello sonatas; Quintet for Wind; Sonata for Violin Solo; Sonata for Cello Solo; Trio, for oboe, clarinet, and bassoon; Trio, for two violins and viola; Trio, for three oboes; Quartet for Brass; Trio, for flute, violin, and viola; Trio, for two violins and piano; Sextet, for wind and piano; Piano Quintet; Octet; Sonata, for recorder and harpsichord; Trio, for recorders; Trio, for flute, violin, and guitar.

Choral Music—Honestum Petimus Usque; Apocalypse, oratorio; Laus Pacis, cantata; Psalm 147; Stultitiae Laus; Te Deum.

Electronic Music—(besides those listed elsewhere): Genèse, Capriccio for violin and electromagnetic sound; Electromagnetic Soundfigures for Soundtracks; Songs, for male chorus and electronic instruments.

Operas—Love Intrigues, comic opera; The Night Watch; Rembrandt; Orestes (radiophonic opera); Asterion (radiophonic opera); Salto Mortale (electronic); Martin Korda, D. P. (electronic).

Orchestral Music—2 symphonies; 4 sets of symphonic variations; 4 violin concertos; 2 cello concertos; 2 flute concertos; Tragic Overture; Heroic Overture; Piano Concerto; Songs of Life and Death, for tenor and orchestra; Overture, 1948; Songs on Texts by Copla, for contralto and orchestra; Ballade: Symphonic Variations on a Dutch Folksong; Organ Concerto; Concerto for Two Violins and Orchestra; Atlantic Dances, for piano and orchestra; Symphonische Klangfiguren.

Piano Music—6 sonatas; 4 sonatinas.

Vocal Music—Three Songs on texts from Boutens' Lentemaan; Three Duets, for soprano, contralto, and strings; Songs, with piano accompaniment; Songs, with organ accompaniment; Seven Songs to Poems of E. E. Cummings.

ABOUT

Backers, C., Nederlandse Componisten; Meulenhoff, J. M., Music in Holland.

Tadeusz Baird
1928–

Tadeusz Baird was born in Grodzisk, Poland, on July 26, 1928. Too young to serve in the Polish army after the Nazis invaded Poland in 1939, Baird was able to pursue his musical education in spite of the war. In 1943 and 1944 he was a pupil of Boleslaw Woytowicz and Kazimierz Sikorski in Lodz. His studies were interrupted when the Nazis interned him in a labor camp until the war's end. In 1947 he settled permanently in Warsaw. For the next four years he attended the Warsaw Conservatory, a pupil of Piotr Rytel and Piotr Perkowski. During this period, between 1948 and 1950, he studied musicology and the history of art at the University.

TADEUSZ BAIRD

In 1949 he affiliated himself with a group of avant-garde composers in Warsaw who identified themselves as Group 49. During this year, he completed two ambitious compositions—a piano concerto and an orchestral Sinfonietta which received a number of noteworthy performances in Poland. Recognition for Baird in Poland came quickly after that. In 1951 he received the Polish State Prize for his first symphony, in C-sharp minor (1950), and in 1952 the Golden Cross of Merit. This symphony was followed by outstanding compositions which gave Baird an impressive

Baird: bârt

standing among Polish composers and which brought him a membership in the Committee of Management of the Polish Composers' Union in Warsaw. These were some of the works: a suite for flute and string orchestra entitled *Colas Breugnon* (1952); *Ouverture Giocosa*, for orchestra (1952); his second symphony (1953); and the *Concerto for Orchestra* (1953).

The style of these works is basically atonal, with strong leanings towards the twelve-tone system which Baird was soon to embrace wholeheartedly.

As a dodecaphonist, Baird was more strongly influenced by Alban Berg than by Webern for, like Berg, Baird combined an extraordinary technical skill with a capacity to endow twelve-tone writing with strong emotional values and a pronounced romantic feeling. Stefan Jarocinski explains that Baird's "submission to the rules of the twelve-tone technique has never been dogmatic and rigid. The melodic factor (motifs, phrases) and its expressive values always have been prominent."

Baird first attracted enthusiasm outside Poland with *Four Essays for Orchestra*, which, in the year of its composition (1958), won the Gregor Fitelberg Composition Contest sponsored by the Polish Radio. Its première took place in Katowice, Poland on August 18, 1958, in a performance by the Polish Radio Symphony conducted by Witold Rowicki (to whom the work is dedicated). Later in 1958, this work was given at the Warsaw Autumn Festival, and in 1959 it was heard in Dresden, Leipzig, and Berlin as well as at the festival of the International Society for Contemporary Music in Rome. The American première followed on January 18, 1961, in a concert at Ann Arbor, Michigan, given by the visiting Warsaw Philharmonic under Rowicki. After that George Szell conducted it in New York and Cleveland. This composition received the Honors of Distinction award from the International Rostrum of Composers in Paris sponsored by UNESCO.

In his informative program notes for the Cleveland Orchestra, Klaus G. Roy described the *Four Essays* as follows: "[It] is music solidly in the mainstream of 'neo-Romantic' musical speech. It builds on the tradition of musical expressivity proposed more than fifty years ago by Gustav Mahler, moves through the expansion of this language by Schoenberg and Berg, and offers a mature and deeply personal experience in musical terms. . . . It conserves traditional and comprehensible means of musical rhetoric in the areas of melody, form, rhythm, and even harmony. Yet it does so without direct imitating of existing models and without falling prey to well-worn conventions."

After the *Four Essays*, Baird received the Honors of Distinction award from the International Rostrum of Composers twice more: in 1963, for *Variations Without a Theme*, for orchestra; in 1966, for *Four Dialogues*, for oboe and chamber orchestra. In addition to these honors, Baird received the Music Prize of the City of Cologne in 1962.

Other significant works of the 1960's were *Erotica*, a cycle of six love songs for soprano and chamber orchestra, texts by Malgorzata Hillar; and *Four Novelettes*, for orchestra, the world première of which took place in the United States at the Congregation of Arts in Dartmouth College on July 16, 1967.

In discussing the general traits of Baird's later works, Bernard Jacobson wrote: "Baird's music is delicate, sensitive, fine-drawn. The influence of Berg is strongly felt in it, but refracted through the prism of Szymanowski's sensuousness. Instead of riveting the ear with decisive gestures, it persuades, cajoles, and even charms, though it does not want for drama of the more inward lyrical sort."

MAJOR WORKS

Chamber Music—String Quartet.
Choral Music—Song of Revolution, cantata; Etiuda, for voices, percussion, and piano.
Orchestral Music—3 symphonies; Sinfonietta; Concerto for Piano and Orchestra; Colas Breugnon, suite for flute and string orchestra; Ouverture Giocosa; Concerto for Orchestra; Cassation; Four Essays; Espressioni Varianti, for violin and orchestra; Variations Without a Theme; Erotica, for voice and orchestra; Epiphanic Music; Four Dialogues, for oboe and chamber orchestra; Four Novelettes.

ABOUT

Lang, P. H. and Broder, N. (eds.), Contemporary Music in Europe.

Sir Granville Bantock
1868–1946

Sir Granville Bantock was born on August 7, 1868, in London. His father, a surgeon, intended him first for chemical engineering, then for the Indian Civil Service. Since Bantock did not at first appear to be particularly musical he did not dispute his father's wishes. A few lessons in harmony and counterpoint at Trinity College, however, convinced him that he wanted to be a professional musician. In 1889 he entered the Royal Academy of Music, where his talent, combined with industry, enabled him after a single term to win the Macfarren Scholarship for composition the first time it was offered.

SIR GRANVILLE BANTOCK

During his student days at the Academy, Bantock completed several works: an Egyptian ballet suite, *Rameses II;* a dramatic cantata based on Moore's *Lalla Rookh* called *The Fire-Worshippers;* and a one-act opera, *Caedmar,* introduced in concert version at the Crystal Palace in London on October 18, 1893. Here the composer anticipated his later passion for oriental subjects.

He was graduated from the Academy in 1892. One year later, on a little less than fifteen pounds, he founded the *New Quarterly Musical Review* which, under his editorship, became a leading journal of musical opinion for the three years of its existence. At this time he supported himself by conducting orchestras for musical shows in the provinces.

On December 15, 1896, Bantock made news by conducting a concert of English music by the younger generation of composers; all the music performed was in manuscript, and was being heard for the first time. The following

May, he once again helped promote unknown English music by arranging a chamber music concert in which only the younger British composers were represented.

In 1897 he became musical director of the Tower in New Brighton, where he conducted band concerts intended for dancing and light entertainment. Bantock added strings and, before long, startled his audiences by including on his programs the serious works of leading British composers; indeed, on several occasions, he even directed all-British programs. In 1898 he founded the New Brighton Choral Society, and some time after that he became the director of the Runcorn Philharmonic Society and the Liverpool Philharmonic.

In 1898 he married Helen F. Schweitzer, a gifted poet, who not only supplied him with the lyrics for some of his best songs but inspired one of his finest works for orchestra, the *Helena Variations* (1899).

It was not until after the turn of the century that Bantock achieved recognition as a composer. It came mainly with *Omar Khayyám,* which he completed in 1909 but which had occupied him for a number of years. This is the composer's most ambitious creation, a monumental three-part setting for solo voices, chorus, and orchestra of Edward FitzGerald's third-edition adaptation of the *Rubáiyát.* The first part had been introduced at the Birmingham Festival in 1906; the second, at the Cardiff Festival in 1907; and the third, at the Birmingham Festival in 1909. Soon after the last of these performances the entire composition was given in London by the London Choral Society, and in 1912 it was successfully performed in Vienna. The rich oriental flavorings of melody and harmony, the striking orchestral colors, and the apt tonal translations of the verses made a profound impression wherever the composition was given.

The oriental influence found in this masterwork is also evident in many other Bantock compositions. But orientalism represented only a single facet of Bantock's polyglot style. A great variety of influences can be found in the extensive repertory of his works: Scottish, in the *Hebridean Symphony* (1915) and the opera *The Seal Woman,* produced in Birmingham on September 27, 1924; pagan, in the choral-ballet, *The Great God Pan* (1915) and the *Pagan Symphony* (1923–1928); biblical, in the

Barber

choral compositions *Christus* (1901), *Vanity of Vanities* (1920), and *The Seven Burdens of Isaiah* (1927); Elizabethan, in some of his songs. Whatever the influence, the style remained both sensuous and exotic, but touched with modern idioms. His music, most of which is programmatic, is richly harmonized and orchestrated, filled with spacious melodies, and always highly imaginative. He always aimed for, and usually realized, poetic beauty. Sidney Grew wrote: "His best music comes at suggestions of evening, heavy odors, aspects of physical beauty, flowers of various types, passion in a state of repose, and languid yearning."

Bantock also distinguished himself as an educator. From 1900 until 1907 he was the principal of the Birmingham Institute of Music. In 1907 he succeeded Edward Elgar as professor of music at the University of Birmingham, a post he held until 1934. In his sixty-fifth year Bantock returned to his alma mater, Trinity College, to join its music faculty. He was knighted in 1930.

Bantock was notorious for his unconventional dress. The newspapers once remarked that he was probably the first man to attend a University faculty meeting in corduroys. He detested formal evening wear. Once when compelled to wear a top hat for a public function, he returned home and smashed it in silent rage. His favorite attire was that of an oriental sheik; visitors coming to see him often found him dressed in oriental splendor from head to foot.

During the last decade of his life, Bantock traveled extensively, making several trips around the world to fill his office as traveling examiner for Trinity College. He made one of these trips in 1938, in his seventieth year, visiting India and Australia among other places. He was back in London just before the outbreak of World War II. He died of pneumonia in London on October 16, 1946.

MAJOR WORKS

Ballets—Egypt; The Great God Pan, choral ballet.

Chamber Music—3 violin sonatas; 2 cello sonatas; Sonata in F major, for viola and piano; Sonata in G minor, for unaccompanied cello; Serenade, for horns; Dramatic Poem, for cello and piano.

Choral Music—The Fire Worshippers, cantata; The Time Spirit, rhapsody; Omar Khayyám; Prometheus Unbound; Atalanta in Calydon, choral symphony; The Vanity of Vanities, choral symphony; Pilgrim's Progress; Christus, oratorio; King Solomon; various songs and suites for unaccompanied men's chorus;

part songs and arrangements for unaccompanied mixed chorus.

Opera—The Seal Woman.

Orchestral Music—Helena Variations; Thalaba, the Destroyer; Hudibras; The Witch of Atlas; Thorvenda's Dream, for narrator and orchestra; Lalla Rookh; Pierrot of the Minute, comedy overture; Dante and Beatrice; Overture to a Greek Tragedy; Fifine at the Fair; Hebridean Symphony; Pagan Symphony; Four Chinese Landscapes, for small orchestra; Aphrodite in Cyprus, symphonic ode; Two Heroic Ballads.

Piano Music—Old English Suite; Dramatic Lyrics and Romances after Browning; Dramatic Poems after Browning; Arabian Nights; Memories of Sapphire.

Vocal Music—Songs of the East (six volumes); Six Jester Songs; Sappho; Three Blake Songs; From Chinese Poets (six series); Songs from Arcady; Dramatic Lyrics (three series); Songs of Shelley; Songs of Childhood; Six Sacred Songs; Songs of the Western Isles; Songs from the Chinese (two cycles).

ABOUT

Anderton, H. O., Granville Bantock.

Musical Opinion (London), December 1946; Musical Quarterly, July 1918; Musical Times (London), November 1946.

Samuel Barber
1910–

Samuel Barber was born in West Chester, Pennsylvania, a town on the outskirts of Philadelphia, on March 9, 1910. He is the nephew of the famous opera contralto Louise Homer. His father was a doctor; his mother, a talented pianist.

Samuel began studying the piano when he was six, with William Hatton Green, a pupil of Leschetizky. One year later he made his first attempt at composition, a piano piece he entitled *Sadness*. When he was ten he planned a full-length opera. Neither of his parents did much to encourage him in his musical interests, preferring to direct him towards participating in sports and in boyish pastimes with friends. He expressed his rebellion in a brief letter to his mother which read: "To begin with, I was not meant to be an athlete. I was meant to be a composer, and will be, I'm sure. . . . Don't ask me to try to forget this and go and play football, *Please*!"

At twelve he found a job as organist in a church in West Chester at one hundred dollars a month. He also played the piano at club meetings and organized a small orchestra in the local high school. While attending high school he performed for Harold Randolph, director of the Peabody Conservatory in Baltimore. Randolph advised Barber to give up his academic schooling and devote himself entirely to music. Randolph also told Barber that a new school of music had just been founded in Philadelphia–the Curtis Institute–and encouraged Barber to apply for enrollment. In 1924, Barber became a charter student there, staying on until 1932, but without leaving high school, from which he was graduated in 1926. At the Curtis Institute, he studied the piano with Isabella Vengerova, composition with Rosario Scalero, and singing with Emilio de Gogorza. In 1928, he received the Bearns Prize for a violin sonata.

SAMUEL BARBER

Barber revealed a strong gift for lyricism in a set of three songs written in the years 1927–1928 to texts by James Stephens and A. E. Housman, as well as in an extended work, *Dover Beach*, for soprano and string quartet, written in 1931 to the poem by Matthew Arnold and introduced in New York on March 5, 1933, by Rose Bampton and the New York String Quartet. Two highly imaginative orchestral works, both completed in 1933, brought him some recognition. The first was the *Overture to the School for Scandal*, heard at the Robin Hood Dell in Philadelphia on August 30, 1933, which brought Barber the Bearns Prize for a second time. The other was *Music for a Scene from Shelley*, inspired by Shelley's *Prometheus Unbound;* its première took place in New York on March 24, 1935, with Werner Janssen conducting the New York Philharmonic.

In 1935 Barber received both a Pulitzer Traveling Scholarship and the American Prix de Rome. He spent several months in Austria and Italy. In Vienna he gave a number of Lieder recitals (he was now an accomplished singer), including on his programs some of his own songs; he also conducted. He then settled at the American Academy in Rome as a Prix de Rome winner. There he completed his first symphony, the *Symphony in One Movement*, which he described as a "synthetic treatment of a four-movement classical symphony." The four sections of the traditional symphony are here compressed into one, constructed from three themes stated at the opening of the work. The première in Rome on December 13, 1936, by the Augusteo Orchestra conducted by Bernardino Molinari was a success. On January 21, 1937, Artur Rodzinski introduced the symphony to the United States in a performance by the Cleveland Orchestra. That same summer, on July 25, Rodzinski conducted it at the Salzburg Festival in Austria–the first time an American symphony was presented there. Barber revised his symphony in 1942, the new version being presented on February 8, 1944, with Bruno Walter conducting the Philadelphia Orchestra.

In 1936 Barber received the Pulitzer Traveling Scholarship a second time. After returning to the United States, he joined the faculty of the Curtis Institute where for a number of years he taught orchestration and conducting.

On November 5, 1938, Barber became the first American composer to be represented on a program of the NBC Symphony Orchestra, Arturo Toscanini conducting. At that time, not one but two of his compositions were played which to this day have remained popular: the *Adagio*, for strings, and the *Essay No. 1*, for orchestra. The *Adagio* was an adaptation of the slow movement of Barber's early String Quartet in B minor – serene, contemplative music built from a single melodic idea which the violins present at the outset of the composition. In the *Essay No. 1*, Barber borrowed a literary form for music to suggest an architectonic structure in which a thought is projected at the opening and then permitted to develop to a logical conclusion in the same way that a central thought unfolds in an essay. *Essay No. 1*, a scherzo, comprises a number of simple themes developed freely, along modest lines. In both the *Adagio* and the *Essay* Barber was the conservative composer paying a good deal of attention to structure and not afraid to give free rein to his melodic inspiration. Simplicity is preferred to complexity, while the main attempt is to seek out a poetic idea. Because this music is neither regional nor national, because it is projected with such sincerity and filled with such beauty, it has enjoyed enormous success in the concert halls of the world and in recordings. Sibelius expressed his delight at the *Adagio*. When the United States was in mourning for President John F. Kennedy, the *Adagio* was played over the radio on a coast-to-coast broadcast as a memorial tribute. The *Essay No. 1* inspired an ovation in Moscow in 1945. Barber wrote a second *Essay* for orchestra in 1942, given for the first time by the New York Philharmonic under Bruno Walter on April 16, 1942.

In 1943 Barber was inducted into the army. A few months later he was transferred to the Air Force where his duties were chiefly musical. He was commissioned to write a symphony in honor of the Air Force, an assignment he completed in 1944. This was somewhat more astringent and dissonant music than Barber had written up to this time, obviously inspired and influenced by Barber's war experiences. It was also more programmatic, since parts suggested in tones the sound of a radio beam and that of a plane spiraling to earth. This work was performed by the Boston Symphony under Koussevitzky on March 3, 1944. One week later it was transmitted by short wave throughout the world by the Office of War Information. Barber revised the symphony extensively in 1947, eliminating all programmatic descriptions of air flight. The new version was introduced in Philadelphia on January 21, 1948, with Alexander Hilsberg conducting the Philadelphia Orchestra.

After his discharge from the Air Force, Barber returned to "Capricorn," his rambling home near Mt. Kisco, New York, acquired before the war with Gian Carlo Menotti, who had been a friend since student days. At Capricorn Barber wrote the major works of the next two decades which gave him a place of first importance among American composers. One of the earliest of these was the Concerto for Cello and Orchestra–introduced by Raya Garbousova and the Boston Symphony under Koussevitzky on April 5, 1946–which earned for its composer a citation from the New York Music Critics Circle. This was followed by the ballet *Medea* (originally called *The Serpent Heart*, then renamed *Cave of the Heart*), commissioned for Martha Graham and her dancers by the Ditson Fund; its world première was given in New York City on May 10, 1946. Two orchestral works derived from this ballet score have since become successful–one was the *Medea Suite*, which Eugene Ormandy first conducted with the Philadelphia Orchestra on December 5, 1947; the other was *Medea's Meditation and Dance of Death*, introduced by Dimitri Mitropoulos and the New York Philharmonic on February 2, 1956.

Other major compositions followed: *Knoxville: Summer of 1915*, text by John Agee, performed by Eleanor Steber and the Boston Symphony under Koussevitzky on April 9, 1948; *Piano Sonata in E-Flat Minor*, commissioned by the League of Composers with funds provided by Richard Rodgers and Irving Berlin and introduced by Vladimir Horowitz on January 23, 1950; *Prayers of Kierkegaard*, a major choral work with the dimensions of an oratorio, presented by the Boston Symphony and the Cecilia Society, with Leontyne Price as soloist and Charles Münch conducting, on December 3, 1954.

Barber's style was now set and established, combining strong lyrical and emotional elements with modern harmonic and rhythmic approaches. Arthur Cohn said of Barber's music: "Lyricism is the dominant feature. . . . He knows how to spin a real melody. . . . His strongest link with the past is in his formal practice: the classical concept of the sonata remains the point of emphasis, even when Barber reshapes it to suit the work at hand." Cohn finds in Barber "more freedom in his harmonic language" without the sacrifice of a "basic romantic accent, even when some salty polytonal words are utilized." And he sums up: "Barber is never academic; he is merely concerned with earlier times, though he is of the twentieth century."

On January 15, 1958, the Metropolitan

30

Opera presented Barber's first opera, *Vanessa*, libretto by Gian Carlo Menotti, who also served as stage director. The setting is a Scandinavian city in 1905. The heroine has been waiting twenty years for the return of her lover, who is dead. Her lover's son, Anatol, turns up instead. He has an affair with Vanessa's niece, Erika, and offers to marry her, but is turned down because Erika knows Anatol does not love her. In the end, Anatol goes off with Vanessa, leaving Erika behind to take Vanessa's place as the forsaken woman waiting in vain for her lover.

In his review in the New York *Times*, Howard Taubman said: "The composer's confidence grows as he finds that he is not only breathing in the strange world but actually absorbed by it. He responds to the adventure, with expanding assurance. He unbends and allows himself a waltz, a country dance, a hymn, a genial aria or two. In the final scene he writes a grand quintet, a full blown set piece that packs an emotional charge and that would be a credit to any composer anywhere today. It is wonderful to behold: By the time he has reached the last act Mr. Barber has learned to write for the lyric theatre with perception and impact. For a man of forty-seven whose work has been largely in absolute music this is an impressive achievement."

Vanessa received the Pulitzer Prize in music. It also made Metropolitan Opera history: as the first world première given during Rudolf Bing's regime as general manager; as the first new American opera mounted at the Metropolitan in eleven years; and as the second American opera to be produced at the Metropolitan for more than two seasons. Still another distinction was earned by *Vanessa*. When it was given its European première at Salzburg in 1958, it became the first American opera ever produced at this world-famous festival.

Barber received a second Pulitzer Prize in music–in 1962, for his Piano Concerto which the publishing house of G. Schirmer had commissioned to help celebrate the centenary of its founding. The concerto was a major attraction during opening week at Philharmonic Hall at the Lincoln Center of the Performing Arts in New York City, where it was presented on September 24, 1962, with John Browning as soloist with the Boston Symphony

conducted by Erich Leinsdorf. In the spring of 1965, this concerto was prominently featured on the programs of the Cleveland Orchestra, conducted by George Szell, during a successful tour of Europe. "It made a decided hit with the audience," reported Harold C. Schonberg in the New York *Times* after the world première, "and it may be that Mr. Barber has supplied a repertory piece. . . . This is a real virtuoso concerto, with some staggeringly difficult writing. It also has a strong melodic profile, a lyric slow movement and a sense of confidence in the entire conception–the confidence that comes only from an experienced composer engaged in a work that interests him."

With the building of a new house for the Metropolitan Opera at the Lincoln Center for the Performing Arts, Rudolf Bing once more called upon Barber–this time to write a new opera to inaugurate the theatre. Barber responded with *Antony and Cleopatra*, its libretto freely adapted from the Shakespeare drama by Franco Zeffirelli, who had also been engaged to stage and design the production. On September 16, 1966, *Antony and Cleopatra* was presented. Bearing in mind the purpose for which the opera was written, Barber created a grand opera along spacious lines, emphasizing the chorus, ballet, and spectacular scenes. To most critics the result proved a disappointment. The libretto had taken far too much liberty with Shakespeare, and not to its advantage; the staging and costuming were often overpretentious with what Harold C. Schonberg called "artifice masquerading with great flourish as art." There were good moments in the Barber score–the dynamic ballet music, some of the eloquent choral episodes, and the affecting closing scene–but not enough to eliminate dullness. Schonberg put it this way: "[The music] was skillfully put together but lacking ardor and eloquence; big in sound but stingy with arresting melodic ideas."

For several years, Barber was the vice president of the International Music Council of UNESCO in Paris. In 1958 he became a member of the American Academy of Arts. In 1959 he received an honorary doctorate from Harvard.

In a revealing personal portrait of Barber, Nathan Broder disclosed that the composer still possesses many of the traits and habits he had as a boy and as a young man. "He is still withdrawn and rather cold, though urbane, when with people he does not know well, but a spring of humor occasionally bubbles to the surface." When Barber is with people he knows and likes "his humor ripples merrily along." Except for playing the piano, he is inept in manual dexterity. Gian Carlo Menotti once said that Barber was probably the only soldier in the United States who never learned to take a gun apart and put it together again. Broder adds: "He is constantly losing things and cannot fry an egg or operate a phonograph."

Among Barber's interests are literature (Stendhal is a particular favorite), art, travel, and food (especially soups). He loves walking in the country. When he was sixteen, his parents gave him a roadster. After he learned to drive and received his license he put the car in a garage and kept it there for a year, preferring to walk.

Barber is a slow and painstaking composer. His search for a precise theme for a musical composition is always arduous. Says Broder: "When he is engaged in such a search he is usually in a bad temper and wanders about, silent and melancholy. He has been seen in a train drawing staves and writing notes in the air with his fingers and erasing them with a sweep of the hand." But once he finds the theme he is looking for his mood changes and he becomes exhilarated.

By the time he has finished a page of manuscript it is—according to his publisher, Hans W. Heinsheimer—"a model of perfection. It is not only checked meticulously for errors, for a wrong or missing rest, for a hemidemisemiquaver that has a hemi too much or a demi too little—it is also written very clearly in an interesting, original, yet very legible hand and it is completely ready for the copyist and the printer. It is the first, and at the same time, the final and definitive draft of the music." Barber's copyist, Arnold Arnstein, has compared the manuscript of a Barber score to an engraving.

MAJOR WORKS

Ballets—Medea (originally named The Serpent Heart, then Cave of the Heart); Souvenirs.

Chamber Music—Serenade, for string quartet; Dover Beach, for soprano and string quartet; Sonata for Cello and Piano; String Quartet; Summer Music, for woodwind quintet.

Choral Music—The Virgin Martyrs; Let Down the Bars, O Death; A Stopwatch and an Ordnance Map; Reincarnations; Prayers of Kierkegaard.

Operas—Vanessa; A Hand of Bridge, one-act; Antony and Cleopatra.

Orchestral Music—2 symphonies; Overture to the School for Scandal; Music for a Scene from Shelley; Adagio, for strings; Essays, Nos. 1 and 2; Concerto for Violin and Orchestra; Capricorn Concerto, for flute, oboe, trumpet, and strings; Concerto for Cello and Orchestra; Medea, suite; Knoxville: Summer of 1915, for soprano and orchestra; Medea's Meditation and Dance of Vengeance; Toccata Festiva, for organ and orchestra; Dei Natali, preludes for Christmas; Concerto for Piano and Orchestra; Mutations from Bach.

Piano Music—Excursions; Sonata; Souvenirs; Nocturne.

Vocal Music—Hermit Songs; Mélodies Passagères; numerous individual songs for voice and piano, including Bessie Bobtail, Daisies, Nuvoletta, The Queen's Face on the Summer Coin, Rain Has Fallen, Sleep Now, and With Rue My Heart Is Laden.

ABOUT

Broder, N., Samuel Barber; Cohn, A., Twentieth Century Music in the Western Hemisphere.

Modern Music, March–April 1945; Musical America, March 1960; Musical Quarterly, July 1948; New York Times Magazine, August 28, 1966; Saturday Review, September 17, 1966.

Henri Barraud
1900–

Henri Barraud was born in Bordeaux on April 23, 1900. While employed on his father's wine farm he began the study of music, first by himself, later with a local teacher. In 1926 he entered the Paris Conservatory but was expelled the same year because of his interest in modern idioms and his refusal to accept textbook rules. He continued to study privately, composition with Louis Aubert and Paul Dukas, fugue with Caussade.

His career as a composer was given a strong boost by Pierre Monteux, who in 1932 presented the finale from Barraud's first symphony, and two years later Barraud's *Poème*. In the latter composition, Barraud revealed an interest in impressionism, but he soon turned to modal writing, stimulated by his fascination for gothicism and neomedievalism. The neomedieval tendency was uppermost in an *opéra comique*, *La Farce de Maître Pathelin*, the

Barraud: bä rō′

libretto for which (by Gustave Cohen) was based on a medieval play. This opera, though completed in 1938, had to wait a decade for its première. It was introduced at the Opéra-Comique in Paris on June 24, 1948. A ballet, *Le Diable à la Kermesse* (1943), was also based on a medieval play.

In July 1936 Barraud married Dénise Parly. A year later he became the director of music at the International Exposition in Paris and the head of a chamber-opera company which specialized in French works.

HENRI BARRAUD

In August 1939, on the day he completed his Concerto for Piano and Orchestra, he was called to rejoin the 17th Infantry Regiment at Mans, which he had previously served as Reserve Lieutenant and which had just been remobilized. Barraud served in the French army during World War II. Following the fall of France he went into hiding in Marseilles. In 1943 he returned to Paris where he became a member of the Front National, an underground organization.

From his World War II experiences emerged a poignant work for orchestra, *Offrande à une Ombre*. This music reflected the grim spirit of the French patriot in time of war and enemy occupation. A correspondent for *Musical America* described this tone poem as follows: "A long melodic line of lovely grace, freely drawn and contrapuntally treated, is followed by a tense, war-like section, evoking the hero's part in the struggle, which ends abruptly with

a drum roll and a tamtam crash clearly depicting the rendezvous with death." Barraud originally intended to dedicate the composition to the memory of Maurice Jaubert, a French composer killed during the war. But Barraud's own brother had been shot by the Gestapo on August 1, 1944, and Barraud extended his dedication to include him as well. On January 10, 1947, *Offrande à une Ombre* received its première performance in the United States, with Vladimir Golschmann conducting the St. Louis Symphony.

Barraud dedicated another work to the memory of his brother: a five-part oratorio, *The Mystery of the Holy Innocents*, based on a text from the third "Mystery" of Charles Péguy. This oratorio was broadcast over the Paris radio on May 8, 1947, Manuel Rosenthal conducting; it was introduced in the United States on December 1, 1950, by Serge Koussevitzky and the Boston Symphony.

Meanwhile, the piano concerto Barraud had completed in 1939 just before he joined the French army was given its first hearing when E. Robert Schmitz performed it in New York on December 5, 1946, with Manuel Rosenthal conducting the New York Philharmonic. This collaboration of Manuel Rosenthal as conductor and Barraud as composer was a sentimental reunion, for it brought together on the stage two musicians who had been comrades-in-arms in the French Resistance movement during World War II. So determined was Rosenthal to present his friend's concerto that not even a delay in the arrival of the master score in New York would tempt him to postpone the performance. Rosenthal hurriedly assembled the individual parts (which had already come to New York) and sat up all night synchronizing them into a single score he could use during rehearsals and at the actual performance. He described the concerto as "impassioned, replete, with a quality best explained as pathos. The second movement is lyrically concentrated, yet warm and sensuous. The third is fiery and impetuous."

In 1948 Barraud was appointed director of the Program National at the Radiodiffusion Française in Paris, supervising the radio presentation of cultural programs, a post he has held since that time.

In the 1950's Charles Münch, conductor of the Boston Symphony, introduced to America

Bartók

two major works by Barraud. One was the *Te Deum*, for chorus and orchestra, written in memory of Serge Koussevitzky. Its world première had taken place at the Venice Festival in September 1956, and the American première followed on April 27, 1957 in Boston. The critic of *Musical America* described this music as "stark and austere, quasi-archaic with steady rhythmic progress and decided power." One year later Münch and the Boston Symphony performed Barraud's Third Symphony in the presence of the composer himself, who had come to the United States as a guest of the State Department. For Harold C. Schonberg, this symphony was a "neo-Honegger work, rather academic sounding, with plenty of rhetoric, anguished horn calls and grim mood." The symphony was also heard in Strasbourg, France, on June 14, 1958, at the festival of the International Society for Contemporary Music.

One of Barraud's most important works after the Third Symphony was his *opera buffa Lavinia*, whose world première took place at Aix-en-Provence on July 20, 1961.

Despite his interest in medieval subjects and his occasional partiality for modal harmonies, Barraud has made effective use of such modern techniques as the twelve-tone system in some of his most ambitious compositions.

MAJOR WORKS

Ballets—Le Diable à la Kermesse; L'Astrologue dans le Puits.

Chamber Music—Concerto da Camera, for thirty instruments; Trio, for oboe, clarinet, and bassoon; String Trio; String Quartet; Sonatina for Violin and Piano.

Choral Music—Deux Chœurs; Le Feu; Le Testament de Villon, cantata; Le Mystère des Saints Innocents (Mystery of the Holy Innocents), oratorio; Cantate pour l'Avènement du Prince de Monaco; Te Deum; Pange Lingua, motet.

Operas—La Farce de Maître Pathelin; Numance; Lavinia.

Orchestral Music—3 symphonies; 2 rhapsodies; Poème; Trois Chansons de Gramadoch, for voice and orchestra; Concerto for Piano and Orchestra; Suite pour une Comédie de Musset; Offrande à une Ombre; Preludes, for strings; Concerto for Flute and String Orchestra.

Piano Music—Preludes (two series); Six Impromptus; Musiques pour les Petits Mains.

Vocal Music—Trois Poèmes; Trois Lettres de Mme. de Sévigné; Quatre Poèmes; Chantefables.

ABOUT

Tempo (London), 1957.

Béla Bartók
1881–1945

Béla Bartók was born in Nagyszentmiklós, Hungary, on March 25, 1881. He was a sickly child, suffering from, among other things, a severe bronchial condition. Prevented from playing with other children, he became a quiet, introspective child who spent his time reading, listening to his mother sing and tell stories, and involving himself in musical activities. He took his first piano lesson on his fifth birthday from his mother, and one month later he was playing four-hand piano duets with her. His mother soon discovered that he had absolute pitch.

BÉLA BARTÓK

When Béla was eight, his father died. His mother took over the financial burden of the family, supporting it by giving piano lessons. After the Bartók family moved to the town of Nagyszollos in 1889, Bartók composed his first piece, a waltz for the piano, and continued his piano studies with a local teacher. There on May 1, 1892, he made his first public appearance as a pianist and composer. Following this concert, the Bartók family moved again, this time to the city formerly known as Pressburg but now identified as Bratislava. Here could be found richer opportunities for young Bartók to develop himself musically. László

Bartók: bŏr′tōk

34

Erkel taught him the piano, and Ernst von Dohnányi (four years Béla's senior) became his friend and adviser. With Dohnányi's encouragement, Bartók went to Budapest in 1899 to enter the Royal Academy of Music. He stayed there four years as a pupil of István Thomán and Hans Koessler. For about two years he did no composing whatsoever, concentrating entirely on developing his piano playing with the hope of becoming a concert virtuoso. He gave a performance at the Academy on October 21, 1901, which led the school reviewer to say: "He plays the piano as thunderously as a little Jupiter. In fact, he is today the only piano student at the Academy who may follow in Dohnányi's footsteps." A public appearance at the Royal Hall followed less than six months later.

Hearing a performance of Richard Strauss's *Thus Spake Zarathustra* lifted him out of his temporary creative stagnation. "At last," he said, "I saw the way that lay before me. Straightway I threw myself into a study of Strauss's scores and began to compose." He also studied Liszt's tone poems which affected him almost as profoundly as did those of Strauss. Still another important influence at the same time was the rising tide of nationalism that swept over Hungary and led to a revival of interest in Hungarian culture. This patriotic movement, in which Bartók was caught up, led him to think for the first time about national music.

During 1902 his first publication appeared: four songs to verses by Lajos Pósa. During the same year he also wrote a scherzo, for orchestra, which he originally intended as a movement of a symphony that never materialized. This scherzo was performed by the Budapest Opera Orchestra on February 29, 1904. His first significant composition was a patriotic tone poem, *Kossuth*–inspired by and modeled after Richard Strauss's *A Hero's Life*. *Kossuth* was a Hungarian "hero's life" in ten tableaux describing the events attending the Hungarian war of independence in 1848–1849 under the leadership of Lajos Kossuth, the revolutionary. When *Kossuth* was performed for the first time (January 13, 1904, by the Budapest Philharmonic under István Kerner), it received an ovation. Later the work was played in Manchester, England, under Hans Richter's direction.

Bartók first became attracted to Hungarian folk music late in 1904. Visiting Kibed, in the Maros-Torda region of Hungary, he heard an eighteen-year-old peasant, named Lidi Dósa, sing an unusual melody, and he was made aware of the existence of a Hungarian folk-song literature quite different from any he had thus far known. In 1905 he made his first journey through Hungary in search of folk songs and came upon a rich lode, which he assembled into *Twenty Hungarian Folksongs*, published in December of 1906. This was his first folk-song publication. For the next eight years he continued his musicoethnological researches, frequently in the company of Zoltán Kodály, writing down music and making recordings. In this way he collected over six thousand melodies. This treasure–dug out of obscurity by Bartók's patient searchings–revealed to the world that authentic Hungarian music was far different from the sentimental tunes formerly popularized by Brahms and Liszt. This music was savage, passionate, barbaric in rhythms, esoteric in melodies, often based on old ecclesiastical modes.

This folk art made a profound impression on Bartók, as he himself explained: "The outcome of these studies was a decisive influence upon my work, because it freed me from the tyrannical use of the major and minor keys. The greater part of the collected treasure, and the more valuable part, was in old ecclesiastical or old Greek modes, or based on the more primitive scales, and the melodies were full of most free and varied rhythmic phrases and changes of tempi, played both rubato and giusto. It became clear to me that the old modes, which had been forgotten in our music, had lost nothing of their vigor. Their new employment made new rhythmic combinations possible. This new way of using the diatonic scale brought freedom from the rigid use of the major and minor keys, and eventually led to a new conception of the chromatic scale, every tone of which came to be considered of equal value and could be used freely and independently."

In his youth, Bartók had been a disciple of Brahms. Later on he profited from Richard Strauss and Liszt. Now, stimulated by his study of Hungarian folk music, he evolved a style of his own in which the basic elements were the same as those found in Hungarian folk songs and dances. "Bartók," said Lawrence Gilman, "steeped his own compositions in the somberness and wildness and humor of this ancient, authentic music of the Hungarian peasantry. . . . Thus the past of his nation lives again in Bartók, amazingly sophisticated and metamorphosed, but charged with its old power and raciness and savor."

"The musical language of a 'national composer' must be as natural to him as his native tongue," wrote Béla Bartók in 1931. "The appropriate use of folksong material, the basis for national music, is not limited to the sporadic introduction or imitation of old melodies, or to the arbitrary thematic use of them in work of foreign or international tendencies. It is rather a matter of absorbing the means of musical expression hidden in them, just as the most subtle possibilities of any language may be assimilated. It is necessary for the composer to command this musical language so completely that it becomes the natural expression of his musical ideas."

The first compositions in which Bartók's creative personality began to emerge were the *Two Portraits*, for orchestra (1907–1908), introduced in Budapest in 1909, and the *Two Romanian Dances*, for piano (1909–1910), which Leo Weiner transcribed for orchestra in 1939. During the next few years Bartók's own severe and austere style slowly crystallized through the exploitation of the primitive rhythms and modal harmonies of Hungarian folk music. With the *Allegro Barbaro*, for piano (1911), Bartók "first comes of age," as Halsey Stevens has remarked. Here a true Magyar style is developed as Bartók releases a savage rhythmic momentum. In 1911 he completed a grim, intense, austere one-act opera, *Bluebeard's Castle*, libretto by Béla Balász. This opera was first performed in Budapest on May 24, 1918; it was given for the first time in the United States by the New York City Opera on October 2, 1952. In 1917, in the second string quartet, Bartók's pronounced individuality asserted itself for the first time within the string-quartet format. Then came the one-act danced pantomime *The Miraculous Mandarin* (1916); the *Dance Suite*, for orchestra (1923); the third string quartet (1927–1928); two rhapsodies, for violin and orchestra (1928); the composer's most important work

for chorus, the *Cantata Profana* (1930); and the Second Piano Concerto (1931).

The increasing complexity of Bartók's writing made performances of his major works few and far between, and most of them when heard made a poor impression. The world première of *The Miraculous Mandarin*, in Cologne on November 27, 1927, was a fiasco—though this was due more to the lurid and realistic libretto set in a city slum than to the music. The second string quartet was decisively rejected at first hearing, in Budapest on March 3, 1918. Nevertheless Bartók did enjoy one or two minor successes, and these came with the premières of his ballet, *The Wooden Prince* (Budapest, May 12, 1917); the opera *Bluebeard's Castle* (1918); and the *Dance Suite*, an orchestral work, first performed in Budapest on November 19, 1923.

The greatest success achieved by Bartók up to this time came with the world première of his Second Piano Concerto, which the composer himself performed in Frankfurt on January 23, 1933, under Hans Rosbaud's direction. Critics in Germany and musical correspondents in Germany praised it highly. The critic for the *Neue Züricher Zeitung* wrote: "Original forces, hardly existent up to now in European music, break out in the earnest first movement—accompanied exclusively by wind instruments—into an elemental *allegro barbaro*; but it is controlled force. A world of higher spiritual order, wonderful plasticity and clarity of form, is built in the slow movement from strict alternation of piano-recitative (with kettledrum) and muted string sound. And what deep originality in the shaping of the presto middle section, what abundance of fantasy in the demonic finale. The piano concerto numbers among the most important, the strongest of the new works." In short order, the Second Piano Concerto was heard in Amsterdam at the festival of the International Society for Contemporary Music, and then in London, Stockholm, Strasbourg, Vienna, Winterthur, Zürich, and Budapest.

In 1907 Bartók assumed the post he was to hold for the next thirty years, that of teacher of piano at the Royal Academy of Music in Budapest, succeeding his own teacher, Thomán. One of his pupils in 1907 was Marta Ziegler, then fourteen years old. The growing attachment that soon developed between teacher and pupil was shown in 1908 when Bartók dedicated to her the first of a series of compositions, *Portrait of a Girl*, the first number in *Seven Sketches*, for piano, op. 9. They were married in 1909; in August 1910, a son, Béla, was born to them. They were divorced in 1923, and the same year Bartók married Ditta Pásztory, a concert pianist, by whom he had another son, Peter.

Bartók's principal works in the 1930's reveal him at the height of his technical and creative powers: the fifth and sixth string quartets (1934, 1939); *Music for Strings, Percussion and Celesta* (1936), introduced in Basel on January 21, 1937; the Second Violin Concerto (1938), performed for the first time in Amsterdam on March 23, 1939; the Divertimento, for string orchestra, world première in Basel on June 11, 1940.

In the New York *Times*, Otto Gombosi singled out the contributions made by Bartók to twentieth century music up to 1940: "What has Bartók given to modern music? First, a richness of new harmonic possibilities. The influence of Debussy did not lead him into coloristic effects, but to an ingenious and daring extension of tonality to the utmost limits. Then he gave to modern music a kind of rhythm which seems to incorporate the elemental powers of nature—a rhythm creating form. He gave to modern music a flourishing melody, which grew up from assimilated elements of folklore to a quite individual richness and originality. He gave examples of formal perfection, growing organically from the material. And finally he gave to modern music a ripe polyphony that has very little to do with neoclassicism and which is formed with an iron consistency that reaches extreme possibilities."

Lawrence Gilman aptly described the Bartók style up to 1940 as "acrid, powerful, intransigeant: the musician of darkly passionate imagination, austerely sensuous, ruthlessly logical, a cerebral rhapsodist; a tone poet who is both an uncompromising modernist and the resurrector of the ancient past."

In the years between the middle 1920's and 1940, Bartók traveled extensively, appearing as pianist in performances of his music. He took his first trip to the United States in 1927,

making his debut in New York City as soloist with the New York Philharmonic, Willem Mengelberg conducting. During that first American tour, Bartók appeared with major orchestras in Cincinnati, Philadelphia, and Boston, and he also performed in piano recitals and with chamber music groups across the country.

In the spring of 1940, Bartók returned to the United States for concert appearances. While he was in America, arrangements were made for him to stay in the country permanently. A research grant was created for him at Columbia University where he could pursue studies in folk music in any way he wished at a yearly salary of three thousand dollars. After returning to Hungary to arrange his affairs, Bartók finally settled down in America on October 29, 1940. Since his appointment at Columbia did not begin until March 1941, he was able to make a transcontinental tour.

Bartók's appointment at Columbia was terminated at the end of 1942. Small though his salary had been, it proved a significant addition to the meager income he could earn from random concert appearances and lectures. Deprived of this regular stipend, Bartók and his wife were thrown into dire financial straits. To make matters still worse, his health was deteriorating alarmingly. He ran a fever almost continuously for a year, and pains in his joints made it impossible for him to walk at times. His spirits were as low as his strength. The fact that his music was being so little heard in America dejected him. And he never became completely acclimated to a new country with foreign ways and a strange language.

The American Society of Composers, Authors and Publishers (ASCAP) was made aware of Bartók's condition and provided the funds to have him hospitalized. The tests that followed failed to provide a clue to the nature of his illness. As Bartók wrote to a friend on June 28, 1943: "The doctors don't know the real cause of my illness—and, consequently, can't treat and cure it! They are groping about as in a darkness, trying desperately to invent the most extraordinary hypotheses. But all of that is of no avail."

While in the hospital, Bartók was visited by Serge Koussevitzky, who brought a commission from the Koussevitzky Music Foundation for an orchestral work. Out of the hospital, Bartók spent the summer months in a New York hotel room working upon the *Concerto for Orchestra* for Koussevitzky. He completed it the same fall–his first new composition written in the United States. Koussevitzky conducted the world première with the Boston Symphony on December 1, 1944, with Bartók present. It scored a major success and has since become one of Bartók's most highly regarded and most frequently performed orchestral compositions.

"The general mood of the work," the composer explained, "represents, apart from the jesting second movement, a gradual transition from the sternness of the first movement and the lugubrious death song of the third, to the life assertion of the last one. . . . The title . . . is explained by its tendency to treat the single instruments or instrumental groups in *concertante*, or soloistic, manner."

When the Concerto was introduced in New York, on January 10, 1945, Olin Downes described it as follows: "It begins with a somber prelude, the theme in the lower strings several times repeated, with a sort of mirage-like reflection of itself in harmonies of the upper strings. Mr. Bartók says that the second movement, scherzo-like, is a jest–though one would say a bitter one–and the third a lamentation. There are references in the fourth movement to the first, and, as a brilliant and entertaining contrast, a joyous whirling finale in the Hungarian style. Often there is the suggestion of dance rhythms and of the sing-song of folk strains–a 'happy' and resolute ending."

In 1944 Bartók also completed one more work, a Sonata for Solo Violin, which Yehudi Menuhin had commissioned and which was introduced by Menuhin in New York on November 26, 1944.

The works Bartók left unfinished were brought to their completion by Bartók's friend Tibor Serly. The first was the Concerto No. 3, for piano and orchestra. Bartók's son Peter, on leave from the Navy, sat by the composer's bedside to rule out the score paper on which Bartók scribbled his music. Bartók looked upon this composition as his spiritual will and testament to the world; he dedicated it to his wife. On the last bar of his sketch copy he wrote the Hungarian word *vege* (the end)– something he had never done before. Ob-

viously, Bartók realized that his life work was over.

Bartók managed to write all but the last seventeen measures of this piano concerto, which Serly was able to develop and orchestrate. The concerto was introduced posthumously on February 8, 1946, with György Sándor as soloist with the Philadelphia Orchestra conducted by Eugene Ormandy. "It is a fine work noble in content," reported Howard Taubman in the New York *Times*. "The ideas in the three movements are bold and original . . . and the writing has the mastery one expects from him. . . . His concerto moves from beginning to end with an undeviating assurance. And there is–most affecting of all–a serenity in the slow movement that could only be the work of a man who had risen above the pains of the flesh."

Bartók also left fifteen unnumbered pages of a draft of a viola concerto which William Primrose had commissioned. To Tibor Serly fell the exacting task of deciphering all these sketches, putting them in a proper sequence, completing the unfinished harmonies, and doing all the orchestration. It took Serly two years to complete this job. William Primrose introduced the reconstructed concerto in Minneapolis–with the Minneapolis Symphony under the direction of Antal Dorati–on December 2, 1949.

With the liberation of Hungary in 1945, the provisional government extended Bartók an invitation to return to his native land. He had every expectation of doing so before the year ended. On September 26, 1945, however, Bartók died of leukemia in a hospital in New York. One of the last things he said was, "The trouble is that I have to go with so much still to say."

By a curious irony, Bartók received in death the general recognition and acclaim in the United States denied him for the most part while he was still alive. Within a few months of his passing, there were forty-eight major orchestral performances of his compositions, twenty-five of them in the months of January and February 1946 alone. Several of his works elicited ovations. Since 1946, performances and recordings have been both frequent and successful. In 1949 the Juilliard String Quartet presented all six of Bartók's string quartets in a cycle of performances in New York City, an event that proved once and for all that Bartók's six quartets were among the most significant contributions to chamber music in the twentieth century. In 1951 the New York City Ballet presented *The Miraculous Mandarin*, and in 1952 the New York City Opera produced *Bluebeard's Castle*. At the same time, Bartók's piano and orchestral music had become basic to the contemporary repertory. Virtually everything Bartók had written has been recorded at least once, and most of his celebrated works have been made available in several different recordings.

In a memorial essay published in a Swiss journal in 1945, Paul Sacher, the distinguished conductor, contributed the following description of the composer: "Whoever met Bartók, thinking of the rhythmic strength of his work, was surprised by his slight, delicate figure. He had the outward appearance of a fine-nerved scholar. Possessed of fanatical will and pitiless severity, and propelled by an ardent spirit, he affected inaccessibility and was reservedly polite. His being breathed light and brightness; his eyes burned with a noble fire. In the flash of his searching glance no falseness nor obscurity could endure. If in performance an especially hazardous and refractory passage came off well, he laughed in boyish glee; and when he was pleased with the successful solution of a problem, he actually beamed. That meant more than forced compliments, which I never heard from his mouth."

Erno Balogh tells us further: "This man, whose music had elemental sweep, barbaric rhythms and penetrating force, never weighed more than one hundred and sixteen pounds and sometimes as little as eighty-seven. His slow, even measured walk was characteristic of his personality. . . . But the small and fragile body was endowed with an iron will and an uncompromising character. . . . He was interested in everything: science, foreign countries, unusual foods, literature, languages, and especially philosophy. He was, in fact, more interested in things than in people. This knowledge of fields other than music was not superficial; he penetrated deeply into a subject and had a strong passion for accuracy. . . . He not only never had luxury but resented the thought of it. He refused to ask favors or to accept help. . . . It was not easy to help him, as he did not want charity."

MAJOR WORKS

Ballets—The Wooden Prince; The Miraculous Mandarin (danced pantomime).

Chamber Music—6 string quartets; 2 violin sonatas; Forty-four Duos, for two violins; Contrasts, for violin, clarinet, and piano; Sonata for Solo Violin.

Choral Music—Three Village Scenes; Cantata Profana; Hungarian, Romanian, and Slovak folk songs.

Opera—Bluebeard's Castle, one act.

Orchestral Music—3 piano concertos; 2 violin concertos; 2 rhapsodies, for violin and orchestra (also for violin and piano); 2 suites; Kossuth; Two Portraits; Dance Suite; Music for Strings, Percussion and Celesta; Divertimento; Concerto for Orchestra; Concerto for Viola and Orchestra (reconstructed, completed, and orchestrated by Tibor Serly); Romanian folk dances, Transylvanian Dances, Hungarian Peasant Songs.

Piano Music—Allegro Barbaro; Sonatina; Suite; Mikrokosmos, six books comprising 153 graded pieces; For Children, four books comprising 85 pieces; Bagatelles, Burlesques, Elegies, Sketches, Hungarian Peasant Songs, Romanian Christmas Songs, Romanian Dances, Rondos, Studies.

Vocal Music—Various songs for voice and piano; various arrangements of Hungarian, Romanian, and Slovak folk songs.

ABOUT

Bátor, V., The Béla Bartók Archives; Bonis, F. (ed.), Béla Bartók: His Life in Pictures; Fassett, A., The Naked Face of Genius: Béla Bartók's American Years; Haraszti, E., Béla Bartók: His Life and Times; Jemnitz, A., Béla Bartók: His Life and Music; Lesznaj, L., Béla Bartók: Sein Leben, Seine Werke; Moreux, S., Béla Bartók; Petzoldt, R., Béla Bartók: Sein Leben in Bildern; Stevens, H., The Life and Music of Béla Bartók; Szabolcsi, B. (ed.), Béla Bartók, Leben und Werk; Szentkirály, J. (ed.), Béla Bartók.

Modern Music, Winter 1946; Musical Quarterly, January 1946.

Leslie Bassett
1923–

Leslie Bassett, the son of a rancher, was born on January 22, 1923, in Hanford, California. His mother gave him piano lessons when he was about five. Two years later the family settled in Fresno, California, where Bassett attended the public schools. There, in his fourteenth year, he began to study the trombone, which became his favorite instrument. In high school, he played the trombone in various jazz combinations and did arrangements for several concert and dance groups. At sixteen he made his first tentative efforts at composition by writing a march for band.

In 1940 he was graduated from Central High School in Fresno with a music award and a scholarship to Fresno State College. His college work was interrupted while he served in the United States Army, during World War II, from 1942 to 1946. He played the trombone with the 13th Armored Division Band in California, Texas, France, and Germany.

LESLIE BASSETT

"I did not dare approach composition with any real hope until after my discharge from military service in 1946," he writes. On December 3, 1946, his first serious attempt at composition–a Suite in G, for orchestra–was introduced by the Fresno Symphony Orchestra.

He received a B.A. degree in music from Fresno State College. His studies, he explains, "were directed toward a broad training in the arts and specific training for the field of instrumental and choral music teaching. I studied most of the instruments, for which I have many times since been grateful. Because of the benefits of the GI Bill I was able to continue my training at the University of Michigan, where I did graduate work in composition. Ross Lee Finney, the teacher (and later colleague) to whom I owe the most, was my tutor for many years." After getting his master's degree in composition from the University of Michigan in 1949, Bassett remained at the University as a teaching fellow. On August 21, 1949, he married Anita Denniston. In 1950, having received a Fulbright grant for a year,

he and his wife went to Paris where he studied composition with Arthur Honegger at the École Normale de Musique, and privately with Nadia Boulanger.

During 1951 and 1952 Bassett taught instrumental music in the public schools of Fresno. In the fall of 1952 he was appointed instructor of composition at the University of Michigan, where he has remained. He is now a professor. The Bassetts make their home in Ann Arbor. They have three children: a daughter born in 1951, and two sons, born in 1953 and 1958.

In the 1950's a number of Bassett's compositions received some measure of recognition through the winning of awards and through performances. His Second String Quartet won a prize at the Concours Internationale pour Quatuors à Cordes in Brussels. The Quartet for Trombones, the Sonata for Horn and Piano, and the Five Pieces for String Quartet received publication awards. The Second String Quartet and the Horn Sonata were performed at a Composers Forum in New York on February 6, 1954, which Bassett shared with Marion Bauer. Bassett's second symphony was given a successful hearing at Asilomar, California, in 1959. On the strength of these achievements, Bassett received the Prix de Rome at the American Academy in 1961. Of the two years spent in Rome he says: "This was a most significant period for me, as it gave me unlimited time to work, outlet for a large number of works, and the chance to compose for a fine symphony orchestra (the RAI Orchestra of Rome)."

Before he left for Rome, Bassett completed the *Five Movements for Orchestra*. This was his first composition for orchestra in five years and, as he explains, it reveals on his part a completely new orientation towards symphonic writing. He says: "I had changed many of my ideas as to what constituted good orchestral writing. As a matter of fact, I had come to realize that most so-called standard orchestration (octave doublings, use of what texts call 'filler material,' overly-cautious ranges, etc.) was offensive to me and needed to be replaced by more effective musical means. I had become interested in the orchestra as color, and I wanted to employ a counterpoint of events or groups even more than of line."

The première of the *Five Movements* took place in Rome on July 5, 1962, with Massimo

Freccia conducting the RAI Orchestra. On February 7, 1964, the work was first heard in the United States, in a performance by the University of Michigan Symphony.

While still in Rome at the American Academy, Bassett completed the writing of the composition which first brought him recognition throughout the music world: the *Variations for Orchestra*. He finished the orchestration in May 1963 and its première, conducted by Ferruccio Scaglia, took place on July 6, 1963, in Rome. The American première followed on October 22, 1965, at a concert of the Philadelphia Orchestra under Eugene Ormandy. The work then went on to win the Pulitzer Prize in music and to receive a grant from the National Institute of Arts and Letters for a recording.

"I wanted to write a large, powerful, single-movement work," Bassett explains in describing his *Variations*, "that would place the listener in the midst of a form he could perceive, and yet at the same time involve him in the gradual unfolding of a thematic-motivic web that would require his most thoughtful attention. The *Variations* are not based upon a theme. The opening motivic introduction consists of four small areas or phrases, each of which is more memorable as color or mood than as theme, and each of which serves in some respect as the source of two variations.... The later variations take up some aspects of the introduction that may have been overlooked or minimized in earlier selections."

In reviewing the American première for the Philadelphia *Inquirer*, Daniel Webster wrote: "Bassett has something distinct to say and surpassing skill in saying it. His big orchestra ... was used to stir up shimmering colors and points of sound.... The instruments were balanced as finely as one finds in chamber music with massed effects sparingly and effectively used.... Its logic was everywhere apparent and its impetus and color were irresistible." To James Felton of the Philadelphia *Evening Bulletin*, the new work proved "attractive, ... laced in wide ranges of instrumental color, and couched in a language spoken by advanced composers.... Although he uses the technique of piling up layers of tone color, he achieves a flow of sound that coheres very well."

In 1964 Bassett received a citation and award from the National Institute of Arts and Letters. The National Council on Arts awarded him a grant for 1966–1967 to allow him time to devote himself exclusively to composition. In 1968 Bassett received a commission from the Koussevitzky Music Foundation for a fifteen-minute chamber music composition. He has also written a work for band which has been frequently performed throughout the country. It is called *Designs, Images and Textures* and was commissioned by the Ithaca (New York) High School, which introduced it on April 28, 1965.

MAJOR WORKS

Chamber Music—3 string quartets; Quartet for Trombones; Trio, for viola, clarinet and piano; Brass Trio; Quintet for Strings with Double Bass; Sonata for Trombone and Piano; Five Pieces for String Quartet; Suite for Unaccompanied Trombone; Woodwind Quintet; Sonata for Violin and Piano; Piano Quintet; Nonet; Music for Saxophone and Piano.

Choral Music—Easter Triptych, for tenor solo, chorus, and instruments; De Profundis; For City, Nation, World, cantata; Moonrise; Remembrance; Eclogue, Encomium and Evocation; Psalm 64; Prayers for Divine Service.

Electronic Music—Three Studies in Electronic Sounds.

Orchestral Music—2 symphonies; Five Movements for Orchestra; Variations for Orchestra.

Organ Music—Toccata; Voluntaries; Four Statements.

Piano Music—Six Piano Pieces.

Vocal Music—Four Songs; To Music.

Marion Bauer
1887–1955

Marion Bauer, in 1948, prepared for the editor of this book the following autobiographical sketch:

"I was born in Walla Walla, Washington, on August 15, 1887, the youngest of seven children, only four of whom were living when I came into the world. My parents were French. My mother was a linguist and a scholar, who spent most of her life with her books. But it was from my father that I inherited my talent and love for music. He had a beautiful natural tenor voice and had the ability to play any of the instruments of the military band.

"After my father's death, in 1890, the family moved to Portland, Oregon. I received my schooling in the public schools of Portland and later at St. Helen's Hall, where for a few years my mother taught. I was graduated from the Hall before I was sixteen. It was somewhat of a problem to decide what career I should follow, for I showed aptness for drawing, for teaching, and for writing, as well as for music. As soon as my school days were over, however, I followed the path of least resistance and went to New York where I began a serious study of music, first with my sister, and then with Henry Holden Huss, who taught me piano and harmony. The gift for musical composition did not assert itself until after I had begun my theoretical studies in New York. I had improvised melodies from the time I was a little girl, but always complained that I didn't know what to do with my left hand!

MARION BAUER

"Almost coincidental with my first harmony lessons, I began writing songs. I was having trouble with my eyes and was making daily visits to the oculist. While waiting to be admitted to his office one morning, I found in a magazine a poem by Gouverneur Morris, and on a piece of scrap paper I scratched a staff and composed my first song. This was followed by two others, one of which, Bourdillon's *Light*, was published by the John Church Company and was sung by Mme. Ernestine Schumann-Heink in 1911.

"Raoul Pugno, the famous French pianist, was touring America in 1906, and he had brought his wife, and his daughter Renée, to this country with him. Renée and I became great friends and I was asked to teach her

English. We made such progress that when it came time for the family to return to France, Mme. Pugno invited me to visit them in their country home at Gargenville (Seine et Oise) to continue Renée's English lessons and to have piano lessons with M. Pugno. He had seen my first little attempts at composition and was very encouraging, telling my sister that he would arrange for lessons in harmony, which he did. I had my own little piano and spent my mornings, after a half-hour walk through the beautiful estate, in practice. My harmony teacher was Nadia Boulanger. I had interesting lessons with Pugno, although I was not technically on par with his other pupils, one of whom was Germaine Schnitzer.

"When I went back to New York, I taught theory and piano, and studied with Eugene Heffley. Mr. Heffley advised me to devote my time and attention to composing and to the study of composition, as he considered that my real musical talent was creative. Until the time of his death, in July 1925, he guided my musical studies, gave my compositions invaluable criticisms, directed me as to what books, musical and otherwise, to read, stimulated my interest in contemporary music, and gave me opportunity to satisfy my desire to understand it.

"It was after my return from France, too, that I met Walter Henry Rothwell, who had come to America as conductor of Henry Savage's production in English of Wagner's *Parsifal*, and who later became conductor of the St. Paul Orchestra. Rothwell was a frequent visitor to our New York home. He found some sketches of mine lying on the piano and immediately became interested in my work and advised my sister to send me to Germany for intensive study. As a result of his advice, I spent a year (1910–1911) in Berlin, studying counterpoint and musical form with Dr. Paul Ertel, and writing a number of songs which were published in 1912 by Arthur P. Schmidt of Boston with whom I signed a seven-year contract. When the St. Paul Orchestra disbanded, due to war conditions, Rothwell established himself in New York, and I became his first composition pupil. I received some of my most valuable training during these years of war, before he was called to Los Angeles to direct the Philharmonic Orchestra.

"In 1921, a small group of young American

composers founded the American Music Guild. Our object was to learn each other's music and to present worthy works by other American composers to the New York public. This organization was short-lived because of lack of funds, but it existed long enough to accomplish its purpose and to open the way for other societies with similar aims, such as the International Music Guild and the League of Composers.

"As a member of the American Music Guild, I had the opportunity to measure my powers and my limitations with those of my colleagues, and to profit by the constructive criticism my works received at their hands. The result was a period of study in Europe. This time I decided that in Paris I would find the kind of work and musical environment for which I was seeking, and I went abroad in May 1923, remaining in France until January 1926, except for brief vacations at home. These were some of the richest years in my life from the standpoint of study and development. I studied fugue with André Gedalge for a season, and met many of the composers and musicians in prominence at the time.

"Before I had been in New York a week, after my return from Europe, I was made a member of the Executive Board of the League of Composers, and of the teaching staff of New York University in the department of music. In 1927, I was made an assistant professor at New York University and, in 1930, when Albert Stoessel resigned as head of the department, I became acting head for a season, with a promotion to associate professor."

In 1932 Miss Bauer was invited by Whitman College in Walla Walla, Washington, to visit her birthplace and receive an honorary master's degree. Fifty years earlier, her mother had been professor of languages at Whitman.

Marion Bauer did not confine her teaching exclusively to New York University. After 1935 she taught at the summer school of Mills College in California and at various other educational institutions including the Carnegie Institute of Technology, Teachers College of Columbia University, and the Juilliard Summer School. After 1940 she was a member of the faculty at the Institute of Musical Art of the Juilliard School of Music (remaining at the Juilliard when the Institute went out of existence) and at the New York School of Music.

These many and varied activities as teacher did not interfere with the flow of compositions, some of which received important performances. In 1936, Zoltán Kurthy and Frank Sheridan introduced her Viola Sonata at a concert of the League of Composers. Her Concertino, for oboe, clarinet and string quartet (commissioned by the League of Composers) was introduced over the CBS radio network in 1940. On August 20, 1941, Albert Stoessel conducted the première of her Suite for String Orchestra, at Chautauqua, New York. On October 25, 1947, Leopold Stokowski directed the New York Philharmonic in a performance of her tone poem *Sun Splendor*, which she had written for the piano in 1926 and later orchestrated.

In the larger forms could be found such impressive compositions as *China*, for chorus and orchestra (text by Boris Todrin), introduced at the Worcester Festival on October 12, 1945; and the Concerto for Piano and Orchestra, first heard in New York City in May 1943 and later published under the title of *American Youth Concerto*. In her larger works, she had what one unidentified critic called "a masculine stride"; her style was vigorous and muscular.

In the field of the art song she showed great variety of style and mood as well as a consummate craftsmanship and the gift of transferring to tones subtle atmospheres and feelings. Among her most successful songs is a set of four to texts by John Gould Fletcher, which Helen Traubel presented in a recital on April 24, 1936.

Miss Bauer collaborated with Ethel Peyser on three books: *How Music Grew* (1925), *Music Through the Ages* (1932), and *How Opera Grew* (1955). She was also the author of *Twentieth Century Music* (1933).

Marion Bauer was vacationing at South Hadley, Massachusetts, when she died of coronary thrombosis on August 9, 1955.

MAJOR WORKS

Chamber Music—String Quartet; Viola Sonata; Suite for Oboe and Clarinet; Five Greek Lyrics, for flute; Sonatina for Oboe and Piano; Concertino, for oboe, clarinet, and string quartet; Trio Sonata, for flute, cello, and piano; Prelude and Fugue, for flute and piano.

Choral Music—Three Noëls; Here at High Morning; A Garden Is a Lovesome Thing; The Thinker; China; At the New Year.

Orchestral Music—Sun Splendor (also for piano); A Lament; Pan, choreographic sketch for chamber orchestra; Symphonic Suite; Concerto for Piano and Orchestra (American Youth Concerto).

Piano Music—Six Preludes; From New Hampshire Woods; Four Piano Pieces; Two Aquarelles; Dance Sonata.

Vocal Music—Various songs for voice and piano including Four Songs to texts by John Gould Fletcher and Songs from Alice in Wonderland.

ABOUT

Howard, J. T., Our Contemporary Composers; Upton, W. T., Art Song in America.

Musical America, September 1955.

Sir Arnold Bax
1883–1953

Sir Arnold Edward Trevor Bax was born in London on November 8, 1883. His interest in music was first awakened when, as a child, he attended Sunday concerts at the Crystal Palace. He began formal study in his thirteenth year, taking violin lessons from an Italian bandmaster. In 1896, when the family moved to Hampstead, Bax attended the Conservatory and began his training in piano, theory, and composition. During this period he served as an accompanist for a chorus led by his father. He spent most of his free hours studying the scores of Wagner's music dramas. At seventeen he enrolled in the Royal Conservatory of Music in London, where he was a pupil of Tobias Matthay (piano) and Frederick Corder (composition). He continually amazed his teachers with his talent for sight reading even the most complex orchestral and operatic scores at the piano.

His interest in Irish folklore and Celtic legends was first stimulated in 1902 through the reading of works by Yeats and was further developed later the same year with his first visit to Ireland. Under this influence he wrote poems and short stories published in Dublin under the pen name of Dermot O'Byrne. In 1904 he completed his first piece of music with an Irish background, *A Celtic Song Cycle* to poems by Fiona MacLeod.

Since he was financially independent, Bax was never compelled to earn his living

Bax: băks

in music. He disdained making appearances as a conductor or pianist, though he showed strong aptitude in both areas. Instead he devoted himself to travel, omnivorous reading, and writing music.

In 1910 he paid a visit to Russia. His impressions of that country were fixed in several piano works, including *May Night in the Ukraine* (1911), *Gopak* (1911), and *In a Vodka Shop* (1915). In 1911 he married and settled in Dublin. Association with Irish literary men—particularly George Russell (Æ)—conversations with leading figures in the Celtic revival, the study of Irish legends, and walking tours in western Ireland intensified his love of all things Irish. The Celtic influence now dominated his musical writing, his compositions continually reflecting the Celtic partiality for mystery, symbolism, dream fantasy, vivid imagery, and pageantry.

SIR ARNOLD BAX

His first major Celtic work was the tone poem *In the Faëry Hills* (1909), based on an episode from *The Wanderings of Usheen*. Two other Celtic compositions followed in 1916 and 1917: *The Garden of Fand* and *Tintagel*. The latter, one of Bax's most famous shorter works for orchestra, evokes the image of Tintagel, a castle-crowned cliff, as seen from the heights of Cornwall.

Bax's First Symphony was completed in 1922 and was introduced in London on December 2, 1922. "It burst like a bombshell upon Queen's Hall," wrote Christopher Whelman. "Even now . . . its impact and rhythmical power remain fresh and startling." Bax wrote six more symphonies after that; the Third, completed in 1929 and introduced in London on March 3, 1930, and the Sixth, heard in London on November 21, 1935, have been the most popular.

"Bax's first three symphonies," says Peter J. Pirie in *High Fidelity*, "form a single process, and are thematically linked: the brutal, curt First, the vast and tragic Second, and the Third, in which the conflict ends, for the time being in supernal peace." Here is how Pirie describes the next three symphonies: "His Fourth is an outburst of almost irresponsible gaiety, and the composer admits an extra-musical inspiration–wild seas bursting over rugged coasts on a windy, sunny day. His Fifth has a legendary aspect, and is beautifully constructed. . . . The conflict at the heart of Bax finally explodes in his Sixth Symphony. In no other work of his does the head-on collision between beauty and brutality express itself more forcibly."

Bax wrote his seventh and last symphony in 1939. This is a work dedicated to the American people; it was introduced in New York City on June 9, 1939. H. G. Sear points out that this work "is simpler in texture, mellower in expression than its forebears. If the first movement expresses struggle, the lyrical slow movement indicates flight to a realm of legend. A land of music, possibly, for, in the finale, Bax finds leisure to state a theme, to work out a set of formal variations, and once more to discover the tranquillity of absolute peace in an epilogue."

Bax also produced an extensive library of music for chorus, for chamber music combinations, for the piano, and for the voice. Whatever medium he chose, Bax was, as Lawrence Gilman said, "the potential dreamer, the visionary, the nature lover" belonging not essentially "to this indurated and brass-bound age, but to an earlier and forgotten world of sensibility and beauty."

Bax wrote little after 1939, and nothing of particular consequence. Two minor items were completed for orchestra in 1943 and 1944, an overture and *Legend*; in 1945 he composed the *Legend Sonata*, for cello and piano; and in 1948 he wrote for Harriet Cohen the Concerto for Piano, Left Hand, which she introduced at the Cheltenham Festival on July 4,

1950. Except for these compositions, and one or two others, Bax concerned himself mainly with functional music. He wrote the scores for two films, one a documentary on Malta in 1943, and the other for the screen adaptation of Dickens' *Oliver Twist* in 1948. He produced a trumpet fanfare for the marriage of Princess Elizabeth and the Duke of Edinburgh in 1949, and a march for the coronation of Queen Elizabeth II on June 2, 1953.

A man of extraordinary modesty, Bax for many years lived in complete withdrawal in the little village of Storrington. Except for annual visits to Dublin and occasional trips to London, this village was his favorite retreat. Here he could indulge in his favorite pastimes: reading (fiction, mysteries, poetry), solving crossword puzzles, playing in an occasional game of snooker, and exchanging small talk with neighbors and friends.

Throughout his career he received numerous honors: in 1931 the Gold Medal from the Royal Philharmonic Society in London; in 1934 an honorary doctorate from Oxford; and in 1937, during the coronation of George VI, knighthood. In 1942 he succeeded Sir Walford Davies as Master of the King's Music.

He was on a visit to Cork in southern Ireland, where he had gone to conduct music examinations at the University, when he died on October 3, 1953.

MAJOR WORKS

Ballets—Between Dusk and Dawn; The Truth About the Russian Dancers.

Chamber Music—3 string quartets; 3 violin sonatas; Piano Quintet in G minor; Elegy, for flute, viola and piano; Four Pieces, for flute and piano; Harp Quintet in F minor; Sonata in G major, for viola and piano; Sonata in E-flat minor, for cello and piano; Piano Quartet in One Movement; Oboe Quintet in G major; String Quintet in One Movement; Nonet; Sonatina in D major, for cello and piano; Octet; Concerto, for flute, oboe, harp, and string quartet; Sonata in D major, for clarinet and piano; Concerto, for bassoon, harp, and string sextet.

Choral Music—Enchanted Summer; Mater Ora Filium, motet; St. Patrick's Breastplate; Walsinghame; The Morning Watch; Te Deum; Nunc Dimittis; Gloria; Epithalamium.

Orchestral Music—7 symphonies; 2 Northern Ballads; In the Faëry Hills, tone poem; The Garden of Fand, tone poem; Symphonic Variations in E major, for piano and orchestra; November Woods, tone poem; Tintagel, tone poem; Phantasy for Viola and Orchestra; Mediterranean, tone poem; Overture, Elegy and Rondo; Overture to a Picaresque Comedy; Winter Legends, for piano and orchestra; The Tale the Pine Trees Knew, tone poem; Concerto in G minor, for cello and orchestra; Rogues Comedy Overture; Concerto in E major, for violin and orchestra; Concerto for Piano Left Hand and Orchestra.

Piano Music—4 sonatas; Sonata in E major, for two pianos; Winter Waters; Dream in Exile; On a May Evening; What the Minstrel Told Us; Whirligig; A Hill Tune; Mediterranean; Burlesque.

Vocal Music—A Celtic Song Cycle; Seven Selected Songs; Five Irish Songs; Three Irish Songs; individual songs for voice and piano.

ABOUT

Bacharach, A. L. (ed.), British Music of Our Time; Bacharach, A. L. (ed.), The Music Masters: v4, The Twentieth Century, by W. R. Anderson [and others]; Bax, A., Farewell My Youth; Hull, R. H., A Handbook on Arnold Bax's Symphonies.

High Fidelity, January 1966; Musical America, November 1, 1953; Musical Quarterly, April 1923.

Conrad Beck
1901–

Conrad Beck, the son of a parson, was born in Lohn, Switzerland, in the canton of Schaffenhausen, on June 16, 1901. At first, he took courses in mechanical engineering at the Technical High School in Zürich. Then, having come to the decision to specialize in music, he enrolled in the Zürich Conservatory where his teachers included Volkmar Andreae and Reinhold Laquai. Upon leaving the Conservatory, he continued his music studies in Berlin and Paris, in the latter city with Ernst Lévy and Jacques Ibert. During his long residence in Paris, from 1923 to 1932, he came into personal association with Arthur Honegger and Albert Roussel, both of whom had a decisive influence on his creative development. His first ambitious works were completed in Paris: five symphonies in the years 1925–1930; a cello concerto, the Concertino for Piano and Orchestra, and the Concerto for String Quartet and Orchestra, all from 1926 to 1929; a cantata, *Der Tod des Oedipus*, text by René Morax (1928); a Requiem, for unaccompanied chorus (1930); and in the years 1925–1928 his third string quartet (which was featured at the festival of the International Society for Contemporary Music at Frankfurt on the Main in Germany on July 2, 1927) and his first string trio. The Third Symphony was given its world première in Boston on February 10,

1928, with Serge Koussevitzky conducting the Boston Symphony. The Concerto for String Quartet and Orchestra was first heard in Chicago in 1929, Leopold Stokowski conducting; this won for him the Elizabeth Sprague Coolidge Award for distinguished contribution to chamber music. The world première of the cantata took place on May 22, 1931, at the concluding concert of the Festival of New Music in Munich.

CONRAD BECK

Discussing the influence of France on Beck's works during this period, Edmond Appra wrote in *Musical America:* "Having lived in Paris for ten years, Beck is one of the rare Swiss composers who has discovered an equilibrium between the Germanic and Latin cultures. His stay in the Capital of Taste and Beautiful Proportion exercised a great effect upon his work. With him, the 'atmosphere of Paris,' may be compared to a spiritual radiance that draws the most sensitive beings towards their deepest insights. . . . His thinking, sometimes hermetic, but never speculative, is the expression of a solitary introspective nature. A distant art, perhaps, but one that is always rich in substance and admirably lucid."

In 1932 Beck returned to Switzerland. He settled in Basel where, from 1938 on, he served as the director of the music section of Radio Basel. There on March 21, 1941, he married Friedel Ehrsam.

He soon adopted a neocontrapuntal style which rejected his earlier romanticism and

French influences for a purely linear form of writing. This tendency, though hinted at in earlier compositions, is found fully realized for the first time in the orchestral overture, *Innominata*, introduced at the festival of the International Society for Contemporary Music at Vienna on June 16, 1932. This composition has been described as a "neoclassical work in dissonant counterpoint." Beck's linear style was further developed in the *Lyrische Kantate* for women's voices and orchestra, with a text by Rilke, first given in Munich on May 22, 1931; in one of Beck's finest works for chorus, the *Oratorio on Verses of Angelus Silesius*, completed in 1934 and introduced soon afterwards in Basel, Paul Sacher conducting; in the Serenade for Flute, Clarinet and Orchestra which Sacher introduced in 1935 in Basel (and which was heard in the United States on November 18, 1938, in a broadcast over radio station WOR); and in the *Kammerkantate*, based on sonnets by Louise Labé, successfully given at the festival of the International Society for Contemporary Music at Warsaw on April 15, 1939. In *Forty Contemporary Swiss Composers*, the *Kammerkantate* is described as "one of the most personal and moving works by Conrad Beck. . . . At first the expression is peaceful, and then it becomes dramatic; the melodic lines of the soprano part are contrasted with the ensemble of flute, piano, and strings." In the Tranquillo section of the work the voice part "takes on the simplicity of a Lied" while the mood of the finale is one of "renunciation and resignation."

Since the end of World War II, Beck has strengthened his position as one of Switzerland's major composers with a number of impressive works. These include his sixth symphony (1950); the Concerto for Viola and Orchestra which Walter Kägi introduced in Baden-Baden in 1951, Hans Rosbaud conducting; his second oratorio, *Der Tod zu Basel* (1953); and his seventh symphony, *Aeneas-Silvius*, first performed in Zürich on February 25, 1958.

In June 1967 Beck visited Expo 67 at Montreal to attend a concert of the Orchestre de la Suisse Romande de Genève conducted by Ernest Ansermet. The program included Beck's *Hommages*, which was then a recently completed composition. Reviewing the concert for the New York *Times*, Raymond Ericson described this music as follows: "Its two short sections, slow and fast, are dense in texture, with chromatic themes contrapuntally treated. The slow section, heavy and plaintive in atmosphere, possessed some individuality on first hearing."

MAJOR WORKS

Ballet—La Grande Ourse.

Chamber Music—4 string quartets; 2 violin sonatas; 2 cello sonatas; 2 string trios; various sonatinas for solo instruments and piano (violin; cello; oboe; viola d'amore); Drei Bilder aus dem Struwwelpeter, for flute, clarinet, and bassoon; Kammerkantate, for soprano, flute, piano, and strings; Gedulden, for voice, violin, viola, and two cellos.

Choral Music—Der Tod des Oedipus; Requiem, for unaccompanied chorus; Oratorio on Verses of Angelus Silesius; Lyrische Kantate; Sommerlied; Three Psalms; Der Tod zu Basel, oratorio.

Orchestral Music—7 symphonies; various concertos for solo instruments and orchestra (cello; piano; violin; flute; harpsichord; viola; string quartet); Kleine Suite, for strings; Innominata, overture; Konzertmusik, for oboe and strings; Rhapsody, for piano, four wind instruments and strings; Vorspiel für Orchester; Chamber Concerto, for cembalo and string orchestra; Hymne; Concertino for clarinet, bassoon, and orchestra; Hommages.

Organ Music—Sonatina; Two Preludes; Choral-Sonate.

Piano Music—2 sonatinas; Klavierstücke I and II; Zehn Klavierstücke für den Hausgebrauch.

Vocal Music—Vocalise; Drei Herbstgesänge; canons; arrangements of folk songs.

ABOUT

Forty Contemporary Swiss Composers; Schuh, W. Schweizer Musiker der Gegenwart.

Musical America, January 15, 1950.

Paul Ben-Haim
1897–

Paul Ben-Haim, Israel's most famous composer, was born Paul Frankenburger in Munich, Germany, on July 5, 1897. His father was a lawyer. Paul received his musical training at the Academy of Music in Munich where his teachers included Friedrich Klose and Walter Courvoisier in composition, and Berthold Kellerman in piano. His studies completed, Paul began his professional life as a conductor, but after 1931 he devoted himself exclusively

Ben-Haim: bĕn кī yēm´

to composition. He began attracting attention in German music circles with three ambitious works in 1931: a tone poem for soprano and orchestra, *Pan*; a Concerto Grosso, for orchestra; and a Biblical oratorio, *Joram*. Though influenced by and at times imitative of some of the modern trends in Central European music, he had already begun to assert his own personality through a poetic, expressive lyricism and a partiality for pastoral moods.

PAUL BEN-HAIM

In 1933, when the Nazis came to power, he left his native land for good and settled in Palestine. He discarded his surname together with his German citizenship, adopting the Hebraic name that means son of Haim. In Palestine he became an arranger and piano accompanist for several folk singers, including the Yemenite artist Bracha Sephira. This association first brought him into contact with, and aroused his enthusiasm for, the varied folk-song and folk-dance literature of Palestine, a literature that was to have a far-reaching influence on his creative growth.

A four-movement string quartet, in 1937, was his first major chamber-music work written in Palestine. "It is," says Peter Gradenwitz, "already permeated with the singular atmosphere of the land. A characteristic pastoral theme of the viola opens the quartet and may be said to dominate all of its movements." Ben-Haim's second important chamber music work in Palestine was the *Variations on a Palestinian Tune*, for piano, violin, and

cello (1939), the main theme of which is of Bedouin origin. In 1941 came what Gradenwitz describes as "the composer's finest chamber music composition of the period"— a quintet for clarinet and strings.

The first major work for orchestra written by Ben-Haim after arriving in Palestine was his first symphony. Begun during the last days of August 1939 when the world hovered on the brink of World War II, it was completed on June 20, 1940, the day on which France collapsed. "It is inevitable," says the composer, "that the work should be influenced by the tragic events of those days; the terrible forces of destruction which tore the ground from under our feet could not fail leaving their stamp on my work, but in spite of this I did not attempt to portray musically any concrete or worldly events." However, Gradenwitz finds that the "tragic-passionate energy of the first movement and the fiery mood of the finale" breathe "something of the character of the fateful period in which the symphony was written." This symphony also has moments of gentle repose, particularly in the slow movement, the main melody of which has the personality of an oriental chant and which concludes with a pastoral cadenza for flute and clarinet.

The First Symphony was introduced by the Palestine Symphony Orchestra on January 5, 1941, the composer conducting. In his second symphony, four years later, the pastoral mood (with which the composition opens in the flute) dominates the entire composition. This work was heard for the first time on February 6, 1947, Georg Singer conducting the Palestine Symphony.

In a good many of his works of the 1940's and 1950's Ben-Haim reveals strong folkloristic influences. In *From Israel*, a suite for orchestra (first performed on January 4, 1953, Georg Singer conducting the Israel Philharmonic), Ben-Haim models his thematic material along the lines of oriental singing and performance, thereby creating a strong Eastern Mediterranean atmosphere. In this work he makes effective use of a Yemenite tune, while in the finale he exploits the rhythms of Palestinian dances. In most of his other compositions, however, Ben-Haim does not resort to quotations. "My use of folk materials," Ben-Haim once told an interviewer, "is a natural language form. I don't take actual melodies. I invent them. It is now my language influenced by my surroundings." Illustrating this practice of deriving rather than borrowing his material from Near Eastern folkloristic sources we find Ben-Haim's piano concerto, which Frank Pelleg introduced with the Israel Philharmonic on February 6, 1950, Charles Bruck conducting; the earlier Concerto for Strings, which Nicolai Malko performed with the Israel Philharmonic on December 3, 1948; and, most significantly, *The Sweet Psalmist of Israel* (1953), a tonal portrait of King David, the musician, text taken from the Bible and scored for soprano and orchestra. This last work owes its origin to Serge Koussevitzky, who had commissioned several famous composers to produce music of Hebraic interest for performance in Jerusalem on the occasion of its three thousandth anniversary. Koussevitzky did not live to complete this project (out of which came such outstanding creations as Milhaud's opera *David* and Arnold Schoenberg's psalm *De Profundis*). But Ben-Haim's *The Sweet Psalmist of Israel*, which was also written for this celebration, turned out to be one of its composer's most successful achievements. It was cited when in 1957 Ben-Haim received the Israel State Prize and it was selected by the International Music Council to represent Israel in an anthology of contemporary music recorded under the auspices of UNESCO. *The Sweet Psalmist of Israel* was introduced in Tel Aviv on October 18, 1956, and in New York City in the spring of 1959 by the New York Philharmonic under Leonard Bernstein. "Mr. Ben-Haim's incorporation of Near Eastern musical devices in his tribute to King David," wrote Raymond Ericson in the New York *Times*, "is deliberate and emphatic, but he does not run the material into the ground. His score . . . is predominantly lyrical, even sweet, and occasionally brooding, until it arrives at the brilliant, dance-like final movement."

On the occasion of the première of *The Sweet Psalmist*, Ben-Haim paid his first visit to the United States. He was described in the New York *Times* as "bespectacled and nearly bald" with a "kindly face and a soft, easy command of English." During his American visit he gave a concert of his music in Pittsburgh, delivered a lecture on Israeli music at Brandeis University, and participated in the International Congress of Cultural Leaders in Washington, D.C. This last event was conducted by the Institute of Contemporary Arts which had sponsored Ben-Haim's visit in collaboration with the America-Israel Cultural Foundation.

Since 1959 a number of major works by Ben-Haim have resulted from commissions. One was the Capriccio, for piano and orchestra, ordered by the Israel Philharmonic for its 1960–1961 tour of the United States, Canada, Mexico, Japan, and India. After its première in Tel Aviv in 1960 this Capriccio was played twenty-two times by the orchestra on its tour. It was heard first in the United States in New York on October 18, 1960, with Pnina Salzman as soloist and the visiting Israel Philharmonic conducted by Carlo Maria Giulini.

Other distinguished compositions include the Sonata for Solo Violin, commissioned by Yehudi Menuhin; a violin concerto, written for the Israeli violinist Zvi Zeitlin at the behest of the America-Israel Cultural Foundation; a cello concerto, for the American cellist Richard Kay; the *Dance and Invocation*, for orchestra, ordered by the Israel Philharmonic Orchestra; *To the Chief Musician*, which the composer described as a "metamorphosis for orchestra," introduced on October 28, 1958, by the Louisville Philharmonic, the orchestra that had commissioned it; and *The Eternal Theme*, for orchestra, the world première of which took place in Tel Aviv on February 12, 1966.

Ben-Haim is active in Israel as a teacher of composition at the Conservatories in Tel Aviv and Jerusalem. He is also a leading figure in the development of musical education in Israel, and in the formation of a musicians' union in that country. For his influential contributions to Israeli music, Ben-Haim was honored in 1945 and again in 1953 with the Engel Prize from the municipality of Tel Aviv.

Ben-Haim has appeared as guest conductor of the Israel Philharmonic. He has made numerous arrangements of oriental and Jewish folk melodies from Yemen, Bokhara, Persia, and other Near Eastern regions.

MAJOR WORKS

Chamber Music—String Quartet; Variations on a Palestinian Tune, for piano, violin, and cello; Clarinet

Benjamin

Quintet; Serenade, for flute, violin, viola, and cello; Sonata in G, for solo violin.

Choral Music—Joram, oratorio; A Book of Verses; Psalm CXXI; Liturgical Cantata, for chorus and orchestra; Vision of a Prophet, cantata; Thanksgiving from the Desert, oratorio.

Orchestral Music—2 symphonies; Pan; Concerto Grosso; Evocation, for violin and orchestra; Concerto for Strings; Concerto for Piano and Orchestra; From Israel, suite; Sweet Psalmist of Israel, for soprano and orchestra; Music for Strings; Three Songs Without Words; To the Chief Musician, metamorphoses for orchestra; Capriccio, for piano and orchestra; Concerto for Violin and Orchestra; Dance and Invocation; Concerto for Cello and Orchestra; The Eternal Theme; Cello Concerto.

Piano Music—Sonatina; Sonata; Suite; Melody with Variations; Music for the Piano.

Vocal Music—Lift Up Your Heads, motet for soprano and eight instruments.

ABOUT

Gradenwitz, P., Music and Musicians in Israel; Gradenwitz, P., The Music of Israel; Holde, A., Jews in Music; Rothmüller, A. M., The Music of the Jews.

Arthur Benjamin
1893–1960

Arthur Benjamin was born in Sydney, Australia, on September 18, 1893, and made his first public appearance as a pianist when he was six. After receiving his preliminary education at the Brisbane Grammar School and his musical training with private teachers, he went to London in 1911. He attended the Royal College of Music there for three years, as a pupil in composition of Sir Charles Villiers Stanford. When World War I broke out, he joined the British army, serving first in the infantry in France and later as a gunner in the Royal Air Force. During one of his missions over Germany his plane was shot down. He was taken prisoner and interned until the war's end; the squadron leader of the German plane that shot him down was Hermann Goering.

After the war, Benjamin returned to Australia. From 1919 to 1921 he taught piano at the Sydney Conservatory. Then, in order to advance his career as pianist and composer, he settled in London. His first important job there was adjudicator and examiner for the Associated Board of the Royal School of Music, an organization founded by the Royal College of Music and the Royal Academy of Music to hold examinations in the British

Isles and the Dominions for scholarship candidates to the two schools. In this capacity Benjamin toured Australia, Canada, and the West Indies. His experiences with local West Indian songs and dances inspired some of his popular pieces of music in later years.

Benjamin's first work to be published, the *Pastoral Fantasy* in A minor, for string quartet, appeared in 1924 and received the Carnegie Award. This was followed in 1926 by *Three Impressions*, for voice and string quartet, and a Violin Sonatina. The latter revealed Benjamin's development, which had achieved "considerable heights of technique and expression," in the opinion of Herbert Howells.

ARTHUR BENJAMIN

Benjamin's first public appearance as a mature pianist took place in 1925 at a Queen's Hall concert directed by Sir Henry Wood. He continued to concertize for a number of years, then abandoned the concert stage to devote himself mainly to composition. Meanwhile, in 1926, he joined the faculty of the Royal College of Music where Benjamin Britten became one of his students.

In his Piano Concerto (1928) and Violin Concerto (1932) Benjamin's style was reserved in feeling, dry and precise in its structural logic. But at times he was also able to tap a rich emotional vein, as in the *Romantic Phantasy*, for violin, viola, and orchestra (1935), introduced in London on March 24, 1938. Other works revealed a gift for gaiety and wit – for example, the farcical one-act opera *The Devil Take Her* (1931). The plot centered on the marriage of a medieval poet in London to a beautiful woman born dumb. Refusing to accept his friend's advice that a dumb wife is worth her weight in gold, the poet arranges to have her operated upon, as a result of which the girl is able to speak. She now turns out to be a noisy shrew; in despair the poet begs the devil to take her. "Benjamin's score," wrote Raymond Ericson in the New York *Times*, "has considerable charm. It frequently elaborates appealingly on folk-like melodies; the harmonies are rich, the orchestral background clever. The text is well set and the singers have opportunities for attractive solos." *The Devil Take Her* was first produced at the Royal College of Music in London in December 1931; a public performance followed in London on November 30, 1932. On August 3, 1963, this gay little opera became Australia's contribution to the International Program Exchange for which CBS Television and eleven foreign television companies reciprocally provided musical or dance productions.

No less merry and spirited, and further enlivened by parody, was Benjamin's second opera, *Prima Donna*, completed in 1933, which failed to get a hearing until sixteen years later when it was mounted at the Fortune Theatre in London on February 23, 1949. Possibly the most successful of Benjamin's compositions was the *Overture to an Italian Comedy*, for orchestra, which has been played in music centers the world over following its première in London on March 2, 1937. The composer had no specific Italian comedy in mind. He sought to depict the bustle and commotion and merriment of Italian life by introducing fragments of Neapolitan folk songs and dances, including a whirling tarantella.

In other successful compositions Benjamin resorted to quotation or adaptation. The most celebrated is *Two Jamaican Pieces* (1938), made up of two numbers: "Jamaican Song" and the now extremely popular "Jamaican Rhumba." In the latter piece a light staccato accompaniment in rhumba rhythm courses nimbly throughout, as the woodwinds present a saucy tune, and the strings an equally dashing countersubject. "Jamaican Rhumba" has become familiar in various transcriptions, including one for two solo pianos.

From San Domingo (1945) and *Caribbean Dance* (1946) are two more orchestral pieces utilizing folk material from the Caribbean. In *Cotillon* (1938), a suite of dance tunes, the melodies are of English origin, found by the composer in a volume, *The Dancing School*, published in London in 1719. In 1955, Benjamin prepared a delightful suite of American square-dance melodies in a work for two pianos and orchestra entitled *North American Square Dances*. This was Benjamin's only attempt to invade the field of American folklore, using eight fiddle tunes once played at old-time square dances. In the suite, local color is introduced through suggestions of footstamping, the plunking of banjos, and the shouts of a caller. This suite was introduced in Pittsburgh on April 1, 1955, with William Steinberg conducting the Pittsburgh Symphony, and the two-piano team of Vronsky and Babin as soloists.

Benjamin also prepared two charming orchestral suites based on the music of other composers. One was the Concerto for Oboe and Orchestra (1942), using material from four harpsichord sonatas by Domenico Cimarosa (1749–1801). The other was the Suite for Flute and Strings (1945), the principal melodies for which came from harpsichord sonatas by Domenico Scarlatti (1685–1757).

Despite his success in adapting popular and folk materials for the concert hall, Benjamin did not neglect writing major works more sober in content, more deeply reflective, more concerned with penetrating thought and personal feelings. His Symphony No. 1 (1944–1945) was successfully introduced at the Cheltenham Festival on June 30, 1948. The *Concerto Quasi una Fantasia*, for piano and orchestra (1949) was first given by the Sydney Symphony on September 5, 1950, with the composer as soloist. In addition, Benjamin completed two important operas. *A Tale of Two Cities*, a romantic melodrama based on Dickens, was heard over the BBC network on April 17, 1953, and won the first prize during the Festival of Britain; its American première took place in San Francisco on April 2, 1960. *Tartuffe*, from Molière, was completed by the composer shortly before his death and was produced posthumously at Sadler's Wells Theatre in London on November 30, 1964.

In 1938, Benjamin left London for Canada,

where from 1941 to 1946 he conducted the Vancouver Symphony. He returned to London early in 1946, and died there on April 10, 1960.

MAJOR WORKS

Ballet—Orlando's Silver Wedding.

Chamber Music—Three Pieces, for violin and piano; Three Impressions, for voice and string quartet; Pastoral Fantasy, for string quartet; Violin Sonatina; Tune and Variations for Little People, for violin and piano; Cello Sonatina; Valse Caprice, for viola and piano (also for clarinet and piano).

Choral Music—Three Mystical Songs; Nightingale Lane; Sir Christmas, for baritone and unaccompanied chorus; Callers, unison song; A Tall Story, two-part song; part-songs.

Operas—The Devil Take Her, one-act; Prima Donna; A Tale of Two Cities; Tartuffe.

Orchestral Music—Concertino for Piano and Orchestra; Light Music Suite; Violin Concerto; Heritage; Romantic Phantasy, for violin, viola, and orchestra; Overture to an Italian Comedy; Cotillon, suite; Two Jamaican Pieces (including Jamaican Rhumba); Prelude to Holiday; Sonatina, for chamber orchestra; Concerto for Oboe and Strings (adapted from Cimarosa); Elegy, Waltz and Toccata, for viola and orchestra (also viola and piano); Symphony No. 1; Red River Jig; From San Domingo; Suite for Flute and Orchestra (adapted from Domenico Scarlatti); Caribbean Dance; Ballade, for strings; Concerto Quasi una Fantasia, for piano and orchestra; Concerto for Harmonica and Orchestra; North American Square Dances.

Piano Music—Odds and Ends, two books; Suite; Three Little Pieces; Chinoiserie; Pastorale, Arioso and Finale; Three New Fantasies; Two Jamaican Street Songs, for two pianos.

Vocal Music—Three Greek Poems; various individual songs for voice and piano.

Richard Rodney Bennett
1936–

Richard Rodney Bennett was born at Broadstairs in Kent, England, on March 29, 1936. He came from a musical family; his mother studied with Gustav Holst. Thus he encountered musical influences from early childhood. He soon revealed an unmistakable bent for music. His creative impulse bore fruit in his boyhood days with the completion of an ambitious cantata, *Put Away the Flutes*. When he was only sixteen, he finished a string quartet. Both of these early works employed a serial technique; in them the influence of Schoenberg, and especially of Webern, is pronounced. Though his serial writing has undergone modifications and transformations through the years, he has remained basically faithful to the method, even in his later sym-

phonies and operas. "It's just a natural way for me to write music," he told an interviewer in 1965, "something I really don't think about at all. And I'm anxious that people should not be conscious of it. . . . The more I use serial technique, the less I am inhibited about making sounds which relate directly to tonality —although it is, of course, not tonal music."

RICHARD RODNEY BENNETT

His academic schooling took place at the Leighton Park School in Reading. During that period he earned part of his expenses by playing piano in jazz ensembles. A scholarship enabled him, in 1953, to attend the Royal Academy of Music in London, where he studied with Lennox Berkeley and Howard Ferguson. This proved a productive period for him since he completed *Five Pieces for Orchestra* (written in 1956 and very well received at the Cheltenham Festival in 1959), a second string quartet (1953), the *Cantata for Voice and Percussion* (1954), and the Concerto for Horn and Orchestra (1956). From 1957 to 1959 he lived in Paris as a recipient of a scholarship from the French government. He studied with Pierre Boulez, who helped to uncover for the young composer new methods and new avenues of expressiveness in the use of serialism. Boulez became a major influence on Bennett's development. In later years other twentieth century composers set for him creative examples which proved vital for his growth; among them were Britten, Dallapiccola, Bartók, and Henze.

In 1958 and 1959 Bennett wrote the background music for two avant-garde films—*Indiscrète* and *The Mark*. He continued to produce music for films, including such highly commercial successes as *Far from the Madding Crowd* in 1967 and *Billion Dollar Brain* in 1968. He also provided background music for a TV series in London.

His main creative activity, however, was the writing of music for the concert hall. After his return from Paris, he established residence in London at 24 Marylebone High Street and worked long and hard on serious composition. Despite the influence brought to bear on him by other twentieth century composers, he soon began to reveal an individuality and personal strength in his rhythmic and harmonic thinking, a thoroughly personal point of view in the kind of material he selected and the way he developed it, and, most significantly, a growing capacity to endow serial writing with emotional impulses and reflective attitudes. This became increasingly apparent in three important compositions completed in 1960: the third string quartet; *The Calendar*, for chamber orchestra; and *Journal*, for symphony orchestra. One year later he made his bow as composer for the stage with a one-act opera, *The Ledge*.

Bennett first attracted world interest with his orchestral compositions, beginning with *Aubade* (1964), which had been commissioned and introduced by the BBC Promenade Concerts and which received critical accolades when performed in Germany. Immediately after that came his First Symphony, which established him as one of the most significant English composers since the end of World War II. The symphony makes use of such unsymphonic instruments as the marimba, maracas, and Chinese blocks, together with the usual instruments of the orchestra. The serial idiom is employed, but with considerable flexibility. "There is considerable freedom in reiteration, permutation and even tonal motives," says Nicolas Slonimsky, "that make the work sound acceptable to untutored audiences."

The symphony had been commissioned by the Peter Stuyvesant Foundation for the London Symphony, which introduced it in London under the direction of Istvan Kertesz on April 3, 1966. The Daily *Telegraph* called Bennett a "lyrical logician, a very unusual constellation of talents" on the basis of this symphony, while the London *Times* described the first movement as "exhilarating," the slow movement as "sultry and amorous with a smashing climax," and the finale as "busy but rather . . . elliptical . . . seen in the end to have absorbed the flavor of the earlier movements and added a firmer streak of its own." American critics were hardly less enthusiastic when the symphony was presented by several major orchestras. On its performance by the Philadelphia Orchestra on January 6, 1967, the critic of the *Evening Bulletin* found the work full of "discernible drama and urgency, vitality, and a fascinating use of instruments," while the critic of the *Inquirer* saw in it "the appeal of a firm direction and contemporary texture . . . a listenable and pleasing new work."

The success of the First Symphony brought Bennett several important commissions. For the City Music Society of London he wrote his fourth string quartet; for the Macnaughton Concerts, his *Sonata No. 2 for Solo Violin;* and for the Leeds Triennial Festival in 1967, the *Epithalamion*, for chorus and orchestra. Probably the most significant commission of all came from the New York Philharmonic to help celebrate its one hundred and twenty-fifth anniversary. For this event Bennett produced his one-movement Symphony No. 2, introduced by the New York Philharmonic under Leonard Bernstein on January 18, 1968. It is scored for a full symphony orchestra, but without clarinets, and the piano plays an all-important role in the orchestration. Three basic tempi are employed in the following succession: allegro, moderato, and vivace. Serialism is used freely and, more than heretofore, expressive and dramatic values are emphasized. To a writer for *Time* magazine, the symphony offered "the proposition that even at the furthest limits of harmony, it is possible to reach a listener with broad melodic lines and ruddy emotionality."

Despite his successes with instrumental music both in Europe and America, Bennett is more partial to opera than to concert music. He has said: "Opera is a way of life." His first important opera was *The Mines of Sulphur*, in three acts, text by Beverley Cross. This is grim drama, set in a small manor house in England in the eighteenth century. The old man who owns the manor is murdered by a criminal and the old man's mistress. Before the murderers can make their escape, a company of strolling players comes to the manor for shelter. The culprits get the punishment they deserve from the players; the leading lady, whom the criminal has kissed, is a carrier of the plague and infects him. The stricken man and his horrified accomplice are left alone on the darkened stage as the final curtain descends.

Bennett confessed that in writing this opera he wanted to create "a tough, violent piece." There was little doubt in the minds of his audiences and critics that he succeeded in achieving his aims. As *Time* said of his music: "His large orchestra churns out great globs of dark-hued atmosphere, over which voices float with wisps of disconnected but curiously memorable melody."

The Mines of Sulphur, which had been commissioned and produced by Sadler's Wells, proved so successful that the company took it on tour to Paris and Zagreb. The opera was also mounted in Cologne and Marseilles, and at La Scala in Milan where it was produced by John Huston, the celebrated American film director. The American première was given in New York by the Opera Department of the Juilliard School of Music on January 17, 1968. Bennett came to the United States to help at rehearsals and to attend the première. On January 18 he was at Philharmonic Hall to hear the world première of his Second Symphony. Had he wished he could have heard another of his scores in New York; the film *Far from the Madding Crowd*, for which he produced excellent and highly atmospheric background music, was then playing in one of New York's leading theatres.

Quite a different kind of opera was the result of a second commission from Sadler's Wells: a comic fantasy, *A Penny for a Song*. The world première of this work took place in London on November 21, 1967. For Bennett the writing of the score to an amusing and at times poignant text by John Whiting proved something of a lark. "I wrote it very quickly, just because it was so enjoyable," he told an interviewer. The theme of the opera is twofold: the futility of war and the frustrations and heartlessness of summer romance. The time is the period of the Napoleonic Wars, the setting a house in Dorset; the entire action takes place in a single day. The opera is filled with whimsical characters each possessing a mania of his or her own, each inhabiting a personal world. One of two eccentric brothers is convinced that Napoleon is about to invade England and bewails the fact that his country is so little prepared to face the menace; the second brother has a neurotic fear of fires. The brothers station a butler atop a tree to look out for either disaster. When the local Home Guard goes through maneuvers, the two brothers are convinced the invasion has begun. One disguises himself as Napoleon to outwit the enemy, while the other goes about busily extinguishing warning signal fires as soon as they are lit. While all this is going on, the young girl of the household falls in love for the first time with a mercenary returning from the actual battlefront. The romance is frustrated when the mercenary comes into conflict with every member of the household because of his radical opinions. By the time dusk has brought the day to a close, the personal life of each member of the household has undergone dramatic change.

To Edward Greenfield, reporting from London to *High Fidelity*, it was not the eccentric characters or the farcical situations in which they placed themselves that made the opera impressive. To him the opera is "an elegiac work of a tender delicacy worthy of a Delius. Laughter at the first performance was scattered rather than universal and the first-night reviews inevitably reflected this disappointment. But, now having seen the piece twice, I am quite sure that it matters not at all whether the audience laughs or not. . . . Once you accept that *A Penny for a Song* is a gentle, whimsical picture of a glorious summer day in Dorset in 1804, and neither a laughter-maker or a social tract, the opera works." *A Penny for a Song* was produced by the Munich Opera in Germany, on January 26, 1968, under the title *Napoleon Kommt*.

In addition to operas Bennett wrote the score for a ballet, *Jazz Calendar*, which enjoyed a spectacular success when introduced by the Royal Ballet at Covent Garden in 1967.

MAJOR WORKS

Ballet—Jazz Calendar.

Chamber Music—4 string quartets; 2 sonatas for solo violin; Sonatina, for flute solo; Four Improvisations, for solo violin; Conversations, for two flutes; Cross-talk, for two clarinets; Trio, for flute, oboe, and clarinet.

Choral Music—Five Carols; Three Verses; Two Lullabies; Epithalamion.
Operas—The Ledge, one-act; The Mines of Sulphur; A Penny for a Song.
Orchestral Music—2 symphonies; Five Pieces for Orchestra; Concerto for Horn and Orchestra; Journal; Calendar, for chamber orchestra; Nocturnes, for chamber orchestra; Aubade; Suite for Small Orchestra (based on The Aviary and The Insect World).
Piano Music—Five Studies; Capriccio, for piano duet.
Vocal Music—Cantata for Voice and Percussion; The Approaches of Sleep, for four voices and ten instruments; London Pastoral, for tenor and chamber orchestra; The Aviary; The Insect World; The Music That Her Echo Is; Five Songs, for tenor and piano.

ABOUT

Time, January 26, 1968.

Robert Russell Bennett
1894–

Robert Russell Bennett was born in Kansas City, Missouri, on June 15, 1894. He has provided the following description of his early life: "Ill health—as a matter of fact, infantile paralysis—caused a shift to the country when I was six. There nine years were passed learning the piano from my mother, and violin, trumpet, and subsequently many other instruments, from my father. Father had a band and orchestra and since some member was usually absent, and the missing member had to be replaced, I was usually called upon as replacement, no matter what instrument. With improved health, I began to study harmony in Kansas City with Carl Busch, then conductor of the Kansas City Symphony Orchestra. During the next four years, a few small compositions of mine were published by Theodore Presser in Philadelphia.

"In 1916, possessed of savings to the amount of about two hundred dollars, a move to New York was accomplished—mostly on nerve. There ensued a period when I was copyist for G. Schirmer, arranger of whatever music I could find to arrange, and then a year in the War. On my return from the Army, on December 29, 1919, I married Louise Edgerton Merrill.

"Not long after that, I began a quiet but lucrative career as orchestrator of musical-comedy scores in New York, which enabled us to bundle up our savings and sail for Paris—again, mostly on nerve. In Paris, I studied with Nadia Boulanger and began my real work as composer—this, rather against my original intention, as I was and am convinced that too much music is written, and I was more anxious at the time to do conducting and possibly critical work than composing. European musicians, however, advised me to write music. In 1927 a Guggenheim Fellowship was won, and, a year later, renewed. With this help, the European stay was extended sufficiently to account for a large list of works."

ROBERT RUSSELL BENNETT

Bennett first came to the notice of the music world when in the season of 1926–1927 a symphonic piece won honorable mention in a contest conducted by *Musical America*. Two and a half years later he received two RCA symphonic awards, for two different orchestral works: *Sights and Sounds* and the *Abraham Lincoln Symphony*. With renown came a greater willingness on the part of leading orchestras and musical organizations to perform his works. On October 24, 1931, the *Abraham Lincoln Symphony* was introduced by the Philadelphia Orchestra under Stokowski. Lawrence Gilman referred to this score as "remarkable" in construction and content. It is in four movements, in each of which (in the composer's own explanation) he has "used two outstanding attributes of Lincoln's character as the inspiration for the themes." The first movement calls forth the atmosphere and backgrounds of Lincoln's home and is contrasted by an elegiac subject suggestive of the man's sadness. The slow movement speaks of "the sentiment of young America of that day," while in the third-movement scherzo Lincoln's weakness for pranks and general devilment is portrayed. The last movement was intended by the composer as a proclamation of what he felt to be "a triumph of a great soul, rich, unbending, inevitable."

Though this symphony is catholic in style and classical in outlook, Bennett's other pieces of this period introduced the jazz idiom into serious musical forms in a novel and intriguing way. In this category belong the *Three Marches* (originally entitled simply *March*), for two pianos and orchestra, first performed on July 8, 1930, by the Los Angeles Philharmonic conducted by Karl Krueger; the *Variations on a Theme of Jerome Kern*, first presented by the New York Chamber Orchestra, Bernard Herrmann conducting, on December 3, 1933; and the Concerto Grosso, for dance band and symphony orchestra, the première of which took place in Rochester, New York, on December 9, 1932, Howard Hanson conducting the Eastman Rochester Orchestra.

Subsequently major works fulfilled the rich promise of the *Abraham Lincoln Symphony*. On April 8, 1935, his opera *Maria Malibran*, with libretto by Robert A. Simon, was introduced at the Juilliard School of Music in New York, Albert Stoessel conducting. The Philadelphia Orchestra under Iturbi presented *Adagio Eroica*, written in memory "of a soldier," on April 25, 1935. *Nocturne and Appassionata*, for piano and orchestra, was played by the Philadelphia Orchestra under Saul Caston, with Milton Kaye as soloist. *The Four Freedoms*, a symphonic suite inspired by four Norman Rockwell paintings, was first heard over the NBC network in a performance by the NBC Symphony under Frank Black on September 26, 1943, and was given in Los Angeles on December 16 of the same year. Louis Kaufman introduced the Concerto for Violin and Orchestra on February 14, 1944. In 1944 Bennett wrote a second opera–this time in one act–entitled *The Enchanted Kiss*, in which Robert A. Simon's libretto was based on a story by O. Henry. It was first given over the Mutual radio network on December 30, 1945. On May 12, 1945, *Water Music*, for string quartet, was featured at the first festival of contemporary music sponsored in New York by the Alice M. Ditson Fund. And one of Bennett's most popular short works for orchestra up to that time–*Overture to an Imaginary Drama*–had its première in Toronto on May 14, 1946, Fritz Mahler conducting the Toronto Philharmonic.

More recent major works by Bennett include *A Commemoration Symphony* which the Pittsburgh Symphony under William Steinberg presented in Pittsburgh on December 30, 1959; the Concerto for Violin, Piano, and Orchestra introduced by Benno and Sylvia Rabinof in Portland, Oregon, on March 18, 1963; and the Symphony, directed by Fritz Reiner in Chicago on April 18, 1963.

Bennett's approach is generally that of a serious musician with a consummate command of his technique, a fine respect for traditional structures, and an approach to esthetic problems that betrays the presence of a sound classicist. At times, however, he reveals an irrepressible bent for the witty and the satiric, even in works not in a jazz idiom. In such compositions, as one unidentified writer said, "he covers every feeling with a bon mot" as if "addressing himself mainly to the smart set."

Bennett has also been active in the field of popular music. In Tin Pan Alley, he is known as one of the most adroit orchestrators in the business. Many of the celebrated musical comedies and musical plays by Gershwin, Porter, Kern, and Rodgers were orchestrated by him, as well as numerous successes by other composers over a period of some thirty years. Among the Broadway triumphs for which he has served as orchestrator were *Oklahoma!, Carmen Jones, Show Boat, Kiss Me Kate, Finian's Rainbow, South Pacific, The King and I, My Fair Lady*, and *The Sound of Music*. His scoring for the motion picture adaptation of *Oklahoma!* earned him the Academy Award in 1955.

"Although I make my living at commercial music," writes Bennett, "I am convinced that the contribution of our lighter composers, authors of what may become American folk songs, is very small. I believe in the deeper thoughts of our better composers to the point of trusting great music to take care of itself against any onslaught of criticism, public reaction, and financial gain for the less cultured (although in many cases equally gifted) writers."

Of his work in the serious field, he says: "I have never made an attempt to exploit my original music; such publications and performances as have taken place were the result of the interest of my friendly contemporaries. Were it not for the restrictions of some of the performing rights societies that I belong to, the whole world could have anything I've written in manuscript, plus my hope that the world will approach my serious efforts in the same spirit that I do."

Bennett was long active in the field of radio. In 1941 he conducted "Russell Bennett's Notebook" over the Mutual network and for the program composed many entertaining and novel features. In 1942 this program earned him the Award of Merit from the National Association for American Composers and Conductors. On December 8, 1944, Bennett launched a new weekly program in which each week he featured a different orchestral fantasy based on American folk tunes. He wrote numerous scores for television documentaries in the 1950's and 1960's and orchestrated Richard Rodgers' music for *Victory at Sea*.

The Bennetts have one child, a daughter, Beatrice Jean. Of his activities other than music, Bennett confesses a passion for baseball and pool, an interest in tennis, and a strange predilection for trying to figure out winners in horse races without making a single bet on his choices (well, hardly ever).

MAJOR WORKS

Chamber Music—Water Music, for string quartet; Hexapoda, for violin and piano; Five Improvisations, for trio; Sonatine, for soprano and harp; Six Souvenirs, for two flutes and piano; String Quartet; Quintet, for accordion and string quartet.
Choral Music—Theme and Variations About a Lorelei; Aux Quatre Coins de Paris; Nietzsche Variations.
Operas—Maria Malibran; The Enchanted Kiss.
Orchestral Music—Charleston Rhapsody; Sights and Sounds; Abraham Lincoln Symphony; Three Marches (originally March), for two pianos and orchestra; American Ballade, fantasia on Stephen Foster's melodies; Adagio Eroica; Concerto Grosso, for orchestra and jazz band; Variations on a Theme by Jerome Kern; Études; Nocturne and Appassionata, for piano and orchestra; Concerto for Violin and Orchestra; The Four Freedoms, symphonic suite;

Classic Serenade, for string orchestra; Overture to an Imaginary Drama; A Dry Weather Legend; Suite of Old American Dances; Concerto in B minor for Piano and Orchestra; Dance Sonata; Rose Variations; Kansas City Album; Ohio River Suite; A Commemoration Symphony; Concerto for Harp, Cello, and Orchestra; Armed Forces Suite; Concerto for Violin, Piano, and Orchestra; Mississippi Overture; Symphony.
Organ Music—Sonata.
Piano Music—2 sonatinas; Tema Sporca con Variazioni.

ABOUT

Goss, M., Modern Music Makers; Howard, J. T., Our Contemporary Composers.
New York Herald Tribune, October 11, 1931; New York Times, November 15, 1942; New Yorker, November 17, 1961.

Alban Berg
1885–1935

Alban Berg was born in Vienna on February 9, 1885, the youngest of four children. His father, a well-to-do merchant, was of Bavarian background; his mother, Viennese. Though musical, Alban Berg had no formal music instruction until his maturity. A sensitive, introspective, self-centered boy, his interest lay in the direction of literature. His literary favorites included Oscar Wilde (to whom, in his manhood, he bore a striking resemblance) and Henrik Ibsen.

His boyhood was cheerful and well adjusted. Winters were spent in Vienna, summers in a villa in Carinthia. When he was fifteen, however, circumstances changed radically. He suffered from a serious bronchial asthma which undermined his health and spirit, and affected him periodically for the rest of his life. Two months later he experienced another setback, this time emotional, in the death of his father, which left the family in precarious financial circumstances. Perhaps these traumatic experiences compelled him to write music, possibly as an escape. Without a lesson in composition, he wrote songs and piano duets; seventy of these items were found in manuscript after his death. His musical gods were Wagner and Mahler, whose influence on him can be perceived in his juvenilia. But intuitively Berg felt that the post-Romantic movement had

Berg: bĕʀк

57

exhausted itself with Mahler and Richard Strauss, that a composer now had to seek out new creative avenues. Until he could come upon these new ways in music he was convinced that, creatively, he had come to a dead end.

ALBAN BERG

A frustrated love affair, combined with a failure in one of his school examinations, led him to attempt suicide when he was eighteen. But by 1904 he had emerged from the depths of his depression and had arrived at a spiritual renewal. This came about as a result of his first meeting with Arnold Schoenberg, which had been arranged for him by his older brother. The bond that first drew the men to each other was their mutual admiration for Mahler. "When Alban Berg came to me," Schoenberg recalled in 1949, "he was a very tall youngster and extremely timid. But when I saw the compositions he showed me—songs in the style of Hugo Wolf and Brahms—I recognized at once that he had real talent. Consequently, I accepted him as a pupil, though at this time he was unable to pay my fee. Later his mother . . . told Alban . . . he could enter the Conservatory. I was told that Alban was so upset by this assumption that he started weeping and could not stop weeping before his mother had allowed him to continue with me."

Berg's lessons with Schoenberg represented his first formal instruction in music. Berg threw himself into study with unparalleled

energy and zeal, sometimes working for hours at his exercises, often late into the night, keeping alert by drinking immense quantities of tea. Schoenberg's independent thinking and high-minded attitudes towards art made a profound impression on the young man. Schoenberg became for Berg not only a teacher but a friend, adviser, inspiration, and model. What the teacher meant to the pupil is revealed in a letter written by Berg to Anton Webern in 1910: "Twice a week I wait for him at Karlsplatz, before teaching begins at the Conservatory, and for fifteen to thirty minutes we walk amidst the hubbub of the city, which is drowned out by the 'roar' of his words. But to tell you about all this is only to increase your suffering and sense of deprivation. . . . How despondent you must be again, far away from all these divine experiences, having to forgo walks with Schoenberg and miss the meaning, the gestures, the cadence of his talk."

Berg studied with Schoenberg for six years. During this period he completed a number of works obviously influenced by his teacher, but traces of Wagnerian and Mahlerian post-Romanticism are still strongly in evidence. These compositions included a piano sonata, op. 1 (1908); Four Songs, op. 2 (1909); and a string quartet, op. 3 (1910).

During his early studies with Schoenberg, Berg combined music lessons with a job as a government official, which he had assumed in 1905. In 1908, a family inheritance enabled him to give up his post and devote himself to the writing of Opus 1. From then on his dedication first to his studies, and next to his compositions, became complete.

In May 1911 Berg married Helene Nahowski. His studies with Schoenberg having ended one year earlier, he now devoted himself assiduously to developing his creative personality. The first work completed following his student association with Schoenberg was the *Five Orchestral Songs*, op. 4 (1912), after postcard texts by Peter Altenberg. The "postcard texts" consisted of terse messages which the Viennese poet Peter Altenberg (whose real name was Richard Englander) used to send to friends and enemies on postcards. Berg, eager to free himself from the bondage of tonality, used Altenberg's unorthodox texts as the medium for his own revolt.

The première of these songs created one of the greatest scandals witnessed in Vienna's concert halls. It took place at a concert of the Academic Society for Literature and Music on March 31, 1913, with a program made up entirely of music by Schoenberg and his pupils and disciples. "If this concert was intended to be a 'memorable occasion' it surely succeeded," reported a dispatch to *Musical Courier* on April 23, 1913, "for it occasioned the greatest uproar which has occurred in a Vienna concert hall in the memory of the oldest critics writing. Laughter, hisses, and applause continued throughout a great part of the actual performance of the disputed pieces. After the Berg songs the dispute became almost a riot. The police were sought and the only officer who could be found actually threw out of the gallery one noisemaker who persisted in blowing on a key for a whistle. But this policeman could not prevent one of the composers from appearing in a box and yelling to the crowd, '*Heraus mit der Baggage!*' ('Out with the trash!'). Whereat the uproar increased. Members of the orchestra descended from the stage and entered into spirited controversy with the audience. And finally the president of the Academic Society came and boxed the ears of a man who had insulted him while he was making an announcement."

Always a slow and fastidious workman, and never a prolific creator, Berg completed only two more works before the outbreak of World War I: *Four Pieces*, for clarinet and piano, op. 5 (1913), dedicated to Schoenberg; and *Three Orchestral Pieces*, op. 6 (1914). In these works Schoenberg's atonal language and his partiality for intricate contrapuntal textures had been assimilated. But whereas Schoenberg was drawing closer to abstraction and further from subjectivity, Berg was bringing to his atonal writing a romantic, intimate approach together with a strong, dramatic viewpoint.

Having been found physically unfit for military service, Berg helped the Austrian effort by working in the War Ministry. Creative work was out of the question. "The urge to be in it [the war], the feeling of helplessness at being unable to serve my country, prevented any concentration or work," Berg told Schoenberg. But when the war had ended, Berg returned to composition by devoting himself to an ambitious project that had occupied his thoughts since 1914. In that year he had seen a performance of Büchner's play *Woyzeck* (Büchner's spelling). He immediately became fascinated by its potential as an opera in an atonal style. He prepared his own text in 1917. With the war over, he concentrated on the music, completing the basic score by 1920 and the orchestration one year later. The first piano score was published in 1921.

Three excerpts from the opera were introduced at the Frankfurt Music Festival in Germany in 1924, Hermann Scherchen conducting. The music created a sensation–violent reactions being expressed both pro and con. The attendant publicity encouraged a stage presentation, despite the formidable production problems. It required one hundred and thirty-seven rehearsals to get the opera ready for the stage. *Wozzeck* was finally seen at the Berlin State Opera on December 14, 1925, Erich Kleiber conducting. Some called it the work of a genius; some even maintained it was the greatest opera since *Pelléas et Mélisande*, a turning point in the development and evolution of the serious musical theatre. But this group numbered mainly the dedicated atonalists of the Schoenberg school. Most others regarded this music as the raving of a madman. Typical of the many denunciations was this review by Paul Zschorlich in the *Deutsche Zeitung*: "As I was leaving the State Opera I had the sensation of having been not in a public theatre but in an insane asylum. On the stage, in the orchestra, in the stalls–plain madmen. I regard Alban Berg as a musical swindler and a musician dangerous to the community. . . . One may ask oneself seriously to what degree music may be a criminal occupation. We deal here, from a musical viewpoint, with a capital offense."

A favorable minority report was handed in by H. H. Stuckenschmidt: "It is difficult to do justice within the limits of a review to the strange perfection and uniqueness of this work. . . . Berg's writing reveals qualities only latent in the libretto, unfolds the most secret psychological details, and testifies to the ingenuity that places him beside the most notable musicodramatists of our time. . . . A meaningful event in the history of music drama."

Even though *Wozzeck* was denounced more often than it was praised, it had aroused so much argument and curiosity that it was widely performed. In ten years' time it received over one hundred and fifty performances in twenty-eight different cities from Amsterdam to Leningrad. It was heard for the first time in the United States when Leopold Stokowski led a staged performance in Philadelphia on March 19, 1931, and in New York on November 24, 1931. Since then, it has been heard in the United States in a concert version in 1951 by the New York Philharmonic under Mitropoulos (which was recorded); it was presented in an English translation by the New York City Opera in 1952; and it was included in the repertory of the Metropolitan Opera on March 5, 1959.

Wozzeck is not only a highly complex and a highly discordant opera but also an opera employing the most novel methods and means. On the one hand it is avant-garde in its persistent use of discords, and in its desertion of melody for a stark, free recitative (*Sprechstimme*, or *Sprechgesang*). On the other hand it goes back to such classical forms as the passacaglia, fugue, suite, march, symphony, invention, and variation. It uses an accompanying orchestra made up of three different ensembles: a chamber orchestra, a military band, and a restaurant orchestra of high-pitched violins. Some of the less conventional instruments used in this orchestra are an out-of-tune upright piano, an accordion, and a bombardon (an obsolete form of tuba).

Büchner's grim story concerns a poor soldier who murders his unfaithful sweetheart Marie and who then meets his own doom in a pool where he has been trying to retrieve the murder weapon. In his eerie, hypertense and discordant music, Berg caught the essence of Büchner's surrealistic episodes, creating, as Martin Cooper pointed out, a unified artistic concept which is more like "the apparent realism of a Kafka story, or a hideously real nightmare than an expression of human feelings." Or, as Alfred Einstein remarked in his criticism of the opera: "The work is full of what lies behind and beneath our ordinary waking life. . . . What makes this work so unique and so convincing is that in this one particular case we have a composer whose technique from the first to the last is in perfect accord with his purpose of giving expression to the poem." Einstein described Berg's music as "drawn

from Wozzeck's poor, worried, inarticulate, chaotic soul. It is a vision in sound. The orchestra is just like a bundle of nerves; at first sight it seems to consist only of confused strands, but it is actually a living organism."

After *Wozzeck*, Berg turned to the writing of concert works, beginning with his Chamber Concerto for Violin, Piano, and Thirteen Wind Instruments, written in 1924 to celebrate Schoenberg's fiftieth birthday. It was introduced in Frankfurt, Germany, on July 2, 1927. In this work the composer indulges his fascination for anagrams. In the opening section, "Epigraphe," he creates a kind of musical anagram out of those letters from the names of Schoenberg, Berg, and Webern–the trinity of atonal music–that could be translated into musical notes in the German notation. Also bearing in mind the trinity of atonal music, Berg built up his structure out of the number three and its multiples.

The *Lyric Suite* (1926)–originally for string quartet, three of its movements were later transcribed by the composer for chamber orchestra–was a six-movement work filled with happy lyrical ideas. Some of the movements are in the twelve-tone technique (before this only a single episode in *Wozzeck* had utilized a twelve-tone row); other movements are in a freer atonal idiom. Unity is achieved throughout the work by having each of the movements repeat a theme from the preceding one.

In 1929 Berg made a setting of three poems by Baudelaire in the concert aria *Der Wein*, which was performed in Königsberg on June 4, 1930. To Robert Craft the three songs are like the three parts of a one-movement symphony, the first serving as exposition and development, the second as a scherzo, and the third (which repeats the first song in a telescoped version) as recapitulation.

One of the few honors Berg enjoyed in his lifetime came to him in 1929 when he was made a member of the Prussian Academy of Arts. At this time he was also offered a teaching post at the Hochschule für Musik in Berlin, which he turned down. After 1932, he divided his year between an apartment in Vienna and a little villa, "Waldhaus," near Velden, on the Worthersee in Carinthia. Both in Vienna and in Carinthia he worked industriously on an opera, his first since *Wozzeck*.

The opera was *Lulu*, on which he labored for

the last seven years of his life and which he did not live to complete. Berg's libretto, which once again he prepared himself, was adapted from two dramas by Wedekind, *Die Büchse der Pandora* and *Erdgeist*. This sordid drama is built from the disagreeable elements of lust, perversion, human degradation, suicide, and death. Its central character is a corrupt woman who destroys one man after another, before becoming a prostitute and being murdered by Jack the Ripper. One unidentified critic in Prague described Lulu as "a heroine of four-dimensional power in her endurance and her suffering, destroying all that she magnetizes. She is a phenomenon of nature, beyond good and evil, a complete cosmos whose secrets, altogether removed from ordinary comprehension, can be revealed only by the music. The way this glowing ball scorches everybody that it touches and finally burns itself out, leaving all life about it extinguished or fading away, has led the metaphysician in the composer to make the transposition to those unearthly spheres, where figures flicker in death like dream images, illumined only by the last dying afterglow of a great irresponsible demon."

In *Lulu*, Berg relies exclusively on the twelve-tone system, the row on which the opera is based appearing at the very beginning. But, as Harold C. Schonberg has pointed out, "Berg's use of the twelve-tone technique is less doctrinaire than that used by today's serialists. There are sections where the music sounds more consonant than anything else . . . and throughout the opera, dissonances and all, the feeling is one of almost romanticism." In another report, Schonberg added: "Rather than being a sharp break from the past, it is a continuation of the main stream of German music from Wagner through Strauss, Mahler and the early Schoenberg."

During 1934 and 1935 Berg interrupted his labors on *Lulu* to complete a commission for a violin concerto for Louis Krasner. As Berg worked on this concerto, he learned of the death of a young friend, the daughter of Gustav Mahler's widow by a second marriage. Berg now decided to transform his concerto into a requiem for this girl. In the first movement her personality is delineated in several graceful themes. The second movement speaks dramatically of the tragedy of death, reaching a climax with a poignant section telling of the deliverance of the girl's soul. In this movement Berg quotes a chorale by Johann Sebastian Bach, *Es ist genug*, to suggest that the soul has finally found peace. Louis Krasner introduced the concerto at Barcelona on April 19, 1936.

The death of a young girl to whom he was devoted was only one of many unhappy circumstances attending Berg's life in the middle 1930's. All his life a sick and frail man, Berg now became physically depleted by his chronic bronchial condition and other ailments. His income greatly reduced because Nazi Germany did not encourage performances of his music, he often did not have enough money for proper medication and attention. For a period he suffered excruciatingly from an infected tooth, unable to pay for dental treatment. One other circumstance added to his misery—his teacher, friend, and mentor, Arnold Schoenberg, had gone off to America. Although the separation had hurt him deeply, he was pained even more by Schoenberg's bitterness towards him because he preferred to remain behind in Austria and continue living under the growing shadow of Nazism.

An orchestral suite which Berg had adapted from *Lulu* was given for the first time in Berlin on November 30, 1934, Erich Kleiber conducting. The reaction was mixed, wavering between excessive enthusiasm and excessive attacks. A performance of that suite in Vienna, on December 11, 1935, was the last concert Berg attended. Though seriously ill, he insisted on helping with the preparation and was also at the concert to receive the enthusiastic response of the audience. He died less than two weeks later, his death caused by blood poisoning brought about by the sting of a bee. Five days before his death he received a blood transfusion. On learning that the blood donor had been a composer of light music, Berg remarked: "I only hope that this doesn't turn me into an operetta composer." Two days later he had a relapse, and on December 23 he remarked prophetically: "This will be the decisive day." He suffered hallucinations late that day, apparently believing he was conducting a performance of *Lulu*. "An upbeat, an upbeat," he kept muttering. He died early on the morning of December 24, 1935.

At the time of his death, only two acts of *Lulu* were completed, together with 268 measures of the third act, and the finale. When *Lulu* received its world première–on June 2, 1937 in Zürich–it was presented with only the first two acts and the finale. In 1953 in Essen *Lulu* was produced with the third act as Berg wrote it filled out with spoken dialogue from the original Wedekind text. This was the first performance of the opera in Germany. The more general practice, since then, has been to include music from the *Lulu* suite to fill out the third act. This is the way the opera was given during its American première at Santa Fe, New Mexico, on August 6, 1963.

Lulu has grown in public acceptance until audiences as well as critics are ready to concede it to be a worthy successor to *Wozzeck* and, in some respects, even superior to it. Performances of *Lulu* have been given throughout Europe. Two of these–one by the Hamburg Opera and the other by the Deutsche Oper in Berlin–were recorded. They were released simultaneously in 1968, supplementing a third recording that Columbia had made a few years earlier. When in June 1967 the visiting Hamburg Opera presented the première New York performance of *Lulu*, the opera scored a tremendous success–probably the greatest accorded any of the operas offered by the visiting troupe. This triumph was repeated soon afterwards when the Hamburg Opera presented *Lulu* at Expo 67 in Montreal.

Paul Pisk described Berg as follows: "Portraits revealing the proportionate symmetry of his features and his tall, lean figure, bear a striking resemblance to those of Oscar Wilde. Even Berg's way of parting his hair, and his manner of dress, resembled those of the poet." In discussing Berg's personality, Pisk said that the composer was a man of good humor and light wit behind which "lay a profound philosophical mind as well as a creative imagination. He inclined towards mysticism. He believed in the symbolism of numbers, and was at home in the study of comparative religion."

Hektor Rottweiler contributes the following additional information about Berg: "He was melancholy and proud, dreamed of happiness and sought pain; fear, and the malice it hides behind, could be read in his eyes. His temperament was gentle, but it had a stamp of steel. . . . His whole attitude would lead one to believe that material reality did not touch him, even from a distance. He wanted many things, but hoped for none, so alone was he. . . . He . . . rejected worldly desires. . . . He treated his own person with prudence and indifference. . . . This clarified a mysterious paradox in Berg's life: he was totally egocentric, and yet entirely detached from himself. He spoke willingly of his works, but without a shadow of vanity. 'It is only when I compose,' he said, 'that I believe myself to be Beethoven; but not after having composed.' "

MAJOR WORKS

Chamber Music—String Quartet; Four Pieces, for clarinet and piano; Chamber Concerto, for piano, violin, and thirteen wind instruments; Lyric Suite, for string quartet (three movements also for chamber orchestra).

Operas—Wozzeck; Lulu.

Orchestral Music—Five Songs, for voice and orchestra; Three Pieces; Der Wein, concert aria for soprano and orchestra; Concerto for Violin and Orchestra.

Piano Music—Sonata.

Vocal Music—Seven Early Songs; Four Songs, op. 2; Schliesse Mir die Augen Beide, two settings; Canon, for four voices.

ABOUT

Ewen, D. (ed.), The New Book of Modern Composers; Leibowitz, R., Schoenberg and His School; Redlich, H. F., Alban Berg; Reich, W., Alban Berg; Reich, W. (ed.), Alban Berg, Bildnis im Wort; Vogelsang, K., Alban Berg, Leben und Werk.

Monthly Musical Record (London), February 1936; Musical Quarterly, October 1936; New York Times, March 30, 1952.

William Bergsma
1921–

William Laurence Bergsma was born in Oakland, California, on April 1, 1921. From the age of six he played the violin in orchestras, "rather badly," he confessed to this editor. His musical interests developed further in Burlingame High School, which boasted an excellent music department and where he was given scope to develop his musical inclinations: "If I wanted to write a piece and copy the parts, the orchestra would play it, and did; my first complete composition was for orchestra and was played at one of its concerts, as were two or three later ones. If I wanted to try conducting, the orchestra was there to experiment on; and, with occasional concerts or incidental music to plays, there even was an audience."

In the summer of 1937, he writes, "I hid my lack of a high school diploma and enrolled in my first formal composition course, at the University of Southern California, taught by Howard Hanson." At the end of a six-week session, Hanson suggested to Bergsma that he send him the composition he was working on. It was the ballet *Paul Bunyan*, planned, says the composer, "rather impractically for puppets and solo dancers." From Rochester Dr. Hanson broadcast an orchestral suite from the ballet. A staged version was produced in San Francisco on June 22, 1939. About twenty-five performances and broadcasts of the orchestral suite followed.

WILLIAM BERGSMA

In 1938 Bergsma entered Stanford University, keeping up his musical activities there by taking courses and composing for ballet groups around the San Francisco area. In 1940, he entered the Eastman School of Music, remaining there four years, first as a student of composition with Howard Hanson and of orchestration with Bernard Rogers, then as a teaching fellow until 1944. "As a composer," he reports, "I was given access to three different orchestras, a ballet group, a small chorus, and virtually any kind of chamber ensemble. There were also specific occasions and inducements in the form of Symposia and Festivals of American Music, as well as other concerts."

Under such stimulating conditions, Bergsma wrote his first string quartet, which the Gordon String Quartet introduced at the Eastman School in 1942. In this composition, which received the Bearns Prize from Columbia University in 1943 and the award of the Society for Publication of American Music in 1945, he reveals for the first time a pronounced tendency towards contrapuntal writing. On May 1, 1942, a ballet, *Gold and the Señor Commandante*, was produced in Rochester, New York; two excerpts from the score were recorded for RCA Victor by the Eastman Rochester Orchestra under Hanson. His reputation grew in 1942–1943 with a Symphony for Chamber Orchestra, commissioned by Town Hall in New York (Rochester, April 14, 1943) and *Music on a Quiet Theme* (Rochester, April 22, 1943), the latter receiving a special award in the Independent Music Publishers Contest. In 1946 Bergsma was commissioned to write *The Fortunate Islands*, for string orchestra, to honor the twenty-fifth anniversary of the League of Composers. Its première took place over the CBS radio network in 1948.

Abraham Skulsky has pointed out that Bergsma's development as a "structural contrapuntist" can be traced in his second and third string quartets. The Second was written in 1944 on a commission from the Koussevitzky Music Foundation, and was introduced on April 24, 1944, by the Gordon String Quartet. Here Bergsma "presents his material with greater economy and contrapuntal development" than he had previously done in his First String Quartet. The Third String Quartet, commissioned in 1953 by the Juilliard Music Foundation, was presented by the Juilliard String Quartet in New York on February 17, 1956. In this composition, "the composer is in full possession of the art of integrating contrasting materials."

However, in Bergsma's first symphony (1949) the treatment is more harmonic than contrapuntal. Skulsky explains that this work resembles a suite more than a symphony, being divided into two large sections (Prologue and March, and Aria and Epilogue) separated by a short Interlude. Its world première took place over the Netherlands Radio, on April 18, 1950, Erich Leinsdorf conducting. It was first heard in the United States in New York during the sixth annual Festival of American Music, with Izler Solomon conducting the CBS Symphony on April 21, 1950.

On February 15, 1956, Bergsma's three-act opera, *The Wife of Martin Guerre*, received its first public performance at the Juilliard School of Music during a festival commemorating the fiftieth anniversary of the school. Janet Lewis's libretto was based on an actual trial that had taken place in sixteenth century France. It involves a man who returns to his wife eight years after he deserted her. The community accepts him as her true husband, but the wife is strongly suspicious he is an impostor. Her fears prove well founded when the real husband finally appears, only to be punished at the gallows.

In the New York *Herald Tribune*, Paul Henry Lang described the opera as "a major event of the American festival." He added: "The music I found interesting and at times admirable. William Bergsma is a sincere lyricist to whom song comes naturally. Nearly all the portions of the work that follow operatic conventions are well set, the mood is faithfully expressed in nicely turned melodies and with an orchestral support that gives the impression of an exquisitely worked-out chamber ensemble."

Commissioned to write an orchestral work for the inaugural week festivities of Philharmonic Hall at the Lincoln Center for the Performing Arts in New York City, Bergsma produced *In Celebration: Toccata for the Sixth Day*. It was introduced on September 28, 1962. Subsequent major works by Bergsma include *Confrontation*, a large work for chorus and twenty-two instruments with text taken from the Book of Job, heard in Des Moines, Iowa, on November 29, 1963; and the *Serenade, To Await the Moon*, for chamber orchestra, which had its première at La Jolla, California, on August 22, 1965.

Abraham Skulsky described Bergsma's style in his fully mature works as "primarily linear; he is both a lyricist and a contrapuntist. He possesses not only melodic inventiveness but also a highly developed organizational ability. Although often poetic and meditative, his music has great structural strength and unity as well as clearly defined logic. One very notable aspect of his music is its character of intimacy."

Early in 1945 Bergsma settled in New York City where, in May, he received a grant from the National Institute of Arts and Letters. In 1946, the year in which he married Nancy Nickerson, he was appointed to the faculty of the Juilliard School of Music, and there he was later named chairman of the departments of composition and of literature and materials of music, as well as associate dean. While affiliated with Juilliard, Bergsma received a Guggenheim fellowship twice, the Columbia Records Music Award, and the Alice M. Ditson Fund Award. In 1963 Bergsma left Juilliard to become director of the School of Music at the University of Washington in Seattle.

MAJOR WORKS

Ballets—Paul Bunyan; Gold and the Señor Commandante.

Chamber Music—3 string quartets; Suite for Brass Quartet; Pastorale and Scherzo; Concerto for Wind Quintet; Fantastic Variations (on a theme from *Tristan*), for viola and piano.

Choral Music—In a Glass of Water; Black Salt, Black Provender; On the Beach at Night; Let True Love Among Us Be; Praise; Confrontation (from the Book of Job), for chorus and twenty-two instruments.

Opera—The Wife of Martin Guerre.

Orchestral Music—Symphony for Chamber Orchestra; Music on a Quiet Theme; The Fortunate Islands, for chamber orchestra (revised, 1956); First Symphony; A Carol on Twelfth Night; Chameleon Variations; In Celebration: Toccata for the Sixth Day; Serenade, To Await the Moon, for chamber orchestra.

Piano Music—Three Fantasies; Tangents, two books.

Vocal Music—Six Songs (to poems by E. E. Cummings); Lullee, Lullay; Bethsabe Bathing.

ABOUT

Reis, C., Composers in America (rev. ed.).

Juilliard Review, Spring 1956.

Luciano Berio
1923–

Luciano Berio was born in Oneglia, near Genoa, Italy, on October 24, 1923. For several generations his family had been musical; some members were composers. Music was an intrinsic part of the activities of the Berio household in Oneglia, and Luciano was subjected to its influence from infancy. His father was his first teacher, instructing him on the organ and piano.

When Luciano was fifteen, he went to Milan to continue his musical education on scholarships at the Milan Conservatory—mainly with Ghedini and Paribeni in composition and Giulini in conducting. He was a brilliant student and upon his graduation received the highest honors.

LUCIANO BERIO

For a short period of time following his graduation, he worked as a coach and conductor in several Italian opera houses. He also did some composing, completing *Due Pezzi*, for violin and piano, in 1951; and, in 1952, *Variazioni* for Piano and *Chamber Music*, for voice, clarinet, cello, and harp, based on poems by James Joyce. Though Berio's writing had a modern profile, it was still in a more or less traditional framework.

In 1952 he paid his first visit to the United States. While attending a concert at the Museum of Modern Art in New York, he heard performances of electronic music for the first time, and it was as if another world had opened for him. On a Koussevitzky scholarship he attended the Berkshire Music Center at Tanglewood that summer and studied composition with Dallapiccola, who introduced him to the artistic potentials of twelve-tone music and serialism. Influenced by Dallapiccola he began to use the serial method, though more in spirit than in letter. "The so-called serial experience . . . has been extremely important," he has said, "and has had an effect on every aware human being, but to

formalize it and settle on it is something else. I feel that I can maintain control without submitting to the label of serialism and control, of course, is the *sine qua non* of composition."

"Controlled" serialism is the term which characterizes the music Berio wrote next—music such as *Variations for Chamber Orchestra* (1953); *Nones*, for orchestra (1954); his first string quartet (1955); and *Allelujah I*, for orchestra (1956). In fact, a highly flexible and free use of serial methods is to be found in almost everything he has written for traditional instruments, outside the field of electronics. However, he did not forget his first listening experiences with electronic music, and he was convinced of the significance and potential of this music. In 1954 Berio returned to Italy and joined the staff of RAI, the Italian Radio in Milan. There he founded the Studio di Fonologia Musicale to experiment with electronic music. Certain of the importance of this new medium, he began to evolve electronic sounds in compositions such as *Mutazioni* (1955), *Perspectives* (1956), *Omaggio a Joyce* (1958), and *Momento* (1958)—music no longer confined to pitched sound but embracing the entire world of sound, including noises of all types. He became particularly interested in opening new areas of expressiveness for the human voice, not only by exploring all the possible gradations of sound between speech and singing but also by uncovering new timbres and sounds through electronic distortions of the voice. He has said: "The traditional singing technique has been to make the voice sound like an instrument—in range, in quality, in all respects. Now we must integrate many more vocal phenomena into the musical structure, particularly those closely related to speech."

One of his most interesting experiments in uncovering new vocal sounds by means of electronics came with *Visage* (1960). Utilizing only a single word, the voice (supplemented by electronic sounds) creates nuances, emotions, and tone qualities never before attempted—at times achieving profound depths of feeling of which formal music is incapable. "*Visage*," Berio has explained, "is a purely radio-program work: a sound track for a drama that was never written. . . . Based on the sound symbolism of vocal gestures and inflections

Berio

with their accompanying 'shadow of meanings' and their tendencies, *Visage* can be heard also as a metaphor of vocal behavior. . . . Thus *Visage* does not present meaningful speech but the semblance of it. Only a single word is pronounced and repeated: the word *'parole'* meaning 'words' in Italian. The vocal events from inarticulated or articulated 'speech,' from laughter to crying and to singing, from patterns of inflections modeled upon specific languages to 'aphasia,' etc. are constantly related to electrically produced sounds."

Another highly important experiment with the voice was made in *Passaggio*, text by Edoardo Sanguineti (1963). This is a work for soprano, two choruses, and a small orchestra. Designated by the composer as a *"messa in scena,"* it requires only a single character on the stage—a woman identified as "Her." A victim of persecution, though who is persecuting her and why is never explained, she gives vent to her agony in the most explosive and electrifying way. One chorus is seated in the audience, interrupting her shrieks and cries with exclamations, insults, and comments—all spoken. A singing chorus is placed in the pit together with an instrumental ensemble made up mainly of winds. The work ends with the woman triumphant over the antagonistic forces in the auditorium, dismissing them from the theatre.

When *Passaggio* received its American premiere, on January 9, 1967, at the Juilliard School of Music in New York, Raymond Ericson, writing in the New York *Times*, called the textual theme "valid enough" but thought "the expressionistic rendering seemed both old fashioned and sophomoric." Yet he found that Berio had made a "quite stunning theatre piece out of it with his brilliant score." And Peter G. Davis, writing in *High Fidelity*, asserted that Berio "invested all this ridiculous material with marvelous entertainment value. The instrumental writing bristles with fascinating sonorities, the various choruses are pitted against each other with exciting aural results . . . and the vocal writing for 'Her' . . . sports some of the most gorgeous avant-garde cantilena I have ever heard."

Visage (1960) was the last piece of music Berio wrote during the period of experimentation with electronics at the Studio di Fonologia Musicale in Milan. Among the electronic pieces he created in Milan perhaps the most interesting is *Omaggio a Joyce* based upon the first forty or so lines from Chapter 11 of Joyce's *Ulysses*. These lines are first read and then translated into electronic sounds—no sound other than the reader's voice being used. A critic for *High Fidelity* finds that "Joyce's words . . . are here progressively released from their semantic contexts and are ultimately transformed into a rich, elaborate, and dramatic polyphony of pure sound."

In 1960 Berio returned to the United States. That summer he was composer-in-residence at the Berkshire Music Center at Tanglewood. The Berkshire Festival that year presented the world première of Berio's *Circles*, for voice, harp, and percussion, to texts by E. E. Cummings. Berio subsequently joined the music faculty of Mills College at Oakland, California, staying two years. After that he went to Cambridge, Massachusetts, and taught courses in music at Harvard. He commuted regularly from Cambridge to New York to teach at the Juilliard School of Music until early in 1967, at which time he gave up his assignment at Harvard to hold a full-time teaching position at the Juilliard School.

The world première of his opera *Laborintus II* took place during the summer of 1968 at the Festival of the Two Worlds at Spoleto, Italy. Earlier the same year, on February 7, a festival of Italian music at the Juilliard School offered the American première of Berio's *Chemins II*, for viola and nine instruments.

Berio considers Boulez and Stockhausen the two most important composers of the twentieth century. He is convinced, as they are, that tonal music is dead. He explains: "In tonal music there were predetermined forms; now we must invent form every time. In tonal music, there was a hierarchy, with melody first, then harmony and finally rhythm taking their places. Now there are no such components—no melody as such. Tonality can still work, of course, for moments of escapism— when one wants to tickle oneself—like with jazz. But for serious art, absolutely *no*." He also believes with Stockhausen that formal concerts as they are given today are a "deadly ritual" and that the present-day concert hall is totally obsolete. Even the newer auditoriums are "national catastrophes," to use his own words.

Among Berio's other achievements in the world of avant-garde music have been the founding and editing of the musical journal *Incontri Musicali* and the organization of concerts of avant-garde music to which he also gave the name Incontri Musicali.

In the New York *Times*, Joan Peyser described Berio as "short, hurried, overbearing, articulate . . . thoroughly Mediterranean, both in his volatile behavior and charming manner."

MAJOR WORKS

Ballet—Mimusique II.

Chamber Music—String Quartet; Serenata, for flute and fourteen instruments; Sequenza, for flute solo; Chemins II, for viola and nine instruments.

Choral Music—Tracce, for two female voices, two choruses, and instruments.

Electronic Music—Mutazioni; Perspectives; Differences, for five instruments and stereophonic tape; Omaggio a Joyce; Momento; Esposizione, for voices, stereophonic tape, and orchestra; Visage, for voice and electronic sounds.

Operas—Passaggio, "messa in scena"; Laborintus II.

Orchestral Music—Nones; Variations for Chamber Orchestra; Allelujah I and II; Tempi Concertati, for chamber orchestra; Quaderni I and II; Epifanie, for mezzo-soprano and orchestra; Sinfonia.

Piano Music—Variations.

Vocal Music—Chamber Music, three songs to texts by Joyce; Circles, to texts by E. E. Cummings; Folk Songs, for voice and instruments.

ABOUT

Lang, P. H. and Broder, N. (eds.), Contemporary Music in Europe; Samuel, C., Panorama de l'Art Musical Contemporain.

New York Times, January 8, 1967.

Leonard Bernstein
1918–

Leonard Bernstein was born in Lawrence, Massachusetts, on August 25, 1918. At that time the Bernstein family lived in Boston, where the father operated a company supplying materials to beauty parlors and barber shops. He and his wife were vacationing with relatives in Lawrence when Leonard, their first child, arrived.

Bernstein's parents were not musical; there was little classical music heard at home. The living room boasted a phonograph, but all that

---

Bernstein: bûrn′ stīn

Bernstein remembers hearing on it were such popular tunes of the day as "Barney Google" and "Oh, By Jingo." Then, when he was eleven, his aunt sent over her upright piano for storage. "I made love to it right away," Bernstein later recalled. He started taking lessons with a local teacher about a month after that. "I knew with finality that I would become a musician," Bernstein says about his first experience with piano lessons. Late one night his family was awakened by Leonard's piano playing. When his father took him to task, the boy replied firmly: "I have to do this. The sounds are in my head and I have to get them out."

LEONARD BERNSTEIN

Bernstein's first important piano teacher was Helen Coates, with whom he studied while attending the Boston Latin School. Under her sympathetic guidance Bernstein developed phenomenally. "He was frighteningly gifted," Helen Coates remembers. "He could read, sing, and memorize anything. He absorbed in one lesson an arrangement that took most of my pupils five or six lessons to learn."

He was completely absorbed with music making. He would borrow scores of symphonies and operas from the library and devour them as if they were detective stories. At a boys' camp, where he spent several summers, he helped produce, write, and direct the camp shows. Once, on a cruise with his father, he proved such a source of entertainment with his piano playing that he was invited to join the ship's permanent staff. In 1934 he attended his first concert, a recital by Rachmaninoff. That was an exciting experience, but nothing to equal the impact made on him when he first heard Prokofiev's *Classical Symphony* and Stravinsky's *The Rite of Spring* on a radio broadcast of the Boston Symphony. He now began seeking out other scores by Prokofiev and Stravinsky and memorizing them; this stimulation led him to write a piano sonata in a discordant idiom. He also began regularly to attend the concerts of the Boston Symphony.

In 1935 he was graduated from the Boston Latin School with honors. He also composed the senior class song. He then matriculated at Harvard, where his music study embraced counterpoint and theory (his first formal contact with these subjects) and music history—with Walter Piston, Arthur Tillman Merritt, and Edward Burlingame Hill. He also continued to take piano lessons privately, this time with Heinrich Gebhard, who gave him a sound introduction to the modern literature of the piano.

His fellow students at Harvard were continually made aware of his amazing musical gifts. As one of them (Irving Fine, later himself a distinguished composer) recalled in *Modern Music*, "His extraordinary memory and his flair for improvisation were almost legendary.... I remember with great nostalgia his appearance as piano accompanist at a series of historical films presented by the Harvard Film Society. *The Battleship Potemkin* rode at anchor to the accompaniment of Copland's *Piano Variations*, excerpts from *Petrouchka*, and Bernstein's own paraphrases of Russian folk songs. Many Harvard Music Club programs would have been lost if Bernstein had not been willing to tackle, almost at sight, anything from the Stravinsky Concerto for Two Pianos to a work by one of his fellow students."

In his last year at Harvard, Bernstein became involved in two ambitious musical projects. One was a production of Aristophanes' *The Birds*, for which he wrote the incidental music. Another was Marc Blitzstein's musical play *The Cradle Will Rock*, for which Bernstein served not only as director and coordinator but also as accompanying pianist and commentator.

In June 1939 Bernstein was graduated from Harvard, *cum laude* in music. Several celebrated musicians, among them Dimitri Mitropoulos, convinced him that he ought to train himself as a conductor. A course in conducting followed with Fritz Reiner at the Curtis Institute in Philadelphia where he also studied orchestration with Randall Thompson and piano with Isabelle Vengerova. He received his diploma from Curtis in June 1941. In the summers of 1940 and 1941 he received scholarships in conducting for the Berkshire Music Center at Tanglewood, where he became a pupil and protégé of Serge Koussevitzky. During 1942 and 1943 Bernstein became Koussevitzky's assistant at the Center, where he was given his first opportunities to conduct an orchestra.

Bernstein's first mature composition, composed during 1941 and 1942, was a sonata for clarinet and piano in the neoclassic idiom of Hindemith. This was Bernstein's first work to be published, and the first to be performed (Boston, April 21, 1942, with David Glazer and Bernstein as soloists).

A far more ambitious work, and one of an entirely different character, followed in 1942, the *Jeremiah Symphony*, Bernstein's first attempt to write for a full symphony orchestra. Bernstein himself led the world première of this work with the Pittsburgh Symphony on January 28, 1944. In this work, as the composer has explained, he did "not make use to any great extent of actual Hebrew thematic material. The first theme of the Scherzo is paraphrased from a traditional Hebrew chant and the opening phrase of the vocal part in the 'Lamentation' is based on a liturgical cadence still sung today in commemoration of the destruction of Jerusalem by Babylon.... As for programmatic meanings, the intention is again not one of literalness, but of emotional quality. Thus the first movement ('Prophecy') aims only to parallel in feeling the intensity of the prophet's pleas with his people; and the Scherzo ('Profanation'), to give a general sense of the destruction and chaos brought on by pagan corruption within the priesthood and the people. The third movement ('Lamentation'), being a setting of a poetic text, is naturally a more literary conception. It is the cry of Jeremiah as he mourns his beloved Jerusalem, ruined, pillaged, and dishonored, after his desperate efforts to save it."

The symphony is spacious in design, Romantic in style, and deeply moving in its emotional intensity and fervor. As the work of a young man in his twenties it was a truly remarkable achievement. Warren Story Smith wrote in Boston: "We do not know whether he will surpass or even equal his first symphonic effort. But no matter. The real point is that one cannot think offhand of any other American composition that has the drive, the poignancy, dramatic strength, and the emotional force of *Jeremiah*." The symphony won the award of the New York Music Critics Circle. It was extensively performed by major American orchestras in 1944 and 1945 and was recorded for RCA Victor.

Thus, by 1944, Bernstein had made his mark as a composer. He had already proved his powers as a conductor as well. In 1943, the music world had been electrified to learn that Artur Rodzinski, then the new musical director of the New York Philharmonic, had selected the young, unknown, and inexperienced Bernstein as his assistant. The wisdom of this choice was dramatically proved on Sunday afternoon, November 14, 1943. The sudden illness of Bruno Walter, guest conductor of the New York Philharmonic, demanded a last-minute substitution. Bernstein was recruited to direct a rigorous program without the benefit of a single rehearsal, and he did so most successfully. Rodzinski, who came in from Stockbridge, Massachusetts, to attend this unscheduled debut, described Bernstein's talent as "prodigious." Koussevitzky, listening to the concert over the radio, wired congratulations. The New York *Times* ran an editorial the following morning. The critics were virtually unanimous in announcing that here was one of the most important baton discoveries in many years.

Bernstein's career as a conductor was launched in triumph. During the next quarter of a century Bernstein developed into one of the foremost conductors of the twentieth century. From 1945 to 1947 he was musical director of the New York City Orchestra. In April 1947 he toured Europe and Palestine in guest performances. In 1953 he became the first American conductor to direct a regular performance (Cherubini's *Medea*) at La Scala in Milan. In 1958 he was appointed director of the New York Philharmonic, with which he

made extensive and remarkably successful tours of the United States, Europe, the Orient, the Soviet Union, and South America. In 1964 he made his debut at the Metropolitan Opera (Verdi's *Falstaff*), and in 1966 he created a sensation when he conducted *Falstaff* at the Vienna State Opera and Mahler's Eighth Symphony with the London Symphony Orchestra in London.

Despite the increasing demands made upon him for guest appearances with America's leading symphony orchestras in the 1940's, he did not relax his efforts as a composer. In 1944 he completed his first ballet score, *Fancy Free*, in which Jerome Robbins made his bow as a choreographer. Produced in New York on April 18, 1944, *Fancy Free* was described in the New York *Times* as a "smash hit . . . a modern ballet in the best sense of the phrase . . . a rare little genre masterpiece." In his book *Ballet*, George Amberg later called it "the first substantial ballet entirely created in the contemporary American idiom, a striking and beautifully convincing example of genuine American style." *Fancy Free* proved so successful that it received 161 performances in its first full season.

The idea of the ballet scenario was the effort of three sailors, on shore leave, to find girls. This same theme was expanded by Bernstein and Jerome Robbins (with the collaboration of Adolph Green and Betty Comden) into a Broadway musical comedy, *On the Town*, opening on Broadway on December 28, 1944. It became one of the hits of the season. The MGM production, released in 1949, starred Frank Sinatra and Gene Kelly, and several of the songs became minor hits. With his later efforts for the Broadway stage, Bernstein became one of the most successful composers the American theatre has known. These included *Wonderful Town* (1953), starring Rosalind Russell; *Candide* (1956); and the epoch-making *West Side Story* (1957), which subsequently became an equally great success in the movies.

In 1946 Bernstein created his second ballet score, *Facsimile*, choreography once again by Robbins. It was introduced in New York on October 24, 1946. Described on the program as a "choreographic observation in one scene," *Facsimile* touched on a subject to which Bernstein was to return in several of his other serious works–the utter loneliness of man, his lack of security in the modern world. This is also the theme of Bernstein's second symphony, *The Age of Anxiety*, based on the poem of the same name by W. H. Auden. The world première was given in Boston on April 8, 1949, with Koussevitzky conducting the Boston Symphony Orchestra and Bernstein performing the piano obbligato.

This symphony was not only one of Bernstein's most complicated compositions but also one of his most eclectic. He had already revealed his eclecticism in his two ballet scores, each of which was stylistically different from the other: *Fancy Free* had been at turns satirical and realistic, abounding with jazz melodies and rhythms; by contrast, *Facsimile* had been high-tensioned, atmospheric, suggestive, and melodramatic, employing idioms and techniques of the serious modern school rather than those of jazz. In *The Age of Anxiety* Bernstein, chameleon-like, continually adapted his style to meet the needs of the varied moods, situations, and intellectual concepts of the Auden poem. Parts of his score were lyrical and romantic; parts exploited unresolved discords and polytonality; a section was in the twelve-tone system; another part used jazz idioms. Yet there was no feeling of disunity present; the various elements were blended with remarkable skill into an entity. The symphony received the Hornblit Prize in Boston, and on February 26, 1950, the music was used for a ballet for which Jerome Robbins created the choreography.

Once again the idea of man's insecurity, the emptiness of his life, his search for an abiding faith and lasting values attracted Bernstein's creative interest–this time in a little one-act opera, a comedy in music, called *Trouble in Tahiti*. It had its world première at Brandeis University at Waltham, Massachusetts, on June 12, 1952. The text, which Bernstein himself wrote, pointed up the domestic quarrels and squabbles of an ordinary married couple in a typical suburban community. As an escape from their unpleasant bickerings, the couple decide to go to the movies to see a picture called *Trouble in Tahiti*. In both text and music, wit and satire predominated, but with them were mixed touches of bitterness and despair. Irving Kolodin described the score in the *Saturday Review* as "crisp and flavorsome,

even witty. . . . The strains designed to give credibility to the personal drama of people involved are often inventive if not precisely moving, possessed of a kind of wistful poetry." *Trouble in Tahiti* was broadcast over a coast-to-coast television network in 1952; it was subsequently produced at Tanglewood and was incorporated into an omnibus production for Broadway, *All in One*.

In 1954 Bernstein wrote *Serenade*, for violin solo, strings, and percussion, on a commission from the Koussevitzky Music Foundation. Bernstein's inspiration was Plato's *Symposium*. Each of the five movements was devoted to one of the Greek philosophers engaged in a discussion of love at the home of the poet Agathon. "The music, like the dialogue," Bernstein has explained, "is a series of related statements in praise of love, and generally follows the Platonic form through the succession of speakers at the banquet. The 'relatedness' of the movements does not depend on common thematic material, but rather on a system whereby each movement evolved out of the elements of the preceding one." *Serenade* was heard at the Venice Festival in Italy on September 12, 1954, with Isaac Stern as soloist and Bernstein conducting. Stern and Bernstein were once again collaborators when the work was first heard in the United States, in New York on April 18, 1956. As had previously happened with *The Age of Anxiety*, the music of *Serenade* was adapted as a ballet score–with the title of *Serenade for Seven* and choreography by Jerome Robbins. Its première took place at the Spoleto Festival in Italy in July 1959.

Following *Serenade*, Bernstein produced two important choral works. The first was his third symphony, *Kaddish*, commissioned by the Koussevitzky Music Foundation. Bernstein was in the process of orchestrating the final pages when he heard the news of President Kennedy's assassination. The "Kaddish" being a Hebrew prayer for the dead, Bernstein felt it appropriate to dedicate his new symphony "to the beloved memory of John F. Kennedy." The world première was given in Tel Aviv, Israel, on December 10, 1963, with Bernstein conducting and Jennie Tourel as soloist. The American première followed on January 31, 1964, in Boston, Charles Münch conducting.

For his text, Bernstein utilized not only the traditional Hebrew prayer for the dead, the "Kaddish," but also a long poem of his own creation in which the narrator (who identifies herself as Lily of Sharon) serves as the embodiment of "that part of man that refuses death," as the composer has explained. This poetic text aroused a good deal of controversy and criticism in Jewish circles, since it establishes an intimate man-God relationship in which man is free to criticize and upbraid God as if He were just another human being. Many regarded such an attitude as blasphemous. But Bernstein took great pains to explain that such an intimate man-God relationship could be found in the biblical story of Job and was rooted in Hebraic folk tradition, particularly with the sect known as Hasidim. Such a tradition, Bernstein maintained, permitted things to be said to God which no other religion might tolerate.

This work is more of an oratorio than a symphony. Unlike the *Jeremiah*, the *Kaddish* never tapped Hebrew music either for quotation or for stylistic imitations. The writing is primarily in the twelve-tone system. Much of the dramatic impact and theatricalism spring from its complex rhythmic patterns, forcefully projected by a large battery of percussion operated by six men and by such devices as hand clapping and monotoned chants.

Bernstein's approach was simpler, and much more lyrical, in his next choral composition, the *Chichester Psalms*, for chorus and orchestra, commissioned by the Chichester Cathedral in England. Using as text three Psalms (Nos. 100, 23, and 131)—with interpolations of lines from other Psalms—Bernstein here produced a score which Raymond Ericson described in the New York *Times* as "extremely direct and simple—and very beautiful. . . . There is a lively, almost jazz, setting for Psalm 100, a plaintive one for boy alto and harp for Psalm 23, in which the theme of violence breaks, and a serenely lovely melody defines most of the final section. The music sometimes consists of the simplest of harmonies, deftly turned to avoid being bland. Some of the melodies are among the sweetest that Mr. Bernstein has written in any context— so sweet and simple that he has taken the risk of being charged with banality. But the charge won't hold because the melodies are so controlled and because the writing has such skill and conviction that the work ends most movingly." The work was first heard in New York City on July 14, 1965, with Bernstein conducting.

In addition to his activities as conductor and composer, Bernstein has distinguished himself as a piano virtuoso in performances of concertos for which he conducts the orchestra in his own accompaniments. He has been a television favorite, particularly in illustrated lectures on a variety of subjects ranging from conducting and jazz to Bach, Beethoven, Mozart, and modern music. He has received several "Emmy" awards, as well as the Sylvania and George Foster Peabody awards for his television work. A number of his television scripts were collected in two books, *The Joy of Music* (1959) and *The Infinite Variety of Music* (1966).

Leonard Bernstein was married to Felicia Montealegre in Boston on September 9, 1951. She was a Chilean-born girl who had come to the United States to advance her career as an actress. She made several well-received appearances over television in the United States and in 1950 was selected by a newspaper poll as the television actress of the year. The Bernsteins have three children. In New York they occupy a sixteen-room apartment that sprawls across the top two floors of a huge apartment house on Park Avenue. They also own a small white house on a hill in Fairfield, Connecticut, where they go on weekends and holidays.

As the editor of this work wrote in his biography of the composer, Bernstein is a perpetual worrier, in spite of his unquestionable success in all areas in which he has engaged, "in continual torment that what he has just done was not good enough or that what he is about to do won't come off as well as he hopes. He (who has always been praised so extravagantly) frets when the critics make some disparaging remark about him. He abhors hearing people call him 'versatile' or telling him he is trying to do too many things. . . . And, strange as it may sound for a man who has already achieved the highest pinnacle of fame, he worries most of all about his artistic future."

Arduous as are his rehearsal mornings with the New York Philharmonic, it is only after the rehearsal that his day's work really begins: "He must now attend numerous conferences with agents, managers, producers; meet newspapermen for interviews; discuss various projects with collaborators; make copious notes on some piece of music he is working on at the moment; plan his TV lectures. When friends come to his apartment for dinner, he will often join them in playing anagrams or discussing books, plays, or politics. Somewhere along the line he finds the time to play with his children, or to join his wife in informal performances of two-piano music."

On concert evenings he eats little and reaches the hall well in advance of the zero hour. At intermission he grumbles over the shortcomings of his performance thus far, pointing out ways in which matters could have been improved. After the concert, he meets friends, colleagues, and fellow musicians who crowd the artists' room to capacity. Then he partakes of his first expansive meal of the day and frequently goes off with his wife to a party.

He has compartmentalized his mind to perform several jobs simultaneously and efficiently. In the same way, he has systematized his day to find the time to do all the many and varied duties that press in on him all the time. His schedule is described in the biography mentioned above: "Whenever he finds a free moment—on a train, in a taxi, at an airport, in hotel lobbies—he also finds the capacity of plunging into work completely oblivious of surroundings or distractions. His powers of concentration are enormous, and with them he possesses an indefatigable vitality. As his wife once said: 'Lenny never does anything in moderation. If we're playing anagrams, he always wants to play till dawn. If we watch the 'Late Show' on TV he always wants to watch the 'Late Late Show' after that. If we go to a movie, he will want to step into another movie right away. If he plays with children, he plays long and hard.' "

Bernstein has received many honors besides those for his television appearances: the Ditson Award; a citation from the National Music Council; a prize from the American Symphony Orchestra League; the John H. Finley Medal for services to New York City. Vice President Nixon presented to him the prize of the Institute of International Education. The Albert Einstein College of Medicine presented

him with the Albert Einstein Commemorative Award in the Arts. Citations have come his way from ASCAP, the Institute of Fidelity Manufacturers, and the New York Newspaper Guild. In 1965, an important foreign award was added to the domestic ones when he received the Danish Sonning Music Prize of over seven thousand dollars.

On November 2, 1966, Leonard Bernstein announced that at the termination of his contract with the New York Philharmonic in the spring of 1969 he would resign as music director. He also explained that he had reached this decision because he wanted henceforth to direct most of his energies to composing: "A time is arriving in my life when I must concentrate on composition and this cannot be done while retaining the great responsibilities inherent in the Philharmonic post, which is a full-time commitment, and, indeed, more than that." At the same time an announcement was made that this did not mean Bernstein's complete separation from the orchestra. A lifetime post as "laureate conductor" had been created for him, in which capacity he would conduct the New York Philharmonic a number of weeks each season and continue to participate in recordings and television broadcasts.

MAJOR WORKS

Ballets—Fancy Free; Facsimile.
Chamber Music—Clarinet Sonata; Elegy for Mippy, for horn and piano.
Choral Music—Hashkivenyu; Chichester Psalms.
Orchestral Music—Jeremiah Symphony; The Age of Anxiety, Symphony No. 2; Serenade, for violin solo, strings, and percussion; Prelude, Fanfare and Riffs, for orchestra; Kaddish, Symphony No. 3; incidental music to Peter Pan and to The Lark.
Piano Music—Seven Anniversaries; Four Anniversaries.
Vocal Music—I Hate Music: Song Cycle of Five Kid Songs; La Bonne Cuisine, cycle.

ABOUT

Briggs, J., Leonard Bernstein; Ewen, D., Leonard Bernstein; Gruen, J., The Private World of Leonard Bernstein.
Esquire, February 1967; Harper's, May 1959; High Fidelity, February 1959; Holiday, October 1959; Life, January 7, 1957; Look, November 11, 1958; Reader's Digest, May 1960; Saturday Evening Post, June 16, 1956; Time, February 4, 1957.

Boris Blacher
1903–

Boris Blacher was born in the town of New-chwang, China, on January 19, 1903 (not January 3, the generally accepted date). His parents were of Estonian-German descent. When Boris was nine, his family moved to Irkutsk, in Siberia, where he studied French and German and took his first lessons in violin and harmony. In 1919 the family went to Harbin, Manchuria. During the next three years Blacher completed his academic school-ing, making significant advances in his musical training through the study of harmony and by conducting the local orchestra. Since or-chestral scores were not readily available in Harbin, Blacher was often required to orches-trate symphonic literature from piano adap-tations. This gave him a valuable apprentice-ship in orchestration.

BORIS BLACHER

In 1922 Blacher settled in Berlin, which became his permanent home. His father en-couraged him to enroll in the Technical High School for the study of architecture, but he soon transferred to the Hochschule für Musik where he studied counterpoint with Friedrich Koch until 1927. After that, he attended classes in musicology at the University of Berlin, where he remained until 1931.

To support himself while going to school,

Blacher: blä′ ᴋer

Blacher performed all sorts of hack duties including playing the piano or harmonium in motion picture theatres, copying music, and orchestrating operettas and popular tunes. In 1926, in collaboration with another young Berlin musician, he completed a two-week assignment to write a two-hour orchestra score for a silent-film biography of Bismarck. In 1929 he produced a serious chamber-music work in the jazz style, the *Jazz Koloraturen*, for saxophone and bassoon. But he imme-diately lost interest in jazz (though he did re-turn to it in 1957 with the *Two Poems*, for jazz quartet) and began writing compositions in modern harmonic and contrapuntal idioms. A suite, for two pianos, heard at the Sing-akademie in 1930, attracted no attention. This was followed by a Concerto for Two Trumpets and Two String Orchestras (1931) and the *Kleine Marschmusik*, for orchestra (1932). The last of these met with some favor after its première in Berlin on November 15, 1932. His reputation was enhanced by a Capriccio for Orchestra (heard over the Hamburg Radio on May 14, 1935) in which he evolved the style of atonal counterpoint which characterizes some of his later important works.

In 1937 Blacher became involved in two creative areas in which he was to prove produc-tive. One was ballet, a medium in which he produced outstanding work. *Fest im Süden* (1935) was a great success and was given in over fifty European theatres. Everett Helm called it "an extremely effective work, pos-sessing great rhythmic vitality; it is pure dance music, based on the abstract movements of the classical ballet rather than illustrating the movements and gestures of pantomimes." Blacher's next ballet, *Harlekinade* (1939), was written on commission from England just before World War II, when Blacher paid a brief visit to London. But the outbreak of the war canceled this première which, instead, took place at Krefeld, Germany, on February 14, 1940.

The second creative area successfully cul-tivated by Blacher was neoclassical music in which he was influenced by Stravinsky. With the *Concertante Musik*, first performed on December 6, 1937, by the Berlin Philharmonic under Carl Schuricht, Blacher began to show an interest in baroque structures, but he filled them with modern idioms and techniques.

The *Concertante* made such a strong impression on the audience that it demanded from orchestra and conductor an immediate repetition of the performance. Blacher's neoclassical style was again evident in the Concerto for String Orchestra (1940); the Partita for Strings and Percussion (1945); and the Divertimento, for trumpet, trombone and piano (1948).

The increasing severity of Blacher's linear writing made him and his music unacceptable to the Third Reich. In the last half of the 1930's Blacher found it increasingly difficult to be performed, or to advance his professional life in music. Nevertheless, several powerful musicians in Berlin used their influence to get him a minor teaching job at the Dresden Conservatory, where he stayed in 1938 and 1939. They also, at infrequent intervals, were able to get some of Blacher's compositions played, including Blacher's Symphony which was performed in Berlin on February 5, 1939. This was the composer's first symphony and his last. On completion of the work he became convinced that the symphonic form had exhausted its potential with Brahms.

During World War II, several important Blacher works were introduced. His first opera, *Fürstin Tarakanova*, was seen in Wuppertal on February 5, 1941, and was generally liked. However, since the text was on a Russian subject, the opera was hurriedly withdrawn after the Nazis attacked the Soviet Union. Blacher drew once again from Russian backgrounds for a second major work, his oratorio *Der Grossinquisitor*, based on a chapter from Dostoevsky's *The Brothers Karamazov*. But this could not be performed in Germany during the war. It was finally presented in Berlin in 1947.

Recognizing the financial and production limitations of opera houses in Germany in the years immediately after war's end, Blacher concentrated his efforts on intimate stage works for which only a small complement of singers, musicians, and stagehands were required. In 1943 he completed his first chamber opera, *Romeo and Juliet*, which was given in a concert version in 1947, the composer conducting; a stage production followed three years later at the Salzburg Festival in Austria. In this opera Blacher developed an operatic technique with which he had experimented in *Fürstin Tarakanova*. Each scene is an entity, thoroughly integrated through the use of some thematic motive or rhythmic pattern that is continually repeated or varied. *Romeo and Juliet* was introduced in the United States in a concert version sponsored by the League of Composers in New York. During the summer of 1955 it received its first American staged presentation, at the Berkshire Music Center at Tanglewood. A few years later, the composer revised his opera extensively. The new version was first heard during the festival weeks in Vienna, on May 22, 1963.

A second opera, *Die Flut* (*The Flood*), was written for radio presentation—Blacher having become the musical director of Radio Berlin in 1945. It was performed for the first time over the Berlin radio on December 20, 1946, and was seen in a stage presentation on March 4, 1947, in Dresden. In *Die Flut* Blacher further develops his technique of dominating each scene with some characteristic motive, melodic or rhythmic, thus making it self-sufficient. Because it was intended for radio, this opera made extensive use of the chorus to explain what was happening; but even on the stage, the opera is best in its choral passages.

Some of Blacher's greatest successes in the middle 1940's came with his orchestral music. The *Variations on a Theme by Paganini* is to this day one of the composer's most popular symphonic works. This is a set of sixteen variations on the melody from Paganini's Twenty-fourth Caprice for solo violin. Blacher's *Variations* was introduced on November 27, 1947, by the Gewandhaus Orchestra in Leipzig. Another successful instrumental work of this period is the Concerto No. 1 for Piano and Orchestra, brilliantly performed at Göttingen on March 20, 1948, by Gerta Herzog, whom Blacher had married in 1945.

With the ballet *Chiarina*, given in Berlin on January 22, 1950, Blacher revealed a new creative strain in his writing, that of satire. The ballet scenario was set in Germany in the 1890's and provided amusing caricatures of the people and the customs of that period. When the Berlin State Opera produced it, the public and critics reacted coldly, mainly because Germans were not attuned to strong satirical overtones either in their ballet or in their serious music. Nevertheless, Blacher continued to tap this satiric vein in the controversial ballet-opera *Preussisches Märchen* (*Prussian*

Fairy Tale) whose première took place at the Berlin Festival on September 22, 1952. The Prussian military and the German love of uniforms are gaily mocked in a text based on Zuckmayer's popular play *Der Hauptmann von Köpenick* and in a score that proved consistently effervescent and highly spiced in harmony and orchestration.

Experiment and innovation characterize many of Blacher's compositions of the 1950's. In compositions such as the *Ornaments* (one set, written in 1950, is for the piano; another, written in 1953, is for orchestra) and in his piano sonata (1951), Blacher evolved a system of rhythmic writing for which he coined the term "variable meters." He perfected a strict arithmetical series for organizing rhythm and meter, sometimes in strict succession (1, 2, 3, 4), at other times evolved by having each subsequent number become the sum of two preceding numbers (1, 2, 3, 5, 8). Blacher originated other rhythmical and metrical systems derived from different progression series (2–3–4, 3–4–5, 4–5–6) and for cyclical variations (2–3–4–5, 5–3–2–4, 3–2–4–5).

In the opera *Abstrakte Oper No. 1* (*Abstract Opera No. 1*) Blacher experimented with abstraction. This opera scandalized Germany when it was first heard (in concert form) at Frankfurt on June 28, 1953. It also caused a furor when staged in Mannheim on October 17, 1953. However, when it was revived at the Berlin Festival in 1957, it met with a more favorable reaction.

The opera was scored for three soloists, chorus, wind, percussion, and piano. Dancers on the stage mimed the action. The libretto (written by the composer Werner Egk) had no plot and very little understandable dialogue. The text consisted mainly of arbitrary and meaningless sounds. Even in places where words were used the meaning remained unintelligible. Most of the action involved two actors in slapstick situations. Each section of the opera bore a title as a clue to the emotion or state of mind presented. The opera begins and ends with "Fear." In between come "Love–I," "Pain," "Negotiation," "Panic," and "Love–II."

"Certain attitudes and situations of universal associative value are put into abstract, surrealistic form," wrote Klaus George Roy in the *Christian Science Monitor*. "Except for

one scene, words and syllables are freely invented to correspond to the emotions of fear, love and sorrow.... The whole thing is enormously funny and affecting, wacky and brilliant."

In Blacher's next opera, *Rosamunde Floris*, his librettist, Gerhart von Westermann, adapted an expressionist play written by Georg Kaiser in 1937. The opera was commissioned for the Berlin Festival in 1960 and introduced there on September 21. "Recitative-like song-speech predominates," says H. H. Stuckenschmidt, "together with spoken episodes.... Pointillistically, the colors of the orchestra create curiously tender and unusual luminosities. Tiny, easily apprehended movement; chordal and color motives underline a dominant idea or situation. A twelve-tone chord breaks into fragments or builds up, as a symbol for the collapse of the dying victims.... Nothing is done conventionally, and yet every measure remains transparent and audible."

Experiment was the keynote in Blacher's next opera: *Zwischenfälle bei einer Notlandung* (*Incidents in Connection with a Crash Landing*), first performed in Hamburg on February 4, 1966. Not only is the structure unusual, but electronic sounds play an important part in the musical score. Both the composer and his librettist (Heinz von Cramer) refused to designate this work as an opera, preferring to describe it as "a commentary in two phases and fourteen situations." In telling about the experiences of eleven survivors of a crash landing, the libretto, as explained by James H. Sutcliffe, does away "with conventional dramaturgy by presenting not a story but rather a series of film-like sequences showing the survivors, trapped in a strange, sinister, even murderous technical world through which they wander, stage by stage, trying to escape what seems to be the treadmill of a nightmare." The electronic elements were used principally "to provide an audible background for scenes illustrating the amazing, sometimes terrifying world of technology. Audience, orchestra and actors were ringed about with twenty-five separate sources for amplified sound, carrying stereophony to such convincing lengths that the conventional orchestral accompaniment sounded almost flat by comparison."

In 1948 Blacher was appointed to the faculty of the Berlin Hochschule für Musik. When the director Werner Egk resigned in 1953, Blacher succeeded him. He has held this post since and is responsible for a reorganization of this renowned school and for inaugurating a fresh, new, progressive curriculum. One of his pupils was Gottfried von Einem, who has since become a distinguished composer.

In 1955 Blacher paid his first visit to the United States to serve as guest professor of composition at the Berkshire Music Center at Tanglewood. During this visit, his chamber opera *Romeo and Juliet* was staged. Blacher returned to the United States during the summer of 1966 to attend the Hopkins Center Congregation of the Arts at Dartmouth College in New Hampshire as composer-in-residence. In the short period between August 10 and August 20 Blacher delivered four lectures and attended four concerts at which his wife made her American debut in the American premières of two of his piano concertos, one written in 1947 and the other (*Variations on a Theme of Clementi*) completed in 1961. Another later work by Blacher heard at these performances was *Five Negro Spirituals for Voice and Chamber Ensemble* (1962). On August 19, 1967, the world première of *Virtuose Musik* took place at the Congregation of the Arts at Dartmouth College.

Blacher wrote the librettos for two operas by Gottfried von Einem: *Dantons Tod* and *Der Prozess*.

MAJOR WORKS

Ballets—Fest im Süden; Harlekinade; Chiarina; Lysistrata; Hamlet; Der Erste Ball; Der Mohr von Venedig (Othello); Demeter; Tristan.

Chamber Music—3 string quartets; Estnische Tänze, for ten wind instruments; Flute Sonata; Violin Sonata; Divertimento, for trumpet, trombone, and piano; Divertimento, for flute, oboe, clarinet, and bassoon; Sonata for Violin Solo; Epitaph, for string quartet; Two Poems for Jazz Quartet; Octet; Virtuose Musik, for solo violin, ten winds, harp, and percussion.

Choral Music—Träume vom Tod und vom Leben; Der Grossinquisitor, oratorio; The Song of the Pirate O'Rourke, cantata; Requiem.

Electronic Music—Study in Black (electronic setting of the spiritual Nobody Knows de Trouble I've Seen); Elektronische Studie.

Operas—Fürstin Tarakanova; Die Flut; Preussisches Märchen; Romeo and Juliet, chamber opera; Abstrakte Oper No. 1; Rosamunde Floris; Fluchtversuch; Zwischenfälle bei einer Notlandung; Zweihunderttausend Taler.

Orchestral Music—3 piano concertos; Concerto for Two Trumpets and String Orchestra; Kleine Marschmusik; Capriccio, for small orchestra; Kurmusik; Divertimento, for wind orchestra; Geigenmusik, for violin and orchestra; Concertante Musik; Symphony; Concerto for String Orchestra; Variations on a Theme by Paganini; Die Nachtschwalbe, dramatic nocturne for voice and orchestra; Violin Concerto; Partita, for strings and percussion; Concerto for Clarinet, Bassoon, Horn, Trumpet, Harp and Strings; Cello Concerto; Ornaments; Studie im Pianissimo; Zwei Inventionen; Viola Concerto; Orchester-Fantasie; Hommage à Mozart; Music for Cleveland; Thirteen Ways of Looking at a Blackbird, for high voice and strings; Musica Giocosa.

Piano Music—2 sonatinas; Suite, for two pianos; Three Pieces; Ornaments; Sonata; Seven Studies in Variable Meters.

Vocal Music—Fünf Sinnsprüche; Four Songs, for high voice and piano; Francesca da Rimini, for soprano and violin; Apreslude; Five Negro Spirituals, for voice and chamber orchestra.

ABOUT

Machlis, J., An Introduction to Modern Music; Stuckenschmidt, H. H., Boris Blacher; Wörner, K. H., Neue Musik in der Entscheidung.

Musical America, June 1953; Score (London), August 1, 1949.

Easley Blackwood
1933–

Easley Blackwood was born in Indianapolis, Indiana, on April 21, 1933. The son of a celebrated authority on bridge, inventor of the famous Blackwood convention, Easley began studying the piano early. He made a number of successful appearances as a prodigy, including one with the Indianapolis Symphony when he was fourteen. During the summers of the period 1948–1950 he attended the Berkshire Music Center at Tanglewood where, in 1949, he studied composition with Olivier Messiaen. From 1949 to 1951 he was a composition pupil of Bernard Heiden at Indiana University and of Paul Hindemith at Yale. In 1953 Blackwood received a Bachelor of Music degree from Yale, followed by a Master's degree in 1954.

Though Blackwood had been writing music since boyhood, he considers the Sonata for Viola and Piano (1953) his first opus. All earlier efforts were discarded. It was followed by a Chamber Symphony, for fourteen instruments. In both compositions he revealed a strong creative gift which earned him in 1954 a Ditson Scholarship for Graduate Studies and a Fulbright grant for study in France. For about two years he worked under Nadia

Boulanger, both in Paris and at the American Conservatory at Fontainebleau; during the summer of 1955 he received the Lili Boulanger Memorial Award.

EASLEY BLACKWOOD

While in France he began working on his first symphony, which he completed in Paris in December 1955. This, his third opus, was introduced in Boston on April 18, 1958, with Charles Münch conducting the Boston Symphony. Münch esteemed this work so highly that he performed it again in Boston the following November, and after that presented it in New York. The symphony was then given the Koussevitzky Music Foundation Prize and recorded under the auspices of the Recording Guarantee Project of the American International Music Fund. One of the members of the distinguished jury selecting Blackwood's symphony for the recording grant was Alfred Frankenstein, who described his reactions to this music in *High Fidelity* magazine: "There were fifty-two entries, and we spent three days listening to them. The Blackwood symphony came along towards the end of the third day, and it all but completely swept the field so far as one member of the auditioning committee was concerned. . . . What captivated us about this symphony was its freshness, its vitality, its dramatic, epical qualities, and the sense of a lively, original uncompromising talent at work. . . . This symphony struck us as being a brilliant, formidable and truly symphonic creation."

Blackwood returned to the United States in 1958 and joined the music faculty of the University of Chicago, where he became assistant professor. In the same year, on a commission from the Fromm Music Foundation of Chicago, he wrote a string quartet, which was successfully performed by the Kroll Quartet and the Budapest Quartet. In 1959, on a commission from the Koussevitzky Music Foundation, he completed a second string quartet as well as a Concertino for Five Instruments.

In 1960 the publishing house of G. Schirmer commissioned him to write a symphony celebrating that company's one hundredth anniversary. Blackwood wrote this, his second symphony, for the Cleveland Orchestra, which introduced it under George Szell's direction on January 5, 1961. "Here," said Paul Henry Lang in the New York *Herald Tribune*, after Szell had directed the New York première, "was a very young composer, mercifully untouched by the lunatic fringe; he is thirsty for music, and the thirsty man does not try to find a reason for his state, he searches for water. In this search, Mr. Blackwood displays a great deal of genuine vitality. . . . The procedure is thematic in the symphonic sense, the quality is rhapsodic. . . . He succeeds in holding the listener's attention to the end."

In his later works—which include concertos, for the violin and for the flute, a *Symphonic Fantasy*, and his third and fourth symphonies—Blackwood makes use of a serial technique, though none of the compositions is a strict serial work. Harold C. Schonberg's description in the New York *Times* of the *Symphonic Fantasy* serves for other later works of Blackwood's as well. "It is," said Schonberg, "dissonant, with wide melodic skips, some serial-sounding textures, unorthodox treatment of instruments, and even some—though not many—conventional tonalities." The Violin Concerto had been commissioned by Yehudi Menuhin for Festival '67 at the Lincoln Center for the Performing Arts in New York City. Menuhin introduced it on July 3, 1967, as soloist with the visiting Bath Festival Orchestra from England.

During the summer of 1968, Blackwood was invited to the Congregation of the Arts at Hopkins Center, Dartmouth College, to be composer-in-residence and to help supervise and direct the lectures and concerts. During his visit, the world première of the Concerto for Flute and Orchestra took place—on July 28, 1968. The year 1968 also witnessed the successful world première of Blackwood's fourth symphony, at the Ravinia Festival, near Chicago.

In a statement on his musical beliefs and principles, Blackwood has written: "Any work which reveals all of its secrets in a single hearing can hardly be considered artistic. The process of discovery and enlightenment upon repeated hearings is an essential part of the true appreciation of good music. It is a composer's duty, therefore, to make the music such that an intelligent listener will want to hear it again.... Ideally, something new should be uncovered each time the work is heard, so that each hearing is a fresh and stimulating experience.... From the composer's standpoint, such a piece is more stimulating to write, both from an intellectual and intuitive point of view, since each problem must be solved on the spot, and all are different. I personally have no dislike for lovely sounds, nor any principles against them.... There are a great many musical elements which are highly desirable, among them lovely sounds; but they cannot all occur in the same composition. It is up to the composer to decide which ones he wishes to maintain, and which ones he is willing to sacrifice."

MAJOR WORKS

Chamber Music—2 string quartets; Viola Sonata; Chamber Symphony, for fourteen instruments; Concertino, for five instruments; Pastorale and Variations, for woodwind quintet; Violin Sonata; Fantasy for Cello and Piano; Music for Flute and Harpsichord; Un Voyage à Cythère, for soprano and ten instruments; Fantasy, for flute, clarinet, cello, and piano; Piano Trio; Trio for Piano, Violin, and Cello.

Piano Music—Three Fantasies.

Orchestral Music—4 symphonies; Clarinet Concerto; Concerto for Orchestra; Symphonic Fantasy; Concertino for Oboe and Strings; Violin Concerto; Concerto for Flute and Orchestra.

Sir Arthur Bliss
1891–

Sir Arthur Edward Drummond Bliss was born in London on August 2, 1891. He received degrees in the arts and in music from Pem-

broke College, Cambridge. In the spring of 1914 he entered the Royal College of Music where his teachers included Ralph Vaughan Williams and Gustav Holst. His musical studies ended after one year when World War I broke out. During the entire conflict, Bliss served in France as a commissioned officer, first with the 13th Battalion, Royal Fusiliers, then with the 1st Battalion, Grenadier Guards. In 1916 he was wounded at the Somme, and two years later he was gassed at Cambrai.

SIR ARTHUR BLISS

During his army service, two of his early chamber music works were performed, and one received a prize at the War Emergency Concerts. Both works were published, but after the war Bliss had the plates destroyed.

Bliss's return to music study was marked by severe self-discipline. In a short period he acquired a sound technique in composition. The first composition he regards as mature was *Madam Noy*, described as a "witchery song," for soprano and six instruments (1918). Between 1918 and 1920 he completed two unusual compositions which brought him to the limelight. The first was the Rhapsody, for soprano, tenor, flute, English horn, and string quartet. This was introspective, poetic music written with simplicity and refinement. The soprano is not so much a vocal soloist as the equal partner of the instrumentalists; in fact she is placed by the composer together with the instruments as she sings a wordless chant to the syllable "ah." The Rhapsody was heard for the first time in London in October 1920, and on August 5, 1923, was successfully featured at the festival of the International Society for Contemporary Music at Salzburg.

One year later Bliss wrote *Rout*, a satiric work scored for soprano and ten instruments. When first heard, in London in December 1920, it was hailed by the critics. It gathered further praise when it was repeated at Salzburg on August 7, 1922. In this composition, as in the Rhapsody which preceded it, the voice is once again assigned meaningless syllables rather than words. Describing *Rout*, Norman Demuth said: "It was like nothing else. Its novel conception and design, its amazing vitality, placed it and its composer immediately in the forefront and stamped him as a highly original mind."

In 1921 Bliss was appointed professor of composition at the Royal College of Music, a post he held only briefly. Since he was financially independent, he soon decided that he preferred devoting himself exclusively to creative work and to those other musical pursuits that stimulated him creatively.

In January 1921 Bliss's *Conversations*—five pieces for a chamber music ensemble—was introduced. The main interest here lies in Bliss's contrapuntal skill. Another composition in 1921 was *Two Nursery Rhymes*, for voice and instruments, whose immediate success was second only to that previously enjoyed by *Rout*. Bliss's partiality for unusual subject matter and for material that lent itself to vivid and pictorial extramusical associations led him in 1922 to write the *Color Symphony*. Here the composer explored the possibilities of relating musical sounds to specific colors while finding a relationship between each color and some specific emotional state. Each movement has not only a tempo marking but also a detailed descriptive title as follows: I. Purple—the Color of Amethysts, Pageantry, Royalty and Death; II. Red—the Color of Rubies, Wine, Revelry, Furnaces, Courage and Magic; III. Blue—the Color of Sapphires, Deep Water, Skies, Loyalty and Melancholy; IV. Green—the Color of Emeralds, Hope, Joy, Youth, Spring and Victory. This symphony had been commissioned by the Gloucester Festival where it was introduced under the composer's direction on September 7, 1922. In 1932 Bliss revised his symphony, removing all program-matic connotations as well as descriptive titles and offering the work as absolute music.

From 1923 to 1925, Bliss lived in Santa Barbara, California, where he occupied himself with composition, lecturing, and conducting. He married an American girl, Gertrude Hoffmann, by whom he has two daughters. He returned to London in 1925. Two major compositions revealed Bliss's growing interest in orthodox, classical procedures together with an increasing partiality for objective rather than subjective expression: Introduction and Allegro, for orchestra (1926) and the Quintet for Oboe and Strings (1927). In a similar classical style and objective approach were the Quintet for Clarinet and Strings, introduced at the festival of the International Society for Contemporary Music at Vienna on June 21, 1932; a Sonata for Viola and Piano (1932), written for and introduced by Lionel Tertis; and *Music for Strings*, first heard on an all-British program at the Salzburg festival during the summer of 1935.

Alec Robertson regards *Morning Heroes* as "the touchstone of Bliss's high qualities as a composer" up to this time. This is a six-movement symphony for narrator, chorus, and orchestra, dedicated to the memory of Bliss's brother, killed in action during World War I. The symphony was introduced at Norwich, England, on October 6, 1930. "Inspired by intense personal emotion," says Robertson, "it shows no trace of either sentimentality or jingoism. The music has the moving restraint, the inward strength and integrity, of great art and, like the words, speaks with a universal language." The words (sometimes spoken, but most often sung) come from various sources: the *Iliad*, Walt Whitman, Li Tai Po, Wilfred Owen, and Robert Nichols.

In 1935 Bliss returned to the United States and wrote the background music for the motion picture adaptation of H. G. Wells's *The Shape of Things to Come*. Four years later, on June 10, 1939, Bliss's Concerto for Piano and Orchestra was introduced; written for the New York World's Fair, it was performed by Solomon and the New York Symphony, conducted by Sir Adrian Boult. Dedicated "to the people of the United States," this concerto is one of Bliss's most lyrical inventions, a work sensitive in its melodic beauty and delicate in expression.

Bliss

Meanwhile, in 1937, Bliss completed his first important work for the stage, his score for the ballet *Checkmate*. First given in Paris by the Sadler's Wells Ballet on June 15, 1937 (during British Music Week at the Paris International Exposition), *Checkmate* became one of its composer's lasting successes. Its scenario, which the composer himself prepared, places the action on a giant chessboard on which the pawns symbolize the cruelty and lust displayed by human beings during the game of life.

When World War II broke out in Europe, Bliss once again visited the United States. This time he served as professor of music at the University of Southern California. In 1942 he returned to England and assumed the post of assistant director of overseas music for the BBC. He went on to become music director of the BBC, retaining this office until 1944. From 1946 to 1950 he was chairman of the Music Committee of the British Council, and from 1954 he served as President of the Western Orchestral Society, Ltd.

One of Bliss's significant works in the postwar era was his first opera, *The Olympians*, libretto by J. B. Priestley. Its world première at Covent Garden on September 29, 1949, was the first new operatic production there since the war's end. The libretto described how gods of antiquity, come upon hard times, descend to earth as strolling actors. Giving free rein to his romantic temperament and his talent for comedy, Bliss here produced one of his most varied and palatable scores. This was an opera, as a cabled report to the New York *Times* said, which was "a good mixture of romance, comedy and extravaganza" and which made for "good entertainment and good art. . . . [In] one episode after another . . . Bliss writes a more lyrical, more spontaneous music than would be expected by those who knew only his sinewy and sometimes astringent style."

Bliss's second opera, *Tobias and the Angel*, was written on a commission from the BBC for television and was introduced on May 19, 1960. It received the Award of Merit at the Salzburg Festival in 1962. Bliss's ballet *The Lady of Shalott* was produced at the Music Festival of the University of California at Berkeley on May 2, 1958. A major choral work, the cantata *The Beatitudes*, was written

for the consecration of Coventry Cathedral, where it was heard on May 25, 1962.

Arthur Bliss was knighted in 1950. Two years after that he was appointed Master of the Queen's Music (in succession to Sir Arnold Bax), and in 1963 he received the Gold Medal of the Royal Philharmonic Society.

Alec Robertson has described Bliss's music as "aristocratic," adding: "Physically, it is entirely healthy and sane; mentally it is distinguished without being aloof; spiritually it is undenominational. It displays unvaryingly fine craftsmanship, a wit that has mellowed with the years, and . . . a note of almost Mediterranean passion and liveliness."

Bliss has summed up his beliefs and principles as a composer: "I believe that the foundation of all music is emotion, and that without the capacity for deep and subtle emotion a composer employs only half the resources of his medium. I believe that this emotion should be called into being by the sudden awareness of the actual beauty seen or by the vision of beauty vividly apprehended. I believe that the emotion resulting from apprehended beauty should be solidified and fixed by presenting it in a form absolutely fitting to it, and to it alone. If I were to define my musical goal, it would be to try for an emotion truly and clearly felt, and caught forever in formal perfection."

MAJOR WORKS

Ballets—Checkmate; Miracle in the Gorbals; Adam Zero; The Lady of Shalott.

Chamber Music—3 string quartets; Madam Noy, for soprano and wind instruments; Rhapsody, for soprano, tenor, and instruments; Conversations, for seven instruments; Oboe Quintet; Clarinet Quintet; Viola Sonata.

Choral Music—A Song of Welcome; The Beatitudes, cantata; Maria Magdala; Golden Cantata; The Beatitudes.

Operas—The Olympians; Tobias and the Angel (television opera).

Orchestral Music—Rout, for soprano and chamber orchestra (also full orchestra); Two Studies; Mélée Fantasque; A Color Symphony; Hymn to Apollo; Introduction and Allegro; Serenade, for baritone and orchestra; Morning Heroes, symphony for narrator, chorus, and orchestra; Music for Strings; Concerto for Two Pianos and Orchestra; The Enchantress, scena for contralto and orchestra; Piano Concerto; Violin Concerto; Meditation on a Theme by John Blow; Edinburgh, overture; Fanfare.

Piano Music—Masks; Two Interludes; Toccata; Suite.

Vocal Music—Three Romantic Songs; The Ballad of the Four Seasons; Two Nursery Rhymes; Seven American Poems.

ABOUT

Bacharach, A. L. (ed.), British Music of Our Time;
Frank, A., Modern British Composers.
Chesterian (London), March–April, 1935.

Marc Blitzstein
1905–1964

Marc Blitzstein was born in Philadelphia, Pennsylvania, on March 2, 1905, of Russian parents. His father was a banker; his mother an amateur singer. Marc showed unusual musical talent, and at the age of three played the piano by ear. Formal piano study was started, and when he was five he gave a public concert. At seven he made his first efforts at composition. At fifteen he appeared as piano soloist with the Philadelphia Orchestra.

MARC BLITZSTEIN

He attended the public schools in Philadelphia, graduating from high school in 1921 with a scholarship to the University of Pennsylvania. He left the University in 1923, after failing in physical education, and enrolled at the Curtis Institute, where he studied composition with Scalero. At the same time he commuted regularly to New York to take piano

Blitzstein: blĭts′ stĭn

lessons with Siloti. In 1926 he went to Europe where he studied composition with Nadia Boulanger in Paris and with Arnold Schoenberg in Berlin.

Upon his return to the United States, he lectured on music at Columbia University and the New School for Social Research. He also composed in the ultramodern idioms of the 1920's. In *Show* magazine, in 1964, Minna Lederman recalled Blitzstein's first important bow as a composer, in New York in 1928, when he performed one of his sonatas: "Barely twenty-three, small and slight, he moved across the stage in an anxious, darting trot, carrying his head forward. His face was pointed and foxlike but the gray eyes held a direct challenge. . . . His sonata was fashionably percussive, the sections separated from one another by a banging down of the piano lid and then a few moments of cold silence. Thus he announced he would 'eliminate padding in transitions'." Miss Lederman added: "It was clear at once that we were meeting a very Angry Young Man. . . . In the late twenties, Marc was simply angry with himself, edgy, mettlesome, sharp-tongued. He looked at everything, he listened to everything, he quarreled with everyone. Brash though he was, he couldn't be ignored."

During this *Sturm und Drang* period, Blitzstein had this to say of his music: "I do not consider my music essentially experimental; for materials I use what has been bequeathed to our generation of composers by the pioneers of the movement called 'modern music'; all my works tend to solve in various ways the problems of a suitable and necessary form for the content." The critics, however, thought otherwise, describing his music as "full of *Donner und Blitzstein*" and calling him a musician more determined to shock than to inspire. One unidentified critic wrote: "Blitzstein's experiments with tones have not always been felicitous. . . . But in his better works Marc Blitzstein is definitely a vigorous and original voice." His better works in this modern style included the ballets *Parabola and Circula* (1929) and *Cain* (1930), the Piano Concerto (1931), and the Serenade, for string quartet (1932). The last of these inspired surprise at the Yaddo Festival in New York in 1932 because the tempo marking of the three movements was "Largo, Largo, Largo."

During this period, in addition to compositions in a highly modern idiom, Blitzstein wrote a little operatic farce, *Triple Sec*, which was produced in Philadelphia in 1928, the year it was written. The text places the audience in a cabaret and assumes that it has imbibed more than one drink, with the result that before long the audience sees the characters on the stage in duplicate, triplicate, or even larger multiples. *Triple Sec* was revived by the New School Opera Workshop in New York in May 1967 and was judged an amusing escapade of a very serious composer on a temporary creative holiday.

Actually, Blitzstein did not realize his identity as a composer, or achieve maturity, until he had embraced the cause of the common man by using his music as an instrument for political and social propaganda. His first such gesture came with the oratorio *The Condemned* (1932), which described the trial and execution of Sacco and Vanzetti. (He was to return to the subject of Sacco and Vanzetti in his last work, an opera, which was left uncompleted.) In *The Condemned*, wrote Henry Brant, "Blitzstein's work reaches a critical stage where his developing interest in expressing a positive social viewpoint is almost directly in conflict with the rigid, impersonal stylization of his musical and literary language. It is significant that during the next three years he composed no major dramatic work."

In 1932 and 1933 Blitzstein traveled in Yugoslavia, Spain, and France. During this period he tried to clarify his aims as a composer. Upon returning to the United States in 1933 he married Eva Goldbeck, a writer (daughter of the famous opera singer Lina Abarbanell). In politics, Eva had pronounced leftist attitudes and her influence on Blitzstein's growing social consciousness was strong. He began thinking in terms of writing music not for an esoteric or highly sophisticated audience but for a mass public—a music whose popular style and simple idiom would make for easy listening and immediate comprehension. He also considered using music to promote his own political and social viewpoints. Soon after the outbreak of civil war in Spain, he completed a work for narrator and piano, *Send for the Militia*. He also wrote a song about a streetwalker, "The Nickel Under My Foot." One evening in December 1935 he played and sang the song for Bertolt Brecht, the German poet and dramatist who had provided Kurt Weill with the text for *The Three-Penny Opera*. Brecht told Blitzstein: "This is very good, but only as far as it goes. Why don't you do a *whole* play about every form of prostitution— the press, the clergy, business, and so forth." One week later Blitzstein started planning an opera on such a subject, using "The Nickel Under My Foot" as one of the numbers.

The writing of his opera occupied him periodically for the next half year. This was a difficult time for the composer since his wife had become seriously ill and was bedridden. Eva died during the summer of 1936. Blitzstein now devoted himself passionately and industriously to his opera, completing the orchestration before the end of 1936.

The opera, called *The Cradle Will Rock*, was scheduled for performance by the WPA Federal Theatre. Dealing as it did with the formation of a steel union and the attempts of a capitalist society to destroy this effort, the opera proved too provocative a subject for the Federal Theatre, which at the last moment withdrew its support. The small audience that had gathered outside the Maxine Elliott Theatre for the opening performance on June 16, 1937, found the auditorium closed. While members of the cast entertained outside the theatre, another theatre, the nearby Venice, was found and the audience was directed there. Since no costumes, scenery, or orchestra were available, the opera was presented in oratorio form, while Blitzstein sat at the piano, played the score, and made informal comments about the action taking place. This novel way of presenting the opera, together with the inherent vitality of the opera itself, created a profound impression. John Mason Brown considered it "the most exciting propaganda tour de force our stage has seen since Clifford Odets' *Waiting for Lefty*." The music critics praised the score for its freshness, wit, and satire. The opera, now financed by private funds, became a success on Broadway and its composer found himself famous.

Though primarily a period piece about the Depression years of the 1930's and the labor strife which this period engendered, *The Cradle Will Rock* nevertheless managed to survive. It was heard on November 24, 1947, in a performance by the New York City Symphony under Leonard Bernstein, the first time the opera was given with an orchestra instead of just a piano. On this occasion Olin Downes referred to the opera as "a work of genius." On February 11, 1960, *The Cradle Will Rock* was produced for the first time as it had originally been planned, with scenery and costumes as well as orchestra. This was the opening event of the New York City Opera's third successive season of American operas. Reviewing this performance in the New York *Times*, Howard Taubman said: "*The Cradle Will Rock* has lost its inflammability as an incitement to the barricades. But it blows up a storm in a theatre that you should appreciate whatever your political allegiance."

Another Blitzstein opera that caused a storm was his *No for an Answer*, introduced in New York on January 5, 1941. This time the opera was written to be presented without orchestra, scenery, or costumes—with the composer once again on the stage playing his score on the piano and making informal comments as he played. *No for an Answer* concerns a group of Greek waiters, seasonal workers at a luxury hotel in a summer resort, who form a social club which soon develops into a union. Dire things happen to the members when an attempt is made to smash the union. "The theme," Blitzstein explained, "is what happens to basic democratic principles in time of stress—what happens to the little people in whose behalf the democratic principles exist, in time of stress." *No for an Answer* was revived by the New York City Opera in 1960.

Soon after the première performance, the license commissioner of New York City prohibited further presentations of this opera on the grounds that the auditorium (Mecca Temple) was guilty of building violations which made the house unsuitable for operatic performances. Since opera had been presented at Mecca Temple many times before this without interference, this move was interpreted as an act of censorship on the part of city authorities against a leftist production.

During this period, in addition to the two operas, Blitzstein wrote a radio song play called *I've Got the Tune* (1937). This has been described as a parable about a modern musician who, having invented a melody, must search for a lyric with a meaning to it. The composer of the melody travels about New York searching for such a lyric; as he goes from one place to the next, his melody changes character. Finally, he appears at a workers' parade. The composer has at last found his place, and the tune has found a lyric. Both composer and tune join the workers' parade.

In 1940 and 1941, Blitzstein was awarded Guggenheim Fellowships. After Pearl Harbor he voluntarily joined the army and was assigned to the Eighth Air Force. There he was given various musical assignments, the most significant being the writing of a symphony, *The Airborne*, dedicated to the Army Air Forces. Scored for narrator, solo voices, male chorus, and orchestra, *The Airborne* was introduced on April 11, 1946, in New York, Leonard Bernstein conducting. The audience gave it an ovation, and the critics were almost as one in describing the score as a major contribution to the modern symphonic repertory. The symphony deals with the history of human flight from the time of Icarus to the end of World War II. A gripping text and score are full of political implications: perhaps no more moving music has been inspired by World War II than the section describing the ruined cities laid low by Fascist bombs, or the salutation to the open sky, symbol of freedom. The symphony received the Page One Award of the Newspaper Guild and was largely responsible for bringing its composer a grant from the American Academy of Arts and Letters.

Critics are generally agreed that Blitzstein's best opera is *Regina*, based on *The Little Foxes*, Lillian Hellman's drama about the disintegration of a decadent Southern family whose members succeed in destroying one another. The characters remain ugly in Blitzstein's opera but, through his music, acquire a new dimension and stature through the infusion of what Leonard Bernstein described as "sweetness and directness." Bernstein went on to show that even Regina herself, one of the most ruthless characters in all opera, is made to sing "melodies of enormous gentility and suaveness precisely at the moment when she is being most unscrupulous and heartless." He concluded by saying that much of the impact of the opera came from this underlying technique of "coating the wormwood with sugar, and scenting with magnolia blossoms the cursed house in which these evils transpire."

The musical fabric of *Regina* is a cloth of

many colors. Sprinkled throughout the opera are numbers that sound like spirituals (sung by the Negro servants) and numbers that have the dynamic pulse of ragtime (played by a Negro band). The score is further made up of Handelian-like recitatives and lilting dance tunes, full-blown operatic arias and recitatives that almost resemble Schoenbergian *Sprechstimme*. There are many sunny choruses, and there are orchestral episodes that have been described as "bitter as gall." But, as Ross Parmenter wrote in the New York *Times*, "the musical flow seems to be unbroken and interconnected. . . . Each of the numbers has a sharply distinctive contour. . . . Mr. Blitzstein wrote music of distinctive profile for each character. . . . He also wrote music that dramatized the group involved."

After trying out in Boston in October 1949, *Regina* opened in New York City on October 30. It has since been revived several times by the New York City Opera.

Juno, produced in New York City on March 11, 1959, was more of a musical comedy than an opera. This was an adaptation of Sean O'Casey's *Juno and the Paycock*. Fitted out with dances, songs, and various other musical episodes, *Juno* had many moments of musical fascination, but as an operatic translation of the O'Casey drama it failed to come off successfully. Brooks Atkinson said: "*Juno* is more earthbound than *Juno and the Paycock*. As a musical work, it does not have the drive, the scorn and the fury of the play."

Blitzstein achieved his most formidable box-office success not with an opera of his own but with the opera of another composer, and not with a musical effort but with a literary one. This success came with his newly revised and adapted libretto for the Bertolt Brecht-Kurt Weill musical play *The Three-Penny Opera*, which had originally been produced in 1928 in Berlin. Weill's musical score was not touched in this new transformation. The new *Three-Penny Opera* was revived in an off-Broadway production on March 10, 1954, to begin a run that extended for six years and some 2,500 performances—the longest of any musical production in the history of the American musical theatre. Two national companies were formed in 1960 and 1961 to tour the United States.

Towards the end of his life, on a grant from the Ford Foundation, Blitzstein was at work on an opera based on the Sacco and Vanzetti case which he had treated in an oratorio thirty years earlier. When the Metropolitan Opera became interested in this new project, considerable stir was aroused in several patriotic and musical groups. The directing board of the National Federation of Music Clubs, for example, adopted a resolution opposing the opera on the ground that its composer had admitted being a onetime member of the Communist Party. Anthony A. Bliss, acting as spokesman for the Metropolitan Opera, replied: "Since Mr. Blitzstein avows that he no longer maintains his past political affiliations we do not feel that we should prejudge the work."

Blitzstein did not live to finish this opera. In January 1964 he went to Martinique for a brief vacation. On January 22 he was attacked and beaten by three sailors in mysterious circumstances never fully clarified. Rushed to a hospital in Fort-de-France, he died twenty-four hours later.

A memorial concert was held at Philharmonic Hall in New York on April 20, 1964. Excerpts from Blitzstein's familiar operas were heard, together with three new songs from operas in progress. The new material included "With a Woman to Be" from the Sacco and Vanzetti project, "How I Met My New Grandfather" from *Idiots First*, and "Then" from *The Magic Barrel*—these last two being one-act operas based on stories by Bernard Malamud which the composer was working on at the time of his death. These premières, said Irving Kolodin in the *Saturday Review*, "ran the gamut from the pseudo-popular vein of 'Then' . . . to a delightful monologue in a Jewish folk vein from . . . *Idiots First*." Describing the aria from the Sacco and Vanzetti opera, Kolodin expressed the opinion that the composer "had penetrated to the heart of his subject."

During the concert an announcement was made that the manuscript of the Sacco and Vanzetti opera had disappeared and presumably was permanently lost. However, several months later, the manuscript was found in the trunk of Blitzstein's car, which had been standing neglected in a garage.

MAJOR WORKS

Ballets—Cain; Show.

Chamber Music—String Quartet; Serenade, for string quartet.

Choral Music—The Condemned, oratorio; Cantatina; Children's Cantata; This Is the Garden, cantata.

Operas—The Harpies, one-act opera; The Cradle Will Rock; No for an Answer; I've Got the Tune (radio opera); Regina; Juno; Sacco and Vanzetti (unfinished); Idiots First, one-act opera (unfinished); The Magic Barrel, one-act opera (unfinished).

Orchestral Music—Concerto for Piano and Orchestra; Variations; Freedom Morning, tone poem; The Airborne, symphony.

Piano Music—Sonata; Percussion Music.

Vocal Music—Four Songs(Whitman); Is 5(Cummings).

ABOUT

Chase, G., America's Music; Copland, A., The New Music: 1900–1960; Goss, M., Modern Music Makers; Mellers, W. H., Music and Society; Thomson, V., The Musical Scene.
Modern Music, July 1946; Saturday Review, May 16, 1959; Score (London), June 1955; Show, June 1964.

Ernest Bloch
1880–1959

Ernest Bloch was born in Geneva on July 24, 1880. His parents were shopkeepers who hoped their son would some day enter the business world. The resolve to become a musician, however, was strongly entrenched in the child. He vowed to devote his life to music, wrote the vow on a piece of paper, placed it under a mound of rocks, and built a ritual fire. Such determination could not be denied. When he was fourteen he began to study solfeggio with Jaques-Dalcroze (creator of eurhythmics), and the violin with Louis Rey. Stimulated by this formal study, he wrote an *Oriental Symphony* and an Andante, for string quartet.

When he was seventeen, Bloch went to Brussels for additional training in music. At the Conservatory he studied the violin with Eugène Ysaÿe, and composition with François Rasse. In 1900 he transferred to Germany to complete his musical education with Ivan Knorr at Frankfurt-am-Main and Ludwig Thuille in Munich. In 1902 he completed his first mature symphony, in C-sharp minor, portions of which were played in Basel in 1903.

Bloch: blôk

Financial reverses at home took him back to Geneva in 1904. On August 13 of that year he married, and supported himself and his wife by working as bookkeeper, salesman, and traveling merchant for his father's shop. "I will write music as I feel I must," he said at the time, "and if it is good it will be heard. Otherwise it will not. Meanwhile I will be a merchant." But business did not absorb all his energies. Each week he lectured on metaphysics at the University of Geneva. In 1909 and 1910 he conducted symphony concerts at Lausanne and Neuchâtel. And during the night he worked on compositions.

ERNEST BLOCH

He completed several impressive works, some Romantic in style, others in an Impressionist vein. One was the sensitive tone-poem *Hiver-Printemps* (1904–1905), first performed in Geneva on January 27, 1906. Another was a set of songs for mezzo soprano and orchestra entitled *Poèmes d'Automne* (1906). Most ambitious of all was an opera, *Macbeth*, on which he labored from 1904 to 1909. He despatched the completed manuscript to the management of the Paris Opéra-Comique which, to his amazement, accepted it for performance. The première took place on November 30, 1910. Some critics were derogatory in their appraisal. A few were enthusiastic. Pierre Lalo called it "one of the most profoundly interesting works which has been given on the operatic stage in these last years; a work in which the singularly powerful nature of a dramatic composer reveals itself." On the whole the opera was successful, receiving sixteen performances in its first season. Then it was neglected until March 5, 1938, when it was given at the San Carlo Opera in Naples. Early in 1953 it was produced at Rome. At both revivals, the opera was acclaimed as a singularly powerful and original conception. Guido Pannain said in *Il Mattino* of Naples: "The composer has assimilated the essence and values of the tragedy. His spirituality, which lives in music, corresponds precisely to that of the play. Bloch has animated what is sculptural and monumental in Shakespeare. He feels the drama in his idiom, which is music. . . . Like Mussorgsky, Bloch renews harmonically the vitality of the word."

One of the critics who believed in Bloch when *Macbeth* was first produced was Romain Rolland. Rolland's interest was aroused when he studied the manuscript of the C-sharp minor Symphony. It was renewed and strengthened by his favorable reaction to *Macbeth*. Rolland made a trip to Geneva to meet and talk to the young composer. He has described his astonishment at finding Bloch sitting behind a high bookkeeper's desk, in his father's store, working patiently over his accounts. On Rolland's urging, Bloch abandoned the shop—and the world of business—to devote himself exclusively to music.

In 1910 came the première of the complete Symphony in C-sharp minor, in Geneva with Bloch conducting. Rolland was in the audience. "Your symphony," Rolland wrote to Bloch, "is one of the most important works of the modern school. I don't know of any work in which a richer, more vigorous, more passionate temperament makes itself felt."

From 1911 to 1915 Bloch earned his living by teaching composition and aesthetics at the Geneva Conservatory. In his compositions he was beginning to turn away from the Romantic or Impressionistic writing that had thus far characterized his writing. He had become convinced of the importance of expressing himself as a Jew in his music and had by now been fired with the ideal of creating a Hebrew music reflecting the history, culture, and ideals of his people. He said: "Racial consciousness is absolutely necessary in music even though nationalism is not. I am a Jew.

I aspire to write Jewish music not for the sake of self-advertisement, but because it is the only way in which I can produce music of vitality— if I can do such a thing at all. . . . It is not my purpose or my desire to attempt a 're-construction' of Jewish music, or to base my work on melodies more or less authentic. I am not an archeologist. I hold that it is of first importance to write good, genuine music—my own music. It is the Jewish soul that interests me, the complex, glowing, agitated soul that I feel vibrating through the Bible."

His first ethnic compositions included the *Two Psalms* (Nos. 137 and 114), for soprano and orchestra (1912–1914); *Trois Poèmes Juifs*, for orchestra, written in memory of his father (1913); and *Psalm 22*, for baritone and orchestra (1914). In 1916 came the *Israel Symphony*, inspired by the holiest day in the Jewish year, the Day of Atonement, when the Jew seeks penance for his sins. This single-movement symphony ends with an eloquent prayer for chorus.

Another work completed in 1916 is still one of Bloch's most frequently heard masterworks, the rhapsody *Schelomo*, for cello obbligato and orchestra. "Schelomo" is King Solomon of the Bible, who is represented by a solo cello.

Bloch's later works of Hebraic interest include the *Baal Shem Suite*, for violin and piano, completed in 1923. This is a three-movement composition inspired by the Hasidic movement founded in Poland in the late eighteenth century by the seer and mystic Baal Shem.

In his Hebraic works, Bloch did not quote actual Hebrew melodies or synagogual chants. He created his own melodies, at the same time utilizing some of the stylistic elements found in Hebrew music, such as its intervallic structure and its rhythmic patterns. The mysticism, spirituality, and over-all melancholy that characterize so much of Hebrew music also pervade Bloch's writing.

Early in 1916 Bloch came to the United States to conduct the Maude Allen dance troupe which had been booked for an extensive tour. The sudden bankruptcy of this venture left Bloch stranded without friends or resources. He made his home in New York City where, in 1917, he joined the faculty of the David Mannes School of Music. Olin Downes (later music critic of the New York

Times) met Bloch at this time. Some years later he described this meeting: "The experience was unique and unforgettable–the scene on an afternoon in a stuffy little bedroom with an upright piano in it, here in New York, where a maniac with blazing eyes, jet-black hair and face lined with suffering and will and vision, sat at the piano, beating it as a madman his drum, and bawling, singing, shouting, released a torrent of music which poured from him like a volcano . . . music bitter, passionate, exalted, and all purple and gold."

Concerts soon helped to familiarize American music audiences with Bloch's music. On December 29, 1916, the Flonzaley Quartet gave the première performance of the First String Quartet. On March 23, 1917, Bloch appeared as guest conductor of the Boston Symphony for the première of his *Trois Poèmes Juifs*. On May 3, 1917, Artur Bodanzky devoted a complete program of the Society of Friends of Music in New York to Bloch, a program that offered the premières of the *Israel Symphony* and *Schelomo*. Bloch's fame was further increased in 1919 when he received the Elizabeth Sprague Coolidge prize of one thousand dollars for his Suite, for viola and piano.

In 1920 Bloch was appointed director of the Cleveland Institute of Music. He was never happy as an administrator, mainly because his ideals and values continually clashed with expediency. Nevertheless, he held this post five years. During this period he completed the first Piano Quintet (1923), in which he experimented with quarter tones in passages calling for high tension, and his first Concerto Grosso (1925). In the latter, Bloch penetrated the world of neoclassicism in order to demonstrate to his pupils at the Conservatory that music did not have to be complex and revolutionary to achieve a modern impact and personality.

In 1924 Bloch became a naturalized American citizen. One year later he left Cleveland to become the director of the San Francisco Conservatory. There, in 1927, he wrote the symphonic rhapsody *America*, which won the first prize of three thousand dollars offered by the magazine *Musical America* in a contest for an American composition for large orchestra. The symphony (submitted, as prescribed by the rules, under a pen name) was the unanimous choice of the judges. It was introduced by the New York Philharmonic on December 20, 1928. The following day it was played simultaneously by major orchestras in Chicago, Philadelphia, Boston, and San Francisco.

In his compositions from the Concerto Grosso to *America*, Bloch had digressed from his former Hebraic ideals and mission by finding his stimulation and inspiration in baroque music, in American backgrounds and history, and in other non-Hebraic subjects. But this digression is not quite so marked as appears on casual inspection. The Piano Quintet, the Concerto Grosso, and *America* may not be Hebraic in intent, but they are the creations of a profound Hebraic consciousness. Isaac Goldberg once made the trenchant observation that the Indians of *America* dance with Hasidic feet. Bloch may have temporarily deserted Hebrew music, but Hebrew music had not deserted him. Some critics even regard the first Piano Quintet, for all its alliance to the classical and romantic traditions of absolute music, as one of his most religious creations–as profound and as deeply moving a voice of Bloch's people as almost anything he had written up to that time.

An endowment by one of San Francisco's patrons enabled Bloch to give up his post in San Francisco in 1930 and devote himself exclusively to creative work. He settled with his family in Switzerland and concentrated his efforts on the writing of *Sacred Service* for the Sabbath morning synagogue prayers. Bloch wanted it to be more than a ritual service; he hoped to create a religious work which would become a monumental song of faith for all humanity. "Though intensely Jewish in roots," Bloch explained, "the message seems to me above all a gift of Israel to the whole of mankind. It symbolizes for me far more than a Jewish service; but in its great simplicity and variety, it embodies a philosophy acceptable to all men."

The *Sacred Service* was written during a critical period in Bloch's life—a period of great spiritual and mental suffering—perhaps the source of its vision, nobility, and eloquence. It is one of Bloch's most high-minded and deeply moving conceptions, in which (to use his own words) "the sacred emotion of the race that slumbers far down in our soul" finds exalted expression in music that passes from tenderness to passion, and from strength to humility.

Upon completing his score, Bloch returned to the United States to direct the American première at a concert of the Schola Cantorum in New York on April 11, 1934; the world première had taken place in Turin, Italy, on January 12, 1934.

With *A Voice in the Wilderness* (1936) Bloch produced a second major work with cello obbligato. Bloch described this new work as a set of six "meditations," all calculated to portray "the unhappy destiny of man." It was introduced by the Los Angeles Philharmonic, Otto Klemperer conducting, on January 21, 1937.

Other major works by Bloch during the 1930's included his Violin Concerto, the first movement of which drew its thematic material from the music of the American Indian (Cleveland, December 15, 1938; Joseph Szigeti, soloist); *Evocations*, a three-movement orchestral suite (San Francisco, February 11, 1938); and a piano sonata (1935).

In 1943 Bloch made his home in Agate Beach, near Portland, Oregon, where he lived in virtual isolation from the outside world in a huge, rambling house on a cliff overlooking the Pacific. Each summer, for a number of years, he left this retreat to teach at the University of California at Berkeley. The rest of the year belonged to composition—and also to such extra-musical activities as reading philosophical tomes, sunning himself on the beach, picking mushrooms, and silent and lonely contemplation. To an interviewer he revealed that in other hours of relaxation he liked "to take a few apples, a bar of chocolate, my camera, and my miniature scores of the Bach 48, and hike into the mountains or on the beach. Also I like to see how rapidly I can write a Bach fugue from memory." Many evenings, before going to sleep, he would read scores of the master composers, to seek out new beauties in thrice-familiar music.

Bloch was uniquely productive during the 1940's and 1950's, possibly more productive than he had ever been, in spite of the fact that in the middle 1950's he suffered severely from cancer, which eventually took his life. In 1953–1954 ne became the first composer ever to receive top awards from the New York Music Critics Circle in two categories: for his third string quartet (1951) and his second Concerto Grosso (1952). He had previously received another Music Critics Circle Award (in 1946) for his second string quartet. In addition to these compositions, he also wrote numerous works for orchestra, or for solo instrument and orchestra, including the Symphony in E-flat, which was introduced in London by the Royal Philharmonic under Efrem Kurtz on February 15, 1956.

In January 1957 Bloch was operated on for cancer. During his convalescence he was visited by Yehudi Menuhin, who commissioned Bloch to write a work for solo violin. Bloch completed this assignment (a solo sonata) on April 17, 1958, receiving from Menuhin such a generous check in payment that he felt impelled to write for the virtuoso a second solo sonata; this he completed in July 1958. These were Bloch's last completed compositions.

Ernest Bloch died of cancer in Portland, Oregon, on July 15, 1959. He was survived by his wife (then seventy-eight) and three children. One of the daughters, Suzanne, achieved recognition as a musical scholar and performer on the lute. Another daughter, Lucienne, became a gifted sculptress and painter. A son, Ivan, is an engineer. Among the honors earned by Bloch were an honorary membership in the Santa Cecilia Academy of Rome and membership in and a gold medal from the American Academy of Arts and Letters.

In a communication to Olin Downes in 1955, on the occasion of Bloch's seventy-fifth birthday, the composer described his musical beliefs and principles as follows: "I have never subscribed to any theories. I have seen so many of them prevail and disappear during my long life. . . . I lived outside of all these currents, alone, a fossil, admiring, without regard to labels, cliques or fads or groups, adoring *music*, when a man has something to say and says it in his own proper way. . . . And so I can enjoy very different styles and conceptions when a Master was able to convey his message. . . . I always made my music as I felt I had to—tonal, atonal, polytonal, chromatic—each work has its own style . . . but I learned all this from the classics. . . . Works written fifty years ago and recent works of mine are different. But not quite consciously. At seventy-five, the psyche-physiology of a human being is different from that of a man of twenty-five (Alas!). My present works are probably less subjective than those I wrote around 1912–1916. . . . They are, perhaps, now more impersonal, now objective, perhaps."

An Ernest Bloch Society was formed in 1937 to promote Bloch's music. When Bloch celebrated his seventieth birthday, the Society presented a six-day festival of his music in Chicago.

MAJOR WORKS

Chamber Music—5 string quartets; 2 suites for string quartet; 2 piano quintets; 2 violin sonatas; 2 sonatas for solo violin; 2 suites for solo cello; Suite for Viola and Piano (also for viola and orchestra); Baal Shem, suite for violin and piano; Four Episodes, for string quartet; Méditation Hébraïque, for cello and piano; From Jewish Life, for cello and piano.

Choral Music—Sacred Service.

Operas—Macbeth; Jezebel.

Orchestral Music—2 concerti grossi; Symphony in C-sharp minor; Hiver-Printemps, tone poem; Poèmes d'Automne, for voice and orchestra; Trois Poèmes Juifs; Three Psalms (137, 114, and 22), for voice and orchestra; Schelomo, rhapsody for cello obbligato and orchestra; Israel Symphony; America, symphonic rhapsody; Helvetia, tone poem; A Voice in the Wilderness, for cello obbligato and orchestra; Evocations, suite; Violin Concerto; Suite Symphonique; Concerto Symphonique, for piano and orchestra; Scherzo Fantasque, for piano and orchestra; In Memoriam; Suite Hébraïque, for viola and orchestra; Sinfonia Breve; Symphony, for trombone solo and orchestra; Symphony in E-flat; Proclamation, for trumpet and orchestra; Suite Modale, for flute solo and string orchestra.

Piano Music—Sonata; various pieces.

Vocal Music—Historiettes au Crépuscule, four songs for soprano and piano.

ABOUT

Chase, G., America's Music; Ewen, D. (ed.), The New Book of Modern Composers; Pannain, G., Modern Composers; Rosenfeld, P., Musical Portraits; Saminsky, L., Music of Our Day; Tibaldi Chiesa, M., Ernest Bloch.

Etude, February 1951; Musical America, February 15, 1956; Musical Quarterly, October 1947.

Karl-Birger Blomdahl
1916–1968

Karl-Birger Blomdahl was born on October 19, 1916, in Växjö, Sweden. His preliminary music study took place with private teachers in Stockholm. Afterwards he became a pupil of Hilding Rosenberg in composition, counter-

---

Blomdahl: blo͞om′ däl

point, and orchestration, and studied conducting with Tor Mann at the Royal High School of Music. His musical education was completed in France, Switzerland, and Italy.

KARL-BIRGER BLOMDAHL

As a young man, Blomdahl affiliated himself with several other young Swedish composers who had been Rosenberg's pupils and who had been influenced by his progressive ideas in music. In short order, Blomdahl became their leading spirit. These young musicians came to be known as "the Monday Group" because they met that day each week to discuss musical problems and clarify their own direction as composers. Their Bible was Hindemith's text, *Unterweisung im Tonsatz*, and their guiding stars were Hindemith, Bartók, and the neoclassic Stravinsky.

The influence of Hindemith and Bartók can be detected in Blomdahl's first important works: his first symphony (1943); the Concerto Grosso, for orchestra (1944); the String Trio (1946); and the Violin Concerto (1947). We confront here a linear style, a frequent recourse to cumulative effect, a concentration of idiom and an economy of means, and an interest in baroque or classical structures.

By the end of the 1940's, Blomdahl had begun showing an increased interest in atonality and expressionism; the influence of Hindemith and Bartók was now being replaced by that of Alban Berg and Anton Webern. Blomdahl's Third Symphony, subtitled *Facetter* (*Facets*), completed in 1950, demonstrated this growing fascination for expressionism. Not strictly in the twelve-tone technique, the work sometimes suggests that technique. The Third Symphony was atonal in the traditions of the early Schoenberg school. It was successfully introduced at the festival of the International Society for Contemporary Music at Frankfurt-am-Main in Germany in 1951 and was performed by major orchestras throughout Europe, bringing Blomdahl international recognition.

Halsey Stevens described the symphony in *Notes:* "Although it is in a single movement, the scope is extensive, the playing time runs to twenty-three minutes – and all of them packed with pertinent and exciting happenings. Blomdahl's materials are jagged and forceful, and he uses them with great economy. . . . The opening is especially touching, with solo flute over a tympani roll, gradually drawing in all the winds to reach a great climax and recede before the violins and violas are called upon. These first fifty bars symbolize the form of the whole work, whose inner sections . . . generate a furious energy which is only slightly tempered by the quieter pages that connect them."

In the early 1950's Blomdahl turned to choral music with gratifying results. In 1952 he completed the oratorio *In the Hall of Mirrors*, based on nine sonnets by Erik Lindegren. Scored for vocal quartet, narrator, basso, chorus, and orchestra, this monumental work was first heard over the Swedish Radio in 1953, then given a public performance in Stockholm on May 29, 1954. Discussing the music, Moses Pergament said in a Swedish newspaper: "The growing power of this music has its own center of nourishment in a visionary tone fantasy which feeds and enfolds an unlimited number of tone pictures of such plasticity, that they not only absorb the poet's macabre orgies of imagination, but also turn them into an enlargement as wide as the cosmic sound of music. With what psychological accuracy, the composer elicits the emotional accents from this esoteric poetry!"

In the Hall of Mirrors is one of three major works in which Blomdahl discusses the plight of man in present-day society. Another was *Anabase*, text by Saint-John Perse. This is a choral composition for narrator, baritone, chorus, and orchestra which Ingmar Bengtsson said in a Swedish newspaper was music with "astringency, force and dynamism," but also with "calm, lyrical warmth and spiritual intensity." The first hearing of *Anabase* took place in Stockholm on December 14, 1956.

The third composition in which the problems of contemporary man are treated is the one that most strongly focused world attention on Blomdahl: his opera *Aniara*, which was produced at the Royal Opera of Stockholm on May 31, 1959, in an initial run of fifty performances in sold-out auditoriums. It was then recorded in its entirety and given an immensely successful German première in Hamburg in the spring of 1960. On May 31, 1967, it was performed by the Stockholm Royal Opera at Expo 67 in Montreal. The published score described the opera as "a revue of mankind in space time." It was the first opera to be inspired by science fiction, the first opera about travel in space, and the first successful opera to make significant use of electronic sounds.

The libretto, adapted by Erik Lindegren from a play by Harry Martinson, tells the story of travelers aboard the space ship *Aniara* bound for Mars. A day before they reach their destination, they celebrate with song, dance, and festivities. They are happy to reach their goal, and jubilant at having left behind a world where so much tragedy and cruelty existed and a homeland which had recently been devastated by an atomic holocaust. But their joy is short-lived. A jam in the steering mechanism causes *Aniara* to drift from its course. It will never be able to reach Mars, nor can it ever return to earth, but must roam about in space indefinitely. It courses through space for some twenty years during which the passengers—overwhelmed by hopelessness and despair and yearning pathetically for some miracle—become disciples of varied and curious cults, sects, and beliefs. They die off, one by one, as the *Aniara* continues its flight through space.

As Martinson explains the symbolism of his text, "The *Aniara* journey can and should . . . be understood as a journey through the destitute and forsaken human soul. . . . *Aniara* is the tragedy of modern man and of his arrogance in the face of matter. . . . *Aniara* seeks to hold up a mirror of art to our modern cosmos in which joy dances in the arms of fear."

Blomdahl's score was a stew of many ingredients—atonality; polytonality; twelve-tone system; folk, church, and dance music; and electronic sounds. In his review for a Stockholm newspaper Curt Berg wrote that the music "ranges from subtlest lyricism to a maniacally lewd dance, from artless love song to depraved ditty, from mournfully recited fairy tale to acid parody on a children's hymn, all the while with the form strictly controlled and with a power of illustrative invention of the most admirable kind." Some of the effective musical episodes consisted of either electronic music or concrete music reproduced on tape, in which eerie sounds helped to heighten tensions, to suggest interstellar atmosphere, to reproduce the sound of supplicating voices coming from enormous distances to describe earthly catastrophes. "The electronic and concrete sections . . . create the strongest suggestion and become towards the end of the opera sublime," reported Erwin Leiser.

The deep-rooted pessimism sounded in *Aniara* reechoed in Blomdahl's next opera, *The Saga of the Super Computer*. This space opera had been scheduled for a world première in Stockholm during the 1969–1970 season. Blomdahl explained that he was writing it, just as he had written *Aniara*, "to shake people, to awaken them to the reality of catastrophes that are closer than they think." However, he did not live to complete the work.

From 1953 until his death Blomdahl was a member of the Royal Academy of Music and from 1960 professor of composition there. In 1955 he visited the United States, devoting most of his time to touring the farmlands of the Middle West where some of his relatives had settled.

Karl-Birger Blomdahl died in Stockholm, June 16, 1968. In an obituary notice in the New York *Times* he was described as a "stocky, ruddy, baldish, cigar-smoking man" who had a deeply pessimistic outlook on life. This pessimism was the reason that he and his wife refused to have any children. "I can't see the meaning of having any," he explained.

MAJOR WORKS

Ballets—Sisyphos; Minotauros.

Chamber Music—2 string quartets; Trio, for oboe, clarinet, and bassoon; String Trio; Suite, for cello and piano; Dance Suite No. 1, for flute, violin, viola, cello, and percussion; Short String Quartet; Dance Suite No. 2, for clarinet, cello and percussion; Trio, for clarinet, cello, and piano.

Choral Music—In the Hall of Mirrors; Anabase.

Operas—Aniara (with electronic sounds); Der Herr von Hancken; The Saga of the Super Computer (unfinished).

Orchestral Music—3 symphonies; Symphonic Dances, Viola Concerto; Concerto Grosso, for chamber orchestra; Violin Concerto; Pastoral Suite, for string orchestra; Praeludium and Allegro, for string orchestra; Chamber Concerto, for piano, wind, and percussion; Forma Ferritonans; Game for Eight, choreographic suite; Fioriture.

Piano Music—Three Polyphonic Pieces.

Vocal Music—Dithyramb, for mezzo soprano and piano; Five Songs, for contralto and piano.

ABOUT

Hartog, H. (ed.), European Music in the Twentieth Century; Lang, P. H. and Broder, N. (eds.), Contemporary Music in Europe.

Pierre Boulez
1925–

Pierre Boulez, the son of an industrialist, was born on March 26, 1925, in Montbrison, department of the Loire. As a child, Pierre sang in the church choir and was given piano lessons by his sister. Additional training in music was given him by private teachers in nearby St.-Étienne. But despite his obvious gift for music, he was directed towards a career in engineering. He completed his preliminary schooling in Lyons and prepared to take the entrance examinations at the École Polytechnique in Paris. But his increasing interest in music, and a providential meeting with Olivier Messiaen, made him change his mind. He decided to forget all about engineering and to specialize in music. "It was a clean break," he later revealed to an interviewer. "I suddenly left one world to enter another. It seems strange to say, but musical life in Paris during the war was much more exciting than it is now. True, there were many restrictions on entertainment, but music, being 'culture,' was allowed by the Germans, of course. People stormed the concert halls, perhaps to get away from it all. Even the modern music of that time was appreciated."

Boulez: boo lĕz′

Boulez

Boulez studied piano and counterpoint with Arthur Honegger's wife, Andrée Vaurabourg. In 1944 he entered Messiaen's harmony class at the Paris Conservatory, where he won first prize in the year of his graduation, 1945. He then studied composition with Messiaen. Strongly influenced by Messiaen's preoccupation with intricate rhythms, including those of Eastern Europe, Boulez completed his first composition, *Three Psalmodies*, for piano (1945). The impact of Messiaen on Boulez was even more noticeable in the Sonatine, for flute (1946). In this composition, as Boulez himself has explained, he "tried for the first time to articulate independent rhythmic structures, of which Messiaen had revealed . . . the possibilities upon classical serial structures."

PIERRE BOULEZ

An even stronger impression was soon made upon him by the twelve-tone system of the Schoenberg school, which he discovered in René Leibowitz's book *Schoenberg and His School* and from hearing one of Schoenberg's compositions. In 1945 Boulez began to study with Leibowitz. Before long he became convinced that the problem of the twentieth century composer was to create a new musical language free from all Romantic associations and that the composer had to be controlled and guided in his creative processes by some "predetermining system." Boulez found that system in the twelve-tone technique. "Since the discoveries by the Viennese, all composition other than twelve tones is useless."

The twelve-tone technique began to dominate his writing and thinking. His first two compositions utilizing a strict twelve-tone row came in 1946–his first sonata for piano and a sonata for two pianos.

In 1948 Boulez was appointed music director of the Parisian theatre run jointly by Jean-Louis Barrault and Madeleine Renaud. In this capacity he conducted a traditional, conservative repertory, for most of which he had neither admiration nor sympathy. (Only once did Boulez himself provide the incidental music for one of the productions–in 1946, when he contributed a score for Aeschylus' *Oresteia*.) He kept the post for a decade, thereby acquiring the financial resources with which to continue his own adventurous creative work without interruption. He also mastered the techniques of conducting which served him well in later years in his promotion of avant-garde music.

With his second piano sonata (1948) Boulez opened up both for himself and for the twelve-tone system new horizons. Boulez himself described his work as representing "a total and deliberate break with the universe of classical twelve-tone writing . . . the decisive step towards an integrated serial work, that will be realized when serial structures of tone colors and dynamics will join serial structures of pitch and rhythm." What Boulez was aiming for was the application of the twelve-tone technique not only to pitch (as had been the case with Schoenberg and Berg) but also to durations, dynamics, and articulation. This represented a break with the more formal twelve-tone school. When the sonata was introduced in Paris by Yvette Grimaud it created a furor, particularly among those dedicated Schoenberg disciples who regarded it as outright heresy. But if Boulez made enemies, he also made disciples. A Boulez clique came into existence, staunchly advocating the serial method and popularizing it among the more radical elements of the twelve-tone school.

Boulez achieved international recognition with *Le Marteau sans Maître* (*The Hammer Without a Master*), probably his most celebrated composition. He wrote it in 1953 and 1954, and it was introduced on June 18, 1955, at a concert of the festival of the International Society for Contemporary Music at Baden-

Baden, Hans Rosbaud conducting. The composition, a setting of three poems by René Char, is in nine movements, scored for contralto and six instrumentalists. At the festival, *Le Marteau sans Maître* caused a sensation. Performances followed in major European cities, as well as in New York and Los Angeles, and a recording was released. "The vocal line," Joseph Machlis explains, "is characterized by wide leaps and the stylized setting we have come to associate with twelve-tone music." But, as Arthur Cohn goes on to say, it is "a far cry from the music of Schoenberg and Webern." What we have here is "pure Boulez—a music of perpetual variation in color and pitch . . . a plastic transformation of strict serial composition."

Here, as in many later works, Boulez gave "the *coup de grâce* to the so-called Western tradition that culminated in Schoenberg," as Harold C. Schonberg wrote in the New York *Times*. "Melody disappeared, deliberately so. Music became athematic, harmonic systems had nothing in common with those of the past, new instrumental and vocal textures had to be devised, new notation invented."

With the financial assistance of Barrault and Renaud, Boulez inaugurated in 1954 a series of avant-garde concerts at the Petit Théâtre Marigny in Paris. This became an annual event, originally called Concerts Marigny but later renamed Domaine Musicale, which moved in 1957 to larger quarters in the Salle Gaveau, and after that to the Odéon. At these performances, avant-garde composers received a hearing. Boulez himself found an opportunity here to get his works played as well as to demonstrate his remarkable gifts as a conductor of new music. His first appearance as a conductor of serious music came about through mere chance. On March 21, 1956, the conductor assigned to direct Boulez' *Marteau sans Maître* at the Domaine Musicale was unable to fill the engagement. Boulez was compelled to replace him and gave an impressive account of himself. Chance again stepped in to bring Boulez to the conductor's platform in 1957—this time in Cologne where his *Visage Nuptial* (1946–50) was being performed. Displeased with the way the conductor was presenting his music, Boulez insisted upon conducting the work himself. Soon after that he was invited to conduct performances at

festivals at Aix-en-Provence in France and Donaueschingen in Germany. In both places he made such a profound impression that guest engagements came readily. In 1960 he received an appointment as principal conductor of the Southwest German Radio Orchestra in Baden-Baden. In 1961 he appeared at the Salzburg Festival with the Vienna Philharmonic; his performance of Stravinsky's *Rite of Spring* elicited an ovation. In 1963 he proved a sensation with his performances of *Wozzeck* at the Paris Opéra and was recalled there the following season not only to perform *Wozzeck* again but also to direct an evening of Stravinsky's ballets.

Boulez has been an indefatigable innovator and experimenter. In 1951 and 1952 he completed a number of provocative works incorporating concrete music (music produced from actual nonmusical sounds recorded on tape, or distortions of such sounds) and electronic music. *Polyphonie x*, for eighteen instruments (1951), created a mild sensation when introduced at the Donaueschingen Festival on October 6, 1951. In a much later work, Boulez combined for the first time electronically reproduced sounds with orchestral tones, in this instance a synchronization of the tones of two orchestras: *Poésie pour Pouvoir*, introduced at the Donaueschingen Festival on October 19, 1958.

Boulez experimented with the rearrangement on the stage of the traditional symphony orchestra in *Doubles*, initially performed in Paris on March 16, 1958. In *Improvisations on Mallarmé*—first given at the festival of the International Society for Contemporary Music at Rome on June 14, 1959—he explored the possibilities of improvisation. From improvisation he progressed to "music of chance" or "aleatory" music—as opposed to creative calculation. His third piano sonata (1961) was made up of five pieces. The printed music permits the interpreter leeway in making his own creative decisions. The performer may omit any of the pieces; may change the sequence of the five pieces; or arrange at will two pairs of four pieces in any order he wishes around a fifth or central piece.

In the spring of 1963 Boulez paid a visit to the United States at the invitation of Harvard University, where he delivered several lectures. He went to New York City on May 25 in conjunction with the presentation of *Le Marteau sans Maître* and explained to the audience his purpose in writing the work. Two years later, at Carnegie Hall, on May 1, 1964, Boulez appeared for the first time in America as a conductor in a BBC Symphony performance of avant-garde music which included the New York première of his *Doubles*. Since then, Boulez has come to be recognized as one of the world's foremost conductors and has made many guest appearances, not only with the major symphony orchestras of Europe and America but also at the Bayreuth Festival in *Parsifal* and with the Bayreuth Festival on its visit to Japan in *Tristan and Isolde*. He also contracted with Columbia Records to make numerous recordings. In 1968 he consummated an unprecedented agreement with the Cleveland Orchestra by signing a five-year contract to appear as a guest conductor for several weeks each season.

In June 1966 Boulez became the center of controversy when he announced he was severing all official connections with the French government and disassociating himself from all its music organizations, including the Domaine Musicale. He had been antagonized by the appointment of Marcel Landowski, a composer with conservative tendencies, as head of a newly established bureau in the cultural ministry.

Boulez maintains a home in Baden-Baden and an apartment overlooking the Boulevard Raspail in Paris. In his liner notes for the Columbia recording of *Le Marteau sans Maître*, Robert Craft reveals that Boulez is "a short man growing slightly stocky, bald, Napoleonic"; that he "smokes cigars, can drink four framboises after dinner with no decline of intellectual focus, and never eats breakfast"; that he is "without religious beliefs, is generous with money, is more attracted to Oriental and Indian cultures than to Italian and Greek and is greatly interested in the Psychological Method"; and that he has "a nervous blink, doesn't date letters, sleeps five hours, is never ill, and has the tiniest handwriting in the world."

Boulez has gathered many of the essays he wrote in the years between 1942 and 1962 into a volume entitled *Notes of an Apprenticeship*. This was published in the United States in 1968 in an English translation.

MAJOR WORKS

Chamber Music—Sonatine, for flute and piano; Le Livre pour Quatuor; Polyphonie x, for eighteen instruments (also for large ensemble); Éclat, for fifteen instruments.

Orchestral Music—Le Visage Nuptial, for two solo voices, chorus, and orchestra; Le Soleil des Eaux, for solo voices and orchestra; Symphonie Concertante, for piano and orchestra; Le Marteau sans Maître, for contralto and orchestra; Poésie pour Pouvoir, for orchestra and electronic sounds; Improvisations on Mallarmé, for voice and orchestra; Pli Selon Pli, for soprano and orchestra; Figures, Doubles, Prismes, for orchestra; Éclat.

Piano Music—3 sonatas; Three Psalmodies; Sonata for Two Pianos; Structures, for two pianos (two books).

ABOUT

Goléa, A., 20 Ans de Musique Contemporaine: De Messiaen à Boulez; Goléa, A., Rencontres avec Pierre Boulez; Hartog, J. (ed.), European Music in the Twentieth Century; Hodeir, A., Since Debussy; Machlis, J., An Introduction to Contemporary Music; Samuel, C., Panorama de l'Art Musical Contemporain.

High Fidelity, May 1966, March 1968; Musical America, February 1957, November 1960; Opera News, January 20, 1968.

Henry Brant
1913–

Henry Dreyfus Brant was born in Montreal on September 15, 1913, of American parents. "I started to compose music at the age of eight, and at twelve wrote my first string quartet," he stated in an autobiographical sketch written for the editor of this book. "Music study began at the McGill University School of Music where my father taught violin. My family moved to New York City in 1928. From 1930 to 1934 I was a scholarship student at the Juilliard School of Music where I studied piano with James Friskin and composition with Rubin Goldmark, and where I won prizes and awards in composition, including the Loeb, Seligman, and Coolidge prizes." After 1934 Brant continued music study privately with Aaron Copland, George Antheil, and Wallingford Riegger.

"Early in my studies," Brant continues, "I adopted the theory that today's composers should be schooled in all the principal contemporary techniques and styles, as well as those of the past. Accordingly, for a time, I wrote deliberately after the manner of Schoenberg, Stravinsky, Hindemith, Bartók, Prokofiev, Milhaud and Weill, as well as in the style of composers of the immediate past, including Debussy, Ravel, Scriabin, Strauss and Mahler. I divided the work of each master into two or three periods, and conscientiously analyzed and imitated each period. I did not go to Europe to learn any of this on the spot; it seemed advisable to cushion the powerful impact of well-established modern European styles as much as possible."

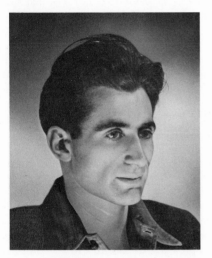

HENRY BRANT

He was early fascinated by experimentation, and at sixteen he wrote *Variations for Four Instruments*, in which he invented the technique of "oblique harmony." This was a scheme of harmonic relationships, as Brant Miller has explained, "between the bass of one chord, the tenor of the second chord, the alto of the third chord, and the soprano of the fourth chord." Another of his early innovations was the use of the variation form in four parts "with no specific instrumentation," Miller notes, "except that they be contrasting colors in which four themes are announced simultaneously or contrapuntally, then all variations directly utilize one of the four themes." Brant has since repudiated these early compositions and has also withdrawn them from publication.

"In the early 1930's," Brant observes, "a composer with Conservatory training who

lacked private means had the choice of supporting himself as a teacher, instrumentalist, arranger, or perhaps critic (but certainly *not* as a 'serious' composer). I went into professional arranging partly with the object of studying the jazz arts and techniques at first hand. It turned out to be much more than that; in the course of many years I have orchestrated almost everything that can be called music, symphonic or popular. This activity afforded me a unique insight into the methods of my American contemporaries. Then, too, in the course of participating in the creation of so much music not one's own, a certain professional tolerance and awareness are acquired, a kind of objectivity towards the rest of the world's music."

Brant earned his living writing or arranging scores for radio and films, and for many years after by teaching orchestration at Columbia University Extension and, beginning in 1947, at the Juilliard School of Music. During the 1930's, he took inordinate delight in writing music for unorthodox combinations of instruments and materials producing sound. In 1932 he wrote *Five and Ten Cent Store*, for violin, piano, and kitchenware. *All Day* (1933) was scored for the flute family exclusively (three piccolos, five flutes, and three alto flutes). *Prelude and Fugue* (1934) was for string quartet and woodwind quintet. In 1938 he wrote *The Marx Brothers*, "three faithful portraits" of Chico, Groucho, and Harpo Marx, scored for tin whistle (or piccolo) and chamber orchestra. During the same period he completed several stage works in a burlesque or satirical style: the two-act burlesque *Dis Chord* (1932), the one-act opera *Miss O'Grady* (1936), the one-act satire *Entente Cordiale* (1936), and a stage work which he described as a "platform opera, earth-rite satire," *Alisaunde* (1940). Also in a satirical vein was his successful ballet *The Great American Goof*, described as a "sort of morality-play fantasy" requiring the dancers to speak as well as dance. With Eugene Loring's choreography and a scenario by William Saroyan, *The Great American Goof* was introduced by the Ballet Theatre in New York on January 11, 1940.

During World War II Brant wrote scores for films produced by the Office of War Information for overseas distribution. Both during and after the war he combined his teaching duties with composing for the radio; in 1944–1945, he wrote background music for the NBC series, "The Eternal Light. " He also was musical director of a dramatic series entitled "Labor–U.S.A.," broadcast over the ABC network; he conducted and composed all the incidental music used on this weekly program. In 1946 (and again in 1955) he was awarded a Guggenheim Fellowship. From 1943 to 1953 he was on the music faculty of Columbia University; he continued teaching at the Juilliard School until 1955. Since 1957 he has been on the music faculty of Bennington College in Vermont.

Several of Brant's major works in the 1940's made extensive use of jazz materials. These compositions include a Concerto for Saxophone and Orchestra, written in 1941 for Sigurd Rascher, who introduced it with the NBC Symphony on May 12, 1945. Another such work was his first symphony, in B-flat (1945). The composer explained that this music is all about "people in the U.S.A. during the 1930's, particularly the generation growing up during those years." The four movements are entitled "Sermon," "Ballad," "Skit," and "Procession," with a jazz tune prominently featured in the second movement and syncopation and the blues basic to the finale. The symphony received its world première on January 30, 1948, with Thor Johnson conducting the Cincinnati Symphony.

In the 1950's Brant interested himself in the new "directional" or "spatial" music. This kind of composition required different groups of performers to be placed in distantly separated positions in the concert hall in order to achieve a stereophonic effect by having the music converge upon the audience from several different directions. *December* (first performance in New York on December 15, 1954) is characteristic of his spatial music. Harold C. Schonberg described it in the New York *Times:* "Mr. Brant . . . spotted singers and instrumentalists all over Carnegie Hall. Trombonists were sporting in the second-tier boxes; choruses sounded from all sides of the house; the tenor soloist . . . and the soprano soloist . . . regarded one another from opposite sides of the dress circle. There also were choral groups, a busy percussionist and a brass orchestra on the stage. The conductor has two podiums, one fore and one aft. . . . Some of

the brass fanfares from the rear–and some of the choruses–were real shockers, as chip-on-shoulderish and dissonantly defiant as anything New York has heard in years."

Another of Brant's experiments used a "polyphony of tempos," in which each of several separated groups plays in its own tempo. *Milennium 2* (1954) boasts as many as twenty-one different tempi, sounded simultaneously, while *Antiphony I* (1953) called for the division of the orchestra into five separate groups, each requiring its own conductor, and each frequently playing in a different tempo. Similarly, spatial music and/or "polyphony of tempos" were further developed by Brant in two large works, *Grand Universal Circus* (1956) and *Atlantis* (1960), the latter described as an "antiphonal symphony."

Brant married Patricia Gorman in 1949; they make their year-round home in Bennington, Vermont. One of Brant's hobbies is collecting and mastering rare wind instruments, such as the Chinese oboe, the Moroccan flute, the Persian oboe, the double ocarina, and varieties of tin whistles. He once claimed that he could execute even difficult virtuoso music on the tin whistle, including Mendelssohn's Violin Concerto and the Paganini Caprices for solo violin.

Brant received the Prix Italia and a grant from the National Institute of Arts and Letters in 1955 and the Alice M. Ditson Award in 1962.

MAJOR WORKS

Ballet—The Great American Goof.

Chamber Music—Variations, for four instruments; Sonata for Oboe and Piano; Oboe Quintet; Poem and Burlesque, for eleven flutes; Five and Ten Cent Store, for violin, piano, and kitchenware; Violin Concerto with Lights, for violin and five electric switches.

Choral Music—Spanish Underground, cantata; Dialogue of the Jungle, for voices, whistles, sirens, and percussion; Atlantis, antiphonal symphony for chorus and orchestra; The Fire Garden, for voices and instruments; Fire in Cities, for chorus, wind instruments, and percussion.

Orchestral Music—2 symphonies; Four Choral Preludes; Concerto for Double Bass and Orchestra; Lyric Piece, for chamber orchestra; Gallopjig Colloquy, ballad for orchestra; Whoopee Overture; Concerto for Clarinet and Orchestra; Concerto for Saxophone and Orchestra; Music for an Imaginary Ballet; The Promised Land; Milennium Nos. 1 and 2; Origins, percussion symphony; Stresses; Signs and Alarms; Antiphony No. 1; Encephalograms; Ceremony; Galaxies, Nos. 1, 2, 3; Angels and Devils; The Grand Universal Circus, spatial theatre piece; Voyage Four, spatial concert piece; Mythical Beasts;

Conversations in an Unknown Tongue, for strings.
Piano Music—Two Sarabandes; Sonata for Two Pianos.

ABOUT

Chase, G., America's Music; Machlis, J., Introduction to Contemporary Music.

Benjamin Britten
1913-

Edward Benjamin Britten was born in Lowestoft, Suffolk, England, on November 22, 1913. He was the youngest of three children. His father was a well-to-do dental surgeon; his mother, an excellent amateur singer. Benjamin was extraordinarily precocious in music; he wrote songs before he could read or write. At nine, he completed an oratorio and string quartet. By the time he left preparatory school (at fourteen) he had produced a symphony, six string quartets, ten piano sonatas, and many smaller works. Years later, in 1934, he gathered some of the melodic ideas from these juvenile efforts into a serious mature work which he called *Simple Symphony*.

His music study began with piano when he was seven and about three years later was broadened to include the viola with Audrey Alston. In 1926 he became a composition pupil of Frank Bridge, who influenced him greatly. "His loathing of all sloppiness and amateurishness set me standards to aim at which I've never forgotten," recalled Britten many years later in the London *Daily Telegraph*. "He taught me to think and feel through the instruments I was writing. . . . In everything he did for me there was perhaps above all two cardinal principles. One was that you should try to find yourself and be true to what you found. The other . . . was his scrupulous attention to good technique, the business of saying clearly what was in one's mind. He gave me a sense of technical ambition. . . . I am enormously aware that I haven't yet come up to the technical standards Bridge set for me."

From 1928 to 1930 Britten attended Gresham's School in Holt, Norfolk. In 1930 a scholarship brought him to the Royal College of Music. There, for three years, he studied composition with John Ireland and piano with Arthur Benjamin and Harold Samuel. Britten was an outstanding student. He won the Ernest Farrar Prize for composition and, as a pianist, he received the title of Associate of the Royal College of Music.

BENJAMIN BRITTEN

Even while attending the Royal College he had some compositions either published or performed. The first to be heard publicly were *Phantasy Quartet* and three two-part songs for female voices (two poems by Walter de la Mare), both performed in London on December 12, 1932. On February 23, 1934, the BBC broadcast the première of Britten's choral variations *A Boy Was Born*, and on April 5, 1934, the festival of the International Society for Contemporary Music at Florence presented Britten's *Phantasy Quartet*. Meanwhile, Britten's first publication, the *Sinfonietta*, for chamber orchestra, was heard in London on January 31, 1933.

The death of his father made it necessary for Britten to earn his living. From 1935 to 1939 he worked at the Government Post Office Film Unit, writing background or incidental music for sixteen documentary films. During this period he wrote music for other films as well, including the full-length commercial motion picture *Love from a Stranger*.

He was not idle as a composer of serious concert music, nor did he lack important performances. On April 21, 1936, the festival of the International Society for Contemporary

97

Britten

Music at Barcelona presented his Suite, for violin and piano. On August 27, 1937, the English String Orchestra conducted by Boyd Neel performed at the Salzburg Festival in Austria Britten's most significant piece of music up to that time: the *Variations on a Theme by Frank Bridge*. The theme Britten used came from the second of Bridge's *Three Idylls*. The ten variations that followed ranged from satire, parody, and burlesque to drama and tragedy. *Variations* was a great success. It was also heard at the festival of the International Society for Contemporary Music at London in 1938, and in a two-year period following the world première it was performed fifty times in Europe and America. In 1949 the music was used for the ballet *Le Rêve de Léonor*, produced by Roland Petit's Ballets de Paris, with choreography by Frederick Ashton.

Still another important work marked Britten's rapidly developing creative powers: his first piano concerto, introduced at a Promenade concert in London on August 18, 1938, with the composer as soloist and the orchestra conducted by Sir Henry Wood. Though this work was received enthusiastically, Britten was dissatisfied with it and put it aside. In 1945 he revised it extensively, the definitive version being given at the Cheltenham Festival in June 1946.

In 1939 Britten went to New York to attend the American première of his *Variations on a Theme by Frank Bridge*. Except for a few months' residence in Brooklyn early in 1940 and a visit to California in 1941, Britten spent almost three years on Long Island, where he worked intensively on several major works. The first was a violin concerto which Antonio Brosa introduced in New York on March 27, 1940, at a concert of the New York Philharmonic, John Barbirolli conducting. Another was *Les Illuminations*, a song cycle for high voice and string orchestra (to poems by Arthur Rimbaud) in which the young composer first proved himself a songwriter of extraordinary invention and versatility; this work received its première in London on January 30, 1940. Possibly the most significant of his American creations was the *Sinfonia da Requiem*, for orchestra, inspired by the death of the composer's father. Utilizing the Latin titles of a Catholic Requiem (Lacrymosa, Dies Irae, Requiem Aeternam), the Sinfonia expressed not only the composer's personal grief over the death of his father but also his despair in seeing the world around him plunge into a cataclysmic war. Since Britten was a passionate pacifist, the impact of the war upon him could hardly be overestimated. The Sinfonia was introduced in New York on March 30, 1941, with John Barbirolli conducting the New York Philharmonic.

While in America, Britten also wrote his first opera, *Paul Bunyan*, with a libretto by W. H. Auden. This opera hardly gave a clue to the composer's later monumental achievements in the musical theatre. Produced at Columbia University in New York in May 1941 it was a failure.

Despite this inauspicious bow as opera composer, Britten received a commission from the Koussevitzky Music Foundation to write another opera. But in 1942, before he began work on the assignment, Britten returned to England, drawn by his desire to help his countrymen in their resistance to the Nazis. He would not bear arms, but he gave numerous concerts in bomb-proof shelters and hospitals. An appellate tribunal officially exempted him from all military duty on the grounds of pacifism and complete dedication to the war effort through music.

The war notwithstanding, Britten continued to write music. He completed two choral works in 1942, the *Hymn to St. Cecilia*, and *A Ceremony of Carols*. In 1943 he wrote, among other works, a Prelude and Fugue for string orchestra, and a Serenade for tenor, horn, and strings, based on poems by Tennyson, Blake, Keats, Ben Jonson, and others.

But the project that occupied him most during the war years was his opera for the Koussevitzky Music Foundation. Montagu Slater prepared the libretto based on George Crabbe's *The Borough*. The opera was *Peter Grimes*, which made Britten a composer of international importance.

Peter Grimes was introduced at Sadler's Wells in London on June 7, 1945, and became one of the memorable musical events of the decade. It was the first new opera given in England in several years; it marked the reopening of Sadler's Wells Theatre after a five-year period of war. These circumstances, dramatic though they were, proved incidental to the salient fact that *Peter Grimes* was an opera of compelling force, originality, and beauty. There was a stirring ovation for the composer when the final curtain descended. The correspondent for the New York *Times* did not hesitate to call the work "a milestone in the history of British opera."

The central theme of *Peter Grimes* was one close to Britten's heart, that of man's cruelty to man. Peter Grimes, a fisherman, is the victim of the fury and intolerance of a mob. He is falsely accused of the murder of his apprentice, and even though he is absolved in court, the townspeople continue to regard him with suspicion. When a second apprentice comes to a tragic end, the people are convinced that Grimes is the murderer. Rather than face the fury of a mob, Grimes commits suicide by going out to sea.

In a long and detailed analysis of the score in the *Sunday Times* of London, Ernest Newman wrote that there were "lyrical episodes . . . a few passages for Grimes or Ellen Orford, the final scene of Peter's madness, the fine recitative 'trio' for the four female characters in the second act. . . . The great part of the stage action is carried out in a sort of song-speech that keeps as faithfully as possible to the accents and rise and fall of the easy flow of ordinary speech, while the orchestra 'points' up what is being said in a curiously effective way. Apart from the lyrical episodes . . . the main burden of intense emotional expression is laid in the orchestra, in a number of interludes which sum up the emotional significance of what has gone before or prepare us for what is to come. They are of great power and masterly musicianship."

The success of *Peter Grimes* finds few parallels in twentieth-century opera. It was heard hundreds of times throughout Europe, in eight translations, before coming to the United States. Its American première took place at Tanglewood, in Lenox, Massachusetts, on August 6, 1946, Leonard Bernstein conducting. It was staged at Covent Garden on November 7, 1947, and at the Metropolitan Opera House in New York on February 12, 1948.

In his next three operas, Britten favored an economical structure of almost chamber music dimensions. *The Rape of Lucretia*, adapted by Ronald Duncan from a play by André Obey, required a cast of only six; the two "choruses" comprised one man and one woman; there were only twelve instrumentalists in the orchestra. A grim drama, *The Rape of Lucretia* is renowned for its effective atmospheric writing, frequently dramatized by discords; at the same time there are many pages appealing for their lyricism. *The Rape of Lucretia* was introduced at Glyndebourne, England, on July 12, 1946, and was so successful that it was presented about one hundred and thirty times in England, as well as in Holland, Belgium, Switzerland, and the United States. The American première took place in Chicago on June 1, 1947. On December 29, 1948, the opera was presented in a Broadway theatre in New York where it had a run of only twenty-three performances. The work was revived in the United States by the New York City Opera in 1958.

Albert Herring (1947) was also modest in design and economical in means. This was a comedy, the libretto by Eric Crozier based on a story by Guy de Maupassant. In the lightness of his musical touch, in his occasional wanderings into broad burlesque, and in his use of formal arias, duets, and ensemble numbers, Britten created an *opera buffa*–but a twentieth century *opera buffa*–for much of his writing is in a modern idiom. *Albert Herring* was first seen at Glyndebourne on June 20, 1947, the composer conducting. Its American première followed at the Berkshire Music Center at Tanglewood during the summer of 1949.

Let's Make an Opera, also in an intimate style, was a functional composition intended to teach children how an opera is written and produced. It was introduced on June 14, 1949, at the Aldeburgh Festival in England (a festival founded by Britten with Peter Pears and Eric Crozier in 1948 and since then an annual event in the Suffolk fishing village). This festival has offered first performances not only of important works by Britten but also of the music of other composers, together with exhibitions of paintings, poetry reading, lectures, and dramatic presentations. When the Aldeburgh Festival celebrated its twentieth anniversary in 1967, still under Britten's artistic direction, it had become one of the most distinguished festivals in England. The twentieth anniversary saw the opening of a new concert auditorium with a ceremony attended by the Queen.

In *Billy Budd* Britten returned to the large

structural dimensions of *Peter Grimes*. This opera was commissioned by the Arts Council of Great Britain for the 1951 Festival of Britain. *Billy Budd* was reminiscent of *Peter Grimes* in several ways. The sea once again became an important setting, and the over-all theme once again was man's inhumanity to man. The new opera was based on Herman Melville's story of the same title, adapted by E. M. Forster and Eric Crozier. Billy Budd, a sailor in the British navy, is the victim of a false charge of treason leveled against him by the master-at-arms, John Claggart. Unable to defend himself, Budd loses his control and kills Claggart; he is court-martialed and hanged.

If the similarities to *Peter Grimes* are important, so are the differences. *Billy Budd* calls for an all-male cast; it has no love interest; and its score dispenses completely with arias and ensemble numbers. With minor exceptions (several chanteys, for example) Britten's writing consists almost entirely of dramatic recitatives, with interest and variety of color and mood focused chiefly on the orchestra. Britten's main concern in this opera is drama rather than music, atmosphere and human compassion rather than effective aural sounds. The result is a work that is "insidiously haunting," as Scott Goddard called it in the London *News Chronicle*. In the *Observer*, Eric Blom said: "Apart from bouncing invention and unfailing technical assurance, there is a riper humanity, a more compassionate understanding expressed in a way impossible to achieve except through music." Such critical samplings show how successful *Billy Budd* was when first introduced at Covent Garden on December 1, 1951. On May 26, 1952, the opera was presented by the British company in Paris as one of the features of the Exposition of Masterpieces of the Twentieth Century. The American première took place over NBC-TV, on a coast-to-coast hook-up, on October 19, 1952. A revised version of the opera, in which the four acts were reduced to two, was presented by Covent Garden in London on April 26, 1963, and in New York by the American Opera Society on January 4, 1966.

One year after the première of *Billy Budd*, Britten became the first composer commissioned to write an opera for a coronation in England. That opera, *Gloriana*, introduced in London on June 8, 1953, was part of the festivities attending the coronation of Queen Elizabeth. It was produced in the United States for the first time in May 1956 at the May Music Festival in Cincinnati.

Gloriana was a failure and has rarely been produced. However, with his next two operas Britten proved he had not lost his sure touch in writing for the musical theatre. In 1954 came *The Turn of the Screw*; Myfanwy Piper's libretto was based on Henry James's celebrated horror story. Britten's high-tensioned music, vivid atmospheric writing, and penetrating characterization produced the same kind of hypnotic effect that James's story had in print. The union of drama and music made for a compelling and unforgettable stage experience. An unusual feature of this opera is the use of an orchestral prelude before each of the sixteen scenes to set the mood, each prelude being based on a twelve-note theme built from the intervals of fourths and thirds. *The Turn of the Screw* was introduced at the Venice Festival on September 14, 1954, and had its American première in New York on March 19, 1958.

Where *The Turn of the Screw* was grim, sober, and frequently realistic, *A Midsummer Night's Dream* (Peter Pears's libretto based on the Shakespeare comedy) was romantic and lyrical. It was first given at the Aldeburgh Festival in England on June 11, 1960. That same summer it was featured prominently at the Holland Festival. On October 10, 1961, it was produced in San Francisco (its American première); in 1963 it was presented by the New York City Opera.

Writing in the New York *Times* in a report from Aldeburgh, Howard Taubman explained that in this opera Britten made no attempt to reproduce the background and atmosphere of Shakespeare's time, through the quotation of folk songs or the imitation of English folk styles: "For the three strands that make up the fabric of the play—the world of the fairies, the concerns of the lovers, the humors of the rustics—Mr. Britten has sought individualized musical idioms. Fairyland is immersed in the musical devices of Impressionism; the rustics have a kind of arioso style that burst into full operatic bloom in the final act in a way reminiscent of the Italian lyric theatre of the early nineteenth century; the lovers are delineated in a conventional neo-Romanticism."

While writing these operas, Britten did not neglect other areas of music. He produced a large library of music of all kinds, much of it as significant as his operas. In symphonic music he produced, in 1945, the *Young Person's Guide to the Orchestra*, one of his most frequently performed symphonic compositions. His purpose here was educational: to teach young people the different instruments of the orchestra. To accomplish this aim he selected a theme by Henry Purcell, following the statement of the theme with a series of variations, each employing different instruments or groups of instruments. The composition ends in a fugue in which the instruments enter one by one, in the same order in which they had been introduced in the variations.

The *Spring Symphony* (1949), commissioned by the Koussevitzky Music Foundation and introduced at the Holland Music Festival on July 14, 1949, was a major work for soloists, chorus, and orchestra. In setting fourteen English poems about springtime, Britten apotheosized the vernal season in music that is poetic and atmospheric, deriving its spirit and personality from English madrigals.

One of the most successful and significant nontheatrical compositions produced by Britten is *A War Requiem* (1962), heard first at Coventry on May 30, 1962, during the celebration of the Consecration of the restored St. Michael's Cathedral. Its American première came on July 27, 1963, at the Berkshire Music Festival at Tanglewood, with Erich Leinsdorf conducting the Boston Symphony.

The text is based partly on the traditional Mass, and partly on poems by Wilfred Owen, who was killed during World War I only a week before the Armistice. The score makes use of three performing groups: the first consists of full chorus, orchestra, and a soprano solo in the presentation of the traditional Mass; the second is a boys' choir; the third uses solo tenor, solo baritone, and a small chamber orchestra in voicing the personal message of the poet.

Much of the impact of the Requiem lies in this marriage of secular and ritual texts: the poet's tragic contemplation of war and death—his protests, sorrow, despair—combined with the outcries and anguished prayers of the Missal text. "The immediate impression," wrote Irving Kolodin in the *Saturday Review*,

"is a work more dramatic than any opera Britten has composed, rising through successive climaxes to a 'Libera Me Domine' ('Deliver Me, O Lord, from Death Eternal'), which can best be described as a frenetic outcry, musically conveyed by resources hitherto unsuspected in the composer. 'Benedictus' is expressively attentive and supplicating, the 'Hosanna,' a frame of light by which it is preceded and followed. Among these violent or tender combinations of large forces, the settings of Owen's poems strike a much more personal, intimate, indeed humanistic note. This is not the tragedy of Everyman, but the anguish of Man."

In the period between 1964 and 1968 Britten wrote the music for three church parables. The first, *Curlew River*, was an adaptation of a Japanese *No* drama which William Plomer made into a medieval miracle play. Sung, played, and acted by a cast of monks, *Curlew River* received its first performance at Aldeburgh on June 13, 1964. "The work is almost hypnotically compelling in its concentration," reported Charles Osborne to the New York *Times*. Britten's second church parable came two years later, also at Aldeburgh, and once again with an all-monk cast. The new work was *The Burning Fiery Furnace*, with a libretto by Plomer. It was presented on June 9, 1966. It retold from the Book of Daniel the story of the three children of Israel and their survival in Nebuchadnezzar's fiery furnace. "This time," said Eric Mason in the London *Daily Mail*, "the action is less severely stylized, more overtly dramatic and, to my mind, more plausible. The music is richer in texture and even more daringly inventive." The third parable, *The Prodigal Son*, introduced in 1968, follows the pattern of the other two.

Between the premières of his first two parables, Britten wrote on commission *Voices of Today* to help celebrate the twentieth anniversary of the United Nations. It was performed on United Nations Day (October 24, 1965), in the General Assembly Building of the United Nations in New York. For the text of the first half of this choral work, Britten went to the New Testament, Sophocles, Blake, Holderlin, Camus, and others for apt quotations on the subject of peace. The second half was a setting of Virgil's Fourth Eclogue, sung in Latin.

Britten

In 1963 the music critics of England selected Britten as "the composer of the year." This is one of numerous honors which Britten has received from all over the world, beginning with the Elizabeth Sprague Coolidge award for distinguished service to chamber music which he received in 1941. He was granted the Companionship of Honor by Queen Elizabeth (for writing *Gloriana*), the Freedom of the Borough of Lowestoft in 1953, and honorary doctorates in music from the University of Belfast in 1954 and Cambridge in 1959. In 1964 he was given the first Aspen (Colorado) Award, a prize of thirty thousand dollars honoring "the individual anywhere in the world judged to have made the greatest contribution to the advancement of the humanities." (Britten used part of his prize money to set up an annual prize at Aspen for British musical compositions.) In 1965 Britten received the Order of Merit, Britain's most coveted award. An honor of a different nature came to him on August 18, 1968, when the Edinburgh Festival was opened with an all-Britten program.

Britten and the tenor Peter Pears toured the United States in joint recitals in 1949, making their American debut on October 23. Since that time they have often appeared in joint recitals both in the United States and Europe. Britten has also been heard extensively throughout Europe as a conductor.

Since 1942 Britten has made his home at Aldeburgh, in East Anglia, Suffolk, twenty miles or so along the coast from the town where he was born. When he was made an Honorary Freeman of the Borough of Lowestoft, he said: "I am firmly rooted in this glorious country." On a later occasion he amplified this theme by saying: "As I get older, I find that working becomes more and more difficult away from home. I plot and plan my music when I am away on tour, and I get great stimulus and excitement from visiting other countries. . . . But I belong at home—there, in Aldeburgh. . . . All the music I write comes from it. I believe in roots, in associations, in backgrounds, in personal relationships. . . . I do not write for posterity. . . . I write music now, in Aldeburgh, for people living there, and further afield, indeed for anyone who cares to play it or listen to it. But my music now has its roots in where I live and work."

He lives in Red House, described by Charles Reid in the New York *Times Magazine*, as a "quasi-manorial pile in rose-colored brick . . . the last word in middle-class taste and comfort. Outside are a sun terrace muscled with vine and a swimming pool where, in warm weather, Britten takes as many as three quick plunges a day, even when deadlines are pressing." Besides swimming, his favorite forms of exercise and relaxation are walking for miles by the North Sea, driving his Alvis car at top speed along the English countryside, and occasionally playing tennis and badminton.

He is unmarried. His daily life is systematically organized and inflexible. Every morning at eight he begins work in a studio over the garage which, except for the grand piano, is furnished with monastic simplicity. He works until it is time for lunch, which often consists of fish as a main course. In the afternoon he takes long walks or drives, during which he works out creative problems. In the late afternoon he returns home for tea and devotes himself to a few more hours of work.

Erich Walter White has singled out several of Britten's personal traits: "His sense of humor (or should one say his sense of proportion?); his brisk, fancy and ambivalent imagination; his fondness for children. He remembers with pleasure his own youth in East Anglia—fêtes and obstacle races, bicycle rides, tennis tournaments, bathing parties, making friends and making music—and projects himself without difficulty into the minds and hearts of young people today."

Britten believes implicitly that "a certain rot, if that isn't too strong a word, set in with Beethoven." He goes on to explain: "Before Beethoven, music served things greater than itself. For example: the glory of God, the greatest of all. Or the glory of the State. Or the composer's social environment. It had a defined social function. After Beethoven, the composer became the center of his own universe. Hence the Romantic school. . . . That tendency is not for me. . . . I try to write as Stravinsky has written, and Picasso has painted. They were the men who freed music and painting from the tyranny of the purely personal. They passed from manner to manner as a bee passes from flower to flower. I try to do the same. Why should I lock myself inside a narrow personal idiom?"

102

MAJOR WORKS

Ballet—The Prince of Pagodas.

Chamber Music—2 string quartets; Phantasy Quartet, for oboe, viola, and cello; Suite, for violin and piano; Lacrymae (Reflections on a song of Dowland), for viola and piano; Six Metamorphoses after Ovid, for solo oboe; Cello Sonata; Suite, for solo cello; Gemini Variations, for piano duet, flute and violin.

Choral Music—A Boy Was Born; Ballad of Heroes; Hymn to St. Cecilia; A Ceremony of Carols; Rejoice in the Lamb, festival cantata; Saint Nicolas, cantata; Spring Symphony; Cantata Academica (Carmen Basiliense); Missa Brevis; Cantata Misericordium; A War Requiem; Voices of Today.

Operas—Peter Grimes; The Rape of Lucretia; Albert Herring; Let's Make an Opera (children's opera); Billy Budd; The Turn of the Screw; Noye's Fludde (miracle play); A Midsummer Night's Dream; Curlew River (religious parable); Crossing the River (religious opera); The Burning Fiery Furnace (religious parable); The Prodigal Son (religious parable); The Golden Vanity.

Orchestral Music—Sinfonietta; Soirées Musicales (adapted from Rossini); Our Hunting Fathers, symphonic cycle for soprano and orchestra; Variations on a Theme by Frank Bridge; Mont Juic; Piano Concerto; Violin Concerto; Canadian Carnival; Les Illuminations, for high voice and string orchestra; Sinfonia da Requiem; Diversions, for piano left hand and orchestra; Matinées Musicales (adapted from Rossini); Prelude and Fugue; Scottish Ballad, for two pianos and orchestra; The Young Person's Guide to the Orchestra; Nocturne, for tenor solo, seven obbligato instruments and orchestra; Symphony for Cello and Orchestra.

Organ Music—Prelude and Fugue on a Theme by Vittoria.

Piano Music—Holiday Diary; Two Pieces, for two pianos.

Vocal Music—On This Island; The Holy Sonnets of John Donne; Canticles, I, II and III; A Charm of Lullabies; Songs from the Chinese; Six Hölderlin Fragments; Songs and Proverbs of Blake; The Poet's Echo, for high voice and piano.

ABOUT

Cohn, A., Twentieth Century Music in Western Europe; Holst, I., Benjamin Britten; Lindler, H. (ed.), Benjamin Britten: Mit Mensch und Musiker; Mitchell, D. and Keller, H. (eds.), Benjamin Britten; White, E. W., Benjamin Britten (rev. ed.).

Musical Opinion (London), July 1949; Musical Times (London), March 1948; New York Times Magazine, October 26, 1962, November 17, 1963; Saturday Review, July 29, 1967; Time, February 16, 1948.

Willy Burkhard
1900–1955

Willy Burkhard was born in Évilard-sur-Bienne, Switzerland, on April 17, 1900. From

Burkhard: bŏŏrk′ härt

1916 to 1920 he attended the Swiss Seminary at Berne. He also studied music at the Conservatory, mainly with Ernst Graf. When Burkhard decided upon music as his profession, he embarked upon a period of intensive training: with Teichmüller and Karg-Elert in Leipzig, Courvoisier in Munich, and Max d'Ollone in Paris. While these studies were going on, Burkhard wrote some songs and choral works with a strong Romantic bent.

WILLY BURKHARD

At twenty-four he returned to Switzerland to launch his professional career by teaching composition, theory, and piano to private pupils in Berne. In his compositions he began to free himself from his former Romantic tendencies. Finding his stimulus in Hindemith and Bartók he adopted a discordant linear style in which he completed his first violin concerto in 1925, his first symphony in 1928, and his first string quartet in 1929.

In 1928 he was appointed to the faculty of Berne Conservatory. He held this post until 1933 when tuberculosis compelled him to seek an extended cure in a sanatorium in Davos. During this period of illness and convalescence he worked industriously on composition, crystallizing a style in which the harmonic language, based on church modes, and a subtle rhythmic pulse were combined with his former linear tendency. An unidentified critic for *Musical America* described this music: "His art reflects in high degree the internal tension Swiss musicians so frequently feel. He feels a compulsion to achieve both moral and intellectual ends in every work. Burkhard is attracted with equal strength by abstract forms and by great lyric and religious themes. . . . In every field of composition he reveals a richness of thought and a compositional assurance that entitle him to be considered a genuine master."

The first work in this mature style was the oratorio *Das Gesicht Jesajas* (*Isaiah's Vision*) written in the period between 1933 and 1935 when the composer was in the sanatorium. It received its world première in Basel in 1936 and is now regarded by many critics as his masterpiece.

The composer has explained how he came to pick the subject of Isaiah and his vision as the material for an oratorio: "The main ideas of Isaiah—the downfall of the unhealthy and the untrue; the hope for the improvement of present chaotic conditions; the signs of a new world order; peace, deliverance, liberation—those religious forces that, in spite of disappointment and reverses, had given a mighty impetus to the intellectual life of all times— these main ideas, do they not form a cross-section of our times and our intellectual life? And these words that were spoken a thousand years ago appeared to me as expressions of the immediate present."

The American première of *Isaiah's Vision* took place in New York on April 3, 1955, in a performance in which the conductor, Paul Sacher, was making his American debut. The composer, then on his only visit to the United States, was in the audience. In his review for the New York *Times*, Olin Downes described the work as follows: "The oratorio is cast in seven parts which alternate 'expressions of imprecation and praise' and 'despair and hope.' . . . The solos are most often in the character of free song. Cantillation is used joyously, sometimes in the manner of a medieval religiousness and occasionally with the cantillation of the East, and the suggestion of Jewish ritual. The orchestra is sometimes austere, like the vocal writing, and at other times it is used massively, explosively."

In 1942 when Burkhard had recovered sufficiently to resume his chores as a teacher, he joined the faculty of the Zürich Conservatory and there he remained for the rest of his life. In 1942 he completed the oratorio *Das Jahr* (*The Year*), inspired by nature and descriptive of the four seasons. When it was first heard in the United States, in New York on February 14, 1964, Howard Klein described the composition in the New York *Times* as a work "of epic breadth" whose "predominant mood was sepulchral owing to its thick textures, massive rhythms and monotonous scoring. . . . Mr. Burkhard's use of church modes and long lines precluded levity."

In 1943 came Burkhard's second violin concerto which Peter Mieg called "a perfect example of Burkhard's style combining free improvisation and thematic rigor." Another important instrumental composition appeared eight years later, a Toccata, for four wind instruments, percussion, and string orchestra, written to celebrate the tenth anniversary of the Collegium Musicum in Zürich. The Collegium, under Paul Sacher's direction, introduced it on December 6, 1951. The style is reminiscent of Bach's toccata methods, though the harmonic writing maintains a twentieth century identity. Slow and fast sections are effectively alternated. A short canonical figure leads to a stirring march-like finale.

Burkhard wrote only one opera: *Die Schwarze Spinne* (*The Black Spider*), with a text by R. Faesi and G. Boner based on a story by Jeremias Gotthelf. The first version of this opera was completed in 1948 and was produced in Zürich in 1949. At that time a critic for *Musical America* wrote that it "created a sensation as much by its audacious scenic conception as by its dramatic intensity. Burkhard's style, often abstract and hard, is humanized in this . . . work, which shows the plenitude of his creative faculties." In 1954 the composer revised the opera.

One of Burkhard's most distinguished compositions in any medium came in 1951, a Mass, for soprano, basso, chorus, and small orchestra. In the *Saturday Review*, Oliver Daniel described it as "intensely moving," adding: "I find it such a poignantly moving work that analytical considerations of the means he employed are irrelevant."

Willy Burkhard died in Zürich on June 18, 1955, from complications following an operation for appendicitis. He was survived by his widow, Marie-Louise, and their two children, a son, Simon, and a daughter, Ursula.

MAJOR WORKS

Chamber Music—2 string quartets; Violin Sonatina; Piano Trio; Suite for Two Violins; Sonata for Solo Viola; Etude Concertante, for cello and piano; Serenade, for flute and guitar; Suite en Miniature, for violin and piano; Canzona, for two flutes (or flute and oboe), and piano (or organ); Cello Sonata.

Choral Music—Till Ulenspiegel, cantata; Vorfrühling, cantata; Te Deum; Spruchkantate; Das Gesicht Jesajas, oratorio; Psalm XCIII; Genug Ist Genug, cantata; Lob der Musik, cantata; Cantate Domino; Heimatliche Kantate; Kreuzvolk der Schweiz; Das Jahr, oratorio; Christi Leidensverkündigung, cantata; Cantique de Notre Terre; Mass; Psalmen-Kantata; various motets, for unaccompanied voices.

Opera—Die Schwarze Spinne.

Orchestral Music—2 symphonies; 2 violin concertos; Fantasy for Strings; Kleine Serenade, for strings; Concerto for Strings; Toccata, for strings; Hymnus; Concertino for cello and strings; Concerto for Organ, Strings and Brass; Konzertstück, for organ and orchestra; Canzona, for two flutes and low strings; Kleine Konzertante Suite; Piccola Sinfonia Giocosa, for small orchestra; Fantasia Mattutina; Toccata, for four wind instruments, percussion, and string orchestra; Sonata da Camera, for strings and percussion.

Organ Music—2 trio sonatas; Variations on Chorale Settings by Hassler; Fantasie; Sonatina; Choral-Triptychon.

Piano Music—Three Preludes and Fugues; Variations on a Minuet by Haydn; Kleine Stücke; Sonatina; Sonata; Weihnachtssonatine.

Vocal Music—Two Rilke cycles, for basso and chamber orchestra, and for soprano and chamber orchestra; Ten Songs; Die Versuchung Jesu, for low voice and organ; Das Ewige Brausen, for basso and orchestra; Magnificat, for soprano and strings; Nine Songs; Psalmenmusik, for soprano and orchestra.

ABOUT

Forty Swiss Composers; Mohr, E., Willy Burkhard: Leben und Werk; Schuh, W., Schweizer Musiker der Gegenwart.

Ferruccio Busoni
1866–1924

Ferruccio Busoni was born in Empoli, near Florence, on April 1, 1866. His father, of Tuscan peasant background, was a clarinetist; his mother, of half-German extraction, was an excellent pianist. When he was four, Ferruccio revealed his talent for music by playing on the piano melodies he had heard his mother perform, and soon after that she became his first teacher. At eight he made his public debut with a recital in Trieste. About a year later he gave a concert in Vienna that was

Busoni: bo͞o zō′ nē

praised by the eminent critic Eduard Hanslick. Busoni included several of his own piano pieces on this program. Then in his twelfth year he directed the world première of his *Stabat Mater*, in Graz.

FERRUCCIO BUSONI

He continued to make appearances as a prodigy, gathering accolades from distinguished musicians, Liszt and Anton Rubinstein included. However, he never took piano lessons with a teacher of recognized standing and experience. He is probably the only world-famous piano virtuoso who can be said to have been self-taught; who developed his technique and his interpretative powers through the years by a long, detailed, and continuous process of self-analysis, and trial and error. (He did, however, study composition in Graz with Wilhelm Meyer-Remy in 1877.) In his fifteenth year he toured Italy as a pianist and composer with such success that he became the youngest musician since Mozart to become a member of the Philharmonic Academy of Bologna. There, in 1883 he conducted a performance of his oratorio *Il Sabato del Villaggio*. In Florence a gold medal was struck in his honor. His travels took him in 1886 to Leipzig where he settled temporarily and came into contact with some of the musicians residing in the city at this time, including Grieg, Tchaikovsky, Mahler, and Delius. In Leipzig, Busoni wrote his first string quartet and made the first of his many celebrated transcriptions for the piano of the music of Johann Sebastian Bach (the D major organ fugue).

In 1889 Busoni was appointed professor at the Helsinki Conservatory where, for a brief period, young Sibelius was his pupil. During this time he married Gerda Sjöstrand, daughter of a well-known Swedish sculptor. (Both sons of the Busonis became celebrated artists.) Later in 1889 he visited St. Petersburg where his *Konzertstück*, for piano and orchestra, received the Rubinstein Prize. In 1890 Busoni was appointed professor of the piano at the Moscow Conservatory. From 1891 to 1894 he lived in the United States, serving on the faculty of the New England Conservatory.

He was so critical of his piano technique and style that he decided to retire temporarily and devote himself to intensive study. He settled in Berlin where he made a fresh start at the piano by restudying everything he had thus far learned and reanalyzing every piece of music he had ever played. From this period of study and analysis he emerged a formidable artist. "Those who never heard him play," said Edward J. Dent, "can have no conception of the prophetic inspiration and grandeur of his performances. His technical achievements in mere speed and strength must have far surpassed anything accomplished by Liszt and Rubinstein." Busoni now made concert tours that took him around the world, performing to universal acclaim. "When he sat down at the piano," recalled Jean Chantavoine in his *Memoirs*, "when he placed his aristocratic hands on the keys, the listeners immediately were aware of his genius: it was like transfiguration."

Though he had started out in his compositions as a child of the German post-Romantic movement (with a particularly strong debt to Liszt, whom he admired excessively), Busoni soon felt impelled to bring to his writing the same kind of penetrating intellectualism he had brought to his piano playing. "Music," he said, "must become so complex and intricate as to kill automatically all dilettantism." But though he was often later to produce works of considerable complexity, he first found his creative stride in a neoclassical style, a movement in which he was the pioneer. Led by his passion for Bach, he became obsessed for a long time with the passion to write music with the clarity, lucidity, and architectonic perfection of the classical masters. "What he sought to achieve," says Edward J. Dent, "was a neoclassicism in which form and expression may find their perfect balance." As early as 1888 he had begun to stray into these neoclassical pastures by completing a symphonic suite whose movements included such baroque dance forms as the gavotte and the gigue. He progressed deeper into neoclassicism with such success that Ernest Krenek is convinced that the whole concept of neoclassicism originated with Busoni (years before the movement became famous with Stravinsky).

As a neoclassicist, Busoni wrote for the orchestra as if it were made up of separate groups of solo players; thus he revived the concertante methods of Handel, Vivaldi, and Bach in their *concerti grossi*. Busoni became partial to small and unusual combinations of instruments, as opposed to the massive forces employed by the German post-Romantics. He reverted to eighteenth century structures, not only to the old dance forms but also to such structures as the toccata, divertimento, and fugue. Like the old Baroque masters, Busoni enjoyed tackling contrapuntal exercises within ambitious designs. He made it a practice to replace passion, ardor, and expansiveness with sobriety, economy, precision, and a strict adherence to classical structure.

One great achievement in the neoclassic idiom was a giant work for piano, *Fantasia Contrappuntistica*—the meeting ground for the polyphonic techniques of Bach and Busoni's intellectualism. He completed the first version in 1910, a second and a third version in 1912, and an adaptation for two pianos a decade after that. This was Busoni's own *Art of the Fugue*, a demonstration not only of his skill in contrapuntal writing but also a testimony that even in the twentieth century polyphony had not exhausted its creative potential. The work opens with a prelude based on the Bach chorale "Glory to the Lord in Heaven." The next four parts consist of four three-part fugues derived from the incomplete final fugue of Bach's *Art of the Fugue* (Contrapunctus No. 19); the last of these used the four notes of Bach's name (in German notation) as its subject. Between the third and fourth fugues he inserted an Intermezzo, three variations, and a cadenza, all of them variations on material from the four fugues.

Neoclassicism, however, represented only one phase of his endeavors as a composer. Another creative facet was his search for new techniques, idioms, and methods—with a daring and an iconoclasm that places him in the forefront of twentieth century modernists. He rebelled against traditional scales exclaiming: "We are tyrannized by major and minor." Experimenting with many different scales he came up with one hundred and thirteen possible ways of arranging whole and half notes within a seven-note series. He evolved a new harmonic system based on these new scales. He experimented with quarter tones and third tones. He devised a new method of notation.

In 1901 and 1902, Busoni gave master classes in piano at Weimar, where he aspired to carry on the traditions of Liszt. A number of years later he combined his world activity as pianist with conducting orchestral concerts in Berlin, having become a passionate protagonist of the new and the unusual in symphonic literature. In 1908 he succeeded Emil Sauer as professor of the piano at the Vienna Conservatory. In 1913 he was appointed director of the Liceo Musicale in Bologna. During the same year he became the third Italian composer to receive the French Legion of Honor (the others were Rossini and Verdi).

The outbreak of World War I interrupted his musical activities. Disgusted and horrified, he fled to America where he once again made an extensive concert tour. Upon returning to Europe, he settled in Zürich. As a protest against the war he refused to make music in any of the warring nations; his musical activities, consequently, became circumscribed. In Zürich, however, he had opportunities to conduct orchestral concerts and play the piano, and he continued to compose. Despite the grimness of the period and Busoni's bitterness and despair, his major achievements at this time included two comic operas. He wrote them in an effort to win back the favor of his Italian compatriots who had accused him of being more German than Italian in his interests, background, and musical orientations. The fact that his native Italy was then at war with Germany was further motivation for writing these comic operas—a creative attempt at least briefly to realign himself with the land of his birth by means of two works in the *opera buffa* style of Rossini and Donizetti.

One was *Arlecchino*, set in eighteenth century Bergamo. The plot spun light-heartedly on the pivot of the love triangle involving Harlequin, Columbine, and Columbine's husband, Matteo. Though Busoni's harmony still reveals solid German foundations, his writing nevertheless is gay and infectious, richly spiced with the condiments of satire and parody. While still working on the opera, Busoni adapted one of its uncompleted sketches into an orchestral piece that gained wide circulation—*Rondo Arlecchinesco*, which Frederick Stock (to whom it is dedicated) introduced in Chicago with the Chicago Orchestra on April 5, 1929.

Arlecchino received its world première in Zürich on May 11, 1917, on a bill that also included Busoni's second comic opera, *Turandot*. The subject of *Turandot* is the same one which Puccini later treated seriously in his last opera—and with such powerful impact and success that Busoni's opera was thrown into permanent shade. In comparing Busoni's *Turandot* with *Arlecchino*, Gerhart von Westerman finds that the former is "the more effective work . . . from the purely musical point of view." He adds: "The merry, grotesque episodes take second place to the lyrical and dramatic events. Though both elements are enchanting in atmosphere, each mood is only lightly touched on, without any real development of the drama or any great attempt to create an oriental setting."

After the War, Busoni returned to Berlin and to his lofty position in German music as a concert pianist, composer, and teacher. The German government appointed him professor of composition at the Academy of Arts. When the collapse of the German mark impoverished Busoni, he tried to rehabilitate his depleted fortunes by going to Paris and establishing himself there as a pianist and teacher. There, in the fall of 1923, his friend Isidor Philipp (professor of piano at the Paris Conservatory) noticed he looked physically frail and spent. On Philipp's urging, Busoni consulted a physician, who diagnosed Busoni's condition as a chronic inflammation of the kidneys and of the muscles of the heart. He warned Busoni to give up drinking and smoking, to both of which Busoni had long been addicted to excess.

Ferruccio Busoni returned to Berlin. He

died there on July 27, 1924, without completing the opera on which he had been laboring for a number of years and which he regarded as his masterwork: *Doctor Faust*. A work of immense scope, *Doctor Faust* was based not on Goethe but on the Faust legend and partly on Christopher Marlowe's *Dr. Faustus*. The theme served to underline Busoni's disenchantment with the world around him, for Busoni identified himself completely with his hero. The opera as a whole is an intellectual rather than emotional tour de force, divorced from sentimentality and reality, and scrupulously avoiding love interest and theatrical effects. To Edward J. Dent, *Doctor Faust* was Busoni's supreme creative achievement, "a work in which he sums up the experiences of a lifetime; it is a drama on a spiritual plane far removed from the normal operatic level."

The opera (completed by Philip Jarnach from Busoni's sketches) was first produced in Dresden on May 21, 1925. It was not successful, and was not heard again for over a decade and a half. Its first important revival took place at the May Music Festival at Florence in 1942. Then, early in 1955, it was revived by the Berlin State Opera, and H. H. Stuckenschmidt concluded his review by saying: "Berlin has had a masterwork restored to it." *Doctor Faust* received its American première in New York on December 1, 1964.

H. W. Heinsheimer gives the following picture of Busoni during the 1920's: "Busoni . . . lived according to a rigid schedule. Clad in silk and velvet, the master would compose during the early morning hours in an inner sanctum that nobody was allowed to enter. (He lived in a huge duplex apartment located in one of the most fashionable sections of Berlin.) At lunch time he would emerge to greet admiring guests, and consume half a bottle of champagne with his food. After the coffee, his guests, aware of the ceremonial of the house, took their departure, and then the pupils began to arrive."

Busoni believed that the function of the creative artist consisted in "making laws, not in following laws ready-made. He who follows such laws ceases to be a creator. Creative power may be the more readily recognized the more it shakes itself loose from tradition. But an intentional avoidance of the rules cannot masquerade as creative power and still less

engenders it. The true creator strives, in reality, after perfection only. And through bringing this in harmony with his own individuality, a new law arises without premeditation."

Busoni was the author of an important theoretical treatise which was translated into English in 1911 under the title *A New Aesthetic of Music*. He also edited many piano masterworks, including Bach's *The Well-Tempered Clavier* and compositions by Liszt.

In the 1940's, an international award was named after Busoni. It was presented by the Santa Cecilia Academy in Rome in alternate years to the one who had made the most notable contributions to modern music. The first recipient, in 1950, was Stravinsky.

MAJOR WORKS

Chamber Music — 2 string quartets; 2 violin sonatas; Albumblatt, for flute and piano; Elegy, for flute and piano.

Choral Music — Primavera, Estate, Autunno, Inverno, for male chorus and orchestra; Il Sabato del Villaggio.

Operas — Die Brautwahl; Arlecchino; Turandot; Doctor Faust (completed by Philip Jarnach).

Orchestral Music — 2 suites; Violin Concerto; Lustspielouvertüre (Comedy Overture); Piano Concerto, with female voices; Berceuse Élégiaque; Nocturne Symphonique; Indian Fantasy, for piano and orchestra; Rondo Arlecchinesco; Concertino for Clarinet and Small Orchestra; Sarabande and Cortège (two studies for Doctor Faust); Divertimento, for flute and orchestra; Tanzwalzer; Romanza e Scherzoso, for piano and orchestra; Zigeunerlied, for baritone and orchestra.

Piano Music — 6 sonatinas; Piano Pieces, two series; Prelude and Fugue; Twenty-four Preludes; Minuetto Capriccioso; Gavotte; Elegien; An die Jugend; Fantasia Contrappuntistica (three versions, and a fourth for two pianos); Toccata.

Vocal Music — Album Vocale; Lied der Klage; Des Sängers Fluch, ballad for contralto and piano; Die Bekehrte; Schlechter Trost; various other songs for voice and piano.

ABOUT

Debussman, E., Ferruccio Busoni; Dent, E. J., Ferruccio Busoni: A Biography; Gray, C., A Survey of Contemporary Music; Nadel, S., Ferruccio Busoni; Pannain, G., Modern Composers; Santelli, A., Busoni; Selden-Goth, G., F. Busoni; Stuckenschmidt, H. H., Busoni; Wasserman, J., In Memoriam Ferruccio Busoni.

Musical Quarterly, January 1917, July 1921, July 1934; Rassegna Musicale (special Busoni issue), January 1940; Score (London), December 1952.

Charles Wakefield Cadman
1881–1946

Charles Wakefield Cadman was born in Johnstown, Pennsylvania, on December 24, 1881 of a musical family. His great grandfather, Samuel Wakefield, a hymnologist, built the first pipe organ west of the Alleghenies. His mother was a singer, a member of the church choir.

When he was thirteen, his family acquired a piano and Cadman took his first music lessons, supplementing his study of the piano with instruction in harmony from Leo Oehmler. Three years later he had a job playing the organ in a church in suburban Pittsburgh.

CHARLES WAKEFIELD CADMAN

When he was sixteen his first piece of music, *The Carnegie Library March*, was published. A two-step in the style of Sousa, it was played by the local band during parades. As soon as it was published, young Cadman presented copies to Andrew Carnegie and Charles M. Schwab, the steel tycoons. Since Cadman's father was a steel-mill employee, the newspapers publicized the story. By selling his sheet music all over town, Cadman made enough money to pay for two years of music study with Emil Paur (conductor of the Pittsburgh Symphony) and Luigi von Kunits.

In or about 1902, Cadman met Nellie Richmond Eberhart, a lyric writer who had moved with her family from Nebraska to Pennsylvania. She interested Cadman in songwriting.

Within a year or so, the collaborators sold about a dozen songs to New York, Chicago, and Philadelphia publishers. Then, in 1907, they conceived the idea of using American Indian themes as a basis for songs, beginning with *Four American Indian Songs*. This cycle of four numbers included "From the Land of the Sky-Blue Water" and "The Moon Drops Low." The latter won a prize in a contest sponsored by the Carnegie Art Institute in Pittsburgh in 1909. In the same year, Lillian Nordica, the prima donna, sang "From the Land of the Sky-Blue Water," and it immediately became such a hit that many important concert singers of that time incorporated the song in their repertory. Another of Cadman's songs written about this time was "At Dawning." For four years it reposed on the shelves of the publishers, the Ditson Company. Then John McCormack featured it on one of his concert tours; before that season was over the song became a best-seller. Both "From the Land of the Sky-Blue Water" and "At Dawning" have each sold about two million copies of sheet music.

In 1909 Cadman spent a summer among the Omaha Indians. He became acquainted with numerous ceremonial songs and flageolet love calls. This experience further intensified his fascination with the music of the American Indian. In subsequent compositions (and in structures larger than the song) he began to make extensive use of American Indian themes, rhythms, and styles. The most ambitious was his opera *Shanewis*, produced at the Metropolitan Opera on March 23, 1918. Sometimes singled out as one of the first truly indigenous American operas, it was also the first American opera to survive more than one season at the Metropolitan. In reviewing it for the New York *Sun*, W. J. Henderson wrote: "Mr. Cadman has handled his material with no mean amount of skill. He has shown a greater command of his technique of opera than any of his predecessors among American composers introduced at the Metropolitan. . . . Good declamation, continuous flow without irrelevant instrumental interruptions, and clear, varied and very discreet orchestration are some of the most valuable traits of the score. The orchestration though simple is not bald. It is full of color, but transparent. The thematic ideas . . . are fluent and melodious,

... the writing for the voices is generally good."

Among Cadman's most distinguished instrumental compositions using American Indian materials is *Thunderbird*, an excellent suite for the piano which he later orchestrated. As an orchestral composition it was introduced in Los Angeles on January 9, 1917. Another work inspired by the Indian was *To a Vanishing Race*, for quintet. So impressed was the critic Henry T. Finck by Cadman's Indian music that he wrote: "Cadman is the most prominent composer who has come forward since the death of Edward MacDowell."

Cadman was not only one of the first composers to utilize successfully in serious composition Indian themes and rhythms, he was also one of the first American musicians to present authentic American Indian music in lecture recitals. In the years between 1909 and 1923 he traveled widely, assisted by the Indian singer Tsianina Redfeather.

Cadman did not devote himself exclusively to American Indian music, though it was the area in which he realized his greatest successes. Also in an American idiom, though not Indian, was an orchestral fantasy, *Dark Dancers of the Mardi Gras*. This was first heard in Milwaukee on March 7, 1934. The composer explained that this work got its name from the Negro side of the Mardi Gras: "The Negroes of New Orleans have a Mardi Gras of their own. The fantasy is supposed to reflect the fantastic, the grotesque, the bizarre spirit of the carnival."

Cadman's second important opera was *A Witch of Salem*, introduced at the Chicago Opera during Mary Garden's regime, on December 8, 1926. It proved so successful that it was kept in the repertory for two full seasons. In 1932 Cadman wrote a delightful short opera for radio, *The Willow Tree*, broadcast over a radio network on October 3.

Cadman's later instrumental works included an excellent Piano Quintet in G minor (1937); the tone poem *Pennsylvania* (Los Angeles, March 7, 1940); *Aurora Borealis*, a major work for piano and orchestra introduced by the composer himself in December 1944, with the Indianapolis Symphony conducted by Fabien Sevitzky; and a lively "American Overture," *Huckleberry Finn Goes Fishing* (1945).

It was Cadman's belief that it was not necessary for a composer to use indigenous material in order to achieve an American identity in his compositions. However, Cadman did acknowledge that the introduction and exploitation of Negro, Indian, cowboy, or Kentucky mountain tunes within a composition contributed greatly to its flavor and local color.

From 1908 to 1910 Cadman was the music critic for the Pittsburgh *Dispatch*. He later moved to southern California. For many years, up to the time of his death, he resided in Los Angeles where he was highly active in its musical life. He served on the Mayor's Civic Music Committee and was one of the founders of the Hollywood Bowl Concerts. In 1923 he received an honorary doctorate from the University of Southern California. He was also a member of the National Institute of Arts and Letters.

He never married. His greatest interest besides composing was to encourage and help develop young musicians and to sponsor their careers. His hobbies were motion picture photography and fishing.

Charles Wakefield Cadman died in Los Angeles of a heart attack, December 30, 1946.

MAJOR WORKS

Chamber Music—Piano Trio in D major; Violin Sonata in G; To a Vanishing Race, quintet; Piano Quintet in G minor; A Mad Empress Remembers, for cello and piano.

Choral Music—Father of the Waters; House of Joy; Indian Love Charms, for children's chorus; The Vision of Sir Launfal.

Operas—Shanewis; The Sunset Trail (operatic cantata); The Garden of Mystery; A Witch of Salem; The Willow Tree (radio opera); Ramala.

Orchestral Music—Thunderbird Suite (also for piano); Oriental Rhapsody; Hollywood Suite; Dance of the Sweet Sister Mary; Dark Dancers of the Mardi Gras; Suite on American Folk Tunes; Symphony; Aurora Borealis, for piano and orchestra; Huckleberry Finn Goes Fishing; Pennsylvania.

Piano Music—Sonata.

Vocal Music—White Enchantment, song cycle; numerous songs for voice and piano including At Dawning, The Moon Drops Low, and From the Land of the Sky-Blue Water.

ABOUT

Hipsher, E. E., American Opera and Its Composers; Howard, J. T., Our Contemporary Composers.

John Cage
1912–

John Milton Cage, Jr., was born in Los Angeles, California, on September 5, 1912. He was the only child of a father who was an inventor, and a mother who was an editor of the Los Angeles *Times*. "My first experience with music," he told an interviewer in 1961, "was through neighborhood piano teachers, and particularly my Aunt Phoebe. She said of the work of Bach and Beethoven that it couldn't possibly interest me, she herself being devoted to the music of the nineteenth century. She introduced me to Moszkowski and what you might call the piano music the whole world loves to play. In that volume, it seemed to me that the works of Grieg were more interesting than the others."

JOHN CAGE

After being graduated from Los Angeles High School in 1928, Cage attended Pomona College in Claremont, California, for two years. He distinguished himself there by winning an oratory contest in southern California. He continued formal piano study with Fannie Charles Dillon, and after leaving Pomona College, traveled in Europe where he had an opportunity to take piano lessons with Lazare Lévy in Paris.

Attracted more and more to the creative phase of music, Cage studied composition intensively with Henry Cowell, Edgard Varèse, Arnold Schoenberg, and Adolph Weiss, all of whom aroused and stimulated Cage's own interest in experiment and innovation. From Schoenberg and Weiss, Cage acquired an interest in nonthematic, nonharmonic procedures of the twelve-tone technique. He became particularly interested in the methods of Anton Webern in reducing themes to fragments and punctuating sound with silences. His early compositions reveal the impact of this influence. *Six Short Inventions*, for seven instruments (1933), *Sonata for Two Voices* (1933), and *Composition for Three Voices* (1934) are three of several works which deal with the problem of "keeping repetitions of individual tones of the superimposed twenty-five tone ranges as far apart as possible," according to the composer, "even though each voice is obliged to express all twenty-five tones before introducing a repetition of any one of them." *Metamorphosis*, for piano (1938), is a five-movement suite in a strict twelve-tone row. The row fragments are never subjected to variation, and the transposition of the fragments was selected according to the intervals of the series.

Stronger even than the effect of the twelve-tone school on Cage was the impression made upon him by Edgard Varèse's experiments in "organized sound" and rhythmic patterns, and of Henry Cowell's early innovations with tone clusters and drawing unusual sounds from the piano by manipulating the strings on the soundboard. More and more, Cage began to gravitate towards percussion music in which melody, harmony, and counterpoint were dispensed with; the form of which consisted exclusively of rhythm and rhythmic units; music in which silences provided dramatic contrasts to sound. All this he regards as a natural evolution from his work with atonality and the twelve-tone idiom. "The theory of percussion is very much akin to atonal music," he said. "No sound any more important than any other comes out of atonal music into organized sound."

In 1936 Cage became a member of the music faculty at the Cornish School in Seattle, Washington. There he began his earliest experiments with percussion music by featuring concerts of percussion instruments. The creative aftermath of these performing experiments was the writing of *First Construction (in Metal)*, in 1939, for a percussion sextet. A *Second*

Construction followed in 1940 in which the instruments were predominantly metal and skin, "with string piano (manually muted and productive of a siren-like sound by means of a cylinder sliding on the strings while a trill is produced on the keyboard)." The *Third Construction* (1941) used rattles, drums, tin cans, claves, cowbells, a lion's roar, cymbal, ratchet, texponaxtle, quijadas, cricket caller, and conch shell. *Imaginary Landscape No. 3* (1942) required not only percussion instruments, tin cans, and a muted gong, but also audio-frequency oscillators, variable speed turntables for the playing of frequency recordings and generator whines, a buzzer, an amplified coil wire, and a marimubla amplified by means of a contact microphone.

Cage's fascination with percussive sound also led him to create the "prepared piano" by stuffing all kinds of material between the strings ranging from nuts and bolts to objects of all types and varieties. By this means he was able to arrive at an altogether new piano sound made up of pings, plunks, thuds, and gong-like resonances. *Bacchanale* (1938) was the first such piece, music intended for a dance performed by Syllvia Fort. Cage wrote extensively for the prepared piano in the 1940's. Among the most significant of these compositions were the *Sonatas and Interludes*, written in the years 1946–1948. These were "an attempt to express in music the 'permanent emotions' of Indian tradition: the heroic, the erotic, the wondrous, the mirthful, sorrow, fear, anger, the odious, and their common tendency toward tranquillity." Here the preparation of the piano is so complex and elaborate that it requires from two to three hours. In discussing Cage's literature for the prepared piano, Virgil Thomson said in the *Herald Tribune:* "His work represents not only the most advanced methods now in use anywhere but original musical expression of the highest poetic quality." Largely as a result of his work with prepared pianos, Cage received in 1949 a Guggenheim Fellowship for creative work in music, and an award from the National Academy of Arts and Letters for having extended "the boundaries of music."

In the early 1950's, Cage became increasingly interested in the potential of noisemakers as a source of new sounds. Anything that was audible became a creative tool. *Imaginary*

Landscape No. 4 (1951) was scored for twelve radios, to be operated by twenty-four players, two players to each radio. *Water Music* (1952) required the performing pianist to use a radio, whistle, water containers, and a deck of cards. Water was poured from a full container to an empty one, with a stop watch regulating the time for the process. A deck of cards was riffled. Static was induced from the radio. "This use of everyday music," Cage has said, "makes me aware of the world around me. Now I go to a cocktail party. I don't hear noise. I hear music."

Williams Mix (1952) is "concrete music" for magnetic tape. Approximately six hundred recordings are necessary to make a version of this composition. City sounds are caught, also sounds produced by the wind, sounds requiring amplification, electronic sounds of all types, and manually produced sounds.

In all three works—and in many others since—the element of chance (aleatory music) enters through a compositional process Cage devised from a process known as I-Ching (the Chinese Book of Changes). With the aid of Chinese dice, Cage developed a prearranged system for all the materials and means of a musical composition. By throwing the dice he gets the materials and means to be used for a given work.

One of Cage's most complex creations in the "chance" method is his Concert for Piano and Orchestra (1957-1958) introduced in New York City on May 15, 1958, with David Tudor as soloist and Merce Cunningham conducting. Tudor, with Cage conducting, introduced the work in Germany over the Cologne radio on September 19, 1958. Cage has explained that "each performance can be different because each individual independently makes his own time program from the material supplied him. Harmonious fusion of sound is not here an objective and, for auditory and visual clarity, the players are separated in space as much as is convenient." The solo pianist not only manipulates the keyboard in the traditional way, but also plunks and plucks the strings on the sound-board, goes under the piano to thump the underside of the instrument, and when not occupied at the piano, produces sounds from electronic instruments. The pianist's part, the composer adds, is a book comprising eighty-four different kinds of compositions, "some, varieties of the same species, some, disparate. The pianist is free to play any of his choice, wholly or in part, superimposed or in sequence. A given performance may be of any length."

In *Variations I* (1958) and *Variations II* (1961), the performers are free to select their own sounds and to improvise them at whatever points in the composition they desire. These are some of the following effects that were used in the performance of the compositions: amplification of the sounds of letter writing, the dropping of cigarette ashes into ashtrays, the untangling of a pile of wires on the floor, the scraping of wires and microphones up and down the strings of the piano soundboard, the putting on and taking off of eyeglasses. A pianist and his partners had microphones attached to their throats to catch the sounds of swallowing, cigarette smoking, coughing, grunting, whining, and so forth. A climax was reached with maximum amplification as microphones were scraped over sheets of glass.

In *Reunion* (1968) Cage evolved a new method for "chance music" combined with electronics. In this work the performers play on an electrified chessboard and the movements of the game determine the sounds of the composition as they pass through the electronic filter. *Reunion* was introduced in New York on May 27, 1968.

Cage has also been a leading figure in the neodada movement of the 1960's. On July 23, 1965, *Variations V* was introduced at the Lincoln Center for the Performing Arts during a festival of French-American music by the New York Philharmonic. This composition required dancers, electronic equipment, and a screen on which distorted images from television and film clips were flashed. At one point the principal dancer, wearing red pants and a gray shirt, rode a bicycle through a mass of electronic transmitters; as he rode, movements of his bicycle impelled the electronic equipment to emit a cacophony of noises which in turn were transmitted throughout the auditorium by loudspeakers.

Theatre Piece, introduced in New York on September 11, 1965, during an avant-garde festival, required a man to hang upside down while wrapped up in a black plastic cocoon. Richard D. Freed in the New York *Times* described some of the other unusual happenings: "a watermelon sliced in the sling that held the upside-down man; a film of Charlotte Moorman playing one of Mr. Cage's other works on the cello as the composer placed a cigar in her mouth and removed it now and then; a tiny Japanese, waving silken banners on a huge bamboo pole; an oil drum rolled down the stairs outside the auditorium; and the usual assortment of balloons, buzzers and electronic sound effects."

The negation of the creative process as that process has been understood through the centuries is, then, a powerful factor in Cage's compositions. What is surely the last word in such a negation—and the ultimate in Cage's experiments with silences as opposed to sound—can be found in a piano piece entitled *Four Minutes Thirty-three Seconds* (1952). This work is in three "silent movements." Throughout, the performer sits at the keyboard without playing.

Cage has held a number of teaching positions since the 1930's. He has been a member of the faculties of Mills College in California, the School of Design in Chicago, the Black Mountain College in North Carolina, the New School for Social Research in New York, and the Center for Advanced Studies at Wesleyan University in Middletown, Connecticut. He has also served as the music director of the Merce Cunningham Dance Company.

On May 15, 1958, at Town Hall, New York, a concert of Cage's music was presented, covering a quarter of a century of his creative experiments. In 1960 this concert was released in a long-playing record album. In 1963 Cage represented the United States at the Zagreb Music Biennale in Yugoslavia where he lectured on his aims and methods and directed a concert of his music. He was "unquestionably the most talked-about figure at the Biennale," reported Gunther Schuller. In 1966 and 1967 he was composer-in-residence at the University of Cincinnati. In 1968 he was elected a member of the National Institute of Arts and Letters.

Cage married Xenia Andreyevna Kashevaroff in 1935; they were divorced a decade later. Cage is an amateur mycologist (founder of the Mycological Society) and finds relaxation from his musical endeavors in periodic field trips in search of various species of mushrooms. He was the author of two volumes of essays and lectures entitled *Silence* (1961) and

A Year from Monday (1968), and with Kathleen O'Donnell wrote *The Life and Works of Virgil Thomson* (1958).

MAJOR WORKS

Audio Visual Music—Water Music; Music Walk; Water Walk; Sounds of Venice; Theatre Piece; Variations V; Reunion.

Chamber Music—Six Short Inventions; Sonata for Two Voices; Clarinet Sonata; Composition for Three Voices; Three Pieces for Flute Duet; Music for Wind Instruments; Six Melodies for Violin and Keyboard; Sixteen Dances; Music for Carillon, I–V; For a String Player; For a Percussionist; Variations I–IV.

Concrete Music—Williams Mix; Fonata Mix; Music for a Marrying Maid; 0'00"; Rozart Mix.

Orchestral Music (also music utilizing sound effects and/or electronic means): Imaginary Landscape, I–V; Construction in Metal, I–III; Credo in US; Amores; She Is Asleep; The Seasons, ballet in one act; Concerto for Prepared Piano and Chamber Orchestra; Speech; Concert for Piano and Orchestra; Cartridge Music; Atlas Eclipticalis.

Piano Music—Metamorphosis; Ophelia; Experiences I; Music of Changes, four volumes; Music for Piano, 1–84; Seven Haiku; Winter Music.

Prepared Piano Music—Bacchanale; Amores; The Perilous Night; A Book of Music; Daughters of the Lonesome Isle; Mysterious Adventure; Three Dances; Sonatas and Interludes; Two Pastorales; Concerto for Prepared Piano.

Vocal Music—Five Songs for Contralto; Forever and Sunsmell; The Wonderful Widow of Eighteen Springs; She Is Asleep; Experiences II; A Flower; Aria; Solo for Voice, I and II.

ABOUT

Chase, G., America's Music; Thomson, V., The Art of Judging Music; Yates, P., Twentieth Century Music.
American Record Guide, August 1960; High Fidelity, April 1960; Musical America, January 1955, June 1958; New York Times Magazine, January 15, 1967; Saturday Review, January 30, 1960; April 30, 1966.

John Alden Carpenter
1876–1951

John Alden Carpenter, a lineal descendant of the John Aldens of Colonial fame, was born in Park Ridge, Illinois, on February 28, 1876. His father was the head of a prosperous shipping-supply firm; his mother was an accomplished singer who had studied in Paris with Mme. Marchesi. She was John's first music teacher. He received more formal instruction in Chicago from Amy Fay (Theodore Thomas's sister-in-law) and W. C. E. Seeboeck, and later from John Knowles Paine at Har-

vard, from which Carpenter was graduated with highest honors and a Bachelor of Arts degree in 1897. After leaving Harvard, he went through several more periods of music study, notably with Edward Elgar for a few months in Rome during the winter of 1906 and, from 1908 to 1912, with Bernhard Ziehn in Chicago. Carpenter always considered this association with Ziehn as the most valuable training he received.

JOHN ALDEN CARPENTER

Upon receiving his degree from Harvard, he went to work in his father's business establishment, of which he ultimately became vice president, continuing in that capacity until his retirement in 1936.

Though his first publication appeared as early as 1904 (a song, "When Little Boys Sing"), it was not until 1912 that he first began to attract attention as a composer. This initial recognition came about through a performance of his Violin Sonata by Mischa Elman. Additional interest in his work was inspired by a song cycle, *Gitanjali*, poems by Tagore (1913), which Felix Borowski wrote "had beauty undisfigured by cheap tunefulness" and whose harmonic subtlety "struck a new note in native composition."

His first major success came with a delightful descriptive suite for orchestra, *Adventures in a Perambulator*, introduced by the Chicago Orchestra under Frederick Stock on March 19, 1915. Though this was Carpenter's first attempt at writing for orchestra, it has remained one of his most frequently played compositions. In six movements, it gives a baby's impressions of the city streets as he is wheeled around in his perambulator by his nurse. The vivid tone pictures are spiced with an engaging sense of humor and with amusing interpolations of quotations from such popular tunes as "Alexander's Ragtime Band," "Ach, Du Lieber Augustin," and "Where, Oh Where, Has My Little Dog Gone?"

With the production of Carpenter's first ballet, *The Birthday of the Infanta*, his fame was further enhanced. Derived by Adolf Bolm from Oscar Wilde's story of the same name, the ballet was introduced in Chicago on December 23, 1919. A symphonic suite, adapted by the composer from the ballet score in 1930, has been frequently played by major orchestras.

Although Carpenter had favored a Romantic style developed along traditional lines, in 1921 he became interested in jazz as a significant tool with which to build an American musical art. He first used jazz in a ballet pantomime, *Krazy Kat*, based on George Herriman's popular cartoon series of that period, which Adolf Bolm produced in New York in 1922. Prior to this performance, on December 23, 1921, the Chicago Orchestra under Stock had introduced an orchestral suite derived from this score.

Carpenter's most celebrated work in the jazz idiom is the ballet *Skyscrapers*. In 1924 Sergei Diaghilev, the artistic director of the Ballet Russe de Monte Carlo, asked Carpenter to write music for a ballet based on American life. Carpenter completed his music late in 1924, but the American tour of the Ballet Russe (for which Carpenter's ballet had been planned) did not materialize. *Skyscrapers*, therefore, received its première performance at the Metropolitan Opera in New York on February 19, 1926. The choreographic and scenic designs were worked out by the composer himself, with the help of Robert Edmond Jones and Sammy Lee.

Skyscrapers was the first successful ballet in a jazz style. But as Oscar Thompson pointed out in his review in *Musical America*, Carpenter's music "more often . . . is of a semi-jazz, than of a real jazz, character; sometimes, as in the episode of the singing Negroes, it is even remote from the spirit of jazz. . . . The work was written for a symphonic orchestra, not a jazz band. Saxophones have parts, but rather minor ones. This is not literal jazz, but jazz as it has filtered through the mind of a musician who thinks in terms of art, and whose purpose was to write an art work, not merely to add to America's storehouse of popular music."

Both in its original version as a ballet and as an orchestral suite featured by America's most important symphonic organizations, *Skyscrapers* helped place Carpenter in the front rank of American composers in the 1920's. He continued to hold that place in the 1930's and 1940's with several major works for orchestra: *Sea-Drift*, a sensitive tone poem inspired by Whitman, introduced by the Chicago Orchestra under Stock on November 30; the violin concerto, which Zlatko Balakovic performed with the Chicago Orchestra on November 18, 1937; the Second Symphony, conducted by Bruno Walter at a concert of the New York Philharmonic in New York, on October 22, 1942; and the symphonic suite *The Seven Ages* (inspired by Jacques' lines in Shakespeare's *As You Like It*), the première of which took place on November 29, 1945, in New York.

W. J. Henderson once pointed out that Carpenter's finest compositions possess a "whimsical fancy, a delicate, even poetic humor, and tender sentiments." Henderson further remarked that Carpenter's melodic invention was "facile and his themes have fluency and grace." But, after 1930 Carpenter's style grew increasingly impressionistic, as he sought to translate into tones deeply poetic impressions and subtle atmospheres. *Sea-Drift* and the Second Symphony reveal this impressionist tendency most strongly.

In 1921 Carpenter was made a member of the Legion of Honor in France. He received honorary degrees from Harvard in 1922, and the University of Wisconsin in 1933. In 1943 he was appointed to the American Academy of Arts and Letters, and on February 13, 1947, he was awarded a gold medal by the National Institute of Arts and Letters "for distinguished services in music" (the first time in nine years that such an honor had been conferred in music).

Carpenter was married twice. The first time was on November 20, 1900, to Rue Winterbotham. She died in 1931, and on January 31,

1933, Carpenter married Ellen Waller Borden, who survived him. He died at his home on Lake Shore Drive in Chicago, April 26, 1951.

MAJOR WORKS

Ballets—The Birthday of the Infanta; Krazy Kat; Skyscrapers.

Chamber Music—Violin Sonata; String Quartet; Piano Quintet.

Choral Music—Song of Faith, cantata.

Orchestral Music—2 symphonies; Adventures in a Perambulator, suite; A Pilgrim's Vision; Piano Concertino; Patterns, for piano and orchestra; Sea-Drift, tone poem; Violin Concerto; Dance Suite; The Anxious Bugler; Seven Ages, suite; Carmel Concerto.

Vocal Music—Improving Songs for Anxious Children; Gitanjali, song cycle; Water Colors, four Chinese songs.

ABOUT

Howard, J. T., Our Contemporary Composers; Seldes, G., Seven Lively Arts.

Musical Quarterly, October 1930.

Elliott Carter
1908–

Elliott Cook Carter, Jr., was born in New York City on December 11, 1908, the son of a lace importer. Elliott revealed a strong bent for music even before he could read or write. Although he did take some piano lessons, his musical interest was not particularly encouraged at home. It was during his last years at the Horace Mann High School that his great love for music was given both encouragement and direction. At that time he was taken to public concerts for the first time by friends whose main interest lay in modern music. Through these friends he came to know Charles Ives, who encouraged him to study music seriously. When he went to Harvard in 1926, Carter had not yet made up his mind to become a professional musician, and so he majored in English literature. He did not abandon music, however. He studied the piano with Newton Swift and solfeggio with Hans Ebell at the Longy School of Music at Cambridge. He attended as many of the concerts of the Boston Symphony as he could, and he sang in the Harvard Glee Club and performed in chamber music ensembles.

It was during his last year as an undergraduate that he decided to become a composer. After receiving his Bachelor of Arts degree in 1930, he continued as a graduate student at the University, taking courses in harmony and counterpoint with Walter Piston. At that time Gustav Holst, the eminent English composer, was a visiting professor at Harvard, and Carter studied composition with him. In 1932, after receiving his Master's degree, he went to Paris at the suggestion of Piston to continue his music study with Nadia Boulanger.

ELLIOTT CARTER

He studied composition privately with Mme. Boulanger from 1932 to 1935. He also took a course in counterpoint at the École Normale de Musique where he received a *Licence de Contrepoint;* sang in a madrigal group led by Henri Expert; and directed a chorus of his own. In 1932, while still in Paris, he composed incidental music for the Harvard Classical Club production of Sophocles' *Philoctetes.* This first performance of his music took place at Cambridge, Massachusetts, in the winter of 1933.

Carter returned to the United States in 1935, settled in Cambridge, and began to hunt for a job—a difficult quest since this was the period of the Depression. While living in Cambridge he wrote incidental music for Plautus' *Mostellaria,* another presentation by the Harvard Classical Club. An excerpt from the score, a Tarantella, was subsequently performed by the Harvard Glee Club during its tour in the fall of 1936 and by the Boston Pops Orchestra under G. Wallace Woodworth in May 1937.

In the summer of 1936 Lincoln Kirstein commissioned him to write a ballet on the subject of Pocahontas. The Ballet Caravan produced the ballet successfully in New York in April 1939. A suite from the score received the Publication of American Music award from the Juilliard Foundation in 1940; more than a quarter of a century after it was written, the suite was recorded by Epic.

In the fall of 1936 Carter went to live in New York, where he was soon writing articles and reviews for *Modern Music*. He also served as the musical director of the Ballet Caravan from 1937 to 1939. In 1938 his choral setting of Robert Herrick's *To Music* won a prize in a contest conducted jointly by the Columbia Broadcasting System, Columbia Records, and the WPA. It was performed in New York by Lehman Engel's Madrigal Singers.

On July 6, 1939, Carter married Helen Frost-Jones, an art critic and sculptor; a son, David Chambers, was born to them in 1943. From 1939 to 1941 Carter was on the faculty of St. John's College in Annapolis, Maryland, where he taught Greek and mathematics and supervised all musical activities. With the collaboration of Scott Buchanan, dean of the college, he devised a new method of teaching music as a branch of mathematics or physics as well as a medium of expression. Carter's article in *Modern Music* (October 1944) provides the details of this innovation in music education.

His duties at St. John's left little time for composition. In 1941 Carter resigned and went to Santa Fe, New Mexico, where he worked on a symphony, completing it in the winter of 1942. This symphony was one of Carter's rare excursions into music with a pronounced American identity. "Underneath the Americana and the folkiness," wrote Eric Salzman in reviewing a recording of the work released in 1961, "there is a kind of elaboration and involvement continually popping up to the surface, an elaboration that goes far beyond the apparently simple pretensions of the music. There is a constant clash between the ideas and technique, between the materials and the way they are set forth. This results in a kind of tension—one might say distention—that is always threatening to explode the work from within." The symphony was introduced by the Eastman-Rochester Symphony under Howard Hanson on April 27, 1944.

After returning East, Carter became music consultant to the Office of War Information in 1943. In this capacity he prepared a large collection of serious-music recordings, European as well as American, for short-wave transmission overseas and to Government posts all over the world. During a vacation at Fire Island, New York, in 1944 he completed the *Holiday Overture*, which was his first orchestral work to gain a certain measure of recognition in Europe, following its presentation by the Baltimore Symphony Orchestra on January 7, 1946. This gay, fast-moving music received a prize of five hundred dollars from the Independent Music Publishers.

In 1945 Carter received a Guggenheim Fellowship, which enabled him to write a piano sonata. Webster Aitken introduced it in New York on February 16, 1947. This work represents a departure from tradition in its use of overtones, produced through pedaling. Virgil Thomson in reviewing the sonata in the *Herald Tribune*, described it as a work "full of power and brilliance. Its relatively quiet moments . . . are not entirely, in feeling, derivative; and as figurations they are quite personal. The brilliant toccata-like passages, of which there are many, are to my ear completely original. I have never heard the sound of them or felt the feeling of them before. They are most impressive indeed."

On March 26, 1947, the Ballet Society of New York presented Carter's second ballet, *The Minotaur*. At the time, he was teaching theory and composition at the Peabody Conservatory in Baltimore. From 1948 to 1950 he was on the music faculty of Columbia University. The acquisition of a second Guggenheim Fellowship in 1950 enabled him to withdraw temporarily from his teaching chores to Tucson, Arizona, where he concentrated entirely on composition. Here he completed his important first string quartet in which he perfected a technique called metrical modulation, by which a continuity is maintained throughout a continual change of tempo, character, and rhythm, with points of rest coming few and far between. This quartet won first prize in the Concours International de

Quatuors à Cordes, in Liège, in which one hundred and fifty composers from twenty countries participated. It was then given its world première in New York in February 1952 in a performance by the Walden Quartet, and in 1954 was performed successfully at the Rome Festival. Alfred J. Frankenstein praised the work as a whole for its "loftiness, grandeur and power"; Paul Henry Lang described it in the New York *Herald Tribune* as "an authentic masterpiece by an American composer . . . one of the handful of truly significant works that open the second half of the twentieth century."

In 1953 Carter received the Prix de Rome, and three years later he was elected a member of the National Institute of Arts and Letters. From 1960 to 1962 he was professor of composition at Yale University, where he wrote his second string quartet (written on a commission from the Stanley String Quartet of the University of Michigan). This composition received the Pulitzer Prize in 1960, as well as the New York Music Critics Circle Award and the first prize from the International Rostrum of Composers sponsored by UNESCO.

The string quartet was performed for the first time in New York by the Juilliard String Quartet on March 25, 1960. In the first line of his review in the New York *Times*, Howard Taubman wrote that this composition established Carter once and for all as "one of the most distinguished of living composers." In a single movement, it further exploits Carter's technique of metrical modulation. But, as Taubman remarked, Carter was not satisfied merely to use a method that had served him so well earlier. "He has set himself new problems, but one of his fundamental concerns has remained the creative use of polyrhythms. The four instruments have been treated with almost rigorous independence, and yet they interact to enrich one another."

This Pulitzer prizewinning quartet was followed by his Double Concerto, for piano, harpsichord, and two chamber ensembles. Commissioned by the Fromm Foundation, the concerto was introduced in New York City on September 6, 1961, and received the New York Music Critics Circle Award. In an interview with Robert Craft, Igor Stravinsky singled it out as the American work which had appealed to him most strongly up to that time. "I like the mood of Carter's concerto," Stravinsky said. "It is full of new-found good spirits. . . . But the success of the piece is due to the listener's immediate satisfaction in its form. . . . I like the shape and sense of proportion in the concerto, the measure of time. . . . But I like the harpsichord and piano writing very much, too." The Double Concerto represented the United States at the festival of the International Society for Contemporary Music in London in 1962.

One of Carter's most significant works is the two-movement Concerto for Piano and Orchestra (1965), commissioned by Jacob Lateiner through the auspices of the Ford Foundation. The Concerto was introduced by Lateiner and the Boston Symphony under Leinsdorf on January 6, 1967. In describing it, the composer said: "Technically the work is based on twelve different three-note groups (triads): six, used exclusively by the piano and concertino, and six by the orchestra. Each triad is associated with one or more tempi and expressive characters. Musical ideas are formed out of constantly changing uses of these fundamental changes."

In 1961 Carter received the Sibelius Medal for Music, in London, and an honorary doctorate from the New England Conservatory in Boston. He served as composer-in-residence at the American Academy in Rome in 1962, and after that he was composer-in-residence in Berlin at the invitation of the Berlin Senate and the Ford Foundation. In 1965 Swarthmore College in Pennsylvania gave him another honorary doctorate in music, and he received the Creative Arts Award from Brandeis University in Massachusetts. For 1967-1968 he served as Andrew D. White Professor-at-Large at Cornell University.

Carter was described by Richard Kostelanetz in *High Fidelity* as "a small and slight man with longish, somewhat unruly gray hair, wide smile and a broad, open, and handsome face. . . . Neither as dominating nor prepossessing as his awesome reputation might suggest, he is at turns lively and reticent, sometimes engaging but usually quite diffident. He speaks animatedly in an indefinite accent, overcoming a slight stutter; yet his sparkling blue eyes tend to turn away, as though he were too shy to look his guest straight in the eye. He frequently moves both hands in symmetrical gestures; yet he often lets the rhythm of conversation disintegrate completely.... More contained than outgoing, he seemingly puts blocks between himself and the world, neither communicating facilely with others nor assimilating easily the information his experience continually throws across his eyes."

Carter spends ten hours a day on composition, relaxing by swimming or walking. His extramusical interests include reading (contemporary poetry and philosophy rather than fiction), travel (he made his first trip to Europe when he was twelve, and since that time has made frequent trips to Europe and the Near East), architecture, and painting. He speaks several languages, some fluently, some haltingly. A victim of insomnia, he spends many of his sleepless hours conjugating irregular Italian verbs.

In a lecture at Princeton University he articulated his ideas on music and the creative process as follows: "Serious music must appeal in different ways. Its main appeal, however, emerges from the quality of the musical material or ideas and perhaps even more from their use in significant continuities, but does not always depend on grasping the logic of the latter on first hearing. There has to be something left for the second time, if there ever is a second time.... The individual effort of the serious composer, as I see it, is not so much in the invention of musical ideas in themselves as in the invention of interesting ideas that will also fill certain compositional requirements and allow for imaginative continuations."

On another occasion he said: "Every piece of mine is a new conception and a new idea—and music must be very living, it must recreate itself in new terms. I usually have a good concept of a piece before I start working, and gradually I get it down, writing large amounts at a time. The character of the music is not thematically developed so much as assembled out of basic materials, such as rhythmic and textual sketches and combinations of intervals in harmonic sounds which stem from a basic idea".

MAJOR WORKS

Ballets—Pocahontas; The Minotaur.

Chamber Music—3 string quartets; Elegy, for viola (or cello) and piano; Quartet for Alto Saxophones; Woodwind Quintet; Cello Sonata; Eight Etudes and a Fantasy, for flute, oboe, clarinet, and bassoon; Two Pieces for Kettledrums; Sonata for Flute, Oboe, Cello, and Harpsichord.

Choral Music—The Harmony of Morning; Musicians Wrestle Everywhere; Emblems.

Orchestral Music—Symphony; Elegy for Strings; Holiday Overture; Variations; Double Concerto for Harpsichord and Piano, with two chamber orchestras; Piano Concerto.

Vocal Music—Various songs for voice and piano including The Dust of Snow, The Line Gang, The Rose Family, Warble for Lilac Time, and Voyage.

ABOUT

Chase, G., America's Music; Cohn, A., Twentieth Century Music in the Western Hemisphere; Mellers, W., Music in a New Found Land.

High Fidelity, May 1968; Musical Quarterly, April 1957; Score (London), June 1955; Time, May 28, 1956.

Alfredo Casella
1883–1947

Alfredo Casella was born in Turin, Italy, on July 25, 1883, to a family of musicians. It is believed that the madrigalist Casella mentioned in Dante's *Divine Comedy* was an ancestor. Alfredo's father was professor of the cello at the Liceo Musicale in Turin; his mother, an accomplished pianist; his uncle, a cello virtuoso.

Alfredo's early contacts with music revealed unusual gifts. He began to study the piano when he was five; only three years later he was able to perform the complete *Well-Tempered Clavier* of Bach. He also studied the cello with his father at the Liceo and made his first attempts at composition. When he was eleven he heard his first opera performance—Wagner's *Götterdämmerung*—which he proceeded at once to memorize from the score.

Music, however, was not his sole interest. He showed such an aptitude for chemistry and electricity that Galileo Ferraris, a friend of the family, insisted that the boy be directed to science. For a while, young Alfredo wavered between science and music, but on the urging of the composer Giuseppe Martucci he finally decided upon music.

In 1896 Casella went to Paris and enrolled in the Conservatory. As a pupil of Diémer, Leroux, and Gabriel Fauré he took prizes in piano playing and harmony. He also came into personal contact with the young Ravel and

Casella: kä sĕl′ lä

the more mature Debussy. Hearing Debussy's *The Afternoon of a Faun* in 1898 was "like a fantastic world perceived for the first time." Despite this admiration for Debussy, Casella took to writing Romantic rather than Impressionistic music. His first two symphonies, written in 1905 and 1909, stem from Mahler and Richard Strauss rather than from the French Impressionists.

Casella's first appearance as a conductor and composer took place in Monte Carlo in 1908 when he led the première of his First Symphony. His first major success came soon after, with the rhapsody *Italia* (1909). It was introduced in Paris on April 23, 1910, in an all-Casella program that also included his Second Symphony and his C major Suite (1910); Casella conducted. In *Italia* the composer skillfully incorporated popular Italian melodies into a romantic texture. As he explained in the published score, his aim was to "picture musically, but without any 'program' whatsoever, Sicilian and Neapolitan life; the first, tragic, superstitious, passionate, as it is found under the scorching sun or in the inferno of the sulphur mines; the second, the turbulent, careless, frenetic existence which may be lived amid the magic of the Gulf of Naples." Among the popular tunes Casella quoted in his rhapsody are "Funiculì, Funiculà," Mario Costa's song "Lariulà," and Tosti's song "Amarechiare." Casella also made use of a song popular with women laborers in the marble quarries; Wolf-Ferrari was to use the same melody in his opera *The Jewels of the Madonna*.

From 1906 to 1909 Casella was the harpsichordist of the Société des Instruments Anciens. In the years 1910–1912 he made a number of guest appearances as pianist and conductor in Western Europe and Russia and he was also the regular conductor of the Concerts Populaires at the Trocadéro in Paris. He was Alfred Cortot's assistant as professor of the piano at the Paris Conservatory from 1912 to 1915, and he wrote music criticism for Clemenceau's newspaper *L'Homme Libre*.

Casella returned to Italy in 1915. There he emerged as one of his country's most dynamic musical forces, whose influence was felt in a number of different directions. He succeeded Sgambati as professor of the piano at the Santa Cecilia Academy in Rome, where for many years he was the teacher of a number of gifted young Italian musicians. He toured extensively as pianist and as conductor distinguishing himself particularly for his performances of contemporary works. He founded the Società Italiana di Musica Moderna, which propagandized new Italian music and young Italian composers. (In 1923 this organization was renamed Corporazione delle Musiche Nuove, becoming the Italian section of the International Society for Contemporary Music.) He devoted himself to musicological research; he issued new editions of piano masterworks by Bach, Mozart, and Beethoven among others; he edited, wrote for, and financed a new musical journal, *Musica d'Oggi;* he wrote critical articles for the Italian papers. He was tireless in devoting his energies to the cause of good music—and, particularly, modern music.

ALFREDO CASELLA

But his many activities did not keep him from composing. In 1913, with *Notte di Maggio* (based on a poem by Carducci), his style evolved from the Romantic to the modern as he showed an increasing interest in unorthodox progressions and tonalities. *Notte di Maggio* was introduced at a Colonne concert in Paris on March 29, 1914. Modern, too, was a tone poem inspired by World War I, the *Pagine di Guerra* (1916), which he had adapted for orchestra from an earlier (1915) work for piano duet. Leon Kochnitzky described this music: "Amidst screeching discords, one could hear shrapnel whistles and blasts, bombs, machine guns and planes. The audience responded as was to be expected by hissing and booing, shouting and howling as only an Italian audience can do." But not all of his music of this period was so advanced in its idiom. He still clung to his earlier Romanticism; for example, the *Pupazzetti*, for orchestra (1918), "five pieces for marionettes" which had a light and graceful touch and a sense of humor.

After World War I, Casella combined modern techniques and idioms with the structures and some of the attitudes of baroque music. He had become a neoclassicist, and in this vein he produced some of his most important compositions. He went to the music of older Italian masters for his melodic material: to Domenico Scarlatti for *Scarlattiana*, for piano and thirty-two instruments, which received its première in New York on January 22, 1927; to Paganini, for *Paganiniana*, a divertimento written to commemorate the centenary of the founding of the Vienna Philharmonic, which introduced it in March 1942. He returned to the old Italian forms in the Partita, for piano and orchestra (first performance in New York on October 29, 1925); in the *Due Ricercari sul Nome di B.A.C.H.* (1932); in the *Sinfonia, Arioso e Toccata* for solo piano (1936); and in various concertos for solo instrument or instruments and orchestra, for string quartet, and for orchestra alone. Indeed, his last orchestral work, the *Concerto for Strings, Piano, Timpani, and Percussion*, was in this neoclassical idiom. Completed in 1943, the Concerto had its world première in Basel, Switzerland, on March 22, 1945. He sought to realize the clarity, precision, objectivity, and purity of the old Italian instrumental masters, but without sacrificing modern devices and modern methods.

His best-known ballet was mainly in a neoclassical style—*La Giara* based on a story by Pirandello and produced for the first time by the Swedish Ballet in Paris on November 19, 1924. The composer explained that he intended in this music "to unite in modern synthesis the old fundamental musical comedy of the Neapolitan school with the elements of Italian folklore, more particularly the Sicilian." In addition to revealing a fine sense for characterization, the score was outstanding for listenable melodies and ingratiating wit.

Alfredo Casella made a triple debut in the United States, as composer, conductor, and pianist, with the Philadelphia Orchestra on October 28, 1921. That season he also made guest appearances with other major American orchestras. He returned to the United States several times—in 1926 to share the conductor's platform of the State Symphony Orchestra in New York with Ernst von Dohnányi; and in the years 1927–1929 to serve as the conductor of the Boston Pops Orchestra. He won two important awards in the United States: a first prize of three thousand dollars from the Musical Fund Society of Philadelphia in 1928 and the Elizabeth Sprague Coolidge Prize in 1934.

Casella's initially tacit, then open, acceptance of the Fascist regime in Italy disappointed many of his colleagues. They could not reconcile Casella's personal integrity, idealism, and cosmopolitan viewpoint with his espousal of dictatorship. His readiness to serve at Fascist festivals and celebrations, they felt, could not easily be condoned. They were particularly disturbed by his readiness to use his own music as a means to propagandize Fascist ideals, as was the case with the one-act mystery *Il Deserto Tentato*, written at the personal request of Mussolini and exalting the Italian conquest of Ethiopia. When it was first performed (at the Florence May Music Festival on May 6, 1937), it was violently denounced by the critics as "pompous" and "grotesque." It proved a fiasco, as bitterly attacked outside Italy for its political orientation as inside Italy for its music. Indeed, one of his personal friends, Leon Kochnitzky, was so upset by this work and by Casella's devotion to Fascism that in writing Casella's obituary a number of years later he could not refrain from remarking that Casella "had more talent as a musician than character as a man."

The last years of Casella's life represented low tide. He was seriously ill, often in pain, having to undergo four difficult operations. Italy's involvement in the war, and the deprivations war brought about for the Italian people, contributed financial problems to Casella's physical ones. Yet in spite of these unhappy circumstances, Casella managed to do a good deal of work. As he wrote to his Parisian friend, Isidor Philipp: "I have written six études for the piano . . . and finished a large edition of the *Well-Tempered Clavier* and the

Castelnuovo-Tedesco

Inventions of Bach; also of the Chopin Études, all of whose works I am to edit. In addition, I have just finished an enormous undertaking: a large Missa Solemnis pro Pace, for soprano, baritone, and orchestra, which I feel to be my best work up to now. You see that I have not been idle despite the adverse circumstances."

Alfredo Casella died in Rome on March 5, 1947. Remembering Casella as he had been before he embraced Fascism, Leon Kochnitzky could describe him with deep affection: "He was magnificent, with his hooked nose, his protruding forehead, and his deep fiery eyes. . . . The man . . . was charming, witty, speaking five or six different languages, including Russian, and extremely warm towards fellow artists." Part of his great charm sprang from his occasional indulgence in whimsy. One day, in his paper *Musica d'Oggi*, he inserted the following advertisement: "For Sale: Well Shaped Symphony in E-flat major, with Scherzo, written in the post-Romantic style by well trained young composer. It consists of a beautiful first part, Allegro assai (twelve minutes) with fully developed theme, bridge passage, and second theme. The second part is an Andante con Variazioni; the Scherzo is pleasant and comfortable. The Finale ends with a solid and thoroughly built fugato. Make offers to Alf. Cas., Box 724, Rome."

In searching for the most salient characteristic of Casella's music, Georges Jean-Aubry came upon the quality of "sensibility." "One must be guarded against the word; those to whom it conveys merely a synonym for sentimentality, will not have grasped its meaning. But those to whom it means the faculty to create a perfect accord between sense and spirit which gives equal pleasure, or at least equal interest to both, will discover the real personality of Casella."

MAJOR WORKS

Ballets—La Giara; La Camera dei Disegni; La Rosa del Sogno.

Chamber Music—2 cello sonatas; Five Pieces for String Quartet; Concerto for String Quartet (also for string orchestra); Serenata, for clarinet, bassoon, trumpet, violin, and cello; Sinfonia, for piano, cello, trumpet, and clarinet.

Operas—La Donna Serpente; La Favola di Orfeo (one act).

Orchestral Music—3 symphonies; Suite in C; Italia, rhapsody; Notte di Maggio, for voice and orchestra; Elegia Eroica; Pupazzetti, pieces for marionettes; Partita, for piano and orchestra; Scarlattiana, for piano and thirty-two instruments; Concerto Romano, for cello and orchestra; Concerto in A minor, for violin and orchestra; Introduzione, Aria e Toccata; Concerto for Trio and Orchestra; Concerto for Orchestra; Paganiniana; Tre Canti Sacri, for baritone and orchestra; Missa Solemnis pro Pace, for soprano, baritone, and orchestra; Concerto for Strings, Piano, Timpani, and Percussion.

Piano Music—Nine Pieces; Sonatina; A Notte Alta (also for piano and orchestra); Deux Contrastes; Due Canzoni Italiane; Due Ricercari sul Nome di B.A.C.H.; Sinfonia, Arioso e Toccata; Sei Studi.

Vocal Music—L'Adieu à la Vie, song cycle.

ABOUT

Bacharach, A. L. (ed.), The Music Masters: v4, The Twentieth Century; Casella, A., Music in My Time: The Memoirs of Alfredo Casella; Cortese, L., Alfredo Casella; D'Amico, F. and Gatti, G. M. (eds.), Alfredo Casella.

Musical Quarterly, July 1947; Rassegna Musicale (special Casella issue), May-June, 1943.

Mario Castelnuovo-Tedesco
1895–1968

Mario Castelnuovo-Tedesco was born on April 3, 1895, in Florence, in the Tuscan hills where his family had lived for four hundred years. "I believe," the composer said, "that I inherited my musical talent from my mother's side, especially from my maternal grandfather, who had encouraged me a great deal in my studies. I knew him to be musical, but not a musician, and it was several years after his death that we found in the recesses of his library, hidden by books, a little notebook in which he had noted by hand music for several Hebrew prayers. The discovery of this little notebook proved one of the deepest emotions of my life, and has become for me a precious heritage." One of Castelnuovo-Tedesco's late compositions was based on his grandfather's themes—*Prayers My Grandfather Wrote*, a set of six preludes for organ.

At the Cherubini Royal Institute of Music, Castelnuovo-Tedesco studied composition with Ildebrando Pizzetti and piano with Del Valle. Pizzetti's influence on the younger man was profound, and was obvious in a piano piece, *Cielo di Settembre*, written at the age of fifteen. Further evidence of Castelnuovo-Tedesco's talent came in 1913 with another piano work,

Castelnuovo-Tedesco: kä stĕl nwō′ vō tā dā′ skō

Questo Fu il Carro della Morte. For many years, Castelnuovo-Tedesco devoted himself only to the shorter forms of music, writing numerous songs and pieces for the piano.

In 1920 he turned to larger forms. The first such important work was *Fioretti*, for voice and orchestra, a setting of verses by Francis of Assisi. Five years later his opera *La Mandragola* (libretto by the composer based on a comedy by Machiavelli) won the Italian Prize. Introduced in Venice on May 4, 1924, it helped establish Castelnuovo-Tedesco's reputation.

MARIO CASTELNUOVO-TEDESCO

One of Castelnuovo-Tedesco's major works was first performed in the United States on April 9, 1930, when Arturo Toscanini led the New York Philharmonic in the world première of the *Symphonic Variations*, for violin and orchestra. In the ensuing decade many significant works by Castelnuovo-Tedesco were presented in America. In New York in 1931 Jascha Heifetz played the *Concerto Italiano* (which had been introduced in Rome on January 31, 1926). Heifetz also performed the world première of Castelnuovo-Tedesco's second violin concerto, *The Prophets*—at a concert of the New York Philharmonic, Toscanini conducting, on April 12, 1933. On January 31, 1935, Gregor Piatigorsky performed the world première of the Cello Concerto, once again with the New York Philharmonic under Toscanini.

Several major influences left a permanent impress on Castelnuovo-Tedesco's music. The composer's passion for Shakespeare is demonstrated by the numerous works inspired by Shakespearean plays: eleven overtures, thirty-three songs, twenty-seven sonnets, numerous duets, and later two operas adapted from Shakespeare's original texts, *The Merchant of Venice* (1956) and *All's Well That Ends Well* (1956–1958). *The Merchant of Venice* won first prize in an international contest sponsored by La Scala and financed by David Campari in which sixty-four operas were entered; the world première took place at the Florence May Music Festival on May 25, 1961, with the American première following in Los Angeles on April 13, 1966.

Another important influence was old Hebrew music, as is evidenced by several of his major works: the *Sacred Service for the Sabbath Eve* (1943); the violin concerto, *The Prophets*, which in three movements characterizes the Biblical prophets Isaiah, Jeremiah, and Elijah; a series of Biblical oratorios including *The Book of Ruth* (1949), *The Book of Jonah* (1951), *The Song of Songs* (1955), and *The Book of Esther* (1962); and the Biblical opera *Saul* (1958–1960).

A third influence was the hills of Tuscany among which the composer was born and reared. As Guido M. Gatti wrote: "The general physiognomy of Castelnuovo-Tedesco's work bears a striking resemblance to the region about his native Florence, rich in soft, undulating lines, all delicately traced by the whole gamut of colors, grays and greens of every value."

When Italy set out on its own anti-Semitic program to prove to the world its solidarity with Nazi Germany, Castelnuovo-Tedesco left his native land and came to the United States. On November 2, 1939, he appeared as soloist with the New York Philharmonic, John Barbirolli conducting, in the first performance of his Second Concerto for Piano and Orchestra.

After settling briefly in Larchmont, New York, Castelnuovo-Tedesco went to California to establish his home permanently in Beverly Hills. He did a great deal of composing for films, frequently under a pseudonym; one of the scores which he acknowledged was that for the René Clair film, *And Then There Were None*. During the last two decades of his life he gradually detached himself from motion pictures to devote himself to teaching. Most of the gifted composers for the Hollywood screen studied with him, and it is no secret in Hollywood that several scores credited to a number of the screen's brilliant young composers are actually the work of their teacher. "I will," he noted wryly, "probably pass on into history as a teacher of jazz composers, although I don't know anything about jazz myself!"

Castelnuovo-Tedesco described himself to the editor of this work as a "quiet, middle-aged gentleman, with white hair, living peacefully in a small bungalow with a tiny garden." He wrote further: "I don't love Los Angeles as I used to love my beautiful city of Florence; but I love the sunshine and the blue sky of California, just as I used to love those of Italy. Sometimes, when I am in my little garden, I feel much like Candide. When at the end of his adventurous career, he cultivates his own garden to earn his living, Pangloss asks him: 'Isn't this the best of all worlds?' 'Yes,' answers Candide, 'but everybody has to cultivate his little garden.'

"I believe I have cultivated my little garden all my life, and honestly. I still enjoy writing music, and I still love (as I did in my youth) great poetry, beautiful books, good paintings; these and the hills, the sea, the flowers, my little family, and a few sincere friends. I have a quiet conscience, and many good memories, and I still believe in God.

"I have several times been back to Italy, and I even own again a small apartment in Florence, overlooking the Arno and the Ponte Vecchio, where I like to spend some months every other year. But America is now my home, where my sons have been educated and my grandchildren are now growing up. And I feel sometimes a little like a cloud suspended between the two continents."

Walter Arlen described Castelnuovo-Tedesco thus: "His slightly bent figure, his gaze from behind thick-lensed spectacles, make him look like a medieval scholar, surrounded as he is by innumerable manuscripts, ancestral miniatures and memorabilia." For several decades Castelnuovo-Tedesco made his home on South Clark Drive, a quiet, tree-lined street in Beverly Hills. His study, where all his composing was done, was dominated by the grand piano upon which rested, said Arlen, "photographs... from another era and another

land.... A large painting by his architect son, Lorenzo, and a draft for a telegram in Gabriele D'Annunzio's boldly oversized handwriting, framed over a desk piled high with correspondence, are the room's only eye-catching accents."

Castelnuovo-Tedesco composed easily and quickly, always in ink, and never at the piano. As Arlen wrote: "Neither musical nor personal struggles—and he has had his share of both—seem to ruffle him. His pervasive, astute intelligence and his penetrating sense of humor are his sharpest, indeed his only, weapons. They have helped him face all situations. Hence his serene, almost constant, smile, and his kindly, almost fatherly bearing toward everyone save the stupid."

Mario Castelnuovo-Tedesco died at Mount Sinai Hospital in Hollywood, California, on March 15, 1968. A day before his death he was apparently in good health and attended to his teaching assignments. But soon after dinner that day he complained of indigestion. His son, a physician, diagnosed the illness as a heart attack and rushed him off to the hospital. He sank into a coma and died the next morning.

MAJOR WORKS

Ballets—The Birthday of the Infanta; The Octoroon Ball.

Chamber Music—3 string quartets; 2 piano quintets; 2 piano trios; Cello Sonata; Sonata Quasi una Fantasia, for violin and piano; The Lark, poem in form of a rondo for violin and piano; Concertino, for harp and seven instruments; Divertimento, for two flutes; Sonata for Violin and Viola; Clarinet Sonata; Bassoon Sonata; Guitar Quintet; Sonata for Viola and Cello; String Trio; Sonata for Violin and Cello; Chorale with Variations, for four horns; Two Sonatas for Trumpet and Piano; Sonatina for Flute and Harp; Sonata for Cello and Harp.

Choral Music—Lecho Dodi; Sacred Service for the Sabbath Eve; Naomi and Ruth, cantata; The Book of Ruth, oratorio; Songs and Processionals for a Jewish Wedding; The Book of Jonah, oratorio; Romancero Gitano, for guitar and chorus; Christina Rossetti Settings; Shelley Songs; Keats Settings; Proverbs of Solomon; The Queen of Sheba, cantata; Lament of David; Song of the Oceanides; Two Motets; The Song of Songs, oratorio; The Fiery Furnace, cantata; Amours de Ronsard; The Book of Esther, oratorio; Tobias and the Angel, scenic oratorio.

Guitar Music—Variations à Travers les Siècles; Sonata; Capriccio Diabolico; Suite; Rondo; Fantasia, for guitar and piano; Escarraman, six pieces after Cervantes; Passacaglia; Platero y Yo, twenty-eight pieces for narrator and guitar; 24 Caprichos de Goya, for two guitars; Sonatina Canonica; Les Guitares Bien Tempérées, twenty-four preludes and fugues.

Operas—La Mandragola; Bacco in Toscana; Aucassin and Nicolette; All's Well That Ends Well; The

Merchant of Venice; Saul; The Importance of Being Earnest.

Orchestral Music—11 concert overtures: Taming of the Shrew, The Merchant of Venice, Twelfth Night, Julius Caesar, A Winter's Tale, A Midsummer Night's Dream, King John, Antony and Cleopatra, Coriolanus, Much Ado About Nothing, As You Like It; 3 violin concertos; 2 piano concertos; 2 guitar concertos; Symphonic Variations, for violin and orchestra; Cello Concerto; Princess and the Pea, for narrator and orchestra; Poem, for violin and orchestra; Serenade, for guitar and chamber orchestra; Indian Songs and Dances; Humoresques on Foster's Themes; An American Rhapsody; Noah's Ark; Concerto da Camera, for oboe and chamber orchestra; Four Dances for Love's Labour Lost; Concerto for Two Guitars and Orchestra.

Piano Music—Cipressi; Alt Wien; Piedigrotta; Le Danze del Re David; Chorals on Hebrew Melodies; Sonata; Preludi Alpestri; Candide; Suite nello Stile Italiano; Evangelion; Six Canons; Six Pieces in the Form of Canons.

Vocal Music—Coplas; Stelle Cadenti; Fioretti di Santo Francesco; 33 Shakespeare Songs; Sonneti di Dante; Heine Lieder; Romances Viejos; Fragments de Marcel Proust; Leaves of Grass; 27 Shakespeare Sonnets; Il Bestiario; Poesia Svedere; Die Vogelweide; numerous individual songs for voice and piano.

ABOUT

Ewen, D. (ed.), The New Book of Modern Composers.

George Chadwick
1854–1931

George Whitefield Chadwick was born in Lowell, Massachusetts, on November 13, 1854. His father was a one-time farmer and machinist who had gone into the insurance business. When George was four, his family moved to Lawrence, Massachusetts, where his musical education began. His older brother taught him piano and harmony; the director of the Lawrence Church gave him singing lessons. Later on, in Boston, Chadwick received organ instruction from Eugene Thayer. In 1872 Chadwick entered the New England Conservatory; there his teachers included Dudley Buck and George E. Whiting. Financial difficulties, however, made it impossible for Chadwick to complete his course of study there. In 1873 he had to take a job as a clerk in the insurance firm where his father was employed. But three years later Chadwick gave up the world of business to become head of the music department of Olivet College in Michigan.

In 1877 Chadwick traveled to Germany where he enrolled in the Leipzig Conservatory,

a pupil of Reinecke and Jadassohn. For his graduation piece he wrote a charming concert overture, *Rip Van Winkle*, introduced on June 20, 1879, by the Conservatory orchestra. After a stay in Munich, where he studied the organ with Rheinberger, Chadwick returned to the United States. He became the organist of the South Congregational Church in Boston and a member of the faculty of the New England Conservatory. He also made his American bow as a composer by directing a performance of his *Rip Van Winkle* with the Handel and Haydn Society in Boston.

GEORGE CHADWICK

In 1885 Chadwick married Ida May Brooks; they had two sons. Chadwick continued teaching harmony and composition at the New England Conservatory until 1897, when he became director, a post he retained until the end of his life. As a teacher he exerted a powerful influence upon many young musicians, including Horatio Parker. He was also active as a conductor; for several seasons he was the music director of the Worcester Music Festival.

His career as composer took a significant step forward in 1886 with the completion of two important orchestral works. One, his third symphony, in F major, whose première was given by the Boston Symphony on October 20, 1894, received a prize from the National Conservatory in New York (directed at that time by Antonín Dvořák). In the first movement the composer makes reference to the first three letters in his own name by building his first theme from the notes "C-H-A" (H, in German musical notation, being B-natural).

Chadwick's second orchestral work in 1886 was the dramatic overture *Melpomene* which the Boston Symphony introduced on December 24, 1887. It has since then become one of the composer's most frequently heard compositions. Chadwick explained: "It was originally intended as a companion piece for my earlier overture, *Thalia*, the full title of which was *Overture to an Imaginary Comedy. Melpomene*, however, somewhat outgrew its original scope, so that it can hardly be called *Overture to an Imaginary Tragedy*, but rather a piece which typifies an atmosphere of tragic poetry in general." The overture opens with a dignified introduction. Strong chords herald the arrival of the elegiac first theme in the strings. The second subject, also in a tragic cast, is presented by the oboe, English horn, and cellos. The work becomes passionate and dramatic but ends with a brooding coda in which material from the introductory section is recalled.

Another of Chadwick's orchestral works still represented on programs today is the *Symphonic Sketches* made up of four picturesque tone poems. The first two sections are particularly popular: *Jubilee* and *Noël*, written in 1895. In 1896 the composer added *A Vagrom Ballad*, which ultimately became the final part; and in 1904 he wrote *Hobgoblin* which became the third part. The work as a whole received its first performance on February 7, 1908, at a concert of the Boston Symphony. *Jubilee*, a picture of a carnival, is made up of two robust themes. The music gains in vitality until a stirring climax is reached. *Noël* has been described as "a little Christmas song," its Yuletide melody being played by the English horn. "Heard today," says Gilbert Chase of these two orchestral pictures, "they have a vitality, a genuineness, a human and emotional quality that takes them out of the category of museum pieces."

Of Chadwick's later works the following are the most notable: *Suite Symphonique* (1911), which received the first prize from the National Federation of Music Clubs; *Aphrodite*, a symphonic fantasy introduced at the Norfolk Festival in 1912; and *Tam o' Shanter*, a symphonic ballad heard first at the Norfolk Festival in 1915.

While he was still alive, Chadwick was regarded as one of America's most important composers. Since his death, however, he has come to be remembered only for a handful of orchestral pieces, in spite of his prolific output. He was a child of the German post-Romantic movement, whose harmonic and orchestral language is derived partly from Wagner but whose descriptive and programmatic writing springs from Richard Strauss. Henry Hadley once wrote: "He had a fine taste and a sure judgment and always chose the richest, the most expressive colors from his musical palette.... In all his works, he constantly achieved startling effects, through peculiarly skillful instrumentation and his profound knowledge of the possibilities of the orchestra."

Chadwick died in Boston on April 4, 1931. His friends described him as a warm-hearted, good-natured, gregarious person, keenly alive to the world around him. He was a voracious reader of history, and a lover of painting and sculpture. He enjoyed the country; some of his happiest times were spent during his summer vacations at Martha's Vineyard.

Chadwick received honorary degrees from Yale and from Tufts College. In 1928 he received a gold medal from the Academy of Arts and Letters.

MAJOR WORKS

Chamber Music—5 string quartets; Piano Quintet.

Choral Music—Dedication Ode; Lovely Rosabelle; The Pilgrims; Phoenix Expirans; The Lily Nymph; Lochinvar; Noël; Aghadoe; The Beatitudes; various choruses for men's, women's, and mixed voices.

Operas—Tabasco; Judith; The Padrone; Love's Sacrifice (operetta).

Orchestral Music—3 symphonies; various concert overtures including Rip van Winkle, Thalia, The Miller's Daughter, Melpomene, Adonais, and Euterpe; Serenade in F, for string orchestra; Sinfonietta, in D; Cleopatra, tone poem; Symphonic Sketches; Angel of Death, tone poem; Suite Symphonique; Tam o' Shanter, ballad.

Vocal Music—Various songs for voice and piano including If I Were You, The Morning Glory, and Time Enough.

ABOUT

Chase, G., America's Music; Howard, J. T., Our American Music.

American Academy of Arts and Letters Bulletin, March 1932; Musical Quarterly, July 1924, January 1935.

Gustave Charpentier
1860–1956

Gustave Charpentier was born in Dieuze, Lorraine, on June 25, 1860. When Germany annexed Lorraine after the Franco-Prussian War, the Charpentier family crossed the French border to Turcoing. There Gustave began the study of music, from the first showing unusual gifts. The necessity of earning a living made it impossible for him to devote himself exclusively to music, and at fifteen he took a job as accountant in a Turcoing factory. His employer, a music lover, recognized the boy's talent and did what he could to encourage it. He helped establish in Turcoing an orchestra and a music society so that young Charpentier might develop his musical abilities. As Charpentier's talent for music became increasingly evident, his employer financed further study at the Lille Conservatory. There Charpentier won several prizes which led to a grant from the town of Turcoing to enable him to enter the Paris Conservatory.

GUSTAVE CHARPENTIER

At the Conservatory, Charpentier, under the guidance of his teacher Massenet, wrote the cantata *Didon*, which won the Prix de Rome in 1887. *Didon*, performed in Paris, Brussels, and Turcoing, brought the young composer his first success.

During his stay in Rome, Charpentier was

Charpentier: shȧr päɴ tyā′

inspired by Italian life and geography to write his first orchestral work—the suite *Impressions of Italy* (1892). This is the only work by Charpentier, apart from his opera *Louise*, which came later, that is still heard. It is a tonal travelogue providing conventional, at times sentimental, pictures of Italy. In it Lawrence Gilman found the "Italy of rustic serenades, brown-bosomed peasant girls, muleteers, warm hillsides under the noonday haze, chimes heard over the hills, the vivid streets of Naples." The work has five sections: Serenade; At the Fountain; On Muleback; On the Heights; and Naples. The suite was introduced at a Colonne concert in Paris in 1892; only one year later, on November 25, 1893, it was heard in the United States with Theodore Thomas conducting the Chicago Orchestra.

After returning to Paris, Charpentier rented a room in Montmartre where he lived the life of a bohemian. He interested himself in socialism, finding an outlet for his political and social ideas in writing songs with orchestral accompaniment to texts propounding Socialist propaganda. In 1900 he helped to found a society to promote the interests of working people, L'Œuvre de Mimi Pinson, an organization which during World War I became an arm of the Red Cross.

The major work to occupy him after he had settled in Montmartre was his opera *Louise*. He prepared his own libretto, based on an incident he himself had witnessed: the illicit love affair of a bohemian painter and a dressmaker faced with parental opposition to their marriage. During the time he labored on his opera he suffered such poverty that he would have gone hungry for days at a time if a friendly grocer had not provided him with credit.

Charpentier named his heroine Louise because, in his early twenties, he had been in love with a girl of that name—Louise Jehan. She was the grand passion of his life. (He never married.) As he revealed later in his life, "We lived happily for two years. Then jealousies began to make us uncomfortable and six months later we parted. Soon afterwards I went to Rome to study. I looked for her when I came back, but without success. I thought she would surely make herself known when *Louise* was produced, but there never was a sign from her until once, during the war, a soldier asked

127

me for seats to a performance of the opera—in the name of his adopted godmother, Louise herself."

Once he had finished his manuscript, in the early 1890's, Charpentier tried to interest managers in it. For almost a decade he took it around to managers who found much to praise in it and would have accepted it if the composer had allowed basic alterations. One manager wanted the time of the opera to be set back a century. Another wanted the realism to be less photographic. A third called for a happy ending. To all such suggestions Charpentier turned a deaf ear, faithful to his original conception.

At long last, *Louise* was produced by the Opéra-Comique in Paris on February 2, 1900. On that occasion, Marthe Rioton sang the title role. The opera was an instantaneous success. Eleven days later, a young and then still unknown Scottish singer took over the part of Louise when Mme. Rioton fell ill. Appearing without the benefit of a single rehearsal, she proved a sensation. Her name was Mary Garden, and from then on the role of Louise and her own name became associated inextricably. She sang the part when *Louise* was heard for the first time in the United States, at the Manhattan Opera House on January 3, 1908.

The opera retained its popularity. It was heard one hundred times in the first season; by 1939 it had been given a thousand times at the Opéra-Comique alone. It went to Covent Garden on June 18, 1909, and it entered the repertory of the Metropolitan Opera on January 15, 1921. The fiftieth anniversary of the opera's première was celebrated at the Paris Opéra on February 28, 1950, before a festive audience that included the President of France. In the final scene, Charpentier—now nearly ninety years old—took over the baton and led the opera to the end when he received one of the greatest ovations the historic auditorium had experienced in its long and rich history. On the occasion of this anniversary, President Vincent Auriol presented him with the grade of Grand Officer of the Legion of Honor.

Louise is an important opera. There is much there that is derivative: a little bit of Wagner (particularly in the use of the Leitmotiv technique) and much more of Massenet. It is a sentimental opera, and its material is of uneven quality. But for all its faults it is a giant achievement in the French lyric theatre. As the first French opera to treat a realistic contemporary subject—and to offer passionate episodes in a naturalistic way—it carried over into French opera the achievements of the Italian *verismo* movement started by Leoncavallo and Mascagni. It was also, for its day, original in its expressive harmonies and in the supple flow and dramatic interest of the recitatives. But beyond its historic importance, *Louise* is an opera that never loses its capacity to enchant audiences. It has a persuasive charm all its own, particularly in the way the city of Paris dominates the work. For it is the personality of Paris, rather than that of its heroine, which gives the opera its unique character and appeal: the sights and sounds and spirit of the city. Paris is caught in the delightful cries of the street vendors which the composer incorporated into his score. It is found in the evocative prelude to the second act, entitled *Paris Awakes*, a miniature tone poem in which the city is portrayed radiantly. In pages like these *Louise* is much more than the tender story of an illicit love affair; it is the song of a city. Charpentier himself once said that *Louise* "is what Paris meant to me—Paris as she looked to the young provincial who had come from the grimy manufacturing town to find things for which he had starved and of which, for so long a time, he had dreamed."

Charpentier wrote a second opera, a sequel to *Louise*. He called it *Julien* (the hero of *Louise*) and it was introduced at the Opéra-Comique on June 4, 1913. It was received poorly, and now is totally neglected. After *Julien*, Charpentier wrote little, having soon become convinced that he had said everything he had to say in *Louise*.

Against the setting which he had used so effectively in his masterwork, that of Montmartre, Charpentier appeared until the end of his life like a character in his opera. He remained true to his bohemian ways – in dress, mannerisms, behavior, long hair, and beard. Until his last days he lived as he had done at the turn of the century, in the same quarters near the Sacré-Cœur he had occupied as a young man. He died there on February 18, 1956, at the age of ninety-five.

Charpentier founded the Syndicate and

Federation of Musical Artists and was its honorary president. In 1912 he became a member of the Académie des Beaux-Arts, in succession to Massenet. In his last year he was awarded a gold medal from the Society of Authors in Paris.

Choral Music—La Vie du Poète, symphonic drama.

Operas—Louise; Julien.

Orchestral Music—Impressions d'Italie (Impressions of Italy), suite; Poèmes Chantés, for voice and orchestra; Impressions Fausses, for voice and orchestra; Sérénade à Watteau, for voice and orchestra.

Vocal Music—Les Fleurs du Mal; Poèmes Chantés; Quinze Poèmes.

Delmas, M., Gustave Charpentier et le Lyricisme Français; Peltz, M. E. (ed.), Opera Lover's Companion; Sere, O., Musiciens Français d'Aujourd'hui.

Musical Quarterly, July 1939.

Carlos Chávez
1899–

Carlos Chávez was born in Mexico City on June 13, 1899. It has often been said of him that he was self-taught in music, but this is not strictly true. He took some lessons from his brother in his tenth year. From 1909 to 1914 he studied the piano with Manuel Ponce, and from 1915 to 1920 with Pedro Luis Ogazón. He also took lessons in harmony from Juan B. Fuentes in 1917 and 1918. Nevertheless, most of what he learned about music came from books and texts; he also learned a good deal about composition by minutely dissecting the works of the masters. He says that much of his later independence as a composer stemmed from the fact that he had been influenced more by texts and published scores than by teachers.

His lifelong interest in musical nationalism began early. When he was sixteen he wrote an article on Mexican music for *Gladios*, though he had not yet done any research in this field. He also wrote some pieces of music in what he thought to be a Mexican idiom, though actually it was in the style of mestizo, Spanish Indian music.

In the years between 1916 and 1918 he com-

Chávez: chä′ vās

pleted several large works, including a symphony and a piano sonata. These were soon followed by a second piano sonata, a piano sextet, and various pieces for the piano. All these were strongly influenced by European classical and romantic traditions, and for this reason Chávez does not include them any longer in any listing of his works.

CARLOS CHÁVEZ

He freed himself from European associations by studying and assimilating the indigenous music of the Mexican Indian. He discovered that there were people in Mexico who still used music in the same way their Indian ancestors had done, as an essential part of communal life. He lived with these people, steeped himself in their music, learned to play their native instruments. Subsequently, his great fascination for native Mexican folk music led him to make difficult trips into the mountains for first-hand studies.

He arrived at his individual style by incorporating the idioms and idiosyncrasies of native Mexican Indian folk music into his own compositions. Thus he managed to produce an authentic Mexican musical art all his own. The first of his works in which native elements were introduced was a ballet, *New Fire* (*El Fuego Nuevo*), written in 1921 on a commission from the Secretary of Education. Linear rather than harmonic, primitive rather than decorative, this music has much of the dynamic pulse and the harsh contrasts that characterize so much of Chávez' later work. A number of years passed before the ballet was produced on November 4, 1928, in Mexico City.

In September 1922 Chávez left for an extended tour of Europe which lasted until May 1923. During this period he first became acquainted with some of the basic tendencies of twentieth century music; in fact for the first time in his life he heard both the names and the music of such masters as Stravinsky and Schoenberg. Returning to his native land he organized and conducted concerts which came to be known as *Música Nueva* and which, from 1923 to 1925, were responsible for introducing to Mexico the works of Satie, Schoenberg, Stravinsky, Poulenc, Manuel de Falla, and other twentieth century composers. In order to study and absorb as much twentieth century music as possible he went to New York in September 1926 and stayed two years. Some of his early compositions were performed there during this period by the International Composers Guild.

On his return to Mexico, Chávez began to assume a position of unrivaled importance in its musical life. In 1928 he organized the first symphony orchestra in Mexico to give a regular series of concerts each year, the Orquesta Sinfónica de México. Not only did this orchestra help to build an audience for symphonic music, it also provided a forum where both the basic orchestral literature and modern music could get a hearing. In a twenty-year period Chávez presented over two hundred and fifty premières (the first performances in Mexico of practically all the prominent modern composers of Europe), and eighty-two premières of compositions by Mexican composers who had never before had performances anywhere. Chávez was the orchestra's principal conductor, but many world-famous conductors were invited as guests, the first time that such eminent musicians had performed in Mexico. The Orquesta Sinfónica was dissolved on March 8, 1949, when Chávez decided to devote himself to composition. However, orchestral music did not die out in Mexico. Chávez persuaded the government to found the National Symphony Orchestra, which has been functioning successfully since late in 1949.

In 1928 Chávez also became director of the National Conservatory of Music, where one year later he founded a chorus, now the major choral group in the country. During the six years that Chávez served as Conservatory director, he reorganized and modernized its curriculum and teaching methods. In 1933, for one year, Chávez was head of the Department of Fine Arts. In 1946, when the National Institute of Fine Arts was organized by Chávez to sponsor and promote cultural activities in Mexico, he became its director, filling this post for half a dozen years.

Through these activities Chávez was responsible for bringing about in Mexico the birth of a significant musical culture. He encouraged younger composers to cultivate folk music and Mexican instruments. He arranged performances of Mexican Indian music on native instruments.

In his own compositions he set a standard for other Mexican composers, with remarkable works whose roots were deep in native Mexican Indian folk art. *Los Cuatro Soles*, a ballet inspired by an ancient Mexican legend with a score based on Aztec musical materials, was written in 1926 and produced in Mexico City on July 22, 1930. A second ballet, *H.P.* (*Horsepower*), inspired by the machine age and described by the composer as a "symphony of the sounds around us, a revue of the times," received its world première in the United States on March 31, 1932, Leopold Stokowski conducting. In this production the scenery was designed by Diego Rivera. The dancers appeared in costumes representing filling stations, pineapples, and objects typifying aspects of Mexican geography. The dances have often been represented on symphony programs and constitute some of the finest pages in the score. Of the music, as a whole, Copland has written that it is "stoic, stark and somber like an Orozco painting."

The orchestral works strongly influenced by Chávez' researches into Mexican music which have become permanent in the twentieth century repertory are his first two symphonies. The first, *Sinfonía de Antígona*, was commissioned by the Department of Fine Arts in 1932 as incidental music for a performance of Jean Cocteau's *Antigone*. As a symphony it was performed in Mexico City on December 15, 1933. *Sinfonía India* was written in 1935 and was first performed over the Columbia Broadcasting System radio network on January 23, 1936. Both works have an almost stark simplicity, reflecting the tendency of Indian music to get down to essentials. As Henry Cowell wrote: "All dross is cut away, every note is meaningful and needed. . . . It has arrived at a point of simplicity in which all unnecessary elements are eliminated." The *Sinfonía India* uses not only authentic Mexican Indian folk themes but even such folk instruments as the water gourd, rasps, rattles, and Indian drums.

In other works Chávez has resorted to a neoprimitive style which reaches back to the early Stravinsky in its exploitation of intricate rhythmic patterns and polyrhythmic designs which, nonetheless, have been influenced by Mexican Indian music. Such a work is *Xochipilli Macuilxochitl* (the name of the Aztec god of music), scored entirely for an ensemble of Indian instruments, most of them popular. This was introduced in New York City on May 16, 1940, with the composer conducting. Another is the *Toccata for Percussion Instruments* (1942), scored for eleven types of percussion instruments, some indigenous to Mexico. The different groups of instruments heard in each of the three movements are used with compelling effect to create dramatic interest. The *Toccata* was heard in Mexico City on October 31, 1947.

Some of Chávez' later symphonies are in an entirely different vein. The fourth (1952)–written on a commission from the Louisville Orchestra in Kentucky, which introduced it on February 4, 1953–is known as "Romantic" because of its strong lyric character. On the other hand, the Symphony No. 5, for string orchestra–introduced in Los Angeles on December 1, 1953, the composer conducting–is neoclassic in its conciseness and objectivity. Neoclassic, too, in spite of its occasional indulgence in rich orchestral sound, is the Sixth Symphony (1963), which was introduced by Leonard Bernstein and the New York Philharmonic on May 7, 1964. Describing this last work, Irving Kolodin said in the *Saturday Review*: "Chávez has managed to create a work that is both freely composed and logically imagined, in a broadly flowing pattern of ideas at once unfettered and strongly disciplined. The ease and purpose with which Chávez moves his musical materials about shows the practiced hand of one who . . . builds with sonority as some may with stone. Indeed, in the forty-three variations of the final passaca-

glia, Chávez has reared a cathedral of sonority. There are scant suggestions in it of the folkloristic elements with which he worked at a prior time though they may merely be more completely assimilated into his idiom than before."

Chávez' first opera was produced in New York City on May 9, 1957, under the title *Panfilo and Lauretta*. It was presented for the first time in Mexico under its original title of *El Amor Propiciado* on October 28, 1959, the composer conducting. The libretto, by Chester Kallman, was based on a tale from Boccaccio's *Decameron* and told the story of four people in the fourteenth century who had gone into retreat in a Tuscan villa to escape the plague. Miriam Gideon explains: "Four plays are improvised as diversions. . . . In these the actual characters of the opera live out their real desires, and preserve their musical identity as well by characteristic melodic styles." Plots within a plot lead to complexity and at times confusion, but the over-all effect is a powerful one. Miss Gideon selects some of the more memorable pages from Chávez' score: "the many-faceted closing chorus of Act I, in which the principals sing of their fate against a bleak and dissonant funeral chant in Latin; . . . contrasting arias (Panfilo's grim portrayal, in acrid dissonances of the plague-devastated city; the aria of the rejected and exploited Elissa, with its wide chromatic leaps; Venus's final aria, 'Look on Love with No Disguise,' in softly curving lines above a romantic triadic harmony); . . . the transparency of the final chorus, 'Time, That Closes Every Eye,' with its concluding section in E major."

Chávez was commissioned by his government to write the music for ceremonies attending the Olympic Games in Mexico City in 1968. *Suite from the Olympic Fire* is an adaptation of parts of this music.

Since 1936 Chávez has often appeared as guest conductor of major American symphony orchestras. In 1938 he received a Guggenheim Fellowship. In 1943 he was appointed a life member of the National College in Mexico City where he gave annual series of lectures until 1949 and concert lectures after 1950. For 1958-1959 he was appointed Charles Eliot Norton Professor at Harvard University; the Norton lectures were published in a book entitled *Musical Thoughts* (1960).

Chávez has been frequently honored by both his own and other countries. His awards and decorations include Chevalier, Legion of Honor, France, in 1932; Commander, Order of the Crown, Belgium, in 1950; Commander, Order of the Polar Star, Sweden, and Officer, Legion of Honor, France, in 1952; the Caro de Boesi Prize in Caracas, in 1954; the Premio Nacional de Artes y Ciencias in Mexico in 1958. He became an honorary member of the American Academy of Arts and Sciences in Boston in 1959 and of the American Academy and National Institute of Arts and Letters in New York in 1960.

Nicolas Slonimsky described Chávez as "solidly built, full of muscular energy, with curly but not unruly hair, and flashing eyes." Slonimsky called him "a man of the world. . . . He is . . . gregarious, is gallant with the ladies, and observes the tradition of kissing their hands. He is a gourmet; his favorite dish is Montezuma pie made of tortillas. . . . He likes wine in moderation. Chávez enjoys conversation on any conceivable subject . . . and on each subject he entertains very strong opinions."

"You cannot eliminate the human element in music and still have art," Chávez told an interviewer in 1960. "I have nothing against the experimenters. That is, I have nothing against them until the boast is made that theirs is a finished art. They have only begun to experiment, and that fact should be understood. . . . It is conceivable that experiments with electronics may lead some day to devices a musician or composer may be able to use creatively. I was once very much interested in such innovations and wrote a book about them. But my mind has turned to other methods of creating new sounds. More valid methods, I believe."

MAJOR WORKS

Ballets—El Fuego Nuevo (The New Fire); Los Cuatro Soles; H.P.; Antígona; Hija de Cólquide (The Daughter of Colchis, or The Dark Meadow).

Chamber Music—3 string quartets; Energía, for nine instruments; Violin Sonatina; Sonata for Four Horns; Cello Sonatina; Two Spirals, for violin and piano; Soli No. 2, for woodwind quintet; Soli No. 4, for trumpet, horn, and trombone.

Choral Music—La Paloma Azul; Canto a la Tierra; Tierra Mojada; El Sol; Prometheus, cantata.

Opera—Panfilo and Lauretta (El Amor Propiciado).

Orchestral Music—7 symphonies (including Sinfonía

de Antígona and Sinfonía India); Sinfonía Proletaria, with chorus; Obertura Republicana; Harp Concerto; Xochipilli-Macuilxochitl, for primitive Indian instruments; Piano Concerto; Toccata, for percussion instruments; Violin Concerto; Resonances; Suite from the Olympic Fire.

Piano Music—6 sonatas; Sonatina; Solo, Blues and Fox-Trot; Ten Preludes; Three Etudes; Invención; Seven Pieces.

Vocal Music—Exágonos; Tres Poemas; La Casada Infidel; Tres Poesías de Pellicer.

ABOUT

Copland, A., The New Music: 1900–1960; Ewen, D. (ed.), New Book of Modern Composers; Morillo, R. G., Carlos Chávez, Vida y Obra.

Chesterian (London), Spring 1956; Musical Quarterly, October 1936.

Samuel Coleridge-Taylor
1875–1912

Samuel Coleridge-Taylor was born in London on August 15, 1875. His father, Daniel Hughes Taylor, was an African who had studied medicine in London and practiced in Croydon. Having become negligent in his medical duties and faced with ruin, Dr. Taylor deserted his wife—an English woman, *née* Alice Hare—and child and returned to his native Sierra Leone. Samuel was raised by his mother.

SAMUEL COLERIDGE-TAYLOR

A friend of the family, Benjamin Holman, gave young Samuel his first music lessons, on the violin. Joseph Beckwith, a local theatre conductor, heard Samuel play one day and was sufficiently impressed to take him on as a pupil. He studied with Beckwith for the next seven years and during that period sang in the choir of St. George's Church in Croydon. "He was a most delightful pupil," the choirmaster, Herbert Walters, later recalled, "quick, eager, and with a wonderful ear." Before long Walters adopted Samuel and in 1890 provided the funds for him to enroll in the Royal College of Music in London. There Coleridge-Taylor studied composition with Charles Villiers Stanford. In 1893 he received a scholarship in composition. During the next year he completed his first ambitious works, including a piano quintet (op. 1), a Nonet (op. 2), and a clarinet quintet (op. 10). In 1896 he completed the Symphony in A minor, with thematic material based on Negro melodies; it was performed that year by the Royal College of Music orchestra conducted by Stanford. The Clarinet Quintet, op. 10, was performed in Berlin the next year by the renowned Joachim Quartet.

Coleridge-Taylor was still a student at the Royal College when he began to write the work that brought him his first major success. It was the *Song of Hiawatha*, based on Longfellow, for solo voices, chorus, and orchestra. The first of three sections, *Hiawatha's Wedding Feast*, was completed in 1896 and introduced at the Royal College of Music on November 11, 1898; the second part, *The Death of Minnehaha*, came a year later and was heard at the North Staffordshire Festival in the fall of 1899; the concluding section, *Hiawatha's Departure*, completed in 1900, was given on March 22 of the same year by the Royal Choral Society in London. Hubert Foss has described the entire work as "astonishing . . . for a man of twenty-three . . . the sheer originality of invention and novelty of scoring have never failed . . . to strike an unfamiliar note on each performance heard again." Foss also said that its success was "unreached by any English composer then living."

In 1898 Coleridge-Taylor was appointed teacher of the violin at the Royal College of Music. In that year he wrote an important orchestral composition, the Ballade in A minor, which was heard at the Three Choirs Festival. A number of critics called it the product of genius. Herbert Antcliffe later described it as follows: "There probably never has been an orchestral work of such importance intrinsically and in its relation to the world of music that has been constructed on so simple a theme of tonality or orchestration."

In 1899, Coleridge-Taylor married Jessie F. Walmisley, whom he had met at the Royal College of Music. They settled down in Croydon where Coleridge-Taylor taught the violin both privately and at the Conservatory. In 1903 he founded an amateur string quartet which gave concerts for a number of years. He extended his conducting activities in 1904 by becoming the director of the Handel Society which, during the next eight years, developed into one of England's important choral groups. He also appeared as guest conductor of orchestral and choral organizations outside England, particularly in performances of his own music. He made three tours of the United States—in 1904, 1906, and 1910—and during his last visit he conducted the première of his last major work, the Concerto for Violin and Orchestra in G minor, at the Norfolk (Connecticut) Festival.

One of Coleridge-Taylor's last compositions proved to be one of his most successful since the *Song of Hiawatha*. It was *A Tale of Old Japan*, for solo voices, chorus, and orchestra, which he completed in 1911 and which was introduced the same year in London by the London Choral Society. This setting of poems by Alfred Noyes, though of smaller dimensions than the *Song of Hiawatha*, revealed the same qualities of "melodic charm, naïvely simple rhythm and glowing orchestral color which had appealed instantaneously as a treatment of Longfellow's verse," as we learn from Grove's *Dictionary of Music and Musicians*. The article describes the music as "picturesque, memorably melodious, variedly harmonized and well orchestrated."

For a number of years, Coleridge-Taylor was professor of music at Trinity College; during his last year he was professor at the Guildhall School of Music. He was also active as a judge in various competition-festivals in Britain, including the Welsh Eisteddfodau.

Samuel Coleridge-Taylor died in Croydon on September 1, 1912. A few moments before his death he sat up in bed singing parts of his Violin Concerto and swinging his arms about as if he were conducting a performance.

Converse

He was a methodical workman, devoting a specified number of hours each day to creative work, and never allowing either his conducting or teaching duties to interfere with this daily activity. He wrote quickly and fluently and produced a sizable library of music, in spite of his strong self-criticism.

Booker T. Washington described Coleridge-Taylor's style as follows: "His work possesses . . . not only charm and power but distinction, the individual note. The genuineness, depth and intensity of his feeling, coupled with his masterly technique, spontaneity and ability to think in his own way, explain the force of the appeal that his compositions make. Another element in the persuasiveness of his music lies in the naturalness, the directness of its appeal, the use of simple and expressive melodic themes, a happy freedom from the artificial."

Samuel Coleridge-Taylor had two children, both of whom became musicians. His son, Hiawatha, conducted the father's *Song of Hiawatha* in London in 1924. His daughter, Gwendolen, was the composer of many songs that were published and performed.

MAJOR WORKS

Chamber Music—Piano Quintet in G minor; Nonet in F minor; Fantasiestücke, for string quartet; Clarinet Quintet in F-sharp minor; String Quartet in D minor; Violin Sonata in D minor; Four African Dances, for violin and piano; Ballade in C minor, for violin and piano.

Choral Music—Morning and Evening Service; A Song of Hiawatha; The Blind Girl of Castel-Cuille; Meg Blane; The Atonement, oratorio; Five Choral Ballads; Kubla Khan; Endymion's Dream; Bon-Bon; Sea-Drift, rhapsody; A Tale of Old Japan.

Operas—Dream Lovers (operetta); The Gitanos (cantata-operetta); Thelma.

Orchestral Music—Ballade in D minor, for violin and orchestra; Zara's Earrings, rhapsody for voice and orchestra; Symphony in A minor; Legend, for violin and orchestra; Ballade in A minor; African Suite; Nourmahal's Song and Dance; Romance in G major, for violin and orchestra; The Soul's Expression, for voice and orchestra; Idyll; Toussaint l'Ouverture, concert overture; Hemo Dance; Four Novelettes; Symphonic Variations on an African Air; Intermezzo; Bamboula, rhapsodic dance; Petite Suite de Concert.

Piano Music—Two Moorish Tone Pictures; Four Characteristic Waltzes; Three Humoresques; Three Silhouettes; Moorish Dance; Cameos; Twenty-four Negro Melodies; Scènes de Ballet; Forest Scenes; Valse Suite, six waltzes.

Vocal Music—Six Children's Songs; Southern Love Songs; African Romances, seven songs; In Memoriam, three rhapsodies for low voice; Six American Lyrics; Three Song-Poems; various other songs for voice and piano.

ABOUT

Bacharach, A. L. (ed.), The Music Masters: v4, The Twentieth Century; Byron, M., Golden Hours with Coleridge-Taylor; Coleridge-Taylor, J., Samuel Coleridge-Taylor: A Memory Sketch; Sayers, W. C. B., Samuel Coleridge-Taylor, Musician: His Life and Letters.

Frederick Shepherd Converse
1871–1940

Frederick Shepherd Converse was born in Newton, Massachusetts, on January 5, 1871. He completed his early academic studies at the Newton public schools while studying the piano with local teachers. He entered Harvard University in 1889 where he continued his musical studies with John Knowles Paine. In 1893 Converse was graduated with honors in music and the additional prestige of having his Violin Sonata performed at the commencement exercises.

FREDERICK SHEPHERD CONVERSE

His father wanted him to consider business rather than music as a career, and so, shortly after graduation, he entered the business world. But he was unhappy there and soon became convinced he belonged to music. For two years he continued music study in Boston with Carl Baermann and George Chadwick. Then, in 1896, Converse went to Europe where he enrolled in the Royal High School of Music

Converse: kŏn′ vûrs

in Munich as a pupil of Rheinberger. On July 14, 1898, his Symphony in D minor was introduced in Munich.

In 1899 Converse returned to the United States and became an instructor at the New England Conservatory. In the year 1901 he was appointed to the music faculty of Harvard, and soon afterward he became an assistant professor.

Several orchestral works in a German post-Romantic style and with the Germanic respect for solid classical structures and formal harmonic designs were successfully performed by the Boston Symphony in the first years of the twentieth century. *Festival of Pan* was heard on December 21, 1900; *Night and Day* (two poems for piano and orchestra), on January 21, 1905. In addition, the Boston Pops Orchestra introduced *Endymion's Narrative* in 1900 and the Philadelphia Orchestra presented the première of one of Converse's most famous compositions, *The Mystic Trumpeter* (based on Walt Whitman), on March 3, 1905.

Converse's reputation was solidly established with the production of his one-act opera *The Pipe of Desire* by the Boston Opera Company on January 31, 1906. The libretto, by George Edward Burton, concerned the magic powers of a pipe which brings doom to a peasant youth, Iolan, and his beloved, Naoia, because he uses it for selfish reasons. "The first impression of Mr. Converse's music—it comes even in the prelude—is almost intoxicating," wrote H. T. Parker in his review. "Mr. Converse has . . . 'feeling,' instinct and imagination. There are twenty tokens of it throughout the opera—in his power of dramatic climax, in his ability to make the vivid, emphasizing, illuminating phrase in voice or orchestra at the poignant moment, in the steady variety of treatment, in the weaving of the voices, instruments, speech and action into a significant, moving and musically beautiful whole; in the skill to summon and maintain communicating atmosphere and mood."

The Pipe of Desire was the first American opera to be produced by the Metropolitan Opera; it was given in New York on March 18, 1910. Soon afterwards, it received the David Bispham Medal.

Besides earning the distinction of being the first American composer represented at the Metropolitan, Converse became the first American to have an oratorio performed in Germany. *Job*, a dramatic poem for solo voices, chorus and orchestra, was heard first at the Worcester Festival in Massachusetts on October 2, 1907, and later in Hamburg on November 23, 1908.

In 1907 Converse resigned from Harvard to devote himself to composition. Then, in 1908, he became vice-president of the Boston Opera Company and went to Europe to scout for singers, settling in Vevey, Switzerland, within convenient traveling distance of Europe's leading music capitals. The selection of *The Pipe of Desire* by the Metropolitan Opera brought him back to the United States early in 1910.

During World War I, Converse joined the Motor Corps of the Massachusetts State Guard as a private. Eventually he was promoted to the rank of captain in the supply department of the 13th Regiment. He industriously promoted music in training camps and conducted community choruses. At the request of the Government he collaborated with John Alden Carpenter in preparing a symphonic arrangement of *The Star-Spangled Banner* which was performed by most of the major American symphony orchestras during the war period.

In 1921 Converse joined the faculty of the New England Conservatory of Music, where for a decade he taught theory and composition. From 1930 to 1938 he served as dean.

Of his major works during the post-World War I era, two symphonies are of particular interest. Symphony No. 1 (the earlier symphony of his Munich days had been discarded) was introduced by the Boston Symphony on January 30, 1920. His Second Symphony was given by the Boston Symphony on April 22, 1922. In both works, Converse still clung to his Romantic past. But after 1927 he became increasingly interested in modern sounds and began to experiment with his harmonic language; at the same time he produced a number of works interpreting American scenes, backgrounds, and experiences. One of these, *Flivver Ten Million*, written to celebrate the manufacture of the ten millionth Ford automobile and generously spiced with discords, was played by the Boston Symphony under Koussevitzky on April 15, 1927. This was followed by "festival scenes" for orchestra entitled *California*, performed by the Boston Symphony on

April 26, 1928, and *American Sketches* (inspired by Carl Sandburg's collection of American folk songs, *The American Songbag*), also heard at a concert of the Boston Symphony, on February 8, 1935.

In 1933 Converse received an honorary doctorate from Boston University, and in 1937 he was elected a member of the American Academy of Arts and Letters. Converse died in Boston on June 8, 1940. His last major work, the Sixth Symphony, was given a posthumous première in Indianapolis on November 7, 1940.

Converse was a fine sportsman, an expert golfer and polo player. His happiest days were spent at his summer home on Lake Sunapee in New Hampshire, where he indulged in shooting, fishing, sailing, and gardening. During the winter months, his favorite hobby was woodcarving; he was also a talented maker of violins.

He always said that he was a thoroughly happy man: happy in his work and play, happy with his teaching duties, happy with his family life. "Life itself," he wrote with an almost religious fervor, "is to me a constant marvel—and I thank God for it."

MAJOR WORKS

Chamber Music—3 string quartets; Cello Sonata; Piano Trio; Concerto for Violin and Piano.

Choral Music—Job, oratorio; The Peace Pipe; The Answer of the Stars; The Flight of the Eagle.

Operas—The Pipe of Desire (one-act opera); The Sacrifice; Sinbad the Sailor; The Immigrants.

Orchestral Music—6 symphonies; Festival of Pan; Endymion's Narrative; La Belle Dame sans Merci, ballad for baritone and orchestra; Night and Day, two tone poems for piano and orchestra (also for two solo pianos); Euphrosyne, concert overture; The Mystic Trumpeter; Hagar in the Desert, dramatic narrative for low voice and orchestra; Ormazd; Ave atque Vale; Fantasia for Piano and Orchestra; Song of the Sea; Elegiac Poem; Flivver Ten Million; California, festival scenes; American Sketches; Concertino for Piano and Orchestra.

ABOUT

Howard, J. T., Our Contemporary Composers.

Aaron Copland
1900–

Aaron Copland was born in Brooklyn, New York, on November 14, 1900. He was the

Copland: kŏp' lănd

youngest of five children, in a family without even remote associations with serious music. Nevertheless, when he was thirteen, inspired by hearing his first concert, a piano recital by Paderewski, he began to think in earnest about a career in music. He started with piano lessons when he was fourteen, and at that time was taught by his sister, Laurine. Soon he demanded and got more professional training. "I distinctly remember with what fear and trembling I knocked on the door of Mr. Leopold Wolfsohn's piano studio on Clinton Avenue in Brooklyn and . . . arranged for piano lessons," he recalls.

AARON COPLAND

In or about 1916, Copland realized that he wanted to be a composer. While attending Boys' High School, he began to study harmony with Rubin Goldmark. Upon graduation in 1918 he renounced college, determined to specialize in music study.

He was already composing, mostly songs and piano pieces. "It soon became clear that Goldmark derived no pleasure from seeing what to him seemed to be 'modernistic experiments.' The climax came when I brought for his critical approval a piano piece called *The Cat and the Mouse*. He regretfully admitted that he had no criteria by which to judge such music." From then on Copland divided his creative activity between the kind of piece he really liked to write and the more conventional kind conforming to textbook rules for submission to his teacher.

One day he read that a music school was being established for Americans in Fontainebleau, France. He applied for enrollment and was accepted as the first student. There he studied composition with Paul Vidal. Sitting in on a session in harmony in Nadia Boulanger's class, he surmised that he had found his teacher. He asked to be taken on as a private pupil in composition and orchestration. For the next three years Copland was Boulanger's pupil (probably the first American she had accepted). Copland has never hesitated to admit that her influence on his development was decisive.

Paris was a stimulating place for a young musician in the early 1920's. It was alive with new musical ideas and new sounds. Copland absorbed all the new music he could hear, especially that which Koussevitzky was conducting at his Concerts—the works of Stravinsky, Prokofiev, Hindemith, the French Six, and Schoenberg. Much of it struck a responsive chord with him. Through Nadia Boulanger he became acquainted with Koussevitzky, the beginning of an association that was to have a far-reaching impact on his career. He was also invited by Boulanger to write a symphony for organ and orchestra which she could perform during appearances with the New York Symphony and the Boston Symphony the following winter.

Copland returned to the United States in June 1924. While employed that summer as pianist with a trio at a resort in Milford, Pennsylvania, he worked on his symphony. That November, at a concert of the League of Composers in New York, two of Copland's piano pieces were performed, *The Cat and the Mouse* and a Passacaglia; this was the first time that Copland's music was heard in America. On January 11, 1925, his first symphony, for organ and orchestra, was introduced by the New York Symphony. Nadia Boulanger was the soloist and Walter Damrosch conducted. When Damrosch had finished his performance he turned to the audience and remarked: "If a young man can write a piece like that at the age of twenty-three, in five years he will be ready to commit murder."

Dr. Damrosch's reaction notwithstanding, the Symphony attracted not only favorable interest in several quarters but also significant support for its composer. The critic Paul Rosenfeld found a generous patron (Alma Wertheim) who stood ready to help support Copland to allow him time to compose. Serge Koussevitzky was so impressed by the symphony that he performed it in Boston on February 20, 1925. He also interested the League of Composers in commissioning Copland to write a new work which Koussevitzky could conduct at a League concert. In addition, Copland received in 1925 the first music fellowship to be granted by the Guggenheim Foundation. The award was extended for an additional year.

Relieved of economic pressures, Copland could devote himself completely to producing a composition for Koussevitzky. "I was anxious to write a work that would immediately be recognized as American in character," he says. "This desire to be 'American' was symptomatic of the period. . . . I had experimented a little with the rhythms of popular music in several earlier compositions, but now I wanted frankly to adopt the jazz idiom and see what I could do with it in a symphonic way." On Rosenfeld's recommendation, Copland was accepted at the MacDowell Colony where, during the summer of 1925, he completed a five-movement suite for small orchestra, *Music for the Theatre*. A sprightly tune in solo trumpet with which the first-movement "Prologue" opens, the nervous rhythms of the second-movement "Dance," and the wailing trumpet in the fourth-movement "Burlesque"—all were rooted in the jazz style and techniques of the 1920's. *Music for the Theatre* was introduced by the Boston Symphony under Koussevitzky in Boston on November 20, 1925; eight days later Koussevitzky conducted it again at a concert of the League of Composers.

Copland made one more attempt to produce a large symphonic work in a jazz style—his concerto for piano and orchestra. It was heard in Boston on January 28, 1927, with the composer at the piano, and Koussevitzky conducting the Boston Symphony. Lawrence Gilman said of the work, in his review in the New York *Herald Tribune*, that it has "an authenticity of life which makes it at once perturbing and richly treasurable. . . . This is music of impressive austerity, of true character; music bold in outline and of singular power."

Copland

"With the concerto," Copland has explained, "I felt I had done all I could with the idiom, considering its limited emotional scope." He completed the *Dance Symphony*, music adapted from an early ballet score, *Grohg*, which received a prize of five thousand dollars in a contest sponsored by RCA Victor Company and was performed by the Philadelphia Orchestra under Stokowski on April 15, 1931. He was now ready to progress from jazz to a complex, objective style in which modern idioms of harmony, tonality, and rhythm predominated.

Copland proceeded to compose a number of major works in which he joined the then advanced school of American composers, with music that had a far greater appeal to the intellect than to the emotions and which, consequently, had only a limited appeal. First, in 1929, came the *Symphonic Ode*, commissioned by the Boston Symphony for its fiftieth anniversary. This was followed by the *Piano Variations* (1930), *Short Symphony* (1933), and the *Statements*, for orchestra (1934).

"During these years," says Copland, "I began to feel an increasing dissatisfaction with the relations of the music-loving public and the living composer. . . . It seemed to me that we composers were in danger of working in a vacuum. . . . I felt that it was worth the effort to see if I couldn't say what I had to say in the simplest possible terms."

Simplification was combined with an easily assimilable style in which folk material often became basic material. The first such work proved an outstanding success and is still one of the composer's frequently played compositions. It was *El Salón México*, based on popular Mexican tunes and inspired by a picture of a popular Mexican dance hall. The première took place in Mexico City on August 27, 1937, Carlos Chávez conducting. After *El Salón México*, Copland wrote the music for two ballets, for which he drew generously from American folk sources, and specifically from the songs of the cowboy. *Billy the Kid* (1938) used such familiar cowboy songs as "Git Along Little Dogie," "Old Chisholm Trail" and "O Bury Me Not." *Rodeo* (1942) was also a cowboy ballet with quotations from American folk songs ("Sis Joe," "If He'd Be a Buckaroo by His Trade," and "Miss McLeod's Reel"). *Billy the Kid* was produced in Chicago on October 16, 1938, by the Ballet Caravan; *Rodeo* was performed by the Ballet Russe de Monte Carlo in New York on October 16, 1942.

This ambition to reach for and relate to a wider audience led Copland at this time to produce a number of interesting functional works. A play-opera, *The Second Hurricane* (1937), and *An Outdoor Overture* (1938) were music for children of high-school age. *Music for the Radio* (1937) was, as the title indicates, a piece for radio broadcast. Scores for *The City* (1939), *Of Mice and Men* (1939), *Our Town* (1940), *The Red Pony* (1949), and *The Heiress* (1949), the last of which received the Academy Award, represented Copland's contributions to screen music; his music for the theatre included the incidental music to *The Five Kings* (1939) and *Quiet City* (1939).

In 1942, on a commission from André Kostelanetz, Copland wrote *Lincoln Portrait*, for narrator and orchestra. The text was based on quotations from Lincoln's letters and speeches; the music quoted two American tunes: Stephen Foster's "Camptown Races" and the folk ballad "Springfield Mountain." Kostelanetz conducted the world première in Cincinnati on May 14, 1942.

The ballet *Appalachian Spring* (1945) was the most important and the most enduring of the scores produced by Copland during this period. It was commissioned for Martha Graham by the Elizabeth Sprague Coolidge Foundation, with a ballet scenario prepared by Miss Graham herself (borrowing her title from a Hart Crane poem) a description of a wedding among the Shakers in the Appalachian mountain region. The ballet was produced in Washington, D.C., on October 30, 1944. In 1945 Copland's music received the New York Music Critics Circle Award. In the spring of 1945 Copland adapted his score into an eight-section orchestral suite which won for the composer his first Pulitzer Prize in music.

In this music Copland borrowed some of his techniques from American folk sources—for example, the brusque rhythms and the open-fifth harmonies of country fiddlers; but with a single exception the thematic material was entirely his own. The exception was a Shaker tune, "Simple Gifts." Virgil Thomson described Copland's score as "pastoral" in style and "blithe and beatific" in spirit.

Though there are no thematic borrowings from folk songs in Copland's Third Symphony (1946), its American personality and spirit cannot be denied. (Copland, however, does quote himself here, by introducing in the first movement a tonal device he had employed in *Appalachian Spring*, and lifting a subject from another of his compositions, *A Fanfare for the Common Man*.) The symphony was commissioned by the Koussevitzky Music Foundation and introduced by the Boston Symphony on October 18, 1946. Koussevitzky, who conducted the première, described it as "the greatest American symphony—it goes from the heart to the heart." The symphony received the Boston Symphony Award of Merit and the New York Music Critics Circle Award. In the New York *Herald Tribune* Virgil Thomson described it as "the reflected work of a mature master" and "a highly personal work." He added: "Nobody else could have written it. It is destined for that very reason, I think, to occupy a niche of some importance in the history of American music.... The nature of the work's expressivity is as plain as a newspaper editorial. It is pastoral and military, the two themes being contrasted through the three movements which do not differ much from one another either thematically or emotionally. They are resolved in the fourth by a transformation of the chief military material into a hymn and of the first theme, hitherto pastoral and meditative, into a sort of triumphal affirmation of faith in the pastoral virtues."

Thoroughly American in both subject matter and personality is Copland's full-length opera *The Tender Land*, commissioned by Richard Rodgers and Oscar Hammerstein II and produced by the New York City Opera on April 1, 1954. Horace Everett's libretto is set in the farmlands of the Midwest during the early 1930's. The love interest involves Martin, a harvester, and Laurie, the girl of the rural household. In the end Laurie is deserted and is left to face the world alone. She chooses freedom over security and leaves her farm to look for her lover. "The music as a whole," reported Ronald Eyer in *Musical America*, "gives a curious impression of being of two distinct varieties simultaneously. The vocal music is relatively simple and is built mostly along conventional diatonic, chromatic and choral lines. It sings easily and well, and Copland's prosody is impeccable. He also handles recitative and parlando with a sure, natural touch. Against this is an orchestral fabric that is far more complex and sophisticated and bears many of the hallmarks of Copland's familiar style of harmonization. Inevitably, there are overtones of *Appalachian Spring* and other more bucolic works, but they are not amiss in this pastoral setting."

Following this première, composer and librettist revised their opera. Parts of their revision were included in a presentation of the opera at the Berkshire Music Center during the summer of 1954. The completely revised opera was produced at Oberlin Conservatory on May 20, 1955. Since then the opera has been revived from time to time: at the Juilliard School of Music in or about 1959; at Philharmonic Hall in New York, in a concert version conducted by the composer, in 1965.

In a discussion of the American identity of Copland's music, Olin Downes wrote in 1950 a tribute on the composer's fiftieth birthday: "Copland's sense of style is that of the American who is of his country, his time, his environment, at the same time he is spiritually a man of the world.... He is neither naïve nor local in his frequent and skillful employment of American folk themes for appropriate expressive purposes.... By the quality of his workmanship, the sincerity and adventurousness of his progress, Copland made himself the spearpoint of the development of the modern American school."

Copland followed his opera with several important compositions: *Canticle of Freedom*, text by John Barbour (1955); *Piano Fantasy* (1957) commissioned by the Juilliard School of Music for its fiftieth anniversary and introduced by William Masselos in New York on October 25, 1957; *Dance Panels*, a ballet in seven movements (1959), whose première took place at the rebuilt Munich Opera House in Germany in December 1963; the Nonet, for nine solo strings (1960), first performance at Dumbarton Oaks, near Washington, D.C., on March 2, 1960; *Connotations*, for orchestra, commissioned by the New York Philharmonic for its opening concert in the new Philharmonic Hall at the Lincoln Center for the Performing Arts where it was introduced on September 23, 1962; *Music for a Great*

Copland

City, for orchestra, which the London Symphony had commissioned for its sixtieth anniversary and which it introduced under the composer's direction on May 26, 1964; and *Inscape*, written for the commemoration of the 125th anniversary of the New York Philharmonic, which introduced it at the University of Michigan on September 13, 1967, under Leonard Bernstein.

Copland lives in Poughkeepsie, New York, in a rambling house atop a wooded hill overlooking the Hudson River Valley. "In physical appearance," wrote Lester Trimble in *Musical America*, "Copland retains the same lean, urban look that has always characterized him. There is no more bulk about his person than there is about his music. The expression on his face may be thoughtful, private, wryly examining or hilariously amused; it is never (at least in public) dark with moroseness or Romantic introspection."

Frequently identified as "the dean of American music," and regarded as something of a spiritual father to an entire generation of American composers, Copland looks very much the part. "He even looks like a patriarch," says Eric Salzman, "with his great head, large even for his tall, upright frame. His features are craggy and forbidding, like those of some giant, extinct bird. All this gives his appearance a kind of Old Testament grandeur.... He dresses with a kind of elegant informality; this might describe his manner, too. He is loose, assured, and easy going—on the surface at least. Beneath an exterior calm, his mind is restlessly in motion."

Copland does his composing at the piano, usually at night. He is not a prolific producer. His compositions come slowly, and in recent years more slowly than ever. "Strangely enough," he confesses sadly, "it doesn't get any easier."

Copland has been tireless in promoting new music and young composers. He was chairman of the executive board of directors of the League of Composers; founder of the Copland-Sessions concerts in New York; director of the American Festivals of Contemporary Music at Yaddo, at Saratoga Springs, New York; organizer of the American Composers' Alliance. He has been a consultant of the Koussevitzky Music Foundation and has been affiliated with the Composers Forum and with the United States section of the International Society for Contemporary Music.

From 1940 until 1965 he was affiliated with the Berkshire Music Center at Tanglewood, serving first as head of the department of composition, then after 1957 as chairman of the faculty. During the summer of 1965 Copland announced his retirement from the Music Center.

Many honors have been bestowed on him. In 1954 he was elected a member of the American Academy of Arts and Letters; in 1956 he received an honorary doctorate from Princeton; in 1964 he was awarded the Presidential Medal of Freedom from President Johnson "for creative talent and demonstrated excellence."

In 1941 Copland toured South America as pianist and conductor. In 1960 he conducted several of his works in the Soviet Union. He has also appeared as a guest conductor throughout the United States, in Europe, and in Israel. He has published several books: *What to Listen for in Music* (1939), *Our New Music* (1941; reissued as *The New Music: 1900–1960*, 1968), *Music and Imagination* (1952), and *Copland on Music* (1960). He has been both the commentator on and the conductor of a series of television programs on the music of the 1920's.

MAJOR WORKS

Ballets—Hear Ye, Hear Ye; Billy the Kid; Rodeo; Appalachian Spring; Dance Panels.

Chamber Music—Vitebsk, trio; Sextet; Violin Sonata; Concerto for Clarinet and Piano; Piano Quartet; Nonet, for strings; Emblems, for wind ensemble.

Choral Music—What Do We Plant?; Lark; In the Beginning; Canticle of Freedom.

Operas—The Second Hurricane (children's opera); The Tender Land.

Orchestral Music—3 symphonies; Music for the Theatre; Piano Concerto; Symphonic Ode (revised 1955); Short Symphony; El Salón México; An Outdoor Overture; Quiet City; Fanfare for the Common Man; Danzón Cubano; Lincoln Portrait; Letter from Home; Preamble for a Solemn Occasion (also for solo organ); Concerto for Clarinet and String Orchestra, with harp and piano; The Red Pony, suite; Orchestral Variations (adapted from Piano Variations); Connotations; Music for a Great City; Inscape.

Piano Music—Piano Variations; Two Children's Pieces; Fantasía Mexicana; Sonata; Four Piano Blues; Piano Fantasy.

Vocal Music—Twelve Poems of Emily Dickinson; Old American Songs, two sets; Dirge in the Woods.

ABOUT

Berger, A., Aaron Copland; Copland, A., The New Music: 1900–1960; Dobrin, A., Aaron Copland: His Life and Times; Downes, O., Olin Downes on Music; Mellers, W., Music in a New Found Land; Smith, J., Aaron Copland.

Chesterian (London), Spring 1958; Esquire, April 1948; Musical America, November 1960; New York Times Magazine, November 13, 1960; Theatre Arts, January 1951; Time, November 20, 1950; Tomorrow, November 1947.

Henry Cowell
1897–1965

Henry Dixon Cowell was born on March 11, 1897, in Menlo Park, California. His father was Irish, the son of the Dean of Kildare; his mother came from an Anglo-Irish farm family in the Middle West. Both parents espoused an educational philosophy of complete intellectual freedom which, coupled with the fact that Cowell was frail and did not go beyond the third grade in school, resulted in an informal education for the boy. He was taught privately, mostly by his mother. He did, however, receive formal violin lessons from his fifth year on, and at seven he performed sonatas by Mozart and Beethoven in recital. At eight, illness obliged him to give up the violin. Since by that time he had decided to become a composer, he gave his instrument away. A piano was not available to him and he had to devise ways of doing his composing mentally. "While my friends were practicing the piano for an hour a day," he recalls, "I'd sit in my room and practice composing by listening to all kinds of sounds that came into my head." He was particularly sensitive to the unusual sounds he heard all around him and tried to concoct methods by which these sounds could be translated into music: the noises of wind and sea; the quality of unusual speech inflections; the singing games of Oriental children.

At eleven, he undertook the writing of an opera based on Longfellow's *Golden Legend*. He never finished it, but one of its melodies was later used for a piano piece, *Antinomy*. From the time he was twelve until his eighteenth year, when his mother died, he earned a living chiefly by raising and selling rare wild plants. By the age of fourteen he had saved enough

---

Cowell: kou′ ĕl

money to buy an old piano. This acquisition encouraged him to experiment at the keyboard, and he eventually discovered tone clusters (chords built on seconds instead of thirds or fourths) and other original tonal effects. Cowell used tone clusters for the first time in a piece entitled *Adventures in Harmony*. Then, invited to write music for a pageant based on Irish legends, he decided that tone clusters would be most effective in describing the sea-god Manaunaun. He played *The Tides of Manaunaun*, as well as *Adventures in Harmony* and several other pieces, at his first public appearance as composer-pianist, at the San Francisco Musical Club on March 11, 1912. *The Tides of Manaunaun* has survived and is one of his most popular piano compositions.

HENRY COWELL

Cowell's name first became known through his tone-cluster compositions. (Many years later he preferred using the term "secundal harmonies" rather than "tone clusters.") He was not the inventor of this technique–among others Vladimir Rebikoff and Charles Ives had previously used groupings of simultaneous seconds–but he discovered the technique independently, without the knowledge that they had done so. In 1913 and 1914 he produced a number of tone-cluster compositions, including *Dynamic Motion*, *Advertisement*, *Amiable Conversation*, and *Antinomy*.

Another method he used to extract unusual sounds from the piano was to adapt conventional violin techniques to the piano strings – harmonics, muted tones, pizzicati. He would play *inside* the piano, that is he would bend over the strings of the piano soundboard and produce all kinds of new sonorities and sounds by manipulating them manually, plucking at them, and at times inserting objects between the strings. *Aeolian Harp* and *The Banshee* are two of several Cowell pieces which use these new effects.

When he was seventeen, Cowell was sent by friends to the University of California to study with Charles Seeger, then head of the music department. At that early age Cowell already had more than a hundred compositions to his credit, but he seemed to Seeger a "very disheveled farm boy." Cowell proceeded to bewilder Seeger by performing pieces on the piano by banging fists and elbows on the key-board. Though Cowell could not matriculate, since he had no formal education beyond third-year elementary school, Seeger was sufficiently impressed to arrange for the boy to be given special status so that he could study theory with E. G. Strickland and composition with Wallace Sabin. In addition Seeger had Cowell visit him once a week for an exchange of musical ideas.

In 1913, under Seeger's influence, Cowell produced a large amount of music in which he experimented with polytonality, atonality, dissonant counterpoint, discordant harmonies, and other idioms. He had no idea that there were composers elsewhere in the world developing the same techniques until Seeger brought him Schoenberg's Opus 11 with the remark: "You might like to see how someone else has handled similar problems."

Cowell continued his music study at the University for three and a half years. He was then made an assistant in the music depart-ment. When the United States entered World War I, Cowell enlisted. He spent the war period conducting a band in Allentown, Pennsylvania. During this period he frequently startled his audiences by having his band play pieces built from tone clusters. When the war ended, Cowell spent two years studying at the Institute of Applied Music in New York.

In the years 1923–1933, Cowell made five European tours and an annual tour of the United States, featuring programs of his own works using avant-garde methods and tech-niques. Paul Rosenfeld, critic and propa-gandist for new music, described his first experience with a Henry Cowell concert thus: "At last the inventor appeared on the platform, a little man with a small, bright, egg-shaped head. Waddling with terrific velocity towards the grand piano at the center of the stage, he promptly sat down at it and applied his entire forearm to the ivories of the dignified instru-ment. A roar arose from the piano, followed by one from the audience, which in turn was followed by still further roars from the piano as the composer again and again struck and released masses of keys now with an arm and now with a fist." Rosenfeld ended by calling these new Cowell effects "stunning."

At his first European concert, in Leipzig in 1923, the police were called to quell the fighting which had broken out in the aisles between the "pros" and the "cons." As the melee subsided, Cowell was discovered at the piano; he had stubbornly continued his per-formance. When he first appeared in Eng-land, a famous review consisted largely of compliments to the makers of the piano which had withstood the onslaught of a composer of tone clusters. A New York editor sent his sports writer to cover the "bout" between "Battling Cowell" and "Kid Knabe" at Carnegie Hall.

By 1926 the astonishment at his unconven-tional piano technique had subsided and the leading liberal critics of Europe and America began to write of Cowell's music with under-standing and admiration, crediting him with seriousness of purpose and integrity, and applauding his gifts. Lawrence Gilman, W. J. Henderson, Percy Scholes, Henri Prunières, Erwin Felber, Adolph Weissman, and Julius Korngold, among others, wrote vigorous appreciations of the strength and significance of Cowell's music and the importance of the new methods he was employing. By 1940 more than two hundred and fifty pianists had publicly performed Cowell's music in America and Europe.

His first Berlin appearance was arranged by the pianist Artur Schnabel, who was suffi-ciently interested in the new technique to learn some of Cowell's pieces himself. Béla Bartók arranged one of Cowell's first Paris performances. Arnold Schoenberg invited Cowell to play his music for Schoenberg's composition class. Cowell also played before

President Tomáš Masaryk and about two hundred members of the Czech Parliament in Prague in 1926.

An interesting feature of a 1928 tour was an official invitation to visit Russia. Cowell was the second American musician to appear in that country following the Revolution; the first was Roland Hayes, the singer. Nikolai Miaskovsky was a member of the Russian State Editions' editorial committee, which sponsored the publication of two Cowell pieces, *Tiger* and *Lilt of Reel*, the first music by an American to be published in the Soviet Union.

Cowell's tone-cluster, or secundal harmony, methods were used successfully not only in piano music but in orchestral music as well. As early as 1915 he wrote highly dissonant pieces for large orchestra, in which massive tone clusters moved polyphonically against each other. Similarly, tone clusters were used in the Sinfonietta for small orchestra, written during the years 1924-1928 and introduced by the Boston Chamber Orchestra under Nicolas Slonimsky on November 23, 1931; in *Synchrony*, for large orchestra, which Slonimsky conducted with the Straram Orchestra in Paris on June 6, 1931, and which the Philadelphia Orchestra under Stokowski introduced in the United States on April 1, 1932. Perhaps the fullest orchestral use of secundal harmonies during this period is found in the Piano Concerto which the composer himself introduced in Havana, on December 28, 1929, with Pedro Sanjuan conducting the Havana Philharmonic.

In 1931 Cowell felt that new directions in musical composition indicated the need for enabling composers to become familiar with complex counter-rhythms. He therefore invented the Rhythmicon, an electric device, which was built by Leon Theremin in accordance with Cowell's suggestions. His interest in the science of sound resulted in the publication in 1919 of a book, *New Musical Resources*, the first American book on contemporary musical theory.

Cowell was always an indefatigable promoter of the music of other living composers; all his organizational activities were directed toward obtaining hearings for a wide range of contemporary works, both in Europe and in the Americas. In 1927 he founded New Music, a cooperative nonprofit organization which issued the only quarterly periodical devoted to the publication of the scores of experimental new music and recordings of the same or similar material. Virgil Thomson said of Cowell's contributions through the *New Music Quarterly:* "No other composer of his time has made, outside of the immediate domain of his own compositional production, so solid a gift to the history of his art as Cowell has done by printing and distributing music of quality that nobody else would print or distribute." In 1940 Cowell was appointed Consultant for the Music Division of the Pan American Union. He also directed the Editorial Project for Latin American Music, under the Pan American Union, in the course of which several thousand manuscripts were examined for recommendation to publishers in the United States. Later he was in charge of the Music Distribution Project, which established loan libraries of scores and records by North American composers in each of the twenty Latin American republics. He also promoted new music as a teacher and lecturer, at the New School for Social Research in New York beginning in 1932, and later at various colleges.

For two years (1943–1945) Cowell acted as consultant in music and chief music editor for the Office of War Information. Partly as a result of the intensive study of non-European folk and primitive music which he had made during the years 1930–1932 under a Guggenheim Fellowship, Cowell was consulted on all music used by the OWI in its broadcasts to both enemy and friendly countries.

Early in 1941 Cowell became interested in a collection of American hymns by old singing-school masters, *Southern Harmony*, edited by William Walker. He had known some of these hymns as a boy. Many were completely unfamiliar to him. They so fascinated him that he began to think of carrying over their style into serious instrumental music. With this in mind he wrote a series of Hymns and Fuguing Tunes for orchestra, which in their general texture were quite new to modern music. This is very plain music, depending for its effect upon its sustained contrapuntal eloquence rather than upon novelty in instrumentation or any current sophisticated and ejaculatory manner. It is an intense and exalted music, of classic simplicity and purity. Cowell's first success in this manner came with his *Hymn and Fuguing Tune No. 2*

(1944), introduced over the radio by the NBC Symphony under Henri Nosco in March 1944; its first public performance was given by the Boston Symphony under Koussevitzky on March 8, 1946. During the next twenty years Cowell produced sixteen hymns and fuguing tunes for various instrumental and vocal combinations. He also incorporated the form into several of his symphonies, notably in Nos. 4, 5, 6, 7, 10, 12, and 15; and into some of his chamber music compositions, such as the String Quartets Nos. 4 and 5, a Sonata for Violin and Piano, and *Set of Five*, for violin, piano, and percussion.

There are two other influences evident in Cowell's music, in addition to secundal harmonies and American rural hymnology. One has been his Celtic ancestry, whose effect is found in such early piano pieces as *Jig*, *The Lilt of Reel*, *The Voice of Lir*, and *The Tides of Manaunaun*. His third symphony (1942) was called *Gaelic*. In later symphonies, such as the Sixth (1955) which the Houston Symphony under Stokowski introduced on November 14, 1955, the scherzo movement is often replaced by music in the style of an Irish jig.

A more recent, and perhaps more significant, development in Cowell's creative growth was his interest in, and adaptation of, the music of the Near, Middle, and Far East. This interest began in his childhood, when he heard a Chinese opera in San Francisco. At that time he lived near the Chinese section and had numerous opportunities to attend concerts of Chinese music, to hear the singing games of Oriental children, and to learn Chinese songs. His first piano piece, *Adventures in Harmony*, contained a section called "Oriental" in which he used the Oriental pentatonic scale. In his maturity Cowell made intensive studies of the theoretic bases of Indian, Chinese, Japanese, and Middle Eastern music. In 1956 and 1957 he heard the varied music of Asia, and particularly the music of the Middle East, on a trip enlarged at the request of the Rockefeller Foundation for a survey of the music of ten Asian countries. This survey was interrupted for three months by an assignment from the United States Department of State to fill a request from the government of Iran to have Cowell supervise the performance of Persian music over the new Teheran radio station. During this stay in the Middle East, Cowell spent ten days at the festival of Madras, India. In 1961 Cowell made another trip to the Near and Far East at the request of the State Department. He represented the United States at the International Music Conference in Teheran and at the East-West Music Encounter in Tokyo. From this trip Cowell brought back a musical instrument resembling a machine gun—actually a Malayan instrument producing tone clusters.

As a natural consequence of this long and intensive immersion in the music of the East, Cowell produced many major works in an Oriental style. Some were based entirely on Oriental musical materials, others utilized Oriental techniques and idioms in an Occidental manner. Among Cowell's Oriental works are the following: the *Persian* Set, for twelve instruments (1957), introduced by the Minneapolis Symphony under Antal Dorati in November 1957; *Ongaku*, two pieces inspired by two different periods of Japanese classical music, commissioned and introduced by the Louisville Orchestra in Kentucky under Robert Whitney on March 26, 1958; *Madras*, Cowell's thirteenth symphony, based on North and South Indian elements and employing Indian instruments, its première taking place in Madras on March 3, 1959; *Homage to Iran* (1959), for violin, piano and Persian drum; the Concerto for Koto and Orchestra (the koto is a native Japanese instrument, in design similar to the ancient European table-harp). The Koto concerto was heard for the first time on December 18, 1964, with Kimio Eto as soloist and Leopold Stokowski conducting the Philadelphia Orchestra.

Discussing his intense preoccupation with the music of the East, Cowell told an interviewer in 1955: "Every musical culture, no matter how strange it may sound to us, will yield its systematic organization to study and experience. Underneath the many strange and unexpected and variously appealing regional musical styles, one will always find a fundamental relationship with all the other music in the world. Differences in style, or regional character, are due to different historical emphasis and different combinations of the same basic elements of music. Of course no man can command all of the forms that man's musical imagination has provided. But a composer today, and especially in America, should be free to appropriate any that he desires. For myself I have always wanted to live in the whole world of music."

Two years later, in 1957, Cowell was quoted as saying: "I place no limitations of period or place on the musical materials I may wish to draw on, for the meaning of music does not depend upon the materials themselves. I believe a composer must forge his own forms out of the many influences that play upon him, and never close his ears to any part of the world of sound."

Discussing Cowell's over-all creative output, Virgil Thomson said: "Henry Cowell's music covers a wider range in both expression and technique than that of any other living composer. His experiments begun . . . decades ago in rhythm, in harmony, and in instrumental sonorities, were considered by many to be wild. Today they are the Bible of the young and still, to the conservatives, 'advanced.' His vast repertory, on the other hand, of choral music for school use and of band music is a model of technical and expressive accessibility. Between these extremes lie . . . [his] symphonies and many other works at once humane of content and original in style. No other composer of our time has produced a body of work so radical and so normal, so penetrating and so comprehensive."

The fiftieth anniversary of Cowell's debut as a composer was commemorated in 1962 with Cowell concerts in New York and elsewhere in the United States; with congratulatory messages from President John F. Kennedy and Governor Nelson A. Rockefeller of New York, among others; with a retrospective exhibit of manuscripts, photos, and memorabilia at the New York Public Library; and with the presentation to Cowell of the Henry Hadley Medal for services to American music by the Society of American Composers and Conductors.

Cowell received two honorary doctorates in music: one from Wilmington College in 1954, the other from Monmouth in 1963. In 1951 he was made a member of the National Institute of Arts and Letters, which in 1961 elected him vice president. Then early in 1963 he received the Lancaster Award for his *Lancaster Overture*, the première of which had taken place on February 5 of that year in Lancaster, Pennsylvania.

With his wife, the former Sidney Hawkins Robertson, whom he had married on September 27, 1941, Cowell shared two homes: an apartment in New York City and a country home in Shady, in the Catskill Mountains of New York. From 1949 to 1965 Cowell was adjunct professor of music at Columbia University. After retiring from Columbia, he spent the last year of his life in Shady. He was working on his twentieth symphony at the time of his death, on December 11, 1965. His nineteenth had been introduced on October 18, 1965, by the Nashville (Tennessee) Symphony. Cowell's last appearance in public took place in New York City on September 22, 1965, at a performance of his choral work *Ultima Actio*, at the Lincoln Center for the Performing Arts.

In collaboration with his wife, Henry Cowell wrote the biography *Charles Ives and His Music* (1954).

MAJOR WORKS

Ballets—The Building of Banba; Atlantis.

Chamber Music—6 string quartets; Romantic Quartet; Quartet Euphometric; Suite, for woodwind quintet; Toccata, for flute, soprano, cello and piano; Hymn and Fuguing Tune No. 7, for viola and piano; Hymn, Chorale and Fuguing Tune No. 8, for string quartet; Hymn and Fuguing Tune No. 9, for cello and piano; Hymn and Fuguing Tune No. 2, for three horns; Violin Sonata; Set of Five, for violin, piano and percussion; Hymn and Fuguing Tune No. 3, for trombone and piano; Septet; Persian Set, for twelve instruments; Prelude and Allegro, for violin and harpsichord; Seven Paragraphs, for string trio; Piano Trio.

Choral Music—Day, Evening, Night and Morning; Ballad of the Two Mothers; Lilting Fancy; If He Please; A Thanksgiving Psalm; The Road Leads Into Tomorrow; Edson Hymns and Fuguing Tunes; Ultima Actio.

Orchestral Music—19 symphonies; Vestiges; Sinfonietta, for small orchestra; Synchrony; Piano Concerto; Old American Country Set; Tales of Our Countryside; Hymn and Fuguing Tune No. 2, for string orchestra; Hymn and Fuguing Tune No. 3; Variations; Music for 1957; Ongaku; Antiphony, for divided orchestra; Concerto for Percussion and Orchestra; Concerto for Koto and Orchestra; Concerto Grosso, for five instruments and orchestra; Lancaster Overture; Hymn and Fuguing Tune No. 16.

Piano Music—Tides of Manaunaun; Dynamic Motion; Advertisement; Amiable Conversation; Antinomy; The Aeolian Harp; The Banshee; The Lilt of Reel; Maestoso; The Harp of Life; Sinister Resonance; Two Ritournelles; Two-Part Inventions; Hymn and Fuguing Piece.

Vocal Music—Rest; Sunset; Vocalise; Sonatina, for baritone, violin and piano; The Pasture; O, Let Me Breathe; Daybreak; The Little Black Boy; Spring Comes Singing; Sunset.

Creston

ABOUT

Chase, G., America's Music; Goss, M., Modern Music Makers; Rosenfeld, P., Discoveries of a Music Critic.

Etude, February 1957; Hi-Fi Systems, Spring 1959; Music Magazine, May 1962; Musical America, March 1962; Musical Quarterly, October 1959; Time, September 23, 1957.

Paul Creston
1906–

Paul Creston was born Joseph Guttoveggio in New York City on October 10, 1906. (He changed his name in 1927.) His father was a housepainter whose meager earnings were hardly enough to provide his family with basic necessities. Paul attended New York public schools, but after two and a half years of high school was forced to abandon his education for a job. It was at this time that he met Louise Gotto, a young dancer, who became his wife on July 1, 1927.

PAUL CRESTON

From childhood on, Creston has been passionately attached to music, which he learned through reading books and studying scores. From time to time, when he could manage the fee, he took piano lessons with a local teacher. Faced during his adolescence with the necessity of earning a living, Creston began to look for jobs in music. His first job, acquired when he was sixteen, was as organist in a motion picture theatre. He lost it when talking pictures became

popular. Then in 1934 he got a job he held for many years—church organist at St. Malachy's Church in New York.

In a communication to this editor he described his early music studies and interests as follows: "The first six years of piano instruction were definitely of mediocre quality. My very first piano teacher was one of those rare individuals who taught all instruments but played none, and my musical fare consisted mainly of operatic transcriptions and the Waldteufel waltzes. Actually, without being aware of it, I was teaching myself by reading many books on music fundamentals and piano playing. At the age of fourteen I began to mingle with other music students and soon realized that my parents were wasting money on a charlatan. I continued music study by myself (not having the financial means for lessons), conducting a thorough investigation of the principles of piano playing from the time of Kullak to Otto Ortmann.

"I began composing soon after the acquisition of my first piano, although I considered it more a pastime than a serious pursuit. This was at the age of eight. My real ambition at the time was to be a concert pianist. But just as I composed for pleasure, I also indulged in poetic creations, my first poem being written at the age of twelve. Consequently, there came a time in my life when I was undecided whether I should follow a musical or a literary career, especially since at the age of seventeen I had three articles published in the *Dance Magazine* besides a number of articles in *Etude*. When I was about twenty-two I reasoned thus: 'In the literary field I am competent in only two phases, poetry and essays. I have tried my hand at short stories and even a novel, and failed miserably. In music, I have a certain degree of facility no matter what the form I choose. Music must be my work.' From that time to 1932 (the date of my Opus 1) I wrote many pieces for piano, some music for the concert dance, experimental fragments, and such, all of which are now resting in oblivion. At the same time I began my unceasing study of harmony, counterpoint, and composition, from the works of the masters, past and present."

His first opus was a set of *Five Dances*, for solo piano (1932). His debut as a composer took place in June 1933 when his incidental music to a play, *Iron Flowers*, was heard in Westchester County, New York. Further encouragement came the same year when Henry Cowell invited him to play his *Seven Theses* for piano at one of the composers' forums at the New School for Social Research. In 1936 Creston's first string quartet was featured at the festival at Yaddo, in Saratoga Springs, New York.

Creston's career as a composer went into high gear in 1938 with two orchestral works: *Threnody*, introduced by the Pittsburgh Symphony under Fritz Reiner on December 2; and *Two Choric Dances*, in a chamber orchestral version heard at Yaddo and an extended version for full symphony orchestra, performed by the Cleveland Orchestra with Arthur Shepherd conducting.

The high point of his career at that time was the First Symphony, which had its première on February 22, 1941, in New York with Fritz Mahler conducting. A major performance followed on March 23, 1943, with Eugene Ormandy conducting the Philadelphia Orchestra in New York. The symphony received the New York Music Critics Circle Award for that year, and in 1952 won first prize in an international competition conducted in Paris. Olin Downes reported in the New York *Times* that this composition was characterized by "clear-cut, straightforward musical thinking . . . by balance of lyrical and contrapuntal elements . . . [and] by general skillfulness and sound worthiness of the instrumentation."

Creston's Second Symphony represented an important step forward for the composer. He explained that the work was conceived as "an apotheosis of the two foundations of all music: song and dance." He arranged the work in the form of an Introduction and Song, and Interlude and Dance. Heard first at a concert of the New York Philharmonic, on February 15, 1945, Artur Rodzinski conducting, the symphony received accolades from the critics who felt that it was skillful in technique, solid in structure, varied in color, romantic in spirit – the work of a sincere and finely equipped musician.

His Third Symphony was commissioned by the Worcester Music Festival where it was introduced on October 27, 1950, with Eugene Ormandy conducting the Philadelphia Orches-

tra. It is subtitled *Three Mysteries* and it draws a good deal of its atmosphere and exoticism from modal writing and its haunting, remote kind of lyricism from the Gregorian chant. This is music of deep religious conviction, its emotion generated by the composer's reaction to the three awesome religious events – Nativity, Crucifixion, and Resurrection.

The emphasis on song and dance – on lyricism and rhythm – returns in the Fourth Symphony, which Howard Mitchell introduced with the National Symphony Orchestra of Washington, D.C., on January 30, 1952. Song and dance are here emphasized most strongly in the second movement, which opens with a pastoral melody, continues with a gay shepherd's dance, and ends with a return of the pastoral tune. Whereas the Third Symphony had been religious, the Fourth was essentially bright, with a good deal of excitement generated in its more vigorous pages. This pitch of excitement is maintained consistently in the last movement.

The keynote of the Fifth Symphony, the composer says, is "intensity, and the feeling is generally one of spiritual conflicts which are not resolved until the final movement." The work was commissioned for the twenty-fifth anniversary of the National Symphony Orchestra, which introduced it under Howard Mitchell on April 4, 1956.

The number of important commissions that have come to Creston through the years attest to the position he has achieved in American music. Out of these commissions and invitations have come other major works besides his Third and Fifth symphonies. The Elizabeth Sprague Coolidge Foundation commissioned his Suite for Cello and Piano in 1956; the Cleveland Orchestra, the Toccata, for its fortieth anniversary (introduced in Cleveland under George Szell on October 17, 1957). The Association of Women's Committees for Symphony Orchestras asked him to write *Janus*, an orchestral work which once again makes use of song (or Prelude) and dance; *Janus* was performed by the Denver Symphony under Saul Caston on July 17, 1959. The Ford Foundation was responsible for the Second Violin Concerto (introduced by Michael Rabin and the Los Angeles Philharmonic under Georg Solti, in Los Angeles, on November 17, 1960). For the Jackson Symphony Orchestra in

Mississippi he wrote *From the Psalmist*, for contralto and orchestra, text taken from the Psalms; it was performed on April 28, 1968.

One of Creston's most significant works during the 1960's was the *Chthonic Ode*, which he wrote in 1966 "in homage to Henry Moore." (*Chthonic* is a term Sir Herbert Read used in referring to Moore's sculpture.) The première of this work took place on April 6, 1967, with Sixten Ehrling conducting the Detroit Symphony Orchestra. "In Henry Moore's sculpture," says the composer, "I see seven qualities which I have striven to incorporate in the music: Vitality, Restraint, Primitiveness, Humanism, Womanhood, Monumentality and Universality. These qualities determined the form of the piece: free sectional form in four distinct but connected sections."

In all of his music, Creston has what Virgil Thomson once described as "musical abundance." He writes fully and richly, and his works are replete with engaging thematic ideas and vitalized rhythmic patterns. His music makes for enjoyable listening since it sounds pleasant and is well constructed and organized. The alternation of lyricism and rhythmic vitality – song and dance – remains a basic feature. Some critics, however, have taken Creston's works to task for lack of contrast or climax; these critics claim that Creston's music is maintained on a single emotional level. But as Henry Cowell wrote in *Musical Quarterly:* "He has deliberately chosen a certain simplicity and delicacy of effect. He prefers sustained lines and it is for this reason that he has eschewed the startling and the violent in contrast, on which both the climactic emphasis and humor depend. Creston's is a temperament that lends itself more easily to warmth and gentility than to the hard surface of wit. . . . His attitude towards music has led him to throw himself into creative activity with every ounce of earnestness and intensity and serious determination of which he is capable."

Here is how Creston has summed up his attitude towards music in general and his creativity in particular: "I look upon music, and more especially the writing of it, as a spiritual practice. To me, musical composition is as vital to my spiritual welfare as prayer and good deeds; just as food and exercise are necessities of physical health, and thought and study are requisites of mental well-being. My philosophic approach to composition is abstract. I am preoccupied with matters of melodic design, harmonic coloring, rhythmic pulse, and formal progression; not with imitations of nature, or narrations of fairy tales, or propounding sociological ideologies. Not that the source of inspiration may not be a picture or a story. Only that regardless of the origin of the subject matter, regardless of the school of thought, a musical composition must bear judgment purely on musical criteria. Its intrinsic worth depends on the integration of musical elements toward a unified whole."

Creston lives with his wife in White Plains, New York. They have four sons. Creston used to be an ardent amateur photographer, but for the past decade or so his hobby has been languages. He has studied Italian, Spanish, French, German, Portuguese, Russian, and Turkish, and he is fluent in the first three.

Numerous honors have been bestowed on him. They include two Guggenheim Fellowships (1938 and 1939); the Citation of Merit from the National Association for American Composers and Conductors (1941 and 1943); the Music Award of the American Academy of Arts and Letters (1943); the Ditson Fund Award (1945); the Citation of Honor from the National Catholic Music Educators Association (1956); and the Christopher Award for his score for the television production *Revolt in Hungary* (1958). From 1956 to 1960 he was president of the National Association for American Composers and Conductors. In 1960 he received a grant from the United States Department of State for travel in Israel and Turkey. In 1961 he was made a member of the board of directors of ASCAP, and in 1962, a Fellow of the International Institute of Arts and Letters. He became a visiting professor of music at Central Washington State College in Ellensburg in the fall of 1967. A year later he was appointed professor of music and composer-in-residence.

MAJOR WORKS

Ballets — A Tale About the Land; Choreographic Suite.

Chamber Music — Three Poems from Walt Whitman, for cello and piano; Suite for Saxophone and Piano; String Quartet; Suite for Viola and Piano; Suite for Violin and Piano; Sonata for Saxophone and Piano; Homage, for viola and piano (also for cello and piano);

Suite for Flute, Viola, and Piano; Suite for Cello and Piano.

Choral Music—Three Chorales from Tagore; Missa pro Defunctis; Dirge; Psalm XXIII; Missa Solemnis; Two Motets; Black and Tan America; The Celestial Vision; Praise the Lord; Lilium Regis; Isaiah's Prophecy; None Lives Forever, for chorus and piano (or organ).

Orchestral Music—5 symphonies; 2 violin concertos; Two Choric Dances; Concertino for Marimba and Orchestra; Prelude and Dance; Saxophone Concerto; A Rumor; Pastorale and Tarantella; Dance Variations, for soprano and orchestra; Fantasy, for piano and orchestra; Chant of 1942; Frontiers; Poem, for harp and orchestra; Piano Concerto; Two-Piano Concerto; Walt Whitman; Dance Overture; Lydian Ode; Toccata; Pre-Classic Suite; Accordion Concerto; Janus; Corinthians XIII; Choreographic Suite; Pavane Variations; Concerto for Alto Saxophone and Orchestra; Chthonic Ode; From the Psalmist, for contralto and orchestra.

Organ Music—Suite; Fantasia; Rapsodia Breve, for organ pedals alone.

Piano Music—Sonata; Five Little Dances; Prelude and Dance, Nos. 1 and 2; Six Preludes; Three Narratives; Metamorphoses.

Vocal Music—Three Sonnets; Three Songs, for high voice and piano; Thirteen French-Canadian Folk Songs; Ave Maria; La Lettre; A Song of Joys; Nocturne, for soprano and eleven instruments.

ABOUT

Chase, G., America's Music; Goss, M., Modern Music Makers.

Musical America, October 1944; Musical Courier, November 15, 1956; Musical Quarterly, October 1948.

Luigi Dallapiccola
1904–

Luigi Dallapiccola was born on February 3, 1904, in Pisino, Istria, then under Austrian rule (later Italian, now Yugoslavian). His father, a professor of classical languages at the local Italian school, was an ardent lover of music who directed his son Luigi to piano study when the child was six. Luigi made remarkable progress and by 1914 was a highly competent performer. When World War I broke out, the Dallapiccolas (together with other Italians) were herded by the Austrian authorities into a detention camp. When the camp closed down, the Dallapiccolas were sent to Austria; they finally settled in Graz early in 1917. In Graz, Luigi continued his academic education at a high school for Italian students. He satisfied his enormous appetite for music by going to the opera, where

the works of Mozart and Wagner aroused his ambition to become a composer.

Toward the end of 1919 his family returned to Pisino, which had become Italian soil. His father became director of a local school. While attending the *liceo*, Luigi studied harmony and piano in nearby Trieste. In 1922 he enrolled in the Cherubini Conservatory in Florence where he continued his piano studies with Ernesto Consolo, receiving his degree in piano playing in 1924. He continued to attend the Conservatory as a student of composition with Vito Frazzi and received his degree in composition in 1931.

LUIGI DALLAPICCOLA

Meanwhile, in 1930, he joined a violinist, Sandro Materassi, in presenting concerts of modern music, an experience that increased and intensified the attraction new music was beginning to have for him. He soon became active as an Italian delegate of the International Society for Contemporary Music and began to adopt in his own works an independent style and unorthodox techniques. Such advanced tendencies in his harmonic, rhythmic, and contrapuntal procedures were first realized meaningfully in a four-movement Partita for orchestra, written in the years 1930–1932. Its première took place in Florence on January 22, 1933; on April 2, 1934, it represented Italy at the festival of the International Society for Contemporary Music in Florence.

Dallapiccola: däl lä pēk′ kō lä

Dallapiccola

Dallapiccola continued to pursue advanced techniques, but still within a tonal framework, in the first set of *Cori di Michelangelo* (1933), in which his writing combined modern idioms with the madrigal-like nature of Renaissance music. Two more sets of choruses to Michelangelo's verses were written in the years 1934–1936. *Divertimento in Quattro Esercizi* (1934), four studies for soprano, flute, oboe, clarinet, viola, and cello, provided a musical interpretation of the four emotions of melancholy, gaiety, joy, and despair. A performance at the festival of the International Society for Contemporary Music in Prague on September 2, 1935, proved an outstanding success. *Tre Laudi*, for soprano and chamber orchestra (1936–1937), demonstrated an increasing skill in writing for the voice along modern lines while retaining Italian ardor and intensity; it was heard at the Venice Festival in 1937.

On April 30, 1938, Dallapiccola, a Roman Catholic, married Laura Coen Luzzato, a Jewish girl. The following September Mussolini embarked on an official anti-Semitic policy. Laura Dallapiccola was dismissed from her post at the National Library in Florence. This act of injustice and persecution stirred Dallapiccola profoundly. "As a man I had to choose either atheism or religion," Dallapiccola told an interviewer many years later. "I chose religion."

A deep religious feeling is found in Dallapiccola's first opera, whose subject touches upon the injustice of fate and the struggle of man against overpowering forces. The opera was *Volo di Notte* (*Night Flight*), libretto by the composer based on Antoine de Saint-Exupéry's famous novel *Vol de Nuit*. Dallapiccola finished this one-act opera in 1939, and its première performance was given in Florence on May 18, 1940.

The problems of persecution and freedom continued to dominate Dallapiccola's creativity. In 1941 he completed the *Canti di Prigionia* (*Songs from Captivity*), a set of choruses with percussion based on prayers of Mary Queen of Scots, Savonarola, and Boethius. The world première took place in Rome on December 11, 1941, the same day that Mussolini announced his declaration of war against the United States. Among the composer's most deeply moving works, these choral songs received a highly successful revival at the festival of the International Society for Contemporary Music in London on July 8, 1946.

The Dallapiccolas remained in Florence until the Nazis entered the city on September 11, 1943. They fled to nearby Fiesole where Dallapiccola completed a cycle of songs on ancient Greek poems, *Sex Carmina Alcaei*. The importance of this work lies in the fact that it was the first by Dallapiccola (in fact the first by any major Italian composer) to be based entirely on the twelve-tone row, a system in which he was to produce some of his major works.

Dallapiccola had first become acquainted with the twelve-tone system in 1924 at a performance in Florence of Schoenberg's *Pierrot Lunaire*, conducted by the composer. "The concert was a scandal of major proportions," Dallapiccola recalls. "Two persons in the audience applauded—myself and Puccini." Dallapiccola remained interested in dodecaphony, even made tentative experiments with that technique in the last movement of his *Divertimento in Quattro Esercizi*, and then used it for certain parts of his *Canti di Prigionia*. But the *Sex Carmina Alcaei* was his first twelve-tone composition. Here, as later, he used the system in a free and highly personal manner. "The twelve-tone method," he has said, "must not be so tyrannical as to exclude *a priori* both expression and humanity."

During the difficult years that the Nazis were occupying Florence—a period in which the Dallapiccolas often had to go into hiding to evade arrest—Dallapiccola worked on a one-act opera whose theme, that of tyranny, persecution, the loss of freedom, was very close to his heart. It was *Il Prigioniero* (*The Prisoner*), libretto by the composer based on a short story by Villiers de l'Isle-Adam and a scene from Charles de Coster's *La Légende d'Ulenspiegel*. The action concerned the imprisonment of a Flemish citizen during the Flemish struggle for liberation from the Spaniards in the period of the Inquisition. In prison he is fired with the hope that the freedom of Flanders is at hand. But upon escaping from prison he discovers he has been deluded. His mind gives way. As he is being dragged off to the stake he mutters the single word *freedom*.

Dallapiccola started to work on his opera on the day in 1938 when his wife lost her position with the National Library. But not until a decade later, on May 3, 1948, was the opera completed. It was performed for the first time anywhere over the Turin radio on November 30, 1949. The first staged presentation took place at the Teatro Communale in Florence on May 20, 1950, during the May Festival; the première in the United States followed on March 15, 1951, in New York. Dallapiccola's score is entirely based on a twelve-tone row. "There are moments," wrote Howard Taubman in his review in the New York *Times*, "when this music rises to heights of tension. For the most part, it is somber, slow-moving, like something through a veil. Dallapiccola reserves his most eloquent writing for the orchestra. He is a master of vivid and moving tonal combinations. And when he combines his orchestra and chorus towards the end, he achieves a shattering effect. . . . In sum, this is a composer and a work of individuality."

How deeply the cause of freedom concerned Dallapiccola became evident in 1944 with the birth of his daughter, who was named Annalibera, because the city of Florence had then been liberated. This concern for liberty and the dignity of man in a free society was reflected in a number of works in addition to *Il Prigioniero*: for example, in the *Ciaconna, Intermezzo and Adagio* for unaccompanied cello, written in 1945 just as the war in Europe had come to a close. The bitter accents of its first movement betray the extent of Dallapiccola's sufferings during the war years, while the closing movement is a gentle prayer of gratitude for the coming of peace. Freedom is also the subject of the *Canti di Liberazione* (*Songs of Liberation*) for chorus and orchestra (1952–1955), based partly on St. Augustine's *Confessions* and partly on a text from Sebastianus Castellio; the première took place in Cologne on June 16, 1960.

In the 1950's, Dallapiccola's adherence to the twelve-tone technique was stricter and purer than it had been up to this point; nevertheless, the Romantic attitudes of his earlier compositions are still prevalent, for he manages to derive from other styles and methods those elements that best serve his artistic needs. As a critic of the New York *Herald Tribune* remarked: "Caring nothing for labels and trends, he takes freely from atonalism for its continuity devices, from impressionism for atmospheric collages, from tonality and consonance for their capacity to chart areas of arrival and departure and to reconcile all tensions and dissonance in repose."

Among Dallapiccola's major works in the 1950's were a sacred drama or oratorio, *Job*, inspired by Jacob Epstein's sculpture *Behold the Man* and first performed in Rome on October 31, 1950; *Tartiniana*, for violin and orchestra, based on melodies from Tartini's sonatas, which the Koussevitzky Music Foundation had commissioned and which was introduced in Berne on March 4, 1952; the *Variations for Orchestra* which the Louisville Orchestra in Kentucky had commissioned and which it introduced on October 3, 1954; the cantata *An Mathilde*, for female voice and orchestra, based on a text by Heine, presented in Donaueschingen, Germany, on October 16, 1955.

Since 1934 Dallapiccola has been professor of the piano at the Cherubini Conservatory in Florence. During the summer of 1951 he paid his first visit to the United States to serve as a visiting professor of composition (the first time he taught composition) at the Berkshire Music Center at Tanglewood. He returned to the Berkshire Music Center during the summer of 1952. On August 16, 1952, he made his American debut as pianist when he appeared as a soloist with the NBC Symphony over the NBC radio network in the American première of *Piccolo Concerto*, for piano and chamber orchestra. Later the same year, on September 22, the first all-Dallapiccola program to be presented anywhere was given in Mexico City, presenting six works from different periods in the composer's career. Similar programs tracing Dallapiccola's creative development were given later in New York, on December 13, 1959, and on November 5, 1964.

In the academic year 1956–1957, and again in the year 1959–1960, Dallapiccola served as professor of music at Queens College in New York. In the 1962–1963 session he occupied the Chair of Italian Culture at the University of California in Berkeley, where he taught composition, delivered lectures, and arranged concerts of his music. While on the campus at Berkeley, Dallapiccola was commissioned by the Committee for Arts and Letters to write *Preghiere* (*Prayers*), three songs for bass baritone and chamber orchestra, based on poems

151

by Murilo Mendes; they were heard at Berkeley on November 10, 1962. *Parole di San Paolo* (for two flutes, two clarinets, bass clarinet, cello, violin, and vibraphone), based on an epistle of St. Paul, received its world première at the Elizabeth Sprague Coolidge Festival of chamber music in Washington, D.C., on October 30, 1964. His first full-length opera, *Odysseus*, was completed in 1968. The world première was given in West Berlin's Opera House, September 29, 1968.

Though Dallapiccola likes to describe himself as "a man of the middle ages," he looks in person the way he writes his music—like a child of the twentieth century. As Edward Downes described him in 1956: "He wore a dark business suit of some elegance and unmistakable twentieth-century cut. The very expression of his face, the questioning, skeptical eyes in features of urbane affability and assurance, the shock of white in his dark hair, all somehow reinforced a distinctly modern impression." He enjoys the theatre intensely; his only form of exercise is walking. His principal hobby is the keeping of a diary, which at this writing numbers almost fifty volumes.

Dallapiccola has received numerous awards through the years from different countries. These include the Carillon at the International Competition in Geneva, Switzerland, in 1935; the Grosser Musikpreis from the German city of Düsseldorf, in 1962; and the Ludwig Spohr Preis in Braunschweig, Germany, in 1964. He is also a member of various cultural and educational academies in Rome, Munich, Berlin, Stockholm, New York, and Buenos Aires.

MAJOR WORKS

Ballet—Marsia.

Chamber Music—Due Studi, for violin and piano; Ciaconna, Intermezzo e Adagio, for solo cello.

Choral Music—La Canzone del Quarnaro; Estate; Cori di Michelangelo, three sets; Canti di Prigionia; Job, sacred drama for narrator, solo voices, chorus, and orchestra; Canti di Liberazione (Songs of Liberation); Requiescant.

Operas—Volo di Notte (one-act); Il Prigioniero (one-act); Odysseus.

Orchestral Music—Partita; Tre Laudi, for soprano and chamber orchestra; Piccolo Concerto, for piano and orchestra; Liriche Greche, for soprano and instruments; Due Pezzi (Two Pieces); Variazioni (Variations); Tartiniana, for violin and orchestra (on themes by Tartini); Piccolo Musica Notturna; An Mathilde, cantata for soprano and chamber orchestra; Cinque Frammenti di Saffo, for soprano and chamber orchestra; Tartiniana Seconda, for violin and orchestra (on themes by Tartini); Concerto per la Notte di Natale dell'Anno 1956 (Christmas Cantata), for soprano and chamber orchestra; Dialoghi, for cello and orchestra; Preghiere (Prayers), for bass baritone and chamber orchestra; Three Questions With Two Answers; Words of St. Paul, for voice and orchestra; Piccola Musica Notturna.

Piano Music—Musica per Tre Pianoforti; Sonata Canonica (on Paganini's Caprices); Quaderno Musicale di Annalibera.

Vocal Music—Divertimento in Quattro Esercizi, for soprano and instruments; Quattro Liriche, three sets; Due Liriche di Anacreonte, for soprano and four instruments; Goethe Lieder, for mezzo soprano and three clarinets; Sex Carmina Alcaei, three cycles; Cinque Canti, for baritone and eight instruments; Parole di San Paolo, for voice and instruments.

ABOUT

Vlad, R., Luigi Dallapiccola.

Musical Quarterly, July 1953, July 1958; Score (London), March 15, 1956.

Claude Debussy
1862–1918

Achille-Claude Debussy was born on August 22, 1862, in Saint-Germain-en-Laye, on the outskirts of Paris. He was the oldest of five children. His father owned a modest china shop which barely provided a living for his family. When a second child was born two years after Claude, the business went into bankruptcy. The impoverished family moved to Paris and settled in the Rue Pigalle, where three more children were born. Poverty compelled the parents to turn over four of their five children to an aunt for upbringing. Claude, however, was brought up by an oversolicitous mother who taught him herself and kept him away from other children. Claude became (as his sister later revealed) "uncommunicative . . . liking neither his lessons nor games. . . . He would spend whole days sitting on a chair, thinking, no one knew what." His main childhood interest seemed to be the collecting of butterflies.

When he was seven, an aunt arranged for Debussy to take piano lessons. His first teacher was an Italian named Cerutti, but he soon was studying with Mme. Mauté de Fleurville, a former pupil of Chopin and a friend of Wagner. When she first heard Debussy play the piano she remarked firmly:

Debussy: dě bü sē′

152

"He *must* become a musician." She gave him his first formal and intensive training at the piano as preparation for the Paris Conservatory, which he entered in October 1873, when he was eleven.

Debussy stayed at the Conservatory eleven years. He was a shy boy, awkward in manner, unsociable, and uneducated, and his teachers and fellow students did not take easily to him. In addition, from the beginning he proved to be an undisciplined rebel in music, searching for new harmonies and unusual tonalities. He constantly amazed pupils and teachers alike by his improvisations which

CLAUDE DEBUSSY

exploited strange progressions and tonal relationships, and contrapuntal lines moving in defiance of textbook specifications. "He astonished us all with his bizarre playing," recalled Gabriel Pierné, Debussy's classmate. "It was all so utterly unorthodox!" exclaimed Debussy's harmony teacher, Durand, on listening to the boy's strange music. Another classmate, M. Emmanuel, later recalled: "One winter evening . . . Debussy went to the piano to imitate the sound of buses going down the street. He played a sort of chromatic groaning, to which his friends . . . listened mockingly. 'Look at them,' Debussy said, turning around. 'Can't you listen to chords without knowing their names?' . . . At the piano we heard groups of consecutive fifths and octaves; sevenths which instead of being resolved in the proper way actually led to the note above

or weren't resolved at all; shameful 'false relations'; chords of the ninth on all degrees of the scale; chords of the elevenths and thirteenths; all the notes of the diatonic scale heard at once in fantastic arrangements. . . . And all this Claude called 'a feast for the ear.' Delibes' class shook with amazement and fear."

Eventually even the diehard academicians had to concede that he had extraordinary talent. Durand gave the boy a prize in harmony before passing him on to Guiraud's class in composition. Marmontel did not hesitate to recommend Debussy for a desirable summer post as house pianist to Mme. von Meck, the patroness who had been Tchaikovsky's friend and benefactor. During the summer of 1880 Debussy traveled with Mme. von Meck and her family to Italy and Austria, and the following two summers he lived at her estate in Russia both as house pianist and as teacher to the children.

Debussy's first compositions were songs, settings of poems by Théodore de Banville, written in 1876 while he was still at the Conservatory. His first impressive compositions were written in the years between 1880 and 1884, after he had become acquainted with the poetry of Paul Verlaine. These efforts consisted of songs to Verlaine's texts (*Mandoline* and *Pantomime*) and were inspired by Debussy's first all-consuming love affair, an affair with a singer named Mme. Vasnier, several years older and married. In dedicating the songs to his beloved, Debussy wrote: "To Mme. Vasnier. These songs which she alone has made live and which will lose their enchanting grace if they are never again to come from her singing lips. The eternally grateful author."

In 1883 Debussy made a bid for the Prix de Rome and got second prize, a fact that caused him considerable disappointment. Nevertheless in 1884 he made a second try and emerged the winner with the lyric scene *L'Enfant Prodigue*. Charles Gounod, one of the judges, described this composition as a work of genius.

Debussy left for Rome on January 27, 1885, to begin a three-year residence at the Villa Medici authorized by the Prix de Rome. He was not happy there. For one thing he was pining for his beloved Mme. Vasnier. For another, he detested everything Italian—the climate, the food, the people, even the music.

Debussy

Finally, he continually chafed under the many restrictions imposed upon him by the academicians of the Conservatory to whom he was required to send back musical works (*envois*). *Printemps*, inspired by Botticelli's *Primavera*, which Debussy sent to Paris in 1887, was severely criticized for its daring harmonic innovations. For the first time the term *impressionism* was used to describe Debussy's music, a term intended as the height of opprobium. "He is an enigma," was Massenet's evaluation of the young composer.

Debussy had had enough of Rome and the Villa Medici. Without waiting for the end of the three-year period he made a precipitate return to Paris in the spring of 1887. There he despatched his last envoi, a composition begun in Rome under the spell of the poems of Dante Gabriel Rossetti, the pre-Raphaelite. Debussy's composition was *La Damoiselle Élue* (*The Blessed Damozel*), a cantata for female solo voices, female chorus, and orchestra based on Rossetti's poem of the same name as translated into French by Sarrazin. The judges found in Debussy's music many things to praise, although they were still disturbed by his fluctuating rhythms and shifting tonalities. The music, they maintained, "still bears the marks of that systematic tendency towards vagueness of expression and form." Because of these defects the judges did not allow the work to be performed. It was not heard until April 8, 1893, at a concert of the Société Nationale de Musique in Paris. A later generation placed it high among Debussy's earlier works, emphasizing that it was here that he gave the first unmistakable indication of coming creative powers. "It exhales," says Léon Vallas, "a curious, delightfully fragrant perfume. . . . There are some attractive and novel effects in the treatment of the female voices, and the instrumentation is light and delicate, though varied throughout."

Debussy set up home in the rue de Londres in Paris with the second of the women who played a vital role in his emotional life—Gabrielle Dupont, whom he playfully dubbed "Gaby of the green eyes." For a decade she was his helpmate and companion; she managed his household; she tended to his every need; and she encouraged him in his creativity.

Debussy was now subjected to several important cultural influences that affected the course he would soon take as a composer. One of these was his personal contacts with the Symbolist poets (Mallarmé, Baudelaire, Verlaine) and the Impressionist painters (Renoir, Manet, Monet, Cézanne, Degas). Through his conversations with these poets and artists, Debussy arrived at musical impressionism—which adapted some of the principles, concepts and aims of these two movements. Debussy now felt that what was all-important in a musical composition was not so much the subject that was being discussed as the impressions the subject aroused in him; that it was not the basic content of a musical work that should command the consideration of the composer, but rather the subtlety of effect, color, nuance, and atmosphere of musical writing. Another influence upon Debussy at this time was that of Erik Satie, the eccentric and iconoclastic French musician whom Debussy met for the first time in 1891 at the café Auberge du Clou. Satie was repelled by the Gargantuan forms and emotional excesses of German Romantic music as well as the ivory-tower attitudes of Romantic composers. He sought a French art that had subtlety of suggestion and understatement, wit and irony and whimsy, all within miniature forms. Satie's fresh approaches, in which old traditions were broken down, made a profound impression on Debussy, just as did Satie's innovations in harmony, changing meters, and barless notation.

In searching for the most subtle effects and the most delicate nuances and atmospheres possible, Debussy rapidly developed a language of his own: unresolved discords; free tonality; exotic melodies derived from old modes, the pentatonic scale, and—most important of all—the whole-tone scale; a rhythmic pulse in which the beat was hidden and the tyranny of the bar line occasionally removed; structures in which an uninterrupted flow was achieved through the breakdown of recognizable landmarks and resting points. Through these and similar means Debussy became music's first great painter—the first to bring to music textures, sensations, images, and sounds it had hitherto not known. He became, as Oscar Thompson once put it, a poet of "mists and fountains, of clouds and rain, of dusk, and of glints of sunlight through leaves."

His first successful attempts to emerge as the

sensitive voice of delicate moods and mysterious landscapes came in the exquisite orchestral prelude to *La Damoiselle Élue* (1888) and the song "Il Pleure dans Mon Cœur," a poem by Verlaine (1888). The first bold harmonic adventure in piano writing was found in *Rêverie* (1890), which more than a half century later became a popular song hit in the United States ("My Revery"). Then came his first masterworks, and with them the first full realization of impressionism. In 1893 he completed the String Quartet in G minor, op. 10, which was introduced by the Ysaÿe Quartet on December 29, 1893, at a concert of the Société Nationale. Most of the critics failed to appreciate that they were experiencing the discovery of a brave new world of sound. But there were some who sensed in this music the presence of genius. Paul Dukas wrote: "Debussy is one of the most gifted and original artists of the younger generation of musicians ... a lyricist in the full sense of the term."

The Quartet was immediately followed by Debussy's first masterwork for orchestra, the *Prélude à l'Après-Midi d'un Faune* (*Prelude to the Afternoon of a Faun*), inspired by the Symbolist poem of the same name by Mallarmé. Here, with the opening measures for solo flute, Debussy magically evoked the gossamer, misty, semi-dream world of a faun, as he is trying to recall past visions and sensations before succumbing once again to sleep and dreams. Introduced on December 22, 1894, at a concert of the Société Nationale, the *Faun* met a lukewarm critical reception. When the work was repeated at a Colonne Concert, Isidor Philipp said in *Le Ménestrel:* "[It] ... is finely and delicately orchestrated; but one seeks in vain any heart or strength. It is precious, subtle, and indefinite in the same way as a work of M. Mallarmé."

The orchestral prelude was followed by an even more ambitious symphonic composition, the *Three Nocturnes*, for orchestra, whose sections are entitled *Nuages* (*Clouds*), *Fêtes* (*Festivals*), and *Sirènes* (*Sirens*). The work as a whole was completed in 1899, and two of the parts were heard at a Lamoureux Concert on December 9, 1900; on October 27, 1901, the entire suite was given. The *Nocturnes* bewildered some of the listeners; but on the whole the work was a success, Debussy's first.

Gaston Carraud called the composer "one of the most original artists of the day"; Pierre de Bréville, while finding that the music "defied analysis," confessed that it was "enchanting."

In 1899 Debussy deserted "Gaby of the green eyes" to marry Rosalie Texier on October 19. She was a dressmaker, unsophisticated and unmusical. But, as Debussy described her, she was "unbelievably fair and pretty." That Debussy loved his "Lily-Lilo" (as he nicknamed her) was proved by the inscription he placed on the manuscript of his *Nocturnes:* "This manuscript belongs to my little Lily-Lilo. All rights reserved. It is proof of the deep and passionate joy I have in being her husband." They made their home in a modest apartment on rue Cardinet—the place where Debussy put the finishing touches on what is generally conceded to be his masterwork, the opera *Pelléas et Mélisande.*

Debussy completed *Pelléas et Mélisande* in 1902. It was introduced by the Opéra-Comique on April 30 of the same year. Scandal preceded the performance; furor attended it. Maurice Maeterlinck, the author of the play that had served as Debussy's libretto, had expected his mistress, Georgette Leblanc, to sing the role of Mélisande. When it was assigned to Mary Garden, Maeterlinck sent a letter to *Le Figaro* vehemently denouncing both the opera and its composer. He said that *Pelléas et Mélisande* "is a piece which has become an almost enemy alien to me. Barred from all control of my work, I am compelled to wish that its failure should be resounding and prompt." Part of the opposition to the new opera, which was articulated in the antagonism of some of the critics and in the open hostility of many in the audience, was the direct result of Maeterlinck's machinations.

But the novel and revolutionary character of Debussy's opera was also responsible for much of the opposition. Here was an opera in which the aria was supplanted by a recitative closely simulating French speech; in which nothing ever happened, but whose effect was dependent on the most sensitive atmospheres and nuances; which was so subdued in dynamics that in all only four fortissimi were noted in the entire score; in which the orchestra, used with the utmost of discretion and economy, provided an exotic background; in which the harmonic writing and the tonality were as iconoclastic as the lyricism. "All I heard," wrote Léon Kerst after the première, "for even when you don't understand a thing you can't go to the theatre without hearing something—well, all I heard was a series of harmonized sounds (I don't say harmonious) which succeeded one another, uninterruptedly, without a single phrase, a single motive, a single accent, a single form, a single outline. And to this accompaniment, unnecessary singers drone out words, nothing but words, a kind of long drawn-out monotonous recitative, unbearable, moribund."

In self-defense Debussy explained his aesthetic aims as follows: "I have tried to obey a law of beauty which appears to be singularly ignored in dealing with dramatic music. The characters of the drama endeavor to sing like real persons, and not in an arbitrary language of antiquated traditions. Hence, the reproach leveled at my alleged partiality for monotone declamation, in which there is no melody. . . . To begin with this is not true. Besides, the feeling of character cannot be continually expressed in melody. Also, dramatic melody should be totally different from melody in general. . . . I do not pretend to have discovered anything in *Pelléas;* but I have tried to trace a path that others may follow, broadening it with individual discoveries which will, perhaps, free dramatic music from the heavy yoke under which it existed for so long."

It was not until four years after its première that Paris acclaimed *Pelléas et Mélisande.* The American première took place at the Manhattan Opera House on February 19, 1908, once again with Mary Garden as Mélisande. The work was produced at Covent Garden on May 21, 1909, and was first heard at the Metropolitan Opera on March 21, 1925, with Lucrezia Bori assuming the leading female role.

Today *Pelléas et Mélisande* is universally recognized as a milestone in twentieth century opera, one of the greatest works ever written for the lyric theatre. Oscar Thompson pointed out three reasons why the opera is unique: "(1) the word setting, which enables the sung text to move with almost the naturalness of speech; (2) the suggestive background of the orchestra, which supplied for the drama what may be termed a tonal envelope, without constituting itself either an accompaniment for the singers or a series of symphonic expansions in competition with them; (3) the mood expressiveness of the score which in its reticence and lack of emotional stress takes on the mystery of the other-worldly, and ends in being profoundly human in its sympathy and pathos."

With the worldwide success of *Pelléas,* Debussy was accepted as France's most famous, as well as most provocative, composer. Oblivious of both adulation and attack he continued to produce works of extraordinary originality, although never again was he to write another opera. His most memorable works for the piano, possibly the most important music written for the instrument since Liszt, came after *Pelléas.* These included the two sets of Preludes (1910, 1913); the *Suite Bergamasque* (1905), which includes "Clair de Lune"; the two sets of *Images,* for the piano, (1905, 1907); the delightful evocation of a child's world in *Children's Corner* (1908); and the two books of Études (1915).

"The creation of the Debussyan piano stands out, like the creation of the Chopin piano, as a unique artistic phenomenon in the history of music," wrote Edward Lockspeiser, "radically changing the musician's whole conception of what the instrument can be made to convey. The instrument Debussy created is unique technically, and it is unique imaginatively."

In 1902 Debussy, weary of his "Lily-Lilo" and her plebeian ways and mentality, fell in love with Emma Bardac, the wife of a banker, and married her on October 15, 1905, as soon as their divorces were obtained. But before that happened, also in 1905, a daughter had been born to them, Debussy's only child. She was Claude-Emma, given the pet name of "Chouchou." It was for her that the composer wrote the *Children's Corner.*

It was about this time that James Gibbons Huneker met Debussy at the Café Riche in Paris. "I was struck by the unique ugliness of the man," he wrote in the New York *Sun.* "His face is flat, the top of his head is flat, his eyes are prominent—the expression veiled and somber—and altogether, with his long hair, unkempt beard, uncouth clothing and soft hat he looked more like a Bohemian, a Croat, a Hun, than a Gaul. His high prominent cheekbones lend a Mongolian aspect to his face. The head is brachycephalic, the hair black."

Alfredo Casella described Debussy this way:

"His color was sallow; the eyes were small and seemed half sunk in the fat face; the straight nose was of the purest classical Roman type; in the thick and jet-black hair and beard . . . years had here and there sown a silver thread. As always with artists of the finer sort, the hands were most beautiful. Debussy's voice was unprepossessing, being hoarse (and this was aggravated by the abuse of tobacco), and he spoke in an abnormal, jumpy way. His dress was scrupulously cared for in every detail. His walk was curious, like that of all men who have a weakness for wearing womanish footgear."

"Debussy was a wit, if perforce a somewhat self-conscious one," said Oscar Thompson. "The virtuosity with which he rolled a cigarette in paper always devoid of glue without spilling the slightest speck of tobacco was a source of wonder and admiration to great and humble alike among the Parisians he encountered day by day. The opera he endured—if only now and then. But the circus! There he would have gladly gone every day. He could admire Mary Garden or Maggie Teyte. But the clowns! Debussy was like a child in his relish of their time-honored slapstick. The card game he enjoyed most was called bezique—Chinese bezique. When he played, Debussy would put his pipe beside him, as a cowboy of American-frontier times might have placed his six-shooter. He would cheat, more or less openly, turning down the tip of a card he might want to put in his hand later."

By the time he reached his fiftieth birthday, Debussy knew he was a victim of cancer. The next nine years was a period of intense physical suffering, aggravated by the financial problems brought on by World War I. Frequently he did not have the money for food or fuel. Yet, in spite of these harrowing circumstances, he continued to write music, including three sonatas in the classical structure of the seventeenth and eighteenth centuries. His last work was the third of these sonatas, for violin and piano, completed in the spring of 1917.

Debussy died at his home in Paris on March 25, 1918, while the city was being bombarded by German machine guns. Only eight days before he had applied for a place then recently vacated in the Académie Française. Because of the war—and the threat of an imminent German invasion of the city—his death went unnoticed. Only about fifty attended his funeral services on March 28, and just a handful followed the coffin to Père Lachaise where Debussy was buried after a single hurried oration. Debussy's body was subsequently removed to the cemetery at Passy.

Debussy was a composer who produced masterworks. He was also a composer whose influence on the music of his times can hardly be overestimated. As Henri Prunières noted, Debussy accomplished "a complete revolution in the musical art. . . . He invented new ways of associating chords hitherto regarded as discords, and used them to produce exquisite and delightful harmonies, and he disengaged the separate timbres of the orchestra by making one accentuate the value of the other, instead of combining them in confused masses. In this respect, his method is that of an Impressionist painter who lays on his canvas primary colors, side by side, instead of mixing them on his palette. Debussy violated all the conventional formulas, replacing them by new ones no less beautiful, and far more suitable for expression of those transient sensations and delicate emotions which he loved above all to portray. He was the incomparable painter of mystery, silence, and the infinite, of the passing cloud, the sunlit shimmer of the waves—subtleties which none before him had been capable of suggesting. His power of expression is not less real for being always restrained and intolerant of excess and over-emphasis, but its force is under the surface."

MAJOR WORKS

Ballets—Jeux; La Boîte à Joujoux.

Chamber Music—String Quartet in G minor; Rhapsody for Saxophone and Piano (orchestrated by Roger-Ducasse); Rhapsody for Clarinet and Piano (orchestrated by Roger-Ducasse); Sonata for Cello and Piano; Sonata for Flute, Viola and Harp; Sonata for Violin and Piano.

Choral Music—L'Enfant Prodigue, cantata; La Damoiselle Élue, cantata.

Opera—Pelléas et Mélisande.

Orchestral Music—Prélude à l'Après-Midi d'un Faune (The Afternoon of a Faun); Nocturnes; Danse Sacreé et Danse Profane, for harp and strings; La Mer; Le Martyre de Saint-Sébastien, incidental music for a "mystery"; Images.

Piano Music—Petite Suite, for piano duet (orchestrated by Henri Busser); Pour le Piano; Estampes; Masques; L'Île Joyeuse; Suite Bergamasque (including Clair de Lune); Images, two series; Children's Corner, suite; La Plus que Lente; Préludes, two books;

Études, two books; En Blanc et Noir, for two pianos; Six Épigraphes antiques, for piano duet.

Vocal Music — Mandoline; Paysage Sentimental; Clair de Lune; Cinq Poèmes de Baudelaire; Ariettes Oubliées; Trois Mélodies; Fêtes Galantes, two series; Proses Lyriques; Chansons de Bilitis; Trois Ballades de François Villon; Trois Ballades de Stéphane Mallarmé.

ABOUT

Dumesnil, M., Claude Debussy: Master of Dreams; Lockspeiser, E., Debussy: His Life and Mind (two volumes); Myers, R., Debussy; Seroff, V. I., Debussy: Musician of France; Thompson, O., Debussy: Man and Artist; Vallas, L., Claude Debussy.

Frederick Delius
1862–1934

Frederick Delius was born on January 29, 1862, in Bradford, England. He was the fourth child, and second son, of Julius and Elise Delius, a German couple who named him Fritz Albert Theodor. His father was the head of a prosperous wool establishment in Bradford.

FREDERICK DELIUS

Delius attended the Bradford Grammar School where he was an indifferent student, more interested in reading mysteries and stories of America's Wild West than in doing his school exercises. Where music was concerned, however, he showed unusual interest, playing the piano by ear and making excellent progress in his study of the violin. His father, however, wanted him to enter the wool

---

Delius: dē′ lĭ ŭs

business and refused to encourage the boy's musical interests. To prepare for a mercantile career, Delius went to International College, in Spring Grove, at Isleworth, which he attended from 1877 to 1880. While at this business college, Delius continued his violin lessons and participated in local musical performances; he also frequently visited London to attend concerts.

He entered his father's business in 1881, first as a bookkeeper, then as a salesman. To enable him to learn as much as possible about the wool business, his father despatched him to Germany to serve an apprenticeship in an important wool establishment in Chemnitz, Saxony. Music, apparently, took up more of his time than business. He made many trips to Dresden, Leipzig, and Berlin to attend performances of operas and orchestral music. A production of Wagner's *Die Meistersinger* made such an impact on him that when he left the opera house he was determined to devote his life to music.

Nevertheless, he remained in his father's business until 1884, making trips to Sweden, Norway, and France. But wanderlust made him restless and the routine of a businessman's life was stultifying. At last Delius decided to set out on his own. He managed to induce his father to provide the funds with which to purchase an orange plantation in Solano, Florida. In March 1884 Delius left for the United States.

Oranges interested him no more than wool had done. He left the running of his grove to a supervisor while he devoted himself to music study and to the writing of his first compositions. He loved the primitive life, the languorous climate, the wild scenic beauty around him, and most of all his detachment from the outside world. He enjoyed the hours he could spend not only on music but also in reading and contemplation, in alligator hunts, in listening to Negroes sing spirituals and watching them dance.

The need for a piano sent him on a three-day journey to Jacksonville where he met Thomas F. Ward, an organist. Delius prevailed on Ward to return with him to Solano. For six months Ward repaid Delius for bed and board by teaching him harmony and counterpoint. Apparently this instruction was profitable for, later in life, Delius confessed: "Ward's counterpoint lessons were the only lessons from which I derived any benefit. . . . He showed wonderful insight in helping me to find out just how much in the way of traditional technique would be useful to me."

Determined to become a composer, Delius realized he had to leave Solano and settle where he could further develop his musical talents. For a short while he lived in Jacksonville, where he sang in a synagogue choir. Then he settled in Danville, Virginia, becoming a member of the music faculty of the Old Roanoke Female School. He also gave local concerts on the violin and accepted rich young ladies as pupils.

With the money he saved, Delius was able to go to Leipzig in 1886 and enroll in its Conservatory as a pupil of Hans Sitt, Reinecke, and Jadassohn. During that first year he completed an orchestral suite, *Florida*. This was an atmospheric four-movement work which included several dance tunes Delius had heard the Negroes perform. When Edvard Grieg visited Leipzig in 1887, he heard *Florida* and was so impressed by the work that he used his influence to encourage Delius's father to provide the young musician with a small but regular stipend.

Following this, Delius made his home in France—first in Croissy, then in the Latin Quarter of Paris where he lived from 1888 to 1896. Freed from financial worries (his father's little stipend was supplemented by generous gifts from an uncle, Theodor, who left him a legacy in 1894), Delius could now concentrate on composition. He wrote a violin sonata and a string quartet. In 1892 *Légende*, for violin and orchestra, became his first published composition, and he completed the writing of his first opera, *Irmelin*, a fairy tale with text by the composer. Though highly praised by Grieg and André Messager, *Irmelin* was not performed during Delius's lifetime. The première took place at Oxford, on May 4, 1953, Sir Thomas Beecham conducting. Irving Kolodin, who attended the performance, described the work as "in essence a tone poem in the form of an opera, a moonlit rhapsody . . . expanded in size and with the addition of vocal parts."

Two more operas followed in the years between 1893 and 1897: *The Magic Fountain*, with text by the composer, and *Koanga*, with libretto by C. F. Keary based on G. W. Cable's novel *The Grandissimes*. *Koanga*, like the *Florida* suite, was inspired by Delius's American experiences. Its action took place on a Louisiana plantation along the Mississippi during the second half of the eighteenth century. Much of the music, particularly some of the choral pages and dance episodes, is based on Negro folk tunes. Still popular from this early Delius opera is the music of "La Calinda," a dynamic West Indian Negro dance. The world première of *Koanga* took place in Eberfeld, Germany, on March 30, 1904.

The last decade of the nineteenth century saw the writing of a fantasy overture, *Over the Hills and Far Away* (1895), the C minor Piano Concerto (1897), and an orchestral nocturne, *Paris: The Song of a Great City* (1899). As if in summation, Delius arranged a concert of his works, which took place in London on May 30, 1899, Alfred Hertz conducting. Most of the critics were severe in their evaluation, regarding Delius's music as the "bizarre affectation of a clever young man" or as "discordant, harsh, and uninviting." Delius's music was not heard again in London until 1907. Germany proved more receptive to him, and it was in Germany that the premières of many of Delius's early works took place.

In 1897 Delius married Jelka Rosen, a painter. They made their home in her villa in the little French town of Grez-sur-Loing (Seine-et-Marne), where Delius lived and worked for the remainder of his life. In 1901 he completed his fourth and most famous opera, *A Village Romeo and Juliet*, whose libretto (by the composer) was based on a novel by Gottfried Keller. The opera was first produced at the Komische Oper in Berlin on February 21, 1907. Thomas Beecham directed the opera's première in England, on February 22, 1910. Both in Germany and in London the opera proved only a mild success. Some critics found things to praise in the music, but most condemned the libretto. An orchestral episode from this score is frequently played today at symphony concerts. It is *The Walk to the Paradise Garden*, described by Philip Heseltine as "an epitome of the whole drama." The writing of this symphonic interlude was almost an afterthought. Delius wrote it during the rehearsals of his opera in England, at the request of Thomas Beecham who needed time to make a change of scenery.

159

Soon after *A Village Romeo and Juliet* came a number of large works for chorus. *Appalachia* (1902), an outgrowth of an orchestral piece originally conceived in 1896, was inspired by Delius's stay in Florida. It was a series of variations on an old Negro slave song. *Sea Drift* (1903) used as text the first verse from Walt Whitman's poem of the same name. *A Mass of Life* (1905) was based on Nietzsche's *Thus Spake Zarathustra*, and *Songs of Sunset* (1907) used verses by Arthur Symons. Of these works, each a product of Delius's maturity, the most significant is *A Mass of Life*. Indeed, Sir Thomas Beecham regarded it as "the climax of Delius's creative achievement . . . the most impressive and original achievement of its genre written in fifty years."

But the works by which Delius is most often represented on concert programs today are the tone poems written in the years 1907–1912, with which he became a leading voice in the post-Impressionist movement. *Brigg Fair* (1907) was an enlargement of the well-known English folk song of that name. *In a Summer Garden* (1908) was an eloquent descriptive tone poem whose program was suggested by two quotations in the published score, a couplet by Dante Gabriel Rossetti and an unidentified German prose poem. *On Hearing the First Cuckoo in Spring* and *Summer Night on the River* are companion pieces, both written in 1912. The first expresses the composer's reaction to the birth of spring; the second evokes the peace and mystery surrounding a misty river at night. The music of all these tone poems is pictorial and atmospheric, their tranquil mood far removed from any suggestions of unrest or turbulence. "It is," wrote an unidentified critic of the London *Times* in discussing the Delius tone poems, "the richly decadent beauty of autumn colors; its feeling is not so much sad as pensive; there is an absence of rhythmic vitality which marks it off sharply from the new music of his younger contemporaries. . . . His is the music of sensibility."

What Bernard van Dieren said of Delius's music in general applies to the famous tone poems as well: "He found the basic material for his music in those of his sensations which appeal to all. Delius is not a Shakespeare and he is the more admirable for his understanding the character of his genius. . . . Delius's art is so completely satisfactory because while being definitely circumscribed it is so justly balanced. His music never undertakes to convey anything that does not belong to the adventures of a very sensitive human spirit. To all that he touched he gave a new meaning, a new color, a new loveliness, and a new poignancy."

In 1907 Henry J. Wood presented the Delius Piano Concerto at a Promenade Concert. Following this, *Sea Drift* was heard at the Sheffield Festival, and *Appalachia*, in London. One of those profoundly impressed by Delius at the time was Thomas Beecham, then a rising young conductor. From that time on Beecham became an indefatigable advocate of Delius's works in England; it was mainly due to his efforts that Delius finally came into his own as a major composer in his native country.

During World War I, Delius lived in England where he completed a major work, the *Requiem*, in memory of young artists who died in the conflict. After the war, back at Grez-sur-Loing, Delius's health began to deteriorate. At first he merely suffered from attacks of fatigue and inertia. By 1922, however, he was paralyzed, and in 1925, blind. Delius accepted the calamity with amazing serenity and fatalism. He sought comfort in listening to his music on recordings and in concert performances broadcast over the radio. He enjoyed being read to, entertaining visitors, eating good food, and composing. He enlisted the services of a young musician, Eric Fenby, who came to live with him and acted as an amanuensis. Painstakingly, Delius dictated to Fenby his last works, note by note: the *Idyll* (1930) and the *Songs of Farewell* (1932), both based on Whitman; the tone poem *A Song of Summer* (1930); and the third violin sonata (1930).

In 1929, though blind and paralyzed, Delius was taken to London to attend a festival of six concerts devoted to his major works. He was finally accorded the full measure of homage he deserved. "The first cheers and noise . . . lasted a full ten minutes," reported Arthur Hutchings, "and all eyes turned to the balcony where Delius lay on his litter surrounded by flowers. For the first time, and the last, his compatriots heard his voice in public. Slowly but clearly he uttered a few sentences of thanks for his reception and for the performance, adding: 'This festival has been the time of my life.' " The festival evoked appreciative articles from England's foremost music critics. The King made Delius a Companion of Honor; Delius's native city of Bradford gave him the Freedom of the City; and Oxford conferred on him an honorary degree.

He never again appeared in public. Back in his villa in France, he dictated his last works. His creativity was finally halted by pains and spasms that had to be assuaged by morphine. Delius died in Grez-sur-Loing on June 10, 1934, and was buried in the town cemetery. A year later his body was transferred to the churchyard in Limpsfield, in southern England. At a nearby church, Sir Thomas Beecham led a concert of Delius's music.

In his admirable personal study of Delius, Eric Fenby singled out the following traits of Delius's character: "His intellectual isolation, his inhuman aloofness, his penetrating truthfulness, wholly indifferent thereby whether he hurt people or not, his utter contempt for the 'crowd' and his all-embracing sufficiency. To these were added his colossal egotism, his dreadful selfishness, his splendid generosity . . . his equal indifference to money and honors, his exceptional refinement." Fenby further pointed out Delius's bent for excess. "If he must smoke, then he must smoke all day; if he must have spinach, then spinach it had to be almost every meal. . . . There were no half-measures with Delius."

MAJOR WORKS

Chamber Music—3 violin sonatas; 2 string quartets; Cello Sonata.

Choral Music—Appalachia; Sea Drift; A Mass of Life; Songs of Sunset; A Song of the High Hills; Wanderer's Song; Requiem; A Poem of Life and Love; Songs of Farewell.

Operas—Irmelin; Koanga; A Village Romeo and Juliet; Fennimore and Gerda.

Orchestral Music—Florida; Piano Concerto in C minor; Over the Hills and Far Away; Paris: The Song of a Great City; Cynara, for baritone and orchestra; Brigg Fair, rhapsody; In a Summer Garden, fantasy; A Dance Rhapsody, Nos. 1 and 2; Summer Night on the River; On Hearing the First Cuckoo in Spring; North Country Sketches; Concerto for Violin, Cello and Orchestra; Violin Concerto; Eventyr, ballad; A Song Before Sunrise; Cello Concerto; A Late Lark, for tenor and orchestra; A Song of Summer; Idyll, for soprano, baritone and orchestra.

Piano Music—Five Pieces; Three Preludes.

Vocal Music—Seven Songs from the Danish; Four Nietzsche Songs; Two Songs for a Children's Album; Four Old English Songs.

ABOUT

Beecham, T., Frederick Delius; Delius, C., Memories of My Brother; Fenby, E., Delius as I Knew Him; Heseltine, P., Frederick Delius; Hull, A. E., Delius; Hutchings, A., Delius.

Norman Dello Joio
1913–

Norman Dello Joio was born in New York City on January 24, 1913. He was descended from a long line of Italian musicians; for three generations his ancestors had been organists in Gragnano, near Naples. His father was also an organist at the Church of Our Lady of Mount Carmel in the Harlem section of New York. Norman's first significant musical impressions came from hearing his father play the organ and listening to the liturgical music at church which aroused his interest in Gregorian chants, an all-important influence in his development as a composer.

NORMAN DELLO JOIO

As a boy, Norman studied the organ with his father, who also gave him lessons on the piano and in theory. When the boy became sufficiently adept at the piano keyboard, he would spend hours with his father playing four-hand arrangements of both classics and modern works. This practice continued for several years, and by the time he was in his early teens, he could, as he reveals, "already play

Dello Joio: dĕl′ ō joi′ ō

anything at sight." Since Italian opera singers often visited the Dello Joio home and made it ring with their renditions of arias, Norman was introduced early to Italian opera. The effect of Verdi on his musical growth proved almost as significant as that of Catholic liturgical music.

At eleven, Norman assisted his father in playing the organ at church. His talent encouraged the father to consider training him as a church organist. When he was fifteen, he studied with Pietro Yon, his godfather, who was the distinguished organist of St. Patrick's Cathedral in New York. He continued his musical education at the Institute of Musical Art in New York with Gaston Déthier as his teacher in piano and organ. His creative talent received some recognition at this time. His Trio for Flute, Cello, and Piano was given the Elizabeth Sprague Coolidge Award in 1939 and was described in the New York *Times* as music of "spirit and grace." Concurrently with his musical activities, Dello Joio pursued his academic schooling at All Hallows Institute in New York, and afterwards for a single year at City College.

To help support himself, Dello Joio held a number of jobs as organist at various churches, beginning with a stint at the Star of the Sea Church on City Island. But he was beginning to think more and more of developing himself as a composer. His first ambitious work—a trio for piano, violin, and cello—received the Elizabeth Sprague Coolidge Prize of one thousand dollars. In 1939 he received a fellowship at the Juilliard Graduate School, where he studied with Bernard Wagenaar. In the summers of 1940 and 1941 he studied composition on a fellowship with Paul Hindemith at the Berkshire Music Center at Tanglewood. It was Hindemith who gave Dello Joio artistic direction by persuading him to seek out a style of writing that was more lyrical, more attuned to his own nature and creative inclinations than the style he had thus far been favoring.

From his sixteenth year on, Dello Joio played the piano in several jazz bands. A number of years later he formed a jazz band of his own which performed extensively throughout the East. Out of these experiences came his enthusiasm for jazz music and his tendency from time to time to incorporate jazz elements

into his writing. The most ambitious of his works in a jazz style came after he had reached full maturity as a composer. This was in 1949 when he wrote a Concertante for Clarinet and Orchestra for the jazz clarinetist Artie Shaw, who introduced it in Chautauqua, New York, on May 22, 1949.

From 1941 to 1943 Dello Joio served as the musical director of Eugene Loring's Dance Players, a ballet company. Out of this affiliation came his first ballet scores, for *Prairie* and *The Duke of Sacramento*, both produced in 1942. The year 1942 also witnessed the winning of the Town Hall Composition Award for his *Magnificat*, for orchestra, which was modeled freely after the style of Gregorian chants. A year later his first piano sonata became his first major work to be published.

Dello Joio was the recipient of Guggenheim Fellowships in 1944 and 1945. In this period he wrote the music for a third ballet, *On Stage!*, produced in Cleveland on November 23, 1945, and a work for orchestra, *Concert Music*, which the Pittsburgh Symphony under Fritz Reiner introduced on January 4, 1946. In 1946 Dello Joio received a grant from the American Academy of Arts and Letters. In 1947 he toured Poland as composer-pianist. From 1944 to 1950 he was a member of the music faculty at Sarah Lawrence College in Bronxville, New York. He returned to teaching in 1956, becoming a professor of composition at the Mannes College of Music in New York City.

In his most significant orchestral works of the mid-1940's, Dello Joio emerged as a neo-classicist who reached back to baroque structures without sacrificing his contemporary identity. In these compositions he also revealed his partiality for the variation form. First came the *Ricercari*, for piano and orchestra, which he performed on December 19, 1945, with the New York Philharmonic conducted by George Szell. The ricercare was a form popular in the sixteenth and seventeenth centuries in which the style of the vocal motet was adapted for instruments, a basic idea or ideas being subjected to fugal treatment. With his own three-movement *Ricercari* Dello Joio retained the classical structure, but he brought to it his own ideas of harmony and rhythm as well as the science of varying the principal theme.

On January 30, 1948, the Pittsburgh Symphony performed the première of his *Variations, Chaconne and Finale*, for orchestra, whose basic material was a theme from a Gregorian chant. When the composition was heard in New York, Olin Downes explained in the New York *Times* that all three movements represented "different concepts of the variation form." He added: "All the forms and developments cluster about the central idea for the oboe announced at the beginning." The *Variations, Chaconne and Finale* received the New York Music Critics Circle Award.

The liturgical element within the variation structure was emphasized strongly in the *Meditations on Ecclesiastes*, for string orchestra, a composition that earned for its composer the Pulitzer Prize in music in 1957. This music started out as a ballet entitled *There Is a Time*, which José Limon introduced in New York in May 1956. Divorced from the dance, and renamed *Meditations on Ecclesiastes*, it was heard in Washington, D.C., on December 17, 1957, in a performance by the National Symphony under Howard Mitchell. As the title indicates, this work interprets the Book of Ecclesiastes (verses from the opening of chapter 3). In twelve sections, it comprises a theme and variations, with each section in a different tonality, and with the basic theme undergoing elaborate transformation.

Dello Joio wrote his first opera in 1949 on a commission from the Whitney Foundation. His subject was Joan of Arc, who had fascinated him from early childhood. Entitled *The Triumph of St. Joan*, and with a libretto by the composer in collaboration with Joseph Machlis, it was introduced at Sarah Lawrence College on May 9, 1950. Olin Downes, in a Sunday feature article in the New York *Times*, described it as a notable achievement, "so interesting and sincere that the listener is held by this piece throughout its length." Despite such kind words—which many other critics echoed—Dello Joio was not satisfied with his opera and withdrew it permanently. "I knew," he explained, "that I had not said what I wanted to about St. Joan."

In 1955 he returned to the subject of St. Joan in another opera. This was a completely new work, with a new libretto and score — though, as he confessed, the temptation to use some of the older material had been great. At first he called the opera *The Trial at Rouen*, the title under which it was given its world première in a telecast over the NBC network on April 8, 1956. It was an opera in the grand manner, consistently lyrical in the Italian manner. After the première, Dello Joio revised it and retitled it *The Triumph of St. Joan*. It was produced by the New York City Opera on April 16, 1959, and received the New York Music Critics Circle Award.

Commissioned by the Louisville Orchestra of Kentucky to produce an orchestral composition, Dello Joio decided to adapt the score of his abandoned first opera about Joan of Arc into a three-movement symphony, calling it *The Triumph of St. Joan Symphony*. At its world première on December 5, 1951, the symphony was used in conjunction with a dance solo by Martha Graham. But since that time the symphony has often been presented by major orchestras without a ballet sequence.

In the period between the two operas about Joan of Arc, Dello Joio completed a delightful one-act opera based on Lord Dunsany's *A Night at the Inn*. He called it *The Ruby*. It was first seen in Bloomington, Indiana, on May 13, 1955. More ambitious in purpose and scope was a two-act opera, *Blood Moon*, written under special grant from the Ford Foundation. Gale Hoffman's libretto, based on the composer's scenario, was built around the colorful personality of the American actress Adah Menken and her frustrated love affair with a handsome young Southerner during the Civil War period. The opera was given in San Francisco by the San Francisco Opera on September 18, 1961.

In 1961 Dello Joio completed an important work for piano and orchestra—*Fantasy and Variations*, commissioned by the Baldwin Piano Company. With Lorin Hollander as soloist, the composition was heard in Cincinnati on May 9, 1962, Max Rudolf conducting. The work is constructed from a four-note cell (G, F-sharp, B, and C), a motive that subsequently is subjected to a set of six variations.

On June 5, 1942, Dello Joio married Grace Baumgold, a dancer. For many years they made their home in Wilton, Connecticut, where they reared three children. A part of each year was spent in an apartment in New York City, and more recently the Dello Joios

163

acquired a summer home at East Hampton, Long Island.

Dello Joio has retained his boyhood enthusiasms for both baseball and jazz. (He was once so adept at baseball that he was offered a job on a professional team.) "He does nothing by halves," said Robert Sabin in *Musical America*. "One senses this quiet intensity in his personality. He is slender, with a thick face dominated by dark, vividly expressive eyes. His voice has the suspicion of a humorous drawl, and his gestures are quiet but always to the point. . . . Dello Joio's youthfulness of spirit is symbolized by the fact that his hair stubbornly refuses to stay combed. It usually looks as if he had just jumped from his desk, running his finger through it, or had just come in from a brisk, breezy walk."

On February 16, 1958, Dello Joio was the subject of a television program, "Profile of a Composer," presented on the CBS network; on this occasion he introduced *A Ballad of the Seven Lively Arts*, for piano and orchestra. A further affiliation with television was the writing of scores for several major productions, including *The Incurable One* and *Vanity Fair*, both seen on the CBS network, and *The Louvre*, presented by NBC; for the last he received an "Emmy" Award in 1965.

In 1958 Dello Joio was given an honorary doctorate from Lawrence College in Appleton, Wisconsin; he received another from Colby College in Waterville, Maine, in 1960. In 1964 he toured the Soviet Union extensively to become acquainted with its musical life and educational facilities. During this visit, students and graduates of the Moscow Conservatory honored him by playing several of his compositions.

MAJOR WORKS

Ballets—Prairie; The Duke of Sacramento; On Stage!; Diversion of Angels; There Is a Time.

Chamber Music—Trio for Flute, Cello and Piano; Sextet, for three recorders (or woodwind) and strings; Fantasia on a Gregorian Theme, for violin and piano; Duo Concertante, for cello and piano; Lamentation of Saul, for baritone, flute, oboe, clarinet, viola, cello and piano (also for baritone and orchestra); Variations and Capriccio, for violin and piano; Colloquies, for violin and piano.

Choral Music—Vigil Strange; The Mystic Trumpeter; A Fable; A Jubilant Song; Madrigal; The Bluebird; A Psalm of David; Song of the Open Road; Song of Affirmation; Adieu, Mignonne; O Sing Unto the Lord; To St. Cecilia; Prayers of Cardinal Newman; A Christmas Carol; Holy Infant's Lullaby; Song's

End; Three Songs of Chopin; Songs of Walt Whitman; Proud Music, for mixed chorus, brass, and organ.

Operas—The Triumph of St. Joan (originally called The Trial at Rouen); The Ruby (one act); Blood Moon.

Orchestral Music—Piano Concertino; Flute Concertino; Sinfonietta; Harp Concerto; Harmonica Concerto; Magnificat; Concert Music; To a Lone Sentry; American Landscape; Ricercari, for piano and orchestra; Variations, Chaconne and Finale; Serenade; New York Profiles; Concertante, for clarinet and orchestra; A Ballad of the Seven Lively Arts, for piano and orchestra; The Triumph of St. Joan Symphony; Epigraphs; Meditations on Ecclesiastes; Air Power; Fantasy and Variations, for piano and orchestra; Antiphonal Fantasy, for organ, brass and strings.

Piano Music—3 sonatas; Prelude: To a Young Dancer; Prelude: To a Young Musician; Nocturnes; Aria and Toccata, for two pianos; Family Album, children's duets; Suite for the Young.

Vocal Music—New Born; There Is a Lady Sweet and Kind; Lament; The Assassination; Six Love Songs; The Listeners; Sonnet of Petrarch; Three Songs of Adieu.

ABOUT

Chase, G., America's Music; Cohn, A., Twentieth Century Music in the Western Hemisphere.

Musical America, December 1, 1950; Musical Quarterly, April 1962.

David Diamond
1915–

David Leo Diamond was born in Rochester, New York, on July 9, 1915. The Diamond family was in modest financial circumstances. The income earned by the father as a carpenter and by the mother as a dressmaker was hardly enough to support a family of four which, besides their son David, included a daughter. The family's poverty prevented David from getting formal instruction in music during his childhood, even though he showed unusual talent early. By the time he was seven, without having taken a single lesson, he had learned to play the violin on an instrument he had borrowed from a friend of the family. He also began putting down on paper original tunes by means of a notation system he had invented. At elementary school while his friends were busy with class problems, he devoted himself to composition.

In 1927 the Diamonds were forced by economic pressures to leave Rochester and live with relatives in Cleveland. There the boy attracted the interest of a Swiss musician residing and teaching in Cleveland, André de

Ribaupierre, who provided the funds to pay for Diamond's first training in music. From 1927 to 1929 he attended the Cleveland Institute of Music, where his violin teacher was his patron, de Ribaupierre. In 1930, after the Diamond family had returned to Rochester, he received a scholarship for the Eastman School of Music, where he studied the violin with Effie Knauss and composition with Bernard Rogers. At the Eastman School Diamond wrote his first large work for orchestra, *Symphony in One Movement*, which was performed by the school orchestra in 1931. This symphony and other youthful compositions which numbered about one hundred were subsequently discarded.

DAVID DIAMOND

Diamond was graduated from high school in 1933 and then attended the Eastman School full time for one year. In 1934 he went to New York City. On a scholarship he attended the New Music School, a pupil of Paul Boepple in improvisation and Roger Sessions in composition. Meanwhile he supported himself by taking any menial job he could find. When he heard that Elfrida Whiteman was sponsoring a competition for young composers, the winner to be financed for two years of study, Diamond entered a Sinfonietta, inspired by poems of Carl Sandburg, with which he won first prize. Later this composition was also withdrawn from circulation.

In 1935 Diamond was commissioned to write music for a ballet, *Tom*, with scenario by

E. E. Cummings and choreography by Massine. Since Massine was then in Paris, Diamond was given the necessary funds to go to France and consult with the choreographer. As it turned out *Tom*, though completed, was never produced. But it was the means by which Diamond made personal contacts with such distinguished Parisian musicians as Ravel and Roussel–a maturing experience which brought him a new perspective and a fresh viewpoint on his own music. In 1937 he returned to Paris and that year began to study composition with Nadia Boulanger. During this time he completed the first works he allowed to survive. These included his first violin concerto, and the *Psalm*, for orchestra, both completed in 1936. The *Psalm* (inspired by a visit to Père Lachaise cemetery in Paris and revealing the influence of the advice and criticism of Igor Stravinsky) was introduced in Rochester on December 10, 1936. From there it went on to win the Juilliard Publication Award in 1937 and to be performed by the San Francisco Symphony under Monteux. Alfred J. Frankenstein praised it for its "fine, granite sensuousness" and its "spare, telling use of the orchestra." Diamond's first violin concerto was introduced by Nicolai Berezowsky in New York on March 24, 1937.

Upon returning to New York, Diamond lived in Greenwich Village, where he became a close friend of the poet E. E. Cummings, and the then little-known artist Willem de Kooning. To earn his living, Diamond worked as a night clerk behind a soda fountain on upper Broadway. For two years he played the violin in the "Hit Parade" orchestra over the radio. His free hours were spent writing music. He was commissioned by the League of Composers to write the Quintet for Flute, String Trio and Piano in 1937. Another composition was inspired by Ravel's death–*Elegy in Memory of Maurice Ravel*, which was performed in Rochester on April 28, 1938.

In the spring of 1938, a Guggenheim Fellowship enabled Diamond to return to Europe, where he continued studying composition with Nadia Boulanger while working on several new compositions. This period saw the writing of *Heroic Piece*, for orchestra (introduced in Zürich on July 29, 1938) and a cello concerto (première in Rochester, on April 30, 1942).

When his Guggenheim Fellowship was extended for a second year, Diamond stayed on in Paris, remaining there until 1939 when the outbreak of World War II brought him back to the United States. On his return he lived for a while at the artists' colony at Yaddo, Saratoga Springs, New York, where he completed several major works for orchestra: *Concert Piece*, given in New York on May 16, 1940; *Concerto for Chamber Music*, a feature of the Yaddo Festival on September 7, 1940; and most significant, his first symphony, which was performed by the New York Philharmonic under Mitropoulos on December 21, 1941. This first symphony, together with his first string quartet (1940), earned him a grant from the American Academy in Rome. And a ballet, *The Dream of Audubon*, with scenario by Glenway Wescott, received the Ballet Guild Award.

In 1943 Diamond won the Paderewski Prize for his Piano Quartet (1938) and in 1944 was awarded a grant from the National Academy of Arts and Letters "in recognition of his outstanding gifts among the youngest generation of composers, and for the high quality of his achievements." In 1958 he received the Guggenheim Fellowship for the third time.

As his reputation grew and his music gained ever wider circulation, Diamond's style underwent a transformation. In his earliest works he had been interested in experimental sounds and thus favored a style that was complex and, at times, discordant. Early in the 1940's a pronounced Romantic feeling penetrated his writing. At the same time, his methods became simpler, clearer, and more consonant. Such a neo-Romantic attitude, with emphasis on lyricism and a strong feeling for the rhythmic pulse, became evident in *Rounds*, for string orchestra, one of Diamond's most popular works up to that time. It was introduced in Minneapolis on November 24, 1944, Mitropoulos conducting. Virgil Thomson described it as "a melodious piece in three movements of which the first two are quite personal and expressive. The third is less so. All are contrapuntal, cleanly thought, stylish, though a little short-lived." *Rounds* received a special citation from the New York Music Critics Circle.

In the years between 1942 and 1948 Diamond completed three symphonies, all of which were given their world premières by the Boston Symphony: the second, on October 13, 1944; the third (1945), on November 3, 1950; and the fourth, on January 23, 1948. His orchestral suite *Romeo and Juliet*, first performed in New York on October 20, 1947, was presented by many major orchestras in the next few years. During this period Diamond also completed his third string quartet. After being introduced at a concert of the League of Composers on March 16, 1947, it received the New York Music Critics Circle Award.

In 1951 Diamond once again left the United States, this time to establish residence in Italy for almost a decade and a half. He made his home in Rome where he was a Fulbright Professor at the University. Later he moved to Florence. During his protracted stay in Italy, he visited the United States several times. On two occasions (in the spring of 1961 and in the fall of 1963) he served as Slee Professor at the University of Buffalo in New York.

In Florence, Diamond completed a number of symphonies and string quartets, as well as choral works and songs. Some were written on commission: for example, *The World of Paul Klee*, for orchestra (1957), was done on a grant from the Rockefeller Foundation; and *This Sacred Ground*, a setting of Lincoln's Gettysburg Address (1962), was written at the request of the Buffalo *Evening News* and radio station WBEN in Buffalo. Other works were written for special occasions: his sixth string quartet (1962), for Milhaud's seventieth birthday; the Nonet, for strings (1962), for Stravinsky's eightieth birthday; the eighth symphony (1960) for Copland's sixtieth birthday; the ninth symphony (1965) in memory of Dimitri Mitropoulos.

In his later works Diamond veered towards abstraction, with an occasional free application of the serial technique. He refuses, however, to be classified as a dodecaphonist. His composition has become drier, more objective, occasionally more cerebral. Yet lyricism is still present, and the former Romantic approaches are not altogether discarded.

Diamond returned to the United States in March 1965. He spent that summer in Aspen, Colorado, as a visiting composer. A program of his works was given there on July 9 to commemorate his fiftieth birthday. This birthday was also celebrated (though somewhat belatedly) on September 23, 1965, by the Philadelphia Orchestra under Ormandy when the composer's *Elegies* was introduced. *Elegies* was written in memory of two writers: William Faulkner and E. E. Cummings. In the fall of 1965 Diamond reestablished his permanent home in New York City where he became a member of the faculty of the Manhattan School of Music.

Honors continued to come to him. His eighth string quartet received the Rheta Sosland Award. ASCAP presented him with the Stravinsky Award. In 1966 he was elected to the department of music of the National Institute of Arts and Letters. On April 28, 1966, Diamond received an unusual tribute when the New York Philharmonic under Bernstein presented the world premières of two of his major works on the same program: a Piano Concerto written in 1959, and his Fifth Symphony, begun in 1947, put aside, and not completed until 1964 after he had written his eighth symphony. Diamond himself conducted the performance of the Piano Concerto. Toward the end of 1967, he was honored by West Virginia University with two concerts devoted entirely to his music. The program on October 29 included the world première of the Quartet No. 10. The composer also delivered two major lectures.

Diamond maintains that in writing his music he has no intention of having "the musical substance represent specific emotional reactions or to conjure up programmatic fantasies. I have a horror of anything as prosaic as that, and since I have never known that method of musical conception, I can only say that the opposite is true. My emotional life and reactions to certain events and situations have worked hand in hand with purely abstract musical conception and manipulation of material and it was always the material that remained foremostly important to me in my working stages."

Diamond is a bachelor. His extramusical interests include painting, cooking, gardening, studying languages (he has now mastered seven), and watching silent movies.

MAJOR WORKS

Ballet—The Dream of Audubon.

Chamber Music—10 string quartets; Violin Sonata; Canticle for Perpetual Motion, for violin and piano; Chaconne, for violin and piano; Quintet, for clarinet, two violas and two cellos; Woodwind Quintet; Piano Trio; Nonet, for strings; Night Music, for string quartet and accordion.

Choral Music—This Is the Garden; Three Madrigals; Young Joseph; This Sacred Ground; Prayer for Peace.

Orchestral Music—9 symphonies; 2 violin concertos; Psalm; Variations on an Original Theme; Elegy in Memory of Maurice Ravel; Heroic Piece; Cello Concerto; Concert Piece; Music for Double String Orchestra, Brass and Tympani; Concerto for Chamber Orchestra; Rounds; Romeo and Juliet, suite; The Enormous Room; Timon of Athens, symphonic portrait; Ceremonial Fanfare, for brass and percussion; Piano Concerto; Ahavah, for narrator and orchestra; Diaphony, for brass, two pianos, tympani and organ; Sinfonia Concertante; The World of Paul Klee; Elegies (one for horn and strings, the other for flute and strings).

Piano Music—Sonata; Sonatina; Concerto for Two Pianos, unaccompanied; Album for the Young.

Vocal Music—L'Âme de Claude Debussy; The Midnight Meditation; We Two; over one hundred individual songs for voice and piano.

ABOUT

Chase, G., America's Music; Goss, M., Modern Music Makers.

New York Times, April 22, 1965; Newsweek, March 18, 1957; Saturday Review, December 2, 1950.

Ernst von Dohnányi
1877–1960

Ernst von Dohnányi was born in Pressburg, Hungary (now Bratislava, Czechoslovakia) on July 27, 1877. His father, a professor of mathematics and physics at the local high school, was also a good amateur cellist and introduced his son to music. By the time he was six, Ernst was playing the piano; at seven he made his first attempts at composition. In 1885, while he was attending school, he became Karl Forstner's pupil in piano and organ. Ernst started giving public concerts when he was nine, and in 1888 made a highly praised appearance in a performance of Schumann's Piano Quintet. By the time he left Pressburg for Budapest, Dohnányi had written a piano sonata, three string quartets, a string sextet, many pieces for the piano, and songs.

In 1894 he entered the Academy of Music in Budapest. During the next three years he studied piano there with Stefan Thomán and composition with Hans Koessler. In 1896 he received the Hungarian Millennium Prize for two compositions, his first symphony, in F major, and the Zrinyi Overture. He also wrote a Piano Quintet in C minor—now designated

Dohnányi: dō′ nä nyĭ

167

Dohnányi

as his opus no. 1—which so impressed Koessler that he sent the manuscript to Brahms. Brahms had the Kneisel Quartet perform it at his summer place at Bad Ischl, then arranged for a public presentation in Vienna at a concert of the Tonkünstler Verein with Dohnányi at the piano. The Quintet was successful, and in 1902 it was published. It is still played today and enjoyed because of its unashamed Romanticism and its rich fund of pleasing melodies. It is so obviously influenced by Brahms (as, indeed, are all of Dohnányi's early compositions) that for a long time it was laughingly referred to as "Brahms's Second Piano Quintet." Brahms did not live long after he had bestowed his blessing on the young composer. At Brahms's funeral, in the early spring of 1897, Dohnányi was chosen to represent the students of the Budapest Academy.

ERNST VON DOHNÁNYI

Dohnányi was graduated in 1897. During that summer he took piano lessons from Eugène d'Albert, who is reported to have told him after the eighth session: "You can go on by yourself now. I have taught you all I can." Dohnányi's debut as a mature concert pianist was made in Berlin on October 1, 1897. On October 24, 1898, he appeared in London in a performance of Beethoven's Fourth Piano Concerto, Hans Richter conducting. On March 22, 1900, he paid his first visit to the United States. Appearing as soloist with the Boston Symphony Orchestra (Wilhelm Gericke conducting), he was described by one of the local critics as "already an artist of high rank."

Up to the time of World War I, he continued to concertize extensively and was acclaimed everywhere as one of the foremost pianists of his time. Indeed, his second concert tour of the United States followed soon after the first—one in November, the other in December of 1900. While thus achieving universal recognition as a virtuoso, Dohnányi also distinguished himself as a teacher of the piano. He joined the faculty of the Berlin High School for Music in 1905, rising to the rank of professor in 1908. In 1915 he resigned his post to return to Budapest. During the war years he taught pupils privately. Then in 1919 he was made associate director of the Academy of Music; and in 1933, principal director.

"As a teacher," wrote the concert pianist Edward Kilenyi, one of his students, "he was extremely noncommittal, preferring to allow the pupil to develop rather than have the teacher do it for him, training the student to such a high degree of musical taste that he himself was conscious of his own errors of interpretation rather than having them pointed out to him by the teacher."

Dohnányi also distinguished himself as a conductor. From 1918 to 1944 he was the conductor of the Budapest Philharmonic and also made guest appearances with the world's foremost symphonic organizations, including those of the United States. In 1925 he was appointed principal conductor of the State Symphony Orchestra in New York, which had only a brief existence.

Despite his varied activities, Dohnányi continued to compose. In 1899 he received the Hans von Bülow Prize from the Bösendorfer piano firm for his E minor Piano Concerto, op. 5. On January 30, 1902, his Symphony in D minor was successfully introduced in Manchester, England. In the years between 1907 and 1913 he completed three works which to this day represent him most frequently on concert programs. In 1907 in Berlin the Klinger Quartet introduced his String Quartet in D-flat. Two years later the Suite in F-sharp minor was written. It was heard first in Budapest in 1910, the composer conducting. In 1913 he completed what is probably his most celebrated work—the *Variations on a Nursery Song*, for piano and orchestra. This is a set of variations on the charming little French tune "Ah, vous dirai-je, maman" (the same melody used in the United States for singing with the alphabet; the same one Mozart also used for variation treatment). Dohnányi's *Variations* was introduced in Berlin on February 17, 1916, with the composer at the piano.

All these are the works of a Romantic who clung to Brahms's coattails. Dohnányi proved himself a true disciple of the master in his respect for classical structures, in his lack of emotional inhibitions, in his partiality for broad-spun melodies and sensuous sweeps of sound, and in his appropriation of some of Brahms's identifiable rhythmic and melodic mannerisms. These early works by Dohnányi may not present the composer in a profile of his own. Nevertheless this music never fails to please audiences with its sound musicianship, poetic materials, fresh lyricism, and overall charm.

In some of his works, Dohnányi made use of the rhythms and melodies of Hungarian folk songs and dances. The most renowned of his national works are the *Variations on a Hungarian Folksong* (1916), which was introduced with the composer conducting in Budapest in 1917; and the *Ruralia Hungarica* (1924), which he originally wrote for the piano and then transcribed for orchestra. The orchestral version of the latter was given by the Budapest Philharmonic under the composer's direction in 1924.

In 1922 Dohnányi received the honorary title of Doctor of Music from the Budapest Academy. In 1930 in grateful acknowledgment of his *Missa in Dedicatione Ecclesiae*, which Dohnányi had written to inaugurate the Cathedral at Szeged, he was presented with a handsome subsidy from the government. In 1931 he received the Corvin Lanz decoration, the highest honor the Hungarian government could bestow in the field of arts and sciences. Also in 1931 he was made head of the Hungarian Broadcasting Service. Later he was appointed Deputy in the Upper House of Parliament and he received the Officer's Cross of the Legion of Honor of France.

Until the outbreak of World War II, Dohnányi was a dominant musical figure in Hungary. As Kilenyi wrote: "The musical life of Budapest centered around him." But Dohnányi did not permit his fame or his many commitments to rob him of the quiet and gracious social life that was a necessity. "Sundays at his country home on the hillside," Kilenyi reveals, "were days of peaceful strolls through the gardens with the few intimate friends who came to visit him—of easy, vivacious conversations about all sorts of subjects—and permeating through it all, the personality of the man himself, his intense interest in everything that went on around him from the flowers which he gardened daily to the newest bulletin just off the press."

The war years, which Dohnányi spent in Budapest, were a time of tragedy. Both his sons died in uniform: his elder son, Hans, in a Nazi prison camp pending execution for his part in the plot against Hitler's life; the other, Matthias, in action with the Hungarian army. The Nazi occupation of Hungary, a period of great trial and suffering for the composer, was followed by the Soviet occupation, which was no better. At last Dohnányi fled from Hungary, found refuge in Austria as a displaced person with the American Army of Occupation, and was able to do some concert work. But unfounded rumors that he had been pro-Nazi and anti-Semitic brought his musical activities in Austria to a sudden halt. The Hungarian government now demanded that the Allied Control Commission return Dohnányi to his country as a war criminal.

The Hungarian government withdrew its charges against Dohnányi following the elections of November 1945. Soon after this Dohnányi was cleared by the American Occupation authorities. He was then given permission to leave Austria. He went to England in the fall of 1947 and gave a number of concerts, including the premières of several major new works. Among these were the Second Piano Concerto in B minor, heard in Sheffield in 1947 with the composer as soloist and Sir Thomas Beecham conducting; and the first version of his Symphony in E major, performed by the Chelsea Symphony in London under Norman Del Mar on November 23, 1948.

The Symphony in E major is one of the important works of Dohnányi's later years. He wrote it during the bitter period of the War, in 1943 and 1944, and its music reflects Dohnányi's preoccupation at the time with the problems of a free life and of death. In the last movement he quotes Bach's chorale

Dresden

Come, Sweet Death. But, as Dohnányi explained, "the movement had nothing to do with the actual death. The words of the chorale tell only of the longing for death of the tired man. The variations alternate between this feeling and the desire to live which finally wins out. Life's victory over Death!" How much this symphony meant to its composer became evident ten years later when he revised it completely. The final version was heard on March 15, 1957, with Antal Dorati conducting the Minneapolis Symphony.

In 1948 Dohnányi came to the United States and appeared in several concerts; one, in Detroit, presented the American première of his Second Piano Concerto. He also held master classes and delivered lectures at several colleges and universities. In 1949 he was appointed to the music faculty of Florida State College in Tallahassee, a post he held until his death. In America, Dohnányi completed his second violin concerto, in C minor, which Frances Magnes introduced in San Antonio on January 26, 1951, Victor Alessandro conducting. He also wrote a Harp Concertino, op. 45 (1952), the Stabat Mater for boys' chorus (1953), and the American Rhapsody, for orchestra (1953).

Dohnányi was in New York arranging recordings of some of his works when he was stricken by influenza. A fatal heart attack followed, and he died in a New York City hospital on February 9, 1960.

Dohnányi was married three times. His last wife, Helen, whom he married in 1949, survived him, as did a daughter from his first marriage.

MAJOR WORKS

Chamber Music—2 piano quintets; 2 string quartets; Cello Sonata in B-flat minor; Serenade in C major, for violin, viola, and cello; Violin Sonata in C-sharp minor; Sextet in C major.

Choral Music—Missa in Dedicatione Ecclesiae; Cantus Vitae; Stabat Mater, for boys' chorus.

Operas—Der Schleier der Pierrette (pantomime); Tante Simona (one-act comic opera); The Tower of the Voivod; Der Tenor.

Orchestral Music—2 symphonies; 2 violin concertos; 2 piano concertos; Cello Concerto; Suite in F-sharp minor; Two Songs, for baritone and orchestra; Variations on a Nursery Song, for Piano and Orchestra; Festival Overture, for double orchestra; Ruralia Hungarica (also for piano); Minutes Symphoniques; Suite en Valse; Harp Concertino; American Rhapsody.

Piano Music—Passacaglia; Four Rhapsodies; Winterreigen; Ten Bagatelles; Humoresken; Three Pieces; Suite im Alten Stil; Six Concert Etudes; Variations on a Hungarian Folksong; Six Pieces; Three Singular Pieces.

Vocal Music—Six Lieder, for baritone and piano; Im Lebenslenz.

ABOUT

Papp, V., Ernst von Dohnányi; Rueth, M. U., The Tallahassee Years of Ernst von Dohnányi.

High Fidelity, December 1957.

Sem Dresden
1881–1957

Sem Dresden was born on April 20, 1881, in Amsterdam, the son of a successful merchant. As a boy he received little formal instruction in music, except for random lessons in harmony from Roeske, in counterpoint from Bernard Zweers, and in composition and conducting from Hans Pfitzner in Berlin. His teachers were all post-Romantics, but they seem to have exerted little influence on him, for his earliest mature compositions were more French than German in style, with a tendency towards Impressionistic writing. These works included the Sonata for Flute and Harp and the Sonata for Cello and Piano, both written in 1918.

In 1914 Dresden founded the Madrigal Society in Amsterdam which he conducted until 1926 and which became one of the finest a cappella choral groups in Europe. This activity as choral conductor was combined with duties as a critic and teacher. In 1918 Dresden became the music critic of the Groene Amsterdammer, and in 1923, of the Telegraaf. His teaching chores began in 1919 when he taught counterpoint at the Amsterdam Conservatory. From 1924 to 1929 he was the director of the Royal Conservatory in The Hague, and from 1929 to 1937 director of the Amsterdam Conservatory. He left Amsterdam and returned to the Royal Conservatory at The Hague in 1937 to become its director but was removed from office in 1940 by order of the Nazi occupation troops. He reassumed his post after the war and was responsible for reorganizing and revitalizing the curriculum. In 1945 he was made president of the State Education Commission.

Beginning with his first string quartet (1924), in which he quoted two old Dutch songs, a strong Dutch element began to penetrate his writing. In several later works he continued to make use of Dutch tunes—for example, his second cello sonata (1942) for which he borrowed the theme of a folk song on the one hand and a medieval hymn on the other; and the Piano Trio (1943), in which he used a popular Dutch children's song. Here, as in his concertos for solo instruments and orchestra, we find a Dutch sobriety of mood, together with rhythmic flexibility (frequent changes of meter, and displacement of accents) and an occasional leaning towards modern contrapuntal writing.

SEM DRESDEN

In *Music in Holland*, J. M. Meulenhoff has pointed out that Dresden often constructed his works from "short, pregnant motives which he varied in a number of ways, thereby subjecting them to inventive play." Dresden's instrumentation "often suggests a kaleidoscope; it is very differentiated, colorful, and sensitive in its sound." These traits are to be found in his *Dance Flashes*, for orchestra (1951), in which he constructed a varied "sound picture" from a single motive. A melody is adapted here for such dance forms as the polonaise, siciliano, waltz, and tarantella. "None of the old dances is fully worked out," says Meulenhoff, "but the elements of the old dance forms are 'touched' in a telling way in a modern style, making use merely of the basic rhythm idea." The *Dance Flashes* received the Leeuw State Prize.

During World War II and the Nazi occupation of Holland, Dresden completed a major choral work in which he expressed the tragic mood of his country and people. It was the *Chorus Symphonicus* (1944), a setting of four psalms with Latin texts. To celebrate the liberation of his country, Dresden produced another important work for chorus and orchestra, the *Psalm 84*, in which, says Meulenhoff, "the old Hebrew prayer is set in a monumental manner." After the war, the writing of large religious works for chorus and orchestra became with Dresden a major preoccupation. These works included an oratorio, *Saint Antoine*, heard at the International Church Music Congress in Augsburg, Germany, in 1955.

Dresden's last work was a one-act opera, *François Villon*, whose text by the composer was derived mainly from Villon's own writings. Dresden had completed only a version for voice and piano when he died. Jan Mul, one of Dresden's pupils, orchestrated it. The opera was produced posthumously at the Holland Festival on July 15, 1958. Howard Taubman, who heard the opera in Amsterdam, reported in the New York *Times* that it had "little action" and that Villon's lines, "glowing though they may be, are not enough to carry the day." Taubman added: "The flaws in the opera must be attributed to Dresden. There is a lack of variety in his musical design. He made an effort to be lyrical, but it had little energy."

Sem Dresden died in The Hague on July 31, 1957. He had been active all his life in promoting the interests of modern music in general, and Dutch music in particular. In 1931 he was elected president of the Dutch branch of the International Society for Contemporary Music.

Dresden summarized his theories on composition as follows: "Each sound, on its own without importance, is transient and only real for a short time; it dies, and in that rapid process of coming and going, the composer has to give it life and importance, far beyond the ephemeral nature of its existence."

MAJOR WORKS

Chamber Music—3 woodwind sextets; 2 cello sonatas; 2 piano trios; Sonata for Flute and Harp; String Quartet; Trio, for two oboes and English horn; Rameau Suite, for sextet; Violin Sonata; Sonata for Cello Solo; Vocalises, for soprano and seven instruments.

Dukas

Choral Music—Chorus Tragicus; O Kerstnacht; Memoriae Judaeorum; Hymnus Matutinus; Assumpta Est Maria; Chorus Symphonicus; Psalm 84; Saint Antoine, oratorio; Saint George and the Dragon.

Opera—François Villon (one act).

Orchestral Music—Various concertos for solo instruments and orchestra (violin; oboe; piano; flute; organ); Theme and Variations; Sinfonietta, for clarinet and orchestra; Dance Flashes, suite.

ABOUT

Meulenhoff, J. M., Music in Holland.

Paul Dukas
1865–1935

Paul Dukas was born in Paris on October 1, 1865. Though he revealed an unmistakable gift for music from early childhood it was some time before he received any formal training. Meanwhile he learned by himself all he could about the piano, solfeggio, and composition.

PAUL DUKAS

He first pursued classical studies at the Lycée Charlemagne at Turgot before concentrating on music. In 1882 he enrolled in the Paris Conservatory, where he stayed six years as a pupil of Mathias (piano), Dubois (harmony) and Guiraud (composition). While still a Conservatory student he wrote two fine orchestral overtures, *King Lear* and *Goetz von Berlichingen*, and in 1886 he won first prizes in counterpoint and fugue. However, when in

---

Dukas: dü kä′

1888 he applied for the Prix de Rome with a cantata, *Velléda*, he received only second prize, thus being denied the opportunity to continue his music studies in Rome.

Military service interrupted his formal study, but this period was not altogether a waste from a musical point of view. Deprived of exercises, textbooks, and teachers, he went to the published scores of the masters for further study, filling in gaps in his musical education. The study and analysis of great works of music gave him both perspective and a more mature understanding of structure and style.

Soon after discharging his military duties, Dukas completed the first of his compositions to attract attention—the concert overture *Polyeucte*, introduced by the Lamoureux Orchestra in Paris on January 23, 1892. The reviewer for the *Guide Musical* wrote that this work was "one of the most remarkable of recent years." Many years later, Martin Cooper said: "*Polyeucte* is distinguished, solidly written, clearly conceived and neatly executed."

More impressive still was his Symphony in C major, first heard in Paris on January 3, 1897, under the direction of Paul Vidal, to whom it is dedicated. Like *Polyeucte*, the Symphony betrays echoes of Wagner, but Dukas's own personality is not altogether submerged. In the clarity of his writing, transparency of harmonic texture, brightness of orchestration, and sensitivity of lyricism, the Symphony made a strong impression. Gustave Samazeuilh wrote: "It is distinguished by a youthful ardor which does not exclude a style of lofty feeling and a strong structure."

The work that first made Dukas famous—and the one, above all others, by which he is today remembered in the world's concert halls—is *L'Apprenti Sorcier* (most accurately translated as *The Sorcerer Apprentice* rather than *The Sorcerer's Apprentice* which is more frequently used). It was heard at a concert of the Société Nationale on May 18, 1897, the composer conducting, and from the beginning it was a success. Less than two years later, on January 14, 1899, Theodore Thomas conducted the American première in Chicago.

This orchestral scherzo is a musical adaptation of a whimsical ballad of Goethe, *Der Zauberlehring*, which in turn was taken from a folk tale. The music describes the program literally, with a most uncommon gift for finding the proper musical equivalent for each development in the delightful story of a sorcerer's apprentice who knows the formula for making a broom animate. He orders it to fetch water, but he does not know the proper incantation with which to halt the routine and a flood ensues. His shrieks summon his master who pronounces the words necessary to make the broom inanimate again and to restore peace and order.

In the years between 1901 and 1903 Dukas completed two important works for the piano. One was the Sonata in E-flat minor which has an almost Beethovenian grandeur. The other, by contrast exquisite and tender rather than spacious and heroic, is the *Variations, Interlude and Finale*, based on a theme of Rameau.

Dukas's only opera, *Ariane et Barbe-Bleue*, came to the Opéra-Comique in Paris on May 10, 1907. Renouncing Wagnerian style and principles, which had so tempted him in his first orchestral pieces, and dispensing with the programmatic realism that had characterized *The Sorcerer Apprentice*, Dukas here created an Impressionist masterwork which some critics regard as second in importance to Debussy's *Pelléas et Mélisande*. Like *Pelléas*, Dukas's only opera uses a text by Maurice Maeterlinck, an adaptation of the Bluebeard legend. And like *Pelléas*, Dukas's opera derives its strength from sensitive atmospheres, understated emotions, subdued colors and dynamics. "This music of Paul Dukas," wrote Gabriel Fauré in *Figaro*, "so clearly delineated, so sharp and eloquent—does it not throw more light on the personages of the drama, who walk in a somewhat imprecise atmosphere and express themselves in a similarly imprecise manner?" The American première of the opera was conducted by Arturo Toscanini at the Metropolitan Opera, on March 29, 1911; Geraldine Farrar appeared as Ariane.

La Péri (1910) was written for the dancer Mlle. Trukhanova; this, too, is the work of an Impressionist. The score designated the composition as a "danced poem"—implying a merger of ballet and tone poem. The score also outlines the basic scenario. The Péri is the descendant of a fallen angel excluded from Paradise until she has done penance. Iskender comes upon her as she is asleep in her jeweled robe and snatches the lotus (symbol of immortality) in her hand. The Péri awakens, dances for Iskender, and thus is able to recover the lotus. She disappears, as darkness surrounds and obliterates Iskender.

La Péri was introduced by Mlle. Trukhanova in Paris on April 22, 1912. The score was heard in the United States on January 7, 1916, with Alfred Hertz conducting the San Francisco Symphony.

Dukas produced few works after 1910. Supercritical of his music, and a little contemptuous of public opinion, he did not try to get his few post-1910 works performed or published. Just before his death he destroyed most of these efforts.

The truth was that after 1910 Dukas regarded himself more as a teacher than as a composer. From 1900 to 1910 he was professor of orchestration at the Paris Conservatory. In 1918 he succeeded Debussy as a member of the Conseil de l'Enseignement Supérieur. From 1927 until his death he was professor of composition at the Conservatory. He was also a music critic for the *Revue Hebdomadaire*, the *Gazette des Beaux-Arts*, and other music journals; and he edited an edition of Rameau's works.

Paul Dukas died of a heart attack in Paris on May 17, 1935. A few months before his death he was chosen to succeed Alfred Bruneau in the Académie des Beaux-Arts.

"Looking at Dukas's art as a whole," says Edward Lockspeiser, "one is left with the impression that his main inspiration came from Beethoven. Probably his music is interesting to us today chiefly because it shows the hidden though binding chain between the musical civilizations of France and Germany."

MAJOR WORKS

Ballet—La Péri, "danced poem."
Chamber Music—La Villanelle, for horn and piano.
Opera—Ariane et Barbe-Bleue.
Orchestral Music—Polyeucte; Symphony in C major; L'Apprenti Sorcier (The Sorcerer Apprentice).
Piano Music—Sonata in E-flat minor; Variations, Interlude and Finale (on a theme of Rameau); Prélude Élégiaque; La Plainte au Loin du Faune.
Vocal Music—Sonnet de Ronsard.

ABOUT

Bacharach, A. L. (ed.), The Music Masters: v4, The Twentieth Century; Fauré, G., Paul Dukas: Sa Vie et Son Œuvre; Indy, V. d', Emmanuel Chabrier et Paul Dukas; Samazeuilh, G., Paul Dukas, Musicien Français.
La Revue Musicale (Dukas issue), May–June, 1936.

Dutilleux

Henri Dutilleux
1916–

Henri Dutilleux was born in Angers, France, on January 22, 1916. His grandfather, Julien Koszul, had been the director of the Roubaix Conservatory. Dutilleux spent his boyhood in Douai where he received his academic education and where he studied harmony and counterpoint with Victor Gallois, director of the local Conservatory. He then attended the Paris Conservatory, where his teachers included Jean Gallon in harmony, Noël Gallon in fugue, and Henri Busser in composition. In 1938 Dutilleux received the Prix de Rome (the last musician to get it before the outbreak of World War II). His stay in Rome was interrupted after a few months when the war compelled him to return to Paris.

HENRI DUTILLEUX

In 1944, following the liberation of Paris, he was appointed head of production of Illustrations Musicales of the French Radio. In this capacity, he wrote music for radio broadcasts. He also contributed scores for motion pictures and theatrical productions. On September 17, 1946, he married Geneviève Joy, a concert pianist.

His first major concert work was a piano sonata (1948), in which a strong individual language based on concentration and economy was couched within a classical structure. The

---

Dutilleux: dü tē yû′

sonata was introduced in Paris by Geneviève Joy at a concert of the Société Nationale de Musique in 1948.

His next significant composition was his first symphony, which Roger Desormière conducted in Paris on June 7, 1951. The composer here intended to portray the birth, development, and death of a dream. He explained: "The music emerges from the shadow in the first movement only to return whence it came in the very last ones. Thus there is established a transition between the real and the imaginary world. It is a little like the inception and unfolding of a dream." The two outer movements are in the form of variations, while the middle movements are a scherzo (in the style of a perpetual motion) and a broadly lyrical lento-intermezzo. Soon after its première, the symphony was used as background music for a ballet, with Léonide Massine's choreography. On January 8, 1954, the symphony was heard in the United States when Charles Münch conducted a performance with the Boston Symphony. Olin Downes said of the work: "It is a powerful conception in a highly modern vein. . . . The symphony has a tragical aspect; fantastical, if not macabre in the scherzo; of a brooding and introspective nature in the slow section movements." When the symphony was recorded in 1957 it received the Grand Prix de l'Académie du Disque Français.

On March 18, 1953, the Paris première of Dutilleux's ballet *Le Loup* (*The Wolf*), was presented by Roland Petit and his company. It was described as the most important new ballet produced in Paris since the end of World War II. The strange scenario (the work of Jean Anouilh and Georges Neveux) tells of a deserted bride who runs away with a wolf, released from its animal trainer's cage. They go off into the forest. "Her initial fright having passed," explain Anouilh and Neveux, "she finds herself attracted to this being, which, unlike men, is incapable of weakness or deception. Accordingly, when the aroused villagers pursue the wolf, she will defend him, and will die with him."

In 1953 Dutilleux received the important Prix du Portique, an award given once every three years to composers under forty years of age for their over-all creative achievements.

Dutilleux's Second Symphony was commissioned jointly by the Boston Symphony

174

(for its seventy-fifth anniversary) and the Koussevitzky Music Foundation. The première took place in Boston, Charles Münch conducting, on December 1, 1959. This is a large work calling for two orchestras: a large one, and a chamber ensemble of twelve instruments. Dutilleux had long been interested in creating such a work; in fact, in his first symphony he had experimented with detaching a small group from the larger body. But he took pains to point out that in writing for a large and small group he was not reviving the old concerto-grosso structure. He assigns equal importance to each, and often uses the two ensembles poly-rhythmically and polytonally. The smaller group is placed in a circle between the conductor and the larger orchestra.

In *Le Point: Revue Artistique et Littéraire*, Antoine Goléa makes note of the significant evolution that took place in Dutilleux's music: "One need only compare the first and second symphonies in order to note to what extent a musician has remained faithful to himself, not without taking into account the great impera-tives of the style of his time, but bending them to the exigencies of his own personality. On the plane of structures of timbre and thematic economy, the Second Symphony . . . takes part in most active fashion in the evolution of music proceeding from the works of Boulez; but while so many young musicians are search-ing—often laboriously—for a form adaptable to their sonorous dreams, Dutilleux does not hesitate . . . to bend the great traditional forms into a sonorous continuum almost entirely new."

Another significant work for orchestra was the result of a commission from the Cleveland Orchestra in the United States: the *Métaboles*, which the Orchestra introduced under George Szell on January 14, 1965. In describing this work the composer explained that he used *métaboles*, a term of rhetoric adapted to musi-cal forms, in order to disclose "the intention of the author in regard to . . . five orchestral pieces: to present one or many ideas in different order and aspects, until—by successive stages—they undergo an actual change of nature. The pieces are linked to one another, and present the following outline: In each, the main motive—melodic, rhythmic, harmonic, or simply instrumental—undergoes successive transformations. . . . At a given stage of

evolution—toward the end of each piece—the distortion is so charged as to engender a new motive which appears as a filigree under the symphonic texture. It is this figure which 'sets the bait' for the next piece, and so forth until the last piece where the initial motive from the beginning of the work is profiled above the coda, in a long rising movement."

In 1959 Dutilleux was awarded the Grand Prix du Conseil Général de la Seine for his contributions to French music. Four years later he retired from his radio work to con-centrate on composition and on teaching composition at the École Normale de Musique. He has been a member of the Conseil Supérieur of the Paris Conservatory; a Chevalier of the Legion of Honor; an Officier des Arts et des Lettres; a member of the French section of the International Society for Contemporary Music; and a member of the executive com-mittee of the Conseil International de la Musique (UNESCO).

In *Les Nouvelles Littéraires*, in 1961, Dutil-leux described his working methods as follows: "I work very slowly. I have an obsession with rigorousness, and I seek always to insert my thought into a formal frame, precise, abstract-ed, strict. On the other hand, I have such a curiosity that I cannot detach myself—before the work in me is completely mature—from all the diverse temptations of form, and often after that which I discover or hear in the course of my search and my work. . . . I am very sensitive to all that occurs in the world, to events, to journals, to books which make their appearance. I can enclose myself in my ivory tower to compose, only when my work has become imperious, that is to say when I have chosen the form it will have. There evident-ly exists a form to each work, according to an interior evolution. The problem of forms, of structures which are far removed from prefabricated frames, preoccupies me more and more."

Jean Roy has noted much inquietude in Dutilleux's music, explaining: "Dutilleux is surely attracted by what is unstable, myste-rious, wavering, by an anguish in the atonality which stamps its contours, effaces the joints. That which is for others a systematic process, a rule of syntax, is for him a climate, a sonorous landscape. He advances, loses him-self, finds himself again."

Egge

MAJOR WORKS

Ballets—La Belle Époque; Le Loup; Salmacis.

Chamber Music—Sonatine, for Flute and Piano; Oboe Sonata.

Orchestral Music—2 symphonies; La Giole, for voice and orchestra; Les Hauts de Hurle-Vent, suite; Sarabande; Concertino, for thirty-eight instruments; Sept Pièces; Cello Concerto; Métaboles.

Piano Music—Sonata.

Vocal Music—Fantasio; Pour une Amie Perdue; Trois Sonnets de Jean Cassou.

ABOUT

Lang, P. H. and Broder, N. (eds.), Contemporary Music in Europe; Roy, J., Présences Contemporaines; Samuel, C., Panorama de l'Art Musical Contemporain.

Klaus Egge
1906–

Klaus Egge was born in Granskerad, in the province of Telemark, Norway, July 19, 1906. He attended the Oslo Conservatory where he studied piano with Nils Larsen and composition with Fartein Valen. His studies in composition were later completed in Berlin with Walter Gmeindel.

KLAUS EGGE

In the first of his three creative periods, Egge was strongly nationalistic in subject matter and in musical materials. Examples of this period include the *Draumkvedsonate* for piano (1934), the first piano concerto (1937),

Egge: ĕg′ gĕ

and the dramatic work for chorus *Sveinung Vreim* (1938). "Both melody and harmony have an unmistakably Norwegian stamp," say Kristian Lange and Arne Östvedt in *Norwegian Music*, "but are presented in modern guise." Lange and Östvedt further point out that a unique distinguishing technical feature in these national compositions results from the composer's adaptation of the Hardanger fiddle. Airs for the Hardanger fiddle are often constructed from a four-note series (tetrachords)—"not infrequently two Lydian tetrachords form the basis of the melody. In tetrachord constructions of this kind there is nothing to prevent the use of a scale which spans two octaves. It may be placed in such a way that it represents the twelve semitones of the octave, but in a diatonic sequence." These combinations provide a melody with an unmistakable Norwegian personality, and Egge fully availed himself of this technique in his early works.

Egge embarked on his second creative period with a Piano Trio (1941) and perfected and crystallized this new style in his first symphony (1942). Bach-like polyphony, but with freedom of movement for the various voices, is a distinguishing trait of this new manner, though the writing does not have the severity of Hindemith's linear counterpoint.

The first symphony was a fruit of the difficult war years. It is dedicated to the "Norwegian seamen who took part in the Great World War" and is in memory of the composer's childhood friend who died in the war. Introduced in Oslo October 4, 1945, the symphony made a deep impression not only for its skillful contrapuntal writing but also for its dramatic and emotional interest. Oscar Hansen wrote in a review: "The symphony is epic in sound. . . . It is in E minor and this is chosen for a reason. This is no preferred key for symphonies, but it is particularly suitable for expressing the elegiac, the passionate, and the past."

This symphony received its American première in Fort Wayne December 4, 1956, in a performance by the Fort Wayne Philharmonic under Igor Buketoff. Monica Agnew described the symphony as follows in the *News-Sentinel*: "There are many short solos for the winds, and the beauty of the plaintive quality of one of these played by solo oboe, bassoon and cello was especially impressive. The composer's use of a drone-like beat on plucked strings of the basses throughout the three movements was interesting. The lovely lyrical character of the second movement, with a chorale-like theme in the winds, which was developed by the various choirs, provided some luscious sounds from the cellos, violas and basses. The third movement rollicked along in contrapuntal style, building a broad climax with much brass and tympani to a final explosive conclusion."

Besides this symphony the most significant product of his second creative period is the second piano concerto (1944), introduced in Oslo December 9, 1946, with Eva Knardahl as soloist. The work consists of a series of seven symphonic variations and fugue on a Norwegian folk song, the same melody used by Grieg in *Norwegian Dances and Songs* for piano, op. 17.

In his third creative phase, Egge developed "a form of music without cadence but with a structure predominantly polyphonic and dissonant, marked by a vigorous emphatic rhythm," according to Lange and Östvedt. Here we encounter greater transparency in the orchestration and a greater economy of means than in Egge's earlier music. Though dissonant, these works are still diatonic, arriving at an individuality of speech through a skillful and at times unusual deployment of tonal relationships.

This third period, the period of Egge's full maturity, produced two symphonies and a violin concerto, among other important works. The second symphony (1947) was given in Oslo December 9, 1949. The third (1957) was commissioned by the Louisville Orchestra in Kentucky which introduced it under Robert Whitney March 4, 1959. The violin concerto (1953) was first heard in a performance by Ernst Glaser in Oslo November 5, 1953, and was later performed by Camilla Wicks and the New York Philharmonic in 1957.

From 1935 to 1938 Egge edited the *Tonekunst* in Oslo. In 1945 he became the music critic of the Oslo *Arbeiderbladet*, president of the Norwegian Composers Society, vice president of the Norwegian Composers Propaganda Committee, and chairman of the Norwegian Artists Council representing twenty-two art groups in Norway. From 1946 to 1948 and again from 1956 to 1958 he was president of the Northern Composers Council. He has also served as Norway's music representative in the Norwegian National Commission for UNESCO, and from 1954 to 1958 as a member of the International Music Council's executive board. For his services to Norwegian music Egge received the Order of King Olaf in 1958. Since 1949 he has received an annual grant from the Norwegian government.

MAJOR WORKS

Ballet — Fanitullen.

Chamber Music — String Quartet; Viola Sonata; Violin Sonata; Wind Quintet; Piano Trio; Woodwind Quintet; Duo Concertante, for violin and viola.

Choral Music — Sveinung Vreim; Noregs-Songen; Den Dag Kjem Aldri; Sanningi.

Orchestral Music — 3 symphonies; 2 piano concertos; Bruresong Yver Heiom, for soprano and orchestra; Fjell-Noreg, symphonic thanksgiving for soprano and orchestra; Draumar i Stjernesno, three songs for soprano and orchestra; Elskhugsvede, for mezzo soprano and strings; Tarn Over Oslo, overture; Violin Concerto.

Piano Music — Draumkvedsonate; Tvoroystes Slatterrytmer; Fantasi; Gukkoslatten; Sonata Patetica.

Vocal Music — Gronlandssanger; Gullharpesongar; Elskhugskvede; Den Myrke Skyfloken; Hovden-Salmar, for voice and organ.

ABOUT

Lange, K. and Östvedt, A., Norwegian Music.

Werner Egk
1901–

Werner Egk was born May 17, 1901, in Auchsesheim, near Augsburg, Germany. He came from old Swabian-Bavarian peasant stock. His strong inclinations for painting and literature, as well as for music, were revealed during his attendance at the local Gymnasium, and it was some time before he chose music as his vocation. Except for piano lessons with Anna Hirzel-Langenhan at Augsburg and later, composition with Carl Orff in Munich, he is completely self-taught.

At nineteen he served as a musical director of the Art Theatre in Schwabing, the Latin Quarter of Munich. In 1924 he went to Italy to convalesce from a serious illness and stayed there several years, absorbing its musical culture. This Italian sojourn crystallized his desire to become a composer and produced

Egk: ĕk

several works. Upon his return to Germany he settled in a suburb of Munich; later, in 1928 and 1929, he lived in Berlin where he first became interested in radio as a medium for composition. Returning to Munich he affiliated himself with the Bavarian Radio there for which he wrote several operas,

WERNER EGK

librettos as well as music. His first radio opera, *Weihnacht*, was broadcast in 1929; his most important one, *Columbus*, was broadcast July 13, 1933. In 1941 Egk adapted *Columbus* for the stage. This version was first produced at the Frankfurt Opera January 13, 1942. Described in the score as a "report and image in three parts," *Columbus* traces the biography of its hero from the time he receives help for his expedition from Queen Isabella, through the time he sets foot in the new world to be greeted by the Indians, and up to the moments of his final disgrace and death in Spain. The story is told, says Gerhart von Westerman, by means of "al fresco pictures in broad, sweeping strokes," with "dramatic moments ... less important ... than epic presentation, which is strengthened through the meditative-choruses." Egk's radio operas were so admirably suited for the medium of broadcasting that he is often recognized as the first outstanding opera composer to have gained both his creative apprenticeship and his first recognition through radio.

One of the earliest of Egk's important concert works was an oratorio, *Furchtlosigkeit*

und Wohlwollen, which he completed in 1931 for a festival in Munich. His first successful concert work was *Georgica* (1934), a delightful suite of four Bavarian peasant pieces for orchestra which had numerous performances both in Europe and in the United States. When this composition was given its world première in the United States, performed by the New York Philharmonic on November 14, 1934, Lawrence Gilman, in his program annotations, described the music as follows by quoting an unnamed source: "Egk, in his own way and with the medium of his own art, attempts to portray the rural life of his own country. One feels in these pieces the prevailing charm of the Upper Bavarian landscape and the naïve simplicity of the age-old Bavarian marches, love songs and dances."

But it is in opera, rather than concert music, that Egk achieved international renown, and he achieved it first in 1935 with *Die Zaubergeige* (*The Magic Violin*), the first opera which he wrote directly for the operatic stage. This work was the consequence of the composer's earlier experiences as a writer of music for puppet shows in Munich. The libretto (by Ludwig Andersen and the composer) was based on a puppet play by Count Pocci. With a fairy-tale text, and with a score brimming over with catchy folk tunes and popular native dance melodies, *Die Zaubergeige* is a Bavarian folk opera which makes an immediate impact on audiences. It enjoyed a huge success when it was introduced by the Frankfurt Opera in Germany May 20, 1935. Geraldine de Courcy said of it at the time: "Egk's delectable concoction may probably rank as the most significant produced in Germany in this sphere of composition since *Arabella* of Richard Strauss." It was widely performed throughout Germany both in its original version and later in a revision which was first seen at the Stuttgart Stadttheater May 2, 1954.

The success of *Die Zaubergeige* brought Egk a commission from the Berlin State Opera which resulted in *Peer Gynt*, libretto by the composer based on Ibsen. It was performed November 24, 1938, the composer conducting. Here Egk departed from the popular idioms and styles of *Die Zaubergeige* to a style that was more subtle, refined, and suggestive. But the gift for melody and extraordinary virtuosity in orchestration revealed in his first stage opera were still evident. Egk successfully conveys in *Peer Gynt*, says Gerhart von Westerman, "the three utterly different spheres in which this drama unfolds: Peer's and Solveig's homeland in the Norwegian mountains, the subterranean kingdom of the Trolls, and the Spanish-American scenes." The American première of *Peer Gynt* took place in Hartford, Connecticut, February 23, 1966—a presentation by Hartt College.

Peer Gynt was followed in 1939 by a *Tanzspiel* (play for dancers) based on the Don Juan theme—*Joan von Zarissa*, introduced at the Berlin State Opera January 20, 1940, the composer conducting.

In the years between 1936 and 1940 Egk served as conductor of the Berlin State Opera. During the war years he worked upon *Circe*, an opera based on Calderón's *El Mayor Encanto Amor*, which the Municipal Opera in Berlin finally produced December 18, 1948. A marriage of *buffa* and *seria* styles—and a curious mixture of farce and mythology—*Circe* failed to make much of an impression. (Fully conscious of the fact that *Circe* had serious artistic shortcomings, Egk rewrote it completely many years later giving it the new title of *17 Tage und 4 Minuten*. The rewritten opera made a far stronger impression when it was introduced in Stuttgart June 2, 1966, than the original had done.) An even more unfortunate fate befell Egk's ballet *Abraxas*, whose première was conducted by the composer at the Munich Opera June 6, 1948. *Abraxas*, based on Heine's dance poem *Doktor Faust* which the composer himself had adapted, reached a climax with an orgy by the demons of hell—an episode that so shocked and outraged the morals and sensibilities of influential officials in Munich that the ballet was forthwith banned by the Bavarian Ministry of Education. The censorship aroused considerable controversy in Munich and fomented much bitterness. As a result of this scandal, Egk decided in 1950 to leave Munich for Berlin where during the next three years he served as the director of the Hochschule für Musik.

By 1953 Egk's outraged feelings had been completely assuaged and he was able to return to Munich. There he wrote a new opera, *Irische Legende*, "five pictures" based on William Butler Yeats's *The Countess Kathleen O'Shea*,

adapted by the composer. The première took place at the Salzburg Festival August 17, 1955, George Szell conducting. The opera received over twenty curtain calls and was regarded as the highlight of the festival. But Egk's greatest success since *Die Zaubergeige* came with the comic opera *Der Revisor*, the composer's text based on Nikolai Gogol's *The Inspector General*. First heard at the Schwetzingen Festival May 9, 1957, *Der Revisor* delighted audiences and critics in spite of the fact that flowing lyricism was abandoned for an austere kind of parlando style. But Egk's music completely captured the merriment and verve of Gogol's satire, with contrasts provided through the interpolation of a Russian folk song and several French chansons. Egk's unfailing sense of good theatre combined with an exceptional skill in writing both for the chorus and for the orchestra made *Der Revisor* an unforgettable operatic experience. "Egk succeeds in keeping things moving from beginning to end," reported Everett Helm in the *Saturday Review*, "and the score employs traditional harmonic and melodic material in a thoroughly witty way, using moderate dissonances freely within a tonal framework. The vocal writing is expert, and the text comes across clearly, supported by a generally transparent and colorful orchestral accompaniment."

Soon after its world première, *Der Revisor* was produced in an English translation in London at the Sadler's Wells Theatre, and also at the Vienna State Opera, the Stuttgart Opera, and the Piccola Scala in Milan. On October 19, 1960, it was introduced to the United States by the New York City Opera, with Egk himself conducting.

The festivities attending the opening of the rebuilt National Theatre in Munich in November 1963 were highlighted by a single world première—that of Egk's *Die Verlobung in San Domingo* on November 27, 1963. Egk's libretto was drawn from a story by Heinrich von Kleist. Reporting his impressions in the New York *Times* Everett Helm said: "The libretto . . . and the score are expertly fashioned; everything 'clicks,' musically and dramatically. The music, couched in a conservative idiom, is effective, grateful for the singers and easy on the audience's ears."

Though Egk makes use of modern idioms, he is essentially a composer with conservative tendencies. "His medium," wrote Henry Pleasants, "is essentially the exploitation of descriptive and graphic devices inherited from Wagner and Richard Strauss. He is distinguished from his contemporaries by his unashamed use of them and his ability to use these particular devices so well."

From 1941 to 1945 Egk was the director of the Composers Union in Bavaria. Since 1952 he has been the president of the Association of German Composers. In 1953 he conceived the idea for and then wrote the libretto for Boris Blacher's avant-garde opera *Abstrakte Oper Nr. 1*.

MAJOR WORKS

Ballets—Joan von Zarissa; Abraxas; Ein Sommertag; Allegria; Die Chinesische Nachtigall; Danza.

Choral Music—Furchtlosigkeit und Wohlwollen, oratorio; Mein Vaterland.

Operas—Die Zaubergeige; Peer Gynt; Columbus (adapted from a radio opera); Circe; Irische Legende; Der Revisor; Die Verlobung in San Domingo; 17 Tage und 4 Minuten; Casanova in London.

Orchestral Music—Georgica, suite; Geigenmusik, for violin and orchestra; Orchester-Sonata; Französiche Suite (based on Rameau); Quattro Canzoni, four Italian songs for high voice and orchestra; Natur, Liebe, Tod, cantata for basso and chamber orchestra; Variationen über ein Altes Wiener Strophenlied, for coloratura soprano and orchestra; La Tentation de Saint Antoine, for contralto, string quartet, and string orchestra; Chanson et Romance, for high soprano and orchestra; Variationen über ein Karibisches Thema.

Piano Music—Sonata.

ABOUT

Lang, P. H. and Broder, N. (eds.), Contemporary Music in Europe; Machlis, J., Introduction to Contemporary Music.

Music Review (London), 1953.

Gottfried von Einem
1918–

Gottfried von Einem was born in Bern, Switzerland, January 24, 1918, the son of the Austrian military attaché. Immediately after the end of World War I, the family settled in Holstein, where Gottfried attended a public school in Plön in which Hindemith had been interested and for which he had written a composition. Interest in modern music and in Hindemith was keen there and helped to stimulate

---

Einem: ī′ něm

Gottfried's own musical inclinations. These interests were further aroused by trips with his father to different parts of Europe which enabled him to hear various performances of operas and orchestral music, including those at the Salzburg Festival. His early contacts with Bruno Walter, Toscanini, and other eminent musicians at the Salzburg Festival encouraged him to develop his own latent talent. At eleven he completed two works for orchestra, one of which, *Helden in Ketten*, he dedicated to Bruno Walter.

GOTTFRIED VON EINEM

For a long time his music study was sporadic, but in 1938 he determined to develop his technique as a composer and went to Berlin hoping to study with Hindemith. The ambition could not be realized: Hindemith had become *persona non grata* to the Third Reich and had left the country. Von Einem studied instead with Boris Blacher.

In 1941 von Einem began his professional career by serving as assistant conductor and coach at the Berlin State Opera and the Bayreuth Festival. This proved to be an important phase in von Einem's creative development by providing him with first-hand experiences in the techniques and methods of opera performances.

Von Einem's first mature compositions were written and performed in the period between 1934 and 1944. Opus No. 1 was the ballet *Prinzessin Turandot*, which Karl Elmendorff conducted in Dresden in 1944 and which

G. D. Fränkische described as "music of scintillating elegance and boundless beauty." Opus No. 2 was a work with which von Einem was first represented on symphony programs in Europe and the United States: *Capriccio*, for orchestra, the première of which took place in Berlin March 12, 1943, Leo Borchard conducting the Berlin Philharmonic. A work of romantic ardor and melodic opulence (particularly in the second movement), *Capriccio* proved a delightful listening experience. The Concerto for Orchestra, op. 4–which Herbert von Karajan introduced with the Berlin State Opera Orchestra April 3, 1944– was welcomed for the same reason. Because of its pleasing lyricism and deeply felt emotion, this concerto was music that was readily assimilable at first hearing. The third movement provides contrast through the spicy intrusion of some jazz material.

Gottfried von Einem's music suffered considerable abuse at the hands of most German critics and Nazi officials because of his undisguised hostility to the Nazi regime. The propaganda ministry was particularly severe in denouncing the Concerto for Orchestra, a fact which discouraged many German and Austrian orchestras from performing it. Von Einem was also personally victimized: at one time he and his mother were seized by the Gestapo and imprisoned for several months.

In 1945 von Einem escaped from Germany. He settled in Salzburg where, in 1946, he married Lianne von Bismarck. They established permanent residence in a medieval watchtower. Their only child, a son, Caspar, was born in 1948. Lianne von Einem died in 1962.

Under the guidance of his teacher, Boris Blacher, von Einem began working on his first magnum opus, the opera *Dantons Tod*. It was based on a play by Georg Büchner (one of whose dramas had provided Alban Berg with the text for *Wozzeck*). The central theme of *Dantons Tod* is the rise and fall of the revolutionary Danton during Robespierre's reign of terror. *Dantons Tod* was introduced at the Salzburg Festival August 6, 1947 (the first year the festival had been resumed since World War II), and its success was enormous. However, the style proved so eclectic that some Austrian wits were tempted to remark: "*Nicht von Einem, sondern von Vielen*"–"Not from one man, but from many."

"The score," wrote Everett Helm in *Musical America*, "is in keeping with his impersonal concept of the story. It is descriptive and it is dramatic, but it is never sentimental. The musical form ... depends directly on the action and is a commentary on it.... Each scene is composed as a separate entity; even the brief introduction with which the opera begins has its own musical material, independent of what follows. The first three and the last three scenes are connected by orchestral interludes, which bridge the changes in mood and cover the changes of scenery.... The vocal writing ... is in keeping with the basic naturalistic-poetic conception.... Most of the opera is written in a kind of melodic recitative that approximates the accents of everyday speech but is still far enough removed from it to preserve the poetic quality of Büchner's language. In the more impassioned passages, von Einem employs an arioso style; but nowhere is there a true aria.... The music is predominantly tonal and is never systematically atonal, but the constant shifting of key often obscures the feeling of a tonal center."

The American première of *Dantons Tod* was given in New York by the New York City Opera in March 1966, with the composer in attendance.

In 1948 von Einem was appointed a member of the board of directors of the Salzburg Festival. On August 17, 1953, the festival once again became the setting for the world première of a von Einem opera, *Der Prozess (The Trial)*. *The Trial* was based on Franz Kafka's symbolic fantasy about a man, tortured by anxieties and guilt feelings he cannot explain, who must stand trial for a crime of which he is totally unaware. The libretto was the work of Boris Blacher and Heinz von Cramer. *The Trial*, like *Dantons Tod*, was an outstanding success. Willi Reich wrote: "We consider *Der Prozess* as one of the most significant musical works of our time for the theatre. After a first hearing, the main impression of von Einem's music is that it creates a completely suitable tonal atmosphere to the action of the stage. It brings the loose dialogue to artistic compact forms. Both vocally and orchestrally, it adds to the sensitivities, thoughts and actions of Kafka's characters things which could not be expressed by the spoken word."

The Trial was given its first American

performance (in an English translation) in New York October 20, 1953, by the New York City Opera. Although some critics found fault with the eclecticism and derivativeness of von Einem's music on the ground that he had tapped sources as varied as Richard Strauss and Stravinsky on the one hand and Kurt Weill and Gershwin on the other, the consensus was that this was forceful theatre and a compelling intellectual experience. Irving Kolodin, although he had some reservations, said in the *Saturday Review:* "Much of *The Trial* testified to his serious purpose, strong sense of orchestral values, constructional powers in developing a scene musically and theatrically." Virgil Thomson called the score as a whole "expressive, distinguished and highly functional."

Early in 1953 von Einem visited the United States for the first time, coming as a guest of the United States Department of State to study the American musical scene. In honor of this visit, the New York Philharmonic presented the American première of *Orchestra Music*, op. 9, written in 1948 and introduced in Vienna on December 21 of that year. In describing the composition, Virgil Thomson also pointed out von Einem's creative identity: "The classical preoccupation . . . seems to be a certain balance between spontaneity and objectivity, between sentiment and drama. This is its real strength, and, for modern German music, its novelty."

On a commission from the Louisville Orchestra, von Einem wrote *Meditations*, for orchestra, which that organization, under Robert Whitney, performed in Kentucky November 6, 1954. Many of von Einem's later orchestral works came about through commissions from the United States: the *Philadelphia Symphony*, from the Philadelphia Orchestra and Eugene Ormandy; *Ballade*, written for the fortieth anniversary of the Cleveland Orchestra; *Night Piece*, contracted for by a New Orleans industrialist, Edward B. Benjamin, who made it a practice to ask leading composers to write "restful music." Neither the *Philadelphia Symphony* nor *Night Music* (both of which had been intended for the Philadelphia Orchestra) were introduced in Philadelphia, nor for that matter in the United States. Both got their first hearings in Vienna— the symphony on November 4, 1961, the *Night*

Piece on April 27, 1963. The *Ballade*, however, received its world première in Cleveland in 1958, just as an earlier von Einem orchestral work—*Symphonic Scenes*—had been given its première in Boston, by the Boston Symphony, on October 11, 1957.

For the theatre von Einem created scores for several successful ballets in the 1950's. *Rondo vom Goldenen Kalb* was produced in Hamburg on February 1, 1952. *Glück, Tod und Traum* was introduced in Alpbach, Austria, in 1954, and *Medusa* at the Berlin State Opera on November 16, 1957. Von Einem subsequently wrote a charming comic opera, *Der Zerissene*, based on Nestroy, which received its world première in Hamburg September 17, 1964.

Gottfried von Einem spends most of the year in Vienna where he shares a comfortable apartment with his son and mother-in-law. Summer holidays are spent in a country home which he has maintained for many years in the Austrian mountains near the Swiss border. His interests other than music include traveling, a carryover from his childhood and boyhood days which he still indulges year after year. He is a voracious reader, and a lover of great paintings. He abhors machinery in all its forms and manifestations. He still does not know how to drive a car, and he is unable to operate his tape recorder.

In 1954 von Einem was made a member of the artistic board of the Vienna State Opera. He was subsequently elected president of the Austrian Music Section of UNESCO and appointed Councillor of the Vienna Konzerthausgesellschaft. In 1960 he was awarded the Theodor Körner Prize and the Prize of the City of Vienna for outstanding contributions to Austrian music. He received the Austrian State Prize for music in 1965.

MAJOR WORKS

Ballets—Prinzessin Turandot; Rondo vom Goldenen Kalb; Pas de Cœur; Glück, Tod und Traum; Princess Zoo; Medusa.

Chamber Music—Hymnus; Das Stundenlied.

Operas—Dantons Tod; Der Prozess (The Trial); Der Zerissene.

Orchestral Music—Capriccio; Concerto for Orchestra; Orchestra Music; Serenade for Double Orchestra; Alpbacher Tanzserenade; Meditations; Piano Concerto; Wandlungen; Symphonic Scenes; Ballade; Von der Liebe, for soprano and orchestra; Dance Rondo; Night Piece (Nachtstück); Concerto in D for violin and orchestra; Cello Concerto.

Piano Music—Four Pieces; Two Sonatinas.
Vocal Music—Eight Songs After Hafis; Five Chinese Songs; Six Japanese Songs; Seven Songs.

ABOUT

Lang, P. H. and Broder, N. (eds.), Contemporary Music in Europe; Machlis, J., An Introduction to Contemporary Music; Rutz, H., Gottfried von Einem und Sein Oper Dantons Tod.

Musical America, May 1951.

Sir Edward Elgar
1857–1934

Sir Edward William Elgar, England's most important composer in two centuries, was born in Broadheath, near Worcester, June 2, 1857. The son of the organist of St. George's Catholic Church who was also proprietor of a music shop, Elgar exhibited a seemingly insatiable appetite for music. He began to study by himself harmony, counterpoint, the violin, and the organ. He spent hours memorizing the scores of symphonies and operas. While attending Littleton House for his academic education, he often substituted for his father as organist. He also wrote, in or about 1869, the music for *The Wand of Youth*, a children's play—two orchestral suites from which he later derived his Opus No. 1. The first suite was introduced at a Queen's Hall concert December 14, 1907, and the second at the Worcester Festival September 9, 1908.

His father wanted him to be a lawyer, and at fifteen Elgar left school to serve as a clerk to a local solicitor. A year later he was sent to London to concentrate on legal studies. After three years, convinced he was not intended for law, he returned home and became absorbed in musical interests and activities. He became the concertmaster of the local orchestra; he played in a woodwind quintet; he gave violin recitals; he played the organ; he orchestrated the works of other composers. In 1879 he went back to London to study the violin with Adolf Pollitzer. Five lessons convinced Elgar that he was not a potential virtuoso. Abandoning all thoughts of invading the concert stage, he turned to other areas of music. For five years he served as bandmaster at the County Lunatic Asylum at Worcester. He also filled various jobs as violinist and

Elgar: ĕl′ gẽr

conductor, and he wrote some functional pieces, one with the droll title of *Quadrille for an Eccentric Orchestra*. A more serious effort was an Intermezzo, for orchestra, performed by Stockley's Orchestra in Birmingham December 13, 1883.

SIR EDWARD ELGAR

In 1885 Elgar succeeded his father as the organist at St. George's in Worcester. Four years later he married one of his pupils, Caroline Alice Roberts, daughter of a major general. She was a woman of extraordinary intelligence, idealism, drive, and devotion. "Her attachment," says F. Bonavia, "was both love and friendship; it had the ardor of the one and the devotion of the other. . . . Not a cloud darkened their life together. She shared his triumphs and his disappointments, often acting as his amanuensis, ruling his music paper, advising, consoling – his inseparable companion."

Her influence on Elgar was far reaching. Her counsel and her complete faith in Elgar's creative potential made him decide, soon after his marriage, to abandon his scattered musical assignments for serious creative work. He set up home in London where, encouraged by his wife, he began to produce works in larger forms and of more ambitious scope than heretofore, including a delightful orchestral concert overture, *Froissart* (1890), which was well received at its first hearing on September 9, 1890. The mood as well as the program of this music was suggested in a motto printed in the published score–a quotation from a poem by Keats: "When chivalry/lifted up her lance on high."

The distractions of a great city were not conducive to sustained and intensive creative work. In 1891 Elgar and his wife moved to Malvern, where they lived for the next thirteen years. There he wrote some ambitious choral compositions. The first was a cantata, *The Black Knight* (1893), based on a poem by Uhland (as translated by Longfellow); its première took place at the Worcester Festival on April 18, 1893. This was followed by the oratorio *The Light of Life* (1896), adapted from the Scriptures, heard at the Worcester Festival on September 10, 1896; and by the cantata *Caractacus* (1898) presented at the Leeds Festival on October 5, 1898.

Elgar achieved international fame with two compositions: *Variations on an Original Theme* (or, as it is now better known, *Enigma Variations*) written in 1899, and *The Dream of Gerontius*, completed in 1900.

In the *Variations* each variation was intended as a portrait of one of Elgar's friends; one variation was a self-portrait. "The enigma," Elgar said, "I shall not explain–its 'dark saying' must be left unguessed." But the enigma is believed by some to be a hidden theme which though never actually heard *could* serve as a source of each of the variations.

The melodic freshness, the emotional exuberance, and at times the affecting tenderness and beauty of the *Enigma Variations* impressed Hans Richter, the celebrated conductor. He introduced the work in London on June 19, 1899, and gave it several performances in other countries. Its success was immediate and outstanding; for the first time the attention of the English music world was focused on Elgar.

Elgar scored an even greater success with his oratorio *The Dream of Gerontius*, based on the poem of Cardinal Newman. Consisting of a series of lyric and dramatic episodes describing the doctrine of purgatory as found in Catholic teachings, the music was filled with mysticism, vivid imagery, and nobility and grandeur. Ernest Newman said of it: "The work is of the first order almost throughout. Its detail work is poignant and convincing, while as a whole it has the homogeneity, the rounded completeness of vision, that only

comes when the artist sees his picture through and through in one white heat of imagination."

The Dream of Gerontius was introduced at the Birmingham Festival on October 3, 1900, Hans Richter conducting. But its success did not come until a year later when the work was given at the Lower Rhine Festival, where it was a triumph. Richard Strauss described it as a masterpiece. From that time on, the oratorio was acclaimed wherever and whenever it was given. It quickly became almost as popular with English audiences as Handel's *Messiah* and Mendelssohn's *Elijah*.

Elgar was now one of England's most celebrated composers. Bernard Shaw went so far as to say that he "holds the same position in English music as Beethoven in German music."

In 1901 Elgar planned to write a set of marches called *Pomp and Circumstance* (the phrase "pomp and circumstance" coming from *Othello*). He completed two of these in 1901, and one each in 1905, 1907, and 1930. The first, in D major, has become as intimately associated with the British Empire as "God Save the King." When Edward VII heard the majestic melody that is the heart of the march (and to which Laurence Housman subsequently wrote the lyric, "Land of Hope and Glory"), he exclaimed: "This tune will go round the world." With the writing of these patriotic marches, Elgar assumed an unofficial position as the music laureate of his country. For the coronation of Edward VII (1901) he was commissioned to write an Ode for solo voices, chorus, and orchestra. This was first performed at the Sheffield Festival on October 2, 1902.

Elgar completed some of his most important orchestral works during the decade between 1901 and 1911. These included the concert overtures *Cockaigne* (1901) and *In the South* (1903); *Introduction and Allegro*, for string quartet and strings (1905); two symphonies, in A-flat major (1908) and E-flat major (1911); and the B minor Violin Concerto (1910). This period also saw the completion of two important oratorios with texts drawn from the Scriptures: *The Apostles* (1903) and *The Kingdom* (1906).

Indicative of the high position Elgar had begun to occupy in English music was the enormously successful three-day Elgar festival that took place in London in 1904, with the

Hallé Orchestra of Manchester conducted by Hans Richter. On this occasion Elgar was knighted. Another evidence of his mounting fame came from Birmingham University which in 1905 appointed him to a chair of music expressly created for him, and which he occupied for one year. In 1911 Elgar was awarded the Order of Merit.

Elgar paid two visits to the United States, the first in 1905 to receive an honorary doctorate from Yale, the second in 1907 to direct a performance of his oratorio *The Apostles* in New York City.

During World War I, Elgar joined the Hampstead Division as special constable; later he volunteered in the Hampstead Reserve. He also enlisted his music in the war effort, setting war poems to music and completing a number of works on martial or patriotic subjects. In addition, to help raise funds for Polish war victims, he wrote a symphonic prelude, *Polonia* (1915).

After the war Elgar returned to more serious creative efforts. He grew increasingly objective in his writing, more reserved in emotion, more partial to concentrated expression and more intimate forms of music. In 1918 came his most important chamber-music works, the E minor String Quartet, the A minor Piano Quintet, and the E minor Violin Sonata. Here we encounter a new economy of means and a new reserve of expression, which also characterized his E minor Cello Concerto (1919), introduced by Felix Salmond in London on October 26, 1919, and now regarded by many critics as one of Elgar's masterworks.

Elgar's wife died in 1920. This was a crushing blow that shook Elgar to the depths. He buried with her tokens of all the honors he had earned, insisting they belonged to her. This gesture aroused a good deal of hostile criticism from those who felt that Elgar was making a public display of sentimentality to the point of sensationalism. But this was actually a sincere act of love and appreciation. How deeply her death affected him was proved even more forcefully when Elgar went into a protracted period of creative silence. Not the persuasion of close friends, not even his appointment as Master of the King's Musick, could bring him back to his work table. He abandoned Severn House in Hampstead, where he and his wife had resided the last

eight years of their life together, and his holiday house at Fittleworth in Sussex, which they had enjoyed since 1917. Instead he began to occupy a modest flat in London at 37 St. James's Place, where he stayed until 1929, when he made his last move—to Marl Bank, Rainbow Hill, in Worcester.

"The tendency to fritter time over trifles, and sometimes with trifling people could not always be resisted," wrote H. C. Colles about Elgar's life in the 1920's. "He was attracted by the idea of himself as a man of many interests of which music was only one, and a minor one at that. This was an innocent pose partly in self-defence against the wiles of lion hunters. The club bore who approached him with musical talk as a gambit could be snubbed with an expression of complete indifference toward the subject. . . . There was everything to divert him from the single-minded concentration of his work which Lady Elgar kept alight in him."

When he finally did return to composition he did so out of patriotism. George V was stricken by a serious illness in 1929. Elgar wrote a Christmas carol as a prayer of recovery. This was the first piece of music he had written in nine years. He now spoke of continuing his work where it had been interrupted, by planning a third symphony. In 1930 he wrote a suite for brass, *Severn*, which he also arranged for orchestra; in 1931 he completed the *Nursery Suite*, for orchestra; in 1932 and 1933 he wrote four compositions for unaccompanied chorus. Meanwhile, in 1931, he received a baronetcy, one of the highest honors that the Crown could bestow.

In January 1934, Elgar suffered from an attack of sciatica which demanded an immediate operation. Though his health degenerated quickly after the operation, he was able to supervise from his bedside a recording session of some of his music. Three weeks later, on February 23, 1934, he died at Marl Bank. One of his last requests was that nobody try to complete or publish his unfinished third symphony. He was buried beside his wife in Malvern; a few days after the burial, a memorial service attended by the great and near-great in English music was held at Worcester Cathedral.

Many critics have pointed out that Elgar was never a highly original composer. He

185

was never the experimenter or the iconoclast. The structures, procedures, and esthetics of the past satisfied him completely. Yet for all his ties to past practices and to older styles he managed to evolve his own musical personality with singular vividness. At best, his music has a charm singularly Elgar's own, together with an affecting lyricism and touching sentiments. J. F. Porte maintained that "his vein of tender sentiment was perhaps the most lovable of all its kind in music, and shared by that of Schubert. Elgar never shows us a soul that is seared or tortured, for while he can feel, he does not despair. An extreme sensitiveness to poetic ideas or reflections is a part of Elgar's thought, but this is always counterbalanced by a breezy reaction, a throwing aside as it were of anything which might lead to doubt; it is the ascendant spirit, the strong faith in himself, the blessing of common pluck, which never failed him."

Elgar had no set method of working. He conceived music at all times, while walking, playing, even while conversing with friends. He was usually scribbling ideas on paper, guarding the scraps carefully, and referring to them when he worked on major compositions. He worked easily and swiftly, ideas came to him copiously, and the task of working out these ideas seemed effortless.

Shaw once described Elgar as a typical English country gentleman. Like many English country gentlemen, Elgar was tall, erect, and well built. He kept himself aloof in the company of strangers, suspicious of people he did not know well. To friends, however, he was open, generous, and warm-hearted. His fine sense of humor (he was especially quick with puns) and his genial disposition were recognized by all who knew him well. He had the English countryman's love of the outdoors. Dressed in informal rough clothing, he often took long walking tours or bicycle trips. He loved flowers, woods, brooks, country paths. Chopping wood and clearing away brushwood was play. He also liked to fish and on occasion he enjoyed handicapping and betting on horses.

MAJOR WORKS

Chamber Music—Violin Sonata in E minor; String Quartet in E minor; Piano Quintet in A minor.

Choral Music—The Black Knight, cantata; Scenes from the Saga of King Olaf, cantata; The Light of Life, oratorio; Caractacus, cantata; The Dream of Gerontius, oratorio; The Apostles, oratorio; The Kingdom, oratorio; various anthems, hymns, and unaccompanied part songs and other choral pieces.

Orchestral Music—2 symphonies; Variations on an Original Theme (Enigma Variations); Pomp and Circumstance, five marches; Cockaigne, concert overture; Introduction and Allegro, for string quartet and string orchestra; In the South, concert overture; Elegy, for string orchestra; Violin Concerto in B minor; Falstaff, symphonic study; Cello Concerto in E minor; Nursery Suite.

Piano Music—Pieces Without Title; Sonatina; Adieu; Serenade.

Vocal Music—Fringes of the Fleet; Sea Pictures; individual songs for voice and piano including Is She Not Fair?, Like to the Damask Rose, Pleading, Rondel, Shepherd's Song, and Speak Music.

ABOUT

Anderson, W. R., Introduction to the Music of Elgar; Cardus, N., A Composers Eleven; Dunhill, T. F., Elgar; José, E. and Cranston, H., The Significance of Elgar; Kennedy, M., Portrait of Elgar; Maine, B., Elgar: His Life and Works; McVeagh, D., Edward Elgar: His Life and Music; Reed, W. H., Elgar; Sheldon, A. J., Edward Elgar; Young, P. (ed.), Letters of Edward Elgar and Other Writings.

Music and Letters (London), Special Elgar Issue, January 1935.

Georges Enesco
1881–1955

Georges Enesco, Rumania's most important composer in the twentieth century, was born in Liveni-Virnav, Dorohoi, August 19, 1881. His father, a farmer, gave him a small violin when he was four. Before long, Georges was playing by ear the gypsy tunes he had heard performed by village musicians. One year later he learned the elements of notation from a local teacher and was able to write down his own tunes. By the time he was seven he had composed several sonatas and rondos for the piano. He had also made considerable progress on the violin, once again with local instruction.

When Georges was seven, his father, fully aware of the boy's talent, took him to Vienna and entered him in the Conservatory. At first, Joseph Hellmesberger, the director, refused to consider one so young for admission, remarking acidly that the Conservatory was "no cradle." But after the child had played for him, Hellmesberger waived rules and personal

Enesco: ĕ nĕ′ skō

prejudices, not only admitting Georges into the Conservatory but taking him in as a member of his own household. At the Conservatory, Enesco studied harmony and counterpoint with Robert Fuchs and violin with Hellmesberger, winning first prizes in harmony and violin in 1892. He made his first appearance as a violinist at a benefit concert at Slanic-Moldova on August 5, 1889. And on January 26, 1892, he made his first appearance as a virtuoso in Vienna.

GEORGES ENESCO

During his student days in Vienna, Enesco became personally acquainted with Brahms. Enesco attended the performance at Hellmesberger's house in which Brahms's Clarinet Quintet was played for the first time anywhere. Admiration for the master soon developed into adulation, an adulation reflected in Enesco's undisguised attempts to imitate Brahms's style and mannerisms in his own compositions.

At the completion of his studies at the Vienna Conservatory in 1893, Enesco was presented with a gold medal. On the advice of Hellmesberger, he then went to Paris to further his violin studies at the Conservatory. He was admitted in 1894 and his teachers included Marsick (violin), Gedalge (counterpoint), and Massenet and Fauré (composition). He won first prizes in violin-playing and harmony.

The first concert devoted entirely to Enesco's music was given in Paris in June 1897. The program comprised the Violin Sonata, op. 2, the Piano Suite, op. 3, and other chamber music works and songs. The Violin Sonata made a particularly good impression on the conductor Édouard Colonne, who asked Enesco for an orchestral composition. Enesco came forward with the *Poème Roumain*, op. 1, which was introduced at a Chatelet concert February 6, 1898. One year later Colonne directed still another Enesco orchestral première, that of the *Fantaisie Pastorale*. The first all-Enesco concert to take place in Bucharest was given on April 11, 1900.

While attracting attention as a composer, Enesco was also launching a successful career as a violin virtuoso. His first important appearance was as a soloist with the Colonne Orchestra on February 11, 1900, when he performed concertos by Beethoven and Saint-Saëns. With appearances throughout Europe he rapidly distinguished himself for his musicianship, taste, penetrating interpretative insight, and complete command of technique. Beginning in 1902 he also appeared in important performances of chamber music, in partnership with Alfredo Casella, pianist, and Louis Fournier, cellist.

During this period in Paris, Enesco achieved renown in another area in music, that of teaching, by conducting master classes in the violin at the École Normale de Musique.

Hand in hand with his growth as a violinist and as a teacher went his development as a composer. In 1900 he completed a significant chamber music work, the String Octet in D major, in which the innovator in him first began to stir. "Although the key is that of C major," explains Nicolas Slonimsky, "it is only teleologically so, for clear C major is not reached until the very end of the work. The changing tonalities are embellished by the multicolored festoons of Enesco's Rumanian scales." Even more Rumanian in style, materials, and personality were the two rhapsodies for orchestra which Enesco completed during 1901 and 1902. First performed in Bucharest on March 8, 1903, the two rhapsodies scored their first major success in Paris when Pablo Casals conducted them on February 7, 1908. The rhapsodies established the composer's fame in Europe. To this day, these spirited, colorful symphonic adaptations of catchy Rumanian dance tunes and folk melodies are

Enesco's most popular compositions, and the most frequently played symphonic works of any Rumanian. The first rhapsody, in A major, is the livelier of the two and the more popular; the second, in D major, is more melancholy.

Though less successful, Enesco's first symphony, in E-flat major, was equally important in his development as a composer and in establishing further his international fame. He completed it in 1905, and its première took place at a Colonne concert on January 21, 1906. Paul Dukas and Eugène Ysaÿe praised it highly. The symphony soon made the rounds of European capitals, and on February 17, 1911, it was heard at a concert of the New York Symphony Society, Walter Damrosch conducting. The symphony is rhapsodic, romantic, and filled with passionate statements; in it Enesco's indebtedness to Brahms is still in evidence.

Just before the outbreak of World War I, Enesco settled in Bucharest. He now became the most influential musician in Rumania. He conducted the Bucharest Philharmonic; he was court violinist to the Queen of Rumania; he gave extended cycles of concerts tracing the history of violin music; he organized concerts of modern music; he established the Georges Enesco Prize for young Rumanian composers.

When the war ended, Enesco established himself again in Paris, spending only a part of each year in Rumania. For the next few decades he occupied a modest apartment on rue de Clichy. During this period he toured the music world in the triple capacity of violinist, conductor, and composer. The first of his many appearances in the United States took place on January 5, 1923, with the Philadelphia Orchestra.

The era between the two world wars saw the writing of a third symphony, in C major, which had its première in Paris on February 26, 1921, Gabriel Pierné conducting. In addition to this work, he completed a string quartet (1921), his third violin sonata (1926), and three piano sonatas (1924, 1927, 1935). His most significant achievement was a "lyric-tragedy" in four acts, *Oedipe* (1932), with a text by Edmond Fleg. The world première took place at the Paris Opéra on March 10, 1936. In 1955 it was successfully revived in Paris.

In 1936 Enesco married Marie Rosetti-Tescano, a Rumanian princess. They had no children. During World War II, the Enescos lived on a large farm in Sinaia, near Bucharest. Those difficult war years found him tending to his farm stock and doing some composing. When the Soviets took over Rumania, they made an exception in Enesco's case by confiscating only two thirds of his farm.

On November 10, 1946, Enesco returned to the United States after an absence of almost a decade. During this tour he received the Grand Cross of the Order of Loyal Service from the Rumanian Ambassador to the United States for his life-long services to Rumanian music. In 1948 Enesco joined the faculty of the Mannes College of Music where he taught a class in the interpretation of chamber music. In his last public appearance in the United States, in New York on January 21, 1950, he appeared with the New York Philharmonic as violinist, pianist, conductor, and composer to commemorate the sixtieth anniversary of his concert debut.

In Paris, in July 1954, Enesco suffered a paralytic stroke that left him an invalid. The Communist Rumanian Embassy invited him to return to his country for good, but Enesco refused to do so, maintaining he had no interest in politics and, therefore, could not fit in gracefully with a Communist regime. He stayed in Paris, working on his last composition, the *Chamber Symphony*, for twelve solo instruments, op. 33.

On May 4, 1955, Enesco died in Paris. In spite of his avowed and open dissatisfaction with the Communist regime in Rumania, that country paid him many tokens of homage following his death. In 1958 it instituted an international festival and competition named for him. (A second one followed in 1961.) Enesco museums were founded at his homes in Livani and Bucharest. The Bucharest Philharmonic added "Georges Enesco" to its name. The town of his birth and a street in Bucharest were also renamed after him.

Enesco produced music in many different styles. An early work such as his first symphony is Brahmsian in its romanticism. His second Suite, for orchestra, is neoclassic. The opera *Oedipe* employs experimental tonalities, even simulations of quarter tones. In discussing the variety of his style, Enesco once said: "People have been puzzled and annoyed because they have been unable to catalogue and classify me in the usual way. They could not decide exactly what type of music mine was. It was not French after the manner of Debussy, it was not exactly German, they declared. In short, while it did not sound outlandish, it did not closely resemble anything familiar, and people are annoyed when they cannot readily classify one. That, I feel sure, comes from the fact that my musical education was not confined to one locality. . . . I was born in Rumania and when I was seven I was studying in Vienna. . . . After years of study in Vienna I came to Paris. . . . I naturally absorbed French influences to a certain extent which, combined with the German, gave further character to my writings."

Enesco is probably best known for those of his works which are based on Rumanian folk idioms—not only the two rhapsodies but also compositions such as his third violin sonata. Utilizing the songs and dances of his native land with virtuosity and freshness, Enesco managed to produce several works indigenous to Rumania yet recognizably Enesco in their skillful deployment of rhythmic and harmonic techniques. But whether Enesco used a national style or a neoclassic one, he was always a musician of impeccable taste, and a sensitive poet. His style was as aristocratic as his personality. Always he served the highest interests of his art faithfully, with humility, without ostentation. This is what Lawrence Gilman meant when he wrote while Enesco was still living: "In a musical era which is increasingly dominated by the spotlight, the wisecrack, and the exhibitionist, Enesco remains, quite naturally and involuntarily, an humble servant of the things that as an artist he reveres and loves. He remains . . . a man of dignity and of gentle ways, modest, and genuine, and simple, magnanimous and poised, wise and humorous and humane, close to the roots of universal things. . . . For years he has gone unpretentiously about his mission, that of fulfilling with devotion the obligations of an artist of intellectual honor and spiritual integrity. He is a composer of depth and power and intensity, an interpreter of insight, a friend of good music and of good musicians."

Enesco pursued his three-fold career in music with intense singleness of purpose. "Nothing else exists for me but work," he once said. "I'm just a musician, and a humble one. My happiness is at the writing table, composing. Outside of my music, I'm like an ostrich that hides under the wing. I have no hobbies. I just happen to live like a bourgeois."

He had this to say about his creative methods: "Melodic ideas come into my heart years, sometimes, before I utilize them. Yet in that time my method of treating them may be very different from what it would have been at their conception. Still I can always put an old idea to account. I compose very slowly because I believe that to be the best way. If you work slowly and carefully, even if you do not achieve great results, you at least achieve sincere ones. . . . Much as I enjoy writing for orchestra, I find no end of pleasure in writing for the piano—writing orchestrally for it, as it were."

MAJOR WORKS

Chamber Music—3 violin sonatas; 2 string quartets; Octet in C major; Aubade, for string trio; Intermezzo, for strings; Dixtuor, for strings and wind; Piano Quartet in D major; Piano Quintet; String Quintet in D minor; Impressions d'Enfance, for violin and piano.

Opera—Oedipe.

Orchestral Music—3 symphonies; 3 suites; 2 Rumanian Rhapsodies; Poème Roumain; Symphonie Concertante, for cello and orchestra; Violin Concerto; Poème Symphonique; Vox Maris, tone poem; Concert Overture on Motifs in Rumanian Character; Symphonie de Chambre.

Piano Music—3 sonatas; 2 suites; Impromptus.

Vocal Music—Seven Songs, op. 15; Three Songs, op. 18.

ABOUT

Enesco, G., and Gavoty, B., Les Souvenirs de Georges Enesco; Kotlyarov, B., Georges Enesco.

Manuel de Falla
1876–1946

Manuel de Falla (Manuel María de Falla y Matheu), Spain's most renowned twentieth century composer, was born on November 23, 1876, in the town of Cádiz, of which both parents were natives. His mother, a thoroughly trained pianist, gave the boy his first music instruction. Two early influences helped mold the later musician. One took place on a visit to Seville when Manuel was ten. There, the

Falla: fä′ lyä

189

Falla

sight of a religious pageant stirred him so profoundly that he never forgot the experience. It awakened his national pride and fed his religious feelings. The second influence was an orchestral concert in Cádiz which was Falla's first contact not only with the orchestra but also with a Beethoven symphony. He later said that he became a musician the day he heard his first Beethoven symphony.

MANUEL DE FALLA

In 1888 he made his first public appearance by performing with his mother a four-hand piano arrangement of Haydn's *Seven Words of Our Savior on the Cross* (which Haydn had written for the Cádiz Cathedral in 1785). Other musical stimulation came through hearing chamber music concerts at the home of a wealthy amateur. For these performances Falla wrote his first pieces of music, which he later destroyed.

He continued his music study in Cádiz with Elois Galluzo (piano) and with Alejandro Odero and Enrique Broca (harmony and theory). During this period he seems to have taken periodic trips to Madrid for special piano lessons. On one occasion, when he was fourteen, he entered a piano-playing competition at the Madrid Conservatory from which he emerged with the first prize. He also wrote a good deal of ambitious chamber music at this time, including a piano quartet and a quintet (for violin, viola, cello, flute, and piano) inspired by Mistral's poem *Mirèio*. None of this music exists any longer.

When he was twenty, Falla enrolled formally in the Madrid Conservatory where he came under the influence of two important Spanish musicians: Felipe Pedrell, the composer and scholar, and the pianist José Tragó. Though Falla won highest honors as a piano student, and though Tragó was convinced the young man had the makings of a virtuoso, Falla preferred creative work. Pedrell encouraged this direction while instilling into Falla his own passionate ideals for a Spanish music based on the foundations of Spanish folk lore, folk song, and folk dance. Pedrell introduced Falla to the wealth of Spanish folk music and inspired him with the artistic mission of interpreting Spain—its geography, culture, history, and people—in a musical art with a strong national identity. In later years Falla confessed: "It is to the lessons of Pedrell and to the powerful stimulation exercised on me by his works that I owe my artistic life."

When Falla completed his course of study in Madrid, he was eager to go to Paris. To raise the necessary funds he composed two Spanish operettas (zarzuelas); one was a failure when produced in 1902, and the other was never mounted. He also taught and played the piano. Meanwhile in 1905 he gave proof of his talent by winning the Ortiz y Cussó prize for piano playing and the first prize in a competition for national operas conducted by the Real Academía de Bellas Artes with his first important work, *La Vida Breve*. In this two-act lyric drama, for the first time he succeeded in realizing Pedrell's ideals for a national musical art. It was a number of years, however, before the opera was produced.

In 1907 Falla bought a seven-week round-trip ticket for Paris. He remained in Paris seven years, a period in which he experienced intense poverty and often had to go without food. But Paris was highly stimulating to a young, sensitive musician who found himself in the vortex of exciting musical adventures. He came into personal contact with many of Paris's leading musicians—including Debussy, Dukas, Ravel, Schmitt, and Roussel—who not only introduced him to their own compositions but also stimulated him with their provocative ideas about music and music making. Falla was able to attend exciting concerts of new music, foreign as well as French, and thus learn about new idioms and techniques. He was absorbing fresh musical impressions all the time. He was also, though slowly, making headway as a composer. In November 1908 his four *Pièces Espagnoles*, for piano, were performed by Ricardo Viñes at a concert of the Société Nationale de Musique and published several months later. In 1909 he completed a set of songs, *Trois Mélodies* (text by Gautier), which was heard at a concert of the Société Indépendante and published in 1910. These two compositions (together with sketches for an ambitious work that in later years were to be used for *Nights in the Gardens of Spain*) were the sum of his creative achievements during his seven-year residence in France. But he had been musically active in other significant ways. In October 1910 he made his Paris debut as pianist in the first concert in that city devoted entirely to modern Spanish music, a program that included his three songs and four piano pieces.

La Vida Breve finally received its world première—not in Spain, but at the Municipal Casino in Nice on April 1, 1913. A year and a half later, on December 13, 1914, it was produced at the Opéra-Comique in Paris. Despite a stilted libretto and serious dramatic shortcomings in Falla's musical setting, the opera was well received, largely because of Falla's success in projecting an authentic Spanish atmosphere. "In this work," says Otto Mayer-Serra, "he shows a strong feeling for regional music in a style highly reminiscent of French lyric opera." *La Vida Breve* is now rarely revived. The Metropolitan Opera produced it on March 6, 1926, but it was removed from the repertory after only four performances. Two Spanish dances from the score survived to become Falla's first pieces of music to gain international recognition.

In 1914, just before World War I broke out, Falla returned to Spain. On November 14 of that year *La Vida Breve* was mounted for the first time in Spain and proved outstandingly successful. For the next few years, from a base in Madrid, he traveled throughout Spain. He was trying to achieve closer identification with Spanish life and backgrounds, particularly those of Andalusia, in order to embody them in his music. As he later explained: "You must go to natural, living sources. . . . You must go really deep, so as not to make any sort of caricature."

In 1915 he completed music for a ballet based on a scenario by Gregorio Martínez Sierra, which in turn derived from an old Andalusian gypsy folk tale. Without ever resorting to musical quotation, Falla here achieved a thoroughly Spanish musical language patterned after the spirit and style of the Andalusian folk song: its throbbing, sensual gypsy melody (a *cante hondo*), its ornamentations, its Oriental colorations, its rhythmic primitivism, its guitar-like accompaniments. Named *El Amor Brujo* (*Love, the Sorcerer*), this ballet was first produced in Madrid on April 15, 1915. It was for the most part a failure. Though it has since had a number of notable revivals—particularly one at the Théâtre des Arts in Paris in 1925—*El Amor Brujo* has never achieved permanence in the ballet repertory. But the score has become a classic through the symphonic suite which circled the music world after it had been introduced in Madrid in 1916 under the direction of Fernández Enrique Arbós. A brilliant, compelling evocation of Spanish gypsy life, *El Amor Brujo* is undoubtedly the most important work of the Spanish nationalist movement since Albéniz' *Iberia*. It is Falla's first masterwork, his "greatest triumph in the purely Spanish manner," says J. B. Trend. One of the dance episodes from this score, the *Ritual Fire Dance*, has become universally popular, particularly in the exciting transcriptions for solo piano and for violin and piano. "For sheer, overwhelming dynamic effectiveness," writes Gilbert Chase, "scarcely anything in modern music can compare with the *Ritual Fire Dance* which Candelas dances at midnight to exorcise all evil spirits."

Falla's next significant composition was *Noches en los Jardines de España* (*Nights in the Gardens of Spain*), for piano and orchestra. He had worked on some of the sketches in Paris in 1909 but did not complete the composition until 1915. The première took place on April 9, 1916, in Madrid, Enrique Fernández Arbós conducting. The titles of the three movements suggest the Spanish pictures the composer had in mind in writing this music. The first movement is entitled "In the Gardens of Generalife"; the second, "A Dance Heard in the Distance"; the third, "In the Gardens of the Sierra de Córdoba." This is one of Falla's most poetic works—"a really wonderful evocation," wrote Joaquín Turina, "although in a sense the most tragic and sorrowful of his works. In the peculiar flavor of the orchestral sonority, one can in fact discern a feeling of bitterness, as if the composer had striven to express a drama of an intimate and passionate nature."

Now recognized as one of Spain's leading composers, Falla was sought out by Diaghilev for a score for a Ballet Russe production. Martínez Sierra provided a scenario based on the satirical novel of Don Pedro Antonio de Alarcón, *The Three-Cornered Hat* (which had previously also been the source of Hugo Wolf's opera *Der Corregidor*). With settings and costumes designed by Pablo Picasso, choreography by Massine, and with Massine and Karsavina as principal dancers, *El Sombrero de Tres Picos*, produced in London on July 22, 1919, was one of the triumphs of the Ballet Russe season and one of the greatest successes the company had known. With its theme stressing broad humor and satire, and with Andalusian peasants as characters, *The Three-Cornered Hat* revealed a new facet in Falla's art. But here, as in his earlier works for the stage, the high point of musical interest was found in the Spanish dances. Three have become fixed in the contemporary symphonic repertory: *The Neighbors*, *The Miller's Dance* (a *farruca*), and *Final Dance* (a *jota*).

In 1922 Falla moved to a house atop a hill in the Cerro del Sol section of Granada. There, removed from the city itself, and only a stone's throw from the Alhambra, Falla made his home for the next seventeen years. A recluse by temperament, Falla rarely left Granada, where his life became routinized. He rose early each morning, took a walk, then attended Mass at the San Cecilio Church. Several hours were then devoted to composition. A siesta followed the noonday meal, after which friends and neighbors came calling. Some work followed later in the evening, and at an early hour Falla retired.

He was a deeply religious man with a strong bent for mysticism. "The spirits with whom he felt closest," says Walter Starkie, "were Saint John of the Cross and the painter Zurbarán, whose ascetic ideals Falla tried to embody in his art." Falla seemed to draw creative strength from solitude and the simple life.

Each year he took what he described to one French interviewer as a "solitude cure," which meant that he went off to some little-frequented Andalusian village, stayed there for two weeks or so, and spoke to nobody for days at an end. In this way, he said, he prepared for work.

He was described by G. Maroto as "slight of build . . . with large expressive eyes—dreamy, melancholy, kind. Sometimes when his voice, always flexible in quality, expressed a subject he felt intensely, he became a stammering child, credulous, timid. . . . On those occasions when doubt or failure assailed his spirit, one might have called him an old man with a slow, grave voice, ready to forfeit his last hopes." Lincoln Kirstein described him thus: "His head was very fine, with a fringe of iron-gray hair like a low tonsure. His skin was waxen brown. . . . His mouth was very narrow. . . . His features were elongated as if by a combination of spiritual discipline and disease."

He had no use for luxuries or the refinements of good living and at times ignored basic comforts. He also renounced personal vanity and self-aggrandizement and abhorred talking about himself or his music. He was a frail man and a hypochondriac.

He worked long and hard on his compositions, but being a most fastidious workman and assailed by a scrupulous sense of self-criticism, he produced only a scattered handful of works after *The Three-Cornered Hat*. But with a single exception, each of these is the work of a consummate master. *El Retablo de Maese Pedro* (*Master Peter's Puppet Show*) was a production for puppets based on scenes from *Don Quixote*. It had three singing characters, all placed in the orchestra pit while the action was performed entirely by puppets. This work, says Gilbert Chase, revealed "Falla's ability to achieve a wide variety of effects—and very subtle and telling effects—with an extreme economy of means." The puppet opera was completed in 1919 and in that year was produced in Seville in concert form. The first staged presentation was seen at the Paris salon of the Princesse de Polignac on June 25, 1923.

The austerity, economy, and objectivity of Falla's writing in the puppet opera are found once again in his Concerto for Harpsichord,

Flute, Oboe, Clarinet and Cello. This neo-classical work drew a good deal of stimulation and guidance from the harpsichord sonatas of Domenico Scarlatti. Falla wrote the Concerto for the harpsichordist Wanda Landowska, to whom it is dedicated. She introduced it at a festival of Falla's music in Barcelona on November 5, 1926, the composer himself conducting.

In the years between 1926 and his death twenty years later, Falla wrote little. *Homenajes*, a four-part suite for orchestra begun in 1920 and completed in 1938, was substandard. It has had little circulation since its world première in Buenos Aires on November 18, 1939, the composer conducting. Much more ambitious in scope, and much more significant in content, was a huge epic work for solo voices, chorus, and orchestra upon which Falla kept working at intervals during the last two decades of his life. It was a "scenic cantata," *La Atlantida*, based upon a great nineteenth century Catalan poem by Mosén Jacinto Verdaguer. It relates how a flood submerged the lost continent of Atlantis and how Spain was saved by Hercules and how the New World was discovered. "It is a grandiose theme," wrote Peter Heyworth in the New York *Times*, "and it drew from Falla a new breadth of musical expression."

Falla did not live to complete the cantata, which was finished by his pupil Ernesto Halffter. *La Atlantida* was heard first in a concert version, in Barcelona on November 24, 1961. As a staged production it was given at La Scala in Milan on June 18, 1962. The American première (in concert version) was conducted by Ernest Ansermet in New York on September 29, 1962.

When civil war broke out in Spain, Falla sympathized with the Franco forces because he saw in the Nationalist movement a check to antireligious activities in Spain. In 1938 Franco appointed him President of the Institute of Spain. But Falla was soon disillusioned by the Franco regime and in 1939 he went to South America where he conducted a number of concerts before settling in Alta Gracia, near Córdoba, Argentina. There, at the Villa del Lago, some twenty-five miles from Córdoba, he spent the last years of his life tended solicitously by his sister, for he was almost continuously ill. His funds were so depleted that he could not afford to buy a piano. Furthermore, he was disturbed by the way the world was going and haunted by strange and inexplicable fears. He insisted that if only he could have just four weeks of peace and physical comfort he would be able to finish *La Atlantida*. But these were denied him—he died of a heart attack in his sleep in Alta Gracia November 14, 1946. His body was brought back to his native city of Cádiz, where funeral services were conducted on January 9. He was buried in the crypt of the Santa María de las Cuevas Church, the inscription on his tombstone being one which he himself had conceived: "Honor and glory belong only to God." On September 8, 1960, a monument by José Menéndez Pidal was unveiled at Falla's grave.

To Edgar Istel, Falla once explained his music credo: "Our music must be based on the natural music of our people, on the dances and songs, that do not always show close kinship. In some cases, the rhythm alone is marked by clapping and drumsticks, without any melody; in others the melody stands out by itself; so that no one should employ vocal melody alone as a manifestation of folk music, but everything that accompanies it or exists without it, never losing sight of the milieu wherein all that has its being."

"Falla's music," wrote J. B. Trend, "is extremely individual. . . . Andaluz on his mother's side, Falla seems to combine the imagination of the Spaniard with the sense of formal perfection of the man of the Mediterranean. To the power of obtaining the subtlest orchestral effects with the simplest means, of seeing where the point is and going straight toward it, is added a power of what the Spaniards call *evocación*—a sense of poetry or suggestiveness . . . something which can be felt rather than explained."

MAJOR WORKS

Ballets—El Amor Brujo (Love, the Sorcerer); El Sombrero de Tres Picos (The Three-Cornered Hat).

Chamber Music—Concerto for Harpsichord, Flute, Oboe, Clarinet, Violin and Cello.

Choral Music—Balada de Mallorca; La Atlantida, scenic cantata (finished by Ernesto Halffter).

Operas—La Vida Breve; El Retablo de Maeso Pedro (for marionettes and singers).

Orchestral Music—Noches en los Jardines de España (Nights in the Gardens of Spain), for piano and orchestra.

Fauré

Piano Music—Pièces Espagnoles; Fantasía Bética.

Vocal Music—Siete Canciones Populares Españolas; Soneto a Córdoba, for voice and harp; Psyché, for voice and five instruments.

ABOUT

Campodonico, L., Manuel de Falla; Chase, G., The Music of Spain; Demarquez, S., Manuel de Falla; Gauthier, A., Manuel de Falla, L'Homme et Son Œuvre; Pahissa, J., Manuel de Falla; Pahlen, K., Manuel de Falla und die Musik in Spanien; Roland-Manuel, Manuel de Falla; Trend, J. B., Manuel de Falla and Spanish Music.

Musical Quarterly, October 1926, January 1943.

Gabriel Fauré
1845–1924

Gabriel Urbain Fauré was born in Pamiers, Ariège, France, May 12, 1845, the sixth and last child of a schoolmaster. As a boy he taught himself to play the organ. He made such an impression on the renowned teacher Niedermeyer that the latter offered to have the boy trained in music without payment. In 1854 Fauré entered the École Niedermeyer in Paris, essentially a school of religious music. Here Fauré was introduced to old liturgical music and to Gregorian chants, an influence which clung to him throughout his later creative development. One of his teachers at the school was Saint-Saëns, who saw to it that the boy received a comprehensive knowledge of piano literature, still another significant influence on young Fauré. In 1863, while Fauré was still at school, his first publication appeared—*Trois Romances sans Paroles*, for piano.

Fauré left school in 1865 with prizes in piano, harmony, composition, and organ. The following year he became the organist of the Saint-Sauveur church in Rennes, Brittany. Though he remained as organist at Saint-Sauveur about four years, he appears to have lost the favor of the church authorities because of his progressive, independent views on the kind of music to be played at services. A pretext to dismiss him was found in 1870 when, late one night after a party, he came to church in evening dress.

Somewhat earlier, in 1868, Marie Miolan-Carvalho sang one of his songs, *Le Papillon et la Fleur*, op. 1, at a recital in Rennes,

---

Fauré: fô rā′

Fauré accompanying her at the piano. *Le Papillon et la Fleur* and other early songs had a tender, wistful loveliness and a sensitive feeling for atmosphere which led Maurice Ravel to write: "The personality of Fauré is apparent in his first songs. The seductiveness of his melodic contour does not cede to the subtlety of his harmony in these pieces."

Early in 1870 Fauré became organist at Notre Dame de Clignancourt in Paris. His work there was interrupted by the outbreak of the Franco-Prussian War, when he joined the service as an infantryman. In 1871 during the Communard disturbances he left Paris for Rambouillet, but after the Third Republic had been established Fauré returned to the capital, this time to play the organ at Saint-Honoré d'Eylau.

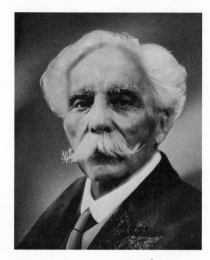

GABRIEL FAURÉ

In 1873 Fauré became acquainted with the celebrated singer Pauline Viardot-Garcia, with whose daughter, Marianne, he fell in love. The romance lasted about four years, ripened into an engagement, and then was suddenly broken off. Some biographers suggest that Fauré finally rejected the idea of marrying Marianne for fear of being compelled, through a closer relationship with Viardot-Garcia, to write operas for her—an assignment for which he had little inclination or affinity. But it is more than probable that the final separation of the lovers was brought about because Marianne was looking for a richer and more successful husband than Fauré.

Fauré's reputation in the world of music was rising. In 1877 he became assistant organist and choirmaster at the Madeleine Church. Liszt became interested in him and helped to draw attention to him. Several important works during this period justified Liszt's high regard. In 1876 Fauré wrote (and had published in Germany) his beautiful Sonata No. 1 in A major, for violin and piano, still one of his most popular chamber-music works. Florent Schmitt said of it that it foreshadowed Franck's violin sonata, which came ten years later, and that its appearance marked "a red-letter day in the history of chamber music." The Sonata was followed in 1879 by the Piano Quartet in C minor with which, it has been said, French chamber music first came fully into its own. In 1881 Fauré wrote his most distinguished work for a solo instrument and orchestra, the *Ballade*, in F-sharp minor, for piano and orchestra.

In 1883 Fauré married Marie Fremiet, daughter of a sculptor. Eric Blom informs us that this was essentially a marriage of convenience "perhaps entered into for domestic tranquillity rather than for material reasons." Blom adds that "nothing much was ever heard of Fauré's wife, either to her advantage or otherwise, except that she made him a good home."

The middle 1880's saw the writing of several major works, including the G minor Piano Quartet, Fauré's most important composition for piano and strings; the stately *Pavane*, for orchestra; and the renowned *Messe de Requiem*, inspired by the death of the composer's father in 1885. By the time this work was introduced, at the Madeleine Church in 1888, it also served as a memorial to Fauré's mother. Fauré's first outstanding creation within a large structure, the Requiem remains one of the most poignant, deeply moving works in French choral music. "Nothing purer, clearer in definition has been written," says Nadia Boulanger. "No exterior effect alters its sober and rather severe expression of grief, no restlessness troubles its deep meditation, no doubt strains its spotless faith, its gentle confidence, and tranquil expectancy."

While successfully pursuing his career as composer and organist, Fauré also distinguished himself as a teacher. He taught his first classes in composition at the École Niedermeyer. In 1895 Fauré took over Massenet's composition class at the Paris Conservatory, and in 1905 he succeeded Dubois as director of the Conservatory, a post he retained for fifteen years. His importance in the classroom can perhaps best be measured by the later success of some of his pupils—Ravel, Schmitt, Roger-Ducasse, Aubert, Nadia Boulanger, Enesco, Charles Koechlin—all of whom expressed their profound indebtedness to him. Here is Koechlin's description of Fauré the teacher: "This 'revolutionary' proved to be a purist as a teacher, to detest clumsiness and carelessness. He himself, and the high standards of his own art, proved in the last resort the most effective spur to his pupils. . . . One would certainly have needed a singular insensitiveness to ask Fauré to listen to anything either banal or pretentious. It happened occasionally and then Fauré would be very calm and quiet, vacant and distant-looking. Having listened to the end, he would turn and ask in a soft voice, with a detached and rather nonchalant air, 'Was there anything else?' Everyone understood what he meant, except of course the culprit who was naturally too thick-skinned."

Fauré continued to tap new veins of poetic expressiveness to the end of his life. In 1898 he wrote incidental music for Maeterlinck's impressionist play *Pelléas et Mélisande* (several years before Debussy's opera); out of this score came Fauré's best-known orchestral suite. In the years between 1908 and 1922 he wrote five piano nocturnes. These contain some of his most eloquent keyboard music. In 1910 he completed the song cycle *La Chanson d'Ève* which, with the cycle *L'Horizon Chimérique* (1922), established him even more solidly as one of France's greatest masters of the art song. In 1913 he completed his most important work for the stage, the lyric drama *Pénélope*, first mounted in Monte Carlo on March 4, 1913. In 1924 came his String Quartet in E minor; of this quartet Émile Vuillermoz wrote: "Never did a creative artist present us with subtler and more powerful achievement."

In his music the spirit of ancient Greece was fused with advanced musical thinking. The serenity, refinement, and beauty of Fauré's writing sometimes make us forget that his style and techniques were highly advanced.

195

Twenty years before Debussy, Fauré suggested some of the syntax of Impressionism, while his harmonic construction is often original and even daring. And yet the Hellenic spirit of his art is ever predominant. Julien Tiersot put it this way: "Perhaps it is not enough to recognize in him a Greek musician revived in the twentieth century; but it is the spirit of Hellenism, as well as its forms, which is reborn in him. . . . He, too, thrusts himself beyond the spheres in order to bring back pure beauty."

In 1909 Fauré was elected to the Académie des Beaux-Arts, and in 1910 he was made Commander of the Legion of Honor. When he retired as director of the Conservatory in 1920 he became the object of a national tribute. A testimonial concert of his music was given by national decree. He was honored by the Sorbonne. He also received the *grand cordon* (designating the Grand Croix, the highest class in the Legion of Honor). To all these honors and official tributes he reacted with his customary humility and modesty.

He spent the last four years of his life in retirement. His health was deteriorating and, although no one knew it until seven years after his death, he was totally deaf. He had suffered from deafness during the last twenty years of his life but had kept his condition secret for fear of jeopardizing his post at the Conservatory. Few outside of his own intimate circle knew of his infirmity.

In the summer of 1924 he went to Annecy for a rest cure. There he worked on his last composition, the E minor String Quartet. Convinced, at last, that he did not have much longer to live, he returned to Paris to spend his last days with his family. Characteristic of his utter simplicity and modesty was the fact that two days before his death he urged his friend and pupil Roger-Ducasse to examine carefully the string quartet which he, Fauré, had just completed. He wanted Roger-Ducasse to assure him that it was worth performing. A few hours before his death he was still thinking about his music. "Have my works received justice?" he inquired. "Have they not been too much admired or sometimes too severely criticized? What of my music will live?" And to these questions he provided his own answer: "But, then, that is of little importance."

Fauré died in Paris November 4, 1924. "All French musicians," says Martin Cooper, "have agreed that no more representative figure has appeared in the French musical world for the last hundred years."

MAJOR WORKS

Chamber Music—2 piano quintets; 2 piano quartets; 2 violin sonatas; 2 cello sonatas; Elegy, for cello and piano; Piano Trio in D minor; String Quartet in E minor.

Choral Music—Les Djinns; La Naissance de Vénus, mythological scene; Madrigal; Pavane; Messe de Requiem; Tantum Ergo; Ave Verum.

Operas—Prométhée, lyric tragedy; Pénélope, lyric drama.

Orchestral Music—Ballade, for piano and orchestra; Romance, for violin and orchestra; Symphony in D minor; Pelléas et Mélisande, suite; Fantaisie, for piano and orchestra; Masques et Bergamasques, suite.

Piano Music—13 Barcarolles; 13 Nocturnes; 9 Preludes; 5 Impromptus; 4 Valse-Caprices; Mazurka; Dolly, six pieces for four hands; Thème et Variations; Huite Pièces Brèves.

Vocal Music—La Bonne Chanson; La Chanson d'Ève; Le Jardin Clos; Mirages; L'Horizon Chimérique; over one hundred individual songs for voice and piano including Après un Rêve, Au Cimetière, Aurore, Les Berceaux, Clair de Lune, En Prière, En Sourdine, Ici-Bas, Lydia, Nell, Noël, Le Parfum Impérissable, Poème d'un Jour, Prison, Les Roses d'Ispahan, Le Secret, Soir, and Tristesse.

ABOUT

Fauré-Fremiet, P., Gabriel Fauré; Fauré-Fremiet, P. (ed.), Lettres Intimes; Fauré, G., Gabriel Fauré; Koechlin, C., Fauré; Rostand, C., L'Œuvre de Gabriel Fauré; Suckling, N., Fauré; Vuillermoz, E., Gabriel Fauré.

Monthly Musical Record (London), May 1945.

Irving Fine
1914–1962

Irving Fine was born Henry Gifford Fine in Boston on December 3, 1914. He attended public schools there and took piano lessons with Frances L. Grover. In 1933 he matriculated at Harvard where he studied theory and composition with Walter Piston, Edward Burlingame Hill, and A. Tillman Merritt. After receiving his Bachelor of Arts degree in 1937 and a master's one year later, he studied composition with Nadia Boulanger, then on a visit to Cambridge. In 1939 he received a grant to continue his studies with Miss Boulanger in Paris. He also studied conducting with Serge Koussevitzky at the Berkshire Music Center at Tanglewood.

Fine's career as a teacher began at Harvard in 1940 when he joined its music faculty. From 1947 to 1950 he was assistant professor of music there, and from 1950 until his death he was the Walter W. Naumburg Professor of Music and Chairman of the School of Creative Arts at Brandeis University. Meanwhile, in the period between 1946 and 1957 he was a member of the faculty at the Berkshire Music Center at Tanglewood, and in the summer of 1950 he was codirector of the Music Seminar at the Salzburg Seminar for American Studies.

IRVING FINE

In the 1940's Fine emerged as a composer with a pronounced neoclassical idiom. His music was influenced most notably by Stravinsky and Hindemith. Several works for chorus (including his incidental music to *Alice in Wonderland* in 1943, the cantata *The Choral New Yorker* in 1944, and *In Grato Jubilo* in 1945), a violin sonata in 1946, and *Music for Piano* in 1947 preceded his first successes. In 1947 he wrote *Toccata Concertante*, for orchestra, introduced by the Boston Symphony October 22, 1948. "The word *toccata*," explained the composer in his published score, "is commonly used to describe improvisatory display pieces for keyboard instruments. It has also been used in connection with concerted music of a fanfare-like character. It is in this latter sense that I used the term." One year later Fine completed the Partita, for wind quintet, which received

the award of the New York Music Critics Circle.

In 1949 and 1950, Fine did research in France on a Fulbright Fellowship, and in 1950 and 1958 he received Guggenheim Fellowships. His first compositions in the 1950's included a string quartet (1951), followed by a *Notturno*, for strings and harp, in which he emphasized lyric content with a romantic approach. The *Notturno*, in three movements, was introduced by the Zimbler Sinfonietta, for which group it was written, on March 28, 1951, the composer conducting.

In some of his compositions during the 1950's, Fine experimented with serial technique. This proved a passing phase between his earlier neoclassic tendencies and his later fully crystallized manner which Nicolas Slonimsky described as "a distinctive style of his own, with a lyrical flow of cohesive melody supported by lucid polyphony, without abandoning the strong rhythmic design."

Important later compositions by Fine included the *Serious Song: A Lament for String Orchestra*, described by the composer as "an extended aria." It was commissioned by the Louisville Orchestra which introduced it in Kentucky in 1955. In the same year Fine also received an award from the National Institute of Arts and Letters.

On March 23, 1962, the Boston Symphony under Charles Münch introduced Fine's Symphony. Fine himself led a performance of this work at the Berkshire Music Festival at Tanglewood on August 12, 1962, just eleven days before his sudden death. Stricken by a heart attack at his home in East Natick, Massachusetts, and rushed to Beth Israel Hospital in Boston, he died on August 23, 1962. He was survived by his wife, the former Verna Rudnick, and three daughters.

In *The Justice*, a publication of Brandeis University, Aaron Copland wrote this about Fine: "The sureness of musical instinct informed his every activity as composer and teacher and performer. He worried considerably about each new work in process of composition. And yet, when we came to know them, they had elegance, style, finish and a naturalness of flow. His problems as composer—of which he had his share—concerned matters of esthetics, eclecticism or influence. These limitations he recognized; they made him modest to a fault. But all his compositions, from the lightest to the most serious, 'sound'; they have bounce and thrust and finesse; they are always a *musical* pleasure to hear."

On October 4, 1962, the New York Philharmonic performed the Adagio from Fine's *Notturno* as a memorial to the composer.

MAJOR WORKS

Chamber Music—Violin Sonata; Fantasia, for string trio; Partita, for wind quintet; String Quartet; Romanza, for wind quintet.

Choral Music—Three Choruses from Alice in Wonderland; The Choral New Yorker; In Grato Jubilo, hymn; The Hour Glass, choral cycle; Choral Music.

Orchestral Music—Toccata Concertante; Diversions, four pieces; Notturno, for strings and harp; Blue Towers; Serious Song: A Lament for Orchestra; Symphony.

Piano Music—Music for Piano, suite.

Vocal Music—Mutability, song cycle.

ABOUT

Cohn, A., Twentieth Century Music in the Western Hemisphere.

Ross Lee Finney
1906–

Ross Lee Finney was born in Wells, Minnesota, December 23, 1906. His mother was a trained musician who gave him his initial instruction. At the University of Minnesota, which he entered in 1924, he studied composition with Donald Ferguson. Later, Finney attended Carleton College from which he received a Bachelor of Arts degree in 1927. He taught cello and the history of music at Carleton until he went to Paris on a Johnson Fellowship to study with Nadia Boulanger in 1928. In 1928 and 1929 he attended Harvard University. In 1929 he joined the music faculty of Smith College where he remained nineteen years. At Smith College he founded the College Music Archives, a series of scholarly publications devoted to old music, and the Valley Music Press for the publication of contemporary American music, and for several years he conducted the Northampton Chamber Orchestra. In 1931–1932 he took a leave of absence from the college to study with Alban Berg in Vienna.

His career as a composer began officially in 1935 when his setting of eight poems by

Archibald MacLeish received the Connecticut Valley Prize and was introduced by Mabel Garrison. This was followed by his first piano sonata (1932) and his Piano Concerto (1934). His first string quartet, which the Gordon String Quartet introduced, received a Pulitzer award in 1937. A concert of Finney's chamber music in 1937 was one of the earliest Composers' Forums sponsored by the WPA in New York City.

ROSS LEE FINNEY

His first Guggenheim Fellowship in 1937 gave him the opportunity to spend another year in Europe, assimilating musical experiences and composing. Several ambitious works followed, the most important being his first works for orchestra alone: *Slow Piece*, for strings (1942); his first symphony (1943); and *Hymn, Fuguing and Holiday* (1943).

These and other works of the period were traditional in their attitudes towards structure and style. Classical forms and romantic feelings were favored, though the harmonic and rhythmic writing had modern colorations and approaches. *Hymn, Fuguing and Holiday* was characteristic. The starting point for Finney's own virile and thoroughly American style was a hymn by William Billings, the fountainhead of American psalmody who is generally recognized as America's first composer. The Billings hymn was sounded by the horns in the first twenty measures. Then Finney embarked on eight variations and two fuguing tunes, concluding with a spirited

"Holiday" section. *Hymn, Fuguing and Holiday* was introduced in Los Angeles on May 17, 1947, Alfred Wallenstein conducting; at that time it received the Alice M. Ditson Award. Finney's revision of the composition was first heard in Miami on January 17, 1966, with Fabien Sevitzky conducting the Greater Miami Philharmonic.

During World War II Finney served with the Office of Strategic Services and was awarded a Purple Heart and a Certificate of Merit. "I was given the Purple Heart," Finney explains, "because I stepped on a land mine. It was my good fortune that the mine was partly defective." Immediately after leaving the service in 1945, Finney completed a new piano sonata, subtitled *Christmastime*, and the *Pilgrim Psalms*. His fourth string quartet (1948) was introduced by the Kroll String Quartet at the Elizabeth Sprague Coolidge Memorial Concert in Cambridge, Massachusetts, after which it received major performances in Germany, Denmark, and South America.

Finney was a member of the music faculty at Amherst College in 1946 and 1947. He received a second Guggenheim Fellowship in 1947. In 1948 he served as visiting professor of composition at the School of Music of the University of Michigan in Ann Arbor and the following year was appointed professor of composition and composer-in-residence. He organized and headed the composition department, created an extensive graduate program in composition, and (on a grant from the Horace H. Rackham School of Graduate Studies) established an electronic music laboratory.

With his sixth string quartet (1950), Finney's musical style underwent a basic change through the adoption of a principle he has described as "a method of complementarity." His large basic structure adhered to tonal traditions; at the same time the details of his writing were ordered on the basis of a twelve-tone technique, in which, as Alban Berg's pupil, he had first become interested almost two decades earlier. Paul Henry Lang, reviewing a performance of this quartet in the New York *Herald Tribune*, said: "This is a quiet and undemonstrative profession of faith. . . . The work deserves to be widely known. It is true chamber music and thoroughly enjoyable, not as an experiment, but as the expression of a mature, thoughtful, and independent mind."

Finney now became more productive than ever, with important works in practically all media except opera. In 1955 the Albeneri Trio introduced his second piano trio, which he had completed a year earlier on a commission from Sigma Alpha Iota. In 1957, on a commission from Yehudi Menuhin, he wrote the *Fantasy in Two Movements*, for solo violin, which Menuhin presented at the World's Fair in Brussels in 1958 before featuring it on his programs throughout Europe. A string quintet, commissioned by the Elizabeth Sprague Coolidge Foundation, was successfully introduced by the Kroll Quartet and Alan Shulman at the Library of Congress in Washington, D.C., in 1958.

In 1959, having been commissioned by the Koussevitzky Music Foundation, Finney completed his most ambitious orchestral work up to this point, his second symphony. It was introduced at Ann Arbor, Michigan, on May 8, 1960, by the Philadelphia Orchestra under Ormandy. In this symphony Finney progresses towards a serial technique, since the entire work is based on a single twelve-tone row which determines not only the pitch but also many aspects of rhythm. The composer described this music as follows: "The dramatic beginning and ending of the symphony seem to me to frame the work in a silence that is intense. Between these high points the work is sometimes tender, sometimes grotesque and bitter, sometimes humorous and capricious. It is futile to describe the emotional intention of this work, but surely the gradual relaxation of the tensions of the beginning into the boisterous confidence of the ending will be felt." The symphony received many performances in the United States and Europe, was recorded, and was chosen to represent the United States at the Rostrum of the International Composers at UNESCO in Paris in 1963. "This is an impressive score," said Louis Biancolli in the New York *World-Telegram*, "fresh, original, boldly conceived and scored, both tonal and atonal in an intriguing fabric of its own and while generally abstract, full of nervous and emotional stir."

Finney's third symphony was dedicated to Eugene Ormandy, who directed the world première with the Philadelphia Orchestra on March 6, 1964. "As I was scoring my Second

Symphony," said Finney in describing the origin of the third one, "a new orchestral work, in many respects the opposite of the one I was writing, evolved in my mind. It was so clear that when I finally found time I composed it in full score in the space of two months. This new symphony was lyric rather than dramatic. It was shorter, less irregular in rhythm, but, like the Second Symphony, very personal in motivation." The symphony was written while Finney was a composer-in-residence at the American Academy in Rome.

Among the many honors and awards that Finney has received are the Boston Symphony Award in 1955, a grant from the Rockefeller Foundation for study in Europe in 1955–1956, and two awards from the Academy of Arts and Letters in 1956. He was elected a member of the National Institute of Arts and Letters in 1962. During the summer of 1962 he worked at the Columbia-Princeton Music Laboratory, an experience that led him to write a number of experimental works for magnetic tape. During the summer of 1965 he was composer-in-residence at Dartmouth College's Congregation of the Arts at Hanover, New Hampshire. In 1967 he was the recipient of the Brandeis Creative Award.

Finney's wife, Gretchen Ludke Finney (whom he married September 3, 1930), is the author of *Musical Backgrounds for English Literature*. They have two sons, one a mathematician, the other a sociologist.

"As a composer," Finney has written, "I never seem to move in the proper direction. Perhaps this independence comes from my Middle Western background and from the fact that my father was a sociologist and writer. I started composing at a very tender age . . . but my father, when he looked at my work, would ask: 'Can anybody else read it?' This remark, though it angered me at the time, challenged me also, and I know it had a strong effect and shaped my concern for communication and craft. I have always felt that art could not be understood from a single viewpoint, that it unfolded, one might say, on two levels, one highly technical and concerned with minutiae, the other emotional and concerned with the grand design."

MAJOR WORKS

Chamber Music—8 string quartets; 3 violin sonatas; 2 viola sonatas; 2 cello sonatas; 2 piano quintets; 2 piano trios; Piano Quartet; Elegy and March, for solo trombone; Fantasy, for solo cello; Fantasy in Two Movements, for solo violin; String Quintet; Divertimento, for woodwind quintet; Divertissement, for piano, violin, clarinet, and cello; Three Studies in Fours, for percussion.

Choral Music—Pole Star for This Year; Oh, Bury Me Not; When the Curtains of Night; Train to Mexico; Pilgrim Psalms; Words to Be Spoken; Spherical Madrigals; Immortal Autumn; Edge of Shadow; Still Are New Worlds; The Nun's Priest's Tale; The Martyr's Elegy.

Orchestral Music—3 symphonies; Violin Concerto; Slow Piece, for strings; Hymn, Fuguing and Holiday; Piano Concerto; Variations; Three Pieces, for strings, wind, percussion, and tape recorder; Concerto for Percussion and Orchestra.

Piano Music—4 sonatas; Nostalgic Waltzes; Variations on a Theme by Alban Berg; Inventions; Fantasy; Sonata Quasi una Fantasia.

Vocal Music—Poems by Archibald MacLeish; Three Seventeenth Century Lyrics; Poor Richard; Three Love Poems; Chamber Music; The Express.

ABOUT

Musical Quarterly, January 1967.

Carlisle Floyd
1926–

Carlisle Floyd was born in Latta, South Carolina, on June 11, 1926. The son of a Methodist clergyman who constantly moved from one parish to another, Floyd attended public schools in various small towns throughout South Carolina. His mother, a proficient pianist, began teaching him the elements of piano playing when he was ten; but most of his piano training came from trial and error and experiments. In fact, it was many years before he received any intensive, formal music instruction, just as it was years before he knew he wanted to become a professional musician. An all-around boy, he showed as much talent for literature and the graphic arts as for music, and he was not quite sure on which field to concentrate his energies. At North High School in the town of North, South Carolina, he revealed his versatility by editing the school paper, serving as vice president of the student body, and playing on the basketball team.

Serious music study began at Converse College in Spartanburg, South Carolina, which he entered on a scholarship when he was sixteen. During his two years there he studied piano with Ernst Bacon. Bacon exerted a strong influence on young Floyd. When Bacon transferred to Syracuse University, Floyd followed him there, continuing his piano studies and receiving in 1946 a Bachelor of Arts degree.

CARLISLE FLOYD

In 1947 Floyd was appointed to the faculty of the School of Music at Florida State University at Tallahassee as an instructor of the piano. He had been specializing in that instrument, having continued his studies with Sidney Foster and Rudolf Firkušny; for a while he contemplated a career as virtuoso. Then, in 1949, granted a temporary leave of absence from Florida State, Floyd returned to Syracuse University to fulfill the requirements for a master's degree in music. During this period he came to the conclusion he preferred composition to performing on the piano.

In 1949 he wrote his first opera—text as well as music, as has since been his practice. He called it *Slow Dusk*. It was produced at Syracuse University in 1949, then was seen at several other universities and opera workshops. A successful revival was given in 1967 by the Opera Repertory Group in Jacksonville, Florida. A second opera, *Fugitives*, received a single performance at Florida State University in 1951.

A suggestion that he write an opera based on the Apocryphal story of Susanna and the Elders brought forth a libretto for his third opera in ten days' time. He wrote the score during the fall and winter of 1953–1954 and completed the orchestration in the fall of 1954. While on a visit to the Aspen Festival in Colorado, he showed some of his music to Phyllis Curtin and Mack Harrell, the singers. They were so impressed with the opera, titled *Susannah*, that they offered to appear in the principal roles. They did so—at Florida State University on February 24, 1955.

Susannah was produced by the New York City Opera on September 27, 1956, once again with Miss Curtin in the title role. It scored one of the greatest successes accorded a new American opera. The critics acclaimed it for the dramatic strength of the text and the forceful impact of the music. In *Tempo* Ronald Eyer described the opera as "a straightforward, unadorned story of malice, hypocrisy and tragedy of almost scriptural simplicity of language and characterization." The opera received the award of the New York Music Critics Circle; it was selected to represent American opera at the World's Fair at Brussels, where it was given its European première on June 25, 1958. It has since then been widely performed in the United States (including numerous revivals by the New York City Opera) and is a staple in the repertory of American opera. It has also been represented on symphony programs through an orchestral suite arranged by Walter Hendl and introduced in 1958 by the Cedar Rapids Symphony in Iowa.

Floyd described his opera as a "musical drama," explaining further that his central theme was "persecution and the concomitant psychological ramifications." The action takes place on a farm in the Tennessee hills in the present time. The heroine is so much the victim of malicious gossip of her neighbors, that, in time, her spirit is broken. Reverend Blitch comes to bring her comfort. He is deeply moved by her agony, and attracted to her physical beauty. Helplessly he begins to make advances to her. Susannah's brother, Sam, discovering what has happened, kills the Reverend. The neighbors now descend upon Susannah to vent upon her their hatred and passion for vengeance. Susannah holds them off with a shotgun. Then, as the curtain descends, she stands alone and forlorn in the doorway of her farm.

Floyd's style is eclectic. A good deal of the

vocal writing is in an effective kind of half-spoken declamation approximating the inflections of speech but regulated in pitch and rhythm and accompanied by the orchestra. But to give his opera a strong American flavor, Floyd also made use of hymns and square dances together with arias that simulated folk songs. At the same time Floyd did not hesitate to employ occasional fully developed arias with the expressiveness of a Puccini, or a Wagnerian Leitmotiv technique, or such modern devices as discords and polytonality.

After *Susannah* came *Wuthering Heights*. The latter was commissioned by the Santa Fe (New Mexico) Opera Association, which presented the world première in Santa Fe on July 16, 1958. The text, by the composer, differed in certain basic ways from Emily Brontë's novel. The time was shifted forward into the nineteenth century, and the telling of the story was done through a flashback technique. The opera at first met with a mixed reaction. The composer then revised it. The new version, introduced by the New York City Opera on April 9, 1959, met with unqualified acceptance. In the New York *Herald Tribune*, Paul Henry Lang said that "from first to last the familiar story is handled in a manner that compels attention and strong sympathy."

Floyd found the textual material for his next opera in the tensions of the post-Civil War period in America. Entitled *The Passion of Jonathan Wade*, it was centered, as the composer explained, "around the theme of a Northern occupation officer caught in a terrible conflict of conscience and duty during the early Reconstruction in the South." Within the frame of a love affair between, and then the marriage of, Jonathan Wade (a high-minded Northern officer) and Celia Townsend (a Southern belle)—and the impact this made upon extremists in both the North and the South—the opera showed how nobility, high ideals, and integrity were destroyed in an atmosphere of intolerance and hate.

The opera was introduced by the New York City Opera, which had commissioned it and which produced it under a Ford Foundation grant—on October 11, 1962. The company, reported Ross Parmenter in the New York *Times*, "chalked up another good deed in the service of American opera.... It aims very high, both morally and dramatically. And it attempts to sweep across a very large canvas." The high point of the opera, for Parmenter, came in the wedding scene in which a Negro servant sings a touching spiritual as the lovers are married. After this, the chorus takes up the touching refrain, and the newlyweds sing a poignant love duet. The affecting lyricism of this scene is matched by several other moments in which Floyd's gift for expressive melody is evident. Parmenter said that "there was so much that was pretty and melodious that one was inclined to wish it had been more purely a love story, and less encumbered with a sense of dramatic history with philosophical overtones."

A commission from the Carolina Charter Tercentenary Commission resulted in a comedy-drama in music, *The Sojourner and Mollie Sinclair*. It was presented as part of the celebration of North Carolina's 300th anniversary on December 2, 1963, in Raleigh. The setting is North Carolina's Cape Fear River Valley; the time, the mid-eighteenth century. The characters are Scottish Highlanders who are torn between their loyalties to their new homeland in North Carolina and to Scotland. Written primarily for television broadcast, *The Sojourner and Mollie Sinclair* was recorded on tape soon after the world première and broadcast over many television stations.

Markheim, with a libretto by the composer based on Robert Louis Stevenson, was produced in New Orleans on March 31, 1966. In this opera, says Harry Wells McCraw, Floyd "has surely produced . . . a work . . . which should excite and satisfy every audience given a chance to see it." McCraw finds that the "score's emotional high point is Markheim's shattering monologue beginning 'His voice still resounds in my ears,' in which he gradually realizes that . . . he has now become a murderer."

Floyd has not confined himself exclusively to opera. His concert works include a piano sonata (1957) which he dedicated to Rudolf Firkušny, who introduced it; a song cycle for baritone and orchestra, *Pilgrimage* (1956), written for Mack Harrell; a cycle of five songs about motherhood, *The Mystery* (1961), which had been commissioned by Phyllis Curtin under a Ford Foundation grant and which she introduced with the San Antonio

Symphony in 1961; and the *Introduction, Aria, and Dance,* for orchestra, the world première of which was given by the New Orleans Philharmonic on April 23, 1968.

In 1956 Floyd received a Guggenheim Fellowship, and in 1957 he earned a citation from the National Association for American Composers and Conductors. The United States Junior Chamber of Commerce named him one of the ten outstanding young men of 1959, pointing to his "memorable contributions through one of the most vigorous of all art forms to the future of American music."

Floyd resides in Tallahassee, Florida, where he is professor of music at Florida State University. In 1958 he initiated there the first accredited course ever given anywhere on the problems attending composers and librettists in the coordination of music and texts in operas.

Here in Floyd's words is his credo: "Opera as a stage genre must be valid and convincing and . . . the first major responsibility for this lies with the book. My first consideration in attempting an opera is whether or not the subject is one in which the emotional, psychological and philosophical conflicts of the story can be externalized through action and visible situation and still retain absorbing, multi-dimensional characters, for the very reason that opera must be primarily externalized. We have veered, too often, I feel, in favor of situation, leaving character development in a rather primitive, elementary state. . . . Also, I feel it is time that we who write operas attempt to make some commentary on time-less human problems in a contemporary way, and that it is not inappropriate that an opera have a 'theme' so long as it is not tiresomely didactic."

On November 28, 1957, Floyd married Kay Reeder, formerly a graduate student in English literature at Florida State University. He has retained his boyhood interest in sports, playing tennis regularly and attending basket-ball and football games.

MAJOR WORKS

Operas—Susannah; Wuthering Heights; The Passion of Jonathan Wade; The Sojourner and Mollie Sinclair; Markheim; Of Mice and Men.

Orchestral Music—Nocturne, for soprano and orchestra; The Pilgrimage, song cycle for baritone, chorus, and orchestra; The Mystery, song cycle for soprano and orchestra; Introduction, Aria, and Dance.

Piano Music—Lost Eden, for two pianos; Theme and Variations, for two pianos; Sonata.

ABOUT

Musical America, February 1957.

Arthur Foote
1853–1937

Arthur William Foote was born on March 5, 1853, in Salem, Massachusetts. He came from an old New England family. His parents were not musical, and they had no intention of encouraging their son in a musical career. The piano instruction he began to receive when he was fourteen was part of an over-all

ARTHUR FOOTE

general education. The curiosity about music aroused by these lessons led him to begin to study harmony with Stephen A. Emery when he was fifteen. In 1870 Foote entered Harvard where he attended the music classes of John Knowles Paine and conducted the Harvard Glee Club. After graduating from Harvard in 1874, he took lessons in piano and organ from B. J. Lang. Foote had planned to become a businessman, but Lang finally persuaded him to switch completely to music. With this in mind, Foote undertook an intensive study of composition with John Knowles Paine. In 1875 he received his Master of Arts degree at Harvard. An honorary degree of Doctor of

---

Foote: fŏŏt

Music was later conferred upon him by Trinity College in 1919, and by Dartmouth in 1925.

During a visit to Europe in 1876 Foote attended the inaugural festival of the Wagnerian music dramas at Bayreuth, an experience he often spoke of with reverence in later years. From 1878 to 1910 Foote was employed as organist at the First Unitarian Church in Boston, and from 1883 to 1933 he pursued a fruitful career as a teacher of piano. In 1881 he organized chamber music concerts in Boston which continued until the end of the century and at which he often appeared as an assisting artist.

His first ambitious, and mature, composition was *The Farewell of Hiawatha*, for men's voices and orchestra, which he completed in 1886. This was followed two years later by another choral work, this time for mixed voices and orchestra, *The Wreck of the Hesperus*. Both betray the impact the Wagnerian music drama at Bayreuth had made upon him.

On February 5, 1887, the Boston Symphony presented Foote's first successful composition for orchestra, the overture *In the Mountains*. This music was also given at the Paris Exposition on July 12, 1889. Later in 1889 (on November 23) the Boston Symphony performed Foote's Suite in D major, op. 21, and on January 24, 1891, his symphonic prologue *Francesca da Rimini*. In the 1890's Foote concentrated on chamber music. His most important works of this period, including the G minor Violin Sonata (1890), the Piano Quartet (1891), the E major String Quartet (1894), and the Piano Quintet (1898), were introduced by the Kneisel Quartet. In these compositions, as in his early symphonic works, the influence is primarily Brahmsian. The emphasis is on broad, stately melodies, rich-sounding harmonies, and rhapsodic moods within clearly defined classical structures.

These qualities do not change markedly in Foote's later works, though an individual style and a more personal attitude are clearly discernible. These later compositions include two that are still heard from time to time: the Suite in E major, for string orchestra, op. 63 (1907), introduced by the Boston Symphony on April 16, 1909, and *A Night Piece*, for flute and string quartet (1918), first heard at a concert of the San Francisco Chamber Society

on January 28, 1919. The latter has also been heard in an orchestral transcription (for flute and string orchestra) which Foote made at the request of Pierre Monteux, who introduced it with the Boston Symphony on April 13, 1923. Foote's last work directly for orchestra was *Four Character Pieces*, after Omar Khayyám (1912)–four orchestral episodes inspired by verses from the *Rubáiyát*.

Olin Downes summed up Foote's style as follows: "Foote cultivated his own garden, musically as well as horticulturally. In an astonishing manner, he found things to say completely, simply, durably his own. His style did not change, but refined and strengthened. It was a remarkable demonstration of the power of sincerity and taste. His scores were never clogged with notes, nor was he tempted by a trick of someone else's style, or an effect of someone else's instrumentation."

In 1899 Foote was elected to the membership of the National Institute of Arts and Letters and was made a Fellow of the American Academy of Arts and Sciences. From 1909 to 1912 he was president of the American Guild of Organists, an organization that he had helped to found.

He spent the closing years of his life in a two-story house in Newton Centre, Massachusetts, where he devoted himself to his music and to his flowers. His studio was filled with books, music, and mementos, and was dominated by an old, battered Chickering piano to which he was deeply attached. He was, as Olin Downes once described him, "spare of build, of less than average height, with rough-hewn energetic features. Only with his intimates was he disposed to many words. . . . He could summon a hot temper and could express himself picturesquely. In other words, he could swear." He was a deeply religious man and held "strong views on all subjects." His wife was the former Kate G. Knowlton of Boston whom he had married on July 7, 1880. They had one child, a daughter.

Foote, who lived to see American music undergoing vast changes of style, had this to say of modern music a few months before his death: "As one of the older generation, I should hardly be expected to feel in the same way about happenings in the past twenty-five years–about polytonality, linear counterpoint, and so forth. Dissonance and consonance seem to me to be complementary; while music entirely consonant becomes monotonous, that which is constantly dissonant is not only tiresome, but, worse than this, unpleasant. Dissonance is not undesirable in itself, but often becomes so because of the unskillful way in which it is used."

On the occasion of his eightieth birthday, the composer was guest of honor of the Boston Symphony, which devoted an entire program to his music.

Foote remained active to the end of his life. The summer before his death, although he was well past eighty, he was busy limbering up his fingers at the piano and rememorizing some of the works he loved most deeply, works mainly by Bach and Brahms. He died of pneumonia, in the Massachusetts General Hospital in Boston on April 8, 1937.

In a eulogy in the New York *Times*, Olin Downes wrote: "There was no one like him, even among his colleagues, no one so simply and unaffectedly absorbed in his task. . . . He never coveted gain, or huge rewards, and lived economically, modestly, absorbed in work. . . . He lived in music and cultivated it in every possible way with intense satisfaction. He respected this privilege, and was fortunate in his devotion."

MAJOR WORKS

Chamber Music—3 string quartets; 2 piano trios; Violin Sonata in G minor; Piano Quartet; Piano Quintet; Cello Sonata; A Night Piece, for flute and string quartet (also for orchestra).

Choral Music—The Farewell of Hiawatha; The Wreck of the Hesperus; The Skeleton in Armor.

Orchestral Music—2 suites (including the Suite in E major); In the Mountains, overture; Francesca da Rimini, symphonic prologue; Serenade in E; Cello Concerto; Four Character Pieces.

Vocal Music—Over 150 songs for voice and piano including I Know a Little Garden Path, Irish Folk Song, It Was a Lover and His Lass, Lad o' the Leal, and The Night Has a Thousand Eyes.

ABOUT

Chase, G., America's Music; Howard, J. T., Our American Music.

Musical Quarterly, January 1937; New York Times, April 18, 1937.

Wolfgang Fortner
1907–

Wolfgang Fortner was born in Leipzig on October 12, 1907. The fact that he grew up in the shadow of St. Thomas Church, where Johann Sebastian Bach had served as cantor, may account for his early interest in polyphony and his strong leanings towards baroque structures.

WOLFGANG FORTNER

From 1927 to 1931 Fortner attended the Leipzig Conservatory, where he studied organ with one of Germany's masters of that instrument, Karl Straube. His teacher in composition was Hermann Grabner, a pupil of Max Reger. Through Grabner, Fortner acquired Reger's partiality for old contrapuntal forms and style, as his early works reveal. His interest in old forms begins with the *Vier Marianische Antiphone*, introduced at the Lower Rhine Festival in Düsseldorf in 1928, and is climaxed by his major choral work, *Eine Deutsche Liedmesse* (1934). His first instrumental works also disclose strong interest in baroque structures and styles. These compositions include the Suite, for orchestra (1930), based on themes of the sixteenth century Flemish master Jan Pieter Sweelinck; two concertos, one for organ (1932) and the other for cembalo (1935); and the Sinfonia Concertante (1937).

Fortner also attended Leipzig University where he combined study in music history and musicology (the latter with Theodor Kroyer) with classes in psychology and philosophy. In 1931 he passed the state examinations as teacher of music in higher education and was appointed to the music faculty of the Institute for Evangelical Church Music, in Heidelberg.

205

Since that time he has lived in Heidelberg and has remained in the teaching profession. From 1954 (when he left the Institute) to 1957, he was professor of composition at the Music Academy in Detmold. Since 1957 he has held a similar post at the High School of Music in Freiburg-am-Breisgau, making the one-hundred-and-fifty-mile drive from Heidelberg to Freiburg once a week to teach his classes.

In *Musical America*, Ernst Thomas singled out two components that prevented Fortner from succumbing to dry academicism in his neo-baroque period: "One was a marked need of sonority, which kept him from allowing the static elements of composition to wither in a puritanically dry vocalism or instrumentalism. . . . [The other] was a sensitivity in harmony that set him on the track of musical expression."

An important change in Fortner's composition, the result of his contacts with the twelve-tone technique, occurred immediately after World War II. Fortner first used a twelve-tone row, though freely, in his third string quartet (1948). But he had been strongly drawn to atonality in his ballet *Die Weisse Rose* (based on Oscar Wilde's *The Birthday of the Infanta*) which was completed in 1945 and produced in Berlin April 28, 1951.

Atonality is used even more extensively in Fortner's Symphony (1947), now considered one of the most important of such works to appear in postwar Germany. Fortner said of this work, which was the first to bring him prominence, that "it renounces any justification through a compositional system and lives solely from a power of conviction of the artistic assertion." This music was strongly affected by the war and postwar conditions in Germany and their impact on Fortner. He has explained that the spiritual background of this music is the conflict between misery and hope. "The atmosphere . . . is one of pathos, immense tension, and sincerity," says K. W. Bartlett. "The thematic material is poignant and concise, the forms employed are concentrated, and harmonically the symphony is of great audacity, the dissonances of the huge climaxes sounding almost aggressive." The symphony was performed for the first time in Baden-Baden on May 2, 1948.

In his mature works Fortner continually exploits twelve-tone rows, and at times se-

rialism, though with far greater freedom and with greater intensity of expression than found in most dodecaphonists. The twelve-tone technique prevails even in a work such as his opera *Die Bluthochzeit* (*The Blood Wedding*), with a text based on a drama by Federico García Lorca (which was also the source of Fortner's dramatic scene for soprano, tenor, baritone, narrator, and orchestra, *Der Wald*). In recognition of the Spanish background, Fortner utilizes in his opera the rhythms of Spanish folk dances, the sensual melodies of Spanish folk songs, and the characteristic Spanish rhythms of clicking castanets and strumming guitars. Nevertheless, the music makes use primarily of a twelve-tone method, and is frequently dramatized by discords and bitonal writing. A dramatic highpoint in the opera comes in the woodland scene in which the hero is killed. The high tensions of this episode are recreated in a twelve-tone canon for two solo violins, accompanied by percussion. *Die Bluthochzeit* received its world première in Cologne May 25, 1957. Fortner subsequently revised both *Der Wald* and *Die Bluthochzeit* and merged them into a single operatic work called *In Seinem Garten Liebt Don Perlimplin Belison*, produced in Schwetzingen May 10, 1962. The musical style of this completely revised opera was described by some German critics as "neo-Webern." From Schwetzingen, Peter Heyworth reported: "The action is conceived in terms of wry humor, and both in shape and subject matter it is ideally suited to operatic treatment. . . . The skill and precision of Fortner's writing is immediately evident and it would be a dull man who could derive no pleasure from the exquisite and variegated sounds that he draws from a chamber orchestra."

Among Fortner's later successful works for orchestra is the *Impromptus*, which had been commissioned by the Southwest German Radio for the Donaueschingen Music Festival in 1957. This composition also utilizes a twelve-tone row. The entire composition is in two contrasting sections, beginning with a vigorous Prelude, and continuing with Theme and Variations. The slow, expressive theme of the second part is played by solo oboe and clarinet, after which the melody is subjected to seven variations, the last one building up to a dramatic, exciting conclusion.

Another noteworthy composition, *Triplum*, for three pianos and orchestra, was introduced at the International Festival of Contemporary Music in Prague on October 4, 1967. Fortner came to the United States to attend the American première of this work, given by the Buffalo Philharmonic under Lukas Foss on January 14, 1968. At that time, John Dwyer, the critic of the Buffalo *Evening News*, described *Triplum* as a three-movement atonal composition with "serial implications in depth, even to the rhythmic combinations for untuned percussion such as the wood-block and light cymbal.... There are apparent conductor's choices in various parts, as to length or repetition of short episodes, and it works up to big, hall-filling fortes, with a sheerly textural thrill in several kinds of pulsating, indefinite clamor. This giant shimmer is made possible by the three mightily grand pianos, in pedaled effects of rolling chaos."

In 1948 Fortner received the Franz Schreker Music Prize of the City of Berlin. In the summer of 1961 he paid his first visit to the United States to teach a master class in composition at the Berkshire Music Center at Tanglewood.

A bachelor, Fortner resides in a California-style house which he had built a number of years ago in a suburb of Heidelberg. He has devoted considerable time and energy to promoting new music and young composers. When he was teaching in Heidelberg, he founded a chamber orchestra there for the express purpose of performing unfamiliar music. After World War II, he organized in Heidelberg the "Musica Viva," a series of concerts providing a hearing for modern composers; and at Freiburg he opened a "studio" where young composers and performers could meet regularly to discuss mutual problems. He has also promoted annual seminars for young composers to exchange ideas and experiences through the Music Institute at Kranichstein. Fortner has been president of the German section of the International Society for Contemporary Music and consultant to GEMA, which is the German equivalent of America's ASCAP or BMI.

MAJOR WORKS

Ballet—Die Weisse Rose.

Chamber Music—3 string quartets; 6 Madrigals, for two violins and cello; Suite, for solo cello; Violin Sonata; Flute Sonata; Serenade, for flute, oboe, and bassoon; Cello Sonata; Trauerode, for clarinet and string quartet; Five Bagatelles, for wind quintet.

Choral Music—Marian Antiphons; Grenzen der Menschheit; Drei Geistliche Gesänge; Eine Deutsche Liedmesse; Nuptiae Catulli; Geistliche Abendmusik; Herr, Bleibe bei Uns!; Die Nachgeborenen; Bertolt Brecht Cantata; Isaac's Sacrifice, oratorio; Song of Birth.

Operas—Die Witwe von Ephesus; In Seinem Garten Liebt Don Perlimplin Belison (a revision of an earlier opera, Die Bluthochzeit, and an earlier dramatic scene, Der Wald).

Orchestral Music—Various concertos for solo instruments and orchestra (organ; cembalo; piano; violin; cello); Suite for Orchestra (on themes by Jan Pieter Sweelinck); Concertino for String Orchestra; Sinfonia Concertante; Concertino for Viola and Small Orchestra; Swabian Folk Dances; Capriccio and Finale; Ernste Musik; Streichermusik II, for string orchestra; Symphony; The Creation, for voice and orchestra; Fantasy on the Name B-A-C-H, for two pianos and orchestra; Aria, for mezzo soprano with solo viola and small orchestra; Movements, for piano and orchestra; Der Wald, dramatic scene for soprano, tenor, baritone, narrator, and orchestra; Impromptus; Aulodie, for oboe and orchestra; Fantasy on B-A-C-H; Triplum, for three pianos and orchestra.

Organ Music—Preamble and Fugue; Toccata and Fugue.

Piano Music—Sonatina; Rondo on Swabian Folk Dances; Kammermusik; Elegies.

Vocal Music—Fragment Maria, chamber cantata for soprano and instruments; Twelve Shakespeare Songs; Two Exercises, for three women's voices and fifteen instruments; In the Midst of Life, cantata for soprano and instruments.

ABOUT

Laux, K., Musik und Musiker der Gegenwart; Lindlar, H. (ed.), Wolfgang Fortner: Eine Monographie.

Musical America, August 1961.

Lukas Foss
1922–

Lukas Foss was born Lukas Fuchs in Berlin on August 15, 1922. His father was a professor of philosophy; his mother, a painter. When Lukas was three years old, he was given an accordion as a Christmas gift. Before many weeks passed, he was able to accompany himself as he sang German folk songs. At the age of seven, he began the study of piano and theory with Julius Goldstein. Goldstein gave the boy a solid grounding in the classic literature so that at first the old masters (particularly Bach and Haydn) became models for emulation. Foss made his first attempts at composition in his seventh year. He asserts that it was a performance of Mozart's *Marriage of Figaro* that led him to become a composer. The opera became such an obsession with him that he learned to sing all the parts and often entertained his family and family guests at the dinner table by giving a one-man performance now of one scene, now of another. In his early teens he undertook the writing of two operas.

LUKAS FOSS

In 1933 he went to Paris, where he attended the Conservatory for two years. His teachers were Lazare Lévy in piano, Noël Gallon in composition, and Felix Wolfes in orchestration. Foss assimilated French music and styles and for the first time became interested in modern idioms and techniques. The music of Paul Hindemith made a particularly strong impression on him, providing him with a new stimulus in his creativity. While pursuing his music study and interests, Foss received an academic education at the Lycée Pasteur.

In 1937 Foss came to the United States which henceforth became his permanent home and where, in 1942, he became a citizen. His musical training continued at the Curtis Institute with Scalero and Randall Thompson in composition, Reiner in conducting, and Vengerova in piano. While still attending the Curtis Institute, he made his debut, at the age of seventeen, as conductor with the Pittsburgh Symphony Orchestra. One year later he was graduated from Curtis with highest honors. He now found American music—particularly the music of Copland and Roy Harris—a source of prime interest, just as he had become fascinated by American life, manners, and ways. "It was a period," he later wrote, "of discovering America for myself, and I felt very passionately part of the country."

Each summer, from 1937 to 1940, he attended the Berkshire Music Center at Tanglewood where he studied conducting with Koussevitzky and composition with Hindemith. He continued his study of composition with Hindemith at Yale University in 1940 and 1941. Strange to say, in view of his long periods of study with Hindemith, Foss was able to discard the strong influence that Hindemith had exerted on him.

The first composition Foss stood ready to acknowledge and to allow to be published (all earlier works having been discarded) was *Four Two-Voiced Inventions*, for piano (1938), whose basic technique was Hindemith's linear counterpoint. A tendency away from Hindemith becomes discernible in the incidental music for Shakespeare's *The Tempest*, commissioned by the Theatre Guild. This production was seen on Broadway on March 31, 1940. An *Allegro Concertante*, performed in Philadelphia and New York, reveals a still sharper break with Hindemith and a growing concern for romantic self-expression. On the strength of these compositions, Foss received in 1942 a Pulitzer Traveling Fellowship.

Two experiences helped Foss fulfill his romantic tendencies as a composer and achieve a new American identity. The first came in 1941 at the Berkshire Music Center, where he conducted a performance of Copland's music from the ballet *Billy the Kid*. Copland's use of cowboy melodies interested Foss and made him think for the first time of the potentiality of this music and the possibility of creating an indigenous American music. The second experience was the reading of Carl Sandburg's epic poem *The Prairie*, in which Foss found echoes and reverberations of his own excitement in America's vitality. "Sandburg's poem," he later recalled, "came to my attention just at the right moment . . . and I proceeded to set this huge epic, the biggest project I ever embarked on. With immense love, I set each word, and with this work developed a musical sensitivity for the English language, and a vocal style born directly out of the 'word.'"

The cantata *The Prairie* brought Foss his

first major success. A symphonic suite derived from the score was introduced by the Boston Symphony on October 15, 1943. This was followed by the première of the complete cantata, performed by the Collegiate Chorale, conducted by Robert Shaw, in New York on May 15, 1944. Later the same year it was selected by the New York Music Critics Circle as the most important new American choral work of the season, and Artur Rodzinski presented it at a concert of the New York Philharmonic. In his description of this work, Robert Strassburg wrote: "It has a broad range of expression. Tender love songs, dance rhythms, driving, aggressive, massed choral effects, clashing sonorities are all controlled and well proportioned. Each movement, growing out of well-defined motives, is filled with the warmth of life, and reveals lyric powers of persuasion that place Lukas Foss in the vanguard of those composers seeking to develop a living art language free of artificial theatricality."

Two orchestral compositions of contrasting emotion revealed Foss's versatility. The Symphony in G, which the Pittsburgh Symphony introduced on February 4, 1945, is a joyful and optimistic piece of music. Opposite in emotional appeal is the *Ode*, dedicated to the men who had fallen in the war, and performed by the New York Philharmonic under George Szell on March 15, 1945. As its dedication suggests, the *Ode* is tragic music inspired by the following line of John Donne: "Any man's death diminishes me." But while the prevailing mood is that of deep sorrow, the work ends peacefully with the optimistic chord of C major as reaffirmation of life. Foss revised this *Ode* in 1958, and the new version was presented in October of that year by the Philadelphia Orchestra under Ormandy.

In 1945 Foss became the youngest composer to win a Guggenheim Fellowship. (He received a second Guggenheim Fellowship in 1960.) This award gave him the time to work on two biblical cantatas for solo voice and orchestra—another stage in his development. As he explained at the time: "I went through an inner metamorphosis. I started studying seventeenth and eighteenth century music with renewed intensity, because it had become apparent to me that the late nineteenth and twentieth century composer commands an increasingly limited field of expression."

In 1945 he completed *Song of Anguish*, for baritone and orchestra, its text derived from the Book of Isaiah. Commissioned by the Kulas Foundation, the score received a dance performance at Jacob's Pillow in Massachusetts during the summer of 1948, the music being performed on the piano. The first presentation as a concert work with full orchestra came on March 10, 1950, with Marko Rothmüller as baritone soloist and the composer conducting the Boston Symphony. Two years later, Foss wrote *Song of Songs*, for soprano and orchestra, which he had been commissioned to do by the League of Composers for the soprano Ellabelle Davis. This was a setting of four of Solomon's songs: "Awake, O Northwind," "Come, My Beloved," "By Night, on My Bed," and "Set Me as a Seal." Ellabelle Davis and the Boston Symphony under Koussevitzky introduced it on March 7, 1947. So highly did Koussevitzky regard this composition that he played it eight times in nine days, in Boston, Northampton, New Haven, Philadelphia, and New York—the first time such a thing had happened to a new work in the history of the Boston Symphony. Cyrus Durgin said in the Boston *Globe:* "The most important thing about the *Song of Songs* is its beauty of emotional expression. From first to last this is a song, and that is unusual in the music of today." Igor Stravinsky wrote Foss: "I find it beautiful, this music of yours . . . an inspiration no longer abandoned to its own fate. Do you remember Braque's statement: 'J'aime la règle qui corrige l'émotion'?"

From 1944 to 1950, Foss was the official pianist of the Boston Symphony Orchestra. From 1950 through 1952 he lived in Rome on a Fulbright scholarship. Two more major choral works occupied Foss in the 1950's. *A Parable of Death* (1952) was a cantata based on a story and poems by Rainer Maria Rilke. The Louisville Orchestra had commissioned it for Vera Zorina, who introduced it with the orchestra in Kentucky on March 11, 1953. In 1956 came *Psalms*, for voices and orchestra (based on Psalms 121, 44, 98, and 23). This was commissioned by the Stockbridge Bowl Association. The première took place on May 9, 1957, with Mitropoulos conducting the New York Philharmonic.

Foss did not confine himself exclusively to choral music. He produced significant works in other media as well. For his second piano concerto (1949), which received its world première at the Venice Festival on October 7, 1951, he was given the Horblit Award following the American première in Boston November 1951. After the composer had revised the concerto in 1953, it received the award of the New York Music Critics Circle. Artur Rubinstein described the revised concerto as "one of the finest pieces written in our time."

Another important work for orchestra was the *Symphony of Chorales* (1958), commissioned by the Koussevitzky Music Foundation and written at the behest of the Friends of Albert Schweitzer in Boston. In this composition, each movement is based on a different Bach chorale. The first performance took place in Pittsburgh on October 24, 1958, with William Steinberg conducting the Pittsburgh Symphony.

In 1950 Foss made his bow as a composer for the stage with a delightful one-act opera, *The Jumping Frog of Calaveras County*, adapted from the Mark Twain story. Foss's score was enlivened through the interpolation of cowboy tunes. The opera was first produced at Indiana University, in Bloomington, on May 18, 1950. Three weeks later it was given in New York, at which time Carter Harmon described it in the New York *Times* as "a thoroughly workable piece of music, unselfconsciously in the 'American' idiom of broad melodic intervals and low emotional tensions."

Foss also wrote a highly successful opera expressly for television: *Griffelkin*, commissioned and produced by the NBC Opera, over the NBC-TV network November 6, 1955. The libretto by Alistair Reid was a child's fantasy about a shy devilkin who gets as a gift for his tenth birthday a day in the world of humans. To help him celebrate that day he is provided with a magic vial. But the kind little devil, instead of cutting up or doing harm, insists on perpetrating a good deed. For this he is banished from the world of devils to become a normal boy in an everyday world. Foss wrote a sprightly, tuneful, effervescent score completely in tune with the light, gay text—a score that includes arias, duets, choral

numbers, as well as a waltz and a canon—a score that blends gaiety with tenderness. This music, says Robert Sabin, is "creative and sincere. Librettist and composer have made their world of childhood wonder seem real, and they have struck those deeper tones that all such fantasies embody. . . . As a whole, it is a glowing and thoroughly successful work."

In 1959 Foss completed a nine-minute opera (libretto by Gian-Carlo Menotti) which was first introduced at the Spoleto Festival in Italy the same year and which the New York Philharmonic under Bernstein performed in New York on May 6, 1960. Entitled *Introductions and Goodbyes*, it called for a single leading character (a baritone), the host at a cocktail party; a chorus represents the other guests. Howard Taubman described this piece as a "diverting trifle."

During the years Foss was the official pianist of the Boston Symphony, he made frequent appearances with the Boston Symphony as solo pianist and had opportunities to appear as a guest conductor with other orchestras. In addition to these chores, Foss initiated a career as teacher by joining the faculty of the Berkshire Music Center at Tanglewood where he was soon elevated to the position of Koussevitzky's assistant. In 1962 he became chairman of the composition department.

In 1953 Foss succeeded Arnold Schoenberg as professor of composition at the University of California in Los Angeles; he also became the director of its symphony orchestra. In 1960 he went on a State Department tour of the Soviet Union and Poland, conducting his own compositions with local orchestras. In 1961 he conducted seven concerts at the Ojai Festival in California and drew the largest audiences in the history of that event; in 1963 Foss was appointed musical director of the festival. In the 1964–1965 season, Foss led a series of concerts of new music in New York, and in 1965 he was the artistic director of the French-American Festival which the New York Philharmonic presented at the Lincoln Center for the Performing Arts.

In 1957 Foss began to interest himself in the possibilities of ensemble improvisation, a new form of music making. Ensemble improvisation is a spontaneous, informal kind of chamber music in which the music is created through a process of improvisation. "It all began very modestly as a means of helping the students," he has revealed, "but suddenly a door opened for me and I saw a vast new territory to explore." He organized an ensemble of four virtuosos who, as the Improvisation Chamber Ensemble, began to perform extensively throughout the United States. Lukas Foss explains: "Improvisation is not composition. It relates to composition, much in the same way a sketch relates to the finished work of art. . . . It is . . . a spontaneous, sketch-like and—incidentally—unrepeatable expression, full of surprises for the listener and for the performer as well."

Foss's most significant work in this improvisational style is his *Time Cycle*, four songs for soprano and orchestra, which he wrote for Adele Addison on a grant from the Ford Foundation. *Time Cycle* received its first public performance in New York on October 21, 1960, with Miss Addison as the soloist with the New York Philharmonic. Participating in this performance was the Improvisation Chamber Ensemble, headed by the composer, who performed an improvised interlude between songs. In this version, *Time Cycle* was recorded for Columbia, received the award of the New York Music Critics Circle, and was choreographed and danced by the Canadian National Ballet. Another version of *Time Cycle* dispenses with improvised interludes and is scored for a chamber ensemble comprising piano, clarinet, cello, and percussion, as accompaniment to the soprano. The composer maintains that these two versions "are too different in their dynamic range to be compared. The latter has the advantage of greater precision. But it neither supersedes the orchestral version nor is it an arrangement of the original. The occasion, the size of the hall, will call for one or the other." The chamber music version was first heard at Tanglewood on July 10, 1961, and was later recorded by Epic.

Later works by Foss either in an improvisational style or in a partially controlled aleatory, or chance, style, include the *Echoi* (1963) and *Elytres* (1964). *Echoi* is a four-part work for piano, percussion, clarinet, and cello which, says Nicolas Slonimsky, applies "stochastic techniques controlled by the drummer striking the anvil to redirect the musical happening, banging on the strings of the piano to stop

the pianist, and so forth." After being introduced in New York in 1964 it received the award of the New York Music Critics Circle.

Elytres can be performed by two different ensembles. One calls for eleven solo instruments. Another is for orchestra with some violins tripled and some percussion doubled. All instruments play only in the high register. Other unusual effects are produced by a percussionist performing on the strings of the piano soundboard with tape-covered vibraphone mallets. Foss has explained that *Elytres* is not aleatory music since "the detail is as controlled as it is in a conventional score, one which does not vary from performance to performance. My own aim was to make multidiversity available without surrendering to chance." *Elytres* was introduced in Los Angeles on December 8, 1964.

Discussing Foss's experiments with improvisation or controlled chance, Brock McElheran explained: "With the new Foss technique the complete composition is written out, the full score appearing quite dense, that is, most of the performing forces seem to be engaged simultaneously. However, by following an intricate diagram, the music is marked so that only a small amount of possible combinations is actually heard at any one time. At another concert different combinations are used."

Another creative procedure that fascinates Foss is using a composition, or part of a composition, by a master as the starting point for works employing his highly individualized modern approaches and techniques. In *Phorion* (first performance in New York on April 27, 1967, with Leonard Bernstein conducting the New York Philharmonic), Foss uses the notes of Bach's Prelude from the Partita in E major, for solo violin, and then subjects them to distortions, modifications, and ultramodern treatments. (*Phorion* in Greek means stolen goods.) In *Non Improvisation* (heard first at the Warsaw Festival in 1967) Foss uses material from Bach's Concerto in D minor, for clavier and orchestra, and juxtaposes it to sounds provided by electric organ and gong. In the *Baroque Variations*, for orchestra (world premiere by the Chicago Symphony Orchestra at Ravinia during the summer of 1967), he takes a movement from a Handel concerto grosso, Scarlatti's Sonata in E major for piano,

Françaix

and a part of Bach's E major Partita and puts them through, in the words of Harold C. Schonberg, "a kind of chemical laboratory in which elements are recognizable . . . but in which they are bent, fractured, refracted, pulverized, stamped on, caressed."

In New York in March 1967 Mstislav Rostropovich introduced Foss's Concerto for Cello and Orchestra—probably the first time that a major Soviet performer gave the world première of an American composition. This proved to be a curious work. As Allen Hughes said, it "begins with the cello and accompanying players circling around one note for three minutes, pits the live cello player against a tape recording he had made previously, has two movements in which the accompaniment for the solos are interchangeable and a fourth movement that makes mincemeat of Bach's Sarabande in C minor."

From 1963 to 1969 Foss was musical director of the Buffalo Philharmonic, whose concerts became under his leadership a vital forum for avant-garde music. With funds from the Rockefeller Foundation, Foss, in collaboration with Allen Sapp, developed in Buffalo the Center for the Creative and Performing Arts where musicians from all over the world could do experimental work.

In October 1951 Foss married Cornelia Brendel, painter and sculptor. With their two children, they make their home in Buffalo.

MAJOR WORKS

Ballets—The Heart Remembers; The Gift of the Magi.

Chamber Music—Violin Sonata; Duo, for cello and piano; Three Pieces, for violin and piano; Capriccio, for cello and piano; String Quartet; Time Cycle, for soprano, piano, clarinet, cello, and percussion; Echoi, for piano, clarinet, cello, and percussion; Elytres, for eleven solo instruments; Sillscapes, for twenty-four wind instruments.

Choral Music—The Prairie; Song of Anguish; Song of Songs; A Parable of Death; Psalms; Fragments of Archilochos.

Operas—The Jumping Frog of Calaveras County (one-act opera); Griffelkin (television opera); Introductions and Goodbyes (nine-minute opera).

Orchestral Music—2 piano concertos; Symphony in G; Pantomime; Recordare; Oboe Concerto; Symphony of Chorales; Concerto for Improvising Instruments and Orchestra; Time Cycle, for soprano and orchestra; Elytres; Discrepancy, for wind instruments; Cello Concerto; Phorion; Baroque Variations.

Piano Music—Three Pieces, for two pianos; Passacaglia; Fantasy-Rondo; Scherzo Ricercare.

ABOUT

Chase, G., America's Music; Goss, M., Modern Music Makers; Machlis, J., Introduction to Contemporary Music.

Melos, December 1954; New Yorker, January 30, 1965; Saturday Review, May 29, 1954; February 26, 1967.

Jean Françaix
1912–

Jean René Désiré Françaix, born in Le Mans, France, on May 23, 1912, comes from a family of professional musicians. His father was the director of the Le Mans Conservatory; his mother was the organizer of a woman's choral group. Jean began the study of music early, from the start showing unusual talent. At the age of four he began improvising on the piano. Before long he was writing his own music. His first published work appeared in 1922, when he was only ten—a piano suite, *Pour Jacqueline*, which had been written one year earlier to celebrate the first walking steps of his little cousin.

JEAN FRANÇAIX

He studied music at his father's Conservatory where he won several prizes. In his tenth year he made regular visits to Paris to study harmony and composition with Nadia Boulanger and piano with Isidor Philipp at the Conservatory. In 1930 Françaix won first prize in piano-playing at the Conservatory.

Françaix: frän sě´

Two of his works received major performances in 1932. On June 21, *Bagatelles*, for string quartet and piano, was introduced at the festival of the International Society for Contemporary Music in Vienna. On November 6, his symphony was presented in Paris by the Orchestre Symphonique, conducted by Monteux. Both compositions were praised. In 1933 came a string trio, still regarded as one of Français's freshest and most spontaneous chamber music works. Hardly past his twentieth birthday, Français was already regarded by some French critics as one of the most important new composers to appear in France since the end of World War I.

Several other significant works fulfilled the promise of these early compositions, among them two important works for piano and orchestra. The Concertino for Piano and Orchestra (1934) was introduced by the composer and the Lamoureux Orchestra under Morel on December 15, 1934. The Concerto for Piano and Orchestra (1936) was first heard in Berlin on November 8, 1936. These were followed by an important ballet (Français's third), *Le Roi Nu*, based on a tale by Hans Christian Andersen, produced in Paris on June 15, 1936, and in London at Sadler's Wells in 1938. In 1937 came a witty chamber opéra-comique, *Le Diable Boiteux* (libretto by the composer based on Le Sage). It called for two male voices and a small orchestra, and it told the story of a limping demon who betrays the foibles and frauds of men to Don Zambullo in return for being liberated from the powers of a magician's phial. When this little opera was revived in New York in 1960, Louis Biancolli wrote in the New York *World-Telegram & Sun:* "Français's pert music points up the mocking satire of the theme, revealing endless ingenuity of phrase and style."

In these compositions he is essentially a neoclassicist influenced by Stravinsky, whom he regards as the greatest composer of the twentieth century (and whom he resembles physically). Français is partial to tersely stated ideas, economical instrumentation, sparing harmonizations. He leans heavily on the French classic tradition. He often interjects into his writing ironic or witty statements. He is at his best when his touch is light, his style graceful, his manner suave.

In 1938 Français paid his first visit to the

United States. He made his American debut in New York on February 11, with the New York Philharmonic, Nadia Boulanger conducting, in a performance of his piano concerto. The wit and sparkle of the music, and the brilliance of his performance, inspired praise from the New York music critics, one of whom described him as "the white hope of French music."

During this visit, Français confided to an interviewer his aims as a composer: "It is important that a composer should be of his country and that he should try to translate the spirit of his country into his music, eliminating the faults and emphasizing the great qualities. In other respects, my ideal is to write music that is absolutely personal, that belongs to myself and not to anybody else. One should not deliberately declare that one adhered to this or that school, or is influenced by this or that composer. One is influenced largely unconsciously, but one's chief conscious interest should be in a personal expression."

Though his best vein is that of wit and irony, which he has tapped freely and frequently, Français has produced an important work in a more sober and majestic style–and with no loss of inventive imagination or technical scale. This is the oratorio *L'Apocalypse de Saint-Jean*, a major work for solo voices, chorus, and two orchestras, which sets texts from the Book of Revelation. He completed his oratorio in 1939, and the première took place in Paris during World War II, on June 11, 1942. Roland-Manuel said of it that it "compels our admiration by its simplicity and nobility, by the serene unity of its construction, the sobriety of its language and mood." The second orchestra used for this oratorio represents Hell, and it makes use of some unusual instruments, including a quartet of saxophones, harmonium, accordion, mandolin, guitar, and xylophone.

In a similar noble and lofty style is the opera *La Main de Gloire* (1945). It was first heard at the Bordeaux Music Festival May 7, 1950. The libretto, based on a story by Gérard de Nerval, was prepared by the composer. Henri Barraud commented: "It is one of the most original stage works produced in France in a long time."

An earlier opera, however, was in the satirical, tongue-in-the-cheek language of his early piano concertino and piano concerto. This was *L'Apostrophe* (1940), text by the composer based on Balzac. Its first performance took place over the French radio in 1947. When it was staged for the first time (at the Holland Music Festival July 1, 1951), it scored a major success. Françaix's wit proved so effective, reported a correspondent for the New York *Times*, that "even the non-French-speaking section of the audience often was lured into laughter by the caprices of the score."

An important later work in which Françaix's gift for wit and levity is predominant is *L'Horloge de Flore*, for oboe and orchestra, completed in 1959. When this composition was recorded in 1967, a critic for the *Saturday Review* described it as "a fanciful sequence of movements (seven in all, played without interruption) derived from a Swedish 'flower clock.' The timekeeper was ornamented with flowers, arranged according to the hour at which they bloomed (3 a.m., poisonberry; 10 a.m., torch thistle; 5 p.m., deadly nightshade; etc.). What precise relationship all, or any, of this has with what Françaix has written is not immediately apparent, but the results are what count, and these are a joy—light, fluent, full of closely fitted instrumental detail."

Françaix has also composed music for ballets. In his first, *Scuola di Ballo* (1933), he made a delightful adaptation of music by Boccherini for a scenario and choreography by Leonide Massine based on a Goldini comedy. *Scuola di Ballo* was produced in Monte Carlo by the Ballet Russe on April 25, 1933. An orchestral suite from this score has often been heard on symphony programs.

One of the best is *Les Demoiselles de la Nuit*, a dramatic ballet with scenario by Jean Anouilh and choreography by Roland Petit. Les Ballets de Paris introduced it in Paris on May 20, 1948, with Margot Fonteyn and Roland Petit as principal dancers. The American première took place at the Metropolitan Opera in New York on April 13, 1951.

Another successful Françaix ballet was conceived by George Balanchine for the New York City Ballet with music taken from the Serenade, for small orchestra, which Françaix had written in 1934. This ballet, named *À la Française*, had its world première in New York on September 11, 1951. John Martin wrote that it was "a delicious little bit of nonsense,

full of style, wit, and excellent invention."

Rollo Myers described Françaix's style: "His music is characterized by engaging spontaneity and great technical proficiency. It is often witty, but rarely profound; not self-consciously neoclassic, but marked on the whole by a classical restraint and sobriety—in a word, by those qualities of clarity, proportion and elegance which have always been the hallmark of the Gallic spirit in the arts."

MAJOR WORKS

Ballets—Scuola di Ballo; Le Roi Nu; Les Malheurs de Sophie; Le Jeu Sentimental; La Lutherie Enchantée; Verreries de Venise; Le Jugement du Fou; Les Demoiselles de la Nuit.

Chamber Music—Bagatelles, for string quartet; Sonata, for two violins and cello; String Trio; String Quartet; Quintet, for violin, viola, cello, flute, and harp; Violin Sonatina; Quartet, for four saxophones; Divertissement, for bassoon and string quartet; Mouvement Perpetuel, for cello and piano; Trio, for woodwind instruments; Quintet, for woodwind instruments; Sonatine, for trumpet and piano; Divertissement, for oboe, clarinet, and bassoon; Piano Trio.

Choral Music—Cinq Chansons pour les Enfants; Trois Épigrammes, for mixed voices and string quintet; L'Apocalypse de Saint-Jean, oratorio; Two Motets; Cantate Satirique, for mixed voices and piano duet; Ode à la Gastronomie.

Operas—Le Diable Boiteux, (chamber opéra-comique); L'Apostrophe (one-act comic opera); La Main de Gloire; La Princesse de Clèves; Paris à Nous Deux (lyric fantasy).

Orchestral Music—Symphony; Piano Concertino; Serenade, for small orchestra; Suite, for violin and piano; Fantaisie, for cello and orchestra; Quadruple Concerto, for flute, oboe, clarinet, bassoon, and orchestra; Piano Concerto; Musique de Cour, for flute, violin, and orchestra; Cantate en l'Honneur de Sully, for baritone, strings, four trumpets, organ, and orchestra; Invocation à la Volupté, for baritone and small orchestra; Rhapsodie, for viola and orchestra; Les Bosquets de Cythère, waltzes; La Douce France; L'Horloge de Fleur, for oboe and orchestra; Cantate de Méphisto, for bass solo and strings.

Piano Music—Scherzo; Cinq Portraits de Jeunes Filles.

Vocal Music—L'Adolescence Clémentine; Cinq Poésies de Charles d'Orléans; Prière du Soir; Chanson, for tenor and guitar.

George Gershwin
1898–1937

George Gershwin was born in Brooklyn, New York, on September 25, 1898. He was a typical American boy who delighted in the games of the street and who looked with scorn upon any boy who had even the remotest connection with music. At the age of six, however, he was fascinated by Rubinstein's *Melody in F*, which he heard in a penny arcade; and when he was nine, he fell in love with a girl because she had a pleasant singing voice.

When he was ten, he attended Public School 25, on the lower East Side of Manhattan, where one of his fellow pupils was a talented young violinist named Maxie Rosenzweig (later known on the concert stage as Max Rosen). Maxie gave a concert in the school auditorium which George refused to attend, preferring instead to play ball in the schoolyard. While running around, he heard the strains of Maxie's violin in Dvořák's *Humoresque*. In spite of himself, George stopped playing ball, drew closer to the window, and listened. The music made so deep an impression on him that he was determined to become a friend of the violinist.

GEORGE GERSHWIN

Maxie's influence on the boy was far-reaching. He revealed to young George the undreamed-of world of great music, playing for George from his violin repertoire. From then on, the streets lost their fascination for George; he had found music, and it brought him his greatest pleasure. One day, on discovering a piano in a friend's house, he started to experiment with the keys. In this way he picked up some of the rudiments of piano-playing and began to compose fragmentary tunes, which he exhibited to his friend. "I'm sorry," Maxie told him, "You haven't got any talent for music. You'd better forget all about it. I know."

From the beginning Gershwin's career was marked by a passionate desire to bring musical significance to American popular music. Even as an adolescent he saw this goal clearly. When, as a boy, he studied the piano with Charles Hambitzer, his first important teacher, he argued tirelessly about the importance of popular music. "I have a new pupil who will make a mark in music if anybody will," Hambitzer wrote prophetically to his sister. "The boy is a genius, without a doubt. He's just crazy about music and can't wait until it is time to take his lesson. ... He wants to go in for this modern stuff, jazz and what not. But I'm not going to let him for a while. I'll see that he gets a firm foundation in the standard music first."

The first piece of music Gershwin wrote was a popular song, "Since I Found You," in 1913; it was never published. The fact that it was a typical Tin Pan Alley tune did not mean that Gershwin had deserted the mission of making the American popular song artistically valid. To help him bring about this ideal he began to search restlessly in the music of the masters for direction. He attended concerts frequently and began to paste the programs and the portraits of the great performers and composers in a gray bookkeeper's ledger he had acquired for this purpose. When, during his adolescence, he worked as a demonstration pianist at Remick's in Tin Pan Alley, he studied harmony and orchestration with Edward Kilenyi. Somewhat later he joined the harmony class of Rubin Goldmark.

Gershwin achieved material success early in life. He published his first song when he was eighteen: "When You Want 'Em You Can't Get 'Em," which was accepted by the firm of Harry von Tilzer. He wrote his first musical-comedy score in 1919, *La, La, Lucille*; this show was produced on Broadway May 26, 1919, ran for over one hundred performances, and yielded a modest hit in the song "Nobody But You." Soon after this, Gershwin produced a smash song hit, "Swanee," which sold millions of copies of sheet music and records, largely because of exploitation by Al Jolson. When he was a little over twenty-two, Gershwin began a four-year assignment writing music for George White's annual revue,

Gershwin

Scandals (one of the most desirable assignments on Broadway), and his songs were interpolated into numerous other successful Broadway productions. Even a London producer ordered a score from him for a major production.

Despite his early success, Gershwin never lost his level-headedness, nor the ability to analyze himself and his purpose. Because he wanted to write outstanding popular music, he impatiently brushed aside his early efforts, however successful they may have been in the musical market place. He wanted an idiom that would be both popular and original. And he worked hard, revising every line and phrase dozens of times. By 1924 he had written several songs which satisfied him: "I'll Build a Stairway to Paradise" for the *Scandals of 1922;* "Do It Again," for *The French Doll;* "Oh, Lady Be Good" for *Lady Be Good!;* "Somebody Loves Me" for the *Scandals of 1924.* With songs like these he had become a master of his trade, and he was fashioning songs that were his personal handiwork.

A handful of farsighted and discerning musicians recognized the touch of genius in these songs. In Tin Pan Alley, Gershwin's stoutest advocates included Max Dreyfus, Irving Berlin, and Jerome Kern—and their praise was unqualified. But even outside Tin Pan Alley there were those who noticed what he was accomplishing. One of these was the American composer and pianist Beryl Rubinstein, who in 1922 startled a newspaper interviewer by speaking of Gershwin as a "great" composer. No one before that time had ever dared to attribute greatness to a composer of popular songs.

In 1923 another serious artist gave a bow of recognition to Gershwin. On November 1, 1923, at Aeolian Hall in New York, the singer Eva Gauthier included four Gershwin songs on a program devoted to great vocal music, with Gershwin accompanying her at the piano in his own numbers. This was the first time American popular music had penetrated a dignified concert hall. "I consider this one of the very most important events in American musical history," wrote Carl Van Vechten. In Boston the music critic H. T. Parker wrote prophetically of Gershwin: "He is the beginning of the age of sophisticated jazz."

Meanwhile, on August 29, 1922, Gershwin incorporated a somber one-act opera, *Blue Monday* (later retitled *135th Street*), into the *Scandals of 1922.* This was not Gershwin's first experiment in writing popular music in a form larger than the song. In 1919 he had written *Lullaby,* for string quartet. (More than forty years later the manuscript of this composition was discovered by the Juilliard String Quartet in the Music Room of the Congressional Library in Washington, D.C., and the belated world première of the work finally took place on December 19, 1967, in Washington in a performance by the quartet.) However, *Blue Monday* represented Gershwin's first tentative attempt to write an opera. It was dropped from the revue after only one performance because George White felt it was too gloomy. But it showed unmistakable talent, and it made a profound impression on the orchestra leader who conducted the work from the pit—Paul Whiteman.

When Whiteman planned a historic jazz concert in New York to draw the attention of the music world to the importance of jazz, he hoped to feature on his program a major jazz work written expressly for the occasion. Immediately he went to Gershwin, who required a good deal of persuasion, for he felt that he was not ready for a major assignment. But Whiteman's flow of arguments and entreaties was irresistible.

On February 12, 1924, Gershwin's *Rhapsody in Blue* was introduced by Whiteman and his orchestra, with Gershwin at the piano, at Aeolian Hall, New York, before an audience of the great and the near-great of the music world. Few musical compositions of our time have won the kind of instantaneous triumph enjoyed by this Gershwin work. Henry O. Osgood wrote that "it is a more important contribution to music than Stravinsky's *Rite of Spring.*" Deems Taylor and W. J. Henderson sang its praises in the press. Henry T. Finck claimed that Gershwin was "far superior to Schoenberg, Milhaud, and the rest of the futurist fellows."

This acclaim was only the prelude. The Rhapsody soon became one of the most famous and profit-making pieces of serious music by an American. It was performed by jazz bands and symphony orchestras, by solo pianists, two-piano teams, and piano ensembles; by solo harmonicas, harmonica bands, and mandolin orchestras; by tap dancers and ballet dancers; by choral groups. It was featured in stage shows and talking pictures. It lent its principal melody to a novel (in which the music was quoted) and furnished the signature for Paul Whiteman.

Its success is understandable. Exciting music at first hearing, it proved even more so with familiarity. It is dramatic, emotional, lyric, rhapsodic; it had the appeal of novelty, and it was American. The music is alive, freshly conceived, full of enthusiasm and spontaneity. Its youthful spirit, its contagious appeal, its cogency assert themselves as forcefully today as they did when the rhapsody was first heard—and not only in the United States but all over the world.

After the *Rhapsody in Blue*, Gershwin consolidated his position as one of America's most admired and most widely performed composers. He wrote one excellent score after another for musical comedies which generally proved to be among the leading successes of their respective seasons. In this field he profited from collaboration with his brother Ira, who provided the songs with deft, skillfully contrived lyrics. *Tip Toes* (1925), *Oh Kay!* (1926), *Funny Face* (1927), *Rosalie* (1928), *Show Girl* (1929), *Strike Up the Band* (1929), *Girl Crazy* (1930)—all these foreshadowed the crowning success of his theatrical career, the political satire *Of Thee I Sing!* (1931) which became the first musical comedy to win the Pulitzer Prize in drama and the first musical to have its text published in book form.

During these years, Gershwin was producing serious music also in the jazz idiom: Concerto in F, for piano and orchestra, commissioned by Walter Damrosch and introduced by the New York Symphony Society under Damrosch, with Gershwin at the piano, on December 3, 1925; the three piano preludes which the composer introduced in New York on November 4, 1926; the tone poem *An American in Paris*, which had its première at a concert of the New York Philharmonic, Walter Damrosch conducting, on December 13, 1928; the *Second Rhapsody*, première by the Boston Symphony under Koussevitzky January 29, 1932; *Cuban Overture*, which Albert Coates first conducted at the Lewisohn Stadium in New York on August 16, 1932; the *Variations on I Got Rhythm*, for piano and orchestra, first performed in Boston January 14, 1934,

with Charles Previn conducting and the composer at the piano; and finally, the opera *Porgy and Bess*, which had its tryout in Boston on September 30, 1935.

"The advance in know-how and musical articulateness during the ten-year period separating his one-act opera *135th Street* and his grand opera *Porgy and Bess* has few parallels in modern music," the editor of this book has said in his biography of Gershwin, *A Journey to Greatness*. "It is an advance from fumbling apprenticeship to full mastery. An examination of his serious works reveals a step-by-step development in technical skill, an increasing self-assurance and *savoir-faire*, a growing command of the materials of his trade. From a structural consideration, the *Second Rhapsody* is notable progress over the *Rhapsody in Blue* in organic unity, compactness of form, adroitness of thematic growth; if the *Rhapsody in Blue* remains the more popular work it is because the basic material is more inspired. The *Cuban Overture* represents a remarkable step forward in the use of contrapuntal means, just as the *Variations on I Got Rhythm* reveals a new virtuosity in thematic variation."

Gershwin's magnum opus was his folk opera *Porgy and Bess*, text by DuBose Heyward based on the play *Porgy* by Heyward and his wife, Dorothy; lyrics by DuBose Heyward and Ira Gershwin. On no other work had he expended so much of his time, energy, and devotion; to no other did he bring such a self-assurance of artistic purpose, such a sureness of direction. It took him twenty months to write and orchestrate his score, a period during which the opera completely dominated his creative thinking. Parts of it were developed in Charleston, South Carolina, where he spent several weeks in a first-hand study of the music and ritual of the Gullah Negroes. It was produced by the Theatre Guild and opened first in Boston on September 30, 1935, then in New York October 10, 1935. The reaction was mixed. Generally speaking, the Boston critics were more enthusiastic than the New York ones, many of the latter regarding it as neither fish nor fowl, neither opera nor musical comedy. In Boston, however, Moses Smith wrote: "It is unique. . . . He has traveled a long way from Tin Pan Alley to this opera." L. A. Sloper considered it "easily as Gershwin's most important contribution to music." But in

Gershwin

New York, Olin Downes wrote that "it does not utilize all the resources of the operatic composer or pierce very often to the depths of the pathetic drama"; Paul Rosenfeld looked upon it as "an aggrandized musical show"; and Samuel Chotzinoff (who had always been Gershwin's strongest booster among the critics) called it "hybrid, fluctuating constantly between musical drama, musical comedy and operetta." Gershwin himself considered it a masterwork and was certain it would survive. Many of the critics who first denounced it later reversed their opinions dramatically, and Gershwin's own faith and optimism were eventually fully vindicated, but not until after his death.

In 1937 *Porgy and Bess* received the David Bispham Medal for distinguished contribution to American opera. It was revived in Los Angeles and San Francisco in 1938, but its success was not firmly established until 1942 when it was revived in New York to enjoy the longest run ever known by a revival in the history of the Broadway theatre. At that time it was given a special award by the New York Music Critics Circle. From 1952 to 1956 an all-Negro American company toured with the opera in Europe, the Middle East, the Soviet Union, and Latin America, to achieve a triumph duplicated by few modern operas. *Porgy and Bess* became the first American opera to be seen at La Scala in Milan; in the 1960's it entered the repertory of the Volksoper in Vienna and the Oslo Opera in Norway; a film version was produced by Samuel Goldwyn in 1959.

Porgy and Bess is a folk opera in the way Mussorgsky's *Boris Godunov* is a folk opera, with broad strokes of realism blended with touches of poetry. *Porgy* is a folk tale told with directness, and in indigenous American accents. The music and the text project Negro humor and pathos, nobility and savagery, wisdom and naïveté without resorting to caricature. *Porgy* is the portrait of a race drawn with sympathetic strokes. And it is filled with wonderful Gershwin melodies: "Summertime," "I Got Plenty O' Nuthin'," "Bess, You Is My Woman Now," "It Ain't Necessarily So," to mention a few.

After completing *Porgy and Bess*, Gershwin went to Hollywood to fulfill commitments for motion pictures. It was his second visit to the film capital for that purpose and his first since 1931, when he wrote the music for *Delicious*. He produced scores for two films starring Fred Astaire: *Shall We Dance* (which costarred Ginger Rogers) and *A Damsel in Distress*. He also worked on the music for a lavish musical produced by Samuel Goldwyn, *The Goldwyn Follies*.

While working on this last-named film, he suddenly collapsed at the studio. It was first believed that he was suffering from the strain of overwork, combined with irritation at the limitations imposed upon his creativity by Hollywood. An exploratory operation at the Cedars of Lebanon Hospital in Hollywood revealed that he was suffering from a cystic tumor in the right temporal lobe. He did not recover from that operation but died at the hospital on July 11, 1937.

Expressions of grief poured in from all over the world. "Like a rare flower which blossoms forth once in a while, Gershwin represents a singularly original and rare phenomenon," said Serge Koussevitzky. Paul Whiteman remarked sadly: "He will never be forgotten, and his place will never be filled." Gershwin's body was brought back to New York. After funeral services at Temple Emanu-El on July 15, Gershwin was buried in Mount Hope Cemetery at Hastings-on-the-Hudson.

In 1945 Warner Brothers presented a successful screen biography of Gershwin, entitled *Rhapsody in Blue*, starring Robert Alda as the composer. Six years later, *An American in Paris* was released by MGM. A picture musical featuring songs by George and Ira Gershwin and the tone poem of the title—used as the score for an extended ballet sequence—it won an Academy Award as the best film of 1951.

Though Gershwin was many times in love, and though on several occasions he contemplated matrimony, he remained single. From 1928 to 1933 he occupied a beautifully furnished penthouse on Riverside Drive, and from 1933 on an even more luxurious apartment on East 72nd Street. (The house on Roxbury Drive that he occupied during his last months in Beverly Hills was rented. It stands next door to the house now occupied by Ira Gershwin and his wife.) Gershwin's New York apartments were his only indulgence in luxury. He owned no expensive jewelry; except for a second-hand Mercedes-Benz acquired in

1927 he never owned a foreign car or yacht; and he never entertained in a baronial manner. He never employed a business representative or a personal press agent and he never kept a lawyer on a retainer. He avoided everything that smacked of display or grandeur, and he abhorred pose of any kind.

As the editor of this book pointed out in his biography of Gershwin, he was "a human dynamo. He rarely walked on the street or the golf-course—he had to run. He rarely walked slowly up a flight of stairs, but leaped a few steps at a time. . . . He was a man of irrepressible enthusiasms, a man who had an extraordinary zest for living and for enjoying. He loved games of all kinds, and he had the capacity for making everything he indulged in a kind of game. When he found a new diversion he went after it with incomparable intensity and passion. When it was golf (his game was in the eighties) he played it every free moment he could, and golf dominated his conversation and thinking all the time. Then it was something else: backgammon, croquet, ping pong, photography, fishing, swimming, horseback riding, roulette. Generally, he preferred pastimes that taxed his muscles. . . . His fine muscular coordination that had made him so splendid a pianist and so good an athlete, also made him an excellent dancer. . . . He used feet, body, and hands with the limpid grace of a trained performer."

Toward the end of his life he began to collect great paintings and he became absorbed in the hobby of painting. He was a remarkably gifted painter whose one-man shows after his death indicated that he might have become almost as important an artist as he was a musician.

MAJOR WORKS

Chamber Music—Lullaby, for string quartet.

Operas—135th Street (one-act opera); Porgy and Bess.

Orchestral Music—Rhapsody in Blue, for piano and orchestra; Concerto in F, for piano and orchestra; An American in Paris; Second Rhapsody, for piano and orchestra; Cuban Overture; Variations on I Got Rhythm, for piano and orchestra.

Piano Music—Three Preludes.

Vocal Music—In the Mandarin's Orchid Garden, concert song.

ABOUT

Ewen, D., A Journey to Greatness: The Life and Music of George Gershwin; Gershwin, I., Lyrics on Several Occasions; Goldberg, I., George Gershwin; Jablonski, E. and Stewart, L. D., The Gershwin Years.

Vittorio Giannini
1903–1966

Vittorio Giannini was born in Philadelphia October 19, 1903. His sister, Dusolina, was a celebrated opera singer, his father a well-known tenor in Italy, and his mother an excellent violinist. His mother began to teach him at an early age. When he was nine, he received a scholarship for the Verdi Conservatory in Milan, where he stayed four years. At fourteen he completed his first opera.

VITTORIO GIANNINI

After returning to the United States, he studied with private teachers before entering the Juilliard School of Music in 1925. There he received fellowships in violin with Hans Letz and in composition with Rubin Goldmark. He was graduated in 1931, and on June 1 of the same year he married Lucia Avella. In 1932 he received the grand prize of the American Academy in Rome. Though this fellowship was originally granted for a three-year period, it was renewed a fourth year because of his exceptional work.

His early chamber music won two publication awards: that of the Juilliard School in 1931 for a string quartet, completed and introduced in 1930; that of the Society for the Publication of American Music in 1932 for a piano quintet (1930). On October 20, 1934, his first opera, *Lucedia*, was introduced in

Giannini: jän nē′ nē

Munich. It was followed by *The Scarlet Letter*, based on Nathaniel Hawthorne, which was successfully introduced at the Hamburg State Theatre on June 2, 1938, with his sister singing the principal soprano role. Next came two radio operas commissioned by CBS, over which network they were introduced—*Beauty and the Beast* (1939) and *Blennerhassett* (1940). Both of these works were subsequently given stage productions.

Commissions were responsible for some of Giannini's later successful compositions. The work he now designates as his Symphony No. 1 was written for the Cincinnati Symphony, which introduced it in 1950. The Cincinnati Symphony also commissioned the *Canticle for Christmas*, for baritone, chorus, and orchestra, performed in 1951. Another major choral work, *Canticle of the Martyrs*, was written for the Moravian Festival and received its première at Bethlehem, Pennsylvania, in 1957. At the request of the Juilliard School of Music he wrote the Prelude and Fugue, for string orchestra, heard in 1956; and for Duke University, the Symphony No. 3, for band. The latter was performed at Duke University in 1959.

On January 31, 1953, the Cincinnati Symphony presented a concert performance of Giannini's opera *The Taming of the Shrew*, which he had written for television. When the opera was staged, on March 13, 1954, it was televised by the NBC Opera Theater over the NBC-TV network. It then received a special award from the New York Music Critics Circle. The New York City Opera produced it on April 13, 1956. At that time, Howard Taubman said in the New York *Times* that "it adorned the season of American opera with the vivacity of its spirits and the boisterousness of its laughter." Giannini's score was described as "the work of a shrewd and skilled musician. It had a vast relish of the opera buffa tradition. There is crispness and point in this music as it speeds the action, and it does not hesitate to pause and sing with sentiment in a shamelessly old fashioned way. . . . The score is instinct with the spirit of Italian lyricism."

On a grant from the Ford Foundation, Giannini wrote an opera, *The Harvest*, which was mounted in Chicago on November 25, 1961. The opera—with a libretto by the composer in collaboration with Karl Flaster—is set on an American farm in or about 1900. Its central character is Lora, who, married to Lem, has a love affair with her brother-in-law Mark and arouses the desires of still another brother-in-law and of their blind father. The emotional conflict ends with the father's strangling of Lora. The drama is Italian verismo to the core, and so is Giannini's music, much of which springs from Puccini.

In *Rehearsal Call*, however, Giannini once again tapped the comic vein. This opera, commissioned by the Juilliard School, which produced it in New York on February 15, 1962, is farce pure and simple, concerned with the often absurd efforts of six young actors (three men and three girls) to attract the interest of a producer who lives in the same apartment house; at the same time all six are emotionally involved. "Giannini's score," reported *Opera News*, "accompanies rather than permeates the action. It is bright and witty. . . . The ambiguous vocal line is fully exposed so that all the laugh lines come across only too well. . . . In the all too infrequent lyric pauses the singers have a breather from their frantic antics and the final octet soars."

One of Giannini's most significant works was written on a grant from the Ford Foundation. This was *The Medead*, a monodrama for soprano and orchestra, first performed in Atlanta, Georgia, on October 20, 1960, with Irene Jordan as soloist. Chappell White, the critic of the Atlanta *Journal*, reported: "Giannini focused on those portions of the drama which could be expanded and articulated in music. He took care to provide for the variety necessary in a large musical structure and to furnish breathing places in the drama, those vital points of lyrical expansion that are the lifeblood of operatic writing. . . . In creating what he calls monodrama, which is more dramatic than the traditional cantata or oratorio, Giannini has blazed a trail that may be followed by others."

Giannini has been described as an "unashamed romanticist," in that he strove for the expression of beauty in, as he put it, "the best manner possible, employing whatever device seems to bring me closer to this goal." His forte was writing mobile melodies, for which he had a genuine gift; consequently, he was probably most successful in writing for the voice.

To an interviewer, Giannini confided: "There's a tremendous difference between 'writing music' and composing. Anyone who has had the proper amount of technical training, which anyone can get if he works hard enough, is able to write music. But to compose, one has to wait for inspiration. The composer's duty is to express what is in him with the utmost sincerity, with no thought of whether it is 'original' and no desire to make an impression by doing startling things. It may sound trite to say it, but there's no denying that beauty must still be the ultimate goal of composition. A composer can say to himself, 'I'm going to write a canon,' or 'I'm going to write a fugue' and do it. But he can't say, 'I'm going to write a melody' and do that. You have to wait for a melody—it has to come to you. Those composers who make a point of avoiding melody are those who, in most instances, couldn't if they wanted to, because it never comes to them."

In 1939 Giannini joined the faculty of the Juilliard School of Music and in 1941 that of the Manhattan School of Music, in the departments of theory, composition, and orchestration. In 1956 he joined the composition department of the Curtis Institute in Philadelphia. He resigned in 1964 to become president of the North Carolina School of the Arts at Winston-Salem. However, he retained his affiliation with the Juilliard by becoming head of a special repertory project financed by the United States Office of Education. He also created an adjunct to the North Carolina School of Arts: a summer music school affiliated with the Chigi Academy in Siena, Italy.

Giannini was found dead in his apartment on West End Avenue in New York City on November 28, 1966. His last opera was *The Servant of the Masters*, libretto by Bernard Stambler based on a comedy by Goldoni. It had been commissioned by the New York City Opera which produced it posthumously as a memorial to the composer on March 9, 1967.

Giannini was married twice. His first marriage ended in divorce in 1951; his second marriage, to Joan Adler in 1953, ended in divorce a decade later. He had no children. His interests included reading (poetry, history, philosophy, detective stories), sports cars, the collection of miniature trains, and cooking dishes from Tuscan recipes.

MAJOR WORKS

Chamber Music—2 violin sonatas; String Quartet; Piano Quintet.

Choral Music—Canticle for Christmas; Canticle of the Martyrs; Three Motets.

Operas—Lucedia; The Scarlet Letter; Beauty and the Beast (radio opera); Blennerhasset (radio opera); The Taming of the Shrew; Christus (tetralogy of four festival operas); The Harvest; Rehearsal Call; Servant of Two Masters.

Orchestral Music—5 symphonies (No. 3, for band); 2 divertimentos, for small orchestra; Frescobaldiana; Concerto Grosso, for string orchestra; Prelude and Fugue, for string orchestra; Trumpet Concerto; Violin Concerto; The Medead, monodrama for soprano and orchestra.

Piano Music—Variations on a Cantus Firmus.

Vocal Music—Various songs for voice and piano including If I Had Known, I Shall Think of You, It Is a Spring Night, and Moonlight.

ABOUT

Howard, J. T., Our Contemporary Composers.

Miriam Gideon
1906–

Miriam Gideon was born in Greeley, Colorado, on October 23, 1906. Her father was professor of philosophy and modern languages at Colorado State Teachers College.

MIRIAM GIDEON

When she was fourteen she went to Boston to live with her uncle, Henry Gideon, an organist and choral director, a major influence of her early years. She studied the piano with Felix Fox and attended the College of Liberal

Arts at Boston University, from which she was graduated with a Bachelor of Arts degree. Later, in New York, she studied composition with Lazare Saminsky and Roger Sessions and received a master's degree in musicology at Columbia University.

In 1939 she went to France and Switzerland for what she hoped would be a protracted stay, but the outbreak of the war aborted these plans. Since then she has made her home in New York City, in an apartment overlooking Central Park, and has combined creative work with teaching. From 1944 to 1955 she was a member of the music faculties of Brooklyn College and City College of New York. Since 1955 she has been on the music faculty of the Jewish Theological Seminary and since 1967 with the Manhattan School of Music.

One of her earliest compositions to attract interest was the *Lyric Piece for Strings* (1941), introduced in April 1944 by the London Symphony, Hugo Weisgall conducting. This is a one-movement work with contrasting sections; in a string-quartet version it was broadcast over WNYC as part of the American Music Festival in 1945, heard on a program of the Forum Group of the International Society for Contemporary Music in May 1946, and recorded in a performance by the Imperial Orchestra of Tokyo, William Strickland conducting.

Greater individuality of style is found in *The Hound of Heaven*, a song cycle for voice, oboe, and string trio based on lines from the poem by Francis Thompson. She wrote it on a commission for the centenary of the founding of Temple Emanu-El in New York. "The texture of this, as of most of Miriam Gideon's works," wrote George Perle in the *American Composers Alliance Bulletin*, "is strikingly personal, characterized by lightness, the sudden exposure of individual notes, constantly shifting octave relationships. The unique quality of the texture, however, is not merely a subjective, idiosyncratic feature, but a consequence of her compositional technique. . . . This is a technique that imposes economy and the exclusion of irrelevancies—a technique that may be indefinitely expanded and within which a composer may grow."

Miriam Gideon has grown as a composer through the cultivation and crystallization of this technique, which characterizes other song cycles, notably the *Sonnets from Shakespeare*, for voice, trumpet, and string quartet (1950); *Sonnets from Fatal Interview*, poems by Edna St. Vincent Millay, originally for voice and piano, later adapted for string trio (1952); and *The Condemned Playground* (1963), for soprano, tenor, flute, bassoon, and string quartet, based on poems of Horace, Gary Spokes and Baudelaire. The last of these works reveals the composer's interest in bilingual settings; Milton's translation of Horace's Latin is integrated into a unified whole that includes a poem of Gary Spokes in English on Hiroshima and lines from Baudelaire's *Litanies of Satan*, in an original French and in an English translation by Edna St. Vincent Millay. Another bilingual treatment can be found in *Mixco* (1957), for solo voice and piano, in which the original Spanish of the Guatemalan poet Miguel Angel Asturias alternates with an English equivalent.

Some of Miss Gideon's most ambitious compositions reveal an attraction for national musical traits, for example her opera *Fortunato* (1958), based on the Spanish play by Serafín and Joaquín Quintero. Here it is not the inflections of national musical speech that are caught, but rather the characteristics of the Spanish people translated into musical terms; authentic folk songs of the Madrid area, the locale of the play, are fused with the composer's own idiom. Interest in ethnic materials is found also in the *Fantasy on a Javanese Motive*, for cello and piano (1958). Here the composer employs a gamelan melody as the basis for a work in which the sonorities of the gamelan orchestra are suggested as well as the intervallic content. "In spite of the very special nature of the work," wrote Milton Babbitt, "those compositional features which are characteristic of the composer's more extended and personal work are present here, in the generation of the total composition from a three-note motive, in the motival identification of linear and harmonic components, and in the construction of an accentually complex rhythmic totality."

Among Miriam Gideon's other significant instrumental compositions are the String Quartet (1946), the Divertimento, for woodwind quartet (1949), the third piano suite (1951), the *Symphonia Brevis* (1953), and the Sonata for Cello and Piano (1961). In addition to the opera *Fortunato*, her dramatic works include *The Adorable Mouse*, a musical fable of La Fontaine for narrator and chamber orchestra (1960).

Miriam Gideon allows each work to dictate its own idiom and organization and has never felt inclined to use any predetermined basis of composition. According to George Perle, she has "assimilated the technical features of nonserial atonality, but her music is not characterized by what, according to some critics, are supposed to be the stylistic features of 'atonality'—'lack of contrast,' 'morbidity,' 'fragmented rhythm,' and so forth. . . . The same concern that the musical sound reveals characterizes her treatment of text. The musical texture parallels the sense of the poem and its intrinsic verbal relationships, rather than external formal features." The vocal works, apart from the sensitive word setting, are concerned with many subtleties of rhythm and instrumental color. The instrumental works are often seemingly rhapsodic, within a highly organized formal structure. Wide, dissonant intervals are employed; melodic lines are usually broad and harmonically oriented; harmonies are intense; there are strong dramatic contrasts, from extreme vehemence to lyric tranquillity.

In 1969 Miss Gideon received one thousand dollars from the National Federation of Women's Clubs and ASCAP—an award to American women composers for contributions to symphonic literature.

MAJOR WORKS

Chamber Music—Lyric Piece, for string quartet; String Quartet; Viola Sonata; Fantasy on a Javanese Motive, for cello and piano; Divertimento, for woodwind quartet; Air, for violin and piano; Three Biblical Masks, for violin and piano; Cello Sonata.

Choral Music—Two Madrigals; How Goodly Are Thy Tents; Adon Olom; The Habitable Earth, cantata; Three Spiritual Madrigals.

Opera—Fortunato.

Orchestral Music—Lyric Piece, for string orchestra; Symphonia Brevis; The Adorable Mouse, musical fable for narrator and chamber orchestra.

Piano Music—5 suites; Sonatina for Two Pianos; Canzona; Six Cuckoos in Quest of a Composer.

Vocal Music—The Hound of Heaven, for voice, oboe, and string trio; Sonnets from Shakespeare, for voice, trumpet, and string quartet; Sonnets from Fatal Interview; Epitaphs from Robert Burns; Mixco; To Music; Songs of Voyage; The Condemned Playground, for soprano, tenor, flute, bassoon, and string quartet; Questions on Nature, for voice, oboe, and piano; Farewell Tablet to Agathocles; Spiritual Madrigals, for vocal trio; Rhymes from the Hill, for voice, marimba, clarinet, and cello.

ABOUT

Stevens, D. (ed.), A History of Song.
American Composers Alliance Bulletin, No. 4, 1958.

Henry F. Gilbert
1868–1928

Henry Franklin Belknap Gilbert was born September 26, 1868, in Somerville, Massachusetts. Since both parents were excellent amateur musicians, he was raised in a musical environment. As a child he was so moved by a concert by Ole Bull, the Norwegian violinist, that he proceeded to manufacture a violin from a cigar box. On this he taught himself to play simple tunes. When he was older he acquired a more formal instrument and received instruction from local teachers. He then began to earn his living by playing the violin in orchestras in hotels and restaurants in Massachusetts and Florida.

HENRY F. GILBERT

When he was twenty he studied composition with Edward MacDowell. At the same time he continued his violin training with Emil Mollenhauer. But financial difficulties compelled him in 1892 to find employment in business. For a number of years he filled a variety of jobs: he worked in his uncle's printing plant; he became a real-estate agent; he served as foreman of a factory; he worked in a Boston publishing house.

In 1901 Gilbert read about the impending world première of Charpentier's opera *Louise* in Paris. This new work so aroused his curiosity and interest that he threw up his job and boarded a cattle boat for France. The première of *Louise* moved him deeply; it convinced him that he was wasting his time in any endeavor outside music.

Typhoid laid him low in Paris. Broken in health (he never recovered fully), he returned to the United States, rented a barn near Cambridge and, in spite of his poverty, concentrated all his efforts on composition. By this time he had become obsessed with the desire to produce music that was thoroughly American and to promote American music. In 1902, with Arthur Farwell, he helped found the Wa-Wan Press to publish music of Americans and to propagandize in every way possible the use of native American elements in the creation of American music. In his own music, Gilbert followed a similar direction by trying to produce major concert works deriving style and idioms from the music of the American Indian or the American Negro. He said: "More than the music of an individual composer, more than the music of any particular school, the folk tunes of the world, of all nationalities, races, and peoples, have been to me a never-failing source of delight, wonder and inspiration. In them I can hear the spirit of all great music. Through them I can feel the very heart-beat of humanity. Simple as these folk melodies are in structure, yet they speak to me so poignantly, and with such a deep sincerity of expression as to be (for myself at least) more pregnant with inspirational suggestion than the music of any *one* composer."

In 1903 Gilbert completed his first major work for orchestra. Originally entitled *Americanesque*, it consisted of a symphonic treatment of three Negro minstrel-show tunes. "Without inquiring too closely into their origin," Gilbert explained, "I have tried to bind together a few scraps into an art form very much in the manner of Edvard Grieg and the folk music of Norway." He renamed the work *Humoresque on Negro Minstrel Tunes*, and the first performance took place in Boston May 24, 1911.

The year 1905 saw the birth of one of Gilbert's most famous compositions, *Comedy Overture on Negro Themes*. The composer himself provided the following information about this appealing composition entirely based on Negro folk songs. "The first movement is light and humorous, the theme being made from two four-measure phrases taken from Charles L. Edwards' book, *Bahama Songs and Stories*. . . . This is followed by a broader, and somewhat slower, phrase. I have here used the only complete Negro tune that occurs in the piece . . . formerly used as a working song by roustabouts and stevedores on the Mississippi River steamboats in the old days. . . . Next comes a fugue. The theme of this fugue consists of the first four measures of the Negro spiritual, 'Old Ship of Zion.' . . . After this, a short phrase of sixteen measures serves to reintroduce the comic element. . . . The piece ends in an orgy of jollity and ragtime."

Comedy Overture on Negro Themes was first heard on August 17, 1910, in New York. A year and a half later it was introduced in Boston by the Boston Symphony and in 1914 it was played in Russia, first in the Crimea and later in Odessa. Olin Downes said of it: "In its rhythmic impulse born of the fragment of the spiritual, its shrewd wit, its infectious laughter, it announces itself as a piece of craft which could have come from nowhere but America."

In 1906 Gilbert's physicians discovered that, as a consequence of his typhoid attack, his heart had been seriously affected. Their prognosis was that he would not survive his fortieth birthday. They urged him to rest as much as possible. He ignored their advice by plunging more deeply than before into composition and working harder than ever. In spite of this, he lived twenty years longer than his physicians had expected.

In the same year in which the doctors prophesied his early death, Gilbert completed one of his most celebrated compositions, the tone poem *The Dance in Place Congo*. This music describes the revels of Negro slaves in Place Congo in New Orleans on a Sunday afternoon. Various Negro songs and dances, together with Creole melodies from Louisiana, form the warp and woof of this musical fabric. On March 3, 1918, a dozen years after it was written, the music was used for a ballet produced at the Metropolitan Opera in New York on the same program with the world première of a new American opera, Charles Wakefield Cadman's *Shanewis*.

At Frankfurt, Germany, in 1927 Gilbert became one of two American composers represented at the festival of the International Society for Contemporary Music, when *The Dance in Place Congo* was performed there on July 1. Though an invalid, Gilbert insisted on going to Europe to attend the performance. His last works were the *Nocturne*, after Walt Whitman (introduced in Philadelphia on March 16, 1928), and the Suite, for chamber orchestra (first given in Boston on April 28, 1928). Gilbert died at his home in Cambridge, Massachusetts, May 19, 1928.

Gilbert, who looked and dressed like a bohemian, was a striking figure—with his flowing hair, Indian profile, and bronzed skin. "His eyes had a glint of humor," Isaac Goldberg once wrote. "They were watery blue, as bland as his voice. There was no compromise in his nose; it came down straight over a strange, wide mouth. His lips, from their lines alone, should have made a scowl, yet despite their droop they usually produced the effect of a genial but watchful smile."

Although Gilbert's music is performed infrequently today, its importance in the development of American music has been recognized. However, it is Isaac Goldberg's opinion that "greater than the legacy of scores will be the rare example of the man's integrity. He was one of the last true New Englanders, in whom the rebel, the philosophic anarchist, the spiritual aristocrat, burned brightly amid the damp darkness of a vanished leadership. He was a Thoreau in tone. Historically, he appeared to have come too late. . . . A genuinely national composer, indeed, may have to retrace some of the ground that Gilbert covered, and may discover that Gilbert came early after all. His Americanism was an organic phase of his sincerity, his independence, his wholeness; these qualities represent, perhaps, his chief meaning for those who are to follow."

Besides his music on Negro melodies, Gilbert also wrote a number of works that derived rhythms and tunes from the American Indian. These included the popular *Indian Sketches*, for orchestra, introduced in Boston on March 4, 1921, and the five *Indian Scenes*, for piano.

MAJOR WORKS

Ballet—The Dance in Place Congo.

Opera—The Fantasy in Delft.

Orchestral Music—Two Episodes; Humoresque on Negro Minstrel Tunes; Salammbô's Invocation to Tänith, for soprano and orchestra; Comedy Overture on Negro Themes; The Dance in Place Congo, tone poem; Strife; Negro Rhapsody; Riders to the Sea; American Dances; Indian Sketches; Symphonic Piece; Nocturne; Suite, for chamber orchestra.

Piano Music—Negro Episode; Two Verlaine Moods; The Island of the Fay (also for orchestra); Indian Scenes; A Rag Bag; Negro Dances.

Vocal Music—Celtic Studies; Pirate Song; various individual songs for voice and piano.

ABOUT

Chase, G., America's Music; Howard, J. T., Our American Music.

American Mercury, November 1928; Modern Music, May–June, 1943; Musical Quarterly, July 1918.

Paul Gilson
1865–1942

Paul Gilson was born in Brussels June 15, 1865. He spent his childhood in Ruysbroeck, on the outskirts of Brussels, where his family moved when he was five. There he received his first instruction in music from the village organist. After returning to Brussels in 1882, he studied piano, harmony, and counterpoint with Charles Duyck. Then Gilson met the eminent Belgian teacher and theorist François Gevaert, who became interested in him and gave him instruction in composition. Largely because of Gevaert's urging, Gilson in 1886 entered the Brussels Conservatory where he remained three years. In his last year at the Conservatory he won the Belgian Prix de Rome with a cantata, *Sinai*, an outstanding success when introduced in Brussels in 1890. Gilson's fame was soon enhanced by the première of his symphonic sketches, *La Mer*, based on poems of Eddy Levis. This composition, in which one of Levis' poems was recited before each of four movements, was heard first at the Concerts Populaires conducted by Joseph Dupont and made a profound impression. It has since remained the composer's most frequently played composition. As early as December 17, 1892, it was heard in the United States, at a concert of the New York Philharmonic conducted by Anton Seidl.

Gilson: zhēl sôn′

Two major works followed *La Mer:* the incidental music to Hiel's drama *Alva*, and the oratorio *Francesca da Rimini;* both were introduced in Brussels in 1895. Two years later Gilson wrote the *Inaugural Cantata* for the Brussels Exhibition. Other choral works included the oratorio *Le Démon*, based on Lermontov; his first ballet, *La Captive*, produced at the Théâtre de la Monnaie in 1902; and his first opera, *Prinses Zonneschijn*, the world première of which took place in Brussels in 1903.

PAUL GILSON

Influenced to a marked degree by the music of the Russian Five, whose works he studied painstakingly, Gilson brought to his writing a strong rhythmic vitality and a highly colorful orchestration, together with solid workmanship and an intensity of expression.

Gilson was appointed professor of harmony at the Brussels Conservatory in 1899, a post he held for two decades. From 1904 to 1909 he also taught theory at the Antwerp Conservatory. In 1909 he became inspector of music for Belgian schools.

From 1901 to 1914 Gilson combined his activities as teacher and composer with the writing of music criticism for Belgian papers: for *Le Soir* from 1906 to 1914; for *Le Diapason* from 1910 to 1914; and for *Le Midi*, a number of years after that. In 1924 he founded the distinguished musical journal *La Revue Musicale Belge*, which he edited.

He exerted an important influence on his younger Belgian contemporaries. He possessed an extraordinary over-all culture, a sympathetic tolerance to all styles in music however progressive, and a natural gift for pedagogy that drew to him some of Belgium's most brilliant young musicians, including Marcel Poot and Francis de Bourguignon.

Gilson was the author of several influential theoretical treatises, among which were *Les Intervalles*, *Le Tutti Orchestral*, *Quintes et Octaves*, and *Traité d'Harmonie*.

He died in Brussels on April 3, 1942.

MAJOR WORKS

Ballets—La Captive; Les Deux Bossus; Légende Rhénane.
Chamber Music—2 string quartets; String Trio; Septet; Scènes Rustiques, for string quartet; Concertstück et Scherzo, for three trumpets; Humoresques, for woodwind and horns.
Choral Music—Sinai, cantata; Francesca da Rimini, oratorio; Le Démon, oratorio; Que la Lumière Soit; Hymne à l'Art; Ludus pro Patria.
Operas—Prinses Zonneschijn; Zeevolk; Rooversliefde; Mater Dolorosa.
Orchestral Music—8 suites; 3 overtures; 3 tone poems; 2 saxophone concertos; La Mer, symphonic sketches; Rhapsodie Canadienne; Rhapsodie Écossaise; Marche Festivale; Variations symphonies; Trois Mélodies Écossaises, for string orchestra; Prélude et Scherzo, for string orchestra; Élégie, for string orchestra; Serenade, for cello and string orchestra; Five Recitations with Orchestra.
Piano Music—Suite Rustique; Suite Nocturne.

ABOUT

Gilson, P., Notes de Musique et Souvenirs.
Music and Letters (London), April 1946.

Alberto Ginastera
1916–

Alberto Evaristo Ginastera was born in Buenos Aires April 11, 1916. His father was a native Argentine of Spanish (Catalan) descent on his father's side and on his mother's side of Italian (Lombardian) background. Neither of Alberto's parents was interested in music; but the child Alberto soon disclosed that he was innately musical. At the age of five he tried to play the Argentine national anthem on a toy flute and, when he could not produce all the notes correctly because the instrument was inadequate for such music, he burst into tears. In 1923 Ginastera began both his academic and his musical training—the former in

Ginastera: hē nȧs tĕ′ rȧ

the elementary school, the latter with private piano lessons. Five years later he enrolled in Conservatorio Williams, where he studied composition with José Gil, piano with Argenziani, and harmony with Piaggio. As a Conservatory student he began to write many small compositions, all of which he later destroyed. After graduating from secondary school in 1935, Ginastera devoted himself to music; a year later he entered the National Conservatory of Music and became a pupil of Athos Palma and José André.

ALBERTO GINASTERA

His first mature work, the score for the ballet *Panambí*, was also the first he allowed to survive. A five-movement orchestral suite from this score was introduced in Buenos Aires on November 27, 1937, Juan José Castro conducting. The ballet, with choreography by Margarita Wallmann, was produced at the Teatro Colón, on July 12, 1940, and received the National Prize. Primitive in its rhythms and modern in harmonies, the score constantly reveals the composer's interest in a national Argentine idiom. For the next few years he continued to pursue this nationalistic tendency, frequently through the exploitation of Argentine folk tunes and dance rhythms. In such a style he produced an excellent piece for the piano, *Danzas Argentinas* (1937), first performed in Buenos Aires October 27, 1937; the *Cantos del Tucumán*, for voice, flute, violin, harp, and two Indian drums (1938), first given in Buenos Aires

July 26, 1938; and *Malambo*, for piano (1940), introduced in Montevideo September 11, 1940.

For his graduation (with honors) from the National Conservatory in 1938, Ginastera wrote his first important work for chorus, *Psalm CL;* it was not heard until April 7, 1945, when Albert Wolff conducted the première in Buenos Aires. Another major work by Ginastera that waited many years for its first performance was his ballet *Estancia*. Commissioned by Lincoln Kirstein for the American Ballet Caravan, it was written in 1941, but the world première, which took place in Buenos Aires, came more than a decade later, on August 19, 1952. Other major works by Ginastera, however, had significant performances soon after they were written: Concierto Argentino, for piano and orchestra, performed in Montevideo on July 18, 1941; also his first symphony, *Sinfonía Porteña*, named after the port of Buenos Aires and introduced there May 12, 1942.

In 1941 Ginastera was appointed to the faculties of the National Conservatory and the Liceo Militar in Buenos Aires. Towards the end of the year, on December 11, he married Mercedes de Toro, a trained pianist. A son was born to them in 1942, and a daughter in 1944. The former is now engaged in the field of electronics; the latter is married to a physician and resides in Paris.

A Guggenheim Fellowship in 1942 provided Ginastera with the funds for a visit to the United States, but the war prevented this. World War II inspired several works, among them *Twelve American Preludes*, for piano, heard in Buenos Aires on August 7, 1944; and *Elegiac Symphony* (1944), dedicated to those who "died for freedom." In 1945 Ginastera became involved in political activity by signing a manifesto with other outstanding Argentine intellectuals defending democratic principles and human rights. Because of this he was relieved of his job at the Liceo Militar. In December 1945 Ginastera finally paid his long-delayed visit to the United States. For a little over a year he lived mainly in New York. There he completed three motets for unaccompanied chorus and the *Suite de Danzas Criollas*, for piano. He also attended two concerts which were devoted entirely to his works, one in New York, the other in Washington, D.C.

Ginastera

During the summer of 1946, Ginastera attended the Berkshire Music Center at Tanglewood to study composition. He was described then as "a chubby youth in horn-rimmed glasses, little looking like one likely to succeed." But Aaron Copland, who taught composition at the Center, became fully aware of the young man's musical potential and encouraged and guided him. They subsequently became close friends, remaining so through the years. Copland, from the beginning of the association, found in Ginastera "a tremendous contrast between the outward personality and the inner man. He is never off the cuff, but speaks always with due consideration for feelings and decorum. . . . A lot goes on inside we don't know about, obviously. He's a very smart cookie, in the best sense." This comment was made many years after Copland had met Ginastera at Tanglewood—at a time when the Argentine had become a world-famous composer.

He returned to Buenos Aires in March 1947 and assumed a dominant place in its musical life. He founded the Conservatory of Music and Dance in Buenos Aires and with several other Argentine composers created the Argentine section of the International Society for Contemporary Music, which he served as secretary general. In 1948 he completed an important work—his first string quartet. It received the prize of the Asociación Wagneriana and was introduced by the Mozart Quartet in Buenos Aires on October 24, 1949. It was subsequently performed extensively in both Europe and America. When it was heard at the festival of the International Society for Contemporary Music in Frankfort in 1951, a German critic writing for *Der Kurier* called it "outstanding," adding: "Of a very personal structure, it shows how the elements of native folklore can be fitted in the sonorous structure and rigidity of actual European musical language."

For a festival of contemporary music in Pittsburgh sponsored by the Carnegie Institute of Technology and the Pennsylvania College for Women, Ginastera was commissioned to write a piano sonata. Johana Harris introduced it November 29, 1952. This proved so successful that it was chosen for the festival of the International Society for Contemporary Music in Oslo in May 1953. The sonata represented a new direction for the composer, towards a freer and more modern idiom with emphasis on polyphony and twelve-tone procedures; but a strong Argentine accent is still evident. His increasing use of modern idiom without a break in national ties is also to be found in two important symphonic works completed in the years 1953–1954. The *Variaciones Concertantes* had been commissioned by the Asociación Amigos de la Música de Buenos Aires. Its first performance took place in Buenos Aires June 2, 1953, Igor Markevitch conducting; in 1957 it received the Cinzano Bicentennial Prize. "These variations," the composer explained, "have a subjective Argentine character. Instead of using folkloristic material, the composer achieves an Argentine atmosphere through employment of his own thematic and rhythmic elements." One of the interesting aspects of the composition is that each variation features a different instrument, or groups of instruments, and each variation reflects the distinctive character of the instruments. *Variations* was used for the ballet *Tender Night* (choreography by John Taras), staged by the New York City Center Ballet in New York on January 20, 1960. Still another ballet based on the *Variations*—entitled *Surazo*—was produced in Santiago, Chile, on July 13, 1961, with choreography by Patricio Bunster.

One year after *Variations* came *Pampeana No. 3*, a three-movement "symphonic pastoral." It had been commissioned by the Louisville Orchestra in Kentucky, which introduced it on October 20, 1954. In June 1956 this work was heard at the thirtieth festival of the International Society for Contemporary Music in Stockholm.

Because of his pronounced anti-Fascist sentiments, Ginastera became increasingly suspect in Argentina during the Perón regime. Finally, in 1952, he was dismissed as director of the Conservatory of Music and Drama which he had founded. Compelled to earn his living elsewhere, he took to writing motion picture scores. In 1955, with the overthrow of the Perón regime, Ginastera was restored to his Conservatory post where he remained until 1958 when he resigned to become director of the new Facultad de Ciencias y Artes Musicales of the Catholic University.

In 1958 Ginastera revisited the United

States at the invitation of the Department of State. He attended the Inter-American Festival in Washington, D.C., where on April 19 his second string quartet received its world première in a performance by the Juilliard String Quartet. This quartet had been commissioned by the Elizabeth Sprague Coolidge Foundation, and it was performed at the festival of the International Society for Contemporary Music in Rome on June 12, 1959. In April 1961, Ginastera again attended the Inter-American Festival in Washington, this time to be present at the premières of his Piano Concerto (commissioned by the Koussevitzky Music Foundation) and the *Cantata para América Mágica* (commissioned by the Fromm Foundation); the former was heard on April 22, and the latter on April 30. The Cantata proved one of Ginastera's most important works up to that time, and it enjoyed a resounding success. "So far as I am concerned," said Irving Lowens in the Washington *Evening Star*, "with this astounding work the Argentine composer conclusively demonstrated yesterday that he is one of the major creators of our day. . . . The result is music of incredible complexity, not only in rhythm but also in melodic contour. Miraculously, the work is already incredibly communicative, even upon first hearing, and it is incredibly exciting." Another highly significant work completed (and introduced) in 1961 was a piano concerto.

To help celebrate the opening season of the New York Philharmonic at the Lincoln Center for the Performing Arts, Ginastera was commissioned to write a violin concerto. Though the composer began working on it in 1962, he did not complete it in time for the introductory season, and the première was delayed until October 2, 1963, when the New York Philharmonic introduced it with Ruggiero Ricci as soloist and Leonard Bernstein conducting. "Delayed or not," said Raymond Ericson in the New York *Times*, "the concerto proved to be a major work, in some respects a magnificent one, worthy of the orchestra and the event that brought it into being." The composer described his concerto as an experiment in the sonorous capabilities not only of the solo violin but also of the individual instruments of the orchestra, and for the work he used the serial technique freely.

The serial technique was also used in Ginastera's first opera, *Don Rodrigo*, one of his most ambitious achievements. This opera was the result of a commission from the municipality of Buenos Aires for the Teatro Colón where it was introduced July 24, 1964. Structurally and stylistically, *Don Rodrigo* is strongly reminiscent of Alban Berg's *Wozzeck*. As did Berg in *Wozzeck*, Ginastera used various instrumental forms: the rondo, suite, scherzo, nocturne, canon, and others. Like *Wozzeck*, Ginastera's opera makes extraordinary use of *Sprechstimme*, or song-speech. "The music is powerful, direct, compelling," says John Vincent, "at times almost overwhelming in its dynamic intensity. . . . One had the feeling that one was witnessing the birth of a work destined to become a landmark similar to *Wozzeck*."

The New York City Opera marked its opening at the Lincoln Center for the Performing Arts by presenting the American première of *Don Rodrigo* on February 22, 1966. "*Don Rodrigo*," reported Ron Eyer in *Life*, "is the most exciting new opera since Alban Berg's *Wozzeck*. . . . It almost brought down the sky-high new roof with the grandeur of its sound. More important it had a lot to say musically. . . . It is a stunningly impressive work that is going to be in opera repertoire for a long time."

In 1962 Ginastera was appointed director of the newly founded Latin American Center for Advanced Musical Studies sponsored by the Rockefeller Foundation for the Instituto Torcuato di Tella in Buenos Aires. The same year Ginastera inaugurated in Buenos Aires an annual festival of modern music.

"If I could write all the works I have in mind," Ginastera told an interviewer in 1962, "I wouldn't stop for the next twenty years. But I am a slow composer. I never start until a work lives completely within me, in my spirit, in my mind. This is what I call the gestation period. Then comes the most painful moment, when I try to put on paper the ideas I have developed intellectually. I compare this moment to that of a child's birth."

Ginastera is a prolific composer. In this he reminds us of Heitor Villa-Lobos, whose successor as South America's greatest composer he is now universally recognized to be; but unlike the prolific Villa-Lobos, who was too often content with the trite and the trivial, Ginastera always maintains the highest possible standards. And, again unlike Villa-Lobos, Ginastera has no interest in popular tunes or folk dance music, preferring ultramodern methods, idioms, means, and materials.

Since 1962, Ginastera's major works have included a Piano Quintet (1963); a cantata for narrator, baritone, and chamber orchestra, *Bomarzo* (Washington, D.C., November 1, 1964); the *Concerto per Corde*, for strings (Caracas, May 14, 1966); *Estudios Sinfónicos*, for orchestra (Vancouver, April 1, 1968); and the Concerto for Cello and Orchestra (Congregation of the Arts at Dartmouth College in Hanover, New Hampshire, July 7, 1968).

The most provocative of his later works— indeed the work that threw the limelight of world attention upon him because of the scandals, arguments, attacks, and counterattacks it aroused—is the opera *Bomarzo*. This composition is not to be confused with the 1964 cantata of the same name, though both texts are the work of the same man (Mujica Lainez). The opera is completely different both in text and in music from the cantata.

The principal character in the opera is Pier Francesco Orsini, Duke of Bomarzo, a hunchback in sixteenth century Italy. Finding life revolting, he goes through violent experiences, many of which are reproduced on stage. His tortured life includes such unpalatable ingredients as homosexuality, narcissism, and impotence, and ends with suicide by poison. Violence, including murder, plays a considerable role in the drama. Male and female nudity, a seduction scene in a bordello, a love scene witnessed by voyeurs, the sight of a young man dying—his head split open on a rock as he dives into a river—a dance by an oversized skeleton, the appearance of ghostly apparitions—these are some of the elements that contributed sensationalism to the opera.

And the opera did cause a sensation, at least in certain quarters, when it received its world première in Washington, D.C., on May 19, 1967. The reaction was such that a scheduled South American première at the Teatro Colón in Buenos Aires on August 9, 1967, was banned by order of the President of Argentina on the grounds that the opera was "obsessed with sex and violence." Despite the immediate response by the Academy of Fine Arts in Buenos Aires that this censorship represented a threat to "artistic freedom," the opera was not shown in Buenos Aires. It was produced, however, with enormous success by the New York City Opera on March 14, 1968; a performance by the same company was recorded in its entirety by Columbia Records.

Most of the major critics in Washington, D.C., in 1967 and in New York in 1968 found little in *Bomarzo* to shock, disgust, or embarrass a twentieth century audience. But they found much to praise. As Irving Kolodin wrote in the *Saturday Review:* "With all the hysterical quotations describing this as a work of 'sex and violence,' and for all the nonsensical ban that has been put upon it in the composer's native Buenos Aires, *Bomarzo* is neither a piece of sensationalism nor a grubby exploitation of contemporary *immores*. It is, rather, a profound, deeply motivated study of an Italian aristocrat . . . a work with a vast amount of sheer ear appeal. It shows Ginastera's command of a remarkably varied range of coloristic and rhythmic devices to the point of complete control at either end of the dynamic scene. . . . He has, with masterful judgment, surrounded his form of serialism with absorbingly varied vignettes that glint and glow with orchestral coloration. . . . Ginastera can be complimented for a sizable success in relation to the resources of his tonal language to the subject with which he is concerned."

Looking at Ginastera personally, one finds it difficult to believe that this is a man who could create an opera condemned for its emphasis on sex and violence. His appearance is that of a simple, mild-mannered man incapable of creating offense in any form whatsoever. According to Howard Klein, Ginastera "has all the rakish personal charm of a bank teller. Of medium height, heavy build, his brown eyes peer placidly through thick black horn-rimmed glasses. His gestures are modest. The interior dynamism of this respected and exciting composer was totally concealed by his unflamboyant manner." According to Donal Henahan, Ginastera "dresses like a bank examiner and thinks like a computer. For several informal talks . . . he wore full uniform: dark blue suit, dark blue socks, black shoes, white shirt with starched collar and small-knotted dark blue tie. Gold cufflinks matched gold tie pin. He spoke in both Spanish and English with excruciating deliberation, precisely and intelligently. Before offering the visitor some sherry, he held up each glass to the light and examined it for cleanliness."

When they are not traveling, Ginastera and his wife occupy a home in the heart of Buenos Aires. "I like very much to be in the center of everything," he explains, "where the people are." Ginastera revealed to Henahan that he lives a routinized existence. Composition is usually done in the mornings; afternoons are devoted to his classes at the Latin American Center for Advanced Musical Studies at the Instituto Torcuato di Tella. "Then," Ginastera continued, "in the evening about seven o'clock, I stop all work and relax. . . . I put on a tuxedo and go out to dinner, or maybe to the cinema." He is, as a matter of fact, a devoted motion picture fan as well as an avid theatregoer. Other interests include collecting African masks and totemic figures, painting, reading, good food, rare wines, and stimulating company.

As the three composers who have influenced him most he names Stravinsky, Schoenberg, and Bartók. As for Ginastera's working habits: "I work directly at the paper but always I have my piano beside me to try out ideas and to release new sonorities," he says. Henahan adds: "His working habits are meticulous, as a glance at a page of music in two stages of evolution showed. The first draft had a couple of disfiguring marks and crossings-out, but looked neater than the final copy turned over by many another composer. Ginastera's own final copy appeared at first to be a page out of a bookkeeper's ledger."

MAJOR WORKS

Ballets—Panambí; Estancia.

Chamber Music—2 string quartets; Duo, for flute and oboe; Pampeana No. 1, rhapsody for violin and piano; Pampeana No. 2, rhapsody for cello and piano; Piano Quintet.

Choral Music—Psalm CL; Three Motets.

Opera—Don Rodrigo; Bomarzo; Beatrix Cenci.

Orchestral Music—Concierto Argentino, for piano and orchestra; Obertura para el Fausto Criollo; Sinfonía Porteña; Sinfonía Elegiaca; Ollantay, symphonic triptych; Pampeana No. 3, pastoral symphony; Variaciones Concertantes, for chamber orchestra; Harp Concerto; Violin Concerto; Sinfonía de Rodrigo, for dramatic soprano and orchestra; Bomarzo, cantata for narrator, baritone, and chamber orchestra; Piano Concerto; Cantata para América Mágica, for soprano and percussion orchestra; Concierto per Corde; Estudios Sinfónicos; Cello Concerto.

Piano Music—Danzas Argentinas; Tres Piezas; 12 American Preludes; Suite de Danzas Criollas; Rondo sobre Temas Infantiles Argentinos; Sonata.

Vocal Music—Cantos del Tucumán, for soprano and instruments; Cinco Canciones Populares Argentinas; Las Horas de una Estancia, song cycle.

ABOUT

Mariz, V., Alberto Ginastera; Suarez Urtubey, P., Alberto Ginastera.

Musical Quarterly, 1957; New York Times Magazine, March 10, 1968; Tempo, Summer 1957.

Umberto Giordano
1867–1948

Umberto Giordano was born on August 27, 1867, in Foggia, Italy. His father, an artisan, wanted him to follow in his trade. But Umberto's talent for music, combined with the protests of music-loving friends, persuaded his father to allow him to study music. Giordano's first teacher was Gaetano Briganti in Foggia. He made excellent progress and in 1881 was sent to the Naples Conservatory, where he stayed five years and where his principal teachers included Paolo Serrao. In 1886 a tone poem, *Delizia*, became Giordano's first composition to receive a public performance.

For a while, Giordano continued to produce instrumental music. Then, in 1888, he completed his first opera, *Marina*, which he entered in the Sonzogno contest. He failed to win the prize (that honor went to Mascagni for *Cavalleria Rusticana*), but he did attract the interest of the powerful publisher Sonzogno, who commissioned him to write another opera. That work, *Mala Vita*, was first seen in Rome on February 21, 1892, and was moderately successful. Giordano subsequently revised the work and retitled it *Il Voto*. In this new version the opera was introduced in Milan in 1897.

Fame came at a time when Giordano had reached the lowest ebb in his fortunes. The operas he had written up to 1896 were either outright failures or meager successes, and they had failed to lift him out of his poverty and obscurity. He was in a state of depression and discouragement. "This is my last card," he said of the opera he was then writing. "If this opera is not a success, I shall play no more."

Giordano: jōr dä′ nō

Giordano

The "last card" proved to be the ace of trumps: *Andrea Chénier*. The effective libretto by Luigi Illica was centered around the character of André Marie de Chénier, a poet who was guillotined during the French Revolution. For this "story with a historical setting," as the composer described his opera, Giordano produced a score that was romantic in the best Italian tradition. He filled his music with large arias, stirring declamations, and big scenes. *Andrea Chénier* was introduced at La Scala in Milan on March 28, 1896. It was a triumph, and overnight Giordano found himself an established composer. Other great houses presented *Andrea Chénier* with immense success: the Academy of Music in New York on November 13, 1896; the Berlin Royal Opera in 1898; and Covent Garden in London in 1904.

UMBERTO GIORDANO

In *Opera News*, Katherine Griffith McDonald described *Andrea Chénier* as "largely an aria opera, for better or worse; even conversations resolve quickly into soliloquies. . . . When the text makes sense, and especially when it moves away from the heroic, Giordano is . . . successful. Moments of ironic humor scattered through the score are underlined by mockingly formal tunes in the eighteenth century manner. . . . Giordano is clearly a musician of action. When he feels compelled to let the singers vocalize, he can turn out grandly lyrical melodies. . . . When, true to his own nature, he lets the music follow the

drama and create its own patterns—as improvisation does—*Andrea Chénier* is fast moving and impressive musical theatre."

Besides making Giordano famous and prosperous, *Andrea Chénier* was responsible for the composer's happy marriage. The authenticated story is as follows: Giordano, while still impoverished and comparatively unknown, was courting the daughter of a Milan hotel proprietor. The latter, a friend of Verdi, confided to the master that his daughter was in love with a composer, adding that he would not object to the match if he could only be sure that the composer had talent. Verdi promised to pass on the merits of the young musician. One day, while Giordano was away in Naples, the hotel proprietor removed from Giordano's room the uncompleted score of *Andrea Chénier* and showed it to Verdi. Verdi later returned the manuscript to the hotel proprietor with the following note: "You may safely confide your daughter to the man who composed a work like this."

Two and a half years after the première of *Andrea Chénier*, there took place the world première of Giordano's second most successful opera: *Fedora*, with a libretto based on the drama by Victorien Sardou. It was seen at the Teatro Lirico in Milan on November 17, 1898. Giordano's passionate, theatrical music was perfectly suited to the dramatics of Sardou's blood-and-thunder play, a fact that explains the enormous popularity enjoyed by the opera at the turn of the twentieth century. It is also the reason why the opera soon became dated and failed to enjoy more than occasional and intermittent revivals. *Fedora* was first produced in the United States at the Metropolitan Opera, on December 5, 1906. It was revived there in 1925 for the prima donna Maria Jeritza.

On January 25, 1915, the Metropolitan Opera presented the world première of another Giordano opera that was to become popular—*Madame Sans-Gêne*, with Toscanini conducting. Like *Andrea Chénier*, the later opera utilized the French Revolution as a background. In fact, *Madame Sans-Gêne*, as Henry Krehbiel remarked in his review in the New York *Tribune*, "in more ways than one . . . harked back to *Andrea Chénier*. . . . The style of writing is there, though applied possibly with more mature and refined skill. We cannot say with as much ingenuousness or freshness of invention, however.... Like all good French music, which it uses and imitates, it is full of crisp rhythms, largely developed from the old dances, and so there is an abundance of life and energy in the score, though little of the distinction, elegance and grace which have always been characteristic of the French school."

Giordano's last successful opera was *La Cena delle Beffe*, produced by La Scala in Milan on December 20, 1924, once again with Toscanini conducting. The libretto was Sem Benelli's popular play, which was set in fifteenth century Florence. Giordano's last opera—*Il Re*, introduced at La Scala on January 10, 1929—was a failure. Though he lived another two decades, Giordano wrote no more, content to rest on his well-earned laurels. He was the recipient of many honors. He was made a Chevalier of the French Legion of Honor, a Commander of the Crown of Italy, and a member of the Italian Academy. He died in Milan on November 12, 1948.

What R. A. Streatfeild said of Giordano is undoubtedly valid: "In his music the usual theatrical tricks for extorting applause too often take the place of a sincere expression of emotion." But it is also true that, together with his obvious partiality for theatricalism, Giordano brought to his operas a rich fund of melody and a sound instinct for building climactic scenes. He was not an original composer, but his best operas represent effective theatre.

MAJOR WORKS

Operas—Mala Vita (revised as Il Voto); Andrea Chénier; Fedora; Siberia; Madame Sans-Gêne; Giove a Pompei; La Cena delle Beffe; Il Re.

ABOUT

Cellamare, D., Umberto Giordano: La Vita e le Opere.
Opera News, March 2, 1963.

Peggy Glanville-Hicks
1912–

Peggy Glanville-Hicks was born in Melbourne, Australia, December 29, 1912. She received her first training in music at the Melbourne Conservatory as a pupil of the director Fritz Hart. She went to London in 1931 where for four years she attended the Royal College of Music on the Carlotta Rowe Scholarship. Her teachers included Vaughan Williams in composition, Gordon Jacob in orchestration, Arthur Benjamin in piano, and Constant Lambert and Sir Malcolm Sargent in conducting. In 1935 the Octavia Traveling Scholarship made it possible for her to travel throughout Europe. During this period she continued her study of composition with Egon Wellesz in Vienna and she concluded it in Paris with Nadia Boulanger.

PEGGY GLANVILLE-HICKS

She had been composing seriously since 1931 when she had completed a number of song cycles, including *Frolic* and *Rest*, to poems by A. E. Housman. Her Sinfonietta, for orchestra, and her first opera, *Caedmon* (text by the composer), came in 1934; her first ballet, *Hylas and the Nymphs*, in 1935. Her initial success came with *Choral Suite*, for women's chorus, oboe, and string orchestra, to poems by Fletcher, which she completed in 1937. Two movements were heard at the festival of the International Society for Contemporary Music in London on June 20, 1938–the first time that music by an Australian composer had been represented at this event.

On November 7, 1938, Peggy Glanville-Hicks married the English composer Stanley Bate. (They were divorced eight years later.) Together, in 1940, they founded Les Trois Arts, a ballet company. For this group, she served in many capacities, including those of assistant business manager, publicity director, assistant conductor, and arranger. She and her husband came to the United States in 1942, establishing permanent residence in New York City; she became an American citizen in 1948. Soon after settling in New York she became affiliated with the League of Composers, serving on the committee arranging concerts of modern music in Central Park in 1943–1944. When the war ended, she joined Dr. Carleton Sprague Smith in founding the International Music Fund to assist European artists displaced by the war to reestablish themselves. In 1948 she became a delegate to the festival of the International Society for Contemporary Music at Amsterdam, where on June 10 her *Concertino da Camera* (1943) was performed. From 1948 to 1958 she served as a music critic for the New York *Herald Tribune*, and from 1950 to 1960 she was director of the Composers Forum which presented concerts of new music by young composers. She was also a member of the Junior Council of the Museum of Modern Art in the early 1950's where she helped organize concerts of avant-garde music.

As a composer she had made her strongest impression up to that time with *Letters from Morocco*, for voice and orchestra (1952), the text of which consisted of excerpts from letters she had received from Paul Bowles, the composer and author. "Miss Glanville-Hicks," said George Antheil, "has set them to music in a series of unusually haunting and different pieces. . . . The Spanish composer Carlos Surinach remarked on first hearing this work that its mood and atmosphere are the most compellingly exotic he has heard since Manuel de Falla and are achieved with neutral materials, without resource to any specifically 'exotic' or 'Oriental' devices, but simply by a deep preoccupation and identification with the texts." *Letters from Morocco* received its first performance in New York on February 22, 1953, with Leopold Stokowski conducting and William Hess as soloist. An early composition for voice and instruments also made use of a most unusual text—*Thomsoniana* (1949), five songs in which the composer provided an amusing musical setting for excerpts from the music reviews by Virgil Thomson in the New York *Herald Tribune*, written as a birthday greeting to the composer-critic.

Letters from Morocco was followed in 1953 by an important opera, *The Transposed Heads*. This was the first opera ever to be commissioned by the Louisville Orchestra in Kentucky (the commission was made possible through a Rockefeller Foundation grant). The composer prepared her own text, based on Thomas Mann's novel of the same name with an Indian setting. The plot has decidedly gruesome overtones, since the two rivals for the love of Sita, her husband and her lover, behead themselves. Then, on a command from the goddess Kali to replace the heads on the bodies, Sita puts the husband's head on the lover's body. When the question as to which of the two is now her legal husband becomes enmeshed in inextricable complexities, all three commit suicide.

But, as Herbert Elwell remarked in the Cleveland *Plain Dealer*, this horror story is "embellished with music of such melodious charm and vitality that the whole work takes on a sort of Mozartean insouciance. The vitality comes not only from the text, but also from the use of various dance tunes, some of which derive directly from Hindu folklore. This is not pseudo-Orientalism, such as Rimsky-Korsakov and other Russian composers indulged in. It is real assimilation of eastern music into an idiomatic fabric that is, all the same, essentially American."

In discussing the Indian sources of her music, Miss Glanville-Hicks said: "It required no great amendment of my own writing method to plan the structure of the work so as to include Indian materials, for over a period of years I have gradually shed harmonic dictatorship peculiar to modernists, and have evolved a melody rhythm structure that comes very close to the musical patterns of the antique world. It was possible, therefore—with a certain selectivity in regard to the scales used—to incorporate Indian folk themes without doing any violence to their unique character, or without altering my own way of writing."

The Transposed Heads was produced in New York in 1958, and was recorded by Columbia.

Another successful opera came in 1961—*Nausicaa*, a feature of the Athens Festival on August 19, 1961. The text, written by the composer, came out of Robert Graves's novel *Homer's Daughter* and is a retelling with modifications and changes of the Homeric legend of Odysseus and Penelope. In the opera,

234

Penelope becomes Nausicaa, and Odysseus becomes Aethon, a shipwrecked Cretan sailor-nobleman. A secondary plot brings up the idea that *The Odyssey* was not the work of Homer at all but of Princess Nausicaa.

"Miss Glanville-Hicks's score," reported the correspondent for the London *Times*, "used musical types from various Greek regions and it was this Greek flavor together with considerations of musical malleability for extended development that guided her choice of material." Peter Gradenwitz said further, in the *Frankfurter Allgemeine Zeitung*: "Style and subject in this opera seem in an odd way timeless. 'Modal' materials are treated at times in a 'serial' spirit, while the sound of the orchestra reveals a master of the modern composer's profession. The effect of *Nausicaa* is not at all that of scientific research work in the fields of history and musical science. It is an opera with an individuality all its own—a work opening vistas to new modern roads in ancient spirit never trodden before."

Glanville-Hicks has produced music successfully for the stage in fields other than opera, notably the ballet. *Masque of the Wild Man* was commissioned by and produced at the first Festival of the Two Worlds in Spoleto, Italy, in 1958. One year later, commissioned by CBS-TV to create a ballet for television, she produced the score for *Saul*.

Peggy Glanville-Hicks received a grant from the American Academy of Arts and Letters in 1953. In the years 1956–1958 she received two Guggenheim fellowships. In 1960 a Rockefeller grant enabled her to do research in the music of the Middle East. And a Fulbright research grant in 1961 gave her the opportunity to explore Hindu folk music and the folk music of the Greek islands.

For many years Peggy Glanville-Hicks made her home in an apartment in Greenwich Village, New York. She now shares her time between New York and a house she owns on the slopes of the Acropolis in Athens.

MAJOR WORKS

Ballets—The Masque of the Wild Man; Saul; Jephtha's Daughter; Tragic Celebration.

Chamber Music—String Quartet; Flute Sonatina; Concertino da Camera, for flute, clarinet, bassoon, and harp; Concertino Antico, for harp and string quartet; Harp Sonata; Sonata for Piano and Percus-sion; Musica Antiqua No. 1, for flutes, harp, marimba, percussion.

Choral Music—Choral Suite; Dance Cantata, for narrator, spoken chorus, and orchestra; Pastoral.

Operas—The Transposed Heads; The Glittering Gate; Nausicaa; Carlos Among the Candles; Sappho.

Orchestral Music—Poem for Chorus and Orchestra; Sinfonietta; Spanish Suite; Piano Concerto; Flute Concerto; Letters from Morocco, for tenor and orchestra; Gymnopedie No. 1, for string orchestra, with oboe and harp; Gymnopedie No. 2, for string orchestra; Gymnopedie No. 3, for string orchestra with celeste and harp; Sinfonia Pacifica; Etruscan Concerto, for piano and chamber orchestra; Concerto Romantico, for viola and chamber orchestra; Tapestry; Drama.

Vocal Music—Frolic; Rest; Come Sleep; Be Still, You Little Leaves; Five Songs from A. E. Housman; Profiles from China; Thirteen Ways of Looking at a Blackbird; Thomsoniana, for soprano and instruments; Ballade.

ABOUT

Bulletin of the American Composers Alliance, vol. 4, no. 1, 1954.

Alexander Glazunov
1865–1936

Alexander Konstantinovich Glazunov was born on August 10, 1865, in St. Petersburg, Russia. His father was a publisher and bookseller, the proprietor of a prosperous establishment which had been founded in Moscow by his own grandfather and subsequently expanded with a branch in St. Petersburg. Both of Alexander's parents were musical. His father played the violin, and his mother was an excellent pianist. Glazunov began to study the piano with his mother when he was nine; at twelve he took instruction from Elenofsky.

"At home we had a great deal of music," Glazunov recalled later in life, "and everything we played remained firmly in my memory so that, awakening in the night, I could construct, even to the smallest details, all that I had heard earlier in the evening." He revealed a gift for recalling a piece of music, note by note, after a single hearing. His aptitude for theory was equally exceptional. Before he was thirteen he was writing chamber and orchestral music. At the same time that all this musical activity was going on, he attended elementary school and technical high school.

When Elenofsky left St. Petersburg in 1878,

Glazunov: glă zōō nôf´

Glazunov

Glazunov went to Balakirev for further musical training. Balakirev was so impressed with him that he brought one of Glazunov's compositions to the attention of Rimsky-Korsakov. The master recalled this event in his autobiography: "It was an orchestral score written in childish fashion; the boy's talent was indubitably clear." Glazunov became a pupil of Rimsky-Korsakov in 1880. "He was a charming boy with beautiful eyes," the teacher wrote. "Elementary theory and solfeggio proved unnecessary for him, as he had a superior ear. . . . After a few lessons in harmony, I took him directly into counterpoint, to which he applied himself zealously. . . . His musical development progressed not by the day, but literally by the hour."

ALEXANDER GLAZUNOV

He had been with Rimsky-Korsakov only a year and a half when he completed his first symphony, in E major. It was introduced at a concert of the Free School of Music, Balakirev conducting, on March 29, 1882. When Glazunov went to the stage to take his bows (a sixteen-year-old boy dressed in a schoolboy's uniform), the appreciative audience was shocked to discover that the symphony had been the work of a youngster. So good was this music (César Cui described it as "frightening in its precocious maturity") that some authorities suspected that it had actually been written by Rimsky-Korsakov. Belaiev, the distinguished Russian patron, not only issued Glazunov's symphony but expressed his interest by offering to publish anything Glazunov wrote. This was an event of considerable significance not only in Glazunov's career but also in all Russian music, since it marked Belaiev's start as the publisher of Russia's leading composers.

Glazunov did not lack for attention after this. Some of the most influential musicians of St. Petersburg sang his praises. Balakirev called him "the little Glinka"; Stassov spoke of him as "our young Samson"; some students at the Conservatory, presenting him with a wreath, designated him as "our Hermann and Cazeneuve"—Hermann and Cazeneuve being two popular magicians of that day. Among Glazunov's compositions of his apprentice period (all published and performed) were two string quartets (D major and F major), the *Overtures on Greek Themes*, and the tone poem *Stenka Razin*. The last of these, completed in 1885, is still heard from time to time. This music was inspired by the seventeenth century Cossack chief who was captured by government troops following his insurrection and put to death. Glazunov's tone poem, which dramatizes the career of the Cossack, is pictorial and descriptive; the celebrated folk song "The Volga Boatman" is quoted.

In 1884 Glazunov went on an extended tour of Europe. In Weimar he completely won the enthusiasm of Franz Liszt, who praised the young man's first symphony effusively. When Glazunov completed his second symphony, in F-sharp minor, he dedicated it to Liszt's memory.

At the Paris Exposition of 1889 this second symphony was performed together with *Stenka Razin*, with enormous success. Glazunov's reputation, thus extended beyond the borders of Russia, circled the globe. In 1892 the Columbian Exposition in Chicago commissioned him to write the *Triumphal March*, for chorus and orchestra. In 1896 he visited England and directed programs of his music, including his still familiar and popular Symphony No. 4 in E-flat, which he had completed in 1893, and which had been introduced in St. Petersburg on February 3, 1894.

Other successful Glazunov compositions before 1900 included his *Five Novelettes*, a suite for string quartet (1888); the fifth symphony in B-flat major, and the two *Valses de Concert*, completed between 1893 and 1895;

the spirited *Carnival Overture* (1894); the Sixth Symphony in C minor (1896); and the ballet *Raymonda* (his first successful work for the stage and one of his most popular), which the Russian Imperial Ballet introduced in St. Petersburg on January 19, 1898, with choreography by Marius Petipa. By 1900 Glazunov was acknowledged to be one of the foremost creative figures not only in Russian music but in all contemporary music; and he was only thirty-five at that time.

Glazunov's most important ballet, *The Seasons*, was completed in 1899 and introduced in St. Petersburg February 23, 1900, once again with Marius Petipa's choreography. The scenario interpreted the four seasons of the year in as many scenes. The ballet was only moderately successful, but the orchestral suite which the composer adapted from his score has become world famous and is now one of Glazunov's most frequently heard symphonic compositions.

Another of Glazunov's works to have retained its immense popularity up to the present time is his Violin Concerto in A minor, which he completed in 1905 and whose world première was given by Leopold Auer (for whom it had been written) in St. Petersburg on March 4, 1905.

In spite of the high standards of works like these, Glazunov's importance as a composer declined sharply after the turn of the twentieth century. Though an acknowledged genius in his youth and a composer of international prestige in his maturity, he became a "has been" during the closing decades of his life. Glazunov wrote his last symphony, in E-flat major, in 1906. Then, for the next sixteen years he wrote sporadically, and little of what he produced had lasting value. His second piano concerto, in B major (1922), his second suite for string quartet (1929), and his seventh string quartet, in C (1931), represent the fruits of a meager crop; none added much to his stature. He was honored in the second decade of the twentieth century as a teacher and as a musical personality. But as a composer he was acclaimed only for a handful of works, most of which were written before 1900, and none after 1910.

Glazunov's career as teacher began in 1899 when he had a class in composition at the St. Petersburg Conservatory. In 1905 he became director of the Conservatory, holding this post until 1928. He exercised a profound influence on his pupils, many of whom were accused of succumbing to "Glazunovchina," or writing in the Glazunov style.

And the Glazunov style represented reaction. As a human being he detested change of every kind. His first biographer, A. W. Ossovsky, noted in a book published when Glazunov was in his middle forties that the composer "has lived and will, it is supposed, continue to live not merely in the same building, but in the very flat in which he first saw the light. He sleeps in the bed on which his birth took place. His father, too, had been born there. His visits abroad had been comparatively rare and brief. While other composers have needed change and a wide experience of life to inspire them, Glazunov has always drawn inspiration from within."

In music, too, Glazunov had no patience with change. He had no sympathy for the new tendencies that were springing up all around him or for composers like Scriabin, Stravinsky, and Prokofiev. A story has been told that when he first heard Prokofiev's *Scythian Suite* in 1916 he rushed out of the concert hall, holding his hands to his ears to drown out the discordant sounds. Figuratively, too, he closed his ears to new styles and techniques.

As a protégé of Balakirev and a pupil of Rimsky-Korsakov, Glazunov inherited the ideals and principles of the national school of Russian composers identified as "The Five." Glazunov's first successful works were for the most part an expression of nationalist ideals—so much so that it may well be said that Glazunov was the last of the famous Russian nationalists.

But even as a nationalist, in the tradition of "The Five," Glazunov lived in the past. Time and again he disappointed Rimsky-Korsakov and the others by his adherence to German structures and German post-Romantic procedures. As he continued writing, Glazunov's music became so increasingly reactionary that it was said of him that he entered the future backwards. He preferred the sound classical forms, traditional melodies and harmonies, and methods and techniques hallowed by the textbook.

Though Glazunov was not in sympathy with the revolution in Russia, he remained in his native land and held several important positions after 1917. For a while he served as a kind of musical emissary in France, Germany, and Austria to send reports on musical activities. He continued as the director of the St. Petersburg Conservatory (renamed Leningrad Conservatory after 1924). He helped organize an opera studio and a students' orchestra, and he did what he could to promote a musical life in the Soviet Union. But the rapid changes brought on first by World War I, and then by the Revolution, oppressed him. He aged far beyond his years. H. G. Wells, who saw him in St. Petersburg in 1920, described him as "pallid and very much fallen away, so that his clothes hang loosely on him." Glazunov complained bitterly that he could not get any music paper, but it was a convenient excuse for his not composing. He had lost his creative will; writing music, which had once come so easily and spontaneously, had become a painful chore.

Growing dissatisfaction with the Soviet Union finally led him to leave his country for good. In 1928 he moved to Paris where he lived for the rest of his life. He visited the United States for the first time in 1929, making his American debut on November 21 as conductor of the Detroit Symphony in a program of his own works. He died in Paris March 21, 1936.

Dmitri Tiomkin wrote the following informal sketch of Glazunov: "Either he was very lively or very silent. Although he inherited considerable wealth from his ancestors that enabled him to live well (up to the time of the Revolution), he was never so happy as in simple bohemian apartments. . . . His particular hobby was his old family coach, a strange-looking vehicle which he used in summer and winter. With a long black cigar, a big black tie and robust figure dressed in the manner of Turgenev's or Tolstoy's novels, he was an outstanding figure. . . . Utter modesty and spiritual democracy were his watchwords at home and in school. As a rule, he spoke little in society, but when he was aroused on a particular subject he could be brilliantly conversational. . . . There was in him much of the hospitable Russian merchant, who loves to entertain his visitors, or, in the good old days, treat them to a glass of tea or vodka."

MAJOR WORKS

Ballets—Raymonda; Les Ruses d'Amour; The Seasons.

Chamber Music—7 string quartets; 2 suites, for string quartet; Novelettes, for string quartet; In Modo Religioso, quartet for brass; String Quintet; Elegy, for string quartet; Quartet for Saxophones.

Choral Music—Triumphal March; Coronation Cantata; Cantata, for women's chorus, soloists, and two pianos; Memorial Cantata; Hymn, for women's chorus; Requiem.

Orchestral Music—8 symphonies; 2 piano concertos; 2 violin concertos; 2 Overtures on Greek Themes; Suite Caracteristique; Stenka Razin, tone poem; The Forest, tone poem; Wedding March; Une Fête Slave, symphonic sketch; The Sea, symphonic fantasy; Rhapsodie Orientale; The Kremlin; Le Printemps, symphonic sketch; Cortège Solennel; Scènes de Ballet, suite; Pas de Caractère; Intermezzo Romantico; Ouverture Solennelle; Ballade; From the Middle Ages, suite; Scène Dansante; Le Chant du Destin, dramatic overture; Two Preludes; À la Mémoire de Gogol, symphonic prologue; Esquisses Finnoises; Introduction et la Danse de Salomé; Karelian Legend; Concerto-Ballata in C major, for cello and orchestra; Concerto in E-flat major, for alto saxophone and orchestra.

Organ Music—2 Preludes and Fugues; Fantaisie.

Piano Music—2 sonatas; Etudes, Impromptus, Preludes and Fugues, Waltzes; Nocturne; Trois Morceaux; Theme and Variations; Idylle; Fantaisie, for two pianos.

Vocal Music—Songs for voice and piano including Golden Spring, Nina's Song, Oriental Romance, and Why Are the Voices Silent?

ABOUT

Bakst, J., A History of Russian-Soviet Music; Calvocoressi, M. D. and Abraham, G., Masters of Russian Music; Fedrova, G., Alexander Glazunov; Leonard, R. A., A History of Russian Music; Montagu-Nathan, M., Contemporary Russian Composers.

Reinhold Glière
1875–1956

Reinhold Moritzovich Glière was born in Kiev on January 11, 1875, of Belgian ancestry. His father was a maker of wind instruments. In 1891 Glière entered the Kiev Conservatory where he remained three years, specializing in violin and composition. When he was nineteen, he enrolled in the Moscow Conservatory, where, under teachers such as Taneiev, Arensky, and Ippolitov-Ivanov, he proved an exceptional student, winning a gold medal in composition. In 1900 he was graduated with honors, having written as a graduation piece a one-act opera-oratorio, *Earth and Heaven.*

Glière: glē ĕr′

During his last year at the Conservatory he completed a number of noteworthy chamber music works that revealed exceptional talent—including his first sextet, his first string quartet, and an octet. He also wrote his first symphony. That symphony, when introduced by the Russian Musical Society in Moscow on January 3, 1903, was criticized so severely that the young composer came to the conclusion he needed more study. For two years, beginning in 1905, he lived in Berlin where he was Oskar Fried's pupil in conducting. The influence of his extended stay in Germany is reflected in his second symphony (1907), which received its world première in Berlin January 23, 1908, at a concert in which the young Serge Koussevitzky was making his bow as a conductor. This symphony is in a Germanic post-Romantic style in contrast to earlier works by Glière which had been pronouncedly Russian in the style of the nationalist school.

REINHOLD GLIÈRE

In 1908 Glière returned to Russia. There he made his debut as conductor. He soon achieved his first success as a composer—with a tone poem, *The Sirens*, influenced by Liszt and introduced in Moscow on January 30, 1906.

When his style finally crystallized, it combined the best features of Germanic Romanticism and Russian nationalism. This is the style which characterizes Glière's most successful composition—his third symphony (sub-titled *Ilia Mourometz*), which is still one of Glière's most frequently played works. He wrote it in the years between 1909 and 1911, and its world première took place in Moscow on March 23, 1912, Emil Cooper conducting. The symphony was highly successful and received the Glinka Prize.

Ilia Mourometz is a hero of Russian legends and epics: a bogatyr who was the son of a peasant. He lived in the twelfth century and performed fabulous deeds in war and peace. Finally defeated in a monumental battle, he fled to the mountains where, according to legend, he turned to stone. Thus the race of bogatyrs came to an end.

The symphony is in an epic style, large in design, rich in orchestral and harmonic colors, filled with stirring climaxes, and at times touched with an exotic Orientalism. The use of an authentic old Russian church chorale as a recurring theme provides not only a strong national flavor but also integration. Sergei Boguslavski in describing the symphony spoke of its "grandiose, majestic structure [achieved] not only by the breadth of its form and the powerful nature of its instrumentation which demands among other things quadrupled woodwind, eight horns, four trumpets and four trombones, but also by the character of its themes and their development." He felt that this "monumental symphony [solved] the difficult problem of a union between program music and the forms of absolute music."

Glière began his career as teacher of composition at the Gnessin School of Music in Moscow in 1900. In 1913 he was appointed professor of composition at the Kiev Conservatory. One year later he became director, and it was largely through his industry and initiative that the institution became the best of its kind in Russia. In 1920 Glière resigned his post in Kiev to become a professor at the Moscow Conservatory; he held that post until the end of his life. He was one of Russia's most distinguished teachers; among his many pupils were Prokofiev, Miaskovsky, and Khatchaturian.

During World War I, Glière was for the most part unproductive as a composer; only a single composition of any importance appeared—a tone poem, *Trizna* (1915). Following the war's end, and the Revolution, Glière allied himself completely with the new regime by becoming head of the musical section of the Moscow Department of People's Education and by organizing concerts for workers. At the same time he wanted his music to glorify the social and political ideals of a workers' state. In 1927 he wrote the first important ballet to employ a revolutionary subject for purposes of propaganda. This ballet was *The Red Poppy*. It achieved remarkable success in the Soviet Union following its triumphant première at the Bolshoi Theatre in Moscow on June 14, 1927. The setting is a Chinese port, where coolies are mercilessly exploited. When a Soviet ship arrives, the captain falls in love with a Chinese girl. Eventually she is killed by the port commander while trying to flee from China aboard the Soviet vessel. With her dying words she urges the Chinese to fight for their liberty, using a red poppy as the symbol of freedom. The "Russian Sailors' Dance" ("*Ekh Yabochko*"), a rousing, spirited piece of music, is the most celebrated excerpt from this score and is often heard at symphony concerts.

An extended period of research into Azerbaijan folklore and folk music, begun in Baku in 1923, resulted in Glière's first opera: *Shah-Senem* (1925). After Glière had revised it radically in 1934, the opera was given its world première in Baku May 4, 1934. In 1938 it was mounted at a festival of Azerbaijan art in Moscow. In the score the composer makes remarkable use of Caucasian folk songs, and particularly the demoniac rhythms of barbaric Caucasian dances. Another period of research into native folk music, this time in the region of Uzbek, resulted in Glière's incidental music for the drama *Hulsara* (1936).

Several significant appointments and awards in the 1930's underscored the all-important place Glière had achieved in Soviet music. He was elected chairman of the management committee of the Moscow Union of Composers in 1937, and two years later he was made chairman of the organizing committee of the Union of Soviet Composers. The same year he was honored with the Order of the Red Banner, and in 1938 with the Order of Merit and the title of People's Artist of the U.S.S.R. In 1940 the degree of Doctor of Sciences was conferred on him for his researches. During these years he produced much functional music, paying tribute to various phases of Soviet life and achievement: *For the Festival of the Comintern* (1924); the *March of the Red Army* (1924); *Happiness of the Fatherland* (1942); *Twenty-five Years of the Red Army* (1943).

During World War II, Glière's music interpreted or extolled the war effort. As he wrote in an appeal to American musicians on July 6, 1941: "We Soviet composers, together with the people, are employing the medium of our art to help the Red Army wage its struggle against the brutal enemy." That year he wrote the orchestral overture *Friendship of the Nations*, a tribute to the collaborative effort of the Allied forces in the war. This was followed by the *War Overture*, a musical declaration of "the fighting principles of the three great powers." He also wrote a patriotic marching song, "Hitler's End Will Come," in anticipation of that event. Finally, *Victory Overture* helped celebrate the defeat of Nazi Germany and was successfully introduced in Moscow on October 30, 1945.

In 1948 Glière received the Stalin Prize for the first time—for his String Quartet No. 4. He won it again in 1950 for the ballet *The Bronze Knight*. This ballet was produced in Leningrad on March 14, 1949. His last complete work was a Horn Concerto, which was heard in Moscow on January 26, 1952; he was working on a violin concerto when he died. A month before his death, Glière made an extended tour of the Soviet Union, conducting concerts of his works in Odessa, Kishinev, and several other cities. He died in Moscow on June 23, 1956.

Because of his pronounced romantic tendencies as a composer, and his strong national spirit, Glière was one of the few outstanding composers to escape indictment by the Central Committee of the Communist Party when, in 1948, it launched its violent attack on "dissonance makers" and "decadent formalists" (see sketch on Prokofiev).

MAJOR WORKS

Ballets—Chrysis, ballet-pantomime; Cleopatra, ballet-mimodrama; Comedians; The Red Poppy; The Bronze Knight.

Chamber Music—4 string quartets; 3 string sextets; String Octet; Eight Pieces, for violin and cello; Ten Duos, for two cellos; Ballad, for cello and piano; Four Pieces, for double bass and piano.

Operas—Shah-Senem; Leili and Mejun; Rachel.

Orchestral Music—3 symphonies (including Ilia

Mourometz); The Sirens, tone poem; Two Poems, for soprano and orchestra; Cossacks of Zaporozh, tone poem; Trizna, tone poem; Zapovit, tone poem; Imitation of Jezekiel, tone poem for narrator and Orchestra; Harp Concerto; Concerto for Coloratura Soprano and Orchestra; Cello Concerto; Horn Concerto.

Piano Music—175 pieces for two or four hands.

Vocal Music—Over 100 songs for voice and piano.

ABOUT

Boelza, I., Glière; Leonard, R. A., A History of Russian Music.

Morton Gould
1913–

Morton Gould was born in Richmond Hill, New York, on December 10, 1913. His musical talent was first recognized during the celebration of the "false Armistice" in 1918 when, hearing a band play Sousa's *Stars and Stripes Forever*, he went over to the piano and proceeded to reproduce the melody accurately. He continued to recreate the melodies he heard and knew, then began to compose tunes of his own. His first published piece, a waltz for the piano, was written when he was six.

MORTON GOULD

At eight he was awarded a scholarship for the Institute of Musical Art; at thirteen he became a pupil of Abby Whiteside; and at fifteen he had completed a two-year course in theory and composition with Vincent Jones at New York University. During this period he made frequent appearances as a child-prodigy pianist and received much publicity.

When he could no longer be classified as a child prodigy, Gould earned his living by accepting whatever job came along. He played the piano in the motion picture and vaudeville houses. He toured the vaudeville circuit as a member of the two-piano team of Gould and Schafter, and sometimes as accompanist for the dancers the De Marcos. He made a few recordings and lectured in colleges and conservatories, where his *tour de force* was an improvisation of fugues on given subjects.

When he was eighteen, he was heard by the movie impresario S. L. Rothafel, better known as "Roxy," who engaged him as staff pianist for the Radio City Music Hall. Three years later, Gould was given his first radio job, conducting an orchestra on a sustaining program for station WOR.

He soon acquired national fame on the radio as conductor and arranger. He combined his energetic and vital performances with the baton with his own arrangements of the popular classics, daring in their exploitation of new effects, brilliant in their use of sonority, and always soundly musical. After seven years on WOR he was selected to direct the *Cresta Blanca Carnival* over a nationwide hookup; with this program he became an outstanding radio personality.

Gould has written many major works for orchestra which have been performed by practically every important orchestra in the United States and by virtually every great conductor. In most of his best works, he has drawn exhaustively from American idioms, backgrounds, and history. Occasionally he has used jazz idioms and techniques with exceptional skill and artistic effect. When he was eighteen he wrote the first such successful work in the *Chorale and Fugue in Jazz*, for two pianos and orchestra, introduced under Stokowski's direction January 2, 1936. After that he wrote a number of other interesting works in a jazz style, among them *Swing Sinfonietta* (1936); *Interplay*, a three-movement work that included a blues (1943); the Concerto for Orchestra (1943), with a finale in a boogie-woogie style; and *Derivations for Clarinet and Jazz Band* (1955), which he wrote for Benny Goodman and which makes an attempt to combine the American jazz vernacular with the old baroque structure of the concerto grosso. The last of these was used as background music for the ballet *Clarinade*, with choreography by George Balanchine, produced by the New York City Ballet on April 29, 1964.

Other successful works used folklore styles or made adept use of American folk idioms. In this category we find *Cowboy Rhapsody* (1942), a symphonic adaptation of such famous cowboy songs as "Trail to Mexico," "Home on the Range," and "Goodbye, Old Paint" introduced by the St. Louis Symphony in March 1944. Others have drawn copiously from the repertory of American popular music: *Foster Gallery* (1941), an orchestral adaptation of several beloved Stephen Foster ballads; *An American Salute* (1942), a symphonic arrangement of the Civil War and Spanish American War song "When Johnny Comes Marching Home"; and a symphony based on well-known marching tunes (1945).

Still other Gould works were inspired by and derive their subject matter from American backgrounds. These include *A Lincoln Legend* (1942), which Toscanini introduced with the NBC Symphony; and *Declaration* (1957), a setting of the Declaration of Independence for narrators, male chorus, and orchestra introduced at the Inaugural Concert in Washington on January 20, 1957.

Gould has also used Latin-American melodies and rhythms for ambitious concert works, notably in *Latin American Symphonette*, for orchestra (1940) and in the ballet *Fiesta*, introduced at Cannes on March 17, 1957.

One of Gould's finest and most successful orchestral compositions, the *Spirituals*, for orchestra, leans heavily on Negro folk songs and has acquired a permanent place in the contemporary American repertoire. Introduced at the American Music Festival in New York on February 9, 1941, the composer conducting, this composition tries to translate into terms of symphonic music the emotional idiom of the Negro spiritual. It simulates the effect realized by a congregation and a choir in a Negro religious service by using a string choir to voice the principal material and using the rest of the orchestra as a kind of accompanying voice.

Gould has produced many works in which the material is entirely his own. Of these, among the best are the Concerto for Orchestra,

introduced by the Cleveland Orchestra under Golschmann February 1, 1945; and the Symphony No. 3, whose première was given by the Dallas Symphony February 16, 1947, the composer conducting. This symphony was subsequently revised, then reintroduced by the New York Philharmonic under Mitropoulos on October 28, 1948.

Gould's most famous ballet, *Fall River Legend*, also uses material exclusively his own. It was presented by the Ballet Theatre in New York on April 22, 1948. The scenario and choreography, both by Agnes de Mille, were based on the double murder committed in Fall River, Massachusetts, in 1892—the story of Lizzie Borden, accused of killing her father and his second wife with an axe, a crime of which she was finally acquitted. The composer said: "The ballet deals with the psychological motivations which led Lizzie Borden to commit murder, and its structure alternates between dramatic sequences and set pieces, so that, in a sense, it combines the qualities of both pure and pantomimic dance." A six-movement orchestral suite derived from the ballet score is sometimes heard at symphony concerts.

Gould's style in these and later works represents a happy synthesis of popular and serious elements of exotic and everyday traits, even of musical elements of the past and those of the present. His polyglot style reveals many different facets, but he uses it with extraordinary effect in the writing of music that, at best, is consistently charming and appealing, alive with an American personality and tempo. Easily assimilable, his music is a favorite at "pop" or promenade concerts; written with consummate musicianship, good taste, and imagination, it is perfectly at ease in the symphony hall.

Gould makes his home in Great Neck, New York with his wife, the former Shirley Banks, whom he married in 1941. They have a son, Eric. Tall and lanky, Morton Gould has an almost perpetually melancholy expression on his face. He confesses he has virtually no hobbies outside music and adds: "I have never taken a vacation, and I wouldn't know what to do with one if I did." However, when pressed to point to a few of his extramusical activities, he reveals that he reads a great deal, occasionally plays ping pong, and dreams of returning to a childhood pastime long abandoned—painting. He is fond of railroads, and keeps a drawer in his desk filled with pictures of trains.

On October 30, 1967, Gould received the Henry Hadley medal for outstanding service to American music, an award made by the National Association for American Composers and Conductors.

Morton Gould composed the scores for the Broadway musicals *Billion Dollar Baby* (1945) and *Arms and the Girl* (1950). For films, he wrote the background music of *Delightfully Dangerous* (1945) and *Cinerama Holiday* (1955); for television, the background music for a twenty-six-installment documentary series, *World War I*, telecast by CBS in 1965–1966.

MAJOR WORKS

Ballets—Interplay; Fall River Legend; Fiesta.

Choral Music—Of Time and the River; Hamariv Arovim.

Orchestral Music—3 symphonies; 3 American Symphonettes; Chorale and Fugue in Jazz; Swing Sinfonietta; Piano Concerto; Violin Concerto; A Lincoln Legend; Foster Gallery; Spirituals; Cowboy Rhapsody; An American Salute; Concerto for Orchestra; Interplay (American Concertette), for piano and orchestra; Viola Concerto; Symphony on Marching Songs; Minstrel Show; Harvest, for harp, vibraphone, and strings; Holiday Music; Philharmonic Waltzes; Serenade of Carols; Family Album; Concerto for Tap Dance and Orchestra; Inventions, for four pianos, woodwinds, brass, and percussion; Dance Variations, for two pianos and orchestra; Showpiece; Declaration, for two narrators, speaking male chorus, and orchestra; Jekyll and Hyde Variations; Dialogues, for piano and string orchestra; Festive Music; Columbia—Broadsides for Orchestra; Concerto for Four Guitars and Orchestra.

Piano Music—3 sonatas.

ABOUT

Howard, J. T., Our American Music; Thomson, V., Musical Scene.

Musical America, December 25, 1943.

Percy Grainger
1882–1961

Percy Aldridge Grainger was born in Brighton, Melbourne, Australia, July 8, 1882. His mother, an excellent musician, discovered her son's musical talent and made every effort to develop it. From his fifth year to his tenth, she sat beside him at the piano two hours a day, guiding his first musical steps with such sympathy and insight that by the time Percy was ten he was able to begin a public career as pianist. He continued to study the piano with Louis Pabst. When he was twelve, Grainger had earned enough money as a prodigy to be able to travel with his mother to Germany to continue piano study with James Kwast and composition with Ferruccio Busoni.

PERCY GRAINGER

It was his mother's influence, too, that directed Grainger toward a career in composition rather than in performance. He composed music from boyhood on, and by the time he was sixteen he was already developing an individual style based partly on his experiments with "beatless music." This was music, as he himself explained, "in which the composer freely uses all intervals, mostly gliding, without being controlled by existing limitations of scale and tonality, and in which all rhythms are free, without beat-cohesion between the various polyphonic parts."

But concert appearances were not abandoned. In 1900 Grainger went to London and made a successful debut. He then proceeded on an extended tour of Great Britain, New Zealand, Australia, and South Africa.

In 1906, in London, Grainger met Edvard Grieg, who was so impressed by the young musician that he invited him to be his guest at his villa, Troldhaugen, in Norway. There Grieg played for Grainger his famous A minor Piano Concerto. At the same time he urged the younger man to perform it at the Leeds

Grainger

Festival in England where Grieg was scheduled to appear as guest conductor. Unfortunately, Grieg's death one month before the Festival deprived the concert of its conductor. But, as the late composer had desired, Grainger performed the concerto and scored a personal triumph.

It was Grainger's friendship with Grieg that encouraged the young composer to begin arranging English folk songs and dances. Grieg had always been interested in Norwegian folk music, and this enthusiasm inspired Grainger to turn his own attention to English folk songs. One result of this interest was a series of orchestral arrangements which brought him his major successes as a composer—among them, *Molly on the Shore*, *Shepherd's Hey*, *Mock Morris*, *Irish Tunes from County Derry*, and *Clog Dance*. His fresh harmonizations and tasteful readaptations of the melodies helped breathe new life into these age-old tunes. "Even when he keeps the folk songs almost within their original dimensions," wrote Cyril Scott, "he has a way of dealing with them which is entirely new, yet at the same time never lacking in taste."

The concerts of Balfour Gardiner at Queen's Hall in London in 1912 first brought Grainger into the limelight as a composer. Here his works for orchestra were introduced, and his compositions became very popular with English concert audiences.

In 1914 Grainger came to the United States. He made a highly successful American debut as pianist on February 11, 1915. He followed it with a performance of the Grieg Piano Concerto with the New York Philharmonic that stirred an ovation. He remained in the United States from that time on; during World War I he enlisted in the United States Army and played in the army band. Besides his extensive concert work, he taught courses in music at the Chicago College of Music from 1919 to 1931 and at New York University, where he was chairman of the music department in 1932–1933.

In 1928 Grainger married Ella Viola Ström in a sensational ceremony at the Hollywood Bowl in California. During these ceremonies there was performed a composition which Grainger wrote expressly for this occasion, *To a Nordic Princess*. The Graingers made their home in White Plains, New York, where Grainger resided up to the time of his death. In 1935 he founded a Grainger museum in Melbourne as a repository of his manuscripts and musical souvenirs.

Speaking of his favorite diversions Grainger once said: "I am passionately fond of football, long walks, wrestling, trotting, swimming, tennis, but find little leisure for any of these pleasures, except trotting, which I do instead of walking on many occasions. I used to be called the 'trotting pianist' in London." Fastidious and methodical about keeping himself physically in shape, Grainger always adhered rigidly to a schedule which called for early hours for sleep and waking, the eating of only the most simple foods, and avoidance of any stimulants. His love of the outdoors often led him to walk from city to city when he was on a concert tour. Once, in South Africa, he walked a distance of sixty-five miles from Pietermaritzburg to Durban, where he was scheduled to give a concert in a few days. At another time, he covered—alone and on foot—the desert of South Australia, completing the eighty-mile distance in three days.

In his concerts he always tried to achieve an engaging informality. He frequently prefaced a performance by making comments to his audience. At one of his recitals he arrived by way of the lobby, entered the concert hall, and proceeded to walk down the aisle—stopping off here and there to shake the hands of friends. Then, after springing to the stage, he went over to the piano to begin his recital.

Though most of Grainger's music reveals the influence of English folk songs, some of his compositions were experimental. His use of beatless music has already been commented upon. He also experimented with unusual polyrhythmic combinations and evolved his own methods of notation. In addition, he always favored colloquial English tempo and dynamic markings in preference to the more conventional ones in Italian.

Percy Grainger died in White Plains on February 20, 1961.

MAJOR WORKS

Chamber Music—Hill Song, Nos. 1 and 2; Walking Tune, for wind quintet; My Robin Is to the Greenwood Gone, for flute, English horn, and six strings; Willow, Willow, for baritone, four strings, and guitar; The Twa Corbies, for baritone and seven strings; Lisbon, for flute, oboe, clarinet, horn, and bassoon.

244

Choral Music—Over 30 settings of Kipling's poems including *The Jungle Book*, cycle; Marching Song of Democracy; The Bride's Tragedy; The Merry Wedding; Father and Daughter; Sir Eglamore; Tribute to Foster; The Lads of Wamphrey; The Lost Lady Found; Marching Tune; I'm Seventeen Come Sunday; County Derry Air; The Three Ravens.

Orchestral Music—In a Nutshell, suite; Molly on the Shore; Colonial Song; Shepherd's Hey; Mock Morris; Irish Tune from County Derry; Handel in the Strand; Youthful Suite; To a Nordic Princess; English Dance; Green Bushes; Blithe Bells; Danish Folk Song Suite; The Warriors.

ABOUT

Howard, J. T., Our American Composers; Parker, D. C., Percy Grainger: A Study; Taylor, R. L., The Running Pianist.

Musical Quarterly, April 1937.

Enrique Granados
1867–1916

Enrique Granados, the son of an army officer, was born in Lérida, Spain, July 27, 1867. One of his father's fellow officers was impressed with his sensitive responses to music and gave him his first lessons. Enrique was still a child when his family moved to Barcelona. There he entered the Conservatory and studied the piano with Pujol and Jurnet, winning first prize in 1883. A year later he went on to Madrid. While earning his living playing the piano in theatre and café orchestras, he attended the Conservatory for three years. His teacher in composition, Felipe Pedrell, was responsible for arousing and stimulating his interest in Spanish folk songs and dances and in the mission of using them as the basis of serious composition.

Provided with funds by a French music patron, Granados went to Paris in 1887 to enter the Conservatory. An attack of typhoid fever prevented him from taking the entrance examinations and enrolling in the Conservatory, and so he took lessons privately with Charles de Bériot while attending some of the Conservatory classes as an auditor. During this period he shared an apartment on the rue de Trévise with the Spanish-born concert pianist Ricardo Viñes.

Granados returned to Barcelona in 1889. On April 20, 1890, he launched his career as concert pianist with a highly successful recital.

Granados: grä nä′ thōs

In 1892 he appeared as soloist with an orchestra and introduced the first of his famous Spanish Dances in a version for piano and orchestra. A set of these, *Spanish Dances* for solo piano, twelve in number, was published in 1893 and included the now celebrated *Andaluza* and *Rondalla Aragonesa*. These Dances were Granados' first important contributions to Spanish national music. More significant still were the two books of piano pieces collectively entitled *Goyescas*, which he introduced on March 11, 1911. These compositions were inspired by the paintings and tapestries of the Spanish painter Goya, as well as by incidents and events in Goya's life and era.

ENRIQUE GRANADOS

Goyescas ranks with Albéniz' *Iberia* as one of the monuments in Spanish piano music and one of the most successful realizations of a native Spanish musical art. Here is what Granados himself once said about Spanish folk music: "The musical interpretation of Spain is not to be found in tawdry boleros and habaneras, in *Carmen*, in anything accompanied by tambourines or castanets. The music of my nation is more complex, more poetic, and more subtle." With specific reference to *Goyescas* he went on to explain: "I intended to give a personal note, a mixture of bitterness and grace . . . rhythm, color, and life that are typically Spanish; and a sentiment suddenly amorous and passionate, dramatic and tragic, such as is seen in the works of Goya."

Granados

In discussing *Goyescas*, J. B. Trend wrote: "What Granados introduced into the music of northern Europe might be described as a gesture. 'Stately Spanish grace' is the first thing that strikes one in such a piece as *Los Requiebros* in the first book. . . . In his way of writing for the piano he owed much to Liszt; the texture of his music is definitely nineteenth century—that is to say, German. Yet his sense of form—or, as some critics hastily conclude, the absence of it—was also new; he rambled on, making his points by repetition (like a Spanish poet) and saying the same things in a number of delightful and decorative ways."

From 1892 to 1898 Granados earned his living by giving piano concerts and teaching. Early in the 1890's he married Amparo Gal. Their first child, Eduardo, born in 1894, became a successful composer. They had five other children.

One of his pupils (and subsequently an eminent interpreter of Granados' piano music) was Joaquín Nin, who left us the following impression of Granados: "I was seduced by his exuberant imagination, his delicious blunders, his unexpected confusion, his nobility, his tragic-comic outbursts, his large eyes always ready to weep, to laugh, to admire, or to show astonishment at everything, the fantastic recitals of his extraordinary adventures, his talks streaked with irony and candor, with refinement and elegance, with contemplation and with activity, with humor and with gravity, with uneasiness and serenity."

To Alicia de Larrocha, one of the most distinguished interpreters of Granados' piano music today, he was a "mixture of child and man, enormously sensitive, full of *prontos*, ready to laugh with tears in eyes. Perhaps it was not for nothing that he inherited the blood of the Antilles from his Cuban father. He was easily influenced by the sounds of music or the glance of a lovely *maja*, quick to respond to the brightness or shadows of life, or to forget its realities. One Granados had a distant look, a mind of dreams and imagination. The other Granados was passionate and involved, capable of profound enthusiasm and strong moods and communicative wit."

On November 12, 1898, Granados' first opera, *María del Carmen*, was successfully produced in Madrid. *Picarol* was given in 1901, and *Follet* in 1903. But it was more than a decade after that before Granados succeeded in writing and having produced an opera to rival his best piano music in artistic distinction.

On April 14, 1914, Granados gave a highly successful piano recital at the Salle Pleyel in Paris in a program made up of his own compositions. On the strength of this triumph he was made Chevalier of the Legion of Honor and given a commission by the Paris Opéra to write a new Spanish opera. To fulfill the assignment, Granados decided to adapt his piano suite *Goyescas*, for the stage; a libretto was prepared for him by Fernando Periquet, set in nineteenth century Spain. The outbreak of World War I prevented production by the Paris Opéra, and it was accepted instead by the Metropolitan Opera in New York.

The opera *Goyescas* was heard for the first time in New York on January 28, 1916, and was a great success. Granados made his first visit to the United States to attend the première, despite the fact that Europe was at war. It is interesting to note that the most famous single musical episode in the entire opera—the ever popular Intermezzo—was written after the opera had gone into rehearsal at the Metropolitan and thus was not part of the original score. The Metropolitan Opera directors felt the need for an orchestral interlude at one point in the opera and suggested to Granados that he write one. The sensuous melody Granados created for his Intermezzo is probably his best-known and is familiar not only in its original version for orchestra but also in numerous and varied transcriptions.

In his review, Richard Aldrich wrote in the New York *Times:* "There is no question that the opera is intensely Spanish in its whole texture and feeling; that it is charged with the atmosphere of the country and vibrates through and through with the musical quality of Spain as does no other opera and no other music heard here. The music is Spanish, coming from the brain and the heart of a real Spaniard. . . . And yet, possessing as it does an intensely national color, what he has written is a personal, individual expression. . . . This music has a haunting power."

During his visit to the United States, Granados was invited by President Wilson to perform at the White House. The invitation compelled Granados to postpone his return to Europe by a week, a decision that proved fatal. He left America full of high hopes for the future, his head teeming with ambitious projects. At Folkstone he boarded the Sussex bound for Dieppe across the Channel. One hour and ten minutes after sailing, on March 24, 1916, the Sussex was torpedoed and sunk by a German submarine. Granados was one of the victims.

Granados was a passionate collector of books, paintings, and firearms. He was also an ardent sportsman whose particular interests included automobile racing and motorcycling.

MAJOR WORKS

Chamber Music—Serenata, for two violins and piano; Piano Trio; Oriental, for oboe and strings; Madrigal, for cello and piano.

Choral Music—Cant de les Estrelles.

Operas—María del Carmen; Petrarca; Picarol; Follet; Gaziel; Liliana; Goyescas.

Piano Music—Bocetos, children's pieces; Cuentos para la Juventud; Danzas Españolas, four sets; Escenas Poéticas; Escenas Románticas; Estudios Expresivos; Goyescas; Libro de Horas; Rapsodia Aragonesa; Valses Poéticos.

Vocal Music—Colección de Canciones Amatorias; Colección de Tonadillas Escritas en Estilo Antiguo; La Maja Dolorosa.

ABOUT

Chase, G., The Music of Spain; Collet, H., Albéniz et Granados; Subira, J., Enrique Granados; Trend, J. B., Falla and Spanish Music; Van Vechten, C. The Music of Spain; Vicens, F., Enrique Granados. High Fidelity, December 1967; Musical Observer, February 1916; Musical Opinion (London), March 1967; Musical Times (London), August 1917, September 1919; Revista Musical Catalana (Granados Number), June 15, 1916.

Alexander Gretchaninoff
1864–1956

Alexander Tikhonovich Gretchaninoff was born in Moscow, on October 25, 1864. His father, who came from a family of merchants, did not believe that music was an essential part of a good education, and for a long time he discouraged musical activity at home. It was not until Alexander was thirteen that he first came into direct contact with music, when a piano was brought into the Gretchaninoff household for Alexander's sister. So belated was the boy's musical education that he was sixteen before he became acquainted with even

Gretchaninoff: gryĕ chŭ nyē′ nôf

the names of Bach and Mozart. He derived a considerable amount of pleasure from the piano, and spent hours improvising. With his mother as ally, he finally succeeded in breaking down his father's resistance to his musical training. In his seventeenth year he entered the Moscow Conservatory where his teachers included Safonov, Laroche, and Arensky. Because of his haphazard and inadequate background he was not a particularly outstanding student. Indeed, Arensky once told him that he had no talent whatsoever and that he should give up all thoughts of becoming a professional musician. "I am not one of those fortunate people whose path of life is strewn with roses," he wrote many years later in a memoir, recalling Arensky's discouraging advice. "Even in my own eyes, I doubted myself. Was I sufficiently gifted, I wondered, to achieve success in life as a creative artist? Such moods were not of long duration, fortunately."

ALEXANDER GRETCHANINOFF

After leaving the Moscow Conservatory, Gretchaninoff went to St. Petersburg to enroll in the Conservatory. There, under the guidance of Rimsky-Korsakov, he suddenly blossomed as an outstanding music student. He fell in love with Vera Ivanova Röhrberg, daughter of an engineer. Vera's father set a condition for his consent to the marriage: that the lovers be separated for a full year. This condition was met. Gretchaninoff and Vera Ivanova were married on February 21, 1891, with Rimsky-Korsakov as best man.

Gretchaninoff

Gretchaninoff's first success as a composer came in March 1893 with the première of his *Concert Overture*, in D minor, performed at the St. Petersburg Conservatory. Three months later he conducted the first performance of *Samson*, a cantata written as a graduation piece. Before the end of 1893 he had completed his first symphony, in B minor, which was heard on January 26, 1895, with Rimsky-Korsakov conducting. The reception to the symphony was lukewarm. But another composition performed that year made a profound impression: *North and South*, the composer's first significant contribution to choral music, the field in which he would henceforth prove uniquely productive.

When his schooling ended, Gretchaninoff lived for six years in St. Petersburg, earning his living by teaching music. He suffered such intense poverty that he finally decided upon a change of scene with the hope of improving his situation. He returned to Moscow where, in 1901, he completed the writing of his first opera, *Dobrynia Nikititch*, which was accepted by the Bolshoi Theatre in Moscow. After numerous postponements that almost broke the composer's heart and spirit, the opera was finally produced on October 27, 1903, with Feodor Chaliapin in the leading role. The opera was a triumph, "such as rarely happens in a composer's life," Gretchaninoff later recalled. "From morning on, a series of congratulatory telegrams from friends and acquaintances poured into my apartment. The trophies of my triumph, wreaths and gifts, were on exhibition in my workroom." Soon after the première, the opera was heard in St. Petersburg and Kiev; and in time it became a part of the regular repertory of every major Russian opera house.

By this time Gretchaninoff had also initiated his career as a composer of sacred music. His first liturgy, *St. John Chrysostom*, op. 13, was completed in 1897. It dissatisfied him, and five years later he wrote a new liturgy, *St. John Chrysostom*, op. 29, introduced in Moscow March 2, 1903. This second liturgy was widely praised. The critic Kashkin called it "a work of genius in its inventiveness, its simplicity, and its superb poetic spirit."

In time Gretchaninoff produced an entire library of sacred music which covered all the services of the Russian Orthodox Church.

His liturgies are among the finest examples of Russian religious music in the twentieth century. Sabaneyev called Gretchaninoff "a perfect master of choral orchestration, if one may use this expression, knowing ideally and to perfection the properties of the human voice . . . extracting from choral masses utterly unexpected and frequently overpowering effects."

The *Missa Oecumenica* is one of Gretchaninoff's most ambitious and most impressive liturgical compositions. He intended it for the religious service, not of any single church but of all churches, embodying as it does a universal concept. Built along spacious lines, it is consistently dramatic and rhapsodical, with powerful climaxes and surges of choral sounds predominating. He wrote the Mass in the period between 1938 and 1943, and it was given its world première in Boston on February 25, 1944, with Koussevitzky conducting the Boston Symphony.

Almost as important as his choral music for the church are his songs, which number over two hundred and fifty. His first opus, written in the years between 1887 and 1892, is a set of five songs. One of these, "Lullaby" or "Cradle Song," is a little masterpiece which is still one of its composer's most popular art songs. A second set of four songs followed in 1893 in which can be found that perennial favorite "On the Steppe." In the more than two hundred songs that followed (Gretchaninoff continued writing songs until the end of his life) he revealed a wide variety of mood and style and a most sensitive feeling for poignant emotion and haunting lyricism. "The main characteristics of Gretchaninoff's songs," wrote M. D. Calvocoressi, "are refinement, easy grace and sentiment which at its best owes little to sentimentality."

Gretchaninoff also produced five symphonies, the finest of which are the last two. The fourth, in C major (1924), was written in memory of Tchaikovsky and was given in New York for the first time anywhere on April 9, 1942, with John Barbirolli conducting the New York Philharmonic. The fifth, in G minor (1936), was heard first in Philadelphia April 5, 1939, Stokowski conducting the Philadelphia Orchestra. Gretchaninoff's choral music and songs were derived mainly from authentically Russian sources; his symphonies, however, are Germanic both as to structure and post-Romantic style.

In recognition of his significant contributions to Russian music, Gretchaninoff was pensioned by the Czar shortly after 1910. The composer was in complete sympathy with the February 1917 revolution—so much so that he wrote *A Hymn to Free Russia* to honor the provisional government of Prince Lwow. But the Bolshevik Revolution of October 1917 was a different matter. From then on he silently opposed the new government and its Communist ideals and waited for the time when he could escape from Russia. Finally, in 1925, he settled in Paris where, for a number of years, he remained active as a composer, conductor, and teacher of singing. In the years between 1929 and 1936 he made five concert tours of the United States. His first appearance in America took place at Carnegie Hall, New York, on January 17, 1929, when he served as pianist in a recital of his songs by Nina Koshetz. On March 25, 1929, he directed in New York a performance of his *Domestic Liturgy* (*Third Liturgy of St. John Chrysostom*) written in 1917. When he returned to the United States in 1939 for his fifth tour, he planned to stay only three months, but the outbreak of World War II intervened and, when France was overrun by the Nazis, Gretchaninoff decided to stay in the United States permanently. He became a citizen in 1946.

In an article on Gretchaninoff, Igor Bazaroff wrote as follows: "Gretchaninoff's personal habits are scrupulous and orderly. He likes his wife to cook for him and rarely eats anywhere but at home. After his dinner at one o'clock he takes a walk in Central Park, and he is so punctual that it is said even the squirrels set their watches by his entrance. His walk takes over forty minutes after which he returns home. At four o'clock he has a cup of tea, then works on his compositions until seven thirty when he has supper. His evenings are usually devoted to visiting his many musical friends."

One of Gretchaninoff's last appearances in public took place on October 26, 1954, in New York in a concert of his compositions honoring his ninetieth birthday. Death came at his home on West Seventy-fifth Street January 3, 1956.

MAJOR WORKS

Chamber Music—4 string quartets; 2 piano trios; 2 violin sonatas; 2 clarinet sonatas; Fifteen Bashkirian Melodies, for flute and piano (also violin and piano); Suite, for cello and piano; 4 Morceaux, for violin and piano; Cello Sonata; Bashkiria, fantasy on Bashkirian themes, for flute and harp; 3 Morceaux, for violin and piano; Brimborions, twelve pieces for oboe and piano; Scherzo, for flute, violin, viola, cello, and harp; Concertino, for two clarinets (or recorders) and piano; Septet (arranged from Sonata No. 2, for clarinet and piano); Poème, for violin and piano; Mélodie, for cello and piano.

Choral Music—Various cantatas, liturgies, Motets, Masses, oratorios, part songs; various a cappella and children's choruses; various vocal quartets.

Operas—Dobrynia Nikititch; Sister Beatrice; The Dream of a Little Christmas Tree, children's opera; The Castle Mouse, children's opera; The Cat, the Fox, and the Rooster, children's opera; The Marriage.

Orchestral Music—5 symphonies; Violin Concerto in C minor; In Modo Antico, for violin and orchestra; Suite, for cello and orchestra; Idylle Forestière, divertissement de ballet (also for small orchestra); Rhapsody on a Russian Theme (also for violin and piano); Concerto da Camera, for flute and orchestra; Triptyque, suite for harp and string orchestra; Six Russian Folk Songs, suite; Poème Élégiaque; Festival Overture; Poème Lyrique; Valse de Concert.

Piano Music—2 sonatas; 2 sonatinas; Arabesques, Aquarelles, Moments Lyriques, Miniatures, Pastels; Children's Album; On the Green Meadow; Pensées Fugitives; Historiettes; Grandfather's Album; Glass Beads; Russian Folk Dances, two volumes; Andrusha's Album; Brimborions; Fragments Lyriques; Promenade au Bois; Suite Miniature; Gouaches; Lettres Amicales.

Vocal Music—Over 250 songs for voice and piano including The Captive, Cradle Song (or Lullaby), Death, Declaration of Love, Dewdrops, Evening Bells, Night, O My Country, On the Steppe, Rain, The Snowdrop, Snowflakes, The Wounded Birch; vocal duos.

ABOUT

Gretchaninoff, A., My Life; Montagu-Nathan, M., Contemporary Russian Composers; Sabaneyev, L., Modern Russian Composers.

Musical Quarterly, July 1942.

Charles Tomlinson Griffes
1884–1920

Charles Tomlinson Griffes was born on September 17, 1884, in Elmira, New York. His interest in music became apparent early in his life. As a child he was able to imitate the sounds of birds with remarkable fidelity. When he was eight, he started to study the piano (his sister gave him lessons), but since he

Griffes: grĭf′ ĕs

detested practicing, he soon abandoned music and directed his innate artistic inclinations to painting. However, after recovering from an attack of typhoid fever, he listened to his sister playing a Beethoven sonata and the experience apparently convinced him that it was music after all, and not art, that appealed most to him. He resumed piano lessons, this time with a local teacher, Mary Selena Broughton, and became a dedicated pupil. He participated in various musical activities in Elmira, playing the organ at the Lutheran church, serving as accompanist for the YMCA chorus, and performing on the piano at concerts arranged by his teacher.

CHARLES TOMLINSON GRIFFES

While attending high school he decided to become a professional musician. In 1903, with funds provided by Miss Broughton, he went to Berlin, where he enrolled at the Stern Conservatory. There he studied piano with Gottfried Gaston and composition with Humperdinck. He gave a number of piano recitals, but, eventually he came to the conclusion that his future lay not in playing the piano but in composing. The first fruits of this decision were a number of songs and piano pieces, all of them, as Norman Peterkin noted, "teutonic in style, rather sentimental in spirit, and the best that one can say of them is that it is the work of a good and sure craftsman."

In 1907 Griffes returned to the United States, where he taught music at the Hackley School in Tarrytown, New York, at a salary of thirty-six dollars a week with room and board. He detested the work and was bored by his pupils. Nevertheless, circumstances compelled him to hold the job for the rest of his life. While performing these teaching chores, he continued to study music assiduously by himself and became an admirer of the music of the Russian national school and that of the French Impressionists. Their influence helped him to arrive at a style of his own, free from Germanic influences—a style in which Impressionism became dominant, accompanied by a partiality for Oriental colors and melodies.

His first significant piano pieces were Impressionist rather than Oriental. They included *The Lake at Evening*, *The Night Winds*, *The Vale of Dreams*, and *Barcarolle*, composed in the years between 1910 and 1913. His most important piano music in an Impressionist style was the *Four Roman Sketches* (1916).

The first movement of *Four Roman Sketches*, entitled "The White Peacock," is regarded by many critics as one of Griffes' greatest works. The inspiration here was a poem by William Sharp describing a white peacock moving in a sunlit garden "as the breath, as the soul of beauty." Griffes orchestrated this piano piece for a choreographic production at the Rivoli Theatre in New York in June 1919. The orchestral version received its first concert performance in Philadelphia on December 19, 1919, Leopold Stokowski conducting the Philadelphia Orchestra.

Impressionism was combined with a strong Oriental strain in another of Griffes' masterworks, the tone poem *The Pleasure Dome of Kubla Khan* (1916). The source was Coleridge's poem, specifically the lines telling of the "stately pleasure-dome . . . a miracle of rare device, a sunny pleasure-dome with caves of ice!" Griffes goes on to explain: "I have given my imagination free rein in the description of this strange place as well as of purely imaginary revelry which might take place there. The vague, foggy beginning suggests the sacred river, running 'through caverns measureless to man down to a sunless sea.' Then gradually rise the outlines of the palace with 'walls and towers . . . girdled round.' The gardens with fountains and 'sunny spots of greenery' are next suggested. From inside come sounds of dancing and revelry which increase to a wild climax, and then suddenly break off. There is a return to the original mood suggesting the sacred river and the 'caves of ice.' "

This tone poem was accepted for performance by the Boston Symphony. Too poor to hire a copyist for the orchestral parts, Griffes did all the work himself, during the hours of night when he was not occupied with his duties as a teacher. Always sensitive in health, he broke down under the strain of this labor. When the Boston Symphony introduced the tone poem in Boston on November 28, 1919, Pierre Monteux conducting, it met with a most enthusiastic response. The *Transcript* described the composition as "music of imagery at almost every turn of the illusion, music throughout of a talent and a temperament taking their own visioning and expressing way, music unlike that of any other composer, yet uncommonly vivid in immediate expression." The *Globe* found that the work exhibited "genuine originality and power of a sort that entitle its composer to be judged by the same standard as men like Ravel, Rachmaninoff and Stravinsky." Olin Downes, then a Boston critic, said: "Mr. Griffes is a man to watch with care.... He is a young American, full of spirit and receptivity, astonishingly progressive, as shown by the texture of a score of a man who has been musically educated in Germany; he has temperament in abundance; he loves to write."

This success was one of the greatest enjoyed by a serious American composer up to that time. As a result, commissions began to pour in for Griffes—for an opera, for a ballet, for new symphonic works. But Griffes had never fully recovered from his physical setback just before the première of his tone poem and during Christmas of 1919 he broke down again, this time a victim of pleurisy. Suspected of having tuberculosis, he was soon sent to a sanatorium in Loomis, New York. There tuberculosis was finally ruled out. But by this time, Griffes was suffering from empyema, abscesses of the lungs resulting from influenza. After an operation on April 5, 1920, that accomplished little to relieve his condition, he died on April 8. Funeral services were held at the Community Chapel of the Church of the Messiah in New York City on April 10. The body was interred in Bloomfield, New Jersey.

Among Griffes' Oriental compositions were several completed in 1917: *Five Poems of Ancient China and Japan;* and two Japanese dance-dramas, *Sho-Jo* and *The Kairn of Koridwen.* In still another composition, written in the years between 1916 and 1918, Griffes drew material from the music of the American Indian: *Two Sketches,* for string quartet.

In one of his finest concert works, the *Poem,* for flute and orchestra, Impressionism is neatly blended with quasi-Orientalism. Griffes wrote his *Poem* for the flutist Georges Barrère, who introduced it with the New York Symphony Society, under Walter Damrosch, on November 16, 1919.

But whatever his idiom, Griffes was a sensitive tone poet. "Like Debussy," says John Tasker Howard, "Griffes was more interested in tints than in solid colors. ... Griffes has occasionally given us harmonies that are exquisite in themselves, dependent on nothing that goes before or that follows. Modes and Oriental scales seem to have held a fascination for him. ... Of Griffes' many gifts, the power of description seems preeminent."

A three-day festival of Griffes' music was held at Elmira College, Elmira, New York, November 20–22, 1964, in commemoration of the eightieth anniversary of the composer's birth.

MAJOR WORKS

Ballets—The Kairn of Koridwen; Sho-Jo.
Chamber Music—Two Sketches, for string quartet.
Choral Music—These Things Shall Be.
Orchestral Music—The White Peacock; The Pleasure Dome of Kubla Khan; Poem, for flute and orchestra.
Piano Music—Three Tone Poems; Fantasy Pieces; Four Roman Sketches (including The White Peacock); Sonata in F.
Vocal Music—Various songs for voice and piano including By a Lonely Forest Pathway, and Lament of Ian the Proud; Two Rondels; Three Poems of Fiona MacLeod; Five Poems of Ancient China and Japan.

ABOUT

Chase, G., America's Music; Howard, J. T., Our American Music; Maisel, E. M., Charles Tomlinson Griffes.

Musical Quarterly, July 1923, July 1943.

Louis Gruenberg
1884–1964

Louis Gruenberg was born on August 3, 1884, in Brest-Litovsk, Russia. When he was two

Gruenberg: gr$\overline{oo}$′ ĕn bûrg

years old he was brought to the United States. He was educated in the New York City public schools and he studied piano with Adele Margulies. His determination to become a serious musician took him to Germany in 1903. He resided in Berlin for a long time and studied piano and composition with Ferruccio Busoni. From time to time he took special courses at the Vienna Conservatory where, in 1912, he was made a tutor. Also in 1912 he made his debut as a pianist, appearing as soloist with the Berlin Philharmonic. At about this time he also completed the writing of his first tone poem, *The Hill of Dreams*, which received a prize of one thousand dollars. He had previously written two operas and some chamber music.

LOUIS GRUENBERG

In 1919 Gruenberg returned to the United States. *The Hill of Dreams* won the Flagler Prize and received its première performance in New York on October 23, 1921. During this period, Gruenberg worked on a new opera, *The Dumb Wife*, based on Anatole France's play. He completed the opera in 1921 only to discover that he could never get it performed since he had failed to clear the rights with Anatole France's executors. He made three trips to Paris to urge them to change their minds but was unsuccessful.

In the early 1920's Gruenberg became interested in the artistic possibilities of jazz and completed several compositions in which this style was effectively used. The best was *Daniel

Jazz (1923), for tenor and eight instruments, which received its première in New York on February 22, 1925. In this composition Gruenberg succeeded in bringing new dimensions to and opening new horizons for jazz idioms. When it is recalled that *Daniel Jazz* was written a year before Gershwin's *Rhapsody in Blue*, its significance as a pioneer experiment in making serious use of jazz materials becomes evident. Other jazz compositions with ambitious structures, intended for concert presentation, included the *Jazz Suite* for Orchestra, which the Cincinnati Symphony introduced on March 22, 1929, and *Jazzettes*, for violin and piano.

In 1930 Gruenberg entered a revised version of his First Symphony, which he had written a decade earlier, in a competition sponsored by the RCA Victor Company. It received a prize of five thousand dollars. (The première took place in Boston on February 10, 1934, with Koussevitzky conducting the Boston Symphony.) But, on January 7, 1933, Gruenberg received national attention when the Metropolitan Opera introduced *The Emperor Jones*, based on Eugene O'Neill's play, with Lawrence Tibbett in the title role. Gruenberg had consulted with O'Neill in Paris concerning the operatic possibilities of his drama. They met at midnight and talked for hours, until Gruenberg was able to persuade O'Neill not only to give him the necessary permission but also to allow him to make some essential changes. Having received O'Neill's blessing, Gruenberg had Kathleen de Jaffa prepare a libretto for him. Then, renting a house in Old Orchard, Maine, he spent fourteen months of intensive work on the opera.

The Emperor Jones is Gruenberg's most important work, and one of the most distinguished operas by an American. Performed at the Metropolitan Opera for two seasons, it was also produced in San Francisco, on November 17, 1933. In 1934 it was given in Amsterdam; and in 1952, in Rome. From time to time, since then, it has been revived in different cities of the United States.

Here is Marion Bauer's analysis of Gruenberg's score: "The mood of Jones, first in his braggadocio, then in his panic as it increases, is mirrored in the music. Gruenberg has achieved a new and original effect in the opera in treating the orchestra as background to the exciting and moving drama. Although incidental, the music, played apart from the opera, would probably be one of the most extraordinary scores of modern times. The composer has lost all sense of personality in the primitive force of the music. Short-breathed phrases follow each other in rapid succession. The deeper-toned instruments are used to create a somber, sinister web over which the highest registers of the woodwinds and violins flare up shriekingly."

Gruenberg (who had edited four volumes of Negro spirituals) was, indeed, only passingly influenced by Negro music in the writing of this operatic score: one such moment is an original "spiritual," *Standin' in the Need of Prayer*, which Brutus Jones sings towards the close of the opera.

Another major work partly influenced by Negro folk music is the Concerto for Violin and Orchestra. It was commissioned by Jascha Heifetz who introduced it with the Philadelphia Orchestra, Eugene Ormandy conducting, December 1, 1944. In the second movement, Gruenberg quotes several measures from two Negro spirituals. In the third movement, however, Gruenberg passes to other bits of Americana when he interpolates some measures from *The Arkansas Traveler* and provides a musical description of a religious revival meeting. Olin Downes described the concerto as "cheerful, melodious, lively, and externally idiomatic."

Gruenberg was for many years active in societies promoting modern music. He was president of the American section of the International Society for Contemporary Music, and was one of the cofounders of the League of Composers in New York. For three years, from 1933 to 1936, he was head of the composition department of Chicago Musical College. Following this he made his home at Santa Monica, California, and for a number of years wrote music for films. On three occasions he received Academy Awards: for *The Fight for Life*, *So Ends Our Night*, and *Commandos Strike at Dawn*. In 1947 he was elected a member of the National Institute of Arts and Letters.

Finally, giving up motion-picture work, Gruenberg lived a solitary and withdrawn life in the 1950's and 1960's at Santa Monica, working hard on compositions. His failure to get these works performed caused him much bitterness, as did the fact that he was rapidly being forgotten by performers and audiences. As he wrote to a friend: "I am working constantly, passionately and carefully, and I firmly believe that I am doing my best work now. . . . I could use a publisher, a record company; but the world of yesterday seems to have forgotten me and the world of today does not know me."

An attempt to lift him out of this undeserved and prolonged neglect was made early in 1964 by means of a concert of his works to help celebrate his eightieth birthday. The cup of Gruenberg's bitterness flowed over when he heard of these plans. He replied angrily: "I'll have none of this eighty-year-old stuff! I was forgotten on my seventieth, my sixtieth and my fiftieth birthdays (where in hell was everybody when I needed this kind of treatment?) but now I don't need anybody. If my stuff is to be played, it will be because it is worthy of being played, and not because I am an old dog who is being thrown a bone!"

The eightieth-birthday concert never took place. Louis Gruenberg died at the Cedars of Lebanon Hospital in Los Angeles June 9, 1964. The work he regarded as his most ambitious was one of his last, the opera *Antony and Cleopatra*.

MAJOR WORKS

Chamber Music—2 piano quintets; 2 string quartets; Violin Sonata; Suite for Violin and Piano; Indiscretions, for string quartet; Daniel Jazz, for tenor and eight instruments; Creation, for baritone and eight instruments; Jazzettes, for violin and piano; Diversions, for string quartet.

Choral Music—A Song of Faith, spiritual rhapsody for narrator, solo voices, chorus, and orchestra.

Operas—The Witch of Brocken; The Bride of the Gods; The Dumb Wife; Jack and the Beanstalk; Emperor Jones; Queen Helena; Green Mansions (radio opera); Antony and Cleopatra.

Orchestral Music—5 symphonies; 2 piano concertos; The Hill of Dreams, tone poem; Enchanted Isle, tone poem; Vagabondia; Jazz Suite; Music for an Imaginary Ballet, two series; Nine Moods; Serenade to a Beauteous Lady; Violin Concerto; Americana, suite; Dance Rhapsody; Music to an Imaginary Legend; Variations on a Pastoral Theme.

Piano Music—Jazzberries; Polychromatics; Jazz Masks; Six Jazz Epigrams; Three Jazz Dances.

Vocal Music—Animals and Insects; Four Contrasting Songs.

ABOUT

Bauer, M., Twentieth Century Music; Chase, G., America's Music; Rosenfeld, P., Discoveries of a Music Critic.

Camargo Guarnieri
1907–

Camargo Mozart Guarnieri was born in Tietê, in the state of São Paulo, Brazil, on February 1, 1907. His father, a Sicilian by birth, was a direct descendant of the Guarnieri family, violin makers of Cremona; his mother belonged to a wealthy and powerful family in São Paulo which had disinherited her when she chose to marry a humble musician. His father, who earned a living playing the flute in theatre orchestras and in the town band, was Camargo's first teacher. "We had a small portable piano which helped to untangle our finances," Guarnieri recalled in an autobiographical sketch. "It was always on loan at the movie house or at a local dance. If I wanted to play, I had to roam with the piano. I continued my piano lessons, dividing my time between music and a passion for collecting spiders and scorpions, which I kept in a drawer until my outraged father threw out the collection."

CAMARGO GUARNIERI

While he was still a boy, the Guarnieri family moved to the city of São Paulo. Camargo continued his study at the São Paulo Conservatory where he was an honor student of Braga and Antonio de Sá Pereira in piano and of Baldi in composition. His studies completed, Guarnieri helped support his family

Guarnieri: gwär nyâ′ rē

by playing the piano in cabarets and motion picture theatres and by working in a music-publishing house. The job with the publisher provided him with an opportunity to become acquainted with a classical library. "I studied [it] starting systematically with the letter *A*. Somewhere along in the *W*'s I got fired because I had been engaged to play dance and not classical music. This was a blow to the family purse: Father and I were the sole family supporters."

In 1927 Guarnieri joined the faculty of the São Paulo Conservatory where he conducted a class in piano; five years later he was promoted to assistant professor. He also became, in 1930, the conductor of a local choral society with which he made several recordings of Brazilian folk songs that were distributed in the United States and found a place in the permanent collection of music at the Library of Congress in Washington. At the same time he was busily engaged in composition. His first publication had been a composition called *Rêve d'Artiste*, issued when he was eleven, long before he had had any systematic training. His creative activity became intensified when he finished his schooling at the Conservatory, and his first taste of success came with *Curuçá*, for orchestra, which was conducted by Villa-Lobos in São Paulo on July 28, 1930. On December 30, 1936, he helped introduce his first piano concerto in São Paulo. Several other compositions won important prizes during this period. One of these was the *Flor de Tremembé*, for fifteen solo instruments and percussion, which he wrote in 1937 to honor a charming young lady from Tremembé whom he married soon afterwards.

Early in 1938 Guarnieri was appointed director of the Cultural Department of the Municipality of São Paulo. During the same year, in a contest sponsored by the Council for Artistic Guidance of the State, he was given first prize which consisted of a three-year scholarship for study in Europe. In Paris he studied composition and orchestration with Charles Koechlin and conducting with François Ruhlmann. When war broke out in Europe, Guarnieri returned to Brazil and became a guest conductor of the São Paulo Orchestra. A violin concerto he completed at this time was awarded first prize in 1940 in an international competition sponsored by the

Fleisher Music Collection in Philadelphia. This award brought him an invitation from the Music Division of the Pan American Union to pay his first visit to the United States. He arrived in 1942, at which time a concert of his works was given in New York under the auspices of the League of Composers. Then, on March 26, 1943, he was invited to Boston to conduct the Boston Symphony in the American première of his *Abertura Concertante*, which had previously been introduced in São Paulo on June 2, 1942. This composition–an overture in classical design, dedicated to Aaron Copland–was Guarnieri's first important orchestral composition heard in the United States. From Boston, Guarnieri went to Rochester to direct the American première of his *Dansa Brasileira*, which had been introduced in São Paulo on March 7, 1941.

Following his return to São Paulo, Guarnieri was appointed musical director of the São Paulo Orchestra. He now completed his first symphony, which received the Luiz Peanteado de Rezende Prize as the best modern symphonic work with a Brazilian identity. This symphony received its world première in the United States, during Guarnieri's second visit, when he directed the Boston Symphony on November 29, 1946. Another important world première of a composition by Guarnieri was heard during this visit–the Piano Concerto No. 2, for which in 1946 he once again received the Luiz Peanteado de Rezende prize in Brazil and which was introduced over the CBS radio network in the United States on April 16, 1947. Later the same year Guarnieri won second prize of five thousand dollars for his Second Symphony in a competition sponsored by the Detroit Symphony Orchestra, and on December 26 he attended the world première of his *Prologo e Fugo*, for orchestra, at a concert of the Boston Symphony directed by Eleazar de Carvalho.

Among the prizes gathered by Guarnieri in later years were those of the Fourth Centennial Contest in São Paulo for his Symphony No. 3 in 1954; and, in 1957, first prize in an international contest held in Caracas–for his *Choro*, for piano and orchestra, first presented at the Caracas Music Festival on March 19, 1957. In 1963 he received two medals from the Association of Theatrical Critics in São Paulo, one for his Concertino for Piano and Or-

chestra and another for his third string quartet.

"Ever since his earliest works," wrote Mario Pedrosa, "Guarnieri has tried to express what is most personal and lyrical and, at the same time, racially, or collectively speaking, most representative of the music of Brazil. This he has done, not through pure tonal impression or harmonic virtuosity, ostentatious or exuberant, superficial or chaotic, but through the mysteries and surprises of counterpoint and the architectural structure of polyphonic composition. Guarnieri is the least impressionistic of contemporary Brazilian musicians and the most lyrical." One authority on Brazilian music, Mario de Andrade, has described Guarnieri as "the best polyphonic composer that our land has produced."

"He has everything it takes," commented Aaron Copland in *Modern Music*, "a personality of his own, a finished technique and a fecund imagination. . . . The thing I like best about the music is its healthy emotional expression–it is the honest statement of how one man feels."

In 1960 Guarnieri returned to the faculty of the São Paulo Conservatory, which he had left in 1938, to teach a course in piano and to occupy a chair in orchestration and composition. From December 1960 to October 1961 he served as the director of the Conservatory. In 1964 he was appointed a member of the faculty of the Municipal Conservatory of Santos to teach composition. The world première of his Fourth Symphony took place in Portland, Maine, on December 5, 1967.

MAJOR WORKS

Chamber Music—6 violin sonatas; 3 string quartets; 2 cello sonatas; Piano Trio; Viola Sonata; Tostão de Chuva, for voice and twelve instruments.

Choral Music—A Morte do Aviador, cantata; Drought, cantata; Coloquio, cantata; Guaná-Bará, cantata.

Opera—Pedro Malazarte.

Orchestral Music—4 symphonies; 3 piano concertos; 2 violin concertos; Tres Dansas, for voice and orchestra; Curuçá; Tres Poemas, for voice and orchestra; Abertura Concertante; Encantamento; Prologo e Fuga; Brasiliana, suite; Choro, for violin and orchestra; Variations on a Northeastern Theme, for piano and orchestra; Fourth Centennial Suite; Choro, for piano and orchestra; Choro, for clarinet and orchestra; Piano Concertino; Choro, for cello and orchestra; Serenade, for piano, xylophone, harp, kettledrum, and string orchestra.

Piano Music—50 Ponteios; 6 sonatinas; Toccata; Toada Triste.

Vocal Music—Various songs for voice and piano.

Haieff

ABOUT

Slonimsky, N., Music of Latin America.
Inter-American Monthly, September 1942; Modern Music, January 1941; Musical Digest, February 1948.

Alexei Haieff
1914–

Alexei Haieff was born in Blagoveshchensk, Siberia, on August 25, 1914. When he was six, his family settled in Harbin, Manchuria, where he received both his musical and his academic education. In 1931 he came to the United States, settled permanently in New York City, and turned with a singleness of purpose to the study of music. After some preliminary training with Constantin Shvedoff, he received a scholarship for the Juilliard School of Music, where for the next three years he studied with Frederick Jacobi and Rubin Goldmark. Subsequently he was a student in composition of Nadia Boulanger both at Cambridge, Massachusetts, and in Paris, and in piano of Alexander Siloti.

ALEXEI HAIEFF

Among his earliest compositions were the Sonatina for String Quartet (1937) and *Three Bagatelles*, for oboe and bassoon (1939). When his music studies were terminated, he embarked on still more ambitious creative endeavors by completing two major works for

Haieff: hī´ ĕf

orchestra—a symphony (1942) and a Divertimento (1944). The latter brought him his first recognition when it was introduced by the Barone Little Symphony on April 5, 1946, and soon afterwards was performed by several major American orchestras, including the Boston Symphony on November 1, 1946. This Divertimento is a five-movement suite which the composer had originally written for the piano and afterwards extended into an orchestral version. "Each movement," Haieff explains, "is dedicated to a different friend of mine." One of the movements, however—the *Lullaby*—was meant for "my friends' babies, who were being born in abundance in 1944."

In 1942 Haieff was awarded the Lili Boulanger Memorial Award and a medal from the American Academy in Rome. In 1946 and 1949 he received Guggenheim fellowships, and in 1947 he was given a grant from the National Academy of Arts and Letters. From 1947 to 1948 he was a Fellow at the American Academy in Rome where in 1952–1953, and again in 1958–1959, he was composer-in-residence. In 1962 he served as Slee Professor of Music at the University of Buffalo in New York, and in 1968 he was appointed composer-in-residence at the University of Utah.

The evolution of Haieff's style can be traced in *Eclogue*, for cello and piano, written in 1947 on a commission from the Koussevitzky Music Foundation; Violin Concerto (1948); and Piano Concerto, introduced in New York City on April 27, 1952, when it received the award of the New York Music Critics Circle. That style became fully crystallized in his Second Symphony, which began in 1955 as a piano sonata and, during residence in Rome on a Fulbright fellowship, was adapted for orchestra. "I tried," he said, "to preserve the transparency of the original writing by avoiding any unnecessary doubling or introducing any new contrapuntal voices, and the discipline of the restriction was inspiring and very gratifying. The only structural change in the whole piece is the final chord which instead of being on the first beat, as in the sonata, now, in the symphony, comes on the second." The second symphony was introduced by the Boston Symphony on April 11, 1958, and received the American International Music Fund Award as one of the two most important new

256

symphonic works heard that season in the United States. In 1963 it was performed by the New York Philharmonic under Josef Krips. After that performance, Harold C. Schonberg described it as follows in the New York *Times*, while pointing to the salient qualities of all of Haieff's mature works: "Like most of Haieff's music, it is delicately turned and exquisitely jeweled. Haieff does not go in for the big utterance. This symphony is a very personal mélange of neoclassicism in general (and Stravinsky, in particular), elements of the French school, and a few suggestions of something Russian lurking in the background."

Wilfred Mellers has pointed out that Haieff "likes to 'build' his pieces geometrically from tiny figures, so that the mosaic metaphor is frequently applicable to his forms."

MAJOR WORKS

Ballets—The Princess Zondilda and Her Entourage; Beauty and the Beast.

Chamber Music—Sonata for String Quartet; Three Bagatelles, for oboe and bassoon; Serenade, for oboe, clarinet, bassoon, and piano; Suite for Violin and Piano, Sonata for Two Pianos; Eclogue, for cello and piano; La Nouvelle Héloïse, for harp and string quartet.

Choral Music—A Short Cantata on a Russian Folk Theme.

Orchestral Music—3 symphonies; Divertimento, for small orchestra; Violin Concerto; Piano Concerto.

Piano Music—Five Pieces; Sonata; Sonata for Two Pianos.

ABOUT

Mellers, W., Music in a New Found Land; Reis, C., Composers in America (rev. ed.).

Howard Hanson
1896–

Howard Harold Hanson was born on October 28, 1896, in the town of Wahoo, Nebraska, of Swedish parents. He received his early musical training in this community, which had largely been settled in earlier days by Swedish pioneers. This influence of heredity and environment greatly affected Hanson's early compositions and is particularly reflected in his *Nordic Symphony* in which he pays homage to the land of his parents' birth.

He received his first music lessons when he was six, his mother giving him instruction on the piano. Before long he also took some lessons on the cello. At eight, he wrote his first composition—a piano trio influenced by Grieg. A year later he became a member of a string quartet in which he played the cello. At Wahoo High School he conducted the school orchestra. While at high school he also attended the School of Music at Luther College for courses in harmony and counterpoint and for advanced study in piano and cello. He made numerous appearances in Wahoo churches, both as pianist and organist and was a member of a church choir.

HOWARD HANSON

In 1912 he was graduated from Wahoo High School and from the School of Music at Luther College. At high school he was the class valedictorian; at the School of Music he was graduated with highest honors. Then, for a year, he was a student at the University of Nebraska in Lincoln. Determined to get additional musical training, he left the university and for about half a year played the cello in various popular orchestras. With the money he saved, he went to New York where he enrolled at the Institute of Musical Art. There he studied piano with James Friskin and composition with Percy Goetschius, completing his course of study in a single year.

Another summer of playing the cello in popular orchestras gave him the wherewithal to enroll in Northwestern University, where he combined his further academic education with musical composition. While he was attending Northwestern, one of his compositions,

257

this time a piece for orchestra, received a major performance, at a concert of the Chicago Symphony under Frederick Stock.

He received his bachelor of arts degree from Northwestern University when he was nineteen. In 1916 he was appointed full professor of theory and composition at the College of the Pacific in San Jose, California. Three years later he rose to the position of Dean of the Conservatory of Fine Arts, becoming the youngest such dean in the United States. He held the post until 1921. During this period he completed several works for orchestra, including *Symphonic Prelude* (1916), performed in San Francisco, and *Symphonic Rhapsody*, introduced in Los Angeles in 1919. The latter performance marked the first time that Hanson appeared as a conductor of one of his own compositions.

In 1921 a competition was created for the American Prix de Rome entitling its winners to reside for three years at the American Academy in Rome. Hanson submitted a tone poem, *Before the Dawn*, and was named one of the three winners of the first competition. During his three-year residence in Rome, he wrote his first important compositions, among them *Nordic Symphony* (1922), introduced by the Augusteo Orchestra in Rome on May 30, 1923, the composer conducting. This is a mature work in which Hanson's later fully developed style can already be detected: his adherence to classical structure; his preference for windswept phrases; his fine feeling for tonal beauty. "The symphony," the composer has explained, "is cyclical, the first movement containing the material upon which the entire symphony is based. This movement, strongly Nordic in character, sings of the solemnity, austerity, and grandeur of the North, of its restless surging and strife, of its somberness and melancholy." Both the style and the subject matter of the symphony inspired some critics to dub Hanson "an American Sibelius." Hanson, however, had no knowledge of Sibelius' music at the time he wrote the work, and the symphony is essentially Anglo-Saxon and Midwestern in personality.

Other works written during this Prix de Rome period include two tone poems for orchestra—*North and West* and *Lux Aeterna*— and a string quartet commissioned for the Coolidge Festival in Washington, D.C.

When he returned to the United States in 1924, Hanson was appointed director of the Eastman School of Music at the University of Rochester. He held the post with distinction for forty years, elevating the school to a place of first importance among America's leading conservatories. He retired as director in 1964, at which time he received an appointment as director of the recently founded Institute of American Music of the University of Rochester.

His first significant work following his return to the United States was *The Lament of Beowulf*, for mixed chorus and orchestra (1925), first given at the Ann Arbor Festival in 1926. Here, as in other works of the same period, his style evolved into a happy union of classical structure and romantic feelings. Hanson described his credo as composer as follows: "I am a 'natural' composer. I write music because I have to write it. Though I have a profound interest in theoretical problems, my own music comes 'from the heart' and is a direct expression of my own emotional reactions." Other works of this period include *Pan and the Priest*, tone poem for orchestra, and the Concerto for Organ, Strings, and Harp, both written in 1926; and Hanson's second symphony, the *Romantic* (1930).

As the composer has explained, the *Romantic Symphony* is "an escape from the rather bitter type of modern musical realism . . . [aiming to be] young in spirit, lyrical, and romantic in temperament, and simple and direct in expression." Commissioned by the Boston Symphony for its fiftieth anniversary, it was introduced by that organization November 28, 1930.

Hanson completed four more symphonies, each a noteworthy contribution to American orchestral literature. The third (1936), like the first, paid tribute to Hanson's Swedish ancestry and to the epic qualities of the pioneers who founded the first Swedish settlement on the Delaware in 1638 and later opened up new territory in the West. The symphony was commissioned by CBS Radio, which introduced three of the movements under the composer's direction on September 19, 1937. The complete symphony was then heard in a performance by the NBC Symphony on March 26, 1938, with the composer conducting.

The fourth symphony (1943) was inspired

by the death of Hanson's father. It is a threnody, the four movements of which assume as titles parts of the Requiem Mass (Kyrie, Requiescat, Dies Irae, and Lux Aeterna). The work was heard first in Boston on December 3, 1943, with the composer conducting the Boston Symphony. It was the first symphony to receive the Pulitzer Prize in music.

Hanson's fifth symphony (1953) is subtitled *Sinfonia Sacra*. Here the composer attempted to interpret the story of the First Easter as recounted in the Gospel according to St. John. The symphony was introduced in Philadelphia on February 18, 1955, with Eugene Ormandy conducting the Philadelphia Orchestra.

The world première of Hanson's Sixth Symphony (1967) was given by the New York Philharmonic on March 4, 1968.

Hanson wrote only a single opera, but that one is numbered among his most ambitious and distinguished achievements—*Merry Mount*. It had its first hearing in a concert version at the Ann Arbor Festival on May 20, 1933, and was staged by the Metropolitan Opera in New York on February 10, 1934.

Eugene Goossens, the composer-conductor, was the one who had persuaded Hanson to try his hand at writing an opera. "It was not until I saw the magnificent libretto of Richard Stokes," explains the composer, "that I decided to cast in my lot with the operatic theatre." Based on Nathaniel Hawthorne's *The Maypole of Merry Mount*, the text was set in Colonial New England. The principal character is Pastor Bradford, who is obsessed with passion for the lovely Lady Marigold Sandys, even though he is betrothed to a Puritan girl. His passion leads him to kill his rival, Gower, and finally sends him and the object of his carnal desires to their death in a church burned by attacking Indians. "The libretto contained everything that I had been looking for," Hanson says. "There was, first, the character of the hero, Bradford, passionate and turbulent; there was the contrast of the Puritan and the Cavalier; the opportunity for using the chorus as the emotional protagonist of a moving and tragic story; and last, the possibility for great scenic effects with the ballet and the orchestra as indigenous parts of the whole."

Hanson described his music as follows: "[It] is essentially a lyrical work, and makes use of broad melodic lines as often as possible. There is less parlando than one might expect to find in a contemporary opera, and a greater tendency toward the old arioso style. The form of each small scene within the larger scene is considered as an entity in itself, a series of small forms within a large form, almost as in symphonic structure. Both harmonically and rhythmically, the listener will hear certain Americanisms. In orchestration, too, use has been made of certain orchestral colors and devices which were born on this side of the Atlantic." A good deal of the writing is modal, especially in the music identifying the Puritans, because the composer felt that the characteristics of such melodic modes as Aeolian, Dorian, Phrygian, and Mixo-Lydian were in keeping with Puritan character.

The opera was an outstanding success, receiving about fifty curtain calls at its world première and being repeated eight more times that season. In his review in the New York *World Telegram*, Pitts Sanborn wrote: "Dr. Hanson's music is most effective in the choral passages, which are plentiful. Take the chant of the men within the church after the impressive choral prelude. . . . Nor has Dr. Hanson failed to assemble lively measures for the Maypole dance or to strike the witching note called for by the wild doings at the 'Hellish Rendezvous.'"

Hanson has not written another opera since *Merry Mount*, but he has produced much instrumental and choral music. In addition to his symphonies, other successful works include *Elegy*, commissioned by the Koussevitzky Music Foundation in memory of Serge Koussevitzky for the seventy-fifth anniversary of the Boston Symphony and first presented in Boston on January 20, 1956, Charles Münch conducting; *Mosaics*, commissioned by the Cleveland Orchestra, which introduced it on January 23, 1958; *Summer Seascape*, commissioned by the New Orleans Philharmonic, and presented in New Orleans on March 10, 1959; *Bold Island Suite*, also commissioned by the Cleveland Orchestra and heard on January 25, 1962; *Four Psalms*, for baritone and orchestra, featured at the Festival of Chamber Music in Washington, D.C., on November 1, 1964; and the *Two Psalms*, for baritone, chorus, and orchestra, heard first at Middletown, Indiana, in April 1968.

259

Hanson's forty years as director of the Eastman School of Music placed him in the vanguard of America's music educators. But his activities in the field of education were by no means confined exclusively to his own school. He has served as president of the National Association of Schools of Music; as chairman of the Commission on Curricula of that organization; as president of the Music Teachers' National Association; as chairman of the Commission on Graduate Study of the National Association of Schools of Music; and as a member of the Examining Jury of American Academy in Rome. In addition, he has served as president of the National Music Council and has been a member of the United States Commission for UNESCO. In 1949 he was a delegate to the Paris Conference of UNESCO; in 1950 he was elected to membership in the American Philosophical Society; and in 1956 he became a member of the National Guild for Community Schools. He was appointed to the advisory committee on the arts of the National Cultural Center in Washington, D.C., in 1960; and to the Concert Advisory Panel of the New York State Council of Arts in 1961. In 1961 he also became a Fellow of the American Academy of Arts and Sciences.

To his importance as a composer and educator must be added his achievements as a conductor, and most particularly as a conductor of modern American music, the first such concert taking place on May 1, 1925. For about a quarter of a century he led an annual festival of modern American music in Rochester. By the time he retired, he had directed over fifteen hundred compositions by some seven hundred composers. An outgrowth of this activity were his mission to Germany as guest conductor of several of its leading orchestras for the Oberlaender Trust of the Carl Schurz Memorial Foundation (his programs were devoted entirely to American music) and a three-month tour from November 1961 to February 1962 with the Eastman School Philharmonic Orchestra throughout Europe, the Middle East, and the Soviet Union under the auspices of the State Department of the United States. Hanson has also appeared as a guest conductor of virtually every major American orchestra.

It would be impossible in a limited space to list all the honorary degrees, honors, and awards which Hanson has gathered through the years. About twenty honorary degrees have been conferred on him beginning with a doctorate in music from Northwestern University in 1924 and extending to one given him by the University of Michigan in 1960. In 1945 he received the Alice M. Ditson Award for outstanding contributions to American music; in 1946, the George Foster Peabody Award; in 1957, a citation from the National Federation of Music and the Laurel Leaf Award from the American Composers Alliance; in 1959, the Huntington Hartford Foundation Award; and in 1962 the annual Medal of Honor from the National Arts Club for "notable and inspired contribution to music."

Hanson married late in life, on July 24, 1946, when he was wed to the former Margaret Elizabeth Nelson, a good amateur musician. For many years Hanson presented a youthful appearance, in spite of stooped shoulders and the chin beard which he has worn since his twenty-fourth year. He is over six feet tall and, as Frederick Fennell has written, "his head is large, with finely chiseled features of a striking Nordic countenance dominated by blue eyes that twinkle or penetrate according to circumstance." The Hansons spend much of their time each year in a home they own on Bold Island off the coast of Maine, which was the inspiration for his *Bold Island Suite*. There he finds ample opportunity to indulge in his favorite outdoor sports of swimming and boating. They maintain a winter residence in Rochester, where Hanson's extramusical diversions include playing with his dogs Peter Bolshoi and Tamara, playing an occasional game of poker or hearts, reading, and mathematics. From time to time he serves as a substitute preacher at the Presbyterian church.

Among the composers of the past, Hanson's favorites are Handel, Beethoven, Palestrina, and Scriabin; among modern American composers, he is most partial to Samuel Barber, Aaron Copland, and Leonard Bernstein. Asked for his preference among his own compositions, he unhesitatingly selected his Fourth Symphony and his opera, *Merry Mount*.

He squirms in discomfort whenever he hears himself called a "prolific" composer. "One of the driving forces of composition," he told an interviewer, "is that it's *so* hard! If only they knew the time I take over deciding between, in a single instance, F-sharp and F-natural!"

MAJOR WORKS

Chamber Music—Piano Quintet in F minor; Concerto da Camera, for piano and strings; String Quartet.

Choral Music—The Lament of Beowulf; Heroic Elegy; Songs from Drum Taps; Hymn for the Pioneers; The Cherubic Hymn; How Excellent Thy Name; Song of Democracy; The Song of Human Rights; Two Psalms, for baritone, chorus, and orchestra; Streams and Deserts, for chorus and orchestra.

Opera—Merry Mount.

Orchestral Music—6 symphonies; North and West, tone poem with chorus; Concerto for Organ, Strings, and Harp; Lux Aeterna, tone poem with viola obbligato; Pan and the Priest, tone poem with piano obbligato; Fantasy for String Orchestra (based on the String Quartet); Piano Concerto; Pastorale, for oboe and strings; Fantasy-Variations on a Theme of Youth; Elegy; Summer Seascape; Bold Island Suite; Four Psalms, for baritone and strings; Dies Natalis.

Piano Music—Four Poems; Sonata in A minor; Three Miniatures; Scandinavian Suite; Three Etudes; Two Yuletide Pieces.

Vocal Music—Three Songs from Walt Whitman; Two Songs from the Rubáiyát; Three Swedish Folk Songs; Three Swedish Songs.

ABOUT

Chase, G., America's Music; Howard, J. T., Our American Music; Goss, M., Modern Music Makers.
Christian Science Monitor, October 14, 1944; High Fidelity, December 1966, June 1968; Modern Music, January-February 1941; Musical America, April 1950; Musical Courier, April 1959; Musical Quarterly, April 1936; Saturday Review, January 30, 1954.

Roy Harris
1898–

Roy Harris was born Leroy Ellesworth Harris in Lincoln County, Oklahoma, February 12, 1898. His parents (of Irish and Scottish descent) had staked a claim in the last of the frontier land rushes, building for themselves a log cabin in which Roy was born. When the boy was about six, sieges of malaria in the county sent the Harris family from Oklahoma to California, where they built a farm in Covina, in the San Gabriel Valley. It was there that Roy spent his boyhood years and attended public school. He showed an unusual interest in books—reading everything that came within his reach from mail-order-house catalogs to Shakespeare. He showed an even greater fascination with music. "My mother taught me how to play; then a teacher came to the house

each week," he recalled later in an autobiographical sketch. "Soon I was performing in public. My father bought us a phonograph—an Edison with cylindrical records. Each new record was an event in our family. We played them nearly every evening—even in the late summer evenings after a long day's work." Besides listening to music he was creating it, performing on the piano, organ, and clarinet, having learned the latter two instruments by himself.

ROY HARRIS

When he was eighteen, Roy Harris acquired a farm of his own. He coupled farm work with the study of Greek philosophy. One year later, America entered World War I, and Harris joined the army as a private. When the war ended, Harris returned to California, abandoned farming permanently, and registered at the Southern branch of the University of California as a special student in philosophy and economics. At the same time he attended classes in harmony, his first contact with music theory. To earn his living during this period he drove a truck for a dairy, distributing each day some three hundred pounds of butter and three hundred dozen eggs. The four years as a truck driver which, he says, "in the annals of events must be termed uneventful," were nevertheless, years "crowded with enthusiasms. Each new harmony, each new melody, each composer discovered was a milestone for me. However, a shadow darkened those years; I couldn't seem to get anywhere as a composer. I never wrote anything. Nobody expected me to. I was just an enthusiastic student and a very apologetic one."

His harmony class at the University had convinced him that he needed more training if he wanted to do serious composing. He took some organ lessons from Charles Demarest and piano from Fannie Charles Dillon. Strengthened in his purpose by this preliminary training, he approached the well-known California musician Arthur Farwell and asked to be his pupil. Farwell took him on because he recognized in the young man a deep musical instinct worth cultivating; this was the first time that Farwell had taken under his wing a student who had had so little background.

Harris worked with Farwell for two years. He was, as Farwell later wrote, a serious pupil eager to absorb all the information he could about music, absorbing his lessons into his sponge-like memory. "I was convinced that he would one day challenge the world," Farwell later commented. Those two years transformed an immature student into a composer. Harris's first composition to be performed was *Impressions of a Rainy Day*, for string quartet, heard in Los Angeles on March 15, 1926. His first written work, however, was an Andante, for orchestra. It came to the notice of Howard Hanson in Rochester, New York, who gave it its world première on April 23, 1926. The following summer, the Andante was also played at the Lewisohn Stadium in New York and at the Hollywood Bowl in Los Angeles. "I knew that the orchestral piece was poor, heavy-footed, fumbling," Harris later said. "It conveyed none of the racy, taut springiness which I felt as I wrote it. I needed knowledge and discipline. But at last something seemed to be expected of me. People said I was a 'fresh talent' but needed technique."

In 1926 Harris went to Paris where he stayed three years (two of those on a Guggenheim Fellowship). He profited immensely from the advice and guidance given him by Nadia Boulanger, but he rejected her efforts to give him a systematic and formal training in counterpoint, harmony, and solfeggio. "She allowed me to go my own way. . . . I subscribed to a series of all the Beethoven string quartets, bought the scores, and studied them in minute detail before and after each concert. . . . Boulanger cooperated with complete

grace, and from this point on life unfolded swiftly and with an exciting logic."

His first major work was the Concerto for Piano, Clarinet, and String Quartet (1927), introduced in Paris on May 8, 1927, and praised by the French critics. He also completed a choral work, *Whitman Triptych* (1927). He seemed well on the way towards achieving his stride as composer—and recognition as well—when misfortune struck. He fractured his spine and became a hospital invalid. Brought back to the United States for a major operation, which proved successful, he was confined to a hospital bed for many months.

Harris has confessed that this accident proved the turning point in his development as a composer. At first it retarded the advance of his career by many months. But in time the accident was to have indirect benefits. For up to that time, he had done all his composing at the piano. His works, therefore, had been basically harmonic, because his fingers had instinctively groped for chord combinations on the keyboard. When, to escape the boredom of hospital routine, he returned to composing, he had to dispense with the piano, and he suddenly found himself artistically liberated. With pencil in hand, and without a piano, he began to write more quickly than before. He could permit his melodic and rhythmic ideas to grow and expand. Most important of all, he began to think and write contrapuntally.

Harris's contrapuntal style became fully crystallized in a number of important works that followed his recuperation from the accident. Having been awarded the Creative Fellowship of the Pasadena Music and Arts Association in 1930 and 1931, Harris completed a string sextet in 1932, *Three Variations on a Theme* for string quartet in 1933, and his first symphony, *Symphony: 1933*. Harris wrote that symphony for Serge Koussevitzky. When Harris had been introduced to the famous conductor for the first time, Koussevitzky said to him: "Copland told me you are the American Mussorgsky. You must write for me a big symphony from the West. I will play." Harris recalls: "He wanted it in September— only four months away. When I brought it to him, he seemed as excited as I. There was a feeling of being about to start a great excursion together." The symphony was given by the Boston Symphony under Koussevitzky on

January 26, 1934. "Koussevitzky's performance was a gala day in my life," Harris says. "Everything had been carefully and sympathetically rehearsed, and the presentation was brilliant. It was a much talked-about event in Boston salons and even drew enthusiastic approval from the dean of American critics, 'hard-to-please' H. T. Parker." The symphony also became the first such work by an American to be commercially recorded.

Commissions for special new works now came to Harris from many different places: from the Boston Symphony, the League of Composers, Westminster Choir, Columbia Records, RCA Victor Records, Elizabeth Sprague Coolidge, and the Columbia Broadcasting Company. Harris had arrived, and quickly.

During the next few years, Harris proved with each succeeding work that his talent was not ephemeral. A concert overture based on the popular American song "When Johnny Comes Marching Home" was performed by the Minneapolis Symphony on January 13, 1935. A Prelude and Fugue, for string orchestra, and a symphonic elegy, *Farewell to Pioneers*, were introduced in Philadelphia in February and March of 1936. A remarkable string quartet, Harris's third (1937), was introduced in Washington, D.C., on September 11, 1939, and then was selected by the Roth String Quartet as the only contemporary American composition to be played at the International Congress of Musicologists in New York. Another extraordinary chamber music work, the Piano Quintet (1937), was hailed as a modern masterwork when introduced in New York on February 12, 1937.

Harris's most important work up to that time—and, in fact, still esteemed as one of his finest creations—is the Third Symphony. When Serge Koussevitzky introduced it with the Boston Symphony on February 24, 1939, a critic wrote in *Modern Music:* "For significance of material, breadth of treatment and depth of meaning; for tragic implication, dramatic intensity, concentration; for moving beauty, glowing sound, it can find no peer in the musical art of America." In short order, the symphony was performed by major orchestras everywhere; it became the first American symphony ever conducted by Toscanini.

By virtue of his Third Symphony—and its immediate successor the fourth or *Folk Song Symphony*, first heard in its entirety in Cleveland on December 26, 1940—Harris revealed the greatest promise for American music. Here is the way Alfredo Casella, the eminent Italian composer and scholar, spoke of him at that time: "In producing a composer such as this master, America has placed herself in the front rank among those nations who are concerned with building a music for the future." By 1940, probably no American composer was performed more frequently or more successfully. Indeed, in a nationwide poll conducted by the Columbia Broadcasting System for an all-request program to be performed by the New York Philharmonic, Roy Harris was given first place among American composers.

Harris's style has not changed radically since 1940, though it has become increasingly subtle in expression and masterly in technique. He likes to describe himself as a "modern classicist." He often writes in the structures, the polyphonic style, and the modal harmonies of the sixteenth century. He remains partial to continuous melodic and polyphonic flow, with long lyric lines, strong asymmetric rhythms, mild dissonances, and the archaic effects of modal harmonies. His music is abstract, usually dependent entirely on its musical logic for its appeal. But whether abstract or programmatic, his music remains recognizably American. Sometimes—though this has been with him an exception rather than a rule—he resorts to quotation to arrive at an American identity, as he did in *When Johnny Comes Marching Home*, in his *Folk Song Symphony*, and in *Kentucky Spring*. Usually all of Harris's material is his own, but his writing here remains as strongly American as those works in which native American tunes are recalled. As we listen to his best works, the choral as well as the instrumental, we are continually made aware of American experiences. His music has the expanse of the western plains. It has the energy and the vitality of a young, growing country. It is music compounded of physical strength and idealism, of optimism and enthusiasm. Even *Modern Music*, a journal not often given to a programmatic approach in interpreting new music, found it best to speak of Harris's works in this way: "Here is music of the bleak and barren expanses of western Kansas, of the brooding prairie night, of the fast darkness of the American soul, of its despair and its courage, its defeat and its triumphs, its struggling aspirations."

Among Harris's later works, perhaps the most significant is his Seventh Symphony. In its first version, completed in 1952, it was awarded the Naumburg Prize. Then Harris revised it extensively. In this new version it received its world première in Copenhagen on September 15, 1955, Eugene Ormandy conducting. Harris describes this music as "a dance symphony," in one sense, and in another sense, "a study in harmonic and melodic variation." He explains further: "In this work I have hoped to communicate the spirit of affirmation as a declaration of faith in Mankind." Nicolas Slonimsky made the following interesting comparison between Harris's first symphony and his seventh, written twenty years apart: "The first symphony was unabashedly effusive, an early revelation of a natural talent striving for self expression. The seventh was philosophical in its cohesive force, and universal in its message. But the kinship between the two works was plain and immediately recognizable. There was the familiar Harrisian exuberance of rhythmic flow, the strong melodic stream, the massive harmonic accumulations where the emotional climax demanded it. In these contrasts, and in these affinities, Harris remains true to himself."

Harris's eighth symphony was introduced in San Francisco on January 17, 1962; his ninth, in Philadelphia on January 18, 1963. Alfred Frankenstein had this to say about the eighth symphony in the San Francisco *Chronicle:* "Seldom have we been given a new symphony that is so incandescent in its illumination: the spirit that breathes through St. Francis' own 'Canticle of the Sun' must have dwelt a while with Harris as he constructed this score. Few of Harris's symphonies move so swiftly. His pace is usually moderate because he has big things to say; this time, however, the music has wings even though it displays the familiar Harris length of line." The ninth symphony, had been commissioned by the Philadelphia Orchestra to help celebrate its sixty-fifth anniversary. "This historic city having been the birthplace of our Constitution," Harris explains, "I selected excerpts from the Preamble for my text, including 'We the people' for the

prelude. The ninth symphony is really a Prelude, Chorale and Fugue. Walt Whitman . . . had bequeathed me three wonderful fragments of poetry for the fugue subjects: 'From life immense in passion, pulse and power'; 'Cheerful for freest action formed under the laws Divine' and 'The Modern Man I Sing.'" Rafael Kubelik, the conductor who gave the symphony its European première, likened the prelude to Breughel and the chorale to "the windows inside of a great cathedral" while describing the fugue as "modern baroque."

Harris's tenth symphony commemorates the centenary of the assassination of Abraham Lincoln. It is called the *Abraham Lincoln Symphony* and it was introduced in Los Angeles on April 14, 1965.

Harris's eleventh symphony was commissioned by the New York Philharmonic for its 125th anniversary. The world première in New York on February 8, 1968, also helped to celebrate (although four days prematurely) Harris's seventieth birthday. The composer had originally planned the symphony as a two-part orchestral piece consisting of a prelude and fugue entitled *War and Peace*. He developed it into a two-part symphony instead, while retaining the programmatic intent. "My theme," Harris explained, "is the conflict facing the entire world. We are about to decide whether or not civilization can save itself, whether problems can be solved without violence." He further described this music as "highly dramatic, almost operatic. It begins in a mood of nervous agitation, dips downward, and ends in an expansive affirmation and optimism."

Harris's twelfth symphony, the *Père Marquette Symphony*, was introduced to the world only fourteen days after the eleventh. It had been commissioned by the Father Marquette Tercentenary Commission to celebrate the three-hundredth anniversary of the voyages in North America of Father Jacques Marquette, the first white man to see the confluence of the Mississippi and Wisconsin rivers. The symphony was first heard on February 24, 1968, in a performance by the Milwaukee Symphony.

From 1934 to 1938 Harris was head of the composition department at the Westminster Choir College in Princeton, New Jersey, and from 1938 to 1943 he was composer-in-residence at Cornell University in Ithaca, New

York. During World War II, he was granted a leave of absence from Cornell to serve in the Overseas Branch of the Office of War Information as chief of the Music Section. Upon leaving Cornell in 1943 Harris became associated with various educational institutions as composer-in-residence, including Colorado College, Pennsylvania College for Women in Pittsburgh, the University of Illinois, and Indiana University. In 1960 he was made director of the International Institute of Music, a division of the Inter-American University in Puerto Rico; at the same time he also served as director of the graduate program of the Philadelphia Musical Academy. In 1961 he was appointed to the faculty of the University of California in Los Angeles.

Through the years he has received numerous awards and honors. These include the Elizabeth Sprague Coolidge Medal for distinguished services to chamber music; the Award of Merit from the National Association for American Composers & Conductors; the first National Committee of Music Appreciation Award. In 1941 he was given an honorary doctorate from Rutgers University. To commemorate his fiftieth birthday, the governor of the state of Colorado presented him with a special citation for distinguished citizenship. In 1958 Harris became the first American composer to conduct his own music in the Soviet Union—when he led a performance of his fifth symphony over the Moscow Radio on October 15. In 1965 he received the Military Order of S. Saviour and of S. Bridget from Sweden.

Harris married Johana (née Beula) Duffey, a concert pianist, on October 10, 1936. They have five children, two of whom helped to form The West Coast Pop Art Experimental Band, a rock "combo" that has made several recordings. All are passionate baseball fans. Harris is angular, slouches slightly, and speaks in a lazy drawl. He habitually gets up before dawn and does his best creative work early in the morning, though he often continues working till noon. In the afternoons, when he is not teaching, he rests, reads, walks, or drives his car at breakneck speed. He is a motoring enthusiast who is always buying new cars. When he is engaged on a major work of programmatic interest, he likes to do intensive collateral reading: in composing his *Abraham Lincoln Symphony*, for example, he went through all the volumes of Carl Sandburg's biography. Except for acquiring automobiles, his pleasures are simple ones: a game of chess; tennis; reading. His tastes in dress and food are equally unpretentious; his favorite meal is steak and potatoes.

His wife has said of him: "In his creative life he is a priest and devil rolled into one bundle of uncompromising drive. . . . It is impossible to carry on a rational word discussion with him since words mean only sound syllables to him. He may not answer—or even hear sentences addressed to him—or he may make nonsense rhyme sequences or rhyme a long chain of unrelated words. . . . Conventional concerts depress him terribly with their worn-out idioms. . . . He is a child who will never grow old. Each new idea, situation, person, book, event, is a new adventure."

"If humanity arrives at a workable solution of international peace," Roy Harris has said, "we will have a great new period of growth in the humanities; and music will again find a proper balance of indigenous melody, harmony, counterpoint, form, and orchestration which will be generated out of the exciting and challenging activity which humanity will experience in building a new world."

MAJOR WORKS

Ballets—Western Landscape; From This Earth; What So Proudly We Hail.

Chamber Music—3 string quartets; Concerto for Piano, Clarinet, and String Quartet; String Sextet; Fantasy, for piano, flute, oboe, clarinet, horn, and bassoon; Piano Trio; Piano Quintet; Soliloquy and Dance, for viola and piano; String Quintet; Violin Sonata; Duo for Cello and Piano; String Quartet in One Movement.

Choral Music—A Song for Occupations; Symphony for Voices; Challenge; American Creed; Alleluia; Fog; Blow the Man Down; Service; Madrigal; Easter Motet; Israel, motet; Mass, for men's voices and organ; Cindy; Festival Folk Fantasy, for folk singer, chorus, and amplified piano.

Orchestral Music—12 symphonies; Chorale, for string orchestra; When Johnny Comes Marching Home, concert overture; Prelude and Fugue, for string orchestra; Farewell to Pioneers, symphonic elegy; Time Suite; Violin Concerto; Accordion Concerto; Two-Piano Concerto; Elegy and Paean, for viola and orchestra; Kentucky Spring; Cumberland Concerto; Piano Concerto; Abraham Lincoln Walks at Midnight, for soprano, piano, and orchestra; Fantasy, for piano and orchestra; Give Me the Splendid Sun, cantata for baritone and orchestra; Canticle to the Sun, for coloratura soprano and chamber orchestra; Ode to Consonance; Epilogue to Profiles in Courage: J. F. K; Jubilation, for chorus, brasses, and piano; Horn of Plenty; Rhythms and Spaces (an expansion of the third string quartet).

Henze

Piano Music—Sonata; Little Suite; American Ballads; Toccata.

ABOUT

Copland, A., The New Music: 1900-1960; Ewen, D. (ed.), The New Book of Modern Composers; Machlis, J., Introduction to Contemporary Music; Mellers, W., Music in a New Found Land.
Etude, December 1956, January 1957; High Fidelity, August 1956; Musical America, January 15, 1957; Musical Quarterly, January 1947; New York Times, February 4, 1968; Stereo Review, December 1968.

Hans Werner Henze
1926–

Hans Werner Henze was born on July 1, 1926, in the Westphalian town of Gütersloh, Germany, where his father was a schoolteacher. At the age of five, Hans began to play the piano; a year later he was studying ballet. When he was seven, he entered the Volksschule in Bielefeld. Later he attended high school in Braunschweig (until 1942) while at the same time he continued his musical training at the State Music School. The war interrupted his music study, and in 1944 he was drafted into the German army. He served in the tank corps and was taken prisoner by the British.

HANS WERNER HENZE

When the war ended, Henze resumed his musical training. In the years between 1946 and 1948 he studied with Wolfgang Fortner at the School for Church Music at Heidelberg

Henze: hĕn′ tsĕ

and completed his musical education in Paris with René Leibowitz. He began his professional life as a performing musician by playing the piano in the State Theatre in Bielefeld. In 1948 he was made musical director of Heinz Hipert's German Theatre in Constance, where he remained two years.

From boyhood Henze had been strongly attracted to the modern idioms of Hindemith, Stravinsky, and Bartók—composers who, while the Nazis were in power, were held in disrepute in Germany and condemned as decadent. "I am proud of having been called a decadent," he later wrote. In such early compositions as the Sonata for Flute and Piano, the Sonata for Violin and Piano, the Chamber Concerto for Piano, Flute, and Strings, and his first symphony—all written before 1948—his interest in the neoclassic methods of Stravinsky and Hindemith and in the advanced harmonic and rhythmic practices of Bartók are strongly in evidence. The Chamber Concerto, performed at Darmstadt on September 27, 1946, was Henze's first composition to receive a public performance. The first symphony received its world première at Darmstadt in 1947; Henze revised this symphony radically in 1963, scoring it for small orchestra.

Influenced by Leibowitz, Henze began to embrace the twelve-tone technique. His first experiment with dodecaphony came with the Violin Concerto, which was introduced at Baden-Baden on December 12, 1948. In *Chor Gefangener Trojer*, a choral work with text from the second part of Goethe's *Faust* (1948), Henze combined a twelve-tone technique with polytonal writing; and in *Piano Variations* (1948) and *Ballet Variations*, for orchestra (1949), he achieved an unprecedented compromise between the twelve-tone system and neoclassicism. His first opera—*Das Wundertheater* (text based on Cervantes), introduced by the Berlin State Opera on May 7, 1949—also employed dodecaphony. In the ballet *Jack Pudding*, first produced at Wiesbaden on June 5, 1951, he experimented with jazz idioms.

Here, then, was a dodecaphonist who was an eclectic. This fact was emphasized in Henze's first opera, *Boulevard Solitude*, introduced in Hanover on February 17, 1952; American première by the Santa Fe Opera on August 2, 1967. The text, a joint effort by the composer and Grete Weil, retold the familiar story of

Manon Lescaut, but in a modern setting and costumes. Michael Steinberg has explained that Henze deliberately chose such a familiar subject for his first opera "to emphasize the newness of his treatment, and to feel freer in using new theatrical techniques to realize the beauty he imagined." The opera was divided into seven scenes, made up in turn of twenty-four musical numbers all derived from a basic set of twelve tones. Nevertheless, the twelve-tone method did not prevent the composer from using whatever other materials he felt would help advance the dramatic line: jazz, formal arias, choral numbers in one of which Massenet was quoted, neoprimitive rhythms, variable meters. "The style of the work is entirely synthetic," said H. H. Stuckenschmidt. "Elements of Schoenbergian and Bergian melody are united by Stravinskyan rhythm and in the last entr'acte with Boris Blacher's . . . three-plus-four-plus-five eighths. Nearly all the possibilities of harmony are employed, from the C major triad to twelve-tone chords, and the vocal writing ranges from the spoken word to arias in the style of Puccini."

Though there were some catcalls and hissing at the première, these were soon drowned out by the applause. The frenzied outcries of denunciation, however, seemed to outweigh the exclamations of enthusiasm when the opera was produced for the first time in Italy—at Naples on March 4, 1954. "Rarely in recent years," reported Michael Steinberg from Italy to the New York Times, "has the introduction of any new music aroused along with the enthusiasm of its admirers such rejection. . . . From the beginning it was difficult to hear the music through the aural fog created by . . . attempts to disturb the performance . . . with name calling, hissing, mock applause, deliberate coughing and all the rest of the ammunition out of the hooligan's arsenal." The enraged protests of the audience, together with the bitter denunciations of the critics, met the opera when it was heard in Rome in April 1954.

For three seasons, beginning in 1950, Henze served as the musical adviser for ballet at the Wiesbaden State Theatre. In this period Henze wrote the scores for his first two ballets, both produced at Wiesbaden in 1951: *Jack Pudding* and *Anrufung Apolls*. During this time he also completed his third symphony—a major success when introduced at the Donaueschingen Festival on October 7, 1951—and a piano concerto which received the Robert Schumann Prize in 1951 and was heard at Düsseldorf on September 11, 1952.

In 1952 Henze—disgusted with so much of the pseudo-intellectual attitudes and approaches and the false values of a *nouveau-riche* society that had come to the fore in his native land—decided to leave Germany and make his home permanently in Italy. He lived for three years at Forio, on the island of Ischia, then for a few years in Naples, and finally in Castel Gandolfo outside Rome. He explained to an interviewer why he had decided to become an expatriate: "In Germany today one is conscious everywhere of an 'establishment of the modern.' Take Frankfurt, as just one example. Before the war the city presented a blend of ancient beauty. . . . Now all this has been replaced by utilitarian modern architecture. The young painter or composer has nothing of the past before his eyes. The present is ugly, and so he is obsessed to create the art of the future. So I have been living in Italy, where the past is still all around, and where the behavior towards the past is natural."

Henze's second opera was *König Hirsch* (*The Stag King*). When introduced in Berlin on September 23, 1956, it aroused a furor—one of the stormiest reactions encountered by any new opera in Germany since the end of World War II—making page one news. The text was prepared by Heinz von Cramer from a fairy tale by Carlo Gozzi. Paul Moor described it as "a fantasy of good and evil, an allegory in which men turn into animals and animals behave with human characteristics." Henze's music is based on the twelve-tone technique only in the first act. After that, the score makes way for a tonal lyricism of an almost Italian nature and a strong romantic style, while the over-all structure—with its profusion of arias, duets, cabalettas, and ensemble numbers—is basically in the Italian manner. In fact, Henze often refers to it as "my Italian opera." Nevertheless there is here a strong emphasis on symphonic writing too. Some of the finest pages in the score are those that are thoroughly symphonic rather than vocal. The writing, says Moor, has "imagination which is, at times, dazzling, slapstick and quite genuinely touching." Despite the furor caused by the audience at the première, some of the critics proclaimed the opera a major work; one of them considered it the most important opera since the days of Richard Strauss.

The American première of *The Stag King* was given by the Santa Fe Opera in New Mexico on August 4, 1965. Reviewing that performance for the New York *Times*, Raymond Ericson wrote: "The moralistic fantasy has inspired Mr. Henze to write a beautiful score. The subject matter suits his style. The music is often highly dissonant, the vocal line sometimes eccentric. But the composer uses a large orchestra with brilliant resourcefulness so that the evocation of a place or mood is immediate."

Whatever tentative romantic and lyrical tendencies were revealed in *The Stag King* were developed further in the ballet *Undine*. This was written for the Royal Ballet of London which introduced it on October 27, 1958, with Frederick Ashton's choreography. The scenario was based on the legend of Undine, the water nymph, who gains her soul through the love of a faithful man. Though the discords of modern writing are here basic to Henze, he frequently reverts to conventional methods of tonality, rhythm, modulations, and so forth. As Everett Helm says, "the emancipated Henze, who now finds the shackles of serial technique too restricting, mixes his techniques with an expert hand and thereby achieves a broad spectrum of expressive and dramatic colors."

For his next opera, *Der Prinz von Homburg*, Henze in his text profited from a German classic, Heinrich von Kleist's play written in 1811; the libretto was written by Ingeborg Bachmann. This was Henze's first attempt to work in opera with a German subject. Its central theme concerns a semi-historical hero, a prince who is charged with treason even though he has led his army to victory. Because of his passion for the lovely Princess Natalie, he neglects his official duties. He is awaiting execution when at the last minute he is freed by the Elector, who restores him to his command. First produced at the Hamburg Opera on May 22, 1960, *Der Prinz von Homburg* was praised not only for its dramatic interest but equally for its strong melodic content. The composer progresses from simple, tonal melodies and harmonies in the first act to textures of increasing complexity in later acts, but without sacrificing lyricism. "As a whole," says H. H. Stuckenschmidt, "the musical language ... is more objective than that of *The Stag King*. Inspiration and exuberant fantasy are subjected to artistic reflection." When the opera received its first performance outside Germany (at the Festival of Two Worlds at Spoleto, Italy, during the summer of 1960), Martin Bernheimer reported: "Upon first hearing, one is most impressed with the expansive lyricism of the love scenes and the big ensembles. ... Harmonically, there is much atonality and a little twelve-tonality; but only seldom does one feel that the composer is following a system at the expense of expression."

Henze's next opera was the most significant he had thus far written. It was *Die Elegie für Junge Liebende* (*Elegy for Young Lovers*), the world première of which took place at Schwetzingen, Germany, on May 20, 1961, when it was given in the German language. It was then presented in its original English text at the Glyndebourne Festival during the summer of 1961. Performances followed later the same year at the Munich Festival and at the Berlin Arts Festival. At the latter it was chosen as "the best new opera production" of the entire festival. The American première (conducted by the composer himself) was given by the Juilliard Opera Theatre in New York on April 29, 1965. An excellent libretto was prepared for Henze by W. H. Auden and Chester Kallman (the same writers who composed the text for Stravinsky's *The Rake's Progress*). The central character is a vain poet whose writings in an Alpine inn are inspired by visions related to him by an elderly woman. When the woman is freed of her hallucinations, the poet turns for inspiration to the story of the love and death of two young people, Elisabeth and Toni, and writes his greatest poem, *Elegy for Young Lovers*.

Peter Davis explained in *Musical America* that the *Elegy for Young Lovers* is an opera of "set pieces: the acts are divided into many small, titled sections, each a self-contained musical unit." Its construction results in a "profusion of arias, duets and ensembles." Davis goes on to say that "perhaps the most striking feature of the score is the spellbinding beauty of its vocal line—positively Italianate in its warmth and spontaneity."

Henze told a Washington, D.C., newspaperman that the *Elegy for Young Lovers* represented for him a turning point in his career as an opera composer. "I had to find my own language—what I wanted from music and what I wanted to do in music. I was not always sure. After *Elegy* I was."

The first opera Henze wrote after the *Elegy* was an *opera buffa* entitled *Der Junge Lord* (*The Young Lord*), first produced at the Deutsche Staatsoper in Berlin April 7, 1965. The hero, the idol of Grünwiesl, turns out to be a dressed-up ape from the circus. This broad comedy (text, the work of Ingeborg Bachmann, adapted from a tale by Wilhelm Hauff) is a satire on German provincialism, and for it the composer produced a score that is consistently tonal, lyrical, and witty. *Die Welt* hailed it as a masterwork and "the rebirth of *opera buffa*." Paul Moor regarded Henze's music as "transparent, almost Mozartean" and proclaimed it a "popular success." This judgment was confirmed when the opera was accepted for immediate performances in Florence, Bologna, Venice, Stuttgart, and Palermo. The American première was given by the San Diego Opera in California on February 17, 1967. Once the darling of the avant-garde, Henze was now embraced by the reactionaries as one of their own. Explaining why he was impelled to produce a more or less traditional *opera buffa*, Henze said: "There comes a point in life when one simply has to laugh."

But Henze did not abandon serious opera, and the following year *Die Bassariden* (*The Bassarids*) received its world première at the Salzburg Festival on August 8, 1966. For this opera, as for the earlier *Elegy for Young Lovers*, the libretto was written by W. H. Auden and Chester Kallman. In this instance the source was Euripides' *The Bacchae*. "The librettists," Peter G. Davis explains, "have updated, cross-dated and back-dated Euripides into a coruscating study of evil, mass hypnosis, and blind, unthinking idolatry." In a single act, lasting about two and a half hours, *The Bassarids* is structurally divided into four symphonic movements. "Although the symphonic structure is largely imperceptible at first hearing," says Davis, "it undoubtedly helped Henze to sustain the musical tension and this he has done with extraordinary skill." For Peter Heyworth, reporting from Salzburg to the New York *Times*,

this score "marks a new restraint in Henze's music"—even though, by the nature of the text, much of the music is "predominantly violent and elaborate." Heyworth finds that Henze has revealed in this new opera a "growing ability to achieve his ends with simple means. This applies to the orchestration as well as the vocal writing. Indeed, the virtuosity with which he has here measured up to a theme demanding both power and subtlety, finally establishes him . . . as the one opera composer of real substance to have emerged from his generation." America first heard *Die Bassariden* in a performance by the Santa Fe Opera on August 7, 1968.

Despite his preoccupation with opera, Henze continued to compose concert music. Since 1961 he has completed two symphonies. The Fourth, subtitled *Il Re Crevo* (so named because the symphony is taken note for note from the second-act finale of the opera *König Hirsch*), was presented successfully by the Berlin Philharmonic on October 9, 1963, the composer conducting. The Fifth was commissioned by the New York Philharmonic orchestra for the opening of Philharmonic Auditorium at the Lincoln Center for the Performing Arts. With the composer in the audience, on his first visit to the United States, the symphony was introduced by the New York Philharmonic under Leonard Bernstein on May 16, 1963. In the fall of the same year, Henze conducted all five of his symphonies with the Berlin Philharmonic on two successive evenings. These performances were then recorded in a single release by Deutsche Grammophon, affording critics an opportunity to study at one hearing Henze's development as a symphonic composer. "Viewed as an entity," wrote Peter G. Davis in *High Fidelity* magazine, "these five works, couched in a colorful, expressive, direct contemporary language, comprise a musical experience as moving and meaningful as anything twentieth century composition has to offer." In the New York *Times*, Howard Klein said: "Listening to the symphonies one is impressed by the integrity of the composer's personality. He writes about the same thing in each essentially, for suffering, striving, anxiety and courage loom from the scores. But each work is true to itself."

Henze produced several highly significant and imaginative concert works other than symphonies. *Musen Siziliens* (*Muses of Sicily*) is a concerto for two pianos, mixed chorus, wind, and tympani, completed in 1966, and performed by the Chicago Symphony on November 2, 1967. The text is based on Virgil's *Eclogues*. The composition has three sections: first, a Pastorale, based on the ninth eclogue, in which young Lycidas tries to get the aging Moeris to sing him some of Moeris's songs; second, an Adagio, text based on the tenth eclogue—the aged Moeris sings his song; third, a section entitled "Silenius," with words from the introduction to the sixth eclogue, the theme of which is artistic creation.

Though *Moralities* (1967)—for narrator, children's voices, orchestra, and solo ensemble—was designated as scenic plays, it is actually a concert work. The text is made up of several of Aesop's fables, adapted by W. H. Auden. This is a highly satirical work, "a cross between witty, harmonically simplified Stravinsky," explains Arthur Darack, "and a three-ring circus. The children's chorus sings nonsense syllables and chants; the narrator declaims his wise, sophisticated comments on foolishness and error. The text also refers to aspects of music history, from the madrigal to electronic music, which is all the excuse Henze needs to give us a whirlwind spoof of the history of music. Henze rails, satirizes, pokes fun at adult music history, while the children storm in with gusto. It is great fun." The world première of *Moralities* took place at the Cincinnati May Festival in 1968.

In the 1960's Henze also produced several shorter works for orchestra (*Los Caprichos Fantasia*, 1963; *In Memoriam: Die Weisse Rose*, 1965; *Three Dithyrambs* and a symphonic fantasy, *Linda Maestra*, both 1967); two concertos, one for double bass and orchestra, the other for oboe, harp, and strings; and three cantatas either for solo voice and chamber orchestra or solo voice and chamber orchestra supplemented by chorus.

In seeking the essence of a musical masterwork—past as well as present—Henze looks for the "timeless quality" which the Italians describe as *concetto*. "You might translate it as 'concept' or 'message,' but that is not quite right," Henze told an interviewer. "The *concetto* is what a piece of music tries to express, and this is what possesses me when I compose. Music cannot express a judgment. It cannot

describe. It is not active in a sociological sense. But it can carry this message of human condition: of love, for example, or forgiveness. I am aware that it is a little dangerous to talk like this. Some regard it as foolish and old-fashioned. But I believe in it wholeheartedly."

Apart from his activities as composer and conductor, Henze has devoted himself to teaching. Since 1961 he has been professor of composition at the Mozarteum at Salzburg. He is unmarried. His hobbies include driving automobiles at terrifying speeds and raising whippets. He has been frequently honored: in 1956 he received the Gold Medal in London; in 1957, the Nordrhein Westphalian Award; in 1959, the Berlin Kunstpreis; and in 1962 the Grand Prize for Artists in Hanover. He is a member of the Berlin Academy of Arts, the Bavarian Academy of Fine Arts in Munich, and the Accademia Filarmonica Romana in Rome. In 1967 he was composer-in-residence at Hopkins Center at Dartmouth College in Hanover, New Hampshire.

MAJOR WORKS

Ballets—Jack Pudding; Anrufung Apolls; Labyrinth; Der Idiot; Tancred und Canthylene; Pas d'Action; Die Schlafende Prinzessin; Maratona di Danza; Undine.

Chamber Music—Flute Sonata; Violin Sonata; String Quartet; Serenade, for cello solo; Wind Quintet; Concerto per il Marigny, for piano and instruments.

Choral Music—Five Madrigals; Chor Gefangenen Trojer; Erde und Himmel; Novae de Infinito Laudes, cantata; Cantata della Fiaba Estrema, for soprano, small choir, and thirteen instruments; Musen Siziliens, for two pianos, mixed chorus, wind, and tympani; Moralities, for narrator, children's voices, and a solo ensemble; The Raft of Medusa.

Operas—Ein Landarzt (radio cantata); Das Ende einer Welt (radio cantata); Das Wundertheater (operatic melodrama); Boulevard Solitude; König Hirsch; Der Prinz von Homburg; Elegie für Junge Liebende; Der Junge Lord, comic opera; Die Bassariden.

Orchestral Music— 5 symphonies; 2 piano concertos; Kranichsteiner Kammerkonzert; Ballet Variations; Violin Concerto; Der Vorwurf, for baritone, trumpet, trombone, and strings; Ode an den Westwind, for cello and orchestra; Quattro Poemi, symphonic suite; Antifone; Symphonische Etuden; Nachtstucke und Arien, for soprano and orchestra; Los Caprichos Fantasia; Epilogue-Adagio; In Memoriam: Die Weisse Rose; Double Bass Concerto; Concerto for Oboe, Harp, and Strings; Three Dithyrambs; Linda Maestra, symphonic fantasy; Essay on Pigs.

Piano Music—Nine Variations; Sonata; Divertimenti, for two pianos.

Vocal Music—Whispers from Heavenly Death, for soprano and eight instruments; Apollo und Hyazinth, improvisations for harpsichord, contralto, and eight instruments; Five Neapolitan Songs, for baritone and chamber orchestra; Being Beauteous, for soprano, four cellos, and harp.

ABOUT

Lang, P. H. and Broder, N. (eds.), Contemporary Music in Europe; Machlis, J., Introduction to Contemporary Music.

High Fidelity, December 1966; New York Times, July 30, 1967; Time, May 24, 1963.

Paul Hindemith
1895–1963

Paul Hindemith, a towering figure in twentieth century music and a leading exponent of the neoclassic movement, was born in Hanau, Germany, November 16, 1895. He was a descendant of Silesian artisans, and the oldest of three children, one of whom, Rudolf, became a concert cellist. His father, a successful decorator and painter, was vigorously opposed to music as a career and did what he could to discourage Paul's early interest in the art. The boy, nevertheless, started to study the violin and viola, revealing an extraordinary gift for both instruments. Though only eleven at the time, he began to earn his living playing in dance bands and the orchestras of cafés and theatres. He enrolled in Hoch's Conservatory at Frankfurt-am-Main where he continued his music studies with Arnold Mendelssohn and Bernard Sekles.

In 1914 he served in the German army. When he was released a year later, he joined the orchestra of the Frankfurt Opera where he became concertmaster. During this period he distinguished himself as a musician in several different ways. He helped found the Amar String Quartet, in which he played the viola, and with which he toured Germany spreading the gospel of modern chamber music. In 1921 he helped to organize the Donaueschingen Festival at Baden-Baden where new composers and new music could get a hearing each year. Hindemith also turned seriously to composition. His first opus was a Trio, for clarinet, horn, and piano. This was immediately followed by his first string quartet, his first cello concerto, and the *Lustige Sinfonietta*, for small orchestra. These and other works completed before 1919 reflect a strong Romantic per-

Hindemith: hĭn′ dĕ mĭt

sonality and the influence that composers such as Brahms and Reger had had upon him. But it was not long before he broke loose from such ties and set out for himself, in opposition to tradition, by continually experimenting with new materials, techniques, approaches, and subject matter and by exploiting the unexpected and the grotesque. *Kammermusik No. 1* quoted a German foxtrot embellished with scale passages in its finale. Mockery, tomfoolery, and satire were given free rein in two one-act operas produced in Stuttgart on June 4, 1921: *Mörder, Hoffnung der Frauen,* and an opera for Burmese marionettes, *Das Nusch-Nuschi.* When Richard Strauss heard some of this music he told Hindemith: "You don't have to write this way, because *you* have talent."

PAUL HINDEMITH

Though he did not discard satire or the grotesque for a number of years, he was beginning more and more to interest himself in polyphonic writing within classical structures—but a polyphony in which the voices moved independently of harmonic relationships. This style, linear counterpoint, is found in his second and third string quartets, op. 10 (1919) and op. 16 (1922); in the second and third *Kammermusik,* op. 36, nos. 1 and 2 (1924, 1925); and in one of his first masterworks, the monumental song cycle *Das Marienleben,* op. 27, verses by Rilke based on the life of the Virgin, introduced at the Donaueschingen Festival on June 17, 1923. This cycle of songs was so close to Hindemith's heart that in

Hindemith

1939 he set four of them for voice and orchestra and in 1948 he issued a completely new version of the entire group with radical revisions (together with an explanatory manifesto pointing up the differences between the earlier and the later set). The very old and the very new, so successfully joined in these and similar works, led one German critic to describe their style as "Bach's Brandenburg Concertos—upside down." In a similar facetious vein, another critic of this period said that Hindemith's music sounded "like Bach played on a nightmare organ, all the pipes of which had been mixed up by some devilish joker."

We now find Hindemith divorced from his earlier Romantic tendencies—"freed from the despotism of a text," as A. Machabey once noted, "from the pre-established plan of program music, from obediences to the caprices and emphasis of sentiment." These are compositions in which "music in itself suffices." We also encounter here a new approach to instrumentation, a new approach to polyphony, a new interest in primordial rhythms, and an increasing partiality to atonal practices. But, commented Alfred Einstein in 1926, "there is nothing at all academic about Hindemith. He is simply a musician who produces music as a tree bears fruit, without further philosophic purpose."

Hindemith's first full-length opera, Cardillac, was produced in Dresden on November 9, 1926. The text was the combined effort of Ferdinand Lion and the composer in adapting a romantic tale by E. T. A. Hoffmann. The main character is a seventeenth century master jeweler who would rather murder his clients than part with the creations he has fashioned for them. Pursued by the police, he finally breaks down and confesses his crimes outside the opera house and is murdered by the avenging crowd. Hindemith's interest in polyphonic writing is here combined with an effort to apply the styles and structures of instrumental music to opera. The action is often interrupted by concert pieces, while different scenes are conceived in terms of such instrumental forms as the fugue, canon, or passacaglia. The result was not completely happy. Dramatic interest was continually sacrificed for musical values. The elaborate polyphonic writing often invited boredom. "In its formal rigidity . . . Cardillac is a perfect ex-

ample of the ideal antiromantic opera as envisaged by musicians in the 1920's," says Gerhart von Westerman. Hindemith recognized the shortcomings of his opera and many years later he completely rewrote both the text and the music so radically that Cardillac emerged as a new opera. In the new version he emphasized both the dramatic and psychological elements in the story, while in his musical writing he supplanted the formerly rigid and formal counterpoint with what Westerman describes as a "flowing, dramatic orchestral language." Effective recitatives alternated with melodic passages "of glowing splendor." In this new adaptation, Cardillac was presented in Zürich on June 20, 1952. It was produced for the first time at La Scala in Milan on January 30, 1964, shortly before the Vienna State Opera revived the original work as seen in 1926. During the summer of 1967 the revised Cardillac received its American première at the Santa Fe Opera.

In 1924 Hindemith married Gertrud Rottenberg, daughter of a conductor of the Frankfurt Opera. The Hindemiths made their home in a picturesque medieval tower which Hindemith had previously acquired and which had become a favorite meeting place for the avant-garde in Frankfurt. In 1927 Hindemith left Frankfurt for Berlin where he had become professor of composition at the Berlin Hochschule für Musik and where he was made a member of the German Academy. With this move Hindemith initiated a distinguished career as a teacher, during which he introduced new pedagogical methods that were to have a far-reaching influence on his many pupils in Europe and the United States. Hindemith eventually clarified his ideas on harmony and composition in a monumental two-volume theoretical treatise (1937, 1939) entitled Unterweisung im Tonsatz (The Craft of Musical Composition)—an attempt to provide a scientific and objective basis for all music from medieval times to the present. In 1954 A Composer's World: Horizons and Limitations was published, emphasizing particularly his own methods, techniques, and outlooks.

His teaching obligations in Berlin did not interfere with composition. He continued to produce work after work with the remarkable fertility of a baroque composer. One of the most controversial of his major works before

1930 was the opera *Neues vom Tage* (*News of the Day*), which created a sensation when produced in Berlin on June 8, 1929. Two works more sharply in contrast with each other than this opera and *Cardillac* would be difficult to imagine. Departing from polyphonic methods and a purely objective approach, Hindemith created in *Neues vom Tage* a modern jazz opera in the spirit of *Zeitkunst* (Contemporary Art), a movement then much in vogue in Berlin. *Zeitkunst* favored modern subjects filled with all kinds of contemporary allusions and references; and its music was partial to a timely style with popular overtones. *Neues vom Tage* was *Zeitkunst* with a vengeance. The text, by Marcellus Schiffer, describes a marital dispute in which the couple become front-page news because of a divorce action. They get so much publicity that they are showered with stage and screen offers. Now rich and famous, they would like to forget the divorce and effect a reconciliation, but the public will have none of this. And so the couple must go through with the divorce.

Much of the music is written with tongue in cheek, as is the libretto. The score includes an aria sung in a bathtub—a hymn to hot water; a chorus in which stenographers are accompanied by clicking typewriters. Where more traditional operas have love duets, this one has a hate duet; where some have wedding marches, this one has a divorce ensemble number. At times the writing is highly realistic, as when the orchestra simulates the sounds of smashing crockery while the principals indulge in one of their noisy brawls; at times, it is spiced with jazz.

In line with *Zeitkunst*, Hindemith during this period also produced a library of pieces for pianola, radio theatre, films, and schools. These pieces too were popular in style and content, intended for mass distribution. For these items, Hindemith himself coined the term "*Gebrauchsmusik*" (practical or functional music). Explaining his purpose, he wrote in 1927: "It is to be regretted that in general so little relationship exists today between the producers and the consumers of music. A composer should write today only if he knows for what purpose he is writing. . . . The demand for music is so great that composer and consumer ought most emphatically to come at last to an understanding." Of particular interest among these functional compositions is an opera for and about children, intended for performance by children—*Wir Bauen eine Stadt*, or *Let's Build a City*, produced in Berlin on June 21, 1930. Besides *Gebrauchsmusik* Hindemith produced some items grouped under the heading of *Hausmusik* (house music). These are pieces written for amateurs to perform at home.

All of his participation in *Zeitkunst*, *Gebrauchsmusik*, and *Hausmusik* might suggest that Hindemith, after going to Berlin, had strayed from his former neoclassic pastures. But this was not so. He continued to produce a great many works in an uncompromising linear style within classic media. These included two more items in the group collectively entitled *Kammermusik*: no. 6, for viola d'amore and chamber orchestra, op. 36, no. 4; and no. 7, for organ and chamber orchestra, op. 46, no. 2. Both were written in 1930. In addition, he completed numerous other works of ambitious dimensions in a linear style. The most significant were the oratorio *Das Unaufhörliche*, introduced in Berlin on November 21, 1931; *Konzertmusik*, for brass and strings, written for the fiftieth anniversary of the Boston Symphony, which introduced it under Koussevitzky on April 3, 1931; and *Philharmonisches Konzert*, commissioned by the Berlin Philharmonic for its fiftieth anniversary and introduced by that organization under Wilhelm Furtwängler on April 15, 1932.

His serious works, his more popular creative endeavors, and his fruitful work as teacher and performer had gained Hindemith universal recognition as one of the foremost and most influential musicians in Germany when the Nazis came to power in 1933. Despite his high position and world reputation, Hindemith came at once to grips with the new regime. He himself was an Aryan, but married to a half-Jewish woman, and he had affiliated himself with Jewish musicians in the performance and recording of chamber music. This would have been enough to make him *persona non grata*. In addition, the Nazis regarded his opera *Neues vom Tage* contemptuously as an expression of the kind of German postwar degeneracy which they had long been fighting; at the same time they considered the cerebralism of Hindemith's serious concert music decadence, with which the Kulturkammer could have little sympathy.

Hindemith

For a while, though held suspect, Hindemith was able to continue his musical activities. Then he became the center of a violent political storm. Wilhelm Furtwängler, the distinguished conductor, planned to present the world première of Hindemith's new opera, *Mathis der Maler*, in Berlin. One of the reasons why the Nazis opposed this première was the sensitive and controversial subject of the text, based on the career of the sixteenth century painter Matthias (Mathis) Grünewald. The text detailed the uprising of the peasants, with Matthias as leader, against the tyranny of the church. Furtwängler, however, insisted that he—and not politicians—ruled the destinies of the Berlin Opera. As a first token of defiance he performed with the Berlin Philharmonic, on March 12, 1934, the world première of a "symphony" derived from the opera score of *Mathis der Maler*. This performance was an extraordinary success, partly because the work is a masterpiece and partly because it provided the audience with an opportunity to express antagonism to the Nazi regime through its enthusiasm for the music. Encouraged by this public reaction, Furtwängler became more determined than ever to mount the opera. On November 25, 1934, he published an open letter, featured on the front page of the *Deutsche Allgemeine Zeitung*, entitled "The Hindemith Case." "It is a shame," he said, "to attempt to defame and drive him [Hindemith] from Germany, since none of the younger generation has done more than he for the recognition of German music throughout the world. In an age that offers so few productive musicians, Germany cannot afford to abandon Hindemith." Late the same night, he was ordered by Hitler to abandon his plans to produce the Hindemith opera. In addition, Furtwängler was disciplined by being removed from his posts with the Berlin State Opera and the Berlin Philharmonic and having his passport withdrawn. It was about a year before Furtwängler was reinstated in the good graces of the government, but by that time Hindemith's music had been officially banned from all German concert programs and Hindemith himself had left the country, in self-imposed exile.

The opera that created this furor and finally drove Hindemith from his country and Furtwängler into temporary banishment is one of the composer's greatest achievements—a masterpiece in each of the two forms in which it has been heard, as an opera and as a symphony. The opera received its world première in Zürich, on May 28, 1938. "It is ironical," remarked H. H. Stuckenschmidt, "that *Mathis*, which can be named beside Beethoven's *Fidelio* and Pfitzner's *Palestrina* in German essence and ethical earnestness, should start its course outside Germany." The opera finally reached Germany in 1946, in Stuttgart; since then it has been produced by Germany's leading opera houses. The American première took place in Boston February 17, 1956. In the opera, as in the symphony, Hindemith's music is evocative of the Reformation with suggestions of Gregorian chant and medieval folk songs; the atmosphere and background of Grünewald's paintings are caught and fixed most subtly in Hindemith's linear writing.

When Hindemith left Germany permanently in 1935, he went to Turkey on an invitation from that country. For one year he helped to reorganize its musical life. In the spring of 1937 he paid his first visit to the United States, on an invitation from Elizabeth Sprague Coolidge. He toured the country as violist in performances of his music, making his American debut at the Coolidge Festival at Washington, D.C., April 10, 1937. During this visit he helped to present the American première of his viola concerto *Der Schwanendreher* (*The Organ Grinder*) at a concert of the New York Philharmonic.

Hindemith returned to the United States for a second tour in 1938–1939. At that time he attended the American première of his ballet *Saint Francis*, performed by the Ballet Russe de Monte Carlo. The score provided the material for one of Hindemith's most exalted works for orchestra, the suite *Nobilissima Visione*, which had its world première in Venice in September of 1938. During this second tour, Hindemith spent the summer of 1939 at Tanglewood conducting a master class in composition at the Berkshire Music Center.

Because of the outbreak of World War II, Hindemith's third visit to the United States, late in 1939, was extended into an indefinite stay. Not only did Hindemith now make his home permanently in the United States, but in 1946 he became an American citizen. In the fall of 1940 he joined the music faculty of Yale

University, where he gave courses in advanced theory and composition and was responsible for the general overhaul of its music curriculum. In 1947 he was named Battell Professor of the Theory of Music at Yale, and in 1950–1951 he served as Charles Eliot Norton Lecturer at Harvard University.

His first return to Europe took place in 1947. At this time he led guest performances of his works in Italy, England, and Holland. In 1949 he went back to Germany, as guest conductor with the Berlin Philharmonic. He was given a royal welcome and urged to return permanently and resume his long-interrupted musical activities. He refused to do so, maintaining that German music had suffered seriously because of the ravages of the Nazi regime and the war. Besides, he added, "I am an American citizen now and have made a new life there. I won't go back to live in Germany."

In America, Hindemith remained extraordinarily prolific, producing major works in all forms and media, most of them of the highest artistic quality. Significant orchestral works included the following: *Symphonic Metamorphoses on a Theme by Carl Maria von Weber*, introduced by the New York Philharmonic January 20, 1944; the Piano Concerto which Jesús María Sanromá presented with the Cleveland Orchestra on February 27, 1947; *Symphonia Serena*, commissioned and introduced by the Dallas Symphony, February 2, 1947. He was also moved by the death of Franklin D. Roosevelt to write one of his most deeply felt choral works, *When Lilacs Last in the Dooryard Bloom'd* (text by Walt Whitman), which received its première in New York on May 14, 1946. In addition to all these works, Hindemith completed a new opera, *Die Harmonie der Welt*, set during the Thirty Years' War, with the astronomer and mathematician Johannes Kepler as principal character. Principal musical episodes from this score were assembled into a three-movement symphony performed in Basel, Switzerland, January 24, 1952. The opera itself was first produced on August 11, 1957, in Munich.

In 1948 Hindemith was appointed a member of the music faculty at the University of Zürich in Switzerland. Nevertheless, he continued to teach at Yale, making the United States his principal home until 1953. In that year he finally decided to reestablish himself in Europe and chose the city of Zürich where he retained his teaching affiliation at the University. From time to time he paid return visits to the United States. In 1963 he attended and participated in a four-day festival in his honor in New York, during which his last opera, *The Long Christmas Dinner* (text by Thornton Wilder), was given its American première; it had previously been introduced in Mannheim, Germany, on December 17, 1961.

Hindemith's last composition was a Mass for *a cappella* chorus, and his last public appearance took place in Berlin November 12, 1963, when he conducted the world première of this composition. He had been ill for several years, a victim of periodic dizzy spells, but had resisted the advice of physicians and friends that he slow down. His health broke down completely while he was visiting his publisher in Mainz, soon after his Berlin concert. When able to do so, he went on to Frankfurt-am-Main to consult his physician. There he was confined to a hospital, where he suffered three strokes. He died in the hospital December 28, 1963. He was survived by his wife Gertrude, who was with him at the time of his death. They had no children.

Many honors were conferred on Hindemith during his lifetime, beginning with a membership in the National Institute of Arts and Letters in 1947. In 1950 he was given the Bach Prize of the City of Hamburg. Twice he received the Award of the Music Critics Circle in New York—in 1953 for his Septet, and in 1960 for *Six Madrigals*. In 1955 the President of Finland presented him with the Sibelius Prize of thirty-two thousand dollars for distinguished services to music, and in 1962 the President of Italy gave him the Balzan Prize of fifty-two thousand dollars.

H. H. Stuckenschmidt described Hindemith in this way: "A friendly boyish head . . . surmounts a lithe, youthful figure. Small in stature, Paul Hindemith likes to make himself smaller still by sitting on a low hassock. He prefers to remain close to earth. From his vantage point, he leads the conversation unobtrusively, a clever, learned, inexorably logical participant, a little malicious, but friendly even in his malice. His knowledge embraces not only music of every age but also the oldest and newest arts of poetry and painting. . . . His fundamental characteristic is a sustained and bantering cheerfulness. Hindemith loves to laugh, but his laughter does not glance off the surface of things. . . . Like Mozart, he can express fundamental verities jestingly. . . . To learn and to teach are his passions.''

One of his earlier hobbies was toy trains. His living room in Berlin, in the years just before Hitler, was usually cluttered with trains, tracks, complex switches of all sorts, miniature tunnels and bridges. When he returned to Germany in 1949 he was amazed to discover that the toy railway system he had built years ago was still in existence, indeed even was in working order. One of his later hobbies was cartooning, at which he was particularly adept. Year after year he would send his friends Christmas cards of his own making and design. The first realization that his friends in America had that Hindemith was seriously ill in 1963 was their failure to receive such a greeting. These diversions, and at times the construction of tables and chairs, were his principal escapes from the supercharged intellectual and musical life he led through most of his waking hours.

Discussing the "new" in music, Hindemith once wrote: "There are . . . periods in the history of music in which an Ars Nova must shake off artistic habits that have grown stale, in order to permit any healthy development to continue. But we have been experiencing such an Ars Nova continually since the death of Beethoven. . . . This 'new,' after a thousand variations, has grown empty, while the ancient striving for the spiritual deepening of music is as new as ever. With all the appreciation that one may reasonably bring to technical innovations, since they should make our work easier, we should nevertheless minimize the word 'new' in the term 'new art' and emphasize rather the word 'art.' ''

MAJOR WORKS

Ballets—Der Dämon, pantomime; Der Plöner Musiktag, pantomime; Triadisches Ballet; St. Francis, or Nobilissima Visione.

Chamber Music—7 string quartets; Kammermusik, Nos. 1 through 7, for various solo instruments and chamber music groups; 3 violin sonatas; 2 sonatas for unaccompanied violin; 2 string trios; various sonatas for solo instruments and piano (flute; oboe; bassoon; unaccompanied viola; unaccompanied cello; clarinet; horn; trumpet; harp; English horn; trombone; cello); Kleine Kammermusik, for wind quintet; Septet; A Frog, He Went A-Courting, for cello and piano; Octet.

Choral Music—Das Unaufhörliche, oratorio; When Lilacs Last in the Dooryard Bloom'd; Apparebit

Repentina Dies; The Demon of the Gibbet, for unaccompanied chorus; Cantique de l'Espérance; Six Madrigals; Mass, for unaccompanied chorus.

Operas—Cardillac (completely revised in 1952); Neues vom Tage; Hin und Zurück; Mathis der Maler; Die Harmonie der Welt; The Long Christmas Dinner.

Orchestral Music—2 piano concertos; 2 cello concertos; Concerto for Orchestra; Konzertmusik, for strings and brass; Philharmonisches Konzert; Mathis der Maler, symphony; Der Schwanendreher, concerto for viola and strings; Trauermusik, for viola and strings; Symphonic Dances; Nobilissima Visione, suite; Violin Concerto; Symphony in E-flat; Cupid and Psyche, overture; Symphonic Metamorphosis on Themes by Carl Maria von Weber; Theme and Variations According to the Four Temperaments, for piano and orchestra; Hérodiade, for chamber orchestra; Symphonia Serena; Clarinet Concerto; Piano Concerto; Concerto for Trumpet, Bassoon, and String Orchestra; Sinfonietta; Horn Concerto; Die Harmonie der Welt, symphony; Pittsburgh Symphony; Organ Concerto.

Piano Music—4 sonatas; Sonata for Two Pianos; Suite; Klaviermusik, op. 37; Ludus Tonalis.

Vocal Music—Die Junge Magd, cycle; Die Serenaden, little cantata; Das Marienleben, cycle (rev. in 1948); Nine English Songs; Bal des Pendus.

ABOUT

Cohn, A., Twentieth Century Music in Western Europe; Collaer, P., A History of Modern Music; Ewen, D. (ed.), The New Book of Modern Composers; Hartog, H. (ed.), European Music in the Twentieth Century; Rosenfeld, P., Discoveries of a Music Critic; Strobel, H., Paul Hindemith (3d ed.); Paul Hindemith, Zeugnis in Bildern.

Musical Quarterly, October 1931, January 1944, July 1964; Musical Review (London), November 1954.

Gustav Holst
1874–1934

Gustav Theodore Holst was born in Cheltenham, England, September 21, 1874. His full name was Gustavus Theodore von Holst; his Swedish ancestors had migrated to England in 1807. Gustav Holst anglicized his first name and deleted the *von* at the outbreak of World War I.

Gustav's father, who was of English birth, was an excellent all-round musician: conductor, pianist, organist, and teacher. One of his pupils was Clara Lediard, a gifted pianist, whom he married. The piano lessons she gave Gustav while he was still a child were soon supplemented by organ lessons with his father.

When Gustav was eight, his mother died and his father remarried. His home life seems to have deteriorated after that. He later

Holst: hŏlst

described his boyhood as both "miserable and scared." He was a sickly, near-sighted, completely neglected boy. His music study—continued while he attended Cheltenham Grammar School—apparently provided him with an escape from life's sterner realities. When he was nineteen he began to earn his living by playing the organ and leading a choir at Wyck Rissington in Gloucestershire.

GUSTAV HOLST

He went to London in 1893 for more intensive music study, enrolling at the Royal College of Music. There he specialized in piano with Herbert Sharpe until he suffered a severe attack of neuritis and transferred to the trombone. In composition he was a pupil of Charles Villiers Stanford, on a scholarship after 1895. While attending the College, he wrote the music for several operettas which reflected his enthusiasm for Sir Arthur Sullivan. The first of these stage pieces was *Landsdown Castle*, performed in Cheltenham on February 7, 1893. At the College he became a friend of Ralph Vaughan Williams who greatly influenced his development through the years.

Holst's creative efforts became more serious as he came under the influence of literature, both English and American. In 1899 he completed a concert overture, *Walt Whitman*. It was followed in 1900 by a symphony, *Cotswolds*, written in memory of William Morris and introduced at Bournemouth in 1902. His first success, though still a minor one, came with *The Mystic Trumpeter*, for soprano and

orchestra, based on Whitman. In 1904 this became Holst's first composition to be performed by the Royal Philharmonic of London.

Upon leaving the Royal Academy, Holst earned his living playing the trombone in the orchestra of the Carl Rosa Opera Company. For a number of years he continued to be a trombonist with major orchestras. At the same time he served for several seasons as organist at the Royal Opera in London. During this period Holst also conducted a choral group. One of the members, a young soprano named Isobel Harrison, became his wife in 1901. A daughter, Imogen, was born to them in 1907.

Two years after his marriage, Holst became a teacher of music at the Edward Alleyn School for Girls in East Dulwich. With this job he embarked upon a career to which he would henceforth devote a good deal of his talent and energy. He became music master at St. Paul's Girls' School in 1905 and at Morley College in 1907, retaining both posts up to the time of his death. From 1919 to 1923 he also taught composition at Reading College; from 1919 on, at the Royal College of Music in London. "His success in this direction," said Edmund Rubbra in *Chesterian*, "was undoubtedly due to his ability to divine all the difficulties that a mind growing into music has to meet and overcome. Holst never dictated the direction in which the pupil's music should grow; rather was it suggested that given such-and-such an idea, the logical development would be so-and-so. But if the pupil did not agree, it was not insisted upon. The usual relationship of master and pupil yielded to a companionship on a voyage of discovery, and the excitements of the journeying were shared by both to an equal degree."

From about 1906 through 1911, Holst's music was strongly affected by the mysticism of Eastern philosophy and poetry, and he began to assume an exotic personality. This was his so-called Sanskrit phase, with his greatest stimulation coming from Hindu epics, particularly the hymns of the *Rig-Veda*. Under this influence, in the years between 1908 and 1911, he wrote four sets of choral hymns to texts from the *Rig-Veda*. In addition, *Sita* (1906), an opera, was based on an episode from the *Ramayana*; and a chamber opera, *Sāvitri* (1908), used material from the *Mahabharata*.

One of his most highly esteemed works in this style was the orchestral suite *Beni Mora* (1910), successfully performed at a Queen's Hall concert in London May 1, 1912.

With the passing of the Sanskrit phase, Holst completed the two orchestral works by which he is today most often represented on concert programs. The first showed the impact made on him by the revival of English folk music, in which he first became interested in 1905. It was a suite for strings, *St. Paul's* (1913), so titled because it was written for the school orchestra of St. Paul's Girls' School, where he was teaching and where it was introduced. In four movements, the music continuously reflects the personality and the modal style of old English songs, two of which are quoted in the finale: "Dargason" (which is repeated thirty times with various harmonic and rhythmic changes) and "Greensleeves" (which serves as a countermelody).

A second orchestral suite, *The Planets*, was completely different in character. This music, as the composer himself explained, "was suggested by the astrological significance of the planets. . . . If any guide to the music is required, the subtitle to each piece will be found sufficient. . . . For instance, Jupiter brings jollity. . . . Saturn . . . not only physical decay but also a vision of fulfillment. Mercury is the symbol of the mind, and so forth." The other movements are Mars, the Bringer of War; Venus, the Bringer of Peace; Uranus, the Magician; and Neptune, the Mystic. *The Planets* was written in the period between 1914 and 1916 and was introduced at a private concert on September 29, 1918. Five of the seven movements were heard publicly on February 27, 1919, and the entire suite was given on November 15, 1920. Brilliant in its orchestration, dramatic in sonorities, picturesque in harmonies and rhythms, and vividly descriptive, *The Planets* enjoyed an immediate and lasting success.

When World War I broke out, Holst tried to enlist but was turned down because of poor health. He spent the war years in a cottage in Essex, composing. Besides *The Planets*, he completed an important choral composition, *The Hymn of Jesus* (1917), text derived from the Apocryphal Acts of St. John. "One feels," says Edmund Rubbra, "that this Gnostic initiation hymn released all pent-up flood of religious feeling in Holst, and yet with what art are the turbulent waters controlled and led into musical channels! The work is perhaps the highest level of Holst's achievement." The Hymn had its first performance in London March 25, 1920.

In October 1918 Holst was dispatched by the YMCA to Salonika, Constantinople, and elsewhere in Asia Minor to help organize musical activities among the British troops stationed there. He was back in England by the end of 1919, resuming his activities as teacher and composer. In February 1923, Holst fell off a platform in Reading, England. The effects of this accident at first seemed negligible, and he did not hesitate to fulfill contractual obligations to deliver several lectures in the United States, at the University of Michigan and at Harvard. This was his first visit to the United States. He returned to England in 1924. His physical condition deteriorated and he had to give up his work as teacher, lecturer, and conductor, and concentrate on composition alone. Fortunately, he was now in a financial position to do so. His opera *The Perfect Fool* (introduced at Covent Garden in London May 14, 1923) had made such a deep impression on one of the listeners that he anonymously sent Holst a large sum of money to enable him to devote himself exclusively to composition. One of the important results of this newly found financial freedom was an opera based on Shakespeare's *Henry IV* entitled *At the Boar's Festival*. It was a major success when produced in Manchester April 3, 1925.

For the next decade Holst lived in comparative seclusion in London. He was frequently in poor health. His daughter, Imogen, described him as "sitting huddled over the fire, sinking lower and lower into a gray region where thought and feeling had ceased to exist and the spirit itself was numb. . . . His mind was closed in gray isolation. He had sunk . . . into that cold region of utter despair." Nevertheless he continued to write music. In 1932 he felt well enough to attempt a second visit to the United States, for the purpose of directing a concert of his works with the Boston Symphony and delivering several lectures at Harvard. But illness prevented him from accepting other engagements. In London he underwent a serious operation that proved fatal. He died there on May 25, 1934, and was buried in Chichester Cathedral. Three years later a Holst Room was opened as a memorial at Morley College.

His separation from the outside world in the 1920's had brought about a radical change of style in his music. His writing became increasingly austere, economical, and objective. He began to experiment with nonharmonic counterpoint and free tonalities. Lean and spare though his music was now, it had lost little of its former poetic sensitivity or expressiveness. In this new vein he wrote the *Twelve Songs*, to lyrics by Humbert Wolfe (1929), and the Concerto for Two Violins and Orchestra, performed in London on April 3, 1930.

"Holst's weaknesses," wrote Ralph Vaughan Williams in *Music and Letters* (July 1920), "are the defects of his qualities—occasionally his magnificent technique masters him and the end gets lost in the means. Sometimes he spoils the noble simplicity of his work by an unnecessary piece of elaboration; at other times, the very individuality of his thought which requires such a personal technique causes a flaw in his work.... But the very fact that these lapses are noticeable only goes to show how individual his music is. As time goes on, the discrepancies get fewer and fewer, and his style gets maturer and maturer, simpler and more individual, and this individuality shows in all his music; whether it is in the extreme harmonic and rhythmic thought of *The Planets* or the absolute simplicity of the *Four Carols*, his signature is plain on every page."

MAJOR WORKS

Ballets—The Golden Goose, choral ballet; The Morning of the Year, choral ballet.

Chamber Music—Quintet for Piano and Wind; Woodwind Quintet; Suite in E-flat; Terzetto, for flute, oboe, and viola.

Choral Music—Four Carols; Choral Hymns, four groups; The Cloud Messenger; Hecuba's Lament; Hymn to Dionysus; Three Festival Choruses; The Hymn of Jesus; Ode to Death; Festival Te Deum; Choral Fantasia; Wassail Song; Six Canons; anthems, choral folk songs, part-songs, psalms, and various a cappella choruses.

Operas—Sita; Sāvitri, chamber opera; The Perfect Fool; At the Boar's Head; The Tale of the Wandering Scholar.

Orchestral Music—Walt Whitman Overture; Cotswolds, symphony; Suite de Ballet in E-flat major; Indra; The Mystic Trumpeter, for soprano and orchestra; Songs of the West; Somerset Rhapsody; Two Songs Without Words; Seven Scottish Airs, for strings with piano; Beni Mora, suite; Phantasies,

suite; St. Paul's Suite; The Planets, suite; Japanese Suite; Fugal Overture; Fugal Concerto, for flute, oboe, and strings; Egdon Heath; Hammersmith, prelude and scherzo; Concerto for Two Violins and Orchestra.

Piano Music—Toccata on Newburn Lads; Christmas Day in the Morning; Nocturne; Jig.

Vocal Music—Various songs for voice and piano.

ABOUT

Holst, I., Gustav Holst; Holst, I., The Music of Gustav Holst; Rubbra, E., Gustav Holst.

Chesterian (London), July–August, 1934; Musical Times (London), July 1934.

Arthur Honegger
1892–1955

Arthur Honegger was born on March 10, 1892, in Le Havre. His parents were Swiss who had left Zürich to set up an important business of café fixtures. Though he was born and lived most of his life in France, Arthur Honegger always retained his Swiss citizenship.

ARTHUR HONEGGER

From his mother, an excellent amateur pianist, he inherited a love of music and acquired a passion for Beethoven's piano sonatas. He soon began to take piano lessons from her, violin lessons from a local teacher, and lessons in harmony and composition from the church organist.

When Honegger was sixteen, he entered his father's business; but his father saw that his

Honegger: ô nĕ gâr'

interest lay elsewhere and sent him to Zürich for additional music study at the Conservatory. There Friedrich Hegar, the director, recognized the boy's talent and was influential in persuading his father to consent to intensive preparation for a professional career. Honegger stayed at the Zürich Conservatory for two years. In 1912 he returned to France and entered the Paris Conservatory, where his teachers included Gedalge (counterpoint), Widor (composition and orchestration), and d'Indy (conducting). In 1914 his studies were interrupted by a year of military service in Switzerland.

While still a student at the Paris Conservatory, Honegger wrote several songs gathered into *Quatre Poèmes*. Some of these were heard in a small hall in Paris on July 13, 1916. One of the songs, *"Prière"* (words by Francis Jammes) was singled out by the composer in his maturity as one of the "best songs, and the most melodious" he had ever written. Several instrumental works followed, among them *Toccata and Variations* for piano, which Andrée Vaurabourg introduced December 15, 1916; the first string quartet (1917), described by Honegger's teacher Gedalge as the "touchstone of a real musician"; the orchestral prelude *Aglavaine et Sélysette*, the composer conducting its première at the Paris Conservatory on April 3, 1917; and the first violin sonata, introduced by Honegger and Andrée Vaurabourg on an all-Honegger program January 19, 1918. The influence of Debussy, Ravel, and Richard Strauss can be detected in most of these apprentice works.

Honegger's name became associated with a group known as Les Nouveaux Jeunes, which drew its guidance from Erik Satie. This group (which also included Germaine Tailleferre, Georges Auric, Roland-Manuel, and Francis Poulenc) made its bow at a concert in Paris January 15, 1918. The Nouveaux Jeunes turned out to be the parent body of the more highly publicized group of young French composers known as The French Six or Les Six. Honegger's identification with this group was responsible for bringing his music a wider circulation than heretofore. The other members of The Six were Darius Milhaud, Louis Durey, Tailleferre, Poulenc, and Auric. (The story of how The Six came into being is told in the sketch of Georges Auric.)

The French Six was not a school of music in the accepted sense–that is, a group of composers with a common purpose and a common ideal. It was a school created artificially by the critic Henri Collet in a review published in *Comoedia* January 16, 1920. Actually, each of the six members produced compositions that had little spiritual or stylistic affinity with the works of the others. But it was also true that all six, at one point or another during the 1920's, produced a number of compositions in a light, catchy, popular style–compositions using music hall tunes and ragtime idioms – in short, compositions which belonged to "everyday music" (*musique pour tous les jours*).

Of the six, Honegger seemed least interested in such adventures into music with tongue in cheek, music that was simple in structure and popular enough in style to attract a large public. Only a scattered handful of Honegger's works can be included in such a category, the only significant one being the Concertino for Piano and Orchestra (1924) which Andrée Vaurabourg introduced in Paris May 23, 1925.

And so, although Honegger's name is included with The Six and although he first gained wide recognition as a member of this group, Honegger had very little in common with the other five composers. Strong-willed and artistically independent, Honegger listened to the esthetic ideals and exchange of ideas of his colleagues, and he admired their music. But he insisted on going in the direction in which his artistic conscience led him.

Characteristic of his independence and his necessity to obey artistic conscience was the fact that his first major success as a composer came with a work that clung to the traditions, structures, and polyphonic style of a past age: the oratorio *Le Roi David* (*King David*), which the composer described as a "dramatic psalm." He completed it in 1921, and its first performance took place at Mézières, Switzerland, on June 11, 1921. The text by René Morat traced the career of the Biblical David from humble shepherd to king and prophet; Honegger's composition comprised three sections which in turn were divided into twenty-eight parts. The music was eclectic, partly Hebraic or Oriental in its intervallic structure, partly polyphonic in the style of Handel or Bach, partly in a simple folk-song idiom. At times his writing was also dramatized by modern harmonies and rhythms. But deep religious conviction was felt throughout the music which, at moments, was also touched by spiritual overtones. *Le Roi David* made a deep impression. In 1923 Honegger reorchestrated it. Reintroduced that year in Winterthur, *Le Roi David* proved an even greater success. The oratorio circled the music world, being heard in Paris in 1924, in New York in 1925, and in Zürich and Rome in 1926.

Le Roi David made Honegger a favorite son of the conservative wing of French composers, just as it caused eyebrows to lift among the more progressive French musicians and critics. But Honegger had no intention of identifying himself permanently with a neo-Handelian or a neobaroque movement. His strong rhythmic language, voice of the twentieth century, distinguished the incidental music he wrote for Paul Méral's *Le Dit des Jeux du Monde*, produced in Paris on December 2, 1921. More vigorous still, and more individual in harmonic and rhythmic treatment, was the "mimed symphony" *Horace Victorieux*, heard in Lausanne October 30, 1921. "*Horace Victorieux*," says Paul Collaer, "surpasses all of Honegger's symphonic works in its expressive power and the homogeneity of its structure"—a truly remarkable appraisal even though it was written before Honegger had produced his last symphonies.

Any doubt that Honegger did not belong in the camp of reaction but stood with the modernists was completely dispelled by *Pacific 231*, an orchestral piece written in 1923 and introduced at a Koussevitzky concert in Paris on May 8, 1924. With realistic strokes, Honegger here described in bold discords and dynamic rhythms the progress of a locomotive traveling at a speed of one hundred and twenty kilometers an hour. Regarded as a musical symbol of the machine age, *Pacific 231* created a sensation, and, together with *Le Roi David*, helped to solidify Honegger's fame.

His reputation was further enhanced by the biblical opera *Judith*, mounted in Monte Carlo on February 13, 1926; and by a cacophonous piece for orchestra describing a soccer game and appropriately named *Rugby*. *Rugby* received a most unusual première on December 31, 1928; it was performed at a soccer stadium in Paris during the intermission of an international rugby match between France and England.

Except for the tongue-in-cheek Piano Concertino of 1925, Honegger's style in the 1920's and early 1930's remained passionate, rugged, freely discordant. It had a strong rhythmic pulse. The contrapuntal writing was often linear. Yet for all this, Honegger also had a bent for lyricism. In analyzing the Honegger music of this period, Guido Pannain noted that lyricism was one of its salient qualities, a lyricism "sometimes instinct with joy and praise, sometimes touched with a melancholy that expresses itself in songs of winged sweetness. The vivid score of *Le Roi David* is steeped in the poignancy of a racial, a national heart cry. The same motive kindles the frenzied vocalism of *Judith*. Honegger in this mood is a poet of the human voice raised in song."

On May 10, 1926, Honegger married Andrée Vaurabourg, the pianist who for several years had been responsible for introducing many of his piano compositions. They made their home in Paris and had one daughter. In 1929 Honegger visited the United States for the first time, appearing as a guest conductor of many major American orchestras in performances of his works.

In the middle 1930's a new artistic dimension was given to his music through a deepening of spiritual values, an increasing mysticism, a new depth of religious feeling. This became evident in what today is regarded as one of his masterworks, the dramatic oratorio *Jeanne d'Arc au Bûcher* (*Joan of Arc at the Stake*), with a mystical symbolic text by Paul Claudel. It was first heard in Basel on May 12, 1938, Paul Sacher conducting and Ida Rubinstein appearing as Joan. Honegger described this work as a "mimodrama," intending it to be produced on the stage with scenery and costumes; but it is often presented as an oratorio. Throughout, the composition presents Joan of Arc fastened to the stake, about to be burned. Her life and career are reviewed in a prologue and eleven scenes through flashbacks described partly by Joan (a speaking role) and partly by Frère Dominique. Comments upon what they narrate are made through choral episodes, choral readings, and orchestral background music. Melody, recitative, and speech are skillfully combined to project the mighty drama of Joan's martyrdom.

Honegger again collaborated with Paul Claudel on an oratorio in 1939, and once again

a work of surpassing majesty was created–
La Danse des Morts (*The Dance of the Dead*).
The première took place in Basel March 2,
1940. Reviewing that performance, Arno Huth
praised Honegger's score for the very same
qualities that had distinguished *Joan of Arc
at the Stake:* "His amazing use of different
media—the speaker, soloists, choruses, orchestra and organ—as well as his sureness of
form, again prove his mastery. No matter how
various the form elements, they are all incorporated into one entity, subordinated to a
dramatic will and used for dramatic effect. . . .
The dance of the dead and the final choruses
have sweeping expressive power, the air is
surcharged with emotion. As a stylistic achievement, the work belongs with Honegger's oratorios, *Le Roi David* and *Jeanne d'Arc* . . .
[and] stands as one of his greatest works."

During World War II Honegger remained
in Paris, active in the Resistance movement.
It is the opinion of Willi Reich that the *Symphony for Strings* (1941) reflects Honegger's
somber moods and intense personal feelings
during this trying period. The symphony was
heard in Basel on May 18, 1942. When it was
introduced in the United States (by the Boston
Symphony under Charles Münch on December
27, 1946), Olin Downes said in the New York
Times: "This score of Honegger's communicates intense feeling that comes from deep
within. . . . What matters in this new symphony
is the composer's emotion which has wrung
from him richly expressive music. For Mr.
Honegger, in these pages, is speaking willy-
nilly from the depths of his heart. . . . He uses
the strings as the most sensitive and expressive
instruments of the orchestra, the one nearest
the human voice."

On October 22, 1944—soon after the liberation of Paris—the world première of Honegger's
Chant de Libération (text by Bernard Zimmer),
commemorating the historic event, was given.
The work had been written long before the liberation—in 1942, during the Nazi occupation,
in anticipation of France's freedom.

Some of Honegger's greatest music after
the war came in the form of symphonies. The
third one, entitled *Liturgique*, was introduced
under Charles Münch's direction in Zürich on
August 17, 1946. This work is made up of three
odes reflecting the emotional content of three
sections of the traditional Latin Mass—the
Dies Irae, the *De Profundis*, and the *Dona
Nobis Pacem*. In the first two, man is in revolt
against God, but in the last section he finds
peace of mind at last. The fourth symphony
makes use of old popular songs from Basel
and is called *Deliciae Basilienses* (Basel Delights); its first performance took place in Basel
on January 21, 1947. Honegger's fifth and last
symphony, which the Boston Symphony under
Münch introduced on March 9, 1951, is integrated through the repetition of a quiet drum
tap in D as the last note of each movement;
it is also dominated in the first movement
by a powerful chorale theme, which the full
orchestra presents in the opening. This chorale
introduces a religious mood, but before the
movement ends, the mood lapses into tragedy
that becomes intensified in the finale. "The
Fifth," says John N. Burk in his program notes
for the Boston Symphony, "is the most poignant, the most inward and deeply felt of his
works." Then, commenting on Honegger's
over-all symphonic production, Burk added:
"It was his symphonies that received his more
direct, deeper, more personal sentiments. As
a symphonist of France he stood pretty much
alone."

Honegger paid a second visit to the United
States in July 1947 to conduct a master class
in composition at the Berkshire Music Center
at Tanglewood. A heart attack made it impossible for him to complete his assignment.
After his return to Paris, his poor health made
further composition extremely trying and difficult. Nevertheless he managed to complete
a number of works, including the fifth symphony, and the *Monopartita*, for orchestra,
heard in Zürich on June 12, 1951. But Honegger
knew that his fifth symphony was his swan
song in that form, as he wrote to Münch in
1951, confessing that he was now far too tired
and too weak to undertake any more ambitious creative projects. He died of a heart
attack in Paris on November 27, 1955.

"He was one of the most pleasant and
charming of men," recalls Everett Helm. "The
gentleness of his demeanor was matched by a
quiet and ready wit. There was no vanity in
his character, nor was he touched by those
feelings of personal ambition or professional
jealousy that all too often mar the tempers of
composers. He was a generous colleague, happy
at the success of his friends and interested in

their works, while modestly belittling the success of his own."

About his aims as a composer Honegger said: "I attach great importance to musical architecture, which I should never want to be sacrificed for reasons of a literary or pictorial order. My model is Bach. . . . I do not seek . . . the return of harmonic simplicity. I find on the contrary that we should use the harmonic materials created by the schools which preceded us, but in a different way—as the base of lines and rhythms."

He also wrote: "Composition is not a profession. It is a mania—a sweet folly. Composition is the most mysterious of all the arts . . . a great part of my work stands outside my own volition. A good composer finds the golden mean between prose and poetry, between craftsmanship and inspiration. I reserve the title of composer for those whose aim is not to cater to the public's taste in everyday enjoyment but, first and foremost, to create a work of art, to express some thought, some emotions, to crystallize their attitude to esthetic or purely human problems."

MAJOR WORKS

Ballets—Skating Rink; Sémiramis, ballet-pantomime; Le Cantique des Cantiques; L'Appel de la Montagne; L'Homme à la Peau de Léopard.

Chamber Music—3 string quartets; 2 violin sonatas; Viola Sonata; Sonatina for Two Violins; Cello Sonata; Sonatina for Violin and Piano; Sonata for Solo Violin.

Choral Music—Le Roi David, oratorio; Cris du Monde; Jeanne d'Arc au Bûcher (Joan of Arc at the Stake); La Danse des Morts; Chant de Libération.

Operas—Judith; Antigone; Amphion; L'Aiglon (with Ibert); Charles le Téméraire.

Orchestral Music—5 symphonies; Pastorale d'Été; Horace Victorieux; Chant de Joie; Pacific 231; Piano Concertino; Rugby; Cello Concerto; Mouvement Symphonique no. 3; Concerto da Camera, for flute, English horn, and strings; Suite Archaïque; Monopartita.

Piano Music—Le Cahier Romand; Hommage à Albert Roussel; Prélude, Arioso et Fughetta sur le Nom de Bach; Souvenir de Chopin; Partita, for two pianos.

Vocal Music—Quatre Poèmes; Poésies de Jean Cocteau; Cinq Mélodies-Minute; Trois Psaumes; individual songs for voice and piano.

ABOUT

Bruyr, J., Honegger et Son Œuvre; Delannoy, M.F.G., Honegger; Feschotte, J., Arthur Honegger, l'Homme et Son Œuvre; Gauthier, A., Arthur Honegger; Gérard, C., Arthur Honegger; Honegger, A., I Am a Composer; Landowski, M., Honegger; Matter, J., Honegger; Reich, W. (ed.), Arthur Honegger, Nach-

klang: Schriften, Photos, Dokumente; Tappolet, W., Arthur Honegger.

Chesterian (London), Winter 1956; Musical America, January 1, 1956; Musical Opinion (London), February 1956; Saturday Review, December 31, 1955.

Alan Hovhaness
1911–

Alan Hovhaness was born in Somerville, Massachusetts, March 8, 1911. His mother was of Scottish descent; his father, a professor of chemistry at Tufts University, was Armenian. Alan's surname was Chakmakjian.

ALAN HOVHANESS

In view of the Oriental character of his later mature compositions, it is interesting that Hovhaness' upbringing was thoroughly American, and that his early musical orientation was exclusively Occidental. When he was five his family moved to Arlington, a suburb of Boston, where he grew up in an American Baptist environment. By that time he had already demonstrated his precocity in music by devising his own method of notation. When he was eight, he began to study the piano with Adelaide Proctor. Heinrich Gebhard, one of the most highly respected piano teachers in Boston, was the next to give him his formal training. Later, in 1932, he went to the New England Conservatory on a scholarship and for two years he studied composition there with Frederick Converse.

Hovhaness: hō vä′ nĕs

Hovhaness

He had been writing music copiously from his boyhood days on, music grounded in Western traditions, music in every possible medium. Most of his writing at this time revealed the conscious influence of Sibelius; in fact, in his ambition to become an American Sibelius he made a trip to Finland to acquaint himself with the country and its culture. Under that influence he completed a symphony in 1933 which was performed by the New England Conservatory Orchestra and received the Samuel Endicott Prize. Hovhaness destroyed this work, and another one, written in 1936, became Symphony No. 1. It received its world première in England on May 26, 1939, in a performance by the BBC Symphony under Leslie Heward. Heward at this time referred to Hovhaness as a genius and described his work as "powerful, virile, and musically solid."

In the years between 1940 and 1947 Hovhaness lived in a small, cramped room in Boston. He supported himself on an income of about forty dollars a month, earned by playing the organ, accompanying, and teaching, while at the same time he continued his music study. In 1942 he attended Bohuslav Martinu's master class in composition at the Berkshire Music Center at Tanglewood (once again on a scholarship).

During this period he found himself ineluctably drawn to Eastern music and Eastern culture. Earlier he had shown an interest in the works of an Armenian composer-priest named Gomidas Vartabed. His interest was later rearoused when he attended a performance in Boston by Uday Shankar and his company in a program of Indian dances and music. As an organist at the Armenian church of St. James in Watertown, Massachusetts, to which he had been appointed in 1940, he came into direct contact with the monodic and modal styles of Armenian liturgical music, which exerted a powerful fascination upon him. This activity coincided with his already fully developed antiquarian tastes for old art, architecture, and music. He now began to study the Armenian language in order to more fully explore the music of Armenia. At the same time, he initiated intensive explorations into the music of the Near East, Middle East, and Far East. For hours he listened to Armenian priests, bishops, and deacons sing the ancient modes with pure intonation. He studied the old

Armenian notations as collected by Father Hagop Mekjian. Now thoroughly dissatisfied with the music he had thus far written, he destroyed some several hundred of his compositions, including seven symphonies, five string quartets, operas, and piano music. At the same time he began to evolve for himself a new manner of writing in which the musical practices and traditions of the Western world were superseded by the individual stylistic and structural character of Armenian music. He began to draw his inspiration for new compositions from Eastern geography, backgrounds, culture, and people.

His first important works in this exotic and Oriental style came in the middle 1940's. The *Armenian Rhapsody No. 2* (1944) makes use of two Armenian dance tunes and an Armenian feast-day melody known as a *dagh. Lousadzak* (*Coming of Light*), a concerto for piano and orchestra (1944), imitates the sound of Oriental string and percussion instruments and is thoroughly Oriental in the way it dispenses with chordal harmonies and achieves climaxes through spiraling melodic lines reaching towards a point of silence. This concerto was given its world première by the Boston Symphony, February 4, 1945. *Elibris* (1944), a concerto for flute and orchestra introduced in San Francisco on January 26, 1950, was named after the god of dawn worshiped by the prehistoric people inhabiting Armenia. Here Hovhaness imitates the sounds of ancient folk music through the free use of the *raga*, a type of melody found in Hindu classical music. *Mihir* (1945), for two pianos, was named after the ancient Armenian fire god and also is Oriental, this time in its series of repeated notes, modal melodies, and intriguing arabesque figures over a cantus. *Arjuna* (1947), Hovhaness' eighth symphony, has all of its melodic material shaped after the contours of Armenian folk songs though the programmatic content is based on an Indian story. On February 1, 1960, thirteen years after its composition, it was heard for the first time in Madras, India; soon after it was extensively played—in Japan, Korea, Germany, France, Hawaii, and Vancouver (on a Canadian Broadcasting Corporation program).

His style now clearly defined, Hovhaness began to produce an immense library of music. Olin Downes described this style as "the repetition or variation of melodic lines; the polyphonic intermingling of figures and arabesques. . . . There is repetition and variation, but not development or architectonics. The modal scale designs are those in the terminology of . . . *ragas* and the fixed rhythmical structure of the *talas*."

Virgil Thomson once provided an even more detailed description of Hovhaness' music by writing in the *Herald-Tribune*: "Hovhaness writes in the early Christian, the medieval and the modern American techniques, possibly even a little in the pre-Christian manner of the ancient and cultivated people. He observes the ancient rules and imitates with modern violins a sizable selection of Near Eastern stringed instruments. He even extends the Oriental grammar of composition . . . held notes against which fluid melodies expand at ease and even quintal counterpoint. . . . The music is at times strophic in phraseology and emotionally continuous, never climactic. Each piece is like a long roll of handmade wallpaper. Its motionless quality is a little hypnotic. . . . Its expressive function is predominantly religious, ceremonial, incantory, its spiritual content of the purest."

Exotic or picturesque or legendary subject matter is a continual source of inspiration to Hovhaness. His ninth symphony, *Saint Vartin* (1948), is a tribute to a national Armenian hero; a fantasy for orchestra, *Anahid* (1945), pays homage to a goddess of pre-Christian Armenia. *Talin* (1952), a concerto for viola and orchestra, was inspired by a ruined Armenian cathedral; the Symphony No. 6 (1962) owes its stimulus, as the composer himself explained, to "the beauty of Korean mountains, the sublimity of Korean traditional music, the wisdom and nobility of Korean people." *Meditation on Zeami* (1964), for orchestra, which Leopold Stokowski introduced with the American Symphony on October 6, 1964, is named after the father of the Japanese No dramas. And *To Vishnu*, Hovhaness' nineteenth symphony—commissioned by the New York Philharmonic for its Promenade concerts and introduced by that orchestra under André Kostelanetz's direction in June 1967—was a tribute to the Hindu god, who, in the composer's words, is "the protector and preserver of the life of the spheres in their endless rotations and spiral motions."

Hovhaness made his first appearance as a conductor of his own music at Town Hall, New York, on June 17, 1945, in a program of his works sponsored by the artists' committee of the Armenian Students Association of America. From 1948 to 1951 he was a member of the faculty of the Boston Conservatory of Music. In 1951 he received a grant from the National Institute of Arts and Letters. This was also the year in which Hovhaness moved permanently to New York City.

In 1953 and in 1955 he received Guggenheim fellowships, and in 1958 honorary doctorates were conferred upon him by the University of Rochester and by Bates College. A Fulbright research fellowship in 1959 made it possible for him to undertake a world tour for research into Oriental music and for the performance of his major works in Oriental countries. He became the first Western composer invited by the musicians of South India to participate at the annual festival of music at Madras; for the event, on commission, he revised his *Madras Sonata*, for piano, which he had written in 1946. Hovhaness also became the first Western composer asked to write music for an orchestra made up entirely of Indian instruments. His composition, entitled *Nagooran* after the great Indian saint of Madras, was given its world première over the All-India Radio in Madras. At some of his Madras concerts, Hovhaness delighted his audiences by performing improvisations on South Indian scales. After one of these performances an Indian musician told him: "You are a priest of music."

Hovhaness achieved another personal triumph when he paid a visit to Tokyo in February 1960. He was greeted by photographers and reporters as though he were a world-famous diplomat. During his visit, he was socially lionized; he was invited by the Japan Philharmonic and the Tokyo Symphony to direct performances of some of his compositions; he appeared on television; he was the recipient of a number of commissions. While in Japan he completed two important chamber music works: *Koke No Niwa* (*Moss Garden*), for English horn (or clarinet), harp, and percussion; and the Piano Quintet. Hovhaness paid a second visit to Japan, during the summer of 1962—this time on a Rockefeller grant for research in the ancient court music of

Japan and Korea. Before this second visit, Hovhaness had served for half a year as composer-in-residence at the University of Hawaii; later, in 1966, he became a composer-in-residence with the Seattle Symphony.

Hovhaness has written music for both ballet and the theatre. *Is There Survival?* was a ballet inspired by a pagan warrior king of Armenian legend, King Vakhaken. Written in 1949, it was produced in 1950 with Jan Veen's choreography. In 1955 the composer revised his score and on this occasion selected several numbers for an orchestral work which has since become one of his most frequently performed compositions. Another ballet score was *Ardent Spring*, written for Martha Graham's tour of the Far East in 1955–1956. This proved so successful that Martha Graham commissioned him to write the music for another ballet, *Circe*, in 1963.

In 1962 the East-West Center in Hawaii commissioned Hovhaness to write a music-dance drama. He fulfilled this obligation by writing both the text and the music for *Wind Drum*, which was first performed at the University of Hawaii Music Festival on May 22, 1962. The rhythmic bodily movements were inspired by Korean dances; the music was constructed from the six-tone scale of Indian music. The entire production was staged with the simplicity of a Japanese No drama. "The standing ovation accorded this . . . presentation . . . attested to the fact that the audience knew it had been in the presence of Beauty," reported the Honolulu *Star Bulletin*.

For the stage, Hovhaness created the incidental music for *The Flowering Peach*, a play by Clifford Odets that opened on Broadway on December 28, 1958.

In commenting on Hovhaness' vast output, Oliver Daniel revealed in the *Saturday Review* that he is writing music all the time and in whatever place he may find himself: "When he does not have a blank music notebook with him, a menu, the reverse side of a bill, or any piece of paper with adequate white space becomes something on which to write his music." Oliver Daniel also contributed the following word picture of the composer's appearance and personality. "Physically he is tall, excessively thin, in fact gaunt. His walk, or one might say gait, is hardly graceful, and his manner, essentially shy, is at times as uncomfortable

as that of a strolling pigeon. He is by nature ascetic; he is a vegetarian and brings his bowl of yogurt to eat in place of a filet mignon. He is a blend of saintly El Greco mysticism, Oriental resignation and Western dynamism." Hovhaness is married to the former Naru Whittington, a pianist. An inveterate traveler, Hovhaness finds that "the nomadic life is a necessity." In addition to his trips to the East, Hovhaness made an extensive tour of France and Germany in 1961 and of the Soviet Union in 1965.

MAJOR WORKS

Ballets—Is There Survival?; Wind Drum; Circe.

Chamber Music—3 string quartets; 2 Quartets, for flute, oboe, cello, and piano; October Mountain, for percussion sextet; Varak, for violin and piano; Saris, for violin and piano; Suite for Oboe and Bassoon; Khirgiz Suite, for violin and piano; Upon Enchanted Ground, for flute, cello, harp, and tam-tam; Orbit No. 1, for flute, harp, celesta, and tam-tam; Hanna, for two clarinets and two pianos; The World Beneath the Sea, No. 1, for saxophone, harp, vibraphone, tympani, and gong; Koke No Niwa, for English horn, percussion, and harp; Wind Quintet; Sextet, for alto recorder, string quartet, and harpsichord (or piano); String Trio; Sonata for Trumpet and Organ; Dance of the Black Haired Mountain Storm, for flute and percussion; Sonata for Flute and Organ; Three Visions of Saint Mesrob, for violin and piano; Sonata for Two Oboes and Organ; Bacchanale, for percussion; Mysterious Horse Before the Gate, for trombone and percussion; Four Bagatelles, for string quartet; Sonata for Flute Solo; The World Beneath the Sea, No. 2, for clarinet, harp, chimes, tympani, and double bass.

Choral Music—From the End of the Earth; Transfiguration; Sing Aloud; Make Haste; Anabasis; Glory to God; Ad Lyram; Magnificat; Gloria; Look Toward the Sea; Psalm 148; Psalm 28; Glory to Man; Fuji; Psalm 23.

Operas—Blue Flame, fairy tale; The Burning House (one-act opera); Pilate (one-act opera); The Spirit of the Avalanche (one-act opera).

Orchestral Music—19 symphonies; 8 concertos for orchestra; 3 piano concertos; 3 Armenian rhapsodies; 2 violin concertos; Psalm and Fugue, for string orchestra; Khrimian Hairig, concerto for trumpet and string orchestra; Anahid, fantasy; Kohar; Haroutouin, aria and fugue for trumpet and string orchestra; Divertimento; Artik; Harmonica Concerto; Talin, concerto for viola and orchestra; Vision from High Rock; Meditation on Orpheus; In Memory of an Artist, suite; Accordion Concerto; Mountain of Prophecy; Variations and Fugue; Floating World; Meditation on Zeami; Fantasy on Japanese Wood Prints, for xylophone and orchestra; The Holy City, tone poem; Praise the Lord with Psaltry.

Organ Music—Dawn Hymn; The Lord's Prayer; O God Our Help in Ages Past.

Piano Music—Twelve Armenian Folk Songs; Artinis; Two Pieces; Vijag, for two pianos; Madras Sonata; Lake of Van Sonata; Shalimar, suite; Sonata; Poseidon Sonata; Child in the Garden, for

286

four hands; Bardo Sonata; Sonatina; Ko-Ola-U, for two pianos; Bare November Day; Dark River and Distant Bell (also for harpsichord).

Vocal Music—Angelic Song; Pagan Saint; Lullaby of the Lake; I Heard Thee Singing; Raven River; Thirtieth Ode of Solomon; Canticle; Live in the Sun; The Stars; Persephone; Dawn at Laona; O Goddess of the Sea; Immortality; I Have Seen the Lord.

ABOUT

Chase, G., America's Music; Cohn, A., Twentieth Century Music in the Western Hemisphere; Mellers, W., Music in a New Found Land.

Musical America, March 1949; Saturday Review, February 22, 1959; Time, March 29, 1958.

Jacques Ibert
1890–1962

Jacques Ibert was born on August 15, 1890, in Paris. His father, a businessman, wanted him to enter the world of commerce, but from his third year on—when he first started to experiment with sounds at the piano—Jacques was drawn to music. In this he was encouraged by his mother, a fine pianist who gave him his first lessons. He made excellent progress. Nevertheless, he soon started to nurse ambitions outside music. Becoming passionately fond of the theatre, he dreamed of becoming an actor. "I have no regret about acting," he later told an interviewer in commenting upon his musical career. "I have learned a lot and though I am a musician, I am still a man of the theatre."

Academic study was completed at Rollin Collège. Only then did Ibert decide to specialize in music. In 1910 he entered the Paris Conservatory where his teachers included Pessard in harmony, Fauré in composition, and Gedalge in counterpoint and fugue. In the last of these classes he was a fellow student of Honegger and Milhaud.

His music study was interrupted in 1914 when, with France at war, he served first in the French Navy and then as an officer in the French Naval Reserve. He spent four years in service, receiving the Croix de Guerre. Although music had to give way to war duties, Ibert managed to complete in 1914 a tone poem for orchestra, *Noël en Picardie*. In 1919 he returned to the Conservatory, entering the composition class of Paul Vidal. His fiancée encouraged him to try for the Prix de Rome,

Ibert: ē bâr′

and Nadia Boulanger prepared him for it. Late in 1919, when he received the prize for the cantata *Le Poète et la Fée*, he married Marie-Rose Veber, daughter of a famous artist and niece of an equally celebrated writer. The Prix de Rome authorities waived their rules against marriage and the Iberts established their three-year residence at the Villa Medici in Rome as prescribed.

JACQUES IBERT

During his residence in Rome, Ibert completed two symphonic works with which he subsequently achieved recognition as a composer. The first was the tone poem *The Ballad of Reading Gaol* (1921), based on three episodes in Oscar Wilde's poem: the march to the gallows by the one who had killed the thing he loved; the phantoms and visions haunting the murderer; and the final prayer and death of the prisoner. *The Ballad of Reading Gaol* was a major success when introduced in Paris at a Colonne concert under Gabriel Pierné, on October 22, 1922.

Escales, or *Ports of Call*, was also written in Rome and achieved an even greater success than the *Ballad*. In writing *Escales*, Ibert was inspired by a Mediterranean cruise he had made with the Navy. The work was a musical travelogue touching the Mediterranean ports of Palermo, Tunis, and Valencia and the town of Nefta. "The composer," André George explained, "allows the musical sensibility to express itself around three popular themes heard in the course of that voyage." The work was acclaimed on its first performance, at a Concert Lamoureux in Paris on January 6, 1924. It soon became one of Ibert's most popular compositions, a fact that eventually caused the composer considerable concern since *Escales* tended to overshadow some of his later works. He told an interviewer sadly: "I have written twenty important works since *Escales*. But always when they speak of Ibert, they talk about *Escales*."

But those twenty works of which Ibert spoke did place their composer among the most highly regarded composers in France. *Angélique* was the first of several operas to be mounted successfully at the Paris Opéra—on January 28, 1927. The orchestral suite *Divertissement*, heard in Paris on November 30, 1930, made the rounds of the music world because of its infectious wit and sparkling satire. Other Ibert works to receive recognition included his flute concerto, given in Paris on February 25, 1934, and a *Concertino da Camera*, for saxophone and orchestra, introduced in Paris on May 2, 1935.

In 1937 Ibert was appointed director of the Academy of Rome; he was the first musician to hold this post. Immediately after World War II, he was appointed assistant director of the Paris Opéra and subsequently spent part of each year in Paris carrying out his duties and devoting the rest of his time to Rome. He resigned from the Academy of Rome in 1955 to become the director of the united management of the Paris Opéra and the Paris Opéra-Comique, from which post he retired in 1957.

Ibert paid his only visit to the United States in 1950 to conduct a master class in composition at the Berkshire Music Center at Tanglewood. At that time, an interviewer for the New York *Times* described him as a "tall, slender man who moves with a litheness that belies his fifty-nine years. He was dressed in bright blue shirt and trousers and his well-shaped features were set off by a white moustache and fringe of white hair."

His presence at Tanglewood brought about the American première of his charming satirical four-act opera, *Le Roi d' Yvetot*, which he had written in 1927 and which had been given its world première at the Paris Opéra on January 15, 1930. Commenting on the American performance, which constituted the first time an Ibert opera had been given in the

United States, Howard Taubman described the score as "gay and resourceful." He added: "Ibert writes with a professional's skill. He can compose sweet tunes and rousing choruses, and his orchestra can support the action as well as weave a magical spell of its own."

Ibert wrote much music for the theatre—not only operas and ballets, but also scores for motion pictures. His love for the stage remained keen to the end of his life. Most of his music for the stage is cast within conventional molds, but at times he experimented with new methods and techniques. This was the case with the ballet *Le Chevalier Errant*, based on *Don Quixote*, presented in Paris on May 5, 1950. This work was a compromise between ballet and opera, and it called for one hundred and twenty singers and a mammoth orchestra. Because of its unusual mixture of drama and dance, of spoken declamation and song, *Le Chevalier Errant* was hailed by some French critics as a successful attempt to evolve a new lyric form.

There are two opposing stylistic tendencies in Ibert's music. One is the satirical. This partiality for levity, flippancy, and satire which distinguishes his opera *Le Roi d' Yvetot* also characterizes his orchestral *Divertissement*, with its witty musical quotations and parodies, is Ibert's lighter side. The more serious Ibert is the neo-Impressionist who produces sensitive compositions filled with subtle nuances and the refinements of Impressionist writing.

But whether he was serious or flippant, Ibert was always, as Henri Prunières once said of him, "a true musician who is acquainted with all the resources, all the subtleties of his art. None better than Ibert knows how to make the most of a melodic idea. He delights in the stark style. . . . Also to be admired . . . is the perfect taste, the tact, which enables him to avoid all shoals."

One of Ibert's last major works for orchestra, commissioned by the Louisville Orchestra in Kentucky, was the *Louisville Concerto*, which was introduced by the orchestra under Robert Whitney, on February 17, 1954.

Ibert was ill when he completed his final composition, *Mouvement Symphonique*, for orchestra, commissioned by the Koussevitzky Music Foundation for the seventy-fifth anniversary of the Boston Symphony. Actually, Ibert had been planning a large work of which the *Mouvement* was to be just a single section, but he never lived to complete the entire project. The single movement was introduced by the Boston Symphony under Charles Münch.

Jacques Ibert died of influenza in Paris on February 5, 1962. He was survived by his widow and their only child, a son.

MAJOR WORKS

Ballets—Les Rencontres; Diane de Poitiers; Les Amours de Jupiter; Le Chevalier Errant.

Chamber Music—Jeux, sonatina for flute and piano; Trois Pièces Brèves, for flute, oboe, clarinet, horn, and bassoon; Pastoral, for four fifes; Entr'acte, for flute and guitar; String Quartet; Trio for Violin, Cello, and Harp; Interludes, for violin and harpsichord.

Choral Music—Chant de Folie; Quintette de la Peur.

Operas—Angélique; Persée et Andromède; Le Roi d'Yvetot; Gonzague; L'Aiglon (with Honegger); Barbe-Bleue (radio opera).

Orchestral Music—The Ballad of Reading Gaol, tone poem; Escales, suite; Féerique, symphonic scherzo; Concerto for Cello and Wind; Divertissement, suite; Paris, suite for chamber orchestra; Flute Concerto; Concertino da Camera, for saxophone and chamber orchestra; Capriccio; Ouverture de Fête; Suite Élisabéthaine; Symphonie Concertante, for oboe and string orchestra; Louisville Concerto; Hommage à Mozart; Bacchanale; Mouvement Symphonique.

Piano Music—Histoires, ten pieces; Toccata à la Mémoire d'Albert Roussel; Suite d'Images.

Vocal Music—Deux Stèles Orientées, for soprano and flute; La Verdure Dorée; Chanson du Rien.

ABOUT

Feschotte, J., Jacques Ibert; Samazeuilh, G., Musiciens de Mon Temps.

New York Times, July 9, 1950; Newsweek, July 17, 1950; La Revue Musicale (Paris), July 1929.

Vincent d'Indy
1851–1931

Paul Marie Théodore Vincent d'Indy was born on March 27, 1851, in Paris. He came from an aristocratic Cévenole family which had made its home in the mountainous region of Vivarais. His mother died in giving him birth, and he was raised by a grandmother, the Countess Reza d'Indy. She was a proud, self-willed matriarch who ruled her family with a strong hand. An excellent musician, she saw to it that each member of the family received sound musical training, and she arranged concerts at home in which family and friends could participate. Vincent's musical tastes as well as

D'Indy: dăN dē′

his critical faculty were therefore early developed; and his interest in music was encouraged. At eleven he began to study the piano with Diémer, with whom he remained four years. At thirteen he studied harmony with Lavignac, and after that theory with Marmontel. An uncle, who had been a pupil of César Franck, continually gave him both encouragement and direction; it was through him that Vincent at sixteen came to know and learn Berlioz' famous treatise on instrumentation. Another important influence on young d'Indy was Henri Duparc, the composer, whom he met in 1869 and with whom he went through a long, laborious period of studying the published masterworks of Bach, Beethoven, and Wagner, among others. As a result of these varied influences, d'Indy became interested in composition. His first two opuses were written when he was nineteen: *Trois Romances sans Paroles*, for piano; and the *Chanson des Aventuriers de la Mer*, for baritone, chorus, and orchestra. The latter is based on a poem by Victor Hugo.

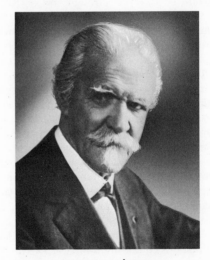

VINCENT D'INDY

With the outbreak of the Franco-Prussian War in 1870, d'Indy enlisted in the 105th Battalion of Guards and saw active service in the battle of Val-Fleuri on December 16, 1870, leading a bayonet charge. He recorded his military experiences in a pamphlet published in 1872.

By the end of 1871 d'Indy was out of uniform. He became a junior member of the

Société Nationale de Musique which promoted performances of new French music in Paris. From 1876 until 1890 he served as secretary and, after César Franck's death, as president. Despite his aptitude for and interest in music, he was led by both his father and grandmother to law. But the death of his grandmother in 1872 relieved him of his obligation to become a lawyer and permitted him to turn completely to music. Introduced to César Franck by Duparc, d'Indy was advised by the master to continue his music study at the Paris Conservatory. D'Indy, however, felt that the routine curriculum at the Conservatory was too stultifying for him. Instead, he became Franck's private pupil. However, when Franck became professor at the Conservatory in 1873, d'Indy entered his class, winning a second *accessit* in 1874, and a first in 1875. From Franck, d'Indy assimilated certain stylistic and structural methods favored by the master—for example, the "cyclic form," in which germinative phrases are developed into full-grown themes and in which unification in a large structure is achieved through the repetition in a final movement of material heard earlier. D'Indy was also strongly influenced by Franck's high-minded idealism and integrity, which he thenceforth tried to emulate. He stood ready at all times to acknowledge the debt he owed to Franck; and he tried to repay that debt partially by writing an authoritative biography of the master, published in Paris in 1906.

During the summer of 1873 d'Indy traveled in Germany and Austria. He spent several days with Liszt at Weimar; he met Wagner in Bayreuth; and he had an unsatisfactory interview with Brahms in Vienna. Back in Paris, he completed an overture for orchestra, *Les Piccolomini*, performed at a Pasdeloup concert in Paris on January 25, 1874. D'Indy later renamed this composition *Max et Thécla*, and used it as the second part of a symphonic trilogy, *Wallenstein*.

In addition to his work as a composer, d'Indy took on various musical activities. From 1872 to 1876 he was organist at the Church of St. Leu, and from 1873 to 1878 he also served as chorus-master and tympanist of the Colonne Orchestra.

In 1876 d'Indy, now a passionate Wagnerite, made a pilgrimage to Bayreuth to attend the world première of the entire *Ring* cycle at the first of the Wagner festivals. For many years after that, up to and including 1891, he returned to Bayreuth from time to time to pay homage at the Wagnerian shrine; in 1882 he heard the world première of *Parsifal*. He became actively involved in the promotion of Wagner's music in 1887 when he assisted Lamoureux in preparing the first performance in Paris of *Lohengrin*.

The first of d'Indy's works now regarded as among his most significant was completed in 1886: the *Symphonie Cévenole*, or the *Symphony on a French Mountain Theme*, introduced by the Lamoureux Orchestra in Paris on March 20, 1887. It was greeted with such enthusiasm that the symphony went a long way towards establishing its composer's reputation. The mountain air upon which this work is based is one heard in the Cévennes region of southern France; the tune itself appears at the beginning of the symphony in the English horn. Variations of the air recur in the other two movements. In discussing this masterwork, René Dumesnil wrote: "Nothing gives us such direct and confidential evidence about the composer: Not that he pours his heart out in lyric and grandiloquent phrases. On the contrary, the qualities of spirit and aspirations of Vincent d'Indy are all revealed in the choice of themes—so simply, expressively and clearly arranged--in the exquisite polyphonic treatment setting them off in classic shape and harmony of proportion. Everything is directly inspired by his native soil."

In the ensuing years, d'Indy contributed several more outstandingly successful and important works to the symphonic repertory. First came *Istar*, symphonic variations first performed in Brussels on January 10, 1897. This music was based on a Babylonian poem, *The Epoch of Izdabar*, in which the daughter of Sin passes through seven gates. Removing at each gate one of her robes, she becomes completely nude at the seventh one. What is particularly interesting about this work structurally is that, unlike most theme-and-variations, the theme here (a broad melody in octaves) is heard *not* at the beginning of the composition but after all the variations have been heard.

The Symphony No. 2 in B-flat major is one of the most important works in that form since Franck and Chausson. In its cyclic form, in the lofty nature of its thematic material, in its spirituality, and in the delicacy and refinement of its over-all atmosphere, the symphony reveals how strong the influence of Franck had been on d'Indy. The d'Indy Symphony was introduced by the Lamoureux Orchestra in Paris on February 28, 1904. One year later, d'Indy completed still another major work for symphony orchestra, a rhapsody for piano and orchestra entitled *Jour d'Été à la Montagne*, or *Summer Day on the Mountain*. This composition at times presents a pictorial, and at times an impressionistic, portrait of nature. It was performed by the Colonne Orchestra in Paris on February 18, 1906.

Just as his orchestral music had been influenced by Franck so his two operas reflected his enthusiasm for Wagner. The first was *Fervaal*, a lyric drama introduced in Brussels on March 12, 1897, with a libretto prepared by d'Indy and derived from a legend from the Cévennes mountains. The two principal characters (Fervaal and a Saracen princess) serve as symbols for the victory of love over barbarism. This opera, noteworthy for its Romantic feelings and its tonal description, made a favorable impression; and so did its operatic successor, *L'Étranger*, produced in Brussels on January 7, 1903.

"It is true," said Philip Hale in his program notes for the Boston Symphony while d'Indy was still alive, "that d'Indy uses his head, not loses it, in composition; that his music will never be popular with the multitude; it lacks an obvious appeal. ... It is not sugary; it is not theatrical. To say that it is cold is to say that it is not effusive. D'Indy does not gush. Nor does he permit himself to run with a mighty stir and din to a blatant climax. ... He respects his art and himself and he does not trim his sails to catch the breeze of popular favor. There is a nobility in his music; there is to those who do not wear their heart on their sleeve true warmth. There is a soaring of the spirit, not a dropping to court favor."

In 1893 d'Indy was invited by the French government to serve on a committee to reform the Paris Conservatory. He proposed such a revolutionary plan that the professors of the institution united against it. The fierce opposition succeeded in frustrating the work of the committee, and as a result d'Indy soon afterwards turned down a professorship in composition at the Conservatory. However, in

1912, after the Conservatory had undergone a radical reform of curriculum, d'Indy accepted an appointment as professor of the ensemble class.

His far-sighted and progressive theories on music education were in fact put into effect in a place other than the Conservatory. In 1894 he helped found the Schola Cantorum, originally created as a school for the study of church music. Six years after its founding, the institution's program was extended to include all phases of music. As one of its directors and principal teachers, d'Indy left an indelible impression on twentieth century French music. Over a period of several decades, many young musicians who studied under him became influential musicians—among them Satie, Honegger, Auric, and Roussel. D'Indy also helped advance musical education in France by serving as inspector of music instruction in Paris, a government appointment he received in 1899.

While he never held a permanent post as conductor, d'Indy was active with the baton, particularly in performances of his own works, and made many tours of Europe as a guest conductor. He paid his first visit to the United States in 1905, making his American debut with the Boston Symphony on December 1 in a program of French music. During this first tour of the United States he also appeared as pianist in performances of his chamber music and delivered a lecture on César Franck at Harvard. D'Indy paid a second visit (his last) to the United States in 1921.

In the years just before World War I, d'Indy spent his winters either teaching in Paris or touring France in concerts of his music. Summers were devoted to composition at his home in Faugs in the Cévennes. After World War I and a second marriage, d'Indy gave up his summer home and spent his vacations in southern France. Of his daily habits, he once wrote: "My life is carefully regulated. I get up early, I work as a matter of fact, I am unable to remain idle for ten minutes. I am orderly, and my manuscripts are rather clean."

Following World War I, d'Indy saw a sharp decline in his artistic fortunes, for he made many enemies, some of them powerful. Max Wald explained this development in the following way: "He was confronted with an array of tendencies with which he was completely out of sympathy. Young men whose ideas clashed with those of their fathers clamored for their day in the sun. Still the crusader in spite of his advanced years, d'Indy wrote hasty, ill-tempered letters to the press, attacking the views and the music of certain young men prominently in the public eye. He was answered with insolence and contempt. It was all very unedifying. . . . The aged man had not lost his talent for making enemies, and these had little difficulty in making him appear, in the eyes of those incapable of judging him at his true worth, as old-fashioned and reactionary. . . . Performances of d'Indy's works became rarer. He took this to heart. . . . Rightly or wrongly he felt that he was being . . . victimized."

Occasionally his far-reaching contributions to French music were still honored, mainly in the form of memberships to academies and artistic societies the world over. One of the last tributes to come his way arrived in January 1931 when he led a performance of his *Symphony on a French Mountain Theme* in Paris and received a tremendous ovation. He died on December 2, 1931, a victim of a heart attack in Paris. On the day he died he had been hard at work on a book about *Parsifal*. His last composition, completed in his final year, was the *Fantaisie sur un Vieil Air de Ronde Française*, for piano.

D'Indy wrote: "An artist must have at least faith, faith in God, and faith in his art; for it is faith that disposes him to learn and by his learning to raise himself higher and higher on the ladder of being, up to his goal, which is God. An artist should practice hope; for he can expect nothing from the present. He knows that his mission is to serve, and to give his work for the . . . generation that will come after him. An artist should be inspired by a splendid charity—'the greatest of these.' To love should be his aim in life; for the moving principle of all creation is divine and charitable love." D'Indy was fond of the following epigram, which he frequently quoted: "Only the heart can engender beauty."

MAJOR WORKS

Chamber Music—3 string quartets; 2 piano trios; Piano Quartet in A major; Trio in B-flat major, for clarinet, cello, and piano; Chansons et Danses, for seven wind instruments; Violin Sonata in C major; Piano Quintet in G minor; Cello Sonata in D major;

String Sextet in B-flat major; Suite, for flute, strings, and harp.

Choral Music—Sainte Marie-Madeleine, cantata; Deus Israël; Sur la Mer; Pour l'Inauguration d'une Statue, cantata; L'Art et le Peuple; Ode à Valence; Six Chants Populaires Français, two series, for a cappella chorus; Le Bouquet de Printemps; Les Trois Fileuses; Chant de Nourrice; La Vengeance du Mari.

Operas—Le Chant de la Cloche, dramatic legend; Fervaal, lyric drama; L'Étranger, lyric drama; La Légende de Saint-Christophe, lyric drama; La Rêve de Cinyras, lyric comedy.

Orchestral Music—3 symphonies; Jean Hunyade; La Forêt Enchantée, symphonic legend; Wallenstein, symphonic trilogy; Symphonie Cévenole (Symphony on a French Mountain Theme); Fantaisie, for orchestra with oboe solo; Tableaux de Voyage; Istar, symphonic variations; Jour de l'Été à la Montagne (Summer Day on the Mountain); Souvenirs, tone poem; Sinfonia Brevis; Le Poème des Rivages; Diptyque Méditerranéen; Concerto for Piano, Flute, Cello, and String Orchestra.

Piano Music—Petite Sonate; Poème des Montagnes; Quatre Pièces; Helvétia; Nocturne; Promenade; Schumanniana; Tableaux de Voyage; Sonata in E major; Menuet sur le Nom d'Haydn; Treize Pièces Brèves; Thème Varié, Fugue et Chanson; Contes de Fées; Fantaisie sur un Vieil Air de Ronde Française.

Vocal Music—Clair de Lune; L'Amour et la Crâne; Lied Maritime; La Première Dent; Mirage; Les Yeux de l'Aimée; Vocalise; Madrigal à Deux Voix, for soprano and cello; also arrangements of folk songs.

ABOUT

Blom, E., Classics: Major and Minor; Borgex, L., Vincent d'Indy, Sa Vie et Son Œuvre; Demuth, N., Vincent d'Indy; Fraguier, M. M. de, Vincent d'Indy; Guy-Ropartz (ed.), Le Centenaire de Vincent d'Indy; Rolland, R., Musicians of Today; Sérieyx, A., Vincent d'Indy; Vallas, L., Vincent d'Indy.

Musical Quarterly, April 1932.

John Ireland
1879–1962

John Nicholson Ireland was born in Bowdon, Cheshire, on August 13, 1879. His father, Alexander Ireland, was the editor of the Manchester *Examiner and Times;* his mother was an author and literary critic. Ireland first revealed an interest in music when he was six; by the time he was fourteen he knew he wanted to become a professional musician. In 1893 he entered the Royal College of Music where he remained eight years and where his teachers included Frederick Cliffe in piano and Stanford in composition. He had just entered the College when his parents died and he was forced to support himself. He continued his music education by winning scholarships and by taking on various little jobs. At seventeen he became an organist at Holy Trinity Church in London and in 1897 he also played the organ at St. Jude's Church in Upper Chelsea.

His music education at the Royal College of Music ended in 1901. He then attended the University of Durham for four years, receiving a Bachelor of Music degree. In 1904 he assumed an organ post at St. Luke's Parish Church in Chelsea, a post he held for the next twenty-two years.

JOHN IRELAND

Ireland began to compose seriously in 1901. His early works included the cycle *Songs of a Wayfarer* (1905), in which is reflected the influence of Brahms and Germanic post-Romanticism. By 1908 Ireland, realizing that his music was derivative, destroyed most of what he had written and refused to allow the remainder to be published, with the exception of a song cycle which appeared in 1912.

Through the rejection of former musical tendencies and the adoption of more modern approaches to melody, rhythm, and harmony, he made a new start in composition. In 1906 he completed the *Phantasy Trio* in A minor, for violin, cello, and piano, which won second prize in a chamber music contest sponsored by W. W. Cobbett. In 1909 the Sonata in D minor, for violin and piano, was awarded first prize in another Cobbett competition which had one hundred and thirty-four entries. With a second violin sonata, in A minor (1917), introduced on March 6, 1917, by Albert Sammons and William Murdoch, Ireland came to full ma-

turity. "Its power is tremendous," wrote Frank Bridge. "Personally I am convinced that it is... a landmark . . . in contemporary music."

Ireland wrote his first mature composition for orchestra in 1913—the prelude *The Forgotten Rite*, introduced at a Promenade concert in London under Sir Henry J. Wood in 1917. It has remained one of his best. "This work," says Rosa Newmarch, "deals with certain mystical aspects of nature, the details of which the composer leaves to the imagination of the hearer. The title, however, seems to point to the infinitely distant ages when certain occult forces of nature were the objects of worship, and if we succeed in adjusting the mind to so vague and remote an atmosphere we shall probably come as near to the meaning of the work as its intentional mysticism will allow."

The Forgotten Rite reveals the influence that Ireland's yearly visits to the Channel Islands (with their ancient ritual associations) had upon him. In *Decorations*, a set of three pieces for piano (1913), he recorded his impressions of a holiday spent in Jersey. Many years later, the Channel Island of Guernsey stimulated the writing of one of his most important compositions for the piano—*Sarnia: An Island Sequence* (1941).

The Channel Islands were one stimulus. Literature was another. Ireland responded particularly to the writings of Arthur Machen. He dedicated to Machen his poignant *Legend* (1933), for piano and orchestra; *The Scarlet Ceremonies* (the third number in the piano set *Decorations*) bears a Machen quotation. Ireland also set to music the poetry of Symonds, A. E. Housman, Hardy, Shakespeare, Blake, Arthur Symons, and Rupert Brooke.

The Concerto for Piano and Orchestra in E-flat major (1930), which Helen Perkin helped to introduce in London on October 2, 1930, is often singled out as one of Ireland's major compositions. It proved so successful at its première that only a few weeks later it was repeated at a Promenade concert under Sir Henry J. Wood, at a concert of the Royal College of Music under Sir Malcolm Sargent, and at a concert of the BBC Symphony. "It is not often one is given an opportunity of becoming so fully acquainted with a new and important work within a short period," remarked Herbert Lambert in *Chesterian*, "and I for one am grateful for this experience, as it has enabled me to confirm the conviction that this composition is destined to take its position as one of the great works of modern music."

Through the years Ireland's music experienced little change. In a letter to Ireland, Philip Heseltine pointed out the "steady development along wholly personal lines" that could be traced in Ireland's music from 1908 on and noted in the later Ireland compositions "the logical development of a style that was already very individual."

Here is how Peter J. Pirie described Ireland's style in *High Fidelity* magazine: "In Ireland the pure Saxon strain—lyrical, evanescent, wistful—tends to be almost his entire matter.... 'The rainbow comes and goes, and lovely is the rose'—the deep pessimism that was a part of Ireland's nature, and which can be heard in his fine Cello Sonata (in G minor, 1923) and in the second of his three piano trios (E minor-major, 1918) found consolation in the beauty of the English countryside; such pieces as the *Concertino Pastorale*, for strings (1939), and the *Dowland Suite*, for brass band (1932), are a distillation of the English spirit. Yet the same countryside has also an atavistic darkness with which Ireland felt an affinity; we see, for instance, the ambiguous, sinister aspect of the Dorset countryside, with its great prehistoric earthworks reflected in the symphonic poem *Mai-Dun* (1921)."

From 1923 to 1939 Ireland was professor at the Royal College of Music where his students included the young Benjamin Britten. He was made Honorary Member of the Royal Academy of Music and of the Royal College of Music in 1924, and in the year 1932 the University of Durham conferred on him an honorary doctorate.

When World War II erupted, Ireland was living in comparative seclusion on the island of Guernsey. He succeeded in escaping from the island in June 1940, just before the Nazis took over, carrying away with him the sketches of his latest but then still uncompleted work for the piano, *Sarnia*. After that he lived mainly in London where, in 1949, there took place at the Royal Albert Hall an all-Ireland concert to honor his seventieth birthday. He died in Washington, Durham, England, on June 12, 1962.

MAJOR WORKS

Chamber Music—3 piano trios; 2 violin sonatas; The Holy Boy, a carol of Nativity for violin and piano; Sonata in G minor, for cello and piano; Phantasy Sonata in E-flat minor-major, for clarinet and piano.

Choral Music—These Things Shall Be; also various hymns and Services for church, unison choral songs with piano, two-part songs with piano, and four-part a cappella songs.

Orchestral Music—The Forgotten Rite, symphonic prelude; Mai-Dun, symphonic rhapsody; Concerto in E-flat major, for piano and orchestra; A London Overture; Legend, for piano and strings; Concertino Pastorale, for strings; Two Pieces, for strings; Epic March, Overture Satyricon.

Piano Music—Decorations; The Almond Trees; Rhapsody; London Pieces; Leaves from a Child's Sketchbook; Sonata; Sonatina; Ballade; Indian Summer; Green Ways; Sarnia; Three Pastels; also various preludes and pieces.

Vocal Music—Songs of a Wayfarer; Marigold; Mother and Child; The Land of Content; We'll Go to the Woods No More; Songs Sacred and Profane; various individual songs for voice and piano.

ABOUT

Bacharach, A. L. (ed.), The Music Masters: v4, The Twentieth Century; Holbrooke, J., Contemporary British Composers.

High Fidelity, January 1966; Music and Letters (London), April 1943; Tempo (London), Spring 1962.

Charles Ives
1874–1954

Charles Edward Ives was born in Danbury, Connecticut, on October 20, 1874. His father, George Ives, an excellent musician, was bandmaster of the First Connecticut Heavy Artillery in General Grant's army, and his music-making won the praise of President Lincoln. A much quoted musical anecdote about General Grant owes its origin to one of George Ives's band performances during the Civil War. After the concert, President Lincoln asked General Grant whether he enjoyed the music. General Grant replied: "I can't tell, Mr. President. I only know two tunes. One is 'Yankee Doodle' and the other isn't."

The elder Ives was an extraordinary musical individual. He experimented with quarter-tone instruments and with acoustics. One day he arranged the men of his band in different places and had the various groups play simultaneously to study the effect. He was always exploring new sound qualities, and from the time Charles was a boy, he encouraged his son to do so, too. One day he had Charles play "Swanee River" in one key while he himself played the accompaniment in an alien one. On another occasion, he had Charles play one melody with the right hand, and a different one in a different key, with the other. "You see, my son," he explained, "you've got to learn to *stretch* your ears." He began to teach Charles music when the child was five, giving him training in harmony, counterpoint, instrumentation, sight reading, and the literature of Bach, Beethoven, and Stephen Foster. He also taught the boy to play the piano, cornet, and organ.

CHARLES IVES

When Charles was thirteen, he was hired as an organist at the Congregational Church in Danbury. Having learned to play the drums, he was also able to join his father's band as a percussion player. One day in 1888 Charles Ives wrote a march, *Holiday Quick Step* (his first composition). His father included it on one of his band programs. At the concert Charles showed for the first time the shyness that haunted him for the rest of his life: he refused to participate in the performance.

His early musical experiences included listening to performances by town bands. Small-town band music was to be the source of some of his later experiments. He was fascinated when two bands approached each other from opposite ends of the street, playing two numbers which were joined in discord when the

bands met. In some of his later compositions he tried to imitate the distant music of two such bands, growing ever louder until they formed a cacophony when the bands came within hearing distance of each other.

Actually, as Ives himself once confessed, he was ashamed of being so deeply involved in music. "Most boys in the country towns of America, I think, felt the same way," he said. "When other boys on Monday mornings on vacation were out driving the grocery cart, riding horses, or playing ball, I felt all wrong to stay in and play the piano." He would have considered himself more normal if he had spent his time like the other boys of his town playing baseball and football—two sports, incidentally, at which he happened to be more than passingly proficient.

Upon graduating from Danbury High School he attended the Hopkins Preparatory School in New Haven. After his father died, Charles continued studying the organ with Harry Rowe Shelley. In 1894 he entered Yale where he attended the music classes of Horatio Parker and Dudley Buck. While attending college, Ives held a part-time job as organist at the Center Church at New Haven. When he was graduated from Yale in 1898 with a Bachelor of Arts degree, he made his home in New York where he shared a West Side apartment with some friends and found a job as clerk in an insurance firm at a salary of five dollars a week. He supplemented this income by playing the organ at the Central Presbyterian Church in New York from 1899 to 1902.

He had begun composing seriously long before he entered Yale. His first song, "Slow March," was written in 1888, when he was fourteen; it is found in the volume *114 Songs*, which he published privately in 1922. He wrote his first symphony in the period between 1896 and 1898, while he was still at Yale. The college years also saw the writing of his first string quartet, *A Revival Service* (1896), and his first choral composition, *Psalm 67* (1898). These early pieces are remarkable for Ives' experimentation with polyrhythms and polytonality, more than a decade before Stravinsky. A composition for organ written in 1898, for example, superimposed a chord in D minor on one in C major. "I found," he later explained, "I could not go on using the familiar chords only. I heard something else."

He continued to explore new sounds and techniques. In 1901 he wrote a short piece for orchestra, *From the Steeples and the Mountains*, requiring two sets of chimes or church bells, each with a high and low part; the only other instruments used were four trumpets and four trombones, each group playing in unison. Since the bells were sounded in different keys, harsh discords predominated while the over-all effect of the composition was distinctly polytonal. The world première of this unique item came sixty-four years after it had been written—on July 30, 1965, with Lukas Foss conducting the New York Philharmonic at the Lincoln Center for the Performing Arts during a festival of French and American music.

In 1901 Ives completed his second symphony, upon which he had been at work for four years. While this music is less discordant and less complex in its rhythmic procedures than some of the other works Ives had written up to that time, it still possessed, as Henry Cowell once said of it, "plenty of devilment . . . especially in the combination of the sacred and profane. Ives is profoundly religious, but he doesn't mind poking a bit of fun at church chords once in a while." This second symphony represented Ives's first significant attempt to make use of authentic American materials. As he himself explained, the symphony "expresses the musical feelings of the Connecticut country around here (Redding and Danbury) in the 1890's, and the music of the country folk. It is full of the tunes they sang and played then." Among the American tunes quoted by Ives are "Columbia, the Gem of the Ocean," "America, the Beautiful," "De Camptown Races" and "Old Black Joe." Country tunes, church hymns, barn-dance melodies are some of the other American ingredients used. "The charm of this melange," said Harold C. Schonberg, "is the unselfconscious way Ives handles the material."

Like all of Ives's other works, his second symphony was not heard until many years after it had been written. It was introduced by the New York Philharmonic under Leonard Bernstein on February 22, 1951.

Ives wrote his Third Symphony in the years between 1901 and 1904; many years later it became one of his most successful works. Here the inspiration was the camp meetings once

popular in Danbury, Connecticut. Many of Ives's themes were based on such old American hymn tunes as "O for a Thousand Tongues" and "Just as I Am." In the second movement, the music describes the games children played at camp meetings while their parents attended the services. "In its deep sincerity," wrote Bernard Herrmann in *Modern Music*, "this symphony is like the great Bach chorales. Its religion has none of the mystic elements of Franck, Elgar or Wagner, but is pure New England."

The Third Symphony did not get a hearing until about forty years after its creation—in New York City on April 5, 1946. The work made a deep impression, the critics describing it as noble and moving. It was singled out for special commendation by the New York Music Critics Circle and in 1947 it received the Pulitzer Prize in music.

In 1906 Ives helped found in New York the insurance firm of Ives and Company, which in 1909 became Ives and Myrick. It had humble beginnings but eventually grew into a highly successful organization, one of the largest of its kind in the United States. For many years Ives served as senior partner. Henry Bellamann pointed out the salient fact that the success of this organization was due to Ives's talent for business, his "hard-headed common sense," and his successful relationships with people in all walks of life. Ives's long career in business provides proof that he was no "wild-eyed revolutionary inhabiting the regions of Bohemia" but a "normal citizen" who for over a quarter of a century "pursued his own way, going to business in the downtown New York district, where many of his associates did not know of his interest in music."

On June 9, 1908, Ives married Harmony Twichell, daughter of a Hartford clergyman. They have an adopted daughter, Edith. His wife encouraged him to pursue his dual existence of businessman by day and composer by night. She understood his creative drive and was tolerant of the fact that he composed "evenings, weekends, and vacations" as she revealed to an interviewer. "He could hardly wait for dinner to be over, and he was at the piano. Often he went to bed at 2 or 3 A.M." Ives himself told a reporter that "we never went anywhere, and she didn't mind." She was also tolerant of the kind of music he was writing, just as she understood his refusal to try to have his music published or performed. Ives often told intimate friends that his wife had been as important an influence upon him as his father had been before her. "Mrs. Ives never once said or suggested, or looked, or thought that there must be something wrong with me," the composer revealed. "She never said, 'Now, why don't you be good and write something nice, the way they like it?' Never. She urged me on my way to be myself and gave me her confidence."

For almost half a century, Ives looked upon his work as a composer as an intimate function that concerned nobody but himself. He was not interested in the applause of audiences or kudos from critics. He never tried to have his music played, just as he never sent his manuscripts to publishers. He wrote as he felt, his only concern being to satisfy his own creative standards. It never seemed to bother him that only his wife and a number of very close friends knew what was contained in those manuscripts that were accumulating in his closet. "It may be," as this editor once surmised in a book on modern music, "that he knew that his writing was much too unorthodox for public consumption. It may have been that his extraordinary reticence, where his creative life was concerned, made him guard his isolation jealously rather than allow public attention to shatter it. The need to work in seclusion, away from the glare of public recognition and freed from all possible affiliations with a listening or writing public, was not just the idiosyncrasy of a strange man. It was an artistic necessity. Only a man who wrote for himself could rid himself as completely of inhibitions as Ives did."

He saw nothing unusual in the fact that he was part businessman and part creator. He often insisted that he drew strength and wisdom as a musician from his business activities. "My business experience revealed life to me in many aspects that I otherwise might have missed," he once told a friend. "I have experienced a great fullness of life in business. The fabric of existence weaves itself whole. You cannot set an art off in the corner and hope for it to have vitality, reality and substance. There can be nothing exclusive about a substantial art. It comes directly out of the heart of experience of life, and thinking about life, and living life. My work in music helped my business, and my work in business helped my music."

In the years between 1903 and 1914 Ives worked on *Three Places in New England* for chamber orchestra. His stimulation here was New England geography, just as New England church hymns had inspired his Third Symphony. The first movement is a picture of the Civil War, the second of the Revolutionary War; the third is an impressionistic tone picture of the Housatonic at Stockbridge. In the first two movements, the harsh, discordant playing of small-town bands is heard; in the second movement a polyrhythmic as well as discordant effect is achieved by having two village bands approach the town from opposite directions, each playing its own melody in a different key and tempo. What is believed to have been the first performance of this set anywhere took place in New York on January 10, 1931, with Nicolas Slonimsky conducting the Chamber Orchestra of Boston.

Ives's most important work for the piano and one of the greatest contributions made to American piano literature by any American was his second sonata, subtitled *Concord*, written in the period between 1909 and 1915. In it, as the composer explained, he tried "to present [one person's] impression of the spirit of the literature, the philosophy, and the men of Concord, Massachusetts, of over half a century ago." The four movements are entitled "Emerson," "Hawthorne," "The Alcotts," and "Thoreau." Some of the most advanced and experimental idioms of rhythm, tonality, and harmony encountered in the music of the time can be found in this work. In the movement entitled "Hawthorne," Ives instructs the performer to use a ruler or a strip of wood in sounding a two-octave tone cluster. In the "Thoreau" movement Ives suggests that "a flute may play throughout the page" because Thoreau "much prefers to hear the flute over Walden." When the sonata was played for the first time in its entirety (in New York on January 20, 1938, by John Kirkpatrick), Lawrence Gilman called it "exceptionally great music—it is, indeed, the greatest music composed by an American in impulse and implication." Almost as remarkable as the music itself is the pamphlet *Essays Before a Sonata* which Ives wrote to explain his music. Ives dedicated the *Essays* to "those who can't stand his music—and the music to those who can't stand his essays; to those who can't stand either, the whole is respectfully dedicated."

In 1916 Ives "completed" a fourth symphony which, in three of its sections, is just an orchestral adaptation of movements from nonsymphonic works. Actually the manuscript of the last movement was so disorganized (parts were found in an old trunk, parts in desk drawers, parts in notebooks) and the notation frequently so undecipherable that it took the painstaking efforts of several musicologists who worked for years after Ives's death to make order out of chaos. What emerged from these efforts was an extremely complex score utilizing an immense percussion section and a subordinate instrumental group, each requiring its own conductor (besides the principal conductor required for the main orchestra). In one section twenty-seven different rhythms are played simultaneously. The symphony as a whole was deemed unplayable until Leopold Stokowski decided to perform it with the American Symphony Orchestra. Before this only the second movement had been performed, in New York on January 29, 1927. A special fund of almost eight thousand dollars from the Rockefeller Foundation was necessary to pay for the rehearsals that were required. Stokowski maintained that it was the most difficult music he had ever played, so difficult that the orchestra had to work out the symphony phrase by phrase, and sometimes measure by measure.

The world première finally took place in New York on April 26, 1965. Audiences and critics found the symphony to be an extraordinary work built up into its monumental design from fragments of various American folk tunes, popular tunes, and hymns, including "Columbia, the Gem of the Ocean," "Turkey in the Straw," "Yankee Doodle," "From Greenland's Icy Mountains," "All Hail the Power," and "Nearer My God to Thee." "From one point of view," reported Irving Kolodin in the *Saturday Review*, "the procedural pattern of double aural image, contrasting counterpoints carried forward with slight concern for consonant discipline, and liberal quotation from every kind of musical experience is standard Ives. But it all flows better, hangs together more consistently, sustains its impulse with greater cumulative power than is most often his case, because it deals with one consistent consideration: the phenomenon of life and the mystery of death."

The first Ives composition to be published was *Concord Sonata*. The composer himself paid for the printing in 1919 and distributed copies free of charge to his friends. Three years after that, Ives collected the songs he had been writing since 1884 and published them, once again at his own expense, for the benefit of his friends, calling the new opus *114 Songs*. The songs were printed chronologically in reverse order: that is, his last song, "Majority" (1921), in which the technique of tone-clusters is used in print for the first time, is the first song, while "Slow March" (1884) appears last. A variety of subjects is treated in these songs, and a variety of styles is exploited: there are romantic songs, cowboy songs, songs in a syncopated ragtime idiom, dramatic songs, sentimental ballads, war songs, humorous songs, hymns, songs in an advanced and ultramodern idiom, and songs in a simple and elementary style. "This volume," the composer explained wryly in his preface, "is now thrown, so to speak, at the music fraternity, who for this reason will feel free to dodge it on its way—perhaps to the waste basket." Then, with characteristic tongue in cheek, he added: "Various authors have various reasons for bringing out a book. . . . Some have written a book for money; I have not. Some for fame; I have not. Some for love; I have not. Some for kindlings; I have not. I have not written a book for any of these reasons or for all of them together. In fact, gentle borrower, I have not written a book at all — I have merely cleaned house. All that is left is out on the clothes-line. . . ." In refutation of a possible argument that some of these songs were unsingable, Ives said: "A song has a few rights, the same as other ordinary citizens. . . . If it happens to feel like trying to fly where humans cannot fly—to sing what cannot be sung—to walk in a cave on all fours—to tighten up its girth in blind hope and faith and try to scale mountains that are not—who shall stop it?"

Lines such as those quoted above point up Ives's sense of humor and his delight in whimsy. He had a Satie-like joy in interpolating into his music all kinds of humorous or absurd suggestions. In one of his orchestral scores he stopped midway in a bassoon passage to add: "From here on, the bassoon may play anything at all." In his Violin Sonata, a theme for trumpet solo makes a sudden, inexplicable appearance; and in a song for voice and piano there is an equally mysterious appearance of a violin obbligato. In his second string quartet he baptizes the second violin "Rollo." There is one point in the music where the second violin gets an extended rest. This leads Ives to say: "Too hard to play, so it just can't be good music, Rollo." And as a footnote to one of his songs he writes: "This song is inserted ... to clear up the long disputed point, namely, which is worse, the music or the words."

After 1928 Ives wrote no more music. He was a victim of diabetes, and his hands trembled so violently that he was incapable of putting notes down on paper. He remained in his insurance business until 1930 when his increasingly poor health sent him into retirement. Then, suffering from a weak heart and cataracts in both eyes, he became a recluse on his Connecticut farm, often avoiding contact even with close friends, and paying only rare visits to New York where he and his wife previously had spent winters in their brown-stone house on East 74th Street. But he was by no means a helpless invalid. He enjoyed taking long solitary walks, and he was even capable of hammering out his music on the piano. He remained completely indifferent to the outside world. He never read the news-papers and not until the last two years of his life did he own either a radio or a phonograph. He was even unaware of news events of world-shaking importance until long after they happened.

He showed the same lack of interest in the way the world of music neglected his works as in what was being said about him. When, towards the end of his life, honors and tributes came to him, he showed no interest. He refused to talk to newspapermen or to pose for photographers; he had no desire to attend performances of his works, which were now becoming frequent and significant. He turned down Leonard Bernstein's invitation to attend the world première of the Second Symphony in 1951, even refusing to be present at a special performance of the work which Bernstein wanted to arrange exclusively for him. (But he did listen to his symphony over his maid's radio

in the kitchen when it was broadcast on Sunday afternoon; and the performance so delighted him that when he came out of the kitchen he did a jig.) Early in 1947 he would not accept the Pulitzer Prize in music which was being bestowed on him for his Third Symphony. He explained angrily: "Prizes are the badges of mediocrity. Prizes are for boys. I'm grown up."

Howard Taubman, then the music critic of the New York *Times*, was one of the few journalists who managed to get access to Ives. This was in 1949. "You drove up to the gracious and simple house high on a hill in Connecticut," reported Taubman in the New York *Times Magazine*, "and Mrs. Ives, gray-haired, gentle and quietly hospitable, was on the porch to meet you.... From inside the house there came a pounding of a cane. Mrs. Ives smiled and nodded, and led you in. Charles E. Ives was standing in a large room which had a high ceiling with the bare beams showing their graceful strength. At first glance he looked like a Yankee patriarch. ... He was gaunt and wiry, and with the help of his cane he stood up straight so that there was only the faintest suggestion of stooping shoulders. The gray, scraggly beard gave his lean face an appearance of roundness. ... He wore rough country clothes—sturdy shoes, blue denim trousers, a faded blue shirt without a tie, an old, darned sweater and a gray tweed jacket. He took off his dark glasses and looked at you, and the eyes were bright and alert."

Ives died at Roosevelt Hospital in New York City on May 19, 1954, of complications following an operation.

Ives's music is remarkable in the way in which it anticipated the advanced and icono-clastic musical practices with which other composers became identified many years later. Before Stravinsky, Ives used polyrhythms effectively; before Bartók and Schoenberg, Ives experimented with atonality; before Stravinsky and Milhaud, he employed polytonality; before Henry Cowell, he was an exponent of tone clusters; and before Alois Hába he worked with quarter-tones. Ives was an ultramodern long before the ultramoderns came into their own.

More noteworthy still is the fact that Ives was an authentically American composer at a time when most Americans were imitating the

Europeans. As the editor of this book has said: "With a sublime disregard for what was taking place across the ocean, Ives was creating music whose spirit and breath reflected American experiences and backgrounds." And Lawrence Gilman wrote: "Ives's music is as indubitably American in impulse as Jonathan Edwards; and like the writing of that true spirit and mystic, it has at times an irresistible veracity and strength and uncorrupted sincerity."

After Arnold Schoenberg's death there was found among his papers a moving tribute to Ives which read: "There is a great Man living in this country–a composer. He has solved the problem of how to preserve one's self and to learn. He responds to [neglect] by contempt. He is not forced to accept praise or blame. His name is Ives."

MAJOR WORKS

Chamber Music—4 violin sonatas; 2 string quartets; Trio for Violin, Clarinet, and Piano; Space and Duration, for string quartet and mechanical piano; All the Way Around and Back, for violin, flute, bugle, bells, and piano; The Innate, for string quartet and piano; Adagio Sostenuto, for English horn, flute, strings, and piano; Piano Trio; Set, for string quartet and piano.

Choral Music—Psalm 67; The Celestial Country, cantata; Three Harvest Home Chorales; General William Booth's Entrance into Heaven.

Orchestral Music—4 symphonies; 3 Orchestral Sets; From the Steeples and the Mountains; Three Places in New England, for chamber orchestra; Calcium Light Night, for chamber orchestra; Central Park in the Dark; The Unanswered Question; Theatre Orchestra Set; Halloween, for piano and strings; The Pond; Browning Overture; The Gong on the Hook and Ladder; Lincoln, the Great Commoner, for chorus and orchestra; Holiday, suite; Over the Pavements, for chamber orchestra.

Piano Music—2 sonatas (including Concord Sonata); Three-Page Sonata; Some Southpaw Pitching; The Abolitionist Riots; Twenty-Two; Three Protests; Three Quarter-Tone Pieces.

Vocal Music—114 Songs.

ABOUT

Chase, G., America's Music; Copland, A., The New Music: 1900–1960; Cowell, H. and Cowell, S., Charles Ives and His Music; Ewen, D., David Ewen Introduces Modern Music; Rosenfeld, P., Discoveries of a Music Critic.

Hi Fi/Stereo Review, September 1964; Listen, November 1946; Modern Music, May–June, 1945; Musical America, February 15, 1954; Musical Quarterly, January 1933; New York Times Magazine, October 23, 1949; Saturday Review, August 28, 1948.

Leoš Janáček
1854–1928

Leoš Janáček, sometimes described as the Mussorgsky of Moravia, was born in Hukvaldy, in northeast Moravia, near the borders of Silesia, on July 3, 1854. He was the ninth of fourteen children, all musical. The father, a schoolmaster, encouraged them to participate in the village festivities, to learn how to play instruments, and to make music at home. Leoš was given music instruction by his father, and from the time he was six he joined his brothers and sisters in musical performances.

LEOŠ JANÁČEK

When he was ten he became a chorister in an Augustine monastery at Brünn where he studied music with the choir director, Father Pavel Krizkowski, until he was fourteen. After leaving the monastery, he continued his music study for four years at the local music school. Then he returned to the monastery to take over Krizkowski's job as music teacher and choir director. Still feeling the need for training, Janáček went to Prague in 1874 and enrolled in the College of Organ Playing. In this period of great hardship, he lived in a perpetually cold attic and had little to eat. Physical discomfort and poverty, however, did not depress him, since he could concentrate on musical activity in which he was making significant progress–he even managed to complete

Janáček: yȧ′ nä chĕk

a three-year course in a single year. Such income as he earned came from teaching music and writing newspaper criticism. When, in one of his reviews, he gave a devastating account of a performance by one of the professors at the Organ College, he was expelled from school for a brief period.

By 1875 he was back in Brünn, to become an instructor at the Teachers' School. In 1876 he was appointed conductor of the Brünn Philharmonic, which he led for a number of years in notable concerts in which the music of such Bohemian masters as Dvořák and Smetana was liberally represented. In the years between 1878 and 1881 he spent a part of each year in Germany and Austria to study educational methods. At the Leipzig Conservatory he studied composition with L. Grill and at the Vienna Conservatory with Franz Krenn.

In 1881 he helped found the Brünn Organ School with which he remained associated for forty years and which he helped to build from a modest school into a large and influential one; it was taken over by the state in 1920. He also became the principal conductor of the Czech Philharmonic, which he directed for seven years. This appointment assured him of a livelihood and enabled him to marry in 1881. The first important stirrings of his creativity took place after his marriage (though he had written a violin sonata in 1879, a string quartet in 1880, and several orchestral works, all of them highly derivative). His first opera, *Šarka*, though not produced until three years after his death, was completed in 1887. The six *Lachian Dances* for Orchestra came in 1890, and a ballet, *Rákoz Rákoczy*, was successfully produced in Prague on July 24, 1891. Under careful study these compositions hint at some of Janáček's developing creative tendencies; but none reveal a high order of inspiration, and none succeeded in gaining for their composer a major place in Bohemian music.

As the years passed several important developments affected Janáček profoundly. In 1896 he made the first of three visits to Russia and became an admirer of all things Russian. He undertook to study the language, and he devoured its literature. The impact of country and culture was reflected in many of his works which now were inspired by Russian backgrounds or subjects.

A second influence was Moravian folk music, which Janáček studied assiduously. As a result of this research, Janáček began to evolve a system of his own, the stylistic elements of which can be found in Moravian folk music. Out of his experiments came Janáček's theories about "melodies of language," theories based on his belief that the melody and rhythm of speech vary with different people and with different backgrounds and conditions. He came to the conclusion that musical expression must be founded upon these positive melodic and rhythmic speech elements.

In a lecture in England, in 1926, Janáček explained the effect Moravian folk music had had in his development: "I have lived among folk songs from childhood. Each folk song contains an entire man: his body, his soul, his surroundings, everything. He who grows up among folk songs, grows into a complete man. . . . There is something else I would like to say. There is not only the folk song, there is also our native tongue . . . and when you put the two together—the source of a folk song and the beautiful language—as well as the whole culture which is behind the language, then I am confident that the real classical music is growing, not the kind which ignores man and his surroundings and sees only the acoustic tone. If I grow at all, then, it is only from the folk song, from human speech, so help me God, and I am confident that I shall grow up."

Janáček's personal style became fully crystallized with the opera *Jenufa*, which he had begun to sketch a quarter of a century or so before he brought the work to completion. Most of the writing was done during a period when Janáček was struck by major tragedy: the death of his son in 1900 and of his daughter in 1903. He assuaged his terrible grief with intense creative effort, ending his work on *Jenufa* late in 1903.

Jenufa is a folk opera which draws material for text and music from Moravian peasant life but whose deeply somber and tragic overtones continuously reflect Janáček's dark mood when he wrote it. "I can only attach the black ribbon of the illness, pain and grief of my daughter, Olga, and of my baby boy, Vladimir, to the score of *Jenufa*," he once confessed. "Here," says Wilfred Mellers, "his tremendous creative power, his pantheistic sympathy with nature, his consciousness of sin, his preoccupation with the melancholy quiverings of conscience and the dark corners of the mind find their consummate fruition in the sinewy flexibility of his line, the complications of his rhythms, the fluidity of his harmonies. With a classical framework, he has created one of the most original idioms in European music."

Jenufa, Janáček's first opera to be staged, was given by the Brünn Opera on January 21, 1904 (under the title of *Jezi Pastorkyna*, or *Her Stepdaughter*). It was a failure. Janáček continued to rewrite the opera during the next few years. On May 26, 1916, it enjoyed a moderate success when it was revived by the Prague Opera; but its ultimate triumph was achieved at the Vienna Opera on February 16, 1918. This was the performance that helped to bring Janáček, a comparatively unknown composer, sudden international fame. Nevertheless, the American première of *Jenufa* at the Metropolitan Opera on December 6, 1924, met with disfavor. Ernest Newman, then serving as a visiting critic for the New York *Post*, called the story "crude" and described the music as "obviously the work of a man who . . . is only a cut above the amateur."

Since 1924 *Jenufa* has come to be recognized not only as its composer's masterwork, but as one of the most original and arresting folk operas of the twentieth century. Though neglected for over a quarter of a century in the United States, *Jenufa* was acclaimed in 1959 when revived by the Chicago Lyric Company and again in 1967 in a production by the visiting Hamburg Opera in New York and at Expo 67 in Montreal. Much of its strength comes from its stark, savage, austere declamation. "Like Mussorgsky," wrote Václav Štěpán, "Janáček rejects all intellectual elements. He uses no polyphony, no thematic construction and development. . . . His passion and dramatic touch, penetrating and concise, accomplish amazing effects especially when the milieu of the drama is so near to him."

His full creative powers now released, Janáček completed his most important song cycle and his most significant symphonic composition before 1920. The song cycle was called *Diary of One Who Vanished*. It comprised settings of twenty-three short poems by an unidentified village youth, describing his frustrated love affair with a gypsy girl. Janáček

set these poems for tenor, contralto, and female chorus, completing his score in 1919. Like *Jenufa*, these songs are tinged with dark colors and suffused with melancholy.

In 1918 Janáček wrote the symphonic rhapsody *Taras Bulba*, now one of his most popular instrumental compositions. Its program was based on Gogol's novel about the fifteenth century Cossack and his two sons, Ostap and Andrey, all of whom meet a tragic end during the struggle between the Ukrainian Cossacks and the Poles. *Taras Bulba* shows extraordinary powers of invention, and it enjoyed great success when introduced in Prague on November 9, 1924.

After World War I and the emergence of Czechoslovakia as an independent republic, Janáček, though an old man, became more productive than ever. "My last creative period," he said, "is a new outburst of the soul which, having already balanced its accounts with the outer world, now desires to be closely related to the simple Czech man."

In the period between 1919 and 1925 he completed four major operas, all of them introduced in Brünn: *Katya Kabanova*, November 23, 1921; *The Cunning Little Vixen*, November 6, 1924; *The Makropoulos Affair*, based on the Karel Čapek fantasy, December 18, 1926; and *From the House of the Dead*, based on Dostoevsky, produced posthumously April 12, 1930. Three of these have been produced in the United States: *Kate Kabanova* at the Empire State Music Festival in New York on August 2, 1960; *The Cunning Little Vixen*, in New York on May 7, 1964; and *The Makropoulos Affair*, in San Francisco on November 22, 1966. Of these *The Cunning Little Vixen* is regarded as the most lyrical. Janáček wrote it after a vacation in the country where he had been inspired and exalted by his proximity to nature and to the sounds of birds and animals. Still reacting to this experience he became deeply moved by an animal fable by Rudolf Tésnohildek in which animals acted like humans and humans like animals. He was particularly attracted to the character of the Cunning Vixen, "the center of the plot," as John N. Burk wrote, "the magnetic pole in whose field all of the other figures move, the symbol of eternal motherhood. She is sensual, coquettish, loving." Thus the opera *The Cunning Little Vixen* came into being, an opera "essentially in praise of nature the regenerator," says Burk. In *High Fidelity*, Robert Silverberg wrote: "It is an opera unlike any other. The numerous animal parts are given to sopranos who must cope with a murderously high tessitura. The musical phrases are elliptical, elusive; so, too, is the story. A mosaic effect is attained by the overlay of brief scenes, strikingly condensed thematic material, high pitched vocalization."

Janáček also made impressive contributions to instrumental and choral music in the 1920's, among them his second string quartet (1923), subtitled *Intimate Pages*, a personal document which he originally planned to name *Love Letters*, since he wrote it for Kamila Stösslova, a woman with whom he had been in love for about a dozen years; a remarkable choral work, *Slavonic Mass*, written to honor the tenth anniversary of the founding of the Czech Republic and introduced in Brünn on December 5, 1927; and what some critics single out as Janáček's most powerful work for orchestra, the Sinfonietta, based on some brass-instrument fanfares written earlier for an open-air athletic meet. The Sinfonietta was introduced as a symphonic work by the Czech Philharmonic on June 29, 1926.

Janáček's seventieth birthday was celebrated both in Prague and in Brünn with cycles of his operas. In 1925 he received an honorary degree from the University of Brünn.

Three years later, a cold, contracted in the Hukvaldy forests, developed into pneumonia, and Janáček died in a Moravian hospital in Ostrau on August 12, 1928.

Ten years after his death extensive cycles of his compositions were performed throughout Czechoslovakia. An even greater tribute was paid to Janáček in 1958 when an international congress of critics and musicologists in Brünn devoted itself exclusively to the life, work, and personality of Janáček. For this occasion, the Brünn Opera (renamed the Janáček Theatre) presented all of the composer's works for the stage; the Brünn Philharmonic performed Janáček's most important concert works, including the *Slavonic Mass*.

The eminent conductor Walter Süsskind, who met Janáček when the composer was in his seventies, described him as follows: "He spoke in short, clipped sentences which resemble the short, nervous phrases that are characteristic of so much of his music. He even pronounced his last name differently, in three quick syllables, although in Czech the second 'a' with its acute accent should be prolonged. He had a habit of repeating his sentences, 'What did he mean? What did he mean?' he would ask in rapid succession. . . . He was a short, stocky man, handsome in a way, with a big shock of silvery hair. Once when I sat behind him at a concert, he sat almost on the edge of his seat, not fidgeting, but listening with high-strung alertness. He walked, too, with an abrupt decisiveness. He was a man of great energy."

MAJOR WORKS

Ballet—Rákocz Rákoczy.

Chamber Music—3 string quartets; 3 violin sonatas; Piano Trio; Youth, for wind instruments.

Choral Music—Amarus, cantata; Na Soláni Čarták; The Eternal Gospel, cantata; Slavonic Mass; various a cappella choruses, part-songs, and motets.

Operas—Šárka; The Beginning of a Romance; Jenufa; Fate; The Excursions of Mr. Brouček; Katya Kabanova; The Cunning Little Vixen; The Makropoulos Affair; From the House of the Dead.

Orchestral Music—Six Lachian Dances; Suite; The Musician's Child, orchestral ballad; Taras Bulba, rhapsody; The Ballad of Blanik, tone poem; Concertino for Piano and Chamber Orchestra; Sinfonietta; Capriccio, for piano (left hand) and chamber orchestra.

Piano Music—Theme and Variations; By Overgrown Tracks, two sets; Sonata; In the Mist.

Vocal Music—Spring Song; Diary of One Who Vanished; Sayings, eighteen couplets for voices, piano and other instruments.

ABOUT

Brod, M., Leoš Janáček; Cernohorska, M., Leoš Janáček; Hollander, H., Leoš Janáček: His Life and Work; Muller, D., Leoš Janáček; Rocek, J., Leoš Janáček; Seda, J., Leoš Janáček; Štědroň, B. (ed.), Leoš Janáček: Letters and Reminiscences; Štědroň, B., The Works of Leoš Janáček; Vogel, J., Leoš Janáček: His Life and Work.

High Fidelity, March 1963; Musical America, January 1963; Musical Quarterly, January 1929, April 1955; Saturday Review, October 15, 1960.

André Jolivet
1905–

André Jolivet was born on August 8, 1905, in Paris. Both parents cultivated the arts, to which André was drawn from his tenth year on. As a boy, he studied the piano with his mother,

Jolivet: zhô lē vĕ′

and cello with Louis Feuillard. For a long while, as he pursued his academic studies through college, his main interest was literature and the theatre. He even dabbled in painting. One day, in trying to set one of his own poems to music, he finally discovered that music was his first love. In 1927 he returned to music study by becoming a pupil of Paul Le Flem in counterpoint, harmony, and fugue. Jolivet's interest in the more advanced tendencies in modern music finally led Le Flem to recommend him in 1931 to Edgard Varèse, with whom Jolivet studied composition, orchestration, and acoustics for three years. During this period, on September 26, 1933, Jolivet married Hilda Gigue; they have three children.

ANDRÉ JOLIVET

Through Varèse, Jolivet became acquainted with the music of Bartók, Schoenberg, and Alban Berg. By adopting some of their techniques in the use of discords and atonality—Jolivet was one of the first Frenchmen to do so—he produced his first important work, a string quartet (1934), in which some of Bartók's methods were emulated. Here, says Abraham Skulsky, Jolivet "shows his concern with the liberation of his music from tonal restrictions."

Jolivet was fascinated by new musical methods and techniques, and in 1935 he formed a musical group which identified itself as "La Spirale"; the other members were Daniel Lesur and Olivier Messiaen. Their aim was to promote new French chamber music,

at the same time effecting a method of exchange with progressive musicians outside France. When, a year after the group was organized, Yves Baudrier joined these three men in a common aim and purpose, the group took the name "La Jeune France" (a phrase borrowed from Berlioz). The aim was now extended to include the cause of modern French music and to emphasize spiritual values which, these composers felt, had been abandoned since the end of World War I. La Jeune France set itself up in opposition especially to the neo-classical tendencies then dominating so much of French music.

To each of the four young composers a return to spiritual values meant something different—Messiaen, for example, was drawn to the mysticism of the Catholic Church. Jolivet, however, interested himself in ancient magic and in the rituals of primitive society which he began to tap for subject matter. He said: "From the technical standpoint, my aim is to liberate myself totally from the tonal system; esthetically it is to give back to music its ancient and original character as the magic and incantational expression of human groups. Music should be a sonorous manifestation directly related to the universal cosmic system."

His first significant excursion into magic and primitive ritual took place with a set of six piano pieces, *Mana* (1935), which Nadine Descouches performed in Paris on December 12, 1935. These are musical descriptions of six statuettes decorating a primitive home. "Mana" is a term found in primitive magic describing a force flowing from a human being towards an object he regards as his fetish and which, in the process, becomes animated.

Ritualism was also the inspiration for several other important Jolivet compositions of the 1930's. These include *Cinq Incantations*, for flute solo (1936); *Cosmogonie*, for orchestra (1938); and *Cinq Danses Rituelles*, also for orchestra (1939). The last is regarded by Abraham Skulsky as "the culmination" of this period in Jolivet's career. "They depict the principal stages in the social and religious life of primitive man. . . . In this work, Jolivet attains an individuality and originality of style characterized by a magic and obsessive atmosphere in the orchestra sound; short melodic ideas, with incessant rhythmic variations; and complexity in harmonic and rhythmic materials." These dances were not heard until December 5, 1944, when André Cluytens conducted them in Paris.

When World War II broke out in 1939, Jolivet was drafted into the French army. He saw action until the fall of France and received the Croix de Guerre. His experiences led him, during the actual conflict, to write a poignant composition for baritone and orchestra in which, to his own text, he described a soldier's despair while identifying himself with his war-torn country. It was named *Les Trois Complaintes du Soldat* (*The Three Complaints of a Soldier*).

In 1942 Jolivet received a grant from the Association de la Pensée Française which enabled him to concentrate on composition. Three years later, however, he accepted an appointment as musical director of the Comédie Française, a post he held until 1958.

Among Jolivet's major works in the 1940's was a tone poem for orchestra, *Psyché* (1946), and the Concerto for Ondes Martenot and orchestra (1947). The Concerto is the first ambitious work to make such extensive use of the Ondes Martenot, though Jolivet had previously experimented with this electronic instrument in various compositions. Ginette Martenot, wife of the inventor of the instrument, introduced the concerto in Vienna on April 23, 1948. *Psyché* is a symphonic movement bearing the following motto: "The downfallen soul, after many a test, unites itself forever with divine love." The music portrays the soul's struggle to free itself from an imprisoning material universe. Rhythmically, the main interest in the composition lies in the way the beat changes constantly from measure to measure—for the composition bears no specific rhythmic indication just as it has no identifying key. One French writer described the work as a kind of symphonic music in which the electronic instrument personifies light, while the orchestra represents chaos and darkness. Gérard Michel, in *Paroles Françaises*, called the première of the concerto "the greatest musical event of the year . . . a total triumph."

Even more important is the Concerto for Piano and Orchestra, introduced in Strasbourg on June 19, 1951 with Lucette Descaves as soloist. Subtitled *Équatoriales*, it has three movements each of which describes some exotic region: Africa, the Far East, and Polynesia. The first movement emphasizes rhythm; the second, unusual and bizarre harmonic colors; the third blends intricate rhythmic processes with exotic harmonizations. Antoine Goléa did not hesitate to describe the concerto as Jolivet's finest work up to that time, referring to it as a modern masterwork. In 1952 the concerto was awarded the Grand Prix of the city of Paris; on January 5, 1953, it received an American première in New York; and in 1958 the music was used by the Paris Opéra-Comique for a ballet, with choreography by Georges Skibine.

Jolivet's first symphony was introduced at the festival of the International Society for Contemporary Music, at Haifa, on May 30, 1954. Five years later came a second symphony, commissioned by the Norddeutscher Rundfunk and featured at the Festival of Berlin on October 3, 1959. In the period between the two symphonies, Jolivet completed an important oratorio inspired by the life of Joan of Arc, *La Vérité de Jeanne*, performed at the Domrémy Festival on May 20, 1956. On September 16, 1956, *Épithalame*, described by the composer as a work for vocal orchestra, was the highlight of the Venice Biennale Festival, at which it received its première. And on January 9, 1962, Jolivet's Symphony for Strings was introduced.

In 1959 Jolivet was appointed Conseiller Technique à la Direction Générale des Arts et des Lettres, and in 1962 he became the president of the Lamoureux Concerts. He is a Chevalier of the Legion of Honor and an Officier des Arts et des Lettres.

MAJOR WORKS

Ballets—Guignol et Pandore; L'Inconnue.

Chamber Music—String Quartet; Trois Poèmes, for ondes Martenot; Cinq Incantations, for flute solo; Petite Suite, for flute, viola, and harp; Chant de Linos, for flute, viola, cello, and harp; Sérénade, for wind quintet with principal oboe; Pastorales de Noël, suite radiophonique for flute, bassoon, and harp; Concertino for Trumpet and Piano; Rhapsodie à Sept.

Choral Music—Kyrie; La Tentation Dernière de Jeanne d'Arc, cantata; La Vérité de Jeanne, oratorio; Épithalame.

Opera—Dolores, one-act opera buffa.

Orchestral Music—2 symphonies; 2 piano concertos; 2 trumpet concertos; Cosmogonie, symphonic prelude; Trois Chants des Hommes, for baritone and orchestra; Cinq Danses Rituelles; Symphonie de Danses; Les Trois Complaintes du Soldat, for baritone and orchestra; Suite Delphique, for wind instruments, ondes Martenot, harp, and percussion; Poèmes

Intimes, for voice and chamber orchestra; Psyché; Concerto for Ondes Martenot and Orchestra; Concertino for Trumpet, Strings, and Piano; Concerto for Flute and Strings; Concerto for Harp and Chamber Orchestra; Suite Transocéane; Symphony for Strings; Bassoon Concerto; Cello Concerto.

Piano Music—Trois Temps; Mana; Études sur des Modes Antiques; Sonata; Hopi Snake Dance, for two pianos.

ABOUT

Samuel, C., Panorama de l'Art Musical Contemporain. Musical America, June 1952.

Joseph Jongen
1873–1953

Joseph Jongen was born in Liège on December 14, 1873. All his musical schooling took place at the Liège Conservatory, from which he received diplomas in solfeggio, harmony, fugue, piano, and organ, and to which he was appointed assistant professor of harmony and counterpoint in 1892. Two years later he received a thousand-franc prize from the Royal Academy of Belgium for his first string quartet. In 1897, two more prizes came his way—one from the Royal Academy for a piano trio; the other, the Belgian Prix de Rome for the cantata *Comala*.

During the next four years Jongen traveled extensively throughout Europe, spending eight months in Rome. In this period he completed his first symphony, introduced at the Concerts Ysaÿe in Brussels in 1900. He also wrote a cello concerto, a violin concerto, and a piano quartet, the last of which was given at a concert of the Société Nationale de Musique in Paris in February 1903.

Upon returning to Belgium in 1903 Jongen was named professor of harmony and counterpoint at the Liège Conservatory and organist at Saint-Jacques Church. He held both posts until the outbreak of World War I. At that time he emigrated to England where he resided during the war years, partly in London, partly in Bournemouth. With Désiré Defauw, Lionel Tertis, and Émile Doehaerd he organized a piano quartet which toured the English provinces and also gave regular performances in London. Jongen gave numerous organ recitals in England during this period.

Jongen: yông′ ĕn

While engaged in these activities, he was writing a considerable amount of chamber, choral, and orchestral music, as well as compositions for the piano and for the organ. In 1916 he achieved a substantial success in London with his second string quartet in A major which *Musical Opinion* described as "one of the finest string quartets of modern times. It is delightful, indeed, to come across music such as this where matter and manner are alike admirable, where the composer's technique is not obtrusive but is subservient to the root musical idea, and in which warmth, intensity of feeling, never develop into extravagance. . . . There is more of Franck than of Saint-Saëns in this quartet, although it has nothing of Franck's tender spirituality; but the chromatic harmonization and the dreamy romantic beauty of much of the first and second movements recall the great Belgian master."

JOSEPH JONGEN

After the war, Jongen resumed his work at the Liège Conservatory. He resigned in 1920 to become professor of counterpoint and fugue at the Brussels Conservatory. In 1925 he became director (a post he retained until 1939, when he was succeeded by his brother, Léon). From 1919 to 1926 Jongen was the conductor of the Concert Spirituel in Brussels and was responsible for introducing many new works by contemporary French, Belgian, and Italian composers.

In 1933 Jongen wrote what many consider

his most distinguished composition: the *Symphonie Concertante*, for organ and orchestra. It is in four movements of which the first is lively and brisk, generating a feeling of excitement, then lapsing into relaxation. The second movement is a light and charming interlude, rhythmically interesting for its rapid changes of time and signature. The third movement is a long, sustained arioso, somewhat mysterious in atmosphere; the fourth is a toccata, dominated by an incessant spinning figure that taxes the virtuoso capacities of the organ.

Jongen completed over one hundred compositions in virtually all media. His music is generally delicate in style, sensitive in feeling, finely wrought, with a personal approach to harmony and rhythm and a masterly command of polyphony. His writing is characterized by subtle suggestions rather than by big impressions and effects. "From the purely expressive point of view," said Charles van den Borren, "he soars, in most of his work (especially in the slow movements) in an atmosphere of nostalgic reverie or cheerful well-being in full accord with his own character and with the idealism of his native soil."

Joseph Jongen died at Sart-lez-Spa, near Liège, on July 12, 1953.

MAJOR WORKS

Ballet—S'Arka.

Chamber Music—3 string quartets; 3 piano trios; 2 violin sonatas; Piano Quartet; Cello Sonata; Two Serenades, for string quartet; Rhapsody, for piano and wind instruments; Concerto for Flute, Violin, Viola, Cello, and Harp; Two Pieces, for four cellos; Quintet, for wind instruments; Two Sketches, for string quartet; Prelude and Chaconne, for string quartet; Duo Sonata, for violin and cello; Quartet for Saxophones; Concerto for Wind Quintet.

Choral Music—La Meuse; Chant Pastoral, for women's voices and piano (or orchestra); La Légende de St. Nicolas, for children's voices and piano (or small orchestra); Hymne à la Meuse, cantata; La Cigale et la Fourmi, for children's voices; Mass; Il Était un Berger, for children's voices and orchestra.

Opera—Félyane (unfinished).

Orchestral Music—Symphony; Violin Concerto; Cello Concerto; Adagio Symphonique, for violin and orchestra; Fantaisie sur Deux Noëls Wallons; Lalla-Rookh, tone poem; Prélude et Danse; Deux Rondes Wallonnes; Impressions d'Ardennes; Concertino for Trumpet and Orchestra; Tableaux Pittoresques; Sarabande Triste; Poème Heroïque, for violin and orchestra; Prélude Élégiaque et Scherzo; Petite Suite; Hymn, for organ and strings; Symphonie Concertante, for organ and orchestra; Passacaille et Gigue; Suite in Olden Style; Triptyque; Ouverture-Fanfare; Alléluia; Ouverture de Fête; Piano Concerto; Bourrée; Harp Concerto; In Memoriam; Ballade: Hommage à Chopin.

Piano Music—Serenade; En Forme de Valse; Suite en Forme de Sonate; Trois Études de Concert; Petite Suite; Pensée Élégiaque; Sonatine; Bourrée; Impromptu and Mazurka; ballades, pieces, preludes.

Vocal Music—Deux Vocalises; Deux Chants sans Paroles; La Musique.

ABOUT

Chesterian (London), December 1923; La Revue Musicale (Paris), July 1923.

Paul Juon
1872–1940

Paul Juon was born in Moscow on March 6, 1872. His father was an insurance official whose family came from the Swiss canton of Grisons; his mother was of German extraction. Juon was a precocious child in music. At sixteen he entered the Moscow Conservatory, where he studied the violin with Hřimaly and composition with Taneiev and Arensky. In 1894 he went to Berlin and attended the Berlin Hochschule für Musik, becoming a pupil of Woldemar Bargiel. He completed his studies there in 1896, having won the Mendelssohn Scholarship. For a year he taught theory at the Baku Conservatory. Then, returning to Berlin, he settled there permanently and devoted himself to teaching and to composition. From 1906 to 1934 he was professor of composition at the Berlin Hochschule.

His compositions attracted the interest of an influential publisher representing the house of Schlesinger. Through this man's efforts, Juon had most of his major works published. One of the earliest performances of Juon's work took place in Meiningen in January 1903 when his Symphony in A major was successfully introduced. After that, performances of his music grew increasingly frequent in Germany, and he achieved particular renown for his chamber music and piano works, which were performed extensively.

Several of Juon's chamber-music compositions were inspired by and were tonal interpretations of Selma Lagerlöf's novel *Gösta Berling*, which had made a profound impression on him. These include a Rhapsody for violin, viola, cello, and piano (op. 37) and a Capriccio, for violin, cello, and piano (op. 39). The latter became particularly well-known

Juon: zhōō ôn'

throughout Central Europe after its introduction by the Russian Trio at the Munich Festival on June 5, 1908. In Germany, says Edwin Evans, this Capriccio was long regarded as "one of Juon's most personal utterances . . . [abounding] with points of melodic and rhythmic interest."

PAUL JUON

One of Juon's highly successful chamber music works, which revealed pronounced Russian national influences, was the second piano quartet in G major (op. 50) which was successfully presented at the Danzig Festival on May 30, 1912. The first movement here has an unmistakably Slavic personality, while the third movement (an elegy) is permeated with Russian melancholy.

"Juon's music," wrote Eberhard Preussner, "is not easily penetrated. . . . His remarkable sense of form is the first of his characteristics. . . . The second characteristic lies in his melodic talent; here he must be grateful to the masters of Russian folk music. Themes, of actual Russian origin, give all of his music an extraordinary charm. . . . Further, his music is characterized by a remarkable rhythmic power."

An unidentified critic for the *Musical Standard* of London said that in Juon's compositions we confront "passages such as Liszt loved to write, breadth and depth as contained in Taneiev's finest work, frenzied dance rhythms such as figure in Sibelius's music. . . . He is often daringly original."

In Juon's music we see a happy marriage of Russian and German influences. "The material is almost invariably Slavic in character," says Edwin Evans, "whilst the treatment is thoroughly German, leaning now towards Brahms, now towards less recent writers of chamber music. His powers of development are strong, and characterized by solidity of thought, whilst the danger of heaviness is cleverly avoided by the use of an exceptional rhythmic ingenuity, probably as Slavic in its origin as the themes he uses."

In 1919 Juon was made a member of the Berlin Academy and also received the State Beethoven Prize. At the outbreak of World War II, Juon left Germany to find a new home in Switzerland. He died in Vevey on August 21, 1940. Juon was twice married: first to Katarina Shalakov, and after her death, to Marie Gunthert.

MAJOR WORKS

Ballet—Psyche.

Chamber Music—3 string quartets; 2 piano quintets; 2 piano trios; 2 violin sonatas; 2 viola sonatas; Sextet in C minor; Octet; Divertimento, for clarinet and two violas; Rhapsody, for piano quartet; Cello Sonata in A minor; Capriccio, for piano trio; Silhouetten, for violin and piano; Piano Quartet in G major; Litaniae, for piano trio; Flute Sonata in F major; Clarinet Sonata in F major; various pieces for violin and piano.

Choral Music—Reiterlied.

Orchestral Music—2 violin concertos; Five Pieces, for strings; Symphony in A major; Vægtervise, symphonic fantasy on Danish folk songs; Serenade; Épisodes Concertantes, for violin, cello, piano, and orchestra.

Piano Music—Tanzrhythmen, three sets for piano duet; Satyre und Nymphen, nine miniatures; Kleine Suite; Ten Preludes and Capriccios; Intime Harmonien, twelve impromptus; Den Kindern zum Lauschen; Zwei Schelmenweisen; Sonata in G major; Jotunheimen, tone poem for two pianos; Kinderträume, fifteen pieces; Kakteen, seven pieces; bagatelles, concert pieces, esquisses, skizzen, waltzes.

Vocal Music—Mörtelweibs Tochter, ballad; various songs for voice and piano.

Dmitri Kabalevsky
1904–

Dmitri Borisovich Kabalevsky was born in St. Petersburg, Russia, on December 30, 1904, the son of a civil servant. Early in his childhood

---

Kabalevsky: kă bă lĕf′ skē

Dmitri revealed a strong inclination to music, playing the piano by ear when he was only six, and soon after that trying to compose. However, intensive music study did not begin until he was fourteen, after his family had moved to Moscow. In 1919 Kabalevsky entered the Scriabin Music School which he attended for six years, specializing in piano; at the same time he studied composition privately with Vassilenko and Catoire. In 1925 he enrolled in the Moscow Conservatory, specializing in piano with Goldenweiser. He remained Catoire's pupil in composition until Catoire's death in 1926, when he entered Miaskovsky's class at the Conservatory. Kabalevsky was graduated in composition in 1929 and in piano in 1930; his name was inscribed on an honor plaque in the front hall of the Conservatory.

DMITRI KABALEVSKY

For a while Kabalevsky taught at the Scriabin School. In 1932 he was appointed instructor of composition at the Moscow Conservatory and subsequently was promoted to full professor.

Kabalevsky had begun serious composition as early as 1922. In 1925, while filling a temporary government post as a teacher in a children's school, he completed some charming pieces for children, among them the *Children's Songs from Pioneer Life*. Four preludes, for piano (1928), his first piano concerto and first string quartet (1929), *The Poem of Struggle* for chorus and orchestra, and a piano Sonatina (1930) showed substantial creative progress,

though their indebtedness partly to Scriabin and partly to Miaskovsky was noticeable.

In 1932 Kabalevsky completed his first symphony, commemorating the fifteenth anniversary of the Russian Revolution. From that time on, Kabalevsky used music to interpret the political and social aims of the Soviet Union. Much of his creativity was stimulated by the historic and cultural traditions of his land and its people. At the same time, while working within a tonal framework and in classical structures, he successfully drew from Russian folk music, and at times even popular sources, to achieve a national identity that linked him with the late nineteenth century "Russian Five" school.

Kabalevsky's first major success was achieved with his Symphony No. 2 (1934). (This was actually his third symphony; a symphony completed in 1933, now designated as Symphony No. 3, subtitled *Requiem for Lenin*, had preceded it.) Though the Second Symphony was essentially absolute music, it attempted in its first movement to suggest man's salvation through his role as a collaborator in the reconstruction of society. The beautiful slow movement spoke of the inner peace and serenity that come when man finds his right place in society; the triumphant finale discusses the ultimate victory of man and his society. The symphony was heard first in Moscow on December 25, 1934. An immediate success, it was soon played throughout the world and had its American première on November 8, 1942, with Toscanini conducting the NBC Symphony over the NBC radio network.

Equally successful was Kabalevsky's second piano concerto, in G minor, completed in 1936. The première performance took place in the United States, on May 9, 1943, with Leo Smit as soloist and Frank Black conducting the NBC Symphony. Intriguing in its lyrical material and masterfully written for the piano, the concerto has remained a favorite with pianists.

The year 1937 saw the completion of another major work, the opera *Colas Breugnon*, based on Romain Rolland's novel. In this work Kabalevsky drew inspiration from French rather than Russian backgrounds; his melodies were modeled after old Burgundian folk songs (two folk melodies are quoted). "My aim," the composer explained, "was to convey the local color and nature of the epoch [sixteenth century Burgundy]." Romain Rolland told the composer: "The folk songs are highly successful. You have grasped their essence perfectly and have given them form in your music." The opera was first produced in Leningrad on February 22, 1938, and proved a great success. Since then its gay little overture has become one of Kabalevsky's most frequently played symphonic compositions.

Also highly popular is the incidental music Kabalevsky wrote in 1938 for a children's play produced in Moscow, *The Inventor and the Comedians*. The basic sections, gathered into a ten-movement orchestral suite renamed simply *The Comedians*, depict the experiences of itinerant comedians as they travel from town to town. The suite was first heard in Moscow in 1940.

Kabalevsky's high position in Soviet music received official recognition in 1939, when he was elected a member of the Presidium of the Organizing Committee of the Union of Soviet Composers. A year later he was admitted into the Communist Party and awarded the Order of Merit. An official publication of the Soviet Union at this time emphasized Kabalevsky's close ties with the common man: "He is always in the very midst of the masses. One can find him at the factory tool room, in *kolkhoz* [collective farm], aboard the ship, in the miners' club, at the newspaper editorial office, and of course in the concert hall."

The war years found him using his music as an instrument for morale and propaganda. Two such major choral works appeared in 1942: the cantata *My Great Fatherland* and the choral suite *People's Avengers*, the latter written in collaboration with the poet Dolmatrovsky, while they were at the war front. Also closely related to the events of the war period was the opera *Before Moscow* (1942), celebrating the twenty-fifth anniversary of the October Revolution.

Kabalevsky won the Stalin Prize three times, the highest award that could come to a Soviet composer during the Stalin era: in 1946 for the second string quartet; in 1949 for the violin concerto dedicated to Soviet youth—since become a staple in the contemporary violin repertory; and in 1951 for an opera describing the Russian struggle in World War II against Fascist invaders, *The Family of Taras*. The

violin concerto received a double première—in both Leningrad and Moscow—on October 29, 1948. The opera was produced in Moscow on November 2, 1947, and in a greatly revised version in Leningrad on November 7, 1950.

Possibly nothing points more strongly to the high esteem with which Kabalevsky was regarded by Soviet officials than the fact that he was one of the very few leading Soviet composers to escape censure by the Central Committee of the Communist Party when it attacked Soviet composers for their "decadence" and "formalism" in 1948. (See sketch on Prokofiev.)

After World War II, Kabalevsky made several tours of Europe in performances of his own works. The production of major works, however, proceeded without interruption. One of his important achievements in the 1950's was his Fourth Symphony, introduced in Moscow in October 1956, then performed over a dozen times in seven Soviet cities from Odessa to Leningrad. Though the composer refused to assign any specific program to the music, he has hinted that it is somewhat autobiographical and that it is mainly an affirmation of life. In a review in the New York *Times* after the American première, in New York on October 31, 1957, with Dimitri Mitropoulos conducting the New York Philharmonic, Ross Parmenter wrote: "The work is an ambitious one. It is laid out on big lines. It uses a massive orchestra, and one felt that the composer, who waited twenty years after his Third Symphony to write this one, wanted his Fourth to be a major work. . . . Basically what he wanted to convey was a man coming through troubled times to a new period of yea-saying. . . . On the expressive plane it did have all the depth and strength it needed to fill out its monumental frame. . . . There was masterly skill in the marshaling of the orchestral resources, it had genuinely songful moments."

Among Kabalevsky's subsequent works, one of the most deeply moving in its emotional content and strongest in musical invention is the Requiem (to words by Rozhdestvensky), which received its world première in Moscow on February 9, 1963. (The American première took place at the Eastman School of Music in Rochester, New York, on December 9, 1965.) Composer and poet dedicated this work to the memory of the Russian heroes who had fallen during World War II. The composition is divided into three long movements, each of which consists of eleven independent episodes. The Soviet critic A. Medvedev explains: "The Requiem arouses in us layer upon layer of feelings, thoughts and images. The work develops not so much on the principle of dramatic contrast between the movements as on the evolution of one leading idea which grows and expands from episode to episode. The idea is the call to *Remember!* It is reiterated throughout the work, now as if spoken by the author, now, uttered by the departed heroes, and again through live and active musical pictures. The general impression from the music of the Requiem is clarity and simplicity."

Another significant composition among his later instrumental works is the Second Cello Concerto, in C minor, which he wrote in 1964 for Daniil Shafran, who introduced it with the Leningrad Philharmonic Orchestra, the composer conducting, in 1965. "This is a showpiece, and an appealing one," wrote a critic for the New York *Times*. "Sometimes the cello sounds like a harp, sometimes like a guitar, but most often it sounds like the most gorgeous, full-bodied, rich-toned and assertive stringed instrument one could imagine. In short, it sounds too good to be true, which is surely the case."

In addition to the above compositions, Kabalevsky completed *Of Our Native Land*, a cantata to words by C. Solodar, commemorating the fiftieth anniversary of the October Revolution. Both the composer and the poet were awarded a prize of the International Radio and TV Association in Prague for this composition.

In addition to his activities as conductor, pianist, teacher, and composer, Kabalevsky has made significant contributions to musicology. He has organized numerous state-music programs and for a period he was the editor of *Soviet Music*. He has never abandoned his early interest in young people and has produced numerous instrumental compositions and songs for them. He corresponds with students of some one hundred and fifty high schools, giving them advice and direction in their musical interests, sending them books and music and recordings, and answering their queries.

Kabalevsky was one of five Soviet musicians

who paid a visit to the United States (his first) in November 1959 on a reciprocal arrangement with the United States Department of State. (The other four were Shostakovich, Khrennikov, Dankevich, and Amirov.) In 1965 Kabalevsky was awarded the Order of Lenin. He serves as head of the music department of the Institute of Art and History at the Academy of Sciences in the Soviet Union.

Juri Jelagin has described Kabalevsky's musical preferences as follows: "At the piano in his small Moscow apartment, surrounded by piles of music, he would play insatiably for hours at a time. His cosmopolitan tastes run from Borodin, whom he considers one of Russia's greatest masters, to the object of his profound veneration, Johann Sebastian Bach."

MAJOR WORKS

Ballets — Vasilek; The Golden Blades of Grass.

Chamber Music — 2 string quartets; Cello Sonata.

Choral Music — 2 Requiems; The Poem of Struggle; My Great Fatherland, cantata; People's Avengers, suite for chorus and orchestra; Songs of the Morning, children's cantata; Leninists, for three choruses; Of Our Native Land.

Operas — Colas Breugnon; Before Moscow; In Flames; The Family of Taras; Nikita Vershinin; Armoured Train; The Encounter with a Miracle, children's opera.

Orchestral Music — 4 symphonies; 3 piano concertos; 2 cello concertos; The Comedians, suite; Violin Concerto; Pictures for Romeo and Juliet, suite; Pathetic Overture; Rhapsody on the theme of the song "School Years," for piano and orchestra; Spring, tone poem.

Piano Music — 3 sonatas; 2 sonatinas; From Pioneer Life; Rondo; various preludes.

Vocal Music — Children's Songs; Sonnets from Shakespeare; Romances.

ABOUT

Bakst, J., A History of Russian-Soviet Music; Danilevich, L., Dmitri Kabalevsky.

New York Times, April 23, 1967.

Aram Khatchaturian
1903–

Aram Ilich Khatchaturian was born in Tiflis, Armenia, on June 6, 1903. Though he early showed an interest in the folk songs and dances of his native land, it was not until comparatively late in life that he was able to receive an adequate musical education. His father, a bookbinder, was too poor to provide such an education for his son. Besides, the boy showed no particular interest in concert music or aptitude for making music. His musical training, consequently, was virtually nonexistent until he was twenty.

ARAM KHATCHATURIAN

In 1920 the family moved from Tiflis to Moscow. One day in 1923 Khatchaturian had an interview with Mikhail Gnessin, an eminent composer and teacher and the founder and head of the Gnessin School of Music. Khatchaturian confessed he knew nothing about music, that he was completely ignorant in both theory and musical literature. Nevertheless, he felt a powerful urge to make music and he wanted to learn how to do so. Gnessin was sufficiently impressed by the young man's sincerity and candor to enroll him in his school on a trial basis. For two years Khatchaturian studied the cello. Then he joined Gnessin's class in composition. Both in cello and in composition he made exceptional progress. He had hardly learned the basic rules of composition when he began writing music. His first piece was a *Dance*, for violin and piano (1926); his second, a *Poem*, for piano (1927). Both were good enough to be published and performed, and in these maiden efforts we can discern qualities that distinguish Khatchaturian's mature style. As Gerald Abraham noted, we here encounter "a fresh and spontaneous vein of melody inspired by the folk music of Transcaucasian peoples, a tendency to loose, rhapsodic structure, a keen rhythmic sense, and a love of warm, colorful sound effects."

In 1929 Khatchaturian transferred from the Gnessin School to the Moscow Conservatory. There, during the next five years, he studied composition with Miaskovsky and orchestration with Vassilenko. During these Conservatory years he revealed greater assurance in the more ambitious structures he was adopting for his writing. Before being graduated in 1934, Khatchaturian completed a violin sonata; a Trio for Clarinet, Violin, and Piano; and *Dance Suite*, his first work for orchestra. In line with the Soviet policy to make music serve the masses, Khatchaturian also produced a good number of functional compositions, including marches, workers' songs, dances, pieces for the balalaika.

His most significant composition while he was still a Conservatory student, and the first work to fulfill his earlier promise, was the Symphony No. 1, which was written in 1932 to honor the fifteenth anniversary of Soviet Armenia. His interest in Armenian folk music, of which he had been making an intensive study for a number of years, is here strongly reflected for the first time, though no actual folk songs or dances are quoted. Khatchaturian's material is unmistakably molded by the melodies, rhythms, and personality of Armenian folk songs, particularly the improvisational method of some of the episodes derived from bardic songs. The symphony was introduced in Moscow in 1932, Eugene Szenkar conducting the Moscow State Philharmonic. For the first time, the limelight of public and critical attention was focused on the young composer. Victor Belaiev said of it: "The three movements . . . are permeated with Eastern color. . . . It is a great work by reason of its contours and proportions; interesting and imposing in its sonority, it is distinguished by the broad treatment of its musical ideas. It revoices the best traditions of the Russian school in their ultimate development."

Khatchaturian's fame outside the Soviet Union was firmly established with his remarkable Piano Concerto (1935), triumphantly introduced in Moscow on July 5, 1937, the composer at the piano. Following its première in the United States (New York, March 14, 1942, with Mario Ajemian as soloist), it became one of Khatchaturian's most frequently played works in America, a favorite with both leading concert pianists and audiences. Its brilliant writing, the folkloristic character of melodies and rhythms, its electrifying vitality combined to make it one of the most appealing piano concertos of the twentieth century. Similarly attractive and popular was Khatchaturian's Violin Concerto (1938), first heard in Moscow on November 16, 1940. For the latter work Khatchaturian received the Stalin Prize.

He was awarded the Stalin Prize again in 1942 for the ballet *Gayane*, produced in the town of Molotov on December 9, 1942. The scene for this ballet is a collective farm where the love affair of Kazakov and Gayaneh is consummated by marriage after Gayaneh's first husband has proved himself a traitor and dies and Kazakov emerges as a hero. The ballet score is studded with lively Armenian folk dances, twelve in number, all gathered by the composer into two orchestral suites which have achieved worldwide popularity at symphony concerts. One of the numbers from the first suite is the *Sabre Dance*. The first time the Suite No. 1 was heard in New York City, the *Sabre Dance* aroused such a demonstration that it had to be repeated. It was mainly through the appeal of this one dance that the Columbia recording of the first suite became the best-selling classical album soon after its release in 1947. *Sabre Dance* was soon heard continually over the radio, in performances by radio and jazz orchestras, and in a piano transcription by Oscar Levant. It became a juke-box favorite, and for many months assumed the status of a nationwide popular hit.

The war years are reflected in Khatchaturian's second symphony, completed in 1942 after the Nazi invasion of the Soviet Union. The composer himself said that "the superhuman suffering caused . . . the Soviet people by the Nazi monsters is portrayed in the third movement." The finale speaks of the heroism and lofty spirit of the Soviet people while prophesying victory. The symphony was heard first in Moscow on December 30, 1943. The composer then revised it, and the new version was heard on March 6, 1944, in the Soviet Union and then given in New York on April 13, 1945, with Leonard Bernstein conducting this first United States performance.

As a leading Soviet composer, Khatchaturian received many honors. He was given the Order of Lenin in 1939 "for outstanding services in the development of music in his native Armenia." Shortly thereafter his name was inscribed on an honor plaque in the hall of the Moscow Conservatory. In the spring of 1943 the government placed a country mansion at his disposal so that he might continue his composing in a setting removed from the harrowing impact of war. He later became the chairman of the Union of Soviet Composers.

Despite his high position—which he maintained after the war with the successful première of his Cello Concerto in Moscow on October 30, 1946—Khatchaturian became the object of vigorous denunciation by the Central Committee of the Communist Party in its wholesale condemnation of Soviet composers on February 10, 1948. (See sketch on Prokofiev.) This attack on Khatchaturian is particularly amazing since his music had always had universal appeal and had always enjoyed great favor with the Russian people. In addition, it was based on folk sources (a demand made by the Central Committee on future works by its composers) and was readily assimilable at first hearing. Khatchaturian's music could hardly be guilty of either "antipopular trends" or "bourgeois formalism" and "decadence," of which he and other Soviet composers were accused by the Committee. Nevertheless, Khatchaturian publicly admitted that the criticism of the Committee was fully justified and promised that henceforth he would write in a more acceptable manner. But late in 1953—a half year after Stalin's death—Khatchaturian published an article in *Soviet Music* condemning the Soviet music policy as proclaimed by the Central Committee in 1948 and urged Soviet composers to free themselves of "tutelage" and to seek out "creative innovation." "A creative problem cannot be solved by bureaucratic means," he stated firmly. The article marked the beginning of the repudiation of the 1948 reactionary music policy and the birth of a new tolerance towards progressive musical techniques. Finally, in 1958, the Communist Party announced officially that the 1948 censure of composers like Shostakovich, Prokofiev, and Khatchaturian had been unjust and that they well deserved to be considered three of the leading composers in the Soviet Union.

In Khatchaturian's music, the folk music

of Armenia is the strongest influence and its stylistic elements have been thoroughly assimilated into his writing. As Dmitri Kabalevsky remarked: "The especially attractive features of Khatchaturian's music are its rootings in national folk fountainheads. Captivating rhythmic diversity of dances of the people of Transcaucasia and inspired improvisations of *ashugs* (bards)—such are the roots from which have sprung the composer's creative endeavors. In the interlocking of these two principles there grew Khatchaturian's symphonism—vivid and dynamic, with keen contrasts, now enchanting in their mellow lyricism, now stirring in their tensity and drama."

Since 1951 Khatchaturian has been professor of composition at the Moscow Conservatory and the Gnessin School of Music. In 1954 his ballet *Spartacus* was awarded the Lenin Prize, even though when first produced, in Leningrad in 1953, it had been a failure and did not improve its position in the performances that followed soon afterwards in Moscow and New York. (However, with new choreography by Yuri Grigorovich, *Spartacus* was revived at the Bolshoi Theatre on April 9, 1968, and proved the greatest success that ballet troupe had enjoyed in some twenty years.) His sixtieth birthday was celebrated throughout the Soviet Union in 1963 with concerts of his major works. He received so many congratulatory letters and telegrams that he was unable to answer them all personally and had to express his gratitude to his well-wishers in the newspaper columns.

Khatchaturian has made a number of tours of Europe conducting his works. On December 5, 1954, there was a concert of his music in London, and in March 1960 he paid his first visit to the United States. In 1960, however, Khatchaturian did not make any public appearances on the American concert stage. His American debut—as conductor-composer—took place on January 23, 1968, when he led a program of his works with the National Symphony Orchestra in Washington, D.C. This concert featured the American première of his *Concerto-Rhapsody*, for cello and orchestra, with Mstislav Rostropovich, for whom it was written, as soloist. This is one of three such works the composer completed in the years between 1963 and 1967, the other two being *Concerto-Rhapsody*, for violin and

orchestra, which came first, and a similar work for piano and orchestra, which came last. In March 1968 Khatchaturian led the American première of his Symphony No. 3 with the Eastman Philharmonic Orchestra in Rochester, New York. Khatchaturian is married to Nina Makarova, regarded by some authorities as the foremost woman composer in the Soviet Union. They first met in 1932 when both attended the Moscow Conservatory. "I loved him and I loved his music," she confided to an interviewer. "That was the main reason we married. But we are very different. He is Armenian—temperamental, strong, and a bit Oriental. I am Russian and lyric."

The Khatchaturians occupy a small apartment in Moscow (in the same building in which Shostakovich and Rostropovich also live), a place too constricted in space to hold more than a single piano. But they also own a country home, and it is there that both do most of their composing—in separate studios, each equipped with its own piano. "It sometimes gets very difficult," Khatchaturian's wife explains, in discussing their separate careers as composers. "We both want to play everything at the same time. It gets very noisy. Besides, somebody has to stop and get dinner."

Khatchaturian bears the honorary title of People's Artist of the U.S.S.R.

MAJOR WORKS

Ballets—Happiness; Gayane; Spartacus.

Chamber Music—String Quartet; Trio for Clarinet, Violin, and Piano; Violin Sonata.

Choral Music—Song about Stalin.

Orchestral Music—3 symphonies; Dance Suite; Symphonie-Poème; Violin Concerto; Solemn Overture; Piano Concerto; To the End of the War; Concerto for Violin, Cello, and Orchestra; Cello Concerto; Masquerade, suite; Russian Fantasy; Overture—Poème; Concerto-Rhapsody, for violin and orchestra; Salutatory Overture; Concerto-Rhapsody, for cello and orchestra; Concerto-Rhapsody, for piano and orchestra; Three Arias Concertante, for voice and orchestra; Flute Concerto.

Piano Music—Poem; Toccata; Scherzo; Dance.

ABOUT

Bacharach, A. L. (ed.), The Music Masters: v4, The Twentieth Century; Khubov, G., Aram Khatchaturian; Martynov, I., Aram Khatchaturian; Schneerson, G., Aram Khatchaturian.

Christian Science Monitor, August 21, 1963; Monthly Musical Record (London), March–April, 1942; New York Times, August 27, 1967.

Leon Kirchner
1919–

Leon Kirchner was born in Brooklyn, New York on January 24, 1919, the son of an art embroiderer. When Leon was nine his family moved to Los Angeles, where he continued the piano study begun in Brooklyn; he also made some tentative attempts at composition. A piano piece he entered in an intramural composition competition when he was sixteen received honorable mention. His piano teacher, John Crown, impressed with his creative potential, introduced the boy to Ernest Toch. Toch, in turn, urged Kirchner to devote himself seriously to composition.

LEON KIRCHNER

Kirchner entered the University of California in Los Angeles to study composition with Arnold Schoenberg, who had just joined the music faculty. Schoenberg was a powerful influence in further persuading Kirchner to become a composer. Nevertheless, Kirchner felt the necessity of completing his academic education. For that purpose he enrolled in the University of California at Berkeley, where he received his Bachelor of Arts degree with a major in music in 1940. One year later he began graduate work in composition with Albert Elkus and Edward Strickland. At the same time he undertook additional studies in

Kirchner: kûrsh′nĕr

composition for a while with Ernest Bloch.

In 1942 his compositions earned him the University's highest music award, the George Ladd Prix de Paris. This entitled Kirchner to go to Europe, a trip made impossible at the time because of the war. Instead of going abroad, Kirchner went to New York City, where he stayed until 1943, studying composition privately with Roger Sessions. In 1943 he completed a choral piece, *Dawn* (to a text by García Lorca), which he regards as his first mature creative effort.

From 1943 to 1946 Kirchner saw active service in the army. In 1946 he returned to Berkeley where he was engaged as a lecturer on music. In 1947 he wrote a one-movement Duo, for violin and piano, which was not performed until March 6, 1949, at which time it was presented at a concert of the League of Composers in New York. "The very first notes were electrifying in their impression of inspiration and originality," reported Carter Harmon in the New York *Times*, "an impression that was heightened as the work progressed." In the fall of 1949, Richard Franko Goldman prophesied a significant future for Kirchner on the basis of this Duo: "Kirchner is already the real thing; he is a composer whose music can stand being heard on programs with the music of anyone writing today."

A piano sonata in 1948 and his first string quartet in 1949 (both influenced by Bartók) confirmed the good impression that the Duo had made. The String Quartet was introduced in New York, received the Music Critics Circle Award in 1950, and was recorded by Columbia. Robert Sabin said of it in *Musical America*: "From the first bar . . . to the last the span of creative tension is never lost."

Kirchner was granted Guggenheim Fellowships in 1948 and 1949, and in 1951 he received an award from the National Institute of Arts and Letters. Meanwhile, in 1949, he married Gertrude Schoenberg, who bore him two children, a son and a daughter. He remained at the University of Southern California in Berkeley until 1951, rising from the post of lecturer to that of associate professor within a four-year period. Then he accepted a professorship at Mills College in Oakland, California. In 1961 he was appointed professor of music at Harvard University.

Alexander L. Ringer, writing in the *Musical*

Kirchner

Quarterly, regards Kirchner's *Sonata Concertante*, for violin and piano (1952) as his "first completely 'settled' composition," the work which represents a crystallization of a "style all his own." "Here," continues Ringer, "energies previously left free to take their wild course are brought under firm control." The work was first heard in New York in November 1952, performed by Tossy Spivakovsky and the composer. When it was performed at the Berkshire Music Center in July 1959 (Kirchner was at the Center as a member of the composition faculty), Jay C. Rosenfeld reported that "the impression is conveyed of tremendous avalanche-like thrusts stemming from irrepressible heroic and romantic compulsion."

On a commission from the Koussevitzky Music Foundation and the Library of Congress, Kirchner completed his first piano concerto in 1953; it was performed on February 23, 1956, at a concert of the New York Philharmonic with the composer as soloist and Mitropoulos conducting. It made such a strong impression that it received the Naumburg Award in 1956 and was recorded for Columbia. "The concerto is not a display piece," wrote Robert Sabin, "although there are some passages of fascinating sonority and harmonic power in it. But it is alive from the first bar to last, and for all its segmentation it has rhythmic drive and structural continuity." The concerto was featured at the festival of the International Society for Contemporary Music in Zürich on June 4, 1957.

A number of major works further emphasized Kirchner's ever growing individuality and creative power: the Toccata, for strings, solo winds, and percussion, commissioned for and introduced by the San Francisco Symphony, on February 16, 1956; the second string quartet, recipient of the New York Music Critics Award after it was introduced by the Lenox String Quartet on November 23, 1959; the Concerto for Violin, Cello, Winds, and Percussion, heard in Baltimore on October 16, 1960; and the second piano concerto, commissioned by the Ford Foundation and receiving its world première in Seattle on October 28, 1963, with Leon Fleisher as soloist.

In 1967 Kirchner received the Pulitzer Prize in music for his String Quartet No. 3, which was introduced by the Beaux-Arts Quartet in New York on January 27, 1967. The unusual feature of this work is that the composer added electronic sounds to those produced by the four stringed instruments. A critic for *High Fidelity* (April 1967) explains: "The electronic element is used conservatively—discreet percussive accents and pitched 'woodwind' sounds mingle with the four strings, extending the textural range of the piece to almost orchestral proportions. At the work's conclusion the two stage loudspeakers take over completely, wresting the thematic material from the human players and turning it into a breath-taking contrapuntal display that mere live performers could never hope to equal. Totally routed, the strings can only answer this outburst with a final pianissimo chord, which sounds a knell of defeat."

Eric Salzman has described Kirchner in the New York *Times* as "tall, well built with characteristically rumpled hair ... [and a] quiet, soft-spoken manner." Kirchner explained to Salzman how he fashions his music: "A few measures, an idea, constitute a gesture; the purpose of the work as a whole is to extend this in time. A phrase sets up the need for balance and extension which is satisfied by what follows. This then constitutes a larger complex which sets up still more implications. The entire piece is built up and forms an entity with infinite implications."

On another occasion, Kirchner expressed his artistic credo as follows: "An artist must create a personal cosmos, a verdant world in continuity with tradition, further fulfilling man's 'awareness,' his 'degree of consciousness,' and bringing new subtilization, vision and beauty to the elements of experience. It is in this way that Idea, powered by conviction and necessity, will create its own style and the singular, momentous structure capable of realizing its intent."

In 1962 Kirchner was elected to the National Institute of Arts and Letters and the National Academy of Arts and Sciences.

MAJOR WORKS

Chamber Music—3 string quartets (third string quartet supplemented by electronic sounds); Duo for Violin and Piano; Sonata Concertante, for violin and piano; Piano Trio.

Choral Music—Dawn.

Opera—Scenes for an Opera.

Orchestral Music—2 piano concertos; Piece for Piano and Orchestra; Sinfonia; Toccata for Strings, Solo

Winds, and Percussion; Concerto for Violin, Cello, Ten Winds, and Percussion.

Piano Music—Little Suite; Sonata.

Vocal Music—Letter; The Times Are Nightfall; Of Obedience; The Runner.

ABOUT

Musical Quarterly, October 1949, January 1957; New York Times, February 21, 1960.

Zoltán Kodály 1882–1967

Zoltán Kodály was born in the town of Kecskemét, Hungary, on December 16, 1882, of a musical family. His father played the violin, his mother the piano, and amateur chamber music performances often took place in the Kodály household. These family concerts were Zoltán's earliest musical experiences. Others consisted of listening to the gypsy orchestra, the only "professional music" available in the town–concerts which may well have been the source of Kodály's later intense interest in folk songs.

ZOLTÁN KODÁLY

His father was a railway official who had to change residence from town to town. From Kecskemét, the Kodály family moved to Szob while Zoltán was an infant. Seven years of Zoltán's early boyhood were spent in Galanta, whose dances he immortalized years later in one of his best known orchestral works. In his tenth year, the family settled in Nagyszombat. There he attended elementary and high school, sang in the church choir, and began to write music, mostly choral pieces (including an Ave Maria) and an uncompleted Mass. A short work for orchestra, an overture, was played at a high school concert in 1897.

In 1900 Kodály went to Budapest where he enrolled in the Royal Academy of Music and became Hans Koessler's pupil in composition. He now heard Brahms's music for the first time, an experience that compelled him to imitation. An Adagio, for violin and piano (1901), was undisguisedly Brahmsian in style. It became one of Kodály's first published pieces and, through its performances in Hungary, his first successful one. The Brahms influence could still be discerned in Kodály's first chamber music works, including sonatas for violin and piano and for cello and piano, and a piano trio.

Music study at the Academy was combined with courses at the University in French culture and Latin humanism, as well as reading classes in German and Hungarian. In 1905 Kodály was graduated from the Academy; and in 1906 he left the University with a doctorate and a thesis entitled *The Strophic Construction in Hungarian Folk Song*.

From 1905 on, Kodály was vitally interested in Hungarian folk music, an enthusiasm stimulated and aroused by Béla Bartók, then his fellow student at the Academy. They made expeditions throughout Hungary, unearthing thousands of folk songs and dances formerly unknown to the rest of the world. Many of these both Kodály and Bartók arranged, edited, and published. To the world outside Hungary, the decorative, sinuous, and sentimental gypsy songs exploited by Liszt and Brahms had long stood for authentic Hungarian folk music. But the researches of Kodály and Bartók proved that the indigenous music of Hungary was far different from gypsy songs and dances. Hungarian folk music had greater virility, was earthier, more brusque, more elemental. Its rhythms had primitive power. Its modal tonalities endowed melodies and harmonies with an exotic personality.

Kodály's studies in Hungarian folk music drew him away from Brahms and helped him to evolve a personal idiom, strongly influenced

Kodály: kō′ däl y'

and molded by the style, techniques, and character of native folk songs and dances. In describing Kodály's style M. D. Calvocoressi wrote: "His music generally has a distinctly narrative character, even when not assuming the form of recitative. Its nature is that of a discourse rather than a meditation: a discourse very definite in tone, broadly and emphatically punctuated with sharp, sudden swerves and forcible repetitions which seem to aim at driving a point finally home before proceeding to the next.... Persistent repetition of a pattern, whether rhythmic or melodic arabesque, is a feature particularly conspicuous in Kodály's music."

An orchestral composition, *Summer Evening* (1906), introduced at a student's concert at the Academy, first gave a true indication of Kodály's style. This is a tone poem, the core of which is an expansive melody with the physiognomy of a Hungarian folk song. In 1929, on Toscanini's request, Kodály revised the composition; the new version received its first hearing in New York on April 3, 1930, Toscanini conducting.

Soon after the original version of *Summer Evening* had been written and performed, Kodály paid a visit to Berlin and Paris; in the latter city he took some lessons in composition from Widor. Upon returning to Hungary, Kodály became professor of composition at the Academy of Music (to which his friend and colleague Bartók had been appointed in the department of piano one year earlier). While devoting himself to teaching, Kodály continued to produce compositions in which his creative personality asserted itself more and more vividly, all the while drawing elements of structure and style from folk song sources. These works included a set of sixteen songs to Hungarian texts (op. 1); his first string quartet (op. 2); nine pieces for the piano (op. 3); and a cello sonata (op. 4). With some of these works Kodály was beginning to get a hearing throughout Europe. The Cello Sonata was introduced on March 17, 1910, in Budapest in a program made up entirely of Kodály's works; the op. 3 piano pieces, performed by Tivadar Szanto, caused a sensation in Paris because of their advanced harmonic and melodic idioms; and the string quartet was featured at a festival in Zürich in 1910, after which it was performed in 1915 in the United States by the Kneisel

Quartet. However, a major success was still a long way off.

In 1910 Kodály married Emma Sándor, who was twenty years older than he and who for the next half century proved to be a most devoted wife and a dedicated believer in his talent; she also served faithfully as his secretary, translator, and business manager. During the years of World War I, Kodály continued his activities as teacher, musicologist, researcher into folk music, and composer. After the war he combined these varied efforts with the writing of criticism for Hungarian journals and for the foreign press. For a seven-month period in 1919 he served as assistant director under Ernst von Dohnányi at the Academy of Music. In 1922 Kodály returned to the Academy to his old post of professor of composition.

Kodály was creatively sterile from 1919 to 1923. Then, in 1923, the city of Budapest commissioned him to write a major work commemorating the fiftieth anniversary of the union of Buda and Pest. He complied with the *Psalmus Hungaricus*, a work for tenor solo, chorus, and orchestra on a sixteenth century Hungarian text. In this music Kodály completely assimilated the styles and idioms of old Hungarian music in constructing a score of surpassing power and eloquence. With a sure hand he combined the old and the new, the characteristics of age-old Hungarian folk song with the techniques and idioms of twentieth century music. He managed to express the old culture of his people without becoming archaic, in fact remaining a voice of his own time. "His musical setting," wrote A. von Toth, "exhausts both the national and subjective elements of the poem and molds them into one perfect and homogeneous unit of great visionary beauty and of great lyric and dramatic strength."

The world première of *Psalmus Hungaricus* took place in Budapest on November 19, 1923; it was an enormous success. On June 18, 1926, the composition was heard in Zürich; in 1927, in Amsterdam, Cambridge (England), and New York. Translated into many different languages, the work was then heard in all parts of the world, giving its composer an international stature for the first time.

Psalmus Hungaricus is one of Kodály's masterworks. Another, this time in the field of opera, is *Háry János* (1925); its successful première took place in Budapest on October 16, 1926. Its hero is a notorious, chronic liar, and the plot describes the many imaginative yarns spun by Háry János about his escapades in peace, war, and love. The score is a veritable mine of fresh, lively folk tunes and dances, but Kodály's personality is never obscured. As Percy Young said: "Kodály's music is an admixture of folk music, other traditional music, and some that is original. That in the first two categories defines the common people; that in the last is courtly. But the antitheses are resolved in Kodály's personal idiom, which, harmonically and instrumentally, enlarges the one and diminishes the other. . . . The presentation of the folk material is colorful and imaginative."

Háry János was produced in Germany, Austria, Switzerland, and the Soviet Union. The American première took place in New York on March 18, 1960. But the music of the opera is best known throughout the world in an orchestral suite which the composer adapted from his opera score and which has become Kodály's most frequently heard symphonic composition. The suite received its world première in New York—in a performance by the New York Philharmonic under Willem Mengelberg on December 15, 1927.

Other strongly national compositions helped place Kodály not only with the leading composers of his own country but with the foremost composers of the twentieth century. They include the delightful *Dances of Marosszék* (1929), which exists in two versions, one for solo piano and the other for orchestra; the orchestral version was introduced in Dresden on November 28, 1930, Fritz Busch conducting. *Dances of Galanta* followed in 1934. This is a work for orchestra made up of gypsy dances popular in the town of Galanta where the composer spent his boyhood years. Though written to commemorate the eightieth anniversary of the Budapest Philharmonic in 1934, *Dances of Galanta* received its world première not in Hungary but in the United States—in Philadelphia on December 11, 1936.

More ambitious than either of these two charming works for orchestra is the Te Deum completed in 1936 to honor the two hundred and fiftieth anniversary of the delivery of Budapest from the Turks. The world première took place at the Budapest Cathedral on September 11, 1936. This is one of Kodály's deeply religious and spiritual creations; nevertheless, religious elements are blended with those of Hungarian folk song and dance. Percy M. Young called the Te Deum "one of Kodály's most vivid works, touching the great points in the European tradition of choral music, yet firmly integrated and individual."

Kodály's style in his finest works was described and analyzed by Béla Bartók: "A strong, broad-flowing melodic invention, a complete grasp of construction, and a certain leaning towards hesitating disintegration and melancholy. The expression of reckless revelry and wild intoxication is foreign to his individuality, which is of a predominantly contemplative nature. . . . Kodály's music . . . is not 'modern' in the current sense of the word. It has nothing in common with atonal, bitonal, or polytonal tendencies: everything remains based upon the principle of balanced tonality. Yet his musical language is entirely new and expresses musical ideas never before heard, thus proving that tonality is not yet completely exhausted."

In 1930, in recognition of Kodály's contributions to Hungarian music, the government honored him with the Order of Merit and the University of Sciences appointed him lecturer, a post he held for two years. His fiftieth birthday in 1932 was celebrated all over Hungary—in villages as well as cities—with programs of his music. In 1934 he was made a member of the National Hungarian Arts Council.

The years of World War II and the Nazi occupation of Hungary were critical for Kodály. He became totally impoverished, and had to survive as best he could. The Nazis put pressure on him to divorce his Jewish wife. This he stoutly refused to do. Instead, he joined an underground movement to help Hungarian Jews escape the Gestapo. When seized for questioning, Kodály stubbornly refused to reveal the identity of his fellow conspirators. Only his enormous popularity with the Hungarian people saved him from a concentration camp.

These difficult times notwithstanding, Kodály managed to complete a number of major works. One was the Concerto for Orchestra which the Chicago Symphony introduced on February 6, 1941. Another was the Missa

Kodály

Brevis, for chorus and orchestra. When the war in Europe ended, Kodály's position in Hungary improved. He played a major role in the rehabilitation of Hungary's musical life and in the revamping of the program of music education in the schools. He was elected president of the National Arts Council and appointed a member of the National Assembly. On his sixty-fifth birthday, he was made a Freeman of Kecskemét and awarded the Grand Cross of the Order of the Hungarian Republic by the Minister of Education. He also received the Kossuth Prize three times.

In 1946–1947 Kodály toured France, Switzerland, Great Britain, and the United States. The visit to America, his first, took place during the winter of 1946 when he came as a delegate to the Congress of the International Confederation of Authors' Societies, held in Washington, D.C. Programs of his compositions were performed in his honor. In Philadelphia, Kodály himself led the Philadelphia Orchestra in the American première of his *Peacock Variations* for orchestra on November 22, 1946. The world première of this work had previously taken place in Amsterdam on November 23, 1939.

During this visit to the United States, Kodály confided to Olin Downes of the New York *Times* some of his musical beliefs: "All music comes fundamentally from popular sources. As the culture of the people advances, the product becomes always more interesting and significant, but when the connection with ancestral sources is lost, the art enters the stage of decadence. . . . One of the most useless things a composer can do is to quote a few folk melodies in his score and think that in so doing he has created something national and genuine. This is no more the case, under such circumstances, than a bunch of flowers cut and put in vases on the shelf is a garden. The garden is made of seeds which have taken growth from the ground."

Kodály's wife died in 1958 at the age of ninety-five. Her illness interrupted a labor that had been absorbing Kodály for many years, the writing of his first symphony. With the return of his equilibrium and peace of mind he went back to his symphony. On December 18, 1959, he married Sara Péczeli, a nineteen-year-old student at the Academy of Music. She was the daughter of one of his earlier pupils.

His original intent had been to adopt her as a daughter, but he changed his mind and married her so that she might inherit his estate without legal complications.

But once again work on the symphony was interrupted when Kodály was stricken with a thrombosis in December 1960. He was able to resume composition two months later, applying himself to his symphony with such intensity and concentrated effort that he was able to complete it in May 1961. The world première took place in Lucerne on August 16, 1961, Ferenc Fricsay conducting; in the United States, it was heard on January 4, 1962, George Szell conducting the Cleveland Orchestra. Percy M. Young in describing the symphony said: "[It] is a credo in the sense that it contains in its form and feeling the philosophy of its composer in respect both of music and the purpose of music. It is Hungarian, but it is not bounded by a territorial frontier. It is comprehensive in allusion (even though the composer himself admits intimate and personal references) and its musical nature shows its affinities with the main symphonic tradition. . . . It is mature music, intellectually powerful and unified in design."

In his old age, Kodály became a venerated patriarch in Hungary, "worshiped," as Alexander L. Ringer noted, "in a manner worthy of a saint. . . . Wherever he appears, walking erect and holding high his impressive head crowned by a long mane of white hair, people of all kinds gather around him, eager to catch a glimpse of the figure to whom they attach so much importance."

Though he now did little composing, he remained active in two areas which for many years had absorbed his interest. One was research in Hungarian folk music. As the director of the Hungarian Academy of Science he supervised the editing and publishing of an encyclopedia of folk songs of which six volumes (over five thousand pages) had been issued by 1966.

The second area was that of teaching music to children through the formation of singing classes and choruses. In 1950 he helped found in his native town of Kecskemét a General School of Singing and Music, in which children were taught sight reading through a novel method he had devised; they were banded together into singing units. The idea spread

320

throughout Hungary and proved a vital influence in developing a musical culture among the very young. "We teach the children with hand symbols," Kodály once explained to an interviewer. "It is like the sign language for deaf mutes. Using the movable 'Do' system—fixed 'Do' is not logical—they rapidly learn to sing any scale step merely by watching the teacher's hand. It's a game to them. They love it. Later they learn to read the notes." He believed firmly in the importance of teaching children to sing—before they begin formal training on an instrument: "Teach them singing first, for free singing without instruments is the school of true and deep musicality. It is better to make musicians before instrumentalists." In *High Fidelity*, Everett Helm, in a report from Budapest, explained: "The children receive six hours' musical instruction a week in the first four grades. They learn to read and write musical notes at the same time they learn the alphabet and word construction. After the fourth grade they have four music classes and two hours of choral singing a week, and they can study instruments as well." Helm's account continued: "What I saw and heard was, indeed, most extraordinary. Particularly interesting was a regular session of what the teacher described as 'one of the less brilliant' classes of eleven- and twelve-year-olds. In the space of forty-five minutes, the following transpired: a short bit of vocalizing in unison, parallel thirds and parallel fifths, with special attention to tone quality, dynamic flexibility and pure intonation; performance of a three-part Palestrina motet; singing of a rhythmic Hungarian folksong (in 7/8 meter) accompanied alternately by pencil tapping, handclapping and footstamping; improvised singing in two parts, following the hand movements of the teacher; singing of another folk song, during which the children marched about the classroom."

Kodály made frequent visits to the schoolroom to see for himself how his singing system was working out. He liked to pose interesting and unusual musical problems to the children and to conduct them in singing performances. The American composer Norman Dello Joio, who attended a conference of the International Society for Music Education in Budapest in 1964, had an opportunity to notice how unflagging was Kodály's energy: "One witnessed his punctual attendance at every session and concert. His grueling day usually started in the early morning, continuing to the close of each evening's performance."

His energy and vitality remained exceptional even in old age. He took daily swims in an open-air pool, winter and summer—swimming having been a favorite form of relaxation and exercise all his life. He also took a daily hike of two miles. Summers were spent at Galyateto, a resort in the Matra mountains, where his day began with a vigorous sprint in the woods—Kodály barefoot, dressed in shorts, and maintaining an even pace.

On Kodály's eightieth birthday, a mammoth celebration took place throughout Hungary. Practically his entire life work was reviewed in concerts of solo, chamber, orchestral, choral, and stage music. The Budapest Opera offered a new production of *Háry János*. At a gala concert sponsored by the Ministry of Culture and the Hungarian Association of Musicians in Budapest, more than one thousand high school children and university students participated in a choral performance. At a concert broadcast by the Hungarian Radio, a new work was performed in which twenty-three of Kodály's students each contributed a variation to a theme from the composer's first string quartet.

Kodály paid his second visit to the United States in July 1965 to serve as composer-in-residence at Dartmouth College, in Hanover, New Hampshire, during the college's third annual Congregation of the Arts. In his honor four concerts of his works were given, including a concert version of his early folk opera *Székelyfonó* (*The Spinning Room*), which had had its world première on April 24, 1932, and his last major work, the symphony. The audiences, which gave him a standing ovation at each of the concerts, saw, in Howard Klein's description, "a small, frail man, [exuding] a saintly magnetism. His white-bearded face is serene, his pale blue eyes calm; he wears his gray hair long, almost to his shoulders."

In February 1967 the Royal Philharmonic Society of London awarded Kodály its gold medal. He planned to go to England to receive the medal personally, but towards the end of February was stricken with a heart attack. He died ten days later, on March 6, 1967, in a

Krenek

hospital in Budapest. His body lay in state at the Academy of Science on March 10, and the following morning he was buried in the Farkasret Cemetery in Budapest.

MAJOR WORKS

Chamber Music—2 string quartets; Cello Sonata; Duo for Violin and Piano; Sonata for Unaccompanied Cello; Serenade for Two Violins and Viola.

Choral Music—Psalmus Hungaricus; Te Deum; Missa Brevis; Kallo, folk dances for mixed chorus and small orchestra; numerous secular and church compositions for chorus.

Operas—Háry János; Székelyfonó (The Spinning Room), lyric scenes based on Hungarian folk songs and dances; Czinka Panna.

Orchestral Music—Summer Evening; Ballet Music; Theatre Overture; Dances of Marosszék (also for piano); Dances of Galanta; Peacock Variations; Concerto for Orchestra; At the Martyrs' Grave; Symphony.

Piano Music—Nine Pieces; Valsette; Zongoramuzsika, seven pieces; Dances of Marosszék; various pieces for children.

Vocal Music—Bicinia Hungarica; various songs for voice and piano; numerous arrangements of folk songs; numerous songs for children and music students.

ABOUT

Eösze, L., Zoltán Kodály; Gray, C., A Survey of Contemporary Music; Mellers, W. H., Studies in Contemporary Music; Weissmann, J. S., Music Today; Young, P. M., Zoltán Kodály.

Etude, April 1951; La Revue Musicale (Paris), February 1947; Saturday Review, July 31, 1965; Tempo (London) June 1946.

Ernst Krenek
1900–

Ernst Krenek was born in Vienna August 23, 1900, the son of an Austrian army officer. At the age of five he began to make up melodies and put them on paper. In 1916 he became a pupil of Franz Schreker. When, in 1920, Schreker left Vienna for Berlin to become director of the Academy of Music, Krenek followed him. He completed his studies with Schreker in 1923. During this period Krenek composed several ambitious works, among them his first three symphonies, which appeared in 1921 and 1922; the *Symphonische Musik* for nine instruments, introduced at the Donaueschingen Festival July 30, 1922; and his first string quartets, written between 1921

Krenek: krĕ′ nĕk

and 1923. Though the influence of Schreker and of French Impressionism can occasionally be detected in these works, they are nevertheless remarkable for the independence of their rhythmic and contrapuntal thought, which attracted both the interest and the enthusiasm of influential critics and musicians.

ERNST KRENEK

In 1923 Krenek left Germany. For two years he lived in Zürich, paying visits to France, Italy, and Austria from time to time. He completed his second opera, *Der Sprung über den Schatten*, produced in Frankfurt-am-Main on June 9, 1924. The first opera had been *Zwingburg*, with a libretto by Franz Werfel, heard in Berlin on October 16, 1924. But in *Der Sprung über den Schatten* he revealed himself for the first time as an exponent of *Zeitkunst*, or Contemporary Art, a movement gaining ascendancy in Germany at the time. He wrote his own text, and he demonstrated a mastery of stage technique and a growing individuality of musical style. Part of that musical individuality came from the way in which atonal writing was combined with jazz style and idioms.

In 1923 Krenek married Anna Justina Mahler, daughter of the composer. Two years later they were divorced. At that time Krenek accepted the post of coach at the Prussian State Theatres in Kassel and Wiesbaden, which he held until 1927. Both theatres were directed by Paul Bekker; through Bekker's influence, Krenek's opera *Orpheus und Eurydike* (text based on an expressionist play by Oskar

Kokoschka) was produced in Kassel on November 27, 1926. In addition Paul Bekker's encouragement was instrumental in the composition of the opera that brought Krenek international fame—*Jonny Spielt Auf!*

Jonny Spielt Auf! was *Zeitkunst* with a vengeance. It had a timely, racy, provocative text by Krenek, in which a Negro bandleader becomes involved with a white woman, his white rival is crushed under the wheels of a train, and the bandleader bestrides the globe, playing jazz tunes on his fiddle while the world below him dances frenetically. In his score, which was largely in a jazz style, Krenek made generous use of parody and satire. In his orchestration, Krenek employed locomotive whistles, automobile horns, sounds from a radio, and the noises of a rattle.

When *Jonny Spielt Auf!* was introduced at the Leipzig Opera on February 10, 1927, it created a sensation. Germany was as delighted with the unorthodox, controversial libretto as it was with the fox-trots and blues in Krenek's vivacious score. The work was soon performed in leading opera houses in more than one hundred European cities and became one of the most highly publicized and most bitterly discussed operas of the early twentieth century. The American première took place at the Metropolitan Opera on January 19, 1929. W. J. Henderson of the New York *Sun* called it "a pretty good musical comedy with some outstanding moments. . . . If you don't take it too seriously you can have a pleasant evening."

The tremendous success of *Jonny Spielt Auf!* made it possible for Krenek to give up his job as opera coach and concentrate on composition. In 1928 he married Berta Herrmann, an actress. They settled in Vienna, where Krenek stayed until 1937, except for occasional tours in Europe as conductor and pianist in programs of his own compositions. For a short while he continued to exploit the jazz idiom in his music—notably in the opera *Leben des Orest*, a modernized version of a Greek drama, mounted in Leipzig on January 19, 1930. But the fascination of jazz soon began to pall. With the song cycle *Reisebuch aus den Österreichischen Alpen* (1929) he returned to romanticism, this time to the romanticism of Franz Schubert.

His extended residence in Vienna brought him into personal contact with the Vienna school of atonalists. He had for some time been interested in the twelve-tone system but had rejected it for his own use. In Vienna he became increasingly interested in the system as a basis of his own composition. In 1932 he planned the opera *Karl V*, a historical drama calling for an austere, atonal musical style; experimenting with the twelve-tone row, he now found that it served his purpose. The twelve-tone work was produced in Prague on June 15, 1938. (It enjoyed a highly successful revival in Munich in January 1965.) "I have been striving," Krenek explained, "for an ever freer and more incisive articulation of musical thought." He had found such an articulation in the twelve-tone system, a technique to which he remained faithful for most of his major works.

Krenek first visited the United States in 1937, as conductor of the visiting Salzburg Opera Guild. The following year Austria was occupied by Nazi forces. Though an Aryan, Krenek was unacceptable to the Nazis, and he decided to leave Austria and make his home permanently in the United States. He arrived in 1938 and in 1945 became an American citizen. From 1939 to 1942 he was head of the music department, later Dean of the School of Fine Arts, at Hamline University in St. Paul, Minnesota. He transferred his home to Los Angeles in 1947. Three years later, he received a special grant to write music for the stage and for television in California. In 1954 he moved to Tujunga, near Los Angeles.

Krenek proved extraordinarily creative in the United States, completing some thirty major works in the years between 1938 and 1948—including operas, symphonies, a ballet, choral works, and various other compositions. Most were in a strict dodecaphonic style. One of the earliest works for orchestra completed in the United States was inspired by an American folk song. He had heard a John Jacob Niles recording of "I Wonder as I Wander" which impressed him, and he used it as a theme for a set of orchestral variations. He wanted, as he explained, "to unfold the feelings of tragic loneliness and passionate devotion by which the solitary wanderer 'under the sky' is animated." This composition, entitled *Variations on a North Carolina Folk Song*, was introduced on December 11, 1942, by the Minneapolis Symphony conducted by Mitropoulos.

Krenek wrote a number of other works of

American interest. Among them was *The Santa Fe Time Table*, for a cappella chorus (1945)—its text consisted of the names of railroad stops between Albuquerque and Los Angeles. Another work with American subject matter was the *George Washington Variations*, for piano (1950).

Krenek's first opera in the United States was *Tarquin*, produced at Vassar College on May 13, 1941. A decade later, his one-act opera *Dark Waters* received its première—on May 2, 1951, at the Festival of Contemporary Arts of the University of Southern California. More significant than either of those operas is *Pallas Athene Weint*, the world première of which took place October 17, 1955, helping to inaugurate the new opera house in Hamburg, Germany. *Pallas Athene Weint*, libretto by the composer, was described by H. H. Stuckenschmidt as "a tragedy on the ideas of democracy.... Pallas Athene wept in this opera over the defeat of Athens, of freedom of thought, of the conception of independent thinking which died with Socrates.... This new opera ... is an expression of the deepest cultural pessimism.... The parallel to our own times is very plain.... In every scene of the opera ... we sense a warning voice, urging us not to abuse the rights of freedom in fighting for freedom and right."

Krenek's later operas included *The Bell Tower*, commissioned by the Fromm Foundation and introduced on March 17, 1957, at the University of Illinois in Urbana as a feature of the Festival of Contemporary Arts; and *The Golden Ram* (*Der Goldene Bock*), which had its world première at the International Congress of Contemporary Music in Hamburg on June 16, 1964. *The Golden Ram*, libretto by the composer, was described by Oliver Daniel as "a magnificent spoof" of the classical legend of the Argonauts. "He has used," said Daniel, "practically every device: taped sounds, amplified off-stage voices, and filtered captions—which flashed across the proscenium like news on the old Times Building on Times Square, adding amusing commentary on the stage happenings.... Musically, the score is brilliant, and Krenek ... has honed his technique to a point of sharp virtuosity." At its world première in Hamburg, the opera caused a furor; indeed, it created what Daniel has described as "one of the wildest demonstrations I have heard since the première of Schoenberg's *Variations* in Berlin more than thirty years ago."

Though he lives in California, Krenek has frequently revisited Europe to conduct performances of his music, to make recordings, and to appear over radio and television. In 1963 he received the Grand Prize of Austria. He has also made important appearances in the United States. On August 22 and 23, 1963, he participated in the Ernst Krenek festival at Raleigh, North Carolina. During the summer of 1965 he was composer-in-residence at Dartmouth College in Hanover, New Hampshire, where an all-Krenek concert was presented on July 7 as part of the Congregation of the Arts. One of the numbers on this program was a world première—*Fibonacci-Mobile*, for string quartet, two pianos, and "coordinator." He returned to Dartmouth College as composer-in-residence during the summer of 1968.

Krenek has expounded his musical beliefs in two books, *Music Here and Now* (1939) and *Self Analysis* (1953). The latter consists of excerpts from an autobiography which Krenek completed in 1950. He deposited the manuscript at the Library of Congress in Washington, D.C., with instructions that it not be opened until fifteen years after his death.

Krenek is an avid student of languages, which he studies as a hobby. Except for mountain climbing—or, failing that, long solitary walks—he has no interest in sports. He is a man of exceptional wit, perception, and wisdom who reveals a trenchant intellect even in casual conversations. He is particularly interested in musico-mathematics, which has motivated him to write various compositions, including *Pentagram*, *Hexaeder*, and *Fibonacci-Mobile*. The last of these is based on the Fibonacci, a mathematical series which consists of a row of numbers each of which is the sum total of its two precedents (1-1-2-3-5-8, and so forth).

At Dartmouth College, in 1965, Krenek described his functions as a composer, and the *raison d'être* of his music, to Conrad L. Osborne: "My composition exists in the dimension of time, just as a mobile exists in the dimension of space. It is there, it exposes itself to view, and people come and look at it, and get from it what they will. I am not responsible for anyone's emotional reaction to it—you may be bored, or think it's funny, or be moved to tears. . . . I would hope that people would come to hear my music without any preconception as to what it should sound like or how it should affect them; if they have preconceptions, they will be disappointed. They should simply listen to see what happens for the interest of it."

Earlier, in 1960, Krenek told Allen Hughes: "I think I work best when I have several things going at once—a new score in the sketching stage, a completed one to copy, an article to write, a lecture to complete. I concentrate on one for a while, then turn to another without ever getting tired of any of them."

MAJOR WORKS

Ballets—Mammon; Der Vertauschte Cupido; Eight Column Line; Jest of Card.

Chamber Music—8 string quartets; Suite for Clarinet and Piano; Suite for Cello Solo; Sonata for Viola Solo; Sonata for Violin Solo; Sonatina for Flute and Clarinet; Violin Sonata; Viola Sonata; String Trio; Parvula Corona Musicalis ad Honorem J. S. Bach, for string trio; Trio for Clarinet, Violin, and Piano; Pentagram, for woodwind quintet; Alpbach Quintet; Hexaeder, six pieces for chamber ensemble; Fibonacci-Mobile, for string quartet, two pianos, and a coordinator; Five Pieces, for trombone and piano.

Choral Music—The Seasons; Von der Vergänglichkeit des Irdischen, cantata; Cantata for Wartime; The Lamentations of Jeremiah; The Santa Fe Time Table, for a cappella chorus; In Paradisum, motet; Missa Duodecim Tonorum; La Corona, cantata; various motets.

Electronic Music—Spiritus Intelligentiae Sanctus, oratorio; San Fernando Sequence.

Operas—Jonny Spielt Auf!; Leben des Orest; Cefalo e Procri; Karl V; Tarquin; What Price Confidence?; Dark Waters; Pallas Athene Weint; The Bell Tower; Ausgerechnet und Verspielt (television opera); The Golden Ram (Der Goldene Bock).

Orchestral Music—5 symphonies; 3 piano concertos; 2 violin concertos; 2 concerti grossi; Concertino, for flute, violin, cembalo, and strings; Seven Pieces for Orchestra; Potpourri; Little Symphony; Theme and Thirteen Variations; Little Music, for wind and orchestra; Symphonic Piece, for string orchestra; Variations on a North Carolina Folk Song; Tricks and Trifles; Symphonic Elegy; Concerto for Two Pianos and Orchestra; Concerto for Violin, Piano, and Orchestra; Concerto for Harp and Orchestra; Medea, for voice and orchestra; Capriccio, for cello and orchestra; Kette, Kreis und Spiegel, tone poem; Eleven Transparencies; Sestina, for voice and chamber orchestra; Marginal Sounds; Quaestio Temporis; From Three Make Seven; Nach Wie vor der Reihe Nach; Perspectives.

Piano Music—6 sonatas; Hurricane Variations; Eight Piano Pieces; George Washington Variations; Zwanzig Miniaturen; Echoes from Austria; Sechs Vermessene; Basler Massarbeit.

Vocal Music—O Lacrymosa; Monolog der Stella; Reisebuch aus den Österreichischen Alpen; Fiedellieder; Die Nachtigall; Das Schweigen; The Night Is Far Spent; The Ballad of the Railroads; Etude; The Flea; Instant Remembered, for soprano and instruments; various Lieder for voice and piano.

ABOUT

Ewen, D. (ed.), The Book of Modern Composers (2nd revised ed.); Machlis, J., Introduction to Contemporary Music; Saathen, F., Ernst Krenek, Ein Essay.

Music Review, February 1948; Musical America, October 1965; New York Times, May 1, 1960; Saturday Review, July 31, 1965.

Benjamin Lees
1924–

Benjamin Lees was born in Harbin, Manchuria, on January 8, 1924, of Russian parentage. He was an infant when his family emigrated to the United States and settled in California. Benjamin became an American citizen when he was seven. It was also in California that Lees received a thorough training at the piano in San Francisco and in Los Angeles. He maintained his home in Los Angeles until the outbreak of World War II, during which he served in the American armed forces from 1942 to 1945. Following his separation from the army, he enrolled in the University of Southern California in Los Angeles and attended classes in theory, harmony, and composition taught by Halsey Stevens and Ingolf Dahl among others. He also took private lessons in composition from George Antheil, a significant influence in directing him towards a career as a composer.

The first significant works by Lees appeared in 1952. These included *Profile for Orchestras*, his first string quartet; and a sonata for two pianos, performed in New York on November 8, 1952. In the years between 1952 and 1955 he completed several more ambitious works: his first symphony; *Declamations*, for piano and string orchestra; and several compositions for solo piano. In 1955 he received a Guggenheim Fellowship for travel in Europe, and there followed a period during which he completed his second string quartet and his first piano concerto. The latter received its world première in Vienna on April 26, 1956. In 1956, he traveled in Finland on a Fulbright grant.

His growing artistic stature became evident

with his Symphony No. 2, commissioned by the Louisville Orchestra, which introduced it on December 3, 1958. No less significant were his Concerto for Orchestra (1959) and his Concerto for Violin and Orchestra (1958). The latter did not receive its world première until 1963 when Henryk Szerying introduced it in Boston as soloist with the Boston Symphony under Erich Leinsdorf. It was particularly well received and within the next few years was performed extensively not only in the United States but also in Germany and France.

BENJAMIN LEES

At this time Lees' style had become crystallized. In addition to revealing a partiality for instrumental music and for the classic forms, he showed a strong preference for polyphonic textures that were frequently complex and sometimes dissonant and for energized motor action. Nevertheless, Lees leans more towards the conservative than the progressive wing of American composers—preferring to speak in a language that is readily assimilable and agreeable to the ear. His music, as Irving Kolodin wrote in the *Saturday Review*, is "neither contrived nor constructed; it is composed, which is to say, evolved with purpose and integrity from a productive premise."

In 1963, on a Ford Foundation grant, Lees composed a piano sonata (his fourth) for Gary Graffman, and it was for Graffman that Lees later produced his Piano Concerto No. 2. The world première took place in Boston on March 15, 1968, Graffman appearing with the Boston Symphony under Leinsdorf. The composer described this important work as follows: "In essence it . . . [is] a vehicle for solo instrument and orchestra . . . with the orchestra assuming as much prominence as the solo instrument. As to structure . . . I chose a modified classical form for this concerto, feeling that the nature of the ideas could be presented with greater clarity in this form." Irving Kolodin found in the concerto derivations from Rachmaninoff, Prokofiev, and Bartók, but considered it "an eminently logical point of departure," since "it sounded . . . like an effort to combine the Rachmaninoff kind of pianistic point of view with certain structural ideas of Prokofiev and the coloristic characteristics of Bartók (especially in the slow movement)."

After absenting himself from the United States for eight years, Lees returned to America in 1962. He subsequently became a member of the Peabody Conservatory in Baltimore. The first major work Lees completed following his return to America was his Concerto for String Quartet and Orchestra, commissioned by the Kansas City Philharmonic, which introduced it on January 19, 1965. It forthwith entered the repertory of several major orchestras. When George Szell conducted the New York première with the Cleveland Orchestra in 1967, Raymond Ericson wrote in the New York *Times* that it was "a very fine work in traditional style. . . . It is well constructed in a lean, direct fashion that is not hard to grasp on initial hearing; its themes are comprehensible without being bland. The novel and tricky task of balancing a string quartet against a full orchestra is carefully worked out, although it presented some acoustical problems to this listener. The business of tossing musical ideas around from a single member of the quartet to full orchestra back to full quartet gives the work a special fascination."

Besides the honors and grants already mentioned, Lees was also the recipient of awards from the Fromm Foundation, the Copley Foundation, and UNESCO, together with the Sir Arnold Bax medal. In 1967, he was invited by the State Department of the United States to tour the Soviet Union where he was a guest of the Union of Soviet composers.

MAJOR WORKS

Chamber Music—2 string quartets; Violin Sonata; Invenzione, for violin and piano.

Orchestral Music—2 symphonies; 2 piano concertos; Profile for Orchestra; Declamations, for string orchestra and piano; Concerto for Orchestra; Violin Concerto; Visions of Poets; Oboe Concerto; Concerto for String Quartet and Orchestra.

Piano Music—4 sonatas; Fantasia; Kaleidoscope; Toccata.

Vocal Music—Three Songs for Contralto; Song Cycle for Evelyn Lear.

Anatol Liadov
1855–1914

Anatol Konstantinovich Liadov was born on May 10, 1855, in St. Petersburg. Many members of his family were distinguished musicians. His grandfather had been the conductor of the St. Petersburg Philharmonic Society, his father the conductor of the Russian Imperial Opera; three uncles filled important professional posts. We learn from Rimsky-Korsakov that Liadov's father was completely irresponsible: "Anatol and his sister had been left to grow up as best they might. Their father, deep in his carousing . . . was never at home and never laid eyes on his children for weeks at a stretch. Though he drew a very good salary, he frequently left his children without a copper so that they had to borrow money occasionally from servants to escape starvation. Of formal education and instruction there could be no question at all." Rimsky-Korsakov further reveals that in his boyhood Anatol used to hover backstage at the Opera, listening raptly to rehearsals and performances: "Glinka he loved and knew by heart. . . . Of singers, chorus and orchestra he had heard enough and more than enough. Amid such surroundings, his boyhood passed and without system."

In 1870 he was enrolled in the St. Petersburg Conservatory where he was a pupil of Rimsky-Korsakov in composition. Despite an innate love of and gift for music, he was a lazy and shiftless student. He often played truant and, when he was in the classroom, his mind was continually wandering. Nevertheless a set of four songs written in 1873 and published three years later showed unusual talent. By 1876,

Liadov: lyà′ dôf

however, the authorities lost patience with him and had him suspended. His pleas and promises to make amends persuaded them to revoke the suspension and permit him to return to school on probation. Liadov now apparently turned over a new leaf and fulfilled his enormous potential. He was graduated with honors in harmony, counterpoint, and fugue. A cantata, *The Bride of Messina* (1877), based on Schiller, was performed and acclaimed.

ANATOL LIADOV

Mussorgsky, who came to know Liadov while the latter was still young, wrote about him as follows: "A new talent has appeared in our midst, a genuine, thoroughly original, thoroughly Russian talent: Constantin Liadov's son. He is bright and unaffected. He has boldness and power. Cui, Borodin and my humble self are delighted with him. Let me describe him—fair-haired, thick-lipped, the forehead not very high but full of character, especially in conjunction with high cheek bones. Irregular little wrinkles run around his nose and mouth. He is extraordinarily nervous and highly strung, and even more extraordinarily taciturn. He will sit listening, uttering not a word; but suddenly the crinkles around his nostrils begin to work and quiver, and that means praise!"

Following his graduation, Liadov was appointed professor of harmony and theory at the St. Petersburg Conservatory. He held this post until the end of his life; among his many pupils there were Prokofiev and Miaskovsky. Beginning in 1885, Liadov also served as professor of theory at the Court Chapel for several years.

In 1884 Liadov married Nadezhda Tolkacheva, who bore him three sons. For the next decade Liadov concentrated on songs and smaller piano pieces, his works including three sets of *Children's Songs* (opp. 14, 18, 22) and a still extremely popular piano miniature, *The Music Box*.

In 1889 Liadov visited Paris where two of his works were given at the Paris Exhibition. In 1894 he became the conductor of the Free School concerts, his programs helping to draw attention to the work of young Russian composers. Soon afterward he was made a member of a committee formed to do research in Russian folk music. Liadov cultivated this field with considerable success, making excellent modern adaptations of many old Russian folk songs.

After the turn of the twentieth century, Liadov—who, thus far, had proved himself an exquisite miniaturist—turned to more ambitious structures and designs in his composition. In the period between 1904 and 1909 he completed a set of three fairy tales (*tableaux musicaux*) for orchestra. These works have proved his most significant contributions to the symphonic repertory. *Baba-Yaga* describes the aerial flight of a witch on her mission of evil; *The Enchanted Lake* (*Le Lac Enchanté*) is an impressionistic portrait of a lake populated by water nymphs; *Kikimora* is about a phantom who is raised by a sorceress in the mountains. These three compositions, says Ellen von Tideboehl, reveal Liadov to be a "true Slav. . . . His fertile imagination gave to his compositions a distinctly fertile Russian character. . . . Liadov's music is entirely national. He continued the work begun by Glinka, the father of Russian music, and his followers."

Still another significant orchestral work by Liadov is a suite of native Russian folk tunes, *Eight Russian Folk Songs*, completed in 1906, the result of the composer's intensive researches into his country's folk music. This modern adaptation of eight folk tunes led Alfred J. Swan to write that here "Liadov's soul . . . blossoms forth, radiates brilliant light. . . . Coupled with elegance, taste and economy,

which is yet exuberant, they make Liadov's settings unique from a purely musical point of view. But, of course, the main charm of them lies in the peculiar spiritual affinity between his genius and the Russian folk song."

When Liadov's health failed in the summer of 1911, he went to the Caucasian watering places for a cure. But he never did recover completely. The outbreak of World War I, for which his son was called to military duty, broke his spirit, and he lost the will to live. He died in Polyanovka, near Novgorod, on August 28, 1914.

Liadov's shyness was neurotic. He hated making public appearances, even at concerts featuring his own compositions, and he was in dread anytime he had to appear in the role of conductor. On the rare occasions when he did enter a concert hall, recalls Lazare Saminsky, his "timid form [would hide] behind some column." He withheld his new score from orchestra and conductor almost up to the time of the last rehearsal and was too retiring to reveal to the conductor how he wanted his music to sound. When a concert was given in his honor in St. Petersburg in 1913, he could not summon the courage to attend.

Because he wrote so many works in the smaller and less exacting forms and because the number of his productions are comparatively few, he has been accused of being inordinately lazy. This was not the case. When he was stimulated creatively he worked long, hard, and painstakingly. However, he refused to write when he did not enjoy his working conditions or when a creative idea would not fire his imagination.

MAJOR WORKS

Choral Music—Bride of Messina; Slava; Chorus for Sœur Béatrice; Chorus in Praise of Stassov; songs for women's voices and piano.

Orchestral Music—2 scherzos; Baba Yaga; The Enchanted Lake; Kikimora; Eight Russian Folk Songs; From the Book of Revelation; Naenia.

Piano Music—Ballades, barcarolles, canons, études, mazurkas, pieces, preludes, variations.

Vocal Music—Songs for Children, three sets; settings of Russian folk songs.

ABOUT

Bacharach, A. L. (ed.), The Music Masters; Calvocoressi, M. D. and Abraham, G., Masters of Russian Music; Zaporozhetz, N., Anatol Liadov: Life and Work.

Chesterian (London), October 1921; Monthly Musical Record (London), January 1915.

Rolf Liebermann
1910–

Rolf Liebermann was born in Zürich, Switzerland, on September 14, 1910. He studied law at the University of Zürich but, having been highly musical from childhood on, combined an academic life with music study at the Academy of Music, mainly with Hermann Scherchen (conducting) and Wladimir Vogel (composition). He began his career as a composer with several scores for pageants and some songs. In 1943 his *Polyphonic Studies*, for chamber orchestra, was performed at a demonstration concert organized at Berne by the Swiss Composers League, and a cantata for baritone and orchestra, *Une des Fins du Monde* (text by Jean Giraudoux), was heard over the Zürich radio. On January 10, 1947, *Suite on Swiss Folk Melodies*, for orchestra, was broadcast by the BBC in London. These early works, more or less traditional in structure and idiom, brought him an award from the municipality of Zürich.

ROLF LIEBERMANN

His interest in the twelve-tone system resulted in his first significant orchestral work, *Furioso*, introduced at the Darmstadt Music Festival in 1947. (Leopold Stokowski conducted it in Dallas on December 9, 1950.) *Furioso* is a three-part composition built from two series of twelve tones, treated rather

Liebermann: lē′ bĕr män

freely. Liebermann's first symphony, heard in Milan in 1949 at the International Congress for Dodecaphonic Music, and his piano sonata (1951) were also in a free twelve-tone idiom.

But it is essentially in the field of opera that Rolf Liebermann made his mark, with a fresh, new approach towards both libretto and music. Liebermann designated his first two dramatic works as *opera semiseria*, a term which indicated the two levels on which the texts progressed—one, intensely serious, humanistic; the other, satiric. The libretto, rather than the music, was Liebermann's prime concern. As he wrote in 1954: "It is high time that all of us opera composers finally take cognizance of the developments that have occurred in the dramatic field during the last three decades.... The composer ... is up-to-date and aggressive; he belongs to the avant-garde and deals with yesterday's problems in tomorrow's language. If we manage to regenerate the musical stage by way of scenic concept, i.e., the libretto, if we achieve congruence of libretto and music in content and expression, and if, finally, we have the courage to bring up problems of our time in opera and to quit the esthetes' beloved ivory tower, then we shall have made decisive contributions towards the solution of the crisis."

Liebermann's first *opera semiseria* was *Leonore 40/45*, libretto by Heinrich Strobel. It was produced in Basel, Switzerland, on March 25, 1952. Later it was presented by several of Germany's leading opera houses. The "Leonore" in the title was intended to suggest the heroine of Beethoven's opera *Fidelio*. Liebermann's opera, like Beethoven's, exalts the power of life. The plot of *Leonore 40/45* concerns the attachment of a German soldier for a Parisian girl during World War II. In a departure from conventional opera, both the German and the French languages are used—sometimes alternately, sometimes simultaneously—to meet the basic needs of the text. Another unusual feature of the opera is the composer's use of quotations from the works of other composers (Wagner, Liszt, Leoncavallo, Stravinsky, Schoenberg, Beethoven); in the last scene, the first four measures of Beethoven's *Fidelio Overture* are sounded to announce the arrival of the guardian angel.

The opera is basically light, ironical, and witty; but it also has deep implications. As

Everett Helm remarked in a review in *Musical America:* "It is by implication the story of European civilization between the years 1939 and 1947. Behind the action on the personal plane are ideas such as mutual understanding and appreciation between so-called enemy peoples; the power of love to conquer the powers of darkness; the necessity of holding to one's ideals in the face of seemingly hopeless odds. But such ideas are seldom openly expressed; they are implied throughout." Of the music Helm said: "The alternating irony, comedy and seriousness of the text are mirrored most skillfully in Liebermann's score, the basis of which is the twelve-tone system."

Penelope (first performed at the Salzburg Festival in Austria on August 17, 1954) is once again an *opera semiseria*, blending profound human values with satire and wit. The text is the old legend translated into modern terms, a tale developed by the librettist, Heinrich Strobel, on two stylistic levels. As he explained, one of these is that of antiquity "which goes to form the outer frame"; the other is the "modern plane upon which the actual tragedy is enacted." Just as the text is a blend of the old and new, so is the music. Sometimes it is baroque in its treatment of recitatives, arias, ensemble numbers, and choruses; sometimes vibrantly contemporary, not only in its use of the twelve-tone system but even in the interpolation of boogie-woogie in an episode in which the friends of Ulysses perform an abandoned dance. "The theatrical talent of Liebermann is among his greatest gifts," reported Max Graf. "He knows how to get results, matching effective music to the stage episodes, and in particular contributing strong endings to his acts."

Liebermann's next opera was of an entirely different character and style. It was *The School for Wives* (adapted by Heinrich Strobel from Molière), commissioned by the Louisville Orchestra which presented the first performance in Louisville, Kentucky, on December 3, 1955. In this opera, Liebermann abandoned the twelve-tone system for a neobaroque style that uses a comparatively small orchestra, a clearly defined classical structure, melodious passages and vocal ensembles interrelated by effective recitatives, and an over-all orchestral and vocal approach reminiscent of Couperin. In spite of all borrowings from the past, the opera

is modern, as Everett Helm noted in his review: "It is decidedly contemporary in spirit. The harmony, which alternates between dissonant and consonant, is always given a twist; and the rhythm, which employs frequent changes of meter, endows the score with a remarkable vitality."

Besides his work for the theatre, Liebermann has produced a number of provocative experiments in instrumental music. One of these, *Concerto for Jazz Band and Orchestra*, had a highly successful première at the Donaueschingen Festival in Germany on October 17, 1954. Another, *Les Échanges*, one of Liebermann's electronic compositions, is scored for fifty-two industrial machines (such as teletypes, cash registers, and staplers) recorded on magnetic tape. It was heard first in Lausanne, Switzerland, on April 24, 1964, at the Swiss Exposition Nationale.

After serving for many years on the music staff of the Swiss Radio Corporation in Zürich, in 1962 Liebermann became director of the Hamburg State Opera, which he helped make one of the most progressive and stimulating opera companies in Europe. This opera company, under Liebermann's direction, paid its first visit to North America in the summer of 1967, giving performances mainly of modern operas both in New York City and at Expo 67 in Montreal. Liebermann himself, however, had previously visited the United States late in 1955 to help supervise the première of *The School for Wives*. At that time he was described by Edward Downes in the New York *Times* as "tall and solidly built, with a tinge of gray in his hair and with mobile features." Early in 1963 Liebermann revisited the United States on a Ford Foundation grant. He returned in June 1967 with the visiting Hamburg State Opera.

MAJOR WORKS

Choral Music—Streitlied Zwischen Leben und Tod, cantata.

Electronic Music—Les Échanges, for fifty-two industrial machines.

Operas—Leonore 40/45; The School for Wives; Penelope.

Orchestral Music—Furioso; Symphony; Polyphonic Studies, for chamber orchestra; Volkslieder Suite (Suite on Swiss Folk Melodies); Une des Fins du Monde, cantata for baritone and orchestra; Chinesische Lieder, for tenor, harp, and strings; Musik, for speaker and orchestra; Concerto for Jazz Band and Orchestra; Geigy Festival Concerto, for Bass

Drum and orchestra; Capriccio, for soprano, violin, and orchestra.

Piano Music—Sonata.

Vocal Music—Chinesische Lied, dramatic scena for contralto, tenor, and piano.

ABOUT

Lang, P. H. and Broder, N. (eds.), Contemporary Music in Europe.

Charles Martin Loeffler
1861–1935

Charles Martin Tornow Loeffler was born in Mulhouse, Alsace, on January 30, 1861. His father was a scientist who adopted the pen name of Tornow for his writings, a name which Charles added to his own later in life. When his father received an appointment to do some scientific work for the government in the province of Kiev, the family settled temporarily in Russia. There Charles absorbed his first important musical impressions—strains of Russian folk and church music which he recalled in some of his compositions.

CHARLES MARTIN LOEFFLER

On his eighth birthday, Loeffler was given a violin, and by the time he was fourteen he knew he wanted to become a musician. By now, the family had made its home in Berlin. There Loeffler studied the violin first with Eduard Rappoldi and then with Joachim; he

Loeffler: lĕf′ lĕr

was also a harmony pupil of Friedrich Kiel. From Berlin, Loeffler went to Paris where he continued to study the violin (with Massart) and composition (with Guiraud).

His studies ended, Loeffler began to earn his living by playing the violin in the Pasdeloup Orchestra. After a year of such activity, he joined the private orchestra of Baron Paul von Derwies at the baron's estates in Lugano and Nice. Upon the baron's death in 1881, Loeffler came to the United States, bearing a letter of recommendation from Joachim. This gave him access to the recently founded Boston Symphony Orchestra, which he joined in 1882. Since this appointment allowed him to accept other engagements, he was able to make a transcontinental tour with the Theodore Thomas Orchestra in 1883. From 1885 to 1903 Loeffler shared the first-violin desk of the Boston Symphony with Franz Kneisel.

Loeffler's first major work, *Les Veillées de l'Ukraine*, a suite for violin and orchestra, was introduced by the Boston Symphony on November 20, 1891. This was a nostalgic musical recollection of the composer's boyhood nights in Russia, inspired by a reading of Gogol. The Boston Symphony continued to introduce other Loeffler compositions: the *Fantastic Concerto*, for cello and orchestra, on February 2, 1894; the Divertimento, for violin and orchestra, on January 4, 1895; *La Mort de Tintagiles*, a dramatic poem derived from the drama of Maurice Maeterlinck, on February 16, 1901; *La Bonne Chanson*, a poem for orchestra inspired by Paul Verlaine, on April 2, 1902.

Loeffler's first masterwork was *A Pagan Poem*, based on the eighth eclogue of Virgil, in which a Thessalian maiden exercises her magical powers in order to bring back the lover who deserted her. Originally, in 1901, Loeffler had written it as chamber music—for piano, two flutes, oboe, clarinet, English horn, two horns, three trumpets, viola, and double bass. In 1903 he arranged it for two pianos and three trumpets. Finally, in 1906, he adapted it for orchestra, the version in which it became famous. This was heard for the first time on November 22, 1907, with Karl Muck conducting the Boston Symphony. Since then it has become one of Loeffler's most frequently performed orchestral works and one of the most important in the repertory of American symphonic music of the early 1900's. The music is not a literal musical translation of Virgil's eclogue, but a musical fantasia based on the poem. Here the composer's former partiality for a post-Impressionist style becomes a basic idiom, an idiom which, as Philip Hale said, is devoted to "tonal impressions rather than . . . thematic development." Hale said further: "He has delicate sentiment, the curiosity of the hunter after nuances, the love of the macabre, the cool fire that consumes and is more deadly than fierce, panting flame."

In 1903 Loeffler resigned from the Boston Symphony to devote himself to teaching and composition. He divided his year between his home in Boston and a farm in nearby Medfield, living for the most part in comparative seclusion. On December 8, 1910, he married Elise Burnett Fay.

He did not produce many works, but what he did complete was of impeccable taste and lofty musicianship, generally permeated with sensitive feelings. Much of his writing remained faithful to French Impressionism, though in one important work, *Memories of My Childhood*, he returned to the modal character of Russian and Ukrainian folk music, and in one or two minor efforts he experimented with jazz.

Memories of My Childhood received the first prize of one thousand dollars in a competition sponsored by the Chicago North Shore Music Festival at which it was introduced May 30, 1924. Loeffler himself provided the programmatic interpretation of this popular work, an account that appears in the published score: "Many years ago, the composer spent more than three years of his boyhood in a small Russian town. . . . He now seeks to express by the following music what still lives in his heart and memory of those happy days. He recalls in the various strains of his music Russian peasant songs, the Yourod's Litany prayer, 'The Happiest of Days,' fairy tales and dance songs. The closing movement of the symphonic poem commemorates the death of Vasinka, an elderly peasant *Bayan*, or storyteller, singer, maker of willow pipes upon which he played tunes of weird intervals and the companion and friend of the boy who now, later in life, notes down what he hopes these pages will tell."

Among other important compositions by Loeffler are *Hora Mystica*, for men's chorus

and orchestra, which received its première with the Boston Symphony under Muck on March 2, 1917; *Canticum Fratris Solis*, for solo voice and chamber orchestra, commissioned by the Elizabeth Sprague Coolidge Foundation, which had its first performance at the Library of Congress on October 28, 1925; and *Evocation*, for women's voices and orchestra, commissioned for the opening of Severance Hall in Cleveland, where it was performed on February 5, 1931.

Charles Martin Loeffler died on his farm in Medfield, Massachusetts, on May 19, 1935. In his last years, one of his favorite diversions was training a boys' church choir in the singing of Gregorian chants.

Loeffler was made Chevalier of the Legion of Honor in 1919, and in 1926 he received an honorary doctorate from Yale University.

In appearance, Loeffler suggested the scholar. He was tall and erect, even in old age, with an air of professorial dignity. He liked to refer to himself as the farmer of Medfield. He loved the country, enjoyed watching the crops grow, and was a great fancier of horses. Many branches of the arts interested him equally— painting, sculpture, and literature. He was engrossed in the American scene in all its facets: he even confessed a liking for good jazz, as a reflection of American experiences and temperament, and expressed the highest respect for Gershwin and Duke Ellington.

Carl Engel, the musicologist, who met Loeffler one year before the composer's death, recorded his impressions in the following paragraph: "He bore the marks of physical suffering. But his razor-blade mind still showed occasionally its flashing edge. His mood was genial, reminiscent. The good things of the table still appealed to him. His wonderful eyes would still twinkle as he unraveled some favorite story, not less amusing for being not altogether new. His precarious cardiac condition did not prevent him from asking the waiter to bring me particularly rich cigars. He acknowledged eagerly how charmed he had been with the person of Arnold Schoenberg. His thoughts roamed the length of contemporary music. . . . From one thing to another, the talk swayed along its circuitous route, not as fast as formerly, but just as absorbing."

What Lawrence Gilman said of *Evocation* might serve as a description of all of Loeffler's music: "radiant, serene, Hellenic, [speaking] with irresistible effect the thought of a mind which has never forgotten that the ultimate ritual of the spirit is the worship of that loveliness which is outside of time."

MAJOR WORKS

Chamber Music—2 Rhapsodies, for oboe, violin, and piano; Octet; String Sextet; Music for Four Stringed Instruments; Quintet, for three violins, viola and cello; Partita, for violin and piano.

Choral Music—Psalm 137, for women's chorus; For One Who Fell in Battle, for mixed a cappella chorus; Beat! Beat! Drums, for unison men's chorus.

Orchestral Music—Les Veillées de l'Ukraine, for violin and orchestra; Fantastic Concerto, for cello and orchestra; Divertimento, for violin and orchestra; La Mort de Tintagiles, dramatic poem; Divertissement Espagnol, for orchestra with saxophone; La Villanelle du Diable, symphonic fantasy; Poem; A Pagan Poem; Hora Mystica, for men's chorus and orchestra; Five Irish Fantasies, for voice and orchestra; Memories of My Childhood; Canticum Fratris Solis, for solo voice and chamber orchestra; Evocation, for women's voices and orchestra.

Vocal Music—4 Melodies; 4 Poems, for voice, viola, and piano; 4 Poems, for voice and piano; The Wind Among the Reeds; The Reveller, for solo voice, violin, and piano.

ABOUT

Chase, G., America's Music; Gilman, L., Nature in Music; Howard, J. T., Our American Music; Rosenfeld P., Musical Portraits.

Musical Quarterly, July 1925, July 1935.

Nikolai Lopatnikoff
1903–

Nikolai Lopatnikoff was born in Reval, Estonia, on March 16, 1903. When he was eleven, he began to study piano and composition. In his youth, he moved on to St. Petersburg, and in 1914 he enrolled in the Conservatory where his teachers included Sacharoff in piano and Schitomirski in theory.

The Revolution ended his musical training. The Lopatnikoff family left Russia, finding a temporary haven in Finland. In Helsinki, his education, both academic and musical, was resumed. In 1920 he went to Heidelberg, where he made considerable progress in music with Ernst Toch, Willy Reberg, and Hermann Grabner. Then, feeling the necessity of undertaking some vocational training so that he might be able to support himself, he entered

Lopatnikoff: lô pät′ nĭ kôf

the Technological College in Karlsruhe, from which he was graduated with a diploma in civil engineering in 1927.

It was during this period that the first performances of some of his compositions took place. These works included his first string quartet, heard in Karlsruhe in 1924, and his first piano concerto, introduced in Cologne November 3, 1925. In 1926 he completed several chamber music works, including a Duo, for violin and cello, and a Sonata, for piano, violin, and snare drum. His first orchestral composition to be performed in the United States was completed at this time: *Introduction and Scherzo*, which the Boston Symphony under Koussevitzky introduced to the world on April 27, 1928.

NIKOLAI LOPATNIKOFF

Lopatnikoff's most important works before 1930 were his second string quartet, which received the Belaiev Prize in 1929, and his first symphony. The latter was heard first at the German Music Festival in Karlsruhe on January 8, 1929, in a performance so successful that it received the German Radio Corporation Prize and drew attention to the composer throughout Germany. When Bruno Walter conducted the symphony in Berlin, the critic of the *Börsen Zeitung* wrote: "Here are to be met qualities rare in new music: youthfulness, invention which has élan, powerful directness and which without pretentiousness looks at the world in a frank and knowing way. Lopatnikoff's slow movement is a beautiful and restrained mirror of our times." Gabrilowitsch conducted the first American performance in 1930 in Detroit, and the first New York presentation was given in 1932 by the New York Philharmonic.

After Lopatnikoff renounced all thought of becoming an engineer to embrace music, he settled in Berlin where, for two years, he served on the board of the Berlin section of the International Society for Contemporary Music. On June 16, 1932, his second piano concerto (which had been introduced in Düsseldorf on October 16, 1930) achieved great success at the festival of the International Society for Contemporary Music at Vienna. This performance impelled Kurt Hermann of Zürich to write: "Lopatnikoff is one of the most striking and self-willed talents of the younger generation. He represents a markedly economical and rhythmically vital linear style."

In 1933 the rise of Hitler and Nazism in Germany caused Lopatnikoff to resume his wanderings. First he returned to Helsinki where he was able to get a residence permit through Sibelius' intervention. Then he went to London where he concertized as composer-pianist. In 1939 he established residence in the United States, becoming a citizen in 1944. Soon after arriving, he joined the faculty of the Hartt Musical Foundation in Hartford, Connecticut. From 1943 to 1945 he headed the department of theory at the Westchester Conservatory in White Plains, New York. He was appointed associate professor of composition at the Carnegie Institute of Technology in 1945, and three years later he was promoted to professor. In 1945 he received the first of two Guggenheim Fellowships. During the summer of 1946 he served as a member of the faculty teaching composition at the Berkshire Music Center at Tanglewood.

His reputation as a composer of symphonic music grew rapidly in the 1940's. His Concerto for Violin and Orchestra was successfully introduced in Boston on April 17, 1942, with Richard Burgin as soloist and Koussevitzky conducting. "On the strength of a single hearing," said the critic of the Boston *Globe*, "Lopatnikoff's Violin Concerto has everything to recommend it. The writing for solo violin is clever: that instrument stands out from the orchestra, and the composer does not demand from it more than the violin is capable of yielding. The solo violin is also treated melodically and in a bright, rhythmic style. It probably will ingratiate itself with all but the most conservative listeners."

On August 2, 1942, his Sinfonietta, a work rich in dramatic contrasts and powerful climaxes, was performed at the festival of the International Society for Contemporary Music in San Francisco. In 1943 Lopatnikoff received a prize of one thousand dollars for the best new work in a contest sponsored by the Cleveland Orchestra to help celebrate its twenty-fifth anniversary. The composition thus honored was the *Opus Sinfonicum*, which Erich Leinsdorf introduced with the Cleveland Orchestra on December 9, 1943. Here the composer tried to produce a short symphonic work free in structure, "a kind of abstract tone poem without program."

On a grant from the Koussevitzky Music Foundation, Lopatnikoff completed in 1944 his Concertino for Orchestra, which the Boston Symphony under Koussevitzky introduced on March 2, 1945. Its poetic slow movement, "Elegietta," was intended by the composer as a memorial to Mrs. Koussevitzky. A memorial of a different kind came in 1945 with the *Variations and Epilogue* for cello and piano (performed by Raya Garbousova and Erich Itor Kahn in New York on January 17, 1947). This was an elegy for Lopatnikoff's first wife, the former Norma Laschinsky, whom he had married on August 17, 1926, and who died in 1945.

Lopatnikoff's productivity was unabated in the 1950's. Major orchestras throughout the United States performed a variety of major compositions including the Concerto for Two Pianos and Orchestra and the Divertimento, both in 1951; the third symphony, in 1954; *Variazioni Concertanti*, in 1958; and *Music for Orchestra*, in 1959. What Frederick Dorian had to say about the Third Symphony, which had its première in Pittsburgh in 1954, was true of many of Lopatnikoff's works: "Lopatnikoff's architecture is one of economy. Everywhere the texture is compact, yet in spite of the tautness of expression, the formal design is spacious. The texture aims at equilibrium between polyphony and harmony; the melody rings at times with Russian overtones, but the thematic design never consciously borders on the folkloristic; it is shaped by a cosmopolitan intellect in the service of melody and polyphony. The feeling of the key is deliberately free."

In 1953 Lopatnikoff received a grant from the National Institute of Arts and Letters. The citation honored him for "his substantial contribution to the literature of symphonic and chamber music in which he proves himself a master of contemporary style and form." A decade later, in 1963, Lopatnikoff was made a member of the Institute.

Among his later works is the opera *Danton*, which took several years to write. Excerpts from this opera were heard for the first time at a concert of the Pittsburgh Symphony, William Steinberg conducting, on March 25, 1967.

On January 27, 1951, Lopatnikoff married Sara Henderson Hay, a poet.

Lopatnikoff feels that the composers who exerted the greatest influence on his early work were Borodin and Mussorgsky. Bach has always been one of his special favorites. Among the moderns he leans most strongly toward Stravinsky and Hindemith.

He writes: "My daily life consists chiefly of composing and teaching; I have given up piano playing because of lack of time, and no longer appear as pianist in my own works. Reading is my principal diversion." He used to be a tennis enthusiast, but more recently he finds greater enjoyment in an occasional game of bridge or chess.

"I am an advocate of no theories at all regarding music," he states, "but only of creative values. I fear more than anything else the danger of academicism and dogmatism in the musical art."

MAJOR WORKS

Chamber Music—3 string quartets; 2 violin sonatas; Duo for Violin and Cello; Sonata for Piano, Violin, and Snare Drum; Cello Sonata; Piano Trio; Variations and Epilogue, for cello and piano.

Choral Music—Vocalise, in Modo Russo.

Opera—Danton.

Orchestral Music—3 symphonies; 2 piano concertos; Introduction and Scherzo; Two Russian Nocturnes; Violin Concerto; Sinfonietta; Opus Sinfonicum; Concertino for Orchestra; Concerto for Two Pianos and Orchestra; Divertimento; Variazioni Concertanti; Music for Orchestra; Festival Overture.

Piano Music—Dialogues; Five Contrasts; Sonata; Variations; Intervals, seven pieces.

ABOUT

Reis, C., Composers in America.

Witold Lutosławski
1913–

Witold Lutosławski was born in Warsaw on January 25, 1913, of a highly cultured family. One of his uncles was a recognized philosopher, and his mother was a successful physician. Witold began studying the piano when he was eleven, and the violin at fourteen. He later attended the Warsaw Conservatory where he studied composition with Witold Maliszewski (a pupil of Rimsky-Korsakov and Glazunov), and piano with Jerzy Lefeld. While still at the Conservatory he completed a number of compositions that were performed, including a piano sonata (1934); and in addition he attended the University of Warsaw where for two years he specialized in higher mathematics. In 1937 he received a diploma in composition from the Conservatory. His first ambitious composition came in 1938—the *Symphonic Variations*, which the Polish Radio Symphony under Gregory Fitelberg introduced on June 17, 1939. He planned to complete his study of music outside Poland but the outbreak of World War II nullified this plan, and in 1939 he was inducted into the Polish army and attached to a Polish unit as chief of a field radio station. During the German military occupation, he lived in Warsaw, supporting himself by playing two-piano music in cafés with Andrezj Panufnik, who later also became a distinguished composer. "We made over two hundred arrangements of classics, all since lost," Lutosławski revealed to an interviewer. "Playing in the café was the only way to stay in music and make money. Naturally, the music was light, café-style. . . . But we arranged clandestine meetings in rooms, daring imprisonment to play chamber music or première some of our things . . . [since] when the Nazis entered Warsaw, Polish music was stopped."

In spite of these unfavorable circumstances, he made every effort to continue composing. In constant fear of deportation—and working hard and late into the night to support himself—he managed to complete some chamber and piano music. The most important was the *Variations on a Theme of Paganini* (1941), a brilliant show piece for two pianos which he

Lutosławski: loō tô släf′ skē

wrote for himself and Panufnik. He was also able to put the finishing touches on the first movement of a symphony, which he succeeded in taking out of Warsaw in 1944 at the time of the Warsaw uprising.

WITOLD LUTOSŁAWSKI

That symphony was Lutosławski's first work to attract attention. Following its première in Katowice by the Polish Radio Orchestra under Gregory Fitelberg on April 6, 1948, it helped to open for the composer a new direction—away from Romantic approaches towards what Zofia Lissa described as "economy and original usage of sounds, an expression of organic connection with folk motives, clarity and originality of style." The main influence on Lutosławski was Bartók — not only Bartók's partiality for discords and atonality, but also the way in which Bartók used folk music as the starting point from which to develop his own idioms, methods, and creative personality. As early as 1945 Lutosławski had written a significant work in folk music style: *Twelve Folk Melodies* for piano. Significant later works in this Bartókian national idiom were *Triptych Silésien*, for soprano and orchestra, introduced in Warsaw on December 2, 1951; Concerto for Orchestra, which received its world première in Warsaw on November 26, 1954; *Five Dance Preludes*, for clarinet, strings, harp, piano, and percussion (1955); and *Miniature Suite*, for orchestra, heard at the first Polish Festival of Contemporary Music in Warsaw in October

1956 and then introduced in the United States in Hartford, Connecticut, on March 26, 1958.

Stefan Jarocinski considers the Concerto for Orchestra Lutosławski's "highest artistic achievement" and "a summit of invention" during the period in which the composer drew his strength and inspiration from Polish folk music. Jarocinski notes that while the Concerto owed its inspiration to folk motives, "both genuine and imaginary," these motives are "worked out in a way that distinctly avoids stylization. Folk motives are used as raw material completely subjected to the larger pattern of the work, and not as a form-determining factor." Jarocinski further recognizes in this music the unity of "two aspects of musical sources," one of which has its source "in the development of a modern musical language," the other of which finds it "in the incorporation of patterns suggested by native folklore."

In *Funeral Music (Musique Funèbre)*, for string orchestra—written in 1958 in memory of Béla Bartók—Lutosławski dabbled with the twelve-tone system, but in a highly individual way which often produced unusual tonal effects. Earlier folk influences were now abandoned. "This is my first word spoken in a language new to me," the composer said when his composition was introduced at Katowice on March 26, 1958, "but it is certainly not my last." *Funeral Music* was successfully repeated in 1959 at the second Warsaw Autumn Festival and at the Venice Festival. "This . . . score was more closely knit than anything he had yet written," said Peter Heyworth in *High Fidelity*. "In particular it achieved a degree of sustained harmonic tension that, like the contrapuntal thinking which underlay it, was new in Lutosławski's music."

Lutosławski was awarded a government prize by Poland in 1955 for his contributions to Polish music. Four years later he was elected to the committee of the International Society for Contemporary Music. In 1962 he was invited to teach a master class in composition at the Berkshire Music Center at Tanglewood. He accepted the invitation even though he had never before done any teaching. He thus became the first important Polish composer to teach in the United States.

Lutosławski's interest in the serial technique waned in 1961 as he became fascinated with the possibilities of aleatory music, or music of chance. "I heard and saw John Cage and his chance music in Darmstadt in 1961," he told an interviewer. "And the experience provided a spark that ignited a powder keg in me. I was a mature composer with many things to express but in fifteen minutes I had an insight into new possibilities open to me by incorporating into my music Cage's ideas." His first adventure with music of chance came with *Jeux Vénitiens*, which received its world première at the Venice Festival on April 24, 1961. A report to the New York *Times* singled out "this fascinating composition" as "one of the most memorable of the entire festival." On August 13, 1965, *Jeux Vénitiens* was heard at the Berkshire Music Festival at Tanglewood, Eleazar de Carvalho conducting the Boston Symphony. In John Burk's program notes for the Boston Symphony we learn that "of the four movements . . . the first and last could be considered the most 'aleatory.' In these two movements especially there is a chance conjunction of playing groups where each keeps its own note values according to a tempo conditioned by an over-all number of seconds. Thus each holds to its own independence which will not necessarily coincide with the music being played by the other group."

Lutosławski further pursued the method of chance in *Trois Poèmes d'Henri Michaux*, for chorus and orchestra (1963), which had been commissioned by the Muzicki Biennale Zagreb; the first performance took place at the Zagreb international music festival on May 9, 1963. A Polish release of the music won the Koussevitzky International Recording Award in 1963, the jury selecting it from eighty-two commercial recordings of symphonic music by living composers. In May 1964 it was also selected as the best composition heard at the International Rostrum of Composers of UNESCO in Paris. A critic for *Holiday*, having heard this work at the Autumn Festival in Warsaw, considered it "probably the most interesting work" heard at this event. "Lutosławski has found the precarious line between the aleatory and the chaotic, and he pursued it in this work with admirable security and effectiveness, allowing the individual choristers a great deal of improvisatory freedom without allowing the work to lose its shape."

A controlled aleatory technique character-izes Lutosławski's String Quartet (1964), which Bernard Jacobson describes as "a masterpiece that would grace any composer's output." He adds: "Much more radical than *Venetian Games* in its application of indeterminate methods—it starts right in with an injunction to 'repeat this phrase till the audience has settled down'—it is nevertheless a powerful, passionate, and withal superbly structured work in which originality of ear and profundity of expression play equal parts."

Lutosławski returned to the United States during the summer of 1966 to serve as composer-in-residence at Dartmouth College in Hanover, New Hampshire, at the invitation of the director of the Hopkins Center Congregation of the Arts. On this occasion, seven of his compositions were performed, four of them for the first time in the United States. Among these four American premières were two late works: the *Postludium*, for orchestra (1963), and *Paroles Tissées*, for tenor and orchestra (1965). The String Quartet (1964) was also represented.

In the New York *Times*, Howard Klein described Lutosławski as "balding, small, sharp-featured, with quick birdlike movements. In conversation the blue eyes and thin lips flash between expressions of worried concern, scolding severity, sportive facetiousness and boyish elation without transition. He speaks without bitterness, his beautiful English tinged with an Oxford accent."

MAJOR WORKS

Chamber Music—Trio, for oboe, clarinet, and bassoon; Dance Preludes, for clarinet and piano (also for clarinet, harp, piano, percussion, and strings); Recitative e Arioso, for violono grande and piano; String Quartet.

Choral Music—Psalms of David; Trois Poèmes d'Henri Michaux; St. Luke Passion; Dies Irae.

Orchestral Music—2 symphonies; Symphonic Variations; Overture, for string orchestra; Musique Funèbre (Funeral Music); Triptych Silésien, for soprano and orchestra; Concerto for Orchestra; Miniature Suite; Threnody—To the Victims of Hiroshima; Jeux Vénitiens; Three Concert Pieces; Postludium; Paroles Tissées, for tenor and orchestra; Sonata for Cello and Orchestra; Postlude.

Piano Music—Sonata; Twelve Folk Melodies; Variations on a Theme of Paganini, for two pianos; Bucolica.

Vocal Music—Five Songs, for female voice and thirty solo instruments.

ABOUT

Lang, P. H. and Broder, N. (eds.), Contemporary

Music in Europe; Lissa, Z., Music in Poland: 1945–1955.

High Fidelity, September 1965; New York Times, August 12, 1962, August 7, 1966; Saturday Review, July 30, 1966.

Gian Francesco Malipiero
1882–

Gian Francesco Malipiero was born in Venice on March 18, 1882. He came from a family that had been prominent in Venice for centuries, and numbered distinguished musicians among its members. His grandfather, Francesco Malipiero, had been a famous opera composer, considered by some a rival to Verdi. His father, Luigi, was a professional musician who married a Venetian countess; Gian Francesco was their first-born.

GIAN FRANCESCO MALIPIERO

Gian Francesco was a musical child who started violin lessons when he was six. In his eleventh year, his family left Italy to live in Germany and Austria for a number of years. During this period, the boy sometimes played in orchestras conducted by his father. In 1898 he entered the Vienna Conservatory for further study of the violin but, failing the examinations, transferred to the harmony class where he did much better. In 1889 he returned to Venice where he became a pupil of Enrico Bossi at the Liceo Musicale Benedetto Marcello. When

---

Malipiero: mä lē pyâ′ rō

Bossi was appointed director of the Liceo Musicale in Bologna, Malipiero followed him, attending the Conservatory. There he wrote his first orchestral composition, *Dai Sepolcri*, successfully introduced at a Conservatory concert in Bologna in 1904.

Two important events early in the 1900's influenced his development as a musician. One was the hearing of Wagner's *Die Meistersinger* which opened up for him new vistas for opera, other than those then being exploited by the Italians. The second, in or about 1902, was his chancing upon manuscripts of old Italian composers. So strongly did he become attracted to the musical art of Italy's past that henceforth he devoted himself assiduously to research in this field; ultimately he became one of the foremost authorities on old Italian music, the editor of definitive editions of the complete works of Monteverdi and various compositions by Vivaldi, Marcello, Cavalli, and other old masters.

"I often wondered what might have become of me if I had not intuitively reached certain decisions which led me where I *had* to go," Malipiero told an interviewer many years later. "I don't know why I went constantly from 1902 on to the Biblioteca Marciana in Venice to study the old composers who were practically unknown to my teachers and fellow students. I copied out not only the works of Monteverdi but also those of many others. To the teaching of the 'Divino Claudio' [Monteverdi] I owe much of my style."

Occupied with his studies of old Italian music, Malipiero found that his own composition was too strongly influenced by old styles. This imitative process was obvious in three symphonies that he completed in the years between 1905 and 1908: the *Sinfonia degli Eroi* (1905), *Sinfonia del Mare* (1906), and *Sinfonia del Silenzio e della Morte* (1908). He felt the need to learn what modern composers outside Italy were thinking and writing; he wanted to study at first hand some of the newer idioms and techniques gaining prominence in Europe. In 1913 (three years after his marriage to the daughter of a Venetian painter) Malipiero went to Paris. There he mingled with the foremost musicians of the day—Debussy, Fauré, Stravinsky, Ravel, Falla, among others. He came into direct contact with the progressive ideas of music and the newer methods. Without completely abandoning his former ways as a composer he now absorbed into his contrapuntal and at times modal writing some of the newer devices, thereby enriching his vocabulary and extending the range of his expressiveness.

Before leaving for Paris, Malipiero had entered five compositions in an Italian contest, four of them under pseudonyms. Four of them won prizes. The discovery that the four winning works were by one man aroused considerable bitterness in Italian music circles, and for a while Malipiero was regarded with hostility by some of his countrymen. When two of his works were publicly performed— the one-act opera *Canossa*, in Rome on January 24, 1914, and the tone poem, *Arione*, on December 12, 1913— a part of each audience had been organized to voice loud opposition and create a disturbance. The failure of both these compositions bothered Malipiero little, for by this time he had disavowed most of his early compositions and had even had the manuscript of *Canossa* destroyed.

Shortly before World War I, Malipiero settled in the little town of Asolo, two hours by automobile from Venice. There his home has since remained. For a while, he found refuge in Asolo from the realities of World War I, but the war finally caught up with him. In October 1917 the retreating Second Army, pursued by the enemy, poured into Asolo. Malipiero and his family fled, and after traveling a difficult and circuitous route arrived in Rome.

The war was responsible for inspiring Malipiero's first major orchestral work, his first success— *Pause del Silenzio*. Made up of seven pieces, each different in character, the work was intended to express the horrors of war. To one Italian critic it represented "shudders... cries, lamentations." Introduced at the Augusteo in Rome on January 27, 1918, Molinari conducting, it was a tremendous success.

In 1919 Malipiero completed the writing of his first important opera, *Sette Canzoni*, with a text by the composer. Actually it was the middle work of an operatic trilogy collectively entitled *L'Orfeide;* but it achieved recognition apart from this cycle and has often been presented independently since its world première at the Paris Opéra, on July 10, 1920. *Sette Canzoni* represented a break with the estab-

lished Italian traditions of Verdi, Puccini, and the "Verismoists." "The melodic declamation as well as the formal structure of this work reminds one immediately of Monteverdi," says Everett Helm. "Recitative-like passages alternate with song-like ones— freely declaimed sections with others that are rhythmically precise. . . . The orchestra plays an integral part structurally and dramatically and counterpoint is used abundantly." This is essentially the style Malipiero favored in many of his subsequent operas. (The world première of the complete trilogy *L'Orfeide* did not take place until 1966, in Italy— at the Florence May Music Festival.)

After the war, Malipiero combined his activity as composer with that of teacher. From 1921 to 1923 he was professor of composition at the University of Parma. In 1923 he returned to Asolo where he lived in comparative seclusion, devoting himself to study, research, composition, editing, and the teaching of a few select private pupils. He emerged from his seclusion once a week to teach composition at the Liceo Musicale Benedetto Marcello in Venice. In 1939 he became director of this Conservatory, holding this post with considerable distinction for about two decades, until he was compelled to retire because of his advanced age.

In 1920 Malipiero's first string quartet, *Rispetti e Strambotti*, received the Elizabeth Sprague Coolidge Prize of one thousand dollars in the United States, and its world première took place at Pittsfield, Massachusetts, on September 25, 1920. Utilizing the structure of two old forms of Italian poetry, and deriving his style from the strophes and cadences of Italian poetry, Malipiero recreated in this one-movement quartet scenes of the Renaissance and the atmosphere of an old Italian world with remarkable effect.

One year later the world première of Malipiero's first major work for chorus was given in the United States: the "mystery," or cantata, *San Francesco d'Assisi*, which the composer completed in 1920. Heard in New York for the first time anywhere on March 29, 1922, this cantata, in four "tableaux," represented a musical interpretation of the personality of St. Francis.

The influence of old Italian music and culture is reflected in many of Malipiero's works:

in operas such as the trilogy *Tre Commedia Goldoniane*, produced in Darmstadt, Germany on March 24, 1926, and *Torneo Notturno*, introduced in Munich on May 15, 1931; in chamber music compositions such as *Ricercari*, *Ritrovari* and *Cantari alla Madrigalesca*, written between 1925 and 1930; and in several of his symphonies and orchestral *Invenzioni*. Like so many of the early Italians, Malipiero, in these works, was more dramatic than lyrical, more contrapuntal than homophonic. His melodies are usually monodic. The classic spirit of the Renaissance—its tranquillity and spirituality—pervades his music, which blends the old and the contemporary in a consistent, coherent fusion. D. Maxwell White described Malipiero's style as "a very free polyphony, in which startling dissonances produced by the interplay of lines are tempered by the free use of consonance. His melody is incisive and when vocal is molded closely on the speech inflections of the human voice. His rhythms are varied and often have a primitive vigor. The instrumentation is sonorous." White also points out that since Malipiero often takes his texts from old poetry, his music frequently "has an archaic ring and this is increased by a perceptible influence of plainsong and free use of the ancient modes."

Though honored by the Fascist regime in Italy as one of the country's leading musicians, Malipiero tried to ignore the political currents around him. On several occasions, however, he came into conflict with the authorities, particularly when his opera *La Favola del Figlio Cambiato* was suppressed soon after its Italian première on March 26, 1934, because it was judged "morally incongruous" with Fascist aims and ideals.

Malipiero did not long remain at odds with the regime. Turning to Shakespeare, he wrote an opera which was judged to be thoroughly Fascist in subject and treatment—*Julius Caesar*, an immense success when produced in Genoa on February 8, 1936. His next opera, another work based on Shakespeare—*Antony and Cleopatra*—was also a major success when it was presented at the May Music Festival at Florence on May 4, 1938.

During World War II, Malipiero involved himself personally in anti-Nazi activity. During the last stages of the Italian campaign he and his wife (she was his second wife, and of British birth) gave shelter to an escaped British aviator who stayed in the bathroom of the attic floor. For several weeks the Malipieros were hosts to their concealed guest until a contact could be established with the partisans, who took the aviator to the hills and arranged for his passage to England.

The war ended almost at his door, and almost miraculously his house escaped destruction. The Second World War, like the first, inspired an important work: the Symphony No. 4, *In Memoriam*, commissioned by the Koussevitzky Music Foundation and introduced by the Boston Symphony under Koussevitzky on February 27, 1948. The tragedy suffered by the Italians during and immediately after the war is touched upon in this symphony in intense and deeply moving music.

Malipiero's nine symphonies are among his most significant contributions to the orchestral repertory. His first symphony had been introduced in Florence on April 2, 1934. His ninth, *Dello Zodiaco*, was performed in Lausanne, Switzerland, almost twenty years later, on January 23, 1952. Malipiero has said that none of his symphonies follow a program, that they "obey an old musical Italian tradition, which is not to adopt, despite its contrapuntal origins, the play of thematic development. The development instead unfolds according to a law peculiarly Latin and is logical because it also corresponds to our way of hearing and of contemplating things created and to be created."

Besides *In Memoriam*, one of Malipiero's most distinguished symphonies is his seventh, *Delle Canzoni*, which was introduced in Milan on November 3, 1949. The composer himself has explained that the work "is essentially linear. Nevertheless, here and there a kind of song emerges, like the voice of a poet of old, singing from the heights of sacred Mt. Grappa, while beyond, far away, always farther, is Venice."

Despite his advancing years, Malipiero has remained—even in old age—extraordinarily prolific, producing major works in all possible media. His own operatic version of the Don Giovanni legend, based on Pushkin's *The Stone Guest*, was produced in Naples on September 22, 1963. Describing Malipiero's one-act *Don Giovanni*, John Ardoin wrote: "It displays a highly personal style in which many elements of the Italian renaissance and baroque music are translated into today's terms and incorporated into a modern idiom." The modern music festival at Venice in 1966 offered the world première of another Malipiero opera, *Metamorfosi di Bonaventura*. Two years later, in September 1968, the festival of contemporary music in Venice offered the first performance of still another Malipiero opera, *L'Aredodese*. Malipiero, however, did not confine himself to opera. *Abracadabra*, for baritone and orchestra, was introduced at the International Festival for Contemporary Music at Venice on April 23, 1963; the same festival featured his second violin concerto two years later; and the *Quartetto per Elisabetta*, for string quartet, was acclaimed at its world première, a chamber music festival in Washington, D.C., in October 1964. Another of Malipiero's instrumental works to receive its première in the United States was *Endecatode*, a chamber symphony. This work was featured at the Congregation of the Arts at Hopkins Center of Dartmouth College, Hanover, New Hampshire, on July 5, 1967.

In describing Malipiero when the composer was in his mid-thirties, Henri Prunières provided a personal portrait that held true for several decades: "His face is emaciated and furrowed. . . . His features are of an astonishing mobility; his abundant auburn hair is slightly silvered; his forehead is straight, his eyes are very blue; his nose is large, thin, and arched; his mouth shows great sensitiveness. In his general appearance, his physiognomy is full of goodness and intelligence, but it appears often contracted, thin, ravaged; under the sway of a moral or physical suffering. Despite the incessant pain caused by his delicate health and sensitive nature, Malipiero keeps joy in his heart."

The editor of this book, who paid several visits to Asolo through the years, wrote in *Twentieth Century Composers:* "He exudes a charm that spreads an atmosphere of warm pleasantness about him, making those near him feel close to him even after a cursory acquaintance. He is a born host, gracious, well poised, solicitous. When he took me by the arm and conducted me about his garden, he stopped at a favorite flower to stroke it affectionately as though it were human. He stopped for a moment in the barn to introduce me to his goat, patting it with tenderness and speaking to it as though it could understand him. When he accidentally stumbled across his dog in the garden, he tipped his hat (in all seriousness) and apologized."

MAJOR WORKS

Ballets—Pantea; La Mascherata delle Principesse Prigioniere; Stradvario; Il Mondo Nuovo.

Chamber Music—4 string quartets; Rispetti e Strambotti, for string quartet; Stornelli e Ballate, for string quartet; Ricercari, for eleven instruments; Ritrovari, for eleven instruments; Sonata a Tre, for violin, cello, and piano; Cantari alla Madrigalesca, for string quartet; Epodi e Giambi, for oboe, violin, viola, and bassoon; cello Sonatina; Quartetto per Elisabetta.

Choral Music—San Francesco d'Assisi, mystery; La Cena, oratorio; La Passione, oratorio; De Profundis; Missa pro Mortuis; La Terra; Mondi Celesti; I Sette Peccati Mortali; La Festa de la Sensa; Cinque Favole; Passer Mortuus Est; Notturno di Canti e Balli; Dialogo VIII.

Operas—L'Orfeide, cycle of three operas (including Sette Canzoni); Tre Commedie Goldoniane, cycle of three operas; Torneo Notturno; La Favola del Figlio Cambiato; Giulio Cesare; Antonio e Cleopatra; Ecuba; La Vita è Sogno; I Capricci di Callot; L'Allegra Brigata; Mondi Celesti e Infernali; Il Figliuol Prodigo; Venere Prigioniera; Il Capitano Spavento; Don Giovanni; Metamorfosi di Bonaventura; L'Aredodese; Gli Eroi di Bona Ventura.

Orchestral Music—9 symphonies; 5 piano concertos; 3 suites; 2 violin concertos; Ditirambo Tragico; Pause del Silenzio; Impressioni dal Vero, three sets; La Cimarosiana; Variazioni senza Tema, for piano and orchestra; L'Esilio dell' Eroe; Concerti; Inni; Sette Invenzioni; Quattro Invenzioni; Cello Concerto; Vergilii Aeneis, symphony for voices and strings; Cinque Favole, for voice and orchestra; Concerto for Two Pianos and Orchestra; Dialoghi; Abracadabra, for baritone and orchestra; Fantasie di Ogni Giorno; Endecatode, chamber symphony.

Piano Music—Risonanze; Maschere che Passano; Tre Omaggi; La Siesta; Il Tarlo; Pasqua di Risurrezione; Preludi a una Fuga; Epitaffio; Omaggio a Bach; Preludi, Ritmi e Canti Gregoriani; Preludio e Fuga; Hortus Conclusus.

ABOUT

Bontempelli, M., Gian Francesco Malipiero; Gatti, G. M. (ed.), L'Opera di Gian Francesco Malipiero; Thompson O. (ed.), Great Modern Composers.

Musical America, April 1962; Rassegna Musicale (Malipiero issue), March 1942; La Revue Musicale (Paris), November 1931.

Frank Martin
1890–

Frank Martin was born in Geneva on September 15, 1890, the youngest of ten children.

Martin: mȧr tăn′

Martin

Love of music was a trait which had existed for several generations in the Martin family. Frank's grandfather had given up a successful career as a manufacturer of textiles to become the first bassoonist of the Musikverein in Geneva and to help found the Geneva Conservatory. Frank's father was a clergyman who encouraged music-making at home and stimulated his children in music study. When Frank was eight years old, he revealed a talent for music by writing little pieces. He also proved so adept at the piano that he was often recruited to provide the accompaniments for vocal and instrumental performances at his home. Intensive music study, however, did not begin until 1906 when he became Josef Lauber's pupil at the Geneva Conservatory. For the next eight years Martin received thorough training in harmony, composition, and orchestration at the Conservatory while his academic studies were also pursued in Geneva.

FRANK MARTIN

Martin's first composition to receive a public performance was *Trois Poèmes Payens*, for baritone and orchestra, based on a text by Leconte de Lisle. It was heard in 1911 at a festival of the Association of Swiss Musicians. The Association immediately took an interest in Martin, and from that time on up to 1925 it performed his works at annual festivals. His compositions during this period were all markedly influenced by César Franck and Fauré, and occasionally by Debussy. The best

of these works were an orchestral suite (1913); *Symphonie pour Orchestre Burlesque* (1915); a violin sonata (1915); and Martin's first major work for chorus, *Les Dithyrambes*, with a text by Pierre Martin (1918). The last of these is described in *Forty Contemporary Swiss Composers* as a "nonreligious oratorio" showing "fine taste, technical mastery, and an esthetic conception akin to that of Ravel."

From 1918 to 1920 Martin lived in Zürich; from 1921 to 1923, in Rome; and from 1923 to 1925, in Paris. The residence in Paris had particular significance since it brought him into contact with the latest French idioms and techniques, an experience that made him increasingly impatient with his former partiality to French post-Romanticism and Impressionism. He became fascinated with the problem of rhythm. In *Trio on Irish Folk Tunes* (1925) and *Rythmes*, for orchestra (1926), he began experimentations with varied rhythmic procedures. The latter was introduced at the festival of the International Society for Contemporary Music at Geneva on April 6, 1929.

In 1926 Martin returned to Geneva where he became involved in varied musical activities. From 1927 to 1937 he served as pianist and harpsichordist for the Société de Musique de Chambre, which he had helped to organize. In 1928 he joined the music faculty of the Dalcroze Institute and later became director. He founded the Technicum Moderne de Musique, which he directed from 1933 to 1939. From 1943 to 1946 he was president of the Association of Swiss Musicians.

In 1930 Martin came under the influence of the twelve-tone system, which he adapted freely to his own esthetic purposes. "I can say that at one and the same time I was influenced by Schoenberg and yet set myself against him with all my musical feeling," he explained at the time. Several of his compositions were in a free twelve-tone idiom: *Guitarre*, for orchestra (1933); a piano concerto (1934); *Rhapsody for Five Strings* (1935); a string trio (1935); a string quartet (1936); and a symphony (1937).

But Martin's creative personality was still in the process of growth and evolution, and it did not become crystallized until after 1938. Beginning with a series of Ballades for various solo instruments and orchestra—the first for saxophone in 1938—Martin began to evolve

342

his own personal style in which he was soon to create the works that brought him recognition. Nicolas Slonimsky has explained that Martin's mature style is "supported by a consummate mastery of contrapuntal and harmonic writing" and reveals a "profound feeling for emotional consistency and continuity." Martin's writing now fused old elements with new, allowing him full freedom to express his ideas independently, yet without deserting established tradition altogether. An exquisite balance is thus maintained between expression and language. When the twelve-tone technique is used, it is modified, as Abraham Skulsky has explained, "to retain only the melodic series and is constructed mainly on the harmonic aggregations of the rhythmic possibilities deriving from the tone row and its intervals." In this way, Martin was able to give free rein to his pronounced gift for lyricism and expressive values.

Le Vin Herbé, a cantata for solo voices, chorus, and eight instruments, revealed Martin as a major creative figure in twentieth century music. It was introduced in Zürich March 26, 1942, in concert form and was produced as an opera at the Salzburg Festival in 1948. The text is based on the legend of Tristan and Isolde, as adapted in 1900 by Josef Bédier; three chapters of Bédier's novel are used. Stylistically, the music stems more from Debussy than from Wagner—in its restraint, understatement, and mystical qualities. It is an intimate work, with the individual voices carrying the story and the chorus providing the commentary. *Le Vin Herbé* was first heard in the United States on February 26, 1961, performed by the Schola Cantorum under Hugh Ross.

In 1943 Martin wrote *Six Monologues from Jedermann*, for baritone or contralto and piano, with a text derived from the mystery play by Hugo von Hofmannsthal; in 1949 Martin orchestrated it. Here, says Henri Gagnebin, "Martin's music expresses all phases of the drama with special intensity: the weight of despondency, the agitation of the man struggling to escape from his destiny, the anguish at the thought of his mother; and prayer which brings him peace. The austere and direct style of Frank Martin is magnificently suited to the theme." An important cantata inspired by World War II followed in 1944. It was *In Terra Pax* which, in the estima-

tion of Oliver Daniel, is music "of deep ecclesiastical conviction . . . that soars with many of the best of the nineteenth century predecessors." While the war was still on, this work had been commissioned from Martin by Radio Geneva so that it might be ready for performance on the day the war ended. He completed the composition in 1945. The text was derived from the Bible.

Two orchestral works brought Martin international recognition in the middle 1940's. The first was *Petite Symphonie Concertante*, for harp, harpsichord, piano, and two string orchestras. It was completed in 1945 and introduced by the Basel Chamber Orchestra in Zürich on May 17, 1946. After that, it was heard throughout the world. The second orchestral work was the Concerto for Seven Wind Instruments, Percussion, and String Orchestra, completed in 1949, and introduced in Berne, Switzerland, on October 25, 1949. His mature compositions are characterized by Jacques de Menasce as music with "broad melodic lines of a chromatic nature, subtle harmonic and rhythmic patterns, and a sustained contrapuntal texture. The common denominator can be described as an organic blend of several methods, which as a composition makes for an idiom that is clearly personal."

Before the 1940's were over, Martin had written a major work for chorus and orchestra—the oratorio *Golgotha*, first heard in Geneva on April 29, 1949, and introduced in the United States on January 18, 1952, by the Dessoff Choirs under Paul Boepple in New York. This monumental work owed its origin to several etchings by Rembrandt which the composer saw in 1945—he was particularly affected by "The Three Crosses" depicting the "three states" of the scene at Calvary. From then on, Martin was fired with the ambition to write an oratorio which, as he said, "would bring the whole of the sacred drama before the audience." He took his text out of the New Testament and from the writings of Saint Augustine, with occasional passages from the Psalms to serve as a commentary. Edward Lockspeiser said: "*Golgotha* is the music of a cultivated man, a man of vision and assurance and originality. . . . There are moments of glacial intensity, as in the final triumphant hymn, and passages of an almost colorless luminosity of an original, neither recognizably

Latin nor Teutonic, yet tense and incisive in effect, like the contours of some wintry landscape."

Martin's first opera, *The Tempest*, was produced in Vienna on June 17, 1956. The text used Shakespeare's play virtually intact, except for some minor deletions and the transformation of Ariel's part into a dancing role, the vocal passages being performed offstage either by a chorus or a single voice. "What tempted me in Shakespeare's *Tempest*," the composer has explained, "apart from its poetic charm which is bound to attract the musician, is the infinite psychological richness of the characters. . . . There are so many different worlds: Ariel's world, the world of Prospero, Miranda and Ferdinand, the world of the courtiers, and finally the drunkards' and Caliban's world— each requiring music entirely different from the others." Ballet and pantomime were skillfully interwoven with the text; theatrical values were understressed so that the work is more like a scenic oratorio than an opera. As Paul Henry Lang noted in his review when the opera received its American première in New York on October 11, 1956: "It has no dramatic power, no action, and nothing to which music can fasten itself with conviction." Declamation often takes the place of song. At times, Lang explains, "the protagonists simply converse and orate." And while the orchestra does help contribute to the over-all atmosphere with tone painting, "dramatically it is neutral and without interest."

A composition of altogether different character received its first stage presentation at the Salzburg Festival in 1960. It was *Le Mystère de la Nativité* (*Mysterium von der Geburt des Herrn*), whose text comprises a dozen episodes describing Christ's birth as depicted in a fifteenth century mystery play. This work originated as an oratorio for radio performance, having been commissioned by Radio Geneva, which introduced it December 24, 1959, Ernest Ansermet conducting. Probably that is why the work, as a staged opera, has such a static quality. "It remained," reported Edward Downes to the New York *Times*, "largely contemplative and lyric. . . . Even the scenes in Hell where he [Martin] confesses to have used a touch of atonality and livelier rhythms, could hardly be called baleful. . . . The score makes the impression of being dominated by melody, particularly vocal melody, of a strongly modal turn. There are echoes of Gregorian chant, folk song and twentieth century arioso styles."

Martin's first attempt at comedy came with the opera *Monsieur de Pourceaugnac*, which the Swiss Radio had commissioned him to write, and which received its world première in Geneva's new Grand Theatre on April 23, 1963. (The following June the opera was successfully featured at the Holland Festival in Amsterdam.) Martin's music for this opera based on Molière's comedy of the same name, adapted by the composer, was found by Everett Helm to "add little to the play itself. At times it even impedes the dramatic progress. There is a great deal of spoken dialogue—free or rhythmic, with or without accompaniment. Some of its vocal sections incline to be either trivial, or, more frequently, heavy footed."

In addition to his operas, Martin has produced several important compositions for the concert stage since 1950. *Études*, for string orchestra, completed in 1956, has been extensively performed throughout Europe and the United States. It was commissioned by the Basel Chamber Orchestra and its conductor Paul Sacher, who introduced it. Another instrumental work that achieved recognition on both sides of the Atlantic is Martin's Concerto for Cello and Orchestra, written during 1965–1966 for Pierre Fournier, who introduced it in Basel in January 1967, Paul Sacher conducting. A Magnificat, for soprano, violin, and orchestra, was a highlight of the Lucerne Music Festival in Switzerland during the summer of 1968; the soloists were Irmgard Seefried and her husband Wolfgang Schneiderhan.

Frank Martin revealed his creative methods in an article published in *Polyphonie*, which Abraham Skulsky summarized as follows: "During the process of composition he is totally involved in translating his will into concrete sounds and rhythms. . . . Only after he has completed it can the composer look upon his work simultaneously as an object and a remembrance. . . . In his own mind he will be able to meditate on his work, knowing better than anyone else its weak and strong points. He will remember the things that came to him without effort and those that caused him trouble. He will seek to understand why certain

344

aspects of the work resisted or misled him. This meditation is precious, because it will help him in his next works. Martin calls this meditation a technique of composition of a very special kind—the technique of inspiration. Acquiring this technique takes a long time; it is the art of provoking discoveries, the art of catching an idea at the right moment. . . .

"In discussing formulation of such meditation, Martin takes us back to the beginning of the creative process. Before he starts, the composer decides the general shape of the work, its dimensions, and its instrumental or vocal means. . . . Sometimes he can foresee certain elements; he may know clearly that the work will be a fugue, a passacaglia, or an allegro. . . . When the composer sits down to work, he looks for melodic and harmonic ideas that are most in accord with his first conception. In the words of Martin, those ideas are the raw materials, which do not depend upon the composer's will. . . . As he brings his technical knowledge to bear upon the initial ideas, the work becomes richer than he had imagined. . . . The success of the work depends upon his adequate use of the right ideas."

In 1946 Martin made his home in Amsterdam, from which city he commuted in the years between 1952 and 1958 to teach at the Cologne Conservatory in Germany. In 1960 he received honorary doctorates from the universities of Geneva and Lausanne.

In the summer of 1967, Frank Martin was composer-in-residence at Dartmouth College's Congregation of the Arts in Hanover, New Hampshire. During the two weeks he spent at Dartmouth, eleven of his compositions were performed, including the American première of *Ouverture en Rondeau*, for orchestra, written in 1958. Martin himself participated at some of these performances. At one he performed his *Eight Preludes*, for piano; at another, he conducted his *Six Monologues from Jedermann*.

MAJOR WORKS

Ballets—Cinderella; Ein Totentanz zu Basel im Jahre 1943.

Chamber Music—2 violin sonatas; Piano Quintet; Piano Trio on Irish Folk Songs; String Trio; String Quartet; Ballade, for flute and piano (also with orchestra); Chaconne, for cello and piano; Ballade, for cello and piano.

Choral Music—Le Vin Herbé, cantata; In Terra Pax, cantata; Golgotha, oratorio; Cinq Chansons d'Ariel; Psaumes de Genève; Pilatus, cantata; Psaumes, oratorio; Le Mystère de la Nativité, oratorio.

Operas—The Tempest (Der Sturm); Monsieur de Pourceaugnac.

Orchestral Music—Various ballades for solo instruments and orchestra (trombone; piano; saxophone; flute; cello); Symphonie pour Orchestre Burlesque; Piano Concerto; Rythmes; Symphonie; Sonata da Chiesa, for flute and orchestra; Sonata da Chiesa, for viola d'amore and orchestra; Six Monologues from Jedermann, for baritone and orchestra; Die Weise von Liebe, for alto and orchestra; Petite Symphonie Concertante; Concerto for Seven Wind Instruments, Percussion, and Orchestra; Violin Concerto; Harpsichord Concerto; Études, for string orchestra; Passacaglia, for string orchestra; Ouverture en Rondeau; Ouverture en Hommage à Mozart; Passacaglia, for large orchestra; The Four Elements; Cello Concerto; Magnificat, for soprano, violin, and orchestra.

Piano Music—Eight Preludes.

Vocal Music—Trois Chants de Noël; Drei Minnelieder.

ABOUT

Machlis, J., Introduction to Contemporary Music; Schuh, W., Schweizer Musik der Gegenwart.

Musical America, August 1949; Musical Quarterly, April 1948; New York Times, January 13, 1952.

Jean Martinon
1910–

Jean Martinon, distinguished equally as a conductor and as a composer, was born in Lyons on January 10, 1910. His father was an architect. He attended the Lyons Conservatory where he specialized in violin, progressing from there on a scholarship to the Paris Conservatory, from which he was graduated with honors in violin playing in 1928. His teachers subsequently included Albert Roussel in composition, and Charles Münch and Roger Désormière in conducting.

He began his musical career with successful appearances as a violin virtuoso. For about fifteen years, he earned his living playing the violin in major French orchestras, but composition interested him far more than performance. He found himself devoting more of his time to creative work and less of it to the concert stage. In the period between 1934 and 1936 he completed his first symphony in C major, and in 1935 he wrote *Symphonietta*, which received a successful première in 1938 at a concert of the Orchestre Philharmonique under Léon Ziguera. Florent Schmitt reported

Martinon: mȧr tē nôn´

Martinon

in *Le Temps* that this music was characterized by "charm and by spontaneous, poetic expression with choice ideas developed with ease and good taste, and a delicate, tasteful instrumentation. In short, this quite delicious piece alone was worth the trip to Salle Pleyel."

JEAN MARTINON

During World War II, Martinon served in the French army. Captured by the Nazis, he was interned for two years in Stalag IX. In the prison camp, he wrote a religious work, the motet *Absolve Domine*, which he dedicated to French musicians fallen in the war; it was performed at Stalag IX on November 2, 1940. He also wrote *Musique d'Exil*, a jazz composition, and an oratorio for narrator, solo voices, chorus, and orchestra, with a text prepared from the 136th Psalm by a fellow prisoner, a French priest. The composition was renamed *Psalm of the Captives* when it was performed in Paris in 1943, Charles Münch conducting, and it received the Grand Prix of the city of Paris by a unanimous verdict of the judges. This moving work, which is now officially entitled *Psalm 136*, went a long way towards establishing Martinon's reputation as a composer. The symbolism of the Hebrew captives lamenting their fate and crying out for vengeance did not escape the Parisians at a time when Paris was occupied by the Nazis, and the audience gave the work an ovation. Its success impelled Martinon to abandon violin playing. When the war ended, he devoted most of his time to composition.

However, he was soon diverted to another musical activity that assumed an importance equal to that of composition. When his first symphony was scheduled for performance in Paris, the conductor insisted that the pressure of other commitments made it impossible for him to rehearse the work properly. He asked Martinon to take over the baton. Martinon did—and though he had never before conducted, he gave such a good account of himself that he was soon invited by other orchestras to lead guest performances. One such invitation came from the London Philharmonic.

Between 1944 and 1946 Martinon served as assistant to Charles Münch with the Société des Concerts du Conservatoire. During that period he led guest performances with other leading French symphony orchestras. In 1946 he was appointed principal conductor of the Bordeaux Symphony, and in 1949 he was made associate conductor of the London Philharmonic. His most important conducting assignment came in 1951 with his appointment as principal conductor of the Lamoureux Orchestra. He retained the post with outstanding success for six years. During that time he traveled extensively throughout South America, Europe, Australia and the Far East as a guest conductor.

The 1940's, which had seen him achieve success as a conductor, also witnessed his growth as a composer. This became apparent with an important symphony (his second), subtitled *Hymne à la Vie* (1944), completed soon after his release from the German concentration camp. The symphony sang the composer's joy at his liberation and at the coming of peace. The three movements of the symphony were described as follows by an unidentified critic: "The music embodies the mysterious processes of human life. In the first part, for instance, the prelude takes shape in a quiet, cosmic mood, expressive of the perennial state in which the individual seems to rally forces from the infinite. This mood changes into a *mouvement perpétuel*, in which we find man in the turbulent stream of human living, its enthusiasms, stresses and joys. This in turn flows into the final section called *Hymne*, which is not as much a hymn of affirmation as a prayer of yearning." The symphony received its first performance in Paris in 1945 at a concert of the Pasdeloup Orchestra.

In works for varied media Martinon extended his fame and solidified his reputation. A composition for narrator, solo voices, chorus, and orchestra—*Ode au Soleil*—received a successful première at the Paris Opéra, under the direction of Louis Fourestier, in the year of its composition (1945). A string quartet (1946) was the recipient of the Béla Bartók Prize in 1948. A ballet, *Ambohimanga*, was produced in 1947 under Manuel Rosenthal's direction. His third symphony, the *Irish* (inspired by several visits to Ireland), was heard in Dublin, over Radio Eireann, in 1949. And his first opera, *Hécube* (1949), with a libretto by Serge Moreux based on Euripides, received its world première as a staged production in Strasbourg on November 10, 1956.

Among Martinon's later works in a large dimension are two violin concertos, a cello concerto, *Three Psalms* for chorus and percussion, the oratorio *Le Lis de Saron* based on *The Song of Songs*, and a fourth symphony, named *Altitudes*, which the Chicago Symphony Orchestra introduced on December 30, 1965, with the composer conducting, as part of its seventy-fifth anniversary celebration. This symphony was inspired by the sport of Alpine mountain climbing, but the work is neither a descriptive nor a narrative composition. On the flyleaf of his score the composer wrote: "For what do they search, these climbers of mountains? Like the pioneers of cosmos, they seek the presence of God! God! The purest and most formidable word that mankind has ever invented." The three movements are entitled: "The Gateway to the Stars," "The Vertical Garden," and "The Crossing of the Gods."

Martinon's style has been largely influenced by Roussel, and to a lesser degree by Schmitt and Bartók. New resources of harmony and tonality are explored, but not at the sacrifice of expressiveness or emotion. Whether he is writing programmatically or producing abstract music, Martinon's writing is full of dramatic intensity.

For two years, beginning in 1957, Martinon was the musical director of the Israel Philharmonic, with which he appeared at the Athens Festival in 1959. On August 1, 1960, he was appointed general music director to the city of Düsseldorf (a post held in former generations by Mendelssohn and Schumann); he was the first French musician to receive so important an appointment in Germany. Meanwhile, on March 29, 1957, Martinon made his American debut as conductor with the Boston Symphony. Numerous engagements followed with other American orchestras. After a very successful appearance with the Chicago Symphony at the Ravinia Festival in 1960, Martinon was invited to Chicago to direct three weeks of concerts in March 1962. This, in turn, brought him an appointment as the musical director of the orchestra, beginning in October 1963. He resigned from this post after the 1967–1968 season and became music director of the Orchestre National de Paris.

Martinon has homes in Düsseldorf and Paris. He has been twice married and has a son by each marriage. His second marriage was to the former Nery Perez in 1958. "He has brush-cut, iron-gray hair and kindly eyes under bushy black brows," wrote Roger Dettmer in *Musical America*. "Away from the stage, Martinon is the polar opposite of conductors who dress in the fashion of a popular singer at a motion-picture première.... He dresses quietly in dark, durable suits, with black or brown shoes. Attached to his jacket lapel is the Légion d'Honneur ribbon. On his right hand is a gold wedding band. When he settles comfortably into an armchair and takes out his pipe ('With your permission, I do not smoke very much, but after a concert I like') Jean Martinon for all the world looks like a prosperous academician. His English is astonishingly fluent and charmingly accented, although he is forever apologizing for a vocabulary and enunciation that are, in fact, superior to the English spoken by a generation of native high-school graduates."

Martinon is a dedicated sportsman. He is particularly adept at skiing and mountain climbing, two sports which he pursues at his chalet in the Alps of southeastern France, where he spends his vacations. He has scaled the peaks of Mont Blanc, the Reigen, the Matterhorn, and the Jungfrau. He also likes to fence, play tennis, and swim.

In 1967 he was awarded the Mahler Medal of Honor.

MAJOR WORKS

Ballet—Ambohimanga (or La Cité Bleue).

Chamber Music—2 sonatinas for violin and piano; 2 sonatinas for solo violin; Wind Quintet; Woodwind

Martinu

Trio; String Trio; Piano Trio; String Quartet; Duo, for violin and piano; Suite Nocturne, for violin and piano.

Choral Music—Trois Chansons de Fernand Marc; Chants Populaires Français; Appel de Parfum, for men's voices; Absolve Domine; Psalm 136; Motet à Saint Jean Baptiste de la Salle; Ode au Soleil; Le Lis de Saron, oratorio; Three Psalms, for chorus and percussion; Cantique des Cantiques, oratorio.

Opera—Hécube.

Orchestral Music—4 symphonies; 2 violin concertos; Symphonietta; Concerto Giocoso, for violin and orchestra; Concerto Lyrique, for string quartet and small orchestra; Les Métamorphoses d'Ovide; Ouverture pour une Tragédie Grecque; Symphonies de Voyages; Prélude et Toccate; Cello Concerto; Rose of Sharon, for soprano and orchestra.

Piano Music—Sonatine; Épilogue d'un Conte d'Amour; En Promenade; Ballade au Soldat Incassable; Introduction et Toccate.

Vocal Music—Humanité; Après Ma Journée Faite; Paysage Antérieur; Les Horizons Perdus Agonisante; Les Vieux Matelots; Sonatine à la Lune Qui s'en Va.

ABOUT

Machabey, A., Portraits de Trente Musiciens Français.
Musical America, November 1963.

Bohuslav Martinu
1890–1959

Bohuslav Martinu was born December 8 1890, in Polička, in eastern Bohemia near the Moravian border. His father was the town shoemaker who had the additional jobs of watching out for fires and ringing the church bells in the tower of St. Jacob's. The church tower represented home for the Martinu family. It was there that Bohuslav was born and it was there he spent a good part of his childhood, usually in isolation.

In 1896 Martinu enrolled in the local school. At the same time he began to study the violin with the town tailor, and within two years he was able to give a concert. By the time he was ten he was composing, completing among other works a string quintet and a string quartet.

Before long he sufficiently impressed some of the town's wealthy citizens so that they raised a fund to send him to Prague for advanced music study. Martinu went to Prague in 1906 and enrolled in the Conservatory where he specialized in the violin. The musical life

Martinu: mär′ tē nōō

of the city exerted a greater influence upon him than his Conservatory studies, for it offered him his first opportunity to become acquainted with symphonic and operatic literature. He also attended the theatre and ballet, growing into an enthusiast of both; and he became a voracious reader. The strict regimen of Conservatory life irritated him; he was impatient with the laws and conventions that inhibited his creativity. Twice he was expelled for minor infractions. After the second time he decided to transfer to the Organ School. Again he grew intolerant of the curriculum and rebelled against textbook rules; he failed his examinations and never received a diploma.

BOHUSLAV MARTINU

In 1913 he joined the violin section of the Czech Philharmonic. When World War I broke out, he was able to avoid military service and continue his musical activities. Towards the end of the war he lived in his native city of Polička where he taught music at the high school and gave private lessons on the violin. He wrote a number of songs to poems by Baudelaire (inspired by a passing love affair) and he celebrated the end of the war by writing the *Czech Rhapsody*, for solo voices, chorus, organ, and orchestra. By 1920 he was back in Prague, resuming his work with the Czech Philharmonic and working industriously on new compositions. A tone poem, *Vanishing Midnight*, and a ballet, *Istar*, were performed in Prague in 1922.

Feeling the need for more study, Martinu

348

reentered the Prague Conservatory and for a while studied composition with Joseph Suk. His lifelong interest in French culture and his now growing enthusiasm for French music finally sent him to Paris. The decision to go was made impulsively while he was performing Albert Roussel's *Poème de la Forêt* with the Czech Philharmonic. Upon receiving a state grant, Martinu left for France in September 1923, intending to stay in Paris only a few months. He remained sixteen years. He made his home in a little room in Montparnasse and devoured all the books and musical scores he could find. He was particularly impressed by Stravinsky's music, much of which he was hearing for the first time. And he was profoundly influenced by Albert Roussel, with whom he studied composition.

The works Martinu completed in Paris reveal how greatly he was affected by his contacts with new French music. His style became leaner and more concise; he avoided sentimentality; he absorbed some of the newer tendencies in harmony and rhythm; and he began to draw his stimulus from the world around him. Paul Nettl notes that the climactic work during this phase of Martinu's development was *Half-Time*, for orchestra, inspired by a football match between French and Czech teams. Described as a "symphony of rhythm," *Half-Time* was given its world première at the festival of the International Society for Contemporary Music at Prague on May 17, 1925. It inspired a good deal of controversy and many differences of opinion.

Similarly concerned with rhythmic procedures was *La Bagarre*, an orchestral picture of a surging, swelling crowd, inspired by Charles Lindbergh's arrival in Paris after his historic solo flight across the Atlantic. "It is not descriptive music," the composer explained. "It is determined according to the laws of composition; it has a chief theme—as the human crowd has its theme of enthusiasm—which directs the movement." *La Bagarre* received its world première in the United States on November 18, 1928, with Koussevitzky conducting the Boston Symphony. It was the first of Martinu's compositions to do so and made such a good impression that it was soon afterwards performed by several other major American orchestras.

His reputation continued to grow. In 1928

his second string quartet was presented at the festival of the International Society for Contemporary Music at Siena, Italy; his string quintet was heard at the Elizabeth Sprague Coolidge festival at Pittsfield, Massachusetts; and on December 14 his Rhapsody, for orchestra, received its world première in Boston.

On March 21, 1932, Martinu married Charlotte Quennehen, a dressmaker. They made their home in a humble attic room and suffered extreme poverty. Martinu would have been unable to pay the hospital bill when his wife was stricken with pneumonia late in 1932 had he not just received from the United States a check for one thousand dollars—the Elizabeth Sprague Coolidge award for his String Sextet.

After 1930 Martinu's writing revealed new facets. A growing lyricism, an increasing expressiveness, and most of all a spiritual kinship with Czech art and lore were increasingly evident in his compositions. While French influences persisted—particularly in the clarity, refinement, and precision of his writing— Czech elements became forcefully evident. In this vein, which Martinu would henceforth tap richly from time to time, he completed a delightful ballet, *Špalíček* (1931), produced in Prague in 1932, and the opera *The Miracle of Our Lady*, with a libretto by Henri Ghéon and the composer (1933), produced in Brünn in 1934. Paul Nettl explains that the ballet was written "in the style of a variety show, with rapid changes of scenes and many colorful portrayals of Czech life, with the text drawn from Czech folk tales." The opera was essentially a medieval miracle play with music, its text often derived from folk legend sources. Here, as elsewhere, Martinu aspired, says Nettl, "to introduce into Czech operatic literature new themes and sources, above all the rich material of Czech folklore, the countless poetic Czech legends."

One of Martinu's distinguished compositions in the 1930's revealed his fondness for utilizing the baroque *concerto grosso* structure. This tendency is found first in the *String Quartet with Orchestra* which Martinu wrote at the request of the Pro-Arte Quartet in 1931— this ensemble introduced it in London, with the London Philharmonic, in October 1932. The juxtaposition of string quartet and orchestra suggested the *concertino* and *ripieno*

Martinu

technique of the old *concerto grosso*. However, the *concerto grosso* form was more completely and recognizably resuscitated in the Concerto Grosso, for chamber orchestra (1937). This composition has had a curious history. It was scheduled for publication in Vienna when the Nazis entered, and one copy of the manuscript was lost. A scheduled performance in Prague was canceled because of the growing political tensions of the time. Its première was then scheduled for Paris in May 1940, but before that concert could take place France fell, and the only other existing copy of the work disappeared. However, the first copy, which had been lost in Prague, was found by George Szell, the conductor, who brought it with him to the United States. The Boston Symphony under Koussevitzky scheduled its performance for January 1941. But copying out the parts proved so difficult that the première had to be postponed until November 14, 1941. Finally performed on that date, the work was found by Olin Downes to be "lusty, swinging music, refreshingly vigorous, simple in texture, though modern in idiom, and driving straight to the final chord."

In September 1938 Martinu paid a visit to Switzerland. It was in this "countryside full of sunlight and the song of birds," as the composer recalled, that he became aware of the signing of the Munich Pact which permitted the Nazi troops to occupy the Sudetenland: "With anguish we listened every day to the news bulletins on the radio, trying to find encouragement and hope that did not come." Martinu's anguish at the sad fate of his country is reflected in a major work he completed at this time, the *Double Concerto*, for two string orchestras, piano, and tympani. "Its notes sang out the feelings and sufferings of all those of our people who, far away from home, were gazing into the distance and seeing the approaching catastrophe," he revealed. "It is a composition written under terrible circumstances, but the emotions it voices are not those of despair but rather of revolt, courage, and unshakable faith in the future. These are expressed by sharp, dramatic shocks, by a current of tones that never ceases for an instant, and by a melody that passionately claims the right to freedom." The Concerto was introduced in Basel, Switzerland, on February 9, 1940, Paul Sacher conducting.

When Paris fell to the Nazis, Martinu lived for a while in southern France and Lisbon. Finally, in March 1941, he came to the United States and made his home in New York, ultimately becoming an American citizen. In America, Martinu proved remarkably productive. So many performances of significant works took place within a few years following his arrival that listing even the most important becomes a difficult process. Between October 28 and November 9, 1943 there were eleven performances of major Martinu compositions in New York, Philadelphia, and Cleveland. During the seasons of 1942–1943 and 1943–1944 he had more new works introduced in the United States than any other composer in the country. Some music critics went so far as to refer to 1943 as the Martinu year. A partial list of these premières includes the First Symphony, introduced by the Boston Symphony under Koussevitzky November 13, 1942; the Second Symphony, presented by the Cleveland Orchestra October 28, 1943; the poignant *Memorial to Lidice*, which Artur Rodzinski directed with the New York Philharmonic on October 28, 1943; the Concerto for Two Pianos and Orchestra, performed by Luboschutz and Nemenoff and the Philadelphia Orchestra under Ormandy November 5, 1943; the Violin Concerto, presented by Mischa Elman and the Boston Symphony under Koussevitzky, on December 31, 1943. These premières came so thick and fast that Martinu was unable to attend them all. While in New York for a performance of his Second Symphony, he had to listen to his Violin Concerto on the radio, in a broadcast from Boston; the world première of his *Memorial to Lidice* took place in New York while he was in Cleveland attending the première of the Second Symphony.

Martinu remained prolific to the end of his life. He wrote four more symphonies, the sixth of which, *Fantaisies Symphoniques* (first heard in Boston on January 7, 1955) became one of his greatest successes. It received the New York Music Critics Circle Award (the second time this honor came to him; the first was in 1951 for an opera, *Comedy on a Bridge*, written in 1936 for radio transmission, introduced in Prague on March 18, 1937, and revised extensively in 1950).

Martinu completed several other operas. *The*

Marriage, based on Gogol, was written for television and was introduced by the NBC Opera company over the NBC-TV network February 7, 1953. His first full-length opera in twenty years was *La Locandiero*, after Goldoni (1954). His last full-length operas were *Mirandolina*, presented in Prague on May 17, 1959, about three months before his death; *Ariadne*, produced posthumously in Gelsenkirchen, Germany, on March 2, 1961; and an *opera buffa*, *Alexander Bis*, also presented posthumously, in Mannheim, Germany, on February 18, 1964. In addition, a major work for solo voices, chorus, and orchestra has been given a staged production: *Greek Passion*, based on the novel of Nikos Kazantzakis, which Jules Dassin had previously made into the successful motion picture *He Who Must Die;* its première took place in Zürich on June 12, 1961, after Martinu's death.

Despite the fact that he had been so prolific, Martinu actually worked on composition only four hours a day, in the morning. His afternoons were usually spent in the pursuit of other interests—mostly, in the study of physics and biology. He enjoyed taking long walks at nighttime. Martinu was an active teacher of music. For five years he was visiting professor of music at Princeton, and he also served on the music faculties of the David Mannes School of Music in New York and the Berkshire Music Center at Tanglewood. He returned to Czechoslovakia in 1946 to become professor of composition at the Master School of the Prague Conservatory, but he held this post only a short time.

In 1957 Martinu served as resident composer at the American Academy in Rome. He died in Liestal, a small town near Basel, Switzerland, on August 28, 1959.

The predominating traits of Martinu's works are clarity, directness, expressiveness, and at times a national identity. He preferred elementary harmonic structures, a fluid and transparent polyphony, and vivid tone colorations. In all his important works we confront great wealth of feeling together with a keen, discerning intellect. The integral unity of his music is particularly noteworthy, just as his melodic writing has a highly personal character. Brief, episodic themes are built into well-arched melodies. Unlike so many other composers, Martinu preferred, rather than to present his fully articulated theme immediately, to suggest melodies and then allow them to develop naturally through the length of a movement.

MAJOR WORKS

Ballets—Istar; Who Is the Most Powerful in the World?; On Tourne; La Revue de Cuisine; Échec au Roi; The Butterfly That Stamped; Špalíček; The Judgment of Paris; The Strangler.

Chamber Music—6 string quartets; 3 violin sonatas; 2 cello sonatas; String Quintet; Piano Trio; String Sextet; Piano Quintet; Piano Quartet; Madrigal Sonata, for flute, violin, and piano; Madrigal Stanzas, for violin and piano; Quartet for Oboe, Violin, Cello, and Piano.

Choral Music—Czech Rhapsody; Madrigals; The Greek Passion; Prophecy of Isaiah.

Operas—The Soldier and the Dancer; The Miracle of Our Lady; Comedy on a Bridge (radio opera); Julietta; The Marriage (television opera); What Men Live By; La Locandiera; Ariadne; Mirandolina, comic opera; Alexander Bis, opera buffa.

Orchestral Music—6 symphonies; 2 piano concertos; Half-Time; La Bagarre; La Rhapsodie; Jazz Suite; Serenade; Partita, for string orchestra; Cello Concerto; String Quartet with Orchestra; Harpsichord Concerto; Les Rondes; Sinfonia, for two orchestras; Suite Concertante, for violin and orchestra; Three Ricercari, for chamber orchestra; Double Concerto; Concerto Grosso; Sonata da Camera, for cello and chamber orchestra; Sinfonietta Giocosa, for piano and chamber orchestra; Memorial to Lidice; Concerto for Two Pianos and Orchestra; Violin Concerto; Toccata a Due Canzoni, for piano and chamber orchestra; Concerto for Orchestra; Intermezzo; Sinfonia Concertante, for solo instruments, piano, and strings; Rhapsody Concerto, for violin and orchestra; Incantation, for piano and orchestra; Variations on a Slovenian Theme; The Rock, symphonic prelude; The Frescoes of Piero della Francesca; Fantasia Concertante, for piano and orchestra; Estampes, suite; Parables.

Piano Music—Czech Dances; Puppets; Les Ritournelles; The Window in the Garden; Fantaisie et Rondo; Mazurka; Etudes and Polkas, three books.

Vocal Music—Children's Songs; Two Songs for Contraltos; Songs on One Page; Songs on Two Pages.

ABOUT

Ewen, D. (ed.), The New Book of Modern Composers; Mihul, J., Bohuslav Martinu; Mooser, R.-A., Panorama de la Musique Contemporaine; Sfranek, M., Bohuslav Martinu.

Pietro Mascagni
1863–1945

Pietro Mascagni was born in Leghorn, Italy, on December 7, 1863. The long-accepted belief that Mascagni's father, a baker, objected to

Mascagni: mäs kä′ nyē

his son's interest in music and that Pietro had to study secretly has been discredited; it is true, however, that the father wanted his son to become a lawyer. Nevertheless, when Pietro entered the Cherubini Institute in Leghorn it was with his father's knowledge and consent, though the latter was given reluctantly. There Mascagni became a pupil of Alfredo Soffredini. Subsequently, Pietro's uncle took the boy into his own household, subsidized his musical education, and encouraged him in his musical pursuits. Under such a stimulus, the boy wrote a symphony for small orchestra and a choral Kyrie, both of which were performed at the Cherubini Institute in 1879. *Filanda*, a Cantata for solo voices and orchestra, received honorable mention in a contest sponsored by the International Exposition of Music in Milan in 1881.

PIETRO MASCAGNI

The death of Pietro's uncle in 1881 brought the boy back home where he continued his musical activities with the full encouragement of his parent. Mascagni now set to music Schiller's *Ode to Joy* (the poem that had served Beethoven for his Ninth Symphony). When performed in Leghorn, this composition received such praise that Count Florestano de Larderel, who was in the audience, stood ready to pay the expenses for the boy's further musical training in Milan.

Mascagni enrolled in the Milan Conservatory, where he was far from happy. Despite the fact that he studied under such notable teachers as Saladino and Ponchielli, Mascagni was oppressed by the exercises and impatient with the rules. He also resented the severe discipline imposed on all Conservatory students. One day, in 1884, he suddenly decided he had had enough of Conservatory life. He abandoned school to join a traveling opera company as conductor. This was a trying period for the young musician, for the hardship of continual travel was combined with intense poverty. In time Mascagni married and settled down in Cerignola where he supported himself by conducting a band which he had helped to organize, by teaching the piano, and by serving as the director of a local music school. He also tried his hand at writing operas. His first, *Pinotta*, though written in 1880, was not produced until half a century later, in San Remo, on March 23, 1932. This was followed a number of years later by *Guglielmo Ratcliff*, which also was not produced until Mascagni had become famous.

He was still a humble and obscure musician when in 1889 he read the news that the publisher Sonzogno was offering a prize for a one-act opera. Strongly attracted to a libretto derived from a tale by Verga, *Cavalleria Rusticana*, Mascagni set to work on an operatic score with such passion that he completed the music in three months. When he finished, he was so dissatisfied with the result that he refused to enter it in the competition. Without his knowledge, his wife dispatched the manuscript to Sonzogno, and it won first prize.

Few operas in music history enjoyed such success at their premières as did *Cavalleria Rusticana*, introduced at the Costanzi Theatre in Rome on May 17, 1890. The composer took about forty curtain calls. Outside the opera house, hundreds waited to cheer him as he left the theatre. Returning home, he found the house besieged by his admirers. He gained entrance by hoisting himself into his apartment through the window.

Cavalleria Rusticana made its composer the man of the hour in Italian music. Parades were held in his honor. Medals were sold with his image. The town of Cerignola made him an honorary citizen, and the king of Italy presented him with the Order of the Crown.

Nor was the success of *Cavalleria Rusticana* a local phenomenon. Before the end of 1890 it had been heard in Hungary, where it was conducted by Gustav Mahler, and it was soon produced throughout Europe. On September 8, 1891, it was first seen in the United States, in Philadelphia. Performances followed immediately in Chicago, Boston, and New York. It was presented at the Metropolitan Opera on December 30, 1891, and, in 1893, the Metropolitan for the first time paired it with Leoncavallo's *Pagliacci* to fill out the evening's bill—a partnership that has since proved more or less traditional all over the world.

This opera was responsible for creating a new trend in Italian opera, identified as *verismo*. In *verismo*, everyday subjects are used, with everyday settings, everyday situations, and everyday characters—as distinguished from historical plots or plots from mythology. *Verismo* was partial to violent, passionate stories treated in a naturalistic way. As far as the music went, *verismo* favored melodramatic arias rather than florid or lyrical ones, while emphasizing choral episodes that helped to establish a mood, orchestral tone painting, and naturalistic recitatives. This operatic movement brought in a period of realism in opera typified by such composers as Leoncavallo and Puccini in Italy and Gustave Charpentier in France.

In his discussion of *Cavalleria Rusticana*, Herbert F. Peyser pointed to its "musical abundance," "emotional turbulence" and the use of contrasts. He added: "Its melodic idiom does not perceptibly owe anything to anyone unless it be to Italian folk song. Indeed, if there is such a thing as an Italian folk opera, *Cavalleria Rusticana* is its very model, Verdi and Rossini notwithstanding! . . . Mascagni grasped the deep artistic truth that action on the stage is not so important as action in music. It is the seething action in the score cunningly punctuated with periods of repose or alleviation that resolves whatever *Cavalleria* may offer."

One unforgettable moment of repose in the opera comes with one of the most celebrated orchestral episodes in all dramatic music—the famous "Intermezzo" in whose serene, almost spiritual measures the composer attempted to catch the spirit of Easter.

Cavalleria Rusticana made its composer wealthy as well as famous. Mascagni was now in great demand as a conductor. In 1895 he was appointed director of the Conservatory

at Pesaro where he remained for seven years.

On October 31, 1891, the première of Mascagni's new opera, *L'Amico Fritz* at the Teatro Costanzi in Rome, attracted interest halfway around the world. This, too, was a success, though not of the magnitude of its predecessor; and it seemed to offer additional hope that a major new opera composer had come into being. *L'Amico Fritz* also represented for its composer a change of creative pace—where *Cavalleria* had been passionate and turbulent *L'Amico Fritz* was refined and idyllic. Italian audiences have remained faithful to it; it is the only other opera by Mascagni to be produced regularly in Italy. But in America—where it was introduced at the Metropolitan Opera in New York on January 10, 1894—it never caught fire and is rarely revived.

Iris, produced in Rome on November 22, 1898, was only a minor achievement and a minor success; and *Silvano* (1895) and *Zanetto* (1896) were failures. Nevertheless, Mascagni's popularity remained undiminished. When he completed the writing of a new opera, *Le Maschere*, its première on January 17, 1901, was given simultaneously in six of Italy's most important opera houses, with Mascagni himself conducting the performance at Rome; a seventh production was offered in Naples two days later. This opera, however, failed to live up to expectations. The work was received coolly everywhere and has since passed out of the repertory.

From then on, Mascagni's fortunes as a composer leveled off. Though he wrote many more operas he never succeeded in achieving anything as popular as *Cavalleria*. As he himself remarked in reviewing a career that practically started at the top and then declined rapidly: "It is a pity I wrote *Cavalleria* first, for I was crowned before I became king."

In 1902 Mascagni came to the United States with a touring opera company which he conducted in his own *Cavalleria* as well as other operas. The tour was badly managed and proved a fiasco. A Mascagni tour of South America in 1911, however, proved a highly successful undertaking.

Much of Mascagni's fame in the 1900's came from his achievements as a conductor, and in 1929 he succeeded Toscanini as the musical director of La Scala. But it was *Cavalleria* alone that continued to place him

Medtner

with the important Italian opera composers of his time. This fact was emphasized in 1929 when he was elected a member of the Royal Italian Academy, upon its inception, and once again in 1940 when the fiftieth anniversary of *Cavalleria* was celebrated with gala performances in Rome, Venice, and Milan, all directed by Mascagni.

Mascagni identified himself closely with the Fascist regime in Italy, and he did what he could to glorify Italian fascism in his works. One of his last operas, *Nerone*—produced at La Scala on January 6, 1935—was a thinly disguised tribute to Mussolini and fascism. With Italy involved in World War II, Mascagni's fortunes hit their lowest ebb. His home was confiscated by the Socialists after the Nazis were driven out of Italy. His persistent arguments that he had never been a Fascist, had never interested himself in politics, and that politicians had been exploiting his name and reputation without his consent failed to make any impression. The last years of his life were spent in poverty and disgrace. He died in Rome on August 2, 1945, of bronchial pneumonia and hardening of the arteries.

MAJOR WORKS

Choral Music—Cantata for the Leopardi Centenary; Requiem in Memory of King Humbert; Inno del Lavoro; Inno degli Avanguardisti.

Operas—Cavalleria Rusticana; L'Amico Fritz; I Rantzau; Guglielmo Ratcliff; Silvano; Zanetto; Iris; Le Maschere; Amica; Isabeau; Parisina; Lodoletta; Il Piccolo Marat; Scampolo; Nerone; I Bianchi ed i Neri.

Orchestral Music—Rapsodia Satanica; Davanti Santa Teresa.

ABOUT

Brockway, W. and Weinstock, H., The World of Opera; Cogo, G., Il Nostro Mascagni; Grout, D. J., A Short History of Opera; Jeri, A., Mascagni; Mascagni, P., Mascagni Parla; Morini, M., Mascagni, the Man and His Music.

Nicolas Medtner
1880–1951

Nicolas Karlovich Medtner, sometimes described as the "Russian Brahms," was born in Moscow on January 5, 1880. His father, who was of German origin, was the director of a factory. A lover of fine literature, the elder Medtner early instilled in his son an apprecia-

---

Medtner: mĕt′nĕr

tion of books. Nicolas' mother was the musician of the family, having been a concert singer, and it was through her influence that Nicolas became interested in music. He learned to play the violin by himself and founded a little orchestra which performed regularly at his home. He also tried his hand at composition. When he was six, he had his first piano lessons, and when he was twelve, he enrolled in the Moscow Conservatory where his teachers included Arensky and Taneiev in composition and Safonov in piano. He did well and received a gold medal in piano when he was graduated in 1900. The same year, he won the Rubinstein Prize in Vienna.

NICOLAS MEDTNER

His first tour (1901–1902) as a concert pianist was very successful. This marked the beginning of a career that continued up to the time of his death and placed him among the foremost pianists of his time. In 1902 he wrote a number of compositions that were published later: his first opus was *Eight Mood Pictures*, and his second, *Three Improvisations*. These were followed by the set *Four Pieces* (1903), and his first piano sonata, in F minor, op. 5 (1904).

It was also in 1902 that Medtner joined the faculty of the Moscow Conservatory where he taught piano. He held this post only one year, preferring to devote his time to composition and to concert work. However, from 1918 to 1921 he resumed teaching at the Conservatory as professor of piano.

354

Though unsympathetic to the revolutionary regime Medtner remained in Russia for several years after 1917 without interrupting his various musical activities. In 1921, however, he decided to leave Russia and make his home in Germany. During this period he undertook a world tour as pianist, performing at his concerts many of his own works. In his American debut in Philadelphia on October 31, 1924, he appeared as soloist with the Philadelphia Orchestra under Stokowski in his own Piano Concerto No. 1 in C minor, which he had completed in 1918. Upon returning to Europe, he lived for some time in Paris. In 1930 he made another extended tour of the United States, this time appearing also in Canada. In 1936 he settled permanently in England, establishing residence in London.

During World War II Medtner and his wife left bomb-stricken London to live temporarily in the Warwickshire home of Edna Iles, a pianist who had long devoted herself to the promotion of Medtner's music. After the war Medtner returned to London, where in 1946 he was soloist in a performance of his three piano concertos with the London Symphony under George Weldon. His second concerto, in C minor, had been written in 1927, and his third, in E minor, subtitled *Ballade*, followed sixteen years later.

In 1948 Medtner acquired a powerful patron in the Maharajah of Mysore, who created a special endowment for the purpose of recording all of Medtner's music, most of it in Medtner's own performances. In reporting this development in the New York *Times*, Joseph Yasser commented: "It is the first case in the annals of music where the entire output of a single composer will be engraved on phonograph records in his own interpretation, so far as his pianistic music is concerned."

Nicolas Medtner died in London, November 13, 1951. Soon afterwards there was a major revival of his music in the Soviet Union.

Though Medtner wrote three violin sonatas and many songs, together with the three piano concertos, he is today remembered mainly for his shorter piano pieces. In some instances he invented his own forms. In his earliest compositions his indebtedness to Brahms is unmistakable. If, in later works, he finally succeeded in freeing himself from his ties to Brahms, he never lost Brahms's respect for

tradition, sound architectural procedures, and post-Romantic attitudes. The newer idioms and techniques of the twentieth century never interested Medtner at all. He preferred to follow the route paved by the German post-Romantic school. He believed in fully developed melodies, harmonies that sound well, deeply felt emotions, and vivid pictorial suggestions. Frequently he introduced into his writing intricate polyphony or complex rhythmic patterns–characteristics that may account for the fact that his music does not always make an immediate contact with audiences.

Ernest Newman wrote: "Medtner is another proof that it is possible to work in the ordinary harmonic medium–develop it in complexity, of course, according to the necessities of the idea–and yet convey an expression of complete originality."

Medtner's most famous works are those shorter Schumannesque pieces to which he has given a variety of descriptive titles and the forms of some of which he himself devised. These include the *Fairy Tales*, the *Musical Pictures*, and the *Romantic Sketches*, as well as Marches, Arabesques, Novelettes, Improvisations, Etudes, Caprices, and Moments Musicaux. Among these forms, he is probably at his best in his *Fairy Tales*. Leonid Sabaneyev wrote in *Modern Russian Composers:* "His creative work is best characterized by this type of composition, invented by him, and partly similar to the old romantic form of the ballad. Medtner's *Fairy Tales* unquestionably belong not only to the best of his creative work, but to the production of romantic inspiration in general. But Medtner's romanticism is peculiar. It is not the romanticism of enchantment, but rather the romanticism of the grotesque. Medtner's fantastic world, which opens for us through the sounds of his *Fairy Tales*, is not the world of elves and witchery, but the poetry of ancient heroic legends, and most of all an echo of the underworld of Nibelungs, gnomes and mountain kings."

"There are certain outstanding qualities in Medtner that combine to make him one of the most striking figures in modern music," wrote Alfred J. Swan. "His style is firm, rigid, somewhat uncouth; his thought concentrated (note his favorite epithet '*concentrando*'), severe, ascetic, graphical, rather than steeped in color, yet of haunting beauty and transparent beauty; his rhythm invariably striking and characteristic."

MAJOR WORKS

Chamber Music—3 violin sonatas; Three Nocturnes, for violin and piano; String Quintet.

Orchestral Music—3 piano concertos.

Piano Music—6 sonatas; Arabesques, Caprices, Elegies, Fairy Tales, Improvisations, Moments Musicaux; Eight Mood Pictures; Three Dithyrambs; Sonata-Triad; Three Novels; Four Lyric Fragments; Forgotten Melodies, three volumes; Three Hymns in Praise of Toil; Romantic Sketches, four volumes; Russian Round Dance, for two pianos; Knight-Errant, for two pianos; Theme and Variations.

Vocal Music—Over 100 songs for voice and piano including Butterfly, To a Dreamer, The Ravens, and Spanish Romance.

ABOUT

Holt, R., Medtner and His Music; Holt, R. (ed.), Nicolas Medtner: A Symposium; Swan, A. (ed.), The Muse and the Fashion; Yakolev, V., Nicholas Medtner.

Music and Letters (London), January 1927; Musical Times (London), January 1915.

Peter Mennin
1923–

Peter Mennin was born Peter Mennini in Erie, Pennsylvania, May 17, 1923. His father, a businessman, was a music lover who enjoyed collecting and listening to recordings, and the phonograph was Peter Mennin's first contact with music. He began music study early—at the age of seven with Tito Spantani, who insisted that the boy learn how to read music before he even touched the piano. Facility in reading and writing music led the boy to create his first piano pieces in the same year he received his first formal instruction; by the time he was eleven he attempted a symphony.

After his graduation from the local high school, Mennin, aged seventeen, entered the Oberlin Conservatory where he studied mainly with Normand Lockwood during the next two years. Before leaving this Conservatory Mennin completed his first symphony, his first string quartet, and some songs.

Early in 1942, during World War II, he was in uniform, doing clerical work with the Air Force at an officer candidate school in Florida. After being separated from the armed forces in the fall of 1942, Mennin worked for a while as a laboratory assistant in a paper

mill before deciding to resume the study of music. He was admitted to the Eastman School of Music in Rochester, New York, on the strength of his first symphony. While studying composition with Howard Hanson and with Bernard Rogers, Mennin completed a number of works performed by the Eastman School Orchestra. The most important was his Second Symphony (1944) which received in 1945 both the Gershwin Memorial Award (for

PETER MENNIN

one of its movements, Allegro, which was performed by the New York Philharmonic under Leonard Bernstein, March 27, 1945) and the Bearns Prize of Columbia University (for the complete work). Other major compositions completed while he still attended the Eastman School included a Concertino for Flute, Strings and Percussion, a Concerto for Orchestra, and the *Folk Overture*, for orchestra. The last mentioned, completed in July 1945, was the first of Mennin's works to receive performances by major orchestras—the New York Philharmonic and the National Symphony in Washington, D.C.—following its première in 1945 by the Eastman School of Music Orchestra under Hanson. Lee Fairley, program annotator of the National Symphony, described this as "a short work possessing a great deal of rhythmic exuberance and strength. The themes are simple and straightforward, perhaps suggesting folk tunes, although no actual folk melodies had been used."

Mennin received his master's degree in music

at the Eastman School in 1946, while holding a fellowship in orchestration. During the summer of 1946 he studied conducting with Koussevitzky at the Berkshire Music Center at Tanglewood.

Mennin's Third Symphony achieved the greatest success of any of his works up to that time. Mennin completed it in May 1946, and its world première was given by the New York Philharmonic under Walter Hendl, February 27, 1947. "It is an accomplished work," reported Virgil Thomson in the New York *Herald Tribune*, "in the sense that its shape holds together and that its instrumentation is professional. Its expressive content is eclectic, ranging from a Sibelius-like sadness to a syncopated animation suggestive of William Schuman. . . . On the whole, the work seemed . . . to represent valid professional accomplishments."

Mennin soon completed two more symphonies. The fourth, called *The Cycle*, enlisted the services of a mixed chorus: the Collegiate Chorale under Robert Shaw introduced it in New York on March 18, 1949. The Fifth was commissioned by the Dallas Symphony, which presented it April 2, 1950, Walter Hendl conducting.

Not yet thirty, Mennin was already a widely recognized and a widely performed composer. A number of important honors had come his way: awards from the National Institute of Arts and Letters and the American Academy of Arts and Letters, in 1946; the first of two Guggenheim Fellowships, in 1949 (the second came eight years later); and in 1950, a centennial citation from the University of Rochester for distinguished service to music.

Among Mennin's later works were two more symphonies. The sixth was commissioned by the Louisville Orchestra which presented the world première in Kentucky on November 18, 1953. The Seventh, named the *Variation Symphony*, was written for the Cleveland Orchestra and George Szell, who introduced it in Cleveland on January 23, 1964. In addition, Mennin completed in 1951 a string quartet (his second), which was first performed by the Juilliard String Quartet on February 24, 1952, and which won the Chamber Music Award from Columbia Records; a piano concerto, commissioned by the Cleveland Orchestra, which performed it, with Eunice Podis as soloist, on

February 27, 1958; and a cello concerto commissioned by the Juilliard Musical Foundation and introduced by Leonard Rose in New York on February 10, 1956.

While still attending the Eastman School of Music for his doctorate, Mennin met and fell in love with Georganne Bairnson, a violin student at the school. They were married August 28, 1947. They have two children, a daughter born in 1958, and a son born in 1960.

After receiving his doctorate from the Eastman School in 1947, Mennin joined the composition faculty of the Juilliard School of Music in New York and remained in the post for a decade. In 1958 he was appointed director of the Peabody Conservatory of Music in Baltimore, where he aroused the admiration of educators for his innovations, such as the American Conductors Project to develop young conductors and the Peabody Art Theatre to train young opera singers. In 1963 he was named to perhaps the most important educational post in American music, that of the presidency of the Juilliard School of Music. He also became president of the Naumburg Musical Foundation. During the summer of 1966 he served as composer-in-residence at the Hopkins Center Congregation at Dartmouth College in New Hampshire. Performances of his major works were heard at three festival concerts. In 1967 he was elected treasurer of the National Institute of Arts and Letters, and shortly thereafter president of the National Music Council.

Mennin's music is complex in idiom and severe in line. It is strong, passionate, and tense rather than emotional or lyrical. It possesses vigor and exuberance to a high degree and generates excitement.

"In writing orchestral scores," Mennin states, "I find that the use of any musical instrument as a medium hampers the natural flow of expression. A blank page of score proves to be a source of mental stimulation. This method of working is greatly aided by the possession of absolute pitch.

"When someone tells me, 'You must keep your audience in mind,' I answer, 'I write music. If audiences do not understand me immediately they will later, maybe never, but first I must satisfy myself.' "

Mennin does his composing chiefly in the early morning hours before he embarks on his

Menotti

administrative duties at the Juilliard School. He is tall (six feet two inches) and always meticulously attired. The New York *Times* described him as follows: "He has gray-blue eyes, a well-groomed moustache, and a gentle, almost diffident manner, although he has always been a human dynamo." His interests outside music include reading and travel, but he hastens to add: "I've almost always been too busy to have any serious hobbies."

MAJOR WORKS

Chamber Music—2 string quartets; Sonata Concertante, for violin and piano; Violin Sonata.

Choral Music—Four choruses on Chinese texts; The Christmas Story, cantata; Bought Locks; Tumbling Hair; The Gold-Threaded Robe; Crossing the Han River; In the Quiet Night.

Orchestral Music—7 symphonies; Folk Overture; Concerto for Orchestra; Concertino, for flute, strings, and percussion; Sinfonia, for chamber orchestra; Concertato (Moby Dick); Fantasia, for string orchestra; Violin Concerto; Cello Concerto; Piano Concerto; Canto.

Piano Music—Five Piano Pieces; Divertimento; Partita; Sonata.

ABOUT

Chase, G., *America's Music*.

Juilliard Review, Spring 1954; Saturday Review, February 26, 1955.

Gian Carlo Menotti
1911–

Gian Carlo Menotti was born to an affluent family in the town of Cadegliano, Italy, on July 7, 1911. He was the ninth of ten children. The Menottis were people of consequence in their town. Gian Carlo's grandfather had been mayor and his father ran a prosperous export-import business, dealing with South American firms. His earliest musical memory is of listening to his mother teach Gregorian chants to neighborhood peasants. Another early influence was the many chamber music performances in the Menotti household, usually with his mother and sister joining in to play classics in four-hand piano arrangements.

His mother gave him his first piano lessons when he was four. At six he tried composition by writing melodies for several erotic poems by Gabriele d'Annunzio. Before many months

---

Menotti: mä nôt′ tē

passed he was an eager participant at family concerts. At nine he revealed his great love for theatre, beginning a lifelong preoccupation. He not only began to write plays, but he also constructed sets, designed costumes, and contrived stage effects for productions with a little puppet theatre which he had received as a birthday gift.

GIAN CARLO MENOTTI

When Gian Carlo was about ten, the family moved to Milan. There he attended both the academic schools and the Milan Conservatory. He frequently heard opera performances at La Scala. Inspired by what he had seen and heard there he wrote an opera, *The Death of Pierrot*, the text of which was distinguished by the fact that all the characters killed themselves in the last act. A few years later he wrote a second opera.

His father died when he was fourteen, leaving the family finances in a state of confusion and entrusting the mother with the responsibility for making all final decisions on Gian Carlo's upbringing and musical education. She consulted Toscanini. The Maestro, aware that the boy by now had become the darling of the Milanese salons, urged her to take him to New York, where he was completely unknown and where he could continue his music studies without being coddled and spoiled.

But first mother and son went to South America to straighten out some of the family business interests there. In 1927 they arrived in New York. There, Tullio Serafin, conductor at the Metropolitan Opera, provided the boy with a letter of introduction to Rosario Scalero, distinguished teacher of composition at the Curtis Institute in Philadelphia. "We were very sad," Menotti revealed to Samuel Chotzinoff, in discussing his first arrival in America. "It was Christmas, and we spent the holidays alone in a hotel. Then we went to Philadelphia to the Curtis Institute of Music where I played some of my things for Scalero. . . . I was given a scholarship. And one rainy afternoon I saw my mother off at the Broad Street Station. Both of us wept. For the first time in my life I was left alone without family or friends. I remember my terror."

Though his loneliness was soon assuaged through his friendship with Samuel Barber, a fellow student at Curtis, and his associations with Barber's family in West Chester, Pennsylvania, the Curtis years were not easy for Menotti. He had to struggle with a new language of which he had not known a single word when first he arrived in Philadelphia. He tried to solve this problem by going to the movies four times a week. He was also unaccustomed to the rigorous discipline of Conservatory life. "I was a bad student," he told Chotzinoff. "I was a puzzle to my teachers. I had to learn in my own way or not at all. I had to develop a private technique. I had to fashion my own instruments, my own weapons, so to speak. And I did. It's a serviceable technique, but it's not the usual equipment." He was graduated from the Institute in 1933.

Menotti developed slowly. First it was the music of Brahms that affected him most strongly. Under the Brahms influence he wrote the *Variations on a Theme of Schumann*, which won the Lauber Composition Prize in 1931. Then he became infatuated with the polyphonic works of the Baroque era, in which Scalero gave him a rigorous training. His fondness for polyphony soon became so great that he developed a hatred of opera and became convinced that his future as a composer lay in choral and instrumental music.

Nevertheless, an idea for a comic opera struck him one day in Vienna, where he had gone for a winter vacation mainly to familiarize himself with the background that had produced a Schubert, a composer who at the moment monopolized his interests. Living in an apartment rented from a Czechoslovakian woman, he greatly admired the owner's beautiful dressing table. "I was so taken with the extravagance and frivolity of this dressing table," he recalls, "that it gave me the idea for my opera, *Amelia Goes to the Ball*. It is really very curious how that dressing table set my mind into motion to write an opera."

He completed the libretto and the music while still in Europe, the libretto being first written in Italian and then translated into English. His imagination fired by that ornate dressing table, he built up a comic little episode from his own boyhood experiences in the salons of the wealthy Milanese. Amelia is a pampered child of such a salon. She has a husband and a lover, and when their angry confrontation threatens to keep her from going to a fashionable ball, she smashes a vase over her husband's head, has her lover arrested as a burglar, and cheerily goes off to the ball with the police officer. It is an amusing little comedy for which Menotti produced a score, à la Wolf-Ferrari, sparkling with wit, rich in melody, and attractively spiced in harmonies. Text and music were in the tradition of *opera buffa*, with its formal arias, ensemble numbers and set pieces. Marriage of words and music, of song and stage action, made excellent comic theatre.

Amelia Goes to the Ball was given its world première in Philadelphia on April 1, 1937, in a production of the Curtis Institute conducted by Fritz Reiner. For the première, George Meade's English translation was used. Less than a year later, on March 3, 1938, it was produced at the Metropolitan Opera. At that time, Pitts Sanborn wrote in the New York *World Telegram* that this little opera was conceived "in the great comic line of *Le Nozze di Figaro*, *Il Matrimonio Segreto*, *Il Barbiere di Siviglia*, *Don Pasquale* and *Falstaff*." One month later, *Amelia Goes to the Ball* was produced for the first time in the Italian language, at the San Remo Opera.

On the strength of *Amelia*, Menotti received important commissions for new operas. One came from NBC, for which he wrote a delightful radio opera, *The Old Maid and the Thief*. It was produced over the NBC radio network on April 22, 1939. A staged presentation followed in Philadelphia on February 11, 1941. Another commission came from the Metropolitan Opera, and it resulted in Menotti's only fiasco—a grand opera, *The Island God*, produced in New York on February 20, 1942. Menotti explains the disaster of *The Island God* by pointing out that "my old German indoctrination came to the surface again. I suffered an illusion of grandeur when I wrote it." It taught him an important lesson: "In it I tackled a subject too heroic for my kind of music. It was then that I realized that the first duty of an artist is to know his limitations. My vein was not heroic. *The Island God* taught me that I was no Wagner." Menotti has withdrawn this opera from circulation. But two symphonic interludes from this score have occasionally been presented at orchestral concerts.

The failure of *The Island God* brought about a depression from which Menotti tried to lift himself by temporarily abandoning stage music for concert music. At this time he wrote his first mature piece of instrumental music, a piano concerto, which Rudolf Firkusny introduced with the Boston Symphony on November 2, 1945. In his concerto the composer tried to capture something of the spirit of the eighteenth century harpsichord master Domenico Scarlatti. "He has given us in terms of modern technique and stylistic expertness a clear, melodic, exhilarating piece of music," reported Olin Downes.

After he had completed the piano concerto, and before it was performed, Menotti created the score for a ballet, *Sebastian*. With choreography by Edward Caton, and with Francisco Moncion and Viola Essen appearing in the leading roles, *Sebastian* was produced in New York on October 31, 1944. Thirteen years later, *Sebastian* returned with new staging and with new choreography by Agnes de Mille, as a production of the American Ballet Theatre in New York on May 27, 1957.

Menotti was appointed to the faculty of the Curtis Institute in the department of composition in 1941. In 1945 he received a grant from the American Academy of Arts and Sciences and the National Institute of Arts and Sciences; a year later he was given the first of two Guggenheim Fellowships. While on the Fellowship, and through a commission from the Alice M. Ditson Fund, Menotti made his return to opera. The idea for his new libretto came to him during a seance. *The Medium*, completed early in 1946, was built around the character of a fake spiritualist who, when confronted by a spirit she cannot explain, loses her self-confidence, renounces her profession, and commits murder.

The Medium was first produced at Columbia University in New York during a contemporary music festival, on May 8, 1946. A grim melodrama, it made a profound impression. Two young enterprising producers then decided to present it on Broadway where it opened on May 1, 1947. The opera stayed on the boards for several months, after which it was seen throughout the United States (as well as in London and Paris) for a total of more than a thousand performances within a few years. In 1955 the opera toured Europe under the auspices of the State Department. It was recorded in its entirety, and in 1951 it was made into a successful motion picture, filmed in Italy under Menotti's direction.

In *The Medium*, Menotti became a disciple of *verismo*, naturalistic opera à la Mascagni, Leoncavallo, and Puccini (see sketch on Mascagni). Robert Sabin has written: "All the elements that constitute Menotti's major contributions to the contemporary musical theatre are found at their best in *The Medium:* a naturalistic and musically adept handling of recitative which blends imperceptibly into heightened melodic expression; a small orchestra employed with such consummate skill that one feels no need for the impact of a gigantic grand-opera ensemble; a fully rounded dramatic treatment in which all minor characters are clearly and lovingly delineated; an intimacy of style and atmosphere more like the theatre than the opera house, but always translated into musical terms."

The Medium was followed by a delightful one-act trifle, *The Telephone*, which has only two characters. First performed in New York on February 18, 1947, it went to Broadway on May 1 to fill out the evening's musical entertainment with *The Medium*. The plot concerns the frantic efforts of a young man to propose to his loved one, efforts made futile by the continual interruptions of the telephone. He finally rushes out to a nearby drug store to telephone his proposal. The entertaining book was brightened by the melodious and witty score.

In *The Consul*, produced on Broadway on March 15, 1950, Menotti returned to *verismo*. This drama, gripping in text and music, is set in an unidentified police state in our own time. A woman is seeking a visa to leave her country, so that she may join her husband in another land. Enmeshed in bureaucratic red tape and haunted by the secret police, she never gets her visa. While she is waiting for it, her child dies. Her husband, who returns from his freedom to join her, is imprisoned. And the heroine can now find escape only in suicide.

The eclectic style which characterized Menotti's writing up to that time served him well in the presentation of his text. Song speech, free rhythms, discords, polytonality—all intensify the terror and frustration that seize the heroine. Soaring lyricism is also present and is responsible for two of the most eloquent moments in the opera: Magda's aria at the close of the second act ("To This We've Come") and the tender lullaby sung by the grandmother to the dying child in the same act. Play and music become a single closely-knit fabric; and both represent extraordinarily effective theatre.

The Consul was a box-office success on Broadway. It received the Pulitzer Prize and the New York Drama Critics Circle Award. Later it was produced in a dozen different countries. The only place it failed to make a good impression was La Scala, in Milan, in 1950 (it was the first opera written and introduced in America to be produced there). Left-wing groups, interpreting the opera as an indictment of Communist countries, staged a demonstration. Patriotic Italians denounced it because Menotti, an Italian, had chosen to become an American, even though he had never given up his Italian citizenship.

Additional proof of Menotti's versatility was provided in *Amahl and the Night Visitors*, which he wrote for television. In place of wit and satire and *verismo* here was a Christmas fantasy, poetic in mood, frequently religious and spiritual in feeling. Menotti wrote this little opera on a commission from NBC, which produced it over its television network on Christmas Eve in 1951. For many years it was an annual television event at Christmas. It also received successful stage productions, including one at the Florence May Music Festival in 1953. *Amahl and the Night Visitors* has historic importance in that it is the first opera written for American television and the first opera whose world première was sponsored by a commercial organization.

The libretto, inspired by Hieronymus Bosch's painting "The Adoration of the Magi," tells the story of a crippled lad who has only one gift to present to the Holy Child—his crutches. He makes that gift to the Three Wise Men, on their way to the Manger in Bethlehem. Because of his generosity he is healed. Much of the musical writing is in an expressive recitative style but, as Olin Downes remarked in his review, "with intensifying beauty at climactic moments, as when the child walks and the king chants of the power and majesty of the Savior." But some of the unforgettable musical episodes are found in the choral sections, particularly those sung by the shepherds.

In *The Unicorn, the Gorgon and the Manticore* (world première in Washington, D.C. on October 21, 1956), Menotti revived the sixteenth century structure of the madrigal sequence in a chamber opera he described as a "madrigal fable." He also completed two other successful operas in *verismo* style, with contemporary backgrounds and realistic treatment. *The Saint of Bleecker Street* was produced on Broadway on December 27, 1954. *Maria Golovin*, commissioned by NBC for the Brussels Exposition in Belgium, received its world première there on August 20, 1958, with the American première following on Broadway on November 5 of the same year.

The Saint of Bleecker Street uses as a setting a street in the Italian section of New York's Greenwich Village. Its heroine is a religious mystic who receives the stigmata on her palms and dies in a frenzy of joy and exaltation during the ceremonies in which she is accepted by the Church as the Bride.

The heroine of *Maria Golovin* is the wife of a prisoner of war whom she has not seen for a number of years. Starved for love, she is drawn to a blind maker of bird cages, owner of a European villa where she has made her home. When her husband, released from prison, comes to claim his wife, the blind bird-cage maker tries to kill him but misses his mark. He is left with the delusion that his beloved and her husband can never be reunited.

Both operas are tragedies in which the torment of the characters is stressed in an eclectic musical style that shifts from the programmatic, realistic and modern to the florid, sentimental, and lyrical. In each opera, Menotti reveals a remarkable feeling and instinct for effective theatre, for arriving at the precise *mot juste* for every requirement of the stage. As the editor of this book has written: "As a man of the theatre he has made his operas not just a vehicle for musical invention, but a vibrant and pulsating stage experience. Perhaps for this reason he has commanded a larger and more varied audience than any other opera composer since 1900." *The Saint of Bleecker Street* was awarded the Drama Critics Award as the best play of the year, the Music Critics Circle Award as the best opera, and the Pulitzer Prize in music—the only Broadway production to have attained this triple crown.

Menotti has always written his own librettos. He even provided another composer with a libretto, for he wrote the text for Samuel Barber's opera *Vanessa*. He also served as his own stage and casting director, and has always involved himself personally in every possible phase and detail of the production. This does much to explain the singleness of concept and projection that has characterized Menotti's operas.

Menotti's most important opera after *Maria Golovin* was *The Last Savage*, which had been commissioned by the Paris Opéra (the first time a non-French composer had been so honored since Verdi). Its world première took place in Paris on October 21, 1963—not at the Opéra, however, but at the Opéra-Comique. The Metropolitan offered it on January 23, 1964. This opera has been described as a "satire of contemporary life" with the foibles of modern civilization as a pet target. "The characters," explains the composer, "are stock figures straight out of the *commedia dell'arte*." Reviewing the opera for the New York *Post*, Harriett Johnson explained: "Menotti spoofs and exposes with good-natured but biting satire, a shower of preposterous contemporary folderol to do with habits, peoples, ideas, concepts—from the cocktail party to the avant-garde painter and the 'electro-dodecaphonic' composer. . . . Menotti's score spouts concerted pieces which include trio, quartet, quintet, sextet and a final septet, with a technique which reflects the composer's skill."

The Last Savage was Menotti's first opera since *Amelia Goes to the Ball* in which he wrote his libretto in Italian. For the world première in Paris he himself translated his text into French; for the American production, how-

ever, the English translation was prepared by George Meade.

Menotti's first opera for television since *Amahl*, named *Labyrinth*, tells the story of a bride and bridegroom come to spend their honeymoon in a hotel. That hotel becomes symbolic of the world, and each character is made to represent an aspect of life. Only after many adventures does the bridegroom manage to convince the hotel desk manager (symbolic of death) to let him have the key to his room. *Labyrinth*, which called for the use of a variety of trick camera shots and effects, was successfully introduced by the NBC Opera Company over the NBC-TV network on March 3, 1963.

Menotti's later works included a dramatic cantata—his first. He called it *Death of the Bishop of Brindisi*, and it was heard on May 18, 1963, at the Cincinnati May Music Festival (which had commissioned it). Here the main action takes place at the death bed of the bishop, who recalls how he sent out an army of infants on a children's crusade that proved disastrous. Much of the effect of the opera springs from the touching music that Menotti wrote for children's voices.

Martin's Lie, introduced at the Bath Festival in England on June 3, 1964, is a one-act opera set in medieval England. It tells of a boy who has to make a choice between truth and his love for another human being. Commissioned by CBS, it was telecast by that network on January 24, 1965.

Menotti also wrote two concert works in the 1960's. One was a set of songs for voice and piano, *Canti della Lontananza*, which Elisabeth Schwarzkopf introduced in New York City on March 18, 1967. The other was the *Triple Concerto*, a concerto for three solo instruments and orchestra, commissioned by the Samuel Rubin Foundation for a world première performance in 1969 by the American Symphony Orchestra under Leopold Stokowski.

Winthrop Sargeant in *Life* describes Menotti as "a handsome, rather rangy Americanized Italian . . . a polished yet boyish and quietly exuberant individual with a poet's absent-mindedness, a fiction writer's irreverence for fact, and an insatiable curiosity about people." Sargeant further tells us that Menotti's "conversation is apt to consist entirely of superlatives"; that "he loves horror stories, magicians, and spiritual mediums"; that he is a "deeply preoccupied driver" who has "collided with numerous roadside warning lights while piloting his car to and from Manhattan"; and that he is also "an occasional and hopelessly incompetent devotee of tennis... [and] a prodigious gossip with an obsessive interest in the private lives of others."

When in New York he shares a rambling eight-room house called "Capricorn," in suburban Mt. Kisco, with the composer Samuel Barber and the poet Robert Horan. Each has a studio in a different part of the house. Menotti's is just about large enough to accommodate him and his grand piano. There he follows such interests as bird breeding, collecting paintings and sculpture, and enjoying heated conversations with stimulating visitors and friends.

He never had much interest in either making money or accumulating it. However, since 1958, when he founded the Festival of Two Worlds in Spoleto, Italy, and as its director made it an annual summer event, he has become more than passingly concerned in ways and means of putting his hands on large sums, since the running of the festival entails enormous expenditures. He also needs money to finance American students in Italy and Italian students in America; to send some indigent child to a hospital, when necessary; to pay bills for some friend fallen upon hard times. "I am terribly conscious of the world around me," is the way he has explained his charitable deeds to Samuel Chotzinoff. "The sense of guilt is, I think, a witness to my character. To satisfy my desire of feeling useful, I waste my time in unending, useless kindnesses. If I weren't a composer I probably would be a nurse in a hospital. . . . Spoleto satisfies my craving to be useful, to help people."

Chotzinoff explains that though Menotti may be a "St. Francis among musicians, distributing his wealth to the needy," he is also "a confessed hedonist." Chotzinoff notes still other contradictions in Menotti's nature. "He is at one and the same time shrewd, tender, worldly, spiritual, unworldly, sensual, and self-critical."

From the time he founded the Festival of Two Worlds in Spoleto, Italy, in 1958, Menotti served as its president and artistic director. In 1967, to relieve himself of many of the administrative duties required for the running of a highly successful annual festival, he created the post of general manager for Massimo Bogianckino and appointed Thomas Schippers musical director. At the same time Menotti retained the post of president. It was under Bogianckino's regime, on July 6, 1968, that an opera by Menotti was produced for the first time at the festival. The opera was *The Saint of Bleecker Street*.

MAJOR WORKS

Ballets—Sebastian; Errand into the Maze.

Choral Music—Death of the Bishop of Brindisi, cantata.

Operas—Martin's Lie (one-act opera); Amelia Goes to the Ball (one-act opera); The Old Maid and the Thief (one-act radio opera); The Island God; The Medium; The Telephone (one-act opera); The Consul; Amahl and the Night Visitors (one-act television opera); The Saint of Bleecker Street; The Unicorn, the Gorgon and the Manticore (a madrigal-fable); Maria Golovin; The Last Savage, opera buffa; Labyrinth; Help, Help, the Globolinks.

Orchestral Music—Piano Concerto; Apocalypse, tone poem; Violin Concerto; Triple Concerto.

Vocal Music—Canti della Lontananza, for voice and piano.

ABOUT

Ewen, D. (ed.), The New Book of Modern Composers.

Holiday, June 1963; New York Times Magazine, March 19, 1950; Theatre Arts, September 1951; Time (cover story), May 1, 1950.

Olivier Messiaen
1908–

Olivier Eugène Prosper Messiaen was born on December 10, 1908, in Avignon, France. His father was a professor of literature who translated Shakespeare into French. His mother, Cécile Sauvage, was a celebrated poet; when her son was born she wrote one of her finest poems, *L'Âme en Bourgeon*.

Messiaen spent his childhood in Grenoble. There he first revealed his exceptional talent for music. He began to compose when he was seven, and soon after began to teach himself to play the piano. Performances of Mozart's *Don Giovanni*, Berlioz' *The Damnation of Faust*, and Gluck's *Alceste*, and the published score of Debussy's *Pelléas et Mélisande* exerted an early

---

Messiaen: mĕ syän′

but important influence on him. Shakespeare's plays also made a deep impression.

When the family moved to Nantes, Messiaen began informal study of harmony. On the advice of Robert Lortat and Louis Vuillemin, he went to Paris in 1919 to enter the Conservatory. For the next eleven years he studied there with Dukas, Dupré, and Maurice Emmanuel, among others. He won every prize available. During this period he made a private and extensive study of rhythm—not only rhythm in Western music but also, as he explained, "Hindu and Greek rhythms, and rhythms of the stars, atoms, bird songs and the human body." Rhythm never lost its fascination for him, and he continually explored all its possibilities. He eventually prepared a rhythm dictionary which incorporated the basic rhythms of the Eastern and Western worlds as well as of ancient Greek music; and in later years he sometimes described himself as a "*rythmicien.*"

OLIVIER MESSIAEN

His first compositions, written while he was still at the Conservatory, contain the seeds of his later mature style and esthetic aims. In 1928 he wrote a twenty-five-measure piece for organ, *Le Banquet Céleste*, in which he first revealed the impact of the Catholic Church and religious mysticism upon his musical thinking and inspiration. This was followed in 1929 by eight preludes for piano which, a year later, became Messiaen's first publication.

He was graduated from the Conservatory

in 1930, and in 1931 he was appointed organist of the Trinité Church in Paris. He first became generally known as a composer on February 19, 1931, at a Straram concert which introduced *Les Offrandes Oubliées*, a highly original orchestral work of strong religious nature. Its three parts (subtitled "The Cross," "The Sin," and "The Eucharist") were based on a program published in the score which began with the following lines: "With arms extended, sad unto death, on the Cross, sheddest Thou Thy Blood. Thou lovest us Gentle Jesus, but we had forgotten."

In a similarly religious vein *L'Ascension*, comprising four "symphonic meditations," is one of Messiaen's most popular works for orchestra. It originated in 1934 as pieces for organ, but soon after was orchestrated. The text, derived from Catholic liturgy and Scripture, describes Christ's prayers to the Holy Father and the responses made by His followers to His words. *L'Ascension* was first given at a concert of the Paris Conservatory Orchestra under Charles Münch in 1945.

Still another profoundly religious work, written for the organ, was *La Nativité du Seigneur* (1935), nine Christmas meditations which, in publication, was preceded by a two-page note outlining some of Messiaen's musical beliefs and aims. (Many of Messiaen's compositions contain similar introductory essays describing his technical and esthetic aims.) Two movements from this organ opus helped to introduce Messiaen to England when he performed them on June 22, 1938, in London at the festival of the International Society for Contemporary Music. Another important organ work of religious character followed in 1939, on the eve of World War II. This was *Les Corps Glorieux*, "seven brief visions," in which Messiaen made important experiments in rhythm and tone color. It was performed for the first time in Paris on April 15, 1945, with the composer at the organ.

By 1939, the strength and originality of Messiaen's music had begun to impress French musicians. One of them was Georges Auric, who wrote: "His fresh inspiration and extremely personal accent at once compelled attention. . . . I shall be much surprised if we have not in Olivier Messiaen one of the future masters of French music."

Meanwhile, in 1936, Messiaen identified

himself with a group of young French composers in a "school" self-styled "La Jeune France," which he helped to organize for the purpose of promoting new French music. This school—which included Daniel Lesur, Yves Baudrier, and André Jolivet, together with Messiaen—made its official appearance on June 3 in a concert at the Salle Gaveau in Paris.

Of the four composers in La Jeune France, Messiaen proved the most original thinker and the most forceful and individual creator. His music became increasingly complex as it began to assimilate polymodal and polyrhythmic devices, intricate rhythm patterns derived from Hindu sources, the modes of plainsongs, and unusual timbres and colors. His main interest lay in rhythm. "The rhythmic pattern of a work is more interesting to me than the melodic or harmonic," he wrote. He delighted in transposing melodic, harmonic, and structural devices rhythmically, thereby writing rhythmic fugues and canons, for example. In some of his works, he had different instruments carry on independent and characteristic rhythmic patterns that appear and reappear in the compositions the way a melodic motive does in a Wagnerian music drama.

From 1936 to 1939 Messiaen taught composition at both the Schola Cantorum and the École Normale de Musique. Messiaen was spending the summer of 1939 in the Dauphine, where he was putting the finishing touches on *Les Corps Glorieux*, when World War II broke out. Called to uniform, he was captured by the Germans and interned for two years as a prisoner of war in Stalag VIII-A in Görlitz, Silesia. In the prison camp he managed to write one of his most eloquent chamber music works, *Quatuor pour la Fin du Temps* (*Quartet for the End of Time*), in eight sections. "Only music," he later revealed, "made me survive the cruelty of the horrors of the camp." The Quartet was performed for the first time at the prison camp on January 15, 1941, with the composer at the piano; some five thousand prisoners were in the audience. "Never was I listened to with such rapt attention and such comprehension," the composer has remarked.

This Quartet was one of the first major works to introduce Messiaen to American audiences. When it was performed in New York on January 30, 1946, Howard Taubman said in the New York *Times:* "Messiaen's talent is

abundant; his musical ideas, like his titles, suggest an overflowing, if restless, mind. . . . This quartet has memorable things—long-breathed passages full of mystery and poetry as well as pages of vibrant, yet controlled, fervor. . . . A richly endowed composer, Messiaen is beyond a shadow of a doubt a man with a voice and personality of his own."

Visions de l'Amen was another important work completed during the war years. This is a seven-movement composition for two pianos (1942), introduced in Paris by the composer and Yvonne Loriod on May 10, 1943. "I know of only one other two-piano work which seems of equal importance," wrote Davidson Taylor in *Modern Music,* "and that is Brahms's *Variations on a Theme by Haydn.*" He described Messiaen's composition as "full of the music of bells, mellow bells and cracked harsh bells like those of Rennes, near bells and distant bells, deep bells, and high and delicate bells."

Upon being released from prison camp and repatriated in 1942, Messiaen resumed his organ post at the Trinité church. At the same time he became professor of harmony at the Paris Conservatory where, in 1947, a special class was created for him in the analysis and esthetics of rhythm. His pupils included Karlheinz Stockhausen and Pierre Boulez. Since that time, he has been giving courses in composition at the Conservatory and has further helped young musicians by founding the Olivier Messiaen piano competition at the Royan Music Festival.

Two large works were completed in 1944. *Vingt Regards sur l'Enfant Jésus*, for piano, is of such vast design that it requires two and a half hours for performance. Messiaen's pupil, later his second wife, Yvonne Loriod, introduced it in Paris on March 26, 1945. This work, extending for some one hundred and seventy-five printed pages, is built from a motto theme, whose theological and musical significance is discussed by the composer in an elaborate explanatory preface. The individual pieces are variants of a simple choral melody. "This theme," explained Olin Downes, "irregularly rhythmed and harmonized in a manner that is self-conscious but certainly not devoid of charm, is the center of arabesques of tone flung about it in a glowing, dreamlike way."

Trois Petites Liturgies de la Présence Divine (1944) was an extension of the composer's experiments with tone colors. Scored for a unison soprano choir, accompanied by celesta, vibraphone, maracas, Chinese cymbals, gong, piano, Ondes Martenot (electronic music), and strings, it achieved its effect through unusual timbres and sound qualities. Introduced in Paris, under the direction of Roger Désormière, on April 21, 1945, the composition aroused considerable controversy.

But Messiaen had not abandoned his experiments with rhythm. In 1948 he completed his most ambitious exercise in rhythmic methods with *Turangalíla*, a ten-movement symphony which he had written on a commission from the Koussevitzky Music Foundation. It received its world première in Boston, December 2, 1949, Leonard Bernstein conducting. The basic element of this mammoth symphony is rhythm. The composer explained that the work was written in "a very special rhythmic language, and makes use of several new rhythmic principles, including nonreversible rhythms, asymmetric rhythms, augmentations with several rhythmic identities, rhythmic modes, and so forth." An immense percussion section is utilized, including temple blocks, wood block, small cymbal, suspended cymbal, Chinese cymbal, gong, tambourine, triangle, maracas, side drum, suave drum, bass drum, and eight tubular bells. In addition to the usual winds and strings, the orchestra is supplemented by the Ondes Martenot and a piano, with extended virtuoso parts written for the latter made up of chord clusters and bird songs. "The orchestra," commented Olin Downes, "is the biggest, oddest, and on occasion, the noisiest, ever."

A few months before the world première of this symphony, Messiaen paid his first visit to the United States to teach a master class in composition at the Berkshire Music Center at Tanglewood. He returned to the United States at the end of the year to attend the première of his symphony.

After writing *Turangalíla*, Messiaen lapsed into a kind of creative fatigue which induced an extended period of silence. This was a time when, in his own words, he felt that "all seemed lost, when the way is no longer clear, when one has nothing more to say." In the *New Statesman*, David Drew explained that this was a period when "his pupils were, so to speak, taking 'the way' from him and continuing it to

a point remote from his own creative ideals." The pupils here referred to included Boulez and Stockhausen, who received their direction and inspiration from Messiaen only to progress in such fresh areas as serial, electronic, and aleatory music. "His near silence at that time," wrote Drew, "when it would have been easy for him to ride the new wave he himself had helped to set into motion, was, I think, one of the most noble gestures in his career. It cost him the dubious advantages of fashionable approval, but it gave him the privacy he needed if he was to reconsider the nature of his art and rediscover its energies."

Creative regeneration came in the middle 1950's. The songs, sounds, and voices of birds which he had first simulated in *Turangalíla* now absorbed Messiaen's interest. More and more he devoted himself to the study of bird songs, even to the point of having regular consultations with an ornithologist. In 1952 his *Organ Book* combined complex rhythmic practices with bird calls. In 1953 came the *Réveil des Oiseaux*, a piano concerto heard at the Donaueschingen Festival in Germany on October 11. In the concerto some thirty different bird songs are used. There followed *Oiseaux Exotiques*, for piano solo, small wind orchestra, and percussion (first performance in Paris on March 10, 1956), in which voices of birds from exotic lands and climes are sounded; and the *Première Catalogue des Oiseaux*, for piano solo, introduced in Paris, April 15, 1959.

Messiaen's most ambitious work inspired by songs and calls of birds is the *Chronochromie*, in seven parts—the title combining the Greek words for "time" and "color" may be translated *Color of Time*. This music is based on materials from bird songs from various lands including those in the Orient; the sounds of waterfalls are also simulated. To David Drew this composition represents the synthesis of Messiaen's creative trend since the middle 1950's. He called it "one of the cardinal works of the postwar years." Then he added: "Its prodigality of harmonic and linear invention is an object lesson to the minor avant-garde. . . . I, for one, have still not found my way through the fantastic forest of the eighteen-part polyphony which forms the crucial penultimate section." It was heard first at the Donaueschingen Festival, October 16, 1960, Hans Rosbaud conducting, and was later presented at the festival of the International Society for Contemporary Music at Vienna, June 19, 1961. Melodic and rhythmic material based on songs and calls of birds also influenced the writing of *Couleurs de la Cité Céleste* (1963) and *Et Exspecto Resurrectionem Mortuorum* (1964).

Messiaen once detailed the influences that helped shape his career: "My mother, the poet Cécile Sauvage; my wife, the composer Claire Delbos (she died in 1959); Shakespeare; Claudel; Reverdy and Éluard; Ernest Hello and Dom Columba Marmion (dare I speak of the Holy Scriptures, which contain the only Truth?); birds; Russian music; the great *Pelléas et Mélisande;* plainsong; Hindu rhythms; the mountains of Dauphine; and, finally, that which pertains to stained glass windows and rainbows."

Though he has concerned himself only passingly with electronic music, and mainly through the exploitations of the Ondes Martenot instrument, and though he has made only a single excursion—with *Timbres Durées* in 1952—into *musique concrète* (concrete music: the composition by tape-recording of freely selected and treated sounds and natural noises into an artistically ordered continuum), Messiaen is convinced of the importance of electronics in musical creativity. He has said: "Each epoch has its own musical language, which dictates the musical means to be used. The music of the Renaissance applied itself perfectly to vocal music and to a cappella choruses; that of the eighteenth century to the orchestra and string quartet; that of the nineteenth, to opera and the piano. The music of the twentieth will probably find its definitive realization in electronic means."

Following the death of his first wife (by whom he had a son), Messiaen married Yvonne Loriod, the concert pianist. She had been one of his first pupils at the Paris Conservatory and the first to perform his *Vingt Regards sur l'Enfant Jésus*. They make their home in Paris, but they are happiest in their little villa, their summer retreat in the Alps. He is Grand Officier de l'Ordre National du Mérite and Commandeur des Arts et des Lettres. In 1963 he received the Prix Florent Schmitt from the Académie des Beaux-Arts.

On December 12, 1967, Messiaen made his New York debut as a performer by participating with his wife in the presentation of his *Visions de l'Amen* at an all-Messiaen program celebrating his fifty-ninth birthday.

MAJOR WORKS

Chamber Music—Theme and Variations, for violin and piano; Fantaisie, for violin and piano; Quatuor pour le Fin du Temps, for violin, clarinet, cello, and piano.

Choral Music—Mass, for eight sopranos and four violins; O Sacrum Convivium; Chœurs pour une Jeanne d'Arc; Trois Petites Liturgies de la Présence Divine; Cinq Rechants.

Opera—Transfiguration.

Orchestral Music—Le Banquet Eucharistique; Simple Chant d'une Âme; Les Offrandes Oubliées; Le Tombeau Resplendissant; Hymne au Saint Sacrement; L'Ascension; Poèmes pour Mi, for soprano and orchestra; Turangalîla; Le Réveil des Oiseaux, for piano and orchestra; Oiseaux Exotiques; 7 Hai-Kai, for piano solo and small orchestra; Chronochromie; Couleurs de la Cité Céleste, for winds, brass, percussion, and piano; Et Exspecto Resurrectionem Mortuorum, for winds, brass, and percussion.

Organ Music—Le Banquet Céleste; L'Hôte Aimable des Âmes; Diptyque; Apparition de l'Église Éternelle; La Nativité du Seigneur; Les Corps Glorieux; Messe de la Pentecôte; Le Livre d'Orgue.

Piano Music—Eight Preludes; Rondeau; Visions de l'Amen, for two pianos; Vingt Regards sur l'Enfant Jésus; Mode de Valeurs et d'Intensité; Neumes Rythmiques; Île de Feu, two volumes; Quatre Études de Rythme; Première Catalogue des Oiseaux.

Vocal Music—Le Mort du Nombre, for soprano, tenor, violin, and piano; Trois Mélodies; Vocalise; Chants de Terre et de Ciel; Harawi, Chant d'Amour et de Mort.

ABOUT

Goléa, A., Vingt Ans de Musique Contemporaine; Goléa, A., Rencontres avec Olivier Messiaen; Messiaen, P., Images; Rostand, C., La Musique Française Contemporaine; Samuel, C., Panorama de l'Art Musical Contemporain; Zinke-Bianchini, V., Olivier Messiaen: Notice Biographique.

Musical Quarterly, April 1950; New Statesman (London), November 9, 1962; New York Times, December 3, 1967; Score (London), December 1954, September and December, 1955.

Nikolai Miaskovsky
1881–1950

Nikolai Yakovlevitch Miaskovsky was born in the fortress of Novogeorgievsk, near Warsaw (then in Russia), on April 20, 1881. His father was an army engineer, a specialist in military fortifications, who wanted his son to follow in his footsteps. Music, therefore, remained a hobby for Nikolai for a long time while he prepared himself for a career in engineering.

Miaskovsky: myä skôf′ skē

He entered the Cadet School in Nizhny Novgorod in 1893. Two years later he enrolled in a military school in St. Petersburg. Upon completing his studies in 1889, he became an army engineer.

NIKOLAI MIASKOVSKY

Meanwhile, music had begun to assume an increasingly significant role in his life. He had been drawn to it from childhood. "The decisive moment arrived when I heard a piano duet of some piece that stirred me profoundly," he told his biographer, Alexei Ikkonikov. "I later found out, not without considerable pains, that it was a potpourri from Mozart's *Don Giovanni*. Then began pleadings for a musical education. We finally hired a piano and my aunt began to teach me."

Upon arriving in St. Petersburg in 1895 he found a piano teacher in Stuneyev, a relative of Glinka's wife. At the same time he began for the first time to study harmony, with N. Kazanli. Stimulated by these lessons and by concerts (a performance conducted by Artur Nikisch in 1896 proved a particularly unforgettable experience), Miaskovsky at fifteen made his first efforts at composition by writing preludes for the piano, mainly influenced by Chopin.

In 1903 he took a six-month course in harmony with Glière, which finally persuaded him to choose music over engineering. With that in mind, for three years he studied theory with Kryzhanovsky, who was responsible for interesting him in some of the more progressive tendencies in music. In 1906 Miaskovsky entered the Conservatory at St. Petersburg where he attended the classes of Liadov and Rimsky-Korsakov.

His creative life was expanding. While still at the Conservatory he wrote some piano, vocal, and symphonic compositions. More important, he made his debut as a composer of symphonies, the first one, in C minor, being written in 1908, although its première did not take place until June 2, 1914, in Pavlovsk. The one-time influence of Chopin had by now been superseded by that of Tchaikovsky, accompanied by occasional excursions into Impressionist writing. On the strength of this symphony he was given a Glazunov scholarship which provided him with the funds to complete his musical education.

After being graduated from the Conservatory in 1911, he completed his Second Symphony, in C-sharp minor, introduced on July 24, 1912. This, and the second piano sonata in F-sharp minor (1912), showed an increasing independence of style and thought. Prokofiev described the sonata as possessing "nobility of material, carefulness of workmanship, and a general attractiveness which render it one of the most interesting sonatas of modern times." A third symphony, in A minor, completed just before the outbreak of World War I, had its première during the war, on February 27, 1915.

When war broke out in 1914, Miaskovsky was called to active service. For three years he was at the front with the Russian army. Wounded and shell-shocked, he was transferred in February 1917 to Reval to work on military fortifications. From 1918 until he was demobilized in 1921, he was a functionary in the Maritime Headquarters in Moscow.

In 1921 Miaskovsky was appointed professor of composition at the Moscow Conservatory, a post he held with distinction until the end of his life. His many pupils included Khatchaturian, Kabalevsky, Muradeli, and Shebalin. He was active in other musical areas as well. From 1921 to 1922 he was assistant director of the music department of the People's Commissariat, and from 1922 to 1931 he was the editor of the Music Publishing House. He subsequently served as consultant for music broadcasts on the All-Union Radio Committee, was on the editorial staff of *Sovetskaya*

368

Muzyka, and held a leading position in the Union of Soviet Composers. The title Artist of Merit was conferred on him in 1926 in conjunction with the sixtieth anniversary of the Moscow Conservatory, and in 1940 he received the honorary degree of Doctor of Arts.

The revolution in Russia had a profound influence on Miaskovsky's creative development. Before that time, his music had been both derivative and completely subjective. After the Revolution he used his music not so much to express personal reactions and emotional responses (a good deal of his writing up to this point had been profoundly melancholy), but primarily to reflect events in his country and the ideologies of the new regime. At the same time, he achieved a greater simplicity of style together with a folk song lyricism. He never embraced the more advanced tendencies of some of his famous colleagues in the Soviet Union, but he was more flexible in his use of harmony and tonality than had previously been his practice.

He produced much instrumental music and many songs, while avoiding the stage. His greatest successes—and his prime importance—came with his symphonies. He wrote twenty-seven in all, thus earning the distinction of having written more works in this form than any other twentieth century composer.

Nicolas Slonimsky has divided Miaskovsky's symphonic output into four distinct periods: "The first period from the First to the Sixth is typical of his pre-Revolutionary moods, introspective and at the same time mystical. . . . His second symphonic period, from the Seventh to the Twelfth Symphony, symbolizes a path from the 'subjective' to the 'objective,' from the individual to the collective. Without trying to be literal in programmatic descriptions of the life in the Soviet Union of that period, he nevertheless went for inspiration to the fields and factories of the country. . . . The third period, from the Thirteenth to the Eighteenth Symphony, represents a synthesis of subjective moods and objective realistic ideas. . . . The Nineteenth Symphony is the beginning of a new phase, almost utilitarian in character. Miaskovsky's symphonic writing here becomes more compact, more directly addressed to the masses."

The first symphony in which his style can be said to have become crystallized is the Sixth, in E-flat minor (1922), first performed in Moscow on May 4, 1924. This music is inspired by such French revolutionary songs as "Ça Ira" and the "Carmagnole," which served to ignite Miaskovsky's own revolutionary ardor—an ardor that expressed itself in passionate, virile outbursts. In the closing movement, in which a chorus is heard in a wordless chant, the composer introduces a quotation from the *Dies Irae*, without ever explaining the reason for the interpolation.

Another important symphony is the Twelfth, in G minor (1932), celebrating the fifteenth anniversary of the October Revolution. Its première took place on June 1, 1932. The most famous of all the Miaskovsky symphonies, the one to gain universal acclaim, is the Twenty-first, in F-sharp minor (1940), which was commissioned by the Chicago Symphony. It received its première, however, not in the United States but in Moscow, on November 16, 1940. (When the work was given by the Chicago Symphony under Frederick Stock, five weeks later, it appeared under the name *Symphonie-Fantaisie*, which has since become the subtitle.) The symphony enjoyed extraordinary success at its première, with the audience shouting for an encore, an occurrence with few parallels in Soviet concert halls. The distinguished Soviet musicologist Gregory Schneerson called it one of the composer's "most noble works." He continued: "The great quality of this composition lies in the combination of impressive beauty of conception with a plasticity of musical images, profundity of content, perfection of form and integrity of structure. . . . In this relatively small work, there is concentrated an enormous life-asserting force, which receives its magnificent expression in the powerful culmination of the development section." On March 15, 1941, the symphony received the Stalin Prize. Its first performance in the United States took place over the CBS radio network on August 23, 1942, with Bernard Herrmann conducting.

Among Miaskovsky's other orchestral compositions, the most popular has been the Sinfonietta for string orchestra (1929), heard in Moscow in May 1930. This is more subjective than most of the works of his later period, a fact that may explain its immediate success. Its rich lyricism is at times tinged with a gentle melancholy.

Miaskovsky

Miaskovsky was also a prolific composer of chamber music, having produced thirteen string quartets. The best of the earlier ones are the second, in C minor (1930), and the fifth, in E minor (1939). Both are characteristic; both seek, says Ikkonikov, "increasingly refined and intricate modes of expression." Ikkonikov regards the fifth quartet with particular favor for "the simplicity of musical ideas, its emotional content and superb form of expression." Of the later quartets, the ninth, in E minor (1943), has had the widest circulation.

When World War II came, it did not interrupt Miaskovsky's creativity. "I worked intensively in those days, even in bomb shelters," he revealed. "After completing three songs and two military marches, I conceived the idea of a Symphonic Ballad. It was finished in October, during the stern days of the Hitlerite offensive against Moscow. . . . Late autumn found me in Kabardino-Balkaria, a small Caucasian republic whose people have a wealth of wonderful songs and dances. Here, in the town of Nalchik, I wrote another symphony, my Twenty-third, whose theme was inspired by Kabardino-Balkarian national music. Then I completed a string quartet in three movements, dedicated to the memory of those who perished for my country. It reflects one thought: the blood which has been spilled has not been in vain."

The Symphonic Ballad Miaskovsky refers to in the quotation above is the Symphony No. 22, heard in Tiflis on January 12, 1942; the Twenty-third symphony commented upon (A minor) was given on July 20, 1942; and the string quartet referred to was his eighth, in F-sharp minor (1942). In addition to these compositions, Miaskovsky produced a cello concerto which has enjoyed high esteem both inside and outside the Soviet Union. It was completed in 1944, was introduced by Sviatoslav Kushentzky on March 17, 1945, and received the Stalin Prize.

Despite the fact that Miaskovsky occupied a place of such significance in Soviet music, both as a composer and teacher, he did not escape censure when the Central Committee of the Communist Party issued its official denunciation of leading Soviet composers in February 1948 (see sketch on Prokofiev). While Miaskovsky's music was not treated so severely as the works of Prokofiev and Shostakovich,

Miaskovsky was criticized for the frequent pessimistic overtones of his writing and for his teaching methods, which, the committee said, injected "inharmonious music into the Soviet educational system."

Miaskovsky died in Moscow on August 9, 1950, a year and a half after this indictment. In announcing his death, the Soviet Council of Ministers described him as "this outstanding Soviet musical worker and people's artist."

Miaskovsky has written as follows about his aims as a composer: "The first thing I demand from music in general is directness of appeal, power, and nobility of expression; music that does not satisfy these three requirements does not exist for me, or if it does exist, then it does so solely for utilitarian purposes. I always consider a piece of music from three points of view: its content, its inner and its outer form. . . . Of the three elements enumerated, I consider the first two to be absolutely essential. I admire good outer form, but I can make allowances for imperfections in it provided the first two elements are beyond reproach."

MAJOR WORKS

Chamber Music—13 string quartets; 2 cello sonatas; Violin Sonata.

Choral Music—Feather Grass; Wings of the Soviets; In Valor's Name; Lenin, cantata; Karl Marx, cantata; Partisans; Kirov Is with Us, cantata; Marching Songs.

Orchestral Music—27 symphonies; 2 Sinfoniettas; Silence, tone poem; Alastor, tone poem; Serenade, for small orchestra; Lyric Concertino in G major, for small orchestra; Concerto for Violin and Orchestra in D minor; Salutatory Overture; Cello Concerto.

Piano Music—9 sonatas; Espiègleries, seven volumes; Whimsies; Reminiscences; Yellowed Leaves; Children's Pieces, three albums; Sonatina in A minor; Rhapsody in B-flat minor.

Vocal Music—Meditations; On the Threshhold; Unseen; Madrigal; Premonitions; At the Close of Day; Faded Garland; various other songs for solo voice and piano.

ABOUT

Ikkonikov, A. I., Miaskovsky: His Life and Work; Sabaneyev, L., Modern Russian Composers; Saminsky, L., Music of Our Day; Shifstein, S. (ed.), Miaskovsky: Articles, Letters, Reminiscences.

American Quarterly on the Soviet Union, April 1938.

Francisco Mignone
1897–

Francisco Mignone was born in São Paulo, Brazil, on September 3, 1897. His father, a flautist, gave him his first music lessons. Subsequently, Francisco received some piano training, following which he was enrolled in the São Paulo Conservatory. During this period he supported himself by playing the piano in a motion picture theatre—"beating out on a piano the staccato rhythm of horses' hoofbeats and the fusillades of bandits trapped in the lair," as he later recalled. From pianist he soon was elevated to the position of conductor and musical arranger of the theatre.

FRANCISCO MIGNONE

He also wrote music. From the first he was attracted to native Brazilian music, and in his writing he utilized Indian, African, and Portuguese elements of Brazilian folk music. In 1918 he officially emerged as a composer when he performed several of his piano pieces at a concert in São Paulo. On December 16 of the same year his father directed the first public performance of one of Francisco's orchestral compositions, the *Suite Campestre*.

A grant from São Paulo, which was extended for seven years, enabled Mignone to go to Milan in 1920. There he studied composition with Ferroni. Influenced by his background, as well as by his visits to La Scala, he com-

Mignone: mē nyō′ nä

pleted a full-length opera set in eighteenth century Brazil, the music strongly influenced by Brazilian folk songs and dances. *O Contratador dos Diamentes* was produced in Rio de Janeiro on September 20, 1924, and proved so successful that a music room was named after Mignone at the São Paulo Conservatory. One of the dance interludes in the opera, "Congada," has since become one of its composer's most frequently played orchestral pieces. It was heard for the first time, under the title *Dansa*, even before the opera was given, in Rio de Janeiro on September 10, 1922, the composer conducting. In 1923 it was performed in Germany, and in 1940 Toscanini conducted it in New York.

A second opera, *L'Innocente*—set in old-world Spain, but with music still derived from Brazilian folk sources—was mounted in Rio de Janeiro on September 5, 1928. In each of the two operas, Mignone used an Italian libretto.

After nine years in Europe, Mignone returned to his native city in 1929. He became professor of harmony and piano at the Conservatory. Later he filled a similar post at the Rio de Janeiro Conservatory, which he had helped to found. In 1941 he played an important role in revolutionizing music education in Brazil when, with the collaboration of Villa-Lobos, he helped revise and modernize the music curriculum of all of the schools of Brazil. In 1942 he toured the United States as conductor and pianist on an invitation from the Department of State, in a cultural exchange of musicians between the United States and South America.

Many of Mignone's works are strongly rhythmical, reminiscent of the Negro dances of Brazil, and are expressive in their lyricism and imaginative in their harmonic structure. Many musicians have come to regard Mignone as the musical voice of his country. The Italian government has conferred upon him a medal for his artistic achievements; and in 1957 the German government invited him to conduct a program of Brazilian music with the Berlin Philharmonic. In the United States among the most successful of his earlier compositions (apart from "Congada") is *Four Fantasias Brasileiras*, for piano and orchestra (1937), music magnetizing in its rhythmic dash and pianistic bravura. Also successful were

Mignone

Momus, a humorous sketch for orchestra introduced in Rio de Janeiro on April 24, 1933; and *Church Windows* (*Festa das Igrejas*), a graphic description of the ideas and emotions inspired by the festivals of the Catholic Church in Brazil. *Church Windows* was heard first during Mignone's visit to the United States in 1942, when he directed a performance with the NBC Symphony over a coast-to-coast radio hookup on April 22. Here we find a trend in Mignone's creativity away from nationalism.

In 1946 Mignone was named Brazil's "best composer of the year," after the successful première of his ballet *Iara*. (*Iara* was introduced in the United States at the Metropolitan Opera in New York by the Russian Ballet in 1946.) He produced a major work for chorus— an oratorio of monumental design—in *Alegrias de Nossa Senhora*, the world première of which took place in Rio de Janeiro on July 15, 1949. He also wrote several works with social messages—for example, his successful *Symphony of Labor* (*Sinfonia da Trabalho*), the four movements of which are given the titles "Song of the Machine," "Song of the Family," "Song of the Strong Man," and "Song of Fruitful Work."

In the years 1950–1952 Mignone completed two symphonies for large orchestra which were never published or performed. But other orchestral compositions after 1950 received important performances and proved very successful. These included his Piano Concerto (first performed in Rio de Janeiro on July 10, 1958) and his violin concerto which received a government prize as the best new symphonic work of the year, following its première in Rio de Janeiro on April 23, 1961. April 7, 1965, saw the première of his *Imagens do Rio de Janeiro*, a set of symphonic impressions written in commemoration of the fourth centennial of the city.

Among other important later works by Mignone are three Masses for mixed chorus (1960, 1963, and 1964); his Second Quintet for Winds (1960), first performed at the United States Embassy in Rio de Janeiro, on July 3, 1960; two piano sonatas (1961, 1965); and a violin sonata (1965) which had its world première in Warsaw on February 15, 1966, in a performance by Arnaldo Estrêla and Mariuccia Iacovino.

As one of Brazil's outstanding composers, Mignone has held numerous important positions. In 1949 and 1950 he was a member of the artistic and cultural commission of the Teatro Municipal, which he served as director from 1950 to 1952. In 1958 he was the principal conductor of the Brazilian Symphony, and from 1962 to 1964 he served as the musical director of the Radio Station of the Ministry of Education and Culture. During 1966 he occupied the chair of full professor at the School of Music of the University of Rio de Janeiro.

He was named "honorary citizen" of Rio de Janeiro in 1954, and he has received honorary professorships from the Institute of Fine Arts of Pôrto Alegre, the Conservatory of Peoltas, and the Santa Cecilia Conservatory at Santos.

In addition to his serious compositions, Mignone has written a number of popular songs and dances to which he affixed the pseudonym of "Chico-Bororo."

MAJOR WORKS

Ballets—Maracatú de Chico-Rei; O Espantalho; Leilão; Batucagé; Babaloxá; Miudinho; Iara; Quadros Amazonicos.

Chamber Music—2 violin sonatas; 2 wind quintets; 2 string quartets; Eight Pieces for violin and piano; Sextet, for piano, flute, oboe, clarinet, bassoon, and horn; Duets for Flute and Clarinet, and for Oboe and Bassoon; Quartet, for flute, oboe, clarinet, and bassoon; Flute Sonata; Viola Sonata.

Choral Music—3 Masses; Alegrias de Nossa Senhora, oratorio; Santa Clara, small oratorio; Six Chorals; Six Short Street-Corner Waltzes.

Operas—O Contratador dos Diamentes; L'Innocente.

Orchestral Music—2 symphonies for large orchestra; Suite Campestre; Caramurú; Congada; No Sertão; Interludo; Suite Asturiana; Notturno-Barcarola; Scenas da Roda; Festa Dionisiaca; Intermezzo Lirico; 4 Fantasias Brasileiras, for piano and orchestra; Momus; Maxixe; Suite Brasileira; Batucagé; Variations on a Brazilian Theme; Sonho de um Menino Travesso; Abertura das Tres Máscaras Perdidas; Sinfonia da Trabalho; Festa das Igrejas (Church Windows); Seresta, for cello and orchestra; Música No. 1; Concertina, for clarinet and small orchestra; Concertina, for bassoon and orchestra; Burlesca and Toccata, for piano and orchestra; Violin Concerto; Imagens do Rio de Janeiro.

Piano Music—3 sonatas; Six Preludes; Six Transcendental Etudes; Lenda Sertaneja; Four Sonatinas; Brazilian Waltz; Six Short Pieces.

Vocal Music—Poema das Cinco Canções.

ABOUT

Slonimsky, N., Music of Latin America.

Darius Milhaud
1892–

Darius Milhaud was born at Aix-en-Provence, in the south of France, on September 4, 1892. His father was a businessman, an exporter of almonds; his mother, a trained singer, was descended from a distinguished Italian family of Sephardic Jews.

DARIUS MILHAUD

Milhaud was attracted to music early. At four he played piano duets with his father; at seven he began studying the violin with Léo Bruguier; and at twelve he performed in a string quartet. "I was a well-behaved but rather neurotic child," he reveals in his autobiography, "continually subject to nervous attacks brought on by the slightest things." Music to this highly sensitive child became, as he notes, "a more and more imperious necessity." When he was thirteen he studied Debussy's String Quartet. He has said that this was "such a revelation to me that I hastened to buy the score of *Pelléas.*" Some lessons in harmony with Hambourg, conductor of a regimental band, stimulated his first creative efforts, and he completed a sonata for violin and piano.

In 1909 Milhaud was graduated from the Lycée Mignet at Aix, where he had specialized in philosophy. He went to Paris, found a room in a boarding house on the Boulevard des

Milhaud: mē lō′

Italiens, and immersed himself in musical activities. He attended concerts and opera performances and became acquainted with the music of Mussorgsky, Stravinsky, and Ravel, all of whom impressed him deeply. He also enrolled in the Conservatory, where his teachers included Leroux (harmony), Gedalge (counterpoint), d'Indy (composition), and Dukas (orchestration). He wrote music constantly. The first work he regards as "worthy of being preserved" was a violin sonata (1911) which received a public performance in Paris in 1913. In 1912 came his first opus, two sets of songs to poems by Francis Jammes. His first string quartet was also written in 1912. It was introduced in 1913. His first opera, *La Brebis Égarée* (text by Jammes), which he had begun in 1910, was finished in 1915, but its world première did not take place until December 10, 1923, when it was produced by the Opéra-Comique. In all of this early Milhaud music the influence of Debussy is evident.

In 1912, while still attending the Conservatory, Milhaud moved to an apartment on the Rue Gaillard. At the time, through Jammes, he met the man whose impact upon him and his musical development was decisive. That man was the poet and diplomat Paul Claudel. Claudel visited Milhaud on the Rue Gaillard one day. Milhaud recalls his own state of mind: "At the idea that the writer I revered more than any other was coming to see me, I was beside myself with excitement. Perhaps I was unconsciously aware that this meeting would decide what my life's work was going to be! ... Between Claudel and me, understanding was immediate, mutual confidence was absolute."

Claudel described to him a new setting of Aeschylus, *L'Orestie*, on which he was then working and suggested the kind of music he would like to have written for it. Milhaud played and sang for Claudel some of his compositions. That day not only was a close friendship sealed, but a new collaboration was born; for both agreed that Milhaud would set *L'Orestie* to music.

Before World War I erupted, Milhaud had not only completed music for *Agamemnon*—the first drama in Claudel's trilogy *L'Orestie*—but had also begun work on another Claudel play, *Protée*, a satiric comedy about the pathetic, hopeless love of an old man for a young girl. In time Milhaud prepared three different versions of the *Protée* score; the first came in 1913; the final one was written six years later.

World War I brought Milhaud's Conservatory schooling to an end. He returned to his native city to await the notice calling him into uniform. Meanwhile, he worked on a number of compositions, including his second string quartet. Upon being rejected for military service on medical grounds, Milhaud returned to Paris, where, in 1915, he received the Lepaulle Prize for composition for his Sonata for Two Violins and Piano ("the only time in my life I ever won an award," he remarks in his autobiography). Most of his creative activity, however, was centered upon the second drama in Claudel's trilogy—*Les Choëphores*—a score which he completed in 1915. This music is particularly notable as the first in which Milhaud made extensive use of polytonal writing, a technique which he developed and which would soon become a basic tool with many young composers. In "Libation," the a cappella chorus from the opera, he wrote in two different keys, one for male and one for female voices.

Another innovation in *Les Choëphores* was that some of the more violent dramatic episodes were spoken in time with the music "while the choruses uttered words or disjointed phrases, the rhythm but not the pitch of which was indicated," as the composer explained. At the same time, to support these "speech elements," Milhaud used percussion instruments with no definite pitch, including such noisemakers as whistles, a whip, and a board and hammer.

Les Choëphores may be said to have been the first of Milhaud's scores in which he emerged as one of the most original and forceful figures in twentieth century French music. The music was first heard in excerpts presented at a concert of the Société pour la Musique in Paris on June 15, 1919. The complete score was given in a concert version in Paris on March 8, 1927, the composer conducting; and the first staged version was presented in Brussels, March 27, 1935. The music was introduced in the United States in a concert version by the New York Philharmonic, November 16, 1950, Mitropoulos conducting.

"It is astounding," reported Robert Sabin in *Musical America*, "that a young man of twenty-three could conceive and execute so mighty a plan as that of *Les Choëphores*. The more one studies the score, the more one marvels at the surety of the style, the economy of means, and above all, the lucid, beautifully integrated texture of the work."

The complete trilogy *L'Orestie*, however, had to wait half a century for its première. This took place in West Berlin at a festival held in April 1963.

In 1916 Claudel became the French ambassador to Brazil. He invited Milhaud to accompany him as an attaché at the Legation. They reached Rio de Janeiro, February 1, 1917, when the city was in the midst of its carnival. Thus Milhaud came at once into contact with Brazilian popular music, folk songs and dances, and this music fascinated him: "There was an imperceptible pause in the syncopation, a careless catch in breath, a slight hiatus that I found very difficult to grasp. So I bought a lot of maxixes and tangos. . . . At last my efforts were rewarded and I could both play and analyze this typically Brazilian subtlety."

Several of Milhaud's compositions written in this period reveal the Brazilian influence. One is the ballet *L'Homme et Son Désir* (text by Paul Claudel), completed in 1918. Another is an orchestral suite of twelve Brazilian dances, *Saudades do Brasil* (1921), a *saudade* being a recollection. In the years following, Milhaud returned many times to melodies and rhythms of Brazilian folk music for major scores.

Towards the end of 1918 Milhaud left Brazil. After a brief stopover in New York in February 1919 (his first visit to the United States), Milhaud finally returned to France. At that time, he became identified with the new "school" of French composers known as "The French Six" (see sketch on Auric, above). His music was performed at concerts devoted to the compositions of the six composers forming the group, but Milhaud's association with the other five, however friendly, was tenuous artistically. He protested at being identified creatively with the others, even though he had the warmest of appreciation for their work and personal affection for each. Milhaud insisted that in writing his own music he had to follow his own path. Indeed, Milhaud was producing works so varied in style and approach that it would be futile to try to assemble them under any single artistic banner, or to identify them with any single school of composition.

Some of his music still remained rooted in Brazilian folk idioms. One of the most important of these works was the ballet *Le Bœuf sur le Toit*, with a text by Jean Cocteau. This music began as an instrumental fantasia in which Milhaud "assembled a few popular melodies, tangos, maxixes, sambas, and even a Portuguese *fado*, and transcribed them with a rondo-like theme recurring between two of them." Originally Milhaud wanted this music to serve as an accompaniment to a Charlie Chaplin movie. Jean Cocteau dissuaded him, however, and offered to prepare a ballet-pantomime scenario which would fit the music better. He did so in short order, using a bar in America during the Prohibition era as his setting and inventing characters and situations which in their absurdity anticipated the dada movement. Introduced in Paris on February 21, 1920, with the famous clown Fratellini in the principal role, *Le Bœuf sur le Toit* aroused interest, curiosity, and discussion. Some time later a now-famous bar in Paris adopted the title for its name.

Other Milhaud compositions were in a jazz idiom and style. In 1920, when Milhaud went to London to attend the performances of *Le Bœuf sur le Toit*, he had his first contact with American jazz, at Hammersmith, a London dance hall where Billy Arnold and his band were performing. After returning to Paris, Milhaud was further fascinated by American jazz through Jean Wiener and his partner Vance at the Bar Gaya on the Rue Duphot. These experiences led to the writing of *Caramel Mou*, a "shimmy," performed by a Negro dancer named Gratton in an avant-garde show produced in 1920.

In 1922 Milhaud made his first tour of the United States as pianist and composer, frequently in performances of his own compositions. He also delivered lectures at Harvard, Columbia, and Princeton universities. In New York, Milhaud visited one of Harlem's night clubs to hear authentic New Orleans jazz. "The music I heard," he declares, "was absolutely different from anything I had ever before heard and was a revelation to me. . . . Its effect on me was so overwhelming that I could not tear myself away. From then on, I frequented other Negro theatres and dance halls." The experience led to the writing of one of Milhaud's most distinguished and best-known compositions in a jazz idiom, the ballet *La Création du Monde* (*The Creation of the World*).

La Création du Monde, a ballet utilizing Negro rhythms (1922), was introduced by the Swedish Ballet in Paris on October 25, 1923. The scenario by Blaise Cendrars describes the world's creation as seen through the eyes of an African aborigine. Milhaud's score incorporates the blues, ragtime, and other elements of New Orleans jazz. One section is a fugue based on a jazz motive. So creative and so symphonic was this treatment of jazz within an ambitious structure that Paul Rosenfeld was led to say that it represented "the most perfect of all pieces of symphonic jazz," and Aaron Copland asserted that jazz here had succeeded in producing "at least one authentic small masterpiece."

Though some of Milhaud's successful works of this period borrowed popular idioms, his own style was reflected in more serious efforts in which he made masterful use of modern techniques and idioms within classical structures—polytonality, polyrhythm, and discordant harmony. These compositions included two important string quartets, Milhaud's fifth and seventh (1920, 1925); a Serenade, for small orchestra (1921); *Five Studies*, for piano and orchestra (1920); a Symphony, for ten wind instruments (1922); a violin concerto (1927); and *Le Carnaval d'Aix*, for piano and orchestra, which he wrote for an American tour and introduced with the New York Philharmonic on December 9, 1926.

Though he was producing works of distinction in all possible media, his richest and finest creativity seemed to be reserved for opera. In *Les Malheurs d'Orphée*, his first chamber opera, as he explains, "the music is stripped to its barest essentials." It is a work of modest dimensions, with a small cast of about a dozen singers and an orchestra of thirteen. Armand Lunel's libretto was a modern adaptation of the Orpheus and Eurydice legend; Milhaud's score—made up primarily of conventional set pieces—was strikingly effective in its deployment of modern rhythmic and harmonic devices and its passionate lyricism. *Les Malheurs d'Orphée* was introduced in Brussels on May 7, 1926. Soon afterward it was heard both over the radio and in the concert hall, with Milhaud conducting the American première at a Pro Musica concert in New York.

More successful still was the tragic one-act opera *Le Pauvre Matelot* (*The Poor Sailor*), with a text by Jean Cocteau. It tells of a sailor's wife who has had no news of her husband for a number of years. When the husband returns, he poses as a rich friend of the family, come to bring distressful news of the husband's sickness and poverty. When the "friend" spends the night in the wife's home, she murders him, hoping to rob him of his money so that she may rescue her husband. Heard at the Opéra-Comique in Paris on December 12, 1927, *Le Pauvre Matelot* became, as Milhaud pointed out, "my most widely performed opera." It had a three-year run in Berlin and was presented in twenty other German cities; it was heard in Vienna, Salzburg, Prague, and Barcelona (in the last-named city, conducted by Milhaud); the American première took place in Philadelphia on April 1, 1937. Reviewing the American première performance, William E. Smith described Milhaud's score as "music which is very modern in melodic line, harmonization (polytonality being generously employed), and orchestration, Milhaud using his means with effectiveness."

From chamber opera, Milhaud graduated to grand opera in *Christophe Colomb*, the world première of which took place in Berlin on May 5, 1930. This was not only Milhaud's most ambitious opera up to this time but also the most experimental. There are many critics who still regard it as one of his masterworks. Paul Claudel's text offers a symbolical, at times allegorical, presentation of Columbus's life—a "vivid mixture," said a reviewer after the première, "of the historical, the mystical and the allegorical, interwoven with the deep ethical strain characteristic of Claudel." The story is told by a narrator reading to a chorus from a book. This chorus represents posterity, which comments critically on what is happening in the drama. The stage is divided into three levels: the front occupied by narrator and chorus, the center serving to present the drama, and the rear consisting of a large screen on which motion pictures are flashed symbolizing what is happening or supplementing the ac-

tion. Darius Milhaud, said Abraham Skulsky in *Musical America*, "attains the height of his powers in this opera. . . . His natural gift of lyric inspiration, the refinement of his polytonal harmonic language, his greatness of conception in monumental scenes, and even his occasional quest for folkloristic elements are all to be found in this work." The American première of the opera took place in a concert version on November 6, 1952, Dimitri Mitropoulos conducting the New York Philharmonic. The first stage production was given by the San Francisco Opera—in an English translation—on October 6, 1968.

Christophe Colomb was the first of three large-scale operas on American subjects, a trilogy which Virgil Thomson once called "a monument of incomparable grandeur." The other two were *Maximilien* (world première at the Paris Opéra on January 4, 1932) and *Bolivar*. The latter, though completed in 1943, was not produced until seven years later, in Paris on May 12, 1950, when it created a scandal, largely promoted by Milhaud's enemies and those who thought the opera too long. Between these two operas, Milhaud completed still another major work for the musical stage, *Médée*, introduced in Antwerp on October 7, 1939. *Médée* was soon afterwards produced in Paris, the last opera heard in that city before the Nazis occupied it in 1940. The last major work written by Milhaud in Paris during the early years of World War II was his first symphony for large orchestra (earlier symphonies had been scored for chamber orchestra). It had been commissioned by the Chicago Symphony, which introduced it on October 17, 1940.

On May 2, 1925, Milhaud married his cousin, Madeleine. They had one child, a son, Daniel, who became a painter. Between the two world wars, husband and wife traveled extensively all over the world. During the summer of 1940 they escaped from Nazi-occupied France to the United States where Milhaud received an appointment on the music faculty of Mills College, in Oakland, California. There he taught composition in the mornings and devoted himself to creative work each afternoon at the home overlooking San Francisco Bay built for him by the University. During that period he completed the opera *Bolivar* and a number of major instrumental compositions, including his second piano concerto (1941), introduced in Chicago on December 18, 1941 with the composer at the piano; the popular *Suite Française*, based on popular French melodies, given its first performance on July 29, 1945, in New York City; two symphonies (1944, 1946), the latter written to commemorate the liberation of France and first performed at a Milhaud festival in Paris on October 30, 1947; and his second cello concerto, which Edmund Kurtz introduced with the New York Philharmonic on November 28, 1946.

In addition to teaching and composing, Milhaud toured the United States and conducted performances of his symphonic compositions with major American orchestras—all this in spite of the crippling arthritis which had begun to affect him in the 1930's. His malady was so advanced that during the early 1940's he could walk only by supporting himself on two canes, and most of the time he had to depend on a wheelchair to get around. In his guest appearances as conductor, he was wheeled to the conductor's stand and assisted into a chair from which, in a seated position, he led the orchestra.

After the war, in 1947, Milhaud returned to France where he became professor of composition at the Paris Conservatory. Despite his infirmity, he henceforth divided his year between the United States and France, assisted in his travels as well as in his daily life by his devoted wife. There was no lessening of his creativity. Now as before he remained one of the most prolific composers of the twentieth century. By the time his seventieth birthday was celebrated at Mills College, he had published over four hundred works in every form and in many different styles.

One style is the Hebraic. As a Jew who all his life had been deeply conscious of his religion, and as a composer partial to folk materials, Milhaud inevitably produced numerous works with a strong ethnic identity. Some of his finest songs are of Hebraic interest, such as the *Poèmes Juifs* (1916) and the *Six Chants Populaires Hébraïques* (1925), the latter described by Edward Lockspeiser as "psychological interpretations of Jewish scenes and characters." In 1939 Milhaud wrote *La Reine de Saba*, a Palestinian air for string quartet which was broadcast over the Jerusalem Radio, and in

1948 he completed a Sabbath Morning Service and the prayer *L'cho Dodi*, both for the synagogue.

The most ambitious of these Hebraic works is the biblical opera *David*, written on a commission from Serge Koussevitzky to commemorate the three thousandth anniversary of Jerusalem as the capital of Judea. The libretto by Armand Lunel traces the life of King David from the time the prophet Samuel visits the house of David's father to the annointment of the boy Solomon as David's successor on the throne of Israel. An interesting feature of this opera is a chorus dressed in twentieth century clothes—identified in the text as "Israelites of the year 1954"—seated outside the stage to comment on the biblical story and provide parallels between ancient and modern history.

The world première took place in Jerusalem on June 1, 1954, in a concert version sung in Hebrew; a distinguished audience, including the President of Israel, attended. The first staged version followed at La Scala in Milan on January 2, 1955, while the American première (once again in a concert version) was performed at the Hollywood Bowl on September 22, 1956. "*David*," reported Walter Arlen, "is full of deeply lyrical passages and dramatic sections in which the composer's sure and experienced hand evokes an atmosphere of uncanny realism without indulging in crass tone painting."

A more recent opera is *La Mère Coupable*, derived from *The Barber of Seville*, one of the two Beaumarchais comedies (the other was *The Marriage of Figaro*) that inspired Rossini and Mozart to write operatic masterworks. Milhaud's new opera was adapted by his wife Madeleine. The world première was given in Geneva on June 13, 1966, and the composer traveled from California to attend the performance. The production attracted celebrities from all over Europe, who failed to be impressed, however, by Milhaud's attempt to interpret an eighteenth century classic in terms of twentieth century music.

Other recent works have proved more impressive. These include his eleventh and twelfth symphonies (1961, 1962); a huge choral symphony, *Pacem in Terris* (text taken from the encyclical of the late Pope John XXIII), the première of which occurred at the opening of

Milhaud

the auditorium of the new building housing Radio-Télévision Française, on December 20, 1963; and a string septet, heard first in Washington, D.C., on October 31, 1964. For the two hundred fiftieth anniversary of New Orleans, Milhaud wrote *Musique pour Nouvelles Orléans*. This work was introduced by the New Orleans Philharmonic Symphony Orchestra on March 12, 1968.

"In a world torn by dodecaphonism and cerebrality, and dragged this way and that," writes Norman Demuth, "Milhaud pursues his own path, unaffected by musical polemics and fashions. His music is as uncompromising as any of that written by the youngest wild tyro, is still debatable, still fascinating."

Milhaud has expressed his convictions as a composer in the following terms: "I have no esthetic rules, or philosophy, or theories. I love to write music. I always do it with pleasure, otherwise I do not write it . . . . Sobriety and simplicity are the best counselors of any composer. A solid and logical construction is indispensable. . . . Anybody can acquire a brilliant technique. The important thing is the vital element—the melody—which should be easily retained, hummed and whistled on the street. Without this fundamental element, all the technique in the world can only be a dead letter."

Edward Lockspeiser has written the following description of the composer: "From a distance Darius Milhaud might almost be taken for Churchill: his great solid bulk has the amplitude of that figure—a big man, a generous-minded man; and you have the same impression as you see him more closely—there is a Churchillian determination about the curl of his lips." To this, Robert Lawrence adds: "The keynote to the man's character is his love of youth and freshness in art and life; his aversion to the static and pretentious. . . . On first meeting you have the sensation of running up against a wall of granite, such are the reserve and feeling of strength that his massive size and crowning shock of . . . hair engender. Later this opening manner may give way to real warmth tinged with an attractive irony. But Milhaud's dignity is the common denominator of the composer and of his music."

The numerous honors gathered through the years by Milhaud emphasize the importance of the place he has won in twentieth century music. These include several honorary degrees from American universities and election to the American Institute of Arts and Letters, the American Academy of Letters and Science, the Santa Cecilia Academy in Rome, and the Music Academy in Sweden. He is a Commander of the French Legion of Honor and an Officer of the Order of the Southern Cross of Brazil.

MAJOR WORKS

Ballets—L'Homme et Son Désir; Le Bœuf sur le Toit; La Création du Monde; Salade; Le Train Bleu; Jeux de Printemps; The Bells; La Cueillette des Citrons; L'Anneau de Pourpre.

Chamber Music—19 string quartets (the 14th and 15th string quartets capable of being played together as an octet); 2 piano quintets; 2 violin sonatas; Pastorale, for oboe and clarinet; La Reine de Saba, for string quartet; La Cheminée du Roi René, for flute, oboe, clarinet, horn, and bassoon; Sonatine, for two violins; Sonatine, for violin and viola; Sonata for Violin and Harpsichord; String Trio; Concertino d'Automne, for two pianos and eight instruments; Élégie, for cello and piano; Suite de Quatrains, for narrator and seven instruments; String Septet.

Choral Music—Cantique du Rhône; Incantations; Sabbath Morning Service; L'cho Dodi; La Naissance de Vénus; Barba Garibo; Cantate des Proverbes; Les Miracles de la Foi; Pacem in Terris.

Operas—L'Orestie (trilogy comprising Agamemnon, Les Choëphores, Les Euménides); Les Malheurs d'Orphée; Le Pauvre Matelot; Christophe Colomb; Maximilien; Médée; Bolivar; David; La Mère Coupable.

Orchestral Music—12 symphonies; 5 piano concertos; 2 violin concertos; 2 cello concertos; 2 concertos for two pianos; Protée, suite; Ballade, for piano and orchestra; Saudades do Brasil (also for piano); Le Carnaval d'Aix, for piano and orchestra; Viola Concerto; Concertino de Printemps, for violin and orchestra; Concerto for Viola and Orchestra; Suite Provençale; Concerto for Flute, Violin, and Orchestra; Clarinet Concerto; Concertino d'Été, for viola and chamber orchestra; Concertino d'Hiver, for trombone and strings; Études, for piano and orchestra; Symphoniette, for strings; Suite Française; Kentuckiana; Symphonie Concertante, for trumpet, bassoon, and chamber orchestra; The Globetrotter Suite; Concertante, for piano and orchestra; Harp Concerto; Ouverture Philharmonique; Aspen Serenade; Murder of a Great Chief of State; A Frenchman in New York; Musique pour Nouvelles Orléans.

Piano Music—2 sonatas; Quatre Romances sans Paroles; Scaramouche, for two pianos; La Muse Ménagère (also for orchestra); Une Journée; Le Bal Martiniquais, for two pianos (also for orchestra); Paris, for four pianos; Jeu; L'Enfant Aimé.

Vocal Music—Poèmes Juifs; Trois Poèmes de Jean Cocteau; Six Chants Populaires Hébraïques; Le Cygne; Chanson du Capitaine; Trois Élégies; Le Voyage d'Été; Quatre Chansons de Ronsard; Rêves; La Libération des Antibes; Ballade-Nocturne; numerous individual songs for voice and piano.

ABOUT

Ewen, D. (ed.), The New Book of Modern Composers;

Collaer, P., Darius Milhaud; Collaer, P., A History of Modern Music; Milhaud, D., Notes Without Music. High Fidelity, March 1961; Musical America, October 1962.

Italo Montemezzi
1875–1952

Italo Montemezzi was born in Vigasio, in the province of Verona, Italy, August 4, 1875. His father, a successful engineer, directed his son toward his own profession. After completing his high school education in Verona, Montemezzi went to Milan to enter the University. En route, he suddenly realized he wanted to become a musician, even though he had little training and had shown no aptitude for music when given piano lessons in his childhood. He took the entrance examinations for the Milan Conservatory three times before he was able to pass them. As a pupil of Saladino in counterpoint and Ferroni in composition he worked hard to make up for lost time, and in 1900 he was graduated with honors. His graduation composition, *Cantico dei Cantici*, for chorus and orchestra, was conducted by Toscanini.

ITALO MONTEMEZZI

For the next few years, Montemezzi lived in semi-seclusion, working on his compositions. His first opera, *Giovanni Gallurese*, was produced in Turin on January 28, 1905, and met

Montemezzi: mōn tä mĕd´ dzē

with such favor that it was repeated seventeen times in the next twenty-nine days. Some critics remarked that its creator must be numbered among the most promising of the younger Italian composers. The American première was given at the Metropolitan Opera House, February 19, 1925.

The success of this opera brought him a contract with Ricordi, the powerful publisher, for a new opera. *Hellera*, mounted in Turin on March 17, 1909, was a failure. But the opera that followed it made him world famous— his masterwork, *L'Amore dei Tre Re* (*The Love of Three Kings*).

"I racked my brains for quite a while before *L'Amore dei Tre Re* came along," Montemezzi once told an interviewer. "It had happened after I had seen a performance of *The Jest*. This would be it! I was so eager to write a score for it that I immediately wrote to Benelli [Sem Benelli, the playwright]. He didn't answer me, of course. He never answers letters. But two weeks later I fortunately ran into him. The news was crushing. The opera rights to *The Jest* had already been sold. Seeing me so disheartened, however, Benelli said, 'But I have another play I am writing and the title of it alone spells success for an opera, *The Love of Three Kings*.'

"For four hours after that we walked about the city, arm in arm, while he told me in great detail about the characters, story, and atmosphere. He hadn't a word written down, but from what he told me I could easily visualize the beauty of his drama, and without delay I took him to Ricordi. We signed a contract then and there—and just six months later *L'Amore dei Tre Re* was produced as a play in Rome."

Two years and three months later both libretto and musical score were completed. On April 10, 1913, the opera was produced at La Scala. It was a major success. In August of the same year it was produced in Cesana where Gatti-Casazza and Toscanini heard it and decided to perform it at the Metropolitan Opera in New York. On January 2, 1914, Toscanini conducted the American première. This, too, was a triumph. After that, the opera could be found in the repertory of every major opera house in the world.

The central character of the opera is the blind King Archibaldo, who is a tragic figure, destroyed by his passion for vengeance. He murders his daughter-in-law when she confesses she loves a man other than her husband; then, after the king has put poison on her dead lips for the purpose of killing her lover, he learns to his horror that he has been instrumental in killing his son as well.

"The union of the music and the text, not only in the expression of the moods but also in the almost intangible reproduction of the literary style, is extraordinary," wrote W. J. Henderson in the New York *Sun* following the American première. At every turn, Montemezzi matched the terror and grandeur of Benelli's drama with music of remarkable emotional impact, expressiveness, and subtle feeling for character and atmosphere. On the one hand it had the symphonic dimensions of a Wagnerian music drama; on the other, it had the soaring lyricism of Verdi. Olin Downes referred to it as "the most poetical and aristocratic of modern Italian operas . . . a tone poem for voices and orchestra made from the patrician verse and the symbolic conception of Sem Benelli, and a wholly exceptional creation it is."

The opera that followed *L'Amore dei Tre Re* further enhanced Montemezzi's position in modern Italian opera. It was *La Nave*, based on the tragedy by Gabriele d'Annunzio, introduced at La Scala on November 1, 1918. It proved such a success that it was selected to inaugurate the 1919–1920 season of the Chicago Opera, with the composer conducting. Two more Montemezzi operas followed. *La Notte di Zoraima* was produced at La Scala on January 31, 1931, and received its American première at the Metropolitan Opera on December 2 of the same year. "The music," wrote Olin Downes, "is in the greater part a distant echo of *The Love of Three Kings*. . . . It is hard to exonerate the composer, for he has sold his birthright for a mess of pottage."

Montemezzi's last opera was *L'Incantesimo*, which had its world première over the NBC radio network on October 9, 1943, the composer conducting. This work was a fantasy whose title, as the composer explained, "refers to that state into which love so often plunges human beings. Story and music are the utmost in simplicity and there is nothing of tragedy about it at all. The music is lyric, not dramatic. I believe there is beauty in it—and that is

the one thing I am interested in projecting."

But *L'Incantesimo* added nothing to Montemezzi's stature, and it has been forgotten. Forgotten, too, have been all the other Montemezzi operas except *L'Amore dei Tre Re*. He remains a one-opera man.

In 1920 Montemezzi married Katherine Leith, an American. At the time of their courtship he knew no English, and she very little Italian. They were married in Paris where a son was subsequently born to them. After 1939, Montemezzi established his home in Beverly Hills, California, where he stayed for about a decade. In 1941 he made a guest appearance as conductor at the Metropolitan Opera in a performance of *L'Amore dei Tre Re*. He returned to Italy in 1949 and died in Vigasio on May 15, 1952.

Montemezzi always felt that melody was the spine of opera, and that music for the theatre must first and foremost be emotional and come from the heart. He once told Verna Arvey: "Anyone can write whatever music he wants, modern or ultra-modern. But if he doesn't have that underlying emotion, it is not music for me. Without emotion, it is just notes. . . . If you do not have melody you do not have music—but the melody need not necessarily be in the strict sense that Donizetti knew it. If you analyze rhythm, you will find that it has a melody of its own. . . . A composer can be modern and melodic, too."

MAJOR WORKS

Choral Music—Cantata in Memory of Ponchielli.

Operas—Giovanni Gallurese; Hellera; L'Amore dei Tre Re; La Nave; La Notte di Zoraima; L'Incantesimo (one-act radio opera).

Orchestral Music—Paolo and Virginia, tone poem; Italia Mia, tone poem; Elegy, for cello and orchestra.

ABOUT

Tretti, L. and Fiumi, L. (eds.), Omaggio a Italo Montemezzi.

Opera News, January 10, 1949.

Douglas Moore
1893–1969

Douglas Stuart Moore was born on August 10, 1893, in Cutchogue, Long Island, New York. "I belong," Moore related, "to the ninth generation of the Moore family to live in this part of the world. My remote ancestor, Thomas Moore, came to Long Island from

Connecticut in 1640 to found what is now the township of Southold, a community rivaled in age on Long Island only by Southampton, also settled in 1640." Moore maintained his residence in the house of his birth, and in 1963 celebrated his seventieth birthday there.

DOUGLAS MOORE

His father was the publisher of *Ladies' World*, one of the earliest women's magazines, and his mother was an editor and a descendant of both Miles Standish and John Alden. His early education began in Brooklyn and at Hotchkiss School. At the latter he met and became a friend of the poet Archibald Mac-Leish, whose verses were the inspiration for a number of Moore's early songs. Later, at Yale University, under the guidance of David Stanley Smith and Horatio Parker, Moore's interests were definitely shifted to music. During his freshman year, Moore composed a popular song about a New Haven waitress, "Naomi, My Restaurant Queen," which was published. Later on, he also composed one of Yale's most famous football songs, "Good Night, Harvard." He received his Bachelor of Arts degree in 1915 and his Bachelor of Music degree two years later.

During World War I, Moore served as lieutenant in the Navy aboard the destroyer U. S. S. Murray, an experience that inspired him to compose a number of rollicking songs that appeared in *Songs My Mother Never Taught Me*, a collection edited by Moore and John Jacob Niles, and a number entitled "Destroyer Life" which became popular. After his demobilization in 1919, he went to Europe for more music study. At the Schola Cantorum in Paris he was a pupil of Vincent d'Indy. He also studied the organ with Nadia Boulanger.

On September 16, 1920, Moore married Emily Bailey; they had two daughters. In 1921 Moore was appointed director of music at the Art Museum in Cleveland where he gave organ recitals, lectured on music, and arranged cultural events. Four art treasures at this museum were the inspiration for his first serious piece of music — *Four Museum Pieces*, originally for organ, then transcribed for orchestra. During this period he studied composition with Ernest Bloch. From 1923 to 1925 Moore was the organist at Adelbert College of Western Reserve University.

In 1925 a Pulitzer Traveling Fellowship in music enabled him to go to Europe to devote himself to creative work and to study with Nadia Boulanger. When he returned to the United States, he became a member of the music department at Columbia University. In 1928 he was made associate professor, and in 1940 he succeeded Daniel Gregory Mason as head of the department. Moore retired from this post in 1962, becoming MacDowell Professor Emeritus. However, he continued to give a course in music appreciation at Columbia.

In 1934 Moore was awarded a Guggenheim Fellowship. This made it possible for him to devote himself to the writing of his first opera, *White Wings*, based on the text of Philip Barry's stage play. Actually, as Moore himself explained, this was not an opera "but an attempt to preserve the values of the play as a play intact." When the world première was given fourteen years later in Hartford, Connecticut — on February 2, 1949 — Allen Bole described the work as "full of charm, color, even beautiful nonsense."

In January 1946 Moore succeeded Arthur Train as president of the National Institute of Arts and Letters; he held the office until 1952. In 1960 he was elected to the American Academy of Arts and Letters and for three years he served as president. He received honorary doctorates in music from the Cincinnati Conservatory in 1946, the University of Rochester in 1948, and Yale University in 1955.

Moore first achieved recognition as a composer with several works for orchestra completed by 1930; all were in a tonal framework, all were melodious and conventional in harmony, and all were effective in their atmospheric, pictorial, or descriptive writing. These compositions included *The Pageant of P. T. Barnum* (1924), *Moby Dick* (1928), and *A Symphony of Autumn* (1930). The earliest of these works became the most popular following its world première in Cleveland on April 15, 1926. The score, which describes five episodes in the life of America's fabulous showman, is rich in wit and American flavor.

Though Moore thus demonstrated a sure touch in writing for orchestra and his successes in this field continued into the 1940's with the Symphony in A major (1945) and *Farm Journal* (1947), he was almost from the beginning of his career especially partial to writing either for the voice or for the stage. "I've always liked setting words better than any other form of composition," he once told an interviewer, "and I've always had a passion for the theatre."

His predilection for writing songs stems from his many friendships with distinguished poets, beginning with his association with Archibald MacLeish in his early school days and continuing, through the years, with his personal contacts with Vachel Lindsay, Elinor Wylie, Padraic Colum, and Stephen Vincent Benét.

It was his friendship with Benét that led him to write his first important work for the stage, the folk opera *The Devil and Daniel Webster*, based on Benét's well-known story. In the tale, the orator-lawyer eloquently and successfully pleads the case for a New Hampshire farmer who has sold his soul to the devil. (The story was made into an excellent motion picture in 1941 starring Walter Huston and Edward Arnold.) Moore prepared his own libretto. First produced in New York on May 18, 1939, *The Devil and Daniel Webster* followed traditional operatic lines by using arias and set numbers and relying on fulsome melodies for its main appeal.

Before progressing to his next opera, Moore completed the writing of a major work for orchestra, his second symphony, in A major, dedicated to Stephen Vincent Benét. It was introduced in Paris on May 5, 1946, with Robert Lawrence conducting the Paris Broadcasting Orchestra. After receiving its American première in Los Angeles on January 16, 1947, the symphony was given honorable mention by the New York Music Critics Circle. The composer explained that his symphony was "an attempt to write in clear, objective, modified style, with emphasis upon rhythmic and melodic momentum rather than upon sharply contrasted themes or dramatic climax. There is no underlying program, although the mood of the second movement was suggested by a short poem by James Joyce which deals with music heard at the coming of twilight."

Moore's next opera was *Giants in the Earth*, produced in New York on March 28, 1951. Arnold Sundgaard's libretto was based on the novel by O. E. Rolvaag, describing the settling of the Dakotas by Norwegians. Moore had been searching for a suitable libretto for more than a decade. What attracted him to Rolvaag's novel was that it had, as he said, "everything—an American theme (and I liked the Norwegian overtones, too), drama, sweep, touches of humor." Describing the opera for the New York *Times*, Olin Downes said: "There is an abundance of concert pieces and dancing, a wedding chorus, a baptismal hymn, and even a fight at the end of the second act which is perfectly legitimate and logical as an incidental feature of the drama. . . . In a number of concerted pieces which call for musical ensemble, Mr. Moore has written dexterously and to the point. And there are moments when the orchestra takes a hand, paints a scene, as in the fine opening stages of the score, with the horn solo and the musical implication of the distances of the boundless plain." *Giants in the Earth* received the Pulitzer Prize in music in 1951. A decade later, librettist and composer revised the opera extensively.

With the American folk opera *The Ballad of Baby Doe*, which entered the permanent repertory of American opera, Moore achieved a noteworthy success. Commissioned by the Koussevitzky Music Foundation to help celebrate the bicentenary of Columbia University, the opera was given its world première in Central City, Colorado, on July 7, 1956. On April 3, 1958 it was produced by the New York City Opera, which since that time has performed it frequently. In 1961 it was presented by an American company in Berlin and

Belgrade. Following its first presentation in New York City, it received the New York Music Critics Circle Award.

John Latouche's libretto is based on an actual event in American history. In Leadville, Colorado, during the gold-rush days of the late nineteenth century, the wealthy and powerful Horace Tabor divorces his wife to marry Baby Doe, a notorious Wisconsin beauty. After he loses both his influence and his money, Baby Doe remains faithful to him until the time of his death in 1899. Then she spends the last thirty-six years of her life in a lonely shack on the grounds of a worthless silver mine left her by her husband, and in 1935 freezes to death there.

"In its re-creation of the spirit of a different age," reported Allen Young in the Denver *Post*, "the production finds the way to speak vividly in bright color and song. . . . There is a heightening of the drama as historical forces blow their frosty winds across the plains into the mountains. . . . The music of Douglas Moore sings with a prodigal variety of moods. It sings songs for the summer night, waltzes and popular tunes of the day. The music communicates to the listener with a directness and freshness that is extraordinary. . . . It is music that could not have been written in another age and it is music which constantly refreshes and delights."

In 1957 Moore wrote a one-act musical trifle, *Gallantry*, with a text by Arnold Sundgaard. This piece satirized the "soap operas" of radio and television. It was given a stage production in New York on March 15, 1958, and a little more than four years after (on August 30, 1962) was telecast over the CBS-TV network on a program entitled *Arias and Arabesques*.

But a return to a more ambitious structure and to a more artistic intent came with *The Wings of the Dove*, a full-length opera in six scenes based on the novel of Henry James, adapted by Ethan Ayer. The New York City Opera produced it on October 12, 1961. "Two hours of the best operatic writing ever done in this country was heard for the first time anywhere at the City Center last night," reported Louis Biancolli in the New York *World Telegram*, and Harriett Johnson said in the New York *Post* that Moore "has created a music drama which is far more sophisticated than his previous operas . . . skillful in structure, sometimes poignant and telling, seldom boring."

Then once again Moore went to American characters and backgrounds for the opera *Carry Nation*, with a libretto by William North Jayme based on the life of the early twentieth century prohibitionist who went around smashing bars and saloons with a hatchet. Jayme's libretto concerns itself mainly with her tragic first marriage to an Army physician who died an alcoholic and thus motivated her to embark on her fiery crusade against liquor. The opera was written for the centenary celebration of the University of Kansas, in Lawrence, where it received its world première on April 28, 1966. The location of the première had relevance, since Carry Nation's first crusade against the evils of drink took place in Kansas, as did her death. In reporting the première to the New York *Times*, Theodore Strongin noted that "Mr. Moore has set all this to eminently singable music, conservative but eloquent. As is proper to opera, characterization develops through singing, through evoking moods through melody." *Carry Nation* was produced by the New York City Opera on March 28, 1968.

Moore made many appearances as guest conductor with major American orchestras. He was the author of *Listening to Music* (1932) and *From Madrigal to Modern Music* (1942).

"The particular ideal which I have been striving to attain," he once said, "is to write music which will . . . reflect the exciting qualities of the life, traditions, and country which I feel all about me." Moore died in Greenport, Long Island, July 25, 1969.

MAJOR WORKS

Chamber Music—Violin Sonata; String Quartet; Quintet for Woodwinds and Horns; Down East, suite for violin and piano; Clarinet Quintet; Piano Trio.

Choral Music—Simon Legree; Perhaps to Dream; Dedication.

Operas—White Wings; The Headless Horseman (high school operetta); The Devil and Daniel Webster; The Emperor's New Clothes (children's opera); Puss in Boots (children's operetta); Giants in the Earth; The Ballad of Baby Doe; Gallantry (satirical one-act opera); The Wings of the Dove; The Greenfield Christmas Tree (a Christmas Entertainment); Carry Nation.

Orchestral Music—2 symphonies; Pageant of P. T. Barnum, suite; Moby Dick, tone poem; Overture on an American Tune; Village Music; In Memoriam; A Farm Journal, for chamber orchestra; Cotillion, for string orchestra.

Nabokov

Piano Music—Museum Piece; Suite.
Vocal Music—Numerous songs for voice and piano.

ABOUT

Chase, G., America's Music; Goss, M., Modern Music Makers; Howard, J. T., Our American Music; Mellers, W. H., Music in a New Found Land.
Modern Music, May 1943; Musical America, August 1963.

Nicolas Nabokov
1903–

Nicolas Nabokov was born in Lubcha, district of Novogrudok, Russia, on April 17, 1903. "Our family estate," he recalls, "was in the corner of Belorussia. . . . The head of the Hasidic community of the village, a wonderful old gentleman, used to come to our house to bind books. He would sit me on his knee and tell me stories of the biblical kings and prophets and sing me songs of the synagogue." One song was quoted by Nabokov many years later (1967) in his Third Symphony. In 1911 his family went to St. Petersburg where he attended the Imperial Lyceum. After the outbreak of the revolution in Russia, he went south, making his home in Yalta, where he continued music study with Rebikov. He finally left Russia in 1920, settling first in Stuttgart, Germany, where he attended the Conservatory from 1920 to 1922 and then in Berlin, where he was a pupil of Busoni and Juon at the Hochschule für Musik. He later lived in Paris for eight years, and in 1926 he received a degree from the Sorbonne.

In Paris he was introduced to Sergei Diaghilev, founder and artistic director of the Ballet Russe de Monte Carlo. Diaghilev commissioned Nabokov to write music for a ballet-oratorio, which the Ballet Russe presented in Paris on June 6, 1928. It bore the elaborate title *Ode, or Meditation at Night on the Majesty of God as Revealed by the Aurora Borealis*. Massine prepared the choreography, Boris Kochno the scenario; the principal dancers were Massine, Danilova, and Lifar. Nabokov's score comprised a dozen separate numbers, including arias, duets, choruses, and instrumental interludes. Since the ballet subject reached back to the poetry and deism of eighteenth century Russia, Nabokov fre-

Nabokov: nă bô′kôf

quently reverted to the style of Glinka, writing with economy and simplicity but also with pronounced Russian flavor. André Schaeffner wrote: "The nakedness, far from being a mark of poverty, becomes the expression of force—the strength of a young composer who knows the value of direct emphasis and of the constant presence in music of song."

NICOLAS NABOKOV

On February 16, 1930, in Paris, Pierre Monteux led the première of Nabokov's first symphony, *Symphonie Lyrique*. This became Nabokov's first major work to be heard in the United States, when Serge Koussevitzky conducted it in Boston on October 31, 1930. An oratorio, *Job*—the composer's first major work for chorus—was heard in 1933. This was an impressive attempt to revive the early monodies of the fifteenth and sixteenth centuries in an oratorio of dramatic character. José Iturbi conducted the work in Mexico City, and on October 4, 1934, it received an American première at the Worcester Festival.

In 1933 Nabokov visited the United States on an invitation from the Barnes Foundation to give a series of lectures on European music. Soon after his arrival, he wrote the score for a new ballet for the Ballet Russe, the idea for which had originated with the poet Archibald MacLeish, who provided the scenario. Entitled *Union Pacific* and covering episodes in the building of the famous railroad, the ballet was Nabokov's first attempt to work with American materials; moreover, it proved to be the first time that Massine was called upon to choreograph an American subject. Into his score Nabokov introduced several native American tunes, including "Monsieur Banjo" (a cakewalk), "Lady Gay," "Butcher Boy," and "Pop Goes the Weasel." *Union Pacific* was introduced in Philadelphia on April 6, 1934. It was a great success and during the next few years was frequently produced by the Ballet Russe both in the United States and in Europe. Commenting on the music, Pitts Sanborn said that it is "modern, the thematic material is effectively employed, and plenty of good red blood courses through its veins."

For about a year and a half Nabokov lived in New York where he devoted himself to teaching, writing, and composition. He became an American citizen in 1939. From 1936 to 1941 he was a member of the music department of Wells College at Aurora, New York. Among the works he completed while serving in this position was an important symphony, the *Sinfonia Biblica*, which was introduced by the New York Philharmonic under Dimitri Mitropoulos on January 2, 1941. Each of the four movements derives its program from the Old Testament and bears an identifying title: Ecclesiasticus (Wisdom); Solomon (Love); Absalom (Fear); and Hosannah (Praise). In this work Nabokov became religious in his feeling, deserting his former tendencies to produce music that had for the most part a strong Hebraic personality. At the same time, he effectively made use of such modern devices as polyharmony and polytonality.

In 1944 Nabokov served as a civilian employee of the United States War Department; he was sent to Europe to serve with the morale division of the Strategic Bombing Survey. For two and a half years he remained in Europe, serving the United States military government as Deputy Chief of Film, Theatre, and Music Control for Germany; as coordinator of Inter-allied Negotiations for Information Media; and also in the capacity of special adviser to Ambassador Robert D. Murphy on cultural and Russian matters.

Upon returning to the United States in 1947, he was invited by the State Department to organize the Russian Broadcast Unit of the Voice of America; for about a year he was its chief. From 1947 to 1952 he taught composi-

tion at the Peabody Conservatory in Baltimore. Then, returning to Europe, he became the secretary general of the Congress for Cultural Freedom in Paris, an office in which he helped to organize the Festival of the Twentieth Century in Paris in 1952. In 1964 he was appointed cultural counselor for the Berlin Festival in West Germany. He resigned four years later but agreed to remain as adviser to the mayor and to the Berlin Senate for the international cultural affairs of the festival. He was then invited by the government of Iran to establish a regular festival in that country to be known as the Teheran Biennale.

Soon after his return to the United States in 1947, Nabokov completed an important work for high voice and orchestra, *The Return of Pushkin*, a three-part elegy given its première in Boston on January 2, 1948, Serge Koussevitzky conducting. The text is a famous Pushkin poem which, as the composer explained, "describes the emotions and reminiscences which arose in the poet when he visited again, in 1835, his family estate. . . . The poem itself is full of longing and melancholy, ending on a note of despair." The composer was stimulated to write this composition by revisiting places in America where he had formerly lived and which he had not seen for a number of years. Describing its musical content, Nabokov said: "In its form, the composition attempts to combine the Russian song form with the larger instrumental forms. The whole structure of the piece is essentially tonal, and the voice is treated as a melodic instrument."

Among his later ambitious compositions are the following: *Vita Nuova*, for soprano, tenor, and orchestra, first heard in Boston on March 2, 1951; a cello concerto called *Les Hommages*, introduced in Philadelphia on November 6, 1953; *Symboli Chorestiani*, featured at the Venice festival in September 1956; and a two-act opera, *The Holy Devil*, commissioned by the Kentucky Opera Association, and introduced by that company in Louisville on April 16, 1958.

In 1967 Nabokov completed his third symphony, subtitled *A Prayer*, which had been commissioned for the 125th anniversary of the New York Philharmonic. The world première took place in New York in January 1968, Leonard Bernstein conducting. The

Nielsen

work was inspired by a prayer of Pope John XXIII begging the Lord's forgiveness "for our blindness in not recognizing the beauty of His chosen people, the Jewish people, for our fault in the suffering inflicted upon them over the centuries, and for our having crucified Him a second time in their flesh." In the symphony Nabokov quotes three melodies—one a Hasidic tune he had heard in his early boyhood, the second a Catholic hymn of oriental origin, and the third from Stravinsky's *Requiem Canticles*. "Of course," the composer has explained, "these are not real 'quotations,' but rather 'approximations.' " Nabokov dedicated his symphony to Pope John XXIII and to Robert Oppenheimer, the scientist. It was the last piece of music Oppenheimer heard before his death.

Stephen Spender wrote the libretto for *The Holy Devil*, using aspects of the Rasputin story. "The subject of course is a natural for Nicolas Nabokov," said Oliver Daniel in the *Saturday Review*. "His Russian background gives him an affinity for such a tale and he evokes the dramatic and characteristic atmosphere of the story effortlessly. It all ends up as real opera." Nabokov revised his opera soon after its première, expanding it into three acts and giving it the new title of *Der Tod des Grigori Rasputin* (*The Death of Gregory Rasputin*). The revision received its world première in Cologne on November 27, 1959.

Nabokov is a cousin of the writer Vladimir Nabokov, the author of *Lolita*. Nicolas Nabokov is himself the author of a delightful book of reminiscences and essays, *Old Friends and New Music* (1951).

In June 1967 Nabokov revisited his native land for the first time since he was fifteen, on the invitation of the Ministry of Culture and the Union of Soviet Composers.

MAJOR WORKS

Ballets—Ode, or Meditation, ballet-oratorio; Aphrodite; Les Valses de Beethoven; La Vie de Polichinelle; Union Pacific; The Last Flower; Don Quixote.
Chamber Music—String Quartet; Bassoon Sonata.
Choral Music—Job, oratorio; Collectionneur d'Échos, for soprano, bass, chorus, and nine percussion instruments; America Was Promise; Symboli Chorestiani.
Opera—The Death of Rasputin (revision of The Holy Devil).
Orchestral Music—Symphonie Lyrique; Piano Concerto; Le Fiancé, overture; Sinfonia Biblica; Three Marches; The Return of Pushkin, elegy for high voice and orchestra; Flute Concerto; Vita Nuova, for

soprano, tenor, and orchestra; Les Hommages, concerto for cello and orchestra; Third Symphony: A Prayer.
Piano Music—2 sonatas.

ABOUT

Nabokov, N., Old Friends and New Music.
High Fidelity, April 1968; Modern Music, November-December, 1934.

Carl Nielsen
1865–1931

Carl August Nielsen was born in Nørre-Lyndelse, on the Danish island of Fyn, June 9, 1865. He was the seventh of twelve children in a family of peasant origin. His father, a house painter, played the violin at local weddings and parties in his spare time.

CARL NIELSEN

While recovering from measles in early childhood, Carl asked for and was given a quarter-size violin. He quickly learned to play a few tunes. For several years he continued learning to play the violin by himself, after receiving some lessons from the local school teacher. Before long he joined his father in playing at public events. When he was fourteen, Nielsen joined a band at the Odense garrison in which he was the youngest member. In Odense, a local tavern pianist introduced him to classical music by performing for him the works of Mozart and Beethoven, among

Nielsen: nēl′ s'n

386

others. This made such an impression on the boy that he managed to get a second-hand piano upon which to learn to play. He also made his first attempts at composition.

A few friends, convinced of his talent, raised a subsidy to send him to Copenhagen for formal musical training. He went there in 1884, presenting himself to Niels Gade, the composer and the director of the Conservatory. Gade, impressed by a string quartet Nielsen showed him as well as by the quality of his violin playing, opened to him the doors of the Conservatory. As a scholarship pupil during the next two years, Nielsen studied with Tofte (violin) and Rosenhoff (composition). In addition he took private lessons in composition from Gade.

From 1886 to 1890, Nielsen earned his living playing the violin in a theatre orchestra. This was the period in which his first opus appeared, the *Little Suite*, in A minor, for strings (1888), performed at the Tivoli Concert Hall. He also wrote several ambitious chamber music works, all of them romantic in style and markedly influenced by Grieg and Gade. These helped to win for him the Ancker stipend, which enabled him to spend a year of travel in Germany, France, and Italy. While in Paris, Nielsen married Anne Marie Brodersen, a young sculptress. They spent their honeymoon in Italy, then returned to Denmark to live in Copenhagen. There Nielsen became a violinist in the court orchestra, remaining in that post until 1905.

In his compositions, Nielsen began to depart from his former romantic ways and to experiment with new procedures. This tendency was already evident in his first symphony, in G minor, written in the years between 1892 and 1894 and revealing unusual harmonic combinations and a new approach towards the intervallic structure of his melodic line. Mark N. Kanny calls it "one of the most daring first symphonies ever written . . . [displaying] much of the tonal and rhythmic incisiveness that characterizes Nielsen at his best." This was the composition which introduced the composer to American audiences; it was performed as early as 1905 by the Chicago Symphony under Frederick Stock. The inclination to try out a new musical language within sound classical structures was continued in a large choral work to a Latin text, *Hymnus Amoris*, which had its world première in Copenhagen on April 27, 1897.

From 1898 to 1901, Nielsen was occupied with writing his first opera, *Saul and David*, produced in Copenhagen on November 28, 1902. Torben Meyer described it as "more of an oratorio than an opera, and resembling somewhat the Greek tragedies and the Gluck operas." The chorus assumes a major role, commenting on the course of the drama and at times participating in the action. From the point of view of musical style, the opera is noteworthy for its polyphonic writing; some of the choral music, says Meyer, "gives the opera an air of nobility and power."

This return to polyphony can also be found in his second symphony, *The Four Temperaments*, first heard in Copenhagen on December 1, 1902. Though the contrapuntal writing reveals a neobaroque tendency, modern expression is still exploited. In the third movement, Nielsen uses polytonality effectively. It is one of the earliest known examples of polytonal writing.

Nielsen wrote six symphonies in all, emerging as Denmark's foremost symphonist, and possibly one of the leading symphonists of the twentieth century. His first major achievement in this category was the third, *Sinfonia Espansiva*, introduced under his own direction in Copenhagen on February 28, 1912. Here his symphonic personality was fully realized. Thenceforth he worked within a classical structure, within a more or less tonal framework, and yet continually exploited modern idioms. Polytonality, unusual key relationships, daring harmonic combinations were all utilized for specific effects. He could create an emotional climate and project extramusical concepts and feelings without becoming specifically programmatic. He was partial to a breadth of design, long-arched themes, and a rhythmic strength, all of which endow his symphonic writing with an epical grandeur that reminds us of Sibelius. "I wanted to protest against the typical Danish soft smoothing-over," is the way Nielsen himself explained the vigor and power of his third symphony. "'Expansive' is indeed the word for this symphony from its first movement through its unself-consciously positive finale," says Richard D. Freed. "Instead of the old 'victory-through-struggle' pattern, the mood is one of unshakable, exultant confidence throughout. It is unashamedly and irresistibly wholesome. A German commentator welcomed the work, when it was new, as 'a mighty animating call from the North.' "

Nielsen's fourth symphony, *The Inextinguishable*, was heard in Copenhagen on February 1, 1916. His most famous symphony, the fifth, was performed in Copenhagen on January 24, 1922. The shadow of World War I hovers over the work, for it is music, as John Briggs has explained, dramatizing "the eternal human conflicts—the clash between man's constructive, progressive instincts and other forces, also human, that are indifferent or destructive." It points up the determination of the human will to survive even in a catastrophe. When this symphony was first given in the United States—by the National Symphony Orchestra under Eric Tuxen on January 3, 1951—Tuxen provided the following description of the music: "The spiritual content ... must be seen against the background of the doubt, anxiety, and unrest that seized the minds of people after World War I. Through its entire evolution, from a quite simple interval movement to the most violent eruptions, the first movement is borne by a peculiar cosmic notion of life. One perceives a gigantic fight between the principles of good and evil, the latter especially being characterized by the snarling and persistent attempts of the snare drum to disturb and tear the melodic structure. The victory of light over the powers of darkness heralded already at the end of the first movement is completed in the second, with its manful belief in will and vitality in all their manifestations."

Nielsen planned his sixth symphony (his last) to be "completely idyllic in character," as he told his daughter, with the same kind of "simple enjoyment of pure sound such as is found in the old a cappella composers." He also revealed that in this symphony he tried writing with the character of each individual instrument in mind: "I think through the instruments themselves, almost as if I had crept inside them." He called the work *Sinfonia Semplice*, or *Simple Symphony*, and conducted the première performance in Copenhagen on December 11, 1925.

In addition to the symphonies, Nielsen completed a number of excellent concertos—one

for the violin (1911), another for flute (1926), a third for clarinet (1928)—and an opera, *Masquerade*, which many consider one of Denmark's most important national operas. It was produced in Copenhagen with outstanding success on November 11, 1906, the composer conducting. Edvard Grieg, who attended the première, wrote Nielsen: "Thank you for last night. It is an amusing and witty work you have created. ... I'm in no doubt that it is the work of a new master who says, 'Here I am!' " The opera is set in eighteenth century Copenhagen, and the principal action takes place at a masquerade at which two people meet and fall in love without realizing that this is the match which their parents had insisted upon and which they had been resisting.

Van Kappel describes Nielsen's style in his major works as follows: "It might, on the whole, be said that the composer did not break with the major-minor mode; he rather built into that system a new melodious feeling akin to church modes. The feeling of pentatonic is extremely strong and distinct in his music. Moreover, chromaticism plays a great part in his more important instrumental compositions. ... A distinctive feature of his instrumental melody is a tendency to allow the tune to weave, for a long time, around a central tone. These new harmonies have some relation to Impressionism, which inspired him, by its combined chords, its unfunctional harmonies, even if the latter contradicted his sense of logic."

Nielsen had a distinguished career as a conductor. From 1908 to 1914 he was the director of the Copenhagen Royal Opera and from 1915 to 1927 of the Copenhagen Musical Society. He also appeared as a guest conductor throughout Europe. In the fall of 1915 he was made director of the Conservatory, where for a while he taught theory; in 1930 he became chairman of the Conservatory's managing committee.

In 1926 in Odense during a concert in which he led a program of his own music, Nielsen suffered a heart attack. He never recovered fully. A second heart attack took his life in Copenhagen on October 2, 1931.

The recipient of many honors, Nielsen was made a Knight of the Dannebrog and a member of the Royal Academy of Stockholm.

But outside Scandinavia his music enjoyed little circulation, a fact that caused him much bitterness in his final years. In fact, not for a number of years after his death did his music receive that full measure of acclaim it deserved. The triumph of his Fifth Symphony at the Edinburgh Festival in 1950, the publication of Robert Simpson's highly laudatory biography in 1952, and the five-day festival of his major works in Copenhagen in 1953, all helped focus attention on him. At about this time his symphonies were recorded. These releases, and a tour of the Danish State Orchestra in 1952, helped to introduce Nielsen to many American music lovers who knew little or nothing about him. But not until the centenary celebration of his birth was there a genuine movement to revive and popularize Nielsen's works, particularly in the United States. Performances of his major symphonies in 1965 by the New York Philharmonic under Leonard Bernstein, the Philadelphia Orchestra under Sixten Ehrling and Eugene Ormandy, the Boston Symphony under Erich Leinsdorf, the Cleveland and Detroit symphonies, and other major orchestras, helped to bring about a healthy re-evaluation of Nielsen's significance.

Two books by Nielsen have been translated into English and were published in London in 1953: *Living Music* and a volume of early reminiscences entitled *My Childhood*. They were originally published in Danish in 1925 and 1927 respectively.

MAJOR WORKS

Chamber Music—4 string quartets; 2 violin sonatas; String Quintet; Serenata in Vano, for clarinet, bassoon, horn, cello, and double bass; Quintet, for flute, oboe, clarinet, bassoon, and horn.

Choral Music—10 cantatas; Hymnus Amoris; Sleep; Fynsk Foraar, lyric humoresque.

Operas—Saul and David; Masquerade.

Orchestral Music—6 symphonies; various concertos for solo instruments and orchestra (violin; flute; clarinet); Helios, concert overture; Pan and Syrinx, tone poem.

Organ Music—29 small preludes; Commotio.

Piano Music—Chaconne; Theme and Variation; Suite; Various pieces.

Vocal Music—Various songs for voice and piano.

ABOUT

Balzer, J. (ed.), Carl Nielsen: Centenary Essays; Simpson, R., Carl Nielsen, Symphonist.

High Fidelity, April 1967; Musical America, November 1, 1952, August 1965; New York Times, September 12, 1965, November 14, 1965; Saturday Review, October 29, 1960.

Luigi Nono
1924–

Luigi Nono was born in Venice on January 29, 1924. He trained for the law, receiving his doctorate in Padua, while at the same time he studied music, mainly with Bruno Maderna, who introduced him to advanced idioms in composition. His later studies with Hermann Scherchen reinforced his earlier interest in modern composition.

LUIGI NONO

Nono's debut as a mature composer came in 1950 with the world première of *Variazioni Canoniche* conducted by Hermann Scherchen on August 27 at the Darmstadt Summer Courses in Music at Darmstadt-Kranichstein. *Variazioni* is an orchestral composition based on a tone row used by Schoenberg in his *Ode to Napoleon* and is entirely in the twelve-tone technique. Thus without too many preliminaries Nono emerged as a dodecaphonist, developing a serial technique in the chamber and orchestral works that followed. *Polifonica, Monodia, Ritmica*, for flute, clarinet, bass clarinet, saxophone, horn, piano, and percussion was directed by Scherchen on July 10, 1951, at the Summer Courses in Music at Darmstadt; some German critics called it one of the most interesting works heard in post–World War II Europe. More important was Nono's *Due Espressioni*, for orchestra, commissioned by the Donaueschingen Festival in Germany and introduced under Hans

Rosbaud's direction on October 11, 1953. William Steinberg introduced it in the United States in 1958 with the Pittsburgh Symphony. *Due Espressioni*, explained Jay S. Harrison in the New York *Herald Tribune*, represents "twelve-tone studies in extreme color and sonority. . . . It is a haunting (and haunted) work that creates an aural landscape from which all easily recognizable objects are banished."

In *Der Rote Mantel*, Nono applied his serial writing to ballet, and produced one of the most provocative dance works seen in Germany in the 1950's. Based on a poem by García Lorca, whose writings had for a long time deeply affected Nono and had stimulated him to write some of his most important works, *Der Rote Mantel* had its world première at the Berlin Festival on September 20, 1954. The critic of the Berlin *Tagesspiegel* described the ballet as a "radical experiment with new methods. . . . The single bowed or mouthed tone gains expressive significance upon the tonal fabrics of rhythm. The melodic shapes are free and floating; they are released from conventional tonality, and, at the same time, tightly controlled . . . [by the observance of] serial principles."

One of Nono's major compositions is the *Epitaph for Federico García Lorca*, a fifty-minute work in three parts for solo voices, chorus, and instruments. The first part (*España en el Corazón*) was conducted by Bruno Maderna at the Darmstadt Summer Courses on July 21, 1952; the second part (*Y Su Sangre Ya Viene Cantando*), by Hans Rosbaud at Baden-Baden on December 12, 1952; and the third part (*Memento*), by Bruno Maderna over the Northwest German Radio in Hamburg on February 16, 1953. Paul Moor, writing in the New York *Times*, did not hesitate to speak of this monumental work in a serial technique as "without question among the major creations of the Schoenbergian school. . . . In the first and last movements, three vocal soloists and chorus speak (in Spanish) and occasionally sing words by the murdered anti-Franco poet and by Pablo Neruda; the middle movement is a passionate concertante for flute and orchestra. For any one who still doubts the twelve-tone technique's potential to convey the most deeply moving human emotions, this work will be a revelation."

One of Nono's most controversial works is the opera *Intolleranza 1960*, which caused a riot at its première at the International Venice Festival of Contemporary Music on April 13, 1961. The text, based on a modern theme with strong left-wing overtones, attacked intolerance in general, and in particular, Fascism, the atom bomb, and segregation; it ends with a symbolic scene in which the world is flooded and wiped out. The music conforms to a strict serial technique, but it also exploits electronic sounds. Neo-Fascists stormed the theatre on opening night to throw stench bombs, to shower the audience with pro-Fascist and pro-Nazi leaflets, and to create such a disturbance that the police had to be called. Since Nono is a member of the Italian Communist Party, Communists also got into the act. However, when *Intolleranza 1960* was introduced in the United States (in Boston, February 22, 1965), it caused only minor disturbances. Some publicity was gained from the fact that at first Nono was refused a visa to help in the production, his entrance denied by American authorities because of his Communist affiliations. But a week later the Department of State rescinded its earlier decision and permitted Nono to enter the country. At the première itself, the only outward sign of disturbance was the sight of a single, lonely picket, representing the Polish Freedom Fighters, who paraded outside the theatre for a while. As for the opera itself, Harold C. Schonberg found it to be an "honest piece of work [which] does not parade party dogmas. . . . Musically the score is a typical example of doctrinaire serial writing. Melodic content is low, the singing line is full of wide leaps. . . . Sequences on magnetic tape . . . are not synthesized electronically. Rather voices are used, for the most part, with a minimum of electronic manipulation."

Scandal again attended a Nono première when on October 19, 1965, his oratorio, *The Representative* (text by the German playwright Peter Weiss) was introduced. Modeled after Dante's *Divine Comedy*, the oratorio, in eleven sections, is concerned with the court proceedings at the trial of Auschwitz guards in Frankfurt, Germany, in 1965. The work features a German judge, nine Jewish witnesses, and eighteen accused Nazi guards. Following the première, which had created a furor more for its inflammable text than for its music, the oratorio was performed in several other German cities, and a shortened version was broadcast over a German TV network.

Minor disturbances broke out at the International Festival of Contemporary Music in Venice in the winter of 1966 at the world première of Nono's *A Floresta e Jovem e Chea de Vida* (*The Forest Is Young and Vital*). The work is a strongly pacifist opera whose title is a quotation from an Angolan guerrilla rebel.

In discussing Nono's style—and setting it apart from that of the other members of the Schoenberg and Webern schools—Martio Bartolotto notes "the cold fire of his instrumental writing, which harbors an incandescent purity, the torrid violence of certain of his percussive explosions, and the singular outpouring of isolated sounds that push towards an aggressive resolution." These qualities, Bartolotto maintains, "are quite alien to the introspection and songlike intimacy that characterize the works of Webern."

Nono is married to Arnold Schoenberg's daughter, Nuria.

MAJOR WORKS

Ballet—Der Rote Mantel.

Chamber Music—Canti, for thirteen instruments; Incontri, for twenty-four instruments; Polifonica, Monodia, Ritmica, for flute, clarinet, bass clarinet, alto saxophone, horn, piano, and percussion.

Choral Music—Epitaph for Federico García Lorca; Il Canto Sospeso: La Terra e la Campagna; La Victoire de Guernica; Liebeslied; Cori de Didone; La Terra Promessa; Songs of Life and Love; The Representative; Sul Ponte di Hiroshima.

Opera—Intolleranza 1960; A Floresta e Jovem e Chea de Vida.

Orchestral Music—Variazioni Canoniche; Composizione, I and II; Due Espressioni; Varianti, for violin solo, strings, and woodwind; Polish Diary (Diario Polacco), for chamber orchestra and percussion; España en el Corazón.

Vocal Music—Canciones a Guiomar, for soprano, guitar, viola, cello, bass, and percussion.

ABOUT

Lang, P. H. and Broder, N. (eds.), Contemporary Music in Europe.

Vitězslav Novák
1870–1949

Vitězslav Novák was born on December 5, 1870, in Kamenice, Bohemia. The death of his

Novak: nô′ väk

father, a physician, placed the burden of supporting the family on him while he was still very young. The necessity of earning a living, however, did not interfere with his education. He attended high school, then enrolled in the University of Prague for the study of law and philosophy. At the same time he attended the Prague Conservatory where his teachers included Antonín Dvořák in composition and Josef Jiránek in piano.

VITĚZSLAV NOVÁK

Dvořák recognized Novák's creative talent and persuaded him to give up law for music. In the intensive period of musical training which followed, Novák began to write music. Some of his early piano works impressed Brahms, who was instrumental in getting them published by the house of Simrock. Novák's opus 1, a Piano Trio in G minor, appeared in 1892; opus 2, a piano ballad, *Manfred*, based on the work of Byron, was presented in 1893. These and the works that came immediately afterwards were influenced by the post-Romantic attitudes of Brahms and Liszt. The most important were the *Serenade*, for small orchestra (1894), and the Concerto for Piano and Orchestra (1895).

Just before the turn of the twentieth century, Novák entered a second creative phase—that of Bohemian nationalism. The influence of Dvořák and Smetana replaced that of Brahms and Liszt, and Novák's writing assumed a Slavic personality, rich in languorous folk melodies and vitalized with dynamic dance rhythms. This national tendency could be found in *Maryša*, an orchestral overture (1898), the piano suite *My Maytide* (1898), and his first string quartet, in G major (1899). And it became fully crystallized in one of the composer's best-known works, *In the Tatra* (1902), a beautiful tone poem of nature in the mountains.

Another fresh tendency, that of Impressionism, can be detected in the song cycle *Melancholy* (1901). Impressionism began to assume ever greater importance in such works as the orchestral tone poems *Eternal Longing* (1904) and *Toman and the Wood Nymph* (1907). Eventually we find the fullest resources of sensitive tone painting employed in a large cantata for solo voices, chorus, and orchestra, *The Specter's Bride* (1913).

Early in 1910 opera began to interest him and he brought to it some of his finest invention and richest imagination. In his first operatic effort, a light one-act comic opera, *The Imp of Zvíkov*, he gave free rein to his natural bent for irony. Written in 1914, it was first produced in Prague on October 10, 1915. His second opera, *Karlstein*—produced in Prague on November 18, 1916—reflected the composer's ardent patriotic feelings, further intensified by World War I. Novák began to seek out texts which echoed the spirit of his country and people and permitted his natural gift for tone painting greater latitude of expression. As a result, he produced two of his finest operas. One was *The Lantern*, produced in Prague on May 13, 1923, which Richard Vesely called "a genre piece depicting the sufferings of the Czechs in the years of their oppression" and which "contains a good many folk tale elements which are treated with subtle humor." The other opera, Novák's last, was *The Grandfather's Heritage*, first performed in Brno on January 16, 1926. In this work, as Vesely pointed out, Novák returns "to his favorite Slovak environment."

In his later years, Novák produced some functional pieces in conjunction with the establishment of the Czechoslovak Republic and later paid tribute to the new pro-Communist regime in such compositions as the *May Symphony* (1943), dedicated to Stalin. These and similar works are of negligible interest. But a few large-scale compositions deserve mention: the *Autumn Symphony*, for men's and women's chorus and orchestra (1934); and the orchestral compositions *South Bohemian Suite* (1937) and *De Profundis* (1941).

Vladimir Helfert noted the following stylistic mannerisms in Novák, regardless of the manner to which he may have been partial at any given time: "Novák invented a new way of using motives which lends to his work an individual character. This characteristic he combined with fresh ideas of harmony, and an original type of melody. These qualities enabled him to enrich Czech music with new forms. In the invention of harmonies, Novák successfully relied on the Impressionism of Debussy. In this respect too he was modern, for he gave Czech music thereby a new orientation. . . . But it would be a mistake to think that Novák merely transplanted French Impressionism to Bohemia. His strong individuality gave this Impressionism other values in quite an individual and original manner. Novák used only the methods of Impressionism in the treatment of his harmonies, but he did not succumb to it in his creative methods in general, for Novák's strictly logical construction has nothing in common with Impressionism. . . . Novák's type of melody, new to Czech music, is based to a great extent on the folk music of eastern Moravia and Slovakia. Even in this respect, however, Novák is original. The great wealth of rhythm and melody contained in Slovak popular music was never before used to any great extent by Czech composers. Novák was the first to do so by consciously using the melodies and rhythmical imagery of Slovak folk songs in his own compositions."

Novák distinguished himself as a teacher of composition and is often regarded as the most important one in twentieth century Bohemia. In 1909 he became professor at the Prague Conservatory. Nine years later, when the Conservatory came under government control and was reorganized, he was made professor at the Master School of the Czech State Conservatory; he held this post until his retirement in 1939. His many pupils through the years included some of Czechoslovakia's most distinguished musicians.

In 1928 Novák received an honorary doctorate from the University of Bratislava, and in 1946 he was given the title of National Artist by the Republic of Czechoslovakia.

Novák died in Skuteč, Slovakia, on July 18, 1949. "It can be said," wrote Jan V. Lowenbach in an obituary tribute, "that in the passing of this vigorous yet sensitive composer three generations of Czechoslovak music had gone at one stroke. For Novák, Dvořák's last and (next to Suk, dead since 1935) most significant pupil and successor, had been as deeply rooted in the spirit of his nation, yet linked to contemporary trends, as his master was. . . . Novák's work embraces a whole development: from the thematic tradition of the Romantics through his own colorful folklore period, to his main and artistically highest achievement of Impressionism. Though a progressive in form and harmony, he never lost his way in amorphousness and atonality. He thus achieved a synthesis which, in addition to the personal stamp, absorbed and integrated the trends of his times."

MAJOR WORKS

Ballets—Signorina Gioventù; Nikotina.

Chamber Music—3 string quartets; Violin Sonata in D minor; Piano Trio in G minor; Piano Quartet in C minor; Piano Quintet in A minor; Three Pieces, for violin and piano; Quasi una Ballata, piano trio; Cello Sonata.

Choral Music—Ballad on Moravian Folk Texts; Six Part Songs, for men's voices; The Storm, cantata; In the Homeland, for men's voices; The Specter's Bride, cantata; Czech Songs, for men's voices; Autumn Symphony; From Life, for men's voices; Twelve Lullabies, for women's voices; The Home, for men's voices; The Stars, for women's voices.

Operas—The Imp of Zvíkov, one-act comic opera; Karlstein; The Lantern; The Grandfather's Heritage.

Orchestral Music—The Corsair, concert overture; Serenade in F major, for small orchestra; Piano Concerto in E minor; Maryša, overture; The Ballad of the Soul of Jan Neruda, for voice and orchestra; In the Tatra, tone poem; Eternal Longing, tone poem; Serenade in D major, for small orchestra; Toman and the Wood Nymph, tone poem; Lady Godiva, overture; Two Romances, for voice and orchestra; In Memoriam, for voice, strings and harp; South Bohemian Suite; De Profundis, tone poem; May Symphony.

Piano Music—Bagatelles, barcarolles, Czech dances, eclogues, Souvenirs, serenades; My Maytide, suite; Sonata Eroica; Songs of Winter Nights; Slovak Suite (also for orchestra); Two Vallachian Dances; Pan; Exoticon, suite (also for orchestra); Six Sonatinas; Youth, twenty-one children's pieces.

Vocal Music—Gypsy Songs; Melancholy; In the Valley of a New Kingdom; Nocturnes; Spring, twenty children's songs; Songs on Moravian Folk Texts; Two Legends; South Bohemian Motives.

ABOUT

Štěpan, V., Novák a Suk.

Chesterian (London), February 1931; Monthly Musical Record (London), July 1950.

Gösta Nystroem
1890–1966

Gösta Nystroem was born in Silvberg, in Dalarna, Sweden, on October 13, 1890. His father was a man of great culture whose interests ranged from botany and science to painting and music. He brought to all his children a love of beauty in art and nature, and his influence on Gösta was far-reaching. A passion for painting and music and a deep-rooted love of nature have been the dominating influences in Gösta Nystroem's life.

GÖSTA NYSTROEM

Gösta received his first piano lessons from his father. He also began study of the organ by the time he was twelve, achieving such proficiency in a short period that while still in his boyhood he was able to substitute for the regular organist at church services. In his fifteenth year music study was seriously begun at the Stockholm Conservatory, where his teachers included Lundberg and Bergenson. Later he studied with Andreas Hallén at the Academy of Music.

For a long time, Nystroem divided his interest and devotion equally between music and painting, revealing a marked gift for both. In Copenhagen and Stockholm he had several exhibitions of his paintings, which were well received. He went to Paris for additional study and work in art, remaining there for twelve years.

Nystroem: nü' strûm

En route to Paris, Nystroem lost all his luggage, which contained virtually all the music he had written. The loss, which at first proved a severe shock, was soon accepted stoically as he began to assimilate new ideas and musical experiences in Paris; suddenly he lost interest in the kind of music he had written. Until his arrival in Paris he had been partial to the post-Romantic style of the late nineteenth century German composers, but his prolonged stay in Paris made him impatient with Romanticism and directed him to Impressionism. This Impressionist phase proved transitory, but it yielded two tone poems, *Ishavet* (1925) and *The Tower of Babel* (1928), among several other compositions. After additional study with Vincent d'Indy and Sabaneyev, Nystroem's style became contrapuntal but with the voices moving independently in a linear style. Greater restraint, objectivity, and purity now entered his writing. The Concerto Grosso for string orchestra (1930) and his first symphony, the *Sinfonia Breve* (1931), revealed, as Moses Pergament wrote, "a simplified style, distinguished by polyphonic texture, greater certainty of forms, and a complete release from vague color effects."

Nystroem returned to Sweden in 1932. In 1933 he became the music critic of a newspaper in Gothenburg, and in 1941 he was elected a member of the Swedish Academy. In the 1930's and 1940's he produced works of full maturity in which the style remains linear, though a romantic spirit is not altogether absent. These mature works include two of his best known compositions, both of them symphonies, the *Sinfonia Espressiva* (1935) and the *Sinfonia del Mare* (1948). The former was first performed at a Scandinavian festival in Gothenburg on February 18, 1937. It had a notable revival at the festival of the International Society for Contemporary Music at Stockholm in June 1956. The latter was introduced in Gothenburg on March 24, 1949.

Discussing the *Sinfonia Espressiva*, Alf Thoor wrote: "The first movement begins with a solo, melodic arabesque which arises, 'out of nothing, undefined, groping,' and out of it the music grows, voice after voice joining in. The development goes slowly, springing up as though guided by inexorable natural forces. Only the strings and tympani are used in the first movement, but the orchestral apparatus is complemented in each movement to reach completeness and might in the fourth and last movement in a concentration of power which meets the demands of the theme."

Thoor found that Nystroem's approach had changed in the *Sinfonia del Mare*. It was now "lighter, free from pain, basically as full of peace as the sea which inspired the composer." To Moses Pergament, this symphony is one of the most important compositions to come out of Sweden: "Inspired by and written close to the sea, it is content to give a suggestive hint of the infiniteness of the horizon and the eternal movement of the sea.... Within such a structure there is ample room for all that dwells in the human heart.... Here is the will to live and struggle for life, but here is also—in profoundly moving elegiac and funereal passages—much in it that expresses intense sorrow over the tragedy of living."

In 1958 Nystroem received an honorary doctorate from the University of Gothenburg. He died August 9, 1966.

MAJOR WORKS

Ballets—Javanese Ballet; Masquerade, ballet-pantomime; Young Men and Six Princesses; Songs at the Sea and Other Songs.

Chamber Music—String Quartet.

Operas—The Blind, radio drama with music; The Treasure of Arne.

Orchestral Music—5 symphonies; Rondo Capriccioso, for violin and orchestra; Regrets, lyric suite; Ishavet (or Arctic Sea), tone poem; The Tower of Babel, tone poem; Lyric Suite; Concerto Grosso, for strings; Hommage à France, concerto for viola and orchestra; Cello Concerto; Overture 1945; Sinfonia Concertante with cello obbligato; Palette Jottings, suite; Partita, for flute, string orchestra, and harp; Violin Concerto; Three Sea Visions; Concerto Ricercante, for piano and string orchestra.

Vocal Music—Various songs for voice and piano.

ABOUT

Music and Letters (London), January 1946; Musical Times (London), December 1928.

Carl Orff
1895–

Carl Orff was born on July 10, 1895, in Munich, Germany, of a noble Bavarian family. Secretive about his personal life, he has permitted only the barest biographical facts about himself to be made public. Orff's father was the commanding officer of the Royal Grenadiers at the Court of the Wittelsbachs. He encouraged Carl to pursue music study early. Orff's first publication, a number of songs, appeared in 1911. In 1914 he was graduated from the Academy of Music in Munich, and for the following four years he was coach and conductor in various German theatres. In 1920 he began another intensive period of study, this time privately with Heinrich Kaminski.

CARL ORFF

In 1925 he helped found the Günther School of Music where he taught for the next eleven years, developing the novel ideas of music education which he eventually elaborated in a five-volume work, *Schulwerk* (1930–1933). He believed that children should begin their musical education during their first year of schooling; that this training should begin with the elements of rhythm rather than melody. The children learn to play various percussion instruments. When they begin using melodies, they are initially taught a few notes. Then they learn to set well-known proverbs, folk rhymes, and sayings to music, in the form of canons, rondos, and so forth. The children are also taught that movements of the body are a part of musical expression. This method was so successfully developed in the Günther School that it was adopted by such educational institutions in Europe as the Mozarteum in Salzburg and the Conservatory in Vienna.

Orff himself has for a number of years conducted a class for public schools over the Munich Radio. "What the Orff approach provides," explains Harris Danziger, "is a bridge between the earliest, spontaneous musical expression of a child and the time when he is ready to undertake the study of a musical instrument. . . . Orff, by meeting the child on his own ground, permits him to use rhythms and melodies that he grasps readily—in fact material that he often creates—and provides him with easily played instruments of beautiful timbre, such as small xylophones, metalaphones and glockenspiels, creating a comfortable musical framework in which spontaneity and fantasy can flourish."

In 1925 Orff's adaptation of Monteverdi's *Orfeo* was successfully produced in Mannheim. He was responsible for two more versions of the old opera, in 1931 and 1941. He also worked on a modern realization of three other Monteverdi compositions in 1925: *Lamento d'Arianna, Ballo delle Ingrate,* and *L'Incoronazione di Poppea.*

Much of his own music was written in traditional structures and with traditional methods—choral, chamber, and orchestral compositions. Yet by the early 1930's he believed that the music of the classical and romantic schools had reached the final phase of development. He also felt that the stage provided an ideal avenue for artistic expression, but only if it stood ready to discard the appurtenances of stagecraft, costuming and scenery and to revert to stage essentials. Convinced of these truths, he disowned almost everything he had written before 1935 and embarked on a completely new road. From that time on he devoted much of his creative energies to the stage, using only the most elementary, even primitive, methods and materials.

His first important work was *Carmina Burana*, which he termed a "scenic cantata." (He scrupulously avoided the term "opera" for his dramatic works, since he was in violent opposition to the established traditions of opera and music drama.) For his text, written partly in medieval Latin and partly in medieval German, Orff went to thirteenth century goliardic poems of unknown authorship which had been discovered in the Bavarian monastery of Benediktbeuern.

The poems describe the activities of wandering students as jesters, singing the praises of nature, love, the tavern, and a free life. There is neither plot nor dramatic action. The composer provides no clue as to how the work is to be staged or costumed, or what scenery is desirable, preferring to leave such matters to the discretion of producers. The music is as barren and as simple as the text. It is scored for soprano and baritone solos, small chorus, and an orchestra made up of an extraordinarily large percussion section which is extremely active throughout the composition. There are no melodies as such, no process of thematic development, no polyphony, and only the most elementary kind of harmonies. Themes are the last word in economy. Sometimes they are reminiscent of Gregorian chants; at other times they consist only of repeated single notes. Repetitive phrases create a kind of hypnotic effect on the listener.

Carmina Burana was first performed in Frankfurt-am-Main in Germany on June 8, 1937, and made a strong impression on audiences and critics. In America, the work first became known through a recording released in 1952. Two years later, on October 3, 1954, the American première took place in San Francisco, and on November 19, 1954, Leopold Stokowski led the East Coast première in Boston. Its acceptance was immediate. Alfred Frankenstein in San Francisco described it as "one of the most vivid, picturesque and richly tuneful choral pieces of modern times." Olin Downes in New York called it "one of the most fascinating and delightful choral works that the century has produced on either side of the water." The New York Music Critics Circle singled it out as the best choral work of the season. *Carmina Burana* has remained popular and is still Orff's most frequently heard composition. Orff himself considers it the real beginning of his work as a composer. After the world première he instructed his publisher: "You can now delete all that I have written before and that you have unfortunately published. With *Carmina Burana* my 'collected works' begin."

Carmina Burana is the first of three "scenic cantatas" which form a trilogy collectively entitled *Trionfi* (*Triumphs*). The second one was *Catulli Carmina* (*Songs of Catullus*), based on Catullus's poems. A simple plot line is developed. Catullus's unhappy love for Lesbia, who betrayed him, is used by the elders to discourage their young ones from too much interest in love-making. The musical accompaniment consists almost entirely of a cappella choruses. Only the prelude and postlude require instruments, and then only four pianos and percussion are used. *Catulli Carmina* was introduced at the Leipzig Opera on November 6, 1943.

The third work of the trilogy was *Trionfo di Afrodite* (*The Triumph of Aphrodite*), which received its world première at La Scala in Milan on February 13, 1953. The text, in Latin and Greek, was derived from a Latin poem by Catullus and Greek poems by Sappho and Euripides. These describe a wedding ceremony in which the couple submit to the laws of Aphrodite. The American première took place in Houston, Texas, on April 2, 1956, Stokowski conducting. As in the two earlier works, rhythm is emphasized and is the source of considerable dynamic appeal. Chant-like recitatives and repetitions of notes, chords, and phrases contribute elemental power.

Commenting on his partiality for texts that reach into the Greek and Latin past, through ancient and medieval poetry, Orff has said: "I do not feel them as old, but rather as valid. The timely element disappears, and only the spiritual powers remain. My entire interest is in the expression of spiritual realities. I wrote for the theatre in order to convey a spiritual attitude."

Even before the last of the trilogy was completed, Orff wrote three delightful works for the stage. Two are derived from fairy tales by the Grimm Brothers; one comes from an old Bavarian legend. The fairy tales are *Der Mond* (*The Moon*) and *Die Kluge* (*The Wise Woman*). The first is described by the composer as a "little world theatre," and the latter as "the story of the king and the wise woman." In each instance, Orff continues to emphasize rhythm, but singable tunes and dance-melodies, together with comic, even burlesque, episodes, contribute considerable popular appeal. Spoken word is as important as sung melody; and pantomime and dance are as prominent as stage action. "Actually," said Jay Harrison about *Der Mond* in the New York *Herald Tribune*, "the work . . . is a combination of oratorio, varsity show, and lyric drama; thus it has something for everybody. Throughout, it alternates dance-hall tunes, statuesque arias, beerstube ballads and even concludes with a nursery air." *Der Mond* was seen first in Munich on February 5, 1939, after which it was often produced in Germany with juvenile casts. Orff revised it some years later, and this version was first produced in Munich on November 26, 1950, then given by the New York City Opera (the American première of the opera) on October 16, 1956. *Die Kluge* was introduced in Frankfurt-am-Main, Germany, on February 20, 1943, and in the United States, in Cleveland, on December 7, 1949.

The little opera based on an old legend was *Die Bernauerin*, subtitled "A Bavarian Piece." "It is a play with accompanying musical effects achieved by a small percussive orchestra and a chorus that sings, chants, hums, and executes involved rhythmic spoken passages with instrumental agility," reported Virginia Pleasants. "For the rest, communication among principal characters is accomplished by unaccompanied dialogue." The text is based on a legend from the Middle Ages and is written in a medieval Bavarian dialect. The first performance took place in Stuttgart, Germany, on June 15, 1947. The American première followed on March 21, 1968, at the University of Missouri at Kansas City.

During the period that the *Trionfi* was being planned and written, Orff also wrote *Antigonae*, a musical play based on Sophocles as adapted by Hölderlin, and it was produced at the Salzburg Festival on August 9, 1949. The response was mixed. Some considered it a work of major importance, in a class with *Carmina Burana*; others regarded the whole work as ingenuous. Everett Helm described Orff's music thus: "The melodic, rhythmic and harmonic means are primary. The major part of the opera consists of a kind of rhythmic declamation, employing repeated notes, a sort of intoned recitative that has nothing to do with traditional free recitative. Some passages are sung without accompaniment (although always in rhythm) or with only an occasional punctuating chord by the orchestra —short rhythmic motives that are repeated many times. Harmonically, the style can be reduced essentially to tonic and dominant, and there are long stretches in which no change of harmony occurs. Dissonance is used sparingly; counterpoint, save of a rhythmic nature, is nonexistent."

Two religious productions came in the late 1950's, one for Easter, the other for Christmas. The former was *Comoedia de Christi Resurrectione* (Stuttgart, April 21, 1957); the latter, *Ludus de Nato Infante Mirificus* (Stuttgart, December 1960). "In both pieces the miraculous event—Christ's birth or resurrection—is not directly depicted," wrote Everett Helm, "but is intimated and described through third persons. In both instances the description is put into the mouths of simple folk. . . . And in both plays the element of darkness is opposed to that of light."

Other Orff works for the theatre included a setting of Shakespeare's *A Midsummer Night's Dream*, introduced in Darmstadt on November 2, 1952; a Bavarian comedy, *Astutuli*, presented in Munich on October 20, 1953; and Hölderlin's setting of Sophocles' *Oedipus —Oedipus der Tyrann—*produced in Stuttgart on December 11, 1959.

Antigonae and *Oedipus der Tyrann* are two works of a trilogy based on Greek dramas. The third is *Prometheus*. Orff used the original Greek text of Aeschylus' *Prometheus Bound* rather than a German adaptation. The world première of *Prometheus* took place at the Stuttgart Opera on March 23, 1968. On April 23, 1968, *Antigonae* was first presented in the United States, in a concert version performed by the Little Orchestra Society in New York, Thomas Scherman conducting.

The following comments by Robert Jackson on *Oedipus der Tyrann* apply as well to the other two works in the trilogy: "Orff's music does not reinterpret the text as much as it reinforces it, accents it, and clarifies it. Most of the lines are sung to convey the dramatically potent dialogue, but a good deal of this is on the level of speech, mixed with patches of spoken dialogue, or areas of rhythmically notated declamation against accompaniment, or still others of melismatic writing. . . . The economic instrumental accompaniment which punctuates and emphasizes this concentrated vocal line relies heavily on percussion."

For many years Orff lived in a modest house in a suburb of Munich. In the middle 1950's he had built for himself and his wife—Luise Rinser, a novelist—a quiet retreat on the Ammersee, an hour's drive from the center of Munich. He prefers seclusion and a static existence. He rarely travels except to participate in performances of his works, although in

July 1962 he crossed the Atlantic for the first time. The purpose of his visit was to attend the Conference on Elementary Musical Education at the University of Toronto, set up primarily to discuss and evaluate Orff's contributions. At that time Harris Danziger described Orff as "a tall, vigorous, good-humored man . . . whose preferred manner of ascending and leaving a platform was to hop on and off. He made two major addresses, participated in all panel discussions and one evening read his verse play, *Astutuli*, acting out all the parts. To hear Orff read is to experience the full meaning of his concept of the unity of rhythm, speech and dramatic gesture."

Orff was honored by the German government with the order Pour le Mérite, for science and art.

MAJOR WORKS

Choral Music—Concerto di Voci; Sirmio; Laudes Creaturarum; Die Sänger der Vorwelt; Sunt Lacrimae Rerum; Naenie und Dithyrambe.

Orchestral Music—Praeludium; Concerto for Wind Instruments and Harpsichord; Entrata (after William Byrd); Bayerische Musik.

Stage Music—Trionfi, trilogy (comprising Carmina Burana, Catulli Carmina, and Trionfo di Afrodite); Der Mond; Die Kluge; Die Bernauerin; Antigonae; Astutuli; Ein Sommernachtstraum (A Midsummer Night's Dream); Comoedia de Christi Resurrectione (Easter cantata); Oedipus der Tyrann; Ludus de Nato Infante Mirificus (Christmas cantata); Prometheus.

ABOUT

Kiekert, I., Die Musikalische Form in den Werken Carl Orffs; Laux, K., Musik und Musiker der Gegenwart; Liess, A., Carl Orff.

Etude, November 1956; Musical America, October 1950; Musical Quarterly, July 1955.

Andrzej Panufnik
1914–

Andrzej Panufnik was born in Warsaw on September 24, 1914, of a highly musical family. His father was a famous maker of lutes and other string instruments; his mother, an Englishwoman, was a gifted violinist. Revealing a strong musical talent in his childhood, Panufnik received his first music lessons from his mother. He then progressed to other private teachers before entering the Warsaw Conservatory where he studied composition

---

Panufnik: pä noof′nēk

with Sikorski. Upon being graduated in 1936, Panufnik went to Vienna where at the State Academy of Music in 1937 and 1938 he was Felix Weingartner's pupil in conducting. "He is a very gifted conductor," Weingartner wrote in a testimonial, "and will certainly make his way." After his studies in Vienna, Panufnik completed his training in conducting with Philippe Gaubert in Paris.

ANDRZEJ PANUFNIK

Though he had written a number of works in Vienna and Paris, he did not achieve a personal style until after his return to Poland during World War II. The first of his orchestral works to reveal a richer and deeper strain than any he had hitherto disclosed was the deeply moving *Tragic Overture* (1942), written during the Nazi occupation. Though completed two years before the Warsaw uprising, its dark and sinister mood and its frequent outbursts of rebellion seem to anticipate the tragedy to come. The work is based on a four-note motive which, Stefan Jarocinski explains, "emerges persistently in an ever-changing harmonic atmosphere often accompanied by sharp polytonal chords resulting from contrapuntal intricacies." Published in 1947, the overture was soon performed all over Europe and became its composer's first successful composition. Leopold Stokowski introduced it in America at a concert of the New York Philharmonic on March 24, 1949.

During the 1940's, Panufnik wrote several works in a national Polish style. One, the delightful *Five Folk Songs*, for children's voices, represented Poland at the festival of the International Society for Contemporary Music in London on July 12, 1946, a few weeks after it had been broadcast over Radiodiffusion Française under the composer's direction. Another national composition was the *Old Polish Suite*, for voice and piano (1949), based on folk airs from Masovia. Most significant, however, was the *Sinfonia Rustica*, derived from folk melodies and rhythms, which received first prize in the Chopin Centennial contest in Warsaw. The symphony enjoyed a highly successful première at a Warsaw festival on May 13, 1949.

Soon after World War II, Panufnik was appointed conductor of the Cracow Philharmonic. His one-year tenure of this post served as the apprenticeship for a far more significant conducting assignment which came his way in 1946 when he became the musical director of the Warsaw Philharmonic. In 1946–1947 Panufnik toured Europe for the first time as a conductor, with successful guest appearances with major orchestras in London, Paris, Geneva, Zürich, and Copenhagen. In 1961 he made his first extended conducting tour of Latin America.

While thus pursuing a career as conductor, Panufnik was making important headway as a composer. *Berceuse*, for twenty-nine instruments and percussion, was performed in Paris on April 26, 1948. In this he experimented with quarter-tones. *Nocturne*, for orchestra—written in 1947 to commemorate the tenth anniversary of the death of Karol Szymanowski, the Polish composer—was awarded first prize in the Szymanowski contest. *Heroic Overture*, written for the Olympiad in Helsinki, received a gold medal and was performed in Helsinki under the composer's direction on July 27, 1952.

In July 1953 Panufnik made a dramatic escape from behind the Iron Curtain with his British-born wife, Scarlett, details of which she described in a book, *Out of the City of Fear*, published in London in 1956. He made his home in England and became a British citizen. During the years from 1957 to 1959 he was the principal conductor of the City of Birmingham Symphony Orchestra.

Panufnik's major compositions in the 1950's included *Rhapsody*, for orchestra, commissioned by BBC and introduced in London on January 11, 1957; *Sinfonia Elegiaca*, the world première of which took place in 1958 in the United States, with Stokowski conducting the Houston Symphony—a work described by the local Houston critics as a "symphonic lamentation" and a "song of mourning" (this music was later adapted for the ballet *Elegy*); and *Polonia*, suite for orchestra, which was commissioned by BBC and first heard in London on August 21, 1959.

In 1963 Panufnik was awarded first prize in a competition sponsored by Prince Rainier III of Monaco which drew one hundred and thirty-three participants representing thirty-eight countries. The winning composition, *Sinfonia Sacra*, had its world première in Monte Carlo in August 1964. In October of the same year the symphony was heard on United Nations Day in Paris during the Semaine Internationale de Paris, and in February 1965 Leopold Stokowski conducted its American première in Rochester, New York. Ossia Trilling of the London *Sunday Times* described the work as "an original and imposing personal statement with unmistakable religious, national, and even erotic musical roots." Bernard Gavoty said in *Le Figaro*: "This is better than just a composition; it is a work of art. . . . It is the prayer between the episodes of battle, devout reflection following the action: an image of life itself, made up of tensions and relaxations."

On November 17, 1968, Leopold Stokowski conducted the American Symphony Orchestra in New York in the world première of *Epitaph for the Victims of Katyn*.

Panufnik lives with his second wife, Camilla, in Twickenham, Middlesex. In 1965 he was awarded the Sibelius Centenary Medal for composition.

MAJOR WORKS

Choral Music—Five Folk Songs, for children's voices; Song to the Virgin Mary.

Orchestral Music—Tragic Overture; Berceuse, for twenty-nine string instruments and percussion; Nocturne; Sinfonia Rustica; Old Polish Suite, for string orchestra; Symphony of Peace; Heroic Overture; Rhapsody; Lullaby; Sinfonia Elegiaca; Polonia, suite; Piano Concerto; Concerto in Modo Antico, for trumpet, tympani, harp, harpsichord, and strings; Autumn Music; Landscape, for strings; Two Lyric Pieces, for small orchestra; Sinfonia Sacra; Elegy; Medieval Triptych, for strings; Epitaph for the Victims of Katyn.

Piano Music—Six Miniature Studies.

Vocal Music—Suita Polska, for soprano and piano; Five Polish Peasant Songs, for soprano (or treble voices in unison) and instruments; Hommage à Chopin, for soprano and piano.

Horatio W. Parker
1863–1919

Horatio William Parker was born in Auburndale, Massachusetts, on September 15, 1863. His father was a distinguished architect; his mother was a linguist who had translated works from Greek and Latin, and an excellent organist. Though there was music all the time in the Parker household, Horatio showed no interest in it until his fourteenth year, when his mother began teaching him the piano and organ. His musical instincts thus awakened, he devoted himself to study and made remarkable progress. As his mother recalled, he would spend "literally whole days at the piano, beginning at daylight and stopping only when his father sent him to bed, perhaps at 11:00 P.M. From that time onwards, he had one objective. Sports and recreation were left out of his life, and the necessary education was with great difficulty imparted in the intervals of music study." When he was fifteen he set to music fifty poems from Kate Greenaway's *Under the Window*, a task that took him only two days. One year later he became principal organist at St. Paul's Church in Dedham and wrote much church music, including hymns and anthems.

Parker studied music intensively with Stephen Emery in theory, George W. Chadwick in composition, and John Orth in piano. Chadwick, who had just opened his studio in Boston and had enrolled Parker as one of his first pupils, later recalled: "He was far from docile. In fact he was impatient of the restrictions of musical form and rather rebellious of the discipline of counterpoint and fugues. But he was very industrious and did his work faithfully and well. His lessons usually ended with his swallowing his medicine, but with many a wry grimace. It was quite natural that before long our relationship should develop from that of teacher and pupil into a warm and sincere friendship."

In 1882 Parker went to Europe to complete his musical education. For several years he studied conducting with L. Abel and organ and composition with Josef Rheinberger. The latter thought so highly of Parker that he asked him to introduce his Concerto in F for organ upon its première in Munich. In Germany, Parker started to write major orchestral works, including a symphony and several overtures, and a number of cantatas which received performances.

HORATIO W. PARKER

After his marriage in Germany on August 9, 1886, to Anna Plössl, daughter of a Munich baker, Parker returned to the United States and received an appointment as organist and music director of St. Paul's Cathedral School in Garden City, Long Island. He also officiated as the organist at St. Andrew's Church and entered a teaching career as a member of the faculty of the National Conservatory, both in New York City.

On May 3, 1893 Parker's first work to gain wide recognition received its première in New York: the sacred cantata *Hora Novissima*, for mixed chorus and orchestra, based on a twelfth century Latin poem by Bernard of Cluny. The performance proved so successful that in 1894 the oratorio was performed by the Handel and Haydn Society of Boston and at the Cincinnati May Music Festival conducted by Theodore Thomas. In 1899 it was given with outstanding success at the Three Choirs Festival in Worcester, England, marking the beginning of Parker's fame and popularity in that country.

Henry E. Krehbiel described this, one of

Parker's most celebrated works, as follows: "It is divided into eleven numbers, including solos for soprano, contralto, tenor and bass, a quartet for the same voices, an unaccompanied chorus in the old style, a capital fugue, a double chorus and four unaccompanied choruses. At the bottom of the composition lies a finely conceived and very pregnant phrase, in the development of which Parker has displayed a degree of learning, a skill, a fluency of musical utterance both vocal and instrumental, a sense of euphony and depth of feeling which redound to the credit, not only of him as an individual, but also of the American school."

In this work, said David Stanley Smith, "Parker's distinctive style is for the first time fully developed. His originality . . . is the more striking in that repetition of treatment has not yet set in. The melody and part-writing are particularly fascinating, and the sentiment, which lies midway between the celestial and the human, responds naturally to the feeling of the thoughtful listener."

In 1893 Parker moved to Boston where he became organist and choirmaster of Trinity Church. One year later he was appointed professor of music at Yale University, a post he retained until the end of his life. He combined his duties as organist and teacher with those of conductor, directing regular concerts of the New Haven Symphony, which he helped to found, and several choral societies.

David Stanley Smith thus described the feverish round of activities that absorbed Parker, following him through a typical week: "Late Saturday afternoon, choir rehearsal in New York; Sunday service, morning and evening; Monday afternoon and evening in Philadelphia for rehearsals of the Eurydice and Orpheus Clubs; night train to New York, thence to New Haven for two classes on Tuesday; Tuesday evening by trolley to Derby for a rehearsal of the Derby Choral Club, arriving in New Haven at midnight; Wednesday, a lecture on the History of Music and a class in composition; Thursday, again two classes; Thursday evening, rehearsal of the New Haven Symphony; Saturday, off again to New York. Naturally these rehearsals culminated in frequent concerts."

Despite this taxing schedule Parker was still able to write a large amount of music which placed him among the leading American composers of his time. An oratorio, *The Legend of St. Christopher*, was introduced on April 15, 1898, by the New York Oratorio Society. A cantata, *A Wanderer's Psalm*, was given by the Hereford Three Choirs Festival in England in 1900. A lyric rhapsody, *A Star Song*, was heard at the Norwich Festival in England in 1902, after winning the Paderewski Prize. In addition, his Concerto for Organ and Orchestra in E minor was performed by the Boston Symphony on December 26, 1902. Pointing up the high esteem with which Parker was regarded in England was the fact that in 1902 he was given an honorary doctorate by Cambridge University.

In 1911 Parker was awarded the first prize of ten thousand dollars in an American opera competition sponsored by the Metropolitan Opera Association in New York. Parker's opera, *Mona*, with a text by Brian Hooker, was produced at the Metropolitan Opera on March 14, 1912, the third American opera ever presented by the company. The setting is Britain during the Roman occupation. Mona, the heroine, is a British princess who falls in love with the Roman governor, one of the detested invaders. Richard Aldrich described Parker's score in the New York *Times* as a "work of remarkable musicianship. . . . It has many elements of beauty, strength and originality." But Aldrich also pointed out that the opera as a whole lacked "lyrical moments . . . [in] passages of really musical climax" and that it was deficient in dramatic impulse.

Parker's next opera, *Fairyland* (text also by Brian Hooker), was awarded first prize in an American opera competition conducted by the National Federation of Women's Clubs. It was introduced in Los Angeles on July 1, 1915. But, as Walter Henry Hall emphasized, Parker's greatest importance as composer does not rest with his operas: "His ventures into opera, while they proved his complete mastery of musical material and enhanced his reputation, also showed that his greatest gift was in the direction of pure choral music."

Parker died of pneumonia at his home in Cedarhurst, Long Island, on December 18, 1919. His last published work was *The Dream of Mary*, a "morality" for solo voices, chorus, children's chorus, and orchestra, introduced

Penderecki

by the Litchfield County Choral Union in Norfolk, Connecticut, on June 4, 1918.

Throughout his life, Parker suffered severely from rheumatism. Notwithstanding this indisposition, he was an enthusiastic participant in several sports. He played golf often, enjoyed cycling, and on occasion indulged in mountain climbing.

"I believe firmly in permanent musical values," he wrote in 1918, describing his musical credo. "I think that those parts of Handel's *Messiah* which now please us most are exactly the ones which made the greatest impression on the very first audience which heard the work sung. I know not whether they are what Handel himself wrote with greatest pleasure or at highest tension, for a composer is at times a partly unconscious instrument who records beauties thrust upon him, flowing through him from heaven to earth. He does not always know what he writes, however perfect it may be. . . . The high aim and the simple integrity of great composers are no accidents. Such men have made themselves perfect instruments by their life work and thought."

MAJOR WORKS

Chamber Music—2 string quartets; Suite, for piano trio; Suite for Violin and Piano.

Choral Music—Hora Novissima; The Legend of St. Christopher; A Wanderer's Psalm; A Star Song; A Song of the Times; Seven Greek Pastoral Scenes; Morven and the Grail; The Dream of Mary; A.D., 1919; various ballads, choruses, odes, and services.

Operas—Mona; Fairyland.

Orchestral Music—4 concert overtures; The Ballad of a Knight and His Daughter; Symphony in C minor; Scherzo in G major; A Northern Ballad; Organ Concerto in E minor; Crépuscule, for mezzo soprano and orchestra; Symphonic Poem.

Organ Music—Sonata in E-flat major; 30 pieces.

Piano Music—Six Lyrics; 12 pieces.

Vocal Music—Six Old English Songs; Swan Songs; various love, sacred, and other songs for voice and piano.

ABOUT

Chadwick, G. W., Horatio Parker; Howard, J. T., Our American Music; Semler, I. P., Horatio Parker: A Memoir for His Grandchildren.

Musical Quarterly, April 1930.

Krysztof Penderecki
1933–

Krysztof Penderecki—probably the most significant Polish composer since Szymanowski and undoubtedly one of the most original in methods and techniques—was born in Debica, Poland, on November 23, 1933. His parents did not plan to make him a musician. Krysztof spent his boyhood years, during World War II, in a little Galician town where he received his preliminary academic education. In 1951 he went to Cracow for higher education. His principal interests were philosophy, art, and literature; music was just a diversion. He taught himself to play the violin and began to write pieces in the style of Bach and Paganini. Before long he became intensely interested in the polyphonic music of composers preceding Bach and began to experiment with polyphonic writing (to which he later occasionally reverted in some of his mature compositions).

His increasing interest in music led him to seek out a teacher in composition. Lessons with F. Skolyszewski convinced him that he wanted to become a composer. In 1954 he entered the Superior School of Music from which he was graduated in 1958 and where his principal teachers were Arthur Malawski and Stanislaw Wiechowicz. Penderecki later became a professor of composition at the same school.

His first serious work appeared in 1958: *Psalms for David*, scored for voices, strings and percussion. This was his first published composition. Within the next year it was followed by *Emanations*, for two string orchestras, and *Strophes*, for soprano, narrator and ten instruments. The three compositions—the *Psalms*, the *Emanations* and *Strophes*—captured the first three prizes in the Young Composers' Competition in Poland. In *Strophes* (texts by Sophocles, Isaiah, Jeremiah, and others) we can already discern Penderecki's later partiality for the most novel procedures, particularly in the unusual way in which he uses instruments and voices to produce new sounds and color combinations. Heard at the third annual Warsaw Autumn Music Festival, *Strophes* caused much controversy.

Penderecki: pĕn dĕ rĕts′ kē

His tendency to attempt the untried and to seek out new effects became even more evident in *Dimensions de Temps et du Silence*, for chorus and orchestra. Here is how Stefan Jarocinski described this work: "Varicolored lines and structures (among others vibrating 'tone areas') are joined by means of permeation; the mixed chorus of forty persons takes over the function of percussion and also serves to produce rustling effects by an appropriate combination of whistling and sibilants."

KRYSZTOF PENDERECKI

From that point on, Penderecki became ever bolder in his novel procedures. Sometimes he embraced serialism (although only tentatively), as in *Anakalis*, for percussion and strings (1960); *Fluorescences*, for chamber orchestra (1962); and the Sonata for Cello and Orchestra (1964). At times he made a brief excursion into the world of aleatory music, though partially controlled. However, electronic music does not interest him at all; for the most part his novel practices are of his own devising. For instance, he wrote for the violins and had the performers rap their bows on their chairs or their fingers on the bodies of their instruments; he had them play behind or on the bridge or on the tail piece; he employed the highest notes possible with indeterminate pitch and had them perform arpeggios behind the bridge. The English critic William Mann, in reviewing *Dimensions de Temps et du Silence*, commented wryly that the composer insisted upon doing everything

possible with the instruments "short of actually playing them." Frequently the composer allowed the players freedom to select whatever notes and rhythmic patterns they chose. In writing for chorus, Penderecki instructed them to shout or whisper or grunt or mutter—as well as sing. In his notation he sometimes deserted conventional notes for unusual markings and designs; Nicolas Slonimsky calls his scores "pictorially startling," explaining that some of the symbols are "hieroglyphic in their visual appearance."

All this may sound quixotic, perhaps even bizarre. But, as Bernard Jacobson has noted, "at his best—which is to say in most of his output—Penderecki uses his chosen methods to produce drama of an intensity and a human impact unmatched by any other composer alive."

Such drama, intensity, and human impact can be found in the first of Penderecki's works to gain him international recognition: The *Threnody for the Victims of Hiroshima* (1960), a memorial on the fifteenth anniversary of the dropping of the first atomic bomb. This composition received first prize in a competition sponsored by the Polish Radio, was introduced in Warsaw, and has since been performed by major orchestras throughout Europe and America. It is scored for fifty-two string instruments. Nicolas Slonimsky, in his program notes for the Los Angeles Philharmonic, explains that this is not "representational music. . . . No attempt is made to convey the impact of the shock wave produced by the atomic bomb . . . but the psychological impact of the music is tremendous, giving an overwhelming sense of distant devastation. One after another, instrumental groups enter at the highest possible pitch, in fortissimo, and form in fifteen seconds a gray cloud of static sound. Suddenly, a microcosmic concert is heard in a wave of disintegrated atomic particles. . . . The polyphony of tapping, rapping, rattling, scraping, sliding, colliding microsounds pervades the scenes; there are silent gaps as if to make a shadowed silhouette of an obliterated human being outlined on the marble slab of a public stairway."

Despite the highly unorthodox procedures and techniques in this *Threnody*, it does have one section (the middle part) in which the composer's early fascination with polyphonic writing is revealed. Penderecki continued to combine polyphony with his iconoclastic methods and sounds in such later major works as the Stabat Mater, for a cappella chorus (1962); the Canon, for fifty-two stringed instruments (1962); and the choral composition that is now generally conceded to be his masterwork, the *Passion According to St. Luke* (1966).

Indeed, there are many critics in Europe and America who regard the Passion as one of the greatest choral compositions created in the twentieth century. It had a tremendous success in Europe, receiving over forty performances in a year and a half, as well as representation at the Venice Festival of Contemporary Music. The American première took place in Minneapolis on November 2, 1967, Stanislaw Skrowaczewski conducting. New York heard it on March 6, 1968, once again in a performance by the Minneapolis Orchestra. Both in Minneapolis and in New York the critics echoed the rhapsodic praises previously voiced in Europe.

The work calls for a narrator (speaking voice), solo voices, chorus, and orchestra. The solo soprano is assigned three arias based on texts from the Psalms, Jeremiah, and the Roman Breviary for Good Friday. The baritone takes the part of Jesus. The basso is called upon to assume several minor parts. The chorus has numerous dramatic as well as spiritual and contemplative passages.

In his review of a recording of this masterwork, Bernard Jacobson called *The Passion According to St. Luke* "a work of shattering dramatic impact and powerfully individual inspiration." He described it as follows in *High Fidelity* magazine: "In musical style, the work is boldly eclectic. Much of the choral and orchestral writing carries on the daring sonic experiments familiar from Penderecki's other works. But alongside these are Gregorian elements, one or two well-distinguished folk elements, and elements from several other styles. . . . Jesus sings mostly in a flexible chromatic style that combines wide post-Webernesque leaps with a recurring cadential tendency." Jacobson adds: "What is most impressive is the way these multifarious elements are made to serve a philosophical and expressive design of exceptional power and coherence. The musical development of the work is indissoluble from its dramatic progress. Thus the choruses gradually become firmer in outline—gradually, as it were, take on flesh—as the inevitability of the Passion story becomes manifest."

Hardly less moving or dramatic is the *Dies Irae*, for solo voices, chorus, and orchestra. The orchestration of this work calls for an air-raid siren. Written in 1967 in memory of those who died in Auschwitz during World War II, the work received its world première in Auschwitz in the year of its composition.

Premières of other major works followed. Two compositions deserving special mention are the Capriccio for Violin and Orchestra and the Concerto for Violono Grande and Orchestra. The latter is unusual because of the instrument for which it was written. The violono grande is a five-string instrument created by Hans Olf Hanson; it is shaped like a viola and it combines the ranges of viola and violin. Penderecki had interested himself in this instrument ten years before he wrote his concerto; in 1959 he wrote *Three Miniatures* for it. However, the Concerto, which had been commissioned by the Swedish government, was his most ambitious attempt to bring artistic validity to the instrument. The world première took place at Dartmouth College, Hanover, New Hampshire, on August 4, 1968. Without abandoning his interest in producing the most unusual sounds and timbres, Penderecki created a composition which one reviewer found to be thoroughly "fascinating. . . . The violono grande came through its maiden voyage triumphantly."

Penderecki paid his first visit to the United States late in 1967 to attend the American première of his *Passion According to St. Luke.* Irving Kolodin described him as a "studious-looking bearded man . . . in his mid-thirties," who "spoke only Polish (in addition to some German)." Though his religious works may suggest strong feelings about Catholicism and though some of his orchestral works hint at an equally powerful political consciousness, Penderecki has refused to acknowledge that either religion or politics has played a significant role in the writing of some of his major works. He explained during an interview in New York: "Well, I am Catholic, but membership in a given church is not really the point. It's rather that I am very much concerned with these topics—Auschwitz, Hiroshima, in my *Threnody*, and the implications of the Passion, which after all is still one of the most topical and indeed universal stories. And I am concerned with these things in an essentially moral and social way, not in either a political or a sectarian religious way."

The year 1968 proved eventful for Penderecki as far as performances went. It witnessed the world premières in Munich of his two operas: *Mother Johanna of the Angels* and *King Ubu*. Among significant local premières of his music in America the same year were the first New York performance of his *Passion According to St. Luke*, the Stabat Mater (by the Bach Collegium and the Kantorei Stuttgart on a visit to New York), and the Capriccio for Violin and Orchestra in Buffalo, New York. In the 1968–1969 season, Penderecki served as composer-in-residence with the Buffalo Philharmonic.

MAJOR WORKS

Chamber Music—Three Miniatures, for violono grande and piano.

Choral Music—Psalms of David; Dimensions de Temps et du Silence, for chorus and orchestra; Psalms; Stabat Mater; Passion According to St. Luke; Dies Irae.

Operas—Mother Johanna of the Angels; King Ubu; The Devils of Loudun.

Orchestral Music—Emanations, for two string orchestras; Anakalis, for strings and percussion; Threnody for the Victims of Hiroshima, for fifty-two string instruments; Polymorphie; Fluorescences, for chamber orchestra; Canon, for fifty-two stringed instruments; Sonata for Cello and Orchestra; Capriccio for Violin and Orchestra; Concerto for Violono Grande and Orchestra; De Natura Sonoris.

Vocal Music—Strophes, for soprano, narrator, and ten instruments.

ABOUT

Lang, P. H. and Broder, N. (eds.), Contemporary Music in Europe.

High Fidelity, April 1967, January 1968; Saturday Review, February 24, 1968.

Vincent Persichetti
1915–

Vincent Persichetti was born in Philadelphia on June 6, 1915. He began to study the piano at five, harmony at eight, and counterpoint at

---

Persichetti: pûr sĭ ket′ tē

nine. When he was eleven, he was already earning money by playing the piano in several local orchestras, experience which he feels helped him greatly in his later compositions for orchestra. At twelve he gave organ recitals and played the double bass in a school orchestra, and at fifteen he was appointed organist and musical director of St. Mark's Reformed Church. He held the post of music director at the Arch Street Presbyterian Church in Philadelphia for sixteen years, beginning in 1932.

VINCENT PERSICHETTI

He received a more systematic training in music at Combs College of Music: composition with Russell King Miller, and piano with Gilbert Raynold Combs and Alberto Jonas. "In those days," he reveals, "Combs College was an active school with a hundred-piece orchestra. I was assistant conductor for several years, then regular conductor for two years. In my early teens, I was restricted to writing in styles that did not go past Debussy. I wrote several volumes of 'forbidden music' of my own: chorales for strings, fugues for woodwinds, dances for brass and 'Passachaconnes' for organ. (I was never able to find out the difference between a passacaglia and a chaconne so I decided to combine the two into a title of my own invention, Passachaconne.) I was caught with this music and thrown out of all classes. From then on, my study was done privately with the faculty."

After receiving his Bachelor of Music degree

from Combs College in 1936, he studied conducting for two years at Curtis Institute with Fritz Reiner. From 1939 to 1941 he held scholarships in piano under Mme. Olga Samaroff Stokowski at the Philadelphia Conservatory of Music; at the same time he studied composition with Paul Nordoff. For the next two summers he studied with Roy Harris at Colorado College. In 1941 he received his master's degree and in 1945 his doctorate, both from the Philadelphia Conservatory.

From 1939 to 1942 Persichetti headed the composition department at Combs College. In this period he served his real apprenticeship as composer, begun with the writing of his first piano sonata and his first string quartet in 1939 and continuing with his first symphony, completed in 1942. The symphony was not heard until 1947, when it was performed in Rochester, New York, on October 21. Most of the compositions he had written before 1938 were discarded.

From 1942 to 1962, Persichetti was the head of the composition department of the Philadelphia Conservatory. In 1947 he joined the composition department of the Juilliard School of Music, and subsequently he became department head.

Persichetti's first important appearance on a concert program took place on April 20, 1945, when Eugene Ormandy conducted the Philadelphia Orchestra in the première of *Fables*, for narrator and orchestra. This was a setting of six familiar Aesop fables, which, the composer explained, "is an emotional parallel of the ageless tales and the text an integral part of the music; no certain instrument is assigned to any one character, but rather a musical equivalent is given the underlying meaning of the fables." The fables used were "The Fox and the Grapes," "The Wolf and the Ass," "The Hare and the Tortoise," "The Cat and the Fox," "A Raven and a Swan," and "The Monkey and the Camel."

Fables made a good impression. The compositions which came immediately after that strengthened the belief that Persichetti was "a personality of great energy," as Rafael Druian described him at the time in *Modern Music*. Particularly impressive was the third piano sonata (1943), which received first prize at the Colorado College of Fine Arts and was heard at the Seventh Annual Festival of Modern Music in Los Angeles. "This substantial work," wrote Rafael Druian, "is built entirely upon a choral motive. It moves from a tragic 'Desolation' to a memorial-like 'Episode,' and culminates in the 'Psalm,' a hope for peace and a hymn of praise."

Noteworthy, too, was Persichetti's Third Symphony, which he had begun in 1942 but did not complete until 1946. Eugene Ormandy conducted the world première in Philadelphia on November 21, 1947.

In the 1950's, Persichetti completed several more symphonies of which the most significant was the fourth, introduced by the Philadelphia Orchestra under Ormandy on December 17, 1954; the Symphony for Strings, commissioned by the Louisville Orchestra, which presented it under Robert Whitney on August 28, 1954; and the Seventh, first performed in St. Louis on October 24, 1959, Eduard van Remoortel conducting. A distinguished chamber music composition was also a fruit of the 1950's, the Piano Quintet which the Kroll String Quartet offered in Washington, D.C., on February 4, 1955.

Persichetti has remained productive, completing major works in all the instrumental forms as well as large works for chorus and numerous songs. Nicolas Slonimsky has described his style as "synthetic" and remarked that it is notable for its "contrapuntal compactness" and the amalgamation of "seemingly incompatible idioms of different historical periods." Thomas Scherman said of Persichetti's creative manner: "Persichetti has synthesized the several features of twentieth century music, but has also retained a connection with the musical culture of the last three hundred years. At the same time his language is sufficiently advanced to allow further exploration of combinations that may bring a new realm of values, not yet realized, into a general musical speech."

Since 1952 Persichetti has combined his activity as head of the composition department at the Juilliard School of Music with the office of editorial adviser for the Elkan-Vogel publishing company in Philadelphia. In 1948 he received a grant from the National Academy of Arts and Letters, and in 1958–1959 a Guggenheim Fellowship. He was honored with a medal from the Italian government in 1958, and in 1964 with a citation from the American Bandmasters Association.

On June 2, 1941, Persichetti married Dorothea Flanagan. With their two children they make their home in Philadelphia. Husband and wife are active in promoting and performing contemporary music in concerts of two-piano and four-hand piano music. Dorothea Persichetti has been a member of the faculty of the Philadelphia Conservatory and has given many performances of her husband's piano compositions.

Boating is a major extramusical interest with Persichetti. He raced sailboats for many years with the Barnegat Bay Yachting Association, most of his sailing having been done in fifteen-foot Snipes, which are international class boats. Indoors, Persichetti enjoys woodcarving and stone sculpturing.

Persichetti is the author of *Twentieth-Century Harmony* (1961). With Frieda Schreiber he collaborated in the writing of a biography of William Schuman (1954).

MAJOR WORKS

Ballet—Then One Day; King Lear.

Chamber Music—8 serenades, for various instruments; 3 string quartets; 2 piano quintets; Suite for Violin and Cello; Sonata for Solo Violin; Concerto for Piano and String Quartet; Fantasy, for violin and piano; Pastorale, for woodwind quintet; The Hollow Men, for trumpet and piano (or organ); Vocalise, for cello and piano; King Lear, septet for woodwind quintet, tympani, and piano; Sonata for Solo Cello; Infanta Marina, for viola and piano; Masques, for violin and piano; Parable, for solo flute; Parable for Brass Quintet.

Choral Music—Magnificat; Three Canons for Voices; Proverb; Hymns and Responses for the Church Year; Seek the Highest; Song of Peace; Mass; Stabat Mater; Te Deum; Spring Cantata; Winter Cantata; Four Cummings Choruses; Celebrations; Pleiades, for chorus, trumpet, and string orchestra.

Orchestral Music—8 symphonies; 2 piano concertos; Concertino for Piano and Orchestra; Dance Overture; Fables, for narrator and orchestra; The Hollow Men, for trumpet and orchestra; Serenade No. 5; Fairy Tale; Introit for Strings; Parable for Brass.

Piano Music—11 sonatas; 6 sonatinas; 2 serenades; Poems, three volumes; Sonata for Two Solo Pianos; Concertino for Two Solo Pianos; Concerto for Piano, Four Hands; Variations for an Album; Parades; Sonata for Harpsichord; Little Piano Book.

Vocal Music—E. E. Cummings Songs; Two Chinese Songs; English Songs; Harmonium, cycle for soprano and piano; Sara Teasdale Songs; Carl Sandburg Songs; James Joyce Songs; Hilaire Belloc Songs; Robert Frost Songs; Emily Dickinson Songs.

ABOUT

Chase, G., America's Music.

American Composers Alliance Bulletin, No. 2, 1954; The Juilliard Review, Spring 1955; Musical Quarterly, April 1957, October 1961; Saturday Review, December 2, 1961.

Goffredo Petrassi
1904–

Goffredo Petrassi was born in Zagarolo, near Rome, on July 16, 1904. Though his musical training came comparatively late, he was early influenced by the choral masterworks of the Roman Baroque era which he sang as a choirboy in various Roman basilicas and at the San Salvatore school in Lauro. From 1918 to 1925 he was employed as a clerk in a music store, an occupation that apparently further stirred his interest in the art; for it was at this time that he began to study the elements of theory and composition during his leisure hours. At the age of twenty, intensive formal training was begun for the first time when he became a pupil of Vincenzo di Donato in harmony. Then, in 1928, he entered the Santa Cecilia Academy, where in 1932 he received a diploma in composition, in the class of Alessandro Bustini. One year later he was also given a diploma in organ, in the class of Fernando Germani.

At about that time he came under the influence of Alfredo Casella, the eminent Italian composer, who aroused in the younger man an enthusiasm for the neoclassic movement, and specifically for Hindemith. Under this stimulus, Petrassi first achieved recognition in 1932 with a remarkable Partita, for orchestra. The work received first prizes in competitions conducted by the Sindacato Nazionale dei Musicisti in Italy and by the Fédération Internationale des Concerts in Paris. On June 13, 1933, it was successfully performed at the festival of the International Society for Contemporary Music at Amsterdam. A neoclassic composition, it is based on three Baroque dance forms (gagliarda, ciaconna, and giga). As Joseph Machlis has noted, it revealed "a musical personality of immense assurance," with its "bold thematic material and lithe contrapuntal writing, powered by driving rhythms."

The neoclassic style that was crystallized in the Partita was further developed in several ensuing compositions, notably the *Preludio, Aria e Finale*, for cello and piano, and the *Introduzione e Allegro*, for violin and piano, both in 1933, and his first orchestral concerto in 1934. But another important influence was

---

Petrassi: pä trä′ sē

soon brought to bear on Petrassi's music, that of Roman Baroque choral music with which he had been familiar in childhood and early boyhood. Baroque structures, the deep religious and spiritual convictions of Baroque music, and the indulgence in polyphonic virtuosity found in that literature are all reflected in several distinguished choral works completed by Petrassi in the years between 1936 and 1941. First, in 1936, came *Psalm IX;* then came a Magnificat, in 1940; finally and most significantly, there followed the "dramatic madrigal" *Coro di Morti* in 1941. The last, acknowledged as one of Petrassi's most important works, was inspired by a poem by Leopardi which suggests that living people may seem as mysterious and terrifying to the dead as the dead are to the living. The *Coro di Morti* was introduced at the Venice Festival in September 1941, the composer conducting. It was performed in several American universities in the late 1940's and early 1950's, among them the University of California at Los Angeles, the University of Illinois, and Indiana University.

From 1937 to 1940 Petrassi was superintendent of La Fenice opera house in Venice. In 1939 he was made professor of advanced composition at the Santa Cecilia Academy and he has held the position since that time with distinction. During the years 1947 to 1950 he served as artistic director of the Accademia Filarmonica in Rome.

During the 1940's, Petrassi completed two operas and two ballets, but they were not in his best creative vein. His first opera, *Il Cordovano*, was a one-act comedy which La Scala produced on May 12, 1949, and which the Turin Opera revived successfully in 1966; his second was *La Morte dell' Aria*, produced in Rome on October 23, 1950. The more successful of the two ballets was *La Follia di Orlando*, seen at La Scala on April 12, 1947.

In the early 1950's, Petrassi departed from his former neoclassical and neobaroque tendencies to embrace the twelve-tone technique and serialism. This new direction, which he was henceforth to pursue, was first found in *Noche Oscura*, a cantata for chorus and orchestra on a text by Giovanni Della Croce, introduced in June 1951 at the Strasbourg Music Festival, Mario Rossi conducting. The twelve-tone system was pursued further in

Petrassi's third concerto for orchestra, *Recréation Concertante*, heard in July 1953 at the Aix-en-Provence festival under Hans Rosbaud. Here, as later, he used the twelve-tone technique with comparative freedom, refusing to adhere rigidly to Schoenbergian principles. As he put it: "I am to some extent a dodecaphonist, but not a dogmatic one."

GOFFREDO PETRASSI

Of particular interest among his orchestral compositions in a free dodecaphonic idiom is his fifth orchestral concerto, commissioned by the Koussevitzky Music Foundation for the seventy-fifth anniversary of the Boston Symphony. That orchestra, under Charles Münch, introduced it on December 2, 1955. The first two movements are based on two fundamental themes, the second of which is derived from the composer's *Coro di Morti*.

From 1954 to 1956 Petrassi was president of the International Society for Contemporary Music. In 1955 he paid his first visit to the United States to attend the première of his fifth orchestral concerto. During the summer of 1956 he conducted a master class in composition at the Berkshire Music Center at Tanglewood. During his visit to Tanglewood his sixth concerto for orchestra was performed by the Boston Symphony under Charles Münch at a Berkshire Music Festival concert. Other Petrassi compositions heard at that time at Tanglewood, in honor of the composer's presence, were the *Coro di Morti* conducted by Hugh Ross and the *Sonata da Camera*, for harpsichord and ten instruments, conducted by Petrassi himself.

When he arrived in the United States, Petrassi was described by John Briggs as a "man of medium stature with slightly Mephistophelean eyebrows and the well-groomed look of a man fresh from the barber shop." A passionate lover of art, Petrassi took advantage of this visit to become acquainted with American art, showing particular interest in the avant-garde styles of Jackson Pollock and Ben Shahn.

Discussing his chamber and orchestral music, the media in which he has proved most influential, Petrassi once said: "My aim is to write in the style of each instrument. . . . My instrumentation is based on the timbres of the instruments themselves. I seek to create new sonorities based on pure instrumental sounds rather than a big, muddy ensemble. It naturally follows that every instrument has its own direct responsibility; it cannot hide behind the other instruments."

Among Petrassi's later important instrumental works are a string quartet (1957), heard at the Vienna Festival of 1958; a serenade for chamber ensemble, featured at the festival of the International Society for Contemporary Music held in Rome on June 11, 1959; his seventh orchestral concerto, heard at the festival of the International Society for Contemporary Music held in Venice in 1965; and *Estri*, a chamber symphony introduced at Dartmouth College at Hanover, New Hampshire, on August 2, 1967.

Petrassi's Serenade, for chorus, was given its première at the Festival of Contemporary Music in Venice in September 1968.

MAJOR WORKS

Ballets—La Follia di Orlando; Il Ritratto di Don Chisciotte.

Chamber Music—Introduzione e Allegro, for violin and piano; Preludio, Aria e Finale, for cello and piano; Sonata da Camera, for harpsichord and ten instruments; Dialogo Angelico, for two flutes; Musica a Due, for two cellos; String Quartet; Serenade, for flute, viola, double bass, harpsichord, and percussion.

Choral Music—Psalm IX; Magnificat; Coro di Morti; Three Choruses; Noche Oscura, cantata; Nonsense; Serenade.

Operas—Il Cordovano (one-act comic opera); La Morte dell' Aria.

Orchestral Music—7 concertos for orchestra; Passacaglia; Partita; Piano Concerto; Quattro Inni Sacri, for voice and orchestra; Invenzione Concertata; Estri, chamber symphony.

Piano Music—Siciliana e Marcetta, for piano duet; Toccata; Eclogue; Invenzioni.

Vocal Music—Colori del Tempo; Vocalizzo per Addormire una Bambina; Benedizione; O Sonni, Sonni; Lamento d'Arianna; Tre Liriche; Miracolo.

ABOUT

Amico, F. d', Goffredo Petrassi; Machlis, J., Introduction to Contemporary Music; Weissmann, J. S., Goffredo Petrassi.

Hans Pfitzner
1869-1949

Hans Erich Pfitzner was born in Moscow on May 5, 1869, of German parents. As a child, Hans was brought back to Germany where his father, who had been a member of the Moscow Imperial Opera orchestra, gained employment as a violinist in the orchestra of the State Theatre in Frankfurt and as director of Hoch's Conservatory. Hans received his first music lessons from him. At seventeen, he entered Hoch's Conservatory where his teachers included Kwast in piano and Knorr in composition. More than a decade later, in 1899, Pfitzner married Kwast's daughter.

In 1892 and 1893, Pfitzner taught piano at the Coblenz Conservatory, and from 1894 to 1896 he was a conductor at the Municipal Theatre in Mainz. In 1893, a concert of his works was heard in Berlin; one of the critics predicted a rich future for the "budding genius."

In 1897 Pfitzner settled in Berlin and was appointed teacher of composition at the Stern Conservatory. From 1903 to 1906 he was the first conductor at the Theater des Westens. In 1907 and 1908 he conducted the renowned Kaim Orchestra in Munich. When he resigned this post, it was to become director of the Strasbourg Conservatory. In 1910 he also became the conductor of the Strasbourg Opera, a post he held until 1916. The University of Strasbourg conferred an honorary doctorate on him in 1913.

He returned to Munich in 1916 and distinguished himself in that city as teacher, composer, and conductor. In 1919 and 1920 he led some of the concerts of the Konzertverein. In 1920 he returned to Berlin to lead the master class in composition at the Berlin Academy of

Pfitzner: p'fĭts' nĕr

Pfitzner

Fine Arts and remained for nine years. The last two decades of his life were mainly spent in Munich, where from 1930 to 1933 he was professor of composition at the Akademie der Tonkunst. After 1933 he made numerous appearances as guest conductor in performances of his own music and occasionally served as piano accompanist in recitals of his songs.

His first opera, *Der Arme Heinrich*, was introduced in Mainz on April 2, 1895, the composer conducting, and was a major success. He was given a dozen curtain calls and bedecked with laurel wreaths. Engelbert Humperdinck wrote in the *Frankfurter Zeitung* that this première was "an event of a significance far transcending local interest." Max Steiner reported in the *Mainzer Tageblatt* that the opera was the most important since those of Wagner. Within a decade it was performed in a large number of German cities, and in 1927 there was a highly successful revival in Berlin.

He did not repeat this success with his second and third operas: *Die Rose vom Liebesgarten*, produced in Elberfeld on November 9, 1901, and *Christelflein*, introduced in Munich on December 11, 1906. But with *Palestrina*, in 1917, he achieved the greatest triumph of his career as a composer. Often described as the last of the German post-Romantic operas, *Palestrina* tells of the legendary saving of the art of contrapuntal music from banishment by the church through the writing of the *Missa Papae Marcelli* by Palestrina. Some writers have pointed out that in this opera the composer identified himself with his protagonist: Pfitzner was using the victory of the sixteenth century Italian over the Council of Trent as symbolic of his own artistic victory over his critics and enemies.

Palestrina was introduced in Munich on June 12, 1917, Bruno Walter conducting. It was so successful that despite the obstacles posed by World War I, it was sent on tour. It was subsequently heard in many of the leading opera houses of central Europe. Disciples of the Wagnerian music drama embraced it; others also praised it for its nobility and spiritual grandeur. "In ethical pathos, in welding poetic and musical talents in a single work, it is the last example of successful Wagnerism," wrote Adolf Weissman. And Edward J. Dent said: "The whole work has a dignity and an asceticism which are rare in modern music."

Palestrina has enjoyed enormous popularity in Germany and Austria, where it has come to be regarded as one of the epochal stage works of the twentieth century. Elsewhere, however, *Palestrina* has made little headway. There is no record of a single performance in the United States or England. A German-language presentation in Amsterdam in February 1939 appears to have been one of the rare performances given outside German-speaking countries. Its archaic identity, its heavy-handed Germanic writing with strong Wagnerian echoes, its complete absence of love interest, and its long stretches of dullness apparently have made the opera unpalatable to all except Germans and Austrians. However, the three orchestral preludes which preface the three acts are occasionally heard at symphony concerts both in the United States and in Europe.

HANS PFITZNER

Pfitzner wrote only one opera after *Palestrina*—*Das Herz*, produced simultaneously in Berlin and Munich on November 12, 1931. But he did produce instrumental music, including two symphonies, several concertos, two string quartets, and a sextet. His greatest successes, however, came with his choral and vocal music, and most notably with a romantic cantata, *Von Deutscher Seele*, written in 1921 and revised for a smaller orchestra in 1937. This is a song cycle for solo voices, chorus, and

410

orchestra; poems by Eichendorff serve as text. H. C. Colles called it "an elaborate score in which the orchestral writing is peculiarly intricate." Its world première took place in Berlin in 1922. During the fall of 1923 it was introduced in the United States at a concert of the Society of Friends of Music in New York, Artur Bodanzky conducting.

Pfitzner received many honors in Germany. In 1920 he was made General Director of Music in Bavaria, and five years later he was decorated with the Award for Merit by the Prussian Academy of Arts and Sciences. Hans Pfitzner societies were organized in several German cities; one of the most important of these was formed in 1938 with Wilhelm Furtwängler, the noted conductor, as president. He remained active as composer and conductor up to the time of World War II. He also wrote several books; a three-volume collection of his writings appeared in the years 1927–1929.

When Hitler came to power, Pfitzner immediately allied himself with the new order. In 1933 he refused to conduct at the Salzburg Festival because of the expressed antagonism of the Austrian Chancellor, Dollfuss, toward Hitler. For a number of years Pfitzner identified himself completely with the ideals—artistic as well as political — of the Third Reich. Official Nazis honored him, and several adulatory books about him were published. In return, Pfitzner wrote compositions honoring Nazis and Nazism, including a festive piece for General Hans Frank, the Nazi governor of Poland who was responsible for numerous atrocities in that country.

By the time World War II broke out, Pfitzner and the Nazis had come to a parting of the ways. On one occasion, Pfitzner refused a Nazi request to write new music for *A Midsummer Night's Dream* to replace that of Mendelssohn. At another time, he was involved in a fierce argument with Field Marshal Goering over some musical matters. He even had unpleasant relations with Hitler. Practically *persona non grata* by the time war erupted, Pfitzner suffered great deprivations. His property confiscated and his ability to earn a living nullified, he was left completely destitute. In 1944 he left Germany for Vienna where he was stricken by a serious illness. He was then removed to a home for the aged in Munich. He was found there after the war by the president of the Vienna Philharmonic, who transferred him to Austria. There he was supported for the remainder of his life by the Vienna Philharmonic.

In 1948 Pfitzner was tried before the Denazification Court in Munich for his Nazi affiliations and was exonerated. He died a year later, in Salzburg, Austria, on May 22, 1949.

MAJOR WORKS

Chamber Music—3 string quartets; Cello Sonata in F-sharp minor; Piano Trio in F major; Piano Quartet in C major; Violin Sonata in E minor; Sextet.

Choral Music—Der Blumen Rache, ballad; Rundgesang zum Neujahrfest; Columbus; Gesang der Barden; Von Deutscher Seele; Das Dunkle Reich; Fons Salutifer; choruses for men's voices.

Operas—Der Arme Heinrich; Die Rose vom Liebesgarten; Christelflein; Palestrina; Das Herz.

Orchestral Music—2 symphonies; 2 cello concertos; Herr Oluf, ballad for baritone and orchestra; Die Heinzelmännchen, for basso and orchestra; Zwei Deutsche Gesänge, for voice and orchestra; Piano Concerto in E-flat major; Violin Concerto in B minor; Lethe, for baritone and orchestra; Duo, for violin, cello, and small orchestra; Kleine Sinfonie; Elegie und Reigen; Fantasie.

Piano Music—Pieces; Studies.

Vocal Music—Numerous songs for voice and piano including Die Einsame, Der Gärtner, Ist der Himmel Darum in Lenz So Blau, Michaelskirchplatz, Nachts, Zum Abschiede Meiner Tochter.

ABOUT

Abendroth, W., Hans Pfitzner; Abendroth, W. (ed.), Hans Pfitzner, ein Bild in Widmung; Bahle, J., Hans Pfitzner und der Geniale Mensch; Müller-Blattau, J., Hans Pfitzner.

Gabriel Pierné
1863–1937

Henri Constant Gabriel Pierné was born in Metz, France, on August 16, 1863 to a musical family. With the outbreak of the Franco-Prussian War, the Piernés went to Paris. There Gabriel entered the Conservatory where he was a classmate of Debussy. His teachers included Lavignac, Marmontel, Franck, and Massenet. During the eleven years he attended the Conservatory he was an outstanding student and won numerous prizes. In 1882 he was awarded the Prix de Rome for a cantata, *Édith*.

Upon his return to Paris from his three-year

Pierne: pyĕr nā´

residence in Rome as required by the Prix, Pierné succeeded Franck as organist at the church of Sainte-Clotilde in 1890, a post he held for eight years. In 1903 he embarked upon a career as a conductor by becoming assistant conductor of Colonne's orchestra. When Colonne died in 1910, Pierné became his successor. For nearly a quarter of a century Pierné directed the concerts of the Colonne Orchestra in Paris and became a major influence in arranging performances of notable new French compositions and bringing recognition to many young French composers. Upon his resignation in 1932, Pierné was made honorary president of the orchestra.

GABRIEL PIERNÉ

On August 24, 1895, Pierné's *opéra comique La Coupe Enchantée* was produced in Royan, France. He wrote two more operas, several ballets, and various instrumental compositions before achieving a major success. This came with the cantata *The Children's Crusade* (*La Croisade des Enfants*), completed in 1902 and successfully introduced by the Colonne Orchestra under Colonne on January 18, 1905. Marcel Schwob's text was based on an old Flemish story of the crusade of Italian children who, without direction or guidance, embarked in the thirteenth century to the Holy Land and were killed at sea during a storm. The cantata won the City of Paris prize of ten thousand francs and was performed throughout Europe. A second cantata, *Children at Bethlehem* (*Les Enfants à Bethléem*) was also well received

when first performed on April 13, 1907, in Amsterdam.

Pierné's most successful work for the stage was the ballet *Cydalise et le Chèvre-Pied*, based on Rémy de Goncourt's *Lettres d'un Satyr* (1913). Here classic mythology is transplanted into French court life of the eighteenth century. The première, long delayed because of World War I, finally took place at the Paris Opéra on January 15, 1923. At that time, Émile Vuillermoz wrote in *La Revue Musicale:* "Pierné has written ... a score of extraordinary youthfulness and allurement. ... The score abounds in coquetries of excellent quality, and is of a vivacity and freshness which will enchant the public."

One of the orchestral episodes in the ballet has since become one of Pierné's most popular compositions. It is the delightfully witty trifle *The Entrance of the Fauns.* Two other slight compositions have also retained enormous appeal through the years: the Serenade in A major, originally written for piano (1875) and known on concert programs everywhere in various transcriptions; and *The March of the Little Lead Soldiers* (*Marche des Petits Soldats de Plomb*), written in 1887. The latter also started out as a piano piece and became popular in the composer's own transcription for orchestra.

As a composer, Pierné was always content to stick to tradition and adhere to accepted methods and styles. He had no interest in experimental techniques or in seeking out fresh or new ways of saying familiar things. He was an outstanding craftsman and possessed the characteristic Gallic qualities of grace, sensitivity, and refinement. "Without pain," said Charles Malherbe, "he has elevated himself to the heights of the subject he handles. ... Endowed with a fertile imagination, with a supple spirit, Gabriel Pierné sketches melodies full of charm, and reveals himself expert in giving these melodies shape and form because within him ... is concealed a very substantial science, together with an intimate knowledge of the classics and a profound understanding of counterpoint."

Pierné's last opera was *Sophie Arnould*, based on the career of the famous singer; the world première took place at the Opéra-Comique in Paris on February 21, 1927. Towards the end of his life, Pierné wrote the scores for three ballets. The last of these, *Images*, was seen at the Paris Opéra on June 19, 1935. He also produced an excellent work for orchestra, *Gulliver au Pays de Lilliput*, which was heard at the festival of the International Society for Contemporary Music at Paris on June 23, 1937.

In 1925 Pierné was elected a member of the Académie des Beaux-Arts, and in 1940 he was made Chevalier of the Legion of Honor. He died while vacationing at Ploujean, in Brittany, on July 17, 1937.

MAJOR WORKS

Ballets—Le Collier de Saphirs; Les Joyeuses Commères de Paris; Bouton d'Or; Le Docteur Blanc; Salomé; Cydalise et le Chèvre-Pied; Impressions du Music Hall; Giration; Fragonard; Images.

Chamber Music—Pastorale Variée dans le Style Ancien, for wind instruments (also for piano); Berceuse, for violin and piano; Caprice, for cello and piano; Canzonetta, for clarinet and piano; Solo de Concert, for bassoon and piano; Variations Libres et Finale, for flute, violin, cello, and harp; Violin Sonata; Cello Sonata; Voyage au Pays du Tendre, for flute, violin, viola, and cello; Introduction et Variations sur une Ronde Populaire, for saxophone quartet; Trois Pièces en Trio, for violin, viola, and cello; Piano Quintet.

Choral Music—La Nuit de Noël de 1870; L'An Mil; La Croisade des Enfants; Les Enfants à Bethléem; Les Fioretti de Saint François d'Assise.

Operas—La Coupe Enchantée (one act opéra comique) Vendée; La Fille de Tabarin; On ne Badine pas avec l'Amour; Sophie Arnould (one-act opera).

Orchestral Music—Ouverture Symphonique; Suite d'Orchestre; Piano Concerto; Marche Solennelle; Pantomime; Scherzo Caprice, for piano and orchestra; Ballet de Cour; Poème Symphonique, for piano and orchestra; Konzertstück, for harp and orchestra; Paysages Franciscains; Divertissement sur un Thème Pastoral; Gulliver au Pays de Lilliput.

Piano Music—Quinze Pièces; Étude de Concert; Album pour Mes Petits Amis; Valse, in G major; Humoresque; Almée; Rêverie; Improvisation; Barcarolle, for piano duet; Valse Impromptu, for piano duet; Ariette dans le Style Ancien; Sérénade Vénitienne; Trois Pièces Formant Suite de Concert; Variations; also bagatelles, mazurkas, nocturnes.

Vocal Music—Contes; Soir de Jadis; Boutique Japonaise; Trois Adaptations Musicales; Trois Mélodies; Six Ballades Françaises; numerous individual songs for voice and piano.

ABOUT

Hill, E. B., Modern French Music; Séré, O., Musiciens Français d'Aujourd'hui; Weber, W., Gabriel Pierné.

Willem Pijper
1894–1947

Willem Pijper was born in Zeist, Utrecht, Holland, on September 8, 1894. He was the only child of a Calvinist laborer who was an amateur violinist. Since Willem was a sickly child, he was not allowed to attend school until he was fourteen. Left to his own devices most of the time, he absorbed himself in reading, studying biology, and experimenting with music. Having learned from his father some of the elements of violin playing, he started to compose little pieces when he was five by devising his own system of notation.

WILLEM PIJPER

When he was fourteen, his health improved sufficiently to allow him to attend secondary school where he amazed his teachers with the richness and variety of his general knowledge gained through reading. School meant association with boys of his own age and it provided him with an opportunity to write music or arrange choral numbers for the school chorus.

He decided to abandon all academic study when he reached his seventeenth year and to concentrate on music. He now became a pupil of Johan Wagenaar in composition at the Utrecht Music School. Willem's father hoped he would become a church organist, but Willem himself had ambitions to be a concert pianist. His teacher Wagenaar

Pijper: pī′ pĕr

413

convinced him that he would do better to concentrate on theoretical studies with the aim of becoming a composer. Though Wagenaar himself was a musical conservative, he did not stand in the way of Pijper's interest in newer practices.

In the period between 1911 and 1913 Pijper produced music for solo instruments and for chorus. His first mature work was a string quartet in 1914, unusual in that it contained several bitonal episodes. He continued to explore the possibilities of polytonality, but at the same time he was strongly influenced by Debussy and Mahler. Debussy's influence is found in Pijper's *Fêtes Galantes*, for voice and piano (verses by Verlaine), which he wrote in 1916. That of Mahler is discernible in Pijper's first symphony, *Pan* (1917). This symphony was a description of nature similar to that in some of Mahler's symphonies but with one essential difference, as J. M. Meulenhoff noted: "While in Mahler's work the relationship between man and nature plays an important part, Pijper's nature symphony contains no human-psychological conflict at all. Pijper tried in his *Pan* symphony to arouse in the listener as directly as possible the heathen, 'animistic' feeling for nature's inspired genius, while leaving aside all human contemplation." Willem Mengelberg directed the world première of the symphony in Amsterdam in 1918.

After 1918 Pijper sharply broke his ties with the recent past. He became increasingly experimental, not only in his use of polytonality and linear counterpoint but also in his departure from what he called "the shackles of the bar lines" through polymetric and polyrhythmic procedures. He also adopted a method of his own, utilizing germinal ideas—he called it the "germ cell theory." A single chord became the basis of his Piano Concerto (1927). The piano sonatinas Nos. 2 and 3 (1925) were both built from the same "germ cell"—the notes A-flat, E-flat, F, and C.

A rising three-note sequence (E-F-A) and two rhythmic motives—the first in a march-like character and the second in a kind of ragtime rhythm—served as the melodic and rhythmic germ cells for Pijper's most celebrated work, the Third Symphony. Completed in 1926, the symphony was given its world première by the Concertgebouw Orchestra in Amsterdam on October 28 of that year. Its emotional climate

is suggested by the quotation from *The Aeneid* which is found on the fly-leaf of the published score: "If I cannot influence the gods, I'll move the powers of hell."

Pijper's style was described by M. D. Calvocoressi as follows: "His themes are definitely tonal or modal, diatonic in character. And although he resorts freely enough to polytonal combinations, his music, in spirit, color and tone, is altogether different from the French polyphonists. It comes no nearer to the atonality school of Schoenberg or that of Bartók. I should incline to say that his incursions into the realm of atonality and polytonality are determined by special purposes of coloration or accentuation, by whims of a moment which the general purpose of the works in which they occur *justifies*."

Pijper was one of Holland's leading music teachers and critics. From 1918 to 1923 he was the critic of the *Utrechts Dagblad*, in which capacity he acted as spokesman for the most important of the younger and more progressive Dutch composers. In 1925 he helped found one of Holland's most important music journals, *De Muziek*, which he edited from 1926 to 1929. His career as a teacher also began early. From 1918 to 1921 he taught harmony and composition at the Amsterdam High School. In 1925 he was appointed professor of composition at the Amsterdam Conservatory. From 1930 to the time of his death he was the director of the Rotterdam Conservatory.

When, in 1928, Pijper was commissioned to write a work commemorating the founding of the Concertgebouw Orchestra, he produced a six-movement work called *Symphonic Epigrams;* all the movements were based on the germ cell of a motive from an old folk song. This was not the first time a folk song had stimulated him. In 1920 he had been inspired by the medieval folk ballad "Heer Halewijn" to create one of his finest choral works—indeed one of the finest choral works in twentieth century Dutch music—*Heer Halewijn*, for unaccompanied eight-part chorus.

He again used this ballad as a source when he wrote his first opera, *Halewijn*, which was produced in Amsterdam on June 13, 1933. The composer liked to refer to this work as a "symphonic drama" or as a "visually perceptive symphony." He implied by this that the drama was built up exclusively through musical means. "The music is indeed completely autonomous," says J. M. Meulenhoff, "and the laws of traditional music drama are only followed in so far as they do not cause the musical demands to suffer."

In his closing years, as he grew increasingly introspective, Pijper sought to simplify his writing; he even reverted at times to a tonal framework. These last works included a cello concerto (1936), a violin concerto (1938), and *Six Adagios*, for orchestra (1940). The last was written for the Freemasons' Lodge and is of particular interest because rhythmically it is based on material found in the opening measures of Mozart's overture to *The Magic Flute*, an opera which originated as a glorification of Freemasonry.

Pijper was working on an opera, *Merlijn*, when he died at Leidschendam, near The Hague, on March 19, 1947; he had been able to complete only the first act. At his death, Paul Sanders wrote of him: "For the first time since the death of J. P. Sweelinck, two centuries ago, was the attention of the world drawn to the creative forces of Dutch music by the appearance of Pijper's work on the international stage."

The distinguished conductor Pierre Monteux wrote the following personal note on Pijper: "He was extremely erudite, and had the profound culture which stems from the classical education common to European schools. He possessed a sharp wit, and his repartee was at times sour and biting if not bitter. He was a great liberal, and an ardent Francophile, loving all things of France—its literature, its music, its paintings. He was a magnificent teacher and many are the young composers in Holland who today owe knowledge of their *métier* to this master. For he was a master, having in music—to my mind—what Erasmus so ably propagated in the world of learning and letters. The reactionaries hated him, and the young of spirit, ardent for the advancement of art in their country, adored him. I can see him now as he came up the walk to our home in Belgium on one of his numerous visits. Tall, pale, and very slender, his face the face of a true ascetic, his eyes seemed to burn with inward enthusiasm for this long awaited moment—the opportunity of talking long hours of music, art and politics with those he knew loved and revered him."

MAJOR WORKS

Chamber Music—5 string quartets (the last unfinished); 2 piano trios; 2 violin sonatas; 2 cello sonatas; Septet; Sextet, for wind and piano; Flute Sonata; Trio, for flute, clarinet, and bassoon; Quintet, for flute, oboe, clarinet, bassoon, and horn; Sonata for Solo Violin.

Choral Music—Spring Is Coming; On the Weaving Loom, for mixed chorus, ten woodwinds, and piano duet; Heer Halewijn; Heer Danielken; Ballads; Of the King of Castile.

Operas—Halewijn, symphonic drama; Merlijn (unfinished).

Orchestral Music—3 symphonies; Orchestral Music with Piano; Fêtes Galantes, for voice and orchestra; Romances sans Paroles, for voice and orchestra; Piano Concerto; Cello Concerto; Violin Concerto; Six Symphonic Epigrams.

Piano Music—3 sonatinas; Three Aphorisms; Three Old Dutch Dances; Sonata; Sonata, for two pianos.

Vocal Music—8 Vieilles Chansons de France; 8 Noëls de France; La Maumariée, two parts; 8 Old Dutch Love Songs; 2 Songs to Dutch Words; Old Dutch Sea Songs, two sets; various individual songs for voice and piano.

ABOUT

Klopenburg, W. C. M., Thematisch-Bibliografische Catalogus van de Werken van Willem Pijper; Meulenhoff, J. M., Music in Holland; Sanders, P. F., Moderne Nederlandsche Componisten.

Gamut (London), July 1928.

Walter Piston
1894–

Walter Hamor Piston, Jr., was born in Rockland, Maine, on January 20, 1894, one of four sons of Walter Hamor Piston, a bookkeeper, and Leona Stover Piston. His paternal grandfather, Antonio Pistone, was an Italian immigrant who had settled in Rockland.

When Walter was eleven, he was taken by his family to Boston, where he received his education, academic as well as musical. While attending the Mechanic Arts High School he studied violin and played in the school orchestra, although his main interest was painting. Upon leaving high school he worked for a while as a draftsman with the Boston Elevated Railway Company. When he was seventeen, he began to study the piano. He played the violin in dance bands and theatre orchestras, but art was still his primary interest. In 1912 he entered the Massachusetts Normal Art School to study drawing and painting.

After graduation from the Art School in 1916, he studied music intensively with private teachers: piano with Harris Shaw; violin with Fiumara, Theodorowicz, and Winternitz. When World War I broke out, Piston joined the Navy. He was stationed at Massachusetts Institute of Technology where he became a member of the aeronautics division band.

WALTER PISTON

When the war ended, Piston decided finally to specialize in music. He entered Harvard in 1920 as a music major. While an undergraduate he became conductor of the Pierian Sodality, a Harvard student orchestra, and served as assistant to Archibald P. Davison, professor of music and conductor of the Harvard Glee Club. On September 14, 1920, he married Kathryn Nason, who had been his classmate at art school. "The only reason I became a composer," he later explained, "was because she painted so much better than I did." Piston was graduated in 1924 *summa cum laude* and with a Phi Beta Kappa key. A John Knowles Paine fellowship made it possible for him to spend two years in Paris where he attended the École Normale de Musique as a pupil of Paul Dukas and studied privately with Nadia Boulanger. In Paris two early Piston compositions were performed, his first public premières—a piano sonata and *Three Pieces*, for flute, clarinet, and bassoon, both written in 1926.

Piston returned to the United States in 1926 and became a member of the music faculty at Harvard. He remained at Harvard for the next twenty-four years, serving as assistant

professor from 1926 to 1938, as associate professor from 1938 to 1944, and as full professor from 1944 to 1959. In 1960 he retired and was made Professor Emeritus. Four books on music theory now extensively used in colleges throughout the country are some of the fruits of Piston's rich career as a teacher. They are *Harmonic Analysis* (1933), *Harmony* (1941), *Counterpoint* (1947), and *Orchestration* (1955).

On March 23, 1928, Piston made his American debut as a composer when Serge Koussevitzky led the Boston Symphony in the première of *Symphonic Piece*. A number of works followed which emphasized Piston's growing importance as a composer. These included his Suite, for orchestra, which he himself conducted with the Boston Symphony on March 28, 1930; the Concerto for Orchestra, first heard in Cambridge, Massachusetts, on March 6, 1934; the Prelude and Fugue, for orchestra, given in Cleveland on March 12, 1936; and his first symphony, introduced in Boston on April 8, 1938, the composer conducting. Two excellent chamber music works also appeared during this period: his first string quartet (1933), successfully performed by the Roth String Quartet; and the Piano Trio (1935), which had been commissioned by the Elizabeth Sprague Coolidge Foundation.

His first major success with public and critics came with his music for the ballet *The Incredible Flutist*, with a scenario written by Piston in collaboration with the dancer Hans Wiener. Wiener and his company introduced the work at a concert of the Boston Pops Orchestra on May 30, 1938. The action takes place in a village marketplace where a circus is entertaining. The company includes a flutist who charms snakes and women with his pipings. An orchestral suite derived from this ballet score, comprising twelve sections, was first played on November 22, 1940, by the Pittsburgh Symphony under Fritz Reiner and soon became one of Piston's most popular compositions.

In 1943, on a commission from the Alice M. Ditson Fund, Piston completed his second symphony, which had its première in Washington, D.C., on March 5, 1944, Hans Kindler conducting the National Symphony. The work received the New York Music Critics Circle Award. "In this symphony," wrote a critic for the New York *Times*, "he is again the master craftsman, while at the same time he has managed to invest the content with a wealth of mood and meaning that defy any censure."

More important still was Piston's Third Symphony, commissioned by the Koussevitzky Music Foundation and introduced by the Boston Symphony under Koussevitzky on January 9, 1948. It brought the composer his first Pulitzer Prize, as well as the Boston Symphony Hornblit Award.

Piston wrote his Sixth Symphony on a commission from the Boston Symphony for its seventy-fifth anniversary season. The world première took place in Boston on November 25, 1955, Charles Münch conducting. "It is a neat, well-made symphony," Howard Taubman said of it, "not in the least problematical. It has some pleasant ideas, flowing and songful in the first and third movements and lively in the second and fourth." The symphony was performed in the Soviet Union in 1956 by the Boston Symphony under Münch. (That Russian tour was the first to be made by an American orchestra.)

Piston received the award of the New York Music Critics Circle a second time in 1959 for his Concerto for Viola and Orchestra. It had been written in 1957 for Joseph de Pasquale, who introduced it with the Boston Symphony under Münch on March 7, 1958. His second Pulitzer Prize in music was for his Seventh Symphony, commissioned by the Philadelphia Orchestra and introduced in Philadelphia, Eugene Ormandy conducting, on February 10, 1962. "It is a typical Piston work," said Harold C. Schonberg, "smoothly constructed, well orchestrated, shapely in form, and always well bred. . . . The melodic material . . . is always to the fore."

In a similarly melodic vein is Piston's Eighth Symphony, which received its world première in Boston, with Erich Leinsdorf conducting, on March 5, 1965. "In this work," the composer explained, "it has been my intention to make music that will be sympathetic to the performers and the listeners, admittedly a quaint and old-fashioned notion."

Among his subsequent significant compositions are the following: the *Variations for Cello and Orchestra*, heard first in New York, March 2, 1967; the Concerto for Clarinet and Orchestra, introduced at the Congregation of the Arts at Hopkins Center, Dartmouth

College, at Hanover, New Hampshire, August 6, 1967; and the *Ricercare*, for orchestra, commissioned for the 125th anniversary of the New York Philharmonic which introduced it under Leonard Bernstein's direction, March 7, 1968.

In a discussion of Piston's style, Nicolas Slonimsky has written: "In the matter of musical form, Walter Piston does not solicit public attention by strange conceits. . . . Generally, he prefers matter-of-fact designations, such as sonata, concertino, or suite. If he refurbishes the old forms, he keeps their recognizable features. In harmony and counterpoint he adopts without partiality such means of musical expression as are suitable to the task at hand. His music is eminently tonal, but when it is his purpose, he ornaments the design with tonal lacery."

Following his retirement from Harvard in 1960, Piston was honored with several concerts of his works. One took place at Cambridge, Massachusetts, in April 1960; another was held in New York on March 30, 1961; a third was given at Aspen, Colorado, on July 21, 1962.

Piston has received many honors and awards besides the two from the New York Music Critics Circle and the two Pulitzer Prizes in music. In 1935 he was given a Guggenheim Fellowship. Three years later he was appointed a member of the National Institute of Arts and Letters. In 1940 he was made a member of the American Academy of Arts and Sciences. He has been the recipient of four honorary doctorates in music, and in 1966 he received the Dickinson College Arts Award for outstanding achievement in music.

The Pistons have a comfortable chalet in Belmont, Massachusetts, and a summer house in Woodstock, Vermont; both houses were designed by Mrs. Piston. They have no children. Piston's principal diversion is chess. He has been described in the *Harvard Alumni Bulletin* as follows: "Shy, witty, affable, Piston has succeeded in synthesizing the most important characteristic of modern music with his own artistry and technical perfection. Like his music, he gives a pleasant, incisive impression, and his Down East twang frankly reveals the American heritage which combines with the Italian warmth of his paternal grandfather."

Pizzetti

Walter Piston has written: "The major problem for the composer must be to preserve and develop his individuality. He must resist the constant temptation to follow this or that fashion. He must find what it is he wishes to say in music and how best to say it, subjecting his work to the severest self-criticism. . . . Strength of will and faith in one's creative gift are essential. . . . The composer must judge for himself in these matters, with self-reliance based on a thorough knowledge of his craft and a capacity for independent thinking as an individual creative artist."

MAJOR WORKS

Ballet—The Incredible Flutist.

Chamber Music—5 string quartets; Piano Trio; Violin Sonata; Quintet, for flute and string quartet; Partita, for violin, viola, and organ; Sonatina, for violin and harpsichord; Divertimento, for nine instruments; Piano Quintet; Duo, for viola and cello; Quintet, for wind instruments; String Sextet; Piano Quartet.

Choral Music—Carnival Song, for men's chorus and brass instrument; Psalm and Prayer of David, for mixed chorus and seven instruments.

Orchestral Music—8 symphonies; 2 violin concertos; Symphonic Piece; Concerto for Orchestra; Prelude and Fugue; Concertino for Piano and Orchestra; Sinfonietta; Prelude and Allegro, for organ and strings; Symphonic Suite; Toccata; Fantasy for English Horn, Harp, and Strings; Viola Concerto; Concerto for Two Pianos and Orchestra; Three New England Sketches; Symphonic Prelude; Lincoln Center Festival Overture; Variations on a Theme by Edward Burlingame Hill; Capriccio, for harp and string orchestra; Variations for Cello and Orchestra; Concerto for Orchestra; Clarinet Concerto; Ricercare.

Piano Music—Sonata; Passacaglia; Improvisation.

ABOUT

Chase, G., America's Music; Goss, M., Modern Music Makers.

Canon, December 1953; Musical America, December 1963; Musical Quarterly, July 1946; New York Times, January 31, 1954; March 26, 1961.

Ildebrando Pizzetti
1880–1968

Ildebrando Pizzetti was born in Parma, Italy, on September 20, 1880, the son of a humble piano teacher. When he was two, his family moved to Reggio Emilia where Pizzetti received his first piano lessons from his father. When music was decided upon as a career, the boy was sent back to his native city. There,

---

Pizzetti: pēt tsät′ tē

when he was fifteen, he entered the Conservatory, a pupil of Righi in harmony and counterpoint. Pizzetti was an exceptional student. During his school years he wrote two operas and several orchestral works. In 1901 he was graduated with honors.

ILDEBRANDO PIZZETTI

The director of the Conservatory at Parma wanted Pizzetti to consider a career as an organist. Since Pizzetti's own interests as a student leaned strongly towards composition, he decided to concentrate on composing while supporting himself by teaching. His early passion was choral music, both the popular kind he heard the peasants sing in the province of Reggio Emilia and the Gregorian chants he heard in a Benedictine monastery. Stimulated by these experiences, he made an intensive study of old liturgical music which led him to experiment with the use of ancient modes in his composition. He began, as D. Maxwell White pointed out, "to envisage a new vocal polyphony as a musical medium free from all contrapuntal clichés and suitable for conveying every shade of emotional expression."

For a brief period following his graduation he was employed as assistant conductor at the Parma Opera. In 1907 he began a long and productive teaching career by serving as professor of theory and composition at the Parma Conservatory for two years. In 1909 he assumed a similar post at the Conservatory of Florence, of which he became director in 1917.

418

In 1924 he was appointed director of the Verdi Conservatory in Milan. In 1936 he succeeded Ottorino Respighi as professor of composition at the Santa Cecilia Academy in Rome, becoming director in 1948. In 1951 he retired and thenceforth devoted himself completely to composition.

In 1905 Pizzetti came upon an excerpt from D'Annunzio's tragedy *La Nave* published in a journal. He set it to music and despatched it to D'Annunzio, who was so pleased that he asked Pizzetti to set several choruses from the same play and to provide the drama with instrumental dances. The incidental music Pizzetti produced in 1905 for *La Nave* marked the first phase of his career as a composer. During that period Pizzetti was strongly influenced by D'Annunzio's writings and was stimulated by them to write incidental music to *La Pisanella* (first performance in Paris on June 11, 1913); a noteworthy song, "I Pastori" (1908); and the distinguished opera *Fedra* (1913), produced at La Scala in Milan on March 20, 1915. *Fedra* was not initially successful, its action being somewhat static while the music seemed cerebral and without emotion. Eventually, however, *Fedra* proved one of Pizzetti's most successful works, receiving repeated performances in leading Italian opera houses after a highly successful presentation in Rome on April 3, 1915. The marriage of play with music that captured the classic beauty of the text now was more easily understood and appreciated. "He rejected the conventional aria," says D. Maxwell White, "and linked poetry and music—the thorniest problem in the composition of an opera—with a new kind of eloquent melodic declamation."

The D'Annunzio phase in Pizzetti's work was succeeded by a biblical period. He completed several choral works and the opera *Debora e Jaele* with texts derived from the Bible. *Debora e Jaele* was introduced at La Scala on December 16, 1922, Toscanini conducting. It is the crowning work of this phase of Pizzetti's creative development. As Guido M. Gatti wrote: "All Pizzetti is in it. . . . In it all sides of his personality have found their highest degree of expression—the poet, the thinker, the man. In this opera is the final fruitage of his conception of art and life; all that was shadowed forth in *Fedra*, but could not find there full expression because fettered by another's words, is here presented in the most convincing manner. The musician was no longer in bondage; we feel that he has freed himself from the shackles he wore in *Fedra*, and that the dramatic conception that found theoretical expression in his writings has passed through the fires of emotion and been made to bend, as regards certain features, to the . . . law of creative genius."

One of Pizzetti's most important choral works during his biblical period was a setting of a fifteenth century morality play by Feo Belcari, *La Sacra Rappresentazione di Abram e d'Isaac*, a score remarkable for its expressive lyricism and serenity of mood. First heard in Florence in 1917, it was later expanded by the composer and performed in the new version in Turin on March 11, 1926.

After the biblical period came one in which the composer was inspired by Italian history. This phase saw the writing and production of what is possibly Pizzetti's most important opera, *Fra Gherardo*, successfully introduced at La Scala on May 16, 1928. The text, by the composer, was based on the thirteenth century chronicles of Salimbene da Parma. The central character is a weaver who rescues a girl from attack, takes her into his home and spends the night with her, and then repents by joining the Flagellant Order. As Fra Gherardo he spearheads a revolt by the Parma citizens against oppressive nobility. The uprising ends suddenly when Fra Gherardo is arrested for heresy and burned at the stake.

Fra Gherardo received its American première at the Metropolitan Opera in New York on March 21, 1929. On that occasion, Lawrence Gilman described the score as "conspicuous for intellectual substance and ingenuity and fine craftsmanship. . . . It is music of the will, of esthetic piety, and good intentions."

Italian history also provided the material for several subsequent operas that enjoyed successful productions. *Orsèolo* (Florence, May 5, 1935) has seventeenth century Venice as a setting; *Vanna Lupa* (Florence, May 4, 1949) was set in fourteenth century Florence. And his most important opera since *Fra Gherardo* has for its background twelfth century England and for its principal character the Archbishop Thomas à Becket, who was assassinated in Canterbury Cathedral. *Assassinio nella Cattedrale*, with a text based on T. S. Eliot's poetic drama *Murder in the Cathedral*, received its world première at La Scala on March 1, 1958, and was a major success; the American première was given in New York City on September 17, 1958.

In *Clitennestra*, seen at La Scala on March 1, 1965, Pizzetti tapped Greek drama, basing his libretto on the *Oresteia* of Aeschylus and *Elektra* of Sophocles. "Quite honestly," reported Claudio Sartori, "it cannot be said that the new opera shows any fresh development in Pizzetti's work for the lyric stage. What it does show is the faith and sincerity that inform the composer's music for the theatre. Particularly impressive is the fact that the artist has recaptured the seriousness of intent that marked his earliest works. . . . Here, once more, the drama is condensed and expressed in the vocal writing, and the various characters are clearly, excitingly limned by music which depicts in masterly fashion the Atridae caught up in the savage vortex of tragedy. The chorus, too, returns to dominate the stage and the score in sensitively managed scenes that are all passion and grief. Once again Pizzetti has given his most sublime music to the chorus."

In his operas, Pizzetti always favored expressive declamation over fully developed, singable melodies. His primary concern was to project the drama, and he molded his music skillfully to the contours of his text while attempting to catch and interpret every shade and nuance of the stage action. As H. T. Parker has said: "With Mussorgsky, Pizzetti agrees that a musical speech can compass the contours, the shadings, the emphasis of the spoken word and so become semi-humanized discourse."

Some of his finest, most stirring pages are those for the chorus. Mario Castelnuovo-Tedesco has written that it is the choral pages of Pizzetti's operas—together with the non-theatrical choral works—which place their composer with the foremost Italian polyphonists since the sixteenth century.

Pizzetti did not neglect instrumental music. His Violin Sonata in A major (1919), the composer's response to the tragedy of World War I, is among the most eloquent of such works in our time. Major orchestral works include the *Concerto dell'Estate*, modeled after the Baroque *concerto grosso*, which received its world première in New York on February 28,

1929, Toscanini conducting the New York Philharmonic; and the *Rondo Veneziano*, also introduced by Toscanini and the New York Philharmonic, on February 27, 1930, after which it was used for a ballet at La Scala on January 8, 1931. In addition Pizzetti produced excellent solo concertos with orchestra, one for the cello (Venice, September 11, 1934), another for the violin (Rome, December 9, 1945). Guido M. Gatti has remarked that Pizzetti's instrumental works are generally characterized by "the vocal nature of the themes, some of which seem to carry a direct suggestion of a sung text."

Pizzetti visited the United States in 1930 when he appeared as pianist and conductor in performances of his compositions. In 1931 he went to South America to conduct *Fra Gherardo* in Buenos Aires. In 1950 he received the international Italia Prize for his one-act opera *Ifigenia* (first performance over the Turin Radio on September 18, 1950). In 1960 he was elected president of the International Society of Composers and Authors in Italy. He also served as a member of the Royal Academy of Music in London and the Académie des Beaux-Arts in Paris.

Pizzetti married twice. After the death of his first wife, Maria Stradivari, in 1920, he wore the dark clothes of mourning, a habit he continued even after marrying his second wife, Signora Riri. He lived in Rome where he assiduously devoted himself to composition every morning, allowing no one and nothing to disturb him, except his pet cat. Partial to cats, he was never without one. He also favored the country over the city; writers of the past over those of the present; a pipe over a cigar or cigarette; and fruit and vegetables over all other kinds of food. He relaxed by going to films, preferably comedies.

He was exceptionally superstitious. He never began a new work on a Tuesday; he never marked the seventeenth page of his scores as "17" but as "16 + 1"; and he adorned his scores with four-leaf clovers.

He liked to have his family around him, including his grandchildren, and for that reason avoided travel. When he was compelled to make a trip, he was always accompanied by his wife.

Ildebrando Pizzetti died in Rome on February 13, 1968.

MAJOR WORKS

Chamber Music—2 string quartets; Violin Sonata in A; Cello Sonata in F; Piano Trio in A.

Choral Music—Lamento; Requiem; De Profundis; Epithalamium; Cantico di Gloria; Due Composizioni Corali a Sei Voci; various sacred choruses and choral songs.

Operas—Fedra; Debora e Jaele; Lo Straniero; Fra Gherardo; Orsèolo; L'Oro; Vanna Lupa; Ifigenia; Cagliostro; La Figlia di Jorio; Assassinio nella Cattedrale; Il Calzar d'Argento, sacred play; Clitennestra.

Orchestral Music—Concerto dell'Estate; Rondo Veneziano; Cello Concerto in C major; Symphony in A major; Violin Concerto in A major; Canzone di Beni Perduti; Preludio a un Altro Giorno.

Piano Music—Sonata; Canti di Ricordanza.

Vocal Music—Various songs for voice and piano including E il Mio Dolore Io Canto, I Pastori, Tre Sonetti del Petrarca.

ABOUT

Ewen, D. (ed.), The New Book of Modern Composers; Gavazzeni, G., Tre Studi su Pizzetti; Gatti, G.M., Ildebrando Pizzetti; La Morgia, M., La Città d'Annunziana a Ildebrando Pizzetti.

Musical America, February 1951; Rassegna Musicale (Pizzetti issue), October 1940.

Marcel Poot
1901–

Marcel Poot was born in Vilvorde, near Brussels, on May 7, 1901, of a highly cultured family. His father was director of the Royal Flemish Theatre in Brussels.

Poot has contributed the following autobiographical information: "Although I was very mediocre, I began studying music at an early age. My father had me join the clarinetists of a local band in which he was saxophonist. Less apt than my young friends, I soon had to give up this position. From then on dates my unpopularity in Vilvorde.

"My father, however, was determined to make me a musician. We then tried the piano. The town organist, Gérard Nauwelaerts, taught me scales and the Czerny exercises. This did not amuse me at all. But the laborious study continued until I was able to play with my professor overtures by Suppé arranged for four hands. My father then decided to enroll me at the Brussels Conservatory. The first time I was turned down. But another period of work with Czerny, and I was finally admitted. There I was a pupil of Sevenants,

Poot: pōt

Lunsens, and Arthur de Greef, after which I took a course in counterpoint and fugue with Mortelmans at the Antwerp Conservatory. The teaching of the academicians did not succeed in making me love my instrument any more than I had up to now. However, from this time on I began to undertake the writing of my first compositions, which I hid.

MARCEL POOT

"We have arrived at the year of 1916. I was introduced to Paul Gilson, an authentic artist with encyclopedic knowledge. He initiated me to the science of orchestration and encouraged me in my composing. My road was now before me. Several hard years of work followed after which I completed my first orchestral work, *Charlot*, in 1926. This comprised three symphonic sketches inspired by the films of Charles Chaplin which I admired greatly and which then exerted a profound influence upon me. More ambitious still was my first symphony in 1929, and a tone poem for large orchestra inspired by Charles Lindbergh's flight across the Atlantic, *Poème de l'Espace;* it was heard at the festival of the International Society for Contemporary Music held at Liège on September 4, 1930.

"Unfortunately, the opportunities for young composers to get heard were virtually nonexistent. Several of my friends decided to band together to protect themselves. This was in 1925. Thus was born the school known as the 'Synthesists.' This title permitted us to exclude all well-determined programs from our music and to work each according to his own temperament but with respect for established forms and traditions. Arthur Prévost consented to direct a concert of our works before an invited audience. That performance made a good impression. From that moment on it opened up for us the doors to other concerts. Most of my companions have since gone their way. If the group is now well scattered, its formation at least permitted several Belgian composers to make themselves known, including De Bourguignon, Bernier among others."

The group dissolved officially in 1930, the year in which Poot received the Rubens Prize and used it to finance a trip to Paris and the study of composition with Paul Dukas. Upon his return to Brussels, Poot began a successful career as a teacher, ultimately becoming professor of harmony, and later of counterpoint, at the Brussels Conservatory. In 1949 he became Conservatory director, a post which he has occupied since that time. During this period he also distinguished himself as a music critic, serving for fifteen years with *Le Peuple*, and from 1944 to 1949 with *La Nation Belge*. In addition, with Paul Gilson, he founded— and at the outset edited—Belgium's most distinguished musical journal, *La Revue Musicale Belge*. In 1943 he became Inspector of Belgian music schools. He has served as a member of the jury of auditions of the Belgian Radio and has also been the president of SABAM, the Belgian society of authors and composers, president of the Union of Belgian Composers, and a member of the Flemish Royal Academy.

Poot has produced numerous compositions, including symphonies, ballets, operas, orchestral and chamber music works, and functional music for radio and motion pictures. In a lighter vein he has written the operetta *The Little Wife of Stavoren* (1928) and *Jazz Music*, an orchestral work utilizing jazz idioms (1933). More serious in intent and within traditional form are a third symphony (1952) and the successful *Symphonic Allegro* for orchestra (1937), in which his writing is vigorous, rich in orchestral and harmonic colorations, and noteworthy for rhythmic vitality. Occasionally, Poot is infectiously witty, as in the delightful *Ouverture Joyeuse* (1935), which received its first American performance in New York on December 14, 1936, Leon Barzin conducting; and in *Mouvement Perpétuel* for

orchestra (1953), which he wrote for the twenty-fifth anniversary of the Palais des Beaux Arts in Brussels.

Charles Van Den Borren has said of Poot: "He never makes use of the remnants of romanticism. He wants to be modern and succeeds without strain, but in a style of his own which rigorously excludes any experimental work. What we like about him is his naturalness and spontaneity. These he has in abundance, and he uses them with admirable conciseness and sobriety—in harmony with his times in rejecting both grandiloquence and decadence. Thus, Marcel Poot has been well able to capture the hearts and spirits of his contemporaries. His music is essentially 'alive,' whatever he has written. . . . He always finds the appropriate tone, with a frankly modernistic note. His works are always tactful, in good taste, and sincerely expressive of a nature which must, above all, be true to itself."

Poot says of his personal life: "I smoke, like beer and wines of all kinds. I love the country, but for a long time now have preferred the city with its vibrant life. I like all normal people. I have a telephone, typewriter, automobile, and I play tennis."

MAJOR WORKS

Ballets—Paris et les Trois Divines; Camera; Pygmalion.

Chamber Music—Sonatine, for violin and piano; Piano Quartet; Trois Pièces en trio, for piano, violin and cello; Cinq Bagatelles, for string quartet; Scherzo, for four saxophones; Divertimento, for oboe, clarinet, and bassoon; Octet, for winds and strings; String Quartet; Ballade, for violin and piano; Sicilienne, for flute and piano; Arabesque, for clarinet and piano.

Choral Music—Le Dit du Routier, oratorio; Icare, oratorio.

Opera—Moretus.

Orchestral Music—3 symphonies; Charlot, three sketches; Poème de l'Espace; Musiquette; Fugato; Jazz Music; Ouverture Joyeuse; Allegro Symphonique; Danse Laudative; Ballade, for string quartet and orchestra; Légende Épique, for piano and orchestra; Triptyque Symphonique; Suite, for wind instruments; Koncertstück, for cello and orchestra; Musique Légère; Sinfonietta; Ouverture Rhapsodique; Mouvement Perpétuel.

Piano Music—Sonata in C; Six Petites Pièces Récréatives; Suite; Variations De Boeck; Étude; Rhapsodie, for two pianos; Sonatine.

Quincy Porter
1897–1966

Quincy Porter was born in New Haven, Connecticut, on February 7, 1897. He was a descendant of early American settlers and a direct descendant of Jonathan Edwards, the colonial theologian. Both Quincy Porter's grandfather and father were professors at Yale.

QUINCY PORTER

Porter began to study the violin in 1907 and for several years was a pupil of Herbert Dittler at the same time that he attended Hopkins Grammar School. In 1914 he entered Yale where he studied composition at the School of Music with Horatio Parker and David Stanley Smith. While still an undergraduate, he gave violin recitals with the pianist Bruce Simonds and revived and conducted the Yale Orchestra.

He was graduated from Yale in 1919 and from the School of Music in 1921. For his graduation exercise he wrote and performed a violin concerto which he himself has described as "Brahmsian" and which received honorable mention in the first American Prix de Rome contest. In two other contests, the Osborne and the Steinert, he won first prizes. In 1920 he went to Paris where he was taught violin by Capet and composition by Vincent d'Indy at the Schola Cantorum.

Following his return to the United States, he resided for a while in New York City,

earning his living by playing the violin in the Capitol Theatre Orchestra while he studied composition privately with Ernest Bloch. When Bloch became director of the Cleveland Institute, Porter followed him there to continue working with his teacher. "Under Bloch's guidance," says Howard Boatwright, "practically every vestige of Porter's early stylistic influences disappeared." Another important influence upon Porter at this time was the polyphonist Orlando di Lasso, from whose motets he derived his ideal "of flowing, almost consistently stepwide melody, and very close-knit continuity of sections."

In 1922 Porter became a member of the faculty of the Cleveland Institute of Music, on Bloch's recommendation, and two years later he became head of the theory department. During this period he played the viola in a string quartet, an experience responsible for arousing his creative interest in chamber music. In the period between 1923 and 1927 he completed his first two string quartets and a piano quintet, as well as orchestral music. *Ukrainian Suite* was introduced in Rochester, New York, on May 1, 1925.

In 1928 Porter resigned from the Cleveland Institute to revisit Paris. He stayed there for three years, two of them on Guggenheim Fellowships. He carried on no formal study but did much soul searching and self-analysis. The works he completed at that time show a growing maturity of concept and sureness of technique. Among them was his first published composition, the second violin sonata (1929); this was also his earliest work to be recorded. In addition, he wrote a clarinet quintet (1929); his third and fourth string quartets (1930, 1931), which were both performed and recorded; and a piano sonata (1930), for Beveridge Webster, who introduced it. Howard Boatwright points out that all of Porter's mature chamber music works find their prototypes in these early compositions written in Paris.

In 1932 Porter became professor of music at Vassar College, where he remained for six years. In this period he wrote a number of orchestral works in which his later symphonic style is not only suggested but even partially realized. The most important is his first symphony, which was introduced by the New York Philharmonic on April 2, 1938, the composer conducting. Later the same year he was appointed dean of the New England Conservatory in Boston. Four years later he succeeded Wallace Goodrich as director. In 1944 he was elected a member of the National Institute of Arts and Letters; in 1964 he became treasurer.

In 1946 Porter resigned from the New England Conservatory to become professor of music at Yale, where he stayed twenty years until his retirement in July 1965.

On October 30, 1943, Porter was awarded the Elizabeth Sprague Coolidge medal in recognition of his "eminent service to chamber music." In commenting upon this award and discussing the Seventh String Quartet (1943), which had been commissioned by the Elizabeth Sprague Coolidge Foundation and performed by the Coolidge Quartet during the ceremony, Ray C. B. Brown, of the Washington *Post*, wrote: "His music is fresh and spontaneous, independent, intellectual, and at the same time emotionally vital. It is contemporaneous in feeling without any indulgence in dissonance. . . . The style is sinewy and lithe, and the formal structure neat in its compactness, while the ideational content is stimulating in its epigrammatic terseness and flashes of wit."

Howard Hanson also drew attention to one of the admirable qualities of Porter's chamber music when, on May 14, 1944, the honorary degree of Doctor of Music was conferred on Porter by the University of Rochester: "In spite of his technical proficiency, his music has not lost the common touch. He has not substituted technique for inspiration or novelty for invention. His strings still weave golden strands of melody, and his harmonies still re-create for the ear of the listener the spirit of beauty."

Porter, of course, also produced major works employing the symphony orchestra, among them the Concerto for Viola and Orchestra and the *Concerto Concertante*, for two pianos and orchestra. The first of these was introduced by Paul Doktor and the CBS Symphony, Dean Dixon conducting, in New York on May 16, 1948. Cecil Smith described this as "an arresting piece and an eloquent one. . . . Mr. Porter has the priceless asset of being able to write the melodies in a vein so personal that there is nothing derivative about them. The Concerto sings from the beginning to end; yet

it also possesses genuine rhythmic verve and a piquant harmonic scheme. . . . It is both entertaining and touching, and is not only one of Porter's best works but a valid addition to the permanent repertory."

The *Concerto Concertante* had been commissioned by the Louisville Orchestra, which introduced it in Kentucky on March 17, 1954, with Dorothea Adkins and Ann Monks as soloists. This work was originally called Concerto for Two Pianos and Orchestra, and as such it was awarded the Pulitzer Prize in music. But Porter soon came to realize that it was not a vehicle for piano virtuosi, that the two pianos were inextricable parts of the orchestral texture; for that reason he decided to rename it *Concerto Concertante*. Describing the work, Harold Boatwright said: "It is an expression of the same psychological atmosphere and approach to musical materials which characterize most other pieces by Porter, except that in this case there is a new polyphonic emphasis, a more brilliant treatment of the orchestra, and a more powerful emotional expression than in any other work except the . . . String Quartet No. 8 (1950). This is, in other words, not just typical Porter, but a real masterpiece in the kind of idiom which he has established for himself."

Porter's *New England Episodes*, a suite for orchestra, was commissioned for the first Inter-American Music Festival in Washington, D.C., where it was introduced on April 18, 1958. One of Porter's last major works for orchestra, his second symphony, received its première with the Louisville Orchestra on January 14, 1964 in Louisville, Kentucky.

From 1958 until his death, Porter served as chairman of the board of directors of the American Music Center, which he had helped to found with Howard Hanson and Aaron Copland in 1939.

Porter married Lois Brown, a violinist, on December 21, 1926. They had two children, a son and a daughter. For many years the Porters lived in the same house in New Haven where Porter had grown up as a boy. Following his retirement from Yale in 1965, the Porters moved to Bethany, Connecticut, eight miles north of New Haven, where they shared the house with a Labrador retriever named Schubert, a gift from Porter's students at Yale. Porter's studio there was designed by his son, William Lyon Porter, an architect. The Porters also maintained a summer home on the side of a hill on Squam Lake in New Hampshire, "a sort of MacDowell colony of my own," said Porter, "but without a colony."

Quincy Porter found relaxation from teaching and composing in such hobbies as photography (he did all his own processing) and printing (he operated his own press). He was for many years an expert in high-fidelity reproduction, and he himself wired his entire house in Bethany for sound. He was also fascinated by toy railway systems; at his summer home he constructed and operated an electrically powered inclined railroad which ran fifty feet from the house to the road.

Porter died of a stroke at his home in Bethany on November 12, 1966.

MAJOR WORKS

Chamber Music—10 string quartets; 2 violin sonatas; In Monasterio, for string quartet; Clarinet Quintet; Suite, for viola solo; Quintet on a Childhood Theme, for flute and strings; Sonata for French Horn and Piano; String Sextet on Slavic Folk Tunes; Four Pieces, for violin and piano; Duo, for flute and harp; Duo, for violin and viola; Duo, for viola and harp (or harpsichord); Divertimento, for two violins and viola; Divertimento, for woodwind quintet; Quintet for Harpsichord and Strings; Oboe Quintet.

Orchestral Music—2 symphonies; Ukrainian Suite, for strings; Poem and Dance; Dance in Three-Time; Music for Strings; Fantasy on a Pastoral Theme, for organ and strings; Viola Concerto; Five Pieces, for strings; Fantasy, for cello and small orchestra; Desolate City, for baritone and orchestra; Concerto Concertante, for two pianos and orchestra; New England Episodes; Harpsichord Concerto; Concertino for Wind Orchestra; Overture on Three American Folk Tunes; Wedding Music for Damaris, for brass, strings, and soprano.

Piano Music—Sonata; Six Miniatures; Day Dreams.

Vocal Music—Twelve Songs for Helen on Nursery Rhymes; This Is the House That Jack Built; Sonnets; Graveyard; Introspections on the Banks o' Doon, for soprano, flute, and piano; Symptoms of Love, song cycle.

ABOUT

Machlis, J., Introduction to Contemporary Music.
Bulletin of American Composers Alliance, No. 3, 1957; Modern Music, Winter 1946.

Francis Poulenc
1899–1963

Francis Poulenc was born on January 7, 1899, in Paris. From his father he inherited not only

Poulenc: poo länk'

affluence, which all his life made it possible for him to devote himself to music without concern for making a living, but also a profound Catholicism which asserted itself strongly in his music after his thirty-sixth year. Poulenc's mother was an excellent pianist, and it was from her that he acquired his own strong interest in music. Her piano playing was his first significant musical experience. Poulenc took his first piano lessons from her when he was five. At eight he studied with Mlle. Boutet de Monvel, César Franck's niece. About this time he heard a composition by Debussy and, as he later confessed, it "awakened me to music." He began to make rapid progress in his studies and by 1915 had decided to specialize in the piano. He became a pupil of Ricardo Viñes, who not only gave him a sound training in the classics but also encouraged his curiosity for and interest in modern music. Already Poulenc had become acquainted with and was deeply moved by the music of Stravinsky and Satie, as well as that of Debussy. Another influence, though this time from the past, was Schubert's song cycle *Die Winterreise*, which he came upon in a music shop. His later passion for writing songs, as well as his strong romantic tendencies and lyrical gifts, was the aftermath of this early association with Schubert's music.

His first compositions were preludes for the piano, written early in 1917. Success came the same year with an unusual work which anticipated the Dada movement, *Rapsodie Nègre*, introduced in Paris on December 11, 1917. The text consisted of a verse from *Les Poésies de Makoko Kangourou*, supposedly the work of a Liberian Negro but actually a hoax; the verse Poulenc set to music in this rhapsody was sheer gibberish. The success of the rhapsody directed public and critical attention to Poulenc for the first time.

Poulenc was drafted into the French army in January 1918. At first he served at the front with an anti-aircraft unit, and later, from July 1919 until his demobilization in October 1921, he worked as a typist in the Ministry of Aviation. While still in the army, he produced a number of compositions in which the tongue-in-cheek attitude of the *Rapsodie Nègre* was maintained. The three *Mouvements Perpétuels*, for piano, introduced by Ricardo Viñes in 1919, were, as Alfred Cortot once said, "reflections of the ironical outlook of Satie adapted to the sensitive standards of the current intellectual circles." Henri Hell wrote: "Spontaneous and most attractively melodious, they display, in the manner of Satie, a genre of the eighteenth century harpsichord composers tastefully spiced with the still new twentieth century notions of dissonance." Once out of uniform he continued his study of music. Despite his established reputation as a composer, for three years, beginning in 1921, he was a composition pupil of Charles Koechlin.

Poulenc's first songs also came in 1919—the cycles *Le Bestiaire* (to poems by Guillaume Apollinaire) and *Cocardes* (to poems by Jean Cocteau). *Le Bestiaire* still reveals the influence of Satie in its wit and gift for caricature; specimens of animal and marine life are described with vivid strokes. *Cocardes* was an ironic imitation of popular songs in which could be found, said Louis Durey, "great musicianship and rich novelty, which often remind us of Mozart by the freshness of their invention, and the elegant and refined sobriety of style."

Poulenc, already well known, was one of the composers whom the critic Henri Collet linked with Milhaud, Durey, Auric, Honegger, and Tailleferre in creating a new "school" of young composers which he baptized "The French Six" (see sketch on Auric, above). Of The Six, Poulenc for a while was the one most faithful to the principles of simplicity, economy, and directness—as well as to the gospel of everyday music for everyday people—all of which represented a reaction to German post-Romanticism and French Impressionism. Influenced on the one hand by Mozart and Schubert, and on the other by Satie and Stravinsky, Poulenc also favored a neoclassic style with strong emphasis on lyricism. In the larger forms, he was, for a decade or so, partial to terse statements, compactness of form, and transparency of texture. Graceful workmanship was combined with charm, spontaneity of expression, ingratiating lyricism, and at times an infectious wit. In this style he produced several important compositions.

The ballet *Les Biches* was Poulenc's first ambitious score, and his first attempt at writing for an orchestra. He was commissioned to write the music by Sergei Diaghilev, the director of the Ballet Russe de Monte Carlo. Diaghilev, impressed with Poulenc's *Mouvements Perpétuels*, wanted him to write music in a similar vein for a witty modern ballet. Poulenc's idea was different. As he put it, he was interested in doing "a sort of contemporary version of the *Fêtes Galantes* in which, as in certain pictures of Watteau, anything one wishes may be seen or imagined." *Les Biches* (*The Does*) was a major success when the Ballet Russe presented it in Paris on January 6, 1924. It has no plot to speak of but details the events at a house party in which

FRANCIS POULENC

the guests move towards one another and in which the hostess tries to form a romantic attachment with one of her young guests. The Poulenc score consists of a suite of dances, each complete and self-sufficient, described by Henri Hell as "exquisite—in the word's precise and original sense. . . . With its ironic and slightly rakish twists, its thoroughly traditional elegance of thought, it goes straight to the point, its one aim being to bring delight."

Other important works—also in a light, graceful, ingratiating vein—followed *Les Biches*. The *Concert Champêtre*, for harpsichord and orchestra, was written for Wanda Landowska, who introduced it with the Paris Philharmonic, under Pierre Monteux, on May 3, 1929. This work was a re-creation in modern musical terms of seventeenth century keyboard music. The Concerto for Two Pianos and Orchestra—first performance at the festival of the International Society for Contemporary Music at Venice on September 5, 1932—is a delightful excursion into levity, its wit projected through a number of popular tunes and rhythms. The Concerto in G minor, for organ and orchestra, was written in 1938 for the Princesse Edmond de Polignac, at whose salon the première performance took place the same year. Here, too, wit is given free rein, along with some solemn, even ominous, passages which portend a new and more serious direction for its composer. This sobriety was also found in his first important religious work for chorus—the *Litanies à la Vierge Noire*, for children's (or women's) voices and organ—and in the Mass in G major, for four-part a cappella mixed chorus, which Poulenc wrote in 1936 and 1937 respectively and in which he gave expression to his deep religious convictions. This music combines humility with sweetness, serenity with spiritual ardor. These traits characterize Poulenc's greatest religious compositions.

In August 1935 Poulenc appeared for the first time as a piano accompanist of Pierre Bernac, the baritone, in song recitals. This event took place at Salzburg, Austria, during the festival season. It was the first of many similar recitals in major music centers in Europe and the United States, the American debut taking place in the fall of 1948 during Poulenc's first visit to the United States. The recitals played a significant role in Poulenc's growth as a composer of art songs. Poulenc himself said that he learned the art of writing songs by accompanying Bernac in the great literature of the German and French schools. From his association with Bernac, Poulenc went on to write songs that have made him one of the greatest composers of such music in the twentieth century. In 1935 he set five poems by Paul Éluard, following this in 1937 with the setting of Paul Éluard's cycle *Tel Jour, Telle Nuit*. From then until 1956 Poulenc wrote about a hundred songs, most of them to poems by Éluard and Guillaume Apollinaire. The best are extraordinary not only for the poetic beauty and sensitivity of their melodies and for the rich invention in the writing of the piano accompaniment, but also for Poulenc's

remarkable gift in projecting subtle feelings, nuances, and atmospheres. As Irving Kolodin wrote in the *Saturday Review*, the "subtle interplay of text and tone certify Poulenc as the inheritor of the great French tradition of Fauré, Chabrier, Debussy and Ravel." Virgil Thomson also considers Poulenc "without a rival as a world master of concert song. . . . No other composer since Fauré has written for voice and piano so copiously, so authoritatively, with such freedom of musical thought, such variety of musical expression."

Poulenc gave up writing songs during the last six years of his life; the poets to whom he was most partial—Éluard, Apollinaire, Max Jacob—were dead. "I understood their poetry extremely well," he explained to an interviewer. "I was able to read between the lines of their poems; I was able to express all that was left unsaid in musical terms. Today, poets do not write in a manner that inspires me to song. . . . To write more would be to force myself in a direction in which I really have nothing more to say."

During World War II, Poulenc was an active member in the French Resistance movement. In the war years his political consciousness invested his music with increasing intensity and expressiveness. In 1943 he wrote a poignant Sonata for Violin and Piano, inspired by and dedicated to the Spanish poet, Federico García Lorca, who was murdered by the Falangists; its first performance was given in Paris on June 21, 1943, by Ginette Neveu, with the composer at the piano. During the same year he completed one of his greatest works for chorus, *Figure Humaine*, to a poem by Paul Éluard. This deeply moving, tragic music was written while Paris was occupied by the Nazis. It expresses not only the suffering of every Frenchman but also his will to resistance; and it concludes with a mighty hymn to liberty.

Expressive lyricism, an exalted spirituality, a deeply moving religious feeling, and shattering tragedy are all to be found in Poulenc's first full-length opera, possibly his greatest single work in any medium: *Les Dialogues des Carmélites*. It was first produced, with outstanding success, at La Scala in Milan on January 26, 1957. The American première followed on September 22 of the same year in San Francisco. In 1958 the opera was telecast over the NBC-TV network and was given the New York Music Critics Circle Award. Georges Bernanos contributed the libretto, based on a novella by Gertrud von Le Fort and a motion picture scenario by Philippe Agostini and the Rev. R. L. Bruckberger. The setting is Paris during the French Revolution. Sixteen nuns prefer to face death at the guillotine rather than dissolve their order. "This is magnificent material for music," reported Christina Thoresby after the world première, "and Poulenc has made full use of the possibilities. . . . He has written a score of rare lyrical beauty, which is clear, flexible, and brilliantly manipulated. It is also frankly tonal and utterly sincere. . . . But this opera also reveals a new Poulenc who is freer and more powerful than had been suspected and who . . . is able to sustain the long line and the complex development of an opera without sacrificing any of the qualities of a sensitive and imaginative miniaturist."

Despite the increasing sobriety and seriousness of purpose in so many of his works in the 1940's and 1950's, he had not altogether deserted the light touch or an iconoclastic attitude. These can be found in compositions such as the Sinfonietta, for orchestra (1947), introduced over the BBC network in London on October 24, 1948; the Piano Concerto, whose world première was given in Boston by the composer and the Boston Symphony on January 6, 1950; and most of all in the *opéra bouffe Les Mamelles de Tirésias*, on a surrealistic libretto by Apollinaire. This little comic opera, which satirizes a French campaign to increase the population, became the center of storm and violent criticism when the Opéra-Comique in Paris introduced it on June 3, 1947. Dismay and shock were caused by some of the items discussed in the text, such as the way in which one of the characters changes his sex, while another gives birth to forty thousand babies. Poulenc's spicy music kept brisk pace with the extraordinary goings-on on the stage. "His music skips along gaily at times," said Howard Taubman. "It has its share of mockery and sentiment, jabs and gibes of irony, broadly comic marches and dances. The composer's touch is everywhere skillful—in the orchestra and in the graceful vocal writing. But somehow the joke palls." The American première took place on June 13, 1953, at the second annual Festival of the Creative Arts

presented in Waltham, Massachusetts, Leonard Bernstein conducting.

Another unorthodox little opera—and a decided *tour de force*, but this time on a note of tragedy—was *La Voix Humaine*, a one-character opera, heard first at the Paris Opéra-Comique on February 9, 1959. The entire libretto, by Jean Cocteau, is a telephone call received by a woman who is being discarded by her lover, who is about to marry another woman. The work ends in utter despair as the woman realizes with finality that the affair is over. Most of the music is in a declamatory style which effectively captures the heartbreak of the deserted mistress.

It is the serious Poulenc, the religious Poulenc, whom we encounter in his last important compositions. One of them was the six-part Gloria, for chorus and orchestra, which the Koussevitzky Music Foundation commissioned and which the Boston Symphony introduced on January 20, 1961. Another was *Sept Répons des Ténèbres*, for orchestra, Poulenc's last work, which he wrote for the New York Philharmonic to help celebrate its opening season at the Lincoln Center for the Performing Arts. The New York Philharmonic introduced it under Thomas Schippers' direction on April 11, 1963. Comparing the two religious compositions, Harold Schonberg noted that while "the prevailing impression of the Gloria was of lyricism" that of the *Ténèbres* was one of "greater depth, passion and mystery."

Francis Poulenc died suddenly at his home in Paris on January 30, 1963. Two evenings before his death he attended a ballet performance at the Opéra-Comique and chatted gaily backstage with Yvette Chauvire, the prima ballerina of that evening.

From 1935, when he first settled in an apartment on the Rue de Médicis overlooking the Luxembourg Gardens, Poulenc spent part of each year in Paris and part in his country house purchased in 1927 at Noizay, in the valley of the Loire River. He never married, and it is believed that he loved only one woman in his life. She was Raymonde Linaissier, with whom he grew up and to whom he was deeply attached, but who died prematurely in 1930. Every Poulenc song in which the word "face" appears is dedicated to her memory.

Poulenc has been described as a "big,

countrified fellow, bony and jovial" who acts like an "overgrown schoolboy." To Edward Lockspeiser, Poulenc's face was "big and doggy," to Jay Harrison, "long and soulful."

"In many ways," added Jay Harrison, "Poulenc is Paris. He is gay like Paris, sad like Paris. And he bustles constantly. His hands wave, his eyebrows arch, he twitches, grins, makes faces. When his mouth talks, all of him talks too. If he is not Paris, he is at least French. Not even a deaf man could doubt that."

In a revealing intimate portrait of Poulenc in *Show*, Allen Hughes disclosed that Poulenc loved "luxury, fine foods and wines, paintings, flowers, and vibrant color. He was really interested only in what could be seen, smelled, touched, or listened to. Except for poetry he seldom read. He found philosophy a bore and thought abstractions abhorrent." Hughes continued: "Poulenc's life was full of paradoxes. He hired the solitude of a hotel and despised solitude, preferring to be surrounded by many people. He did not like the country very much, but maintained a home in the middle of it. He adored Paris and could not bear to stay there for more than a few weeks at a time. He did not like to walk, but neither drove nor owned a car. He was enough of a gourmand to enjoy eating pastries before lunch but he was given to restricting himself to the strictest of diets. He loved dogs . . . but would not allow himself to have one in his later years." Hughes also described how superstitious Poulenc was: "Whenever it was time to leave the house in the country to go to Paris or elsewhere, he placed postage stamps in a special little box on his writing table and played on both pianos (an upright and a grand) just before he went out of the door for the last time. The pianos were closed after his departure, never before. All this was to insure a safe return."

In his introduction to Henri Hell's biography of Poulenc, Edward Lockspeiser contributes this over-all evaluation of the composer as distinguished from the man: "No composer of our time has so consistently worked in the purest form of diatonic harmony. . . . Poulenc has shown that the special magic of diatonic harmony, modulation, uncluttered by wrong notes, can sometimes, even today, make an effect as poignant as in Schubert himself. . . . Sweetness, however, can pall. . . . Occasionally,

therefore, some kind of terrifying specter is made to burst through Poulenc's lyrical facade."

MAJOR WORKS

Ballets—Les Biches; Les Animaux Modèles.

Chamber Music—Various sonatas for solo instruments and piano (two clarinets; clarinet and bassoon; horn; trumpet and trombone; violin; cello; flute; oboe; clarinet); Trio, for piano, oboe, and bassoon; Aubade, choreographic concerto for piano and eighteen instruments; Sextet, for piano and wind; String Quartet.

Choral Music—Sept Chansons; Litanies à la Vierge Noire; Petites Voix; Mass in G major; Sécheresses, cantata; Quatre Motets pour un Temps de Pénitence; Exultate Deo; Salve Regina; Figure Humaine; Un Soir de Neige; Chansons Françaises; Quatres Petites Prières; Stabat Mater; Quatre Motets pour le Temps de Noël; Ave Verum Corpus, motet; Gloria.

Operas—Les Mamelles de Tirésias; Les Dialogues des Carmélites; La Voix Humaine.

Orchestral Music—Concert Champêtre, for harpsichord (or piano) and orchestra; Concerto in D minor, for two pianos and orchestra; Concerto in G minor, for organ, strings, and tympani; Sinfonietta; Concerto for Piano and Orchestra; La Dame de Monte Carlo, lyric scene for soprano and orchestra; Sept Répons des Ténèbres.

Piano Music—Trois Mouvements Perpétuels; Sonata, for piano duet; Suite in C; Napoli; Pastourelle; Deux Nouvellettes; Trois Pièces; Hommage à Albert Roussel; Huit nocturnes; Douze Improvisations; Villageoises, pieces for children; Feuillets d'Album; Intermezzo in C major; Intermezzo in D-flat major; Suite Française; Les Soirées de Nazelles; Bourrée d'Auvergne; Mélancolie; Thème Varié; Sonata, for two pianos.

Vocal Music—Rapsodie Nègre, for baritone, piano, string quartet, and clarinet; Le Bestiaire; Cocardes; Poèmes de Ronsard; Chansons Gaillardes; Vocalise; Airs Chantés; Épitaphe; Quatre Poèmes de Guillaume Apollinaire; Cinq Poèmes de Max Jacob; Le Bal Masqué, cantata for baritone (or mezzo soprano) and instruments; Huit Chansons Polonaises; Cinq Poèmes de Paul Éluard; À Sa Guitare; Tel Jour, Telle Nuit; Trois Poèmes de Vilmorin; Deux Poèmes d'Apollinaire; Miroirs Brûlants; Le Portrait; La Grenouillère; Ce Doux Petit Visage; Bleuet; Fiançailles pour Rire; Banalités; Chansons Villageoises; Métamorphoses; Deux Poèmes d'Aragon; Le Pont; Trois Chansons de F. García Lorca; Mais Mourir; Le Disparu; Main Dominée par le Cœur; Calligrammes; La Fraîcheur et le Feu; Parisiana; Rosemonde; Le Travail du Peintre; Deux Mélodies; Dernier Poème.

ABOUT

Audel, S., Moi et Mes Amis; Hell, H., Francis Poulenc; Rostand, E., Francis Poulenc: Entretiens avec Claude Rostand.

Chesterian (London), November-December 1935; Musical America, April 1960, February 1963; New York Times, November 7, 1948; Saturday Review, February 23, 1963; Show, June 1963.

Sergei Prokofiev
1891–1953

Sergei Sergeevich Prokofiev was born in Sontzovka, near Ekaterinoslav (now Dnepropetrovsk), in the Ukraine, on April 23, 1891. His father, a graduate of the Academy of Agriculture and the manager of estates, was in comfortable financial circumstances. His mother was an excellent pianist. Sergei was their only living child; two daughters, born before Sergei, had died at birth.

SERGEI PROKOFIEV

In an autobiographical sketch, Prokofiev revealed that "from the day I was born I heard music. . . . One day, when mother was practising exercises by Hanon, I went up to the piano and asked if I could play my own music on the two highest octaves of the keyboard. To my surprise, she agreed, in spite of the resulting cacophony. This lured me to the piano. Soon I began climbing up to the keyboard all by myself and would try to pick out some little tune. One such tune I repeated several times, so that mother noticed it and decided to write it down. My efforts at that time consisted of either sitting down at the piano and making up tunes which I could not write down, or sitting at the table and drawing notes which could not be played. I just drew them like designs, as other children drew trains and people, because I was always seeing notes on the piano stand.

Prokofiev: prŭ kôf′ yĕf

One day, I brought out my papers covered with notes and said: 'Here, I've composed a Liszt rhapsody.' I was under the impression that a Liszt rhapsody was a double name of a composition like sonata-fantasia. Mother had to explain to me that I couldn't have composed a Liszt rhapsody because rhapsody was a form of composition, and Liszt was the name of a composer who had written it. Furthermore, I learned that it was wrong to write music on a staff of nine lines without any divisions, and that it should be written on a five-line staff with division into measures. . . . I actually began to write down little songs which could be played."

He wrote his first piece of music when he was five—Galop Hindou, for piano, motivated by a famine in India which he had heard his parents discuss. Six months later he wrote a rondo, a march, and a waltz. After that he was taken by his father to see an opera, an experience that led him to try writing one. He completed words and music of The Giant in his ninth year. From 1900 to 1902 he was occupied by a second opera, Desert Islands. By the time he was twelve he had completed a symphony, for four hands, a set of twelve piano pieces, and a third opera, Feast During the Plague.

Despite this extraordinary activity in music, and the remarkable talent it revealed, Sergei's parents were determined to develop the boy along other lines. He was encouraged to indulge in sports, was taught to ride horseback, swim, play croquet. His father gave him lessons in Russian and arithmetic, and his mother encouraged him to become interested in gardening. He began to play chess, a pastime that later in his life would develop into a passion. He also indulged in boisterous childish games with peasant children.

But music—both the playing of the piano and composition—was his main interest. One day, he brought some of his music to Taneiev, who told him: "You must develop a more interesting harmony. Too much of your music employs the tonic, dominant and subdominant." But Taneiev recognized Prokofiev's talent and advised the boy to take lessons in composition with Glière.

When Prokofiev was thirteen he entered the St. Petersburg Conservatory. There, for the next decade, he studied composition with Rimsky-Korsakov, Nicolas Tcherepnin, and

Liadov, and piano with Annette Essipov. All the time he was writing music, mainly for the piano. Some was influenced by Reger, some by Scriabin; in a good many of his pieces he ventured towards goals of his own. In the years between 1907 and 1909 he completed several études and pieces for the piano, including the *Suggestion Diabolique* which later became successful and which, amazingly enough, reveals some of his later personal creative attitudes. He also wrote his first piano sonata and his first orchestral composition (a Sinfonietta). These and others of his compositions came to the attention of A. V. Ossovsky, a musicologist, who in turn informed the publisher Jurgenson: "I have absolutely no doubt that this young musician—composer, pianist and conductor—is unusually gifted. To judge by the way he has begun, he has a great future in front of him." As a result of such a recommendation, Jurgenson bought several of Prokofiev's compositions. Prokofiev's first opus was his piano sonata; his second, third, and fourth were collections of piano pieces.

On December 31, 1908, Prokofiev made his first public appearance as a pianist, performing several of his own compositions including the *Suggestion Diabolique*. The discords, the percussive way in which the piano was played, the original manner in which the melody moved—all this caused shock. One critic declared: "If one regards these rather unintelligible compositions as trials of the pen, so to speak, one can perhaps discern a trace of talent in them." One of those present who was particularly impressed—who even went so far as to call the pieces "remarkable" and "full of personality"—was young Igor Stravinsky.

In 1909 Prokofiev received diplomas in composition and piano playing, but he remained at the Conservatory for another five years. During that period he grew increasingly ambitious in his compositions, completing his second piano sonata, his first two piano concertos, and his first opera since childhood (*Magdalene*). In these works he experimented further with discords and unorthodox modulations and tonalities. Some of his teachers were horrified by the kind of music he was producing. In one of his pieces he used unresolved seconds; in another, two different keys were employed simultaneously. When Taneiev saw some of this music, he was shocked. "I have merely followed your advice," Prokofiev told him. "I proceeded to develop a more interesting harmony, just as you advised me." Nevertheless, the first piano concerto, which Prokofiev introduced in Moscow on August 7, 1912, was generally well received, even though the distinguished critic Sabaneyev described the music as "coarse, primitive cacophony scarcely deserving the name of music."

In the spring of 1914, Prokofiev was graduated from the Conservatory with highest honors in piano playing and conducting. For his graduation exercise on May 24, he played his First Piano Concerto (he had already written a second one, introduced at Pavlovsk on September 5, 1913, but it had received unfavorable notices). Glazunov ran out of the Conservatory auditorium, cupping hands over ears to drown out the sounds. Some of the professors, however, thought the work had extraordinary merit and presented its composer with the coveted Rubinstein Prize.

Soon after leaving the Conservatory, Prokofiev went on a holiday to London. There he met the impresario of the Ballet Russe, Sergei Diaghilev, who commissioned him to write a ballet score for his company. Meanwhile, World War I broke out. As the only son of a widow, Prokofiev was exempt from military service and on his return to Russia was able to devote himself to composition.

The ballet Prokofiev was writing for Diaghilev utilized a text in which the characters were the ancient Scythians and their gods. This did not appeal to Diaghilev and he rejected it. Prokofiev, however, was so taken with the theme that he decided to use it for an orchestral suite. The four-movement *Scythian Suite* was introduced in St. Petersburg on January 29, 1916, Prokofiev conducting. The music was too advanced in style for the tastes of both critics and audience. One of the violinists in the orchestra was quoted as saying to a friend: "My wife is sick and I must buy medicine, otherwise I would never consent to play this crazy music."

The *Scythian Suite* involved Prokofiev and the critic Sabaneyev in a scandal which created considerable stir at the time. The work had originally been scheduled for an earlier performance, but at the last moment had been withdrawn from the program. Sabaneyev, who did not attend the concert, wrote a review violently attacking the new Prokofiev work, calling it "barbaric music" and stating categorically that it had given him neither "pleasure or artistic satisfaction." The fact that there existed only a single copy of the score, and that the copy was in Prokofiev's possession, emphasized the amusing point that Sabaneyev had written his attack without having heard or become familiar with a note of the music. This incident was widely publicized and created a furor; it did much to bring the composer a great deal of attention and sympathy.

There was another major disappointment. Albert Coates, conductor of the Maryinsky Theatre, had asked Prokofiev to write an opera. He composed *The Gambler*, based on the Dostoevsky novel, but when he submitted his score, it was found unsingable and unplayable. *The Gambler* had to wait more than a decade for its première, which finally took place at the Théâtre de la Monnaie in Brussels on April 29, 1929. It was not well received and for a long time was neglected. On April 5, 1957, it was revived in New York City, and on August 28, 1962, it was produced at the Edinburgh Festival by the visiting Belgrade Opera. On the latter occasion, Peter Heyworth reported: "The intention was that music and drama move on an equal footing and thus avoid artificialities of opera. The trouble is that in the absence of sustained melody on the one hand and of sustained symphonic interest on the other, the libretto inevitably shapes the opera, and the score is thus reduced to underlining and illustrating the text. Often Prokofiev does this with great brilliance and resource."

If Diaghilev had been unsympathetic to the subject of the Scythians, he was more partial to another ballet text with which Prokofiev was engaged. Steeping himself in Russian folklore, Prokofiev came upon a whimsical tale of a buffoon, which he adapted into a ballet scenario. He completed his score in 1915, calling it *Chout*. The war delayed the première for six years. When *Chout* was introduced by the Ballet Russe in Paris on May 17, 1921, it was a great success. A twelve-movement suite for orchestra, drawn from the ballet score, was introduced in Brussels in 1924; this was also well received.

Prokofiev's style, so long foreshadowed in his earlier works, was fully crystallized in the composition of his first violin concerto, completed in 1913, which received its world première in Paris on October 18, 1923; the already commented upon *Scythian Suite;* his first symphony, called *Classical*, because it was a twentieth century adaptation of the classical symphonic style and structure of Haydn and Mozart and one of the earliest examples of the neoclassic movement (first performance in St. Petersburg on April 21, 1918); and the third and fourth piano sonatas (1917).

"After the publication of the First Violin Concerto," wrote Nicolas Nabokov, "little has changed in either the style or technique of Prokofiev's music." Nabokov then went on to analyze Prokofiev's highly personal creative methods: "Prokofiev loves, for instance . . . to play a little game of melodic construction which could easily be discovered in any one of his pieces. The game consists of taking a conventional rhythmic figure, tying it up with a conventional melodic pattern, so obvious as to border sometimes on triviality, and then afterwards forcing this melodic line into a harmonic frame which seems disconnected, surprisingly arbitrary, and produces the feeling that the melody has been refreshed by having been harmonically mishandled. Another little game in Prokofiev's thematic structure is the abruptness and unexpectedness of his leaps. . . . These characteristics contribute a great deal to the joking, sarcastic nature of much of his music. . . . In a certain sense a similar game is carried on within his harmonic texture. Chords, generally very simple chords, are related in such an entirely unexpected fashion that the ear has always a new element of harmonic surprise to cope with."

Soon after the revolution in Russia, Prokofiev was provided with funds by the publishing house of Serge Koussevitzky to undertake an American tour. He came by way of Siberia, Japan, and Honolulu, making his first American appearance in a piano recital in New York on November 20, 1918. The critics liked his playing, but not his piano works, which some of them described as "Bolshevism in art" and "Russian chaos." James Gibbons Huneker called him a "musical agitator." Richard Aldrich saw in the finale of one of Prokofiev's piano sonatas "visions of a charge of Mammoths on some vast immemorial Asiatic plateau."

In Chicago, Prokofiev presented the world première of one of his most celebrated works, the third concerto, in C major—on December 16, 1921, with Frederick Stock conducting the Chicago Symphony. Prokofiev was also commissioned to write a new work for the Chicago Opera. He completed the assignment—*Love for Three Oranges*—on schedule, but the opera house director found the work too difficult to perform and mount and refused to live up to his contract. Two years later, however, Mary Garden took over the direction of the opera company and produced *Love for Three Oranges* on December 30, 1921. This is a satirical opera with a fairy-tale text by the composer based on an eighteenth century tale by Gozzi which passes from nonsense to whimsy and from wit to broad burlesque. Prokofiev's music was tart, ironic, discordant; the opera was badly received both in Chicago and, a week later, in New York. "Without tunes, what is the use of an opera?" lamented one of the critics. Not until its revival by the New York City Opera on November 1, 1949, was this sparkling and delightful fantasy fully appreciated. Olin Downes wrote that it was "really something to write home about. It is . . . a most original piece. The opera is a parody of operas, but it is also a most distinguished work of art. . . . The orchestra is simply amazing all the time, in its soft and mordant commentary, its scherzo movements, which are the quintessence of fantasy and humor."

By the time Prokofiev left the United States in 1922 he had married Lina Llubera, a young Cuban singer he had met in California. They first went to live in the picturesque Bavarian town of Ettal. But in October 1923 Prokofiev set up a permanent home in Paris, leaving the city for a few months each year to make concert appearances. In January 1927 he returned to his native country, for the first time since he had left it in 1918, to give a number of highly successful concerts.

In Paris, Prokofiev continued writing major works in a provocative modern style which became increasingly discordant; their premières were events of first importance. The Concerts Koussevitzky introduced his cantata, *Seven, They Are Seven* on May 29, 1924, and his second symphony on June 6, 1925. On June 7, 1927, in Paris, the Diaghilev Ballet Russe performed the première of Prokofiev's proletarian ballet, *Le Pas d'Acier* (*The Age of Steel*)—the composer's first attempt to give an artistic interpretation to Soviet life by glorifying the growth and development of industrialization in Russia. The ballet was received apathetically in Paris where it was described as "the apotheosis of machinery." But in London, the following July, it made such a good impression that it was performed eight times. "As an apostle of Bolshevism, he has no peer," commented one newspaperman.

Other major works of this period included the third symphony (Paris, May 17, 1929); the ballet *L'Enfant Prodigue* (Paris, May 21, 1929); the fourth symphony, written in 1930 to commemorate the fiftieth anniversary of the Boston Symphony (Boston, November 14, 1930); the fourth piano concerto, for the left hand only, which though completed in 1931 did not receive its première until 1956, in West Berlin; and the fifth piano concerto, which the composer himself introduced in Berlin on October 31, 1932.

Late in 1933 Prokofiev decided to return permanently to Russia and become part of its social and political revolution. He was given a hero's welcome and placed among the most honored leaders of Soviet culture. Though his basic musical style remained unaltered in the Soviet Union, Prokofiev found a new direction and purpose as a creative artist. He dedicated his music to Soviet ideologies, creating works intended to propagandize Soviet principles and aims and glorifying Russian backgrounds and traditions. One of his first important successes following his return came with delightful incidental music for a motion picture, *Lieutenant Kijé*—music which has since become universally popular through the orchestral suite adapted from the score and introduced in Paris, under the composer's direction, on February 20, 1937. *Lieutenant Kijé* was a broad satire on military heroism and bureaucracy in the time of the Czars, and it inspired Prokofiev to write some of his brightest and wittiest music.

The period 1935–1936 was marked by two large works: the second violin concerto (first performance by Robert Soetens in Madrid on December 1, 1935) and the ballet *Romeo and Juliet*, completed in 1936 and produced in Leningrad on January 11, 1940. Other Prokofiev works drew inspiration from the well of Russian backgrounds and history, the most significant being the cantata *Alexander Nevsky* which, like *Lieutenant Kijé*, was adapted from incidental music for a motion picture. This cantata was introduced in Moscow on May 17, 1939. It is a highly descriptive and at times realistic portrayal of the career of Prince Alexander Nevsky, the hero who mustered an army and defeated the Knights of the Teutonic Order when they invaded Novgorod in 1242.

Prokofiev also took to writing music for children. In 1935 he completed some charming piano pieces, and later he wrote some ingratiating children's songs. The most successful and important of his children's music came in 1936 with a symphonic fairytale, *Peter and the Wolf*, intended to teach the young the instruments of the orchestra. Each character in the fairytale is identified with a different orchestral instrument and by a subtle use of a leading motive for each. *Peter and the Wolf* is full of youthful gaiety, wit, and spontaneity; its success became worldwide, following its première in Moscow on May 2, 1936.

In 1939 Prokofiev and his wife were divorced. Less than two years later, Prokofiev married again. His second wife (who survived him) was Mira Alexandrovna Mendelson, a highly gifted student in languages at the Institute of Literature.

When the Nazis invaded the Soviet Union in 1941, Prokofiev was living in a Moscow suburb and working on his music for the ballet *Cinderella*, which was finally presented in Moscow on November 21, 1945. The life-and-death struggle of his land and people led him to dedicate himself to the war effort through the writing of military marches and songs on anti-Fascist texts. "But soon events assumed such gigantic and far-reaching scope," he told an interviewer, "as to demand larger canvases." The *Suite: 1941* for orchestra reflected the impact of the war on his musical thinking. Works ambitious in scope and monumental in design followed, all inspired by events in the war-torn Soviet Union. In the years between 1940 and 1944, Prokofiev completed three piano sonatas inspired by the war: the sixth, in A major; the seventh, in B-flat major, known as the *Stalingrad Sonata;* and the eighth, in B-flat major. The most successful of these was the seventh, in which the immense power and high tensions of the music suggest the heroic defense of the city of Stalingrad by the victorious Red Army. Svyatoslav Richter introduced it in the Soviet Union in 1943 and it brought Prokofiev his first Stalin Prize.

On January 13, 1945, there took place in Moscow the première of Prokofiev's Fifth Symphony, his first such work in fifteen years. Dedicated to the spirit of man, a spirit ennobled by the harrowing experiences of invasion and war, this symphony is one of its composer's noblest works. He himself considered it the culmination of a large period of his creative life. Many critics agreed with him. Olin Downes said: "The symphony is certainly one of the most interesting and probably the best that has come from Russia in the last quarter of a century. It is unquestionably the richest and the most mature symphonic score that the composer has produced. There are new spiritual horizons in the serenity of the opening movement and wonderful developments that come later." Serge Koussevitzky, who introduced it to the United States in Boston in November 1945, called it one of the greatest works of the twentieth century and broke a precedent by performing it twice in the same season in New York.

The most ambitious and the largest of all Prokofiev's works during the war period was his opera *War and Peace*, almost as epical in concept and projection as the Tolstoy novel on which it was based. The libretto was the work of Prokofiev's wife, who concentrated on the Napoleonic invasion in 1812. The opera called for sixty characters and was so long that it required two nights for performance. Particularly effective are the mass scenes, including the chorus of the Smolensk refugees and the staging of the battle of Borodino; Prokofiev's orchestral writing is eloquent in the tone poems describing the ruined Moscow, the spring nocturne of the first scene, and the battle of the partisans and the French. The opera was seen first in Leningrad on June 12, 1946. But just before his death, Prokofiev revised it extensively. This definitive version was later produced in Leningrad, on March 31, 1955.

Following the end of the war, Prokofiev was regarded, and justly so, as one of the country's foremost cultural figures. He received many honors. Then, at the peak of his fame and at the height of his creative powers, he was suddenly and inexplicably the object of a violent attack by his own government. He became a victim of a new music policy, adopted by the Central Committee of the Communist Party on February 10, 1948.

Three months earlier, a new Soviet opera, *Great Friendship*, by Vano Muradeli, had been given its première. Muradeli's cacophonous music aroused the displeasure of Stalin, who made his feelings known. Taking their cue from Stalin, leading government and music officials headed by A. A. Zhdanov demanded a new orientation on the part of Soviet composers: away from modernism or cerebralism towards simplicity, away from the esoteric and towards a musical language that derived its character and inspiration from the Russian past. In the public resolution of February 10, 1948, the Central Committee vigorously denounced some of the leading Soviet composers of the time—not only Prokofiev, but also Shostakovich, Khatchaturian, and Miaskovsky, among many others—for what was described as "decadent" tendencies in their musical thinking. The official phrase was "decadent formalism." In the words of the resolution, these composers were condemned for "the negation of the basic principles of classical music" and for preaching "a sermon for atonality, dissonance and disharmony, as if this were an expression of 'progress' and 'innovation,' in the growth of musical compositions which transform into cacophony, into a chaotic piling of sounds."

One week after the promulgation of this resolution, Prokofiev hotly exclaimed to a neighbor composer at a meeting of Soviet musicians in Moscow: "They should stick to politics and leave music to musicians." But as it became increasingly apparent that the new tendency in Soviet thinking would not pass, Prokofiev wrote a long and detailed apology to Tikhon Khrennikov, head of the General Assembly of Soviet composers: "Elements of formalism were peculiar to my music as long as fifteen or twenty years ago. Apparently the infection caught from contact with some Western ideas." He concluded that in the future he intended to take a new direction towards melody, simplicity, and polyphony and away from discord and cerebralism. "In my new opera, *A Tale of a Real Man*, I intend to introduce trios, duets and contrapuntally developed choruses for which I will make use of some interesting northern Russian folk songs. Lucid melody, and as far as possible, a simple harmonic language are elements which I intend to use." However, when this new opera was privately performed in Leningrad on December 3, 1948, it did not please the authorities. Khrennikov condemned it for its "modernistic and antimelodic style." Prokofiev's Sixth Symphony, heard in Leningrad on October 11, 1947, was also harshly criticized.

But eventually Prokofiev was able to regain his previous position in the cultural life of the Soviet Union. He wrote an oratorio, *On Guard for Peace*, a condemnation of the Western "war mongers" and a paean to the Soviet "international peace movement." He also wrote a vocal-symphonic suite, *Winter Bonfire*, which adopted some of the realistic and readily assimilable style demanded by the new Soviet esthetics. Both works were heard at a concert in Moscow on December 19, 1950, and both were responsible for bringing Prokofiev the Stalin Prize in 1951. To further emphasize Prokofiev's return to the good graces of the authorities, there took place on April 23, 1951, a special concert celebrating his sixtieth birthday. Prokofiev, who was ill at a resort (he had previously suffered two strokes), could not attend, but he heard the concert over the radio. When his Seventh Symphony was heard in Moscow on October 11, 1952, it was hailed by audience and critics as a masterwork embodying the greatness of Soviet art. The composer, who attended the performance, was given a tremendous ovation. However, when this symphony received its American première on April 10, 1953, the critics found the work to be substandard Prokofiev.

When Prokofiev made his last tour of the United States, in 1938, he was described as follows by Alice Berezowsky in her book *Duet with Nicky:* "He was tall and bald-headed and looked exactly like a well-to-do businessman. His suit was a conservative English tweed; his tie, a small patterned foulard. His unremarkable face was clean-shaven. Prokofiev sat eating and talking with a minimum of motion and without changing his poker-face expression. . . . Judged by his looks, Prokofiev might have been the author of the President's Annual Report of the Consolidated Utilities

Corporation. There was an air of authority about him and the evidence of seasoned judgment in his remarks. Prokofiev is a man who knows exactly what he wants, formulates his aims with absolute clarity and has the talent, healthy vitality, and capacity for hard work to achieve them."

He has further been described by his friends as a hard-headed and practical man who was always efficient, neat, and punctual. His method of writing music—as reported in *Time* magazine—provided still another insight into his personality: "He composes with the cold matter-of-factness of a mathematician, and keeps stacks of copybooks in which he hoards themes for future compositions. He jumps from bed to jot one down; they occur to him while taking walks, and especially while riding trains. . . . When he has saved up enough little scraps of melody, he works out an idea for a large composition to use them in. . . . He works regularly between the hours of ten and noon every day. When he is seriously at work, he never listens to anybody else's music."

Away from music his principal interest was chess. Occasionally he liked to participate in a game of bridge or, when partners were not available, double solitaire. He did not drink or smoke, but ate a good deal of candy. By his first marriage he had two sons, neither of whom is musical.

Prokofiev died in Moscow on March 5, 1953 (the same day that Stalin died). His last major work was the ballet *Tale of the Stone Flower*, rehearsals of which began on March 1. A revision of the music for a needed pas de deux was made by Prokofiev in a few minutes on the afternoon of March 5. Immediately afterward, he suffered a cerebral hemorrhage that proved fatal. The première of *Tale of the Stone Flower*, delayed for almost a year, was given in Moscow on February 12, 1954.

MAJOR WORKS

Ballets—Chout; Le Pas d'Acier; L'Enfant Prodigue; Sur le Boristhène; Romeo and Juliet; Cinderella; Tale of the Stone Flower.

Chamber Music—2 string quartets; 2 violin sonatas; Overture on Hebrew Themes, for clarinet, string quartet, and piano; Quintet in G minor, for wind and strings; Sonata in C major, for two violins; Sonata for Solo Violin in C minor; Sonata in D major, for flute and piano; Sonata in C major, for cello and piano.

Choral Music—Seven, They Are Seven, cantata; Mass Songs; Cantata for the Twentieth Anniversary of the October Revolution; Songs of Our Days;

Alexander Nevsky, cantata; Ballad of the Unknown Boy, cantata; Thirtieth Anniversary of the October Revolution; Winter Bonfire; On Guard for Peace, oratorio.

Operas—The Gambler; Love for Three Oranges; The Flaming Angel; Simeon Kotko; Betrothal in a Convent; Tale of a Real Man; War and Peace.

Orchestral Music—7 symphonies; 5 piano concertos; 2 violin concertos; Scythian Suite; Le Pas d'Acier, suite; American Overture; L'Enfant Prodigue, suite; Divertimento; Symphonic Song; Cello Concerto; Lieutenant Kijé, suite; Romeo and Juliet, three suites; Summer's Day; Peter and the Wolf, for narrator and orchestra; Russian Overture; Suite: 1941; Ode on the End of the War; Cinderella, three suites; Anniversary Poem; Pushkin Waltzes; Summer Night, suite; Wedding Scene, suite; Gypsy Fantasia; Ural Rhapsody; The Volga Meets the Don; Poem of Fatherland; Sinfonia Concertante in E minor, for cello and orchestra.

Piano Music—9 sonatas; 2 sonatinas; Études; Pieces (including Suggestion Diabolique); Toccata in C major; Sarcasms; Visions Fugitives; Tales of an Old Grandmother; Things in Themselves; Pensées; Children's Music; Carnival, for two pianos.

Vocal Music—The Ugly Duckling; Three Children's Songs; Three Pushkin Romances; Five Songs Without Words; various songs for voice and piano; various children's songs for voice and piano.

ABOUT

Abraham, G., Eight Soviet Composers; Ewen, D. (ed.), The New Book of Modern Composers; Hanson, L. and Hanson, E., Prokofiev; Nabokov, N., Old Friends and New Music; Nestyev, I., Sergei Prokofiev: His Musical Life; Samuel, C., Prokofiev; Schlifstein, S. I. (ed.), Serge Prokofiev: Materials, Documents, Reminiscences; Seroff, V., Sergei Prokofiev, a Soviet Tragedy; Streller, F., Sergej Prokofjew; Slonimsky, N., The Symphonies of Prokofiev.

Atlantic Monthly, July 1942; Musical Quarterly, October 1944; New York Times, March 15, 1953; Time, November 19, 1945.

Giacomo Puccini
1858–1924

Giacomo Antonio Domenico Michele Secondo Maria Puccini, the most celebrated Italian opera composer since Verdi, was born in Lucca on December 22, 1858. For several generations, the Puccinis had distinguished themselves as professional musicians in Lucca. Giacomo's mother determined early to have her son follow in the family tradition. Fortunately, the boy revealed from the beginning an uncommon gift. After receiving some elementary instruction from an uncle and some lessons on the organ from his father, young Puccini, aged six, took over his father's post as choirmaster and organist of San

Puccini: pōot chē′ nē

436

Martino church when his father died in 1864. A preliminary period of organ study with Carlo Angeloni was followed by his entrance into the Pacini Institute at Lucca for training in theory and church music. Puccini then held various posts as organist in churches in nearby villages. He also did some composing. A cantata, *Juno*, submitted in a local competition did not win but was performed in Lucca; and a motet for the feast of Santa Paolina was also well received in a local performance.

GIACOMO PUCCINI

He might have been satisfied to remain a reputable Lucca musician, playing the organ and writing church music, if he had not heard a performance of Verdi's *Aida* in Pisa. What he heard in that theatre to which he had walked, a distance of thirteen miles, stirred him so deeply that for the first time he saw his future clearly: He, too, would write operas. But first he would have to study. Financial assistance came from a granduncle; supplemented by a modest subsidy from Queen Margherita, it enabled him to go to Milan in the fall of 1880 to take the entrance examinations for the Conservatory, which he passed easily. Puccini attended the Conservatory for three years as a pupil of Bazzini and Ponchielli.

"I like Milan," he wrote his mother once he got used to city life. "I am not hungry. I eat a great deal, and I fill up on substantial soup. My appetite is satisfied. In the evenings I go to the Gallery for a stroll, then come home footsore. Reaching my room, I do a little counterpoint. I do not play the piano because it is not allowed at night. After that, I go to bed where I read seven or eight pages of a novel. This is my life."

Upon graduation in 1883, he had one of his compositions, *Capriccio Sinfonico*, for orchestra, performed at a Conservatory concert. It had been written for his final examination. It made such a good impression that it was accepted for publication and was even given an additional performance by the orchestra of La Scala conducted by Franco Faccio. Yet, even though he had achieved a measure of recognition with an orchestral piece, he had not forgotten his ambition to write for the stage. In this aim he found strong support in his teacher Ponchielli, already renowned as the composer of *La Gioconda*. Ponchielli urged Puccini to write a one-act opera for a competition sponsored by the publishing house of Sonzogno. The opera Puccini wrote, *Le Villi*, did not win the prize, but it did attract the interest of Arrigo Boito, the distinguished librettist and composer, who raised the necessary funds for its production. Given at the Teatro dal Verme in Milan on May 31, 1884, *Le Villi* was so successful that La Scala accepted it for production the following season and Ricordi contracted for its publication. In addition, Ricordi commissioned young Puccini to write an opera, paying him an advance of three hundred lire a month for a two-year period.

It was during this period that Puccini met and fell in love with the woman destined to share his life. She was Elvira Gemignani, the wife of a local merchant. For a while their affair was secret; then Elvira decided to leave her husband and live openly and permanently with Puccini. Though a son, Antonio, was born to them on December 23, 1886, Puccini and Elvira were never able to marry. Antonio was legitimated by the courts as Puccini's son only after the composer died.

The opera that resulted from Ricordi's contract, *Edgar*, was a failure when produced at La Scala on April 21, 1889, mainly because of its incredibly poor libretto. "I am terribly hard up and I don't know how I can go on," Puccini wrote to his brother in South America after this fiasco. "I'm piling up debts. Presently the crisis will come and then, God help me!"

But with his third opera came a dramatic change of fortune. Collaborating with three librettists, Puccini completed *Manon Lescaut*, based on the celebrated romance of Abbé Prévost which Massenet had already made into a successful opera. *Manon Lescaut*, introduced at the Teatro Regio in Turin on February 1, 1893, was a triumph. The audience, reported the *Gazzetta del Popolo*, was "stunned and overcome by emotion." Another Milan journal called the new opera "the work of a genius, conscious of his powers, master of his art, a creator and perfecter of it."

It is with *Manon Lescaut* that Puccini's career as Verdi's successor began. Here, as D. C. Parker wrote, we find "some of the most vigorous and spontaneous melody which Puccini has given us.... The Puccini 'manner'... is not absent. Indeed, considering the chronological position of the opera, it is surprising that there is so much of the mature Puccini in it." And George R. Marek has written: "It is fresh and fragrant. It is impulsive and ardent. Neither time nor the advancing sophistication of music has taken from the opera its piquancy."

Manon Lescaut was the first Puccini opera to spread the composer's reputation outside Italy. When produced in London, a year after its Turin première, it received praise from George Bernard Shaw, who remarked prophetically: "Puccini looks to me more like the heir of Verdi than any of his rivals." The American première of the opera took place at the Grand Opera House in Philadelphia on August 29, 1894.

While visiting Paris for the French première of *Manon Lescaut*, Puccini worked on *La Bohème*, an opera based on Henri Murger's popular novel *Scènes de la Vie de Bohème*. The report that another Italian composer— Leoncavallo, creator of *Pagliacci*—was fashioning an opera on the same subject sent Puccini to work at white heat. It was Puccini's *La Bohème* which was heard first—at the Teatro Regio in Turin on February 1, 1896, Toscanini conducting. At first it seemed that Leoncavallo would emerge victor in this competitive bid to bring the Bohemians of Paris to the operatic stage, for Puccini's opera was received apathetically, and at times even with hostility. Some objected to its realism and simplicity; others, to the fact that it did not have the kind of big scenes, spectacles, and climaxes they demanded of grand opera. A critic of *Stampe* felt that Puccini's score was written too hurriedly "with very little labor of selection and polishing" and prophesied that the opera would "leave no great trace upon the history of our lyric theatre." Only one Italian critic, a man named Pozza, seemed to recognize its true merit and insisted that before long connoisseurs would embrace it.

It was at the third presentation of *La Bohème*—in Palermo, late in 1896—that Pozza's prognostication was realized. Though that performance took place on Friday the thirteenth and the conductor of that evening, Leopoldo Mugnone, was notoriously superstitious, the opera achieved a great success. The audience, delirious with delight, refused to leave the auditorium until Mimi's death scene had been repeated. *La Bohème* went on to become Puccini's best loved opera and one of the favorites in the Italian repertory. By the time Leoncavallo's opera was produced, Puccini's *La Bohème* had so solidly established itself that nobody had an ear for a second opera on the same subject. Leoncavallo's *La Bohème* went into permanent discard. For this, Leoncavallo never forgave Puccini, detesting him openly and thoroughly until the end of his life.

La Bohème placed its composer in the vanguard of the opera composers of his generation. "There are few operas in the past fifty years or so," said H. F. Peyser, "in which the score mirrors so exactly and sensitively the changing moods of the text and is so filled with the true spirit of the piece. Its various arias, duets, quartets and other concerted pieces are recognizable and easily detachable from their context, yet the opera is a thoroughly modern work such as no Italian composer of fifty years earlier would have thought of writing."

The success of *La Bohème* made Puccini wealthy as well as famous. He built a beautiful Florentine villa at Torre del Lago, where he could indulge in his favorite pastimes of hunting, driving high-powered cars at maximum speeds, joining his friends in good food, wines, and witty conversations, and leading the life of a *grand seigneur*. He was strikingly handsome and dapper, always meticulously dressed, and always attractive to and attracted by women.

The erotic nature in Puccini was, as George R. Marek points out, only one facet of the composer's personality. The other was his "ever present and unreasonable melancholy." Puccini himself once said, "I have always carried with me a great sack of melancholy," and one of Puccini's intimate friends, Renato Simoni, remarked that Puccini possessed "the sadness of Tuscans." "We should not try to explain this melancholy by definite causes, such as his diabetes," Marek explains. "It was indeed unreasonable and inborn—and permanently adolescent."

He was not essentially a cultured man, and his reading experience was neither wide nor discriminating. He had little interest in either religion or politics and enjoyed perpetrating practical jokes and telling off-color stories and sprinkling his conversation with vigorous profanity.

Despite his worldwide fame, Puccini was for the most part an extremely shy and modest man. "It was only among friends that he was unbuttoned," says Marek. "He was most comfortable with people who were intellectually his inferiors and from whom he feared no competition."

After *La Bohème* came another masterwork—*Tosca*, based on Sardou's successful drama, introduced at the Teatro Costanzi in Rome on January 14, 1900. Like *La Bohème*, it was not at first successful; but, also like *La Bohème*, it did not wait long for worldwide recognition. In less than five years after its première, *Tosca* had been produced and acclaimed in Paris, London, and New York, and had gained permanent status in the repertory of all the principal opera houses in Italy. The first American *Tosca* was produced by the Metropolitan Opera on February 4, 1901.

In 1903, while his car was being driven at high speed—with a chauffeur, not the composer, at the wheel—Puccini was involved in a serious accident. He was almost killed, and for the next year he suffered excruciatingly from a fractured right tibia.

Though confined for months to an invalid's chair, and often in pain, Puccini managed to work on a new opera, *Madama Butterfly*. When produced by La Scala on February 17, 1904, the new work was booed and hissed. The oriental subject and characters, the at times equally exotic musical materials, the absence of a major tenor aria, and the subdivision of the opera into two acts of uneven length—all created a decidedly unfavorable impression on the first-night audience. To the shouts of disapproval, Puccini bellowed back: "Louder, you beasts. Shriek at me, yell. But you will see who is right. This is the best opera I have ever written."

Despite his confidence in his opera, Puccini altered it extensively, on the advice of Toscanini. The revised version was given in Brescia on May 28, 1904, and won an unqualified victory. After the first act, Puccini was given another great ovation. "I have never seen anything like it," he remarked.

Puccini paid his first visit to the United States late in 1906 on the occasion of the American première of *Madama Butterfly* at the Metropolitan Opera, on February 11, 1907. Here, too, Puccini enjoyed a triumph. Richard Aldrich wrote in the New York *Times:* "The delicacy, the shifting pictorial beauty, the completely penetrating atmosphere give perhaps greater delight in this opera of Puccini's than in any of his others. In nothing else has he so completely identified the music with the action, the sentiments, the passions and the surroundings that are shown upon the stage. Puccini has wrought his music into the very substance and spirit of the drama. It is his subtlest and most highly finished score, and denotes an advance over his previous operas in the matter of fine detail as well as the powerful effect of orchestration and the manipulation and development of his themes."

His favorable reaction to America and Americans led Puccini to search for an American text for his next opera. He found it in a Broadway play by David Belasco, adapted from a story by John Luther Long, *The Girl of the Golden West*. The Metropolitan Opera commissioned him to do the opera. With a brilliant cast headed by Caruso, Destinn, and Amato—and with Toscanini conducting—the Metropolitan Opera presented the world première on December 10, 1910. The evening was a gala one, attracting a brilliant audience, and the reaction to the new opera was for the most part highly enthusiastic. "There is much that is significant and interesting to be noted in the score," said Richard Aldrich in a review in the New York *Times*. Nevertheless, the opera did not retain its popularity and today it is only occasionally revived.

For the next seven years Puccini wrote no operas. He emerged from this temporary retirement in 1917 with *La Rondine*, an opera in a vein lighter than that he had previously employed. *La Rondine* was introduced in Monte Carlo on March 27, 1917. It was followed by a trilogy of one-act operas (*Il Trittico*) comprising *Il Tabarro*, *Suor Angelica*, and *Gianni Schicchi*. The first, *The Cloak*, is a highly realistic drama; the second, *Sister Angelica*, has religious and mystical overtones; the third is an *opera buffa*. The three operas were given their world premières on the same evening at the Metropolitan Opera House, on December 14, 1918. Of the three, the comic opera, which Puccini deliberately and successfully wrote in the manner and traditions of Rossini and Wolf-Ferrari, has remained the most popular.

Puccini's last opera, *Turandot*, like *Madama Butterfly*, had an oriental setting and oriental characters. It is Puccini's most original and most modern score, sprinkled with discords, unorthodox tonalities, and unusual timbres. Yet the characteristic Puccini lyricism—sweet, tender, and expressive—is never sacrificed. "In this complex score," explain Herbert Weinstock and Wallace Brockway, "Puccini never forgets that he is creating a musico-dramatic work, and is almost always the master of his materials. Yet it is Puccini all the way through, with a genius for tragic utterance that reaches its height in the music he gave to the pitiable Liù."

Puccini did not live to complete *Turandot*. In 1924 in Brussels he underwent an operation for cancer of the throat. A heart attack followed the operation, and he died on November 29, 1924. News of his death reached Milan while a performance of *La Bohème* was taking place at La Scala. The opera was interrupted for a short announcement of the sad news and a performance of Chopin's Funeral March by members of the orchestra. The audience stood in silent homage. Puccini's body was brought back from Brussels to be buried in his native city of Lucca.

When *Turandot* was given its world première at La Scala on April 25, 1926, Toscanini conducting, it was played unfinished as Puccini had left it. Puccini had confided to Toscanini that should the opera be left incomplete, the composer would like to have it produced that way. When the music stopped, the curtain remained raised, and the characters remained on the stage. Toscanini turned to the audience, his eyes swelling with tears. He said softly: "Here the Maestro put down his pen." Subsequently another Italian opera composer, Franco Alfano, completed *Turandot*, and that is the way the opera is now performed. In the Alfano version it received its first United States performance at the Metropolitan Opera on November 16, 1926.

Puccini himself once said: "I love small things, and the only music I can or will make is that of small things . . . so long as they are true and full of passion and humanity, and touch the heart." His canvas, as he himself knew, was undoubtedly limited, but he had the gift to fill that canvas with a wondrous beauty that never loses its effect. "There is never anything coarse or vulgar or effusively banal in his approach," wrote Richard Specht, "but always a noble and fastidious delicacy, the quintessence, so to speak, of exquisite music. . . . His ideas are full of an inimitable elegance, a quivering grace, and a sure feeling for artistic tact and grace which colors even the smallest phrase with his personality. . . . He has his own peculiar, unforgettable, note, and further, a bitter-sweet, gently irritating aroma that is all his own, not only in his orchestration, but also in pure tone and harmony."

MAJOR WORKS

Chamber Music—String Quartet in D major; Fugues, for string quartet; I Crisantemi, for string quartet.

Choral Music—I Figli d'Italia Bella; Motet in Honor of San Paolino; Mass in A major; Diana; Inno a Roma.

Orchestral Music—Capriccio Sinfonico; Preludio Sinfonico; Marches.

Operas—Le Villi; Edgar; Manon Lescaut; La Bohème; Tosca; Madama Butterfly; La Fanciulla del West (The Girl of the Golden West); La Rondine; Il Trittico (The Triptych), a set of three one-act operas comprising Il Tabarro, Suor Angelica, and Gianni Schicchi; Turandot (completed by Franco Alfano).

Vocal Music—Various songs for voice and piano including Allor Ch'io Sarò Morto, Noi Legger, Romanza, and Spirito Gentil.

ABOUT

Carner, M., Puccini; Del Fiorentino, D., Immortal Bohemian: An Intimate Memoir of Giacomo Puccini; Greenfield, E., Puccini: Keeper of the Seal; Marek, G. R., Puccini: A Biography; Marotti, G., Giacomo Puccini; Puccini, G., Letters; Sandlewski, W., Puccini; Sartori, C., Puccini; Specht, R., Giacomo Puccini.

Henri Rabaud
1873–1949

Henri Benjamin Rabaud was born on November 10, 1873, in Paris. His father, Hippolyte, was professor of the cello at the Paris Conservatory, which Henri attended as a pupil of Massenet and Gedalge. In 1894 Rabaud received the Prix de Rome for his cantata *Daphne*. During his three-year residence in Rome he completed a tone poem (*Andromède*), an oratorio (*Job*), and a string quartet which was performed in Vienna. He also helped to found orchestras in Rome and Vienna.

HENRI RABAUD

In 1895 he wrote his first major work, the Symphony No. 1 in E minor. Four years later he achieved success with the tone poem *La Procession Nocturne*, based on a portion of the Faust legend as retold in a poem by Nikolaus Lenau. Rabaud's composition is a sensitive portrait of Faust as, on a midsummer night, he watches a religious procession. The music is impressionistic, distinguished for subtle atmosphere and a sure structural logic. Introduced by the Colonne Orchestra in Paris on January 15, 1899, it was acclaimed and since then has been one of the most popular of Rabaud's works for orchestra.

Two operas by Rabaud were performed before he duplicated in the theatre the success

Rabaud: rà bō′

he had won in the concert hall with his tone poem. His first opera, *La Fille de Roland*, was produced at the Opéra-Comique on March 16, 1904. This was followed by *Le Premier Glaive*, in Béziers in 1908. Then, on May 15, 1914, the Opéra-Comique in Paris presented Rabaud's masterpiece, *Marouf, Savetier du Caire* (*Marouf, Cobbler of Cairo*). This delightful comic opera was based on a story from *A Thousand and One Nights*. Marouf, a cobbler, takes to the sea to escape from a humdrum life with a shrewish wife. He encounters many adventures. Posing as a wealthy merchant in Khaitan, he is given the run of the palace by the Sultan, and in time he even marries the Sultan's daughter. When his identity is discovered, the princess continues to love him, and they flee from the kingdom. When the pursuing Sultan and his men find them in the desert, the Sultan is ready to forgive and forget.

Camille Bellaigue called this operatic gem "the last smile of French music before the war." Much of the charm of Rabaud's music comes from his subtle use of oriental-type melodies and instrumental colors. A highly effective climax is provided by the sensuous oriental ballet in the third act. *Marouf* was first presented in the United States, at the Metropolitan Opera on December 19, 1917. At that time, W. J. Henderson described the work as "one of fancy, humor and sentiment, without a touch of the tragic.... His voice parts move wholly in arioso. There are no sharply defined song or aria forms. Oriental color is laid on not merely with a brush but with a palette knife. And the greatest amount of illustrative and descriptive detail is inevitably given to the orchestra.... The greatest pleasure ... will be obtained by regarding the music as a colorful background for a legendary comedy."

Though Rabaud wrote several more operas— it was his habit to complete an opera once each decade—and though he wrote some fine orchestral compositions, including a second symphony, his reputation is based almost exclusively on *La Procession Nocturne* and *Marouf*. He wrote music for several plays and motion pictures. Among the latter are *Le Miracle des Loups* which on November 14, 1924, became the first film ever shown at the Opéra-Comique. Rabaud's last opera, *Le Jeu de l'Amour et du Hasard*, was completed a

441

year before his death and was produced post-humously in Monte Carlo in 1954.

His compositions revealed an elegant, refined style, an impeccable taste, and occasionally wit. He combined, says André Cœuroy, "intelligence and flexibility" with a "penetrating mind, energetic, without rigidity, bold without braggadocio, marvelously balanced, and certain enough of its strength to indulge in every curiosity."

In 1908, with his appointment to the conducting staff of the Paris Opéra and the Opéra-Comique, Rabaud began a long and distinguished career as conductor. He became principal conductor of both organizations in 1914. Two years later he was appointed musical director of the Concerts du Conservatoire. In 1918 he resigned from his posts in Paris to become principal conductor of the Boston Symphony when Karl Muck was interned as an enemy alien; Rabaud stayed in Boston one season.

Describing Rabaud as a conductor, an unidentified writer for *Musical America* said: "The impression one gains of Mr. Rabaud as he stands at the conductor's desk is one of calm authority. Tall and angular, almost ungainly in appearance, his figure gains poise and dignity by his sincere, unaffected manner. His beat is simple and straightforward, unornamented by any of the sensuous gyrations which ofttimes weaken an otherwise convincing beat. In spite of his French birth, training and experience, he looks every inch the native-born Vermonter of pre-Revolutionary ancestry."

Pitts Sanborn contributed the following additional comment: "Others who remember M. Rabaud at that time would hardly speak of him as ungainly. Tall he was, and thin, but he carried himself with an unobtrusive dignity and his simplicity on the podium was noteworthy. He wore a full beard, at that time like his hair iron-gray. There was a definite suggestion of New England about him, if not specifically of Vermont. To the eye he might have been a Unitarian minister in a tranquil elm-shaded town."

In 1922 Rabaud succeeded Gabriel Fauré as director of the Paris Conservatory, retaining this post until 1941. He died in Paris, after a prolonged illness, on September 11, 1949.

MAJOR WORKS

Chamber Music—String Quartet; Allegro de Concert, for cello and piano.

Choral Music—Job, oratorio; Psaume IV; Hymne à la France Éternelle; L'Été.

Operas—La Fille de Roland; Le Premier Glaive; Marouf, Savetier du Caire; Antoine et Cléopâtre; L'Appel de la Mer; Rolande et le Mauvais Garçon; Le Jeu de l'Amour et du Hasard.

Orchestral Music—2 symphonies; La Procession Nocturne, tone poem; Églogue; Le Sacrifice d'Isaac; Flute de Pan; Divertissement Grec; Au Village; Poème sur le Livre de Job; Divertissement sur des Chansons Russes; Suite Anglaise; Concertino for Cello and Orchestra.

ABOUT

Hill, E. B., Modern French Music; Ollone, M. d', Rabaud.

Le Ménestral (Paris), February 17, 1928.

Sergei Rachmaninoff
1873–1943

Sergei Vassilievich Rachmaninoff was born in Onega, in the district of Novgorod, Russia, on April 1, 1873. His grandfather, Arkady, had been a famous piano virtuoso; his father, Vasili, was a happy-go-lucky dilettante who loved music and enjoyed playing the piano. Vasili's inherited wealth was augmented by several estates which his wife had brought him as a dowry. However, he dissipated his fortune and by the time Sergei was nine the family was destitute; when Vasili deserted his family, they went to live with Sergei's grandmother, who supported them.

Sergei's first piano lessons came from his mother and were followed by three years of study with Anna Ornazkaya, a graduate of the St. Petersburg Conservatory. When he was nine he entered the St. Petersburg Conservatory on a scholarship. Though he possessed extraordinary precocity and perfect pitch, he was lackadaisical about his studies and indolent in his habits. Instead of going to class he went roller skating, swimming, or boating, or wandered about aimlessly.

Several early musical experiences affected him profoundly. One was the singing of his sister, Elena, who first acquainted him with Tchaikovsky's music, which moved him deeply.

Rachmaninoff: rŭk mä′ nyĭ nôf

Another was the services at church. Yet these experiences failed to lift him out of his lethargy and indolence. He disliked practicing the piano, and he disliked studying music theory even more. Only his natural gifts made it possible for him to keep in comfortable stride with his fellow pupils at the Conservatory with the minimum of effort he expended.

SERGEI RACHMANINOFF

His grandmother had faith in the boy's talent and became convinced that a change of scene, and a change of teacher, might prove beneficial. The boy was sent to Moscow and placed with Sverev, a severe disciplinarian and an inspiring teacher. Sverev carefully nursed the spark of the boy's inherent love and gift for music, fed it with the fuel of tactfully presented lessons, and then permitted the spark to burst into full flame. For two years, between 1883 and 1885, Rachmaninoff worked with his teacher not only in piano but also in languages, literature, and history. Then the boy was ready to undertake a full curriculum at the Moscow Conservatory. In 1885 he entered the piano class of Siloti and the composition classes of Arensky and Taneiev. His interest and enthusiasm aroused, Rachmaninoff now became a brilliant pupil. Alexander Goldenweiser, who was Rachmaninoff's fellow pupil at that time, later recalled: "Rachmaninoff's musical gifts... surpassed any others I have ever met, bordering on the marvelous, like those of Mozart in his youth. The speed with which he memorized

new compositions was remarkable. . . . It was his practice to memorize everything he heard, no matter how complicated it was." At one of his examinations, Rachmaninoff played his own *Song Without Words* to a jury that included Tchaikovsky; the master praised him highly for both the composition and its performance. In 1892, as a graduation exercise in composition, he wrote (in seventeen days) a one-act opera, *Aleko*, based on Pushkin's *The Gypsies*. Though strongly influenced by Tchaikovsky's *The Queen of Spades*, it had enough freshness and originality to bring its young composer the Conservatory's highest honor, the Gold Medal for composition.

Rachmaninoff's remarkable talent as composer attracted the attention of Karl Gutheil, who became his publisher. Thus began a sympathetic and friendly, as well as a business, arrangement that lasted until Gutheil's death. Opus 1 was Rachmaninoff's First Piano Concerto in F-sharp minor, completed in 1891, while he was still a Conservatory student, and introduced by the composer himself at a Conservatory concert on March 17, 1892; Opus 2 was *Two Pieces*, for cello and piano (1892); Opus 3 was *Five Pieces*, for piano (1892). The last of these included the Prelude in C-sharp minor, a composition that achieved a tremendous success in the music world, made its composer's name known universally, and became one of the most popular pieces for the piano written in the twentieth century. Rachmaninoff himself introduced the prelude in a Moscow recital on September 26, 1892. Many descriptive programs have been devised to interpret this vividly dramatic composition, but Rachmaninoff disavowed them all, preferring to consider his piece simply as absolute music. Though the composition yielded a fortune through the sale of the sheet music, Rachmaninoff gained nothing for himself. He had sold the piece outright to his publisher for a few rubles.

Aleko was mounted at the Bolshoi Theatre in Moscow on May 9, 1893, and was a great success. The audience gave the young composer a rousing ovation, and one of the most enthusiastic listeners was Tchaikovsky.

Despite these early triumphs, Rachmaninoff's career did not progress without major setbacks. The most serious came with the

Rachmaninoff

première of his First Symphony in D minor, on March 27, 1897. It was a fiasco, mainly because of a performance which Rachmaninoff himself described as "beneath contempt," with parts of the symphony "completely unrecognizable." But as Rachmaninoff himself realized as he listened to his own work, the symphony had serious deficiencies which became evident to him from the first rehearsal. He fled from the hall in horror and wandered about in the streets. "The despair that filled my soul would not leave me," he later explained. "My dreams of a brilliant career lay shattered. My hopes and confidences were destroyed. . . . This was the effect of my own Symphony on myself. When the indescribable torture of this performance had at last come to an end, I was a different man."

Following that first performance, the manuscript of the symphony disappeared and for many years was considered lost. But a two-piano version was found in the Soviet Union after Rachmaninoff's death. This led to an intensive search for the orchestral parts, which were finally located in the library of the Leningrad Conservatory. In 1945 the symphony was once again performed in the Soviet Union, and on March 19, 1948, it was introduced in the United States by the Philadelphia Orchestra under Eugene Ormandy. Both in the Soviet Union and in the United States audiences received the work more courteously than enthusiastically.

After the failure of the First Symphony, Rachmaninoff succumbed to a despair from which he was unable to free himself for several years. He refused to work; he could not contemplate either the present or the future with hope or confidence. He became obsessed with psychopathic fears that he was a failure, a musician without talent. At times he lapsed into a stupor. His friends, fearful that this increasing morbidity might become chronic, urged him to visit a Dr. Dahl, who effected cures through the powers of autosuggestion, as Émile Coué, French exponent of autosuggestion, had in his day. As Rachmaninoff lay in his office in a kind of semistupor, Dr. Dahl constantly repeated the formula: "You will begin to work again. You will compose a concerto. The concerto will be good." Dr. Dahl continued this treatment day after day, week after week, until Rachmaninoff, almost magically, felt a return of vitality and self-confidence.

It was with renewed spirit and creative strength that he went to work and found ideas coming to him in abundance. He wrote his Piano Concerto No. 2 in C minor in a white heat of inspiration. This concerto, dedicated to Dr. Dahl, was first performed on November 9, 1901, by the Moscow Philharmonic, with the composer as soloist. With its outpouring of rich, sensuous melodies, its passionate moods, its dramatic episodes, and its telling climaxes, it had an overpowering impact. "The piece resembles a romantic costume drama of the late nineteenth century," says Richard Anthony Leonard in his *History of Russian Music*, "with a leading role that is an actor's dream. The pianist, like the actor, enjoys all the choice scenes designed for melancholy brooding, impassioned love making, furious conflict, and final triumph. The light plays constantly upon all the facets of his heroic conduct and all his changes of costume."

This concerto has become Rachmaninoff's most celebrated composition in a large structure; it is perhaps not excessive enthusiasm to call it the most popular concerto written in the twentieth century. One of its melodies became an American popular song hit, "Full Moon and Empty Arms," and numerous motion pictures, including Noël Coward's *Brief Encounter*, have used it either as background music or as an integral part of the story line.

The Second Piano Concerto marked Rachmaninoff's return to success. Almost as a token of his reborn faith in himself and his powers, on April 29, 1902, he married his cousin and sweetheart, Natalie Satina, a young pianist who had graduated from the Moscow Conservatory. He now began to make more extensive tours as a concert pianist; and shortly after the turn of the century he became recognized as one of the supreme concert performers, one of the strongest box-office attractions, of the time. He also distinguished himself with the baton, having made his conducting debut on October 12, 1897, in a performance of Saint-Saëns's *Samson et Dalila*. During the period from 1904 to 1906 he was the conductor of the Bolshoi Theatre.

Rachmaninoff was now one of Russia's most celebrated and sought-after musicians. His salon became a gathering place for the leading figures in the musical and intellectual life of Moscow. Finding that his social obligations—and his conducting chores at the Bolshoi Theatre—severely encroached upon his creativity, Rachmaninoff resigned as conductor and in 1907 left Russia to live in Dresden. There, in semiseclusion, he completed his two most important works for symphony orchestra alone: his Second Symphony in E minor and the tone poem *The Isle of the Dead*, inspired by the famous painting by Böcklin. He himself directed the premières of both compositions—the symphony in St. Petersburg on February 8, 1908; the tone poem in Moscow on May 1, 1909.

Rachmaninoff paid his first visit to the United States in 1909 in the triple role of composer, conductor, and pianist. His American debut took place at Smith College in Northampton, Massachusetts, on November 4, 1909. In New York City on November 28 he was heard in the world première of his Third Piano Concerto, in D minor, at a concert of the New York Symphony, Walter Damrosch conducting.

During the early years of World War I, Rachmaninoff gave concerts in Russia for soldiers and refugees. He also tried to escape in composition from the grimness of war. He produced some songs; he completely rewrote his First Piano Concerto; and he worked upon his Fourth Piano Concerto, in G minor. Then came the first phase of the Russian Revolution, in February 1917. "Almost from the beginning of the Revolution," he told his biographer Oskar von Riesemann, "I realized that it was mishandled. Already by March of 1917 I had decided to leave Russia, but was unable to carry out my plan, for Europe was still fighting and no one could cross the frontier." But the excesses of the revolution, as they mounted, revolted Rachmaninoff. He realized he would have to seek a permanent home elsewhere. The offer of a concert tour of Scandinavia provided an avenue of escape. With only a small suitcase in hand and no more than a few hundred rubles in his pocket, Rachmaninoff left Russia in December 1917, never to return.

He stayed in Scandinavia about a year, then came to the United States to begin on December 8, 1918, a new tour as pianist. From then on he concentrated his activities as an interpreting artist at the piano rather than with the baton. Few pianists anywhere had the kind of following he attracted, or gathered such critical accolades. From 1918 to 1935 his permanent home was in Switzerland, on the banks of Lake Lucerne; after 1935 his main home was in the United States, first in New York City, then in Beverly Hills, California. Just a short time before his death he became an American citizen.

Rachmaninoff used to quote an old Russian proverb in self-criticism: "If you hunt three hares at one time, how sure can you be that you will kill even one of them?" Rachmaninoff's career in America was marked by his hunting of three hares at once. In the winter of 1939 the Philadelphia Orchestra presented a monumental three-concert cycle in Philadelphia and New York in which Rachmaninoff appeared as pianist, composer, and conductor. If it had ever been doubted, it was certainly proved eloquently during this festival that when Rachmaninoff hunted three hares, he could also kill them all. As a pianist, he performed three of his concertos with a command of the piano, an aristocracy of style, and an immaculateness of taste that placed him with the greatest performing artists of all time. As a conductor, he directed his own music, bringing to his works authority, musicianship, and an infallible instinct; he was not just another composer conducting his music with more enthusiasm than technique, but a scrupulous artist who knew what he wanted and how to achieve it efficiently.

The third Rachmaninoff was, to be sure, the composer, whose major works spread over three full programs. This was probably the greatest Rachmaninoff of all. After leaving Russia, Rachmaninoff produced only a handful of works, but all have the distinction of style, the emotional appeal, the sincerity that brought his earlier masterworks their universal acceptance. The most notable of these later works are the following: *Rhapsody on a Theme by Paganini*, the composer's last work for piano and orchestra, a series of variations on the theme of Paganini's Caprice No. 24 (world première in Baltimore on November 7, 1934, the composer appearing as soloist with the Philadelphia Orchestra); the Third Symphony, in A minor (introduced by the Philadelphia Orchestra on November 6, 1936); the

445

Rachmaninoff

Symphonic Dances, for orchestra (heard in Philadelphia on January 3, 1941).

Rachmaninoff opened no new worlds of music as a composer. He was content to live in the one that had been dominated by Tchaikovsky. Like Tchaikovsky he wore his heart on his sleeve. The works overflow with Russian lyricism and romanticism, just as they are seized and held by Russian melancholia. What an unidentified critic said of Rachmaninoff's Second Symphony, when it was heard in the United States on November 26, 1909, holds true for all of Rachmaninoff's music: "If Tchaikovsky voices the passionate, the somber, the tragic, the swift ecstasy of beauty . . . Rachmaninoff prefigures the brooding, the somber, reflective state of soul. He endures the sight of the dark aspects of Russian life, of all life, but rather as the seer than as the rebel. There is almost a Tolstoyan resistance to evil in his attitude. The world that he looks out upon is a somber world of dim distances, of golden lights and shadows, and steady motion. His attitude towards it is impersonal and dispassionate. His creed is moderation."

All his life, Rachmaninoff was a sad, lonely man, but never more so than when he cut his ties with the land of his birth. As an exile, he was never quite able to adjust himself completely to a new life in new surroundings, with a new language. He always felt himself in isolation, separated from settings, things, and people that had meant so much to him both as an artist and as a man. He confessed his homesickness openly at all times, but it was not necessary to hear such a confession. His homesickness cries out from the best pages of his later compositions.

Rachmaninoff was a methodical man who practiced the piano, ate his meals, and took his periods of relaxation and rest at the same hours each day. Breakfast was eaten early in the morning, lunch at one, dinner at six; meals were generally simple, with dinners featuring Russian dishes. Between meals he liked munching on an apple and always took a bag of apples with him when he was traveling. Except for an occasional glass of wine, he imbibed no alcohol. His favorite nonalcoholic beverage was strong tea drawn from a samovar. He also drank coffee, but usually only before and during his concerts. He was a chronic smoker, salving his conscience by using a denicotined brand and a cigarette holder stuffed with absorbent cotton. After breakfast he took a long walk, his favorite form of exercise; and after lunch he napped. Even on concert evenings he partook of a full dinner. Always meticulously punctual, he arrived at the concert hall half an hour before the time of performance. When he was free, he liked to spend his time quietly, reading or conversing with personal friends. He rarely attended parties and scrupulously avoided elaborate public events.

He preferred composing during the summer, when he had no concerts to give. "When I compose, I am a slave," he said. "Beginning at nine in the morning, I allow myself no respite until after eleven at night. A poem, a picture, something concrete, helps me immensely. There must be something definite before my mind to convey a definite impression, or my ideas refuse to appear."

To the editor of this book, Rachmaninoff once dictated a statement concerning his art, which reads in part: "I try to make music speak simply and directly that which is in my heart at the time I am composing. If there is love there, or bitterness, or sadness, or religion, these moods become part of my music, and my music becomes either beautiful or bitter or sad or religious. . . . I am not a composer who produces music to the formula of preconceived theories. Music, I have always felt, should be the expression of a composer's complex personality; it should not be arrived at cerebrally, tailor-made to fit certain specifications."

Rachmaninoff was in poor health the last few years of his life. Conscious that he probably did not have much longer to live, he was eager to make one last extensive concert tour of the United States. That tour started on February 8, 1943, but it ended abruptly in New Orleans, where he collapsed. Taken back to Beverly Hills, he died there on March 28, 1943.

MAJOR WORKS

Chamber Music—Trio Élégiaque in D minor; Cello Sonata in C minor.

Choral Music—The Spring, cantata; Liturgy of St. John Chrysostom; The Bells, choral symphony; Vesper Mass; Three Russian Folksongs.

Operas—Aleko; The Miserly Knight; Francesca da Rimini.

Orchestral Music—4 piano concertos; 3 symphonies; The Rock, symphonic fantasy; The Isle of the Dead, tone poem; Rhapsody on a Theme by Paganini, for piano and orchestra; Symphonic Dances.

Piano Music—2 sonatas; 2 suites, for two pianos; Études-Tableaux, Moments Musicaux; Pieces; Preludes; Variations on a Theme by Chopin; Variations on a Theme by Corelli.

Vocal Music—Numerous songs for voice and piano including The Answer, Before My Window, Christ Is Risen, Daisies, Fate, How Fair This Spot, The Lilacs, In the Silent Night, The Little Island, Sorrow in Spring, To the Children, Vocalise.

ABOUT

Bertenson, S. and Leyda, J., Rachmaninoff; Culshaw, J., Rachmaninoff: The Man and His Music; Lyle, W., Rachmaninoff; Riesemann, O. von, Rachmaninoff's Recollections; Satin, S. (ed.), In Memory of Rachmaninoff; Seroff, V., Rachmaninoff.

Musical Quarterly, January–April 1944; Tempo (London), Rachmaninoff Issue, Winter 1951–1952.

Maurice Ravel
1875–1937

Maurice Joseph Ravel was born in Ciboure, near Saint-Jean-de-Luz, in the Basque region of France on March 7, 1875. He was the first child of a Basque mother and a Swiss-born father, an engineer. When Maurice was three months old, the Ravel family left the Basque country to set up home in the Montmartre district of Paris. Encouraged by a highly cultured father, Maurice began to study music early. He was only seven when he took piano lessons with Henri Ghis, who is best remembered as the composer of *Amaryllis*, sometimes known as *Air Louis XIII*. Four years later, Ravel studied harmony with Charles René. In 1889 he entered the Paris Conservatory where he was placed in the preparatory piano class. The next fifteen years were spent at the Conservatory with such distinguished teachers as Pessard, Gedalge, Charles de Bériot, and Fauré. In de Bériot's class he became a fellow student of Ricardo Viñes, who later became a distinguished interpreter of Ravel's piano music. In 1893, in Pessard's harmony class, Ravel wrote his first two compositions. Both pieces were for the piano: one markedly influenced by Alexis Chabrier (*Sérénade Grotesque*); the other, a song, influenced by Satie ("Ballade de la Reine Morte"). Ravel's first published composition, also for the piano,

Ravel: rá věl'

followed in 1895: *Menuet Antique*. Another work completed in 1895 but not published was the *Habanera*, for two pianos, a movement in a suite entitled *Sites Auriculaires*. The *Habanera* was subsequently orchestrated by the composer and incorporated into his *Rhapsodie Espagnole*. "In embryo," Ravel said of his *Habanera*, "I consider that it embodies many of the elements which were to dominate my later compositions." Roland-Manuel called it an "unforgettable work . . . [with] the strength of a prophecy assured of its fulfillment."

MAURICE RAVEL

Though Ravel respected the classical rules taught him at the Conservatory and was a consistently brilliant student, he did not hesitate to indulge in harmonic explorations beyond the periphery established by the textbook. His teachers with one exception were impatient with his iconoclastic attitudes. The exception was Gabriel Fauré, who understood the young man's restlessness and impatience with tradition and encouraged his original bent for new idioms. Thus encouraged, Ravel completed his first composition to be performed. It was *Les Sites Auriculaires* for two pianos, introduced on March 5, 1898. This was followed by Ravel's first work for orchestra, an overture entitled *Shéhérazade*, which the composer conducted at a concert of the Société Nationale de Musique on May 27, 1899.

Success came with two piano pieces: *Pavane pour une Infante Défunte* (1899) and *Jeux d'Eau* (1902), both introduced at a concert of the

Ravel

Société Nationale in Paris on April 5, 1902. The *Pavane* helped make Ravel a household name, and it has remained one of his most popular compositions, particularly in an orchestral adaptation prepared by the composer. Yet it is a slight work, formal and sentimental, and completely uncharacteristic of Ravel. The composer himself had no high opinion of it and explained its great success by the programmatic interpretations fixed to the music by annotators because of its picturesque title, a title Ravel chose because of its alliterative sound. Ravel did not hesitate to pick out its faults: "The influence of Chabrier is much too glaring," he wrote in 1912, "and the structure is rather poor."

But *Jeux d'Eau* is quite another story. This composition is remarkable for its unusual resonances, extraordinary exploitation of piano sonorities, and its brilliant use of the upper register of the keyboard. Though revealing the influence of both Liszt and Fauré, it opened a new world of haunting sounds and timbres for piano writing; certainly it opened them up for Debussy who, from the moment he became acquainted with it, began to write for the piano in an entirely new manner.

The *Jeux d'Eau* was Ravel's first piano masterwork. His first masterwork in the field of chamber music was the Quartet in F major, performed by the Heyman Quartet in Paris on March 5, 1904. Roland-Manuel described the Quartet as a "miracle of grace and tenderness, a marvelous jewel of polyphony which knew how to submit to the requirements of the classical form without manifesting any of its restrictions." The Quartet was immensely successful and was responsible for placing its creator among the most important new composers to emerge in the new century.

Because of his passionate dedication to innovation and experiment, Ravel joined several other progressive young musicians in Paris (including Florent Schmitt, Stravinsky, and Manuel de Falla) to form the Société des Apaches. *Apache*, a term applied to ruffians and criminals, was adopted by the young musicians to describe their own position as outlaws. The members met regularly in a studio in Auteuil to discuss music, to play their own compositions, and to exchange new ideas. The influence of the Apaches strengthened Ravel's own penchant for the unortho-

dox, leading him to ever greater experimentation in idiom and originality of musical thought. His three "poems" for voice and orchestra entitled *Shéhérazade*, not to be confused with the earlier orchestral overture of the same name, originated in the circle of the Apaches. So did one of Ravel's piano masterworks, *Miroirs*, which he himself played for the first time anywhere at an Apache gathering. About *Miroirs*, the five movements of which are each dedicated to a different member of the Apaches, the composer had this to say: "It represents such a considerable change in my harmonic development that even musicians who were accustomed to my manner up to then were somewhat disconcerted." Ricardo Viñes gave the première performance on January 6, 1906. The fourth movement, *Alborada del Gracioso*, subsequently became famous as a symphonic composition in Ravel's own orchestration.

During this period in his life, Ravel was somewhat of a dandy. He was elegantly attired, usually with a flower in his lapel, and his manners were most meticulous. He sported a beard and side whiskers (both of which he would soon dispense with) and his fellow Apaches and his closest friends called him "Rara." "I can see him now," recalls Léon-Paul Fargue, "like a sort of debonair wizard, sitting in his corner at the Grand Écart or the Bœuf sur le Toit, telling endless stories which had the same sort of elegance, richness and clarity as his compositions. He could tell a story as well as he could write a waltz or an Adagio. One of the most remarkable traits of this curious Pyrenean was his passion for perfection. This man, who was profoundly intelligent, versatile, precise and as learned as it was possible to be and who did everything with a facility which was proverbial, had the character and the qualities of an artisan—and there was nothing he liked better than to be compared to one. He liked doing things, and doing things well."

Much of Ravel's fame came from the high quality of his early compositions and from their successful presentations, but much of it was due to the storms that raged through musical Paris—storms of which he was the center. The first came in 1905 when he made his fourth attempt to capture the Prix de Rome. He was even denied the right to sit in for the

448

preliminary examination. Many leading French musicologists and musicians, including Romain Rolland, were shocked that a composer as gifted as Ravel should have been denied the prize; they violently condemned the judges for their partiality to other, far less worthy, men, as well as for their prejudice against Ravel. The battle was fought bitterly in newspapers and pamphlets. The "Ravel affair," as it came to be known, developed into a public scandal. Théodore Dubois, director of the Paris Conservatory, was compelled to resign his post; he was succeeded by Fauré, who instituted major reforms. Only then did the furor die down.

A second "Ravel affair" dominated the French press in 1907 after the première of Ravel's *Histoires Naturelles* on January 12, 1907. This was a satiric composition with text by Jules Renard consisting of caustic poems about a peacock, kingfisher, guinea hen, and cricket which Ravel set to sardonic and mocking music. Many critics were vituperative: Pierre Lalo described the music as "a café-concert with ninths," others found the work "labored and unmusical" or just a "collection of laborious rarefied harmonies—and successions of involved and complicated chords." What created a veritable tempest, however, was Pierre Lalo's insistence that Ravel was nothing more than an imitator of Debussy, a plagiarist. Some musicians concurred. Others, however, jumped to Ravel's defense, pointing out that Ravel was not an imitator of Debussy but his artistic heir, that Debussy had been the point of departure for Ravel's music, which was completely different from Debussy's Impressionist style. They pointed to Ravel's classical order and symmetry, clarity, precision, wit, masculinity, intellectualism—qualities not to be found in Debussy. For months, the question involving Ravel and Debussy was argued in the papers. If it accomplished nothing else, it helped make Ravel one of the most publicized composers in France.

A succession of important works soon proved the case for Ravel's defenders. In 1907 he completed two compositions reflecting his lifelong fascination with Spain. The *Rhapsodie Espagnole* was the composer's first important work for orchestra in which he revealed his extraordinary gift for instrumentation. It was heard at a Colonne concert in Paris on March 15, 1908, and was such a success that one of its selections, the Malagueña, had to be repeated.

Soon after finishing the orchestral rhapsody, Ravel completed another masterwork on a Spanish subject, the brilliant one-act opera *L'Heure Espagnole* (*The Spanish Hour*). Its witty text, the work of Franc-Nohain (Maurice Legrand), detailed the extramarital escapades of a clockmaker's fickle wife in eighteenth century Toledo. The opera waited four years for its première, which finally took place at the Opéra-Comique in Paris on May 19, 1911— and it was a failure. But in the period following World War I audiences and critics developed a new perspective enabling them to become enchanted with this light-hearted, tongue-in-cheek gem. The American première occurred in Chicago, January 5, 1920. When the opera was produced at the Metropolitan Opera on November 7, 1925, Olin Downes said that it "accomplished perfectly its purposes.... Every event of the Spanish hour ... is depicted ... with humor as adroit as it is inspired in craftsmanship."

In the period between 1907 when *L'Heure Espagnole* was written and 1911 when it was first produced, Ravel completed several other major works. These included the orchestral suite *Ma Mère l'Oye* (*Mother Goose*), which had originated as a four-hand piano suite and which, following its transcription for orchestra by the composer, was heard on January 21, 1912; and the *Valses Nobles et Sentimentales*, for piano, inspired by Schubert's waltzes (first performance in Paris on May 9, 1911, by Louis Aubert).

What is generally singled out as Ravel's greatest work is the ballet *Daphnis and Chloe*, written on a commission from the Ballet Russe de Monte Carlo, which presented it in Paris on June 8, 1912, with Nijinsky and Karsavina as principal dancers. The initial reaction was mixed, but a few perceptive critics were aware that this was a major work. Jean Marnold said in his review: "The score abounds in tableaux of the most exquisite plastic beauty; among these the appearance of the gracious nymphs in the twilight shadow of a dream is a page without precedent or model in the whole of music. . . . Never has the magic of picturesque sonority reached such an intensity." Since its première *Daphnis and Chloe* has been recognized as one of the peaks in twentieth century music. Edward Burlingame Hill said of Ravel's music: "He has attained large contours, breadth of mood and impressive climaxes with the same continuity of development and richness of detail as in his shorter pieces. Throughout, the music achieves a graphic delineation of character, and furthermore has a plastic quality which incites mimetic response." Symphonic literature has been enriched through two orchestral suites, or "series," which the composer adapted from the ballet score—the second one being more popular than the first.

When World War I came, Ravel tried to enlist in the army and in the air corps, but his poor health made him unacceptable. He then served at the front with a motor corps, an experience which profoundly affected his nerves. In memory of the war dead, Ravel wrote the piano suite *Le Tombeau de Couperin*, a musical tribute structurally influenced by the distinguished eighteenth century French composer François Couperin le Grand. Ravel's suite received its première in Paris in January 1920, and an orchestral transcription by the composer was heard in Paris on February 28 of the same year.

Ravel's partiality for the Viennese waltz, already reflected in his *Valses Nobles et Sentimentales*, once again became evident in a major work for orchestra, *La Valse*. Here the source of Ravel's inspiration was Johann Strauss II rather than Schubert. Ravel's intention was to present "a kind of apotheosis of the Viennese waltz linked in my mind with the impression of a fantastic whirl of destiny." The published score contributed the following descriptive material: "Whirling clouds give glimpses through rifts of couples dancing. The clouds scatter, little by little. One sees an immense hall peopled with a twirling crowd. The scene is gradually illuminated. The lights of the chandeliers burst forth, fortissimo. An imperial court, in or about 1855." The first performance on December 12, 1920, proved a great success. Several years later the music was used for a choreographic conception by Ida Rubinstein.

In 1921 Ravel bought a villa, "Le Belvédère," in Montfort-l'Amaury, in the Île-de-France region. Here, he lived out the remainder of his life in comparative retirement, working assiduously on his compositions and finding diversion by tending to his garden and entertaining friends. He was patiently and solicitously attended by a servant, Mme. Revelot, who regarded him more as a son than an employer. He never married. He found delight in the company of a family of Siamese cats to whom he was particularly devoted and to whom he talked in a cat language which he insisted they understood.

Among the important works completed in the 1920's was a charming stage fantasy, *L'Enfant et les Sortilèges*, text by Colette, which was produced by the Monte Carlo Opera on March 21, 1925; a rhapsody for violin and orchestra, *Tzigane*, written for the virtuoso Yelly d'Aranyi, who introduced it in London on April 26, 1924; and what is perhaps the most popular single work Ravel ever wrote and one of the most famous in twentieth century symphonic music, the *Boléro*. Commissioned by Ida Rubinstein, who introduced it in Paris on November 20, 1928, it created a sensation, which was repeated in other performances, even when presented by symphony orchestras without the benefit of dance. In America it was introduced by the New York Philharmonic under Toscanini on November 14, 1929. Every major orchestra performed it, and it became a "hit." Six different recordings were issued simultaneously; it was played in movie theatres and over the radio both in its original symphonic form and in numerous transcriptions. It was used in a Broadway revue and its title was bought for a Hollywood film. Built on a single theme in two sections, *Boléro* is a stunning tour de force with an inescapable kinetic appeal as the melody grows in dynamics and changes in orchestral color, until a thunderous climax erupts in full orchestra.

Ravel's last two major works for orchestra were two piano concertos: one in D major for the left hand alone, in a jazzlike idiom; the other for both hands, in a more classic style. The Left-Hand Concerto was introduced by the one-armed pianist Paul Wittgenstein, for whom it was written, on November 27, 1931, in Vienna; the two-hand concerto, in G major, was given in Paris on January 14, 1932, with Marguerite Long as soloist.

Ravel's last composition was a song cycle for baritone and orchestra to poems by Paul Morand: *Don Quichotte à Dulcinée*, which Martial Singher and the Colonne Orchestra under Paul Paray introduced in Paris on

December 1, 1934. Here, as in some of his earlier masterworks, the background and inspiration are Spanish; the musical material is often derived from Spanish folk sources.

In the fall of 1932, while riding in a Paris taxicab, Ravel suffered an accident which caused him to lose his powers of coordination and become partially paralyzed. He never recovered fully. He found some diversion in the society of friends and even in travel, but he was incapable of writing music any longer. "I no longer have any music in my head," he confided to a friend. "I'm finished."

His worsening condition required an operation for a tumor on the brain, which took place in mid-December of 1937. After eight days in a semicoma, he died in the hospital, in the Auteuil section of Paris, on December 28, 1937. Three days later he was buried in the family tomb in the cemetery at Levallois. "With Maurice Ravel," wrote Émile Vuillermoz, "has disappeared the greatest French composer of our age. Since the deaths of Gabriel Fauré and Claude Debussy, it was in his hands that the torch of our national art was kept alight. . . . He dominated from afar all the musicians of his time."

Ravel paid only one visit to the United States, in 1928, when he toured the country in concerts of his own works. When he arrived in New York, early in January, he expressed a desire to visit Harlem, to see Edgar Allan Poe's house in the Bronx, and to meet George Gershwin. All this he succeeded in doing. His American debut took place in Boston, with the Boston Symphony, on January 12, 1928.

Ravel once expressed his musical credo to the editor of this book: "I am not a 'modern composer' in the strictest sense of that term because my music, far from being 'revolution' is rather 'evolution.' I belong to no school of music and adhere rigidly to no current musical styles. I try to create beautiful ideas in music and attempt to develop them to their logical, perhaps inevitable, end. Great music must always come from the heart; great music must always be beautiful. . . . Music, I feel, must always be emotional first, and intellectual second. . . . A composer should not compose his music to theories. He should create musical beauty directly from the heart, and he should feel intensely what he is composing."

Ravel, then, was not interested in innovation or experiment for its own sake. As Virgil Thomson noted in the New York *Herald Tribune*, "for all its complexity of texture, wealth of invention and profound technical originality, his work presents fewer difficulties of comprehension than that of any other great figure of the modern movement." Thomson added: "Maurice Ravel was not interested in posing as a prophet. . . . He was no sybil, no saint, no oracle nor sacred pythoness. He was simply a skilled workman who enjoyed his work. . . . Always he worked objectively, with the modesty of an architect or a jeweler, but with the assurance of a good architect or a good jeweler. He was equally master of the miniature and of the grander lay-outs. At no necessary point does his expression lack either subtlety or magnitude. . . . Ravel was a classical composer because his music presents a straightforward view of life in clear and durable form."

A fastidious, even exquisite, workman, Ravel continually produced beautiful music with sensibility, grace, and refinement. He had an extraordinary virtuosity in composition. His music was always the last word in skillful construction. But it was, of course, far more than just skillful technique. He had a manner, a charm all his own. He was perhaps at his most delightful and most original in the make-believe world of enchantment—of fairies and animals and puppets and children—as in the *Mother Goose Suite* or the fantasy *L'Enfant et les Sortilèges*. But whether he wrote in this vein or in a Spanish idiom or in the spirit of the Viennese waltz, he was a creator who could always give voice to surpassing beauty. He was, says Guido Pannain, "the spiritual heir to the last half-century's poetic feeling in France, and at the same time . . . he is a connoisseur of contemporary life, of that Parisian quality of richness and evanescence in thought."

In her biography of Ravel, Madeleine Goss presents the following personal picture of the composer: "Ravel was . . . precise in every detail. Small, both in stature and in build, his slender figure was always dressed in the latest and most irreproachable style. No effort was too great for him to make in achieving the effect he sought, whether this was a matter of matching ties, socks and handkerchiefs to a certain suit, or of working out the intricate detail of a composition. . . .

451

Rawsthorne

"As a whole, his life was colorless, almost devoid of so-called human interest; no violent emotions or overwhelming passions clouded the clear mirror which reflected his art. . . .

"As a story-teller, Maurice Ravel . . . was clever and amusing; he expressed himself well, with simple elegance and a certain dramatic ability. Everything he did, even to the relating of anecdotes, was influenced by his desire for perfection. He had an unusual gift for imitation, and could produce the call of birds and animals in a singularly realistic way. If someone paid him a compliment he would try to conceal his pleasure and embarrassment by turning aside with a humorous bird or animal cry. . . . Ravel's innate reserve and shyness left him only when he was with children or animals."

MAJOR WORKS

Ballet—Daphnis and Chloe.

Chamber Music—String Quartet in F; Introduction and Allegro, for harp, string quartet, flute, and clarinet; Piano Trio in A minor; Sonata for Violin and Cello; Tzigane, for violin and piano (also for violin and orchestra); Violin Sonata.

Operas—L'Heure Espagnole (one-act comic opera); L'Enfant et les Sortilèges (one-act fantasy).

Orchestral Music—Shéhérazade, for voice and orchestra; Alborada del Gracioso (also for piano); Rhapsodie Espagnole; Ma Mère l'Oye, or Mother Goose Suite (also for piano, four hands); La Valse; Boléro; Concerto in G major, for piano and orchestra; Concerto in D major, for piano left hand and orchestra; Don Quichotte à Dulcinée, for baritone and orchestra.

Piano Music—Pavane pour une Infante Défunte (also for orchestra); Jeux d'Eau; Sonatina; Miroirs; Gaspard de la Nuit; Valses Nobles et Sentimentales; Le Tombeau de Couperin.

Vocal Music—Histoires Naturelles; Cinq Mélodies Populaires Grecques; Chants Populaires; Trois Poèmes de Mallarmé; Deux Mélodies Hébraïques; Ronsard à Son Âme; Rêves; individual songs for voice and piano.

ABOUT

Bruyr, J., Maurice Ravel; Demuth, N., Ravel; Fragny, R. de, Maurice Ravel; Gerar, M. and Chalupt, R. (eds.), Ravel au Miroir de Ses Lettres; Goss, M., Bolero: The Life of Maurice Ravel; Jankélévitch, V., Maurice Ravel; Myers, R. H., Ravel: Life and Works; Onnen, F., Maurice Ravel; Roland-Manuel, Maurice Ravel; Seroff, V. I., Ravel.

La Revue Musicale (Paris), Ravel issue, December 1938.

Alan Rawsthorne
1905–

Alan Rawsthorne was born in Haslingden, Lancashire, England, on May 2, 1905. He planned to become a dentist and did not begin to study music seriously until he was twenty-one. In 1926 he entered the Royal Manchester College of Music where for four years he was a pupil of Frank Merrick (piano), Carl Fuchs (cello) and Keighley (composition). In 1930 he went to Berlin where he took piano lessons with Egon Petri. His studies ended, in 1932 Rawsthorne was appointed to the staff of Dartington Hall, in South Devon, where for two years his varied musical duties included the writing of music for the School of Dance Mime.

ALAN RAWSTHORNE

In 1935 he married Jessie Hinchliffe, a violinist. They settled in London where Rawsthorne concentrated on composition. The year 1936 saw the writing of the first compositions in which his later mature style was foreshadowed: a concerto for clarinet and strings and a trio for flute, oboe, and piano. He achieved recognition throughout Europe with two works heard at festivals of the International Society for Contemporary Music: *Theme and Variations*, for two violins, performed in London on June 18, 1938, and the *Symphonic Studies*, for orchestra, performed in Warsaw on April 21, 1939.

From 1941 until the end of the war, Rawsthorne served in the British Army where his principal task was the writing of music for army films. Serious creativity, however, was not neglected. His Piano Concerto No. 1 was performed by Louis Kentner in London in 1942 at a Promenade Concert which was conducted by the composer, who was given a forty-eight-hour leave from his army base in Wales to fill the engagement. This work was a new adaptation of a concerto for piano, strings, and percussion written in 1939. In 1945 Rawsthorne completed a major orchestral composition, *Cortèges*, heard at a Promenade Concert in London on July 23, 1945. A violin concerto, which he had begun in 1940, however, had to wait until the end of the war for its completion. The preliminary sketches were lost during an air raid and the composer had to reconstruct what he had thus far prepared. War duties delayed much of the writing. Eventually completed in 1947, the concerto received its world première at the Cheltenham Festival one year later and proved to be the composer's most mature and individual creation up to that time. Rawsthorne has explained that his intention in this music was "to combine the rhapsodical style of expression with the brilliance of a solo instrument." Hubert J. Foss described the work as "the now gentle, now disturbing, now friendly, now menacing Violin Concerto." It is dedicated to the composer William Walton, from whose oratorio *Belshazzar's Feast* a theme is quoted.

All of Rawsthorne's music up to this point had a severity of melodic line and a freedom of tonality that might suggest disrespect for tradition. Yet, as Wilfred Mellers remarked, Rawsthorne owed a great debt to the music of the past. From a formal standpoint, Mellers says, Rawsthorne "is unequivocally a baroque composer with his roots in the formal conceptions of Corelli and Bach. . . . His notions of form are architectural and decorative and have two main prototypes in the baroque music of the seventeenth and eighteenth centuries—the variation and the *concerto grosso*, the latter comprising toccata technique . . . cantilena, or aria, fugal elements related to the old fantasia technique, and the formalism of the dance. . . .

"While the chaconne of the First Piano Concerto is naturally the clearest example of Rawsthorne's connection with the baroque technique, the two-violin Variations, the string-

quartet Variations and even . . . the *Symphonic Studies*, are more freely based on the same notion of the variation form. In all, the principle of development is cumulative over an harmonic skeleton that is hardly more than latent; and in all, it is this skeleton which gives such tautness to the often very passionate melodic and figurative elements.

"About the nature of Rawsthorne's aria technique . . . his aria-like movements manifest always his combination of lyrical fervor with balanced architectural discipline."

After World War II, Rawsthorne received two commissions which resulted in major works. First, in 1950, came the symphony commissioned by the Royal Philharmonic, which introduced it on November 15, 1950. This symphony attracted much praise for its solid workmanship and its individual harmonic approaches. The second commission, from the Arts Council for the Festival of Britain, produced the Piano Concerto No. 2, which was a triumph when introduced by Clifford Curzon and the London Symphony under Sir Malcolm Sargent on June 17, 1951; since that time it has come to be recognized as one of Rawsthorne's most important achievements. "The Concerto has burst out on us not only as an exhilarating feat of creative technique," wrote Eric Blom, "but with a forceful emotional impact." Dyneley Hussey said: "It is most cunningly constructed and its themes are straightforward but not commonplace." And Martin Cooper called the work an excellent example of Rawsthorne's "delicate, tough-but-tenuous style of writing and very personal orchestration."

Subsequent works added to his international fame. These included his second string quartet (1954), his second violin concerto (1956), his second symphony (1959), the concerto for ten instruments (1962), and the *Improvisations on a Theme by Constant Lambert*, for orchestra (1961).

In describing the second symphony, whose première took place in Birmingham on September 29, 1959, the composer said that it sprang from "the various sensations aroused by life in the country, though this, I imagine, and perhaps hope, will not be apparent to anyone else." The composer also explained that the third movement was a country dance with "sinister elements appearing from time to time, as so frequently happens during rustic pursuits." In the final movement, Rawsthorne has set for voice and orchestra a poem about spring by the sixteenth century poet Henry Howard, Earl of Surrey. When this symphony was first heard in the United States (with John Barnett conducting the National Orchestral Association in New York on May 1, 1961), Raymond Ericson noted in the New York *Times:* "In four movements, lasting almost twenty minutes, the music reflects the pastoral atmosphere in an alternating brooding and lyrical fashion. The alternation can be pinpointed in the English composer's overlay of major and minor triads for his harmonic and melodic material, in his use of a march-like theme as an interruption of the rhapsodical movement."

According to Colin Mason, writing in Grove's *Dictionary of Music and Musicians*, the most distinctive element in Rawsthorne's style is its harmony: "He dispenses with key signatures, and his music is in a real sense atonal." Mason describes the harmony as "spare, frequently in two parts only," while the tonal ambiguity "arises from the endlessly changing succession of false relationships and the liberal use of the tonally indefinite augmented triad."

Rawsthorne makes his home in a quiet village in Essex, with his second wife, Isabel Lambert, a painter, whom he married in 1954.

MAJOR WORKS

Chamber Music—3 string quartets; Viola Sonata; Theme and Variations, for two violins; Quartet, for clarinet, violin, viola, and cello; Cello Sonata; Violin Sonata; Concerto for Ten Instruments; Piano Trio; Quintet for Piano and Wind; String Quartet; Tankas of the Four Seasons, for tenor, oboe, clarinet, bassoon, violin, and cello.

Choral Music—Four Seasonal Songs; A Canticle of Man, cantata; Canzonet, for soprano solo and mixed chorus; Lament for a Sparrow, for tenor, chorus, and harp; Carmen Vitale, for soprano, chorus, and orchestra.

Orchestral Music—3 symphonies; 2 piano concertos; 2 violin concertos; Concerto for Clarinet and String Orchestra; Symphonic Studies; Street Corner, overture; Cortèges; Oboe Concerto; Concerto for String Orchestra; Concertante pastorale, for flute, horn, and strings; Practical Cats, for speaker and orchestra; Hallé, overture; Improvisations on a Theme by Constant Lambert; Medieval Diptych, for baritone and orchestra; Divertimento, for chamber orchestra; Elegiac Rhapsody, for string orchestra; Cello Concerto.

Piano Music—Sonatina; Bagatelles; The Creel; Four Romantic Pieces.

Vocal Music—Two Songs (to poems by John Fletcher); We Three Merry Maidens; Carol.

ABOUT

Frank, A., Modern British Composers.

Monthly Musical Record (London), February 1948; Music and Letters (London), January 1951; Music Review (London), May 1951; Musical America, February 1952.

Gardner Read
1913–

Gardner Read was born on January 2, 1913, in Evanston, Illinois. He was the youngest of three children of a music-loving insurance broker and a mother who played the piano. As a boy of ten he sang with the choir of St. Luke's Church in Evanston, but he received no music instruction until 1928, when he entered the Evanston Township High School where an arts major had just been instituted. He took courses in music while studying the piano and organ with private teachers, and he enrolled as a private composition student at the School of Music of Northwestern University. While still a high school student he completed *Opus One*, a composition inspired by frequent visits to the movies; it is made up of some fifty melodic themes to accompany varied episodes in silent motion pictures. When in 1932 Read wrote the senior song for his graduating class, the number of his compositions reached eighteen.

Read spent the summer of 1932 at the Interlochen National Music Camp where he studied conducting with Vladimir Bakaleinikov. There he met Howard Hanson, who encouraged him to apply for a scholarship to the Eastman School of Music. He was awarded that scholarship, and he kept it for four years. His teachers included Edward Royce, Paul White, Bernard Rogers, and Hanson himself. In 1936 he was graduated with the degree of Bachelor of Music, and in 1937 he received a master's degree in composition.

While spending the first of several summers at the MacDowell Colony in 1936, he completed his first symphony, which he entered in a contest sponsored by the New York Philharmonic. He won the first prize of one thousand dollars and the symphony was performed by the New York Philharmonic under Barbirolli on November 4, 1937. The critic of the New York *Herald Tribune* called Read a "composer of consequence" adding: "The musical ideas are well defined, he is well acquainted with the orchestra and its possibilities, and in addition to many measures revealing a richly colored and impressive use of the hues of the instrumental palette, the symphony has passages of appealing lyric eloquence."

GARDNER READ

In 1938 Read was awarded the two-thousand-dollar Cromwell Fellowship for travel abroad; it was renewed the following year. He toured most of Europe and the Near East; during this time he received some instruction in composition from Jean Sibelius in Finland and Ildebrando Pizzetti in Italy.

Upon his return to the United States, Read was appointed professor of composition at the National Music Camp at Interlochen (Michigan) for the summer of 1940. The following summer he received a fellowship to study composition with Aaron Copland at the Berkshire Music Center in Massachusetts. In the fall of the same year he joined the faculty of the St. Louis Institute of Music where he taught for two years. Then in 1943 he was made head of the department of composition at the University of Missouri (Kansas City) Conservatory of Music.

His second symphony, completed in 1942, received the Paderewski Prize of one thousand dollars and a world première on November 26, 1943, with the composer conducting the Boston

Symphony. Hans Rosenwald described the style of this work as based "more upon dynamics and sonorities than the pursuit of conventional melodic formulas." According to Dr. Rosenwald, the composer evolved "through his studies in polyphony a harmonic idiom of his own, and this idiom is the most significant contribution of his new symphony."

Important performances of other orchestral compositions followed. An early work, *Prelude and Toccata* (written in 1937, and first introduced by the Rochester Philharmonic under Howard Hanson on April 29, 1937) was played by the Pittsburgh Symphony under Fritz Reiner in 1945. *Pennsylvaniana*, a suite inspired by the folk music of Western Pennsylvania, received its world première by the Pittsburgh Symphony under Reiner on November 21, 1947. Earlier the same year, on May 4, *Partita*, for small orchestra, had been heard at the annual festival of American Music in Rochester.

Here, as in later compositions, the musical world of Gardner Read is definitely of the twentieth century. As Nicolas Slonimsky has written: "His individuality is unmistakably stamped on his technique. . . . The basic harmony in Read's music is always tonal. As the music progresses and emotional tension grows, the harmony forms its own excrescences, and at climactic points expands into polyharmonic combinations." Slonimsky points out that an important element in Read's creative concept is "the tone color of instrumental groups. He likes to contrast the opposite registers; the somber coloring of the brass in low register is thrown into relief against the higher notes in the strings. . . . The percussion section frequently plays an important part in Read's orchestration. Often the kettledrums are given episodic solos, which contribute to the picturesque quality of the orchestration and often suggests a programmatic design without explicitly stating it."

The number of his compositions exceeds one hundred and twenty-five, and he has written in all forms. Among his later works are two more symphonies, the third and fourth; the former was successfully performed by the Pittsburgh Symphony under William Steinberg on March 2, 1962. Two other successful orchestral compositions resulted from commissions: the *Toccata Giocosa*, written for the

Louisville Philharmonic which performed it on March 13, 1954; and *Vernal Equinox*, introduced by the Brockton Symphony in Massachusetts on April 12, 1955. One of Read's most ambitious works—one to which he is particularly partial—is a large opus for solo voices, chorus, and orchestra entitled *The Prophet*, based on a text by Kahlil Gibran, completed in 1960. "When I was writing it," says Read, "it just flowed out, poured out. It was finished in only two months." Another ambitious work is his first opera, *Villon*, in four acts, completed in 1967. The libretto is by James Forsyth and is based on Forsyth's play.

In commenting on his own work Gardner Read has said: "Every new work constitutes a challenge, principally to solve a problem of form and structure. But as a foil to this seemingly intellectual approach, my music is basically romantic in mood. Some works are neoromantic, some neoclassic, some quasi-impressionistic. I feel it is a greater test of a composer's technique and abilities to cultivate as many different styles as he feels necessary rather than pursue only one."

From 1945 to 1948 Read headed the composition department of the Cleveland Institute of Music. In 1948 he was appointed composer in residence and professor of composition at Boston University College of Music, where he has since remained. Boston University celebrated Read's fiftieth birthday on March 27 and 28 of 1963 with a festival of his music which ranged chronologically from an early choral piece, *To a Skylark* (1939), to the world première of a large choral work, *The Reveille*, completed in 1962. In the academic year 1957–1958 Read lectured at Harvard. In 1966 he served as visiting professor of composition at the University of California in Los Angeles.

Gardner Read met his wife, the former Vail Payne, in 1940, while he was teaching at Interlochen, where she worked in public relations. They were married on September 17, 1940, in the chapel of the University of Chicago. The Reads, together with their only child (Cynthia Anne), live at Manchester-by-the-Sea, Massachusetts, throughout the year; Read commutes to Boston one hour each way to fulfill his teaching commitments at Boston University.

In 1957 and again in 1964 Read received grants from the United States Department of State to lecture and conduct in Mexico; in 1960 and 1965 he was given a summer resident fellowship at the Huntington Hartford Foundation in Pacific Palisades, California. He is the author of the *Thesaurus of Orchestral Devices* (1952) and *Music Notation* (1963).

MAJOR WORKS

Chamber Music—Suite, for string quartet; Piano Quintet; Sonata Brevis, for violin and piano; Songs to Children, for mezzo soprano, flute, harp, and string quartet; Nine by Six, for wind sextet; String Quartet No. 1; Sonoric Fantasia, for celesta, harp, and harpsichord.

Choral Music—The Golden Journey to Samarkand; Mountain Song; To a Skylark; Sister Awake; The Golden Harp; The Prophet, oratorio; The Reveille; Chants d'Auvergne.

Opera—Villon.

Orchestral Music—4 symphonies; The Painted Desert, tone poem; Four Nocturnes, for voice and orchestra; From a Lute of Jade, for voice and orchestra; Fantasy, for viola and orchestra; Prelude and Toccata; Suite, for string orchestra; Passacaglia and Fugue; Pan e Dafni; American Circle; First Overture; Songs for a Rainy Night, for voice and orchestra; Night Flight; Threnody, for flute and strings; A Bell Overture; Partita, for small orchestra; Pennsylvaniana Suite; Quiet Music for Strings; Dance of the Locomotives; The Temptation of St. Anthony, dance symphony; Toccata Giocosa; Vernal Equinox; Jeux de Timbres; Sonoric Fantasy No. 2, for violin and chamber orchestra; Sonoric Fantasia No. 3, for wind instruments.

Organ Music—Passacaglia and Fugue; Suite for Organ; Eight Preludes on an Old Southern Hymn; Variations on a Chromatic Ground.

Piano Music—Three Satirical Sarcasms; Sarabande; Passacaglia and Fugue, for two pianos; Driftwood Suite; Sonata da Chiesa; Touch Piece; Five Polytonal Studies.

ABOUT

Chase, G., America's Music; Howard, J. T., Our American Music.

Max Reger
1873–1916

Max Reger was born in Brand, Bavaria, on March 19, 1873. His father, the village schoolmaster, was a competent organist. When Max was a year old, the family moved to Weiden where he later attended public school. At the same time he received some instruction on the piano and in harmony from his father, and lessons on the organ and in composition from Adalbert Lindner. Reger gave excellent performances on both the piano and the organ

Reger: rā′ gĕr

when he was only thirteen. From 1886 to 1889 he was the organist of the Catholic church at Weiden. In addition, he wrote many compositions, mostly pieces for the organ and for the piano, and songs.

MAX REGER

It was intended that he pursue a career as schoolmaster, but after passing his examinations, he decided to sidestep teaching and concentrate on composition. A powerful influence in bringing about this decision was Wagner's *Die Meistersinger* and *Parsifal*, heard at Bayreuth. The operas made such an impression on him that Reger wrote a tone poem, *Héroïde Funèbre*, in a Wagnerian style. He despatched some of his manuscripts to Hugo Riemann, the distinguished teacher and theorist, who forthwith invited Reger to Sondershausen to live with him and be a member of his class at the Conservatory. When Riemann transferred to Wiesbaden in 1891, Reger followed him there, attending the Wiesbaden Conservatory for four years. During the year 1895–1896, he taught piano and organ in the same city.

In 1896 Reger was required to enter military service. This ordeal broke his health and spirit to such an extent that for a number of years following his release from military duties he was an invalid. While convalescing, he lived with his parents in Weiden, devoting all his time to composition. He produced a prodigious library of instrumental music at that time.

In 1901 he went to live in Munich where he married Elsa von Bagensky, whom he had met and fallen in love with in Wiesbaden. He earned his living by conducting and by playing the piano. His concert appearances in Germany, Austria, and Switzerland during this period were highly successful. In 1905 and 1906 he combined his concert activity with the teaching of counterpoint at the Music Academy in Munich and with the conducting of a choral group, and at the same time he continued to write music. In 1904 he completed his eighty-sixth opus, the *Variations and Fugue on a Theme by Beethoven*, a composition still heard from time to time. Originally a work for two pianos, it became successful in the orchestration made by the composer in 1915. In this work Reger borrowed a melody from Beethoven's Bagatelle in B-flat major, op. 119, which he then subjected to eight skillful variations, revealing above all else an extraordinary contrapuntal technique. The composition culminated in a monumental fugue, the subject of which is not the Beethoven theme but a theme by Reger himself. At a climactic point, however, the Reger and Beethoven themes are combined contrapuntally.

His varied activities overtaxed his highly sensitive nervous system, and in 1906 he suffered a stroke that brought on partial paralysis. He spent several months at Lake Chiem where he completed his *Introduction, Passacaglia and Fugue*, for two pianos. Upon recovery he undertook a tour of Russia as pianist and conductor.

In 1907 Reger became director of music at the University of Leipzig and the conductor of its chorus, jobs he kept only one year. From 1907 until his death (and even while holding various other important posts) he taught counterpoint at the Leipzig Conservatory. From 1911 to 1915 he was the principal conductor of the Meiningen Orchestra. In 1911 he was given the honorary appointment of Hofrat (privy councilor) and in 1915 music director of the city of Jena. Through these years recognition of his achievements came with the presentation of honorary degrees by several universities and the honorary title of professor by the king of Saxony.

Some of Reger's most important works were written before World War I. In 1910 he completed his Piano Concerto in F minor, introduced in Leipzig on December 15 of that year; Artur Nikisch conducted the Leipzig

Gewandhaus Orchestra, and Frau Kwast was soloist. This work was so well received that it was given thirty performances in various centers of Europe. It was not heard in the United States until November 16, 1945, when Rudolf Serkin performed it in Minneapolis. Serkin has since kept the work alive in the modern repertory through repeated performances.

On October 11, 1912, the *Romantic Suite*, for orchestra, inspired by verses by Joseph Freiherr von Eichendorff, was heard in Dresden. A year later, one of Reger's most frequently performed orchestral compositions received its world première: the *Four Tone Poems after Böcklin*, which the composer himself conducted in Essen on October 12, 1913. As the title suggests, this is a musical interpretation of four paintings by Arnold Böcklin, one of which (*The Isle of the Dead*) was also the inspiration for the famous tone poem by Rachmaninoff, written in 1907.

Variations and Fugue on a Theme by Mozart, another of Reger's distinguished works for orchestra, was written in 1914 and introduced in Berlin on February 5, 1915, the composer conducting. For his theme, Reger went to the opening movement of Mozart's A major Piano Sonata, which Mozart himself used for variation treatment. Nine variations follow—the ninth being a fugue, the subject of which is the Mozart theme stated by first violins and answered by second violins.

With the coming of World War I, Reger tried to enlist in the German army but was turned down because of poor health. He was found dead in bed, in Leipzig, on May 11, 1916, a newspaper in his hands and a cigar in his mouth; he was the victim of a heart attack.

Paul Rosenfeld once said that Reger looked like a "swollen myopic beetle with thick lips and a sullen expression." The violinist Adolf Busch, a longtime friend of Reger's, called him "humorous, generous, impulsive, [one] who could not bear restraint or hear of anyone else being oppressed." All his life, Reger struggled to overcome his addiction to alcohol. "When he tried to cut down, he had to go through the motions at least," Busch reveals. "He would drink eight cups of bouillon as he sat talking. Once he got sick on too much lemonade."

Pessimistic to the point of bitterness about the fate of composers and their music, Reger used to say: "The life of a composer is work, hope and bicarbonate of soda"; and he would comment that people enjoyed "composers and pigs only after their deaths."

Reger was one of the most scholarly musicians of his generation. He favored abstract music over programmatic and was partial to a contrapuntal style which he handled with the most extraordinary skill and variety. His god was Bach, whom he regarded as the be-all and end-all of musical existence, and his aim frequently was to arrive at a creative reinterpretation of Bach's methods along Romantic lines. This devotion to Bach and polyphonic methods—and to such baroque structures as the toccata, passacaglia and fugue—led many of his contemporaries to denounce him as a stuffy academician. "Seated at his work bench of a musical mechanic, in a shop whose windows were rarely opened to the outside world," wrote André Cœuroy, "he manufactured, like a shoemaker his shoes, fugues and more fugues. He did not wish either to dazzle or impress; he created problems, and found their solutions. He personified abstract music; he was the man of Bach's polyphony and of the old forms brought back to life." But despite Reger's partiality to the past, the complexity of his polyphonic writing, the unevenness of his voluminous production, he was capable of nobility, grandeur and a richness of invention that make his finest works, at least, highly rewarding listening.

Nevertheless, Eric Blom is of the opinion that it is not for these achievements that Reger is remembered most often but because of his "tenacious upholding of the great traditions in composition, based mainly on a study of Bach's art in all its bearings." In this return to Bach, Reger—along with Busoni—was an early significant pioneer of the neoclassic school that was soon to flourish in the works of Hindemith.

A Max Reger Society to promote his music was founded in Germany in 1920, and some years later another such society was created in Austria. In 1947 Reger's widow opened a Max Reger Institute in Bonn to perpetuate the memory of the composer through performances of Reger's works and those of composers influenced by him. Annual prizes were given in Reger's name both for new music and for musicological studies; the first such award was presented on the seventy-fifth anniversary of Reger's birth. In 1954 the German publishing house of Breitkopf & Härtel initiated a monumental project: to issue everything Reger had written.

MAJOR WORKS

Chamber Music—5 string quartets; 2 piano quartets; 2 piano trios; 2 string trios; 9 violin sonatas; 3 violin suites; 4 sonatas for unaccompanied violin; 14 preludes and fugues for unaccompanied violin; 4 cello sonatas; 3 suites for unaccompanied cello; 3 clarinet sonatas; Piano Quintet; Clarinet Quintet.

Choral Music—Psalm C; Die Nonnen; Die Weihe der Nacht; Römischer Triumphgesang; cantatas, choral arrangements, folk songs, hymns, motets, sacred songs, songs for male chorus, songs for mixed chorus.

Orchestral Music—Sinfonietta; Serenade; Variations and Fugue on a Theme by J. A. Hiller; Symphonic Prologue to a Tragedy; Comedy Overture; Concerto in the Olden Style; Romantic Suite; Four Tone Poems after Böcklin; Ballet Suite; Variations and Fugue on a Theme by Mozart.

Organ Music—6 trios; 2 suites; Fantasy and Fugue on B-A-C-H; Symphonic Fantasy and Fugue; Variations and Fugue on an Original Theme; choral fantasies, choral preludes, preludes and fugues, variations.

Piano Music—4 sonatinas; Variations and Fugue on a Theme by Telemann; Variations and Fugue on a Theme by Bach, for four hands; Variations and Fugue on a Theme by Beethoven, for two pianos (also for orchestra); Passacaglia and Fugue, for two pianos; Bunte Blätter; Charakterstücke; Fantasiestücke; canons, etudes, intermezzi, pieces, waltzes.

Vocal Music—Schlichte Weisen, six books; Sacred Songs, with organ; Nursery Rhymes; various individual songs for voice and piano; vocal quartets.

ABOUT

Braungart, R., Freund Reger: Erinnerungen; Brock, C., Max Reger als Vater; Eberhard, O., Max Reger; Habbe, K., Max Reger, Entwicklungsgang eines Deutschen Meisters; Reger, E., Mein Leben mit und für Max Reger; Reger, M., Briefe eines Deutschen Meisters; Stein, F. W., Max Reger: Sein Leben in Bildern; Taube, L., Max Regers Meisterjahre: Wehmeyer, G., Max Reger als Liederkomponist.

Musical Times (London), June 1925.

Ottorino Respighi
1879–1936

Ottorino Respighi was born in Bologna on July 9, 1879, of a musical family. His grandfather had been a violinist and organist in a Bologna church; his father taught the piano at the Liceo Musicale.

Ottorino's father instructed him in the elements of music. When he was twelve, Respighi

Respighi: rä spē′ gē

entered the Liceo Musicale where he was taught the violin by Sarti. He also received instruction in composition from Torchi and Martucci. By the time he was graduated in 1899, he had already given some proof of creative talent with *Symphonic Variations*, performed successfully at a Liceo concert.

OTTORINO RESPIGHI

A period of travel followed Respighi's graduation from the Liceo. In 1900 he lived in St. Petersburg where he played the viola in the Opera orchestra and studied orchestration and composition with Rimsky-Korsakov. Later he visited Berlin.

From 1903 to 1908 Respighi played the viola in the Mugellini String Quartet in Bologna. However, his main interest was composition, and important performances of ambitious works soon made him known in the early 1900's. In 1902 came his Concerto for Piano and Orchestra, heard in Bologna. On March 12, 1905, *Re Enzo*, a comic opera, was produced, also in Bologna. On January 6, 1905, *Notturno*, for orchestra, was heard in New York City, and on November 20, 1910, *Semirama*, a lyric tragedy inspired by Richard Strauss's *Salome*, was successfully mounted in Bologna.

Now a recognized composer, Respighi was appointed professor of composition at the Santa Cecilia Academy. Mario Labroca, a pupil at Santa Cecilia during this period, says: "He was not very tall, and with his frank eyes set widely apart, he strangely reminded me of

Beethoven. His pupils talked about him with enthusiasm because he had a profound knowledge of music, and especially because he based his teachings on roots deeper than those currently known, ranging beyond those earlier examples of Italian instrumental music which only he and a few of his contemporaries had been among the first to approach." One of Respighi's pupils at Santa Cecilia was Elsa Olivieri-Sangiacomo, a talented singer and composer whom he married in 1919.

Respighi's first orchestral masterwork was heard on March 11, 1917, when the Augusteo Orchestra in Rome gave the première of his tone poem *The Fountains of Rome* (*Fontane di Roma*), a set of four nature pictures, each inspired by one of Rome's famous fountains seen at different times of the day. In the published score, the composer explained that his aim was "to give expression to the sentiments and visions suggested . . . by four of Rome's fountains, contemplated at the hour in which their character is most in harmony with the surrounding landscape, or in which their beauty appears most impressive to the observer." In this music, Respighi revealed for the first time an extraordinary gift for pictorial writing as well as a remarkable talent for orchestration.

In 1924 Respighi completed a second set of orchestral impressions of Rome, *The Pines of Rome* (*Pini di Roma*), heard in Rome on December 14, 1924. In this work Respighi was interested not in nature pictures but in expressing memories and visions aroused by familiar Roman scenes. A novel feature of this composition is the interpolation of a phonograph recording of a nightingale's song as part of the instrumentation.

A third set of Roman pictures, *Roman Festivals* (*Feste Romane*) was written in 1928 and was introduced on February 21, 1929, by the New York Philharmonic conducted by Toscanini.

In his symphonic trilogy on Rome, the composer's most celebrated creations, he "realized a personal form of symphonic poem," wrote G. A. Luciani, "in which the descriptive and colorful element blends intimately with the lyrical and sentimental element, and in a line which persistently maintains its classicism in spite of a very modern technique." Several elements go into the shaping of Respighi's

musical speech: Debussy's Impressionist harmony, Richard Strauss's vivid pictorialism, Rimsky-Korsakov's orchestration. But this mixture has been made with such extraordinary skill that a highly personal product is achieved.

Vivid pictorialism, calling for the fullest resources of orchestration in the manner of Richard Strauss and Rimsky-Korsakov, is only a single facet of Respighi's varied creative output. He also wrote many compositions in a neoclassical style. Some of these works make use of old modes and plain chants within classical structures. The violin concerto *Concerto Gregoriano* (1921), for example, used Gregorian chants, while the Piano Concerto (1924) was written in the Mixolydian mode. Other compositions are similarly rooted in the past. They include *Old Airs and Dances for the Lute*, two series transcribed for orchestra (1917, 1924), and the orchestral suite *The Birds* (1927), based on pieces by such old masters as Pasquini, Jacques de Gallot, and Rameau. Here, as in his popular pictorial tone poems, Respighi proved a powerful influence in helping bring about a renaissance of symphonic music in Italy.

Though he emphasized instrumental music, Respighi did not desert opera. After his apprenticeship in the musical theatre, he created a comic work, *Belfagor*, which La Scala produced on April 26, 1923. The New York *Times* in its obituary of Respighi, remarked that the general characteristics of Respighi's talent "are united in this opera. . . . Respighi had no intention in this work of solving the musical problems of the day. He merely wished to write a musical comedy without losing himself in unfruitful experiments. While abstaining from writing uninterrupted arias and duets, he nevertheless duly indicated in *Belfagor* the singing and recitative arts."

Belfagor was followed by *La Campana Sommersa* (*The Sunken Bell*), text derived from a play by Gerhart Hauptmann; it was produced in Hamburg on November 18, 1927, and received its American première at the Metropolitan Opera on November 24, 1928. "Mr. Respighi spins a multicolored tonal web," reported Lawrence Gilman. "He has the Mediterranean instinct for song, and his lyric line is buoyant and sustained. The reservations that one must make are that his music lacks profile and that he is never quite as eloquent as his subject cries for him to be—as you keep wanting him to be."

An opera of quite a different character—a triptych "mystery" with deeply religious and mystic overtones—came with *Maria Egiziaca* (*Mary of Egypt*). The world première took place in New York City in a concert version, on March 16, 1932, with Toscanini conducting the New York Philharmonic, and for this performance a stage spectacle was devised utilizing the background of a triptych in the manner of an old religious painting. After the overture had been played by a small orchestra placed on one side of the stage, curtains were parted by two young women attired as angels. Then the performance continued in a concert presentation by the Philharmonic.

In 1923 Respighi was appointed the director of Santa Cecilia, as successor to Enrico Bossi. He held this post only two years, preferring to concentrate on his own creative work and on teaching a few select classes in composition. In the 1925–1926 season he made the first of several tours of the United States, his American debut taking place in New York City on December 31, 1925, when he was heard with the New York Philharmonic (Willem Mengelberg conducting) in the world première of his piano concerto. He returned to the United States in 1928 and again in 1932 to attend performances of his operas *The Sunken Bell* and *Maria Egiziaca*.

In 1932 Respighi was appointed to the Royal Academy. In the same year he was one of ten leading Italian composers who signed a manifesto condemning the growing trend in twentieth century music away from human and emotional content and toward cerebralism. The manifesto read in part: "In the musical world reigns the biblical confusion of Babel. For twenty years the most diverse and disparate tendencies have been lumped together in a continual chaotic revolution. . . . We are against this art which cannot have and does not have any human content and desires to be merely a mechanical demonstration and a cerebral puzzle. . . . A logical chain binds the past and the future—the romanticism of yesterday will again be the romanticism of tomorrow."

Respighi was working on his last opera, *Lucrezia*, when in 1936 he was stricken with a heart attack. Confined to bed, he continued to work industriously on the opera, but he did not live to complete it. He died in Rome on April 18, 1936. His wife, Elsa, completed the opera, which was produced posthumously at La Scala February 24, 1937.

Respighi's funeral was attended by the king, Premier Mussolini, and most of the leading statesmen and musicians of Italy. A Mass by Palestrina was sung by the Augusteo Choir at the funeral services at the Chiesa di Santa Maria. Respighi's remains were taken for burial to his native city of Bologna.

MAJOR WORKS

Ballets—Scherzo Veneziano; La Boutique Fantasque (based on music by Rossini); Belkis, Regina di Saba.

Chamber Music—String Quartet in D major; Five Pieces, for violin and piano; Violin Sonata in B minor; Deità Silvane, for voice and eleven instruments; Il Tramonto, for mezzo-soprano and string quartet; Quartetto Dorico, for two violins, viola, and cello.

Choral Music—La Primavera, lyric poem for solo voices, chorus, and orchestra; Lauda per la Natività del Signore, for solo voices, chorus, and orchestra.

Operas—Re Enzo, comic opera; Semirama, lyric tragedy; Marie Victoire; La Bella Addormentata nel Bosco, musical fable; Belfagor, lyric comedy; La Campana Sommersa (The Sunken Bell); Maria Egiziaca, mystery; La Fiamma; Lucrezia (completed by Elsa Respighi).

Orchestral Music—Notturno; Sinfonia Drammatica; Fontane di Roma (Fountains of Rome), tone poem; Antiche Arie e Danze per Liuto (Old Airs and Dances for the Lute), two sets; Ballata delle Gnomidi; Concerto Gregoriano, for violin and orchestra; Concerto in Mixolydian Mode, for piano and orchestra; Pini di Roma (Pines of Rome), tone poem; Vetrate di Chiesa (Church Windows), symphonic impressions; Impressioni Brasiliane; Trittico Botticelliano, for small orchestra; Gli Uccelli (The Birds), suite; Toccata, for piano and orchestra; Feste Romane (Roman Festivals), tone poems; Metamorphoseon Modi XII; Concerto à Cinque, for oboe, trumpet, violin, double bass, and piano, with strings.

Piano Music—Three Preludes on Gregorian Melodies; Six Pieces for Children, for four hands.

Vocal Music—Various songs for voice and piano.

ABOUT

Bacharach, A. L. (ed.), The Music Masters: v4, The Twentieth Century; Rensis, R. de, Ottorino Respighi; Respighi, E., Respighi: His Life Story.
Rassegna Musicale, April 1933.

Silvestre Revueltas
1899–1940

Silvestre Revueltas was born in Santiago Papasquiaro, in the state of Durango, Mexico,

Revueltas: rä vwĕl′ täs

on December 31, 1899. At the age of eight he began to study the violin, and in 1913 he went to Mexico City where he attended the Conservatory for three years. There he continued his violin study with José Rocabruna while receiving his first lessons in composition from Rafael J. Tello. During this period he played the violin in public bars and movie houses and in this way became familiar with Mexican popular music; some of the stylistic elements of Mexican popular music later were incorporated into his own compositions.

SILVESTRE REVUELTAS

Revueltas came to the United States in 1916. For two years he attended Saint Edward College in Austin, Texas; then, for another two years, he was a pupil of Felix Borowski and Samatini at the Chicago Musical College. He returned to Mexico for a short period in 1920, long enough to make his debut as concert violinist. But he soon returned to the United States for additional violin study, this time mainly with Ševčik.

From 1924 to 1926 he joined forces with Carlos Chávez in promoting modern music in Mexico through concerts of violin and piano music in an attempt to break down the musical insularity of his countrymen. "The reaction was violent," he later recalled, "and we were soon personally introduced to the encouraging hisses, foot stamping, insults and aggressive indignation of a backward and lazy public."

Returning to the United States in 1926, he spent the next two years conducting orchestras in Texas and Alabama. Chávez then called him back to Mexico to become assistant conductor of the newly founded Orquesta Sinfónica de México, of which Chávez was principal conductor. This proved for Revueltas an important affiliation, not only in advancing his career as conductor, but also in providing him with the means of getting his compositions rehearsed and performed.

It was due mainly to Chávez' advice and influence that in 1931 Revueltas involved himself seriously with composition. From the outset Revueltas interested himself in writing music about Mexican streets and byways, resort towns and dives, marketplaces and places of amusement. Though he made extensive use of native instruments, he was not interested in national music as such, nor was he drawn to research in old Mexican and Indian musical lore.

His career as composer began officially with an orchestral piece, *Esquinas* (*Street Corners*), whose première he himself conducted in Mexico City on November 20, 1931. "It would be amusing to find in the music the noise of taxi horns, street cars and trucks," the composer explained, "but unfortunately there is nothing of that in it. Rather it is the sound, or perhaps the silence, of the inner traffic of the souls passing by. Conventional analysis may discover in the music some definite form, binary, ternary, song form and so on. That is of no consequence. The traffic of which I speak is multiform, without visible coherence. It is subordinated to the rhythm of life, not to the distance from one side of the street to the other."

The tones of mockery which perhaps can be detected in the above programmatic note can also be found in the composer's descriptions of his other works of this period. About *Ventanos* (*Windows*), which he conducted on November 4, 1932, he said: "It is a composition without a program. When I composed the music, I may have intended to convey a definite idea. Now that several months have elapsed, I no longer recall what it is." With *Cuauhnahuac* (first performance on June 2, 1933), Revueltas produced his first composition to receive a significant hearing in the United States. "Cuauhnahuac" is the ancient Indian name for the Indian resort town of Cuernavaca. But, as the composer explains,

462

"this is music without tourism. In the orchestra, an Indian drum (*huehuetl*) is used as a means of national propaganda. Other instruments in the score are even more nationalistic, but no attention should be paid to them; it is all just anticapitalist agitation." In *Janitzio*, (première on October 13, 1933), Revueltas again turned to Mexican geography, saying: "Janitzio is a fisherman's island in Lake Patzcuaro. Lake Patzcuaro is filthy. The romantic travelers have embellished it with verses and music of the picture-post-card type. Not to be outdone, I, too, added my grain to the sandpile. Posterity will undoubtedly reward my contribution to national tourism." And for *Caminos* (first heard on July 17, 1934) Revueltas once again found stimulation and inspiration in the tortuous byways and streets of Mexico.

Addicted to alcohol, Revueltas composed much of his music while partly or wholly inebriated; often he did not later remember what he had originally put down on paper. When he first rehearsed his *Caminos*, he took the bass clarinetist severely to task for playing something he, Revueltas, had not written. When the musician proved that he had played the music exactly as it was found on the manuscript, Revueltas exclaimed: "My God!" Then he whistled the way he really wanted the passage to sound.

Revueltas' most frequently performed composition is *Sensemayá*, an orchestral tone poem originally scored for voice and small orchestra in 1937, then in 1938 rescored for large orchestra without voice. This is a setting of a poem by the Afro-Cuban poet Nicolas Guillen, *Chant to Kill a Snake*. Revueltas' sister has disclosed that the poem's title is "simply a fanciful, whimsical name; it has no interpretation and no sense. The poet used it solely as an idiomatic rhythm in the poem . . . and this poem inspired Revueltas to compose his tone poem of the same name." A strong pulse courses throughout the composition. Cross rhythms imposed on the basic beat, exciting syncopations, and rapidly changing meters all help to create hypertension and to build up primitive force.

While still carrying out his duties as assistant conductor of the Orquesta Sinfónica, Revueltas became in 1933 a member of the faculty of the National Conservatory in Mexico City, whose concerts he conducted. In 1936 he resigned from his post with the Orquesta Sinfónica to form an orchestra of his own—the Orquesta Sinfónica Nacional—but its life span was brief.

When civil war broke out in Spain in 1937, Revueltas went to that country to join the Loyalist cause and work in its music section. On October 7, 1937, he led the world première of his orchestral suite *Redes* (adapted from a score he had written for a motion picture). This performance took place at a concert meeting of the Committee Against War and Fascism in Barcelona. This music was later choreographed by José Limón for the Ballet Mexicano.

After returning to Mexico, Revueltas resumed his varied musical activities. But a lifetime of intense poverty, heavy drinking, and dissipation exacted a heavy price. Stricken with pneumonia, Revueltas was too weak to fight the disease. He was found lying unconscious in the street and died soon afterwards in a hospital, on October 5, 1940. Only a few hours before his death there took place in Mexico City the highly successful première of his ballet *El Renacuajo Paseador*.

Revueltas' music is characterized by its "deep lyrical strain," according to Nicolas Slonimsky. "The forms are agglutinative, the ideas following one another in free succession governed only by the laws of contrast and recurrence." Even though he never used folk material, his music was unmistakably Mexican, since his melodies and rhythms were often derived from popular Mexican sources.

"My music," Revueltas wrote, "is functional architecture, which does not exclude sentiment. Melodic fragments derive from the same impulse, the same emotion as in my other works; they sing in persistent rhythms, ever in motion; they produce sonorities that may seem strange because they are not common. My rhythms and sonorities are reminiscent of other rhythms and sonorities, just as building material in architecture is identical with any building material, but it serves for constructions that are different in meaning, form, and expression."

Revueltas' music is simpler, more direct, more romantic than that of his more celebrated compatriot Carlos Chávez. Paul Bowles wrote: "There is none of the preoccupation with form or conscious establishment of individual style that makes Chávez's music an intellectual product." Unfortunately, there took place a sharp cleavage in Mexico's musical life created by the disciples of Chávez and Revueltas, a musical conflict which continued up to the time of Revueltas' death and which often embarrassed both Chávez and Revueltas.

Revueltas' music never enjoyed wide recognition while he was alive. It is true that a small band of younger composers—including Galindo and Contreras—grouped themselves around him and were inspired by him, creating a camp of their own in direct opposition to Chávez and his followers. But public performances of Revueltas' works were infrequent, and the general public did not welcome him. For one thing, Revueltas was generally disliked for his sharp, satirical tongue, which knew neither discipline nor tact. For another, he was often an object of ridicule because of his excessive drinking.

After his death, however, his music assumed increasing importance in Mexico. The critics publicized his life and work extensively, and all-Revueltas concerts—the first on December 13, 1940—began to draw attention to his creative powers.

Revueltas wrote the music for a number of Mexican films. His last work, a ballet, *La Coronela*, was left unfinished. It was completed by Galindo and Huízar, and produced posthumously on November 20, 1941.

MAJOR WORKS

Ballets—El Renacuajo Paseador; La Coronela (completed by Galindo and Huízar).

Chamber Music—3 string quartets; Feria, for string quartet.

Orchestral Music—Esquinas; Cuauhnahuac; Ventanas; Janitzio; Colorines; Caminos; Toccata, for violin and orchestra; Sensemayá; Homenaje a Federico García Lorca; Redes.

Piano Music—Canción; Allegro.

Vocal Music—Dos Canciones; Siete Canciones.

ABOUT

Contreras, G., S. Revueltas; Slonimsky, N., Music of Latin America.

Musical America, February 1958; Musical Quarterly, April 1941.

Wallingford Riegger
1885–1961

Wallingford Riegger was born in Albany, Georgia, on April 29, 1885. His father, who was engaged in the lumber business, had been a choirmaster when he was only fourteen; later on, he learned to play the violin and as a married man participated with his children in performances of chamber music at home. Wallingford's mother was an accomplished pianist.

WALLINGFORD RIEGGER

When Riegger was three, the family moved to Indianapolis where the boy was given lessons on the violin until 1900, when the Riegger family moved to New York. Wallingford now changed from violin to cello in order to fill out the complement of the family string quartet, which for a number of years gave weekly performances.

In 1904 Riegger entered Cornell University on a scholarship. He was there only one year when he decided upon music as his profession. He then enrolled in the Institute of Musical Art in New York City where he studied composition for the first time, mainly with Percy Goetschius. Goetschius prophesied at that time that Riegger would develop into a "master" if he could only free himself from "modern" influences.

Riegger became a member of the first

Riegger: rē′gĕr

graduating class of the Institute of Musical Art in 1907. He continued his music studies in Berlin for a number of years. At the Berlin High School for Music he studied the cello with Robert Hausmann. Privately, he continued his cello study with the distinguished Dutch virtuoso Anton Hekking, and he also took an intensive course in composition and counterpoint with the American composer Edgar Stillman Kelley, who was then resident in Berlin.

Upon returning to the United States in 1910, Riegger married Rose Schramm, a former high school acquaintance. For the following three years he earned his living playing the cello in the St. Paul (Minnesota) Symphony.

In 1914 Riegger went back to Germany. There he conducted opera performances in Würzburg and Königsberg and orchestral concerts in Berlin. In 1917, only three days before America entered World War I, Riegger returned to the United States with his wife and three daughters to become head of the departments of theory and cello at Drake University in Iowa. This was the first of many teaching posts.

Riegger's first opus was a piano trio in B minor which received the Paderewski Prize in 1922 but was not performed until March 21, 1930. A. Walter Kramer described it as "the best trio to date by an American composer, and one of the best modern trios by any composer." In 1923 Riegger received honorable mention for his *American Polonaise* in a competition conducted by the Lewisohn Stadium Concerts, and the following year he was given the Elizabeth Sprague Coolidge award for his setting of *La Belle Dame sans Merci*. This was the first native American composition to be so honored. At its première, at the Coolidge Festival in Pittsfield, Massachusetts, on September 19, 1924, it was given an ovation.

The *Rhapsody for Orchestra*, composed in 1925 but not given a hearing until Erich Kleiber conducted it with the New York Philharmonic on October 29, 1931, was Riegger's first significant attempt to write in an atonal style. In 1927 he produced another ambitious work in a strictly atonal idiom, the *Study in Sonority*, in ten parts, for violins. The genesis of this composition is an interesting one. At that time Riegger was the head of the

cello and theory departments at Ithaca Conservatory, where he led a student orchestra. During the summer the orchestra was reduced to violins only, and the necessity of finding something the violin-orchestra could play led him to write a composition which he originally called *Caprice* and in which each of the violins had a separate part to play. When *Study in Sonority*, as *Caprice* was subsequently renamed, was given its first public presentation (Leopold Stokowski conducting the Philadelphia Orchestra on March 30, 1929), not ten but forty violins were used. The critics were divided in their reactions. One called it "masterful, written with skill and power"; another said it was "aurally horrible." Henry Cowell described it as a "choiring of angels" while Samuel Chotzinoff insisted it had "nothing to say." Later judgments, however, were mainly positive. Of these, that of William Soskin is typical. He found it to be an "immensely exciting composition" in which dramatic use is made of a theme "built upon an arbitrary tonic chord, atonal though it may be, and thrown against several highly effective backgrounds."

The *Study in Sonority*, while atonal, is still not in the twelve-tone system. That system was first used (though only partly) in *Dichotomy*, for chamber orchestra (1932), introduced in Berlin on March 10 of that year. It is one of the earliest compositions by an American in a dodecaphonic style.

In 1928 Riegger left Ithaca to settle in New York City, where he held teaching posts at the Institute of Musical Art, Teachers College at Columbia University, and the Metropolitan Music School. He writes: "I got to know the pioneers of the modern movement in America, and spiritually akin to them, I cast my lot with them. These included Henry Cowell, Charles Ives, Carl Ruggles, and Edgard Varèse. We had rejected the neoclassicism of a war-weary Paris and had struck out for ourselves, each in his own way. We formed the Pan American Association of Composers (which included Latin Americans) and gave, at a tremendous expense of time and energy, numerous concerts both there and abroad.

"Meanwhile, I had become an admirer of the matchless art of Martha Graham, through whom I was drawn into a new sphere of creative activity: writing for the modern dance.

Riegger

I had not been impressed with the prettiness of the ballet, so alien to the American scene but so generously patronized. The modern dance, being vital and expressive—and an American product—fascinated me.

"A lot of music I turned out for the dance was of necessity episodic in structure, so that only a small portion of it could be rescued for concert purposes. I salvaged the finale of the *New Dance*, composed for Doris Humphrey, which I arranged for two pianos, for violin and piano, for band, and for symphony orchestra; also fragments from *Chronicle*, written for Martha Graham, which I converted into an orchestral piece; and a part of *Candide*, prepared for Charles Weidman, which I put into my first symphony."

Of the three works mentioned above by Riegger as having been adapted from ballet scores into concert works, the most successful was *New Dance*, introduced by the Pittsburgh Symphony under Fritz Reiner on January 30, 1942. It was admired for its rhythmic cogency and was soon performed by other major American orchestras.

Concerning his music for the dance Riegger commented: "[I] found the twelve-tone technique entirely compatible with my own idiom, although generally I would abandon it in the course of a movement or composition." The Second String Quartet (first performed at the Yaddo Festival in New York on September 8, 1940) follows the twelve-tone technique "in its most rigorous form, that is, without transposition and the many modifications and derivations that have come into use."

Two orchestral compositions that attracted attention were not, however, in a dodecaphonic style but rather transferred other modern devices of harmony, rhythm, and tonality into strictly baroque structures. *Canon and Fugue* was heard at the festival of the International Society for Contemporary Music at Berkeley, California, on August 1, 1942. The canon was a piece of music Riegger found in 1941 among his student compositions. A friend urged him to make use of it, and he did so by adding a fugue to it—"for needed contrast and dimension," as he noted. This work was extensively performed in the United States, Europe, and Latin America, not only in its original version for strings but also in a later adaptation for full symphony orchestra.

A successor to *Canon and Fugue* came with the *Passacaglia and Fugue* for orchestra, the world première of which took place in Washington, D.C., on March 19, 1944, with Hans Kindler conducting the National Symphony. This composition had begun a year earlier as a work for band and as such was performed by the Goldman Band in New York on June 16, 1943. Here, as in the earlier *Canon and Fugue*, Riegger revealed a gift for creating muscular music of a highly individualized personality within the formal patterns of a baroque structure and in a polyphonic style.

Acceptance also came for Riegger's third symphony which had been commissioned by the Alice M. Ditson Fund and was given its world première on May 16, 1948, Dean Dixon conducting. The critics were almost unanimous in praising it for its technical skill, subtlety of artistic expression, and creative imagination. For this work the New York Music Critics Circle gave Riegger its annual award; a second award was received from the Naumburg Foundation, which paid for the recording (it was the first time a major Riegger work had been recorded). Riegger revised the symphony twice. After the second revision had been heard in New York (on December 7, 1964), Louis Biancolli said: "This is Riegger at his most individual. The idiom is spare and knotty, the development original and compact, the final fugue an intellectual teaser to performer and listener." Richard Franko Goldman called it one of the half-dozen or so best symphonies by an American.

Riegger wrote a fourth symphony, this time on a commission from the Fromm Music Foundation for a festival held in 1957 at the University of Illinois in Urbana. It was heard on April 12. Although not in Riegger's more usual atonal style, and with frequent discords, this music is aurally palatable because of its rich fund of lyricism, conventional rhythms, and colorful scoring. One of its most deeply moving sections is the second movement, material which Riegger had adapted from a ballet score he had produced in 1936 for Martha Graham (*Chronicle*) and which had been inspired by the agony and tragedy of the Spanish civil war. Klaus G. Roy is of the opinion that this movement was the point of departure for the entire symphony and dictated both the form and style of the other movements.

Reviewing the symphony, the Boston critic Cyrus Durgin wrote: "It is, upon first acquaintance, a work of much technical and orchestral stature, and of a great deal of expressive power. This is a Symphony which has both head and heart appeal, and whose texture ranges from free-flowing melody to grinding dissonance, with a good amount of mild and tonal harmony in between."

Riegger's seventy-fifth birthday in 1960 was celebrated with significant performances of major works. The Kansas City Philharmonic invited him to conduct an entire program of his compositions, and the Contemporary Music Society in New York devoted a program to him on April 27. At a concert of the National Orchestral Association in New York Riegger led a performance of his *Festival Overture*, a composition in a more or less Romantic style which had been commissioned for the Conference on the Creative Arts in Boston, where it was first heard, on May 4, 1957. In 1960 Leonard Bernstein conducted the New York Philharmonic in a presentation of Riegger's *Variations for Piano and Orchestra*. Within the restricted framework of this twelve-tone composition, he managed to be whimsical and even jazzy.

What Herbert Elwell wrote in the Cleveland *Plain Dealer* about Riegger's *Music for Orchestra*—after its première in Cleveland on March 22, 1956—serves well to characterize the nature of the composer's creativity over a period of some forty years: "Riegger is . . . an advanced and highly independent musical thinker, who speaks his piece with terse, uncompromising language, that says exactly what it means and stops at the right place, when it has no more to say. There is no false emotionalism in Riegger, no academic padding, no pompous and untested certitudes that drive blindly toward vague conclusions." Elwell found in this music the same qualities to be found in the man, namely his "simplicity, his wit, his catholicity of taste, and his passion for social justice. These things come out in his music to give it color, pungency and a disturbing but fascinating sense of the dangerous revolutionary realities of our time."

After the death of his wife in 1957 (to whose memory he dedicated his fourth symphony), Riegger lived with his daughter, Ruth, in an apartment on West 113th Street in New York.

In late March 1961 he was taking a walk on Amsterdam Avenue when he tripped over a leash while two dogs were fighting. This accident necessitated an operation on the brain from which Riegger never recovered. He died in a hospital on April 2, 1961. Just before his death he was awarded the Brandeis Creative Arts Award by Brandeis University.

In an eloquent obituary of Riegger in the *Musical Quarterly*, Richard Franko Goldman said in part: "Riegger's qualities of honesty, kindness, and humor will not be forgotten by those who knew him. He was a serious and devoted person, humble towards his art and unassuming in his relations with his colleagues. Like all serious people, he was able to laugh at himself. He viewed life with passion and accepted his difficulties with patience. He had conviction and faith, and at heart an unquenchable optimism about art and about people. . . . In any history of American music, Riegger's name must have an honored place."

To the editor of this book Riegger remarked that his avocations for many years included "fussing and landscaping" at his summer place in Holland, Massachusetts. "One summer I built a toolshed," he continued, "and painted it, too. I confess to liking bridge and detective stories, which supply a wonderful excuse for not getting at my composing." All his life he had a strong political and social consciousness, and stood in the vanguard of left-wing activities in the United States. In 1957 he was questioned by the House Subcommittee on Un-American Activities, at which time he invoked the Fifth Amendment, refusing to state whether he was then or had ever been a member of the Communist Party.

MAJOR WORKS

Ballets—With My Red Fires; Chronicle; Candide; Trend; Case History; Trojan Incident; Machine Ballet.

Chamber Music—2 string quartets; Piano Trio; Whimsy, for cello and piano (or violin and piano); Suite for Flute Solo; Three Canons, for woodwind; Divertissement, for flute, harp, and cello; New Dance, for violin and piano; Music for Voice and Flute (or two flutes); Duos for Three Woodwinds; Violin Sonatina; Music for Brass Choir; Piano Quintet; Nonet for Brass; Woodwind Quintet; Concerto for Piano and Woodwind Quintet; Variations, for violin and viola; Movement for Two Trumpets, Trombone, and Piano; Introduction and Fugue, for four cellos.

Choral Music—In Certainty of Song, cantata; Eternity; From Some Far Shore; Easter Passacaglia; Who Can Revoke?

Riisager

Orchestral Music—4 symphonies; American Polonaise; Rhapsody; Study in Sonority, for violins; Fantasy and Fugue, for organ and orchestra; Dichotomy, for chamber orchestra; Scherzo; Evocation, for percussion and strings; New Dance; Consummation; Canon and Fugue, for strings (also for large orchestra); Passacaglia and Fugue (also for band); Processional (also for band); Music for Orchestra; Variations for Piano and Orchestra; Variations for Violin, Viola, and Orchestra; Overture; Preamble and Fugue; Dance Rhythms; The Dying of the Light, for voice and orchestra; Festival Overture; Introduction and Fugue, for cello and orchestra; Variations, for violin and orchestra; Quintuple Jazz; Sinfonietta; Introduction and Fugue; Duo for Piano and Orchestra.

Piano Music—Scherzo, for two pianos; Evocation, for two pianos (also for piano, four hands); The Cry, for two pianos (or piano, four hands); New Dance, for two pianos (also piano solo); New and Old, twelve pieces; Variations, for two pianos.

Vocal Music—La Belle Dame sans Merci, for solo voices and instruments; Music for Voice and Flute; Two Bergerettes, for soprano (or tenor) and piano; A Shakespeare Sonnet; Ye Banks and Braes o' Bonnie Doon.

ABOUT

Rosenfeld, P., Discoveries of a Music Critic.

American Composers Alliance Bulletin, November 1956; Etude, October 1956; HiFi/Stereo Review, April 1968; Modern Music, November–December 1942, Winter 1946; Musical America, May 1955; Musical Quarterly, January 1950, July 1961; New York Times, April 9, 1961.

Knudåge Riisager
1897–

Knudåge Riisager was born in Port Kunda, Estonia, on March 6, 1897. His father was a successful Danish engineer. In 1900 the Riisagers returned to Denmark, where Knudåge received his early academic education and took violin lessons from Peder Moller. Riisager studied political economy at the University of Copenhagen, receiving his Bachelor of Arts degree in 1921. While attending the University, he studied composition with Otto Mallering, director of the Copenhagen Conservatory, and Peder Gram, a well-known composer. In these years Riisager began composition. He completed a string quartet which was introduced by the Peder Moller Quartet on November 10, 1919, and an orchestral overture, *Erasmus Montanus*, which was completed in 1920 and introduced four years later.

Upon graduation from the University of

Riisager: rē′ sä ēr

Copenhagen, Riisager went to Paris to continue his music study with Paul Le Flem and Albert Roussel. He was completely enthralled by the new currents in music that flowed so freely in Paris in the 1920's, and he paid two more visits to that city to keep in close contact with all the new developments. After his third stay in the French capital, Riisager was transformed from a traditionalist composer into a revolutionary one. He now became a passionate advocate of many of the new and advanced tendencies in contemporary music, not only in his own compositions but also in his critical writings for journals and newspapers. At first he aroused considerable opposition among leading Danish musicians; it was a number of years before his progressive attitudes were tolerated.

KNUDÅGE RIISAGER

Beginning with the *Introduzione di Traverso* and his first symphony—both written in 1925—Riisager began to make extensive use of polyrhythms and polytonality. This music was so complex in technique, and so brusque and harsh in sound, that audiences and critics rejected it. Nevertheless, recognition for Riisager was not altogether lacking, and in 1925 he received the Wilhelm Hansen Prize for composition. Favorable reviews came for his *Variations on a Theme by Mezangeau*, for orchestra in 1926, and for his *Shrove Time* overture, introduced in 1932. A piano sonata, completed in 1931, was heard in Copenhagen in 1932 and represented Denmark at the

468

festival of the International Society for Contemporary Music held at Florence on April 3, 1934.

Meanwhile, Riisager was earning his living as a government official, having become secretary of the Ministry of Finance in 1926 and in 1939 chief of the section. He resigned in 1950 to concentrate on composition. In 1956 he was appointed by the Ministry of Culture as director of the Copenhagen Conservatory, a post he has occupied since then. He is also the director of the Royal Opera Academy, a training center for opera singers.

In 1930 Riisager received the Ancker Endowment, enabling him to visit Leipzig and study counterpoint there with Hermann Grabner. Elements of baroque style now penetrated his austere modern idiom, though some of the advanced tendencies of twentieth century music were not abandoned. Within a classical structure, Riisager completed the Concertino for Five Violins and Piano and the Concerto for Trumpet and Strings. Both were heard at festivals of the International Society for Contemporary Music: the Concertino in Baden-Baden in April 1935; the Concerto in London on June 20, 1938. Even more successful was the ballet *Qarrtsiluni*, first heard as an orchestral suite in 1938 before the ballet itself was presented by the Royal Danish Opera on February 21, 1942. The term *qarrtsiluni* comes from the Eskimo language and means "something that is about to burst." The ballet text, set in Greenland, was based on *The Gift of the Feast* by Knud Rasmussen, the Arctic explorer. In his score, Riisager combined primitive Eskimo rhythms and melodies with sophisticated harmonies and orchestration. The music is in turn demoniac in its strength and ecstatic in its intensity. "The ballet," wrote Peter William, "is one of the most original and thrilling works I have seen in years . . . perhaps the most exciting work in the whole Danish repertory." It was successfully produced at the festival of the International Society for Contemporary Music at Palermo in 1949, at Covent Garden in London in 1952, and at the Paris Opéra in 1961.

In 1942 Riisager received a prize from the Danish Ministry of Education. The Nazi occupation of Denmark was responsible for bringing into Riisager's writing a strong national feeling. During the war he wrote the stirring *Danish Psalm*, to a sixteenth century text (first performance in Copenhagen on September 18, 1945); the *Summer Rhapsody*, based on Danish folk melodies; and a national *opera buffa*, *Susanne*, which was produced at the Copenhagen Royal Opera on January 7, 1950. "Such a change of style," wrote Sigurd Berg, "does not necessarily have to be an indication of artistic cleavage, but may be regarded as a slowly developing inner strength, anchored in the soil from which the best in Danish music has sprung."

Some of Riisager's most important music after World War II was for the ballet. His score for *Étude*, which the Royal Opera produced on January 15, 1948, was based on the music of Carl Czerny. This ballet has had wide acceptance, having been produced frequently at the Paris Opéra since 1952, by the London Festival Ballet in 1954, and by the American Ballet Theatre in 1963. It was on the program of the Munich Festival in 1963 and has found a permanent place in the repertory of the Dutch Ballet in Amsterdam.

Two other Riisager ballets have had extensive performances throughout Europe and the United States, both of them choreographed by Birgit Cullberg: *The Lady from the Sea* (1950) and *The Moon Reindeer* (1958). After being introduced by the Royal Opera in Copenhagen, both ballets were given by the American Ballet Theatre, the Royal Opera in Stockholm, the Oslo Opera, and the Cologne Opera. In addition to these scores Riisager arranged, orchestrated, and adapted Lully's opera-ballet *Le Triomphe de l'Amour* for production by the Royal Opera in Copenhagen in 1962.

From 1928 to 1962 Riisager was president of the Danish League of Composers. In 1961 he was named Commander of the Order of Dannebrog, by appointment of the King of Denmark.

MAJOR WORKS

Ballets—Benzin; Qarrtsiluni; Phoenix; Étude; The Lady from the Sea; The Moon Reindeer.

Chamber Music—6 string quartets; 2 violin sonatas; Sonata for Flute, Violin, Clarinet, and Cello; Music for Wind Quintet; Concertino for Five Violins and Piano; Serenade for Flute, Violin, and Cello; Concertino for Oboe, Clarinet, and Bassoon; Quartet for Flute, Oboe, Clarinet, and Bassoon; Divertimento, for flute, oboe, horn, and bassoon; Sonata for Two Violins; Piano Trio.

Rivier

Choral Music—Danish Psalm; Song for the Sun.

Opera—Susanne, comic opera.

Orchestral Music—4 symphonies; Erasmus Montanus, overture; Suite Dionysiaque, for chamber orchestra; Introduzione di Traverso; Variations on a Theme by Mezangeau; Shrove Time, overture; Suite, for small orchestra; Marche Tartare; Concertino for Trumpet and Strings; Little Overture, for strings; Primavera, concert overture; Sinfonia Concertante, for strings; Three Danish Carols; Partita; Targut Dance; Final Galop; Summer Rhapsody; Tivoli-Tivoli; Sinfonietta, for small orchestra; Archaeopteryx; Sinfonia Serena, for strings and tympani; Chaconne; Violin Concerto.

Piano Music—Quatre Épigrammes; Sonata; Two Pieces; The Merry Trumpet; Sonatine.

ABOUT

Berg, S., Knudåge Riisager.

Jean Rivier
1896–

Jean Rivier was born in Villemomble, near Paris, on July 21, 1896. Both parents were excellent musicians. His father was a flutist; his mother, a pianist. When Jean was still a boy, his family moved to the Latin Quarter of Paris. There Jean began his academic schooling. Though he started to play the cello and to compose when he was still quite young, Rivier had very little training, and for the most part had to shift for himself in his music-making.

The completion of his academic education coincided with the beginning of World War I and Rivier enlisted in the French Army. While serving at the front, he felt such an acute need for musical expression that he completed a cello sonata on whatever scraps of paper he could find. He was gassed in action and spent three years after his demobilization in army hospitals. For his bravery in action he was awarded the Croix de Guerre. By 1922 he had recovered sufficiently to enter the Paris Conservatory and receive his first formal instruction. He remained there four years, winning prizes in counterpoint and fugue as a pupil of Caussade.

His musical schooling over, he married Marie Peyrissac on February 16, 1920. He now began composition in earnest, and several important conductors soon became interested in him. Albert Wolff was responsible for Rivier's receiving his first public performance for an

Rivier: rē vyā´

orchestral work when the *Chant Funèbre* (1927) was heard at a concert of the Pasdeloup Orchestra in Paris in 1928. (It was repeated at the festival of the International Society for Contemporary Music at Liège on September 6, 1930.) Walter Straram and Pierre Monteux also gave important premières of Rivier's music: *Trois Pastorales* (1928); *Burlesque*, for violin and orchestra (1929); the orchestral overture *Don Quichotte* (1929); and *Adagio for Strings* (1930). The most significant as well as the most ambitious work of this period was his first symphony, in D major, heard in Paris on January 29, 1933, after which it was featured at the festival of the International Society for Contemporary Music held at Warsaw on April 14, 1939.

JEAN RIVIER

Together with Henri Barraud, Rivier helped found a "school" of young French composers who identified themselves as the "Triton." From 1936 to 1940, Rivier was chairman of the group. These young men chose to travel on the path of moderation—between the group that was writing in the twelve-tone system or in the mystical style of Messiaen on the one hand and the neoclassicists on the other. Actually, in the works Rivier completed as a member of the Triton, he achieved a compromise between impressionism and neoclassicism. In this vein he wrote *Psaume LVI*, for soprano, chorus, and orchestra (1937); the second and third symphonies (1937, 1938); the Violin Sonatina (1937); the second string quartet (1940); and the Piano Concerto in C major (1940).

The Third Symphony is characteristic. It was commissioned by the French government and introduced in Paris on November 25, 1940. Here all the principal thematic subjects utilize a single motive (a descending interval of a fifth). Pastoral moods alternate with vigorous ones within a soundly classical structure which includes a fugal passage in the finale. At turns romantic and dynamic, this symphony represents that middle-of-the-road policy which goes a long way towards explaining its popularity with audiences. In the United States it became one of Rivier's most frequently heard compositions, following its American première in Hartford, Connecticut, in 1939, Leon Barzin conducting.

If any principles govern Rivier's style, they are those of conciseness, economy, and objectivity—all-important elements in his creative process. He believes that a musical work must be only as long as its idea warrants—the shorter, the better. He avoids involved developments and elaborate recapitulations, preferring to state each idea succinctly and then progress to the next thought. His passion for brevity was once vividly revealed at a rehearsal of one of his trios, when Rivier continually deleted nonessentials from his music until the performing artists (the Pasquier Trio) were afraid that nothing would be left; thereafter, they rehearsed Rivier's works only in his absence.

"Jean Rivier's temperament," wrote Henri Sauguet, "dictates all manner of emotional gradations, from the climactic to the intimate and tender, and he is not notable for any special selectivity in his style, either idiomatically or formally. His formal métier is most unspecific: he will compose in any form from operetta to oratorio with equal assurance, following his own caprice and humor of the moment without inhibition."

Later important works by Rivier include a Requiem (1951), which was featured at the festival of Vichy in August 1952; and his sixth and seventh symphonies (1958, 1960), subtitled respectively *Les Présages* and *Les Contrastes*. The sixth, subtitled *Les Présages*, was introduced on December 11, 1958, and the seventh on January 9, 1962—both in Paris. To Antoine Goléa, the sixth symphony "shows

to what an extent its author is capable of self renewal in the direction of ever-growing concentration on the means of expression." The American première took place on March 3, 1967, with Georges Prêtre conducting the Philadelphia Orchestra.

In 1947 Rivier became a deputy for Darius Milhaud in the department of composition at the Paris Conservatory where, since 1962, he has been full professor of composition. He is a Chevalier of the Legion of Honor.

Rivier resides in a modern apartment, his home filled with exotic plants, paintings, and objets d'art. His wife is a talented musician and their son is a physician. Rivier has always been vitally interested in all the arts; indeed he has long felt that it is impossible to understand music maturely without an intimate acquaintance with the allied arts. He is an avid sportsman, interested in rugby, tennis, swimming, skiing, roller-skating, and ping-pong.

MAJOR WORKS

Ballet—Divertissement.

Chamber Music—2 string quartets; String Trio; Suite, for oboe, clarinet, and bassoon; Sonatina for Viola and Cello; Grave e Presto, for four saxophones; Improvisation et Finale, for oboe and piano.

Choral Music—Psaume LVI; Requiem.

Opera—Vénitienne, one-act operetta.

Orchestral Music—7 symphonies; 12 concertos; Chant Funèbre; Danse du Tchad; Trois Pastorales, for small orchestra; Burlesque, for violin and piano; Don Quichotte, overture; Adagio, for strings; Ouverture pour une Opérette Imaginaire; Le Voyage d'Urien; Paysage pour Jeanne d'Arc, symphonic tableau; Piano Concertino; Piano Concerto; Viola Concertino; Ballade des Amants Désespérés; Divertissement dans le Style Opérette for chamber orchestra; Rhapsodie Provençale; Violin Concerto; Ouverture pour un Drame; Concerto Brève, for piano and strings; Concerto for Saxophone, Trumpet, and Strings; Concerto for Flute and String Orchestra; Musique pour un Ballet; Concerto for Clarinet and Strings; Drames; Concerto for Strings and Percussion.

Piano Music—Cinq Mouvements Brefs; Musiques; Trois Pointes Sèches.

Vocal Music—Various songs for voice and piano.

ABOUT

Musical America, October 1948.

Ned Rorem
1923–

Ned Rorem was born in Richmond, Indiana, on October 23, 1923, of Norwegian heritage. He was raised as a Quaker. His boyhood and youth were spent in Chicago where he attended public schools and, from 1940 to 1942, Northwestern University. Even as a boy he showed an interest in music, making his first attempts at composition when he was nine. In Chicago he studied composition with Max Wald. "When I was young," he told an interviewer, "it was a toss-up whether I would be a composer or a writer, so I became a little of both." In 1942 he specialized in music after receiving a scholarship for the Curtis Institute in Philadelphia, from which he was graduated in 1947. From 1944 on, while continuing his music study, he lived in a small apartment on East 12th Street, New York. In 1947 he studied composition with Bernard Wagenaar at the Juilliard School of Music where he received a master's degree in music in 1949. During the summer of 1947 he attended the Berkshire Music Center at Tanglewood near Lenox, Massachusetts, as a pupil of Aaron Copland in composition. He also studied composition with Virgil Thomson, receiving lessons in return for his services as a copyist.

In 1948 he received the Music Libraries Association Award for his song "The Lordly Hudson," and a year later he was given the Gershwin Memorial Award for his Overture in C, which was performed by the New York Philharmonic. In the spring of 1949 he went to Paris where he remained during the next six years, except for intermittent vacations in Morocco. Encouragement came from various sources: from the Vicomtesse de Noailles, at whose eighteenth century mansion he frequently resided; from the winning of the Lili Boulanger Prize in 1950; from a Fulbright Fellowship in 1951–1952 for the study of composition with Arthur Honegger. And it also came from performances of his compositions. In 1951 his first symphony was introduced in Vienna; his *Six Irish Poems*, for voice and orchestra, was broadcast over the French radio by Nell Tangeman; his ballet *Melos* received the Prix de Biarritz; and his second piano sonata was introduced by Julius Katchen.

Encouragement brought on extraordinary creativity. Between the time he arrived in Paris and the end of 1951 he had produced a symphony, a string quartet, a piano sonata, violin sonata, a piano concerto, an opera, five song cycles, fifty songs, three ballets, and many other pieces. In 1952 a ballet, *Dorian Gray* (scenario

and choreography by Jean Marais) was introduced in Barcelona where, as he confesses, it "flopped ignominiously." In 1953 there took place in Paris a concert devoted entirely to his music. In 1954 he was presented with the Eurydice Choral Award.

NED ROREM

Ned Rorem first achieved recognition with his songs, and some critics stood ready to acclaim him as one of the leading songwriters of his time. Here is William Flanagan's description of Rorem's songs in his liner notes for a Columbia recording: "Rorem's music—his superb art songs, in particular—is *pretty*, terribly pretty. And the expressive intent that lies behind the merger of words and music is, almost invariably, immediate, clear and above all, right. And while no one who knows the composer's music at all could miss its singularly personal tone, the musical language is direct, uncomplicated, even . . . familiar."

Rorem produced a whole library of songs which have been extensively performed and recorded. This sometimes obscures the fact that he has worked just as often, and just as successfully, in the larger forms.

Following his return to the United States in 1955, the Louisville Orchestra presented on May 28 the world première of his *Designs*, for orchestra. His second symphony was introduced in La Jolla, California, on August 5, 1956; his third symphony was performed by the New York Philharmonic on April 19, 1959,

Leonard Bernstein conducting. A major choral work, *The Poet's Requiem*, was heard in New York on February 15, 1957; its text was eight contemporary poems. A tone poem, *Eagles*, was performed by the Philadelphia Orchestra on October 23, 1959. And an opera, *The Robbers*, was produced in New York on April 14, 1958. Meanwhile, in 1957, he received a Guggenheim Fellowship.

In his fully mature compositions, Rorem is the follower of no system. He is, as Dillard Gunn once said of him, "the first successful modern romanticist"; he places importance on both lyricism and emotion. Rorem himself has explained in his book *Paris Diary*: "After ten years of chattering every known musical speech, of imitating now one and then another school, of wanting to become famous by writing like the famous, I've decided now to write again the way I did at age eleven when I knew no one: my music from my heart with my own influences. It's important to be 'better than' not 'different from' and everyone has forgotten how to write nice tunes." He also said: "If I am a significant American composer it is because I've never tried to be New."

In 1960 Rorem was commissioned by the New York City Opera, on a Ford Foundation grant, to write an opera. Rorem planned to adapt Du Bose Heyward's *Mamba's Daughters*, but by the time he had finished one sixth of his score, Heyward's widow died, complicating the problem of acquiring the necessary rights. He then turned to an original libretto entitled *The Cave*. "After I had finished the whole thing," Rorem confesses, "nobody knew what it was about, including me." It was shelved in favor of Colette's *Chéri*, but the rights to that were not available. Thus, after a long, circuitous route, Rorem arrived at August Strindberg's *Miss Julie*, the libretto prepared by Kenward Elmslie. "Kenward," explains Rorem, "reduced the play to a skeleton for which music could provide the flesh. He split the one-act play down the middle to make a two-act opera and underplayed the master-slave theme in favor of sensuality. We added four subsidiary characters and a chorus. Otherwise it is pure Strindberg."

Miss Julie was produced in New York on November 4, 1965. Harriett Johnson in the New York *Post* called it "the work of an experienced, sensitive composer" who during the

first act "knowingly blends realism with dreaming." Nevertheless, Miss Johnson felt that the score as a whole was "not strong enough to stand up to Strindberg." In the New York *Times* Harold C. Schonberg complained of "blandness. ... All was very polite and innocuous."

From 1959 to 1961 Rorem was composer in residence and Slee Professor in composition at the University of Buffalo. In the 1965–1966 academic year he was composer in residence at Utah University.

In 1966 Ned Rorem's *Paris Diary*, an account of some of his experiences in Paris between 1949 and 1955, was published. In the preface to this book, Robert Phelps said this about its author: "He is gifted, good looking, and in the circles in which he moves, celebrated for both. Besides being a composer, he is an imaginative social climber . . . an earnest narcissist. He is also an intellectual, a hero worshipper, an excessive drinker of alcohol, and a lover." Other books by Rorem are *The New York Diary, Music from Inside Out*, and *Music and People*.

MAJOR WORKS

Ballets—Melos; Ballet for Jerry; Dorian Gray; Early Voyagers; Eleven by Eleven; Antics for Acrobats; Excursions; Lovers.

Chamber Music—2 string quartets; Concertino da Camera, for harpsichord and seven instruments; Mountain Song, for flute and piano; Violin Sonata; Lento for Strings; Sinfonia, for fifteen wind instruments; Pilgrims, for strings; Eleven Studies, for eleven players; Trio for Flute, Cello, and Piano; Lovers, narrative for harpsichord, oboe, cello, and percussion; Trio, for flute, cello, and piano.

Choral Music—The 70th Psalm; The Ascension; Paris Journal; The Poet's Requiem; A Sermon on Miracles; Two Psalms and a Proverb; Votive Mass of the Holy Spirit; He Shall Rule, for chorus and organ; various works for a cappella chorus.

Operas—A Childhood Miracle, for six singers and thirteen instruments; The Robbers; Miss Julie; Last Day, monodrama.

Orchestral Music—3 symphonies; 2 piano concertos; Designs; Eagles; Ideas; Lions; Six Irish Poems, for voice and orchestra; Sun, for female voice and large orchestra; Water Music; Ideas for Easy Orchestra.

Piano Music—3 sonatas; Toccata; A Quiet Afternoon; Barcarolles; Sicilienne, for two pianos; Burlesque; Slow Waltz.

Vocal Music—Penny Arcade; Flight for Heaven; Another Sleep; To a Young Girl; Cycle of Holy Songs; From an Unknown Past; Eclogues; Poèmes pour le Paix; Anacreontics; King Midas; Three Poems of Tennyson; Poems of Love and the Rain; Two Poems of Plato; Hearing; Some Trees; numerous individual songs for voice and piano.

Rosenberg

ABOUT

North, W. S., Ned Rorem: A Twentieth-Century Song Composer; Rorem, N., New York Diary; Rorem, N., Paris Diary.

Opera News, November 6, 1965.

Hilding Rosenberg
1892–

Hilding Constantin Rosenberg was born in Bosjökloster, Sweden, on June 21, 1892, the son of a gardener on a country estate. Much of his boyhood was spent helping his father tend the grounds and gardens. The boy's first musical impressions came from hearing his mother sing and were reinforced when he joined the church choir at the age of eight; he soon earned the privilege of ringing the tower bells on Sundays and holy days. His musical gifts were revealed by his ability to play the violin and piano without the benefit of a single lesson, and despite the lack of formal training he developed into a capable musician. In 1909 he passed examinations for organist and precantor at Kalmar, impressing his examiners particularly with his facility at improvising on given themes. Soon afterward his family moved to Trelleborg, where he played the violin in an orchestra, gave concerts on the piano, and wrote some functional compositions.

He was aware of his technical limitations, and in 1914 he applied for admission to the Stockholm Conservatory, presenting as his credentials a recently completed violin sonata. He was accepted, and began to study composition there with Ellberg. He had the good fortune at the time to make an impression on one of the Conservatory professors, Richard Andersson, who took him under his wing. Andersson introduced Rosenberg to the great musical literature of the past and present and saw to it that Rosenberg became acquainted with philosophy and classical writings. Another significant influence on Rosenberg was his friendship with Vilhelm Stenhammar, a leading figure in Swedish music.

Hearing Sibelius' Fourth Symphony impelled Rosenberg to write a symphony of his own. He did not like the final product, even though Stenhammer found much to commend,

---

Rosenberg: rō′ zĕn bĕr y′

and discarded three of the movements completely. However, he permitted the slow movement to survive as an independent composition under the title of its tempo marking, *Adagio non Troppo*. He was more satisfied with his next symphony (1919), which he designated as his first. The discarded work had been written in imitation of Sibelius, but the Symphony No. 1 was derivative from the German post-Romantics.

HILDING ROSENBERG

Instinctively Rosenberg was unhappy with the kind of music he was producing. He sensed that there were fresher, newer ways of writing music. To seek out what the younger composers of other lands were doing, he went to Dresden in 1920. There he studied theory and counterpoint with Buchmayer and Striegler, and there he first heard and became impressed with the atonal compositions of Schoenberg, which opened up new worlds for him. From Dresden, Rosenberg proceeded to Paris. There he became familiar with other advanced musical tendencies of the time and was particularly influenced by Stravinsky. From that point on, Rosenberg abandoned his romantic compositions to search for a new, fresh musical language.

He assumed an advanced style of writing for the first time in his first string quartet (1920). How revolutionary this work sounded to Swedish ears can best be gauged by a short review that appeared after the première performance: "With the last item, the portals of Hell were opened for the whole audience. Neither personal authority nor public sympathy can be increased by four performers impersonating inmates of Konradsberg [a mental hospital in Stockholm] and interpreting barbarous and obscure fantasies of a fifth."

But Rosenberg still was not satisfied with his music. He wanted simplicity, lucidity, compression. Without abandoning such progressive tendencies as atonality or linear counterpoint, he pursued conciseness within modest structures. It was in this style that he produced his first mature works, and the first to gain recognition. They included the eloquent *Sinfonia da Chiesa*, Nos. 1 and 2 (1923–1924); the first piano sonata (1923); the second and third string quartets (1924, 1926); the majestic *Sinfonia Grave*, a composition he had begun in 1928 but did not complete until seven years later; and the *Sinfonia Concertante*, heard at the festival of the International Society for Contemporary Music held in Paris on June 22, 1937.

For a brief period after returning to Sweden from Paris, Rosenberg was a music critic in Gothenburg. Then he settled permanently in Stockholm, where from 1932 to 1934 he was a coach and assistant conductor at the Royal Opera; in 1934 he became first conductor.

Always a devotee of the stage, Rosenberg began to write incidental music for various plays (including the Greek dramas *Medea*, *Antigone*, and *Oedipus Rex*), and he composed his first opera and his first ballet. The opera was *Journey to America*, an *opera buffa* about a young Swede come to America to make his fortune and then returning home to claim his sweetheart. The première took place in Stockholm on November 24, 1932. In 1938 Rosenberg completed a score for a fantastic ballet, *Orpheus in Town*, which received its première by the Stockholm Opera in 1938 and proved his greatest success up to that time. The ballet scenario describes how Carl Milles' famous statue of Orpheus, which stands outside the Stockholm Concert Hall, comes to life and goes in search of his Eurydice; he believes he has found her in the form of a beautiful society lady at a night club. A seven-movement orchestral suite from the ballet score has been widely performed throughout Europe and the United States.

The music for this opera and ballet, as Andrew McCredie has written in *Musikverein*, "quickly established those features which were to be so characteristic of Rosenberg's later operas—an effective vocal declamatory style, a resourceful use of orchestral forces, of however limited dimensions, a real sense of harmonic color and a flare for beautiful choral writing."

Of his later works Rosenberg's two most successful operas were *The Island of Bliss* (produced by the Stockholm Opera on February 1, 1945) and *The Portrait* (first performed at the Stockholm Opera on March 22, 1956). The first was a fantasy combining legend, folklore, mysticism, and symbolism. It provided, as Olin Downes reported, "much opportunity for dancing, exotic scenery and vocal display as well as dramatic action that passes in a never-never land of illusions and deceptions in the search for love." *The Portrait* was based on a tale by Gogol in which a disillusioned young painter sells his soul for money, only to end impoverished and mad. This score, we learn from Ingrid Sandberg, is more distinguished for its symphonic writing and impressive choruses than for its lyricism: "Fine orchestral music is contained in all the short interludes separating the scenes. Due to the dramatic intensity of the libretto, the composer has set much of the text in a near recitativo style which allows the words to stand clear."

All his life, Rosenberg had been drawn to religious subjects, an area in which he produced some of his most ambitious writing. *The Holy Night* (1936) is an exquisite setting of poems by Gullberg; this work became an annual Christmas feature over the Swedish Radio. Symphony No. 4, *The Revelation of St. John*, was described by Moses Pergament as one of Rosenberg's "mightiest and most comprehensively authoritative compositions." Pergament adds that the "apocalyptic visions are arrayed in musical apparel of convincing dramatic effectiveness. The work also contains a large number of chorales for a cappella choir, as exemplary in their linear purity as in their original but entirely ecclesiastical harmonic style, not to mention their great atmospheric value. I do not hesitate to describe this work as one of the most significant in the international musical literature of the twentieth century." On May 11, 1948, during his first visit to the United States, Rosenberg directed the American première of this fourth symphony in Chicago.

The opera-oratorio *Joseph and His Brethren*, derived from the epic novel by Thomas Mann, is of even more expansive design than the fourth symphony: it is made up of four oratorios which require eight hours for performance. "A whole world takes place in this music," says Pergament, "just as it did in the poetic work: a world of thought and dreams, experience and wisdom, of good and evil wills. It is a world whose stupendous radius and teeming life give a good idea of the extent of the spiritual evolution which must lie behind the composer's determination to express all this in music." Rosenberg himself conducted the world première of the final portion of the oratorio in Stockholm on March 23, 1948.

The line of Rosenberg's creative development can clearly be traced in his string quartets, beginning with his initial break with romanticism and his excursion into experimental areas with his first quartet, and concluding with his later quartets, written in the twelve-tone system—the first time Rosenberg employed this technique. The sixth string quartet (1953) received a prize after being performed at the festival of the International Society for Contemporary Music in Stockholm in June 1956. Then in the spring of 1958 the Swedish Broadcasting Corporation commissioned Rosenberg to create a mammoth chamber music project: six quartets. He completed the assignment in 1959 and the entire cycle was heard over the Swedish Radio. "In these six quartets," says Alf Thor in *Musikverein*, "Rosenberg meditates, broods, plays, propounds theses, appeals, and provokes. It is a richly flowing music, spontaneous, strong in form—music in extended strands, delineated with expression, grace and an ever untiring artistic dedication. . . . Every quartet is unique through its message, but technique has not influenced his language; his idiom, countenance and gestures remained unchanged."

In 1957 Rosenberg received the honorary degree of Doctor of Music from Uppsala University.

MAJOR WORKS

Ballet—Orpheus in Town.

Chamber Music—12 string quartets; Sonata for Solo Violin; Trio, for flute, violin, and viola; Suite in D major, for violin and piano; Sonatina for Flute and Piano; Violin Sonata; Trio, for oboe, clarinet, and bassoon.

Choral Music—The Holy Night; Golgotha, oratorio; Joseph and His Brethren, four opera-oratorios.

Operas—Journey to America, opera buffa; Marionettes; The Two Princesses; The Island of Bliss; The Portrait.

Orchestral Music—6 symphonies; 4 orchestral concertos; various concertos for solo instruments and orchestra (violin; trumpet; violin, cello, and piano; cello; viola); Sinfonia da Chiesa, Nos. 1 and 2; Threnody for V. Stenhammar; Sinfonia Concertante; Overtura Piccola; Overtura Bianca-Nera; The Louisville Concerto.

Piano Music—4 sonatas.

ABOUT

Pergament, M., Hilding Rosenberg: A Giant of Modern Music.

Music and Letters (London), July 1947; Musikverein (Stockholm), No. 3, 1960.

Albert Roussel
1869–1937

Albert Charles Paul Marie Roussel was born in Tourcoing, France, on April 5, 1869. Both parents died while he was still a child, and he was raised first by a grandfather and then by an aunt. At his aunt's house, when he was about eleven, he was given his first music lessons: instruction at the piano from the organist of the Notre Dame church in Tourcoing. But from the time he spent his holidays at a sea resort in Belgium, Roussel's first love was the sea, his crowning ambition to become a sailor. In 1884 he entered the Stanislas College in Paris to prepare for entrance into the naval academy. There he was a brilliant student in mathematics, a subject which continued to fascinate him for the rest of his life. During that time he attended opera for the first time, and he was initiated by the local organist into the instrumental literature of Bach, Mozart, and Beethoven. In 1887 he enrolled as a cadet in the Naval School at Brest. After completing his nautical studies, he sailed for a number of years on various gunboats or cruisers, the last time as a sublieutenant on the gunboat Styx bound for Siam. His experiences aboard ship to foreign ports awakened his love for nature, and he often said later that his best musical ideas

Roussel: rōō sĕl'

came to him in the open spaces of the country.

He was already beginning to write music. His first composition to be performed was an Andante, for string trio and organ, given in Cherbourg on December 25, 1892. By 1894 he had decided to resign his naval commission, abandon the sea, and begin music study in earnest. He rented a small flat in Paris where he began a period of instruction in organ and theory with Eugène Gigout. Under Gigout's guidance he completed two madrigals. They were submitted in 1897 in a competition sponsored by the Société des Compositeurs, and both were selected to share first prize. On May 3, 1898, Roussel led the première of these choral pieces. That same year also saw the publication of his first opus, *Des Heures Passent*, a suite for piano.

ALBERT ROUSSEL

In 1898 Roussel began a nine-year period of study at the Schola Cantorum where he came under the influence of Vincent d'Indy. Other professors there criticized him for insisting on breaking the established rules of composition. Nevertheless, guided and inspired by d'Indy, Roussel was a brilliant student. In 1902, while still an undergraduate, he was appointed professor of counterpoint, a post he occupied until 1914.

He was making noticeable headway as a composer. Much of the chamber music he wrote while attending the Schola Cantorum he later destroyed, but a piano trio written in 1902 became his Opus No. 2. Several of his orchestral pieces were performed under Alfred Cortot's direction at concerts organized to give public presentations of new compositions, and in 1906 the critic Jean Marnold wrote an enthusiastic review in the *Mercure de France* of Roussel's *Rustiques*, a piano suite.

Roussel was graduated from the Schola Cantorum in 1908, a year which also saw his marriage, on April 7, to Blanche Preisach, and, on March 22, the first public presentation at a Concert Populaire in Brussels of his first symphony, *Le Poème de la Forêt*. Impressionist in style, this composition clearly reflected the composer's intense love of nature.

During the winter of 1909–1910, Roussel yielded once again to the call of the sea. This time he and his wife sailed as passengers for the East, where he visited India, Ceylon, Singapore, and Saigon. Exploring exotic places provided him with a new direction and new subject matter for his compositions. Oriental backgrounds and elements of oriental music now became tools of his creative trade. The first work to reveal this new tendency was a symphonic triptych with chorus and solo voices, *Évocations*, each movement of which described a different place in India. Heard in Paris on May 18, 1912, at a concert of the Société Nationale, *Évocations* was an outstanding success. Georges Jean-Aubry later wrote: "*Évocations* is one of seven or eight symphonic works composed during the past twenty years which will insure, for a long time to come, the future of French music."

The ballet-opera *Padmâvatî* (vocal score completed in 1914) was another work inspired by the trip to India. While exploring some ruins in that country, Roussel came upon the setting where, in the thirteenth century, the legendary tragedy of the Hindu heroine Padmâvatî was supposed to have taken place. The story made such an impression on him that he asked Louis Laloy to adapt it as a libretto. The ballet-opera was produced at the Paris Opéra on June 1, 1923—almost a decade after it was written. Basil Deane described it as a "spectacle containing related dramatic scenes," and commented that "accepted on this basis, *Padmâvatî* is an impressive achievement. Roussel performs the difficult feat of presenting this world, remote not only in time and place, but also in its assumptions and attitudes, with sincerity and conviction."

But even before he had begun to work intensively on his ballet-opera, Roussel had completed the score for a ballet which is now his most celebrated composition: *Le Festin de l'Araignée* (*The Feast of the Spider*), scenario by Count Gilbert de Voisins inspired by Fabre's *Studies of Insect Life*. The ballet was presented on April 3, 1913, at the Théâtre des Arts, which had commissioned it; it was immediately successful. An orchestral suite prepared by the composer (and heard for the first time in New York on October 23, 1914, Walter Damrosch conducting) has become one of Roussel's most frequently heard works. "Using a miniature orchestra," wrote Edward Burlingame Hill, "he has yet found the means to illustrate the action, characterize its personages with delicate and pungent humor and yet rise to tense moments."

During World War I, Roussel tried to reenlist in the navy but was turned down for reasons of health. He did manage eventually to get a commission in the artillery and for a while served as a transport officer at Verdun. These war experiences further undermined his health and brought about his release from the service in January 1918.

He acquired a villa in Vasterival, perched on a promontory on the Normandy coast, with a view of his beloved sea. This became his yearly summer retreat for the rest of his life; here he did some of his most important creative work. His reputation was growing rapidly and some of his compositions were heard at festivals of the International Society for Contemporary Music in the period between 1923 and 1925. His Second Symphony, in B-flat major, was given a successful première in Paris on March 4, 1922. On June 1, 1923, the première of the ballet-opera *Padmâvatî* finally took place, at the Paris Opéra. An all-Roussel concert was heard at the Paris Festival of the Société Musicale Indépendante in 1925 and repeated in London.

After 1925 Roussel's style went through another major transformation. He discarded once and for all his early interest in impressionism and his subsequent partiality for orientalism and became a neoclassicist. In this idiom he produced one of his finest works, the Suite in F major, an orchestral work written for and dedicated to Serge Koussevitzky. Koussevitzky led its world première with the Boston Symphony on January 21, 1927. Within such baroque structures as the prelude, sarabande, and gigue, Roussel created music which effectively alternated energetic movement with graceful, restrained episodes. Here, as in his subsequent neoclassical works, Roussel carefully resolved, as Arthur Hoérée pointed out, "the classical problem of equilibrium between form and style. His constant evolution, a sign of vitality, does not preclude a fundamental unity which is in itself esthetic."

Roussel's sixtieth birthday in 1929 was celebrated in Paris with a four-concert festival of his works. At the same time the Opéra-Comique revived the ballet *Le Festin de l'Araignée*, and *La Revue Musicale* devoted an entire issue to him. All this helped to emphasize that Roussel was now a major creative figure in French music, a fact recognized by the Santa Cecilia Academy in Rome in 1931 when it conferred membership upon him, and by the Senate of Hamburg, Germany, when in 1933 it awarded him the Brahms Centenary Medal. Roussel's eminence was also recognized by Koussevitzky, who commissioned him to write a symphony commemorating the fiftieth anniversary of the Boston Symphony. This symphony—Roussel's Third, in G minor—was successfully introduced in Boston on October 24, 1930. The composer, on his first visit to the United States, was in the audience. He had come on an invitation from Mrs. Elizabeth Sprague Coolidge to participate in a festival of chamber music in Chicago where his Trio, for flute, viola, and cello (op. 40), was being presented.

The year 1931 brought further successes. On May 22, 1931, a new Roussel ballet, *Bacchus et Ariane*, his first stage work on a classical subject, was produced at the Paris Opéra. Henri Prunières described it as "one of the happiest and most original productions of the Gallic school in this genre during these many years. It gripped us at the very opening measures and did not cease to hold us until the very end. The hand of the master in full possession of his powers is felt here." From this score, as previously from *Le Festin de l'Araignée*, the composer extracted basic episodes for a symphonic suite whose first performance was given in Paris on November 26, 1936, Charles Münch conducting.

With the favorable reactions to *Bacchus et Ariane* still ringing in his ears, Roussel paid a visit to London to attend the British première of his *Psalm 80* at the festival of the International Society for Contemporary Music on July 28. This psalm, one of its composer's most distinguished works for chorus, had a resounding success in London, just as it had enjoyed one at its world première in Paris on April 25, 1929.

Roussel's interest in *la musique pure*, or "pure music," as the French liked to describe classicism and objectivity, was emphasized in the major compositions that came towards the end of his life: the D major string quartet (1932); the Prelude and Fugue, for piano (1934); the Sinfonietta, for string orchestra (1934); the Fourth Symphony (1934); and Roussel's second ballet on a classic subject, *Aeneas*, completed in 1935 and produced in Brussels on July 31 of the same year, Hermann Scherchen conducting.

The Fourth Symphony, in A major, one of its composer's masterworks, was introduced in Paris on October 19, 1935, at a Pasdeloup concert, Albert Wolff conducting. The audience reaction was so enthusiastic that the scherzo movement had to be repeated. It was frequently played in the United States following the American première in Boston late in 1935, Koussevitzky conducting. Albert Bernard spoke of the symphony's "perfect balance" and "its eloquence as considered as it is expressive." He added: "Force, vigor, sanity, act as ballast in a light and translucent edifice of sound. It is hard to tell what draws one most in this work of art—its luminous simplicity, its absence of artifice, its qualities of wit, of emotion, the certainty of its metier, or the aptness of its thought."

Roussel remained productive to the end of his days. Not even a serious illness (pneumonia) kept him from his work bench. In 1936 he completed the *Rhapsodie Flamande* and the Cello Concertino. His last complete work, the String Trio, op. 58, was finished in July 1937. He was working on still another trio, this time for woodwinds, when death came in Royan on August 23, 1937. Four days later, following his wishes, he was buried in a cemetery not far from his Vasterival villa. A half year after his death, on April 4, 1938, an all-Roussel concert was given in Paris to honor his memory. His last opus, the string trio, was heard for the first time at this concert.

Roussel was the president of the music section of the Paris International Exhibition and a member of the French committee of the International Society for Contemporary Music. He remained passionately devoted to the promotion of new music to the end. Though weak and ill, he insisted in 1937 on studying all the French scores submitted for the International Society for Contemporary Music festival. It was characteristic of his unselfishness that when an attempt was made to include his Fourth Symphony at the 1937 festival he stoutly refused to give permission, insisting that his place on the program belonged to some younger and less famous French composer who was in need of encouragement and recognition.

Here is Hoérée's description of Roussel: "I seem to see before me a portrait of Velázquez. A long face, straight forehead, small keen eyes, thin nose, drooping moustache and short pointed beard, courteous manners, moreover, and a profound aristocracy."

In his biography of Roussel, Basil Deane detailed a typical day for the composer: "Roussel rose early and began either by playing the piano (preferably the music of his favorite composers, Bach and Chopin) or by tackling a mathematical problem. After that, the morning belonged to composition. Roussel liked to spend the afternoon outdoors, in long walks near the sea if he was at his summer villa. Winter time was spent in Paris or in travels."

Besides mathematics Roussel was fascinated by astronomy and enjoyed reading scientific treatises in other areas as well. "I love the sea, forests, life in the country in preference to the enervating life of cities," he once revealed. "I also love to discover in old cities, treasures which their artists of many centuries ago have left behind as a heritage."

MAJOR WORKS

Ballets—Le Festin de l'Araignée (The Feast of the Spider); Bacchus et Ariane; Aeneas.

Chamber Music—2 violin sonatas; Joueurs de Flûte, for flute and piano; Duo for Bassoon and Cello; Serenade, for flute, violin, viola, cello, and harp (or piano); Trio, for flute, viola, and cello; String Quartet in D major; Trio for Strings.

Choral Music—Two Madrigals; Évocations; Madrigal aux Muses; Le Bardit des Francs; Psalm 80.

Operas—Padmâvatî, opera-ballet; La Naissance de la Lyre, one-act opera; Le Testament de la Tante Caroline, comic opera.

Rubbra

Orchestral Music—4 symphonies; Pour une Fête de Printemps, tone poem; Suite in F major; Piano Concerto in G major; Concerto for Small Orchestra; Petite Suite; Sinfonietta, for strings; Rhapsodie Flamande; Cello Concertino.

Piano Music—Des Heures Passent; Rustiques; Sonatina; Prelude and Fugue; Trois Pièces.

Vocal Music—Odes Anacréontiques; Jazz dans la Nuit; Deux Idylles; Mélodies; Poèmes Chinois; various individual songs for voice and piano.

ABOUT

Bernard, R., Albert Roussel; Deane, B., Albert Roussel; Demuth, N., Albert Roussel: A Study; Hoérée, A., Albert Roussel; Pincherle, M., Albert Roussel.

Modern Music, November–December 1937; Musical Quarterly, October 1938; La Revue Musicale (Paris), Roussel Issue, May–June 1929.

Edmund Rubbra
1901–

Edmund Rubbra was born in Northampton, England, on May 23, 1901, to a family of modest means. His father was a laborer who, at the time of Edmund's birth, was employed in a factory. Both parents loved music; his mother was for many years a leading soprano in a choir in Northampton. She gave Edmund his first piano lessons when he was eight; when he was eleven he made his first attempts at composition. Music soon became such a passion with the boy that whenever he could accumulate a few shillings he would spend it on sheet music, particularly the works of his two favorite composers, Debussy and Cyril Scott.

In his fourteenth year, Edmund was compelled by the straitened financial condition of his family to leave school and find a job. He became an office boy in a shoe factory, later a clerk in a railway office. His spare time was always filled with music study, mainly without professional guidance, and with writing compositions. When he was fifteen, he set to music several poems by Sir Walter Scott and even made plans to write an opera based on *The Lady of the Lake*; in the latter attempt he was frustrated by his inadequate technique.

In 1916 Rubbra gave a piano recital in Northampton devoted entirely to Cyril Scott's compositions. Scott heard about the performance and offered to teach Rubbra composition. Rubbra took advantage of this generous offer,

Rubbra: roo ′brĕ

making regular journeys from Northampton to London once every two weeks over a period of almost two years. Through Scott, Rubbra came to know Evlyn Howard Jones, a distinguished pianist, who in 1919 encouraged Rubbra to apply for a scholarship in composition at Reading University. Rubbra supplemented this study with lessons in piano with Evlyn Howard Jones and in composition with Gustav Holst. Holst proved a particularly decisive force in Rubbra's development at this time. One year later, Rubbra was awarded an open composition scholarship at the Royal College of Music, where he remained for four years, a pupil of Vaughan Williams and John Ireland.

EDMUND RUBBRA

After leaving the Royal College of Music, Rubbra settled in a small town in the English countryside to devote himself to composition. His first opus, *The Secret Hymnody*, for chorus, came in 1921, followed by a number of songs, several more compositions for chorus, and *Double Fugue* for orchestra (1924). A piano concerto (1931), his first string quartet (1933), and his first symphony (1936) revealed not only increasing sureness in the handling of large forms but also an enrichment of melodic imagination and lyrical expressiveness and a growing skill in polyphonic writing.

In 1933 Rubbra married Antoinette Chaplin, a French violinist; they have two children. Four years after his marriage, he received his first recognition as composer when he was

480

given the Collard Fellowship of the Worshipful Company of Musicians. During World War II he served first in the Royal Artillery, then in the Army Music Unit. After the war he gave numerous performances over the radio and in concerts with the Rubbra-Gruenberg-Pleeth Trio. In 1947 he was appointed lecturer in music at Oxford. A year later he joined the Roman Catholic Church and assumed the second Christian name of Dominic. Rubbra has received several honorary degrees, and in 1963 he was elected Fellow of Worcester College at Oxford.

Rubbra's most distinguished works are his symphonies and concertos. His first symphony was introduced on April 30, 1937, by the BBC Symphony. The same orchestra presented his second symphony on December 16, 1938. Here certain stylistic traits, characteristic of later works, are already evident, such as his interest in contrapuntal methods and his partiality for conciseness and precision in his writing. These two symphonies, Arthur Hutchings has noted, "show the composer at great labor not to overcrowd his canvas, to write contrapuntally, but in large, gracious periods which allow certain moments to stand out as high spots."

There is even greater concentration in his fourth and fifth symphonies (1941 and 1948 respectively). But this music does not lack emotional content. "Now and again there comes a work with the power to make one fall in love with music all over again," wrote Herbert Howells in a letter to Rubbra. "In such a mood I found myself when listening to your symphony." He was talking about the fifth, which Wilfred H. Mellers regards as "the culmination" of Rubbra's symphonic output. "While the clarity of the third and fourth had not been achieved without some sacrifice of the intensity and grandeur of the second," says Mellers, "in the fifth, Rubbra has written a work which expresses an experience as complex as that of the second, with a lyrical lucidity comparable with that of the third and the fourth."

Rubbra's style has often been modeled, though more instinctively than consciously, after the lyrical polyphony and free rhythms of the Elizabethan composers. If he is faithful to any belief it is in the "generating power of melody," as he wrote to the editor of this book,

"and in the diatonic system that the Western European music has used for centuries." But he took pains to emphasize that he is by no means a reactionary.

Rubbra's concerto literature embraces works for the piano, the viola, the violin, and the cello. Mellers remarks that in his concerto writing, Rubbra does not follow the classical traditions of engaging the soloist and the orchestra in "a quasi-dramatic dialogue." Instead, Rubbra assigns to his solo instrument the task of acting "as the mainspring of the lyrical impulse."

In conjunction with the American première of Rubbra's Viola Concerto, which William Primrose had commissioned in 1952 and introduced in London on April 15, 1953, Rubbra paid his first visit to the United States in the fall of 1959. At that time Eric Salzman described him as "a short, bearded, gray and benign-looking man." Rubbra has revealed that his extra-musical interests include gardening, painting, and the reading of poetry and of books on philosophy and general literature.

MAJOR WORKS

Ballet—Prism.

Chamber Music—3 string quartets; 2 violin sonatas; Five Spenser Sonnets, for tenor and string quartet; Cello Sonata; The Buddha, suite for flute, oboe, violin, viola, and cello; Lyric Movement, for string quartet and piano; Piano Trio; Fantasia on a Theme by Machaut, for recorder (or flute), string quartet, and harpsichord (or piano); Two Sonnets by William Alabaster, for baritone (or contralto), violin, and piano; Cantata Pastorale, for high voice, treble recorder, harpsichord, and cello; Oboe Sonata; Variations on a Phrygian Theme, for solo violin; Meditation on a Byzantine Hymn, for unaccompanied viola; Veni Creator Spiritus, for voice and brass.

Choral Music—Madrigals, motets; Missa Cantuariensis; The Morning Watch, motet; Magnificat; The Dark Night of the Soul; Missa in Honorem Sancti Dominici; Te Deum; Tenebrae, Nine Lamentations of the Soul; Festival Gloria; Lauda Sion; Autumn; Cantata di Camera Crucifixus Pro Nobis; The Beatitudes.

Opera—Bee-Bee-Bei.

Orchestral Music—7 symphonies; 2 piano concertos; concertos for various solo instruments and orchestra (viola; violin; cello); Double Fugue; Triple Fugue; Sinfonia Concertante, for piano and orchestra; Rhapsody, for violin and orchestra; Fantasy for violin and orchestra; Improvisations on Virginal Pieces by Farnaby; Soliloquy, for cello, strings, two horns, and tympani; Festival Overture; Five Medieval Latin Lyrics, for baritone and string orchestra; Improvisation, for violin and orchestra.

Piano Music—Introduction and Fugue; Introduction, Aria, and Fugue (also for harpsichord).

Vocal Music—Rune of Hospitality; A Duan of Barra; Soontree, a lullaby; Three Psalms; The Jade Mountain, five songs to Chinese words; Salve Regina, for counter-tenor (or contralto, or baritone) and harpsichord (or piano, or organ); various individual songs for voice and piano.

ABOUT

Bacharach, A. L. (ed.), British Music of Our Times; Frank, A., Modern British Composers; Mellers, W. H., Studies in Contemporary Music.

Musical Quarterly, January 1942; Musical Times (London), February–March, 1945.

Carl Ruggles
1876–

Carl Ruggles was born on March 11, 1876, in Marion, Massachusetts. He is a descendant of New England whalers and seafaring folk; Ruggles Street in Boston is named after one of his ancestors.

At an early age Ruggles was taught the violin. He was a prodigy, and at the age of nine, dressed in short velvet pants and a white shirt with Buster Brown collar, he gave a private performance for President Cleveland. After studying with Joseph Claus and Christian Timner, former concertmaster of the Concertgebouw Orchestra of Amsterdam, Ruggles went to Boston. There he took courses in music with Walter Spalding and John Knowles Paine. On April 27, 1908, he married Charlotte Snell. While pursuing his music studies, Ruggles supported himself and his wife by playing the violin in theatre orchestras and tutoring students for their entrance examinations at Harvard.

In 1912 Ruggles went to Minnesota. There he founded the Winona Symphony, which he directed for five years, and taught at the Winona Conservatory. During that time he began his career as a composer, although he later disavowed most of his early compositions. The first piece of music he was willing to acknowledge in later life was "Toys," a song written in 1919. In his early period, Ruggles' style was homophonic with a strong inclination for extended melodic lines. This tendency continued with important modifications and changes in his next work, *Men and Angels* (1920), a symphonic suite for five trumpets and bass trumpet. This is high-tensioned music, strongly dissonant, with a melodic line that is severe and angular, music in which Ruggles'

subsequent partiality for dissonant counterpoint first became evident.

Ruggles arrived in New York in the early 1920's. He helped Edgard Varèse organize the International Composers Guild, which gave its first concert on December 17, 1922. This program featured the world première of Ruggles' *Men and Angels*, the first time that one of his compositions received a significant hearing. The work represented the United States at the festival of the International Society for Contemporary Music in Venice on September 8, 1925. Revised, rescored, and renamed *Angels*, the work received a second première in Miami on April 24, 1939. The new version impressed Virgil Thomson in 1949 as an "extraordinary and secretly powerful work. . . . Complete avoidance of the dramatic and picturesque gives to the work a simplicity and nobility rare in the music of our time. Its plain nobility of expression and utter perfection of workmanship place Ruggles as one of our century's masters, perhaps the one among all from whom the young have most to learn now."

Ruggles' singular individuality and courageous iconoclasm were even more strongly in evidence in the three-movement orchestral suite *Men and Mountains* (1924). Here the composer experimented further with dissonant counterpoint and drifted more and more towards atonality. This composition was inspired by Blake and carries the following line: "Great things are done when men and mountains meet." It was first heard as a work for chamber orchestra in New York City on December 7, 1924. Rescored for large orchestra it was heard in New York on March 19, 1936. At that time Lawrence Gilman said that it was music of "a natural mystic, a rhapsodist, a composer who sees visions and dreams favorite dreams."

Portals, for orchestra, followed in 1926, introduced in New York on January 24. This composition carried in its published score a quotation from Walt Whitman: "What are those of the known but to ascend and enter the unknown?"

Several biographical notices on Ruggles carry the information that he wrote an opera based on Gerhart Hauptmann's drama *The Sunken Bell* (the same play which Ottorino Respighi used for his own opera of the same title). This opera no longer exists, for the good reason that Ruggles destroyed it. He had worked on it laboriously in the 1920's. Since the Ruggles family was then living in a small, cramped apartment, his wife would take their son, Micah, out each day for several hours, regardless of the weather, to give Ruggles the quiet and the space in which to work. When Ruggles had completed two acts he submitted them to the Metropolitan Opera, which then fixed a date for the opera's world première. Then, one day, back from her daily stroll, Mrs. Ruggles found the apartment floor completely covered with litter; Ruggles had come to the conclusion that his opera was not very good, and he had torn up the score.

Sun-Treader, for large orchestra, is sometimes singled out as Ruggles' most significant composition. He completed it in the early 1930's, and its world première took place in Paris on February 25, 1932, Nicolas Slonimsky conducting. A motto from Robert Browning's poem *Pauline* serves as the clue to the intent of the music: "Sun-treader—life and light be thine forever." This is hypertensioned music in a discordant, atonal style. On April 22, 1936, it was heard at the festival of the International Society for Contemporary Music at Barcelona; it was also performed in Berlin. But it did not have its American première until January 24, 1966, at which time the Chicago Symphony under the direction of Jean Martinon performed it in Portland, Maine, during a Charles Ruggles festival.

In 1937 Ruggles was appointed to the faculty of the School of Music at the University of Miami in Florida and he remained there for approximately a decade. After that Ruggles and his wife divided their year between an apartment at the Chelsea Hotel in New York and a summer place in Arlington, Vermont, where they occupied a reconverted schoolhouse. When Ruggles' wife died in October 1957, he went into seclusion the year round in Arlington.

Small towns and people from small towns have always fascinated Ruggles; large cities have always incurred his dislike. In Arlington he has become a friend of the local traffic cop, the village house painter, the village carpenter.

Ruggles' last composition was *Organum*, for large orchestra (1945), introduced by the New York Philharmonic on November 24, 1949.

After *Organum* Ruggles gave up composition and turned to painting, for which he revealed a marked gift and in which he was to achieve a moderately successful career.

CARL RUGGLES

In 1953 Ruggles received an award from the National Association of American Composers and Conductors for his creative achievement, and in 1954 he was elected a member of the National Institute of Arts and Letters. On his ninetieth birthday, Bowdoin College in Maine presented a two-day festival honoring Ruggles. His music was performed; his life, works, and achievements were discussed; and his paintings were put on exhibit. It was on this occasion that the orchestral work *Sun-Treader* received its American première.

Ruggles' method of preparing his manuscripts was unique. Henry Cowell has given the following amusing description: "On my first visit to Ruggles, he took me immediately into his living room and began unwinding a huge roll of pieces of butcher paper, pinned together with safety pins to make a whole which almost covered the entire floor of the room. Drawing his own huge staves, he had written down his ideas, borrowing his baby son's colored crayons for that purpose, each on a separate piece of paper; then he had pinned them together. This carpet of musical creation was spread out over the floor and we got down on our hands and knees to study it. He had begun to write on this Gargantuan scale at a time when he was having trouble with his eyes and couldn't see notes smaller than table-spoons; after a few years of this it somehow seemed silly to return to ordinary notes when his eyes improved.

"Along the margins and over the staves, Ruggles was accustomed to comment with vigorous crayon scribbles, and he added a few more adjectives ('Superb!,' 'Stinks!,' 'Putrid!,' 'Sublime!') each time he went over his work."

In other ways, too, Ruggles' method was uniquely his. Cowell tells of the time he visited Ruggles and found him at the piano, singing a single tone at the top of his voice, and banging out a single chord over and over again. He continued to do this for about an hour. Unable to suppress his curiosity any longer, Cowell asked Ruggles what he was doing. Ruggles replied: "I'm trying over this damned chord to see whether it still sounds superb after so many hearings . . . I'll give the chord the test of time right now. If I find I still like it, after trying it out several thousand times, it'll stand the test of time all right."

In a monograph on Ruggles, privately published and privately distributed in 1946, Lou Harrison evaluated Ruggles the composer as follows: "As a creative mind Ruggles is definitely of the individualist persuasion. His way of working over a long period of time towards ultimate clarity and precision of a particular musical formation is an indication of this attitude. So, too, is the over-all coherence, stylistically, which his output presents. . . . He is surely one of the most astonishing among the composers of his time. None other that I know of has pursued to quite so great a degree the constant clarification, and, still further, the ultimate right form for work."

MAJOR WORKS

Chamber Music—Angels, for four violins and three celli (or four trumpets and three trombones).

Orchestral Music—Men and Mountains, for chamber orchestra; Portals, for string orchestra; Sun-Treader; Organum.

Piano Music—Evocations.

Vocal Music—Toys.

ABOUT

Chase, G., America's Music; Goss, M., Modern Music Makers; Harrison, L., About Carl Ruggles; Rosenfeld, P., An Hour with American Music.

Musical Quarterly, October 1932; New York Times, October 12, 1958; Score (London), June 1955.

Harald Saeverud
1897–

Harald Saeverud was born in Bergen, Norway, on April 17, 1897. He has revealed that his birth took place in a churchyard, explaining: "My house was built on its grounds—the churchyard was very ancient and in disuse for some time. It is possible that there exists a relation between the morbid churchyard atmosphere and the plaintive sad music which at the time was my entire repertory." As a child he used to perform an old "passion-chorale" with a decidedly lugubrious mood, as well as other melancholy numbers. His preoccupation with sad music was finally broken when he came upon a simple children's melody which captivated him. It was at that time that he decided he wanted to be a composer. By the time he was fifteen he had written enough orchestral music to be able to conduct a concert of such works in Bergen, on December 12, 1912. His first published composition, however, did not appear until 1919. Opus one was *Five Capricci*, for piano; it was followed by the *Appassionata*, overture, opus 2.

During these early years he received a sound training in piano and harmony at the Musical Academy in Bergen, mainly with Holmsen. In 1920 he went to Germany where he remained a year, attending the Berlin Hochschule für Musik as a pupil of F. E. Koch; he also studied conducting with Clemens Kraus.

His formal training finished, Saeverud returned to Bergen. He earned his living playing the piano and teaching, while devoting himself more and more intensively to composition. In the period between 1923 and 1926 he completed two symphonies, together with several concertos and various piano compositions. Works completed in the early 1920's, influenced by his one-year stay in Germany, were in the German post-Romantic style of Brahms and Bruckner. This tendency soon ran its course and by the middle 1920's he deserted his Romantic interests to experiment with atonality and other modern attitudes. In this new idiom he produced his third symphony, in B-flat minor (1926), and a piano suite and a cello concerto as well. The symphony was described by Richard Hove as "absolute and delicate

---

Saeverud: sā′ vĕr üd

music . . . created by a strongly intellectual attitude combined with an unusually high degree of musical inventiveness."

With *Fifty Small Variations*, for orchestra (1931)—a composition that takes only five minutes to perform—Saeverud entered a new phase. He turned to extended tonality while emphasizing polyphonic practices. This vein was tapped for the first of his works to gain attention outside Norway—the *Canto Ostinato* (1934), enthusiastically received at the fourth International Festival at Baden-Baden in April 1939. Reviewing this work at the time, Fred Hamel called it "the most interesting composition of the whole festival. . . . This was a very original and powerful work. From a structural point of view it was a passacaglia, not quite according to conservatory rules, but with constantly surprising ideas, with extraordinary tone combinations and fantastic effects of orchestration." In a similar style were the fourth symphony (1937), an oboe concerto (1938), and his first Divertimento (1939). Giving free rein to his creativity was largely made possible through a state grant in 1933 which enabled him to give up all other professional activities for composition. The grant also made it possible for him to visit the United States in 1934. There, at New York's City Hall, he married Marie Hvoslef, whose parents were of Norwegian birth but of American citizenship.

Kristian Lange and Arne Östvedt remark in *Norwegian Music* that Saeverud's *Canto Ostinato* of 1934 "reminds us to some extent of Norwegian folk music" because of its use of the modes of old Norwegian church music. Musical nationalism comes sharply into focus in Saeverud's works in 1940 and is evident in some of his most famous compositions. The impetus driving him to musical nationalism was the Nazi invasion of Norway. "I felt that my work must be a personal war within the war with Germany," he said. A distinctly Norwegian style begins to emerge in his orchestral *Shepherd's Tune Variations* (1941). Musical nationalism was further developed in a symphonic dance, *Festa Campestre* (1942), and it arrived at full maturity in the *Sinfonia Dolorosa* and the *Symphonic Dances*, both completed in 1942; *Dances and Country Tunes from Siljustöl*, a series of five volumes (1943–1945); and the *Ballad of Revolt* (1943), which

the composer had adapted for orchestra from one of the piano *Dances and Country Tunes*.

The bitterness and tragedy of the war are reflected in both the *Sinfonia Dolorosa* and the *Ballad of Revolt*. The symphony was the composer's sixth, introduced in Bergen on May 27, 1943. "The whole work," reported a critic for *Dagens Nyheter*, "expresses so clearly horrified sorrow and powerless fury that one is left in no doubt as to the 'message'. . . . The result is perhaps not beautiful music in the classical sense, but may be—and has in this case become—expressive, caustic, harrowing." The *Ballad of Revolt*, dedicated to the "great and small heroes of the underground movement," was described by a critic for the London *Daily Telegraph* as "pithy and terse," encompassing "the events of Norway's war-time oppression" and rising "from uneasy mutterings in the depths to a colossal climax, typifying the shaking-off of the shackles."

HARALD SAEVERUD

A lighter mood prevails in the five volumes comprising the *Dances and Country Tunes from Siljustöl*, one of its composer's most celebrated creations, and the one in which his use of Norwegian folk materials is most effective. The word *Siljustöl* in the title refers to the composer's home surrounded by silver birches, which he has maintained for many years outside Bergen, where he and his wife reared three sons and where he still resides. Graham Carritt described these pieces in the *Monthly Musical Record* of London as follows: "The piano works . . . are of moderate length and have picturesque titles, sometimes flower names, which are intended both to stir the imagination of the listener and to help the right interpretation for the player. . . . A clear-cut melodic line with unusual harmonies that are sometimes surprisingly bitter, a marked rhythmic pattern, and usually a remarkable clarity distinguish this music. The harmonies or background are quite often intended not to obtrude but to be shadowy and rather elusive."

Another score which helped to enhance Saeverud's reputation was his incidental music to Ibsen's *Peer Gynt*. The director of the Norwegian Theatre in Oslo invited Saeverud to write music for a new production of the Ibsen play. Saeverud was long hesitant to invade a province so long dominated by Grieg. But as he thought about the project it occurred to him that perhaps Grieg's Romantic music, good as it was, was not altogether in tune with the somewhat harsh spirit of the Ibsen play. Saeverud began to feel that a more dramatic, non-Romantic approach was called for. This realization gave Saeverud the courage to begin work. The play, with Saeverud's music, was produced in Oslo on March 2, 1948, with great success. After that, an orchestral suite based on the music began to circle the musical world. When it was first heard in the United States (in New York on February 25, 1957), Howard Taubman said: "Mr. Saeverud's music . . . has thrust and violence and tenderness that does not become sweet. The thematic ideas are fundamentally conservative, but they are treated with a full awareness of the theatrical uses in the resources of brittle rhythms, acrid harmonies, and imaginative orchestration."

In the 1950's Saeverud's principal works included a second piano concerto and his eighth symphony, *Minnesota* (1958). The latter had been commissioned for the Minnesota Centennial and was introduced on October 18, 1958, with Antal Dorati conducting the Minneapolis Symphony. In the 1960's Saeverud produced his first score for ballet, *Bluebeard's Nightmare*, the world première of which was given by the Norwegian Opera on October 4, 1960. His ninth symphony was heard at the Bergen International Festival on June 12, 1966. In addition to these works, Saeverud wrote the *Entrata Regale*, for orchestra, to open the Ber-

gen festival in 1960 (he revised the composition extensively in 1964); the *Haakonshallen*, festival music for the reopening of the thirteenth century King Haakon's Hall in Bergen in 1961; and the *Marcia Solenne*, for orchestra, officially introduced in April 1967 but actually played one year earlier on the organ during the wedding ceremonies of the composer's son Sveinnung.

Virgil Thomson said of Saeverud's music: "It sounds like no other music today. It is at once comical and poetic, touching of sentiment and at the same time stimulating by its realistic treatment of folk ways and of symphonic instruments."

Since 1955 Saeverud has been receiving a handsome yearly grant from the government in recognition of his status in Norwegian music. Other honors include membership in the Swedish Musical Academy, conferred in 1952, and knighthood (Order of Saint Olaf, first class), conferred in 1957.

MAJOR WORKS

Ballet—Bluebeard's Nightmare.

Chamber Music—Romanza, for violin and piano.

Choral Music—Shepherd's Farewell.

Orchestral Music—9 symphonies; 2 piano concertos; Overtura Appassionata; Siljustöl March; Fifty Small Variations; Canto Ostinato; Oboe Concerto; Rondo Amoroso; Lucretia Suite; Shepherd's Tune Variations; Divertimento No. 1; Festa Campestre; Little Bird's Waltz, for chamber orchestra (also for piano); Her Last Cradle Song, for strings; Ballad of Revolt; Peer Gynt, two suites; Violin Concerto; Vade Mors; Entrata Regale; Haakonshallen; Bassoon Concerto; Marcia Solenne.

Piano Music—Five Capricci; Sonata in G minor; Suite; Countryside Festival; Six Sonatinas; Six Small Piano Pieces; Dances and Country Tunes from Siljustöl, five volumes.

ABOUT

Lange, K. and Östvedt, L., Norwegian Music.

Nordisk Musikkulture (Oslo), No. 4, 1952.

Erik Satie
1866–1925

Erik Alfred Leslie Satie was born in the town of Honfleur, near Le Havre, France, on May 17, 1866. His mother, Jane, of Scottish descent, was a gifted musician who wrote pieces for the piano; his father, Alfred, was a ship's broker.

Satie: så tē′

Erik was their first child. Born a Catholic, he was nevertheless baptized in the Anglican Church. However, in his sixth year, at the demand of his grandparents, he was rebaptized a Catholic.

ERIK SATIE

The Saties moved to Paris while Erik was still a child. When Erik was six, his mother died, and he was sent back to Honfleur to be reared by his grandparents. There he began his academic education, as well as the study of music with the local organist, Vinot. Vinot taught him the piano and at the same time introduced him to the music of the Gregorian plain chants to which Satie remained partial all his life and by which he was strongly influenced in his first compositions. The study of the piano was later continued with another local teacher, and lessons in harmony began with a musician named Mathias. In later years, Satie remarked sardonically that his piano teacher thought he had a remarkable gift for composition but his harmony teacher was convinced his talent lay with the piano.

In 1878 Satie rejoined his father in Paris. Five years later he entered the Paris Conservatory, where he continued his interest in old modal music and medieval plain chants while at the same time revealing an inquisitiveness about new idioms and techniques. He frequently startled his teachers with exercises that wandered off into discord and unorthodox tonalities. Some of his teachers regarded him as indolent and had a low opinion of his talent;

Satie had small sympathy either for the Conservatory curriculum or for his teachers. He remained at the Conservatory only one year. After that, he shifted for himself in whatever musical direction an unbridled and undisciplined temperament led him.

He began composing in 1885 with two little pieces for the piano entitled *Valse-Ballet* and *Fantaisie-Valse*. When they were published in 1887 he designated them opus 62—his first excursion into whimsy. This publication was immediately followed by a setting of three poems by De Latour, which his father (now a music publisher) issued privately.

Possibly because he was dissatisfied with the kind of music he had thus far been writing, Satie returned to Gregorian plain chants. His deep study of medieval music and Gothic art produced a set of four piano pieces collectively called *Ogives* (1886) in which Satie made a conscious attempt to convey in sound a Gothic atmosphere. *Sarabandes* followed in 1887, *Gymnopédies* in 1888, and *Gnossiennes* in 1890, all of them for the piano. In these compositions Satie began to exploit not only unusual subject matter but also new idioms and techniques. Uncommon progressions and harmonic combinations abounded in *Gymnopédies*, a set of three dances (the title comes from *gymnopedia*, an ancient Spartan festival in which naked youths worshiped their gods with song and dance). In *Sarabandes*, the use of chords of the ninth anticipated Debussy by some fourteen years; in *Gnossiennes*, Satie experimented for the first time with barless notation. Equally significant were the precision and economy of style. Jean Cocteau once remarked that in these pieces Satie showed the greatest audacity of all—the audacity of being simple. This was a conscious rebellion against the excesses of post-Romanticism; the impact of this rebellion upon French musical thought can hardly be exaggerated.

For a brief period in 1886, until he was released from uniform following an attack of bronchitis, Satie fulfilled the duties of military service required of all Frenchmen. During his convalescence he read the writings of Joséphin Péladan, leader of the Rosicrucian Society, whose mysticism and occult philosophy made a deep impression upon him. In 1890 Satie came into personal contact with Péladan and shortly afterwards assumed the unofficial position of composer to the cult. His music became steeped in mysticism—beginning with the incidental music he wrote for three of Péladan's plays. This music was also strongly imitative of early church music, and particularly of the Gregorian plain chant. But, as Everett Helm noted, "these are given a very personal touch. The simplicity of the musical expression and the clarity of the texture are typically Satie."

During these years Satie supported himself by playing music hall tunes in such cabarets as Le Chat Noir and the Auberge du Clou. He made his home in Montmartre, on the Rue Cortot, in a room he furnished with only the barest necessities. He became a familiar figure in Montmartre's cafés, where he did much of his composing, and in its streets, where he was known for some of his eccentricities. He always wore a bowler hat and carried an umbrella under his arm. His face was bearded, and his keen eyes peered through a pince-nez. An enormous clay pipe stuck out of his pocket. He never used a public conveyance, always traveling by foot however great the distance, carrying a hammer in his pocket for nighttime protection. He was known never to wash himself with soap, preferring pumice stone. He was usually solitary and withdrawn, and he had no interest in women. "I am a man whom women just don't understand," he used to say.

It was at the Auberge du Clou, in 1891, that Satie first met Debussy. Debussy was impressed by Satie's novel ideas, particularly by his revolt against Wagner and post-Romanticism and his idea for a music firmly grounded in French spiritual and intellectual values. As Satie later wrote: "I explained to Debussy the necessity for a Frenchman to disassociate himself from the Wagner 'adventure' which was uncongenial with our national aspirations. I made it clear to him that . . . we should have our own music—without sauerkraut if possible." Satie's music fascinated Debussy, who orchestrated two of the pieces from *Gymnopédies*. It was Satie's influence that enabled Debussy to crystallize his own aims and purposes as a composer as well as to adopt some of the newer idioms and techniques. Debussy himself conceded that Satie had been "decisive for the esthetic concept underlying *Pelléas et Mélisande*."

Freeing himself at last from the mysticism of the Rosicrucians and from his musical dependence on old church music, in 1895 Satie lapsed into a period of creative silence. He was going through a period of reevaluation, of seeking out a new direction. He found that direction in 1897 with the set of piano pieces called *Pièces Froides*. From that point on he favored whimsical titles for his compositions and found delight in interpolating into his music amusing or outlandish instructions or explanations to the performer. His quixotic titles included *Desiccated Embryos*, *The Dreamy Fish*, *Flabby Preludes for a Dog*, *Sketches to Make You Run Away*, *Three Pieces in the Shape of a Pear*. The last of these was inspired by a casual remark made by Debussy, who said that Satie's music had no form to speak of.

Within these pieces Satie inserted all kinds of curious comments. In one place he advised the pianist to put his hands in his pockets. He suggested that one of the phrases should be played "dry as a cuckoo, light as an egg," while another should sound like a "nightingale with a toothache." In one of the piano pieces he quoted Chopin's *Funeral March* but identified it as a Schubert Mazurka.

But the rebel was interested in humor and whimsy not only for their own sakes; he was a dedicated artist fighting against the Romantic tradition that composers must take themselves and their art with religious seriousness. He was an artist in conflict first with the pretentious structures and the even more pretentious style of Wagner and Mahler, and second with the preciousness of Debussy and his Impressionist followers. With his economical writing in slight structures, and with his odd titles and odder comments, he was parting company with the excessive emotionalism, the pompous attitudes, and the elaborate thinking processes of his immediate predecessors and many of his contemporaries. Through his novel approaches Satie was preparing the way for the neoclassicists, for the dadaists, for the popularists, and for those French composers who wanted to make music a more human and direct esthetic experience for large audiences. He was promoting an "everyday music" (*musique de tous les jours*) for everyday audiences—music that was down to earth, simple, and unpretentious, often making use of popular tunes. In this he set the stage for the emergence of the school of young French composers known as The French Six (see sketch on Auric).

In 1898 Satie moved out of Montmartre to Arcueil, a suburb of Paris. For the remainder of his life he occupied bleak, drab lodgings over a bistro, on the second floor of a house on the Rue Cauchy known as "Les Quatre Cheminées." He permitted no one to set foot in his quarters. The first time any of his friends invaded his rooms was after his death; they were appalled by the bleak poverty and disorder. Satie did all his own housecleaning. Each evening he went down to the square to draw a pitcher of water—dressed from head to foot in gray velvet, a garb which earned him the sobriquet the "velvet gentleman." Once, when he received a modest bequest, he lost no time in spending all his money in the purchase of a dozen velvet suits and numerous stiff collars and waistcoats.

His eccentricities both as a composer and as a man made him notorious. But if there was any doubt about the seriousness of his purpose as a creative artist, and of his highmindedness, it was dispelled in 1905 when, at the age of forty he decided to return to the music school-room. He was not altogether pleased with what he had written, feeling the need to broaden his approach. He was convinced his technique was inadequate. To help himself acquire the tools with which to build larger and more ambitious structures, he enrolled in the Schola Cantorum. For three years he attended the classes of Vincent d'Indy and Albert Roussel. He was a most conscientious pupil, and Roussel described him as a "prodigiously endowed musician."

This period of Conservatory study provided Satie with the technique and confidence he needed to undertake assignments larger than a piano piece. Within such larger forms he once again proved himself a pioneer and an iconoclast, and his thinking and planning became even more fanciful and grotesque than before.

In 1913 he wrote the music for a satirical stage work, Le Piège de Méduse, in which a stuffed monkey danced between scenes. Other nonsensical situations involved a Baron (who was made up to look like Satie), his daughter Frisette, and her lover Astolfo. Frisette and Astolfo will get the Baron's permission for marriage only if they can answer a preposterous question. The absurd text and the impish wit

of the music (scored for seven instruments) is pure dadaism—even though that movement had not yet been born.

In 1916 Satie's masterwork, the ballet Parade, was written—scenario by Jean Cocteau, sets and costumes by Picasso. It was produced by the Ballet Russe de Monte Carlo in Paris on May 18, 1917, causing a scandal. The critics proved so hostile that Satie was provoked into sending Jean Poueigh an insulting letter. Sued by the infuriated critic, Satie was sentenced to eight days in jail for "public insults and defamation of character," but the sentence was suspended. "The performance of Satie's Parade," wrote Darius Milhaud some years later, "will stand in the history of French music as a date equally important with that of the first performance of Pelléas et Mélisande."

Parade was years ahead of its time in several different ways. In its staging, in the animated pictures created by Picasso, and in the thematic structure of Satie's music (the piling up of lyrical ideas as if they were so many cubes), it helped introduce cubism to the musical stage. Satie's score also represented one of the earliest successful attempts to use ragtime with serious artistic intent. In addition, the musical background included the sounds of sirens, typewriters, dynamos, discharged revolvers, airplane motors—anticipating by some years experiments in mechanistic music and the use of noise within the context of serious musical compositions.

Parade was one of Satie's chief works in the period following his studies at the Schola Cantorum. Another was the three-part symphonic drama Socrate, for four sopranos and orchestra (1918), with a text based on three dialogues of Plato. The singing voice is almost entirely recitative, while the orchestral background seems to move independently of the voice, often consisting of just melodic or rhythmic patterns. The writing is linear, once again anticipating a later significant idiom in twentieth century music.

Socrate is a work of extraordinary simplicity, directness of expression, and abstraction of thought. "Those who don't understand the work," Satie wrote in the program for the première, which took place in Paris on February 14, 1920, "are requested by me to adopt an attitude of complete submission and complete inferiority." Wilfred Mellers has written:

"In this work Satie has had the moral courage to present, without the protection of irony, the 'negation' of his life. . . . Thus *Socrate*, which is usually supposed, with a certain amount of truth, to be so completely abstract a work, is really a more personal document than any other single work of Satie's. . . . It has a quality of oddly sinister inhumanity; it is extremely disturbing music with something of the 'unpleasantness of great art.' It is the expression of a spiritual loneliness so complete as to be almost without consolation."

Satie wrote the music for two more ballets: *Mercure* and *Relâche*, both produced in Paris in 1924, the former on June 15, and the latter on November 29. *Mercure*, like *Parade*, was a collaboration between the composer and Picasso: the treatment of the subject matter and the cubistic quality of staging and costuming were reminiscent of *Parade*. *Relâche*, Satie's last completed composition, was a fresh adventure into dadaism, with overtones of surrealism. It includes a dance with a wheelbarrow and another with a revolving door; men and women dress and undress on the stage. All the action takes place against a background of phonograph discs piled up in a solid wall practically up to the proscenium. One of the scenes calls for a motion picture in which action on the screen is accompanied by constantly repeated musical phrases which bear no direct relation to the screen images. Another scene features a strip tease.

In 1920 Satie became involved in still another artistic experiment—*musique d'ameublement* or "furnishing music." The term was devised by Matisse to designate an art form as comfortable as an easy chair, one that created no distraction of any kind. On March 8, 1920, an exhibition of paintings took place in the Faubourg St. Honoré. On that occasion, Satie's music was performed in a gallery while the public concentrated on the pictures. The program for this event explained: "We present for the first time . . . furnishing music. . . . We beg you to take no notice of it and to behave . . . as if the music did not exist." It exasperated Satie to find some of the people actually stopping in their tracks and concentrating on the music; he ran over to them and begged them to continue what they had been doing, either talking to friends, or walking around looking at the pictures. Many people in Paris regarded the whole thing as a joke or a stunt, but Satie was deadly serious in his endeavor to try something new. Actually, *musique d'ameublement* might well be regarded as the forerunner of background music for motion pictures or television productions in which the music is expected to be ignored while the attention is fixed on story, dialogue, and action.

Just as he continued to open new areas for music, so did Satie continue to exert a vital influence on young composers. In 1923 he helped to organize a new "school" of young composers who named themselves "École d'Arcueil" after the neighborhood in which Satie lived. This group, whose members included Sauguet and Desormière, made a fetish of austerity and simplicity.

Constant Lambert analyzed Satie's traits as a composer: "Melodically speaking we find the juxtaposition of short lyrical phrases of great tenderness with ostinatos of extreme and deliberate bareness. Harmonically speaking, Satie's methods differ as much from Debussy's static use of chords for their own sake as they do from Liszt's rhetorical use of chords as so many points in a musical argument. His harmonic sense . . . is rich and pleasing, but, like his lyrical sense, displays a curiously objective and unatmospheric quality. The strangeness of his harmonic coloring is due not to the chords themselves, but to the unexpected relationships he discovers between chords which in themselves are familiar enough. . . . His progressions have a strange logic of their own but they have none of the usual sense of concord and discord, no trace of the *point d'appui* that we usually associate with the word progression. They may be said to lack harmonic perspective in much the same way that a cubist painting lacks a special perspective."

On July 1, 1925, Erik Satie died in a hospital in Paris after a six-month illness. The few friends who were at his side said that he died as he had lived, with a smile on his lips. In *Notes Without Music*, Darius Milhaud described the intense poverty of Satie's last years: "This man . . . owned almost literally *nothing*; a wretched bed, a table covered with the most incongruous objects, one chair, a half-empty wardrobe. . . . On the ancient, broken-down piano, with its pedals tied up with string, there was a parcel whose postmark proved that it had been delivered several years before."

Olin Downes, who met Satie in the closing year of the composer's life, described him as "an amusing old man, a dilettante of the future, who wore a blue, shiny suit, a gleaming eyeglass, and misleading whiskerage, and who ate his food in a mincing and derisive manner."

MAJOR WORKS

Ballets—Parade; Mercure; Relâche.

Piano Music—Ogives; Sarabandes; Gymnopédies (two movements orchestrated by Debussy); Gnossiennes; Danses Gothiques; Pièces Froides; Trois Morceaux en Forme de Poire, for piano duet; Trois Préludes Flasques; Aperçus Désagréables, for piano duet; Descriptions Automatiques; Embryons Desséchés; Peccadilles Importunes; Heures Séculaires et Instantanées; Avant-Dernières Pensées; Études; Enfantines, three sets of pieces for children; Sports et Divertissements; Les Pantins Dansent.

Stage Works: Geneviève de Brabant, for marionettes; Le Piège de Méduse, lyric comedy; Socrate, symphonic drama for four sopranos and small orchestra.

Vocal Music—Trois Mélodies; Trois Poèmes d'Amour; Quatre Petites Mélodies; Ludions.

ABOUT

Mellers, W. H., Studies in Contemporary Music; Milhaud, D., Notes Without Music; Myers, R. H., Erik Satie; Templier, P. D., Erik Satie.

Hi Fi/Stereo Review, October 1967; High Fidelity, December 1963; Music and Letters (London), October 1923; Musical America, November 15, 1950; La Revue Musicale (Paris), Satie Issues, March 1924, June 1952.

Henri Sauguet
1901–

Henri Sauguet was born on May 18, 1901, in Bordeaux. The plain chants he sang as a choirboy in a local church first stimulated his interest in music. But his most important boyhood musical experience came in his fifteenth year upon hearing a Debussy piano prelude, *The Girl With the Flaxen Hair*. "This was the *coup de foudre* determining my career," he said. "Henceforth, my one all-abiding ambition was to become a composer. From this time on, too, I was fascinated by all contemporary music, sometimes to the exclusion of the classics."

He started to study the piano and organ with local teachers, and when he was sixteen he took lessons in composition with Joseph Canteloube. Faced with the practical problem

Sauguet: sō gĕ′

of having to earn a living, he filled various jobs: salesman in a department store, secretary to an Oriental company, staff worker with an oil company. Not until his twenty-sixth year was he able to concern himself exclusively with music.

HENRI SAUGUET

Several songs and piano pieces by Sauguet were brought to the attention of Darius Milhaud. "The talent revealed in them was still not very sure of itself," Milhaud later recalled, "but had an authentic poetry of its own." He invited Sauguet to come to Paris for a visit and to attend some concerts. Sauguet arrived in 1921 and stayed with Milhaud. "We were all captivated by Sauguet's charm of manner, his subtle, refined intelligence, his profound culture, and his love of life," says Milhaud. One of the musical experiences in Paris to move Sauguet most profoundly was the hearing of Schoenberg's *Pierrot Lunaire*.

In 1922 Sauguet returned to Paris. He underwent a period of study with Charles Koechlin. A meeting with Erik Satie led him to join Roger Desormière, Max Jacob and one or two others in forming a "school" of composers calling itself "École d'Arcueil." The dean was Satie, who resided in the Arcueil district of Paris at that time. Through his affiliations with Satie, Sauguet became familiar with some of the more advanced tendencies of French music. Nevertheless, as a member of the group Sauguet dedicated himself to simplicity and austerity.

He wrote both the libretto and music of a one-act *opera bouffe militaire* produced at the Théâtre des Champs-Élysées on April 24, 1924. This was Sauguet's first work to receive a major presentation. Success came in 1927 with *La Chatte*, a ballet with choreography by George Balanchine, produced by the Ballet Russe de Monte Carlo. This was so well received that it was given over a hundred performances in less than two years, providing Sauguet with the financial resources to give up his extra-musical jobs and devote himself entirely to composition. In 1928 he wrote the music for *David*, a ballet introduced by Ida Rubinstein at the Paris Opéra in the same year. Still another ballet, *Night*, choreography by Serge Lifar, was produced successfully in London in 1930.

In the 1930's Sauguet wrote a good deal of incidental music for various theatrical and motion picture productions. His most significant serious creation of this period was his four-act opera *La Chartreuse de Parme*, with a libretto by Armand Lunel adapted from the Stendhal novel. The opera was produced on March 16, 1939. "The music," said Milhaud, "is marvelous, often light-hearted, tender and broad in its treatment, but rising in the last act to genuine heights of emotion." Milhaud confessed he was so drawn to this opera that he attended not only all of the final rehearsals but even the first seven performances.

Sauguet's first major work for orchestra was a product of World War II: *Symphonie Expiatoire*, written in 1945 in memory of innocent war victims. This composition, we are told by the composer, was his attempt "to relieve one's conscience, to expiate in the original sense of the word, and to reflect the helplessness during the Nazi occupation of France." The concluding movement is a moving lullaby to the dead. The symphony was introduced in Paris after the end of the war, on February 8, 1948.

During the war, Sauguet also wrote the music for an important ballet: *Les Forains*, with choreography by Roland Petit, first performed in Paris in March 1945. This depicts strolling players, describing what happens to one such group in a city street. George Balanchine says: "The overture . . . blares out with trumpets, drum rolls, and crashing cymbals—appropriate music for a parade, a vaude-

ville show, or a circus. The ballet that follows is something like all of these." *Les Forains* was seen in the United States on October 8, 1950, in a performance by Les Ballets de Paris in New York.

Sauguet's ballet *Cordélia* received its world première on May 9, 1952, at the Exposition of Twentieth Century Arts in Paris. In reviewing the première, Edward J. Pendleton explained that the story involves a "young girl martyrized by her parents, but to whom love offers an escape." About the music, he said this: "This adorable story is . . . accompanied by music as sympathetic and lovely as the subject itself. M. Sauguet possesses the gift of finding the exact color and the most appropriate musical matter for his ballets; he obtains thereby a rare unity." A later ballet, *La Dame aux Camélias*, was successfully introduced at the Berlin Exposition on September 29, 1957.

Sauguet's principal orchestral compositions of the 1950's included one commissioned by the Louisville Orchestra in Kentucky: *Les Trois Lys*. In this three-section work the three elements of harmony, melody, and rhythm are represented by the three lilies that once symbolized the French monarchy and that were incorporated into the symbol for the city of Louisville. The composition was heard in Louisville on September 25, 1954.

Sauguet's style is often a compromise between impressionism and medievalism. His sensitive atmosphere is derived from Debussy, while his esoteric melodies and modal harmonies come from the plain chant. Occasionally, the influence of Poulenc or Honegger can be detected. Sauguet has occasionally employed modern idioms, though sparingly; some of his later works show an interest in the twelve-tone system. "What is happening in our time is to me the most exciting of all," he says.

Sauguet has been an influential music critic for *L'Europe Nouvelle* and *Echo de Paris* among other journals. He also helped found several literary magazines, including the *Revue Hebdomadaire*, *Candide*, and *Tout à Vous*.

Sauguet first visited the United States in the spring of 1953. On April 23, the International Society for Contemporary Music sponsored an all-Sauguet concert in New York. This program included the American premières of his music for the ballet *La Nuit*, his second string quartet (1948), *Bocages* (three caprices for wind and harp, 1949); and the song cycle *La Chèvre-Feuille*. "The native wit and movement, the Gallic point and esprit, and the warm, directly melodic nature of Mr. Sauguet's art were extensively revealed," reported Olin Downes. Sauguet returned to the United States during the summer of 1962 to help supervise the American premières of his Third Symphony and a delightful one-act comic opera, *La Contrebasse*, based on Chekhov.

Sauguet's apartment on the Boulevard de Clichy in Paris is cluttered with collections of exotic fabrics, statuettes, and paintings and objets d'art. Next to music, Sauguet's greatest interest lies in art; his personal collection is a testimony to his discriminating taste. Another of his interests is acting. He has made several successful stage appearances, including a notable performance in Molière's *Tartuffe* in 1945.

Much of Sauguet's popularity springs from the success of the many distinguished scores he has written for motion pictures; one of the most highly esteemed is that for the comedy *The Scandals of Clochemerle*.

MAJOR WORKS

Ballets—La Chatte; David; La Nuit; Fastes; Cartes Postales; La Cigale et la Fourmi; Image à Paul et Virginie; Les Mirages; Les Forains; La Rencontre; Pas de Deux Classique; Cordélia; La Dame aux Camélias.

Chamber Music—2 string quartets; Flute Sonatina; Divertissement de Chambre, for flute, clarinet, viola, bassoon, and piano; La Voyante, a suite for soprano and instruments; Suite for Clarinet and Piano; Madrigal, for soprano and five instruments; Cinq Images pour un Saint-Louis à Damiette, for flute, oboe, trumpet, and harpsichord; Six Interludes, for organ, two guitars, and tambourine; Dix Images pour une Vie de Jeanne d'Arc, for flute, oboe, clarinet, bassoon, horn, trumpet, and piano; Bocages, three caprices for wind and harp.

Choral Music—Enigme, ballad; Les Ombres du Jardin, cantata; Ma Belle Forêt; Bêtes et Méchants.

Operas—Le Plumet de Colonel, one-act opéra bouffe militaire; Un Amour du Titien, operetta; La Contrebasse; La Chartreuse de Parme; La Gageure Imprévue; Les Caprices de Marianne; La Dame aux Camélias.

Orchestral Music—3 symphonies; 2 piano concertos; Chant Funèbre pour de Nouveaux Héros, for tenor and orchestra; Stèle Symphonique; Portraits de Paris, suite; Orphée, for violin and orchestra; Les Trois Lys; Concerto in C major, for cello and orchestra.

Piano Music—Sonata in D major; Feuillets d'Album; Les Jeux de l'Amour et du Hasard, five pieces for two pianos; Pièces Poétiques, two sets of pieces for children; Valse Brève, for two pianos; Espièglerie, for children; Suite Royale, for harpsichord.

Vocal Music—Six Sonnets de Louise Labé; Quatre Poèmes de Schiller; Deux Poèmes de Shakespeare; Deux Poèmes de l'Intermezzo; Cinq Poèmes de Hölderlin; Chanson de Marins; Deux Poèmes de Tagore; Six Mélodies des Poèmes Symbolistes; Force et Faiblesse; Les Pénitents en Maillots Roses; Deux Mélodies de Valéry; La Chèvre-Feuille; Mouvements du Cœur; numerous other songs for voice and piano.

ABOUT

New York Times, April 19, 1953.

Florent Schmitt
1870–1958

Florent Schmitt was born in Blâmont, in the department of Meurthe-et-Moselle, France, on September 28, 1870. His parents were devoted amateur musicians. His father gave Florent his first lessons in piano and organ; the boy did not seem especially interested. He also insisted that Florent get a thorough academic training, and so Schmitt was raised on the classics and German Romantics. His favorite subjects at school were Latin, geography, and algebra.

FLORENT SCHMITT

When he was seventeen, he came upon Chopin's music, which awakened his latent musical talent. He returned enthusiastically to piano study, and his progress convinced him he wanted to become a musician. He attended the Nancy Conservatory to prepare for entrance examinations for the Paris Conservatory, studying with Henri Hess (piano) and Gustave Sandré (harmony). In 1889 he enrolled in the Paris Conservatory, where he

Schmitt: shmēt

became a pupil of Dubois, Lavignac, and Gedalge until he was called for military service, a period during which Schmitt played the flute in a band. When his service ended, Schmitt reentered the Conservatory, this time in the classes of Massenet and Fauré. In 1896 he tried for the Prix de Rome and failed. One year later he gained second prize. Finally, in 1900, first prize became his with the cantata *Sémiramis.*

Schmitt spent the years between 1901 and 1904 in Rome. He said: "I distinguished myself by the fact that I got into more trouble than probably any other holder of the Prix de Rome." Nevertheless, he sent back to the authorities in Paris several compositions (known as "*envois*"). One of these proved to be his first important piece of music, *Psalm 47* (Psalm 46 in the Vulgate), for chorus, soloists, and orchestra, completed in 1904.

After his residence in Rome ended, Schmitt spent two years traveling in Europe, Scandinavia, North Africa, and the Near East. In 1906 he settled in Paris, where, on December 27, the first concert devoted exclusively to his compositions was given. On this program *Psalm 47* received its world première. At that time, some critics condemned the music for its advanced idiom, its discords, and its unusual modulations. One or two were perceptive enough to realize its true value— M. D. Calvocoressi, for example, described it as powerful, even grandiloquent, music. Since that time, this *Psalm* has come to be regarded as one of Schmitt's finest compositions and a major contribution to French choral music.

A year after the première of the *Psalm*, two more of Schmitt's distinguished creations were heard: the ballet *La Tragédie de Salomé* and the Piano Quintet in B minor. The Quintet, begun in 1901, was not completed until seven years later. When it received its première at a concert of the Société Nationale in Paris on March 27, 1908, M. D. Calvocoressi called it "one of the most moving . . . and revealing creations of the past few years." *La Tragédie de Salomé*, inspired by a poem of Robert d'Humières, was a "mute drama," performed by the dancer Loie Fuller on November 9, 1907. Schmitt then adapted the music first into a symphonic suite for chamber orchestra, and later into a suite for large orchestra. The last version is the definitive one. First heard at a Colonne concert in Paris on January 8, 1911, it has become one of Schmitt's most frequently played compositions. Sensual in style, romantic in its fervor, and exciting for its emotional surges and exotic colorations, *La Tragédie de Salomé* never fails to make a strong impression.

Schmitt took an active part in the musical life of Paris, particularly in promoting new developments. In 1909 he helped found the Société Musicale Indépendante, serving on its executive committee. He was also an active member of the Société Nationale. He continually used his expanding influence to further the cause of new music and experimental techniques, never hesitating to hurl himself into the maelstrom of every *cause célèbre* on the side of an attacked composer. He was one of the first important musicians in Paris to speak enthusiastically about Satie; he defended Stravinsky loudly and belligerently during the tempestuous world première of *The Rite of Spring;* and he sided with Schoenberg when the *Five Pieces for Orchestra* caused a furor in Paris.

Nevertheless, in spite of the staunch way in which he promoted new music, he never identified himself with the Debussyites (then so much in vogue) or with the avant-garde, beginning to emerge. In his musical writing as in his thinking he remained singularly free of schools, trends, or vogues.

Schmitt's music, wrote M. D. Calvocoressi, is "free from the abstract intellectualism and formalism that are so dangerous to all arts, and reveals a temperament loving sounds and rhythms for their own intrinsic beauty; it possesses that inwardness, that effusive lyricism through which it at times differs from the music of the Impressionist school. . . . He does not scruple to use, at times, the simplest and so to speak the most massive dynamic effects; he shuns neither grandiloquence, nor insistence, nor any of the plain, if effective, means of classical art, never to be met with in the works of a Debussy or a Ravel. But with him they are never mere rhetorical expedients and nowise resemble the stereotyped airs and graces of the postclassicists. In fact, that straightforward idiom, that epic diction, being natural to Schmitt in some of his moods, appear in his music alive and original."

From 1922 to 1924 Schmitt was the director of the Lyons Conservatory. In 1932 he visited the United States, appearing on November 25 as soloist with the Boston Symphony in the world première of his *Symphonie Concertante*, for piano and orchestra. Two days later he went to New York to participate in a Florent Schmitt program sponsored by the League of Composers. Four years later Schmitt was elected a member of the French Academy. He was also made Commander of the Legion of Honor.

During the period before World War II, Schmitt served as music critic for *Le Temps*. After the war, he spent his winters in Paris (at the home of Mme. Moreau, who guarded him jealously from the distractions and annoyances of the outside world). In the summer he occupied his own house in St. Cloud. His diversions included travel, long walks, attending the five o'clock teas at the homes of friends, and going to the theatre and films. He possessed extraordinary vitality even in old age and revealed an endless reservoir of enthusiasm, good humor, and capacity for work. In his middle eighties he completed the writing of his first symphony, attending its world première at the festival of the International Society for Contemporary Music at Strasbourg, France, on June 15, 1958. He died soon after, in the Paris suburb of Neuilly, on August 17, 1958. A year before his death he was awarded the Grand Prix in Music by the City of Paris.

MAJOR WORKS

Ballets—La Tragédie de Salomé; Le Petit Elfe Ferme-l'Œil; Oriane la Sans-Égale.

Chamber Music—Piano Quintet in B minor; Lied et Scherzo, for double wind quintet; Sonate Libre en Deux Parties Enchaînées, for violin and piano; Suite en Rocaille, for flute, violin, viola, cello, and harp; Hasards, suite for piano, violin, viola, and cello; Quartet for Saxophones; String Trio; Quartet for Flutes; Quartet for Three Trombones and Tuba; String Quartet.

Choral Music—Psalm 47; Three a Cappella Choruses; Danse des Devadasis; Five Motets; Chant de Guerre; Hymne à l'Été; Trois Chants en l'Honneur d'Auguste Comte; Six Choruses for Women's Voices; Fête de la Lumière; En Bonnes Voix; L'Arbre entre Tous.

Orchestral Music—La Tragédie de Salomé, suite; Tristesse au Jardin, for voice and orchestra; Trois Rapsodies; Scherzo Vif, for violin and orchestra; Rêves; Légende, for violin (or viola, or saxophone) and orchestra; Kerob-Shal, for voice and orchestra; Enfants, for small orchestra; Quatre Poèmes de Ronsard, for voice and orchestra; Trois Chants, for women's voices and orchestra; Janiana, for string orchestra; Habeyssée, for violin and orchestra; Trois Monocantes; Scène de la Vie Moyenne; Symphony.

Piano Music—Soirs, ten preludes; Trois Valses Nocturnes; Pupazzi; Pièces Romantiques; Crépuscules; Ombres; Mirages; Trois Rapsodies, for two pianos; Trois Danses; Suite sans Esprit de Suite; Clavecin Obtempérant, suite.

Vocal Music—Various songs for voice and piano.

ABOUT

Ferroud, P. O., Autour de Florent Schmitt; Hucher, Y., Florent Schmitt, l'Homme et l'Artiste; Marceron, M., Florent Schmitt.

Chesterian (London), March 1932.

Arnold Schoenberg
1874–1951

Arnold Schoenberg, apostle of the twelve-tone technique, was born in Vienna on September 13, 1874. Although his parents were highly musical and introduced him to good music when he was young, it was several years before he revealed any particular aptitude for the art. For eight years he attended the Realschule in Vienna where, when he was eight, he started to study the violin. At twelve he made his first attempt at composition, writing several duets for the violin which he played with his teacher. "All my compositions," he later said of his juvenile efforts, "were merely imitations of such music as I had access to."

Although the death of his father, when Arnold was sixteen, forced him to earn a living, he continued his music. While working as a bank clerk, he studied the cello by himself and frequently participated in performances of chamber music. He also continued to compose. One of his works was brought to Alexander von Zemlinsky, eminent Viennese composer and teacher. Convinced of the young man's talent, Zemlinsky took him under his wing, taught him counterpoint (the only formal instruction in theory Schoenberg ever received), and got him a job as cellist in an orchestra Zemlinsky was then conducting. For a brief period, in 1895, Schoenberg also conducted an amateur chorus.

Through Zemlinsky, Schoenberg became acquainted with a group of progressive-minded musicians who infected him with their own enthusiasm for Wagner. Under this influence Schoenberg completed in 1897 the String Quartet in D major, the first of his works to be performed. It was received enthusiastically

Schoenberg: shûn′ bĕrĸ

at a concert of the Tonkünstler Verein in Vienna in the winter of 1898. (The score of this quartet was long thought lost, but when Schoenberg came to the United States he brought a copy with him and it was revived at a concert at the Library of Congress in Washington, D.C., on February 8, 1952.) Following the quartet Schoenberg wrote some songs (1897) which were assembled in his first publications (opp. 1, 2, 3). Professor Gärtner introduced a few in a recital in Vienna in December 1900. They were failures. "And from that time on," Schoenberg once commented, "the scandal never ceased."

ARNOLD SCHOENBERG

Still under the spell of Wagner, Schoenberg completed during a three-week period in 1899 a sextet, *Transfigured Night* (*Verklärte Nacht*), a musical setting of a poem by Richard Dehmel, *Weib und die Welt*, describing a walk taken in the moonlight by a man and woman. The woman confesses she is about to have a child by another man. Her companion understands and forgives. They fall into each other's arms and resume their walk in the moonlight. The music is sensual, atmospheric, and pictorial in the style of the post-Romantic school—richly harmonized and consistently melodic. Nevertheless, it was a failure when first heard in Vienna on March 18, 1902. In 1917 Schoenberg transcribed the work for chamber orchestra. As such it became famous —the most frequently performed of all of Schoenberg's compositions. On April 8, 1942,

the Ballet Theatre in New York presented a dance setting entitled *The Pillar of Fire*, with choreography by Antony Tudor. In 1943 Schoenberg once more revised the orchestral version.

Under the impact of post-Romanticism— and particularly of the music of Richard Strauss, Mahler, and Wagner—Schoenberg began in 1900 to work on a monumental cantata, *The Gurre-Lieder*. This was a setting of a cycle of poems by Jens Peter Jacobsen narrating the love affair of King Waldemar of Denmark with Tove in the Gurre castle. Most of the music was written by the end of 1901, but the final chorus and the orchestration had to wait a decade.

On October 7, 1901, Schoenberg married Mathilde Zemlinsky, the sister of his teacher. Soon after the marriage, impelled by the need to support his wife, Schoenberg moved to Berlin where he found a job as a conductor in a smart cabaret. He also orchestrated operettas and wrote potboilers. During the early years of his marriage, the probability of a performance of the *Gurre-Lieder* being remote, he continued to delay its completion, instead undertaking other creative projects. Late in 1902 he wrote the tone poem *Pelleas und Melisande*, based on Maurice Maeterlinck's Impressionist drama. Since Debussy's opera on the same text had been performed on April 30, 1902, causing a furor, it is reasonable to assume that Schoenberg knew of its existence; he might even have been influenced by Debussy, since the concluding pages of the Schoenberg tone poem employ the whole-tone scale. But where Debussy's opera was Impressionistic, Schoenberg's tone poem was a richly textured and programmatic composition in a post-Wagnerian style, calling for a huge orchestra. Its première came in Vienna on January 26, 1905. "For the whole fifty minutes," reported Ludwig Karpath in *Die Signale*, "one deals with a man either devoid of all sense or who takes his listeners for fools. . . . Schoenberg's opus is not merely filled with wrong notes . . . but is itself a fifty-minute-long protracted wrong note. This is to be taken literally. What else may hide behind this cacophony is impossible to ascertain."

In 1902, through the influence of Richard Strauss, Schoenberg was given the Franz Liszt stipend. A year later he returned to Vienna, to divide his time and activity between composition and teaching. He now began to gather around him a group of students, some of whom were eventually to be numbered among his most fervent disciples, the nucleus of a "school" of composition which would follow and glorify his principles and carry on his traditions. These students included Alban Berg, Erwin Stein, Anton Webern, and Egon Wellesz. As Anton Webern said: "Schoenberg . . . is our master in the highest sense of the word. He developed our personality to the point of self-expression."

Among the compositions he completed soon after returning to Vienna were a set of six songs, op. 8 (1904); the first Kammersymphonie, op. 9 (1906); the string quartet in F-sharp minor, op. 10 (1907); the pieces for the piano, opp. 11 and 19 (1908, 1911); and *Five Pieces for Orchestra*, op. 16 (1908). With these works Schoenberg permanently broke his ties with post-Romanticism. He was now striving for condensation, precision, objectivity—the reduction of music to essentials. He had also come to the conclusion that the old harmonic methods and the old tonal system were obsolete. He was now increasingly partial to short forms. More and more he began to abandon a tonal center and a unifying key signature, to drift more and more towards nontonality (Schoenberg always opposed the term "atonality" as applied to his music). The second string quartet in F-sharp minor, op. 10, was the last composition in which he used a specific key signature for a period of more than three decades. Its finale is his first piece of completely atonal music. He favored discords, refusing to recognize any longer a distinction between consonance and dissonance. "It is not lack of invention or technical skill that has urged me in this direction," Schoenberg explained in 1909. "I am following an inner compulsion that is stronger than education, and am obeying a law that is natural to me, therefore, more powerful than any artistic training."

At the same time he worked sporadically at the *Gurre-Lieder*. When completed in 1911, it proved to be a work of enormous dimensions, scored for narrator, five solo voices, three male choruses, an eight-part mixed chorus, and an immense orchestra of one hundred and forty instruments. In writing out the parts, Schoenberg had to use a special forty-eight-stave music sheet devised for him. The *Gurre-Lieder* became the apotheosis of Schoenberg's post-Romantic period (which by 1911 he had long since outgrown). It was, therefore, still the old Schoenberg with strong ties to accepted tonal practices and unifying key signatures. Introduced in Vienna on February 23, 1913, Franz Schreker conducting, the *Gurre-Lieder* was warmly received, one of the few successes Schoenberg was destined to enjoy in his lifetime. But, unable to forget the hostile treatment his non-Romantic compositions had been receiving, Schoenberg refused to acknowledge the ovation.

Ignoring the public reception of the *Gurre-Lieder*, he proceeded with his atonal work, becoming increasingly bolder in his experiments and independent in his thinking. In 1912 he wrote *Pierrot Lunaire*, a setting of Symbolist poems by Albert Guiraud for narrator and instruments. The absence of tonality and the presence of discords now became basic to Schoenberg's methods. In addition, he devised a new kind of lyricism which has come to be known as *Sprechstimme* or *Sprechgesang* (song speech—a declamation structurally characterized by its free rhythms and unequal measures, with the singer indicating the pitch of a note rather than singing it, then sliding either up or down to the next note). With *Pierrot Lunaire*, Schoenberg crossed the threshold of musical expressionism by creating an absolute music so completely divorced from extramusical connotations that frequently the music played by the instruments was completely irrelevant to the sung text: for example, in one of the songs, "Serenade," the text refers to a viola but the instrument participating is a cello.

Because of the newness of its speech, *Pierrot Lunaire* needed forty rehearsals before it could finally be performed. That performance took place in Berlin on October 16, 1912, and inspired a major scandal. The audience bellowed out its disapproval at the strange, discordant sounds. Fistfights broke out between these dissidents and Schoenberg's followers. The critics were poisonous. Otto Taubman wrote: "If this is music, then I pray my Creator not to let me hear it again."

Jeering, catcalls, fistfights also attended the world première of *Five Pieces for Orchestra*, which took place in London on September 3,

1912. Ernest Newman reported: "It is not often that an English audience hisses the music it does not like; but a good third of the people at Queen's Hall the other day permitted themselves that luxury. . . . Another third of the audience was not hissing because it was laughing, and the remaining third seemed too puzzled either to laugh or to hiss." The critic of the London *Daily Mail* inquired: "Why, then, should the ears of the Promenade audience be tortured with scrappy sounds and perpetual discord?"

An even greater furor erupted on March 31, 1913, when Schoenberg and his disciples presented a concert of their works in Vienna; on this occasion, Schoenberg's *Kammersymphonie No. 1*, op. 9 received its first hearing. Here is the report of the event in the *Musical Courier:* "If this concert was intended to be a 'memorable event' it surely succeeded, for it occasioned the greatest uproar which has occurred in a Vienna concert hall in the memory of the oldest critics writing. Laughter, hisses and applause continued throughout a great part of the actual performance of the disputed pieces. . . . The police were sought and the only officer who could be found actually threw out of the gallery one noisemaker who persisted in blowing on a key for a whistle. But this policeman could not prevent one of the composers from appearing in the box and yelling to the crowd, 'Out with the baggage!' Whereat the uproar increased. Members of the orchestra descended from the stage and entered into spirited controversy with the audience."

The hostility which Vienna had shown for Schoenberg's music drove him back to Berlin in 1911. He became instructor of composition at the Akademie für Kunst and lecturer on esthetics at the Stern Conservatory. But he returned to Vienna before World War I broke out. Despite the fact that he was now past forty he was twice mobilized into the Austrian army—from December 1915 to September 1916, and from July to October 1917. During this trying period he taught at the Seminary for Composition, which he had founded in Vienna in 1915.

The prolonged period of creative silence led Schoenberg to reevaluate his aims and to clarify his direction for himself. He came to the realization that his complete rejection of tonality had led not to freedom but to anarchy.

He felt the need for some kind of discipline and order: a new set of principles, a new musical grammar and syntax to replace the old ones he had discarded. Slowly and methodically he began to work out a system which eventually had worldwide repercussions and which made him the leading figure in the avant-garde movement in music. This was the twelve-tone technique or row (dodecaphony), an altogether new approach to the chromatic scale. Another Austrian composer, Josef Matthias Hauer, had preceded Schoenberg in formulating a twelve-tone technique, both in theoretical writings and in a piano piece published in 1912 (*Nomos*). But it was Schoenberg who developed the idea from a mere suggestion into one of the most influential techniques in twentieth century music and endowed it with artistic significance.

In *Since Debussy*, André Hodeir succinctly sums up the essential facts about the twelve-tone technique: "The twelve-tone row system proclaims that all notes are equal. . . . Since the twelve notes have been arranged in a given sequence, the entire work (or fragment of a work conceived as an entity) will necessarily derive from this row, from its eleven possible transpositions on the various degrees of the chromatic scale, or from its inverted, retrograde, and retrograde-inverted forms. Thus in the course of the work as a whole, the generating idea—which by itself is neither a theme nor a mode—may assume as many as forty-eight forms without affecting the fundamental unity of the musical discourse. Within a given constituent cell, none of the twelve notes which go to make up the row may be sounded twice until all the eleven others have been heard; this is to avoid 'polarizing' the melody, or harmony, as the case may be."

There are a number of stylistic elements found in twelve-tone compositions by Schoenberg and his school. Unusual sonorities are produced through glissandos, trills, flutter tonguings, harmonics, muted passages. Constructive rhythm is exploited—which means that a rhythmic pattern is given the same importance in the unfolding of a movement as a melodic figure. The interval of the fourth is employed in a melodic idea, while the interval of the seventh is used for high tension. Intricate contrapuntal structures are favored, whereas classical forms to which atonalists are partial (fugue, suite, passacaglia, sonata, invention) are condensed and compressed. Condensation and compression of material are also sought after.

Schoenberg used a twelve-tone row in the concluding number (the waltz) of his *Five Pieces*, for piano, op. 23 (1923), and in the fourth movement (a setting of a sonnet by Petrarch for baritone) of his *Serenade*, op. 24 (1923). The first Schoenberg composition built entirely from a twelve-tone row was the *Suite for Piano*, op. 25 (1924). The twelve-tone row became a system which Schoenberg used with extraordinary skill, ingenuity, and variety in succeeding works: the third string quartet, op. 30 (1926), first performance in Vienna on September 19, 1927; *Variations for Orchestra*, op. 31 (1928), first performance in Berlin on December 2, 1928; *Two Pieces* for piano, opp. 33a, 33b (1932); Violin Concerto, op. 36 (1936), first performance in Philadelphia on December 6, 1940; and the second *Kammersymphonie*, op. 38 (1939), first performance in New York on December 15, 1940.

In these compositions, as Hans Gutman noted, Schoenberg "drove expressionism in music to the furthest possible point. He completely unraveled the individual voices and so shattered the harmonic groundwork that nothing further remained to be accomplished in this direction." These were the creations of a highly analytical brain, cold and calculating, divorced of all human feeling. This was not the kind of music capable of winning the enthusiasm of audiences and critics at first hearing. There was, therefore, no end to the antagonism created by first performances of Schoenberg's music. To counteract the lack of sympathy and understanding, at least in Vienna, Schoenberg in November 1918 founded the Society for Private Performances so that the new music of his followers could be performed in a favorable environment. All critics were barred; only those who were understanding and appreciative of the new style gained admission. Applause was taboo. Except for these concerts, Schoenberg stubbornly refused to attend performances of his compositions.

In the era between the two world wars, Schoenberg divided his time each year between his home in Mödling, a Viennese suburb to which he moved in 1918, and Berlin, where in 1925 he was appointed professor for life at the Academy of Arts in succession to Busoni.

His wife Mathilde died in 1923, and in 1924 Schoenberg remarried. His second wife was Gertrud Kolisch, sister of the first violinist of the Kolisch String Quartet. Schoenberg had two children by his first wife and three by his second.

Despite the antagonism aroused by public performances of Schoenberg's compositions, his eminence both as a theorist and as a composer was universally accepted. His sixtieth birthday in 1934 was, consequently, celebrated in Austria. But Schoenberg was no longer a resident of that country. In 1933 he saw the birth of Nazism in Germany. He recognized its implications when in May of that year the German Ministry of Education dismissed him from the faculty of the Prussian Academy of Fine Arts, a life appointment. Though born a Jew, he had been converted to Christianity in 1921. Nevertheless, his Jewish birth—as well as his experimental music, which the Nazis regarded as decadent—made him *persona non grata* in Germany. Realizing that it could not be long, now, before Austria would be submerged under the wave of Nazism, Schoenberg decided to leave Europe permanently. He went to Paris where, in May 1933, he went through a religious ceremony in a synagogue reinstating him in the Jewish faith. The following autumn, on October 31, he arrived in the United States. On April 11, 1941, he became an American citizen.

For a number of months after coming to America, Schoenberg was on the faculty of the Malkin School of Music in Boston. During this period he occupied an apartment on Beacon Street in Brookline. Poor health (he had chronic asthma) compelled him in 1934 to seek a warmer climate; he moved to the Brentwood section of Los Angeles, where he lived for the rest of his life. In 1935 he was appointed professor of music at the University of Southern California. A year later he assumed a similar post at the University of California in Los Angeles, which he held until 1944. After that, he confined his teaching activities to a few select private pupils (about eight in all) until a month before his death.

He remained creatively productive, though the major works completed in America demonstrated an altogether new orientation not only to his own system, but to the world around him and to the political events that had shaken him to his roots. His return to Judaism impelled him to write a number of works with Hebraic background. These included an adaptation of the celebrated synagogal Yom Kippur prayer *Kol Nidrei*, for narrator, chorus, and orchestra (1938) and Psalm CXXX, for unaccompanied chorus, with a Hebrew text (1950); and a monumental biblical opera, *Moses und Aron*, two acts of which were completed in 1932 and to which, after a hiatus of almost two decades, he returned just before his death.

Other compositions were inspired by events of the times. When Schoenberg first became conscious of the world around him, he tried to express that world in subjective music in the *Ode to Napoleon*, for speaking voice, piano, and string orchestra (1943). He used Byron's poem to protest against the tyranny of dictatorship. Byron's final invocation to George Washington became in Schoenberg's setting a mighty hymn of praise to democratic freedom. The *Ode* was first heard in New York on November 23, 1944, with Artur Rodzinski conducting the New York Philharmonic.

In *A Survivor from Warsaw*, a cantata for narrator, men's chorus, and orchestra (1947) Schoenberg was inspired both in his text and in his music by the suffering of his fellow Jews in the concentration camps of Nazi Germany. With grim realism Schoenberg described the horrors perpetrated by the Nazis on their victims, and in doing this he brought to his atonal writing human values rarely before encountered in his music. This cantata is one of his most deeply moving creations. Commissioned by the Koussevitzky Music Foundation, it was given its world première on November 4, 1948; Kurt Frederick conducted the Albuquerque Civic Symphony.

In these and other late works, Schoenberg became more flexible than ever in his use of the twelve-tone system. He no longer felt the necessity for conforming to it rigidly. He now used it when his subject called for it; otherwise he used it sparingly, or not at all. His new flexibility allowed for the infusion of human feelings, even a return of some of his early Romantic ardor. It also helps explain why so many of his last works proved so successful at first hearing.

For Schoenberg was no longer a prophet without honor. Indeed, accolades, tributes, and testimonials of all kinds began to accumulate. In 1947 the National Institute of Arts and Letters presented him with the Special Award of Distinguished Achievement. All-Schoenberg concerts throughout the United States helped to commemorate his seventy-fifth birthday. Premières of his new works drew ovations from the audiences and effusive praise from the critics. Schoenberg's lofty station in twentieth century music—and the extraordinary influence he had exerted on his generation—was the subject of numerous articles.

To Schoenberg—so long dishonored, abused, vilified—these victories proved hollow. He could not forget his earlier struggles, and he remained bitter. When he received the prize of the National Institute of Arts and Letters, he replied with a violent attack on those who had misunderstood him and his music for so many years, suggesting that the award should have been bestowed on his enemies, since it was they who were responsible for his fame and worldwide acceptance.

When his seventy-fifth birthday was being celebrated in many cities of the United States, Schoenberg sent his friends a message bearing the words "To be recognized only after his death," which further demonstrated how bitter he had become. It opened with the following thought: "For many years I have resigned myself to the fact that I cannot hope for a full and appreciative understanding for my work—for what I have to say as a musician."

His feud with Thomas Mann, late in 1948, was also testimony to his bitterness. Mann had written a novel, *Doctor Faustus*, whose central character was a composer employing the twelve-tone technique. In an introductory statement, Dr. Mann published the following explanation: "It does not seem supererogatory to inform the reader that the form of musical composition delineated in Chapter XXIII, known as the twelve-tone row or system, is in truth the intellectual property of a contemporary composer and theoretician, Arnold Schoenberg. I have transferred this technique in a certain ideational context to the fictitious figure of a musician, the tragic hero of my novel. In fact the passages of this book that deal with musical theory are indebted in numerous details to Schoenberg's *Harmonielehre*."

Any other composer, however distinguished,

might have been flattered to find a Nobel Prize winner devoting a novel to a method he had made famous. But Schoenberg, a lifetime victim of persecution, saw only victimization in having his system used in a work of fiction. He sent a vitriolic letter to the *Saturday Review* attacking Mann for taking advantage of "my literary property"; expressed indignation at the "consequences of ascribing my creation to another person which, in spite of being fictitious, is represented as a living man"; foresaw the dire possibility of having some encyclopedist of the year 2060 ascribing "my theory" to Thomas Mann!

But as Robert Breuer remarked in the *Saturday Review*, "in the mild atmosphere of his waning days, he became reconciled with his fate. With a touching warm gratitude he accepted the honors awarded him by his native city. He wanted to pay a visit to Vienna, but never regained enough physical strength to do so."

Arnold Schoenberg died at his home in Brentwood on July 13, 1951. He had been seriously ill for several months. Nevertheless he had been hard at work on his biblical opera, *Moses und Aron*, which he had abandoned after two acts in 1932. He did not live to complete it. The world première of the two acts was given over the Hamburg Radio on March 12, 1954, with a staged version following in Zürich on June 6, 1957, during the festival of the International Society for Contemporary Music. The conductor Hermann Scherchen, who regarded the opera as one of the epochal achievements of our century, was then responsible for directing performances of the opera in Milan, Vienna, and Paris. When it was produced at Covent Garden in London on June 28, 1965, *Moses und Aron* created a sensation—not for its austere twelve-tone style; but because the staging called for an orgy scene depicting naked virgins and the sacrifice of live animals. The American première of *Moses und Aron* took place in Boston on November 30, 1966.

In summing up the general reaction to *Moses und Aron*, Hans F. Redlich wrote in *Opera*: "Its very sound—mysterious, visionary, frenzied, triumphant in turns—is as unique as its mixture of opera, oratorio, and cantata, serving together in the transmission of a tremendous religious experience. When the music ebbs away prematurely at the end of Act II—

with Moses despairing of his vocation in a moving passage combining instrumental melody and *Sprechstimme*—an artistic and a human experience has reached its consummation, which may well represent to future generations the musical high-water mark of the century."

Though he was one of the foremost innovators in twentieth century music, Schoenberg detested being called a revolutionary. "What I did was neither revolution, nor anarchy, but evolution," he insisted. He also disliked fixing any kind of label to his compositions. "My music," he once wrote Roger Sessions, "must be listened to in the very same way as is any other music—forget the theories, the twelve-tone method, the dissonances, and so forth, and may I add: if possible, try to forget the composer, too. I once said in a lecture: 'A Chinese poet talks Chinese, but what does he say?' To this I add: It is my own private business to write in this or that style, to use one or another method—this should not be of interest to the listener. But I do want my mission to be understood and accepted."

In a personal portrait written during the composer's later years in California, Lou Harrison said: "Schoenberg . . . as an American citizen . . . is singularly well adjusted, amiable, inquisitive. He has enough energy today to supply several twenty-year-olds. He seems in much better health and much younger than when he arrived in this country. Limping into the classroom, one day, he explained that his toe had been injured in an accident at his workshop. He had been building furniture. His hobby-habit, perhaps, contributes much to his excellent vigor and helps appease an insatiable curiosity. That curiosity is, of course, proverbial. It has made him the most reliable compendium of musical knowledge in existence. He said one day that many accused him of being a mathematician. There was a moment's silence; then he mock-maliciously remarked that he couldn't help it if he could think better than others. One must agree."

Dika Newlin adds the following personal information: "No picture of Schoenberg would be complete without recollections of his home life in Brentwood, California. The big Spanish-type house, set in spacious enclosed grounds, was always a lively place to visit, what with three young children [his grandchildren] and assorted pets ranging from dogs, through Angora rabbits, to Easter chicks." Miss Newlin also reveals that Schoenberg was an ardent believer in numerology. In spite of the fact that he was born on September 13, he regarded the number "13" as unlucky. "But this did not keep him from celebrating the date in grand style. Never to be forgotten are his birthday parties with good food and drink, plenty of informal music making, and the master of the house everywhere at once doing everything from playing tennis or Ping-pong to singing (?) his own parody on 'Wien, Wien, nur du allein.' . . ."

Schoenberg produced several important theoretical treatises. These included the *Harmonielehre* (1911) which appeared in an English translation as *Theory of Harmony* in 1947; *Models for Beginners in Composition* (1942); *Style and Idea* (1950).

MAJOR WORKS

Chamber Music—4 string quartets; Verklärte Nacht, or Transfigured Night, for string sextet (also for chamber orchestra); Serenade, for clarinet, bass clarinet, mandolin, guitar, violin, viola, cello, with baritone voice; Quintet, for flute, oboe, clarinet, horn, and bassoon; Suite, for two clarinets, bass clarinet, violin, viola, cello, and piano; String Trio; Fantasia, for violin and piano.

Choral Music—Friede auf Erden; Gurre-Lieder; Kol Nidrei; A Survivor from Warsaw; De Profundis; Die Jacobsleiter (unfinished).

Orchestral Music—2 Kammersymphonie; Pelleas und Melisande; Five Pieces; Accompaniment Music to a Cinematographic Scene; Suite in G, for strings; Violin Concerto; Piano Concerto; Theme and Variations; Ode to Napoleon, for speaker, strings, and piano.

Piano Music—3 Klavierstücke; 6 Kleine Klavierstücke; 5 Klavierstücke; Suite; 2 Klavierstücke.

Vocal Music—Das Buch der Hängenden Gärten; Herzgewächse; Pierrot Lunaire, for Sprechstimme, piano, flute, clarinet, violin, and cello; various songs for voice and piano.

ABOUT

Armitage, M. (ed.), Schoenberg; Collaer, P., A History of Modern Music; Ewen, D. (ed.), The New Book of Modern Composers; Hartog, H. (ed.), European Music in the Twentieth Century; Hodeir, A., Since Debussy; Leibowitz, R., Schoenberg and His School; Newlin, D., Bruckner, Mahler, Schoenberg; Rufer, J., The Works of Arnold Schoenberg; Stein, E. (ed.), Arnold Schönbergs Briefe; Stuckenschmidt, H. H., Arnold Schoenberg; Wellesz, E., The Origin of Schoenberg's Twelve-Tone System.

Musical Quarterly, October 1951; New York Times Magazine, September 11, 1949; Saturday Review, January 30, 1960.

Franz Schreker
1878–1934

Franz Schreker was born of Austrian parents on March 23, 1878, in Monaco, where his father was employed as court photographer. His father died when Franz was ten, and his mother, a descendant of Austrian nobility, took her family of four to Vienna where they lived in abject poverty. This condition did not interfere with Franz Schreker's musical development, once he had demonstrated that he had unusual talent. He received a scholarship for the Conservatory, where he studied the violin with Arnold Rosé and theory with Fuchs and Grädener. At eighteen he wrote and had performed *Psalm 116*, a choral work, and an *Intermezzo* for strings which won a prize. Despite these accomplishments, and his brilliance as a student, Schreker often came into conflict with the school authorities. On one occasion, he broke the rules against extra-curricular activities by organizing a music society to give public concerts. At other times, he antagonized his teachers by his enthusiasm for music with modern idioms.

After completing his studies, Schreker worked for a year in 1907–1908 at the Volksoper. In 1908 he helped organize the Vienna Philharmonic Choir, whose programs were open to the more advanced representatives of modern music, and in 1911 he became its principal conductor. In this office he gave the world première of Schoenberg's *Gurre-Lieder* in 1913. Besides his work as conductor, Schreker also pursued an active career as teacher, having been engaged in the department of composition at the Akademie der Tonkunst in 1912.

His first opera, *Flammen*, was written when he was twenty. It was never published, and the only performance took place in 1902 with piano accompaniment. Schreker worked six years on his second opera, *Der Ferne Klang* (*The Distant Tone*), for which he wrote his own libretto—a practice he pursued in all subsequent operas. *Der Ferne Klang*, completed in 1909, was produced at Frankfurt-am-Main on August 18, 1912. Though its indebtedness to Wagner placed it solidly in the post-Romantic camp, Schreker was already revealing a

---

Schreker: shrā′kĕr

personal identity. His application of instrumental forms to opera made a powerful impression on Alban Berg, who arranged the vocal score for publication. There is small doubt that Berg's use of a similar practice in *Wozzeck* was the result of his interest in Schreker's opera. Schreker's frequently modern harmonies, sometimes suggesting Debussy, brought a nod of approval from Schoenberg in his *Harmonielehre*. And Schreker's first experiments with symbolism made him use sound as "the embodiment of ideal, mystic forces," as Donald J. Grout noted.

When *Der Ferne Klang* was heard in Paris for the first time, Henri Quittard recognized its originality by saying in *Le Figaro:* "It is certain that the composer must be counted from this day as one of the most original and most interesting writers of our epoch."

If Vienna had failed to appreciate fully *Der Ferne Klang*, it did not deny its recognition or enthusiasm to Schreker's first ballet, *Der Geburtstag der Infantin*. This adaptation of Oscar Wilde's popular story *The Birthday of the Infanta* was successfully produced in 1908. Fifteen years later he revised it and renamed it *Spanisches Fest*. The symphonic suite based on the ballet score retains the original title of *The Birthday of the Infanta* and is one of Schreker's most frequently played orchestral compositions.

Die Gezeichneten (*The Stigmatized*) was Schreker's first completely successful opera. Schreker wrote it in the period between 1912 and 1915, and its première took place at the Frankfurt Opera on April 25, 1918. The libretto used a Renaissance setting, with a love interest involving a beautiful girl and a cripple with a beautiful soul. For this quasi-symbolic, quasi-expressionist drama, Schreker produced a truly remarkable score which still drew deeply from the reservoir of Wagner. But Wagnerism was blended with an eroticism reminiscent of Richard Strauss, and naturalism was blended with mysticism. The dramatic element was emphasized without sacrificing expressive lyricism. The harmonies are strong, frequently daring. The orchestration is at times orgiastic and at other times extremely sensitive.

Schreker's next two operas added further to his fame in Central Europe. *Der Schatzgräber* (*The Treasure Digger*) was produced by the Frankfurt Opera on January 21, 1920. It

was followed by a one-act "mystery," *Das Spielwerk*, which actually was a revision of a three-act opera written before World War I and produced simultaneously at the Vienna Royal Opera and the Frankfurt Opera on March 15, 1913: *Das Spielwerk und die Prinzessin*. The one-act revision was seen in Munich on October 30, 1920. Both *Der Schatzgräber* and *Das Spielwerk* represent a drift away from Wagner and towards an increasingly modernized harmonic idiom that edges ever closer towards expressionism. Schreker was now embraced by the progressive factions in Germany and Austria. He even became something of a cult. By 1924, his operas had been given more than two hundred performances throughout Central Europe.

FRANZ SCHREKER

In 1920 he became director of the Berlin Hochschule für Musik, and many distinguished German and Austrian composers came under his influence there, including Ernst Krenek, Karol Rathaus, Alois Hába, and Jascha Horenstein. But by 1930 Schreker had lost his influence and his following, as new movements came into vogue. Schreker's last operas were failures when introduced in Berlin and Freiburg.

His reputation as a teacher also suffered, not only because he had lost his following as a composer, but also because he was notoriously lackadaisical about administrative duties. Under pressure from Chancellor Franz von Papen, Schreker finally resigned his post as director of the Berlin Hochschule für Musik in 1932; but in compensation he was assigned a master class in composition at the Prussian Academy of Arts. With the rise of the Nazis, in 1933, however, Schreker was denied even his class in composition. Out of step with the new regime, Schreker became more removed than ever from the musical life of his country. This tragic turn of affairs broke his health and spirit. Before the end of 1933 he had suffered a stroke, and he died in Berlin on March 21, 1934—by that time a completely neglected, underrated, and in some instances forgotten composer. He was survived by his wife, Marie (who had once sung leading female roles in his operas), and their two children, Ottilie and Emanuel.

MAJOR WORKS

Ballets—Der Geburtstag der Infantin (The Birthday of the Infanta); Rokoko (Four Pieces in Olden Style); Der Wind, dance allegory.

Choral Music—Psalm 116; Schwanengesang.

Operas—Flammen; Der Ferne Klang; Das Spielwerk und die Prinzessin (revised as Das Spielwerk); Die Gezeichneten; Irrelohe; Der Singende Teufel; Der Schmied von Gent; Christophorus.

Orchestral Music—Ekkehard, symphonic overture; Phantastische Ouvertüre; Romantische Suite; Vorspiel zu einem Drama; Kammersymphonie, for twenty-three solo instruments; Kleine Suite, for chamber orchestra; Two Lyrical Songs from Whitman's Leaves of Grass, for high voice and orchestra; Vom Ewigen Leben, to poems by Walt Whitman, for soprano and orchestra.

Vocal Music—Various songs for voice and piano.

ABOUT

Bekker, P., Franz Schreker; Kapp, J., Franz Schreker; Neuwirth, G., Franz Schreker.

Musikblätter des Anbruch (Vienna), special Schreker issue, 1928.

Gunther Schuller
1925–

Gunther Schuller was born in New York City on November 22, 1925, of a family of musicians. His grandfather had been a conductor and music teacher in Germany. His father, Arthur Schuller, was violinist with the New York Philharmonic for forty-one years.

Brought up in such a family, Gunther heard classical music from his earliest childhood, and he responded to it sensitively. He recalls how

Schuller: shoo′ lĕr

one day when he was only six he and his brother sang through the entire *Tannhäuser* overture, imitating the sound of all the instruments of the orchestra. In his twelfth year, Gunther became a boy soprano at the St. Thomas Church Choir School conducted by T. Tertius Noble and discovered that he had a gift for sight reading. About that time he also began to study the flute, but when he was fourteen he shifted to the French horn.

GUNTHER SCHULLER

His academic education took place in the public schools of the city simultaneously with his first systematic training in theory at the Manhattan School of Music. With his graduation from Jamaica High School in 1942, his academic education came to an end. And after he left the Manhattan School of Music the same year, he was mainly self-taught in music.

In January 1943 Schuller became a horn player in the Ballet Theatre orchestra, which toured the country. Before the year was over, he was appointed first horn of the Cincinnati Symphony. It was with this orchestra, conducted by Eugene Goossens, that Schuller made his official bow as composer, by appearing as a soloist in the première of his Concerto for Horn and Orchestra in 1944. By the end of 1945 he had written a cello concerto, a suite for woodwind quintet, and a tone poem for orchestra entitled *Vertiges d'Éros*.

As a member of the faculty of the Cincinnati College of Music, where he taught the horn, Schuller met a young student of voice and piano, Marjorie Black, whom he married in New York City on June 8, 1948. They have two sons.

Another significant event in Schuller's life took place in Cincinnati: his first hearing of Duke Ellington and his orchestra, an experience that made him an Ellington enthusiast. He listened to Ellington records by the hour and set for himself the task of orchestrating several of Ellington's compositions. Some of Schuller's symphonic adaptations of Ellington's music were heard at "pop" concerts of the Cincinnati Symphony. This interest in Ellington also led him in 1955 to compose his *Symphonic Tribute to Duke Ellington.*

Largely as a result of his admiration for Ellington, Schuller soon became a jazz devotee. Eventually he arranged jazz concerts, performed jazz music, worked on a musico-analytical study of jazz, used jazz within the framework of some of his serious compositions, and in 1968 published a book, *Early Jazz.*

From 1945 to 1959 Schuller played the horn in the orchestra of the Metropolitan Opera in New York, filling the position of first horn nine of those years. This period saw the production of much chamber music for various instruments (mostly winds); his *Symphony for Brass and Percussion*, introduced in the year of its composition (1950) by the Cincinnati Symphony and presented at the Salzburg Festival in Austria in 1957; and the *Dramatic Overture* for orchestra (1951), successfully performed in Darmstadt, Germany, in 1954 and by the New York Philharmonic in 1958.

One of his most significant works up to that time was his first string quartet (1957), which had been commissioned by the Fromm Music Foundation for the 1957 Festival of Contemporary Arts at the University of Illinois at Urbana. When the work was performed by the Claremont String Quartet in Pittsfield, Massachusetts, during the summer of 1963, Ross Parmenter described it as follows in the New York *Times:* "It opens and closes with slow movements, and most of it is muted. Yet such is its tension and expressiveness that it had a deep effect. It has many long, drawn-out quiet sounds that provide a basis from which the other sounds emerge, now like the sharp cries of anguish, now like mysterious night sounds, and occasionally in snatches of intense lyricism."

Schuller's first important experiments in combining jazz with modern serious musical resources came in 1955 with the previously mentioned *Symphonic Tribute to Duke Ellington* and with *12 by 11*, for chamber orchestra and jazz improvisation. In 1957 Schuller coined the term "third stream" to describe a union of the rhythm and improvisations of jazz and such advanced idioms of twentieth century music as serialism. He said: "I believe that the serial technique is the most meaningful method so far discovered to organize present-day musical resources. I believe also that jazz has developed, through the improvisational method, a natural, strongly individual, basically unnotable feeling and spontaneity which has an extraordinary communicative potential. I believe that these two forces (serial technique and jazz) will primarily determine the course of music in the next several decades." In line with such thinking he wrote the Concertino for Jazz Quartet and Orchestra, which the Baltimore Symphony introduced in 1959; the *Variants on a Theme by Thelonius Monk;* and the *Variants on a Theme by John Lewis.* His most ambitious score exemplifying third-stream music is the ballet *Variants*, which he completed in 1960, and which (with George Balanchine's choreography) was seen in New York on January 4, 1961. This music called for an orchestra in the pit and a jazz ensemble on the stage—and Schuller conducted both groups. Schuller also promoted third-stream music as a member of the Modern Jazz Quartet, which has appeared publicly in numerous concerts throughout the United States.

Schuller's experimentation was not confined exclusively to jazz. In writing *Spectra*, for orchestra, he was concerned with two problems. The first related to structure. Feeling that conventional classical forms could no longer serve the twentieth century composer, Schuller here constructed a one-movement composition which, as he explains, "had no preconceived formal mold into which the music could be poured. In terms of form, the work in a real sense unfolded itself." The second problem was of a physical-acoustical nature. His many years of experience as a performer in orchestras made Schuller conscious of the inadequacy of the conventional orchestral seating plan to meet the demands of

505

twentieth century orchestration: "It occurred to me that the anachronistic seating arrangement must be altered if the demands of newer orchestral techniques are to be met. I therefore devised a seating plan which conforms more to the variegated color possibilities of the modern orchestra." The seating plan for *Spectra* split the orchestra into seven groups—five of them of various chamber-music dimensions; each group could be joined with the others or could operate independently. The title *Spectra*—related to the color spectrum—refers "to the use of various color series as an important all-pervading structural element of the work. The composition, completed in 1958 on a commission from the New York Philharmonic and Dimitri Mitropoulos, was introduced by that organization on January 14, 1960. Commenting on this acoustical experiment, Irving Kolodin said in the *Saturday Review:* "Whether to the palate or the ear, the proof of the pudding is the tasting; and Schuller's musical upside-down cake had a distinctive flavor of its own."

In 1959 Schuller completed the orchestral composition with which he achieved one of his major public successes. It was the suite *Seven Studies on Themes of Paul Klee*, which he wrote for the Minneapolis Symphony under a grant from the Ford Foundation in conjunction with the American Music Center. The work received its world première in Minneapolis on November 27, 1959, Antal Dorati conducting. The reflection of the visual arts in musical sound was a subject that had long interested Schuller. In his *Seven Studies* he tried to relate seven Klee paintings to musical tones: "Antique Harmonies," "Abstract Trio," "Little Blue Devil," "The Twittering Machine," "Arab Village," "An Eerie Moment," and "Pastorale." "Each of the seven pieces bears a slightly different relationship to the original Klee picture from which it stems," the composer has explained. "Some relate to the actual design, shape or color scheme of the painting, while others take the general mood of the picture or its title as a point of departure." Despite the fact that the work uses the serial technique, it became a major success and was soon performed by leading orchestras throughout the United States. It was also heard at the festival of the International Society for Contemporary Music

at Cologne on June 12, 1960. Wherever it has been presented, it has won enthusiastic audience approval, as well as high praise from the critics. When it was heard in New York, Howard Taubman reported: "It is not often that a new piece wins such hearty applause at a first performance." Herbert Elwell said after the Cleveland performance: "It has been said of Klee's work that it has a 'childlike freshness.' That is exactly what the music possessed. To me it was fascinating in its clarity and simplicity of texture, its humor, its total lack of platitude, and its variety of moods and colors."

American Triptych: Three Studies in Texture (1964) was another successful attempt by the composer to find a correlation between painting and music. Here Schuller's point of departure was three American paintings: "Four Directions" by Alexander Calder; "Out of the Web" by Jackson Pollock; and "Swing Landscape" by Stuart Davis. By trying to translate into sound the texture of each of the paintings, Schuller progressed one step beyond his *Seven Studies*. When the work was first heard (in New Orleans on March 9, 1965, the composer conducting), Frank Gagnard remarked in the New Orleans *Times-Picayune:* "Since Schuller here deals with two non-objective artists and one abstractionist, there is not as much specific pictorial reference. . . . The composer is not literal but he is evocative in a highly sophisticated way."

Another major work for orchestra, though not concerned with visual arts, is Schuller's first symphony, the première of which was conducted by Donald Johanos in Dallas on February 8, 1965. Once again the symphony proved that a composition written in a serial technique could provide a welcome listening experience even for the general public. What impressed John Rosenfeld in the Dallas *News* was Schuller's gift "for placing instruments in their most euphonious and most inviting registers. There is little in the instrumental resource that doesn't exploit sensibly and to musical purpose." To Irving Lowens, in the *Musical Quarterly*, this symphony is "the product of a creative mind of the highest order. It is at its best when it is most approachable through the ears alone. And it is a pretty convincing demonstration that melody and the most advanced serial techniques are by no means incompatible."

The successes Schuller had enjoyed up to 1966, substantial though they were, were merely the preface to a triumph which few American composers have known, and certainly no others in the American avant-garde movement. That triumph came with the opera *The Visitation*, Schuller's first. He wrote it in Berlin on a Ford Foundation grant as composer-in-residence, and a commission from Rolf Liebermann, the director of the Hamburg Opera. The excitement and enthusiasm aroused during and immediately after the world première on October 12, 1966, with the composer conducting, have few parallels in the twentieth century. The work received a twenty-two-minute ovation and fifty curtain calls. The German newspapers the next morning were unanimous in hailing it as a work of major significance, and several did not hesitate to call it a masterwork. One critic described Schuller as the "Puccini of twelve-tone opera." To Rolf Liebermann *The Visitation* was the most important opera since *Wozzeck*.

Three companies cabled for the recording rights. Invitations poured into the office of the Hamburg Opera to visit major capitals with the new opera. The two major American opera companies asked for performing rights, and so did a festival planned for Urbana, Illinois. Two German opera houses sent Schuller commissions for new operas; the BBC asked him to do a television opera. Schuller was an international celebrity, and his opera—without a single note having been heard outside Hamburg—was world famous.

However, when *The Visitation* received its American première (performed by the visiting Hamburg State Opera in New York on June 28, 1967), it was rejected by the opening-night audience—some hissed, others left the theatre before the opera was over. It was severely criticized in the press as "naïve," filled with "embarrassing clichés," and lacking "in heart and soul." The general reaction was far better when the opera was given by the San Francisco Opera in October. "The opera made impressive dramatic impact," reported the critic of the San Francisco *Chronicle*, "and established itself as an important work, but it likely deserves neither the extravagant European enthusiasm of last fall nor the disappointed New York reaction of last June."

Schuller wrote his own libretto, based on Kafka's drama *The Trial* which Gottfried von Einem had previously made into an opera. Schuller transplanted the setting to the United States, used Negroes as principal characters, and racial problems as the basis of his drama. The text describes the tragedy of Carter Jones, a Negro University student, who was rejected by his own Negro society without being assimilated into a white one. He is accused and found guilty of crimes he has not committed and in the end is lynched. "The opera traces his attempts to find justice in a nightmare world of corruption and misunderstanding," explained James H. Sutcliffe in a cable to the New York *Times*.

The music is in the third-stream style devised by Schuller to combine twelve-tone writing with jazz. The latter is played by a seven-man jazz ensemble. "The jazz combo was able to swing, even when they were playing the tone row that is one of Schuller's innovations," said Sutcliffe, who described the score as a whole as "sensitive and expressive, always interesting and theatrically effective despite its complexity."

Schuller has distinguished himself both as a conductor and as an educator. In 1963 and 1964 he led a series of concerts entitled "Twentieth Century Innovations" in New York City, and since then he has appeared as a guest conductor of major American symphony orchestras. As an educator, he has been a member of the faculty of the Manhattan School of Music, which he joined in 1950; the Berkshire Music Center at Tanglewood, where from 1963 to 1965 he was acting head of the composition department, and, after that, head; Yale University, where, in 1964, he was appointed associate professor; and the New England Conservatory in Boston, of which he was made president in 1966.

Schuller was responsible for a radio series comprising one hundred and fifty broadcasts called "Contemporary Music in Evolution"; the series was eventually heard over seventy-seven stations of the National Association of Educational Broadcasters. In 1962 he became music director of the First International Jazz Festival, held in Washington, D.C.

He has been honored many times. In 1960 he received the National Institute of Arts and Letters Award and the Brandeis University Creative Arts Award. In 1961 he became the first American to be commissioned to write a work for the modern music festival at Donaueschingen, Germany; the work was *Contrasts*, for orchestra, introduced on October 22, 1961. In the years between 1962 and 1964 he was awarded Guggenheim Fellowships, and he was chosen by the Department of State to become a special visitor to Yugoslavia, Poland, and West Germany. He received the Darius Milhaud Prize for the best film score of the year in 1964—the Polish film *Yesterday in Fact*. In 1966 he received the Hornblit Award.

In 1967 Schuller was commissioned to write a new orchestral work for the opening of Powell Symphony Hall, the new home of the St. Louis Symphony. He himself conducted the composition, *Fanfare for St. Louis*, on January 24, 1968.

MAJOR WORKS

Ballet—Variants.

Chamber Music—2 string quartets; Suite for Woodwind Quintet; Cello Sonata; Oboe Sonata; Fantasia Concertante, for three oboes and piano; Quartet for Doublebasses; Trio for Oboe, Horn, and Viola; Quintet for Four Horns and Bassoons; Symphony for Brass and Percussion; Fantasy for Unaccompanied Cello; Fantasy, for four cellos; Five Pieces, for five horns; Music for Violin, Piano, and Percussion; Recitative and Rondo, for violin and piano; Quartet for Flute and Strings; Variants on a Theme by Thelonius Monk; Variants on a Theme by John Lewis; Woodwind Quintet.

Opera—The Visitation.

Orchestral Music—Horn Concerto; Cello Concerto; Vertiges d'Éros, tone poem; Dramatic Overture; 12 by 11, for chamber orchestra and improvisation; Symphonic Tribute to Duke Ellington; Contours; Concertino for Jazz Quartet and Orchestra; Seven Studies on Themes of Paul Klee; Spectra; Contrasts; Piano Concerto; Movements for Flute and Strings; Symphony; American Triptych; Composition in Three Parts; Gala Music; Diptych, for brass quintet and orchestra; Five Bagatelles; Triplum; Fanfare for St. Louis; Concerto for Double Bass and Orchestra.

Vocal Music—Meditations; Five Shakespearean Songs; Seven Songs; Six Renaissance Lyrics.

ABOUT

Machlis, J., Introduction to Contemporary Music.
Musical Quarterly, April 1965; Saturday Review, November 12, 1966.

William Schuman
1910–

William Howard Schuman (named after William Howard Taft) was born in New York City on August 4, 1910. His grandfather had come from Germany to the United States during the Civil War and served in the Confederate Army. His father fought in the Spanish American War, then earned his living as a bookkeeper and later became vice president of the firm. Although William did not reveal unusual talent for music in his boyhood, he began to take violin lessons with a local teacher because at that time his ambition was to perform with his school orchestra. However, he was reluctant to practice and his progress was slow. Nevertheless, he did participate in modest concerts, usually of semiclassical music, in his own home; from time to time he performed little violin pieces at public concerts. His real passion was baseball and he dreamed of becoming a major leaguer. His other athletic interests were swimming and boxing. In the arts he preferred the drama and tried his hand at writing a play; it was produced at Speyer Junior High School, which he was then attending.

As a student at George Washington High School, he formed a jazz ensemble called Billy Schuman and his Alamo Society Orchestra; it performed at dances and other functions. With this group, Schuman played the violin and banjo, and sometimes he appeared as vocalist. During the summer, as a guest at a boys' camp, he wrote music for stage productions mounted by the campers, and it was at the camp that his first piece of serious music, a tango for violin written when he was sixteen, was introduced.

While still at high school, he began to write music for popular songs, some of which were published. None were hits, but a few were used as special material by vaudeville and night-club performers. One was "In Love With You," a song which deserves a special place in the history of popular music because the lyrics were the work of young Frank Loesser, who later became one of America's greatest songwriters, and this number was Loesser's first publication.

Schuman: shoo′ măn

After graduation from high school in 1928, Schuman enrolled at New York University School of Commerce to prepare for a business career. In spite of his ventures in popular music, the idea of making a living through music never seriously entered his mind. One day, April 3, 1930, his sister took him to his first concert—a performance by the New York Philharmonic—an event that changed the course of his life. Convinced he must become a serious musician, he left New York University, resigned his job with an advertising agency, and enrolled in the Malkin School of Music for a course in harmony. "I could see there was something burning there," his harmony teacher, Max Persin, later recalled. Persin not only taught Schuman harmony but also introduced him to the wealth of musical literature by having him study scores by the hour. Schuman then took lessons in counterpoint from Charles Haubiel.

Realizing he must find a way of supporting himself, Schuman entered Teachers College at Columbia University in 1933 and received a Bachelor of Science degree two years later. After a summer studying conducting at the Mozarteum in Salzburg, he joined the music faculty of Sarah Lawrence College in Bronxville, New York, in the fall of 1935. There he conducted the chorus, which performed compositions by students, and commissioned works from established American composers. Under Schuman's direction the chorus achieved such fame that, following a tour, the college newspaper stated: "Our chorus is our football team. Notre Dame has Knute, but we have Bill." On March 27, 1936, he was married to Frances Prince.

By this time composition had begun to absorb him completely. In 1933 he wrote four chorale preludes for mixed a cappella voices. These settings of four poems by Edna St. Vincent Millay, Countee Cullen, Carl Sandburg, and Alfred Tennyson were published under the title *Four Canonic Verses*. They were sung at Teachers College at Columbia University on May 3, 1935. In 1934 he also wrote two other compositions: a *Canon and Fugue*, for piano trio; and *Choreographic Poem*, for seven instruments.

While in Europe attending the Mozarteum, Schuman began to plan a symphony with material he had used in the *Choreographic Poem*. He completed it towards the end of 1935. On October 21, 1936, it was introduced in New York City at a WPA concert which also included the *Four Canonic Verses* and Schuman's first string quartet.

WILLIAM SCHUMAN

This symphony attracted the interest of Roy Harris, then teaching composition at the Juilliard School of Music. Harris became Schuman's teacher, the two-year period of instruction exerting a far-flung influence on the student. Harris's interest in polyphony, in medieval modes, in polyharmony, was passed on to Schuman, who began to adopt such methods in his own writing. These traits became discernible in Schuman's second symphony (1937), first performed at a WPA concert in New York on May 25, 1938. Aaron Copland heard the performance and persuaded Serge Koussevitzky to conduct the symphony in Boston in February 1939. Boston critics were almost unanimous in denouncing the work. The exception was Moses Smith who wrote in the Boston *Transcript*: "Dr. Koussevitzky, far from having made a mistake in placing it on one of his programs, is actually disclosing to Boston audiences a genuine American talent."

Schuman was dissatisfied not only with his second symphony but also with his first symphony and first string quartet. He withdrew them all from further performance. New creative projects proved more satisfying, and in July 1939 he completed his first composition to remain in the repertory, the *American Festival Overture*, for orchestra. This brisk, vivacious music opens with a three-note phrase intended to simulate the call "wee-awk-eem" which New York City boys used to convoke the gang for play. "This call," Schuman explained, "very naturally suggested itself for a piece of music written for a special occasion—a festival of American music." Introduced by the Boston Symphony under Koussevitzky on October 6, 1939, in an American music festival sponsored by ASCAP, the overture was a great success.

Recognition now came to Schuman from several different directions. He received Guggenheim Fellowships in 1939 and 1940. In 1941 he was given the Award of Merit from the National Association of American Composers and Conductors, and in 1943 the award from the National Institute of Arts and Letters. His Third String Quartet was the first composition commissioned jointly by the League of Composers and Town Hall in New York; the Coolidge String Quartet introduced it in New York on February 27, 1940. His Third Symphony—world première in Boston on October 17, 1941, Serge Koussevitzky conducting—received such critical acclaim that it made Schuman a national figure in music; for it he received the New York Music Critics Circle award. Olin Downes said: "It takes the position of the best work by an American of the rising generation." The *New Yorker* referred to Schuman as "the composer of the hour by virtue of the popular and critical success of his Third Symphony."

Schuman was becoming the composer not of the hour but of the year 1943. After his fourth symphony was presented by Artur Rodzinski with the Cleveland Orchestra on January 22, 1942, it was successfully performed in New York and Philadelphia. On January 13, 1943, an entire program of his works was heard at Town Hall, New York. One month later, on February 13, 1943, the Pittsburgh Symphony under Reiner performed Schuman's short and deeply moving symphonic piece *Prayer in Time of War*. On March 26, 1943, the Boston Symphony under Koussevitzky presented the world première of a secular cantata *A Free Song* (text by Walt Whitman), which received the first Pulitzer Prize in music. The Koussevitzky Music

Foundation commissioned him to write a new symphony, *Symphony for Strings*, which was heard in Boston under Koussevitzky on November 12, 1943. On the occasion of this première the critic of the Boston *Herald* remarked that Schuman was "well on his way to becoming the foremost American-born composer of the day."

His identity as a composer was now crystallized. He had begun to free himself from whatever polyphonic and modal influences of Harris had clung to his earlier music; he was achieving a melodic style, and harmonic and rhythmic procedures, that were basically his own. His writing was lyrical, yet it had the strength and momentum that led Leonard Bernstein to praise it for its "buoyancy," "energetic drive," and "vigor of propulsion." Paul Rosenfeld, singling out a prominent quality of Schuman's style, pointed to his "force, originally fixed and deadly, which is subjected to a new incarnation and finally moves joyously unified and with a gesture of embrace towards life."

In 1945 Schuman resigned from Sarah Lawrence College to become director of publications of G. Schirmer. It was probably the first time that an important composer held such a position in a major publishing house. But though he had signed a three-year contract, Schuman was not destined to hold his post long. Hardly had he settled into his job when he was called to fill a bigger one, that of president of the Juilliard School of Music. Schirmer released him from his contract but retained his services as chief adviser of publications for the next seven years.

When Schuman, at thirty-five, took over his new office at the Juilliard School, one of its trustees remarked: "This will either be the greatest thing that ever happened to Juilliard or the most colossal error of our collective lives." It was not an error. In the years that followed, and almost from the moment he took over, Schuman overhauled the school's curriculum, changed its personnel, instituted major reforms, and succeeded in making it one of the most progressive conservatories in the world. He combined the Juilliard School with its junior affiliate, the Institute of Musical Art, into a single organization. He founded remarkable festivals, was responsible for important premières and revivals performed by school forces, and helped to create the Juilliard String Quartet, which has since become one of the most prominent chamber music ensembles in the world. In recognition of Schuman's far-reaching contributions to music education, as well as his importance as an American composer, the University of Wisconsin conferred on him an honorary doctorate in music in June 1949; he was the youngest man ever to be thus honored in the century-old history of the University.

At Juilliard, Schuman proved a remarkable executive—practical, hard-working, extremely efficient, systematic, and outstandingly capable of getting along with people of varying temperaments, interests, and backgrounds. He seemed to have a natural gift for resolving chaos into order. His executive duties, demanding though they were, did not restrict his creativity. From the time he took on his manifold tasks at Juilliard, he made it a practice to devote two hours each morning to composition at his home in New Rochelle. "I am a very tough disciplinarian—with myself that is," he told an interviewer in 1960. "I compose four hundred hours during the school year; that's an average of ten hours a week. Some weeks I do a little less, some a little more. I keep track of the hours on a desk pad so that I am sure to make it come out. Then I put in two hundred hours during vacation; so I get six hundred hours in all. It shocks a lot of people that a creative artist would work on such a regimen. But after all, if I'm a composer, I must write music."

His production during his first five years at Juilliard proved how successfully he could combine the lives of an executive and a creator. He completed two ambitious scores for ballets, both written for Martha Graham: *Night Journey*, introduced at Harvard on May 1, 1948; and *Judith*, which Martha Graham presented with the Louisville Orchestra under Robert Whitney, on January 4, 1950. *Judith* received the New York Music Critics Circle Award. In addition to these scores he completed a new symphony, his sixth, commissioned by the Dallas Symphony, which introduced it under Antal Dorati on February 27, 1949. He wrote his fourth string quartet on a commission from Elizabeth Sprague Coolidge to commemorate the one hundred and fiftieth anniversary of the Library of Congress. And he

produced a violin concerto which Isaac Stern performed with the Boston Symphony on February 10, 1950.

He subsequently completed three more major symphonies. The seventh received its world première on October 21, 1960, in Boston with Koussevitzky conducting. The eighth received its first performance in New York on October 4, 1962, under Leonard Bernstein. The ninth, entitled *Le Fosse Ardeatine* (after the cave in which 335 Italians were slain by the Nazis in an act of reprisal in 1944) was given for the first time on January 10, 1969, by the Philadelphia Orchestra. Schuman also contributed an additional ballet score for Martha Graham, *The Witch of Endor*, which she introduced in the fall of 1965; a work for cello and orchestra, *Song of Orpheus*, first performance in Indianapolis under Izler Solomon on July 4, 1961; a threnody for Martin Luther King and Senator Robert Kennedy, *To Thee Old Cause*, introduced by the New York Philharmonic under Leonard Bernstein on October 3, 1968; and a major work for chorus in 1958, *Carols of Death* (text by Walt Whitman), which a reviewer for *High Fidelity* described as "certainly a masterpiece by a composer whose immensely distinguished contribution to choral literature has never been properly acknowledged."

Schuman has enriched orchestral literature with imaginative adaptations of music by other composers. His *New England Triptych*, which André Kostelanetz commissioned in 1956 and introduced in Miami on October 28 of that year, utilizes three hymns by William Billings, America's first important composer. These hymns serve as a point of departure for an extremely successful symphonic cycle. Almost a decade later, Schuman, in similar fashion, worked with the music of Charles Ives in *Variations on America*, for organ.

In their biography of Schuman, Flora Rheta Schreiber and Vincent Persichetti wrote: "If there is more of one ingredient than another in the rich mixture of William Schuman's music it is the strong-fibered energy that generates a constant boil of motion. There is motion stirred by boldness and intensity, movement that pushes forward resourcefully and seriously, and beneath even the quietest pages a restless current that will eventually surface in a rush."

Among the later honors conferred upon Schuman, in addition to honorary degrees, are the Bicentennial Anniversary Medal from Columbia University and the first Brandeis University Creative Arts Award in music, both in 1957. In 1967 he was given the Concert Artists Guild award for his "distinguished achievements in the development of our musical life and sponsorship of talented young artists." In addition he was made Fellow of the National Institute of Arts and Letters and an honorary member of the Royal Academy of Music in London.

Further recognition of his powers in administration and organization came in January 1962 when he was appointed president of the Lincoln Center for the Performing Arts in New York, as successor to General Maxwell D. Taylor. Under Schuman, the Lincoln Center grew into a giant complex comprising concert and opera auditoriums, the Juilliard School of Music, theatres, a library of the performing arts, and other affiliated institutions. The first of these buildings, Philharmonic Hall, was opened on September 23, 1962. During the next five years came the New York State Theatre, the Vivian Beaumont Theatre, the Library-Museum of the Performing Arts, the Metropolitan Opera House, and the Juilliard School of Music. In December 1968 Schuman announced that he was resigning as president but would remain available for consultation and to serve as chairman of the Carnegie Study of the Lincoln Center educational program.

Schuman maintains his home in New Rochelle where he and his wife live with a son and a daughter. Here he built a studio where he does his composing and outdoor and indoor swimming pools where he can indulge his passion for swimming the year round. He is still vitally interested in baseball and combines this pastime with voracious reading of books and periodicals; going to the theatre, films and concerts; using gadgets of all sorts; and experimenting with different food combinations. He is tall (just under six feet), slim, nearly bald, with "a narrow face" (Harold C. Schonberg's description), "prominent features, a look of intelligence so pronounced that it can almost be touched, a perpetually eager expression, and a quality of quivering suppressed excitement." Schuman is a meticulous dresser and expects all those who work with him to be similarly well groomed. He has been described by some of his friends as "a radical with conservative ideas." Schonberg adds: "He is, for instance, almost prissy about the amenities of living, and sees no reason why people should not always conduct themselves with decorum."

About his credo as a composer he has said: "The time-honored verities of artistic creation still seem to be basic. The *sine qua non* is an inner urge that knows no denying. A composition must have two fundamental ingredients— emotional validity and intellectual vigor.... Works of merit in our times, as in times past, have been composed through a variety of approaches and techniques encompassing the gamut of known devices, plus the invention of new ones.... I am not much impressed with categories, but prefer rather to judge each work on its own terms."

MAJOR WORKS

Ballets—Undertow; Night Journey; Judith, choreographic poem; The Witch of Endor.

Chamber Music—4 string quartets; Quartettino for Four Bassoons (also for clarinets or saxophones); Amaryllis, variations for string trio.

Choral Music—Pioneers!; This Is Our Time; Requiescat; Holiday Song; Te Deum; Four Rounds on Famous Words; The Lord Has a Child; Carols of Death.

Opera—The Mighty Casey.

Orchestral Music—9 symphonies; American Festival Overture; Piano Concerto; Credendum; New England Triptych (based on William Billings); Violin Concerto; A Song of Orpheus, for cello and orchestra; To Thee Old Cause.

Piano Music—Three-Score Set; Voyage; Three Piano Moods.

ABOUT

Chase, G., America's Music; Ewen, D. (ed.), The New Book of Modern Composers; Goss, M., Modern Music Makers; Schreiber, F. R. and Persichetti, V., William Schuman.

Juilliard Review, Winter 1955; Modern Music, November–December 1944; Musical Quarterly, January 1945; Saturday Review, November 1, 1947.

Cyril Scott
1879–

Cyril Meir Scott was born in Oxton, Cheshire, England, on September 27, 1879. His father, a Greek scholar, directed him early towards academic studies. His mother, an amateur pianist, was a deeply religious woman who would have liked to see the boy prepare for the clergy. But Cyril's passionate interest in and talent for music from childhood on persuaded both parents to allow him to develop along his own lines. When he was twelve, Cyril was sent to Germany where because of his unusual talent he was accepted as a pupil of the piano at Hoch's Conservatory in Frankfurt-am-Main, even though he was below the prescribed age for admission. At fourteen he went back to England to resume his general education, while continuing piano study with Steudner-Welsing in Liverpool. At sixteen he returned to Hoch's Conservatory where he remained three years, most of that time attending the composition class of Iwan Knorr.

CYRIL SCOTT

In 1898 Scott settled in Liverpool to begin his professional career in music by teaching and playing the piano. There his lifelong interest in writing poetry was stimulated further by his friendship with Charles Bonnier, the distinguished professor of French literature at the University of Liverpool. By 1900 Scott began to divide his time between writing poems and composing music. As a composer he made significant headway with the première early in 1900 of his first symphony, conducted in Darmstadt by Willem de Haan. A year later his *Heroic Suite* was introduced in Liverpool under Hans Richter's direction. Both compositions, however, he subsequently destroyed, together with a number of other early works. More representative of the kind

of music he wanted to write were the Piano Quartet in E minor, introduced in London in 1901 by an ensemble that included Fritz Kreisler as first violinist; and the Second Symphony, the première of which was conducted by Henry J. Wood in London at a Promenade concert on August 25, 1903. Shorter orchestral pieces were also being heard. Among these were *A Christmas Overture*, performed in London on November 13, 1906, and the overture to Maeterlinck's *La Princesse Maleine*, played in London on August 22, 1907.

Scott was now also writing and publishing some of the songs and smaller items for the piano which made him famous. The best known of the piano numbers were *Danse Nègre, Water Wagtail,* and *Lotus Land;* among the most famous songs were "Lullaby," "Blackbird's Song," and "Daffodils." These became so popular that for a long time Scott was erroneously believed to be exclusively a composer of miniatures.

But it was with his larger, more ambitious, compositions that he made a definite impact on contemporary music. He was one of the first English composers to use a pronounced modern style, beginning with the Piano Sonata (1909) and the Violin Sonata (1910). His works were characterized by a daring use of shifting meters, discords, unorthodox modulations, unusual progressions adventurous for those years. In some compositions he dispensed with a key signature; in others he assumed a complicated method of irregular barring in order to get a more precise accentuation for his long-flowing melodic line. Many composers of that day were influenced by the kind of music he was creating and expressed their indebtedness. "When I first went to London around 1900," wrote Percy Grainger, "Cyril Scott seemed to me to be the leading English compositional thought. It was largely his musical ideas and innovations that his fellow composers discussed and drew esthetic nourishment from." Eugene Goossens said: "Cyril Scott was the first English composer who was at once truly English and truly modern." And Claude Debussy wrote: "His rhythmic experiments, his technique, even his style of writing may at first appear strange and disconcerting. Inflexible severity, however, compels him to carry out to the full his particular system of esthetics and his only."

His fame spread beyond England in 1913 when he was invited to Vienna by Gustav Mahler's widow. There his overture *La Princesse Maleine* proved so successful that plans were made to present some of his large choral compositions in Vienna the following year. World War I, however, frustrated these plans. But in England presentations of his major compositions knew no interruption. At a festival organized by Sir Thomas Beecham in London, Cyril Scott was heard in the world première of his piano concerto on May 15, 1915. A year after that Beecham led the first performance of Scott's *Two Passacaglias on Irish Themes*. Another major work of that period was a choral setting of Keats' poem *La Belle Dame sans Merci*, introduced in 1916 and successfully revived at the Leeds Festival in 1934.

Scott toured the United States in 1920, appearing as soloist in a performance of his own piano concerto with the Philadelphia Orchestra on November 5, 1920. The program also included his *Two Passacaglias on Irish Themes*, which he himself conducted. When the program was repeated in New York a few days later, Richard Aldrich wrote in the New York *Times:* "He is one of the most 'modern' of English composers of the present day. . . . Like most others of the advanced school, he is apparently more concerned with color, instrumental and harmonic, with effects of sonority, contrasts of timbre and resonance, with rhythmic complexities and the superimposition of incommensurable rhythms than with melodies, and the musical resources of dramatic development."

After returning to England, Scott worked upon his first opera, *The Alchemist*, writing his own libretto as well as the music. It was produced in Essen on May 28, 1925. Two later operas were never given.

In 1933 his *Festival Overture* (a revision of his early *La Princesse Maleine*) received the Daily Telegraph Prize. *Ode to Great Men* was heard at the Norwich Festival in 1936; a harpsichord concerto was introduced in April 1938; and an oboe concerto was performed in September 1948. In 1961 he completed an important chamber work—Trio, for flute, cello, and piano; and in 1962, an orchestral Sinfonietta.

Here is George Lowe's description of Scott's style: "The vocabulary in which he chooses to express himself is one of considerable originality both rhythmically and harmonically. He has no belief in imprisoning himself within the bounds set by theorists, but believes that art should be allowed to articulate freely, and he takes all sorts of licenses so long as they are not incompatible with his ideas of good taste."

Scott expounded his musical beliefs to the editor of this book: "I consider that music without some sort of melody or motive cannot be lasting. The secret of satisfactory musical creation and form lies in variation. Moreover, musical form cannot be dispensed with. As to narrowing down musical creation to theories and labels, this in my opinion denotes a lack of inspiration and a backward step.

"Although the dictum must be taken with some reservation, for opinions differ as to what is beauty and what is ugliness, yet the true artist is he who succeeds in inventing new forms of beauty. It is not very difficult to invent new forms of ugliness but far from easy to invent new forms of beauty as did the masters of music. Of course, for the sake of variety and strength, it is essential to have periods of discordancy as a foil to the concordant parts, especially in operatic creations, but where there is nothing but discordancy the result is monotony. For my own part, in my more serious creations, I have not been afraid of discord, but neither have I been afraid of melody as a necessary contrast."

Scott believes that people who have no interest in sport or games should seek their recreation in a change of work. He himself has turned to writing poems during periods of rest from music. He has also translated into English a large number of verses by the German poet Stefan George, whom he met for the first time when he was studying music in Frankfurt and who subsequently became a lifelong friend. Scott occasionally also likes to "play about with colors," as he puts it, by way of stimulating his imagination.

Since his twenty-fourth year he has devoted himself to the study of mystical and occult philosophy, which has affected both his life and outlook, and he has written several books on the subject. He is a pronounced mystic with a strong leaning towards Yoga, theosophy, and Vedanta.

Scott has written *Music: Its Secret Influence*

Throughout the Ages (1933, revised 1950), and an autobiography, *My Years of Indiscretion*.

MAJOR WORKS

Chamber Music—2 piano quintets; 3 string quartets; 4 piano trios; 2 string trios; 3 violin sonatas; Piano Quartet; Tallahassee, suite for violin and piano; Ballad, for cello and piano; Sonata Melodica, for violin and piano; Piano Trio in One Movement; Aubade, for recorder and harpsichord; Trio, for clarinet, cello, and piano; Cello Sonata; Clarinet Quintet; Rondo Serioso, for viola d'amore and piano; Trio Pastorale, for flute, cello, and piano; Flute Sonata; Sonata for Two Violins and Piano.

Choral Music—Mirabelle, cantata; La Belle Dame sans Merci; Nativity Hymn; Mystic Ode; Summerland; Ode to Famous Men; Hymn of Unity, oratorio.

Operas—The Alchemist; The Shrine; Maureen O'Mara.

Orchestral Music—3 symphonies; 2 piano concertos; La Princesse Maleine, overture (revised as Festival Overture); Aubade; Noël, a Christmas overture; Two Passacaglias on Irish Themes; Violin Concerto; Early One Morning, poem for piano and orchestra; Irish Serenade, for string orchestra; Rima's Call to the Birds, scena for high soprano and orchestra; Summer Gardens, suite for small orchestra; Concerto for Harpsichord and Chamber Orchestra; Oboe Concerto; Hourglass, suite for small orchestra; Russian Fair; Sinfonietta, for strings, organ, and harp; Sinfonietta, for string orchestra.

Piano Music—3 sonatas; Handelian Rhapsody; Deuxième Suite; Impressions from the Jungle Book; Five Poems; Egypt, five impressions; Ballad, variations on a troubadour air; Rondeau de Concert; Variations on an Original Theme, for two pianos; Russian Fair, for two pianos; Pastorale Ode; over one hundred short pieces including Danse Nègre, Lotus Land, Water-Wagtail.

Vocal Music—Numerous songs for voice and piano including Blackbird's Song, Daffodils, Lullaby.

ABOUT

Hull, A. E., Cyril Scott; Scott, C., My Years of Indiscretion.

Alexander Scriabin
1872–1915

Alexander Nikolaievich Scriabin was born on January 6, 1872, in Moscow. His father was a lawyer who had entered the consular service; his mother was an accomplished pianist, a pupil of Leschetizky and a graduate of the St. Petersburg Conservatory.

Alexander's mother died when he was still an infant. Since his father's consular duties sent him to distant Near Eastern posts, the

---

Scriabin: skryȧ′ byĭn

child was placed under the care of his grandmother and an aunt. They allowed him to develop academically and musically according to his own inclinations. The boy learned by himself to read and write. His aunt, however, gave him his first piano lessons, from which point he went on to learn as much music as he could through trial and error at the keyboard. Once, when he was five, after attending an opera performance, he built a little theatre with which he performed miniature dramas of his own writing by taking all the roles.

ALEXANDER SCRIABIN

Both his grandmother and his aunt pampered and spoiled him. They were so over-solicitous about his welfare that one or the other had to be with him all the time. He was not permitted to play with other children; in fact, he was not allowed to go out alone into the street until he was fourteen. Aunt and grandmother were in constant terror of possible illnesses, accidents, danger. Scriabin's later hypochondria, hypersensitivity, and obsessive fears—as well as his egocentricity—surely owe their origin to this strange early upbringing.

His devotion to music was extraordinary, so much so that all other interests receded into the background. The piano became something of an obsession. He would kiss it as if it were human, and he would be emotionally disturbed whenever it was tuned. He disliked formal lessons and exercises, but improvisations so absorbed his interest that he would stay at the keyboard for hours at a time. His technique, therefore, left much to be desired, and his ability to read music was sorely deficient. Nevertheless, when Anton Rubinstein heard him play he remarked: "Let the child develop in freedom. Everything will come out in time."

In 1882 at his own request he was enrolled in the Military School in Moscow, where he was an excellent student, popular with both classmates and teachers. At this time he began to study the piano intensively with G. E. Conus; later, he continued his piano lessons with Zverev.

By the time he had completed his education at the Military School he knew he wanted to become a professional musician rather than enter the army. In 1885 he studied composition privately with Taneiev. Three years later he entered the Moscow Conservatory where he attended the classes of Safonov, Arensky, and Taneiev. He devoted himself with such slavish industry to developing his piano technique that the muscles of his right hand became paralyzed. This, however, did not keep him from winning the gold medal in piano playing when he was graduated from Safonov's class in 1892. In studying theory, however, he was less fortunate; Arensky regarded him as a "scatterbrain." When Scriabin failed his examinations, he left the Conservatory without a diploma in composition.

Nevertheless he had already produced much music for the piano which revealed considerable creative talent, though the influence of Chopin could be readily detected. The publisher Jurgenson thought so highly of his music that he accepted some of these compositions. Scriabin's first opus was the Waltz in F minor; the second, a set of three pieces including an etude, a prelude, and an impromptu; the third, a set of ten mazurkas.

In 1894 Scriabin appeared in a piano recital in St. Petersburg in which he featured some of his own compositions. Belaiev, the powerful publisher and patron, who was in the audience, was so impressed both with Scriabin's pianism and with his compositions that he decided to take the young musician in hand. He offered to publish everything Scriabin wrote. More than that, he decided to finance Scriabin's career by subsidizing his tours as a concert pianist. Scriabin's first compositions published by Belaiev appeared in 1895. Hs first concert

tour of Europe, in the 1895–1896 season, was highlighted by a recital in Paris, the entire program of which was devoted to his own compositions. The critic of *Libre Critique* described him as "equally great as composer and pianist . . . an enlightened philosopher." So successful was this tour that Belaiev arranged a special annuity of over five hundred rubles to enable Scriabin to devote more of his time to composition. Rimsky-Korsakov, also impressed by Scriabin's gifts, called him a "star of the first magnitude, newly risen in Moscow."

In 1897 Scriabin married Vera Isakovitch, a pianist. She made several appearances with her husband in joint recitals; in her solo appearances she performed Scriabin's music extensively. On January 31, 1898, they gave a successful recital in Paris presenting an all-Scriabin program.

Scriabin's first compositions through op. 8, which was the twelve Etudes, are Chopinesque in their poetic moods, in exploitation of piano timbres and textures, and in the use of extended melodic lines of romantic interest. Alfred J. Swan, however, took pains to point out that Scriabin was no mere imitator: "He is Chopin's rightful successor, and, as such, carried to an extreme certain peculiarities of Chopin's style. What lay in the background with Chopin comes to the fore with Scriabin; the music grows in nervousness. . . . The tissues become closer and more compact, the writing neater and more scrupulous than even Chopin's."

After op. 8, Scriabin's writing, for a period, became more Lisztian than Chopinesque, more expansive in style, more brilliant in virtuoso effects. These characteristics are evident in the Piano Concerto in F-sharp minor, which received its world première in Odessa with the composer as pianist on October 23, 1897, Safonov conducting the Odessa Philharmonic; and the third piano sonata, in F-sharp minor (1897). By 1900 his creative ambition had sufficiently expanded to permit him to undertake his first symphony, op. 26, its choral ending sounding like a religious paean to art.

This religious glorification of art indicated the direction in which Scriabin was now drifting. At the turn of the century, Scriabin became deeply involved in mysticism. He was impressed by the writings of Prince Sergei Nikolaievich Trubetskoi, who promulgated the idea of the oneness of love and God; at the same time he became convinced of the validity of Wagner's belief that art cannot exist for its own sake alone but must serve to direct and uplift mankind. From these premises he progressed to the ultimate conviction that art must become a "transformer of life," a means of converting life into a "kingdom of God on earth." To his thinking Nietzsche contributed the concept of the superman, with whom he soon identified himself. He even planned an opera about the superman, a Siegfried-like hero who conquers through the power of art. Scriabin now became intoxicated with the power, invincibility, and omnipotence of the ego, the creative "I."

Mysticism, pantheism, theosophy, self-deification, solipsism all gave a new purpose to his music. His writing grew increasingly involved and rarefied as he attempted to make his art express his mystical concepts. He even evolved a system all his own the better to achieve his purpose, the basis of which was the so-called "Mystery Chord," constructed from intervals of the fourth, a practice first foreshadowed in his fourth piano sonata in F-sharp major, op. 30 (1903), and fully realized in his third symphony. That symphony, in C major, was subtitled *The Divine Poem*. In it the composer described the evolution of the human spirit through pantheism to the affirmation of the divine ego. Completed in 1904, the work was introduced in Paris under Artur Nikisch's direction on May 29, 1905. "A piece of wonderful music " is the way A. Eaglefield Hull described it, "full of rich themes, well developed, and combined with mastery of counterpoint and modern harmony of a hue the like of which had not been heard before. It is musically logical, full of contrast, design, and color. At times the texture is quite simple; at other moments, of great complexity. Altogether it is a work of great originality and high poesy— an epoch-making work in the handling of modern harmony."

In his next symphony, in C major, *Poem of Ecstasy*, Scriabin described the ecstasy of unfettered creative activity. The work was built upon five melodic subjects symbolizing yearning, protest, apprehension, will, and self-assertion. He completed it early in 1908, at which time he played parts of it to a group of distinguished musicians. One of them, Rimsky-

Korsakov, said: "He's half out of his mind." After it had been introduced in New York under Modest Altschuler on December 10, 1908, and repeated one month later in St. Petersburg, the symphony received the second Glinka Prize and found many supporters.

His personal life, like his creative one, was changing radically. He had been a member of the faculty of the Moscow Conservatory from 1898 to 1903, in the piano department. He never liked teaching and resented the way it kept him from composing. In 1903 he decided that he had had enough of the classroom. On January 10, 1904, his publisher and benefactor, Belaiev, died, bringing to an end the annual subsidy he had been receiving. This, combined with the fact that he was no longer drawing a salary from the Conservatory, would have spelled poverty but for the fact that one of his wealthy pupils came to his rescue as a patroness to endow him with a comfortable yearly income.

In 1903 Scriabin deserted his wife and four children for a young pianist, Tatiana Schloezer, the sister of the eminent music critic Boris de Schloezer. She stood ready to worship him, just as she shared his passion for theosophy and Nietzsche. They lived together, unable to marry since Scriabin's wife stubbornly refused to grant him a divorce. The situation led to serious complications late in 1906 when Scriabin came to the United States for his first concert tour. He made his American debut in New York on December 20, 1906, appearing as soloist with the Russian Symphony under Altschuler in a performance of his own piano concerto. Scriabin then embarked on a tour in which he was joined by Tatiana. A scandal developed when the public became informed that Scriabin and Tatiana were not legally married. To avoid prosecution on grounds of moral turpitude, Scriabin and Tatiana left the United States suddenly without completing the scheduled engagements.

In 1908 Scriabin met the young, brilliant, and wealthy conductor Serge Koussevitzky, who was also the director of a new publishing house devoted to the issue of new Russian music. Since Belaiev's death, Scriabin had been looking for a new publisher and patron; and young Koussevitzky was on the lookout for an exciting new music personality to promote. Their meeting and friendship solved the problems of both. Koussevitzky proposed to publish all of Scriabin's music henceforth and to propagandize Scriabin's orchestral music through performances at the Koussevitzky Concerts. In 1910, when Koussevitzky left with his orchestra on his famous trip along the Volga, Scriabin went along with him, appearing eleven times as soloist in his piano concerto. On March 15, 1911, Koussevitzky gave in Moscow the world première of Scriabin's last symphony, *Prometheus*, which the composer had written for Koussevitzky. This was a complex and not often clear musical delineation of the struggle of Man against the Cosmos, with Man endowed by Prometheus with the creative will through a divine spark. An involved work, it was made all the more complex by its requirement for a color-keyboard to throw colors on a screen while the music was being played. The color apparatus was not used when Koussevitzky introduced the work, but it was used at its American première in New York on March 20, 1915, Altschuler conducting. Since that time the symphony has been played without benefit of colors.

A rupture between Scriabin and Koussevitzky developed soon after this première. It was inevitable. Each was too much the egotist, too much the individualist, too convinced of his own importance and greatness, too combustible, for a harmonious relationship to exist indefinitely. The rift proved permanent. In spite of this, Koussevitzky never relaxed his efforts on behalf of Scriabin's music and performed it repeatedly, not only in Russia but, later, in Paris and in Boston.

After *Prometheus* Scriabin began to evolve a Gargantuan scheme: the creation of a monumental world philosophy to which he gave the name "The Mystery." His Mystery was to consist of a union of social, religious, philosophic and artistic thought summing up the history of man from the dawn of time to the final, inevitable cataclysm. (After the cataclysm, Scriabin felt, a new era would come, breeding a nobler race of men.) Every means was to be used: not only sight and sound but also smell; Scriabin even planned to employ a new language of sighs and exclamations to express the heretofore inexpressible. To Scriabin, his Mystery was the last will and testament of a dying civilization before the emergence of a new and greater one.

Scriabin planned his Mystery for many years. He wanted it performed in India in a special temple built for that purpose. He wanted worshipers as the audience. He went to a travel agency to get all the information he could about accommodations in India. But all that Scriabin succeeded in writing of the Mystery was the text and some musical sketches for a preamble which he called "Propylaea"—Propylaea being the entrance to the Acropolis in Athens.

When the war broke out in 1914, Scriabin was jubilant, for he was convinced that this was the cataclysm that he had so long foreseen and that he was delegated by Fate to become the new Messiah, leading the way out of the cataclysm to a brave new world. His premature death brought these grandiose visions to a sudden end.

In 1914 Scriabin visited London where he made a number of appearances in performances of his work. Back in Russia he gave a piano recital in St. Petersburg on April 15, 1915. This was his last public appearance. Returning to Moscow, he developed a carbuncle of the upper lip which he neglected and which developed into gangrene. He died on April 27, 1915. He had three children by Tatiana, who were legitimated after Scriabin's death.

Scriabin was known to be an eccentric, a man of strange contradictions. Though fearful of climatic changes, he never wore a hat, since he was convinced that to do so caused depilation. He was always taking medicines of all kinds, including quack remedies, to ward off sicknesses, real and imagined, and he wore gloves as a protection against germs. He had a neurotic fear of being alone and was a man given to excesses of emotion. Listening to one of his own compositions induced in him a kind of rapture. "I have seldom seen a composer's face and figure so mobile while listening to his own music," once commented Leonid Sabaneyev.

Scriabin and Tatiana had a son Julian, who was an extraordinary musical prodigy. When he was eleven, as Nicolas Slonimsky (who knew him) informs us, Julian wrote piano preludes which "were direct continuations of his father's last opus numbers." One summer day in 1919, Julian and his friends went on an excursion to an island in the

Dnieper River. Wading in the water, Julian, a poor swimmer, came upon a sudden drop and was unable to save himself. Slonimsky was with a group of professional seamen who found the boy's body at dusk.

In addition to his symphonies Scriabin produced a library of music for the piano including sonatas, etudes, and preludes. The growth of his style can be traced from Romanticism through harmonic and rhythmic experimentation to its final refinement and mysticism. During the period of experimentation, "his innovation consisted mainly in creating new chords," says Leonid Sabaneyev. "This enthusiasm was a sort of sport with him. Scriabin wished to outdistance his contemporaries in creating chords with the greatest number of notes." In the last period, Scriabin's style, continues Sabaneyev, reached "an extraordinary exquisiteness and refinement, his harmony a rare complexity along with a saturation of psychological content. Side by side with this, we observe a dissolution of rhythm, a reduction of melody to the minimum, a severance of the musical web and line which turns into a series of spasmodic exclamations and destroys the impression of unity and wholeness."

MAJOR WORKS

Orchestral Music— 5 symphonies (including The Divine Poem, The Poem of Ecstasy, and Prometheus); Piano Concerto in F-sharp minor.

Piano Music—An entire library of piano music including 89 preludes, 26 etudes, 21 mazurkas, 10 sonatas, 6 impromptus, 2 nocturnes, together with sundry other pieces.

ABOUT

Bakst, J., A History of Russian-Soviet Music; Bowers, F., The Enigma of Scriabin; Brook, D., Six Great Russian Composers; Calvocoressi, M. D. and Abraham, G., Masters of Russian Music; Hull, A. E., Scriabin; Leonard, R. A., A History of Russian Music; Sabaneyev, L., Scriabin; Swan, A. J., Scriabin.

Roger Sessions
1896–

Roger Huntington Sessions was born in Brooklyn, New York, on December 28, 1896. Most of his ancestors were New England clergymen, and when he was four, his family returned to Massachusetts, where Roger was brought up. At the age of five, he began to study the piano with local teachers. His mother, an accomplished pianist who had

studied at the Leipzig Conservatory, took over the instruction when Roger reached twelve. At thirteen, fired by his enthusiasm for Wagner, whose music he had recently heard, he made an attempt at writing an opera based on Tennyson's *Lancelot and Elaine*. At the age of fourteen, upon hearing a performance of *Die Meistersinger*, he decided that he wanted to be a composer.

ROGER SESSIONS

Extraordinarily precocious in all his studies, both academic and musical, Sessions was graduated with highest honors from Kent School in Connecticut in 1911 and entered Harvard College, though he was still under fifteen. Musical experiences began to accumulate as he attended the concerts of the Boston Symphony and made his first contact with modern music through the scores of Stravinsky and Schoenberg. In addition, he became the editor of the *Harvard Musical Review*, for which he wrote critical essays.

He was graduated from Harvard with a Bachelor of Arts degree when he was eighteen. His parents encouraged him to go to France to study with Ravel, but the war made this impossible. Instead, Sessions entered the Yale School of Music, where he became Horatio Parker's pupil. There he wrote a movement for a violin sonata and a composition he was planning as a movement of a full-length symphony but presented as a self-sufficient composition called *Symphonic Prelude*. This orchestral work was heard at a concert at the

Yale School of Music and received the Steinert Prize. In 1917, after getting his Bachelor of Music degree at Yale, Sessions became an assistant in music at Smith College where he served as instructor from 1919 to 1921.

Ernest Bloch, impressed with Sessions' talent, became his teacher. When Bloch was appointed director of the Cleveland Institute of Music in 1921, Sessions followed him there. After an additional period of study, Sessions became Bloch's assistant.

During this period Sessions composed incidental music for *The Black Maskers*, a play by Leonid Andreyev, which was given at Smith College in June 1923. Five years later Sessions adapted the score into an orchestral suite that was introduced in Cincinnati on December 5, 1930. Stokowski conducted the work with the Philadelphia Orchestra in 1933, and since then it has been played by major orchestras throughout the United States. This was Sessions' first success as a composer, and he achieved it with music in a decidedly Romantic style and with traditional methods.

When Bloch resigned his post in Cleveland in 1925, Sessions withdrew from his job in protest, since Bloch had had a violent disagreement with the Conservatory authorities. For the next eight years, Sessions lived in Europe, mainly in Florence, on the funds of two Guggenheim Fellowships, a two-year fellowship at the American Academy in Rome, and a Carnegie grant. While in Europe he completed in 1927 his first symphony, in E minor; it was successfully introduced by the Boston Symphony under Koussevitzky on April 22, 1927. Sessions returned to the United States for this event. Upon visiting the United States one year later, he collaborated with Aaron Copland in founding the Copland-Sessions concerts in New York, which were devoted to the presentation of new music. His activity in promoting modern music brought him to the board of directors of the League of Composers in 1933. The following year he became president of the United States section of the International Society of Contemporary Music.

He was living in Berlin when the Nazis came to power in 1933. The rapid course of events in Germany convinced him that the time had come for him to leave Europe and reestablish himself permanently in the United States. He assumed a number of teaching posts beginning with an appointment at the School of Music in Boston. After serving on the faculty of the School of Music at Boston University, he went to Princeton in 1935 as instructor in music. He was promoted to assistant professor in 1937 and associate professor in 1940. For a seven-year period, beginning in 1945, he was professor of music at the University of California at Berkeley. Then, in 1953, he returned to Yale to accept the Conant Professorship of Music, holding this post until 1965. In 1966 Sessions joined the faculty of the Juilliard School of Music in New York, where he taught composition twice a week. Among the many Americans who have studied under him over the years are David Diamond, Leon Kirchner, Milton Babbitt, Hugo Weisgall, Paul Bowles, and A. Lehman Engel. In 1968 he was appointed Charles Eliot Norton Professor at Harvard University, in which capacity he delivered six lectures.

The Violin Concerto in B minor is the first work which Sessions himself believes embodies the basic attributes of his later style. He began to write it in 1931, completing it four years later. It was first performed at an all-Sessions concert at the New School for Social Research in New York in 1935, with Serge Kotlarsky as soloist, accompanied by the composer at the piano. The first orchestral performance followed January 8, 1940, with Robert Gross as soloist for the Illinois Orchestra conducted by Izler Solomon. In this composition Sessions' modern idiom is realized in music that is often discordant, music in which the melodic line has Spartan austerity. An unusual feature of its orchestration is that it dispenses altogether with violins while enlarging the wind section and splitting up the violas and cellos into subdivisions. The reason for this practice is to allow the tone of his solo instrument to be heard to best advantage. The writing for the solo instrument is complex. Indeed, this work makes such stringent technical demands on the performer that the violinist for whom it had originally been intended insisted that it was "unplayable." Sessions reveals that when he finished the concerto he took the score to Alfredo Casella to inquire if the work needed simplification. Casella shook his head, maintaining that nothing could be done. "You see," Casella said, "it was *born* difficult." To which Sessions later added: "My music comes the way it *has* to come."

Despite the complexity and cerebralism of his writing, Sessions realized a major success with his second symphony. The Alice M. Ditson Fund had commissioned it, and it took two years to write. On January 9, 1947, it was introduced in San Francisco with Pierre Monteux conducting. While the composer was working on the symphony, President Roosevelt died, a tragedy that finds reflection in the somber mood of the third-movement Adagio. But the composer revealed that "this deeply affecting and fateful event," while being inextricably "associated in my mind with this movement in particular" also colors parts of the first and last movements. Alfred J. Frankenstein described the symphony as "big . . . challenging . . . important . . . austere . . . fiendishly difficult . . . a complex of forceful and fruitful ideas which can be studied for a long time before they yield all their secrets." Sessions regards this symphony as a milestone in his own development, the goal he had been reaching for since his Violin Concerto. After the symphony was played by the New York Philharmonic under Mitropoulos, it received the New York Music Critics Circle Award and was recorded under a grant by the Naumburg Foundation.

The year 1947 saw the production of Sessions' first opera, *The Trial of Lucullus*, performed at the University of California in Berkeley on April 18, 1947. The text had been written in 1939 by Bertolt Brecht as an anti-Hitler play for radio production. To this one-act opera, Sessions brought much of the complexity and austerity of his second symphony. There is little melody here. The score is an elaborate texture in which words and action and music are interwoven inseparably into a single unified conception. As the composer explained: "I have sought to have each character speak in accents that should be his or her own, while at the same time a part of a convincing musical whole." Alfred J. Frankenstein remarked in his review that "the most remarkable feature of the opera from a purely esthetic point of view is the unparalleled suppleness of its declamation. . . . Through an exquisitely perfect adjustment of tone and word, Sessions achieves an incredibly clear-edged musical characterization of individuals, so that the music of each role projects its personality with the utmost definition and point."

Most of Sessions' major works since the 1950's have been written on commission from major organizations, a testimony to his significant place in American music. His third symphony was written to commemorate the seventy-fifth anniversary of the Boston Symphony, which introduced it on December 6, 1957. His fourth symphony, written for the Minnesota Centennial Commission for the 1958 state celebration, was given its première by the Minneapolis Symphony under Antal Dorati on January 2, 1960. His fifth symphony was ordered by the Philadelphia Orchestra and Eugene Ormandy, who presented it on February 7, 1964. His sixth symphony, heard on January 19, 1966, in a performance by the New Jersey Symphony under Kenneth Schermerhorn, was written at the joint request of the orchestra and the State of New Jersey. And his eighth symphony was written on commission for the 125th anniversary of the New York Philharmonic, which introduced it under William Steinberg on May 2, 1968. In addition, the Piano Concerto helped celebrate the fiftieth anniversary of the Juilliard School, which offered it at its American music festival on February 10, 1956; the *Idyll of Theocritus*, for soprano and orchestra, was written for the Louisville Orchestra (première in Louisville on January 14, 1956); and Psalm 140, for soprano and orchestra, was composed for soprano and organ in 1963 for the sesquicentennial anniversary of the Princeton Theological Seminary, with the first performance of the orchestral version taking place in Boston on February 11, 1966, Erich Leinsdorf conducting the Boston Symphony.

One of his most ambitious achievements of these later years is the three-act opera *Montezuma*, in which he employs the twelve-tone system, though freely and often intuitively. This is a work which Sessions had been planning for almost thirty years, for which G. A. Borgese had completed a libretto in 1941, and on which Sessions began to work intensively in 1960. On April 19, 1964, the opera was produced in Berlin. Peter Maxwell Davies reported to the New York *Times* that "there is little doubt that this is Sessions' masterpiece;

it is also his most problematic and difficult work." The opera's theme is the conquest of Mexico by the Spanish under the leadership of Hernando Cortez in the early sixteenth century. The Aztec emperor Montezuma is sympathetic to and cooperates with Cortez, an act for which he pays with his life when the Spanish invaders defy Cortez and proceed to plunder and murder. "The work," said Heinz Joachim in *Musical America*, "is not so much an opera as it is epic music theatre. . . . Without dramatic action, the historical material is treated as a monumental chronicle. . . . The harsh and austere sound of the score surprisingly complements the exotic coloration and the sacerdotal rigidity of the scenery." The Boston Opera Company arranged to present the American première of *Montezuma* in Boston in May 1969.

Mark A. Schubart has written that "Sessions' development as a composer is unusual in that his works do not fall into 'periods' or 'styles.' . . . His growth has been a consistent evolution, combined with an expanding concept of harmonization and a refinement and crystallization of melodic materials." For the most part, Sessions' music follows "the German conception of music as a grandly expressive art, rather than the French conception of it as a sensuous or a coloristic one."

Sessions himself has written: "I am first and foremost a composer, and all my ideas (even about teaching) derive their essence from my experiences as a composer, and my first-hand knowledge of a composer's psychology. . . . It is the most fundamental principle with me that only music counts; ideas or intentions do not count at all apart from the music. In other words, my ideas can prevail only in so far as my music prevails."

In 1958, as part of the cultural, educational, and technical exchange agreement between the United States and the Soviet Union, Sessions visited the U.S.S.R., where his music was played and acclaimed. Sessions is a member of the National Institute of Arts and Letters, the American Academy of Arts and Letters, and the American Academy of Arts and Sciences. He is also a foreign member of the Berlin Akademie der Künste. In 1964 he received an honorary doctorate from Harvard, the latest of a number of honorary degrees, and in the presentation was described as "a distinguished

composer and teacher whose work communicates the loneliness and loftiness of artistic experience."

From January 27 to 29, 1961, inclusive, Northwestern University in Evanston, Illinois, in cooperation with the Fromm Foundation, held a Roger Sessions festival in which more than half of Sessions' lifetime output was heard. Later the same year an all-Sessions concert in New York City helped to celebrate the composer's sixty-fifth birthday. "It is a little staggering in retrospect, to comprehend that nearly all of the large works stand today, and seem likely to stand forever, among the principal monuments of American music," wrote Benjamin Boretz in *Musical Quarterly* on the occasion of Sessions' sixty-fifth birthday. "This is certainly a profound tribute to the qualities of mind, determination, and native gift that Sessions has brought to bear on his work, which has now brought him to the status of an old master, who unburdened by any necessity to struggle furiously to the head of the mainstream, is content simply to cast one masterwork after another into its midst." His seventy-first birthday was also celebrated with an all-Sessions concert in New York, on March 3, 1968.

Sessions has been married twice. His present wife is the former Elizabeth Franck, whom he married on November 26, 1936. They have two children, a daughter and a son. Their son, John, is a member of the music faculty of Smith College and a cello virtuoso. Roger Sessions and his wife make their home in Princeton, New Jersey.

MAJOR WORKS

Chamber Music—2 string quartets; Duo, for violin and piano; Sonata for Violin Solo; String Quintet; Six Pieces, for cello and piano.

Choral Music—Turn O Libertad; Mass.

Operas—The Trial of Lucullus; Montezuma.

Orchestral Music—8 symphonies; The Black Maskers, incidental music; Violin Concerto; Idyll of Theocritus, for soprano and orchestra; Divertimento, for percussion, harp, and strings; Piano Concerto; Psalm 140, for soprano and orchestra; Cello Concerto.

Piano Music—3 sonatas; From My Diary.

Vocal Music—On the Beach of Fontana.

ABOUT

Chase, G., America's Music; Mellers, W., Music in a New Found Land.

Musical America, September 1957; Musical Quarterly, July 1959, July 1961; Perspectives, Summer 1956; Saturday Review, June 26, 1954.

Arthur Shepherd
1880–1958

Arthur Shepherd was born in Paris, Idaho, on February 19, 1880, of English parents who had emigrated to the United States as converts to the Mormon religion. His earliest musical influences came through family interests: both parents and several uncles and aunts participated regularly in the singing of part songs and English glees, performances in which the boy soon joined. He received his first instruction in music on the melodeon (a small reed organ) and a few years later was taught the piano. One of his teachers, Martin Haenisch, recognized his talent and prevailed on his father to obtain for him the best possible instruction. There was some hesitation before a choice could be made between Leipzig and Boston. In the end, the American city prevailed, and Shepherd entered the New England Conservatory in September 1892. There he studied piano with Dennée and Carl Faelton, composition with Chadwick and Goetschius. He rounded out his Conservatory years as president of the graduating class and received a silver seal of honor on his diploma.

Following his graduation, in 1897, the Shepherd family moved to Salt Lake City. There Arthur Shepherd devoted himself to composing, teaching, performing on the piano at public concerts, playing the organ in churches, and organizing and conducting the Salt Lake City Symphony. The most venturesome exploit of this period was his first serious attempt at orchestral composition, the *Ouverture Joyeuse* which won the Paderewski Award in 1902 and was soon performed in New York City by the Russian Symphony under Modest Altschuler.

At about this time, Shepherd participated in a music publishing venture—the Wa-Wan Press—founded by Arthur Farwell in 1901 at Newton, Massachusetts. For five years Shepherd submitted to its editorial committee several of his compositions, a few of which were published. These included the *Theme and Variations* for piano, which became the composer's opus 1, and his opus 2, the *Mazurka and Prelude*, also for piano.

In 1908 Shepherd moved to New England; for a while he lived at Arthur Farwell's home in Newton. During that year he won two prizes

from the National Federation of Music Clubs: for his piano sonata, op. 4, and for a song, "The Lost Child." In 1910 he brought his wife and their three children to Boston, where he became teacher of harmony and counterpoint at the New England Conservatory. In 1913 he won another prize, for a rather turgid though ambitious work for baritone, chorus, and orchestra, *The City in the Sea;* it was performed under Frederick Stock's direction at an annual meeting of the National Federation of Music Clubs.

ARTHUR SHEPHERD

In or about 1916 he wrote a work of clearer texture and firmer craftsmanship, the *Fantaisie Humoresque,* for piano and orchestra, introduced at the New England Conservatory on February 8, 1918, with Lee Pattison as soloist and the composer as conductor. This work subsequently received major performances by the Cleveland Orchestra and the Boston Symphony.

During the period immediately following America's entrance into World War I, Shepherd became the conductor of the Cecilia Society in Boston serving during 1917–1918. This and other musical activities in Boston were interrupted when he enlisted in the army to become bandmaster of the 303rd Field Artillery Regiment Band in France.

In 1920 Shepherd went to Cleveland to serve as assistant conductor of the newly founded Cleveland Orchestra of which Nikolai Sokoloff was principal conductor. For six years

Shostakovich

Shepherd combined this work with the writing of the program notes for all the orchestra's concerts. Among the compositions he completed during the period were *Overture to a Drama* (first performance in Cleveland, March 27, 1924); a symphony entitled *Horizons* (introduced in Cleveland on December 15, 1927); and *Triptyque*, for high voice and string quartet, to poems by Tagore (1926).

In 1927 Shepherd severed his association with the Cleveland Orchestra to become a member of the faculty of Cleveland College as lecturer on music appreciation. Shortly thereafter he was appointed professor of music at the Graduate School of Western Reserve University, from which he retired in 1950. He served as the music critic of the Cleveland *Press* from 1929 to 1932. In 1938 he received an honorary doctorate in music from Western Reserve University and was elected to membership in the National Institute of Arts and Letters.

One of Shepherd's most successful later works for orchestra found him making one of his rare excursions into the realm of American folk tunes: the *Fantasy on Down-East Spirituals*. This work was commissioned by the Indianapolis Symphony to help celebrate its tenth anniversary and was introduced by the orchestra on November 2, 1946, Fabien Sevitzky conducting. Shepherd found his thematic material in spirituals collected by the folklorist George Pullen Jackson, drawing from that source four tunes: "Experience," "End of the World," "Last Trumpet," and "Sweet Messenger."

Later works by Shepherd included his second symphony, which the Cleveland Orchestra performed on March 7, 1940; a violin concerto (1947); and *Theme and Variations*, for orchestra, first performed in Cleveland on April 9, 1953.

Shepherd's style in his earlier works reveals an eclecticism rooted in the romanticism of the late nineteenth century, but with a closer affinity with French and Russian practices than with traditional German idioms. Even in a work as early as his first piano sonata (1907) he revealed an independent trend towards the use of indigenous materials and a probing for personal expression. By reason of his British lineage and his cradling in the Rocky Mountains of America's West, Shepherd showed a natural predilection for the folk type of melody. At times there emerges an almost atavistic affinity for tunes with a Celtic cast. Shepherd's technique in later works evidenced an increasing concern with a free contrapuntal texture and a plastic rhythmic syntax. Throughout all the more representative works, early and late, there is no indication of stylistic or idiomatic experimentation.

Arthur Shepherd died in Cleveland, Ohio, January 12, 1958.

MAJOR WORKS

Chamber Music—3 string quartets; 2 violin sonatas; Piano Quintet; Praeludium Salutatorium, for wind and strings; Divertissement, for wind ensemble.

Choral Music—Song of the Sea Wind; The Lord Hath Brought Again Zion, motet; The City in the Sea, cantata; Ballad of Trees and the Master; Song of the Pilgrims, cantata; Grace for Gardens; Build Thee More Stately Mansions; Psalm 42; Drive On.

Orchestral Music—2 symphonies; Overture Joyeuse; The Festival of Youth; Fantaisie Humoresque, for piano and orchestra; Overture to a Drama; Choreographic Suite; Fantasia Concertante; Fantasy on Down-East Spirituals; Violin Concerto; Theme and Variations.

Piano Music—2 sonatas; Gigue Fantasque; Exotic Dances; Capriccios.

ABOUT

Howard, J. T., Our Contemporary Composers.
Musical Quarterly, April 1950.

Dmitri Shostakovich
1906–

Dmitri Dmitrievich Shostakovich was born in St. Petersburg (now Leningrad) on September 25, 1906. Both parents were intellectuals and ardent music lovers: his father, an engineer, worked in the Office of Weights and Measures before becoming the manager of a large estate; his mother was a trained pianist, a graduate of the St. Petersburg Conservatory. When Dmitri was five he was taken for the first time to the opera—to hear a performance of Rimsky-Korsakov's *Tsar Saltan;* the next morning he was heard singing some of the arias. Nevertheless, in later years, he insisted: "I had no particular inclination for music. I cannot recall a single instance when I evinced any interest in, or listened to, music when someone was playing at home. I became a musician by pure accident. If it had not been

Shostakovich: shŭ stŭ kô′ vyĭch

524

for my mother, I should probably never have become one."

His mother began to teach him the piano when he was nine. In a few months' time he was playing works by Haydn and Mozart. He demonstrated an unusual gift for reading music at sight and revealed a remarkable musical memory and an unusual imagination. He delighted in associating musical sounds with extramusical images. Otherwise, maintains Nicolas Nabokov, Shostakovich's childhood was "very much like that of any other child of his milieu. He went to school through the milky fogs and drizzly rains of St. Petersburg; he was a pale, frail boy coddled and adored by his parents, and surrounded at home by a studious and serious atmosphere."

DMITRI SHOSTAKOVICH

He continued his music study at the Glasser School of Music where he wrote his first piece of music—*Theme and Variations*, for piano. The piece was never actually put down on paper. But a number of years later, when Shostakovich gave piano recitals, he sometimes played it as an encore. Other early compositions were influenced by the Revolution, which had broken out in Russia when Shostakovich was ten—among them *Hymn to Liberty* and the *Funeral March for the Victims of the Revolution*. Despite the physical hardships that beset the Shostakovich family (fuel and food were scarce), Dmitri's musical training continued without interruption. In September 1919 he enrolled in the St. Petersburg Conservatory

where his teachers included Nikolayev (piano) and Maximilian Steinberg (composition). Shostakovich had been at the Conservatory barely a year when he wrote his first composition for orchestra, a scherzo, followed by eight piano preludes. Glazunov, the director of the Conservatory, said of him: "The boy's gifts are phenomenal, comparable to Mozart's."

He continued to write music while attending the Conservatory. His first published work was *Three Fantastic Dances*, for piano (1922). To Ivan Martynov, this composition is characteristic of the later Shostakovich in "the lightness of touch and graceful humor as well as the imagery: the drollery of the first dance, the lyrical capriciousness of the second, and particularly the grotesque 'zig-zags' of the third. The 'galloping' miniature rhythms, the unexpected harmonic changes and turns of melody anticipated many a later page of Shostakovich."

The death of Shostakovich's father in February 1922 plunged the family into difficult financial circumstances, only partially relieved when his mother found a job as typist in the Department of Weights and Measures. Dmitri tried to help support the family by playing the piano in a motion picture theatre, but he was soon fired, since too often he became so fascinated by the movie that he completely forgot to play. Poverty, however—and the many deprivations and sufferings caused by the revolution—was not the only thing to trouble young Shostakovich. He was suffering from tuberculosis of the lymph glands, a condition that necessitated repeated operations and visits to a sanatorium. These problems interrupted his studies and musical activities from time to time but they could not arrest his development. He made a number of appearances as pianist, frequently performing his own compositions on the program, and a newspaper in St. Petersburg noted: "He played . . . with a clarity of artistic intention that showed him to be a musician who deeply feels and understands his art. Shostakovich's compositions . . . are fine examples of serious musical thought."

Shostakovich was graduated in piano from the Conservatory in the spring of 1923, and in composition in 1925. For his graduation exercise in 1925 he completed his first symphony, in F major (marked opus 10, though it was only the composer's second published work). On May 12, 1926, Nikolai Malko conducted it at a concert of the Leningrad Philharmonic. "All went more than brilliantly," reported Shostakovich's mother in a letter, "a splendid orchestra and magnificent execution! But the greatest success went to Mitya [Dmitri]. The audience listened with enthusiasm and the scherzo had to be played twice. At the end, Mitya was called to the stage over and over again. When our handsome young composer appeared, looking almost like a boy, the enthusiasm turned into one long thunderous ovation."

A few months later the symphony was heard in Moscow during a series of concerts in which Shostakovich was making his bow in that city both as composer and pianist. As in Leningrad, so in Moscow: the symphony was acclaimed. "It is a symphony which reflects all that a composition can give of the most important in the artist," said the critic of the Moscow *Evening Radio*. In 1927 Bruno Walter directed the symphony in Berlin in its first performance outside the Soviet Union, and on November 2, 1928, Leopold Stokowski conducted its American première at a concert of the Philadelphia Orchestra. After that, the symphony was heard the world over, bringing the young composer international recognition.

Though derivative—partly from Tchaikovsky, partly from Prokofiev—this symphony is a truly remarkable achievement for a composer only eighteen years old. It is remarkable for its rhythmic vitality, freshness of melodic material, and virtuosity of orchestration. It has the infectious spontaneity, enthusiasm, and even brashness of youth. There are some critics who today regard it as Shostakovich's best symphony; certainly it has remained one of his most popular ones.

The success of the First Symphony was followed by a one-year period of creative silence. "Once my studies were completed," he revealed in an autobiographical sketch, "there came the necessity of assorting a large portion of the musical baggage which I had acquired. I grasped that music is not merely a combination of sounds arranged in a certain order, but an art able to express by its own power the most diverse ideas or feelings. This conviction did not come to me without travail. Let it suffice that during the whole year of 1926 I did not write a single note, but from 1927 I have never stopped composing."

Upon returning to composition in 1927, Shostakovich identified his music with the ideas and ideals of the Soviet Revolution. He had become a politically conscious composer, using music as the means by which to express Soviet ideology. He said: "The aim which I assign to my work is that of helping in every way to enlighten our remarkable country." He also said: "There can be no music without ideology.... Even the symphonic form ... can be said to have a bearing on politics. Good music ... is no longer an end in itself but a vital weapon in the struggle."

His Second Symphony, in B major (1927), commemorated the tenth anniversary of the October Revolution; its final movement was a setting of a text by Lenin. His Third Symphony, in E-flat major, *May Day* (1929), was dedicated to the working class. Despite their popular political and social attitudes, both symphonies were failures—the Second, after being introduced in Leningrad on November 6, 1927, and the Third following its première in Leningrad on January 21, 1930.

A three-act satirical opera, with the composer's own libretto based on Gogol's *The Nose*, proved an even greater failure when produced in Leningrad on January 13, 1930. It was condemned in the Soviet press as a product of "bourgeois decadence" and was soon removed from the repertory. The two symphonies and the opera were thrown into discard—the two symphonies permanently. However, *The Nose* was belatedly revived in Düsseldorf on June 27, 1963, and became an outstanding success, with Paul Moor reporting in the New York *Times* that "it crackles with sardonic humor from beginning to end." When *The Nose* received its American première on August 11, 1965, performed by the Santa Fe Opera Company in New Mexico, Raymond Ericson wrote: "The score has bite and gusto.... It is sardonic and has youthful boisterousness. Wheeling piccolos, whining violins, sneering trombones poke fun at situations. The result is acidulously funny at times."

Shostakovich once again tapped a vein of satire, in a ballet, *The Golden Age*, a sardonic commentary on capitalist society. It had received first prize in 1929 in a competition conducted in the Soviet Union for a ballet on a

Soviet subject, and its première took place in Leningrad on October 27, 1930. Shostakovich's music was liked far more than the ballet itself. The orchestral suite of five movements, which the composer adapted from his ballet score, achieved enormous popularity on symphony programs everywhere. This music revealed the composer's unusual gift for wit and satire, a gift that he would reveal again and again in his later compositions. Two movements have gained particular favor. The "Polka," a satire on the Geneva Peace Conference, highlights a saucy tune for xylophone and a brass-band melody for tuba and trumpets. Brass-band music is caricatured in "Danse Russe," with its accordion-like harmonies and its piquant use of percussion instruments.

During the next few years Shostakovich established his position as one of the most successful and highly regarded composers in the Soviet Union. A second ballet, *The Bolt*—once again a satire—was a major success when introduced in Leningrad on April 8, 1931. His artistic importance was again recognized when he introduced in Moscow on May 24, 1933, his twenty-four preludes, op. 34, and when his first piano concerto proved a triumph at the world première given in Leningrad on October 15, 1933, with the composer appearing as the soloist.

On May 13, 1932, Shostakovich married Nina Varzar, a physicist, whom he had met five years earlier. "He was a very bashful, modest young man," Nina recalled in later years, "but with all this he was already fully matured as man and musician." They have two children: a daughter, Galina, born in 1936; and a son, Maxim, born two years later. "Dmitri has been very devoted to his family, especially to our children," Nina has revealed.

Shostakovich's most ambitious work in the early thirties, the opera *Lady Macbeth of Mzensk*, was produced in Leningrad on January 22, 1934. The libretto, the work of the composer in collaboration with A. Preis, was based on a story by Leskov, a realistic, even lurid, drama, compounded of lust, adultery, murder, and suicide—a sordid picture of provincial middle-class life in old Russia. The heroine is the helpless victim of a "decadent and foul bourgeois milieu." She is treated sympathetically, the tragedy of her life (ending when she murders her rival and commits

suicide) built up with powerful dramatic impact. However, much in the opera is also treated satirically, and the music provides a humorous or sardonic comment on whatever is happening on the stage.

At its world première in Leningrad and in productions in Moscow and other Russian cities, the opera proved a tremendous success. The conductor Samosud hailed it as "a work of genius, and I am convinced that posterity will confirm this estimate." Other critics called it a "great masterpiece," the "first monumental work of Soviet musical culture." One critic, conscious of the contradiction between the satire and the tragedy in the opera, saw in it "a new genre of satiric tragedy." The opera was kept on the boards in the Soviet for two years.

While the opera was still riding high in popularity in the Soviet Union, it was introduced in the United States—in Cleveland on January 31, 1935, and soon after that in New York. The critical reaction was decidedly negative. Olin Downes called it "lurid . . . naïve . . . puerile . . . immature." W. J. Henderson described it as "bed-chamber opera" and regarded its creator as the "foremost composer of pornographic music in the history of the art."

And then, in Russia one day in January 1936, Stalin attended a performance and expressed revulsion at the entire production. Immediately a tirade of abuse was heaped on Shostakovich and his opera by the Soviet press. The barrage began with an article in *Pravda* on January 28, 1936, entitled "A Pandemonium Instead of Music." It said in part: "The music quacks, grunts, growls, suffocates itself in order to express the amatory scenes as naturalistically as possible. . . . Some critics call this glorification of merchant lust a satire. But there is no satire here." Music critics took the cue and began to condemn Shostakovich's music as "crude, primitive, vulgar" and "fidgety, screaming, neurotic." The opera was withdrawn and shelved. Shostakovich publicly conceded that he had made a serious mistake in his treatment of the Leskov story.

In the post-Stalin era, Shostakovich removed this opera from the shelf and revised it by deleting from the text some of its more lurid episodes and making some alterations in the music. With a new title, *Katarina Ismailova*, it was successfully revived in the Soviet Union, after which it was produced in London, San Francisco, and New York, and then made into a Soviet film. "It is music," now wrote Alexander Fried, "only a man of vital, masterly gifts and craftsmanship could have written. And more than once it attains inspired beauty."

But in 1936 the attack on *Lady Macbeth* was succeeded one week later by equally vitriolic denunciations of Shostakovich's new ballet, *The Limpid Stream*, which had been introduced in Leningrad on April 4, 1935. "It jingles, it means nothing; the composer apparently has only contempt for our national songs," wrote a Soviet editorialist. It was now quite obvious that Shostakovich had fallen from grace with the Soviet authorities, a fact further emphasized in 1936 when Shostakovich's latest symphony, the Fourth, in C minor, was summarily dropped after a rehearsal and denied a performance. It was not heard until January 20, 1962.

Shostakovich's return to success and popularity was almost as dramatic as his sudden downfall. In 1937 he completed his Fifth Symphony, in D minor, to celebrate the twentieth anniversary of the Soviet Republic. Introduced in Leningrad on November 21 of that year it was given a thunderous ovation. The critics, who for two years had been ignoring Shostakovich when they did not attack him, were unanimous in singing his praises. One of them, Andrei Budyakovsky, described the symphony as "a work of great depth . . . a milestone in the composer's development." The Fifth is, to be sure, one of Shostakovich's most powerful and consistently inspired compositions. In place of his usual attitudes of satire and grotesquerie we confront in this music wind-swept emotions, intense feelings, a majesty of concept, all within a structure of cathedral-like spaciousness. Its slow movement is one of the most moving pieces of music Shostakovich wrote up to 1937.

Having thus reestablished himself as a successful composer, Shostakovich lost no time in solidifying his position in Soviet music. In 1940 he won the Stalin Prize for the first time, for his Piano Quintet in G minor (first performance in Moscow on November 23, 1940). Then, following the invasion of the Soviet

Union by the Nazis in 1941, he became something of a national hero. He joined the fire-fighting brigade at the Conservatory (he had tried to join the army but had been turned down), and at the same time he enlisted his music in the war effort.

One of his first creative endeavors during the war and one of his most ambitious works was a symphony interpreting the impact of the conflict on the Soviet people, and specifically the effect of the siege of Leningrad on its people. He completed the symphony—his seventh, subtitled *Leningrad*, in C major—in the town of Kuibishev, to which the government had been transferred from Moscow. There, on March 5, 1942, the symphony was introduced before an audience including diplomats, high Soviet officials, army officers, and representatives of the American military and diplomatic corps. The symphony was a triumph and brought its composer a second Stalin Prize.

The symphony was heard and acclaimed throughout the Soviet Union and then traveled around the free world. In the United States it was introduced over the NBC radio network on July 19, 1942, Arturo Toscanini conducting, and shortly after was played by virtually every major orchestra in America. Much of the overpowering thrust of the work at that time was due to the stirring way in which the music reflected the mood of the era. The first movement described the effect of the war upon a happy and confident people and included a requiem for the war dead. The two middle movements were intended as an intermezzo confirming "life in opposition to war," as the composer explained: "I have tried to express the thought that art, literature and science must advance in spite of the war." The third movement spoke of the love of life and the beauties of nature, and the fourth gave a forecast of the inevitable victory of "light over darkness, wisdom over frenzy, lofty humanism over monstrous tyranny."

Shostakovich's Eighth Symphony, in C minor, came one year later. This work emphasized the positive values of life but, since the Soviet Union was still at war, it had tragic overtones as well. Introduced in Moscow on November 4, 1943, it had only a moderate success.

The optimism, the faith in life and its blessings, which Shostakovich had hoped to put into his Eighth Symphony, is found in the Ninth, in E-flat major, heard in Leningrad on November 3, 1945. This is one of Shostakovich's happiest pieces of music; the feeling of joy and gaiety it exudes is truly intoxicating. Nevertheless, the Soviet critics did not like it, dismissing it for "ideological weakness."

But an attack of a much more serious nature was about to strike Shostakovich again. On February 10, 1948, the Central Committee of the Communist Party severely took to task most of the leading Soviet composers for their "subservience to bourgeois decadence" and their "formalism" (see sketch on Prokofiev). Shostakovich also came under fire.

With perhaps none too commendable resiliency, Shostakovich proceeded to change his esthetic aims and musical style to conform with the new principles being laid down by the Central Committee demanding a simpler and more melodious music, a music grounded in Russian folk songs. He made a public confession that he had been guilty of the faults pointed out by his accusers and he promised to mend his ways. This attitude helped to restore him to favor with the authorities. In March 1949 he was made a member of a committee of seven representing the Soviet Union at the Cultural and Scientific Conference for World Peace held in the United States. This was his first visit to America, and it was not altogether a happy one: on the public platform he gave statements that had obvious propaganda slants; away from the platform he proved to be shy, close-mouthed, uncomfortable. He hoped to make a tour of the country, but the State Department refused to grant him permission and he left for home after a single week.

A few months after his return to his native land he received the Stalin Prize a third time. It was given to him for two compositions: an oratorio praising the Stalin reforestation plan, *Song of the Forests*, introduced in Leningrad on November 15, 1949; and the background music for the motion picture *Fall of Berlin*.

Shostakovich's Tenth Symphony, in E minor—completed in 1953 and introduced in Leningrad on December 17 of that year—was in the class of his First and Fifth. Indeed, to Olin Downes, it proved to be "the first score in the symphonic form that proclaims the complete independence and integration of his genius." Thoroughly Russian in personality, without resorting to folk-song quotations, the symphony was, as Raymond Ericson said in his review, "touching in its spirit, and often beautiful in its melodic pathos." Following its American première in New York, on October 14, 1954, Dimitri Mitropoulos conducting the New York Philharmonic, the symphony received the New York Music Critics Circle Award.

In his Eleventh Symphony, in G minor (first performance in Moscow on October 30, 1957), Shostakovich paid tribute to the 1905 political insurrection in Russia; in the Twelfth Symphony, subtitled *Lenin* (première in Leningrad on October 1, 1961), he glorified the Revolution of 1917. Both were well received, the Eleventh bringing him the Lenin Award. But with his Thirteenth Symphony (introduced in Moscow on December 18, 1962) Shostakovich once again came into conflict with the authorities. Following the death of Stalin greater latitude had been given composers in the selection of their subjects and in the kind of style they favored, and Shostakovich's Thirteenth Symphony (dedicated to the heroic fight of the Soviet people against Nazi Germany during World War II) had as a text for the closing movement *Babi Yar*—the controversial poem by Yevtushenko that is a violent indictment of anti-Semitism in the Soviet Union (Babi Yar being a vale near Kiev where hundreds of Jews were killed and buried during the war). When Shostakovich's symphony was first heard, it was received by the audience in frigid silence. The press, reflecting the disapproval of political authorities, subjected it to severe criticism. Shostakovich then made important changes in the Yevtushenko text, with the poet's consent, and the new version of the symphony, given in February 1963, proved highly successful.

Whether he is extravagantly praised or just as extravagantly denounced—and both reactions have been (politics aside) justifiable on occasion—Shostakovich is one of the most significant composers of the twentieth century. It is true that he lacks the gift of self criticism and that he often combines powerful creation with second-hand ideas and clichés. It is also true that he is too ready to stoop in order to conquer. But if a composer is to be judged by his best music, Shostakovich is a powerful and original voice. He has a scintillating irony and an infectious wit; and in moments of greater repose, he can be noble and genuinely majestic. His greatest works, as Ivan Martynov has written, are "allied to the best and most progressive works of Western European art.... The significance and timeliness of their content, their refreshing originality, eloquence of expression and progressive character place the mature works of Shostakovich among the most outstanding creations of world culture."

On the occasion of his fiftieth birthday, in 1956, Shostakovich was decorated with the Order of Lenin, and in 1958 he was given the International Sibelius Prize for his contributions to music. In November 1959 he paid a second visit to the United States as part of the cultural exchange program agreed upon in Geneva between President Eisenhower and Premier Khrushchev. The increasing tolerance in America towards representatives of Soviet culture helped to create a more favorable climate for Shostakovich's return than had prevailed a decade earlier, and during his extensive tour he was acclaimed. In the summer of 1962, he attended the Edinburgh Festival in Scotland where a series of concerts was devoted to his major works, including eight of his string quartets and almost all of his symphonies. At the White Nights festival in Leningrad in the summer of 1966, a comprehensive cross-section of Shostakovich's creative career was presented in concerts which offered not only all of his major works but also several compositions by some of his pupils.

In celebration of Shostakovich's sixtieth birthday, in 1966, he was awarded the title of Hero of Socialist Labor, the first musician to receive the highest honor a Soviet citizen can receive from the government. On March 16, 1967, he was presented by Chancellor Josef Klaus with the Great Insignia of Honor for services to the Austrian Republic.

When Shostakovich came to the United States in 1959 he was described in the New York *Times* as "slim (though he is now putting on weight), serious-looking, bespectacled, with a lock of hair generally falling over one eye.... Mr. Shostakovich has retained the boyish look he had during Conservatory days." He is a chain smoker, a devotee of sports (soccer particularly), addicted to driving

automobiles at breakneck speeds, and a proficient chess player. He reads a good deal; his favorite authors are Chekhov, Gogol, and Maupassant. Whatever he does is done with extraordinary zest and enthusiasm.

Shostakovich's first wife, Nina, died in 1954. Two years later he married Margarita Kainova. His son Maxim, by his first marriage, was a concert pianist; it was for him that Shostakovich wrote his second piano concerto, which Maxim introduced in Moscow on May 10, 1957. In 1968 Maxim Shostakovich announced that he would give up the piano to become a conductor specializing in his father's music.

When he was sixty, Dmitri Shostakovich had a heart attack. Two years later he suffered a broken leg. In 1968 he decided, for reasons of health, to resign as head of the Composers Union of the Russian Federation, a post he had held since 1960. However, he consented to become secretary of the Russian Composers Union and he holds the same post with the Soviet Composers Union, which is a larger organization.

His first wife described Shostakovich's work habits as follows: "He demands no 'special' working conditions. He just sits down at his writing desk and writes—morning, noon, evening.... If it isn't singing or shouting, noises do not affect him at all. The door of the room where he works is usually open.... He composes swiftly, writing the score straight through, usually without changes or deletions. Dmitri has a great capacity for work and once having started a composition he is wholly engrossed.... Once the work is finished he cools down, so to speak, to warm up again and become entirely engrossed with the next work. He almost never reverts to what he has already written and therefore already experienced. It is far simpler for him to write a new than to remold a finished work."

MAJOR WORKS

Ballets—The Golden Age; The Bolt; The Limpid Stream; School of Ballet.

Chamber Music—10 string quartets; 2 piano trios; Two Pieces, for string octet; Cello Sonata; Piano Quintet; Three Pieces, for unaccompanied violin.

Choral Music—Leningrad; Song of the Forests; Democratic Vistas; Ten Songs on Revolutionary Texts; Two Russian Songs.

Operas—The Nose; Lady Macbeth of Mzensk (revised as Katarina Ismailova); Moskva Tcheremushki, light opera.

Orchestral Music — 14 symphonies; 2 cello concertos; 2 piano concertos; 2 violin concertos; Ouverture de Fête; Overture on Russian and Kirghiz Folk Themes; The Execution of Stephen Razin, vocal tone poem for basso, chorus, and orchestra; Poem of Mourning and Triumph; Concertino for Two Pianos.

Piano Music — 2 piano sonatas; 48 preludes and fugues; Six Children's Pieces; Concertino for Two Pianos.

Vocal Music — Four Songs to Texts by Pushkin; Six Songs, for basso and piano; Two Songs on Texts by Svetlov; From Jewish Folk Poetry, eleven songs; Two Songs to Texts by Lermontov; Five Songs to Texts by Dolmatovski; Four Monologues; Spanish Songs; Five Satires; Seven Songs to Words by Alexander Blok.

ABOUT

Danilevich, L., Our Contemporary: The Work of Dmitri Shostakovich; Ewen, D. (ed.), The New Book of Modern Composers; Hofmann, M. R., Dmitri Shostakovich; Martynov, I., Shostakovich: The Man and His Work; Nabokov, N., Old Friends and New Music; Sahlberg-Vatchadze, M., Shostakovich; Seroff, V. I., Dmitri Shostakovich: The Life and Background of a Soviet Composer.

Musical Quarterly, October 1942.

Jean Sibelius
1865–1957

Jean (originally Johan Julius Christian) Sibelius, the most celebrated Finnish composer, was born in the town of Tavastehus (Hämeenlinna) on December 8, 1865. The son of a regimental doctor, he was a shy and sensitive child who avoided group activities and preferred the company of a single friend. He began school at the age of eight, attending a Swedish-language elementary institution, but he was a dreamer who was impatient with academic discipline and found it difficult to keep his attention on the lessons. When he attended the Finnish Model Lyceum which he entered at the age of eleven, his teacher often remarked: "There goes Sibelius into another world." His first love was nature; his favorite pastimes included collecting plants, chasing butterflies, wandering in the forests.

He started piano study in his ninth year but soon shifted to the violin, which remained his favorite instrument. From the beginning he showed a marked aptitude for improvisation and, before long, an interest in composition. When he was ten he wrote his first piece of music, *Water Drops*, a duet for violin and cello. By the time he was fifteen he was

---

Sibelius: sĭ bā′ lĭ o͝os

studying the violin seriously with Gustav Levander, a local teacher, and receiving lessons in theory. He also absorbed theoretical knowledge by studying a treatise on musical composition. These studies made it possible for him to extend his creative efforts to the writing of several trios and other chamber music compositions.

JEAN SIBELIUS

Upon leaving the lyceum, when he was twenty, Sibelius entered the University of Helsinki (Helsingfors) to study law. At the same time he studied the violin at the Institute of Music. Law books bored him; after a single year at the University he decided to concentrate exclusively on music. Soon he had made sufficient progress on the violin to appear publicly in solo performances and with chamber music groups. At the Institute, his teachers included Ferruccio Busoni (then on a visit to Finland) and Martin Wegelius, director of the Institute. Busoni became Sibelius' close friend; the two spent hours at a time in local cafés and restaurants talking about music. Several other young men also became intimates and significantly influenced his intellectual and musical growth: the music critic Karl Theodor Flodin; the conductor Robert Kajanus, who later became one of the most distinguished interpreters of Sibelius' music; the writer Adolf Paul; the composer-conductor Armas Järnefelt. To one of them, Adolf Paul, young Sibelius appeared "a handsome, slender youth of medium height with bright eyes, a blond moustache, and an impressive head of dark blond hair falling over an imposing forehead."

Stimulated by these associations, Sibelius wrote more music. In 1888 his first publication appeared—a song entitled "Serenade." The same year his *Theme and Variations*, for string quartet, was performed at the Institute. A string quartet, in 1889, drew this praise from Flodin: "With this composition, Mr. Sibelius has given such excellent proof of an original musical talent that we can expect the greatest things from him."

Sibelius completed his course of study at the Institute in the spring of 1889 and received a state grant which enabled him to continue his training in Germany. As a composition pupil of Adolf Becker in Berlin, Sibelius completed only one composition, a piano quintet. Sibelius returned to Finland briefly in 1890 to become engaged to his sweetheart, Aino Järnefelt, the daughter of the composer. This mission accomplished, Sibelius traveled to Vienna to complete his music study with Robert Fuchs and Karl Goldmark. Contact with the post-Romantic traditions then so popular in Vienna led Sibelius to write several compositions in a similar vein: these included an overture and a ballet scene, both for orchestra. They were performed in Helsinki by an orchestra conducted by Robert Kajanus, but neither attracted any interest or inspired unusual comment.

Sibelius deserted these post-Romantic tendencies soon after returning to his native land in 1891. During the closing decade of the nineteenth century Finland was suffering oppression at the hands of its Russian rulers. The ruthless despotism of Nicholas II robbed the Finnish people of their freedom. Newspapers were suppressed; patriots were imprisoned. This effort to crush the Finnish people aroused their patriotic ardor. Underground movements were formed to harass the Russians and to bolster national pride. The spirit of the times infected Sibelius and in it he found his mission as a composer: to make his music serve the cause of Finnish liberation and to give voice to his own intense national feelings. He joined a group of patriots, "Young Finns." He also began work on the first of his compositions to derive its text from the *Kalevala*, Finland's national epic. Out of the *Kalevala*, Sibelius lifted the exploits of the hero Kullervo, which he adapted into an ambitious

work for solo voice, chorus, and orchestra. *Kullervo* was completed in 1892 and was introduced in Helsinki on April 28 of that year. "With this work," wrote Oskar Merikanto after the première, "Sibelius had taken a big step forward and at the same time brought Finnish art towards a more promising future." In 1916 Erik Furuhjelm wrote: "*Kullervo* is, for its time, an extraordinarily daring and powerful work. . . . It must be viewed as epoch-making." Thus, at the introduction of this work, and for some years thereafter, Finnish critics and writers did not hesitate to regard *Kullervo* as a Finnish masterwork. In spite of this, *Kullervo* was never again heard in its entirety during Sibelius' lifetime. He withdrew the work, intending to make extensive revisions, but he never completed this project. He did, however, permit individual movements to be played from time to time, but only on condition that the program make it clear that this music dated from 1892.

On June 10, 1892, Sibelius married Aino Järnefelt. They spent their honeymoon in Karelia and then set up their home in Helsinki. Aino eventually bore him six daughters, one of whom died in infancy. Family obligations, heightened by the imminent birth of the first child, intensified the long-existing need to earn a living, and Sibelius found a job as teacher of theory, composition, and violin at the Institute of Music and at the Orchestra School. At the same time he accelerated his creative activities. In 1892 he completed his first exclusively orchestral work inspired by Finnish legends, *En Saga*. Its first performance—in Helsinki on February 16, 1893, the composer conducting—was more or less a failure. Sibelius hurriedly withdrew his composition and waited nine years to revise it extensively. With notable changes in the orchestration, *En Saga* emerged as a masterwork—Sibelius' first to survive. Through the broad, passionate theme in bassoons over string arpeggios and the quiet pastoral episode midway highlighted by a clarinet solo, this tone poem sounded a new note—not only for its composer but also for Finnish music.

Soon after he had completed writing the first version of *En Saga*, Sibelius wrote the *Karelia Overture* and the *Karelia Suite*, both for full orchestra (1893). Much more significant, however, was *Four Legends*, for orchestra, completed in 1895. This was a suite inspired by the *Kalevala*, centering around the mythical exploits of the hero Lemminkäinen. The work includes one of the most poignant and frequently heard of Sibelius' tone poems, *The Swan of Tuonela* (now performed independently of the other three legends). The following program note appeared in the published score to describe the music: "Tuonela, the land of death, the hell of Finnish mythology, is surrounded by a broad river with black waters and rapid currents, on which the swan of Tuonela floats majestically." Unforgettable is the way the swan is evoked by a sensitive song for English horn accompanied by muted strings and drum rolls. *The Swan of Tuonela* was first heard in Helsinki on April 13, 1896, the composer conducting.

The most popular work produced by Sibelius before 1900 was the patriotic tone poem *Finlandia*. He wrote it during a new wave of tyranny in Finland in 1899. As a reaction to this oppression, a series of entertainments was organized to raise money and to voice a protest. For these entertainments, Sibelius wrote a suite called *Finland Awakes*, the last section of which was named *Suomi*, the Finnish word for Finland. Under the new title of *Finlandia*, this last section was performed in Helsinki on July 2, 1900. It caused a furor. Finnish people identified themselves and their political aspirations with this vitally national music, the main melody of which, carried by the woodwind, expressed the hope for liberation that stirred so restlessly in every Finnish heart. Because this tone poem was so thoroughly Finnish in feeling and mood, many suspected that Sibelius had quoted Finnish folk tunes; but all the melodic material is Sibelius' own. Incidentally, the long accepted belief that the Russians did not allow the tone poem itself to be heard under the title *Finlandia*—or for that matter that the composition was for a while even suppressed—is apocryphal, a legend Sibelius himself helped to create. *Finlandia* was the title used at the concert in 1900, and it is the title found in those subsequent performances which might have been frowned upon by the Russians but were not forbidden.

Finlandia is the most famous musical composition to come out of Finland. It has been said that it accomplished more than all the fiery pamphlets and speeches combined to bring about Finnish independence. In the world outside Finland it has more often been associated with Finnish national pride and purpose than the Finnish national anthem. During World War II, after Finland was invaded by the Soviet Union, *Finlandia* was played around the world to propagandize the new Finnish struggle for freedom.

In spite of its enormous popularity—perhaps because of it—*Finlandia* has often been seriously criticized by musicologists as blatant and pompous music that wears its emotions all too obviously on its sleeve. No doubt it lacks subtlety, but in his biography of Sibelius, Harold E. Johnson makes the following salient comment: "What is ignored is that *Finlandia* is a first-rate example of hack writing by a composer who happened to be in a highly exalted patriotic mood." If this was functional music—and this is precisely what the composer intended—then it was functional music that fulfilled its purpose with extraordinary success.

The immense success of *Finlandia* made Sibelius Finland's foremost living composer. His own country had acknowledged that fact even before *Finlandia* was written. In 1897 Sibelius became the first Finnish composer to be given an annual government subsidy to enable him to give up most of his teaching assignments. In 1900 he toured Scandinavia, Germany, Holland, and France with the Finnish Philharmonic Orchestra in programs that included some of his compositions.

Finlandia was not the only important piece of music Sibelius produced in 1899. Another was the First Symphony, in E minor, which was heard on an all-Sibelius program conducted by Kajanus on April 26, 1899. The Second Symphony, in D major, was completed in 1901, with its première taking place in Helsinki on March 8, 1902. One of the most important symphonists of the twentieth century was making his bow with two works highly derivative, mainly from Tchaikovsky, works supercharged with dramatic and emotional electricity. Although the composer's personality had not yet been clarified, the impact of the two symphonies on audiences was obvious everywhere they were performed. Though hardly representative of the mature Sibelius, these works have never lost their popularity; in fact, they have remained the most frequently heard of all Sibelius' symphonies.

Greater restraint of feeling, an increasing economy of means, a more tight-lipped control are found in the symphonies Sibelius wrote after 1902. These are combined with a new concept of symphonic structure in which the binary form of the classic symphony is replaced by a more pliant mold into which Sibelius poured terse, concentrated statements which he built up, like pieces of a mosaic, into a unified tonal picture. The Third Symphony, in C major, came in 1907 (first performance in Helsinki on September 25, 1907); then the Fourth, in A minor (Helsinki, April 3, 1911); the Fifth, in E-flat major (Helsinki, December 8, 1915); the Sixth, in D minor (Helsinki, February 19, 1923); and the Seventh, in C major (Stockholm, March 24, 1924). The Seventh Symphony was Sibelius' last, even though he lived another thirty-four years. For a decade or more after 1923 there had been rumors that he was working on an eighth symphony, but this was not the case. Sibelius had spoken his last symphonic word in the Seventh.

In the symphonies, from the third through the seventh, Sibelius achieves that full mastery of technique, sublimity of concept, powerful conciseness of speech, and subtle national identity which are the characteristic traits of his symphonic style. "For any parallel to the mature symphonic work of Sibelius," wrote J. H. Elliott, "one turns to the sagas of the Northern races, so naturally and deeply is the music informed by the spirit, national and heroic, from which the legends arose. The general atmosphere is that of the wild, solitary, fabulous; and even where the moods of the music are predominantly triumphant—as, for instance, in the Third and Fifth Symphonies—the bursts of barbaric splendor and the building-up of powerful and vivid climaxes retain a certain austerity not to be accounted to the conscious joys of victory. Rather do they appeal as an exaltation in the abstract of some noble impulse which has striven and achieved. . . . Sibelius gives each symphony an individual character while sustaining the whole compass of his art upon a level that is remote, noble and aloof."

Constant Lambert once remarked that Sibelius advanced "the symphonic form more than any composer since Beethoven. Unham-pered by the oppressive tradition which has virtually driven the Germans from a sentimental diatonicism to its mechanical reaction of intellectual atonality, he has produced a series which would, one imagines, be far more acceptable to Beethoven himself than the elaborate scaffoldings the Germans have erected in his name."

It is generally conceded that Sibelius' best symphonies are the Fourth and the Seventh. Gerald Abraham has said that the Fourth is the work "in which the composer is most completely himself, in which his symphonic methods are most uncompromisingly employed." Cecil Gray has spoken of the Seventh Symphony as "one of the highest summits to which music has yet attained." He compared its "sheer constructive mastery and intellectual power" to the first movements of Beethoven's *Eroica* and Ninth symphonies. "It is not merely a consummate masterpiece of formal construction, however, but also a work of great expressive beauty, of a lofty grandeur and dignity, a truly Olympian serenity and repose which are unique in modern music."

Illness, and the fear of illness, shadowed much of Sibelius' life. From 1901 to 1905 he suffered severely from a disease of the ear which, for a while, threatened total deafness. Hardly had he been relieved of this fear, when another obsessed him. A growth in his throat was diagnosed as cancerous. He underwent an operation in Berlin in May 1908 which, he recalled, was "tedious and painful." He recovered, but the fear that the malignancy might return haunted him for years.

This may be the reason why some of the music he wrote in the years between 1900 and 1910 is filled with melancholy, at times even despair. *Valse Triste*, the highly popular salon piece, was written in 1903 and introduced in Helsinki on April 25, 1904, the composer conducting. This slow, lugubrious melody in three-quarter time is a tonal picture of death as it comes to claim a woman who recalls feverishly the gaiety of a ball; but its deep-rooted pessimism reflects some of Sibelius' own morbid feelings at a time when he thought he was going deaf. To this grim period also belongs one of his most personal creations, the string quartet *Voces Intimae* (*Intimate Voices*), completed in 1909. Still another major work of the early 1900's is his only concerto—that in D minor, for violin and orchestra, which Carl Halir introduced in Berlin on October 19, 1905, in its revised and definitive version.

In 1913 Carl Stoeckel, an American music patron, commissioned Sibelius to write a new orchestral work and conduct its première at the Norfolk music festival in Connecticut. Sibelius' American debut took place on June 4, 1914, in an all-Sibelius program including the world première of *The Oceanides*, which he had written for the occasion. Two weeks later Yale University conferred on him the honorary degree of Doctor of Music. In making the presentation, the president of the University said: "Still in the prime of life, he has become, by the power and originality of his work, one of the most distinguished living composers. What Wagner did with Teutonic legend, Dr. Sibelius has done in his own impressive way with the legends of Finland as embodied in her national epic. He has translated the *Kalevala* into the universal language of music, remarkable for its breadth, large simplicity, and the infusion of a deeply poetic personality."

The period of World War I was difficult for the composer and his family. His publishers, being German, could not send him his royalties, and he suffered severe financial hardship. Performances of his compositions in the Western world brought him no income whatsoever, since Finland was not a signatory to the Berne convention. Inflation had sadly depleted the purchasing power of the annual government grant of fifty thousand marks awarded to him in 1915 on his fiftieth birthday. (The grant was doubled to one hundred thousand marks in 1925, but by then it was worth roughly only twenty-five hundred dollars.) To support his family, Sibelius had to do hack work, and even so his income was a meager one. Other problems beset him. Immediately after the Revolution in Russia, civil war broke out in Finland between the "red" and "white" guards. The Red Army twice invaded Sibelius' home, terrifying its occupants. "I did have a revolver hidden in a room," he later revealed. "My house porter, who was present during the search, knew of this, and if he had betrayed me, my life would not have been worth much."

After the war, Sibelius toured Europe conducting concerts of his works. After 1924 he went into complete retirement. Henceforth he traveled little, except for periodic visits to Helsinki, and he wrote less. His last composition—a set of piano pieces, *Esquisses*, op. 114—was issued in 1929.

He secluded himself in his beautiful two-story villa, "Ainola," in the little town of Järvenpää, twenty miles from Helsinki, which had been his permanent home since 1904. Here, surrounded by the forests he loved, he found amid scenes of incomparable natural beauty the privacy and seclusion he needed for contentment. Up to the time of World War II, pilgrims from all parts of the world beat a path to Järvenpää to pay homage to Sibelius. They needed no address to reach their destination. They merely boarded the train headed north out of Helsinki and told the conductor they were visiting Sibelius; to accommodate them, the train would make a special stop at Järvenpää—a town too small to have a station.

To his visitors Sibelius always proved a gracious host. He loved to be surrounded by people, and he enjoyed hearing first-hand news of the outside world. But these visits proved so taxing that, after the end of World War II, Sibelius' wife protected him from his admirers. In this she was aided by her countrymen, who did what they could to discourage visitors from going to Villa Ainola. When a conductor on the train was asked to stop at Järvenpää, the passenger was told politely but firmly that visitors were no longer received at the Sibelius home.

Henry Askeli pictured Sibelius as he appeared to friends and visitors in the 1930's: "Outwardly he is a powerful man, rather large in size, with good posture and healthy appearance.... The color of his expressive face is ruddy; his marine-blue eyes under scanty eyebrows are set off by strange, vertical wrinkles. His nose and sensitive mouth are well proportioned to each other. His head which, until some years ago, had a crop of brown unruly hair, is now shaven clean. There is a combination of the old Roman Imperator and the modern English gentleman about him. He radiates nobility of mind and powerful personality."

He was always neatly and meticulously dressed, usually in whites and blues. But, since he insisted on physical comfort and freedom of movement, he always wore suits that hung loosely, collars that were several sizes too large, and shoes that were especially made for him in Berlin. Essentially a simple man, he nevertheless was partial to three indulgences: gourmet dishes, expensive cigars, and excellent brandy. When, in his sixties, he feared a recurrence of cancer, he gave up cigars and alcohol completely for fifteen years. Then, convinced that he was well, he returned to both with renewed zest.

He once explained his addiction to cigars: "The odor of cigars brings to memory so much of my childhood. When my father died and I was given many of his possessions, I was spellbound by the strong odor of cigars. His books, his papers, everything had the same fragrance, which became almost holy to me. Now, when I smoke, my childhood inundates me. . . . The smell of a cigar (only a good cigar) is to me the return of carefree times."

His greatest joy seemed to come from walking in the forests near his villa or sitting on a balcony, looking at the beautiful vista stretching before him for miles. "I love the mysterious sounds of the fields and forests, water and mountains," he said. "Nature has truly been the book of books for me." He was a man who loved his home, his wife, his children, and the society of close friends. Before World War II he liked to visit the local tavern and surround himself with neighbors, enjoying his brandy and cigars while exchanging small talk and colorful stories.

The years of World War II, like those of the preceding war, were trying ones. Once again the flow of royalties was temporarily arrested and the Sibelius household was hard put to make ends meet. Musical groups in England wanted to help relieve his situation by arranging benefit concerts, but he stubbornly refused to encourage them, insisting his own condition was no worse than that of his countrymen. He also would not consider the possibility of seeking safety abroad. Far more painful to him than his own personal deprivations was to see his beloved land attacked by superior Soviet forces. Frequently, when Soviet planes zoomed overhead, he would rush out of his house and direct an angry fist at them.

After the war he went into almost complete isolation at Villa Ainola. He had by now become recognized not only as Finland's greatest composer but also as a national hero.

A performing string quartet, a museum, a park, and streets were named after him; so was the Music Institute he had once attended. In 1940 an attempt was made to erect a statue in his honor, but this project had to be abandoned when Sibelius protested loudly. However, he did allow the Finnish government to issue a postage stamp with his picture, on the occasion of his eightieth birthday, the first time a living composer was thus honored. In 1951 the government of Finland and the city of Helsinki combined to sponsor an annual festival of Sibelius' music. His ninetieth birthday was celebrated throughout Finland with festive concerts and other events.

Jean Sibelius died of a cerebral hemorrhage at his home at Villa Ainola on September 20, 1957. His body was brought to the Church of St. Nicholas in Helsinki in a slow, solemn procession. Less than three hours after it arrived, some twenty thousand Finns had filed past his coffin. Fifty thousand students stood silently outside the church during the funeral services, conducted by the Archbishop of Finland. The streets of Helsinki were lined with many more thousands of mourners as the coffin returned to Villa Ainola. Sibelius' widow, Aino, died in 1969 at the age of ninety-eight.

To help commemorate the fiftieth anniversary of Finnish independence a huge abstract metal sculpture (the work of Eila Hiltunen) was unveiled in Helsinki on September 7, 1967. It weighs twenty-eight tons and is twenty-six feet high and thirty-two feet long, with a depth of nineteen feet. This memorial to Sibelius aroused much controversy in Finland, because the abstract designs of five hundred and eighty silvery pipes appeared to have no relation either to the composer or to his music. A compromise was reached with the placement of a large metallic sculpture of the composer's head at the site.

"Music is for me music and nothing else," he said. "If someone writes about my music and finds, let us say, a feeling of nature in it, all well and good. Let him say that, as long as we have it clear for ourselves, we do not become a part of the music's innermost sound and sense through analysis. . . . Compositions are like butterflies. Touch them even once and the dust of hue is gone. They can, of course still fly, but are nowhere as beautiful. . . .

Greater sureness makes one more and more prone to scorn solutions that come too easily, that follow the line of least resistance. One is always faced with new problems. The thing that has pleased me most is that I have been able to reject. The greatest labor that I have expended, perhaps, was on works that have never been completed."

MAJOR WORKS

Chamber Music—Voces Intimae, string quartet; Violin Sonatina; Novelette, for violin and piano; 5 Danses Champêtres, for violin and piano; various pieces for violin and piano, and for cello and piano.

Choral Music—The Origin of Fire; Song of Väinö; various cantatas.

Orchestral Music—7 symphonies; Scènes Historiques, two suites; Kullervo, tone poem; En Saga, tone poem; Karelia, suite; Four Legends from the Kalevala (including The Swan of Tuonela); Christian II, suite; Finlandia, tone poem; Valse Triste; Pelléas et Mélisande, suite; Violin Concerto in D minor; Belshazzar's Feast, suite; Pohjola's Daughter, symphonic fantasy; Night Ride and Sunrise, tone poem; In Memoriam, funeral march; The Bard, tone poem; The Oceanides, tone poem; The Tempest, two suites; Suite Caractéristique, for small orchestra; Tapiola, tone poem.

Piano Music—3 sonatinas; bagatelles, impromptus, pieces, rondinos; Sonata in F major; Six Finnish Folksongs; Pensées Lyriques; Kyllikki; Four Lyric Pieces.

Vocal Music—Numerous songs for voice and piano including Flower Song, From an Anxious Heart, Hymn to Thaïs the Unforgettable, In the Field a Maiden Sings, O Were Thou Here, Slow as the Sunset Colors, and The Tree.

ABOUT

Abraham, G. (ed.), The Music of Sibelius; Ekman, K., Jean Sibelius; Gray, C., Sibelius; Hannikainen, I., Sibelius and the Development of Finnish Music; Helasvuo, V., Sibelius and the Music of Finland; Johnson, H. E., Jean Sibelius; Layton, R., Sibelius; Parmet, S., The Symphonies of Sibelius; Ringbom, N. E., Sibelius; Tanzberger, E., Jean Sibelius; Törne, B. de, Sibelius: A Close-Up.

Elie Siegmeister
1909–

Elie Siegmeister, the son of a surgeon, was born on January 15, 1909, in New York City. He was brought up in Brooklyn, where his family moved when he was six. He was no child prodigy in music. His boyhood interests included baseball in sandlots, playing with his friends in the streets, the writing of poetry, mathematics, chess. In his ninth year, while

Siegmeister: sĕg′ mĭ stĕr

attending grade school, he began to study piano; but, as he has remarked, this proved more of an annoyance than a pleasure, probably because of the unsatisfactory instruction he was receiving. It was his father who awakened in the boy a strong love for music by taking him to the Sunday afternoon concerts of the New York Philharmonic and to performances at the Metropolitan Opera. At fourteen Elie was an expert on the *Leitmotive* in Wagner's *Ring* cycle and a passionate admirer of the symphonies of Beethoven and Tchaikovsky. At fifteen he studied piano with his first influential teacher, Emil Friedberger, a pupil of Leschetizky. Friedberger further stimulated Siegmeister's musical interests by analyzing for him the masterworks of Bach and Beethoven.

ELIE SIEGMEISTER

At Boys High School, in Brooklyn, Siegmeister was a member of the championship mathematics team and of the chess team; he was also president of the Physics Club. Precocious in his studies, Siegmeister was only fifteen when he was graduated from high school and matriculated at Columbia College. At Columbia he majored in psychology and philosophy before switching to music. From 1924 to 1927 he was in Seth Bingham's composition class for which he wrote sonatas and fugues, showing an increasing aptitude for composition. In 1926 he studied composition with Wallingford Riegger.

Upon graduating from Columbia in 1927,

with a Phi Beta Kappa key, Siegmeister went to Paris where he lived for the next five years, studying composition with Nadia Boulanger. During this period, in 1930, he married Hannah Mersel. "The early years of study in Paris were valuable for training received in some areas," he now reveals, "but not the total blessing one might imagine. I never quite felt at home in Europe, did not care for the precious and somewhat effete atmosphere of 'society' musicians clustered around the Boulanger studio." Nevertheless, in Paris, he felt for the first time an urge to discover an American voice in music. For a while he experimented with jazz idioms in compositions like *Saturday Night*, for saxophone, and his first violin sonata (1931) which included a second theme in a Charleston rhythm. Several songs to poems by Robert Frost (1930) he now regards as "the first completely achieved personal pieces I have written." When they were revived in 1962, Siegmeister confessed being "very happy with them" and would not have been displeased "to write some more like them today."

It was soon after his return to the United States that he arrived at a new concept of the role of the composer. Previously he had tried to write comparatively esoteric works appealing to a limited, sophisticated audience. He now became convinced that a composer must be rooted, personally and musically, in the life of his nation and its people; that a composer had to reach out to people everywhere and speak to them, directly and simply, through his music. A powerful stimulus in arriving at such conclusions was his interest in the music of Charles Ives, about which he has remained passionately enthusiastic. "Ives shed light on the path I wanted to follow," says Siegmeister, "and have followed ever since. He was a glorious ancestor to whom one can always look back, and know that a great man has charted the course."

At this time Siegmeister organized a chorus composed of shipping clerks, house painters, stenographers, and students which gave concerts of new American music wherever an audience could be found. They appeared in lofts and empty stores in the Bronx and Brooklyn. These concerts provided Siegmeister with an opportunity to introduce some of his vocal and choral compositions,

including *Strange Funeral in Braddock*, for voice and piano or orchestra (1933), and *John Henry* (1936), for chorus. He also composed music for the dance, for the theatre, for amateur groups, and for children—in a continuous effort to achieve a direct personal contact with as many people as possible, including many who never attended concerts of modern works.

It was not long before Siegmeister became intimately associated with the field of American folk music, a development that had an immeasurable influence on his career as a musician and composer in the 1930's and 1940's. As a youngster, he had been extremely fond of Negro spirituals. When Aunt Molly Jackson sang to him some folk tunes from Harlan, Kentucky, she opened up to him the whole varied vista of the musical creation of the American people. He began to travel throughout the United States, listening to the folk songs of various regions and putting them down on paper. He made numerous arrangements and free fantasies on folk themes. The fruits of his intensive research can be found in his anthology, *A Treasury of American Song*, edited in collaboration with Olin Downes, and in the musical play *Sing Out Sweet Land!*, produced on Broadway by the Theatre Guild of New York in 1944, the score of which is made up of American folk songs.

From 1935 to 1938 Siegmeister studied conducting on a fellowship at the Juilliard School of Music. In 1939 he founded the American Ballad Singers, a group which he led in numerous concerts both in New York and on tour throughout the United States. He also conducted all the performances on Broadway of *Sing Out Sweet Land*!

The influence of American folk idiom upon his creative thinking can be discovered in his first successful works for orchestra, which many of America's leading symphony orchestras performed in the 1940's. All these compositions were definitely American—in rhythm, texture, orchestration, and especially in their straightforward lyricism. Siegmeister's interest in people led him to range over the entire American scene. In various compositions he depicted people at work and at play in their historic growth or everyday experiences. *Ozark Set* (first performance in Minneapolis on November 7, 1944, Dimitri Mitropoulos conducting) portrays moments in the life of the people of the Ozark Mountains, with effective re-creation of a religious camp meeting and a Saturday night square dance. The traditions of the Midwest are glorified in *Wilderness Road* (introduced in Detroit in June 1945) and in *Prairie Legend* (première in New York on January 18, 1947, Leopold Stokowski conducting). *Lonesome Hollow* (given in Columbus, Ohio, in 1948) reflects the more thoughtful and poetic aspects of American character through the portrayal of a man walking through a lovely valley in the lonely hills, his reveries interrupted by the strains of a village dance heard from a distance. In *Western Suite* (introduced by Arturo Toscanini and the NBC Symphony on November 24, 1945) actual folk songs are woven into Siegmeister's orchestral texture. And *Sunday in Brooklyn* (introduced by the NBC Symphony, on July 21, 1946) portrays life in the composer's home borough, the whole reflecting the spirit of the city streets through popular tunes.

The employment of either folk or popular materials and the presentation of American backgrounds, scenes, and experiences represent only one of several creative areas cultivated by Siegmeister. He has also produced much absolute music that is modern, adventurous, sometimes dissonant, at times complex; much that is personal and introspective. Among these are such important works as his first string quartet (1935), three symphonies (1947, 1950, 1957), the second string quartet (1960), the second violin sonata (1959), and the second piano sonata (1964). Though fully exploiting some of the resources of modern writing, Siegmeister prefers to work within an expanded tonal framework, his musical ideas tightly bound together by the architectonic structure. Basically, Siegmeister is a Romantic who believes that music springs from inner experiences, feelings, and thoughts. As a Romantic he leans heavily on expressive lyricism. Lyricism is what impressed Virgil Thomson in Siegmeister's Second Symphony, which was heard in New York on February 25, 1952: "Its songful material is of the utmost beauty.... Its tunes are lovely, its tone is serious and its emotional content is all the more for that." Yet there is strength as well as romantic ardor in this music. A critic for the daily *Oklahoman* said of the Third Symphony when the Oklahoma City Symphony

introduced it under Guy Fraser Harrison's direction in February 1959: "Rhythm was predominant, strong rhythm, double and triple rhythm, sometimes in conflict, sometimes in agreement, all pure Siegmeister. His melodies were utterances of faith that were second cousin to a Shouting Methodist's. But it was Siegmeister's use of the resources of the orchestra that gave the piece its ultimate character of *joie de vivre*."

Still another creative area that has proved fruitful for Siegmeister is that of dramatic or theatre music, music that is tuneful, rhythmic, and fully aware of its stage responsibilities. Since *Sing Out Sweet Land!* Siegmeister has produced nothing directly for the Broadway stage. But he has written two one-act operas that make for delightful theatre: *Darling Corie*, libretto by Lewis Allen (1952), an opera based on the life of mountain people of the Southern Appalachians; and *Miranda and the Dark Young Man*, libretto by Edward Eager (1955), a kind of Shavian parody on traditional romantic opera which, nonetheless, succeeds in being romantic in its own right.

Siegmeister considers his full-length opera *The Plough and the Stars* (1963), based on Sean O'Casey's play, his most ambitious work and artistically his most successful. Here the various levels on which he has been working find common ground. "It has all of my music in it," says Siegmeister, "from the serious and the abstract to the theatrical and the folk; even some ragtime rears its head from time to time." When the opera was heard for the first time—in St. Louis on May 15, 1963—a critic for the *Globe-Democrat* described it as "powerful musical theatre" and "an intense dramatic utterance. ... Siegmeister's score is an intricate and demanding one for both voice and orchestra.... It contains a wide variety of musical expression ranging from bawdy music-hall ditties to gentle, tender love songs. Moments of low humor balance and accent the irony and the tragedy."

Since 1949 Siegmeister has been a member of the music faculty of Hofstra University on Long Island, where in 1965 he became a full professor and in 1966 composer-in-residence. He has also been the conductor of its symphony orchestra. During the summer of 1967 he was composer-in-residence at the Haverford Chamber Festival. Siegmeister has lived in Great Neck, Long Island, since 1954. He has two daughters, both married, and both intensely musical, though not professionally so. Apart from music, Siegmeister's interests embrace reading, going to the theatre, and engaging in stimulating conversations. For physical exercise he prefers tennis and swimming. Siegmeister helped to organize the American Composers Alliance. He is a member of the board of directors of the American Music Center, the official United States Government information agency for music. He wrote the background music for the motion picture *They Came to Cordura*, starring Gary Cooper and Rita Hayworth, released in 1959.

MAJOR WORKS

Chamber Music—2 string quartets; 3 violin sonatas; Two Pieces, for saxophone and piano; Song for a Quiet Evening, for violin and piano; Soliloquy, for solo cello; Fantasy, for solo cello; Sextet, for brass and percussion; Two Pieces, for solo cello.

Choral Music—John Henry; Abraham Lincoln Walks at Midnight; Song of Democracy; The New Colossus; Anne Rutledge; Freedom Train; Christmas Is Coming; This is Our Land; In Our Time; I Have a Dream, cantata for baritone, narrator, chorus, and orchestra.

Operas—Darling Corie, one-act opera; Miranda and the Dark Young Man, one-act opera; The Mermaid in Lock 7, one-act opera; The Plough and the Stars.

Orchestral Music—3 symphonies; American Holiday; Ozark Set; Prairie Legend; Wilderness Road; Western Suite; Sunday in Brooklyn (also for piano); Funnybone Alley, for voice and orchestra; Summer Night; Lonesome Hollow; From My Window (also for piano); Divertimento; Clarinet Concerto; Three Symphonic Sketches (Cordura Suite); Flute Concerto; Five Fantasies for the Theater; Dick Whittington and His Cat, a symphonic story for children.

Piano Music—2 sonatas; Theme and Variations, Nos. 1 and 2; Serenade; The Children's Day; Folkways U.S.A., three books; American Kaleidoscope; Three Preludes; Lonesome Song.

Vocal Music—Refugee Road; The Crime Took Place in Granada, song cycle; The Lincoln Penny; Johnny Appleseed; Euclid; A New Wind a-Blowin'; Street Cleaner Man; Lazy Afternoon; Lonely Star; For My Daughters, song cycle; Madam to You, song cycle; Songs of Experience; The Face of War, song cycle; Four Songs to Poems by Eberhart.

ABOUT

Ewen, D., Complete Book of 20th Century Music.

Christian Sinding
1856–1941

Christian Sinding was born in Kongsberg, Norway, on January 11, 1856. After studying

---

Sinding: sĭn′ dĭng

piano and harmony with Lindemann in Trondheim, he went in 1877 to the Leipzig Conservatory where he was a pupil of Reinecke in orchestration, Schradieck in violin, and Jadassohn in theory. Upon his return to Norway, Sinding settled in Christiania (now Oslo) where he earned his living teaching the piano and making a number of concert appearances. In 1880 a modest government stipend enabled him to return to Germany to devote himself to further study and composition. At this time he completed his first symphony, the world première of which took place on March 25, 1882, in Oslo. Upon hearing Sinding play the first movement of this symphony on the piano Grieg wrote: "It was magnificent. It was in the spirit of the first movement of the Ninth, yet it was all Sinding not Beethoven." During this period Sinding also wrote his first opera, *Titandros* (1884), which was frankly imitative of the Wagnerian music drama and was never produced; and a Piano Quintet (1884), which became his first major work to be published and which was heard in Oslo in 1885 and in Leipzig in 1888. On December 19, 1885, the first all-Sinding concert given anywhere was heard in Oslo. His Piano Concerto in D-flat, introduced in Berlin on February 23, 1889, placed him firmly in the camp of the German post-Romantics influenced by Brahms and Wagner.

In 1890 Sinding received a new government stipend, this time large enough to make it possible for him to give up all activities except composition. This was testimony to the high position he was beginning to occupy in the musical life of his native land. He continued to work in the larger forms, producing a piano trio in 1893, a violin sonata in 1894, and a violin concerto in 1898. But his fame became international through some of his shorter works for the piano which were issued in the 1890's; these included several sets of pieces (*Stücke*), opp. 24, 25, 31, 32, and 33 in 1896. It is here that we find the most popular single piece of music Sinding ever wrote—the perennial favorite of piano students and salon orchestras, *Frühlingsrauschen* (*Rustle of Spring*), the third number in op. 32. This is probably also the most popular composition written about the vernal season. Influenced partly by Wagner—the Wagner of the Forest Music in *Siegfried*—Sinding here created a sentimental melody filled with the wonder and magic of nature's rebirth at springtime. The melody is placed over a repeated accompanying figure suggesting spring's rustle. Among other popular piano pieces by Sinding are *Marche Grotesque*, from the same set; the Minuet and Serenade from op. 33; the Chanson, from op. 34; the Humoresque, from op. 49. Eugen Stegnitz singled out for praise in such pieces "the way in which the thematic material as a nursery of new musical organisms is turned to best advantage, the luxuriantly flowing, ever expressive and refined melody, and finally the spontaneous but always highly interesting themes."

When Grieg died in 1907, Sinding was generally acknowledged to be Norway's leading composer, and he maintained this position up to the end of his life with a prolific output. His second symphony was conducted in Berlin by Artur Nikisch on March 22, 1907. His opera, *Der Heilige Berg*, was introduced in Dessau on April 19, 1914. This work was successfully revived in Oslo in 1931, in a concert performance, with Kirsten Flagstad singing the principal female role.

In 1915 the Norwegian government awarded Sinding a life pension of four thousand crowns a year; and in 1916, in celebration of his sixtieth birthday, he was awarded an additional thirty thousand crowns. For many years Sinding spent a part of each year in Berlin where he was held in high esteem and where he served as a member of the Academy of Arts. His third symphony received its world première in Berlin on January 10, 1921. From 1921 to 1923, Sinding was a member of the faculty of the Eastman School of Music in Rochester, New York. On January 11, 1936, his eightieth birthday, his fourth symphony, *Vinter og Vaar*, was given its world première in Oslo.

Christian Sinding died in Oslo on December 3, 1941.

Jenö Arbo has written that Sinding's music is "independent of any school. His style has often a Scandinavian strain, . . . [though it is not] always possible to characterize it as specifically Norwegian; but its sharp-cut rhythms, bold harmonies and vigorous tendency are characteristic of his Norwegian temperament. . . . Sinding's music is more epic than dramatic. He favors a heroic *fresco* style

which is manly and passionate in its form of expression. Side by side with the typical Sinding characteristics (restless modulation, violent harmonic movements, rhythmic monotony) we see the influence of Wagner, especially as regards melody and harmonization."

CHRISTIAN SINDING

M. M. Ulfrstad makes an interesting comparison between Sinding and his distinguished predecessor Grieg: "Grieg's style was a combination of national melody with Schumann technique. Sinding's style became a combination of national melody with Wagnerian technique. His music is optimistic, virile, and of epic strength and breadth. Whilst Grieg's music was an echo from the mountains, thin, mournful moods and poetic idylls, Sinding's is an echo from the sea that dashes against the rocks. In his music are heard the storm, the thunder of the waves, and the daring of the Vikings."

MAJOR WORKS

Chamber Music—3 piano trios; 4 violin sonatas; 4 violin suites (including Suite in the Old Style); Piano Quintet in E minor; Scènes de la Vie, suite for violin and piano; String Quartet in A minor; Cantus Doloris, variations for violin and piano; Three Capricci, for violin and piano; Nordische Ballade, for cello and piano.

Choral Music—Til Molde; various cantatas.

Opera—Der Heilige Berg.

Orchestral Music—4 symphonies; 3 violin concertos; Piano Concerto in D-flat major; Suite in A minor, for violin and orchestra; Épisodes Chevaleresques, suite; Rondo Infinito; Legende, for violin and orchestra;

Romanze in D major, for violin and orchestra; Abendstimmung, for violin and orchestra.

Piano Music—Variations in E-flat minor, for two pianos; Suite; Fifteen Caprices; Burlesques; Mélodies Mignonnes; Morceaux Characteristiques; Studien und Skizzen; Sonata in B minor; Fatum, variations; Nordische Tänze und Weisen, for four hands; numerous Pieces and Characteristic Pieces; etudes, intermezzi, waltz.

Vocal Music—Homecoming, cycle; about 250 songs for voice and piano.

ABOUT

Lange, K. and Östvedt, A., Norwegian Music; Monrad-Jorganssen, D., Christian Sinding.

Charles Sanford Skilton
1868–1941

Charles Sanford Skilton, whose best works are based on the musical idioms of the American Indian, was born in Northampton, Massachusetts, on August 16, 1868. He was graduated from Yale University with a Bachelor of Arts degree in 1889; during his junior year there he composed his first serious work, *The Burial of Moses*. In the year of his graduation, he wrote incidental music to *Elektra*, which was performed at Smith College in Northampton. Upon leaving Yale, he went to New York to study organ with Harry Rowe Shelley and composition with Dudley Buck. In 1891 he traveled to Berlin where his musical training was continued to 1893 at the Hochschule für Musik with Albert Heinz in organ and Bargiel in composition.

Upon returning to the United States in 1893, he was appointed director of music at the Salem Academy and College in Winston, North Carolina. During this period he also conducted the Salem Philharmonic. He left Salem in 1896 and for a year lived in New York where he attended the Metropolitan College of Music. From 1898 to 1903 he was the music director at the State Normal School in Trenton, New Jersey. There, in 1900, he founded the Monday Morning Musical Club. In 1903 Skilton was appointed Dean of the School of Fine Arts at the University of Kansas, occupying this post until 1915; he also served as professor of organ and music history for most of the remaining years of his life.

Though he composed continuously through these years, winning first prizes for several compositions in competitions sponsored by the

Kansas Federation of Music Clubs, he did not arrive at a full crystallization of his personal style until he became interested in the music of the American Indian. This happened in 1915 when an Indian pupil offered to teach him tribal songs in exchange for music lessons. Skilton, fascinated by this initiation into a new world of music, decided to explore it even further. Haskell Institute, a government school for Indians, located at Lawrence, Kansas, made possible a more detailed study of the subject of Indian music.

CHARLES SANFORD SKILTON

His first important compositions on American Indian subjects and in an American Indian style came quickly. In 1915 he wrote *Two Indian Dances*, for string quartet. Soon after he orchestrated this work and made it the first of a two-part composition for orchestra entitled *Suite Primeval*. The première of the first part was heard in Minneapolis on October 29, 1916; the second part, on November 13, 1921. *Two Indian Dances* became a popular work and was performed by major orchestras throughout the United States. Later works in a similar Indian vein included the *Sioux Flute Serenade*, for small orchestra (1920); and *Shawnee Indian Hunting Dance*, for orchestra, introduced by the Detroit Symphony on December 11, 1930. An opera, *The Sun Bride*, was given its world première in a radio broadcast on April 17, 1930. A second opera, *Kalopin*, though never produced, received the David Bispham Memorial Medal of the

American Opera Society of Chicago in 1930.

While his Indian works have achieved the greatest popularity, Skilton by no means restricted himself to the use of Indian materials. His compositions, embracing nearly all forms of musical presentation, show his interest in developing musical styles independent of European sources. In addition to the works using Indian themes, many of his compositions are deeply rooted in the American scene. In Skilton's compositions one recognizes first of all a sincerity of musical expression combined with the sterling craftsmanship of a gifted, scholarly musician. His works are rarely conventional in makeup but are written for the most part in a fresh and sophisticated style.

Skilton spent the year 1937–1938 in Europe, chiefly in Vienna, where he orchestrated Handel's Suite No. 4, for clavier, which received important performances as the Suite in E minor. He also composed an important chamber music work, the String Quartet in B minor. His final composition was a group of songs for soprano, *Zoo Fantastique*.

Charles Sanford Skilton died in Lawrence, Kansas, on March 12, 1941.

His chief recreations were reading, walking, and telling stories to children, whom he delighted in entertaining. A deeply religious man, he was also of scholarly inclination and rarely permitted a day to pass without spending some time in reading classics in Greek, French, Italian, German, or English. Despite these scholarly qualities, he thoroughly enjoyed baseball, Western movies, and a good detective story.

He spent many summers composing at the MacDowell Colony in Peterborough, New Hampshire. Loving the outdoors, he found the Colony an ideal spot for his creative work.

MAJOR WORKS

Chamber Music—2 violin sonatas; Violin Sonatina; Sarabande, for wind instruments; Two Indian Dances, for string quartet (also for orchestra as Part I of Suite Primeval); Sioux Flute Serenade; String Quartet in B minor.

Choral Music—The Witch's Daughter, cantata; The Guardian Angel, oratorio; From Forest and Stream; Midnight; The Fountain; Ticonderoga, cantata.

Operas—Kalopin; The Sun Bride; The Day of Gayomair.

Orchestral Music—Suite Primeval, two parts; Autumn Night; Shawnee Indian Hunting Dance; A Carolina Legend, tone poem; Mt. Oread, overture; Sioux Flute Serenade, for small orchestra; American Indian Fantasie, for cello and orchestra.

Piano Music—Three Indian Sketches.
Vocal Music—Zoo Fantastique.

ABOUT

Howard, J. T., Charles Sanford Skilton.

Leo Sowerby
1895–1968

Leo Sowerby was born in Grand Rapids, Michigan, on May 1, 1895. Both parents were British, his father coming from England and his mother from Canada. When Leo was four, his mother died, and three years later his father remarried. It was his stepmother who became a vital influence in his life by turning him to the study of music. At the age of seven, Sowerby began taking lessons on the piano with Mrs. Frederick Burton, who remained his teacher until he was graduated from elementary school. The study of harmony was begun in his eleventh year after he had procured a textbook and learned the rudiments of theory by himself. When he arrived in Chicago, at the age of fourteen, he had to his credit a number of interesting compositions. In Chicago, Sowerby attended Englewood High School and at the same time studied the piano with Calvin Lampert and Percy Grainger and theory with Arthur Olaf Andersen.

In his fifteenth year Sowerby decided to learn the organ. He had about six lessons with Lampert but was unable to practice as much as he desired because it cost him twenty-five cents an hour to use the organ and he could little afford it at the time. One day, on his way home from a lesson, he stopped off at a meat market and procured a large sheet of tough brown wrapping paper. Having already supplied himself with a foot rule and pencil, he proceeded to visit a church. There he made as accurate a sketch of the organ pedals as he could. This he took home and placed under the front of his piano to use as a pedalier for daily practice until he acquired a bit of foot technique. At the same time, he obtained books on organ construction, including the mechanism of action, touch, and stops, all of which he memorized. His love for the organ as a means of expressing himself grew with his urge to compose.

Sowerby: sō´ ẽr bē

Sowerby

In his eighteenth year Sowerby made his official debut as a composer when his Concerto for Violin and Orchestra was performed by Glenn Dillard Gunn on a program of American music. (Sowerby rewrote this work in 1938, and the new version was introduced in Rochester, New York, by Jacques Gordon.) His first successful composition—the first work to remain in the repertory—is a delightful concert overture for orchestra, *Comes Autumn Time* (1916). The effervescence, ebullience, and youthful energy of this music make for delightful listening, its point of departure being a poem by Bliss Carman, *Autumn*. Another charming orchestral work was written in 1916, the suite *Irish Washerwoman*. This was followed in 1917 by *Set of Four*, a suite "of ironics" for orchestra, introduced in Chicago on February 15, 1918.

LEO SOWERBY

Sowerby made his debut as a concert pianist in 1917, just before America's involvement in World War I. This performance took place at the Norfolk Music Festival in Connecticut and was followed by appearances in recitals and as soloist with symphony orchestras. On December 8, 1917, Sowerby enlisted in the American army and was rushed into the 86th Division, stationed at Camp Grant, Rockford, Illinois, as a raw recruit in the 332nd Field Artillery. He became a member of its band and then was promoted to bandmaster; he also received a commission as second lieutenant. In the summer of 1918 he went to France with his regiment; on March 1, 1919, he was honorably discharged. Following his separation from the army, Sowerby completed the writing of a piano concerto, the world première of which took place in Chicago on March 5, 1920, with the composer as soloist.

His talent was recognized in 1921 when he became the first American to be awarded the Prix de Rome established by the American Academy in Rome. Sowerby did not compete for this fellowship; it was awarded to him unanimously after all the manuscripts which had been submitted had been rejected. The three years in Rome were important in his artistic development. During that time he wrote several compositions, the most important of which was *King Estmere*, a ballad for two pianos and orchestra, introduced in Rome on April 8, 1923.

After returning to the United States in 1924, Sowerby proceeded to advance his career not only as concert pianist and composer but also as organist and educator. In 1925 he joined the composition department of the American Conservatory of Music in Chicago, where he remained until 1962, most of those years as head of the department. From 1927 to 1962 he was organist and choirmaster of St. James's Cathedral (Episcopal) in Chicago.

As a composer he made notable strides in the 1920's and 1930's. Of particular interest are his second symphony (world première in Chicago on March 29, 1929); a tone poem, *Prairie*, first heard at Interlochen, Michigan, on August 11, 1929; and a concerto for organ and orchestra introduced in Boston on April 22, 1938. The most interesting feature of these works is the versatility of their style. As a critic of the Boston *Transcript* wrote: "There is probably no factor in modern musical method that Sowerby has not at one time or another explored."

Two more symphonies came in the 1940's. The third was commissioned by the Chicago Symphony which introduced it on March 6, 1941; the fourth was heard in Boston on January 7, 1949. In between these two major works, Sowerby produced in 1943 *The Canticle of the Sun*, a major work for chorus and orchestra based on Matthew Arnold's translation of the St. Francis canticle. Following its world première in New York on April 16, 1945, it received the Pulitzer Prize in music.

For the fiftieth anniversary of Washington Cathedral in Washington, D.C., Sowerby was commissioned to write *The Throne of God*, an extended anthem for chorus and orchestra. This was performed on November 18, 1957. In September 1962, he became the first director of the newly formed College of Church Musicians at the Washington Cathedral.

During the summer of 1968 Leo Sowerby was teaching at Camp Wa-Li-Ro, a summer music school on Middle Bass Island near Port Clinton, Ohio, when he was suddenly taken ill. He was rushed to Magruder Hospital in Port Clinton and a few days later, on Sunday July 7, died there.

Sowerby said of himself: "I find diversion mostly in the diversity of the work I do: composer, organist, choirmaster, teacher, lecturer. When this palls, I try contract bridge. I have never been interested in sports."

During his life he received honorary doctorates from the University of Rochester and from the American Conservatory of Music. He was made an honorary Fellow of Trinity College in London, and he was a member of the National Institute of Arts and Letters.

MAJOR WORKS

Chamber Music—3 violin sonatas; Serenade, for string quartet; Quintet for Flute, Oboe, Clarinet, Bassoon, and Horn; Pop Goes the Weasel, for flute, oboe, clarinet, bassoon, and French horn; Symphony for Organ; Suite for Organ; String Quartet in G minor; Clarinet Sonata; Poem, for viola and organ; Trumpet Sonata; Ballade, for English horn and organ.

Choral Music—Vision of Sir Launfal; Great Is the Lord; Te Deum in D minor; Song for America; Forsaken of Man; Canticle of the Sun; Christ Reborn; The Throne of God; The Ark of the Covenant; also many compositions for Episcopal church service.

Orchestral Music—4 symphonies; 2 piano concertos; 2 cello concertos; Comes Autumn Time, concert overture; Irish Washerwoman, suite; Set of Four, suite; King Estmere, ballad for two pianos and orchestra; Money Musk; Medieval Poem; Prairie; Concerto for Organ and Orchestra; Theme in Yellow; Concert Overture; Fantasy on Hymn Tunes; Classic Concerto for Organ and Strings; Portrait, a fantasy in triptych; Organ Concerto.

Piano Music—From the Northland, suite; Cantus Heroicus; Fisherman's Tune; Synconata, for two pianos; Florida Suite; Toccata; Sonata; Suite, for four hands.

Vocal Music—With Strawberries; Prayer of the Singer; Three Psalms, for basso and organ; Three Psalms, for contralto or baritone and organ; Songs of Faith and Penitence, for soprano and organ.

ABOUT

Howard, J. T., Our Contemporary Composers.
Musical Quarterly, April 1938.

William Grant Still
1895–

William Grant Still was born in Woodville, Mississippi, on May 11, 1895, with a racial background of American Indian, Negro, Irish and Spanish blood. He was, he reports, strongly influenced by members of his family: "My father, who was musically inclined, passed on when I was three months old. My mother then moved to Little Rock, Arkansas. I owe her very much, for she taught me to curb a strong and rather unruly will, and aroused in me a strong and permanent interest in the various branches of art. My maternal grandmother, who resided with us in Little Rock, taught me many of the songs sung by Negroes in the days of slavery; this was my apprenticeship in the field of music. From my grandmother, too, I learned the value of faith in God."

WILLIAM GRANT STILL

His grammar and high school education was pursued in Little Rock, and when it was completed he entered Wilberforce University. He was then sixteen years old.

"My mother's plan," he recalls, "was for me to study medicine after finishing college, and she strongly opposed my desire to study music despite the fact that she had provided for me to receive instruction in the art of playing the violin quite a few years before I entered college. But I loved music, and was willing to make sacrifices for the sake of gaining a musical education."

After acquiring training in theory and composition at Oberlin Conservatory, Still was given a special course in composition with George W. Chadwick at the New England Conservatory. He completed his study of composition with Edgard Varèse in New York.

While pursuing this formal study, Still earned his living playing various instruments in orchestras in Columbus, Ohio. After his studies were over—and following service in the Navy during World War I—he wrote arrangements of popular music for W. C. Handy and for Paul Whiteman and his orchestra. He also did arrangements for and directed the programs of the "Deep River Hour" over radio station WOR, in New York. His experiences in this commercial field, together with his studies, combined to form a basis for Still's later musical individuality. His first public appearance as a serious composer was made with dissonant compositions. In a few years' time, however, he drew sharply away from ultramodernism and used his experience with modern idioms in forming his own style.

He first found his creative identity with music that was intensely racial, strongly melodic, and vibrant with emotion. One of the earliest of such works was *From the Dark Belt*, for orchestra (1926). This was followed by *Darker America* and his first major success, the *Afro-American Symphony*. The latter two works for orchestra were introduced in Rochester, New York: *Darker America* on November 21, 1927, and the symphony on October 29, 1931. When the symphony was performed in Germany, several German critics regarded it as one of the most characteristically indigenous works to come out of the United States. The symphony was also performed in Budapest, Paris, and Panama, and in several cities in England. In this, and in other compositions of the 1930's, Still did not interest himself in tonal experiments. He was concerned mainly in expressing the gamut of his experiences within musical sounds; and he did this with sincerity, frequently with poignancy.

The 1930's were an unusually productive period for Still. Receiving the Guggenheim and Rosenwald fellowships, both of which were renewed, enabled him to launch the writing of several major works. These included two operas, *Blue Steel* in 1935 and *Troubled Island*

in 1938; a ballet, *Lenox Avenue*, in 1937; and various works for orchestra. He also made music history in America by becoming the first Negro to conduct a major symphony orchestra, the Los Angeles Philharmonic, which he led in 1936 in the performance of several of his compositions at the Hollywood Bowl. Nineteen years later he also became the first Negro to lead a major orchestra in the deep South, by appearing in 1955 with the New Orleans Philharmonic at Southern University.

During the period of World War II, Still was led by his growing social consciousness to write music with strong social and racial implications. *And They Lynched Him On a Tree*—for narrator, contralto, chorus, and orchestra—was heard in New York on June 25, 1940. Here he departed from descriptive music of racial interest to attack social injustice. He followed this with a stirring patriotic composition, *Plain Chant for Americans*, for baritone and orchestra, introduced in New York on October 23, 1941. Orchestral compositions, some of which gained wide circulation in the 1940's, also reflected his deep social and racial consciousness. *In Memoriam: The Colored Soldiers Who Died for Democracy* was a brief requiem which tried to say in music what so many Negro fighters said during the war through heroic deeds; its first performance was heard in New York on January 5, 1944. In the *Poem for Orchestra* (first performance in Cleveland on December 7, 1944) he pointed to the rebirth of a war-desolated world through a stronger belief in God. Not on a racial theme, but nevertheless a highly successful piece for orchestra during the 1940's, was the *Festive Overture* which Eugene Goossens introduced with the Cincinnati Symphony on January 18, 1945. It was awarded first prize of one thousand dollars in a competition sponsored by the Cincinnati Symphony to commemorate its fiftieth anniversary.

Still's opera *The Troubled Land*, which was written in 1938, was finally given its world première by the New York City Opera on March 24, 1949. Langston Hughes's libretto tells the story of the rise to power and the tragic ending of Jean Jacques Dessalines, the first emperor of Haiti and the founder of Haiti's independence. Negro choruses, voodoo dances, haunting vocal episodes carrying reminders of spiritual music, and dynamic rhythms springing out of New Orleans jazz—all contributed a strong and unique flavor. Olin Downes said: "There is enough that is broadly melodious, enough that supplies dramatic movement on the stage, enough of operatic architecture to make the opera as a whole entertaining and to justify . . . a good number of repetitions." *The Troubled Land* brought Still in 1949 a citation from the National Association for American Composers and Conductors for "outstanding service to American music."

Highway No. 1, a later Still opera, was produced in Miami on May 11, 1963, at the University of Miami's fourth annual festival of American music. The libretto, written by Verna Arvey, was set in a filling station on Route No. 1 that runs from North to South, and depicted dramatic episodes in the lives of Bob and Mary, a typical small-town southern couple.

In 1961 Still won first prize for his orchestral composition *The Peaceful Land*, in a competition sponsored by the National Federation of Music Clubs. Its world première took place in Miami on October 22, 1961, with Fabien Sevitzky conducting.

To help celebrate the two hundred and fiftieth anniversary of the founding of New Orleans, Dillard University presented the New Orleans Philharmonic in a special all-Still program on April 16, 1968. Two months earlier, on February 25, Still had been honored in Washington, D.C., at the Awards Luncheon of the Association for the Preservation and Presentation of the Arts.

"In composing," Still has informed the editor of this book, "I often use material that I have had in my notebook for a number of years. Just as often I rely on inspiration for the material needed. One of the most interesting things about composing is the way musical themes change as they are being worked out into a composition. When a melody occurs to me, it is immediately recorded. Then when there is a chance to use it in a new composition, I begin to work with it. The process of change is so gradual that it is not until months after I have finished the composition and have looked back over the theme in its original form and in its new form that I can understand what happened to it. Sometimes the change is so marked that an outsider would scarcely recognize any similarity."

Since 1939 Still has been married to Verna Arvey, distinguished writer and critic, who has provided the texts for several of her husband's operas and other compositions. This is Still's second marriage, the first one having taken place in 1915 to Grace Dorothy Bundy. Still has three children by his first marriage and two by his second. For many years the Stills have lived in Los Angeles where Still finds diversion in gardening and making toys for his grandchildren. He is deeply religious and never begins to work on a new composition without prayer. All of his compositions bear this inscription: "With humble thanks to God, the Source of Inspiration."

MAJOR WORKS

Ballets—La Guiablesse; Sahdji; Lenox Avenue.

Chamber Music—Incantation and Dance, for oboe and piano; Suite, for violin and piano; Pastorela, for violin and orchestra.

Choral Music—And They Lynched Him On a Tree; Caribbean Melodies; Those Who Wait; Wailing Woman.

Operas—Blue Steel; Troubled Island; A Bayou Legend; Miss Sally's Party; A Southern Interlude; Highway No. 1; Costaso; Mota; Minette Fontaine.

Orchestral Music—5 symphonies; Darker America; From the Black Belt; Africa; A Deserted Plantation; Kaintuck', for piano and orchestra; Dismal Swamp; Ebon Chronicle; Can't'cha Line 'Em; Plain Chant for America, for baritone and orchestra; Old California; In Memoriam; Festive Overture; Poem; Archaic Ritual Wood Notes; Rhapsody, for soprano and orchestra; The American Scene, two series of suites; Patterns; The Peaceful Land; Prelude for Strings and Piano.

ABOUT

Arvey, V., William Grant Still; Embree, E., Thirteen Against the Odds; Hare, M. C., Negro Musicians and Their Music; Locke, A., The Negro and His Music.

Karlheinz Stockhausen
1928–

Karlheinz Stockhausen was born in Mödrach near Cologne, on August 22, 1928. From 1947 to 1950 he attended the Musikhochschule in Cologne where he studied the piano with Hermann Schroeder. When the distinguished

Stockhausen: shtôk′ hou zĕn

Stockhausen

Swiss composer Frank Martin came to Cologne in 1950, Stockhausen studied composition with him for about a year. In 1951 Stockhausen went to Paris for additional music study with Milhaud and Messiaen. Neither of these teachers had an appreciable influence upon him. But this was not the case with Pierre Schaeffer, creator of *"musique concrète"* (music consisting of selective sounds, or distortions of sounds, recorded on tape). Schaeffer initiated Stockhausen into the world of electronic music and opened up for him new horizons. From 1952 to 1954 he attended the University of Bonn where, as a pupil of Werner Meyer-Epler, he took courses in physics and acoustics. In 1953 he affiliated himself with the radio station in Cologne, where he helped found a laboratory of electronic music and began his first experiments; in 1954 he issued the first published text on electronic music.

KARLHEINZ STOCKHAUSEN

For a while, in his compositions, Stockhausen worked with conventional instruments, sometimes even in a conventional way. In 1951 he wrote *Kreuzspiel*, for oboe, bass-clarinet, piano, and percussion; his concern with sound values led him to give specific instructions on the placement of the four performers on the platform and on the height of the individual platforms upon which they were to sit. *Spiel*, for orchestra, and *Schlag Quartet*, for piano and three tympanists, both appearing in 1952, further demonstrated his intention to control rigidly his compositional materials while re-

vealing as well his later tendency to employ complex contrapuntal methods, discords, free rhythms, and percussive sounds.

With *Kontrapunkte No. 1*, for ten instruments (1953), he adopted the serial technique which he used with uncompromising rigidity. This is a one-movement composition with no development, no contrast, no repetition, no variations. Individual tones are used the way a pointillist painter uses dabs and spots of color and become what Arthur Cohn has described as a "vibrating color image."

In the *Klavierstücke*, Nos. 1 through 9 (1952–1954), he continued to exploit the resources of serialism. Then the problem of "music in space" or the "spatial dimension in music" engaged his interest. In 1957 he completed a "spatial" work for three orchestras—*Gruppen*, introduced in Cologne on March 24, 1959. As he explained, he began with this composition "a new development of instrumental music in space. Three self-sufficient orchestras surround the audience. They play (each under its own conductor) partially independently, in different tempi; from time to time they meet in common rhythm; they call to each other and answer each other; one echoes the other; for a whole period of time one hears only music from the left, or from the front, or from the right. The sound wanders from one orchestra to the other." Thus what Stockhausen has called a "new musical time-space" was created.

With *Carré*, scored for four orchestras and choruses, each orchestra and chorus placed in a different part of the auditorium, Stockhausen further pursued his experiments with "spatial music." *Carré* was first performed in Hamburg on October 28, 1960.

But, in 1956, Stockhausen also began to experiment with aleatory music, or music of chance. *Zeitmasse*, for flute, oboe, English horn, clarinet, and bassoon (first performed over the Munich radio in November 1956) was written in a rhythm that was relative rather than absolute. As Arthur Cohn explains: *"Zeitmasse* is like no other musical composition in its disordered tempo and abrogation of metric continuity." Chance enters when the performer at will can slow down or increase the speed in contrast to, and sometimes in combination with, metronomically set speeds. Chance also enters into cadenza-like passages in which the performer's improvisation, although controlled, is nevertheless not set down rigidly.

Elements of chance enter even more strongly into *Klavierstück No. 11* (1956), introduced in New York by David Tudor on April 22, 1957. This composition is in what the composer chooses to designate as "open form." The work consists of nineteen fragments which the pianist can play in whatever order he wishes, and each fragment can be played in any one of six specified tempi, dynamics, and type of touch. When the performer has gone through one fragment three times, the piece has ended. Similarly in *Zyklus*, for one percussion player (1961), controlled chance plays a significant role. The percussion player is instructed that he can begin on any page he wishes. But once he starts he must continue from that point on until he reaches and plays the first stroke of the passage with which he had begun.

Another fruitful area for Stockhausen's creative investigations has been electronic music or, as he terms it, "sound objects." In *Gesang der Jünglinge* (1956), heard at an international convention of musicology in Cologne in 1958, Stockhausen combines human voice (a boy soprano) with taped sounds. This composition uses a text from the Book of Daniel, the song of praise which Shadrach, Meshach and Abednego sing in the fiery furnace. "The human voice," Arthur Cohn explains, "also undergoes tape arrangement-disarrangement, and the fragmentation gives startling effects. The expressive assortment includes intelligible words, a sweetness jelling with the very opposite."

Later important electronic compositions by Stockhausen include *Kontakte*, for piano, percussion, and electric sonorities (1959); *Momente*, for soprano, four choruses, and thirteen instruments (1962); and Mikrophonie I and II (1964, 1965). *Kontakte* (heard at the International Festival for Contemporary Music at Cologne, June 11, 1960) has been described as a contest between electronic sound and the sounds of percussion and the piano. However, while some performances present this composition with live musicians playing traditional instruments, others are completely electronic in that the performers have previously recorded their parts on tape so that their music is also electronically produced. *Mo-*

mente, first performed in Cologne in 1962, is a choral work with thirteen traditional instruments. But the score also exploits extramusical sounds produced by monkey wrenches, plastic refrigerator containers filled with air-gun pellets, cardboard tubes, and other equally unusual instruments. According to Theodore Strongin, *Momente* impinges "on all sorts of universes at the edge of one's consciousness, hinting at them rather than articulating them. A definite arch of organized experiences takes shape: excitement, threat, fear, even grandness."

In some of his electronic works, Stockhausen continued to experiment with the spatial dimension in music. The *Gesang der Jünglinge* is meant to be played through a five-channel stereophonic system; the sounds of *Kontakte* come to the audience from four different parts of the auditorium. And the chorus in *Momente* is arranged in four separated groups, each comprising sixteen singers.

Kontakte was used by the composer as the background music for a neodadistic play with music called *Originale*, seen in New York on September 8, 1964. The stage action included such bizarre happenings as a man standing on a chair spraying himself with shaving lather from a can while he is ducking himself in water and drinking from a shoe, a chimpanzee playing the cymbals, someone dropping eggs on a plastic sheet from the top of a ladder, a recitation of Allen Ginsberg's poems by the poet himself, and a girl playing the cello while sitting astride a balcony railing.

An unusual amalgamization of electronic sounds and chance music was achieved by Stockhausen in the ballet "X," written in 1967 on a commission from the Bremen Radio. Here the sounds created by the movements of the dancers are picked up by contact microphones and serve as background music. In this way the background music is actually created not by the composer but by the dancers themselves, though Stockhausen provides the dancers with major cues on electronic tape. J. Marks explains that the dance is performed "in an environment of selective 'junk' capable of specific kinds of sounds: egg shells, foil, piano strings strung across 2 by 4 rubber tubing, etc. The dancers ... move across surfaces which create sound: they ... use their arms and legs like bows to produce sound on the piano strings and on other materials." In short, in the ballet "X" Stockhausen has produced a work "in which dance is made audible."

Just as extraordinary in its use of chance methods is *Aus den Sieben Tagen*, completed in 1968. In writing this unusual composition (which the composer refers to as a "meditative exercise") Stockhausen lived for a week without food or sleep to get into the proper creative frame of mind. For the work he used no musical notes, nor any symbols—just a series of verbal lines telling the performers what they are expected to do. In Peter Heyworth's translation some of the lines read as follows:

> Think nothing.
> Wait until it is absolutely still in you.
> When you have reached that
> Begin to play.
> As soon as you start to think, stop
> And try to reach
> The condition of thinking nothing
> Then continue to play.

With this as a guide, the instrumentalists then improvise their music.

Karlheinz Stockhausen appeared in New York on January 6, 1964, in a lecture recital featuring a number of his works (including *Kontakte* and *Zyklus*) and explaining his aims and methods. In the academic year 1966–1967 he was visiting professor at the University of California at Berkeley. Stockhausen is one of the editors of *Die Reihe*, a quarterly journal devoted to serial music. A collection of his essays published in Cologne in the year 1963 bears the same title as his electronic composition *Momente*.

In his liner notes for the Columbia Records release of *Zeitmasse*, Robert Craft describes Stockhausen as a "tall man . . . who smokes a pipe . . . and is inclined to think and write in metaphysical terms." Stockhausen is a strongly religious man (a Catholic) with pronounced domestic leanings.

It disturbs Stockhausen very much to be described by so many of his colleagues as a "circus performer" or "sensationalist." To Theodore Strongin he complained: "Most listeners' first contact with my music is not the music but the 'paraphernalia'— the 'spectacle,' to put it negatively. I don't quite know how to deal with this misunderstanding. I must put up with being labeled 'sensationalist,'

'out to create shock,' or even 'cabaret clown,' before understanding of the purely musical range of problems of tone-color composition sets in. Even when one no longer sees anything at all—in other words, when listening to loudspeakers—extra-musical associations possess many listeners."

And to J. Marks he said: "The extramusical activities which I sometimes draw upon have nothing to do with external purposes. They develop out of purely musical criteria, as part of that organic process which differentiates music from mathematics. I am a product of many influences; naturally I draw upon them freely and sometimes unconsciously. My music makes sense to me. I can't ever understand why it poses problems for others."

MAJOR WORKS

Ballet—"X."

Chamber Music—Schlag Quartet, for piano and three tympanists; Zeitmasse, for flute, oboe, English horn, clarinet, bassoon; Zyklus, for solo percussionist; Refrain, for three instruments (piano and percussion).

Choral Music—Carré, for four orchestras and four choirs.

Electronic Music—Studie I and II; Kontakte; Gesang der Jünglinge, with boy's voice; Prozession; Mikrophonie I and II; Telemusik; Solo; Prozession.

Orchestral Music—Kreuzspiel, for oboe, bass clarinet, piano, and percussion; Spiel; Kontrapunkte; Gruppen; Momente; Hymen.

Piano Music—Klavierstücke, Nos. 1–11.

ABOUT

Cohn, A., Twentieth Century Music in Western Europe; Hodeir, A., Since Debussy; Lang, P. H. and Broder, N. (eds.), Contemporary Music in Europe.

Saturday Review, September 30, 1967.

Richard Strauss
1864–1949

Richard Strauss was born in Munich on June 11, 1864, in a household made gracious by wealth, culture, and a sophisticated and professional appreciation of music. He was the only son, the older of two children. His mother was the daughter of the prosperous Munich brewer Pschorr. His father, Franz, was a celebrated horn player who was in the orchestra when Wagner helped to rehearse *Tristan und Isolde* for its world première. It is interesting to point out—in view of the son's

Strauss: shtrous

later espousal of Wagner and the music dramas—that Franz Strauss detested Wagner's music and did whatever he could to discredit it. Many intrigues in Munich against Wagner were organized and led by Strauss. On one occasion he openly revealed his contempt by suddenly leaving the orchestra in the middle of a Wagner rehearsal and remarking bitterly that he would not play such music. Wagner once told him, in appreciation of Strauss's remarkable horn playing: "You play my music too well to be anti-Wagnerian." When Wagner's death was announced to the men of the orchestra, they all rose in silent tribute, but Franz Strauss remained seated.

RICHARD STRAUSS

Richard's mother began to teach him the piano when he was only four but soon turned him over to August Tombo for more formal instruction. By the time he was six, he was composing music, his first efforts being a Christmas song and *Schneiderpolka* for piano. From then on, he was often found sketching tunes on scraps of paper, even at school. His obvious gift for and interest in music called for an extended program of study. In 1872 he became a violin pupil of Benno Walter, concertmaster of the court orchestra, and from 1875 to 1880 he studied composition with F. W. Meyer, the court orchestra conductor.

While thus involved in music study, Strauss received a comprehensive academic education, and in 1882 he enrolled in the University of Munich. By that time, though he was only eighteen, some of his compositions had already received important performances. In 1880 three of his songs were performed in Munich by Frau Meysenheim, a distinguished singer—the first time Strauss was heard in public. On March 14, 1881, his string quartet in A major, op. 2, was played in Munich by an ensemble headed by his teacher Benno Walter. Less than three weeks later, on March 30, Hermann Levi conducted in Munich the première of Strauss's first symphony, in D minor. In 1880 a *Festival March* for orchestra, which Strauss had written when he was twelve, became his first published work.

He spent a year at the University of Munich specializing in philosophy and esthetics before deciding to devote himself completely to music. During that year he continued to write ambitious works without interruption; the performances of these added to his rapidly growing reputation. The Serenade in E-flat major, for thirteen wind instruments, was heard in Dresden on November 27, 1882. On February 8, 1883, came the world première in Munich of his violin concerto in D minor. Before the year 1883 was over, an orchestral concert overture and a cello sonata in F major had also been played. In addition, Strauss's second symphony, in F minor, was given its world première in New York City on December 13, 1884, Theodore Thomas conducting.

Partly because he had received his basic training in music from conservative teachers and partly because of the influence of his father, Strauss's early works were firmly grounded in tradition. Classical models were used. The principal influence upon him was the music of Brahms, whose creative mannerisms filtered into his own writing. Yet, derivative though these works were, and without a personal viewpoint, they were remarkable as the creations of one so young—sure in technique, mature in thought, articulate in expression, appealing in honest emotion.

Strauss's Serenade in E-flat major, for thirteen wind instruments, attracted the interest of Hans von Bülow, then the conductor of the Meiningen Orchestra. He performed it in 1882, then invited Strauss to write several orchestral works for him. Strauss complied first with his Horn Concerto No. 1, in E-flat major (first performance in Meiningen, on

March 4, 1885). In October 1885 Strauss was appointed assistant music director in Meiningen by von Bülow, and in 1886 he succeeded von Bülow as principal music director. This marked the beginning of Strauss's long and rich career as a conductor.

In Meiningen, Strauss befriended Alexander Ritter—poet, philosopher, and musician—who was largely responsible for opening up to the young composer new creative vistas by inflaming him with his own enthusiasm for Wagner. Strauss was already drawn to Wagner when he first met Ritter. A performance of *Tristan und Isolde* in Munich, followed by a visit in 1882 to Bayreuth, where he heard *Parsifal*, were powerful forces in destroying his earlier prejudices about the music dramas. But it was only after his personal association with Ritter that he finally broke the Brahmsian influence and became a true believer of the Wagner gospel. Ritter, who was the husband of Wagner's niece and had been Wagner's friend, convinced Strauss that the time had come for him to desert his Brahmsian tendencies and embrace Wagnerian principles. He wanted Strauss to become a follower of "the art of the future," to write music that was dramatic and programmatic (*Musik als Ausdruck*, or Music as Expression, was a favorite slogan of the Wagnerians), instead of pure and absolute music. He tried to convince Strauss that the old classic structures of symphony and sonata and concerto had outlived their usefulness and had to make way for a new, more flexible mold more receptive to expressive musical ideas and extramusical connotations. Ritter was thinking specifically of the tone poem as developed by Liszt.

Strauss listened to Ritter, was impressed, and turned in a new direction as composer. "His influence," he later confessed in discussing Ritter, "was in the nature of a storm wind."

In 1886, after a brief trip to Italy, Strauss completed his first work in the new manner: a symphonic fantasy, *Aus Italien*, a dramatic and poetic account of his impressions of Italy. For the first time he used discord in an attempt to achieve greater tonal realism. At the same time he deserted the formal structure of the symphony for a more supple, elastic mold. Introduced in Munich on March 2, 1887, *Aus Italien* was a fiasco. Strauss's father was indignant, and Hans von Bülow was frankly puzzled. The latter asked: "Does my age make me so reactionary? I find that the clever composer has gone to the extreme limits of tonal possibilities (in the realm of beauty) and in fact has even gone beyond those limits without real necessity."

But there was no turning back for Strauss, however much audiences, critics, and friends might reject his new approaches. On the contrary, he now proceeded with greater daring and independence in the direction he had chosen. In 1887 came his first tone poem, *Macbeth* (first performance in Weimar on October 13, 1890). During the decade that followed, Strauss completed half a dozen other tone poems that now startled, now shocked, and now excited the entire world of music. They made their composer the most provocative figure in the music of his time—famous and notorious at one and the same time. These tone poems proved Strauss to be one of the freshest, most inventive, and most original composers of his era, with a daring imagination, a virtuoso technique at composition, and a wizardry at orchestration matched by few. They have remained Strauss's most celebrated works for orchestra and to this day are among the most significant contributions to the symphonic literature of the post-Wagnerian era. *Don Juan*, based on a poem by Nikolaus Lenau, was heard in Weimar on November 11, 1889. It was followed by *Tod und Verklärung* (*Death and Transfiguration*) in Eisenach on June 21, 1890. *Till Eulenspiegels Lustige Streiche* (*Till Eulenspiegel's Merry Pranks*) was introduced in Cologne on November 5, 1895; *Also Sprach Zarathustra* (*Thus Spake Zarathustra*), based on Nietzsche, in Frankfurt on November 27, 1896; *Don Quixote*, symphonic variations based on Cervantes, in Cologne, on March 8, 1898; and *Ein Heldenleben* (*A Hero's Life*), in Frankfurt on March 3, 1899. In the last of these tone poems Strauss identified himself with the hero by quoting some of his own music in the section devoted to the hero's achievements.

As Lawrence Gilman once wrote, these tone poems "intruded into the smug and homely milieu of the concert room of the nineties with somewhat the effect of a lightning bolt at a family reunion." There was always, in Strauss's music, the unusual, the bold, the unexpected: the jarring discords; the amazing use of realistic effects; the rich orchestration which sometimes called for instruments rarely found in the traditional symphony orchestra, and sometimes even of Strauss's own invention; the sensual harmonies; the complicated way in which melodic ideas were transformed and developed. Music such as this inevitably inspired either indignation or satire. César Cui said: "This is not music but a mockery of music." Debussy once described one of the tone poems as "an hour of music in an asylum." One music critic characterized *Till Eulenspiegel* as "a vast and corruscating jumble of instrumental cackles about things unfit to be mentioned."

The surprise and the shock are, of course, gone. Neither Strauss's cacophony nor his realism can startle today's audience, long since accustomed to far greater indiscretions by more daring iconoclasts. But the wonder of his music remains, its pages of luminous poetry and exalted speech, its fire and passion. In these tone poems, Strauss seemed "to touch life with generous daring," as Lawrence Gilman wrote, "and at every side—at its loveliest and noblest, at its most disordered and pitiable and grotesque. He had learned how to convey experience still drenched in its essential colors, pungent with veritable odors, rich with all its implications. But Strauss, the orchestral tone poet, concerned himself less with the voicing of elemental emotions through heroic types than with the expression of human experience through the most direct and realistic processes of musical psychologizing. Unlike Beethoven in his dramatic overtures, Liszt and Tchaikovsky in their symphonic tone painting, Strauss was little concerned with the voicing of elemental emotions through symbolic figures. It was not Grief or Desire that engrossed him, but Don Quixote's grief, and Don Juan's desire."

Even before Strauss began to write these remarkable tone poems he was already producing some of his finest Lieder. He was only in his teens when he wrote and had published *Eight Songs*, op. 10, to poems by Hermann von Gilm. This publication, which appeared in 1882, included three gems: "Allerseelen," "Zueignung," and "Die Nacht." In these three songs we find that soaring and expressive lyric line, that dramatic piano accompaniment of an almost orchestral texture which

would henceforth characterize Strauss's songwriting. Before the century ended, Strauss had completed a library of songs which placed him beside Schubert, Schumann, Brahms, and Hugo Wolf as one of the foremost creators of Lieder. Among these were such masterworks as "Morgen" (1886), "Ständchen" (1886), "Ruhe, Meine Seele," (1894), "Heimliche Aufforderung" (1894), and "Traum durch die Dämmerung" (1895).

Even while he was becoming world famous as a composer during the closing decade of the nineteenth century, he was also developing as an important conductor of operatic and symphonic music. From 1886 to 1889 he conducted the Court Opera at Munich; from 1889 to 1894 he was the first conductor of the Weimar Court Orchestra. In 1894 and 1895 he led symphonic concerts with the Berlin Philharmonic, and in 1891 he directed performances of *Tannhäuser* at Bayreuth. In 1898 he was appointed music director of the Berlin Royal Opera where he remained a dozen years and distinguished himself as one of the supreme interpreters of his time of the works of Mozart, Beethoven, and Wagner as well as of his own music. He made frequent appearances throughout the world conducting his own scores: in 1896, in Belgium, Russia, and Germany; in 1897, in Holland, France, England, and Spain. In 1903 he conducted a Strauss festival with the Concertgebouw Orchestra in Amsterdam. His American debut as conductor came in 1904 when he toured the United States with the Wetzler Orchestra, his first appearance taking place in New York on February 27. One month later, on March 21, he presented in New York the world première of his *Symphonia Domestica*, which shocked audiences and critics with its realistic effects and candid autobiographical sidelights.

Having written his most notable tone poems and songs by 1900, Strauss now went on to dominate a new world of music, that of opera. He had written his first operas in the closing decade of the nineteenth century. The first was *Guntram*. Strauss's own libretto, based on an old German legend, pointed up the theme of redemption, a subject dear to Wagner's heart. Wagnerian, too, was Strauss's use in his score of chromaticism, the leitmotiv technique, and the sensual orchestration. *Guntram*, produced in Weimar on May 10, 1894, was a failure.

553

So was its successor, *Feuersnot*, produced in Dresden on November 21, 1901. In this opera the composer once again identified himself as a hero.

Strauss's third opera was his first masterwork for the stage: *Salome*, based on Oscar Wilde's play, introduced in Dresden on December 9, 1905. With it Strauss once again became one of the most controversial figures in music. The première in Dresden was an immense success; Strauss had to take more than twenty curtain calls. The critics were rhapsodic in their praises of Strauss's extraordinary dramatic power and elemental passion. But such acclaim gave way before long to a tempest that erupted in many different parts of the world. In Berlin, *Salome* was first barred by the Kaiser himself; then, when performed, it was described as degenerate and disgusting. In London, the censors would not permit its performance. In New York, at the Metropolitan Opera, where it was produced on January 22, 1907, it aroused such moral indignation that it was removed from the repertory after a single performance. "Richard Strauss's music is esthetically criminal or at least coarse or ill-mannered," wrote W. J. Henderson. "His music often suggests a man who comes to a social reception unkempt. . . . No boor ever violated all the laws of etiquette as Strauss violates all the laws of musical composition." The opera also drew such violent protests in Chicago that there, too, it was withdrawn.

But *Salome* has outlived its attackers. Time has made possible a more tolerant view towards Wilde's decadent play about the desire of Salome for John the Baptist and her lascivious love play with his decapitated head when it is brought on a tray. Listeners, now, are better attuned to Strauss's realistic and at times orgiastic score. It is now apparent that in *Salome* we have one of the most vital and original works of the post-Wagnerian period and that its emotional impact on audiences is overwhelming. As Olin Downes wrote in the New York *Times* when the Metropolitan Opera revived *Salome* on January 13, 1934, for the first time since its provocative American première: "The opera, as an opera, aside from its sensational reputation . . . fascinated and impressed the audience. Its effect no longer lies in its novelty but in something quite else, namely, its convincing intensity and inspiration."

With his next opera, *Elektra*, Strauss collaborated for the first time with the distinguished Austrian poet and dramatist Hugo von Hofmannsthal, who was to provide the librettos for many of his operas. With even greater realism than in *Salome*, music and text portrayed the neurotic and demoniac Elektra in an artistic work that was at turns morbid and passionate, gruesome and spellbinding. When *Elektra* was first produced—in Dresden, on January 25, 1909—a correspondent for the New York *Times* reported: "It is a prodigious orchestral orgy. . . . The marvelous imitative effects of the orchestra are blood-curdling, drastic and gruesome to the last degree. It is fortunate for the hearers that the piece is no longer, or else it would be too nerve-wracking." Some of the German critics regarded the work as "lurid," "violent," "harrowing." But a few recognized and acknowledged its intrinsic power. Alfred Kalisch remarked that "the mind has to travel far back to search for anything at all comparable to it in musical mastery and almost elemental emotional power." The American première of *Elektra* was given at Oscar Hammerstein's Manhattan Opera House on February 1, 1910. Once again, as they had done for *Salome*, the critics denounced it violently for its sensational content.

Elektra, like *Salome*, is one of the towering peaks in twentieth-century opera. It is the apotheosis of musical realism, in which every resource at Strauss's command is summoned to point up atmospheric, psychological, and dramatic implications. He uses a far larger orchestra than in *Salome*, with emphasis on low ranges and somber colors; at the same time he splits up his strings into subdivisions to heighten the sensuality of sound. Far more than in *Salome* he makes use of discords, bitonal harmonies, special effects.

Their next operatic collaboration, *Der Rosenkavalier*, represented for Strauss and von Hofmannsthal a radical change of pace. Strauss had long wanted to write a comic opera in the light, ingratiating style of either Mozart or Johann Strauss II. Von Hofmannsthal met Strauss's need by providing him with a witty, nostalgic book set in the Vienna of Maria Theresa. For this play Strauss composed one of his most ingratiating, melodic, infectious, and at times deeply moving scores—neither Mozart nor Johann Strauss, but hroughout pure Richard Strauss. The waltzes from this opera have Straussian sensuousness—Richard Straussian, that is; they have become a favorite at symphony concerts in an adaptation made by the composer. The composer also prepared a symphonic suite based on musical episodes from the opera. However, the waltzes for all their popularity are by no means the outstanding pages in the opera. The Marschallin's first-act monologue in which she contemplates approaching advanced age, the beautiful Serenade in eighteenth-century bel canto style, the love duet of Sophie and Octavian, the Schubert-like trio that closes the opera—these represent Strauss at the peak of his powers. This is the most human of all Strauss operas, possessing "a quality of sentiment as immemorial as the heart of mankind," says Herbert F. Peyser, "emotions which are age-old and unbesmirched, a spirit of humor which, so often ribald and gross and of dubious taste, is of its time and indeed of the earth. . . . Through all its inflated abundances there runs a tragic element which is the common lot of humankind."

Der Rosenkavalier was introduced in Dresden on January 26, 1911; Max Reinhardt was the stage director. It reached America on the stage of the Metropolitan Opera on December 9, 1913.

Der Rosenkavalier pointed a new direction for Strauss—away from realism, complexity, and sensationalism towards simplicity, and even a classical approach. In this vein he completed in 1912 delightful incidental music for von Hofmannsthal's adaptation of Molière's *Le Bourgeois Gentilhomme*, which drew its melodic material from Lully. The score was heard first when *Le Bourgeois Gentilhomme* was produced in Stuttgart on October 25, 1912, in a Max Reinhardt production. One of the interludes from the incidental music was elaborated by the composer into a charming opera, *Ariadne auf Naxos*, with text by von Hofmannsthal, and produced by the Vienna State Opera on October 4, 1916. Intimate in style (a small chamber orchestra is used), economical in means, and light-fingered in touch, *Ariadne* was a marked contrast to Strauss's earlier Wagnerian practices and procedures, particularly in the way he emphasized the voice over the orchestra.

With the outbreak of World War I, Strauss, his wife, and their only child—a son, Franz—sought refuge in their villa in Garmisch-Partenkirchen in the Bavarian Alps. His wife was Pauline de Ahna, a famous singer, whom he first met at a summer resort in Bavaria in 1892 and whom he married on September 10, 1894. In 1895 she starred in Strauss's opera *Guntram*. She was a strong-willed, efficient woman, who ruled not only her household but also her husband. She arranged his social program, advised him on all his business affairs, and methodically planned his day. The marriage was a happy one, henpecked though Strauss was, as Pauline never spared energy or effort to provide her husband with the proper surroundings and the conditions in which he could work to best advantage.

The war years saw the completion of his first symphonic work since the *Symphonia Domestica*. It was the *Alpensinfonie*, descriptive of a day in the Alps, introduced in Berlin on October 28, 1915. With this work Strauss briefly returned to his old realistic ways of tonal writing by introducing a wind machine and a thunder machine to simulate an Alpine storm. The *Alpensinfonie* was not well received, and it has never become popular. The war years also saw the completion of a new opera, *Die Frau ohne Schatten*, text by von Hofmannsthal. Introduced at the Vienna State Opera on October 10, 1919, it was a failure. However, revivals of this opera after Strauss's death helped to bring about a reevaluation which placed it with the composer's masterworks. A symbolic work in which Strauss reverted stylistically to his old Wagnerian ways, *Die Frau ohne Schatten* contains a good deal that finds Strauss at the height of his creative powers. As Irving Kolodin remarked, after the opera had been given a triumphant revival by the Metropolitan Opera at the Lincoln Center for the Performing Arts in October 1966: "Strauss drenched the subject with some of the freshest, sweetest, most heartfelt music he ever wrote."

Though he had produced few successful works since *Der Rosenkavalier*, Strauss was fully recognized in the post-World War I period as the most celebrated composer of the twentieth century. The city of Vienna presented him with grounds near the Belvedere Palace so that he might build a home for himself while fulfilling his duties as co-director with Franz Schalk of the Vienna State Opera from 1919 to 1924. To this palatial home, as well as to his home in Garmisch-Partenkirchen, pilgrims from all over the world came to pay him homage. He was also honored with pomp and ceremony whenever he gave guest performances. On his second visit to the United States, which began in New York on October 31, 1921, he appeared as guest conductor of the Philadelphia Orchestra in a program of his compositions. "He was greeted," reported Richard Aldrich, "with a roar of applause that persisted till he had bowed many times. . . . The applause was greater after each number; and after the second one, there were extensive tributes of flowers and a wreath tied up with little flags of black, white and yellow laid upon the stage."

In the period between the two world wars, Strauss concentrated his creative activity mainly on the stage. He wrote eight more operas, beginning with a comic trifle, *Intermezzo*, described as a "domestic comedy." Its text, by the composer, was based on an episode in his married life; the opera was introduced in Dresden on November 4, 1924. Two more operas followed, with texts by Hugo von Hofmannsthal. *Die Ägyptische Helena* (introduced in Dresden on June 6, 1928) proved a dismal failure when the Metropolitan Opera mounted it for the American première on November 6, 1928. More appealing and more successful was *Arabella*, first performed in Dresden on July 1, 1933. This work is regarded as a kind of companion piece to *Der Rosenkavalier*. Like its predecessor it has Vienna for a setting (but a Vienna of a different time and milieu) and some infectious waltz tunes. Like *Der Rosenkavalier*, it reveals a light musical touch and an enchanting mood. But the subtler and profounder values of *Der Rosenkavalier* are lacking. As Harriett Johnson said at the American première of *Arabella*, which was given by the Metropolitan Opera on February 10, 1955, this was an opera "to be trifled with, like the Sachertorte flown from Vienna, which enhanced the sweetness of the Metropolitan stage. . . . *Arabella* is unrelieved froth." Yet in spite of the misgivings of some critics, *Arabella* has become the most popular of the Strauss operas dating from the period following *Der Rosenkavalier*.

Arabella was the last opera for which Hugo von Hofmannsthal provided the libretto; he died on July 15, 1929, a few days after completing the *Arabella* text. "Hofmannsthal," said Strauss, "was the one and only poet who besides his strength as a poet and his gifts for the stage, had the sympathetic ability to present a composer with dramatic material in a form suitable for setting to music—in short, the ability to write a libretto that was simultaneously stageworthy, satisfying at a high literary standard, and composable."

When the Nazis came to power in 1933 Strauss embraced the new order. He was made president of the Third Reich Music Chamber and he served as president of the German Federation of Composers. He offered no resistance to the policies of the Chamber of Culture when it removed non-Aryan musicians from Germany's musical life. Upon the ejection of Bruno Walter from his post with the Leipzig Gewandhaus Orchestra, Strauss assumed his place on the podium. He also conducted in Bayreuth after Toscanini withdrew. But the honeymoon of Strauss and the Nazis was short-lived. The Nazis were displeased by the fact that Strauss's daughter-in-law was Jewish. They were unhappier still when Strauss insisted on writing an opera (*Die Schweigsame Frau*) to a libretto by Stefan Zweig, a Jew. Because Strauss was a world figure, the Nazis allowed *Die Schweigsame Frau* to be produced in Dresden on June 24, 1935. But three weeks later, Strauss was deposed from his official positions in German music and encouraged to go into quiet withdrawal and retirement in his villa at Garmisch-Partenkirchen. He lived there and in Switzerland during the turbulent years of World War II, part of that time subjected to house arrest because of his objection to the war. With his royalties choked off and his foreign income impounded, Strauss and his family suffered severe poverty during the war years.

Despite the hardships and the mental torment, Strauss managed to remain creatively productive in the years just before and during the war. Even though he was under a political cloud, two of his operas were produced in Nazi Germany before World War II, both to texts by Josef Gregor. They were *Friedenstag* (introduced in Munich on July 24, 1938) and *Daphne* (Munich, October 15, 1938). During the war he finished two more operas—*Die Liebe der Danae*, libretto by Gregor; and *Capriccio*, text by Clemens Krauss. The latter, Strauss's last opera, was heard in Munich during the war, on October 28, 1942. *Die Liebe der Danae*, however, had to wait until the war's end; it was presented at the Salzburg Festival on August 14, 1952.

Capriccio, described as "a conversation piece for music in one act," is a fascinating curiosity in that the text has very little dramatic action and is actually hardly more than an extended discussion by the characters on the relative importance of words and music in an opera. When the opera was first produced in America (New York, April 2, 1954), Robert Sabin described it as "an esthetic drama." He added: "No composer has left a more moving testament than this, for it sums up the best of Strauss. There is no striving for lurid effects.... *Capriccio* does not seek to stun the listener with forceful climaxes, to keep him tense with dramatic suspense, to tease him constantly with sentimental themes of human interest."

During the war, Strauss also wrote some instrumental compositions, including two concertos—one for the horn, the other for the oboe—in which he reverted to the romantic tendencies as well as the classical structures he had abandoned in early manhood. Less traditional, however, was *Metamorphosen*, which was introduced under Paul Sacher's direction in Zürich on January 25, 1946. Though essentially a study in string sonorities (it is scored for twenty-three solo instruments), this is music touched with tragedy; it makes effective use of a quotation from the funeral march of Beethoven's *Eroica Symphony*. Strauss developed this music while Germany was collapsing at the end of the war. With Germany defeated and the Allied forces occupying the country, Strauss felt that his native land had perished. Recognizing this fact, he wrote the words *In Memoriam* at the end of his manuscript.

When Strauss visited London in 1947, after the war had ended, to conduct a concert of his works at a Strauss festival, he was given an ovation. On June 8, 1948, a denazification court in Munich cleared him of collaboration with the Nazis. His eighty-fifth birthday was celebrated throughout the world with festive concerts; his position in Germany as the *grand homme* of German music was reaffirmed.

Strauss's last work was *Four Last Songs*, with orchestra (1948), to verses by Hermann Hesse and Josef von Eichendorff. This was Strauss's swan song, and he knew it. It is no coincidence that for the fourth song he chose "Im Abendrot," the last line of which asks: "Is this death?" *Four Last Songs* received a posthumous première in London on May 20, 1950, with Kirsten Flagstad as soloist and Wilhelm Furtwängler conducting.

When Richard Strauss died of uremia in his villa in Garmisch-Partenkirchen on September 8, 1949, the Bavarian government proclaimed national mourning. Strauss's remains were taken to Munich for cremation. During the rites, Dr. Hans Ehard, Bavarian Minister-President, called Strauss "one of the few creative composers of this century." Music by Beethoven and selections from Strauss's *Der Rosenkavalier* were played. Strauss's ashes were returned to Garmisch-Partenkirchen for burial in his garden.

Walter H. Breuer, who visited Strauss after World War II, recorded his impressions in *Musical Digest:* "I was surprised at the magnificent physique of Richard Strauss at his age. He is very tall, hardly bowed and still has a very distinguished and handsome appearance. As we talked, he would get up and move around the room with great agility, picking up photographs to show me. Occasionally, he became exceedingly animated in his conversation, in which his wife, Pauline, assisted. ... Strauss has long slender hands of a remarkable blend of physical and spiritual beauty, terminating in probably the longest fingers I have ever seen. In contrast to most musicians' more or less well rounded heads, Strauss has an unusually elongated shape of head with a well developed frontal portion. Like most outstanding personalities, Strauss's eyes have a striking fascination about them. ...

"Strauss still dresses in excellent taste and reflects the unobtrusive nonchalance of the *grand seigneur.* ... There is a sincere, convincing politeness in his manner. ... He is still vitally interested in the happenings of the music world. ... In his ardent interest in the goings-on of the modern world and his flexibility in accepting completely revolutionary ideas, Strauss is a fine example of a mellowed wisdom and adaptability of a great mind that has succeeded in remaining young in spirit and, thus, is still able to cope with and derive from a young, modern life at the culmination of his own times."

There were two Strausses, each diametrically opposed to the other. One was the lord of the music world, the aristocrat who lived in the grand manner, and who impressed those around him with his immense culture as well as refinement and impeccable taste. The other Strauss was known only to his most personal friends, a man capable of pettiness and opportunism, fantastically parsimonious, a man who allowed himself to be dominated by his wife and was, in fact, in continuous fear of her.

Strauss once explained his method of composition as follows: "I compose everywhere ... walking or driving, eating or drinking, at home or abroad, in noisy hotels, in my garden, in railway carriages. My sketch book never leaves me, and as soon as a motive strikes me I jot it down. One of the most important melodies for my opera (*Der Rosenkavalier*) struck me while I was playing a Bavarian card game. ... But before I improvise even the smallest sketch for an opera, I allow the texts to permeate my thoughts and mature in me for at least six months so that the situation and characters may be thoroughly assimilated. Then only do I let my musical thoughts enter my mind. The subsketches then become sketches. They are copied out, worked out, arranged for piano and rearranged as often as four times. This is the hard part of the work. The score I write in my study, straightway without troubling, working at it twelve hours a day."

He wrote down his ideas on loose sheets, all of them stored in a closet as "people put their savings in a bank." Strauss added: "With the flight of time, interest accumulates. Likewise as time flies, the outlined ideas develop within me. One fine day I take all the sheets out of the closet and an opera grows out of it."

MAJOR WORKS

Ballets—Josephslegende; Schlagobers.

Chamber Music—2 sonatinas for sixteen wind instruments; String Quartet in A major; Suite for Thirteen Wind Instruments; Sonata in F major, for cello and piano; Serenade in E-flat major, for thirteen wind instruments; Piano Quartet in C minor; Violin Sonata in E-flat major; Metamorphosen, for twenty-three solo string instruments.

Choral Music—Wanderers Sturmlied; Zwei Gesänge; Taillefer; Bardengesang; Eine Deutsche Motette; Cantate; Die Tageszeiten; Austria; Soldatenlied; Die Göttin im Putzzimmer; various choruses for unaccompanied men's voices.

Operas—Guntram; Feuersnot; Salome; Elektra; Der Rosenkavalier; Ariadne auf Naxos; Die Frau ohne Schatten; Intermezzo; Die Ägyptische Helena; Arabella; Die Schweigsame Frau; Friedenstag; Daphne; Die Liebe der Danae; Capriccio.

Orchestral Music—2 horn concertos; Violin Concerto in D minor; Symphony in F minor; Burleske, for piano and orchestra; Aus Italien; Don Juan; Macbeth; Tod und Verklärung (Death and Transfiguration); Till Eulenspiegels Lustige Streiche; Also Sprach Zarathustra (Thus Spake Zarathustra); Don Quixote; Ein Heldenleben (A Hero's Life); Symphonia Domestica; Festliches Praeludium; Eine Alpensinfonie; Le Bourgeois Gentilhomme, suite; Divertimento, for small orchestra (based on Couperin); Parergon on Symphonia Domestica, for left hand piano and orchestra; Oboe Concerto; Duet Concertino, for clarinet, bassoon, strings, and harps; various songs for voice and orchestra (including Four Last Songs).

Piano Music—Five Pieces; Sonata in B minor.

Vocal Music—Numerous songs for voice and piano including Allerseelen, Befreit, Cäcilie, Du Meines Herzens Krönelein, Freundliche Vision; Heimkehr, Heimliche Aufforderung, Ich Trage Meine Minne, Morgen, Die Nacht, Ruhe Meine Seele, Ständchen, Traum durch die Dämmerung, Wiegenlied, and Zueignung.

ABOUT

Brandl, W., Richard Strauss, Leben und Werk; De Mar, N., Richard Strauss: A Critical Commentary on His Life and Works; Fabian, I., Richard Strauss; Krause, E., Richard Strauss: Gestalt und Werk; Lehmann, L., Five Operas of Richard Strauss; Mann, W., Richard Strauss; Mann, W., Richard Strauss: A Critical Study of His Operas; Marek, G. R., Richard Strauss: The Life of a Non-Hero; Petzoldt, R. and Crass, E., Richard Strauss: His Life in Pictures; Pfister, K., Richard Strauss: Weg, Gestalt, Denkmal; Rolland, R., Souvenirs sur Richard Strauss; Rostand, C., Richard Strauss.

Igor Stravinsky
1882–

Igor Fedorovich Stravinsky was born in Oranienbaum, near St. Petersburg, on June 17, 1882. He was the third child of Fedor Stravinsky, the principal basso of the St. Petersburg Opera. Though the young Stravinsky had rich and frequent associations with music, he did not reveal any exceptional gifts for the art. He began piano study when he was nine. As soon as he had acquired a basic technique he avoided formal exercises for improvisations, a fact that disconcerted his teacher. This bent for improvisation was only one of

Stravinsky: strȧ vĭn′ skĭ

several ways in which he revealed his interest in music. Another was to spend hours in his father's well-equipped library, studying operatic scores. Thus he came upon Glinka's *Ruslan and Ludmila* and *A Life for the Czar*, both of which moved him deeply. Hearing these two operas in actual performance intensified his enthusiasm. His adoration of Glinka was a significant factor in his decision to become a musician. Another was hearing Tchaikovsky's *Symphonie Pathétique*, performed in memory of the recently deceased master. Tchaikovsky, like Glinka, was from that time on one of Stravinsky's favorite composers.

IGOR STRAVINSKY

Probably convinced that young Stravinsky's interest in music was greater than his talent, his father decided against a musical career for him. Igor went through academic schools (which he detested) as preparation for a career in jurisprudence; then he entered the University of St. Petersburg for his law studies. He did not, however, neglect music. With a private tutor he began to study harmony, for which he could summon little enthusiasm—perhaps, as he later explained, "owing to the pedagogical incompetence of my teacher . . . and perhaps . . . to my inherent aversion to any dry study." From a textbook he acquired the elements of counterpoint, which appealed to him far more than harmony did. He also continued working at the piano, mostly without the benefit of formal instruction.

In 1902, through the intercession of Rimsky-Korsakov's son, who was Stravinsky's fellow student at the University, Stravinsky was able to meet the composer-teacher in Heidelberg. He recalls the meeting: "I told Rimsky-Korsakov of my ambition to become a composer and asked his advice. He made me play some of my first attempts. Alas! the way he received them was far different from what I had hoped. Seeing how upset I was, and evidently anxious not to discourage me, he asked if I could play anything else. I did so, of course; and it was only then that he gave his opinion." Rimsky-Korsakov took pains to urge Stravinsky not to abandon law. However, he also encouraged the young man to develop his knowledge of harmony and counterpoint through private teachers and self-study, avoiding the more formal curriculum of the Conservatory.

Stravinsky followed the master's advice. While continuing to attend the University, he often visited the Rimsky-Korsakov household where he came into contact with stimulating artists, writers, and musicians. Through some of the more progressive young musicians he came to know the music of Chabrier, Franck, and Debussy for the first time, and was particularly impressed by Debussy for his "extraordinary freshness and freedom of technique." Although at the same time he took some lessons in theory from Kalafti, he received most of his education in theory from the study of textbooks. "These self-imposed exercises," maintains Eric Walter White in his biography of Stravinsky, "opened up a wider vista in the domain of musical composition and did more than anything else at this period of his life to stimulate his imagination and desire to compose, and to lay the foundations of his future technique."

Under these varied stimuli, Stravinsky began to write a piano sonata in 1903. The problems that this, his first ambitious work, posed made him seek out Rimsky-Korsakov for guidance. Rimsky-Korsakov gave it generously, at the same time giving young Stravinsky some instruction in instrumentation. The sonata was finally completed in 1904, but it was never published. Rimsky-Korsakov then carefully guided Stravinsky through the writing of his first symphony, in E-flat major, and a song cycle for mezzo-soprano and orchestra on poems by Pushkin, *Le Faune et la Bergère*.

Stravinsky

These were Stravinsky's first two opuses and his first compositions to be performed. They were presented at a private concert arranged by Rimsky-Korsakov in St. Petersburg in the spring of 1907. The symphony and *Le Faune* received their first public hearing in St. Petersburg on February 5, 1908. The symphony made very little impression; it was too strongly derivative from Rimsky-Korsakov, Tchaikovsky, and Wagner. But the song cycle was a huge success. Eventually, Stravinsky revised his symphony; the new version had its first hearing in Montreux, Switzerland, on April 2, 1914, Ernest Ansermet conducting.

In 1905 Stravinsky completed his course of study at the University. On January 11, 1906, he married a cousin, Catherine Gabrielle Nossenko. The couple made their home in Ustilug, in Volhynia, on an estate belonging jointly to Stravinsky's wife and his sister-in-law. Encouraged by his wife to give up all thoughts of law and specialize in music, Stravinsky spent the next few years at Ustilug working on various compositions. He also made periodic visits to St. Petersburg to consult Rimsky-Korsakov, as well as to continue his associations with the city's musical activities.

Among the compositions completed in 1908 were two for orchestra: *Scherzo Fantastique*, op. 3, and *Feu d'Artifice* (*Fireworks*), op. 4. The latter was intended as a wedding gift to Rimsky-Korsakov's daughter and was dispatched as a surprise to the master. Rimsky-Korsakov, however, never saw the music; he died a few days before the parcel arrived.

Both the *Scherzo Fantastique* and the *Fireworks* were performed for the first time in St. Petersburg on February 6, 1909, at a Siloti concert that proved a turning point in the young composer's career. The reason was the presence of Sergei Diaghilev, the extraordinary dilettante and promoter of the arts, who at that time was in the process of creating the Ballet Russe. With his unusually keen instincts for detecting genius in the raw, Diaghilev recognized a powerful creative potential in these two early Stravinsky pieces, in spite of their indebtedness to Rimsky-Korsakov (and, in the case of *Fireworks*, in small measure to Dukas). These compositions convinced Diaghilev that Stravinsky was a major composer in the making. He decided then and there to have this dynamic musician affiliated with the Ballet Russe.

The first assignment Diaghilev gave Stravinsky was to orchestrate two Chopin pieces (a nocturne and a waltz) for *Les Sylphides*, which the Ballet Russe presented on June 2, 1909, during its first season. But Diaghilev had a much more important assignment in mind for the young composer, a complete and original ballet score. This commission opened up for Stravinsky a medium he had never before considered, a medium in which he was to achieve greatness.

Diaghilev had commissioned Liadov to write music for a ballet based on the old Russian legend of the Firebird. Liadov, who was notoriously lazy, delayed so long in writing the score that Diaghilev had to seek out another composer. He decided to pin the assignment, important though it was, on the still obscure and inexperienced Stravinsky. Fokine was to prepare the choreography, Golovine and Bakst, the scenery and costumes; and Tamara Karsavina would appear as the Firebird to Fokine's Prince Ivan.

Stravinsky completed his score in May 1910, and on June 25 of that year *L'Oiseau de Feu* (*The Firebird*) was introduced in Paris. It was a triumph, not only ushering in a new era for the modern dance but also bringing recognition to Stravinsky. Henri Ghéon wrote: "*L'Oiseau de Feu*, being the result of an intimate collaboration between choreography, music and painting, presents us with the most exquisite miracle of harmony imaginable, of sound and form and movement. The old-gold vermiculation of the fantastic back-cloth seems to have been invented to a formula identical with that of the shimmering web of the orchestra. And, as one listens, there issues forth the very sound of the wizard shrieking, of swarming sorcerers and gnomes running amuck. When the bird passes, it is truly the music that bears it aloft."

The story of the Firebird relates how Prince Ivan captures and releases the Firebird and how in gratitude the bird presents him with one of its feathers. With the feather the Prince is later able to free thirteen beautiful girls held captive by the ogre Kastchei in his castle. One of the thirteen becomes the Prince's bride.

This is the kind of tale to which Stravinsky's

teacher, Rimsky-Korsakov, would have been partial; and there is in the Stravinsky score much of Rimsky-Korsakov, especially the Rimsky-Korsakov of *Le Coq d'Or*. But there is also much of Stravinsky, especially in the extraordinary rhythmic vitality of some of the music. "The Dance of the Kastchei," for example, represents a primitivism that was new to sophisticated music, a primitivism that Stravinsky was to cultivate and develop into a musical style that changed the writing of music throughout the world. No wonder that Diaghilev remarked after one of the rehearsals: "Mark that man Stravinsky! He is on the eve of celebrity." No wonder, too, that immediately after the première, Debussy rushed backstage to embrace the composer.

With *Petrouchka* Stravinsky became the favorite son of the avant-garde. The younger European artists and musicians used it as the spearhead to attack tradition and orthodoxy. The futurist Marinetti paraded the streets of Rome with a banner reading: "Down with Wagner! Long live Stravinsky!"

Petrouchka was produced by the Ballet Russe in Paris on June 13, 1911. Once again the choreography was by Fokine; the principal dancers were Nijinsky as Petrouchka and Karsavina as the Ballerina. Picturesquely set in a Russian carnival, *Petrouchka* tells the story of the frustrated and tragic love of Petrouchka, the hero of a puppet show, and a puppet ballerina, who is interested in a Moor. The Moor kills Petrouchka, to the horror of the carnival audience, until it is reminded by the policeman that the victim is not a human being, after all. *Petrouchka* was a tremendous success. Serge Lifar regarded it as "one of the peak points, if not the peak of the Ballet Russe's first epoch."

For Stravinsky, *Petrouchka* represented a giant forward step in the clarification of his creative personality. He had finally broken his ties with Rimsky-Korsakov, though not with his Russian past, its background and folk music. As the editor of this book has written in *David Ewen Introduces Modern Music:* "Stravinsky's score was at turns vividly pictorial (the depiction of the bustle and gaiety of carnival life), subtle and revealing in its characterization (as in the gentle portrait of the puppet-ballerina by the piano, later joined by flute), humorous and sardonic (as in the amus-

ing picture of the heavy-footed dance in the tuba), and vividly national (the Russian dances of the coachmen, and the music for the gypsies). Bolder than ever was Stravinsky in his use of unresolved dissonances. His experiments with polytonality were both so brilliant and successful that from here on in this technique would be favored by many modernists. The long, flowing melodies of *The Firebird* now made way for terse statements, loosely strung together. This was the music of the future, bold and free."

Stravinsky's next ballet placed him with the foremost modernists of his generation. It made him the high priest of a neo-primitive cult in music that influenced composers throughout the Western world and ushered in a new era and a style for the twentieth century. That ballet was *Le Sacre du Printemps* (*The Rite of Spring*), first performance by the Ballet Russe in Paris on May 29, 1913. Choreography was by Nijinsky; scenery and costumes were designed by Nicholas Roerich. The première inspired one of the most notorious scandals in the musical-performance history of our times.

Carl Van Vechten, who was in the audience, recorded what took place at the time: "A certain part of the audience was thrilled by what it considered to be a blasphemous attempt to destroy music as an art and, swept away with wrath, began, very soon after the rise of the curtain, to make cat-calls and to offer audible suggestions as to how the performance should proceed. The orchestra played unheard except occasionally, when a slight lull occurred. The young man seated behind me in a box stood up during the course of the ballet to enable him to see more clearly. The intense excitement under which he was laboring betrayed itself when he began to beat rhythmically on the top of my head with fists." Some famous musicians yelled out that the music was a great bluff; others shouted in retaliation that it was the work of a genius. One woman spat in the faces of several demonstrators. The Princesse de Pourtalès left her box in a huff exclaiming: "I am sixty years old, but this is the first time that anyone has dared to make a fool of me!" And throughout the entire pandemonium, Debussy pleaded with the audience to remain quiet and listen patiently to the music.

561

Stravinsky

Le Sacre established Stravinsky as a world figure in music, one of the most publicized and fiercely debated figures in the music of our generation. Eventually, the world of music came to accept this score—which had become famous as a symphonic suite—as one of Stravinsky's greatest. When Cecil Gray wrote, in 1929, that *Le Sacre* is "one of the most conspicuous landmarks in the artistic life of our period" he was echoing the opinion of most discriminating musicians.

Subtitled "scenes of ancient Russia," *Le Sacre* describes a pagan ritual; the adoration of Nature by primitive man; a conflict between two groups in gymnastics and battles; the consecration of the earth; ritual dances; and finally a sacrifice in which a young girl dances to her death. For these sequences Stravinsky produced a score that brought his neoprimitive style to complete fulfillment. Never before was he so daring in his use of discords and polytonality, so lavish in the handling of orchestral sonorities, timbres, and contrasting dynamics. But it was in his rhythmic writing that he proved himself a virtuoso. With his rapidly changing meters, polymeters, polyrhythms, displaced accents—and with his emphasis on the percussion instruments—he emancipated rhythm and gave it an importance it had never previously known.

Stravinsky continued to pursue the neoprimitive cult and to use Russian backgrounds and culture with several additional compositions. Among these was *Le Chant du Rossignol (The Song of the Nightingale)*. This composition exists in three versions: as an opera (1909–1914); as a ballet (1914); and as a tone poem (1917). The last version is the one now most familiar.

Les Noces (The Wedding), "choreographic Russian scenes" which Stravinsky wrote between 1914 and 1917, was one of his more unconventional creations of this period. This is a cantata with dances describing a primitive wedding in old Russia. The orchestra consists entirely of percussion, including four pianos. The singers are placed in the orchestra pit with the instrumentalists. "Dealing with primitive folk," Nicolas Slonimsky explains, "the composer succeeds in presenting the village types in their illiteracy. If the music seems jerky and the phrases short, the listener must be reminded of the immature minds predominant in an atmosphere of primitive culture." *Les Noces* was produced by the Ballet Russe in Paris on June 13, 1923.

In 1919 Stravinsky left his native land to take up residence on the outskirts of Paris. For the next decade and a half France was his adopted country and his permanent home. He became a French citizen on June 10, 1934. With the change of environment, there also came about a change of artistic viewpoint and a change in musical methods. Stravinsky began to lose interest in Russian subject matter and he freed himself from his ties to Russian folk music. At the same time he rejected his neoprimitive practices, veering sharply away from his former preoccupation with rhythm, brilliant orchestration, rich sonorities, and sharply contrasted dynamics. He became French in his search for refinement, clarity, precision, symmetry, and objectivity. He sought music more concerned with contrapuntal procedures than with rhythmic ones, music that deserted pictorial and programmatic interests. The desire to produce such music led him back to the classical structures of the concerto, symphony, oratorio, Mass, *opera buffa*, and stylized eighteenth century *opera seria*.

Stravinsky's neoclassical period became fully crystallized after he had settled permanently in France. But even before 1919 he had begun to move from complexity to simplicity, from primitivism to classicism, from subjectivity to objectivity. In 1918 he completed the score for *L'Histoire du Soldat (The Story of a Soldier)*, introduced in Lausanne, Switzerland, on September 28, 1918. This is an intimate ballet with only seven instruments in the orchestra, three performers, and a narrator. Still another work pointing towards Stravinsky's later neoclassical tendencies is *Pulcinella*, a ballet in which Stravinsky reached into the classical past to use melodies by the eighteenth century composer Pergolesi. Stravinsky completed the score in 1919 before settling in France permanently; and the Ballet Russe introduced it in Paris on May 15, 1920, after Stravinsky had made France his home.

After one or two compositions, including the *Symphonies of Wind Instruments* (1920), Stravinsky finally achieved the neoclassic idiom for which he had been groping. He achieved it with the Octet, introduced in Paris on October 18, 1923. Aaron Copland, who attended that performance, has described how shocked the audience was on hearing the music. The people had come expecting to hear the neoprimitive Stravinsky but instead were confronted with music in a classical structure and in a contrapuntal style. Many in the audience, including most of the critics, criticized the Octet severely. They could hardly have guessed at the time that Stravinsky was now entering a creative phase that would last some forty years.

During the French period of Stravinsky's neoclassic years, he completed numerous works the importance of which is now readily acknowledged. These included the following: the opera-oratorio *Oedipus Rex*, text by Stravinsky and Jean Cocteau based on Sophocles (first performance in Paris on May 30, 1927); the ballet *Apollon Musagète*, commissioned for a festival at the Library of Congress in Washington, D.C., where it was produced on April 29, 1928, with Adolph Bolm's choreography; *Capriccio*, for piano and orchestra, which the composer himself introduced with the Paris Symphony on December 6, 1929; the *Symphony of Psalms*, written to commemorate the fiftieth anniversary of the Boston Symphony, first performed not in Boston but in Brussels on December 13, 1930; the melodrama *Perséphone*, text by André Gide, world première in Paris on April 30, 1934; and a number of concertos, including one for the piano and wind instruments (1924), another for violin and orchestra (1931), a third for two solo pianos (1935), and a fourth, *Dumbarton Oaks*, for sixteen instruments (1938).

Stravinsky paid his first visit to the United States in 1925, making his American debut as guest conductor of the New York Philharmonic on January 8 in a program of his own compositions. He then toured the country. He returned to the United States on several occasions for guest performances. In 1939 he made a permanent change of residence—this time to Hollywood, California—and subsequently a change of citizenship, becoming an American on December 28, 1945. In America he served as Charles Eliot Norton lecturer at Harvard University in 1939 and 1940. His first wife died in 1939, and Stravinsky married Vera de Bossett, an artist, in April 1940. By his first wife Stravinsky had four children, one of whom, Soulima, is a concert pianist and a member of the music faculty at the University of Illinois; another son, Theodore, has distinguished himself as a painter.

One of the first compositions completed by Stravinsky after coming to the United States was his Symphony in C, his first symphony in thirty-three years. He wrote it to honor the fiftieth anniversary of the Chicago Symphony, which introduced it on November 7, 1940. Another symphony was completed in 1945, the *Symphony in Three Movements*. Stravinsky conducted the première with the New York Philharmonic on January 24, 1946. His first important liturgical music, a Mass for mixed chorus and ten wind instruments, was given in Milan on October 27, 1948. Earlier the same year (April 28) a classic ballet, *Orpheus*, had been produced by the Ballet Society in New York and it had received a special citation from the New York Music Critics Circle.

Before Stravinsky's neoclassic period had run its course, he had written his first full-length opera, *The Rake's Progress*, libretto by W. H. Auden and Chester Kallman based on Hogarth's drawings. While working on the score he listened endlessly to the music of Mozart, and especially to Mozart's opera *Così Fan Tutte*. Mozart was Stravinsky's model for this opera set in eighteenth century England, though he was also influenced partly by Gluck and partly by Handel. *The Rake's Progress* is in the *style gallant*, and its structure is a classical *opera buffa* with sequences of arias, recitatives, ensemble numbers, and choruses. *Opera buffa* wit and lyricism are emphasized. In reviewing the world première which took place in Venice on September 11, 1951, Howard Taubman said in the New York *Times*: "But even in passages that seemed such excellent imitations that they struck one as quotations, there are touches that are pure Stravinsky. In short, like a superb eclectic, he has drawn inspiration from all these sources but has made the final result a product of his own individuality." Taubman found that the music as a whole had "gaiety and tenderness, simplicity and brilliance, incisive wit and honest feeling." The American première took place at the Metropolitan Opera, February 14, 1953.

With *The Rake's Progress*, Stravinsky's neoclassic period came to a close. As had been the case with the earlier neoprimitive compositions when first heard, Stravinsky's neoclassic music aroused divergent opinions. Some critics felt that in this period Stravinsky produced many of his enduring masterworks, music of the utmost purity and objective beauty. Other critics were of a different mind, insisting that this was decadent music, devoid of feeling and thought, incapable of arousing anything more in the listener than a studied appreciation of its craftsmanship.

By the time he had passed his seventieth birthday, Stravinsky stood ready to embrace an entirely new compositional idiom: dodecaphony. He began to explore the possibilities of the twelve-tone system, even if only tentatively, in the *Cantata on Four Poems by Anonymous English Poets of the 15th and 16th Centuries*, heard in Los Angeles on November 11, 1952; in the Septet, which though written in 1952 was not given until January 24, 1954, in Washington, D.C.; and in a ballet for seven dancers, *Agon*, which he completed in 1956 and which was performed in Los Angeles on June 17, 1957. From these experiments with the twelve-tone system he immediately progressed to the serial technique to which he henceforth remained faithful. This development was found in a composition for tenor, baritone, chorus, organ, and orchestra praising the city of Venice and its patron, Saint Mark: *Canticum Sacrum ad Honorem Sancti Marci Nominis*, introduced in Venice on September 11, 1956.

Many of Stravinsky's subsequent works in the serial technique followed the lead of the *Canticum* by treating either religious or biblical subjects, reflecting Stravinsky's deep and lifelong religious convictions. *Threni*, for solo voices, chorus, and orchestra, was based on the Lamentations of Jeremiah from the Vulgate (first performance at the International Festival of Contemporary Music in Venice on September 23, 1958). *A Sermon, a Narrative and a Prayer* was a religious triptych for contralto, tenor, speaker, chorus, and orchestra commissioned by Paul Sacher, who conducted its world première in Basel, Switzerland, February 23, 1962. *Noah and the Flood*, a biblical spectacle to be narrated, mimed, sung, and danced, was written on a commission from NBC, which telecast it over its network on June 14, 1962. *Abraham and Isaac*, a sacred cantata for baritone and chamber orchestra, with a Hebrew text taken from Genesis, had its world première in Jerusalem on August 23, 1964. And the *Requiem Canticles*—for four voices, chorus and orchestra—was commissioned by Princeton University for an all-Stravinsky concert on October 8, 1966. The last-mentioned of these works was used by George Balanchine for a ballet in memory of Dr. Martin Luther King, Jr.—introduced in New York on May 2, 1968.

The latest stage in Stravinsky's creative evolution has proved as much a shock to the world of music at large as when the composer first renounced post-Romanticism for neoprimitivism and then rejected neoprimitivism for neoclassicism. Perhaps even more so. For many years Stravinsky had expressed his lack of interest in, if not outright opposition to, the twelve-tone system. There was little personal contact between Stravinsky and Arnold Schoenberg, though they lived only a few miles apart in Los Angeles. Yet with Schoenberg dead—and despite the fact that Stravinsky was entering the dusk of life—he suddenly discovered a new language for himself in dodecaphony.

Stravinsky's attitude toward the severe public and critical reaction to his new development is typical of him: a combination of indifference and hostility. He had long since written that the public "cannot and will not follow me in the progress of my musical thought. What moves and delights me leaves them indifferent and what still continues to interest them holds no further attraction for me. For that matter, I believe that there was seldom any real communion of spirit between us. If it happened— and it still happens—that we liked the same things, I very much doubt whether it was for the same reasons. . . . Their attitude certainly cannot make me deviate from my path. I shall assuredly not sacrifice my predilections and my aspirations to the demands of those who, in their blindness, do not realize that they are simply asking me to go backwards. It should be obvious that what they wish for has become obsolete for me, and that I could not follow them without doing violence to myself. But, on the other hand, it would be a great mistake to regard me as an adherent of *Zukunftsmusik*— the music of the future. Nothing could be more ridiculous. I live neither in the past nor in the future. I am in the present. I cannot know what tomorrow will bring forth. I can know only what the truth is for me today. That is what I am called upon to serve, and I serve it in all humility."

Old age has not curtailed Stravinsky's creativity, nor has it compelled him to curtail his heavy program of guest appearances as conductor of his own music throughout the world. In August 1962 he toured Israel and then paid his first return visit to the land of his birth in almost half a century. Severely criticized in the Soviet Union during the Stalin era, Stravinsky was welcomed as a hero when first he put foot on Russian soil on September 21 and when in Moscow on September 26 he conducted his first concert in Russia.

When not on tour, Stravinsky and his wife live in a modest house on North Wetherly Drive in Hollywood. It is a crowded house, for besides the two Stravinskys the ménage includes a cook, a gardener, Stravinsky's daughter (who often serves as Stravinsky's chauffeur), and Robert Craft. Craft is a brilliant musician and journalist who for more than a decade has been serving as the master's right hand. He performs the hundred and one menial jobs and obligations that overwhelm the daily routine of a world figure in music; he helps Stravinsky at rehearsals, and shares his program at concerts. He is painstaking in making a record of Stravinsky's conversations and opinions which he has gathered into several books.

Stravinsky composes for a few hours in the afternoons, then the same evening plays over what he has written for his wife and Robert Craft. The next morning he reviews and revises what he has done the day before. His day is a full one. In addition to composing, he pays a daily visit to his doctor, goes through and replies to his voluminous mail, pores over books (he is a voracious reader), entertains visitors and friends. Relaxation comes from playing Scrabble or solitaire, walking about the patio at the back of his house, partaking of afternoon tea with family and friends, listening to recordings, doing physical exercises, and taking a seemingly infinite variety of medicines either to relieve a physical discomfort or to prevent one.

John McClure has written that Stravinsky gives the immediate impression of "slightness," of being "as frail as a bird." McClure goes on to give the following word picture of the composer: "His voice is deeply pitched and resonant with a persistent Russian accent. . . . Stravinskian is a kind of unblended Esperanto made from English with *subito* French and German spiked with Italian, and the conversation in his polyglot household will switch without warning into any of them. . . . His use of English is both precise and fresh, and he has the philologist's love of finding and tracing new words and new meanings. . . . Stravinsky's eagerness for the new or the next, whether music or book, concert or country, makes his critics by comparison look like testimonials to the art of taxidermy. . . . He loves to know, to taste, to touch, and to see, as much as to hear."

A world figure in music for over half a century, Stravinsky has gathered numerous awards and honors. In 1951 he received the gold medal in music from the National Institute of Arts and Letters; in 1954 the Royal Philharmonic presented him with its highest honor, the Gold Medal. In 1955 he received the Sibelius Gold Medal given once every five years for distinguished services to music. Four years later the Sonning Foundation of Denmark presented him with its first international music award. In 1963 an international prize, named after Sibelius and valued at twenty-seven thousand dollars, was given Stravinsky by the Finnish Fund for Arts and Sciences.

Stravinsky's eightieth birthday in 1962 was celebrated throughout the world with festivals of his works. On that occasion he was invited to the White House as a dinner guest of President and Mrs. John F. Kennedy; he also received a gold medal from Secretary of State Dean Rusk, at ceremonies held at the State Department. From June 30 to July 23, 1966, the New York Philharmonic presented a ten-concert Stravinsky festival at the Lincoln Center for the Performing Arts. Each of the programs served to illustrate the relationship between Stravinsky's music and that of the composers who either influenced him or were influenced by him.

Columbia Records, under the artistic direction of John McClure, has undertaken the recording of all of Stravinsky's compositions, as many of them as possible under Stravinsky's own direction.

MAJOR WORKS

Ballets—L'Oiseau de Feu (The Firebird); Petrouchka; Le Sacre du Printemps (The Rite of Spring); Le Chant du Rossignol (The Song of the Nightingale); Pulcinella (based on music by Pergolesi); Les Noces (The Wedding); Apollo Musagète; L'Histoire du Soldat (The Story of a Soldier), for narrator and seven instruments; Le Baiser de la Fée (based on music by Tchaikovsky); Jeu de Cartes (Card Party); Perséphone, melodrama; Orpheus; Agon; Noah and the Flood; Variations.

Chamber Music—Ragtime, for eleven instruments; Three Pieces, for clarinet solo; Concertino, for string quartet; Octet, for wind instruments; Duo Concertant for violin and piano; Suite Italienne, for violin and piano; Élégie, for viola solo; Septet; Epitaphium, for flute, clarinet, and harp; À la Mémoire de Raoul Dufy, for string quartet; Elegy for J. F. K., for baritone, two clarinets, and corno di bassetto.

Choral Music—Pater Noster; Symphony of Psalms; Credo; Ave Maria; Mass; Babel, cantata; Cantata on Four Poems by Anonymous English Poets; Canticum Sacrum ad Honorem Sancti Marci Nominis; Threni; Monumentum pro Gesualdo; A Sermon, A Narrative and a Prayer; Requiem Canticles.

Operas—Le Chant du Rossignol; Renard, comic opera; Mavra, comic opera; Oedipus Rex, opera-oratorio; The Rake's Progress.

Orchestral Music—2 suites; Symphony in E-flat major; Fireworks; Scherzo Fantastique; L'Oiseau de Feu, three suites; Petrouchka, suite; Le Sacre du Printemps, suite; Four Studies; Le Chant du Rossignol, tone poem; Pulcinella, suite; Symphonies of Wind Instruments; Piano Concerto, Capriccio, for piano and orchestra; Violin Concerto in D; Divertimento; Concerto in E-flat (Dumbarton Oaks), for chamber orchestra; Symphony in C major; Danses Concertantes; Four Norwegian Moods; Ode; Scènes de Ballet; Scherzo à la Russe; Symphony in Three Movements; Concerto in D, for strings; Movements, for piano and orchestra; Variations; T. S. Eliot, In Memoriam; Canon on a Russian Tune.

Piano Music—2 sonatas; Serenade in A; Concerto for two solo pianos; Two-Piano Sonata.

Vocal Music—Four Russian Songs; Three Songs from William Shakespeare; In Memoriam Dylan Thomas; Elegy for J. F. K.; Abraham and Isaac, sacred cantata.

ABOUT

Armitage, M. (ed.), Igor Stravinsky; Corle, E. (ed.), Igor Stravinsky; Onnen, F., Stravinsky; Siohan, R., Stravinsky; Stravinsky, I., Conversations; Stravinsky, I., Dialogues and a Diary; Stravinsky, I., Expositions and Developments; Stravinsky, I., Memories and Commentaries; Stravinsky, I., Stravinsky: An Autobiography; Stravinsky, I., Table Talk; Strobel, H., Stravinsky; Tansman, A., Igor Stravinsky; Vlad, R., Stravinsky; White, E. W., Stravinsky.

Encounter (London), June 1963; The Gramophone (London), June 1962; Musical America, January 1963; Musical Quarterly, 1962; New York Times Magazine, June 16, 1957; June 10, 1962; Newsweek, May 21, 1962; Saturday Review, June 16, 1962; Score (London), Stravinsky Issue, January 1957.

Joseph Suk
1874–1935

Joseph Suk was born in Křečovice, Bohemia, on January 4, 1874. His father, a schoolteacher and choirmaster, gave him his first music lessons and enrolled him in the Prague Conservatory when he was eleven. Under Anton Bennewitz's instruction he made excellent progress on the violin, and he studied theory with Foerster and Stecker, piano with Jiránek. After passing his final examinations in 1891, he stayed on at the Conservatory for an additional year to study composition with Dvořák. Dvořák inspired his pupil with enthusiasm for his own methods and style; the Dvořák impress is strong upon the compositions Suk wrote while still attending the Conservatory. These included the Piano Quartet in A minor, op. 1, and the *Dramatic Overture*, op. 4, both written in 1891; and the Serenade in E-flat major, for strings, op. 6 (1892). As Richard Veseley remarked, however, there is also much of Suk in this music: "He is far more tender and intimate and melancholy than Dvořák; his rhythm is not so racially elementary, therefore richer; his breadth of melody is not so greatly concerned with periodicity." In the *Dramatic Overture*, Suk displayed a partiality for tragic utterance characteristic of so many of his later compositions.

In 1892 Suk helped found the Bohemian String Quartet, composed of Suk and three fellow students at the Conservatory. The group gave its first concert on October 22. For about a decade, Suk was second violinist of this distinguished chamber music organization which set a new standard in Bohemia and gave a hearing to deserving Bohemian composers. It was largely due to this organization that Smetana's string quartet *From My Life* achieved recognition. Suk's long association with this ensemble influenced his creative development by giving him that intimate understanding of chamber music style that served him so well when he wrote his G minor Piano Quintet (1893, revised 1915), and his two string quartets, opp. 11 and 31 (1896, revised 1915; 1911).

In 1898 the relationship between Dvořák and Suk became closer than just that of master

Suk: sŏŏk

and disciple. In that year Suk married Dvořák's daughter, Otilie. It was about this time that Suk first began to attract attention as a composer. On November 25, 1899, there took place in Prague the highly successful world première of his Symphony No. 1 in E major. The symphony revealed a wealth of lyricism and sentiment which Suk had also drawn upon in the charming incidental music written in 1898 for a fairy tale by Zeyer, *Radúz and Mahulena*, performed in Prague on April 6, 1898. From the latter score, Suk extracted salient material for an orchestral tone poem rich in fantasy; he called it *A Tale*.

JOSEPH SUK

One of Suk's most celebrated compositions is the *Fantasy for Violin and Orchestra*. He wrote it in 1903, and it was first heard in Prague on January 9, 1904, with Karel Hoffmann as soloist. This work has biographical interest; many commentators find in its elegiac beauty and deeply moving pathos a presentiment on the part of the composer of impending tragedy. Double tragedy struck Suk, first with the death of his father-in-law, Dvořák, in 1904, and then the death of his wife, Otilie, in 1905. He became extremely morbid and soon after suffered a nervous breakdown. When he returned to composition, following recovery, a funereal atmosphere began to pervade his writing. His melodies grew increasingly poignant, his mood increasingly lugubrious. Otakar Šourek put it this way: "He took up the struggle forced upon him by destiny. The range of his work expands

from the narrow sphere of the individual to embrace the sterner problems of humanity, and he now strives to show how grief and suffering may be overcome through faith in life and in the individual will, while in his boldest flights he hymns universal love, the love of all."

He came back to composition with his second symphony in C minor, which he called *Asrael*. Completing it in 1906, he dedicated it to the memory of his father-in-law and his wife. This work, first heard in Prague on February 3, 1907, is steeped in gloom and indicates how far into the abyss of despair the composer had plunged. Once he touched bottom emotionally, however, he was able to lift himself back towards resignation and peace of mind. That feeling is found in his orchestral tone poem *A Summer Fairy Tale*, a tonal portrait on nature, heard in Prague on January 26, 1909.

The outbreak of World War I aroused Suk's patriotism and led him to write several works in which his troubled emotions of the period are reflected. When he was most concerned over the fate of his country, he wrote *Meditation on the St. Venceslas Chorale* (originally for string quartet, but subsequently transcribed for string orchestra). Following his country's liberation Suk wrote a deeply moving tribute to the war dead in *Legend of Dead Victors*. And, in 1920, for the seventh Sokol festival, he produced *Towards a New Life*, an orchestral march, which with the addition of lyrics by Křička, became identified as the "Marseillaise" of Czechoslovakia. In Veseley's words, these three compositions together "may be considered as a symphonic trilogy of Suk's zealous patriotism."

During the closing decades of Suk's life still another major transformation took place in his writing. He began to show an interest in modern techniques as well as an increasing subtlety in his harmonic and contrapuntal methods. All this became evident in one of his most striking works for orchestra, the tone poem *Maturity* (1917), introduced in Prague on October 30, 1918.

In a discussion of Suk's music, Hans Hollander remarked how strongly the composer had been influenced by Dvořák, especially in his chamber and piano music: "These works reveal the intimacy of his voluntary kinship with Dvořák. . . . Even after Suk had turned his attention to program music . . . this exuberant melodist and reveler in tone color still faithfully cherished the spiritual legacy of the departed Dvořák, a legacy closely in keeping with the distinctively subjective character of his own artistry."

In 1922 Suk was appointed professor of composition at the Prague Conservatory. He became its director eight years later. His last major work was *Epilogue*, for baritone, women's voices, chorus, and orchestra, which he had begun in 1920 but which he did not complete until twelve years later.

Joseph Suk died in Benešov, near Prague, on May 29, 1935. Two years before his death he was elected a member of the Santa Cecilia Academy in Rome. Suk's grandson, also named Josef (Dvořák's great grandson) has distinguished himself as a concert violinist. He made his American debut on January 23, 1964, as soloist with the Cleveland Orchestra.

MAJOR WORKS

Chamber Music—2 string quartets; Piano Quartet in A minor; Piano Trio in C minor; Piano Quintet in G minor; Four Pieces, for violin and piano; Elegy, for violin and cello, string quartet, harmonium, and harp; Allegro Giocoso, for string quartet; Bagatelle, for flute, violin, and piano; Melody, for two violins.

Choral Music—Mass in B-flat major (Křečovice Mass); Ten Songs, for women's voices; Four Songs, for men's voices; Three Songs, for mixed voices with piano; Epilogue.

Orchestral Music—2 symphonies; Dramatic Overture; Serenade in E-flat major, for strings; A Winter's Tale, overture; A Tale; Under the Apple Trees; Fantasy, for violin and orchestra; Fantastic Scherzo; Prague, tone poem; A Summer Tale, tone poem; Maturity, tone poem; Meditation on the Chorale St. Venceslas (also for string quartet); Legend of Dead Victors; Towards a New Life.

Piano Music—Polish Fantasy; Humoresque; Suite in G major; Moods; Two Cycles of Pieces; Slumber Songs; Friendship; Episode.

ABOUT

Berkovec, J., Josef Suk; Květ, J. M. (ed.), Joseph Suk: A Symposium; Štěpán, V., Novák a Suk.

Musical Quarterly, July 1934.

Heinrich Sutermeister
1910–

Heinrich Sutermeister was born in Feuerthalen, in the canton of Schaffhausen, in

Sutermeister: soo tĕr mī′ stĕr

Switzerland, on August 12, 1910. In his early years he had no idea of becoming a professional musician and received a comprehensive academic education at the University of Basel and in Paris, specializing in philology and the arts. At the University of Basel he attended Karl Nef's class in music history, and in 1931 he decided to study music. In 1932 he attended the Academy of Music in Munich where he became a pupil of Carl Orff and Walter Courvoisier among others and where he specialized in composition and conducting. Upon leaving the Academy he worked in 1934 and 1935 as coach and accompanist at the Municipal Theatre at Berne. But he soon began to concentrate his energies on compositions, which were significantly influenced by the music of Honegger.

HEINRICH SUTERMEISTER

In 1934 he completed *Sechs Barocklieder* for chorus, in which he revealed for the first time his interest in Baroque texts. He followed this in 1936 with *Jorinde und Joringel*, a chamber oratorio based on Grimm, and in 1937 with a Divertimento for string orchestra. His first important work was a cantata for a cappella chorus, *Andreas Gryphius*. Here, as Pieter Mieg notes, is the "announcement of the real quality of this composer, which is to express his joy in music." Here, too, Sutermeister's basic style becomes developed. Mieg explains: "Sutermeister remains attached to the tonal system and concentrates mainly on the possibilities of diatonic harmonies and pure melody. Nevertheless, his development in the field of rhythm and sonority shows how much these elements have become conscious and constructive."

Sutermeister first attracted world attention with an opera, *Romeo and Juliet*, which enjoyed a remarkably successful première in Dresden on April 13, 1940. Adapting his libretto from Shakespeare and concentrating on the love interest, Sutermeister realized a concentrated work which was unafraid of emotion and broad melodies. "When the brilliant fanfares of Capulet's party give way to the delicate notes of the solo violin which accompanies the lovers' first shy conversation," writes Gerhart von Westerman, "a lyrical atmosphere is created which, because it is truly operatic in conception, is also strongly dramatic. This same applies to the poetic, ecstatic garden duet and to the final scene." Following its première, the opera was produced in twenty-two European opera houses.

For his second opera, Sutermeister went to Shakespeare's *The Tempest*, which he renamed *The Magic Island* (*Die Zauberinsel*). It was produced in Dresden on October 30, 1942. But Sutermeister's greatest success after *Romeo and Juliet* came with *Raskolnikoff*, with a libretto by the composer's brother based on Dostoevski's *Crime and Punishment*. This opera was given in Stockholm on October 14, 1948. Writing in *Musical America*, Edmund Appia maintained that *Raskolnikoff* "confirmed his [Sutermeister's] emotional gifts. Sutermeister reacts equally against post-Wagnerian Romanticism and the decadent refinements of Impressionism. He employs a simple, direct language, in which harmony plays no more than a structural role, while rhythm and melody regain their primitive power of incantation. Fully aware of contemporary technical resources, he writes music that may be described as primitive-modern."

Sutermeister has also demonstrated his talent for comedy in *Titus Feuerfuchs*, produced in Basel on April 14, 1958. This is a burlesque opera based on Nestroy's farce *Der Talisman*. Parody, satire, and good humor overflow in a score that derives much of its infectious appeal from the skillful use of dance rhythms. *Titus Feuerfuchs* represented Switzerland at the World's Fair held in Brussels during the summer of 1958.

Seraphine, based on Rabelais, was another felicitous comic opera; it was produced in Zürich, June 10, 1959. His later operas include *The Red Boot*, introduced at the Lausanne Festival in Switzerland on May 14, 1964, and *Madame Bovary*, first produced by the Zürich Opera at the International June Festival on May 26, 1967. Sutermeister has also written operas for radio and television broadcasts. One of the most successful of his radio operas was *Die Schwarze Spinne*, based on a story by Jeremias Gotthelf, broadcast in 1936. A dozen years later the composer adapted this opera for the stage, a version seen at St. Gall on March 2, 1949. In 1965 Sutermeister won first prize in Salzburg for a television opera, *The Ghost of Canterville*.

Though most famous for his operas, Sutermeister has also produced much distinguished concert music. In 1953 he completed a Requiem Mass which was heard throughout Europe following its world première in Basel on June 11, 1954. The reaction of a critic for the *Stuttgarter Zeitung* is typical: "Few contemporary compositions of sacred music can be put on a par with this work. . . . It contains a great many magnificent ideas worked out in a masterly way. The dramatic parts . . . move everyone by their force and vividness. A deeply religious fundamental mood penetrates this work throughout." Other noteworthy concert works include his second and third piano concertos (1953, 1961) and a cello concerto (1956).

Heinrich Sutermeister has expressed his credo as an opera composer in the following way: "I am absolutely convinced that the modern opera composer must also devote his attention to the fields of broadcasting and cinema; he has much to learn there. Only then can he gain in clarity about his position in the culture of today. The situation is not hopeless, once he realizes that today's public must be stirred and shocked with means radically different from those of earlier times. The musical idiom may certainly be as modern as possible, as long as there is tangible evidence of a will of almost 'evangelistic' fervor harsh and uncompromising in showing up the eternal relations to which we are subject and the will to say yes or no."

Since 1942 Sutermeister has made his home at Vaux-sur-Morges, a little village on Lake Geneva in Switzerland. In 1947 he married

Sydeman

Verena-Maria Renker. Since 1963 he has conducted a class in composition at the State High School for Music in Hanover, Germany.

MAJOR WORKS

Ballets — Das Dorf unter dem Gletscher.

Chamber Music — Suite, for four wind instruments; Serenade, for two clarinets, trumpet, and double bassoon; Konzertstück, for trumpet and piano; Capriccio, for clarinet solo; Gavotte de Concert, for trumpet and piano; Serenade, for flute, oboe, clarinet, bassoon, horn, and trumpet.

Choral Music — 7 cantatas; Sechs Barocklieder; Jorinde und Joringel, chamber oratorio; Requiem Mass; Mass in E-flat; Zwei Barocklieder; La Route Est Belle; Drei Lieder.

Operas — Die Schwarze Spinne, radio opera; Romeo and Juliet; Die Zauberinsel; Niobe; Raskolnikoff; Die Füsse im Feuer, radio ballad (also staged as opera); Fingerhütchen, radio melodrama (also staged as opera); Titus Feuerfuchs, comic opera; Seraphine, comic opera; Das Gespenst von Canterville (The Ghost of Canterville), television opera; The Red Boot (Der Rote Stiefel); Madame Bovary.

Orchestral Music — 3 piano concertos; 2 Divertimenti; Sieben Liebesbriefe, for tenor and strings; Die Alpen, fantasy on Swiss folk songs; Marche Fantasque; Orazione per Orchestre, for piano and orchestra; Cello Concerto; Poème Funèbre pour Paul Hindemith.

Piano Music — Sonatina in E-flat; Bergsommer, eight pieces; Hommage pour Arthur Honegger.

Vocal Music — Four Songs; Psalms 70 and 86, for low voice and orchestra.

ABOUT

Forty Contemporary Swiss Composers; Lang, P. H. and Broder, N., Contemporary Music in Europe.

William Sydeman
1928–

William Sydeman was born in New York City on May 8, 1928. He was educated at the Hunter College Elementary School, at Blair Academy in 1944–1945, and finally at Duke University from 1951 to 1953. At the same time he was industriously pursuing the study of music at the Mannes College of Music in New York where he was a pupil of Salzer and where he received a bachelor of science degree in 1955. During 1954 and 1955 he studied composition privately with Roger Sessions, continuing during the summer of 1955 at the Berkshire Music Center at Tanglewood. He returned there the following summer to study composition with Goffredo Petrassi. In 1958 Sydeman received his master's degree in music

Sydeman: sīd′ măn

from Hartt College of Music at the University of Hartford in Connecticut.

From his seventeenth year on, he had been composing four hours a day, six days a week. With his musical training completed and his career as a composer beginning to develop rapidly, he discarded everything he had written before his twenty-seventh year and almost everything he had produced before 1958. The survivals from his apprentice period included a Quartet, for clarinet, violin, trumpet, and double bass (1955); a Woodwind Quintet (1955); a Concertino for oboe, piano, and string orchestra (1956); Variations, for piano (1958); *Orchestral Abstractions* (1958); and Concerto da Camera for Viola and Seven Instruments (1959). They received their first performances between 1961 and 1963; the most successful of these compositions was the Concerto da Camera, which won the Pacifica Foundation Award in 1960 and was heard in San Francisco on July 12, 1962.

WILLIAM SYDEMAN

On the strength of several distinguished works completed between 1959 and 1962, Sydeman received an award in May 1962 from the National Institute of Arts and Letters. The citation described Sydeman's music as "clearly conceived, colorful, and cleanly contrapuntal . . . the honest and straightforward music of an outstanding young talent." Attention was further focused on Sydeman on November 22, 1963, when the Boston Symphony, under Erich Leinsdorf, presented the world première of his *Study for Orchestra, No. 2*, which had taken him four years to complete. This is a one-movement composition in which, as John N. Burk, the program annotator for the Boston Symphony, explained, "the thematic material . . . is continually evolving from section to section, as if one were looking at the same subject from numerous different perspectives and in ever-changing contexts." For this work Sydeman was given the Boston Symphony Merit Award in 1964.

On October 15, 1965, the Boston Symphony under Leinsdorf introduced *Study for Orchestra, No. 3*, a two-part composition which, as the composer has revealed, interests itself in the orchestra as a whole: "For the most part, colors remain pure—winds, brass, percussion, and strings function as individual colors and are rarely mixed. Rather they are often swiftly juxtaposed in kaleidoscopic fashion." Reviewing this music for the New York *Times*, Raymond Ericson said: "The composer has a flair for this kind of writing. More than many of his colleagues, he seems to know what will sound well, and he works for some remarkably attractive, pure textures. Even when he builds a shatteringly dissonant climax for full orchestra, its elements can be heard clearly."

The Boston Symphony was also responsible for the première of Sydeman's *In Memoriam—John F. Kennedy*, which had been commissioned for the orchestra by Mrs. Ruth Kaufmann and which was performed in Boston on November 4, 1966, Leinsdorf conducting. This is a two-movement composition for narrator and orchestra (the narrator at the première was E. G. Marshall). Sydeman developed his text from several of President Kennedy's speeches, from a poem by Stephen Spender, from a selection from Ecclesiastes, and from remarks about President Kennedy by Theodore Sorensen and Arthur M. Schlesinger, Jr. "The text," the composer informs us, "is not only integral to the general form and 'sonority' of the work, but is the basic element of the work, with which the music functions to clarify, delineate or make dramatically more effective." Into his musical texture Sydeman has woven quotations from the funeral march of Beethoven's *Eroica* symphony. The reason for the interpolation is that, on the afternoon of November 22, 1963, immediately following the world première of Sydeman's *Study for Orchestra, No. 2*, in Boston, Erich Leinsdorf came to the stage to announce that President Kennedy had been assassinated that morning; following the announcement, Leinsdorf led a performance of the Beethoven funeral march. "It is impossible for me to think of the tragedy without recalling this movement," says Sydeman, "and so I have incorporated and developed at length fragments of two elements of the *Eroica*, the opening bar with its heavy dotted rhythms, and the initial phrase of the second theme with its heroic sweep up and its subsequent, resigned, stepwise descent."

The Lament of Elektra (1964) is still another important work by Sydeman, a setting of a text by Sophocles for contralto, quintuple chorus, and chamber orchestra. Commissioned by Samuel Wechsler, it was given its first performance at the festival of American music at Tanglewood, August 10, 1964. Here Sydeman makes use of the serial technique with such effect that, as Howard Klein noted in his review, "the work managed to convey both particular moods and a sense of growth in a large and very logical design."

In discussing his style and creative outlook with Allen Hughes of the New York *Times*, Sydeman said in 1965: "I am something of a musical hybrid, split between the traditional urge to 'say something' and the twentieth century materials, which have so long been associated with impersonality and abstraction. . . . I wed a traditional esthetic to a contemporary technique. If I engage in any form of serialism, it is never as an end in itself, but as a means of ordering my musical material discreetly so as to sound sensible. If I utilize some aleatoric procedure, it is because a specific musical problem I have encountered during the course of composition is best solved by improvisatory methods. If my 'sound' or rhythmic vocabulary is contemporary, it is because the cliché offends me as much as the world of creative imagination delights me."

During the summer of 1966, Sydeman toured Eastern Europe under the auspices of the cultural exchange program in connection with his *Study for Orchestra, No. 2*, heard at the Prague Spring Festival in a performance by the Czech Philharmonic under Leinsdorf. During the same summer, on August 7, the world première of Sydeman's *Music for Viola, Winds and Percussion* took place at the

Congregation of the Arts at Hopkins Center of Dartmouth College.

In 1959 Sydeman joined the faculty of the David Mannes College in New York where he teaches composition and conducts a course in modern music. He lives in a house on Old Broadway in Hastings-on-the-Hudson, New York, with his wife and three children. He has converted half of his garage into a studio where he does his composing every day, usually from eight in the morning until noon.

MAJOR WORKS

Chamber Music—3 Concerti da Camera, for solo violin and instruments; 2 woodwind quintets; Quartet, for violin, clarinet, trumpet, and double bass; String Quartet; Study, for two flutes and piano; Divertimento, for flute, clarinet, bassoon, and string quintet; Fanfare and Variations, for brass quartet; Trio, for violin, clarinet, and double bass; For Double Bass Alone; Seven Movements for Septet; Tower Music, for brass quintet; Variations, for oboe and piano; Variations, for violin and piano (or harpsichord); Quintet, for clarinet, French horn (or trombone), piano, percussion, and double bass; Concert Piece, for French horn and organ; Music for Flute, Viola, Guitar, and Percussion; Homage to L'Histoire du Soldat; Oboe Quartet; Quartet, for violin, flute, clarinet, and piano; For Clarinet Alone; Trio, for flute, double bass, and percussion; Brass Quintet; Trio for Contra Bassi; Fantasy and Two Epilogues, for flute, violin, cello, and piano; The Affections, for trumpet and piano; Trio, for treble instruments; Sonata for Solo Violin; various duos for solo instruments and piano.

Choral Music—Reflections Japanese; The Lord's Prayer; Prometheus, cantata; Lament of Elektra; The Defiance of Prometheus.

Orchestral Music—Studies, Nos. 1, 2, and 3; Concertino, for oboe, piano, and string orchestra; Orchestral Abstractions; Concert Piece, for chamber orchestra; Largo, for cello and string orchestra; Oecumenicus, concerto for orchestra; In Memoriam–John F. Kennedy, for narrator and orchestra; Music for Viola, Winds, and Percussion; Concerto for Piano Four Hands and Chamber Orchestra.

Piano Music—Two Pieces; Variations; Sonatina; Prelude; Fantasy Piece, for harpsichord.

Vocal Music—Japanese Songs; Julia's Clothes; Spider; Songs, for soprano, flute, and cello.

ABOUT

Musical Quarterly, September 1964; New York Times, November 21, 1965.

Karol Szymanowski
1882–1937

Karol Maciej Szymanowski was born in Timoshovka, near Yelisavetgrad (now Kirovo-

Szymanowski: shĭ mä nôf′ skē

grad), in the Polish Ukraine, on October 6, 1882. He was the third of five children. (The long accepted birth date of September 21, 1883, which the composer himself believed to be accurate, has since his death been proved erroneous through the discovery of new certificates.) His father, a wealthy Polish landowner, and his mother, a baroness of Swedish extraction, were both musical and made their home the rendezvous for leading artists and scholars. In his childhood and boyhood, Karol moved about in a setting in which the love of music, literature, and art was encouraged and nurtured.

KAROL SZYMANOWSKI

When Karol was four, he suffered injuries from a fall which affected one leg; for years it was impossible for him to walk without the help of a stick. Consequently, he was unable to join other children either at school or at play, and his education took place privately at home. His was a lonely boyhood. He sought diversion in such solitary pastimes as playing music, reading, and introspection. Music attracted him particularly. Without any formal instruction he began to play the piano. Before long he received some lessons from his father, and after that from an aunt. Later on, Gustav Neuhaus, a local teacher (and a distant relative), began to give him some instruction in theory. A performance of Wagner's *Lohengrin*, which he heard in boyhood, inspired him with the ambition to become a composer. He purchased all the Wagner piano scores he could put his hands on and then studied them painstakingly.

By 1900 he had completed a number of works for the piano, including two sonatas and various etudes and preludes. A set of nine preludes became his first opus when it was issued in 1906, six years after its composition. Szymanowski's model was Chopin, for whom his admiration was boundless. Zdzislaw Jachimecki said of these early preludes: "The lyric sincerity, the charmingly poetic ideas, the beauty of his melodic invention, the harmonic variety, and, finally, the elegance of technique and finesse commanded universal attention."

Convinced of their son's talent for music, the Szymanowskis decided to send him to Warsaw for more study. He arrived in the Polish capital in 1901 and soon after that began to take music lessons with Zawirski and Noskowski. Under the latter's guidance, Szymanowski completed a piano sonata in C minor which won first prize in a Chopin competition in Lemberg. While still in Warsaw, Szymanowski also wrote his first large work for orchestra—the *Concert Overture* (1905).

A significant influence in his development was his friendship with several other young, brilliant Polish musicians in Warsaw. In the fall of 1905 these young men formed the Association of Young Polish Composers (later identified as "Young Poland in Music") to advance the interests of young Polish musicians. It was through the efforts of this group that Szymanowski's first ambitious works received an important hearing: on February 6, 1906 Gregor Fitelberg directed the Warsaw Philharmonic in Szymanowski's *Concert Overture*. At the same concert Harry Neuhaus performed Szymanowski's *Variations*, for the piano, op. 10 (1904) and the Etude in B-flat minor, op. 4, no. 3 (1902). The Etude is the composition that Paderewski later made famous throughout Europe with repeated performances. Szymanowski's music made a deep impression. One eminent critic, Alexander Polinski, wrote: "On hearing yesterday the works of Karol Szymanowski I did not doubt even for a moment that I was faced with a composer whose talent is of no common order. Everything he writes bears the stamp of genius."

The Association of Young Polish Composers established its headquarters in Berlin,

and Szymanowski followed it there early in 1906. On March 30, 1906, the Association presented a concert of music by Polish composers in Berlin, with Gregor Fitelberg conducting the Berlin Philharmonic. This event, however, attracted little attention.

Szymanowski spent two years in Germany. During that period he was absorbed in the study of music by Wagner, Richard Strauss, Reger, and Mahler. The influence of German post-Romanticism penetrated the writing of Szymanowski's first symphony, in F minor, which was completed in 1907 and introduced in Warsaw on March 26, 1909. Apparently aware of how derivative this music was, the composer finally decided to withdraw it from general circulation.

In 1908 Szymanowski left Berlin to divide his time during the next few years between his native city and foreign capitals. He completed a second symphony, in B-flat major, in 1909 and a second piano sonata, in A minor, in 1910. The symphony was heard in Warsaw on April 7, 1911, but was given a poor reception. In the 1930's the composer revised this work with the help of Gregor Fitelberg, and it was given a better reception. In 1967 the conductor Stanislaw Skrowaczewski made further changes and performed the symphony successfully with the Minneapolis Symphony, in Minneapolis and on tour. The sonata was extensively performed in Europe by Artur Rubinstein, who thenceforth did all he could to promote Szymanowski's piano music. In both of these works, the earlier German Romantic influence had been superseded by that of Scriabin, not only in the harmonic language but also in the expression of rapturous, ecstatic moods.

From 1912 to 1914, Szymanowski lived in Vienna. There he became interested in exotic subjects and idioms. His fascination with oriental and Near Eastern philosophy and mysticism and with Near Eastern backgrounds and culture led him in 1913 to write a one-act opera, *Hagith*, which had to wait a decade before it had a hearing in Warsaw; and the *Love Songs of Hafiz*, a set of songs for voice and orchestra (1914). Two of these *Hafiz* songs were heard at a concert of the festival of the International Society for Contemporary Music at Salzburg, on August 4, 1923.

An important shift in musical values came about in 1914 through an extended visit to

France where Szymanowski became impressed with Ravel's post-Impressionism. The lush harmonies and the sensuous moods and melodies of German Romanticism and Scriabin were now replaced by the subtler nuances, suggestions, and atmospheres of the Impressionist school. In this new manner Szymanowski produced his first major works. They were written during the harrowing period of World War I, which the composer spent mainly in Poland but partly in Russia, where he had gone to give several concerts with the violinist Paul Kochanski in 1916. These Impressionist compositions include the *Métopes* for piano and an important suite for the violin, *Mythes*, both in 1915. The latter contains *The Fountains of Arethusa*, which is probably the most popular piece of music Szymanowski wrote and which has often been performed apart from the other movements of the suite. The war years also saw the writing of a third symphony (1916), a work which still showed some traces of Szymanowski's former oriental interests. The symphony, subtitled *Song of the Night*, engages a tenor and a mixed chorus for a setting of poems by the thirteenth-century Persian mystic Jalal-ad-din Rumi (better known as Jalal). Its première took place in London on October 24, 1921, Albert Coates conducting.

The Russian Revolution had far-reaching repercussions in Poland, and Szymanowski was personally affected. The Szymanowski estate was plundered; all the family belongings were confiscated. Destitute, Szymanowski lived for a while with relatives until they, too, were stripped of their possessions. Then, in 1919, Szymanowski went to live in Warsaw, where he tried to make a living through music. But the reaction to his compositions was frigid. As he wrote bitterly to his friend Jachimecki in 1920: "I am a stranger, incomprehensible and probably even useless to the general structure of Polish music. . . . The European atmosphere of my art is almost indigestible to such provincialism." He did much better on tour, often appearing as pianist in the presentation of his own compositions. He was heard in Paris and London; and then, in 1921, he paid his first visit to the United States.

During the next few years Szymanowski began to make some headway in his own country. In 1922 his first string quartet, in C major (1917), received an award from the Polish Ministry of Education; its first performance in Warsaw in 1924 was a success, and one year later it represented Poland at the festival of the International Society for Contemporary Music at Venice. The year 1922 also witnessed the world première of Szymanowski's opera *Hagith*—on May 13, 1922, in Warsaw. And on June 19, 1926, a full-length opera, *King Roger*, was given an ambitious presentation by the Warsaw Opera.

In 1921 Szymanowski had spent a few months in the Tatra ranhes of the Carpathian mountains in Poland where he heard native folk songs and dances and was delighted with the local customs. The experience impelled him to write music embodying the style and spirit of Polish folk music. As he remarked on first adopting a national idiom: "The law has worked itself out in me according to which every man must go back to the earth from which he derives. Today I have developed into a national composer, not only subconsciously, but with a thorough conviction, using the melodic treasures of the Polish people."

His first major work in a national style was the song cycle *Slopiewnie* (1922), lyrics by Julien Tuwim. This music, says H. H. Stuckenschmidt, is "a unique synthesis of primitive and subtle elements." It was followed by an even more significant national achievement, the ballet *Harnasie* (1926), which helped place its composer with the foremost creative figures in twentieth century Polish music. The scenario was based on a Polish legend about robbers from the Tatra mountains, and the music emulated the shifting tonalities, the modal character, the languorous melodies, and the strong rhythms of Tatra peasant music. "The music," says Stuckenschmidt, "conjures up with the pose of genius, the wild and lonely landscape of the Carpathians. . . . [It shows] Szymanowski as a masterly manipulator of nationalist melody of intricate Slavonic rhythms." *Harnasie* was produced in Prague on May 11, 1936. It was Szymanowski's first unqualified masterwork.

However, it was the *Stabat Mater* (1926), text in Polish by Jankowski, that brought Szymanowski his first great success in Warsaw. This religious work was the composer's first attempt at liturgical music, and like *Harnasie* it has its roots embedded in nationalism. The composer here combines the melodies and rhythms of his country with sixteenth century polyphonic methods in a vividly pictorial and dramatic way. When *Stabat Mater* was introduced in Warsaw on January 11, 1929, it was a triumph, Szymanowski's first major work to be honored in such a decisive way in his own country. "Szymanowski," Stuckenschmidt has written, "here devised a modern choral texture which gloriously resurrects the great traditions of Eastern church music, yet wholly renounces the strict polyphonic forms of canon and fugue."

In 1926 Szymanowski was appointed director of the Warsaw Conservatory. His always delicate health deteriorated sharply and in 1929 he suffered a nervous breakdown. Resigning his post at the Warsaw Conservatory, he went to a sanitarium. Refreshed and strengthened by his stay there, he was finally able to resume his musical activities. He became president of the Academy of Music in Warsaw. He also completed two major works which rank with his greatest: the *Symphonie Concertante*, for piano and orchestra (1932), and his second violin concerto (1933). In the former he himself was the soloist at the world première in Poznan on October 9, 1932; the violin concerto was introduced in Warsaw on October 6, 1933, by Paul Kochanski, the virtuoso for whom it was written.

Szymanowski's health broke down again in 1936 and he was confined once more to a sanitarium, this time near Lausanne, Switzerland. Only a few months before his death, ill though he was, he attended a successful production of *Harnasie* at the Paris Opéra. He died of laryngeal tuberculosis on March 28, 1937. His body was entombed in a vault reserved for famous men at Skalka Church in Cracow.

"The work of Karol Szymanowski," wrote his compatriot and fellow composer Alexander Tansman, "does not merely mark a glorious page in Polish music; it has attached itself incontestably to the artistic heritage of the entire world, as very precious material; it is a robust branch of the musical tree of Europe. It is quite certain that the music of Szymanowski cannot please everyone; lovers of the 'picturesque,' of 'local color,' of extravagant sonorous effects will relish it only slightly; but for real musicians it presents a genuine interest by its very existence, because its undeniable originality imposes itself upon musicians of a different esthetic. Freeing himself from a certain heaviness which weighs down his earlier works, Szymanowski learned to forge for his ideas a musical language that is very personal. He belongs, without doubt, to the group of the greatest musicians of our time."

Almost thirty years after Szymanowski's death, on December 11, 1965, the new Grand Opera House in Warsaw was opened with a revival of *King Roger*.

MAJOR WORKS

Ballets—Mandragora, pantomime; Harnasie.

Chamber Music—2 string quartets; Violin Sonata in D minor; Romance, for violin and piano; Notturno e Tarantella, for violin and piano; Mythes, three poems for violin and piano; Berceuse d'Aitacho Enia, for violin and piano.

Choral Music—Agave; Stabat Mater; Veni Creator; Litany; Kurpian Songs.

Operas—Hagith, one-act opera; King Roger.

Orchestral Music—3 symphonies; 2 violin concertos; Concert Overture; Penthesilea, for soprano and orchestra; Love Songs of Hafiz, for voice and orchestra; Symphonie Concertante, for piano and orchestra.

Piano Music—3 sonatas; Fantasy in F minor; Métopes; Masques; Four Polish Dances; etudes, mazurkas, preludes.

Vocal Music—The Songs of the Fairy Princess; Four Songs to Tagore; Songs of the Foolish Muezzin; Slopiewnie; Children's Rhymes; Five Songs to Joyce.

ABOUT

Bacharach, A. L. (ed.), The Music Masters: v4, The 20th Century; Golachowski, S., Karol Szymanowski; Lobaczewska, S., Karol Szymanowski; Maciejewski, B. M., Karol Szymanowski: His Life and Work; Pannain, G., Modern Composers.

Chesterian (London), November 1927; The Listener (London), May 22, 1947; Musical Quarterly, January 1922; La Revue Musicale (Paris), May 1922; Slavonic and East European Review, July 1928.

Alexander Tansman
1897–

Alexander Tansman was born on June 12, 1897, in Lodz, Poland. He began the study of music at the Lodz Conservatory with Gawronski. He was only fifteen when one of his compositions, the *Symphonic Serenade* for orchestra, was performed by the Lodz Symphony.

Tansman: täns′ män

Tansman

Intending to make law his career, he went to Warsaw to attend the University. Music was not neglected; Tansman studied composition privately with Piotr Rytel and piano with Lütschg. Music soon became such an all-consuming interest that he decided to leave the University.

ALEXANDER TANSMAN

When, during World War I, Poland became an independent state, Tansman joined the Polish army. He continued writing music while in service. In 1919 he entered two compositions in a national Polish competition, winning both the first and second prizes. When the war ended, he participated in two concerts of chamber music devoted exclusively to his works, one in Lodz, the other in Warsaw. The proceeds enabled him to visit Vienna. Then he settled in Paris, which remained his permanent home, and in 1938 he became a French citizen.

His first years in Paris were marked by poverty and trying personal deprivations. But he was not unhappy, for the vitality of Paris's musical life exhilarated him. He associated with some of the most prominent French musicians of the day, including Ravel and Schmitt, and was stimulated by them to find a new direction in his musical writing. Up to that time he had been most strongly influenced by Chopin, but in Paris, as Irving Schwerké noted, "Tansman found . . . the form, the order and logic of thought, the linear refinement his music needed, and learned there to

remove from himself all *a priori* modern tendencies in order to give free course to his natural musical emotion. In becoming a master of French *savoir faire*, he lost nothing of the sensitive side of his art."

Vladimir Golschmann, then a young and influential conductor, recognized Tansman's talent and arranged a concert of Tansman's piano works in Paris on February 17, 1920. A year later, Golschmann directed the première of Tansman's *Impressions* and *Intermezzo Sinfonico*, both for orchestra. For many years after that, Golschmann continued to promote Tansman's music and was largely responsible for bringing it recognition. Many of the orchestral works were either introduced or performed by Golschmann both in the United States and in Europe; and some of them were written for him.

Despite the infiltration of French influences into Tansman's writing, a Polish identity was not altogether obfuscated. A strong national strain continued to assert itself in his compositions. The rhythm of Polish dances became an integral part of his idiom, and he wrote many polonaises and mazurkas for the piano. He also produced orchestral compositions, such as the *Four Polish Dances* (1931), introduced at a Pasdeloup concert in Paris on December 12, 1933, the four movements of which comprise a Polka, a Kujawiak, a Dumka, and an Oberek (the last is a kind of mazurka). In his Symphony No. 2 in A minor (1926)—first performance in Boston on March 18, 1927, Koussevitzky conducting— the rhythms of Polish dances can be found in the scherzo movement.

One of Tansman's most successful shorter works for the orchestra in the 1920's was *Danse de la Sorcière*, first heard in Brussels on May 5, 1924, and subsequently extensively performed elsewhere. It was featured at the festival of the International Society for Contemporary Music in Zürich, June 22, 1926. This piece went a long way towards establishing Tansman's reputation as one of the most vital of the younger Polish composers. His reputation was enhanced by a series of concert tours, in which he appeared in the triple role of composer, conductor, and pianist. In 1926 he visited Austria, and one year after that, Germany. On December 28, 1927, he made his American debut as soloist with the Boston

576

Symphony in a program that included the world première of his Second Piano Concerto. An extensive tour of the United States followed. In 1933 he toured the Far East.

To the rapidly expanding Tansman repertory two important compositions for orchestra were added in the 1930's. *Triptych*, for orchestra, introduced in St. Louis under Golschmann's direction on November 6, 1937, was in the French-Polish style characterizing so many of Tansman's major works. The *Sonatine Transatlantique* (1930), however, was music of a different character. It represented Tansman's first successful use of jazz rhythms and harmonies. The *Sonatine* was introduced in the United States by Walter Gieseking, but many other pianists performed it extensively in Europe and the United States in the 1930's. Kurt Jooss used this music for a ballet entitled *Impressions of a Big City*, produced in Cologne on November 21, 1932.

In 1941 Tansman left Europe to settle temporarily in the United States after some harrowing experiences in France eluding the Nazis. On October 30 of that year he received the Elizabeth Sprague Coolidge medal for distinguished service to chamber music. He remained in the United States through the war years. Soon after his arrival, several of his works written during the trying period in war-torn France and reflecting his emotional disturbance at that time were performed successfully in the United States. One of them was the *Polish Rhapsody*, inspired by the heroic defense of Warsaw during the first weeks of the war. When the rhapsody was introduced in St. Louis on November 14, 1941, Vladimir Golschmann conducting, Reed Hynds wrote in the St. Louis *Star-Times:* "It is alive in every bar. Tansman . . . had written it to catch the spirit of Poland; to give a sense of the country's tragedy; to celebrate the return of hope to that unhappy people. He has succeeded signally well by clothing essentially simple Polish songs and dances in the finest symphonic garb. All of those aspects of Polish culture, from the polonaise and the mazurka, to a certain mordant melancholy observed in Polish art, are evoked by Tansman's imaginative work."

Tansman wrote many new works in the United States. They included three symphonies. The fifth (1942), introduced in Baltimore on February 2, 1943, once again made use of jazz techniques. He also wrote piano pieces for children, a variety of other works for different media, and several scores for motion pictures.

In 1946 Tansman returned to Paris where he has since lived and where he has continued to be creatively productive. In 1951 he completed a major choral work, the oratorio *The Prophet Isaiah*, which Alfred J. Frankenstein described as a "monumental structure, translating into music the breadth of scale and grandeur of rhythm that characterize the biblical prose he uses." An opera, *Le Serment*, was successfully produced in Brussels on March 11, 1955. *Capriccio*, for orchestra, which had been commissioned by the Louisville Orchestra in Kentucky, was performed by that orchestra on March 6, 1955. A ballet, *Resurrection*, was produced in Nice in 1962, the year of its composition. And *Psalms*, for tenor solo, chorus, and orchestra, was successfully performed at the International Week of Music Festival in Paris in 1962.

This is Edward Lockspeiser's appraisal of Tansman: "A lyric quality is one of his salient characteristics. His melodic inventiveness, particularly in the slow movements, has a warmth and sensitiveness which are truly his own; and it is in the Lied (aria form), often employed by him for the Andante in works of the sonata type, that his melodic gifts are severely tested. . . . Tansman has rhythmic dynamism to a remarkable degree, but this powerful virility, sometimes brutal, but never vulgar, does not in any way detract from the beauty of the lyricism which helps to characterize his manifold personality."

To the editor of this book Tansman explained his musical credo thus: "Musical composition is an independent and self-sufficient art and should, as far as symphonic music is concerned, be motivated exclusively by musical elements of melody, harmony, rhythm, and form, without trying to express literary or pictorial subjects. I think that before anything else, a composer has to follow his own ideas without any conscious concession to temporary theories (esthetic or technical), tastes or publicized trends. I am not a partisan of the utilitarian concept of music. It is fortunate for a composer if his work is pleasing. But the purpose of a composition should not be influenced in advance by this effort to please; the task of the composer is to say what he *must* say and not to follow an *à la mode* pattern. This does not mean that music has to be complicated or enigmatic to be original. On the contrary: simplicity goes hand in hand with honesty. But *artificial* simplicity often results in vulgarity and is often more 'fabricated' and contrived than the most complex modern score.

"The development of musical composition goes more and more to the melodic outline, which after all is the basis of the music, the melody being shaped by its rhythmic design. The harmony remains as always a temporary means of expressing the musical idea; and the constructive element of form, unfortunately so often neglected in our time, is of primary importance. It does not matter if the form is classical, or a derivation from classicism; but it has to be present, seriously worked out. In my last works, I take very great pains with my constructive element without which, I feel, music remains improvisation rather than art."

In 1937 Tansman married Colette Cras, daughter of Jean Cras, an admiral in the French Navy; she died in 1953. They had two daughters. Tansman maintains his home on the Rue Florence Blumental in Paris. He is an avid traveler and an admirer of films (his second piano concerto is dedicated to Charles Chaplin). His other diversions include tennis, billiards, reading, and collecting ancient statuettes and bronze pieces. He is a recipient of the Jiji Shimpo medal from Japan.

MAJOR WORKS

Ballets—Sextuor; Lumières; La Grande Ville; Bric-à-Brac; Le Roi Qui Jouait le Fou; Ballet Mexico-Américain; The Emperor's New Suit; Resurrection.

Chamber Music—8 string quartets; 2 string trios; 2 string serenades; Violin Sonata; Suite Divertissement, for violin, viola, cello, and piano; Flute Sonata; Cello Sonata; Serenade, for piano, violin, and cello; Septet; Danse de la Sorcière, for woodwind quintet and piano; Deux Mouvements, for four cellos; Nous Jouons pour Maman, for violin, cello, and piano; String Sextet; Divertimento, for oboe, clarinet, trumpet, cello, and piano; Sonatine, for violin and piano; Tombeau de Chopin, for string quartet.

Choral Music—The Prophet Isaiah, oratorio; Four Prayers; Psalms.

Operas—La Nuit Kurde; La Toison d'Or; Le Serment; Sabbatai Zevi, le Faux-Messie.

Orchestral Music—7 symphonies; 3 serenades; 2 piano concertos; 2 partitas for piano and orchestra; Danse de la Sorcière; Sinfonietta; Ouverture Symphonique; Suite, for two pianos and orchestra;

Toccata; Triptyque, for strings; Symphonie Concertante; Deux Moments Symphoniques; Four Polish Dances; Piano Concertino; Deux Pièces; Partita, for strings; Viola Concerto; Adagio, for strings; Rapsodie Hébraïque; Fantasy, for cello and orchestra; Fantasy, for violin and orchestra; Variations on a Theme by Frescobaldi; Polish Rhapsody; Études Symphoniques; Lied et Toccata; Musique pour Cordes; Musique pour Orchestre; Ricercari; Sinfonia Piccola; Capriccio; Concerto for Orchestra; Partita, for cello and orchestra; Chamber Symphony; Six Études; Six Movements, for strings.

Piano Music—5 sonatas; 3 sonatinas; Four Polish Dances; Five Impressions; Les Jeunes au Piano; Pour les Enfants, four volumes; arabesques, ballades, intermezzi, mazurkas, polonaises, preludes.

ABOUT

Schwerke, I., Alexander Tansman.

La Revue Musicale (Paris), February 1929.

Deems Taylor
1885–1966

Joseph Deems Taylor was born in New York City on December 22, 1885, and educated in the New York City public schools, at the Friends' School, and at the Ethical Culture School, from which he was graduated in 1902. He attended New York University, receiving his bachelor of arts degree in 1906. After college, Taylor enjoyed a brief career in vaudeville, once being offered top billing in a comic act involving a variety of hats. Then he found an editorial post first with the *Nelson Encyclopedia* and after that with the *Encyclopaedia Britannica*.

Music interested him from childhood on. He was only ten when he wrote his first piece of music, a waltz. When he was eleven he began to take piano lessons, but he dropped them after eight months. He never again took another piano lesson. From 1908 to 1911 he studied harmony and counterpoint with Oscar Coon, but after 1911 all his training in composition, theory, and orchestration came from reading textbooks. At college he wrote music for four campus shows, one of which, *The Echo*, was produced on Broadway in 1909, starring Bessie McCoy.

In 1913 he won a prize for *The Siren Song*, a tone poem he had written one year earlier. In 1914 he completed two ambitious choral works, the cantatas *The Chambered Nautilus*, to the text of the poem by Oliver Wendell Holmes, and *The Highwayman*, based on the poem by Alfred Noyes. This year also saw the appearance of Taylor's first publication, a song, "Witch Woman." From that time on he was determined to be a serious composer, but he had no intention of surrendering those extra-musical activities that earned him a living. He put it this way: "I tried teaching and found it an intolerable bore. No one would dream of hiring me as a conductor, and I am a dreadful pianist. So I hit on a fourth choice: I subsidized. I, the composer, would be supported by me, doing other things."

DEEMS TAYLOR

The "other things" included a stint as assistant editor of a trade journal from 1912 to 1916. In 1916 he was appointed assistant Sunday editor of the New York *Tribune*, and from 1916 to 1918 he was the war correspondent for that newspaper. He later became the assistant editor of *Collier's Weekly*.

In 1921 he was appointed the music critic of the New York *World*. He held this post with distinction for four years, proving himself at once one of America's wittiest and most tolerant commentators on the music scene. As relaxation from newspaper work, Taylor expanded and adapted for symphony orchestra a suite that he had written in 1917–1919 for a chamber music ensemble and that had been introduced on February 18, 1919: *Through the Looking Glass*, based on Lewis Carroll's tale. The revised, expanded version was heard on March 10, 1923, in New York with Walter Damrosch conducting the New York Symphony. It became an immediate favorite, and since then has been extensively performed.

Composition began to assume such an important role in Taylor's life that in 1925 he resigned from the *World* to devote himself completely for the first time to creative work. During his four years as a critic his creativity had been channeled into the theatre, with incidental music for nine plays including Molnar's *Liliom* and *Beggar on Horseback*, by George S. Kaufman and Marc Connelly; the latter contained an extended musical sequence for a pantomime entitled *A Kiss in Xanadu*.

Taylor's first significant work following his retirement from the *World* marked his return to the concert hall. It was the tone poem *Jurgen*, based on James Branch Cabell's satirical novel. The work had been commissioned by Walter Damrosch, who introduced it at a concert of the New York Symphony on November 19, 1925. Music generously spiced with wit and satire, *Jurgen* revealed Taylor's exceptional gift for musical characterization.

The talent shown in *Jurgen* brought Taylor to the attention of the Metropolitan Opera, which commissioned him to write an opera. In 1926 Taylor went to Paris where, in collaboration with the distinguished American poet Edna St. Vincent Millay, he worked on the opera which made him a composer of international importance. On February 17, 1927, that opera, *The King's Henchman*, was given its first performance at the Metropolitan Opera, a widely publicized première that proved to be one of the major events of that musical season. Though Miss Millay's libretto bears a striking similarity to that of *Tristan und Isolde* and though Taylor's score has some obvious Wagnerian overtones (particularly in its chromatic harmonies and use of the Leitmotiv technique), *The King's Henchman* was by no means an imitative opera. The music was Taylor's own—refined, cultured, sensitive, often beautiful. Lawrence Gilman referred to it as "the best American opera we have ever heard," the work of "an expert craftsman, an artist of sensibility and warm responsiveness." Olin Downes said: "From the perspective of other American operas heard or read in score . . . it is clear that Mr. Taylor and Miss Millay have produced the most effective and artistically wrought American opera that has reached the stage." The audience liked the opera, too, with the result that the work was performed fourteen times in three seasons. This was the first time an American opera had achieved such a success. In the fall of 1927 it was broadcast on a coast-to-coast network program to launch the Columbia Broadcasting System.

The Metropolitan Opera now commissioned Taylor to write a second opera. This time the composer went for his subject to *Peter Ibbetson*, a novel of Du Maurier. Taylor himself prepared the libretto in collaboration with the actress Constance Collier. Introduced on February 7, 1931, *Peter Ibbetson* was given a mixed reception. Most critics felt it was not the equal of *The King's Henchman*. Nevertheless a number of orchestral episodes were singled out for praise: the first-act waltzes, the second-act inn music, and the third-act dream music. Despite the reservations of the critics, *Peter Ibbetson* actually turned out to be an even greater box-office attraction than *The King's Henchman*. It was given sixteen times in four seasons and enjoyed the distinction of inaugurating the 1933–1934 opera season at the Metropolitan, the first American opera to open a season. On July 22, 1961, it was successfully revived at the Empire State Music Festival in New York. Two orchestral suites arranged by Taylor from the opera score have been performed by major orchestras.

From 1927 to 1929, Taylor was editor of *Musical America* and in 1931–1932 he was the music critic of the New York *American*. With the growth and development of radio broadcasting, Taylor affiliated himself with the new medium. He made his radio debut as commentator in 1927 when his opera *The King's Henchman* was heard over the CBS network. In 1931 he broadcast over NBC a series of talks on the history of opera. After that, for a number of years, he was the program commentator for broadcasts of the New York Philharmonic concerts and performances from the Metropolitan Opera. He also served as master-of-ceremonies on numerous sponsored programs and was a frequent guest on the popular program *Information Please!* His musical commentaries over the radio provided the material for three books on music: *Of Men and Music* (1937), *The Well-Tempered Listener* (1940), and *Music to My Ears* (1949). In 1940 Taylor also served as the commentator for the

Walt Disney motion picture production *Fantasia*, in which animated cartoons served to illustrate a number of musical masterworks conducted on the soundtrack by Leopold Stokowski.

Taylor wrote two more operas after *Peter Ibbetson*. *Ramuntcho* was based on the novel of the same title by Pierre Loti, adapted into a libretto by the composer himself. Its setting was a Basque village at the turn of the present century, and Taylor's score made considerable use of Basque folk songs. The opera was introduced in Philadelphia on February 10, 1942, and was described by Robert A. Simon as "an effective and strikingly melodious score, full of singable music." His last opera was *The Dragon*, a fantasy based on a play by Lady Gregory, which received its première in New York on February 6, 1958. Intended for intimate performances by college workshops and small opera companies, *The Dragon* was structurally of modest proportions, requiring a comparatively small orchestra and no ballet or chorus.

During these years Taylor had not abandoned symphonic music. On November 14, 1942, the New York Philharmonic under Howard Barlow introduced *Marco Takes a Walk*, inspired by Dr. Seuss's story in verse *And to Think that I Saw It on Mulberry Street*. This music described the adventures of an imaginative little boy on the way to school; the structure is a theme and variations. Later symphonic works included *A Christmas Overture* (introduced in New York on December 23, 1943, the composer conducting); *Elegy*, inspired by the death of an Egyptian princess who died at the age of twelve (heard in Los Angeles on January 4, 1945); and the *Restoration Suite* (première in Indianapolis on November 18, 1950).

In his last years, Taylor was crippled by arthritis. Despite his infirmity, he made a trip to Miami in December 1963 to attend a performance of an orchestral adaptation of *Peter Ibbetson* arranged by Fabien Sevitzky, who conducted the work with the University of Miami Symphony. It was one of Taylor's last public appearances. He died in a hospital in New York City on July 3, 1966.

Taylor was married three times: to Jane Anderson in 1917 (the marriage ended in divorce a few years later), to Mary Kennedy in 1921 (they were divorced in 1934), and to Lucille Watson-Little in 1945 (the marriage was annulled in 1952). Taylor had only one child, a daughter by his second marriage, with whom he lived during his last years.

From 1942 to 1948 Taylor was president of the American Society of Composers, Authors and Publishers (ASCAP).

MAJOR WORKS

Chamber Music—Portrait of a Lady, for eleven instruments; Lucrece, suite for string quartet.

Choral Music—The Chambered Nautilus, cantata; The Highwayman, cantata.

Operas—The King's Henchman; Peter Ibbetson; Ramuntcho; The Dragon, one-act opera.

Orchestral Music—Through the Looking Glass, suite; Jurgen, tone poem; Circus Day, suite; Marco Takes a Walk; A Christmas Overture; Elegy; Restoration Suite.

ABOUT

Grout, D. J., A Short History of Opera; Howard, J. T., Deems Taylor.

Alexander Tcherepnin
1899–

Alexander Nikolaievich Tcherepnin was born in St. Petersburg on January 20, 1899, the son of the celebrated Russian composer and conductor Nicolas Tcherepnin. From 1908 to 1917 Alexander attended elementary and high school, but his attendance was frequently interrupted by illnesses and long periods of rest and recuperation in the Crimea.

As a child Alexander received some piano lessons from his mother; but his father, though ready with advice and guidance, refused to give him any formal instruction. Extraordinarily precocious, Alexander wrote a comic opera when he was twelve, a ballet when he was thirteen, and several piano sonatas at fourteen. He also made an appearance as pianist in his fourteenth year in a concert featuring a number of his own compositions. Some of his boyhood piano compositions were included many years later in his Bagatelles, op. 5, *Pièces sans Titre*, op. 7, and *Episodes* (no opus number).

In the spring of 1917 Alexander was graduated from high school. Determined to specialize in music, he submitted some of his piano compositions to the directors of the St. Petersburg Conservatory. Later in 1917 he was admitted to the Conservatory and for a few months was a pupil of Sokolov in harmony and Kobiliansky in piano. Then, in 1918, when his father became director of the Tiflis Conservatory, Alexander went to the Caucasus. Life there was both difficult and primitive; at one time he suffered an attack of typhus. Nevertheless, he managed to attend classes in philosophy at the university while studying piano with Ter-Stepanova and counterpoint with Th. de Hartmann. He also became involved in various musical activities, such as giving piano recitals in Georgia and Armenia, writing music criticism for newspapers, and composing and conducting incidental music for theatrical productions.

ALEXANDER TCHEREPNIN

When the Red Army occupied the Caucasus, the Tcherepnins—unsympathetic to the new Bolshevik regime in Russia—fled by ship to Marseilles. From there, they made their way in 1921 to Paris, where they established their home. Alexander continued music study at the Paris Conservatory, principally composition with Gedalge, counterpoint with Vidal, and piano with Isidor Philipp. One day, Philipp had occasion to read through several of Tcherepnin's manuscripts and was so impressed that he henceforth used his authority

Tcherepnin: chĕ rĕp′ nēn

to further the young man's career. Upon leaving the Conservatory, Tcherepnin found influential sponsors ready to promote his concert career. In September 1922 he gave a successful piano recital in London in a program made up of his own music. This marked the beginning of a career at the keyboard that in the next decade or so would span the globe. In the dual capacity of pianist and composer Tcherepnin made his debut in Monte Carlo in 1923 in the première of his first piano concerto, which he had completed three years earlier.

In 1923 Tcherepnin was asked by Anna Pavlova to write music for a ballet based on material she had gathered in India. The ballet, *Ajanta Frescoes*, was introduced at Covent Garden in London on September 10, 1923, with outstanding success. Pavlova continued to feature the work in her repertory for the remainder of her career; after her death, it was mounted by various other ballet companies throughout central Europe.

Two major concert works of this period added to the composer's growing reputation. *Rapsodie Georgienne*, for cello and orchestra, was one of several works to reflect the composer's interest in the music of the Caucasus with which he had become acquainted in Tiflis. The rhapsody does not quote any actual folk songs but it does make extraordinarily effective use of their varied rhythms and unique harmonic structures. It was heard early in 1924 in Bordeaux, after which it received a successful hearing in Paris, both times with André Hekking as soloist.

Tcherepnin's second piano concerto followed the rhapsody. In one movement, this work showed a perceptible advance over the first piano concerto in the composer's skill in writing for the keyboard and in his enriched invention in rhythm and variation. The concerto received its world première in Paris on January 26, 1924.

His growing self-assurance now permitted Tcherepnin to undertake ambitious structures other than the concerto. On October 29, 1927, his first symphony was heard in Paris. It was followed less than three months later by the première of his first opera, *Ol-Ol*, in Weimar, on January 31, 1928. The opera was based on Andreyev's *The Days of Our Life*, which the composer himself fashioned into a libretto.

Willi Reich wrote: "The text . . . is a lively picture of student and soldier life in old Russia. To this material, Tcherepnin added some striking music admirably adapted in the willful primitiveness to the action in hand, and spreading around the tragic conflict of life the true atmosphere of peasant thought and peasant ways." This opera was performed in Vienna, Prague, and Bratislava before being staged in New York City in 1934.

In 1933 Tcherepnin undertook a world tour as composer-pianist. He made his first coast-to-coast tour of the United States in 1934. (His first brief visit had been in 1927.) From 1934 to 1937 he made extended tours to the Orient during which he became deeply interested in oriental music and composers, helping to promote the careers of promising young composers by founding a publishing house for them and editing collections of Chinese and Japanese music in Western notation. On August 24, 1937, he married a Chinese girl, Lee Hsien-ming, a concert pianist; they have three sons.

With the coming of the Sino-Japanese War, Tcherepnin left the Orient and came to live for a year in the United States. He returned to Paris in 1938, remaining there during the war years. Following the liberation of Paris he gave numerous concerts for American troops in France and after the war resumed his travels as composer-pianist with appearances in Europe and the Near East.

He returned to the United States in 1948. After conducting a master class in piano at the San Francisco Music and Art Institute, he served on the faculty of the De Paul University Music School in Chicago from 1949 to 1964. He was also a member of the faculty at the Académie Internationale d'Été in Nice and at the Mozarteum in Salzburg. In 1958 he became an American citizen. During these years he divided his time between Paris and Chicago. In 1964 he gave up all his teaching assignments to concentrate on composition and concert tours. At that time he moved from Chicago to New York; he also maintained a second home in Paris.

On August 13, 1952, the world première of his opera *The Farmer and the Fairy*, with text based on an ancient fable, took place at the Aspen Music Festival in Colorado. In reviewing the opera for *Musical America*,

Quaintance Eaton wrote: "Tcherepnin has employed the pentatonic scale for his fable, exemplifying, as he says, an uncomplicated way of life.... To tell the simple story the composer has devised a set of songs connected by orchestral tissue of the colorful texture provided by a large percussion section, used in the five-tone manner, which gives oriental flavoring throughout, plus the occasional Slavic reference that seems to be inescapable. The narrative is sometimes humorous.... The Tcherepnin opera provided considerable visual amusement." This opera received the David Bispham medal in 1960.

Much of Tcherepnin's music is touched with Russian colors; but much of it has also been influenced by his attraction to the Orient. Always technically assured, his music exploits modern rhythmic and harmonic devices freely, so that even in his quasi-oriental music a twentieth-century identity is not lacking. An unusual technical feature of his music is the use of a nine-tone scale which he invented—adding two hexachords (the second being an inversion of the first)—and with which he is identified. This scale is particularly effective in voicing grotesque or satirical situations or anguish.

Hand in hand with the use of a nine-tone scale goes a contrapuntal technique which Tcherepnin has designated as "interpoint." Willi Reich explains this method as follows: "The composer's aim is to construct polyphonic form chiefly in broken, intersected lines, the thematic insertions being evoked and made clear simultaneously by breaks in part-writing."

The nine-tone scale, "interpoint" writing, and a Russian personality can all be found in Tcherepnin's fourth symphony, which Charles Münch commissioned for the Boston Symphony. Its world première took place in Boston on December 5, 1958. Cyrus Durgin described the symphony in the Boston *Daily Globe* as "a work of large stature, solid substance, much imagination in melody and harmony, and, above all, original. There is constant motion, and the music lives and breathes in every measure." The symphony was awarded the historically important Glinka Prize.

In May 1967 Tcherepnin visited his native land, touring the country in performances of his own compositions. This was his first return in half a century.

MAJOR WORKS

Ballets—Fresques d'Ajanta; Training; Der Fahrende Schüler mit dem Teufelsbannen; Trepak; La Légende de Rasin; Déjeuner sur l'Herbe; Chota Roustaveli; La Colline des Fantômes; Jardin Persan; Nuit Kurde; La Femme et Son Ombre; Aux Temps des Tartares.

Chamber Music—3 cello sonatas; 2 string quartets; Piano Quintet; Ode, for cello and piano; Elegy, for violin and piano; Le Violoncelle Bien Tempéré, twelve preludes for cello and piano (two with drum added); Suite for Cello Solo; Mouvement Perpétuel, for violin and piano; Sonatina, for kettledrum and piano; Sonatine Sportive, for bassoon and piano; Andante, for tuba and piano; Trio, for flutes; Marche, for three trumpets; Quartet, for flutes; Sonata da Chiesa, for viola da gamba and organ.

Choral Music—Vivre d'Amour, cantata; Pan Kéou; Le Jeu de la Nativité; Six Liturgical Songs, for mixed a capella chorus; Four Russian Folksongs, for mixed a capella chorus; Mass, for three equal a capella voices.

Operas—Ol–Ol; Die Hochzeit der Sobeide; The Farmer and the Fairy.

Orchestral Music—5 symphonies; 6 piano concertos; Rapsodie Georgienne, for cello and orchestra; Concertino, for violin, cello, and orchestra; Magna Mater; Russian Dances; Three Pieces, for chamber orchestra; Mystère, for cello and chamber orchestra; Concerto da Camera, for flute, violin, and chamber orchestra; Concertino, for violin, cello, piano, and strings; Divertimento; Suite Georgienne; Fantaisie, for piano and orchestra; Suite Japonaise; Evocation; Suite; Harmonica Concerto; Oraison Symphonique; Capriccio; Symphony-Prayer; Serenade, for string orchestra; Bagatelles, for piano and orchestra.

Piano Music—2 sonatas; Sonatine Romantique; Toccata; Préludes Nostalgiques; Autour des Montagnes Russes; Badinage; Le Monde en Vitrine; La Quatrième; Expressions; Suite, for harpsichord; arabesques, bagatelles, etudes, inventions.

ABOUT

Reich, W., Alexander Tscherepnin.

Randall Thompson
1899–

Randall Thompson was born in New York City on April 21, 1899, of New England stock. At Harvard he studied music with Spalding, Hill, and Davison. He was graduated with a bachelor of arts degree in 1920, and two years later received his master's degree, *summos honores*. During this period (1920–1921) he studied composition privately with Ernest Bloch in New York. In 1933 he received his doctorate in music at the School of Music of the University of Rochester.

In 1922 a fellowship enabled him to attend

the American Academy in Rome where he stayed three years. Two short works for orchestra were introduced in Rome at this time: the tone poem *Pierrot and Cothurnus*, on May 17, 1923; and the symphonic prelude *The Piper at the Gates of Dawn*, on May 27, 1924. Returning to the United States, Thompson contributed several songs and an instrumental number to the successful stage revue, *The Grand Street Follies of 1927*, which opened on Broadway on June 25, 1926. During the same year he also wrote incidental music for *The Straw Hat*, another Broadway show. This interest in American popular music carried over into his serious writing a year and a half later with *Jazz Poem*, for piano and orchestra, performed in Rochester, New York, on November 27, 1928, with the composer at the piano.

RANDALL THOMPSON

On February 26, 1927, Thompson married Margaret Quayle Whitney, by whom he has four children. In 1927–1928 he served as professor of music theory, organist, and choral director at Wellesley College, to which he returned for the academic year 1936–1937. In 1929 he delivered several lectures at Harvard. A Guggenheim Fellowship in 1929 gave him the opportunity to complete his first symphony, whose world première took place in Rochester, New York, on February 20, 1930. The fellowship was renewed in 1930.

For one season, 1931–1932, Thompson was the conductor of the Dessoff Choirs in New York. From 1937 to 1939 he was a member of the music faculty of the University of California in Berkeley; from 1939 to 1941 he served as director of the Curtis Institute of Music in Philadelphia; and for a five-year period, beginning with 1941, he was head of the School of Fine Arts at the University of Virginia. After two years as professor of music at Princeton, Thompson was appointed professor of music at Harvard in the fall of 1948 and served as chairman of the music department 1952–1957.

Thompson's first major success as a composer came with his second symphony, which he wrote in Gstaad, Switzerland, in the period between July 1930 and September 1931. The first performance of this work was given in Rochester, New York, on March 24, 1932, Howard Hanson conducting. Simple and direct in both vocabulary and emotion, occasionally drawing inspiration and material from Negro folk songs, and passing lightly and gracefully from romantic moods to those in a lighter vein, the symphony had an immediate appeal. "He has not hesitated at times to be obvious," reported Lawrence Gilman. "He has not strained, he has not constricted his fancy and his feeling; he has not been afraid to sound quite different from Schoenberg. His music has humor and warmth and pleasantness; many will find it agreeable and solacing." His symphony was extensively performed after that, not only in the United States but also in England, Italy, and Germany. Within a decade it had received over five hundred performances.

Some of Thompson's most important works were written for chorus. *The Peaceable Kingdom* was commissioned by the League of Composers and was introduced in New York on March 29, 1936. The text was taken from Isaiah; but the composer's strongest inspiration came from Edward Hicks' allegorical painting *The Peaceable Kingdom*, depicting William Penn making peace with the Indians and Daniel surrounded by lions.

Thompson achieved a tour de force with his *Alleluia*, for mixed chorus, in 1940. He wrote it on a commission from Serge Koussevitzky for the opening-day ceremonies of the first session of the Berkshire Music Center at Tanglewood and had three weeks in which to complete the assignment. Using for his text the single word *Alleluia*, Thompson produced a remarkably stirring piece of festival music that soon became a favorite in the choral repertory.

No less significant is *The Testament of Freedom*, composed to honor the two hundredth anniversary of the birth of Thomas Jefferson. With four passages from Jefferson's writings as a text, this four-movement work is a stirring patriotic paean which many critics considered one of the most eloquent expressions in music of our national spirit and traditions. The work was first heard on April 13, 1943, at the University of Virginia in a performance broadcast over the CBS network and transmitted by the Office of War Information overseas to the armed forces. Later it was performed by the Harvard Glee Club and also by the Boston Symphony under Koussevitzky. When, on April 14, 1945, Koussevitzky dedicated a program of the Boston Symphony to the memory of the recently deceased President Roosevelt, he included a performance of this Thompson choral work.

In 1941 Thompson received the Elizabeth Sprague Coolidge Award for distinguished contributions to music. One year later, on a commission from the Columbia Broadcasting System in conjunction with the League of Composers, Thompson wrote a radio opera, *Solomon and Balkis*, libretto based on a story by Kipling. The première took place on March 29, 1942; the performance was repeated over the radio the following fall. The first staged production had occurred in Cambridge, Massachusetts, on April 14 of the same year.

Thompson's third symphony was the result of a commission from the Alice M. Ditson Fund of Columbia University. He began to make sketches in 1944, but the symphony was not completed until 1949. It was first heard at the American Music Festival at Columbia University on May 15, 1949, Thor Johnson conducting. Noel Straus wrote in the New York *Times:* "Mr. Thompson's symphony had nobility, real depth of feeling, and each of its four movements had a definite message to impart. Tragic in its implications, this was music that was at once markedly sincere, spontaneous and moving."

Commissions were also responsible for many of Thompson's major later compositions. *The Last Words of David* (1949) was written at the request of Serge Koussevitzky for the Berkshire Music Center and heard at Tangle-

wood on August 12, 1949, following which it was featured in a documentary film about Tanglewood made available by the State Department for foreign distribution. The Koussevitzky Music Foundation commissioned the writing of *A Trip to Nahant*, an orchestral fantasy performed in Philadelphia on March 18, 1955; the University of California asked for the Requiem, one of Thompson's most ambitious choral works, introduced at the Berkeley Festival of Music on May 22, 1958; and Christ's Church in Cambridge contracted for still another choral work, the oratorio *The Nativity According to St. Luke*, world première, March 28, 1965.

In an essay on Randall Thompson in the *Musical Quarterly*, Elliott Forbes made the following evaluation: "The music of Randall Thompson is first of all American in spirit; the bulk of it has been written for American needs and has been inspired by the native artistic environment of this country. While the end is contemporary American, the means are made up of an assimilation and incorporation of values in music dating back to the sixteenth century. His music places him, then, to borrow Thompson's own terminology, among both the Nationalists and the Eclectics."

MAJOR WORKS

Chamber Music—String Quartet; The Wind in the Willows, for string quartet; Suite, for oboe, clarinet, and viola.

Choral Music—Five Odes of Horace; Pueri Hebraeorum; Rosemary; Americana; The Peaceable Kingdom; Tarantella; The Lark in the Morn; Alleluia; The Testament of Freedom; The Last Words of David; Ode to the Virginian Voyage; Requiem; The Passion According to St. Luke, oratorio.

Orchestral Music—3 symphonies; Pierrot and Cothurnus, tone poem; The Piper at the Gates of Dawn, symphonic prelude; A Trip to Nahant, fantasy; Jazz Poem, for piano and orchestra.

ABOUT

Chase, G., America's Music; Howard, J. T., Our Contemporary Composers.

Modern Music, May–June 1942; Musical Quarterly, January 1949.

Virgil Thomson
1896–

Virgil Garnett Thomson was born in Kansas City, Missouri, on November 25, 1896, of southern Confederate stock, one of whom was among the first settlers of Jamestown, Virginia. His father, who worked as a clerk in the post office, was of Scottish ancestry; his mother, of English-Welsh origin. Virgil grew up in Missouri with his sister Ruby, who was eleven years his senior. He took his first piano lessons when he was five and was soon also studying the organ and theory with local teachers. By the time he was twelve he was playing the organ at the services of the Calvary Baptist Church in Kansas City and giving piano recitals. He went to the local public schools and to the Kansas City Polytechnic Institute and Junior College, where he founded a magazine and also formed a literary society.

VIRGIL THOMSON

In 1917 he enlisted in the army; he was trained as a radio engineer and was commissioned a second lieutenant in the Military Aviation Corps. After the Armistice, Thomson completed his studies at the Junior College in Kansas City and then entered Harvard, where, along with regular academic classes, he attended composition and other music courses given by Davison and Hill. His career as a composer began during his college years, in July 1920, with the writing of *De Profundis*, for chorus, and a song, "Vernal Equinox," to a poem by Amy Lowell. During the summer of 1921 he was a member of the Harvard Glee Club that gave concerts in Europe. When the Glee Club set sail for home, Thomson remained behind in Paris where, for the next year, he

studied privately with Nadia Boulanger on a John Knowles Paine Traveling Fellowship.

He returned to Harvard in 1922, supporting himself during his final undergraduate year by holding a job at college as assistant instructor and playing the organ at the King's Chapel in Boston. In addition, he taught some courses and performed French music at the Harvard Music Club. In 1923 he was graduated with a bachelor of arts degree. For about a year he lived in New York, studying counterpoint with Rosario Scalero at the David Mannes School of Music and conducting with Chalmers Clifton. Several compositions for piano together with some choral works and songs and minor pieces for orchestra represented the sum of his creative achievements during this period—notable among them were *Two Sentimental Tangos*, for orchestra (1923), and the *Missa Brevis*, for male voices (1924).

For a while he taught at Harvard as assistant instructor, supplementing his income by writing articles on music for *Vanity Fair*. Then, having accumulated five hundred dollars, he decided he must devote himself exclusively to composition, and to accomplish that, he went to Paris in September 1925 to establish permanent residence. In February 1926 he completed his first chamber music work, a *Sonata da Chiesa*, for clarinet, trumpet, viola, horn, and trombone. This was a three-movement composition comprising a Chorale, a Tango, and a Fugue. More important was his first major work for orchestra, *Symphony on a Hymn Tune*, begun in 1926, but completed two years later. The basis of the four-movement work was a hymn tune in the pentatonic scale which became virtually the theme song of the Southern Baptist Convention: "How Firm a Foundation, Ye Saints of the Lord." The composer's intention was to evoke a picture of nineteenth century American farm life in the Midwest through simple, folk-style music. He realized his mission so successfully that Paul Rosenfeld likened the symphony to a Currier and Ives print. The symphony waited almost two decades for its première, being heard in New York on February 22, 1945, with the composer conducting the New York Philharmonic.

During his long residence in Paris, Thomson established firm friendships with Picasso, Gide,

Cocteau, Hemingway, Gertrude Stein, Scott Fitzgerald, and most of the leading French composers. Moreover, he became interested in the provocative, spicy, everyday manner of writing music once propagandized by Erik Satie and then promoted by The French Six. In this idiom and with the aim of creating "everyday music" Thomson set several of Gertrude Stein's poems: "Susie Asado" in April 1926, and in February 1927 "Preciosilla" and "Capital, Capitals." Then, in 1928, he wrote the music for an opera with a text Gertrude Stein wrote expressly for the purpose, but fashioned into a workable libretto by Maurice Grosser. The opera was *Four Saints in Three Acts.* In keeping with the obscure and undecipherable text and often unintelligible dialogue, the opera is actually not in three acts but in four and there are more than four saints in the cast. The birth of the opera is described in Gertrude Stein's *Autobiography of Alice B. Toklas:* "Virgil had asked Gertrude Stein to write an opera for him. Among the saints there were two saints whom she had always liked better than others, Saint Theresa of Avila and Ignatius Loyola, and she said she would write an opera about these two saints. She began this and worked very hard at it all spring and finally finished *Four Saints in Three Acts* and gave it to Virgil to put to music. He did. And it is a completely interesting opera, both as to words and music."

Four Saints in Three Acts was first performed by a cast of Negroes in Hartford, Connecticut, on February 8, 1934, sponsored by "the Friends and Enemies of Modern Music." Taken to New York and conducted by Alexander Smallens, the opera enjoyed a successful six-week engagement, beginning on February 21, 1934. It was also performed soon after that in Chicago. What perhaps surprised critics most was to find that, in spite of Stein's dada-like text, there was nothing avant-garde in Thomson's score, which was filled with engaging tunes and hymn-like melodies, pleasing harmonies, and a most winning wit. "It may be said," wrote Lawrence Gilman, "that it is deceptively simple, a little self-consciously candid and naïve, actually very wily and deft and slick, often subtly and wittily illusive, distinguished by an artful banality. This is a suave and charming score."

After the Broadway presentation, *Four Saints in Three Acts* was heard in a concert performance on a coast-to-coast radio broadcast and was recorded by RCA Victor. As a stage production, it was revived with an all-Negro cast in New York on April 16, 1952; at that time Cecil Smith wrote that, after eighteen years, the opera "remained a masterpiece—wayward and ambiguous, alternately profoundly serious and tongue-in-cheek, but worthy of respect and affection as a piece far superior to the mere temper of the time in which it was first produced." This production was transferred to Paris later in 1952 for the Masterpieces of the Twentieth Century festival.

Thomson's concert music in the 1930's included a *Stabat Mater,* for soprano and string quartet (1931); his second symphony (completed in 1931 but not performed until November 7, 1941, in Seattle); and his second string quartet (1932). In 1936 he wrote background music for a documentary motion picture produced by Pare Lorentz, *The Plow That Broke the Plains,* a discussion of America's waste of its natural resources. A six-movement suite adapted from the score, rich in the use of American folk materials, became Thomson's first successful work for orchestra. In 1937 he produced another distinguished score for a motion picture documentary, *The River,* once again a Pare Lorentz production.

Thomson's first ballet score was heard in 1938: *The Filling Station,* choreography by Lew Christensen and book by Lincoln Kirstein; it was first produced by the Ballet Caravan in Hartford, Connecticut, on January 6, 1938. This was a "first" not only for Thomson but also for American ballet—the first successful ballet on an American theme, the first created and performed exclusively by Americans. The setting was an American filling station; the action concerned the attempt "to discover an American hero," as George Balanchine has explained, "a hero equivalent to the heroes of classical European ballets." He turned out to be Mac, a filling-station attendant, who foils an attempted holdup and helps to apprehend the criminal. When the ballet was successfully revived in New York in 1953, Walter Terry had this to say of the Thomson music: "Virgil Thomson's score, delightful to the ear and an invitation to dance, is based upon the popular rhythms (invigorated by some powerful folk memories) of the day."

587

While living in Paris in the 1930's, Thomson was a correspondent for *Modern Music*, the journal of the League of Composers in New York. He also wrote lively and provocative articles on music for other magazines and newspapers, and a book, *The State of Music* (1939, reissued in 1962). These activities as a writer on musical subjects proved a valuable apprenticeship. Soon after the outbreak of World War II, Thomson left his Paris home to reestablish himself permanently in New York. During his long stay in Paris he had made frequent visits to the United States. In the fall of 1940, he succeeded Lawrence Gilman as music critic of the New York *Herald Tribune*. Thomson soon became one of the most widely discussed and most controversial writers on music in America, a critic who continually proved himself to be independent, fearless, and forceful. He later collected the best of his criticism into three books: *The Musical Scene* (1945), *The Art of Judging Music* (1948), and *Music Right and Left* (1951). In 1954 he retired from the *Herald Tribune* to devote himself more intensively to composition and conducting.

Thomson composed a second opera to a text by Gertrude Stein, commissioned to do so by the Alice M. Ditson Fund of Columbia University. This opera, *The Mother of Us All*, was produced at Columbia University on May 7, 1947. The Steinesque libretto, based on the career of Susan B. Anthony and her crusade for woman suffrage, once again suited Thomson and inspired him to create a melodious score rich with American flavors. According to Olin Downes, Thomson here produced a work "of more substance and firmer grip than the more stylistic and symbolic *Four Saints*. . . . The score has tunes closely related to America's past and even present. One is reminded of old waltzes and sentimental songs, and there is a hymn tune, excellently conceived in the style of old American hymns . . . which constitutes a really moving commentary on the scene of a wedding and, without sentimentalizing, brings home a certain pathos, and not only pathos of the past. . . . In the sum of it, the textual setting is very adroit, entertaining and expressive."

One month following the première, the opera received a special citation from the New York Music Critics Circle, since it was ineligible for a regular award because Thomson was a member of the Circle. In 1964 the opera was revived in New York by the American Opera Company. A four-movement symphonic suite derived from the opera score was introduced by the Knoxville Symphony on January 17, 1950.

In 1948 Thomson wrote music for *Louisiana Story*, a documentary film produced by Robert Flaherty. It described an oil development in Louisiana and the effect it had on a French family, all seen through the eyes of a fourteen-year-old child. Drawing his musical material from Cajun dances of the Acadian region (which he had found in Louisiana in *French Folk Songs*, edited by Irene Therese Whitefield), Thomson here created one of his best and most successful orchestral scores. The music of *Louisiana Story* became the first motion picture score ever to win the Pulitzer Prize for music. A symphonic suite derived from the score (introduced in Philadelphia on November 26, 1948) has become Thomson's most frequently played symphonic work. This suite quotes only a single folk tune; but a second suite, entitled *Acadian Songs and Dances*, makes more copious use of folk material.

An important later choral work reveals still another facet of Thomson's many-sided creative talent. The *Missa Pro Defunctis* is deeply devotional music, even though the composer still finds some of his germinal ideas in such popular idioms as the tango, waltz, and boogie-woogie. "Within the religious framework," explains John Gruen, "these Thomsonian devices have been placed on the side of the angels as it were, and have been given reverential status. . . . The demands of the Requiem text are monumental in scale. They are met with the kind of mastery that only a composer who has reached the pinnacle of his career is able to produce." The Requiem was heard first at the Annual Spring Festival of the Arts at State University College (which had commissioned it) in Potsdam, New York, on May 14, 1960.

Commissioned by the New York Philharmonic to produce a work honoring its one hundred twenty-fifth anniversary, Thomson wrote *Shipwreck and Love Scene*, for tenor and orchestra (text derived from Byron's *Don Juan*). Leopold Stokowski led the première in New York on November 1, 1968. Two other significant symphonic works of the 1960's are

The Feast of Love, for baritone and orchestra (based on anonymous Latin poetry of the second and fourth centuries A.D. translated into English by the composer), heard first in Washington, D.C., at the Coolidge Festival on November 1, 1964, and *Fantasy*, for orchestra, the première of which took place in Kansas City on May 28, 1966.

Thomson was one of the founding fathers of the New York Music Critics Circle in 1941 (disbanded in 1965). In 1947 he was made an Officer of the French Legion of Honor. In 1948 he was elected to membership in the National Institute of Arts and Letters, and in 1959 to the American Academy of Arts and Letters. In 1966 the National Institute of Arts and Letters presented him with its highest award, the Gold Medal, in recognition of his service to music. He received honorary degrees from Syracuse University in 1949 and Rutgers in 1956.

Since settling in New York, Thomson has lived at the Hotel Chelsea described by Kathleen Hoover as "the last of Manhattan's plush inns of the hansom cab era. . . . In these surroundings, and behind the telephonic Maginot Line of the Chelsea's answering service, he works in splendid isolation." Thomson is a bachelor. His favorite diversion is cooking, but most of the meals at the Thomson household are prepared by a professional cook. What he enjoys most, away from music, is to entertain his wide circle of friends as dinner guests and to participate with them in lively conversations. He regularly holds evenings of chamber music at his home which Kathleen Hoover says "have a prewar Viennese authenticity."

In 1963 Thomson was visiting professor of music at the University of Buffalo. He was named Andrew Mellon Professor of Music at the Carnegie Institute of Technology in September 1966. In 1968 he received the Creative Arts Award Medal from Brandeis University. He has written a volume of memoirs entitled *Virgil Thomson*, published in the fall of 1966.

MAJOR WORKS

Ballet—Filling Station.

Chamber Music—2 string quartets; Sonata da Chiesa, for clarinet, trumpet, violin, horn, and trombone; Five Portraits, for four clarinets; Violin Sonata; Four Portraits, for violin and piano; Serenade, for flute and violin; Sonata for Solo Flute; At the Beach, for trumpet and piano.

Choral Music—Missa Brevis No. 1 and No. 2; Scenes from the Holy Infancy; Hymns from the Old South; Kyrie; Song for the Stable; Missa Pro Defunctis; Crossing Brooklyn Ferry; Dance in Praise.

Operas—Four Saints in Three Acts; The Mother of Us All; Lord Byron.

Orchestral Music—2 symphonies; 2 suites; The Plow That Broke the Plains, suite; The River, suite; Portraits; The Mayor La Guardia Waltzes; Canons for Dorothy Thompson; The Seine at Night; Louisiana Story, suite; Acadian Songs and Dances (from Louisiana Story); Wheatfield at Noon; Cello Concerto; Five Songs after William Blake, for voice and orchestra; Sea Piece with Birds; Fugues and Cantilenas, suite; Concerto, for flute, strings, and percussion; A Solemn Music; Concertino for Harp and Strings; Feast of Love, cantata for baritone and chamber orchestra; A Joyful Fugue; The Feast of Love, for baritone and orchestra; Fantasy; Shipwreck and Love Scene, for tenor and orchestra.

Piano Music—4 sonatas; 2 sets of etudes; over 40 portraits; etudes, inventions.

Vocal Music—Stabat Mater, for soprano and string quartet; Chamber Music, for soprano and piano; La Belle en Dormant, for soprano and piano; Four Songs to Poems by Thomas Campion; Mostly About Love; Collected Poems (Koch); Mass, for solo voice, or voice and piano.

ABOUT

Copland, A., Our New Music; Hoover, K. and Cage, J., Virgil Thomson: His Life and Music; Thomson, V., Virgil Thomson.

Musical Quarterly, April 1949.

Sir Michael Tippett
1905–

Sir Michael Kemp Tippett was born in London on January 2, 1905, of Cornish descent. He spent his first fifteen years in a small village in Suffolk where he attended grammar school and took weekly piano lessons. This was, he confesses, a lonely and withdrawn existence which encouraged in him a good deal of introspection and soul-searching. Growing up in the post World-War I period, he was a moody boy who early became obsessed with social problems and disenchanted with the world around him.

When he was eighteen Tippett went to London to study music intensively. At the Royal College of Music he studied composition with Charles Wood and R. O. Morris, and conducting with Sir Malcolm Sargent and Sir Adrian Boult. When he was twenty-nine he completed his first symphony, in B-flat major, which he later discarded. This was followed by his first string quartet (1935); his first work for chorus, *A Song of Liberty*, words by William Blake (1937); and an ambitious composition for the piano, *Fantasy Sonata* (1938). In these, as in his discarded symphony, romanticism was stressed strongly; the symphony further revealed the influence of Sibelius. With the exception of the string quartet, which he revised in 1943, all of Tippett's compositions written before World War II are regarded by him as efforts of his apprenticeship, a period which he prefers not to be represented on concert programs any longer. His first mature work combined his strong bent for romantic expression with skill in contrapuntal writing, evident in his *Double Concerto*, for string orchestra (1939), introduced in London in April 1940, the composer conducting.

SIR MICHAEL TIPPETT

In 1940 Tippett was appointed music director of Morley College in London, a post filled for many years by Gustav Holst, and he remained there until 1951. During World War II he became a conscientious objector, preferring prison to abandoning his pacifist ideals. His strong humanitarian feelings and his lifelong sympathy for a suffering mankind found voice in the oratorio *A Child of Our Time* (1942), performed in London on March 19, 1944, Walter Goehr conducting. The theme of the oratorio (text by the composer) was the shooting of a Nazi diplomat in Paris by a persecuted Jewish youth in November 1939. But as a critic for the London *Times* pointed out, "This single incident in the long story of man's inhumanity to man is treated symbolically as representing the ascendancy of evil which mankind hopes to be temporary." To heighten the religious mood of the music—and to call attention to another persecuted people—Tippett interpolated into his score five Negro spirituals; but the writing is also a skillful mixture of jazz, madrigals, polyphony, and complex rhythmic structures.

The deeply personal note Tippett had sounded in so many pages of *A Child of Our Time* is stressed even more strongly in *Boyhood's End* (1943). This cantata to a text by W. H. Auden, which Peter Pears and Benjamin Britten introduced in London in 1943, had a highly successful revival at the festival of the International Society of Contemporary Music in London in 1962. Melody and youthful passion are here predominant, but Tippett's strong feeling for rhythm is not underplayed.

In Tippett's first mature symphony, introduced by the Liverpool Philharmonic under Sir Malcolm Sargent on November 10, 1945, rhythmic and contrapuntal processes are ascendant over lyrical ones. When first heard, the symphony was a failure. So was Tippett's first opera, *The Midsummer Marriage*, a three-act comedy with libretto by the composer, completed in 1952 and produced at Covent Garden on January 27, 1955. The failure was due mainly to its libretto which most critics found to be obscure, confusing, too symbolic. But one or two reviewers found much to praise in Tippett's music, which was lyrical, skillful in its choral and orchestral writing, and powerful. For example, Cecil Smith described the libretto as "a snarl of symbolism and half intelligible mysticism," but maintained that the music revealed Tippett as "a composer of first stature." He added: "His melodic fund is unfailing; his harmonic sense is as organic as Hindemith's and as subtle as Fauré's; his instrumentation is deft, warm and varied, and only rarely overburdened the singers. The work as a whole grows cumulatively and possesses the quality of apparent inevitability." Tippett revised the opera extensively and the première of the new version (at Covent Garden in the spring of 1968) drew accolades from the critics. Thomas Heinitz regarded it as "not merely Tippett's masterpiece but one of the richest and most beautiful operatic scores which this century has produced."

For his second opera, which the Koussevitzky Music Foundation commissioned, Tippett went to the *Iliad* to fashion his own libretto, retelling the story of the Trojan War, of Helen's seduction by Paris, and of Paris's ultimate tragic destiny. This opera, called *King Priam*, was produced at Coventry Cathedral in England on May 29, 1962; performances at Covent Garden followed in June. The work, before its revision, appeared to reverse the strength and weakness of Tippett's first effort at opera: its libretto was the strong suit, the music found wanting. Peter Heyworth reported: "The trouble is that his technical resources do not always measure up to the demands of his powerful imagination. He has always responded strongly to words, and the declamatory vocal writing . . . has for the most part great strength of purpose. But the orchestral writing is less consistently convincing. As the vocal idiom grows more declamatory, so inevitably does the ear look to the orchestra for musicality, continuity, and shape." Heyworth added that nevertheless when Tippett managed "to give his ideas a long-term substance, the results are often magnificent."

One of those magnificent pages can be found in the trio of Paris, Priam, and Hector which comes towards the end of the second act. "As it rises to its climax of false triumph," notes Heyworth, "it is rudely shattered by the blood-curdling war cry of the avenging Achilles. The hour of doom has struck and the act comes to a close with one of the opera's most terrifying curtains. This is the fruit of genius, and it measures the potency of Tippett's inspiration when he has found adequate means of expressing it."

The more significant and more successful of Tippett's later concert works include the following: the piano concerto written in 1955 on a commission from the City of Birmingham Orchestra in conjunction with the John Feeney Charitable Trust, first performance by Louis Kentner and the City of Birmingham Orchestra in October 1956; the second symphony, commissioned by BBC, first performance in London on February 5, 1958, Sir Adrian Boult conducting; the one-movement second piano sonata, introduced by Margaret Kitchin at the Edinburgh Festival in 1962; the *Concerto for Orchestra*, commissioned by the Edinburgh Festival and heard there on August 26, 1963;

and *The Vision of Saint Augustine*, a major choral work with text based on two mystical experiences related by St. Augustine in his *Confessions*, world première in London on January 19, 1966. These last works, *The Vision of Saint Augustine* particularly, find the composer supplementing his former interest in lyricism, rhythm, and counterpoint with a new concern for resonance and sonority, a concern which achieves remarkable richness and variety of substance and texture through the use of an extended percussion section.

During the summer of 1965 Tippett paid his first visit to the United States. He was invited by the Music Festival at Aspen, Colorado, where his early oratorio, *A Child of Our Time*, was performed. He returned to the United States for the 1967–1968 season, to serve as guest conductor of the St. Louis Symphony. Tall, thin, almost dour in appearance, looking more like a Breton sailor than a composer, Tippett appeared much younger than his almost sixty years. His sixtieth birthday was celebrated in England with performances of major works. In June 1966 he was knighted by the Queen.

MAJOR WORKS

Chamber Music—3 string quartets; Sonata for Four Horns.

Choral Music—A Song of Liberty; A Child of Our Time, oratorio; Plebs Angelica; The Weeping Babe; The Source, motet; The Windhover, motet; Crown of the Year, cantata; The Vision of Saint Augustine; Lullaby; Magnificat and Nunc Dimittis.

Operas—The Midsummer Marriage; King Priam.

Orchestral Music—2 symphonies; Concerto, for double orchestra; Fantasy on a Theme by Handel, for piano and orchestra; Suite in D major; Little Music, for strings; Fantasia Concertante on a Theme by Corelli, for strings; Divertimento on Bellinger's Round, for chamber orchestra; Piano Concerto; Praeludium, for brass, bells, and percussion; Concerto for Orchestra; Fantasia Concertante.

Piano Music—2 sonatas.

Vocal Music—The Heart's Assurance, for high voice and piano.

ABOUT

Kemp, I. (ed.), Michael Tippett: A Symposium on His 60th Birthday.

Musical Quarterly, October 1964.

Ernst Toch
1887–1964

Ernst Toch was born in Vienna on December 7, 1887, to a middle-class family, none of whose members were particularly musical. As a child, Toch learned to read music by watching his friends play the piano and correlating the sounds with the printed notations. Toch said he revealed an enormous interest in timbres of all kinds: "I can remember as a child listening to the stonecutter while he was making cobblestones and taking great pleasure from different qualities which the ear perceived each time the hammer struck a fresh blow. I can also remember playing tunes for hours on the wooden boards of graduated lengths which formed the gate to our country garden in Vienna."

ERNST TOCH

He began to compose when he was six, ruling out his own manuscript paper for the purpose. Later he acquired some technical knowledge of composition by copying out the music of Bach, Mozart, and Beethoven. He continued this process of self-instruction in music while in elementary and high school. In spite of his lack of formal training he was able to complete a number of chamber music works including his first string quartet, in A minor (1905), which the renowned Arnold Rosé Quartet introduced in Vienna.

Toch: tōK

His father insisted that he be trained for some profession, so after graduation from high school in 1906, Toch entered the Vienna University as a medical student. During his three years there he continued to devote leisure hours to music study and to composition. In 1909, on the recommendation of Max Reger, he was awarded the Mozart Prize in composition, providing for a year of study at Hoch's Conservatory in Frankfurt-am-Main. The prize permanently changed Toch's life, impelling him to abandon medicine for music. In Frankfurt, Toch studied the piano with Willy Rehberg. In 1910 he received the Mendelssohn Prize, and soon after that the Austrian State Prize for composition—the latter four times consecutively, for various orchestral and chamber music works including an orchestral scherzo and his third string quartet, in D-flat major, published in Leipzig in 1909 and 1911 respectively.

In 1913 Toch was appointed teacher of theory at the Hochschule für Musik in Mannheim. During World War I, he served in the Austrian army. He married Alice Babette Zwack on July 23, 1916. With the cessation of hostilities, Toch returned to Mannheim to resume his pedagogical activities and his work as composer. He also resumed and concluded his music study, receiving a doctorate in music at the University of Heidelberg in 1921. His thesis, *Melodielehre*, was published in Germany in 1923, after which it was translated into Russian and Spanish.

Until about 1918, Toch's music was influenced most strongly by Brahms and revealed a strong Romantic bent. An important step towards a more individual style was taken with his String Quartet in C major (1919) in which a greater freedom was allowed for the movement of the melodic line and a stronger and more independent manner of harmonic and rhythmic writing was evidenced. But his former Romantic tendencies, with emphasis on emotion over intellect, were by no means deserted. When his style finally became established, he wrote a number of works that brought him public and critical recognition for the first time. At the German Tonkünstlerfest in Kiel on June 17, 1925, Toch's Concerto for Cello and Orchestra, performed by Emanuel Feuermann, was singled out by Hugo Leichtentritt as "the most remarkable work heard at the festival." A piano concerto was first performed in Düsseldorf on October 8, 1926, proving so successful that it was repeated in Berlin, featured at the festival of the International Society for Contemporary Music at Frankfurt in 1927, and given at a Koussevitzky Concert in Paris in 1928. A delightful comic opera, *Die Prinzessin auf der Erbse* (*The Princess and the Pea*), based on the familiar fairy tale, was acclaimed at the Festival of Modern Music at Baden-Baden on July 17, 1927, and heard in New York a decade later.

By the time Toch settled in Berlin in 1929 he was acknowledged one of Germany's leading composers. In the spring of 1932 he paid his first visit to the United States, touring the country in performances of his chamber music and piano music. On March 25, he appeared as soloist with the Boston Symphony in a performance of his piano concerto and the *Bunte Suite*, for orchestra. At that time an unidentified critic for the New York *Times* described the concerto as "one of the most mettlesome and arresting scores of the modern German school."

The political upheaval in Germany which brought Hitler to power sent Toch permanently out of that country. He arrived in London in 1933, and in the fall of 1934 he came to the United States where, for a while, he taught composition at the New School for Social Research. He settled in California in 1936 and from 1940 on lived in Santa Monica, where he received his American citizenship.

Soon after his arrival in the United States, Toch completed a number of orchestral compositions which solidified his fame in America. One of these was *Big Ben*, a set of orchestral variations on the Westminster Chimes. Though the idea for the music had come to Toch in London, he did not write it down until after reaching New York. The framework of the piece is the melody of the clock, which is developed into a strongly rhythmic main theme. This, in turn, becomes the basis of a series of intriguing and ingenious variations. Introduced in Cambridge, Massachusetts, on December 20, 1934, by the Boston Symphony under Koussevitzky, *Big Ben* enjoyed immediate success and was soon afterwards performed by other major American orchestras.

The brilliant comedy overture *Pinocchio*, subtitled *A Merry Overture*, also gained wide circulation. Toch was inspired to write this sprightly music in 1936 after coming upon an illustrated copy of Collodi's *Pinocchio*. The overture was performed by the Los Angeles Philharmonic under Otto Klemperer on December 10, 1936.

In 1938 Toch completed one of his most important chamber music works, the Quintet for Piano and Strings which had been commissioned by Elizabeth Sprague Coolidge. The first performance was given by the Roth Quartet, with Toch at the piano, in Pittsfield, Massachusetts, on September 23, 1938. Soon afterwards it was recorded for Columbia. The composer provided for each of the four movements a descriptive word suggesting its mood: "Lyrical," "Whimsical," "Contemplative," and "Dramatic." Nicolas Slonimsky has said of this music that it "displays his best qualities of rhythmic drive, romantic and elegiac melody, lucidity of contrapuntal technique, economy and richness of harmony and—last, not least—his practical knowledge of instrumental writing."

In 1940 Toch joined the faculty of the University of California in Los Angeles as professor of composition. For more than a decade he combined teaching with the writing of scores for many motion pictures.

In the early 1950's Toch returned to Europe, making his home mainly in Switzerland, where he wrote his first and second symphonies. Both were introduced in Vienna, the first on December 20, 1950, and the second on January 11, 1952. During these years in Europe he traveled extensively, lecturing and participating in performances of his works. He made a number of return visits to the United States to assume teaching or lecturing assignments at various universities. In 1954 he was visiting composer at the Berkshire Music Center at Tanglewood. In 1957 the government of the West German Republic presented him with the Grand Cross of the Order for Merit.

In 1956 Toch received the Pulitzer Prize in music for his third symphony, which the Pittsburgh Symphony had introduced under William Steinberg's direction on December 2, 1955. Suggested by a line from Goethe's *The Sorrows of Werther* ("Indeed I am but a wanderer, a pilgrim on earth—what else are you?"), the symphony is divided into two sections. The first is lyrical; the second, dramatic. Unusual effects are achieved through the interpolation of instruments not generally encountered in symphonic music, such as a Hammond organ, a pipe organ, a glass harmonica, and tuned glass bells. In addition, other novel sounds were produced offstage by a tank of carbon dioxide which produced hissing noises through a valve, and a wooden box in which croquet balls produced unique noises after being set into motion by a rotating crank.

In reviewing a recording of this symphony (released by Capitol), a reviewer for *Musical America* said: "Externally, the symphony is marked by brilliant orchestra color in a wide spectrum, an equally wide scope of dynamic expression, and frequent recourse to exotic effects. . . . It must not be assumed from this that the symphony is merely a trick piece, depending upon instrumental novelties for its effect. The odd instruments are used sparingly. The music as a whole has a nostalgically oriental quality. It is tonal and substantially melodic with a good deal of emotional expressiveness."

In 1957 Toch was elected a member of the National Institute of Arts and Letters. One year later he reestablished his home at Santa Monica where he stayed for the rest of his life. His seventy-fifth birthday in 1962 was celebrated throughout the music world with commemorative concerts and recordings of representative works by various companies. On December 16, Toch was a guest of honor at a birthday luncheon tendered him by the American Society of Composers, Authors and Publishers (ASCAP). In 1963 the Austrian government presented him with its Cross of Honor for Science and Art.

Toch's fifth symphony, completed in 1963, received its world première on March 13, 1964, with Erich Leinsdorf conducting the Boston Symphony. This composition was noteworthy for the prominence it gave to four solo violins—in one place in the score the number was expanded to six. Several important works were completed in Toch's last year, including *Symphony for Strings; Three Pantomimes*, for orchestra; a Quartet, for oboe, clarinet, bassoon, and viola; and music for a puppet show entitled *Enamored Harlequin*.

Ernst Toch died in a hospital in Los Angeles October 1, 1964, following abdominal surgery.

Toch always believed that the most significant single element in music is form: "There must be form—the outer shape, dictated by a work's inner organic life. That form will present, in some aspect, a struggle between different concepts. There must be a curve as inevitable as the trajectory of a shell."

"There can be no doubt," comments Nikolai Lopatnikoff, "that perfect form and finish are two of the outstanding qualities of Toch's art. Yet his expert craftsmanship and facile mastery of all technical problems should not lead us to underevaluate the inner content of his work and the deep ethical tenor of his language."

Toch was the author of *The Shaping Forces of Music* (1948), which was reissued in a paperback edition on his seventy-fifth birthday.

MAJOR WORKS

Chamber Music—13 string quartets; Duos, for two violins; Serenade, for three violins; Spitzweg Serenade, for two violins and viola; Dance Suite, for flute, clarinet, violin, viola, double bass, and tympani; Two Divertimenti, for string duo; Violin Sonata; Cello Sonata; String Trio; Piano Quintet; Five Pieces for Wind Instruments and Percussion; Sonatinetta, for flute, clarinet, and bassoon; Three Improvisations, for violin, viola, and cello; Quartet, for oboe, clarinet, bassoon, and viola.

Choral Music—Das Wasser, cantata; Valse, for speaking chorus; Geographical Fugue, for speaking chorus; Der Tierkreis; Cantata of the Bitter Herbs; The Inner Circle, six choruses; Phantoms; Walt Whitman.

Operas—Die Prinzessin auf der Erbse (The Princess and the Pea); Egon und Emilie; Der Fächer; The Tale Is Told, one-act opera.

Orchestral Music—6 symphonies; 2 piano concertos; Scherzo; Five Pieces, for chamber orchestra; Cello Concerto; Divertimento, for wind orchestra; Comedy for Orchestra; Bunte Suite; Little Theatre Suite; Music for Orchestra and Baritone; Big Ben, variations; Pinocchio, overture; The Idle Stroller; Hyperion, dramatic legend; Dedication, for string orchestra (also for string quartet); Notturno; Circus Overture; Peter Pan, a fairy tale; Short Story; Intermezzo; Epilogue; Capriccio; Three Pantomimes.

Piano Music—Reminiscences; Burlesken; Die Jongleur; Klavierstücke; 5 Capriccietti; Tanz und Spielstücke; Sonata; Kleinstadtbilder; Etuden; Profiles; Ideas; Diversions; Sonatinetta; Three Little Dances; Reflections; Sonata for Piano, Four Hands.

Vocal Music—Die Chinesische Flöte; Neun Lieder; Poems to Martha; There Is a Season for Everything; Vanity of Vanities.

ABOUT

Musical Quarterly, October 1938.

Vincenzo Tommasini
1878–1950

Vincenzo Tommasini was born on September 17, 1878, in Rome. Since his father, a well-known historian, had respect for a well-rounded education, Vincenzo had to combine the study of music (for which he showed a marked aptitude from early childhood) with academic training. He attended the Santa Cecilia Academy where he studied composition with Falchi and violin with Pinelli. His academic education was completed at the University of Rome, where he specialized in philology and Greek literature. While attending the University, he wrote scholarly articles for philological journals and an introduction for a new edition of Xenophon's *De Re Equestri*.

VINCENZO TOMMASINI

In 1902 Tommasini left Italy for a long, extended trip. He spent a year in Berlin studying with Max Bruch and then visited Paris, London, and New York. During this period of travel he produced his first compositions. An orchestral overture to Calderón's *La Vida Es Sueño* was written in 1904. On April 8, 1906, his first opera, *Medea*, was produced in Trieste. These and other early compositions were both conventional and derivative; they failed to make much of an impression.

A new creative point of view, and a new

Tommasini: tōm mä zē′ nē

direction, were evident in the String Quartet in F major (1909). Here imitation gave way to a personal style that combined a strong romantic personality with an equally robust modern spirit. Guido M. Gatti said of this composition: "The themes of the first movement are really beautiful. . . . They always retain their drive; their emotion is always alive and vivid." *Poema Erotico*, for orchestra, and a one-act opera, *Uguale Fortuna*, followed immediately. The opera won first prize in a national competition sponsored by the city of Rome in 1913; it was successfully produced at the Teatro Costanzi in Rome the same year. On November 16, 1916, Toscanini conducted in Rome the first performance of one of Tommasini's major works for orchestra, *Chiari di Luna*. This sensitive tone picture rich with poetic imagery placed its composer in the forefront of those younger Italians who concerned themselves with the writing of symphonic music.

Tommasini achieved international renown with the ballet *Le Donne di Buon Umore* (*The Good-Humored Ladies*). With choreography by Léonide Massine, it was produced by the Ballet Russe in Rome on April 12, 1917. The scenario was based on Goldoni's comedy of the same name. For his music, Tommasini adapted several of Domenico Scarlatti's sonatas for the harpsichord which suited the time, the setting, and the plot frivolities of the scenario admirably. The ballet achieved a major success throughout Europe; so did the music which Tommasini adapted into a five-movement symphonic suite.

In the 1920's Tommasini made other significant additions to the Italian symphonic repertory: *Paesaggi Toscani* (*Tuscan Landscapes*), a rhapsody based on Tuscan folk melodies, introduced in Rome in December 1923; *Prelude, Fanfare and Fugue*, performed in Rome in 1927 with Victor de Sabata conducting; and the orchestral variations *Il Carnevale di Venezia* (*Carnival of Venice*), written in the style of Paganini, which had its world première in New York on October 10, 1929, Arturo Toscanini conducting the New York Philharmonic.

Alfredo Casella emphasized Tommasini's importance in Italian music by saying that his works summed up "the whole of the movement which has given to Italy a characteristic school of instrumental music. Like his contemporaries, Respighi, Pizzetti, Malipiero . . . he had to wage war against the persistent and exclusive devotion of the Italians to operatic music, which, having accomplished the destruction of the native instrumental tradition, violently opposed every attempt to revive a nonoperatic style. . . . In this movement, Tommasini played a considerable part.

"His first compositions were based on classic examples. He was next influenced to some extent by French Impressionists, but eventually freed himself from their sway, and his latest works are typically Italian in style and character. The nationalism is perceptible even in the earlier ones, and is especially manifested in certain features common to all modern Italian music, chief of which are (1) a scheme of construction so absolutely one with the fundamental idea as to appear its logical and inevitable development; (2) a harmony which arises from the free movement of the parts; (3) musical ideas which tend to be contained within a melodic line. These three characteristics are almost invariably found in Tommasini's compositions."

In analyzing the style of Tommasini's most important works, M. Zanotti-Bianco finds that they are "dreamy, melancholy, restrained in emotion, graceful, light, and ironical. In the combination of these qualities, lies his personality. He is not an innovator, but he remains in the current of new achievements. He constructs his music with sureness and with technical knowledge that is free from pedantry, and his art is essentially Italian."

Tommasini had many and varied interests ranging from horses to classical literature. He produced some skillfully wrought verses in Greek. Of his method of writing music he said: "I am in the habit of reworking each thing I compose many times. Sometimes I will put aside a work for several months before beginning to work upon it anew. I find that I can achieve the most felicitous expression only through constant revision."

Tommasini died in Rome, December 23, 1950.

MAJOR WORKS

Ballets—Le Donne di Buon Umore (The Good-Humored Ladies); Le Diable s'Amuse; Tiepolesco.

Chamber Music—3 string quartets; Violin Sonata; Harp Sonata; Due Macchiette, for cello and piano.

Operas—Medea; Uguale Fortuna, one-act opera.

Orchestral Music—La Vita è un Sogno; Poema Erotico; Inno Alla Beltà; Chiari di Luna; Il Beato Regno; Paesaggi Toscani (Tuscan Landscapes); Nápule, fantasy; Violin Concerto; Quattro Pezzi; Rondo Scherzoso; Concerto for String Quartet; La Tempesta, symphonic study; Concerto for Orchestra, with cello obbligato; Duo Concertante, for piano and orchestra.

ABOUT

Chesterian (London), February 1923; Musical Times (London), November 1921; Rivista Musicale Italiana (Rome), October–December 1951.

Joaquín Turina
1882–1949

Joaquín Turina was born in Seville, Spain, on December 9, 1882. He studied theory in his native city with Evaristo García Torres, the organist and choirmaster of the Cathedral, and piano with Enrique Rodríguez, before entering the Madrid Conservatory where he specialized in piano with José Tragó. In 1905 Turina went to Paris and enrolled at the Schola Cantorum where he was a pupil of Moszkowski in piano and Vincent d'Indy in composition. The latter exerted a particularly strong influence upon his musical development.

Turina remained at the Schola Cantorum until 1914. His close association with leading French composers led him to imitate their creative mannerisms. For a while he was addicted to the Franckist school of which d'Indy was a major spokesman; he adhered to the basic creative methods of César Franck and his followers in his early chamber music compositions, which included a violin sonata and several quartets. The G minor Piano Quintet, Turina's first published work, was heard in Paris in 1907.

The drift away from French influences came about through his friendship with such Spanish nationalist composers as Albéniz and Manuel de Falla, both of whom were in Paris at this time. After the première of Turina's G minor Piano Quintet, Albéniz and Falla took Turina to a café on the Rue Royale where a passionate discussion persuaded him to join the Spanish nationalist movement in music. "I realized," the composer later said in recalling this incident, "that music should be an art, and not a

Turina: tōō rē′ nä

diversion for the frivolity of women and the dissipation of men. We were three Spaniards gathered together in that corner of Paris and it was our duty to fight bravely for the national music of our country."

In becoming a nationalist, Turina began to combine Spanish folk idioms and materials with the sensitivity and refinement, and at times mysticism, of French music to which he had formerly been so partial. His first successful creation in a Spanish national style was *La Procesión del Rocío*, a musical description of a religious procession in Seville. Completed in 1912, the work had its world première in Madrid on March 30, 1913. Likened by Debussy to a luminous fresco, *La Procesión* was responsible for placing Turina solidly in the camp of the Spanish nationalist composers. To this day it is one of his most distinguished and frequently heard works.

In 1913 Turina returned to Spain, settling in Madrid. From then on, until his death, he was a major force in the musical life of his country. He played the piano in an important chamber music ensemble, the Quinteto de Madrid. He served as professor at the Madrid Conservatory. He led performances of the Ballet Russe in Spain. He wrote music criticisms for *El Debate*. He was a member of the Spanish Academy of Arts.

But his greatest importance lay in his own compositions. His place with the foremost Spanish nationalists was never seriously disputed, particularly after the world première of his opera *Margot* in Madrid on October 10, 1914. He continued to produce numerous works which are numbered among the richest achievements of the Spanish nationalist school. He was prolific, but from the huge mass of his production a number of compositions stand out today in bold relief.

One of these is *Mujeres Españolas*, for piano, the first set of which was completed in 1917, a second one following fifteen years later. This is a series of tonal portraits of three women in music that is authentically Andalusian in melodic and rhythmic identity. One of the women has a classic personality; another is sentimental; a third is a coquette. In 1920 Turina completed *Danzas Fantásticas*, originally for the piano, but later scored for orchestra. These dances are all based on the pulsating throb and beat of Andalusian dance rhythms.

During the same year, 1920, he won first prize in a competition held by the San Sebastian Casino for a picture of life in Seville. Turina's winning work was the *Sinfonía Sevillana*, for orchestra, the world première of which took place in San Sebastian on September 11, 1920.

JOAQUÍN TURINA

Turina's most celebrated chamber music work is *La Oración del Torero*, for string quartet (1925). This music is striking for contrast of mood and color in the description of a bullfighter's prayer. A distinguished work for the piano followed in 1930, the first set of *Danzas Gitanas*, a series of sketches of Granada—its landscapes, gypsy life, and dances. Turina composed a second set of such sketches in 1934.

Pedro Morales divided Turina's music into three groups: "First, those bearing no distinctive mark of nationalism; second, those in which it predominates; and third . . . [those] in which the idiom is a blending of Spanish and foreign elements."

According to Leigh Henry, Turina was "a musical impressionist of fine sensibility, both spiritually and musically. His music, however, differs in constructive methods from that of those generally termed Impressionists. He tends towards the rather literary type of poetic expression exemplified in Albéniz's *Iberia* or in *Images* of Debussy, but his treatment of sound and rhythm is more objective in the strictly aural sense, and more full of feeling for pure musical design than that of the elder Spaniard. Viewed as a whole, the general character of

Varèse

his work is subjective and impressionistic and has a certain flavor of romanticism."

During the turbulent years of the Spanish Civil War, Turina continued to pursue his varied musical activities, seemingly oblivious of the hazards and torments of that time. He continued to make public appearances in Madrid until the end of his life. He died in Madrid on January 14, 1949.

MAJOR WORKS

Chamber Music—2 piano trios; 2 violin sonatas; Piano Quintet in G minor; String Quartet in D minor; Escena Andaluza, for viola, string quartet, and piano; El Poema de una Sanluquena, for violin and piano; La Oración del Torero, for string quartet (also for string orchestra); Piano Quartet in A minor; Variaciones Clásicas, for violin and piano; Serenata, for string quartet; Círculo, for violin, cello, and piano.

Operas—Margot, lyric comedy; Jardín de Oriente, one-act opera.

Orchestral Music—La Procesión del Rocío, tone poem; Evangelio, tone poem; Danzas Fantásticas (also for piano); Sinfonía Sevillana; Canto a Sevilla, cycle of songs for voice and orchestra; Rítmos, six dances; Rapsodia Sinfónica, for strings.

Piano Music—Sevilla; Sonata Romántica; Coins de Séville; Tres Danzas Andaluzas; Recuerdos de Mi Rincón; Album de Viaje; Mujeres Españolas, two sets; Cuentos de España, two sets; Niñerías, two sets; Sanlúcar de Barrameda; El Cristo de la Calavera; Jardines de Andalucía; La Venta de los Gatos—Leyenda Becqueriana; El Barrio de Santa Cruz; La Leyenda de la Giralda; Dos Danzas Sobre Temas Populares Españoles; Verbena Madrileña; Mallorca; Evocaciones; Recuerdos de la Antigua España; Viaje Marítimo; Ciclo Pianistico; Miniaturas; Danzas Gitanas, two sets; Niñerías, two sets; Tarjetas Postales; Jardín de Niños; El Circo; Silhuetas; En la Zapatería; Fantasía Italiana; Rincones de Sanlúcar; Bailete; Preludios; Fantasía Sobre Cincos Notas; Concierto sin Orquesta; En el Cortijo.

Vocal Music—Poema en Forma de Canciones; Tres Arias; Dos Canciones; Corazón de Mujer; Tríptico; Tres Sonetos; Saeta en Forma de Salve; Vocalizaciones; Tres Poemas; Homenaje a Lope de Vega.

ABOUT

Chase, G., The Music of Spain; Sopeña, F., Joaquín Turina.

Chesterian (London), April 1949.

Edgard Varèse
1883–1965

Edgard Varèse was born in Paris on December 22, 1883. (A close friend of the family revealed at the time of Varèse's death that the long-accepted birth year of 1885 for the com-

Varèse: vä rĕz′

poser was due to a mix-up in the birth records.) When Edgard was nine, his family moved to Turin where the boy's early education in mathematics and science began. He also showed a strong interest in music, beginning composition at the age of eleven without training. At twelve he completed the writing of an opera, *Martin Paz*, based on a story by Jules Verne. Varèse's father was opposed to music as a career, insisting that the boy must train himself to become an engineer. When, in 1904, Edgard abandoned his preparations for entering the École Polytechnique to concentrate on music, he left home permanently. In the same year he entered the Schola Cantorum for his first formal study of music. His teachers included Vincent d'Indy and Albert Roussel. Later Varèse entered Widor's master class at the Paris Conservatory where he received the first Bourse Artistique offered by the city of Paris. He also founded and directed a chorus and organized a series of public concerts.

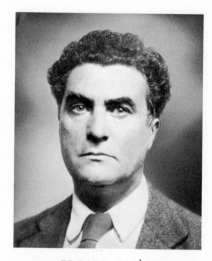

EDGARD VARÈSE

A rebel in music from the beginning, Varèse had no tolerance for academicism. Many years later he revealed to Edward Downes that even in his youth he dreamed of a music "made of sound set free." Even then he was fascinated by Helmholz's experiments with sirens and before long started to make some modest experiments of his own: "I found I could obtain beautiful parabolic and hyperbolic curves equivalent for me to the parabolas and hyperbolas in the visual domain. From then on I knew that somehow I would some day realize a new kind of music that would be spatial."

His interest in new sounds and his impatience with the status quo in music led him to abandon both the schoolroom and Paris to go to Berlin in 1907. There he founded and conducted the Symphonischer Chor which specialized in the performance of the polyphonic music of the past but also participated in some of the stage productions directed by Max Reinhardt. Varèse's friendship and association with such distinguished composers as Richard Strauss, Mahler, and Busoni proved a powerful stimulus in his own development as an independent musical thinker. He worked on an opera with a text by Hugo von Hofmannsthal which was lost in a fire. Other compositions of this period he subsequently destroyed, since he was no longer sympathetic to his one-time Romantic or Impressionistic tendencies. Instead he began to seek out new timbres, new sonorities, new sounds. A tone poem, *Bourgogne*, which was introduced in Berlin in 1910, was described by the critic Bruno Schrader as "infernal noise, cat music."

After successful guest appearances as the conductor of the Prague Philharmonic, an extensive tour was arranged for him, but the outbreak of war in 1914 brought an end to the project. Varèse returned to France to enter the army but was discharged one year later because of his poor health.

In December 1915, Varèse came to the United States to conduct a performance at the Hippodrome in New York of Berlioz' *Requiem* in honor of the war dead of all nations. He soon decided to make New York his permanent home, ultimately becoming an American citizen in 1926. Almost at once he became active in New York as an advocate of modern music, founding the New Symphony Orchestra to introduce the works of contemporary composers who were seldom represented on American symphony programs. The first concert of the New Symphony took place in New York on April 11, 1919. Varèse resigned as the conductor a season later, when the orchestra's directors decided on a change of artistic policy that placed less emphasis on the moderns. In 1921, with Carlos Salzedo, he founded the

International Composers' Guild, the first American organization devoted exclusively to new music. Its opening concert took place on December 17, 1922, and included compositions by Honegger, Ravel, and Carl Ruggles among others. For six years, Varèse guided the destinies of this organization, introducing to New York the works of over fifty modern composers, many of whom (including Schoenberg and Webern) thus received a hearing in New York for the first time. In 1926 he created the Pan American Society to promote the new music of all the Americas.

This strong interest in new music was now reflected in his own compositions which began to set a new path away from the accepted procedures of the classicists and romantics. His academic background led him to seek out novel subject matter for musical description in which science and mathematics were married to music. The old creative methods held no interest for him any longer. He was even bored by most of the traditional music of the formal concert hall and opera house. And so he sought a new kind of structure with new kinds of music-making. He now preferred abstract designs to formal ones. He dispensed with melody and consonance by using repeated notes or fragments and concentrating on discords. He became fascinated with new sounds, many of them extramusical, many of them the kind that could have best been produced electronically if such means had then been available. He emphasized percussion and rhythm, building up his effects through an accumulative process. He introduced all kinds of noises and noise-makers into his scores. He began to think more and more in terms of spatial music. He soon baptized his kind of music as "organized sound." He tried, as Nicolas Slonimsky once said of him, to reach "into the field of musical infinities, and to explore extreme registers and sonorities." Varèse himself explained: "I try to fly on my own wings."

In 1923 Varèse began to excite, annoy, and frequently amuse audiences and critics with his compositions. *Hyperprism*, scored for winds and percussion (including sleigh bells), was introduced in New York on March 4, 1923. It reminded Olin Downes of "election night, a menagerie or two and a catastrophe in

599

a boiler factory." *Octandre*, heard on January 13, 1924, led W. J. Henderson to write: "It shrieked, it grunted, it chortled, it mewed, it barked—and it turned all the eight instrumentalists into contortionists. It was not in any key, not even in no key. It was just a ribald outbreak of noise." *Intégrales*, for small orchestra and percussion (introduced on March 1, 1925), sounded to Ernest Newman, visiting critic for the New York *Post*, "a good deal like a combination of the early morning in the Mott Haven freight yards, feeding time at the zoo, and a Sixth Avenue trolley rounding a curve, with an intoxicated woodpecker thrown in for good measure." *Arcana* (first heard on April 8, 1927, at a concert of the Philadelphia Orchestra, Leopold Stokowski conducting) called for five choirs of percussion. It plunged Oscar Thompson "into morasses of sound which seemingly had little relation to music. . . . There was no mercy in its disharmony, no pity in its succession of screaming, clashing, clangorous discords."

In spite of such hostile reactions, Varèse continued to explore new worlds of sonorities and sounds. One of his most provocative works was *Ionisation*, which had its première in New York on March 6, 1933. This composition was written for an orchestra comprising forty-one percussion instruments and two sirens; among the percussions were friction and sibilation instruments of undetermined pitch. Varèse attempted in this work to produce the kinds of sounds which later composers would achieve electronically.

As soon as electronic instruments became available, electronic music began to fascinate Varèse. The invention of the Thereminvox, one of the pioneer electronic instruments, led Varèse to use it in *Equatorial*, heard on April 15, 1934. In 1936 Varèse told an interviewer: "The future composer of symphonies will consult the scientist in his laboratory instead of the violin maker in his garret."

Although sound was to Varèse the basis—the "raw material"—of his compositions, he felt in the 1920's and 1930's that the wrong emphasis had been attached to the character of sounds he was using. He said: "Form is the dominating factor in any work of art, and my chief preoccupation in composing is the form, the structure of the work I have conceived. The form of a work results from the density of the content. Even the most beautiful phrase goes into the discard if it is not structural, if it is only an imaginative vagabond. As for the timbres of the instruments, their personality, their standardized attributes, they are of purely anecdotal value. But the individual timbres and their combinations are useful ingredients of the tonal compound—coloring and isolating the various planes and volumes and thus from being incidental, they become part of the form. I do not use sounds impressionistically as the Impressionist painters used colors. In my music, they are an intrinsic part of the structure."

In 1937 Hanya Holm used Varèse's *Octandre* and *Ionisation* for a dance creation entitled *Trend*, which received from John Martin the New York *Times* Award as the best dance production of the year. Varèse's *Intégrales* was the inspiration for Martha Graham's ballet *Shapes of Ancestral Wonder*.

Following his work in the thirties, Varèse was creatively quiescent for a period of almost twenty years. He was brought back to creativity—and to experiment—by the rapid growth and development of electronic music. In the early 1950's he acquainted himself with the developments in *musique concrète* in Paris. In 1954 he collaborated with several technicians in creating a huge work, *Deserts*, for wind instruments, percussion, and sounds produced on magnetic tape. The première in Paris on December 2, 1954, created a scandal. Thematic material was here reduced to figures of one or two repeated notes and intervals. Three interpolations of electronically produced noises were integrated into the over-all context. The bridge between the sounds created by the wind instruments and those produced on magnetic tape was made by the percussion instruments with complex rhythmic projections.

For the Philips Pavilion at the Brussels Exposition during the summer of 1957, Varèse developed his ideas on spatial music—music that had long been fascinating him. *Poème Électronique* was a composition Varèse had worked out in collaboration with the architect Le Corbusier. Four hundred and twenty-five loud speakers were required to project this eight-minute work, recorded on tape. The sounds accompanied lights devised by Le Corbusier and flashed on the curved ceiling of the pavilion. No attempt was made to correlate the sounds with the lights, each being independent. Without the lights, the *Poème Électronique* was given in New York in November 1958, arousing such enthusiasm that the composition was repeated.

Varèse's last composition was *Nocturnal*, completed in 1960. In this work electronically produced oscillation sounds were supplemented by a soprano, men's voices, and a chamber orchestra. The world première took place in New York on May 1, 1961.

Subjected to attack in the 1920's and 1930's, ignored and virtually forgotten in the 1940's, Varèse lived long enough to find himself acclaimed as a prophet who had anticipated a good many of the avant-garde developments of the 1950's and 1960's. Columbia Records issued a volume of his compositions in 1960. When a concert of his works was given in New York on May 1, 1961, the audience rose to its feet to cheer him. "This remarkable tribute from people who were miles away from being beatniks," remarked Ross Parmenter in the New York *Times*, "proved the extent to which Mr. Varèse has won his points. These people accepted him as a modern master." Still another all-Varèse concert was heard in New York on September 3, 1964, and earlier that year Leonard Bernstein, conducting the New York Philharmonic, revived *Deserts*. On May 21, 1963, Varèse was honored at a dinner in New York at which he was the recipient of the first Koussevitzky International Recording Award. In 1965 he was given the Edward MacDowell medal. Three years earlier, in 1962, he had received the Brandeis University Award in music.

On October 27, 1965, Varèse underwent intestinal surgery. Suffering a relapse, he died in a New York hospital on November 6, 1965.

From the early 1920's to the end of his life, Varèse occupied two floors of a four-story brownstone house he owned at 188 Sullivan Street in New York's Greenwich Village. He lived there with his wife, Louise, a distinguished translator of French works, whom he had married in 1921. The Varèse home was described by Theodore Strongin: "The upper floor bears the mark of Louise, Varèse's studio is downstairs at garden level. The largest object in the room is a grand piano, but every inch is so teeming with something or other that one scarcely notices the piano. The desk is covered with a profusion of pens, pencils, knives, clothespins (to use as paper clips), drafting equipment, stop watches, old scraps of paper.... Elsewhere in the room are scientific journals, Chinese gongs, a suspended cymbal, several sizes of drum. On the wall is the photograph of the eye of a hurricane; also, paintings by Braque, Miró, Calder; various drawings (even one of Beethoven)."

Edward Downes described Varèse as a "stocky, vigorous figure, with strong, florid features, and a crown of thinning gray hair that stands up like an aureole around his head."

MAJOR WORKS

Chamber Music—Octandre, for flute, oboe, clarinet, bassoon, horn, trumpet, trombone, and double bass; Density 21.5, for unaccompanied flute.

Electronic Music—Equatorial, for bass voice, trumpet, trombones, organ, percussion, and Thereminvox; Deserts, for wind instruments, percussion, and electronically produced sounds; Poème Électronique: Nocturnal, for soprano, men's voices, chamber orchestra, and electronically produced sounds.

Orchestral Music—Offrandes, for voice and small orchestra; Hyperprism, for wind instruments and percussion; Intégrales, for small orchestra and percussion; Amériques, for large orchestra; Arcana, for large orchestra; Ionisation, for forty-one percussion instruments and two sirens; Metal, for soprano and orchestra; Espace, for chorus and orchestra.

ABOUT

HiFi/Stereo Review, September 1954; Juilliard Review, Fall 1954; Modern Music, January–February 1928; Musical Quarterly, April 1966; New York Times, November 16, 1958; La Revue Musicale (Paris), January 1956; Score (London), March 1957; Time, December 12, 1955.

Ralph Vaughan Williams
1872–1958

Ralph Vaughan Williams was born in Down Ampney, Gloucestershire, on October 12, 1872. He was the second son and the youngest of three children of the rector of Christ Church in Down Ampney, who died when Ralph was two and a half. The three children were reared by their mother, who moved to Surrey to live with her sister, Sophie Wedgwood. (They were related to the Wedgwood family of pottery makers.) Sophie Wedgwood gave Ralph his first music lessons by teaching him the rudiments of the piano. After Ralph, at six, had written his first piece of music— a four-measure composition for the piano entitled *The Robin's Nest*—his aunt began to teach him thorough bass. Some violin study was started when Ralph was seven; when he was eight he took a correspondence course in music from the University of Edinburgh, passing two examinations. Music study continued at a preparatory school at Rottingdean, which he entered in 1882 and where his piano teacher introduced him to the music of Johann Sebastian Bach. At this time, Vaughan Williams made his first public appearance as a violinist. In 1887 he entered Charterhouse, where he played the violin in the school orchestra and joined some of his fellow students on Sunday evenings to perform Italian baroque compositions. He also took some lessons on the viola and organ, and completed a piano trio in G minor which was performed at a school concert on August 5, 1888. "All I remember about it," Vaughan Williams recalled many years later, "is that the principal theme was distinctly reminiscent of César Franck."

RALPH VAUGHAN WILLIAMS

In the summer of 1890 Vaughan Williams vacationed in Germany where he heard his first Wagnerian music drama, *Die Walküre*. This experience sparked an interest in Wagner that persisted throughout his life. Partly as a result of this experience, and partly because of his expanding musical activities, he decided to delay entering Trinity College, Cambridge, in order to concentrate on music study. In 1890 he enrolled in the newly founded Royal

College of Music in London, studying composition with Hubert Parry, who subjected him to a rigorous theoretical study of the classics. Hearing performances of great music extended his musical horizon. Verdi's *Requiem* and Wagner's *Tristan und Isolde* made a particularly deep impression upon him.

In October 1892 Vaughan Williams finally matriculated at Trinity College. There he continued his music study with Charles Wood in composition and Alan Gray in organ, at the same time participating in all of Cambridge's musical activities. He became a member of the University Music Club, which not only performed music but subjected all performed compositions to detailed discussions. He founded and led a small chorus that concentrated on Schubert's Masses. Yet, for all his interest in music, he was no shining light; on the basis of some songs and choral pieces he had written, his teacher Charles Wood was of the opinion that he had no talent as a composer.

In 1894 Vaughan Williams returned to the Royal College of Music for additional intensive study. As a pupil of Charles Stanford he completed, in 1894, a Serenade, for small orchestra, which his teacher described as a "most poetical and remarkable work." Stanford's influence was significant, but even more so was that of a fellow student, Gustav Holst, who later became a famous composer. As fast friends, Vaughan Williams and Holst exchanged compositions, dissected them, and profited from one another's point of view. This relationship continued as long as Holst lived.

While attending the Royal College, Vaughan Williams helped support himself by serving as organist at St. Barnabas, South Lambeth, at a salary of fifty pounds a year. He disliked the work, feeling that he was an incompetent performer. Consequently, soon after he had married Adeline Fisher, on October 9, 1897, he resigned his organ post. With his bride he left for Germany, where for a number of months he absorbed new musical experiences by attending performances of concerts and operas in Berlin and, for a brief period, studied composition with Max Bruch. Back again in England, he set up home in Westminster in London. For seven years he earned his living playing the trombone in various orchestras and bands. At the same time he continued his studies and in 1899 he completed them, passed his examinations, and submitted a Mass for double chorus and orchestra as an exercise for a doctorate in music at Cambridge. For some reason never explained, he did not get this degree officially until May 23, 1901.

By 1901 he had completed several compositions for chamber music combinations, for chorus, and also for orchestra. A Quintet in D major, for clarinet, horn, violin, cello, and piano, was heard in London on June 5, 1901. *Heroic Elegy and Triumphal Epilogue*, for orchestra, was conducted by Stanford at the Royal College of Music on March 5, 1901. *Bucolic Suite*, for orchestra, was given at Bournemouth on March 10, 1902. These and similar works revealed more craftsmanship than individuality, with the influence of Brahms omnipresent. At almost thirty years of age Vaughan Williams gave little evidence of outstanding creative talent. In fact, his most important musical achievement up to 1904 was the editing of a hymnal. He was fully aware of his shortcomings. As he himself later confessed: "I wondered if I was wasting my time. The years were passing and I was adding nothing to the sum total of my musical invention."

The turning point in his career as a composer came in 1904 when he joined the Folk Song Society, which had been founded in 1898. This was not Vaughan Williams' first contact with English folk music. As early as 1893 he had come across an English folk song, "Dives and Lazarus," in a volume entitled *English County Songs* published in 1892. The song aroused for the first time his interest in English folk music and its modal style. He had discussed this interest with some of his teachers at the Royal College, and in 1900 found a powerful ally in Cecil Sharp, who was a passionate advocate of going out into the field to ferret out folk songs of various regions and of collecting these songs in publications. Vaughan Williams had done some exploration of his own and by 1903 had published his first edition of folk songs. His affiliation with the English Folk Song Society in 1904 gave a new impetus to these endeavors and led him to intensify his researches. He worked industriously in Essex, Norfolk, Sussex, Yorkshire, and Wiltshire, uncovering a wealth of material that he edited, harmonized, and published.

His revitalizations brought world recognition to and admiration of such gems as "The Turtle Dove," "Down in Yon Forest," "The Dark-Eyed Sailor," and "We've Been Awhile Awandering."

His immersion in English folk music led Vaughan Williams in a completely new direction. He now aimed to incorporate the folksong material into ambitious structures while molding his own melodic and harmonic idiom after the patterns found in old English folk songs. Thus, in 1906, he completed *Norfolk Rhapsodies*, three works embodying folk melodies native to King's Lynn in Norfolk. The first such rhapsody, in E minor, has survived following its première performance in London on August 23, 1906. Four folk songs are quoted: "The Captain's Apprentice," "A Bold Young Sailor," "The Basket of Eggs" and "On Board a '93.'" The second rhapsody, in D minor (first performance in Cardiff on September 27, 1907) used tunes like "Young Henry the Poacher" and "The Saucy Bold Robber"; the third, in G minor and major (first performance at the Cardiff Festival on September 27, 1907) quotes among other folk songs "The Lincolnshire Farmer," "Ward the Pirate," and "The Red Barn." The second and third rhapsodies were withdrawn by the composer and have not been heard since 1914. The first rhapsody enjoyed a minor success.

Towards the Unknown Region, for chorus and orchestra, based on Walt Whitman, enjoyed a major success when introduced at the Leeds Festival on October 10, 1907, the composer conducting. Herbert Thompson wrote in the *Yorkshire Post:* "The music moves along with a certain spiritual form. . . . The very striking work, original and showing a homogeneity that very little of the British school reveals, met with immediate and hearty approval." A London *Times* critic reported that the work marked "the composer as the foremost of the younger generation . . . already a master."

In spite of these successes and favorable critical evaluations, Vaughan Williams felt the need for additional study. For that purpose he went to Paris in 1908 and for several months studied there with Maurice Ravel. "I learned much from him," Vaughan Williams said at one time. "For example, that the heavy contrapuntal Teutonic manner was not necessary. '*Complexe, mais pas compliqué,*' was his motto. He showed me how to orchestrate in points of color rather than in lines. It was an invigorating experience to find all artistic problems looked at from what was to me an entirely new manner."

Study with Ravel gave Vaughan Williams greater skill and self-assurance both in orchestration and harmonization. The first compositions completed after his return to England reveal this new self-confidence: the song cycle *On Wenlock Edge*, to poems by A. E. Housman, which Gervase Elwes introduced in London on November 15, 1909; and his first symphony, *The Sea Symphony*, a large work for solo voices, chorus, and orchestra with text derived from Walt Whitman, first performed at the Leeds Festival on October 12, 1910.

In 1910 came Vaughan Williams' first masterwork, *Fantasia on a Theme by Thomas Tallis*, for string quartet and double string orchestra. Introduced at the Three Choirs Festival in Gloucestershire on September 6, 1910, the work made little impression; a critic for the *Musical Times* even thought it was "overlong for the subject matter." The composer withdrew it. In 1921 he deleted some of the material, including the closing section, and revised the rest. The critical reaction changed sharply. "The work is wonderful," now wrote J. Fuller-Maitland in the London *Times*, "because it seems to lift one into some unknown region of musical thought and feeling." Taking a tune from the *Metrical Psalter* of the sixteenth century English church composer Thomas Tallis, Vaughan Williams created an impassioned work for strings in which the antiphonal character of sixteenth century church music is revived.

Major works completed between 1910 and the beginning of World War I solidified for Vaughan Williams a lofty place in English music: *Phantasy Quintet* for strings (heard in London on March 23, 1914); *Fantasia on Christmas Carols*, for baritone, chorus, and orchestra (introduced in Hereford, September 12, 1912); and most significantly, *A London Symphony*, completed towards the end of 1913 (world première in London on March 27, 1914). Though the composer originally avoided a program for this symphony, he did not discourage later annotators from providing a detailed description in which the four movements became four pictures of London life. "The Westminster chimes hum on the air and suddenly London wakes," wrote Scott Goddard. "Then turn to the uneasy sighs at the end of the Scherzo or to the rending wail that begins the last movement. This is a different London and a musician not viewing it but pondering over it. It is a town haunted by the countryside it devours. The Nocturne (the second movement) recalls walking home along Piccadilly in the small hours of a summer's morning when, petrol fumes at their weakest, the light winds from the country blow across the Green Park. . . . The errand boy whistles tunes such as Swift might have heard while bathing in the Thames, before his house in Chelsea, tunes that have a country air and a folk-song turn of phrase."

A London Symphony was rewritten a number of times. It was reconstructed in 1915 because the score had been lost en route to Germany in July 1914. Then on three different occasions the composer revised it. The final version was heard on February 22, 1934, Sir Thomas Beecham conducting.

Vaughan Williams was forty-two years old when World War I broke out. Though he was exempt from military service because of his age, he enlisted in the Territorial Royal Army Military Corps and for three years served as an orderly in hospitals in France and Macedonia. Determined to take a still more active part in the war, he took and passed examinations for a commission in the Royal Garrison Artillery and saw service with the First Army in France.

After the war, Vaughan Williams returned to musical activity and assumed a leading position in English music. He joined the faculty of the Royal College of Music, with which he remained affiliated until his death, teaching composition. He was appointed conductor of the Bach Choir, which he directed from 1920 to 1928.

An uninterrupted succession of major works during the period between the two world wars made Vaughan Williams the logical successor to Sir Edward Elgar as England's foremost composer when Elgar died in 1934. This fact was emphasized in 1935 when Vaughan Williams received the Order of Merit. The rich harvest of Vaughan Williams compositions included two symphonies: the gentle and bucolic *Pastoral Symphony* introduced in London on January 26, 1922, and—by contrast—the dynamic and highly rhythmic, at times discordant, Symphony No. 4 in F minor, heard in London on April 10, 1935. In addition, Vaughan Williams completed a poetic romance for violin and orchestra, *The Lark Ascending* (1920), and a violin concerto (1925); *The Shepherds of the Delectable Mountains*, a "pastoral episode" based on John Bunyan's *Pilgrim's Progress*, world première in London on July 11, 1922; a romantic ballad opera, *Hugh the Drover*, introduced in London on July 11, 1924; *Flos Campi*, a suite for solo viola, wordless chorus, and small orchestra (1925); the four-act opera *Sir John in Love*, based on Shakespeare's *The Merry Wives of Windsor*, first performance in London on March 21, 1929; *Job*, a masque for dancing inspired by Blake's illustrations for the Book of Job, produced in London on July 5, 1931; and various works for chorus and for orchestra, as well as many adaptations of English folk songs.

Philip Heseltine characterized the Vaughan Williams style in these works: "[They have] strong melodic invention and a most original fund of contrapuntal resource in which there is nothing even faintly reminiscent of scholasticism. With the purely harmonic development of the twentieth century, Vaughan Williams shows little sympathy. . . . We certainly find extremely novel combinations of sounds in some of the later compositions, but they are almost invariably conditioned by the movement of the individual parts, of which the line is often seen in a higher dimensional aspect, so to speak, through the addition to each note of the two other notes necessary to complete the common chord."

As Scott Goddard remarked in *Music and Letters*, this music had a far-reaching impact on Vaughan Williams' contemporaries: "Vaughan Williams has influenced English composers in various directions and in varying degrees. His inclination towards folk song . . . his singularly downright use of contrapuntal devices, the richness of the resultant harmony—all these he has increased in intensity and made personal to himself; and their effect on his contemporaries is undoubted."

The common denominator of Vaughan Williams' music is, of course, its English identity, its deep-rooted nationalism. He himself has written: "Many young composers make the mistake of imagining they can be universal without at first having been local. Is it not reasonable to suppose that those who share our life, our history, our customs, our climate, even our food, should have some secret to impart to us which the foreign composer, though he be perhaps more imaginative, more powerful, more technically equipped, is not able to give us? This is the secret of the national composer, the secret to which he only has the key, which no foreigner can share with him and which he alone is able to tell his countrymen."

The nationalism of Vaughan Williams, in the words of Hubert Foss, "grows from the earth. It comes from the people; its roots are in what they wanted to sing then, though it may not be what they want to hear now. His nationalism is not negative; sometimes it is more positive than his esthetic thought and his musical appeal to the public. It is never superimposed; not once in his career has he been an Englishman consciously. There is no pastiche, no strutting, no attitudinizing. Vaughan Williams does not deliberately mispronounce foreign words."

Vaughan Williams was an outspoken foe of Fascism and Nazism, and his music was banned in Nazi Germany just before World War II. During that war—too old to put on a uniform again—he served his country by driving a salvage truck and performing various other war duties in a civilian capacity, including service on the Dorking Committee for Refugees from Nazi Oppression. Though his country was in its darkest hours, it nevertheless managed to pay Vaughan Williams the homage of celebrating his seventieth birthday in 1942 with six concerts of his works broadcast over BBC and with performances of compositions written by several English composers in his honor.

The war years did not arrest his creativity. In his Fifth Symphony in D major (1943) and the Concerto for Oboe and Strings (1944) we encounter a serenity and repose startling for music written during the grimmest years of the war; it was almost as if the composer were fleeing from reality to the peace and contentment of an inner life. His Sixth Symphony in

E minor (1948), one of his greatest works in any form, has greater turbulence in the first three movements, together with a feeling of tragedy; but the concluding movement is perhaps the most tranquil music ever put down on paper. "The symphony progresses deeper and deeper to the inmost recesses of consciousness," wrote Olin Downes. "We know of no other symphony whose finale is so sensitive and intimate in its nuances, so completely of the spirit. . . . It was as if the reveries of centuries had amassed themselves about his heart."

Though an old man, and the victim in his last years of deafness, Vaughan Williams remained productive until the very end. He completed three more symphonies: *Sinfonia Antartica* (1953); Symphony No. 8 in D minor (1956); and Symphony No. 9 in E minor (1958). The last of these is, for the most part, music of utter despair, rising in the finale to a pitch of pessimism that seems to bewail the futility of life; in fact, after the final bar, the composer added the word *niente* (nothing).

In addition to his symphonies, Vaughan Williams produced a masterwork for the stage: an opera (or, as the composer designated it, a "morality"), *Pilgrim's Progress*, text based on John Bunyan; the première took place at Covent Garden in London on April 26, 1951. The score, with its blending of mysticism and deep poetic feeling, was regarded by Vaughan Williams as the culminating point of his creative life. As if to emphasize this point, he interpolated into it portions of his earlier compositions, including the one-act pastoral *The Shepherds of the Delectable Mountains*, which he had written in 1922. Reviewing *Pilgrim's Progress* in the London *Daily Express*, Cecil Smith wrote that it was "the noblest new work produced on any of the world's lyric stages since the end of the war."

Vaughan Williams paid three visits to the United States, the first in 1922 when he was invited to direct a concert of his works at the Norfolk Music Festival in Connecticut. This concert took place on June 7 and included the American première of his *Pastoral Symphony*. A second visit followed in 1932, when he delivered several lectures on national music at Bryn Mawr College. His last appearances in America, in the year 1954, included lectures

at Cornell and Yale universities and guest appearances as conductor in several of his major works.

His eightieth birthday was celebrated throughout the music world with commemorative concerts. Four months after this birthday, on February 7, 1953, Vaughan Williams married his secretary, Ursula Woods. His first wife had died in 1951.

The following personal portrait of Vaughan Williams was written by Stephen Williams for the New York *Times* while the composer was still alive: "He looks like a farmer. Indeed, one commentator has likened him to 'a large shaggy sheepdog, lovable, kindly, intelligent and untidy.' He is a man entirely without self-consciousness: a big, heavy, lumbering figure, usually dressed in rough tweeds, who looks as though he is on his way to judge the short horns at an agricultural show."

Michael Kennedy had this to add after Vaughan Williams' death: "To the end of his life his pale skin was fresh, his face unlined. No ravages of time or struggle of spirit showed here. Humor and serenity, kindliness and candor were his habitual expressions, with occasional flashes of sudden anger. . . . At the end of his life he rejoiced in new suits and ties and was rather amused to be called a dandy by his friends." Kennedy also noted Vaughan Williams' "extraordinary range of . . . knowledge on a tremendous number of subjects" and his "sense of humor which at times was Rabelaisian and at other times wickedly witty."

Vaughan Williams' last public appearance took place on August 5, 1958, when he attended a performance of his Ninth Symphony at a Promenade Concert in London. On the day before his death, he was at his desk working on a setting of carols scheduled for performance during Christmas. He died at his home in London on August 26, 1958. Two days later he was cremated, and on September 19 his ashes were buried in the North Choir aisle of Westminster Abbey.

MAJOR WORKS

Ballets—Old King Cole; On Christmas Night; Job, a "masque for dancing"; The Bridal Day, a "masque for dancing."

Chamber Music—2 string quartets; Phantasy Quintet; On Wenlock Edge, song cycle for tenor, string quartet, and piano; Six Studies in English Folksong, for cello and piano (also violin and piano, viola and piano, and clarinet and piano); Household Music, three preludes on Welsh tunes for string quartet; Suite for Pipes; Sonata in A minor, for violin and piano.

Choral Music—Anthems, canticles, carols, hymns, motets, part songs, Services, Te Deums; Toward the Unknown Region; Willow Wood; Five Mystical Songs; Fantasia on Christmas Carols; Flos Campi, with viola solo; Sancta Civitas, oratorio; Mass in G minor; In Windsor Forest, cantata (adapted from the opera Sir John in Love); Magnificat; Dona Nobis Pacem; Five Tudor Portraits; Folksongs of Four Seasons; The Sons of Light, cantata; Oxford Elegy; A Cotswold Romance, cantata; Epithalamion, cantata; This Day, cantata.

Operas—The Shepherds of the Delectable Mountains, pastoral episode (incorporated into Pilgrim's Progress); Hugh the Drover, ballad opera; Sir John in Love; The Poisoned Kiss; Pilgrim's Progress, a "morality."

Orchestral Music—9 symphonies (including London, Pastoral, and Sinfonia Antartica); Norfolk Rhapsody No. 1 in E minor; Overture to The Wasps; Fantasia on a Theme by Thomas Tallis; The Lark Ascending, romance for violin and orchestra; Violin Concerto in D minor (originally Concerto Accademico); Piano Concerto in C major (also for two pianos and orchestra); Suite for Viola and Small Orchestra; Fantasia on Greensleeves (arranged from Sir John in Love); Serenade to Music; Oboe Concerto; Concerto Grosso, for string orchestra; Bass Tuba Concerto in F minor.

Piano Music—Canon and Two-Part Invention; Valse Lente and Nocturne; Hymn Tune Prelude; Suite of Six Short Pieces; Introduction and Fugue.

Vocal Music—Songs of Travel; numerous songs for voice and piano including Linden Lea, Orpheus with His Lute, and Silent Noon; numerous arrangements of folk songs.

ABOUT

Day, J., Vaughan Williams; Dickinson, A. E., Vaughan Williams; Foss, H., Ralph Vaughan Williams: A Study; Howes, F., The Music of Vaughan Williams; Kennedy, M., The Works of Ralph Vaughan Williams; Pakenham, P. M., Vaughan Williams; Vaughan Williams, U., R. V. W.: A Biography of Ralph Vaughan Williams; Young, P. M., Vaughan Williams.

Heitor Villa-Lobos
1887–1959

Heitor Villa-Lobos was born in Rio de Janeiro. His birth date has been pinpointed by recent research as March 5, 1887. For a long time the year listed most frequently for Villa-Lobos's birth was 1881, though other years between 1881 and 1891 were occasionally offered. Villa-Lobos himself did not seem to know what the correct year was; whenever

Villa-Lobos: vĕ′lä lō′ bŏosh

anybody asked him for it, he would select at random now one year, now another.

Villa-Lobos's father was an amateur cellist. It was from him that Heitor received music lessons when he was six, first on the cello, later on the piano. He was from the beginning an undisciplined pupil who rebelled against formal exercises and instruction. After his father's death in 1899, Heitor abandoned all schooling. He earned his living playing in theatre orchestras and in restaurants. At the same time he continued to study the piano by himself and learned by trial and error how to perform on various wind instruments.

HEITOR VILLA-LOBOS

He was fascinated and strongly influenced by the popular music of Brazil—the kind that he played in restaurants and theatres and the kind he heard sung or strummed on guitars in the streets. Popular idioms were those Villa-Lobos favored when he began to write his own music, for example his first published piece, *Salon Waltz*, for piano, which appeared in 1908. Popular tunes and rhythms also characterized *Canticos Sertanejos* (*Country Songs*), published in 1909.

He became interested in Brazilian folk music when he made an expedition to the northern states in 1905 to seek out local songs and dances. This adventure was so successful that it kindled in him a lifelong enthusiasm for autochthonous folk songs and dances. Less successful was his attempt to get back to formal schooling. In 1907 he entered the

National Institute of Music. The discipline made him restive, and the strict curriculum irritated him. He soon left school, preferring to learn music in his own haphazard way, picking up technique and information as he went along.

His personal experiences proved far more valuable to him than textbooks and class-rooms. In 1912 he traveled to east Brazil, where he came into contact with the native songs, rites, myths, and customs of Bahia, Espirito Santo, and Pernambuco. His appetite whetted by these contacts, he traveled later the same year with Romeu Donizetti into the interior of Brazil in search of Indian folk songs. For three years he continued these expeditions up the Amazon and its tributaries, gathering authentic examples of all types of Brazilian folk and popular music as he went. His rewarding discoveries made a powerful impact on him; in fact, they served as the decisive turning point in his career as a composer. Burle Marx put it this way: "For a temperament like that of Villa-Lobos, inclined to the strange, fantastic and exotic, such direct contact with a primitive culture would lead naturally to a new path and a new goal. . . . Villa-Lobos not only recorded, learned and absorbed but he merged what he found with what he recognized as his own. The result was a fusion of all the elements in his own nature."

At that time Villa-Lobos began to write music strongly influenced by Indian melodies, rhythms, instruments, and legends. In 1914 he completed *Dansas Africanas*, for orchestra, which carried the subtitle "Dances of Mestizo Indians of Brazil." This set of three dances was the first of his compositions to give a clue to his later mature creative personality, particularly in his skillful use of syncopated tunes and complicated rhythms, the latter utilizing several percussion instruments indigenous to Brazil. Villa-Lobos's exploitation of novel instrumental effects became evident in *Amazonas*, in 1917, one of several tone poems based on Indian mythology. *Amazonas*, which describes an Indian girl pursued by gods and monsters in a tropical jungle, features such unusual techniques as harmonics-glissandos and string instruments played below the bridge. Indian legend and the jungle are also basic to the tone poem *Uirapurú*, another work composed in 1917 (Uirapurú is the legendary enchanted bird whose nightly song lures Indians into the jungle). *Dansas* and *Amazonas* waited almost fifteen years for their premières, both of which took place in Paris: *Dansas* on April 5, 1928, and *Amazonas* on May 30, 1929. *Uirapurú* was adapted for a ballet that was produced in Buenos Aires on May 25, 1935.

On November 13, 1915, there took place in Rio de Janeiro the first concert devoted entirely to Villa-Lobos's music. It made a good impression. Villa-Lobos now settled in Rio de Janeiro, married Lucilia Guimarães, a concert pianist, and began a new period of formal study with Francisco Braga.

Then in 1919 Villa-Lobos was discovered by the celebrated concert pianist Artur Rubinstein. Rubinstein had gone to Rio de Janeiro to give a concert and entered a motion picture theatre in which one of Villa-Lobos's compositions was being played. The music impressed him, and he made it his business to seek the composer out. Soon after their initial meeting, Villa-Lobos visited Rubinstein at his hotel, bringing an orchestra with him. Then and there he conducted for Rubinstein a program of his works. This performance further assured Rubinstein of Villa-Lobos's great talent. Rubinstein now began to use his influence to gain for the composer a government stipend for study abroad. A number of years later, in 1926, Villa-Lobos repaid Rubinstein by writing *Rudepoema*, a brilliant and rugged virtuoso piece for the piano intended as a portrait of Rubinstein's personality and one of Villa-Lobos's finest works for the keyboard. He orchestrated it in 1932 and in its orchestral version it was introduced in Rio de Janeiro on July 15, 1942, under the composer's direction.

The government stipend enabled Villa-Lobos to go to Paris in 1922 and stay a number of years. He explained that he had gone to France not to learn about French music but to teach Paris about his own works. Performances of his compositions indeed attracted considerable interest. In 1927, a Villa-Lobos festival was presented in Paris, and in 1929 the Lamoureux Orchestra devoted an entire program to him. In fact, Villa-Lobos's international fame can be said to have started in Paris in the 1920's. The new trends in music with which Villa-Lobos became acquainted in Paris interested him; but they left little impression on his creative personality. In Paris, as earlier in Rio de Janeiro, he remained himself—an original.

After returning to Brazil, Villa-Lobos combined his work as a composer with an important assignment as an educator. In 1930 he became the director of music education in São Paulo, and in 1932 he transferred to Rio de Janeiro to assume a similar post. He set out to revolutionize the teaching methods in Brazil. In time he introduced the teaching of Brazilian folk songs and dances into the public schools; devised methods of hand signals with which to train musical illiterates to read music; founded choruses all over the country and directed them yearly in massed performances sometimes numbering as many as twenty-five thousand children at once. Dr. Francisco Curt Lange, the Uruguayan musicologist, called Villa-Lobos's work in music education "the world's greatest achievement in the field of musical pedagogy." All this he accomplished while continuing to be extraordinarily prolific in composition.

He also conducted extensively, appearing with Brazil's leading orchestras as well as in other countries. In November 1944 he paid his first visit to the United States, making his American debut in Los Angeles late that month as guest conductor of the Werner Janssen Symphony in a Villa-Lobos program. For the next few months he toured America in guest appearances with leading orchestras. The League of Composers in New York set aside an entire week in February 1945 as Villa-Lobos Week. The Koussevitzky Music Foundation commissioned him to write a new symphonic work—the tone poem *Madona*, world première in Rio de Janeiro on October 8, 1946, the composer conducting. He returned to the United States for tours in 1947 and 1957. In the latter year, his seventieth birthday was celebrated in New York—first on March 4, when he was cited at City Hall in New York for his achievements as composer and music educator and given a scroll by the mayor; and again on March 28, when he appeared as guest conductor of the New York Philharmonic in a program that included three of his own compositions.

Villa-Lobos was one of the most prolific composers of the twentieth century. He is believed to have written well over two thousand compositions, the exact number uncertain because he was careless about his manuscripts and allowed some to go astray or to be picked up as souvenirs by admirers. Since he was an eclectic, the more than two thousand works are in many different styles and idioms and in every possible medium. From his lifelong studies in Brazil's native music he derived his powerful rhythmic momentum as well as his tendency towards improvisation; from his fascination with Brazil's popular tunes he drew fresh and singable lyricism. Frequently, too, he made use of native Brazilian instruments, and just as often he resorted to quoting folk and popular tunes. Most of the time, however, the material is his own, even if it invariably derives both its physiognomy and its personality from native Brazilian folk or popular sources.

"His music," says Burle Marx, "is a continuous, spontaneous, abundant pouring forth. He is perhaps the only modern composer who creates with complete abandon and unself-consciousness. Not at all perturbed by rigid innovations, or by problems of style and form, he creates like a god—without question and with sure confidence. Each work has a form, a color, a style, and a vigor of its own. It is possible perhaps that such an amalgamation of contending forces—indigenous, primitive, Portuguese, European, African—could spring only from a country like Brazil with its great unexplored forests, its mountains, its rivers and vast skies. Whatever the sources, the music is Villa-Lobos."

Villa-Lobos himself devised two forms of composition as a means of bringing greater artistic and universal appeal to Brazilian songs and popular tunes. Some of his finest works use these forms. One he called *Chôros*, a popular Brazilian dance tune played by a street band. Villa-Lobos wrote fifteen of these—for solo instruments, for various combinations of instruments, for chorus, for orchestra, and for band. Popular Brazilian music is here exploited in compositions that are at turns infectiously lyrical and restlessly rhythmic. One of the most celebrated of these compositions, *Chôros* No. 5, for solo piano, is entitled *Alma Brasileira*. The sixth (for orchestra, guitar, and native instruments) and the tenth (for chorus and orchestra) are also representative.

The other form devised by Villa-Lobos is

the *Bachiana Brasileira*. This is a suite in a contrapuntal style which tries to achieve a marriage of Bach's counterpoint with some of the rhythmic and melodic tendencies of Brazilian folk music. Villa-Lobos produced eight such compositions. The second and fifth are particularly popular: the second, for a toccata movement entitled *The Little Train of Caipira* which picturesquely recreates the progress of a little Brazilian train; the fifth, for its opening "Aria" movement, a sensuous folk song for voice and an orchestra of cellos.

Villa-Lobos's enormous output also includes a dozen symphonies; operas and operettas (one of the latter, *Magdalena*, was produced in Los Angeles and New York); ballets; choral works, large and small; tone poems; concertos for various solo instruments and orchestra (even for such unusual instruments as the guitar and the harmonica); fifteen string quartets together with numerous other chamber music works; piano pieces; song cycles and songs. Two of his later compositions were commissioned by the Louisville Orchestra in Kentucky: *Erosion, or the Origin of the Amazon River*, heard in Louisville on November 7, 1951; and *Dawn in a Tropical Forest*, performed in Louisville on January 23, 1954. Villa-Lobos's last symphony, his twelfth, was also given its world première in the United States—at the Inter-American Music Festival in Washington, D.C., on April 20, 1958. Another of his later orchestral works was written for Israel—*Odyssey of a Race*, heard at the International Festival of Contemporary Music at Haifa on May 30, 1954.

He wrote quickly, effortlessly—all the time, any place, and almost under any stimulus. In 1957 while dining at the home of the Brazilian deputy consul in New York, Villa-Lobos was so delighted with a Brazilian delicacy that then and there he wrote a composition in praise of the dish. He called it *A Fugue Without End*, and named each of its four movements after one of the main ingredients of the recipe: "Farina," "Meat," "Rice," and "Black Beans." Always interested in unusual methods and techniques he wrote *The New York Skyline* for the New York World's Fair in 1940 by finding the equivalents in pitch, tempo, and rhythm for the contours of New York's skyscrapers drawn on graph paper; he conducted this piece at the opening of the Fair. On another occasion he traced the outline of a mountain range in Brazil on graph paper and proceeded to translate the rise and ebb of the line into musical terms. He often used graph paper, in place of music sheets, in an attempt to achieve in music the geometric contours of drawings.

Though seriously ill in his last years, he did not slow down his activities, nor did he curtail his travels. In his last year and a half he made a concert tour of Europe and the United States. He died of uremia in Rio de Janeiro on November 17, 1959.

Nicolas Slonimsky, who knew Villa-Lobos well over a period of many years, wrote the following personal sketch when the composer was still alive:

"There is nothing peculiarly Brazilian, savage, or jungle-like in Villa-Lobos's appearance and behavior. In fact, he looks and acts very much like a professional musician, and speaks French with a characteristic Parisian cadence. In his office, in a brand new skyscraper near the Opera House, the door is always open, and people drop in without ceremony. Villa-Lobos presides at his desk, cluttered up with manuscripts, notebooks, photographs, and miscellaneous objects. At another desk, his faithful secretary copies his music and answers telephones. At a third desk, a huge office typewriter rattles along. Villa-Lobos is not disturbed by noises. . . . He can compose in the midst of pandemonium. . . .

"His artistic credo is paradoxical. 'I am a sentimentalist by nature,' he says, 'and at times my music is downright sugary, but I never work by intuition. My processes of composition are determined by cool reasoning. Everything is calculated, constructed.' Whereupon he produced a curious exhibit, a sheet of graph paper, with the chromatic tones marked in the vertical, and the rhythm values, a sixteenth note to each square, in the horizontal line. 'This is how I compose,' he said. He does not have to wait upon inspiration. Any outline, any graph can serve him for a melody. . . .

"Villa-Lobos is very fond of charts, formulas, neologisms. He has made a chart to indicate the position of Brazilian music in the world of art. Each country is designated by a sort of zodiac sign, and arrows lead from one country to another, with Brazil in a whirlwind center of musical influences, but strong in its own primeval independence. Villa-Lobos is nationalistic. He says he places civic duties as a Brazilian musician even before the international fellowship of all artists. . . .

"Villa-Lobos possesses an incredible store of physical energy. He can carry on for hours, talking, playing, conducting, without showing signs of fatigue. One afternoon, after a full day's work at the office, he got out the huge score of his as yet unperformed *Chôros No. 11*, for piano and orchestra, and read it through, standing at his desk, gesticulating, imitating the instruments, barking out the rhythms. That evening, Villa-Lobos was not too tired to play, rather unpianistically, his pieces for the benefit of his friends and visitors at his home. Villa-Lobos also plays billiards, quite professionally, beating all amateurs hands down."

MAJOR WORKS

Ballets—Uirapurú; Dansa da Terra.

Chamber Music—17 string quartets; 2 Brazilian String Quartets; 4 Sonate-Fantaisies, for violin and piano; 3 piano trios; 2 cello sonatas; Piano Quartet; Piano Quintet; Quartet, for harp, celesta, flute, and saxophone, with women's voices; Mystic Sextet, for flute, clarinet, saxophone, celeste, harp, and guitar; Trio, for oboe, clarinet, and bassoon; Chôros No. 2, for flute and clarinet; Nonetto; Chôros No. 7, for flute, oboe, clarinet, saxophone, bassoon, violin, and cello; Quintet, for flute, oboe, English horn, clarinet, and bassoon; Bachiana Brasileira No. 1, for eight cellos; Bachiana Brasileira No. 5, for voice and eight cellos; Bachiana Brasileira No. 6, for flute and bassoon; Trio, for violin, viola and cello.

Choral Music—Chôros No. 3, for male chorus and seven wind instruments; Canção da Terra; Chôros No. 10, Rasga o Coração; Chôros No. 14, for chorus, band, and orchestra; Vidapura, oratorio; As Costeiras.

Operas—Zoé; Malazarte; Magdalena, light opera.

Orchestral Music—12 symphonies; various concertos for solo instruments and orchestra (piano; harp; cello; guitar; harmonica); Dansas Africanas; Amazonas; Uirapurú; Vitória; Paz; Chôros Nos. 6, 12, 13, 14; Chôros No. 11, for piano and orchestra; Momo Precoce; Bachianas Brasileiras Nos. 2, 4, 7, 8; Bachiana Brasileira No. 3, for piano and orchestra; Montanhas do Brasil; America; Bachiana Brasileira No. 9, for strings; Rudepoema (also for piano); Madona; Descobrimento do Brasil, four suites; Mandú-Carará; Erosion, or The Origin of the Amazon River; Dawn in a Tropical Forest; Odyssey of a Race; Poem of Itabira, for voice and orchestra.

Piano Music—Prole do Bébé, two suites; Historia da Carochinha; Lenda do Caboclo; Dansa Infernal; Cirandinhas; Chôros No. 5, Alma Brasileira; Saudades das Selvas Brasileiras; Francette et Pia; Ciclo Brasileiro; As Três Marias; Poema Singelo.

Vocal Music—Noite do Luar; Mal Secreto; Fleur Fanée; Il Nome di Maria; Sertão no Estio; Canções Tipicas Brasileiras; Historiettes; Épigrammes Ironiques et Sentimentales; Suite, for voice and violin; Poème de l'Enfant et de Sa Mère, for voice, flute, clarinet, and cello; Serestas; 3 Poemas Indigenas; Modinhas e Canções.

ABOUT

De Paula Barros, C. M., O Romance de Villa-Lobos; Giacomo, A. M. de, Villa-Lobos: Alma Sonora do Brasil; Mariz, V., Heitor Villa-Lobos; Muricy, J. C. de A., Villa-Lobos; Slonimsky, N., Music of Latin America.

Modern Music, October–November 1939.

Sir William Walton
1902–

William Turner Walton was born in Oldham, Lancashire, England, on March 29, 1902, of a family of musicians. Both parents were singing teachers; his father was also the choirmaster of the Oldham Church. William joined the choir when he was five; at the same time he received his first instruction in music from his father. At ten, he was awarded a scholarship for Christ Church Cathedral Choir School at Oxford. Here his musical talent attracted the interest of the Cathedral organist, who, in turn, recommended the boy to Sir Hugh Allen, professor of music at Oxford. Sir Hugh became Walton's teacher in composition, instruction which the boy soon supplemented by studying texts on theory. Walton also made his first attempts at writing music by producing several choral numbers and songs.

In 1918 Walton became one of the youngest men ever to receive a bachelor of music degree at the Choir School. This marked the end of his formal training in music, and except for subsequent advice from such eminent musicians as Busoni, Edward J. Dent, and the conductor Ernest Ansermet, Walton never again had a music teacher.

Dr. Thomas Banks Strong, Dean of Christ Church, was impressed with Walton's talent and used his influence to get the boy admitted to Christ Church, Oxford, even though he was under age. This was an unhappy choice. Entering Christ Church when he was sixteen, Walton applied himself so completely to his musical studies and interests that he neglected other subjects in the curriculum and was expelled.

By that time he had written two chamber music works of more than passing interest. One was a string quartet, completed when he was seventeen and eventually performed successfully at the festival of the International Society for Contemporary Music at Salzburg on August 4, 1923. In 1924 an even more important composition, his Piano Quartet, completed in 1919, received the Carnegie Trust Award, which provided funds for its publication; the award citation described it as a "work of real achievement." Certain derivative influences can be noted in both compositions, principally Brahms and Fauré; nevertheless both were strongly individual creations, the first in which Walton's own Romantic tendencies find full, free expression.

SIR WILLIAM WALTON

At Oxford, Walton met Sacheverell Sitwell. Upon leaving Oxford and finding residence in London, Walton moved frequently with the Sitwells, the remarkable literary family that included Osbert and Edith as well as Sacheverell. For a while Walton even lived with the Sitwells, who came to regard him as "their adopted or elected brother." Their sophisticated literary and artistic judgments and their progressive attitudes towards all the arts made a strong imprint on the young, impressionable composer.

In *Laughter in the Next Room*, Sir Osbert Sitwell described how the seventeen-year-old William Walton appeared to him at first meeting. He found Walton to be a "rather tall, slight figure, of typically northern coloring, with pale skin, straight, fair hair, like that of a young Norwegian or Dane. The refinement of his rather long, narrow, delicately shaped head, and of his bird-like profile showing so plainly above the brow the so-called bar or mound of Michelangelo that phrenologists claim to be the distinguishing mark of the artist—especially the musician—even his prominent, well-cut nose, scarcely gave a true impression of his robust mental qualities or of the strength of his physique. Sensitiveness rather than toughness was the quality at first most apparent in him."

The immediate artistic result of Walton's friendship with the Sitwells was the writing of an unconventional, provocative piece of music, rich in humor and satire, with which Walton first attracted attention. This work, called *Façade*, was originally scored for reciting voice and seven instruments, and consisted of settings of abstractionist or dadaistic poems by Edith Sitwell. Walton completed his score in 1922, at which time it received a private performance at the Sitwell home in Chelsea. A public performance followed at Aeolian Hall in London on June 12, 1923, inspiring a good deal of amusement, ridicule, and discussion. Two years later, Walton revised and expanded the work. The new version was introduced at the New Chenil Galleries in London on April 27, 1926. Unseen, Edith Sitwell recited her nonsense verses, her voice emerging from a megaphone-shaped mouth painted on the curtain; the instrumentalists were also concealed—and Walton's music was just as unconventional as the presentation. It revealed an uncommon gift for burlesque, humor, mock sentimentality, whimsy, and parody. It was wonderful fun, and it caused a sensation. "As a spirited and lively work," wrote Hubert J. Foss, "it is without a modern English rival, so full of pace and vivacity and humor is it. Its chief technical interest lies first in its brilliant rhythmic pattern which, touched by the tricks of jazz writers, far exceeds mathematically anything they have ever heard of; and secondly, in its ability to state a plain and obvious melody in a significant way without accompaniment. . . . *Façade* is an amusement of the high-jinks kind, but well shows that music to be amusing must first be satisfactory and (particularly) skillful as music."

Subsequently, *Façade* was presented at the festival of the International Society for Contemporary Music at Siena, in 1928; was twice used as material for ballets; and has often been heard at symphony concerts in two suites which the composer extracted from his score.

In 1925 Walton completed a breezy concert overture, *Portsmouth Point*, describing a waterfront scene with lively nautical-sounding tunes and dances. Its première took place at the festival of the International Society for Contemporary Music at Zürich on June 22, 1926; after that it was performed by major orchestras in Europe and the United States.

Sobriety began to invade Walton's writing with two ambitious compositions for solo instruments and orchestra. The *Sinfonia Concertante*, for piano and orchestra, was given in London on January 5, 1926, with York Bowen as soloist and Ernest Ansermet conducting; the Viola Concerto was introduced by Paul Hindemith at a London Promenade concert on October 3, 1929, the composer conducting. The former revealed a new facet of Walton's musical personality which was not at first fully appreciated; but the Viola Concerto was a triumph. Here we find Walton in full mastery of the tools of his trade, as gifted in the projection of poetic and expressive moods as he had been in the writing of light, satiric tunes for *Façade*. The concerto was chosen for the festival of the International Society for Contemporary Music at Liège in 1930.

Even more successful than the concerto was the oratorio *Belshazzar's Feast*, which had been commissioned for the Leeds Festival in England and was introduced there on October 10, 1931. Osbert Sitwell had prepared the text from the Bible, dramatizing the principal narrative of the fifth chapter of the Book of Daniel, and combining it with verses from Psalms 137 and 81. Though this was Walton's first mature exercise in writing for chorus, he produced a score distinguished for nobility of style, spaciousness of design, and felicitousness in writing dramatic or expressive episodes. "If Walton never again wrote a note, good, bad, or indifferent he has in *Belshazzar's Feast* definitely staked a claim to a position of first importance," wrote J. H. Elliot. "No words could do justice to this music; its force and power, its unhesitating rightness as musical and dramatic statement and, above all, the blazing artistic conviction which drives the whole conception forward, mark it as one of the most remarkable achievements of any English composer."

As a result of the success of *Belshazzar's Feast*, Walton's music was now in demand—so much so that his first symphony was performed even before it was finished. When three movements had been completed, Sir Hamilton Harty introduced them with the London Symphony on December 3, 1934—the fourth movement had still to be written. When it was completed, the symphony was given another première, on November 6, 1935.

Walton wrote still another major work before World War II, the Concerto for Violin and Orchestra, which Jascha Heifetz had commissioned. Walton paid his first visit to the United States to discuss this project with Heifetz. He planned to return for the concerto's world première in Cleveland on December 7, 1939; but the war broke out in Europe two months before the première and Walton's return visit to America was indefinitely postponed.

In his first symphony and violin concerto Walton had evolved an eclectic style that ranged freely and flexibly from romanticism to modernism. His method, as Edwin Evans pointed out, was "to surround his material with a wealth of contrapuntal arabesques and a profusion of rhythms. But it is such clear writing that clarity suffers but rarely.... Walton has acquired [such] confidence that, when he is so disposed, he can allow a subjective emotion to rise to the surface without any fear that it will float there like a stain."

During World War II, Walton served in the Ambulance Corps in London. While in uniform, he was assigned to write the music for several documentary films. At that time he also completed a comedy overture, *Scapino* (a return to the lively and tuneful manner of *Portsmouth Point*), on commission from the Chicago Symphony to celebrate its fiftieth anniversary. The Chicago Symphony introduced it on April 3, 1941, Frederick Stock conducting. In addition, two ballet scores were written during the war years: for *The Wise Virgins*, in 1940, Walton adapted and orchestrated music by Johann Sebastian Bach; and in 1943 he wrote an original score for *The Quest*, a Spenserian ballet with choreography by Frederick Ashton, produced by Sadler's Wells. In recognition of his achievements, Oxford University conferred an honorary doctorate upon him in 1942. During the forties he also wrote important film scores— *Major Barbara*, *Henry V*, and *Hamlet*—and incidental music for the Gielgud stage production of *Macbeth*.

When the war was over, Walton toured the Scandinavian countries as conductor in programs of his own works. Back from these engagements—with which his career as conductor of his music began officially—he plunged into new creative assignments. In 1947 he completed his first chamber music work in two decades—his first major concert work in almost a decade—the String Quartet in A minor, which the Blech String Quartet introduced over the BBC radio on May 4 of that year. "In the new Quartet was heard the mellowest music he had yet composed," said Kenneth Avery, who found that much of the harshness that had persisted in the violin concerto and the first symphony had disappeared completely.

On November 19, 1947, Walton received the Gold Medal of the Royal Philharmonic Society of London, the presentation being made by Ralph Vaughan Williams. In 1949 Walton married Susana Gil Passo in Buenos Aires. Made financially independent through the generous bequest of a friend, Walton eventually established himself on the island of Ischia where he has since lived the year round in a comfortable villa; favorable investments in property further enhanced his position. New and greater honors came hand in hand with affluence: in 1951 he was knighted, and in 1953 he was invited to write a Te Deum for the coronation of Queen Elizabeth II.

Walton's first opera was completed in 1954, after seven years of concentrated effort. It was *Troilus and Cressida*, libretto by Christopher Hassall based on Chaucer's adaptation of the medieval romance. The world première took place at Covent Garden in London on December 3, 1954. It was a truly gala performance, "by all odds," reported Cecil Smith in *Musical America*, "the most brilliant musical event of the autumn season in London. The boxes were full of peers, knights and their ladies." The opera rose majestically to the occasion. Utilizing an almost Italian style, the music proved melodious, emotional, and powerfully dramatic. "The long-lined vocal idiom . . . provides a strong element of characterization as

well as sentiment," continued Smith. "There are arias, beautiful ones, for all the main singers and expertly written ensembles." *Troilus and Cressida* became the first opera since Britten's *Peter Grimes* in 1945 to win the unanimous approval of the public, professional musicians, and critics. It was also acclaimed in America when it received its première in San Francisco on October 7, 1955, and again at its New York première on October 21, 1955, with the composer at both presentations. Harriett Johnson wrote in the New York *Post:* "There is . . . no doubt that the Walton opera is a highly impressive and frequently deeply moving work, created by a composer who knows how to fuse the materials of music into a dramatic synthesis."

Walton's second opera was in a completely different style. A one-act comic opera entitled *The Bear* (based on a story by Chekhov), it was introduced at the Aldeburgh Festival during the summer of 1967. The text deals with the efforts of a landowner to collect rent from a widow. They engage in a fierce battle of words but end up in love with each other. Walton produced a sardonic, satirical, quasi-whimsical score for the opera, including a parody of his own serious musical style in *Troilus and Cressida*. *The Bear* was first presented in the United States at Aspen, Colorado, on August 15, 1968.

A cello concerto (first performance in Boston on January 25, 1957, with Gregor Piatigorsky as soloist and Charles Münch conducting); a *Partita* for orchestra (written on commission for the fortieth anniversary of the Cleveland Orchestra, which introduced it on January 30, 1958, George Szell conducting); a second symphony (first performed at the Edinburgh Festival in Scotland on September 2, 1960, John Pritchard conducting the Liverpool Philharmonic); *Variations on a Theme by Hindemith* (written for the one hundred and fiftieth anniversary of the Royal Philharmonic of London which performed it on March 8, 1963 in London); and *Philharmonic Overture* (commissioned by the New York Philharmonic, the orchestra which performed the world première on December 7, 1968, André Kostelanetz conducting)—all these works are the late harvest of a slow and careful workman. Composing has never come easily to Walton. Major works have arrived only after a long period of gestation. But each work, when finally released, has been the product of a supreme craftsman who has always found ready at hand the tools and materials he needs to build impressive architectonic structures and to fill those structures with a variety of striking ideas, emotions, and moods.

Except for books (Walton is an avid reader) and paintings (of which he owns a modest collection), he has few interests outside music. He does not care for sports either as a participant or as a spectator. He has no hobbies. He finds no interest in games of any kind, whether of skill or of chance. For physical exercise he takes long walks and goes swimming. He is not indifferent to the benefits his wealth has brought him. He likes fine clothes, good food, expensive cars, and beautiful surroundings. Dallas Bower finds him to be a "tough, shrewd, North-country Englishman gifted with a sardonic wit and at times a Rabelaisian humor." But he also notes in Walton, though sometimes carefully concealed behind an austere exterior, "kindness, compassion, and consideration for others." Bower adds: "The cool, impassive objectivity of his approach to affairs, the rather slow-moving and dignified, but never pompous, manner of his bearing, give an impression that Walton would have made a success in any walk of life he had cared to follow."

Walton made his first American appearance as conductor in 1955 when he led a performance of his *Crown Imperial March* (1938) at the United Nations. On August 8, 1963, he conducted an all-Walton program at the Lewisohn Stadium in New York.

MAJOR WORKS

Ballets—The Wise Virgins (based on music by Johann Sebastian Bach); The Quest.

Chamber Music—2 string quartets; Piano Quartet; Façade, for narrator and seven instruments (also for large orchestra); Toccata, for violin and piano; Violin Sonata.

Choral Music—Belshazzar's Feast; Te Deum; Gloria.

Opera—Troilus and Cressida; The Bear, one-act comic opera.

Orchestral Music—2 symphonies; Portsmouth Point, concert overture; Façade, two suites; Sinfonia Concertante, for orchestra with piano; Viola Concerto; Violin Concerto; Scapino, comedy overture; Music for Children; Partita; Johannesburg Festival Overture; Cello Concerto; Variations on a Theme by Hindemith; Philharmonic Overture.

Piano Music—Music for Children, two books; Duets for Children.

Vocal Music—Three Songs to Poems by Edith Sitwell; Under the Greenwood Tree; Song for the Lord Mayor's Table.

ABOUT

Bacharach, A. L. (ed.), The Music Masters: v4, The Twentieth Century, by W. R. Anderson [and others]; Cohn, A., Twentieth-Century Music in Western Europe; Ewen, D. (ed.), The New Book of Modern Composers; Howes, F. S., The Music of William Walton.

Music and Letters (London), January 1947; Musical America, February 1952; Musical Quarterly, October 1940.

Robert Ward
1917–

Robert Eugene Ward was born in Cleveland, Ohio, on September 13, 1917. He was one of five children of a father who owned a moving and storage business. While attending public schools in Cleveland, Robert took lessons on the piano with Ben Burtt for two years and wrote his first compositions. In 1935 a scholarship took him to the Eastman School of Music in Rochester, New York, where he specialized in composition with Bernard Rogers, Howard Hanson, and Edward Royce. By the time he was graduated from the Eastman School in 1939 with a bachelor of music degree, several of his works had been introduced under Howard Hanson's direction. These included *Fatal Interview*, for soprano and orchestra (1937); *Slow Music* (1938); and *Ode for Orchestra* (1939).

Upon leaving Rochester, Ward entered the Juilliard School of Music on a composition fellowship. There he continued to study composition with Frederick Jacobi for one year, following this with a year of conducting instruction with Albert Stoessel and Edgar Schenkman. During the summer of 1941 he attended the Berkshire Music Center at Tanglewood as a composition student of Aaron Copland. While attending the Juilliard School, he was for one year a member of the music faculty of Queens College in New York. His first symphony (1941) received the Juilliard Publication Award and was introduced in New York on May 10, 1941.

Soon after Pearl Harbor, Ward was inducted into the United States Army. Stationed at Fort Riley in Kansas, he wrote the basic score for an all-soldiers' show, *The Life of Riley*.

Then he became the conductor of the 7th Infantry Band in the Pacific area, touring army installations throughout that theatre of the war. He and his band were cited for outstanding service. At that time he also founded and directed a jazz ensemble. For meritorious service during a Japanese attack on Attu in the Aleutians, Ward was decorated with a Bronze Star.

ROBERT WARD

The writing of music was not altogether abandoned during his years in the service. Two orchestral works completed during the war years subsequently received numerous performances from major American orchestras. They were the *Adagio and Allegro*, written in 1943 while the composer was stationed in Hawaii (and introduced in New York in May 1944); and *Jubilation*, an overture sketched during the Leyte and Okinawa campaigns but completed in New York in March 1946 and introduced in Los Angeles on November 21, 1946.

While still in the Army, in 1944, Ward received the Alice M. Ditson Fellowship from Columbia University. And in the same year, on June 19, he married Mary Raymond Benedict, a teacher. They have five children.

"The years in the Army," he later said, "proved most beneficial musically, in that I came into close contact with several phases of musical activity which otherwise I might have never known." He was discharged from the Army in December 1945 with the rank of war-

rant officer, junior grade. He returned to the Juilliard School where he completed his courses in conducting with Schenkman and received a postgraduate study certificate in May 1946. The same year he received a grant from the American Academy of Arts and Letters.

His studies concluded, Ward resumed his career as a teacher of music by joining the faculty of the Juilliard School, where he remained for a decade, and by giving courses at Columbia University from 1946 to 1948. He was the music director of the Third Street Music Settlement from 1952 to 1955, and from 1954 to 1956 was assistant to the president of the Juilliard School. Upon the death of Vittorio Giannini in 1967, Ward assumed Giannini's post as president of the North Carolina School of Arts at Winston-Salem.

Ward gained recognition for himself as a composer with his second symphony (1947), heard first in Washington, D.C., on January 25, 1948, later at the annual festival of contemporary American music sponsored by the Alice M. Ditson Fund at Columbia University in New York. Jazz elements, which had been evident in *Jubilation*, appeared in this symphony to contribute rhythmic vitality and a strong American flavor—particularly in the slow movement, which is a blues; otherwise the symphony followed traditional procedures. Irving Kolodin said in the New York *Sun:* "Ward's work is frisky in its energy, assured in its prodigious breeziness."

In 1949–1950 and again in 1951–1952, Ward received Guggenheim fellowships. He continued to produce music for orchestra and to enjoy extensive performances and favorable critical comment. He produced two more symphonies: the third, heard in Washington, D.C., on March 31, 1950; and the fourth, written for and introduced at the La Jolla Festival in California eight years later. Both reveal the composer's concern with a strong lyric line and demonstrate impressive growth in the techniques of orchestration and polyphony. Such development can also be found in several other compositions for orchestra: *Euphony* (1954); *Divertimento*, commissioned by the Portland Junior Orchestra in Oregon (1961); *Music for a Celebration*, commissioned by Broadcast Music, Inc., for its twentieth anniversary (1963); and the Piano Concerto whose world première took place in Washington, D.C., at the Inter-American Music Festival on June 23, 1968.

Despite his successes in instrumental music, Ward's most impressive achievements have come in opera. His first was *Pantaloon*, produced at Columbia University on May 17, 1956. This is a setting of Andreyev's play *He Who Gets Slapped*, with a libretto by Bernard Stambler. In reviewing the opera, Howard Taubman said that it made "effective use of the lyric theatre. . . . The work is dramatic and lyrical; it holds the attention and engages one's sympathies. . . . The libretto moves and gives the composer opportunity for music." When the New York City Opera revived the work on April 12, 1959, the original Andreyev title was restored and became definitive.

With *The Crucible*, Ward emerged as an American opera composer of outstanding importance. *The Crucible* is the play by Arthur Miller dealing with witchcraft accusations in New England and focusing on the Salem trials of 1692. Working closely with Miller, Bernard Stambler as librettist created a taut drama which loses none of the original stark terror, violence, penetrating characterizations, incisive dialogue. Relying more strongly on the voice than the orchestra in projecting the drama, Ward successfully met the many exacting challenges of his text. "He has built his music drama as relentlessly as Miller molded his play," commented Miles Kastendieck in the New York *Journal American*. "The result is an opera with tremendous impact." Winthrop Sargeant said in the *New Yorker:* "His music, though quite accessible to the average listener, is everywhere dignified and nowhere banal. It is continuously expressive, and it intensifies all the nuances of the drama, from anguish and despair, to heroic nobility. Most remarkable of all, it is eminently singable, and though it contains only a few brief passages that might be described as arias, it restores the human voice and deft vocal melody to the controlling position these things must assume in all true opera."

Following the world première staged by the New York City Opera on October 26, 1961, *The Crucible* received the Pulitzer Prize in music and a citation from the New York Music Critics Circle. Ward became the first American composer to direct the German première of an American opera when, in 1963,

he led *The Crucible* at the State Theatre in Wiesbaden.

On a commission from the Central City Opera House Association in Colorado, Ward wrote the opera *The Lady from Colorado*, which had its world première in Central City on July 3, 1964. The libretto (the work of Bernard Stambler, based on a novel by Homer Croy) has a Colorado setting. The action takes place in the mountain town of Elkhorn in the late nineteenth century. It traces the careers of an Irish immigrant girl who runs the local laundry and her husband, an expatriate English nobleman. The score also has local interest, since one number after another sings the praises of the Mountain State in operetta style. The opera proved a great success, selling out for all of its fifteen performances. Sandor Kallai, in the Kansas City *Star*, said that it "captures the spirit and the lawless excitement of the old West. . . . There is an absolute abundance of singable melody and earthy humor, which should assure the work a lasting place on the light opera stage."

Since 1956, Ward has been the executive vice president and managing editor of the Galaxy Music Corporation and the Highgate Press. In 1955–1956 he was chairman of the American Composers Alliance, and subsequently he served as chairman of its board of directors. In 1963 Sioux City honored him with an entire weekend of festivities, lectures, and concerts featuring his compositions. In 1964 Ward was selected to serve on the Joint Committee of the Contemporary Music Project for Creativity in Music Education, administered by the Music Educators National Conference.

MAJOR WORKS

Chamber Music — Violin Sonata; Fantasia for Brass Choir and Tympani; Arioso and Tarantella, for cello (or viola) and piano.

Choral Music — Earth Shall Be Fair, cantata; With Rue My Heart Is Laden; Concord Hymn; Let the Word Go Forth; That Wondrous Night of Christmas Eve; When Christ Rode into Jerusalem.

Operas — He Who Gets Slapped (originally entitled Pantaloon); The Crucible; The Lady from Colorado.

Orchestral Music — 4 symphonies; Fatal Interview, for soprano and orchestra; Ode; Yankee Overture; Adagio and Allegro; Jubilation Overture; Concert Music; Night Music, for chamber orchestra; Jonathon and the Gingery Snare, for narrator, small orchestra, and percussion; Euphony; Prairie Overture; Divertimento; Hymn and Celebration; Piano Concerto.

Webern

Vocal Music—Ann Miranda; As I Watched the Ploughman Ploughing; Epithalamion; Rain Has Fallen All the Day; Sacred Song for Pantheists; Sorrow of Mydath; Vanished.

ABOUT

American Composers Alliance Bulletin, May 1962.

Anton Webern
1883–1945

Anton Webern, one of the trinity of twelve-tone composers which included Schoenberg and Alban Berg, was born in Vienna on December 3, 1883. He was the second son of a mining engineer. The Weberns were a titled family which, since the early nineteenth century, had owned a small estate in Preglhof, in the Carinthian section of Austria. As a member of the nobility Webern for many years prefixed the title *von* to his last name, but he dropped this practice late in his life.

ANTON WEBERN

Webern's preliminary schooling took place in the Austrian towns of Graz and Klagenfurt. Music study (piano, cello, and theory) began in Klagenfurt in 1893 with Erwin Komauer. In 1902, Webern entered the University of Vienna as a student of philosophy. There he enrolled in the musicology class of Guido Adler. In 1906 he received his doctorate in music at the University.

Composition had begun early for Webern;

Webern: vā′ bĕrn

as a discovery in 1961 of numerous Webern manuscripts revealed for the first time, some songs were written when Webern was only fifteen. While still attending the University he completed a ballad for voice and large orchestra, *Siegfrieds Schwert* (1903), together with a composition for large orchestra, *Im Sommerwind* (1904). These and other apprentice efforts revealed that Webern, like so many other young composers in Vienna, was following the lead of, and in many instances imitating, Wagner and Richard Strauss. *Im Sommerwind* was a particularly recognizable child of post-Romanticism and Wagnerism, when it belatedly received its world première in Seattle, Washington, on May 25, 1962.

Another influence could, however, be found in *Im Sommerwind*, that of Arnold Schoenberg—the Schoenberg of *Verklärte Nacht* and *Gurre-Lieder*, still faithful to the Wagner cult. In the year that Webern wrote *Im Sommerwind*, he met Schoenberg for the first time. A four-year period of study with Schoenberg followed. As a disciple of his teacher, Webern was led away from the subjectivity of post-Romanticism to the objectivity of atonality.

Webern's first composition to bear an opus number appeared in 1908, the year in which Webern's study with Schoenberg came to an end. The work was the *Passacaglia*, for orchestra, the première of which was conducted by the composer in Vienna in the year of its composition. The structure was in the traditional baroque manner, a theme subjected to contrapuntal variations. Webern's polyphonic skill and his gift of building up to moments of dramatic interest suggest that he might have had one eye on the C minor Passacaglia of Bach and another on the finale of Brahms's Fourth Symphony. Nevertheless, in this work, certain idiosyncrasies of Webern's later style already come into focus, such as his tendency to reduce larger thematic thoughts to fragments and the tendency to exploit themes with wide intervallic leaps.

As Schoenberg was drawn more and more to atonality, Webern followed him with unswerving allegiance. The period between 1909 and 1911 saw the completion of two compositions in which Webern's break with post-Romanticism became complete. Brevity, compression, high tension, objectivity, the reduction of materials to basic essentials—all

618

these can be found in the *Five Pieces for String Quartet*, op. 5 (1909); the *Four Pieces*, for violin and piano, op. 7 (1910); and the *Five Pieces for Orchestra*, op. 10 (1911). One movement in the *Five Pieces for String Quartet* was only thirteen measures long. Although the *Four Pieces*, for violin and piano, still adhered to a tonal scheme, the tonality was flexible enough to allow the epigrammatic subjects to move about freely with more concern for variation than for development or repetition.

In the *Six Pieces for Orchestra*, op. 6 (1910), the *Five Pieces for Orchestra*, op. 10, and the *Six Bagatelles*, for string quartet, op. 9 (1913) Webern continued more boldly towards brevity and concentration. The six orchestral pieces take only ten minutes to perform. In the *Five Pieces*, op. 10, only one movement requires more than a minute, the shortest one lasts only fourteen seconds. The *Six Bagatelles* extend only for fifty-eight measures in all, with the longest movement (the fifth) only thirteen measures long. At the same time Webern reduced the dynamics to such a point that the *Five Pieces* started out pianissimo and ended almost inaudible, with only a single climax (for eight instruments) to vary the sonority. The large orchestra is treated as if it were just a small and intimate ensemble. Thematic material is reduced to fragments with no harmony to speak of, fragments described as "melodies in one breath." Thematic development and repetition were by this time abandoned. Discussing Webern's methods in his *Bagatelles*, Erwin Stein further points out that "almost every note of a melody is given to a different instrument, and each one in a different tone color (harmonics, pizzicato, col legno, and so forth). This, together with a rhythm that often lays stress on the weak beat of a bar, imparts to these pieces something unusually glistening and fluid."

Webern (like Schoenberg and Berg) was at his first performances the victim of hostility and attacks from both audiences and critics. When the *Six Pieces for Orchestra* was introduced—in Vienna on March 31, 1913—the audience expressed its violent opposition in no uncertain way. A despatch from Vienna to the Boston *Evening Transcript* described what happened: "Before ten measures of that slow, groaning, wheezing music . . . had been played,

there were grins. Then somebody giggled. The next moment, a good quarter of the hall was in open-hearted laughter. . . . Inimical hisses spread to the high-priced seats and war began. . . . From that time on the pieces were played mostly amid laughter."

In the period between 1908 and 1913, Webern conducted theatre orchestras in Bad Ischl, Vienna, Teplitz, Danzig, and Stettin. On February 22, 1911, in Danzig, he married Wilhelmine Mörtl, by whom he had four children, three of them girls. During World War I, Webern enlisted in the Austrian Army but was soon released because of defective vision. In 1917 he lived in Prague, where he conducted orchestral concerts.

In June 1918, Webern settled in the Mödling section of Vienna, near Schoenberg. That year he helped Schoenberg found the Society for Private Musical Performances in Vienna and for several years was its co-director. This organization was devoted to the performance of music by the Schoenberg school, performances at which audiences were asked to refrain from applause and from which all critics were barred. On May 1, 1924, Webern received public recognition as a composer for the first time, when he was given the City of Vienna Prize in music. During these years he expanded his activities as conductor by directing the Workers' Symphony Concerts in Vienna (1922–1934) and the Vienna Workers' Chorus (1923) and by serving as music director of the Austrian Radio (1927). In addition, he made occasional appearances as guest conductor in European cities outside Vienna, notably in London in 1929 and in Barcelona in 1932.

When Schoenberg embraced the twelve-tone technique in 1924, Webern followed suit. The twelve-tone idiom first appears in Webern's music in the *Three Spiritual Folk Songs*, for voice, violin (or viola), clarinet, and bass clarinet, op. 17 (1924). And it is pursued with Schoenbergian rigidity in the *Three Lieder*, for voice, clarinet, and guitar, op. 18 (1925); the *Two Goethe Songs*, for chorus, celesta, guitar, violin, clarinet, and piano, op. 19 (1926); and the String Trio, op. 20 (1927).

In the middle 1920's Webern was commissioned by the League of Composers in New York to write a symphony (op. 21, 1928). It is here—in what some musicologists now describe as the most influential single work of the twentieth century—that Webern suggests the technique of serialism. In serialism, the twelve-tone technique applies not only to pitch, but also to dynamics, rhythm, tone color. This represents the last word in creative discipline—the ultimate reduction of music to abstraction. When the Symphony was first heard (in New York City on December 18, 1929, Alexander Smallens conducting), the critics were appalled by what they heard. Olin Downes asserted that Webern had achieved "the perfect fruition of futility," and he added: " 'The Ultimate Significance of Nothing'—this would be the proper title of the piece." Oscar Thompson wrote: "What the audience heard suggested odd sounds in an old house when the wind moans, the floors creak, the shades rattle, and the doors and windows alternately croak and groan." Samuel Chotzinoff compared the work to "the fractional music uttered at night by the sleeping inhabitants of a zoo."

Webern perfected the methods of the Symphony in subsequent works: Quartet, op. 22, for saxophone, clarinet, violin, and piano (1931); the Concerto, for nine solo instruments, op. 24 (1934); *Piano Variations*, op. 27 (1936); and String Quartet, op. 28 (1938). Here, as Ernest Krenek once noted, the composer withdraws more and more "into the detached, cool, miraculous and exciting world of the musical patterns, where the abstract spirit of music seems to have its own enigmatic life, sufficient unto itself," with the texture thinned out so that "in many places the musical flow is reduced to the tenuous strand of a single tone line."

Some official recognition came to Webern early in the 1930's. On April 13, 1931, there took place in Vienna a concert devoted exclusively to his music. This event inspired favorable reactions from one or two of Vienna's more progressive critics. A little more than a year after that, Webern was given the City of Vienna Prize in music for the second time.

In 1933 Webern became active for the first time as a teacher of composition by accepting several private pupils. From that time on, teaching was his main source of income. When the Nazis rose to power in Germany, Webern had high hopes that the new regime might

create a climate in that country more receptive to his music. He was, of course, soon disenchanted. The Nazis denounced his music as "cultural Bolshevism" and banned it from German concert halls.

After the Nazis marched into Austria, Webern was reduced to dire financial circumstances, as all sources of income were suddenly cut off. He became, as Krenek wrote, "a quiet, friendly man, but given to sudden terrifying tantrums. Such outbursts of frightful anguish were undoubtedly caused by pent-up feelings of frustration and bitterness, natural to a man who knew his worth and could convince nobody of it." Much of Webern's depression at this time sprang from the fact that his two distinguished colleagues were no longer near him to give him strength and hope: Alban Berg was dead; Arnold Schoenberg had left Europe for good. To still another colleague, Egon Wellesz, Webern wrote sadly in 1939: "Yes, my dear fellow, things have taken a turn quite different from what we expected."

During World War II, tragedy struck the Webern household when Webern's only son was killed during a bombing raid. With the war edging ever closer to Vienna, Webern fled with his wife and one of his daughters to Mittersill, in the Austrian Tyrol. He lived, as a neighbor, Cesar Bresgen, has since revealed, in rooms that were "as humble as could be, but hospitable." Bresgen recalled that Webern was "repeatedly busy at a shabby little table with pencil and compass, occupied with geometrical figures or lines and signs." At that time Webern was suffering acutely from stomach disorders, which could not be treated properly because of the war. Nevertheless, he was still busy with composition—at work on a third cantata which he never completed. He sometimes attended concerts in the local church. Sometimes he visited his daughter and son-in-law, who lived nearby. Most of all, he liked taking long walks in the forests. "Webern's very touching joy in the little wonders of nature," says Bresgen, "especially in the world of vegetation, was known to all who came close to him. Characteristic was the long contemplation of things, the immersion of himself in them; thus when he observed a fern or mountain flower, it was preferably in its habitat."

After the German capitulation in May 1945,

American troops occupied Mittersill. On the night of September 15, at about ten o'clock, Webern took a stroll outside his son-in-law's house, smoking a cigar. While walking in the darkness, Webern was shot and killed by an American sentry. The circumstances surrounding this tragedy long remained confused by contradictory reports. One early report accused the son-in-law of the murder. Another stated that an American sentry, seeing Webern in the darkness, ordered him to stand still and that Webern, failing to comprehend, had continued his walk and thus brought about his own death.

Not until fifteen years after Webern's death were the circumstances surrounding it clarified once and for all, thanks to the painstaking researches in Mittersill of Hans Moldenhauer, a dedicated Webern admirer. What had happened in 1945 was this: Webern's son-in-law had been involved in black market operations in Mittersill, a fact known to the occupying American troops. Two soldiers were despatched to the house of the son-in-law to question him, on an evening when Webern had been invited there for dinner. Webern enjoyed that evening tremendously, an evening topped off by a gift from his son-in-law of an American cigar. At 9:45 P.M. Webern went out of the house to enjoy his cigar. While he was out, two American soldiers had arrived to place the son-in-law under arrest. Confronting a dark figure outside the house, the first American suspected serious trouble, drew his gun, and fired. The composer staggered into the house and collapsed. His last words were: "It is finished." The son-in-law was convicted and jailed for a year. The soldier who had fired the fatal shot was tormented for the rest of his life by recollections of the tragedy. In fact, the soldier's wife insisted that her husband's premature death in 1950 from alcoholism was the result of a tormented conscience.

Webern was convinced that ultimately the world would recognize his creative importance. He said: "In fifty years at the most everyone will experience this music as *their* innate music; yes, even for children it will be accessible. People will sing it."

The day when children will sing Webern's music may still be far in the future. Nevertheless, it cannot be doubted that since his death the importance of Webern and his music has become an accepted fact. Erntes Krenek has said that Webern represented the most complete break with musical tradition in centuries; and Pierre Boulez has written that all music written before Anton Webern is dead tissue. Boulez, Stockhausen, Gunther Schuller and other avant-garde composers—jazz as well as classical—have used Webern as their point of departure. Young composers the world over—and some composers, such as Stravinsky, in their old age—have adopted Webern's serial method as a basic technique.

Posthumous recognition has come to Webern in several stages. In 1957 Columbia Records issued Webern's complete works in an album directed by Robert Craft. In May 1962 the School of Music at the University of Washington, in Seattle, held a three-day Anton Webern Festival arranged and led by the distinguished Webern authority Hans Moldenhauer. An immediate result of this event was the formation of the International Webern Society with one hundred and sixty-eight founding members from eleven countries. In 1965 a second international Webern festival was held at Salzburg, Austria, during the festival season. A fourth event, held to commemorate the twentieth anniversary of his death, followed in Mittersill, where Webern had been shot. Plaques were set up on the house where he died and on the church that had been used as his morgue. In 1964 two annual Webern festivals were inaugurated, one in Buffalo, New York, the other at the Congregation of the Arts at Hopkins Center at Dartmouth College. A ballet entitled *Episodes*, with choreography by George Balanchine, was set to Webern's music and produced at the Lincoln Center for the Performing Arts in New York. In 1969 the Harkness Ballet introduced *Moments*, the music for which came from Webern's *Six Bagatelles*.

In 1961 Moldenhauer discovered a treasure-trove of Webern manuscripts in the possession of Webern's oldest daughter. His find included not only compositions but also a stage play, diaries, and other valuable writings. All the material was purchased for the Webern archives at the University of Washington in Seattle. Moldenhauer found another Webern collection in an attic of an old house near Vienna in 1965. This included several compositions (some of them very early ones) the existence of which even Webern authorities had not suspected.

MAJOR WORKS

Chamber Music—Five Pieces, for string quartet; Four Pieces, for violin and piano; Six Bagatelles, for string quartet; Three Little Pieces, for cello and piano; String Trio; Quartet, for violin, clarinet, saxophone, and piano; Concerto, for nine instruments.

Choral Music—2 cantatas; Entflicht auf Leichten Kähnen; Two Goethe Songs; Das Augenlicht.

Orchestral Music—Passacaglia; Six Pieces; Five Pieces; Symphony; Variations.

Piano Music—Variations.

Vocal Music—Der Siebente Ring; Five Songs, op. 4; Songs, op. 8; Four Songs, op. 12; Four Songs, op. 13; Six Songs, op. 14; Fünf Geistliche Lieder; Three Canons; Drei Geistliche Volkslieder; Three Songs, op. 18; Viae Inviae; Three Songs, op. 25.

ABOUT

Anton Webern, zum 50 Geburtstag; Anton Webern: Dokumente, Bekenntnisse, Erkenntnisse, Analysen; Kolneder, W., Anton Webern; Leibowitz, R., Schoenberg and His School; Moldenhauer, H. (comp.), Anton von Webern Perspectives; Moldenhauer, H., The Death of Anton Webern; Reich, W., Anton Webern: The Man and His Music; Wildgans, F., Webern.

Musical Quarterly, January 1967; Musical Times (London), October 1940; Saturday Review, May 28, 1966; Score (London), September 1955.

Kurt Weill
1900–1950

Kurt Weill was born on March 2, 1900, in Dessau, Germany. Since his father was a cantor in a synagogue and his mother was a fine amateur pianist, there was always good music in the Weill household. Though the child seemed receptive to music, he did not get any formal music lessons until he was fourteen. At that time he began to study the piano with Albert Bing. Bing soon detected signs of creative talent in the boy and urged him to train himself as a composer. His father agreed. After receiving preliminary training in theory, he went to Berlin in 1918 and enrolled in the Berlin Hochschule für Musik, where his teachers included Humperdinck and Krasselt. Weill's studies were temporarily interrupted when he served as an opera coach and conductor at Dessau and Lüdenscheid, but from 1921 to 1924, once again in Berlin, he studied composition pri-

Weill: vīl

vately with Busoni, supporting himself by playing the piano in beer halls.

Busoni's influence led Weill to write instrumental works advocating and reflecting the advanced musical thinking of the day—abstract and frequently discordant compositions catering to a sophisticated minority. In this style he completed a symphony in 1921 (long thought lost, but recovered in 1958); *Fantasy, Passacaglia and Hymn*, for orchestra; *Frauentanz*, for soprano, viola, flute, clarinet, horn, and bassoon, featured at the festival of the International Society for Contemporary Music at Salzburg on August 6, 1924; and a violin concerto (1924), heard at the Zürich Festival on June 23, 1926. This concerto was neglected for the next thirty years, until in 1955 it was revived by Anahid Ajemian to receive its American première in Indianapolis, Izler Solomon conducting. In the 1960's a second symphony was recovered; it had been written in 1933.

KURT WEILL

While working on such serious, complex works with strictly limited appeal, Weill was beginning to question his values. In 1922 he wrote the music for a children's ballet, *Die Zaubernacht*, which had so great an appeal for audiences old and young that Weill began to think for the first time of writing compositions for a new public, a public that could not understand or respond to his complex and esoteric works. He was becoming convinced that composers had too long occupied an ivory tower by addressing themselves only to a negligible handful of musical *cognoscenti*. It was to be several years before Weill abandoned the writing of such music, but meanwhile he was thinking at this time in terms of a musical art with a broad base, an art as meaningful to the masses and as contemporary in subject matter as the daily newspaper—music deriving its appeal through the exploitation of popular tunes and idioms. He was contemplating the writing of an opera with a vital subject treated forcefully and realistically, set to music that was spirited, tuneful, and readily assimilable. "Do you want to become a Verdi of the poor?" Busoni asked him. Weill replied with a question of his own: "Is that so bad?"

While searching about for a suitable subject for his first opera, Weill came upon a one-act play by the German expressionist playwright Georg Kaiser—*Der Protagonist*. This was a surrealistic play about an actor who confuses real life with the stage and commits murder while performing in the theatre. Weill asked Kaiser for permission to set the stage piece to music. On March 27, 1926, *The Protagonist* was introduced in Dresden with tremendous success. The eminent musicologist Oskar Bie called it a perfect fusion of text and music. As for the music, its main interest lay in its pleasing lyricism and dramatic strength.

The success of *The Protagonist* led the Berlin Kroll Opera to commission Weill to write music for a new opera, this time with text by Ivan Goll. It was called *The Royal Palace* and was an experimental work in which pantomime and motion picture sequences were combined with stage action. Its première took place on March 2, 1927. Many years later, on October 5, 1968, the American première was performed by the San Francisco Opera.

Next came a satirical opera, *The Czar Has Himself Photographed*, the text of which was the first that Georg Kaiser wrote for the musical stage. It was presented in Leipzig on February 18, 1928. This opera carried Weill well along the path he had been pursuing, cautiously using popular German and American jazz styles—in fact one German critic described it as a "jazz opera." The intelligentsia in Germany felt that Weill was betraying his artistic trust and condemned him for it. Weill, however, knew what he wanted. Explaining his aims in no uncertain terms, he told an interviewer at the time: "I want to reach the real people, a more representative public than any opera house attracts. I write for today. I don't care about writing for posterity." And the general public was attracted to his new kind of opera. *The Czar Has Himself Photographed* was an enormous box-office success—within a short period it was heard in some eighty theatres in Germany.

The turning point in Weill's career and his emergence as the leading spokesman of *Zeitkunst*, a new esthetic cult then sweeping Germany, came simultaneously. *Zeitkunst* represented an art that is contemporary in theme and appeal, dealing with modern subjects, interpreting the modern spirit, and rooted deeply in modern sources. Weill first became an apostle of *Zeitkunst* with a little one-act sketch with music, *Mahagonny* (1927), which was Weill's first collaboration with Bertholt Brecht. *Mahagonny*, a satire on modern society (produced on July 17, 1927), proved an epoch-making achievement not only for *Zeitkunst* but also for Weill. With it he finally broke his ties with the traditional forms of opera and established a new form he called "song play." Popular songs replaced formal arias. Jazz became basic to the vocabulary. "Nothing like it had ever been tried by a serious composer," said H. W. Heinsheimer, "and it had the effect of a bombshell."

Having finally arrived at the kind of structure and style best suited to his purpose, Weill was now ready to create his masterwork, *The Three-Penny Opera* (*Die Dreigroschenoper*), for which Brecht once again provided the libretto. The work, which had its world première on August 31, 1928, is a twentieth century adaptation of John Gay's famous eighteenth century ballad opera, *The Beggar's Opera*. Gay's text gave Brecht ample opportunities to voice his own leftist social and political thinking by pointing up the corruption of German society in the 1920's. He produced a text that is satirical, cynical, at times even bitter. And Weill's music is a masterly fusion of classic and popular idioms: the opera opens with a blues and ends with a mock chorale. In between come such varied musical items as music-hall tunes, a shimmy, and a fox-trot, on the one hand, and a canon and opera-like arias and choruses, on the other.

The Three-Penny Opera caused a furor. From its Berlin première it went on to become possibly the most successful musical production in Germany in the era between the two world wars. In its initial year it received over four thousand performances in a hundred German theatres. After five years, it had been given ten thousand times in Central Europe, in eighteen languages. It was made into an artistic cinema production by G. W. Pabst, the eminent motion-picture producer; this was the first of several screen adaptations. Several of the principal melodies, especially "Moritat," became hit songs. A bar named Dreigroschenoper was opened in Berlin and no other music was played there but excerpts from the opera.

The star of *The Three-Penny Opera* was Lotte Lenya, who played the part of the prostitute. By 1928 Lotte Lenya had become Mrs. Kurt Weill. They had met in 1924 when Weill paid his first call on Georg Kaiser. At that time, she was living with the Kaiser family and had been despatched to the railroad station to meet Weill. "What struck me was his voice," she later recalled, "very quiet, very soft, and very deep. We fell in love soon after that." They were married on January 28, 1926.

Lotte Lenya returned to the role which she had originated when *The Three-Penny Opera* was revived off-Broadway on March 10, 1954, with the text newly adapted by Marc Blitzstein but with Weill's music untouched. This was not the American première of the opera, however. That had taken place in New York City on April 13, 1933, and the opera had lasted only thirteen performances at that time. The 1954 revival, however, established *The Three-Penny Opera* as one of the most successful musicals ever produced in the United States; it ran for six years in New York, and two national companies toured with it throughout the country in 1960 and 1961. The song "Moritat"—or "Mack the Knife" as it is now better known—was recorded in forty-eight versions and sold over ten million discs; it reached the top rung of the Hit Parade in 1955.

The Three-Penny Opera was followed by *Der Jasager*, intended for school production. Brecht's libretto was based on a Japanese No play. This little work was produced in over five hundred educational institutions in Germany. In 1929 Weill and Brecht wrote *Happy End*, an opera about gangs in Chicago. From the score comes "The Bilbao Song," a tune that achieved hit status in the United States in 1961.

On March 9, 1930, *The Rise and Fall of the City of Mahagonny*—an expansion of the 1927 one-act opera *Mahagonny*—was introduced simultaneously at the Leipzig Opera and the Frankfurt Opera. The Brecht libretto is at times an obscene, and always an irreverent, satire on decadent capitalist society. Mahagonny is a fictional town in Alabama where three ex-convicts build a new society in which people are free to do what they wish without consideration of ethics or morality. The hypocrisy, corruption, duplicity of modern society—together with the drives and rivalries of capitalism—are here laid bare. With a musical score that makes extensive use of popular tunes and jazz, *The Rise and Fall of the City of Mahagonny* is, in H. H. Stuckenschmidt's description, "a document of its times. The atmosphere of the Berlin of the 1920's has found no more anguished expression than in this opera." One of the songs from the score became an outstanding hit in Germany in the 1930's, "Alabamy Song"—(title in English because the lyrics are in a gibberish English).

Because of the success of *The Three-Penny Opera* and *The Rise and Fall of the City of Mahagonny*, Weill became not only the leading spokesman of *Zeitkunst* but also the foremost European composer to utilize popular idioms within opera. His last success in Germany was *Die Bürgschaft*, produced in Berlin on March 10, 1932; it was adapted from a parable by Herder and used the chorus as narrator. Banned by the Nazis in 1933, *Die Bürgschaft* was not seen again for another quarter of a century; it was revived by the Städtische Oper in Berlin during the Berlin Festival in the fall of 1957.

On February 18, 1933, *Der Silbersee* (text by Georg Kaiser) opened in eleven German cities. A week later the Reichstag in Berlin was aflame, setting into motion a chain of events that put the control of Germany in the hands of the Nazis. The fact that *Der Silbersee* had a song called "The Ballad of Caesar's Death," an indictment of Hitler and Nazism, was not the only thing that now made Weill's situation in the new Germany perilous. He was a Jew. Moreover, the Nazis had long considered him a "Kultur Bolshevist," the voice of a decadent Germany; even in 1930, the Nazis had released stink bombs and started fist fights in Leipzig and Frankfurt at the premières of *The Rise and Fall of the City of Mahagonny*.

Warned by friends that his life was in immediate danger, Weill and his wife fled from Germany. For two years they lived in an old stone house in Louveciennes, outside Paris. There Weill composed the score for a ballet, *The Seven Deadly Sins* (*Die Sieben Todsünden*), produced in 1933 by Les Ballets in Paris and London, with George Balanchine's choreography, starring Tilly Losch. He also completed the score for a musical play, *Marie Galante*, text by Jacques Deval. One of its songs, "*J'Attends un Navire*," became a favorite song of the French underground movement during World War II. In 1935 Weill wrote the music for a stage satire produced in London, *A Kingdom for a Cow*.

In September 1935, on an invitation from the distinguished stage director Max Reinhardt, Weill came to the United States, where he lived for the rest of his life. Reinhardt was then planning a mammoth production in New York—a pageant of the Jewish people called *The Eternal Road*, with text by Franz Werfel—and called upon Weill to write the music. Since the opening of *The Eternal Road* was delayed several times, Weill's debut as a composer for the American theatre had to come with another play—*Johnny Johnson*, a bitter antiwar "musical fable" by Paul Green, which opened on Broadway on November 19, 1936. *The Eternal Road* was finally produced in 1937.

Beginning with *Knickerbocker Holiday*, which starred Walter Huston and which opened in New York on October 19, 1938, Weill became one of Broadway's most successful and highly esteemed composers. A complete account of his career in the American theatre does not come within the scope of this volume since it involves his popular music, but the scores are worth noting: *Lady in the Dark*, by Moss Hart (1941); *One Touch of Venus*, by S. J. Perelman and Ogden Nash (1943); *The Firebrand of Florence*, a musical based on the life of Benvenuto Cellini, by Edwin Justus Mayer (1945); *Street Scene*, by Elmer Rice, based on his own play of the same title (1947); *Love Life*, by Alan Jay Lerner (1948); *Lost in the Stars*, by Maxwell Anderson, based on Alan Paton's novel *Cry, the Beloved Country* (1949). Most of these productions belong in the category of musical comedy. Two (*Street Scene* and *Lost in the Stars*) were musical plays in which Weill's score outgrew the more limited confines of the popular theatre to assume ambitious artistic dimensions. Howard Taubman, for example, did not hesitate to call *Street Scene* "an American opera, if you emphasize the adjective more than the noun." He added: "For it is a congeries of musical idioms. It has some genuine operatic writing, in the sense that the music furnishes the emotional core of a scene." To Olin Downes, *Lost in the Stars* was also more of an opera than a musical comedy. In line with such thinking, *Street Scene* was produced by the Düsseldorf Opera in Germany in the winter of 1955 and by the New York City Opera on April 2, 1959; *Lost in the Stars* entered the repertory of the New York City Opera on April 11, 1958.

One of Weill's last works for the American stage was an American folk opera intended for production by schools and other nonprofessional groups. It was *Down in the Valley* (text by Arnold Sundgaard), introduced at Indiana University on July 15, 1948. In this work Weill makes ample and effective use of a number of Kentucky mountain folk songs, including "Sourwood Mountain," "Down in the Valley," and "The Lonesome Dove."

"Ever since I started working for the theatre," Weill once wrote to the editor of this book, "I have considered myself a theatre composer. I believe that the musical theatre is the highest, the most expressive and the most imaginative form of theatre, and that a composer who has a talent and a passion for the theatre can express himself completely in this branch of musical creativeness. Through my work for the theatre I have arrived at the conclusion that the distinction between 'serious' and 'light' music is one of the misconceptions of the Wagnerian period in music. The only distinction we should make is the one between good and bad music. I believe that new forms of musical theatre can be developed in close connection with the living theatre and the fundamental ideas of our time, and that these new forms can take the place of the traditional opera or operetta. Most of my own works for the theatre in Europe and this country have been experiments in different forms of musical theatre. Broadway seems to me a perfect place to develop a musical theatre which, in time, will become to this country what opera was to Europe."

Kurt Weill died in New York City on April 3, 1950. In a eulogy in the New York *Times*, Olin Downes wrote: "Weill's position among modern composers is exceptional. It involved his evolution from the status of a composer of 'highbrowed' and formidably educated variety to one whose art has the widest public appeal. It includes in this perspective an artist who came here from Germany and assimilated remarkably the American scene and viewpoint, and expressed these things significantly in his later music. And there is another important angle to the business, which is Weill's significant contribution to forms of modern opera. . . . He stands as a sovereign example of the forces that merge in the American 'melting pot' toward a national expression, and the forces of this period which are working to create new forms of operatic expression in our theatre."

Since Weill's death, his widow, Lotte Lenya, has promoted his music in recitals, over television, in the theatre, and in recordings.

Kurt Weill was a short, somewhat stocky man with a cherubically round face that had a perpetually owlish expression, due to his enormous eyes. Because he preferred living on the outskirts of a great city, he made his home during his last years on a large farm in New City, in Rockland County, New York. He liked to work—indeed, he did his best work—under pressure, finding neither noise nor company any distraction when he was busy. When not composing, he read much—sometimes Shakespeare, and always all the newspapers he could put his hands on. He was a lover of paintings, of which he became a collector. He was careless about his dress, selecting his clothes more for comfort than for appearance.

MAJOR WORKS

Ballet—Die Sieben Todsünden (The Seven Deadly Sins).

Chamber Music—String Quartet; Frauentanz, medieval songs for soprano and instruments; Vom Tod im Walde, ballade for basso and ten instruments.

Choral Music—Recordare; Das Berliner Requiem;

Lindbergh's Flight, radio cantata; The Ballad of Magna Carta; Walt Whitman Songs.

Operas (and/or musical plays): The Protagonist; Royal Palace; Der Zar Lässt Sich Photographieren (The Czar Has Himself Photographed); Happy End; Die Dreigroschenoper (The Three-Penny Opera); Aufstieg und Fall der Stadt Mahagonny (The Rise and Fall of the City of Mahagonny); Die Jasager; Die Bürgschaft; Der Silbersee; Street Scene; Lost in the Stars; Down in the Valley, one-act opera.

Orchestral Music—2 symphonies; Rilke-Lieder, two sets for voice and orchestra; Der Neue Orpheus, for soprano, solo violin, and orchestra; Fantasy, Passacaglia and Hymn; Quodlibet; Violin Concerto.

ABOUT

Ewen, D., Complete Book of the American Musical Theater; Ewen, D., The Story of America's Musical Theater; Green, S., The World of Musical Comedy.

Herald Tribune, April 9, 1950; Melos (Berlin), May 1950; New York Times, April 9, 1950; Tomorrow, March 1948.

Jaromir Weinberger
1896–1967

Jaromir Weinberger was born in Prague on January 8, 1896. Of peasant origin, he spent his boyhood years on the farm of his grandparents, where he had an opportunity to hear the folk songs and dances of his native land, a musical experience he never forgot. In his youth he attended the Prague Conservatory where he studied with Krička and Hofmeister. His compositions at this time were influenced by the French Impressionists. He was aware of the derivativeness of these early works, and eventually he destroyed them.

One of the first compositions he regarded with sustained favor was *Puppet-Show Overture*, written when he was seventeen. A lively, tuneful piece, it had a number of successful performances in Europe. This success notwithstanding, Weinberger felt the need for more instruction. In 1915 he became Max Reger's private pupil in composition in Leipzig.

Weinberger paid his first visit to the United States in 1922 when he became professor of composition at Ithaca Conservatory in New York State. He remained in America four years before returning to Europe to hold several minor musical posts in Bratislava and Eger in Czechoslovakia.

During that time his style as a composer was going through a radical transformation. He

Weinberger: vīn′ bĕrg ẽr

had long since abandoned the French composers to return to the musical heroes he had admired as a boy—Dvořák and Smetana. A renewed acquaintance with their music led him straight to musical nationalism. Weinberger now felt an overpowering attraction for the songs and dances of his native land and ambitious to create music in an authentically Bohemian style.

JAROMIR WEINBERGER

It was as a nationalist that he achieved his identity and realized his first major successes. In fact, his fame assumed international proportions in 1927 when his opera *Schwanda, der Dudelsackpfeifer* (*Schwanda, the Bagpipe Player*), was introduced at the National Theatre in Prague on April 27. The libretto—adapted by Miloš Kareš from a play by Josef Tul which, in turn, was rooted in Bohemian legend—is a delightful mixture of humor, fantasy, satire, and realism. It tells of the futile attempt of the bandit Babinsky to win the lovely Dorota away from her husband, Schwanda. Weinberger's music is filled with catchy folk tunes and dance rhythms that make for easy, pleasurable listening. *Schwanda* became his most famous opera.

Schwanda was not particularly successful, however, at its première. Yet when it was revived in Breslau, Germany, on December 16, 1928, it was a sensation. From there it went on to capture the opera world. In the years between 1927 and 1931 two thousand performances were given in Europe. On November

7, 1931, the American première took place at the Metropolitan Opera. There were few, indeed, to doubt that *Schwanda* was the most successful opera to come out of Bohemia since Smetana's *The Bartered Bride*. In addition to its formidable popularity in the theatre, the music of *Schwanda* gained permanence in the symphonic repertory by virtue of two highly popular orchestral excerpts, the Polka (from Act II, scene 2) and the fugue (closing scene).

Otto Erhardt explained the enormous success of *Schwanda* as follows: "First of all, *Schwanda* is a thoroughly pleasant fellow. . . . Secondly, it is quite an unproblematic work and takes no shame in working with the established means which the opera has recognized since the time of *The Magic Flute*. In the third place, the author of the text and the composer have given to the theatre what belongs to the theatre. In the fourth place, there is the general admixture of the realistic and the fantastic which seldom fails to have its effect on the wide public. Even the grotesque and the burlesque elements have their place, without descending to caricature. Thus the taste of the time is catered to and yet the work is not burdened with features of only temporary value."

We also find the Bohemian influence in several of Weinberger's works for orchestra written soon after *Schwanda*. *Overture to a Knightly Play* is a vivid musical description of a knight who combines characteristics of Don Quixote, Falstaff, and Casanova. The music makes extensive use of Bohemian folk melodies. And so does the work *Six Bohemian Songs and Dances*, for orchestra, which was highly successful when introduced in Darmstadt in 1930.

Weinberger completed three more significant operas in the 1930's. *The Beloved Voice* was produced in Munich on February 28, 1931; *The Outcasts of Poker Flat*, libretto based on the Bret Harte story, was introduced in Brünn on November 19, 1932; and *Wallenstein*, based on Schiller, was seen in Vienna on November 18, 1937. None of the three was as successful as *Schwanda* nor did any of them have its charm and popular appeal, but all three possess sound dramatic values. All are imaginative and at times original, and all contain musical episodes of permanent interest.

"In examining these operas," wrote Paul Nettl, "we can trace the path of Weinberger's artistic development. Though *Schwanda* is strongly influenced by Czech legendary themes, and *The Beloved Voice* follows the patterns of Czech-Yugoslavic folklore, the two succeeding works already depart from the canons of style dictated by folklore tendencies. In *Outcasts of Poker Flat*, a new dramatic principle is introduced and developed. We have in this work a combination of opera and melodramatic portrayal: that is, realistic dialogue is spoken while, on the other hand, the emotional outbursts of the leading characters are portrayed musically, both of these being accompanied by the orchestra, to which is entrusted the task of describing the psychological situation and painting a background. By way of this experiment Weinberger arrived (in his *Wallenstein*) at a new form of dramatic technique which is quite novel in essentials though it has roots in older models. Where Wagner uses the leitmotiv to accompany the various characters as they appear on the stage, Weinberger uses definitely formed motives to characterize specific emotional situations."

In 1939, after a visit to England, Weinberger traveled to the United States. He subsequently became an American citizen and established permanent residence in St. Petersburg, Florida. Soon after arriving in the United States he completed his most popular work for orchestra (with the exception of the *Schwanda* excerpts). It was *Under the Spreading Chestnut Tree*, a set of variations on a popular English tune. The idea came to him at Juan-les-Pins during the summer of 1938. Attending a newsreel theatre, he saw a film of the King of England visiting a summer camp and being serenaded by the youngsters with a popular English song. Weinberger was so taken with the tune that he decided to use it for a series of variations providing a picture of historic English scenes, landscapes, and backgrounds. The work was heard first at a concert of the New York Philharmonic, John Barbirolli conducting, on October 12, 1939.

In 1941 Weinberger wrote the *Czech Rhapsody*, in which he once again became a Bohemian nationalist composer. Its première took place in Washington, D.C., on November 5, 1941. However, Weinberger's residence in the United States brought about another change of creative values—Bohemian-inspired music gave way to works with a strong American identity and American subject matter. He said at the time: "I now feel that to compose Czech music is to cultivate a patch of ground too limited and restricted. That was very good when my viewpoint on cosmic matters was limited."

The American influence is found in a number of orchestral works written and performed in the 1940's: *Prelude and Fugue on Dixie; A Lincoln Symphony; The Legend of Sleepy Hollow*. But Weinberger soon outgrew the American influences just as he had formerly outgrown the Bohemian ones. He now aspired to produce music with a broad humanitarian base. "I can no longer speak of any one country in my music," he said. "I must speak to all people everywhere, and in an idiom that they will understand. I now feel that music should be humanitarian in its approach and message; it should be universal in scope. To achieve this is to attain the highest realms of true art. That is what I hope my music will now become. The day of nationalistic music is over; music should now aspire to be international, speaking to, and of, all races, creeds, and countries."

Of his subsequent compositions the most significant are the *Préludes Religieuses et Profanes*, for orchestra, introduced in Rotterdam in 1955; and the *Five Songs from Des Knaben Wunderhorn*, which received its première at the Vienna Festival Weeks in Austria in 1962.

His failure to obtain performances for his major works in America—indeed, his feeling that he was no longer a part of the mainstream of American music—led to a profound melancholia. On August 6, 1967, Weinberger committed suicide by taking an overdose of pills at his home in St. Petersburg, Florida.

MAJOR WORKS

Choral Music—Bosnian Rhapsody; The Ecclesiastes; 150th Psalm; The Way to Emmaus.

Operas—Schwanda, der Dudelsackpfeifer (Schwanda, the Bagpipe Player); The Beloved Voice; The Outcasts of Poker Flat; A Bed of Roses, light opera; Wallenstein.

Orchestral Music—Puppet Show Overture; Christmas; Bohemian Songs and Dances; Overture to a Knightly Play; Passacaglia, for organ and orchestra; Colloque Sentimental, for violin and orchestra; Under the Spreading Chestnut Tree, variations; Song of the High Seas; Czech Rhapsody; A Lincoln Symphony; The Legend of Sleepy Hollow; From Tyrol; Eine Walzerouverture; Préludes Religieuses et Profanes;

Des Knaben Wunderhorn, song cycle for voice and orchestra.

Piano Music—Gravures; Sonata; Etude.

Vocal Music—Songs of Faith.

ABOUT

Ewen, D., Complete Book of 20th Century Music.

Hugo Weisgall
1912–

Hugo Weisgall was born in Ivančice (Eibenschitz), Czechoslovakia, on October 13, 1912. His father was a singer who gave up a career in opera to become a cantor in the synagogue. When Hugo was eight, the family moved to the United States, settling in Baltimore. Hugo's interest in the theatre, which later made him so successful in the writing of operas, revealed itself early. When he was about ten, he gathered the neighborhood children to act in a play about the Knights of the Round Table which he himself prepared and in which he played the part of King Arthur. When, somewhat later, he became interested in the story of Robinson Crusoe, he used his backyard as a setting for the enactment of the tale, digging up dirt to create a realistic setting for the performance.

While attending public schools in Baltimore, Weisgall began the study of music. In 1927 he entered the Peabody Conservatory on a Boise Fellowship. There, for the next three years, he studied with Florette Gorfine, Alexander Sklarevski, and Louis Cheslock. During that period he was also an undergraduate at Johns Hopkins University and received his degree in 1931. From 1936 to 1939 he studied conducting with Fritz Reiner and composition with Rosario Scalero at the Curtis Institute in Philadelphia. After that, until 1941, he studied composition privately with Roger Sessions. Meanwhile, he also returned to Johns Hopkins University for graduate work in 1937, and he received his doctorate in German literature three years later.

Composition had begun for him in 1930 with the writing of a piano sonata. In 1931 he wrote *Four Impressions*, for voice and piano; and in 1932, a one-act opera, *Night*. *Four Impressions* received the Bearns Prize from Columbia University. Weisgall's opus no. 1 was *Four Songs*, for voice and piano,

to texts by Adelaide Crapsey (1934). In this work he progresses from the diatonic and consonant language of the first three songs to the chromaticism and dissonance of the fourth song, but without sacrificing lyricism. While taking his graduate courses at Johns Hopkins, Weisgall wrote scores for two ballets, *The Quest* (1937) and *One Thing Is Certain* (1939).

During World War II, Weisgall enlisted in the United States Army. He served as assistant military attaché to the Allied Governments in Exile, in London and Prague. The impact of the war is reflected in the song cycle *Soldier Songs*, for baritone and orchestra, written in 1944 and 1945. It comprises nine songs on texts by various poets and reveals Weisgall "as a dramatic composer of the greatest magnitude," according to Abraham Skulsky. "It also shows him in full possession of his compositional powers and of all the peculiarities of his style as they will appear later in his operas."

During the war, on December 28, 1942, Weisgall married Nathalie Shulman, by whom he has two children, a daughter and a son. Upon leaving the Army, Weisgall returned to Baltimore where he started to earn his living by teaching music privately. He also involved himself actively in Baltimore's musical life, by serving as director of the Baltimore Institute of Musical Arts in 1948–1949; by founding in 1949 the Chamber Music Society of Baltimore, which he directed for many years; and by organizing and directing the Hilltop Musical Company. From 1953 to 1955 he lectured on music at Johns Hopkins, and from 1953 to 1956 he was the conductor of its orchestra. He also promoted modern music. In 1946–1947 he was a member of the international jury of the International Society for Contemporary Music at its festival in Copenhagen, and he performed a similar service in 1957 for the festival in Zürich.

While serving as a cultural attaché to the American Embassy in Prague in 1946–1947, Weisgall wrote the music for *The Outpost*, a ballet commissioned by the National Theatre of Prague. The dances from this score became Weisgall's first composition to get a significant hearing when he conducted it on January 11, 1947, at a concert of the National Symphony in Washington, D.C.

It was in opera, rather than orchestral

music, however, that Weisgall achieved both success and importance. His opera *The Tenor* (1949), based on a play of Wedekind, was produced in Baltimore on February 11, 1952, under the composer's direction. This was followed in 1952 by *The Stronger*, from a play by Strindberg, first performance (with orchestra) in Westport, Connecticut, on August 9, 1952. These two short one-act works, each a commendable achievement, served to prepare the composer for the writing of his most ambitious opera up to that time, the three-act *Six Characters in Search of an Author*, based on Pirandello. Commissioned by the Ditson Fund of Columbia University, it was written between 1953 and 1956 and was introduced by the New York City Opera on April 26, 1959.

"Like the play," wrote Howard Taubman in the New York *Times*, "the opera functions on many levels. It seeks to be learned and satirical, fantastic and farcical, intellectual and emotional. . . . Mr. Weisgall's music has no end of skill and cleverness."

Abraham Skulsky has observed that in Weisgall's first three operas, he develops towards "the total unification of the musical and dramatic elements. Just as in his musical context he attains a very personal style through the combination of seemingly contradictory elements such as diatonism and chromaticism, the elements of Mahler and consequently Berg with that of Stravinskyan classic rhythm, the almost Verdian quality of his melodic line with that of a tight structure, so does he approach the operatic problem and through a combination of various concepts he attains a marvelous unity. . . . Another factor in Weisgall's successful approach to opera is his ability to establish a well-defined mood either for the different characterizations or as basis for the entire work. . . . Each of his operas contains both the elements of comedy and tragedy."

Purgatory (1959)—first performance at the Library of Congress in Washington, D.C. on February 17, 1961—is a word-for-word setting of William Butler Yeats's allegory of youth, age, and motherhood. The critical consensus was that the composer had only partly realized his goal; that too frequently the music did not rise to the exacting and subtle demands of Yeats's poetry.

In 1960 Weisgall was commissioned by Thomas Scherman and the Little Orchestra Society to write an opera which that organization could present in concert form. The work he created was *Athaliah*, with a text by Richard Franko Goldman based on Racine's tragedy. Its world première took place in New York City on February 17, 1964. Harold C. Schonberg called it "a dignified, serious, well-wrought score that in philosophy and treatment stems from Berg's *Lulu*. It is dissonant, has some dodecaphonic textures, a leaping melodic line that more often than not is a parlando (or 'talking') line and an orchestral background that comments strongly on the action." On October 9, 1968, the New York City Opera presented the première performance of *Nine Rivers from Jordan*, which the composer had written on a grant from the Ford Foundation.

HUGO WEISGALL

Weisgall left Baltimore in 1959 to make his home in Great Neck, Long Island. Since 1953 he has been on the faculty of the Juilliard School of Music, and since 1960 he has been professor of composition at Queens College in New York. From 1952 to 1962 he was also chairman of the faculty at the Cantors Institute and Seminary College of Jewish Music of the Jewish Theological Seminary of America in New York.

In 1954 Weisgall received a grant from the National Institute of Arts and Letters. In 1955, and again in 1959, he was given Guggenheim fellowships.

MAJOR WORKS

Ballets—The Quest; One Thing Is Certain; Outpost.
Choral Music—2 Choral Etudes; Five Motets, Hymn; Two Children's Choruses; Nine Choral Pieces.
Operas—The Tenor, one-act opera; The Stronger, one-act opera; Six Characters in Search of an Author; Purgatory; Athaliah; Henry IV; Nine Rivers from Jordan.
Orchestral Music—Overture in F; A Garden Eastward, cantata for high voice and orchestra; Soldier Songs, for baritone and orchestra.
Piano Music—Variations; Fugue and Romance, for two pianos.
Vocal Music—Four Songs; I Looked Back Suddenly; Two Madrigals.

ABOUT

American Composers Alliance Bulletin, No. 2, 1958; Etude, December 1956.

Ermanno Wolf-Ferrari
1876–1948

Ermanno Wolf-Ferrari was born in Venice on January 12, 1876. His mother was Italian; his father, German. From his father, a famous painter, Wolf-Ferrari appeared to inherit a gift for art. Determined to have the boy follow in his own footsteps, the father despatched young Ermanno to Rome for art study. Eventually, Wolf-Ferrari succeeded in producing several noteworthy canvases.

Wolf-Ferrari had begun music study by himself when he was fifteen. His progress was so rapid that in 1893 he was permitted to go to Munich, where for two years he studied with Rheinberger. At the same time he wrote his first compositions. A pilgrimage to Bayreuth, the shrine of Wagnerian music drama, convinced him that he wanted more than anything else to be a composer and made him abandon art for music. However, in view of his passion for Wagner, it is interesting to note that a later hearing of *Siegfried* brought on what has been described as a "psychosomatic shock." A serious illness followed. When Wolf-Ferrari recovered, he became almost pathologically opposed to Wagner.

Upon returning to Venice he received his first major hearing as a composer with the performance of a biblical cantata, *La Sulamite*, in 1899. On February 22, 1900, his first opera, *Cenerentola*, was introduced in Venice, but with little success. When the opera was re-

---

Wolf-Ferrari: vōlf′ fär rä′rē

peated in Germany in 1902 under the title of *Aschenbrödel*, it made a far more favorable impression.

His talent for the musical theatre first became evident with two works in an *opera buffa* style. The first was *Le Donne Curiose*, a farce based on a Goldoni play, introduced in Munich on November 27, 1903. This was followed by *I Quattro Rusteghi*, in Munich, on March 19, 1906. In both scores, Wolf-Ferrari revealed a light and graceful touch, a gift for soaring melody, a flair for the comic, and great charm. These qualities established him as a worthy twentieth century successor to the long line of famous Italian *opera buffa* composers that had begun with Pergolesi.

ERMANNO WOLF-FERRARI

Le Donne Curiose was introduced in the United States at the Metropolitan Opera on January 3, 1912. At that time Richard Aldrich wrote: "[Wolf-Ferrari] is a master of moods in musical representation, and sentiment expressed with direction and without sentimentality. . . . The scoring is very light with subtle refinements; it is an example of what a master can do with comparatively few resources."

I Quattri Rusteghi had to wait almost half a century for its American première, which was given in New York on October 18, 1951, by the New York City Opera. "The unostentatious craftsmanship and transparent instrumental and vocal writing of Wolf-Ferrari made the score a pleasure to listen to, whatever deeper merit it may lack," reported Cecil Smith.

Wolf-Ferrari

From 1902 to 1907, Wolf-Ferrari was the director of the Liceo Benedetto Marcello in Venice. After that, he taught for a while at the Mozarteum in Salzburg. Settling in a suburb of Munich, he finally relinquished his teaching commitments to concentrate on composition. And he created his two operatic masterworks, one in an *opera buffa* style, and the other an *opera seria*. The comedy was an engaging little one-act opera, *The Secret of Suzanne* (*Il Segreto di Susanna*), which was introduced triumphantly in Munich on December 4, 1909. A silly little sketch, revolving around Suzanne's terrible secret that she smoked cigarettes, inspired Wolf-Ferrari to write one of his freshest and most spontaneous scores. Upon receiving its American première in New York, on March 14, 1911 (in a performance by the visiting Chicago Opera), *The Secret of Suzanne* was heard for the first time in the Italian language. (The world première had been sung in German.)

In marked contrast to the levity of *The Secret of Suzanne* is *The Jewels of the Madonna* (*I Gioielli della Madonna*), presented in German in Berlin on December 23, 1911. In this work the composer revealed a remarkable change of pace by producing a tragic opera in the *verismo* style in which the music is outstanding for its realism, tension, and dramatic impact.

In 1918 William Saunders contrasted the strengths and weaknesses of Wolf-Ferrari's two celebrated operas as follows: "His airs do not display a great power of melodic invention, but interspersed as they frequently are in a welter of discordant cacophony, they actually sound to better advantage than they would otherwise have done. A great fault in these melodies of his, also, is a too frequent use of cadence. His clever borrowings and employment of popular airs and folk themes, on the other hand, supply a welcome variety. . . . His writing and scoring of dance themes, also . . . falls little, if at all, short of genius. His choral writing, again, is seldom at fault and generally reminds one of the best examples of Verdi. . . . And lastly he is a past master of orchestration."

In 1912 Wolf-Ferrari paid his first visit to the United States to supervise the American première of *The Jewels of the Madonna* at the Chicago Opera on January 16, 1912—the first time that the opera was to be heard in its original Italian. Less than two months later, on March 5, the composer attended the first production of his opera at the Metropolitan Opera House, in a performance by the visiting Chicago Opera Company. The first Metropolitan Opera Company production took place on December 12, 1925.

On December 4, 1913, came the world première of another Wolf-Ferrari *opera buffa*, *L'Amore Medico*, based on Molière's *L'Amour Médecin*, produced in Dresden. In this opera, too, the composer's talent for melody and comedy was ascendant.

For twelve years Wolf-Ferrari wrote no operas. He returned to the stage with *Gli Amanti Sposi*, based on a comedy by Goldoni, produced in Venice on February 19, 1925. Neither in this work nor in the six operas that followed was Wolf-Ferrari able to duplicate either the quality or the success of his earlier operas.

Wolf-Ferrari also wrote much instrumental music, but his gift was essentially operatic, and few of his concert works have survived.

Wolf-Ferrari died in Venice on January 21, 1948.

MAJOR WORKS

Chamber Music—2 violin sonatas; 2 piano trios; Piano Quintet; String Quartet.

Choral Music—La Sulamite, cantata; The Daughter of Jairus, mystery; La Vita Nuova, oratorio.

Operas—Cenerentola; Le Donne Curiose; I Quattro Rusteghi; Il Segreto di Susanna (The Secret of Suzanne); I Gioielli della Madonna (The Jewels of the Madonna); L'Amore Medico; Gli Amanti Sposi; Das Himmelskleid; Le Vedova Scaltra; Il Campiello; La Dama Boba; Gli Dei a Tebe.

Orchestral Music—Chamber Symphony; Serenade, for string orchestra; Idillio, concertino for oboe, string orchestra, and two horns; Suite Concertino, for bassoon, two horns, and string orchestra; Suite Veneziana; Arabeschi; Divertimento; Kleines Konzert, for English horn and orchestra.

ABOUT

Grisson, A. C., Ermanno Wolf-Ferrari; Stahl, E. L., Ermanno Wolf-Ferrari.

Rivista Musicale Italiana (Rome), July–September 1949.

Eugene Zádor
1894–

Eugene Zádor was born in Bátaszék, Hungary, on November 5, 1894. "At first, my father was a teacher in Bátaszék," he writes. "Later, when the family grew to encompass eight children, of which I was the seventh, Father looked for a more lucrative business and opened a small leather factory. When I was six, we moved to the city of Pécs, where I began my piano lessons. My first compositions, influenced by Schumann and Verdi, were all for the piano. But when, in Budapest, I heard a work by Richard Strauss, I came under his spell; and especially his orchestration had a magical effect on me.

EUGENE ZÁDOR

"The most interesting reminiscence from my boyhood days came when I was fifteen. I studied composition with the head of the Conservatory in Pécs. But only three short years later, in Vienna, the same man studied with me. Another memory is from high school. When the kind French teacher saw that I was composing in class, he stopped teaching until I had finished the piece. His son is a cellist with the New York Philharmonic."

In 1911 Zádor entered the Vienna Conservatory, where he studied composition for two years with Richard Heuberger, whom he describes as "a mediocre composer but a good

Zador: zä′ dōr

teacher." Two years later he studied composition with Max Reger in Leipzig, "a mediocre teacher but a good composer." He also took courses in musicology with Hermann Abert and Arnold Schering. During this period he wrote music reviews for five years for a Hungarian newspaper in Pécs. In 1918 he completed his first mature work, *Bánk Bán*, an orchestral tone poem introduced in Budapest in 1919. His study of musicology, with Fritz Volbach, was completed in 1921 at the University of Münster, from which he received his doctorate in music.

In 1921 he settled in Vienna, becoming professor of composition at the Conservatory. His career as a composer developed rapidly, with the writing of his first symphony, the *Romantic* (1922), and the world première of his first opera, *Diana*, produced at the Budapest Royal Opera on December 22, 1923. Five years later, on March 29, 1928, the Budapest Royal Opera introduced the opera *The Isle of the Dead*, and on February 15, 1936, *Asra*.

Zádor completed several important and highly successful instrumental compositions in the 1920's and 1930's. *Variations on a Hungarian Folksong* was well received when it was introduced in Vienna on February 9, 1927. It was followed by the *Rondo*, for orchestra (first performance in Vienna in 1934). This work was given extensive hearings in Europe. Donald Francis Tovey said of it: "It admirably represents the style of a master who, being versed in every form of classical technique, has devised a pleasantly humorous modus vivendi with every modern tendency that does not display a conscientious objection to mastery."

Even more successful was the *Hungarian Caprice*, for orchestra, which had its first hearing on February 1, 1935, in Budapest, with Carl Schuricht conducting the Budapest Philharmonic. Since that time, the composition has had hundreds of performances in Europe and the United States, under such distinguished conductors as Stokowski, Ormandy, Monteux, Wallenstein, Szell, and Barbirolli. More than any of his other works, it served to focus world interest on its composer. Helpful, too, in establishing his reputation was his Piano Quintet, which was given the Hungarian National State Prize in 1934. Recognition of his growing stature as a composer and as a teacher came from both sides of the Atlantic Ocean in 1935, when he was given the honorary title of professor by the Royal Academy of Music in Budapest, and an honorary doctorate by the New York College of Music.

In 1939 Zádor came to the United States. He stayed in New York for about a year, supporting himself by teaching, and by serving as an orchestrator for the Ford radio hour. His opera *Christopher Columbus*, which he had completed in 1939, received its world première at the Centre Theatre in New York City on October 8 of that year. In 1940 Zádor left for California, set up home in Hollywood, became an American citizen, and for a quarter of a century (until 1963) orchestrated over a hundred scores for motion pictures. Three of these scores—*Spellbound*, *A Double Life*, and *Ben-Hur*—received Academy Awards.

Despite his Hollywood obligations, Zádor was able to maintain a steady pace of creativity as a serious composer with particularly notable contributions to symphonic literature. He is basically a middle-of-the-road composer who avoids new techniques and experiments for their own sake, refuses to remain bound by any system, and yet does not avoid unusual sounds or intervals as long as they conform to a tonal framework. He comments: "I wonder whether today it does not take more courage to write a tonal piece which the composer feels is sincere than to write in the convenient and not always controllable fashion of the twelve-tone composer or electronic music." His writing is always strongly melodic, always euphonious, always constructed and orchestrated with skill and ingenuity. His Hungarian background is probably the greatest single influence on his style. Some of his most frequently performed works reveal their national identity in melodies that simulate the sensuousness and languor of gypsy tunes and rhythms that are a carry-over from gypsy dances. But Zádor does not believe in quotations or adaptations; all the materials he uses, however derivative, are exclusively his.

One of his most widely played compositions was written soon after he had settled in the United States: the thirteen-minute *Children's Symphony*, in four movements, first performed in New Orleans in 1940. Almost two decades later, Zádor rewrote the work, the new version receiving its première in Beverly Hills, California, on October 17, 1960. The composition later received over one hundred performances in the United States, England, Austria, Ireland, Germany, the Philippines, and Israel. Partly programmatic (three of the four movements describe respectively a fairy tale, marching soldiers, and a day on the farm), the symphony uses simple procedures and melodies; the work as a whole has the charm, freshness, and vivacity of childhood.

Biblical Scenes (originally named *Biblical Triptych*) was inspired by Thomas Mann's series of novels dealing with the character of Joseph. This composition for large orchestra was successfully introduced by the Chicago Symphony on December 10, 1943. Dr. Mann, to whom the work is dedicated, wrote to Zádor: "You have succeeded admirably in doing with musical tone that which I attempted to do with words, namely, to unite primitive, oriental sound with modern sensibility and understanding. It is a real satisfaction for me to know that my story has inspired a master in the art which has ever been very dear to me, to create a work of such beauty and so full of the promise of permanency."

Several of Zádor's compositions in the 1950's were of Hungarian inspiration. They include the *Élégie* and the *Rhapsody*, both for orchestra, both strongly influenced by Hungarian folk songs and dances. The former received its première on November 11, 1960, with Eugene Ormandy conducting the Philadelphia Orchestra; the latter was introduced on February 12, 1961, in Los Angeles, in a performance by the Los Angeles Philharmonic.

Other recent Zádor compositions display a keen-edged wit, a love of gaiety and laughter, and a light and graceful touch in the projection of humorous episodes. In such a vein he produced *Five Contrasts for Orchestra*, which had its world première on January 8, 1965, Eugene Ormandy conducting the Philadelphia Orchestra. Reviewing the composition, Daniel Webster said in the Philadelphia *Inquirer*: "Zádor is a composer of more than usual wit, and his five concise sections were alive with the spirit, humor, and a sardonic strain not unlike that of his countryman Bartók." Equally delightful in its calculated levity is the *Overture on a Merry Theme*, first performance in Birmingham, Alabama, on January 12, 1965.

On December 10, 1964, during festivities

attending the opening of the new Los Angeles Music Center, the Los Angeles Philharmonic under Zubin Mehta introduced Zádor's *Festival Overture*, written for the occasion. In the Los Angeles *Times*, Albert Goldberg described it as "a resounding affair . . . replete with fanfares and orchestral pageantry, and with a more serious middle section to balance and give it weight."

Another orchestral work by Zádor to receive its world première at the Los Angeles Music Center is the *Aria and Allegro*, which the Los Angeles Philharmonic performed under the direction of Hans Schmidt-Isserstedt on March 2, 1967.

In areas outside orchestral composition, Zádor has completed two one-act operas: *The Virgin and the Fawn*, produced in Los Angeles in 1965, and *The Magic Chair*, performed at Louisiana University in 1966. A full-length opera, *The Scarlet Mill* (based on Molnar's *The Red Mill*), was introduced in Brooklyn, New York, on October 26, 1968. For chorus, Zádor has completed a *Triptych* (1964), comprising three chorales; the first describes an ancient church; the second is based on a simple, touching French folk tale; and the third is a joyful invocation of a wanderer enjoying the beauties of the countryside.

Zádor lives in Hollywood, California with his wife and their two children, a boy and a girl. His wife is the former Maria Steiner, whom he married in Geneva on November 9, 1946. He has no hobbies, no interests outside music, except reading. "I spend sixteen hours each day either listening to music or writing it," he reports. His only exercise is walking—for two or three hours every day around the block where he lives. "I stay on my block," he explains, "because when I am thinking, I might get killed if I tried to cross the streets." Some of his best musical ideas come to him during these daily strolls, but, he adds, "using the legs is also important."

MAJOR WORKS

Ballets—The Machine Man; The Jury.

Choral Music—Three Rondels; Cantata Technica; Scherzo Domestico; Triptych.

Operas—Diana, one-act opera; The Isle of the Dead; X-Mal; Rembrandt; The Awakening of Snow White; Azra; The Inspector General; Christopher Columbus; The Virgin and the Fawn, one-act opera; The Magic Chair, one-act opera; The Scarlet Mill.

Orchestral Music—4 symphonies (including Children's Symphony); 2 rhapsodies; Bánk Bán, tone poem; Variations on a Hungarian Folksong; Scherzo; Biblical Scenes (originally entitled Biblical Triptych); Elegy and Dance; Divertimento; Fugue Fantasia; Elegie; Suite for Brass; Ode to Peace; The Remarkable Adventures of Henry Bold; Festival Overture; Variations on a Merry Theme; Five Contrasts; Aria and Allegro; Trombone Concerto.

ABOUT

Tovey, D. F., Essays in Musical Analysis, vol. 6.

Appendix I

Aleatory Music (Chance Music): Boulez, Cage, Foss.

American Indian Music: Cadman.

American Nationalism: Copland, Cowell, Ives, Siegmeister.

Arcueil, École d': Satie, Sauguet.

Armenian Nationalism: Khatchaturian.

Atonality: Schoenberg, Berg, Webern.

Bohemian Nationalism: Janáček, Martinu, Weinberger.

Brazilian Nationalism: Villa-Lobos.

Cante Hondo: Falla.

Chance Music: *See* Aleatory Music.

Concrete Music (Musique Concrète): Boulez.

Directional Music (Spatial Dimension): Brant, Stockhausen.

Dodecaphonic Music: *See* Twelve-tone System, Serialism.

Electronic Music: Babbitt, Boulez, Cage, Stockhausen.

English Nationalism: Vaughan Williams.

Everyday Music: *See* Musique de Tous les Jours.

Fauvism: *See* Neo-primitivism.

Finnish Nationalism: Sibelius.

Formalism, or "Decadent Formalism": Prokofiev, Shostakovich.

French Six: Auric, Honegger, Milhaud, Poulenc.

Gebrauchsmusik (Functional Music): Hindemith.

Germ Cell Theory: Pijper.

Hebrew Music: Bloch.

Hungarian Nationalism: Bartók, Kodály.

Impressionism: Debussy, Delius.

Italian Nationalism: Casella.

Jazz: Carpenter, Copland, Gershwin, Gould.

La Jeune France: Messiaen.

Linear Counterpoint: Hindemith.

Melodies of the Language: Janáček.

Metrical Modulation: Carter.

Mexican Nationalism: Chávez.

Musique Concrète: *See* Concrete Music.

Musique d'Ameublement (Furnishing Music): Satie.

Musique de Tous Les Jours (Everyday Music): Satie.

Naturalism or Realism: Charpentier, Strauss.

Neo-classicism: Busoni, Reger, Hindemith, the middle Stravinsky.

Neo-dadaism: Cage.

Neo-mysticism: Messiaen.

Neo-primitivism (Fauvism): Stravinsky.

Neue Sachlichkeit (New Objectivity): Reger.

Norwegian Nationalism: Sinding.

Nouveaux Jeunes: Honegger.

Open Form: Stockhausen.

Opera Semiseria: Liebermann.

Organized Sound: Varèse.

Polish Nationalism: Szymanowski, Tansman.

Polymeters: Ives, Stravinsky.

Polyrhythm: Ives, Stravinsky.

Polytonality: Ives, Milhaud, Stravinsky.

Post-impressionism: Ravel.

Post-romanticism: Scriabin, Strauss.

Prepared Piano: Cage.

Proletarian Music: Blitzstein, Prokofiev, Shostakovich.

Rumanian Nationalism: Enesco.

Secondal Harmonies: *See* Tone Clusters.

Serialism (Serial Technique): Babbitt, Boulez, the late Stravinsky, Webern.

Société des Apaches: Ravel.

Song Play: Weill.

Sound Synthesizer: Babbitt.

Spatial Dimension: *See* Directional Music.

La Spirale: Jolivet.

Swedish Nationalism: Alfvén, Atterberg.

Synthesists: Poot.

Third Stream: Schuller.

Time Fields: Stockhausen.

Tone Clusters (Secondal Harmonies): Cowell, Ives.

Triton: Rivier.

Twelve-tone System (Dodecaphony): Berg, Schoenberg, Webern.

Variable Meters: Blacher.

Verismo: Mascagni, Puccini.

Whole-tone Scale: Debussy.

Zeitkunst (Contemporary Art): Weill.

Appendix II

A SELECT BIBLIOGRAPHY

Abraham, Gerald. Eight Soviet Composers. Oxford University Press (London). 1943.

Austin, William W. Music in the 20th Century: From Debussy Through Stravinsky. Norton. 1966.

Bacharach, A. L. ed. British Music of Our Times. Pelican Books. 1946.

Bacharach, A. L. ed. The Music Masters; vol. 4: The Twentieth Century, by W. R. Anderson [and others]. Cassell (London). 1957.

Bakst, James. A History of Russian-Soviet Music. Dodd. 1966.

Bauer, Marion. Twentieth Century Music; How It Developed, How to Listen to It. new ed. rev. Putnam. 1947.

Brook, Donald. Composers' Gallery. Rockliff (London). 1946.

Brook, Donald. Five Great French Composers. Rockliff (London). 1946.

Calvocoressi, M. D., and Abraham, Gerald. Masters of Russian Music. Knopf. 1936.

Chase, Gilbert. America's Music. 2d rev. ed. McGraw-Hill. 1966.

Chase, Gilbert. The Music of Spain. 2d rev. ed. Dover. 1959.

Cohn, Arthur. The Collector's Twentieth-Century Music in the Western Hemisphere. Lippincott. 1961.

Cohn, Arthur. Twentieth Century Music in Western Europe: the Compositions and the Recordings. Lippincott. 1965.

Copland, Aaron. Our New Music. McGraw-Hill. 1941.

Ewen, David. David Ewen Introduces Modern Music; a History and Appreciation from Wagner to Webern. Chilton. 1962.

Ewen, David, ed. The New Book of Modern Composers. 3d ed. rev. & enl. Knopf. 1961.

Ewen, David. The World of 20th Century Music. Prentice-Hall. 1968.

Foulds, John H. Music To-day. Nicholson (London). 1934.

Graf, Max. Modern Music. Philosophical Library. 1946.

Hansen, Peter Sijer. An Introduction to Twentieth Century Music. Allyn. 1961.

Hartog, Howard, ed. European Music in the Twentieth Century. Praeger. 1957.

Hodeir, André. Since Debussy: A View of Contemporary Music; tr. by Noel Burch. Grove. 1961.

Howard, John Tasker. Our Contemporary Composers. Crowell. 1941.

Howard, John Tasker. This Modern Music. Crowell. 1942.

Lang, Paul Henry, and Broder, Nathan, eds. Contemporary Music in Europe: A Comprehensive Survey. Schirmer. 1965.

Leibowitz, René. Schoenberg and His School. Philosophical Library. 1949.

Machlis, Joseph. Introduction to Contemporary Music. Norton. 1961.

Mellers, W. H. Music in a New Found Land: Themes and Developments in the History of American Music. Knopf. 1965.

Mellers, W. H. Studies in Contemporary Music. Dobson (London). 1947.

Mitchell, Donald. The Language of Modern Music. 2d ed. Faber (London). 1966.

Moisenco, Rena. Realist Music: 25 Soviet Composers. Meridian (London). 1949.

Newlin, Dika. Bruckner, Mahler, Schoenberg. King's Crown Press. 1947.

Salazar, Adolfo. Music in Our Time. Norton. 1946.

Salzman, Eric. Twentieth-Century Music: An Introduction. Prentice-Hall. 1967.

Slonimsky, Nicolas. Music Since 1900. 3d ed. rev. & enl. Coleman-Ross. 1949.

Yates, Peter. Twentieth Century Music. Pantheon Books. 1967.

Picture Credits